CENSUS OF INDIA 1891

Census of India 1871-1951, 9 Sets In 384 Bindings (9788121258876) Rs. 700000

Census of India 1891, 28 Vols. In 49 Bindings (978-81-212-7129-5) Rs. 125000

1. General Report (9788121269834) Rs. 1450
2. General Tables For British Provinces And Feudatory States (9788121269810) Rs. 2710 (Vol. I)
3. General Tables For British Provinces And Feudatory States (9788121269797) Rs. 950 (Vol. II)
4. Assam - Report (9788121269773) Rs. 2390 (Vol. I, V.1)
5. Assam - Tables (9788121269759) Rs. 2210 (Vol. II, V.2)
6. Assam - Provincial Tables (9788121269735) Rs. 1310 (Vol. II, V.3)
7. The Lower Provinces of Bengal and their Feudatories - The Report (9788121269711) Rs. 1660 (Vol. III)
8. The Lower Provinces of Bengal and their feudatories - The Administrative Tables (9788121269698) Rs. 4200 (Vol. IV)
9. The Lower Provinces of Bengal and their feudatories - The Caste Tables (9788121269674) Rs. 2600 (Vol. V, Pt. 1)
10. Lower Provinces of Bengal - The Provincial Tables (9788121269650) Rs. 1980 (Vol. V, Pt. 2)
11. Berar or the Hyderabad Assigned Districts (9788121269636) Rs. 3360 (Vol. VI)
12. Bombay and Its Feudatories - Report (9788121269612) Rs. 4010 (Vol. VII, Pt. 1)
13. Bombay And Its Feudatories - Imperial Tables (9788121269599) Rs. 790 (Vol. VIII, Pt. 2)
14. Imperial Series - Burma Report (9788121269575) Rs. 2320 (Vol. IX-V.1)
15. Imperial Tables - Burma Report (9788121269551) Rs. 3360 (Vol. X-V.2)
16. Provincial Tables Burma Report (9788121269537) Rs. 3510 (Vol. X-V.3)
17. Provincial Tables Burma Report (9788121269513) Rs. 3630 (Vol. X-V.4)
18. The Central Provinces And Feudatories - The Report (9788121269490) Rs. 2290 (Vol. XI, Pt. 1)
19. The Central Provinces And Feudatories - Imperial tables and supplementary returns (9788121268936) Rs. 2010 (Vol. XII)
20. Madras The Report On The Census (9788121269476) Rs. 2870 (Vol. XIII)
21. Madras - Tables I to XVII-C, British Territory (9788121269452) Rs. 3490 (Vol. XIV)
22. Madras - Tables A TO E, British Territory. Tables for feudatory States and A Caste Index (9788121269438) Rs. 2820 (Vol. XV)
23. The North Western Provinces and Outh - Report and Provincial Tables (9788121268912) Rs. 3100 (Vol. XVI, Pt. 1)
24. The North - Western Provinces and Oudh- Imperial Tables (9788121269414) Rs. 2000 (Vol. XVII, Pt. 2)
25. The North - Western Provinces and Oudh- Imperial Caste Tables (9788121269391) Rs. 3020 (Vol. XVIII, Pt. 3)
26. Punjab and Its Feudatories - The Report on the Census (9788121269377) Rs. 2710 (Vol. XIX, Pt. 1)
27. Punjab and Its Feudatories - Imperial Tables and Supplementary Returns for the British Territory (9788121269353) Rs. 1370 (Vol. XX, Pt. 2)
28. Punjab and Its Feudatories - Imperial Tables and Supplementary Returns for the Native States, Together With A Caste Index (9788121269339) Rs. 4910 (Vol. XXI, Pt. 3)
29. Report on The Census of The Districts of Ajmere-Merwara (9788121269056) Rs. 720 (Vol. XXII)
30. His Highness The Nizam's Dominions - Report (9788121269315) Rs. 2240 (Vol. XXIII, Pt. 1)
31. His Highness The Nizam's Dominions - Report (9788121269292) Rs. 2410 (Vol. XXIII, Pt. 2)
32. His Highness The Nizam's Dominions - Imperial And Supplementry Tables and Caste Index (9788121269278) Rs. 3390 (Vol. XXIII, Pt. 3)
33. Baroda - Report (9788121269254) Rs. 3810 (Vol. XXIV, Pt. 1)
34. Baroda - Tables (9788121269230) Rs. 2620 (Vol. XXIV, Pt. 2)
35. Mysore - Report (9788121269216) Rs. 2590 (Vol. XXV, Pt. 1)
36. Mysore - Imperial Tables (9788121269193) Rs. 1600 (Vol. XXV, Pt. 2)
37. Mysore - Tables (9788121269179) Rs. 5320 (Vol. XXV, Pt. 3)
38. Mysore - Supplementary Tables (9788121269155) Rs. 3590 (Vol. XXV, Pt. 4)
39. Mysore- Supplement to the Mysore census report of 1891 being a list of villages in the Mysore province and : comparing the population as per Censuses of 1891, 1881 & 1871 (9788121279024) Rs. 5350 (Vol. XXV, Pt. 5)
40. Rajputana - The Report, Imperial Tables And Supplementary Returns (9788121269131) Rs. 2330 (Vol. XXVI, Pt. 1)
41. Rajputna - The Provincial Tables and Remarks (9788121269117) Rs. 550 (Vol. XXVI, Pt. 2)
42. Central India (9788121269094) Rs. 2000 (Vol. XXVII)
43. Kashmir State - The Report on the census and Imperial and supplementary Tables (9788121269070) Rs. 2290 (Vol. XXVIII)
44. The Census of Calcutta (9788121269032) Rs. 890
45. Report on the census of Cochin (9788121269018) Rs. 790 (Pt. 1)
46. Report on the census of Cochin - The Final Census Tables with Appendices (9788121268998) Rs. 910 (Pt. 2)
47. Report on the Census of Coorg (9788121268974) Rs. 730
48. Report on the census of Travancore -Report (9788121274029) Rs. 4220 (Vol. I)
49. Report on the census of Travancore -Appendix (9788121268950) Rs. 5300 (Vol. II)

Owing to the antiquity and rarity of this book, certain pages are regrettably absent, and readability is compromised due to the blurring of the original text. If you possess any insights regarding the availability of these missing sections, kindly inform us. Your assistance is crucial in ensuring the completion of this significant work for the benefit of future generations.

CENSUS OF INDIA, 1891

BOOK-38: VOLUME XXV

MYSORE

PART IV.—SUPPLEMENTARY TABLES,
A TO **E**
AND
SPECIAL (LOCAL) TABLES **A** TO **D**

V. N. NARASIMMIYENGAR

GYAN

Published by

GYAN

Gyan Publishing House
5, Ansari Road
Daryaganj, New Delhi-110002
Phone: 011-47034999, 9811692060
E-mail: books@gyanbooks.com

Distribution Network
gyanbooks.com
India, USA, Canada, UK, Australia

ISBN: 978-81-212-7129-5 (Set) 28 Vols. In 49 Bindings
978-81-212-6915-5 (PB) Book-38, Vol. XXV, Pt. IV

First Published, 1894

2nd Impression 2024

Printed at: Gyan Press, Delhi.

CENSUS OF INDIA 1891

Census of India, 1891.

VOLUME XXV.

MYSORE.

PART IV.

SUPPLEMENTARY TABLES, A TO E,

AND

SPECIAL (LOCAL) TABLES, A TO D

BY

V. N. NARASIMMIYENGAR,
PROVINCIAL SUPERINTENDENT OF CENSUS OPERATIONS IN MYSORE.

BANGALORE:

PRINTED AT THE GOVERNMENT CENTRAL PRINTING OFFICE.

1894.

CONTENTS

OF

PART IV.

SUPPLEMENTARY TABLE A.

PART I.

CHRISTIANS BY SECTS.

SUPPLEMENTARY TABLE A.

Christians by Sects.

PART I.

SECTS.

	District.	Total Christians.			Distribution by Sect.															
					Roman Catholic.								Greek Church.							
					Total.		Foreign (European, &c.)		Eurasian.		Native.		Total.		Foreign (European, &c.)		Eurasian.		Native.	
		Total.	Males.	Females.	Males.	Females.	Males.	Females.	Males.	Females.	Males.	Females.	Males.	Females.	Males.	Females.	Males.	Females.	Males.	Females.
	1	2	3	4	5	6	7	8	9	10	11	12	13	14	15	16	17	18	19	20
1	Bangalore	6,107	3,141	2,966	2,334	2,073	23	25	49	54	2,262	1,999	...	...	...	...	...	...	...	...
2	Kolar	2,996	1,712	1,284	1,137	908	30	13	88	60	969	835	23	...	23	...	...	...	...	...
3	Tumkur	743	401	342	111	139	...	...	5	7	106	132	...	...	...	...	...	...	...	...
4	Mysore	2,947	1,471	1,476	1,072	1,201	14	112	70	46	988	1,043	...	...	...	...	...	...	...	...
5	Hassan	3,296	1,710	1,586	1,337	1,267	20	...	41	44	1,276	1,223	...	...	...	...	...	...	...	...
6	Shimoga	1,651	1,034	617	985	589	5	3	13	2	967	584	...	...	...	...	...	...	...	...
7	Kadur	2,209	1,556	653	1,247	492	69	34	82	25	1,096	430	...	...	...	...	...	...	...	...
8	Chitaldurg	284	166	118	98	79	9	...	3	5	86	54	...	...	...	...	...	...	...	...
	Total......	20,233	11,191	9,042	8,321	6,753	220	187	351	246	7,750	6,330	23	...	23	...	...	...	...	...
	The Civil and Military Station, Bangalore	17,902	9,115	8,787	5,422	6,022	601	411	510	650	4,311	4,951	1	3	...	...	...	...	1	3
	GRAND TOTAL......	38,135	20,306	17,829	13,743	12,775	821	598	861	896	12,061	11,281	24	3	23	...	...	...	1	3

SUPPLEMENTARY TABLE A, PART I.—*Continued.*

	District.	Church of England. Total. Males.	Church of England. Total. Females.	Church of England. Foreign (European, &c) Males.	Church of England. Foreign (European, &c) Females.	Church of England. Eurasian. Males.	Church of England. Eurasian. Females.	Church of England. Native. Males.	Church of England. Native. Females.	Church of Scotland. Total. Males.	Church of Scotland. Total. Females.	Church of Scotland. Foreign (European, &c) Males.	Church of Scotland. Foreign (European, &c) Females.	Church of Scotland. Eurasian. Males.	Church of Scotland. Eurasian. Females.	Church of Scotland. Native. Males.	Church of Scotland. Native. Females.	St. Paul's Church. Total. Males.	St. Paul's Church. Total. Females.	St. Paul's Church. Foreign (European, &c) Males.	St. Paul's Church. Foreign (European, &c) Females.	St. Paul's Church. Eurasian. Males.	St. Paul's Church. Eurasian. Females.	St. Paul's Church. Native. Males.	St. Paul's Church. Native. Females.
		21	22	23	24	25	26	27	28	29	30	31	32	33	34	35	36	37	38	39	40	41	42	43	44
1	Bangalore	**144**	135	**61**	45	**62**	72	**21**	18	...	51	..	20	...	23	...	8	**1**	1	...	...	**1**	1	...	...
2	Kolar	**104**	39	**66**	8	**31**	24	**7**	7	**1**	...	**1**	...	...	...	...	...	...	...	...	...	...	...	...	...
3	Tumkur	**12**	8	**10**	8	**1**	...	**1**	...	...	...	...	...	...	...	...	...	...	...	...	...	...	...	...	...
4	Mysore	**34**	23	**13**	7	**14**	16	**7**	...	...	...	...	...	...	...	...	...	...	...	...	...	...	...	...	...
5	Hassan	**32**	14	**25**	13	**3**	...	**4**	1	**6**	...	**4**	...	**2**	...	...	...	...	...	...	...	...	...	...	...
6	Shimoga	**6**	2	**5**	2	**1**	...	...	...	...	...	...	...	...	...	...	...	...	...	...	...	...	...	...	...
7	Kadur	**129**	63	**42**	21	**28**	23	**59**	10	...	...	...	...	...	...	...	...	...	...	...	...	...	...	...	...
8	Chitaldurg	**18**	2	**6**	2	**12**	...	...	...	...	...	...	...	...	...	...	...	...	...	...	...	...	...	...	...
	Total	*479*	*286*	*228*	*106*	*152*	*135*	*99*	*45*	*7*	*51*	*5*	*20*	*2*	*23*	...	*8*	*1*	*1*	...	...	*1*	*1*	...	...
	The Civil and Military Station, Bangalore	**2,763**	1,838	**2,145**	1,007	**464**	630	**154**	201	**21**	26	**14**	7	**5**	11	**2**	8	...	...	...	...	...	...	...	...
	GRAND TOTAL	**3,242**	**2,124**	**2,373**	**1,113**	**616**	**765**	**253**	**246**	**28**	**77**	**19**	**27**	**7**	**34**	**2**	**16**	**1**	**1**	...	...	**1**	**1**	.	...

SUPPLEMENTARY TABLE A. PART I.—*Continued*

District	Distribution by Sect.																							
	St. James' Church.								Protestant.								Methodist.							
	Total.		Foreign (European, &c.)		Eurasian.		Native.		Total.		Foreign (European, &c.)		Eurasian.		Native.		Total.		Foreign (European, &c.)		Eurasian.		Native.	
	Males.	Females.	Males.	Females.	Males.	Females.	Males.	Females.	Males.	Females.	Males.	Females.	Males.	Females.	Males.	Females.	Males.	Females.	Males.	Females.	Males.	Females.	Males.	Females.
	45	46	47	48	49	50	51	52	53	54	55	56	57	58	59	60	61	62	63	64	65	66	67	68
1 Bangalore	4	2	...	...	...	...	4	2	87	170	3	...	10	43	74	157	32	32	2	...	4	3	26	29
2 Kolar	...	...	...	...	...	...	...	...	113	83	24	6	18	16	71	61	62	23	6	...	8	...	48	23
3 Tumkur	...	...	...	...	...	...	...	...	139	77	4	...	2	2	133	75	...	...	...	...	...	...	...	...
4 Mysore	...	...	...	...	...	...	...	...	128	79	37	27	8	9	83	43	...	...	...	...	...	...	...	...
5 Hassan	...	...	...	...	...	...	...	...	56	45	32	20	1	...	23	25	...	...	...	...	...	...	...	...
6 Shimoga...	...	...	...	...	...	...	...	...	7	2	...	...	...	...	7	2	...	...	...	...	...	...	...	...
7 Kadur	...	...	...	...	...	...	...	...	116	71	27	3	16	33	73	33	...	...	...	...	...	...	...	...
8 Chitaldurg	...	...	...	...	...	...	...	...	17	13	...	...	...	...	17	13	...	...	...	...	...	...	...	...
Total......	4	2	...	...	...	...	4	2	663	540	127	56	55	75	481	409	94	55	8	...	12	3	74	53
The Civil and Military Station, Bangalore......	...	...	...	...	...	...	...	...	44	54	25	20	1	1	18	24	11	17	8	7	2	10	1	...
GRAND TOTAL......	4	2	...	...	...	...	4	2	707	594	152	85	56	76	499	433	105	72	16	7	14	13	75	52

SUPPLEMENTARY TABLE A. PART I.—*Continued.*

District.	Distribution by Sect.																							
	American Methodist.								Baptist.								Wesleyan.							
	Total.		Foreign (European, &c.)		Eurasian.		Native.		Total.		Foreign (European, &c.)		Eurasian.		Native.		Total.		Foreign (European, &c.)		Eurasian.		Native.	
	Males.	Females.	Males.	Females.	Males.	Females.	Males.	Females.	Males.	Females.	Males.	Females.	Males.	Females.	Males.	Females.	Males.	Females.	Males.	Females.	Males.	Females.	Males.	Females.
	69	70	71	72	73	74	75	76	77	78	79	80	81	82	83	84	85	86	87	88	89	90	91	92
1 Bangalore	...	...	...	...	...	...	...	...	7	8	2	3	5	5	...	...	25	11	7	5	10	1	8	5
2 Kolar	27	37	...	...	...	...	27	37	3	...	...	...	...	...	3	...	79	14	53	2	9	2	17	10
3 Tumkur	...	...	...	...	...	...	...	...	...	...	...	...	...	...	...	...	54	54	2	3	...	...	52	51
4 Mysore	...	...	...	...	...	...	...	...	...	...	...	...	...	...	...	...	78	20	1	...	4	3	73	17
5 Hassan	...	...	...	...	...	...	...	...	...	...	...	...	...	...	...	...	5	6	3	1	2	4	...	1
6 Shimoga	...	...	...	...	...	...	...	...	...	...	...	...	...	...	...	...	19	18	7	10	...	...	12	8
7 Kadur	...	...	...	...	...	...	...	...	...	...	...	...	...	...	...	...	3	5	...	...	3	5	...	...
8 Chitaldurg	...	...	...	...	...	...	...	...	...	...	...	...	...	...	...	...	5	...	...	...	...	...	5	...
Total.....	27	37	...	...	...	...	27	37	10	8	2	3	5	5	3	...	268	128	73	21	28	15	167	92
The Civil and Military Station Bangalore.....	...	...	...	...	...	...	...	...	47	64	23	27	13	25	11	12	368	397	186	94	51	101	131	202
GRAND TOTAL.....	27	37	...	...	...	...	27	37	57	72	25	30	18	30	14	12	636	525	259	115	79	116	298	294

SUPPLEMENTARY TABLE A. PART I.—*Continued.*

	District.	Distribution by Sect.																							
		London Mission.								German Mission.								Presbyterian.							
		Total.		Foreign (European &c.)		Eurasian.		Native.		Total.		Foreign (European &c.)		Eurasian.		Native.		Total.		Foreign (European &c.)		Eurasian.		Native.	
		Males.	Females.	Males.	Females.	Males.	Females.	Males.	Females.	Males.	Females.	Males.	Females.	Males.	Females.	Males.	Females.	Males.	Females.	Males.	Females.	Males.	Females.	Males.	Females.
		93	94	95	96	97	98	99	100	101	102	103	104	105	106	107	108	109	110	111	112	113	114	115	116
1	Bangalore	9	11	1	1	6	4	2	6	...	...	...	...	...	...	...	...	8	6	3	2	...	...	5	4
2	Kolar	...	...	...	...	...	...	...	...	...	...	...	...	...	...	...	...	...	...	...	...	...	...	...	...
3	Tumkur	...	...	...	...	...	...	...	...	...	...	...	...	...	...	...	...	...	...	...	...	...	...	...	...
4	Mysore	...	...	...	...	...	...	...	...	...	...	...	...	...	...	...	...	...	2	...	...	...	...	...	2
5	Hassan	...	...	...	...	...	...	...	...	1	...	...	...	...	...	1	...	13	...	8	...	...	...	5	...
6	Shimoga	...	...	...	...	...	...	...	...	...	...	...	...	...	...	...	...	...	...	...	...	...	...	...	...
7	Kadur	...	...	...	...	...	...	...	...	...	...	...	...	...	...	...	...	...	...	...	...	...	...	...	...
8	Chitaldurg	...	...	...	...	...	...	...	...	...	...	...	...	...	...	...	...	...	...	...	...	...	...	...	...
	Total......	*9*	*11*	*1*	*1*	*6*	*4*	*2*	*6*	*1*	...	...	...	...	...	*1*	...	*21*	*8*	*11*	*2*	...	...	*10*	*6*
	The Civil and Military Station, Bangalore......	...	...	...	...	...	...	...	...	...	...	...	...	...	...	...	...	212	86	183	52	21	25	8	9
	GRAND TOTAL......	9	11	1	1	6	4	2	6	1	...	...	...	...	...	1	...	233	94	194	54	21	25	18	15

SUPPLEMENTARY TABLE A. Christians by Sects.

SUPPLEMENTARY TABLE A. PART I.—*Continued.*

District.	Distribution by Sect.																							
	Congregationalist.								Lutheran.								Episcopalian.							
	Total.		Foreign (European &c.)		Eurasian.		Native.		Total.		Foreign (European &c.)		Eurasian.		Native.		Total.		Foreign (European &c.)		Eurasian.		Native.	
	Males.	Females.	Males.	Females.	Males.	Females.	Males.	Females.	Males.	Females.	Males.	Females.	Males.	Females.	Males.	Females.	Males.	Females.	Males.	Females.	Males.	Females.	Males.	Females.
	117	118	119	120	121	122	123	124	125	126	127	128	129	130	131	132	133	134	135	136	137	138	139	140
1 Bangalore	32	42	...	...	...	...	32	42	33	1	7	...	25	...	1	1	...	...	...	...	...	...	...	...
2 Kolar	...	...	...	...	...	...	...	...	1	...	1	...	...	...	...	...	79	112	7	4	6	4	66	104
3 Tumkur	...	...	...	...	...	...	...	...	...	...	...	...	...	...	...	...	...	...	...	...	...	...	...	...
4 Mysore	...	...	...	...	...	...	...	...	...	...	...	...	...	...	...	...	...	...	...	...	...	...	...	...
5 Hassan	...	...	...	...	...	...	...	...	...	...	...	...	...	...	...	...	5	3	...	...	...	...	5	3
6 Shimoga	...	...	...	...	...	...	...	...	...	...	...	...	...	...	...	...	...	...	...	...	...	...	...	...
7 Kadur	...	...	...	...	...	...	...	...	...	...	...	...	...	...	...	...	...	...	...	...	...	...	...	...
8 Chitaldurg	...	...	...	...	...	...	...	...	...	...	...	...	...	...	...	...	...	...	...	...	...	...	...	...
Total......	*32*	*42*	...	...	...	...	*32*	*42*	*34*	*1*	*8*	...	*25*	...	*1*	*1*	*84*	*115*	*7*	*4*	*6*	*4*	*71*	*107*
The Civil and Military Station, Bangalore......	32	45	2	6	3	2	27	37	60	71	1	5	12	2	47	64	57	63	36	41	14	19	7	3
GRAND TOTAL......	64	87	2	6	3	2	59	79	94	72	9	5	37	2	48	65	141	178	43	45	20	23	78	110

SUPPLEMENTARY TABLE A. PART 1.—*Continued.*

	District.	Distribution by Sect.																							
		Unsectarian.								Non-Conformist.								Plymouth brethren.							
		Total.		Foreign (European &c.)		Eurasian.		Native.		Total.		Foreign (European &c.)		Eurasian.		Native.		Total.		Foreign (European &c.)		Eurasian.		Native.	
		Males.	Females.	Males.	Females.	Males.	Females.	Males.	Females.	Males.	Females.	Males.	Females.	Males.	Females.	Males.	Females.	Males.	Females.	Males.	Females.	Males.	Females.	Males.	Females.
		141	142	143	144	145	146	147	148	149	150	151	152	153	154	155	156	157	158	159	160	161	162	163	164
1	Bangalore	1	9	1	3	...	6	...	...	...	...	...	...	...	...	...	...	...	...	...	...	...	...	...	...
2	Kolar	2	...	2	...	...	...	...	...	...	...	...	...	...	...	...	...	...	...	...	...	...	...	...	...
3	Tumkur...	...	...	...	...	...	...	...	...	...	...	...	...	...	...	...	...	...	...	...	...	...	...	...	...
4	Mysore	...	...	...	...	...	...	...	...	...	...	...	...	...	...	...	...	...	...	...	...	...	...	...	...
5	Hassan	3	...	1	...	...	...	2	...	...	...	...	...	...	...	...	...	...	...	...	...	...	...	...	...
6	Shimoga...	...	...	...	...	...	...	...	...	...	...	...	...	...	...	...	...	...	...	...	...	...	...	...	...
7	Kadur	...	...	...	...	...	...	...	...	...	...	...	...	...	...	...	...	...	...	...	...	...	...	...	...
8	Chitaldurg	...	...	...	...	...	...	...	...	...	...	...	...	...	...	...	...	...	...	...	...	...	...	...	...
	Total......	6	9	4	3	...	6	2	...	...	...	...	...	...	...	...	...	...	...	...	...	...	...	...	...
	Civil and Military Station, Bangalore......	37	54	26	39	9	15	2	...	10	16	2	2	...	...	8	14	1	1	1	1	...	...	...	...
	GRAND TOTAL......	43	63	30	42	9	21	4	...	10	16	2	2	...	...	8	14	1	1	1	1	...	...	...	...

SUPPLEMENTARY TABLE A. PART I.—*Continued.*

District.	Distribution by Sect.																							
	Open Brethren.								Theist.								Salvationis to.							
	Total.		Foreign (European &c.)		Eurasian.		Native.		Total.		Foreign (European &c.)		Eurasian.		Native.		Total.		Foreign (European &c.)		Eurasian.		Native.	
	Males.	Females.	Males.	Females.	Males.	Females.	Males.	Females.	Males.	Females.	Males.	Females.	Males.	Females.	Males.	Females.	Males.	Females.	Males.	Females.	Males.	Females.	Males.	Females.
	165	166	167	168	169	170	171	172	173	174	175	176	177	178	179	180	181	182	183	184	185	186	187	188
1 Bangalore	...	...	...	...	...	...	...	...	...	...	...	...	...	...	...	...	...	...	...	...	...	...	...	...
2 Kolar	...	...	...	...	...	...	...	...	...	...	...	...	...	...	...	...	...	...	...	...	...	...	...	...
3 Tumkur	...	...	...	...	...	...	...	...	...	...	...	...	...	...	...	...	...	...	...	...	...	...	...	...
4 Mysore	...	...	...	...	...	...	...	...	...	...	...	...	...	...	...	...	...	...	...	...	...	...	...	...
5 Hassan	...	...	...	...	...	...	...	...	...	...	...	...	...	...	...	...	...	...	...	...	...	...	...	...
6 Shimoga	...	...	...	...	...	...	...	...	...	...	...	...	...	...	...	...	...	...	...	...	...	...	...	...
7 Kadur	...	...	...	...	...	...	...	...	...	...	...	...	...	...	...	...	...	...	...	...	...	...	...	...
8 Chitaldurg	...	...	...	...	...	...	...	...	...	...	...	...	...	...	...	...	...	...	...	...	...	...	...	...
Total...	...	...	...	...	...	...	...	...	...	...	...	...	...	...	...	...	...	...	...	...	...	...	...	...
The Civil and Military Station, Bangalore......	...	1	...	1	...	...	...	...	1	...	1	...	...	...	...	...	2	4	2	4	...	...	...	...
GRAND TOTAL......	...	1	...	1	...	...	...	...	1	...	1	...	...	...	...	...	2	4	2	4	...	...	...	...

SUPPLEMENTARY TABLE A. PART I.—*Continued.*

District.	Distribution by Sect.															
	Others.								Not stated.							
	Total.		Foreign (European &c.)		Eurasian.		Native.		Total.		Foreign (European &c.)		Eurasian.		Native.	
	Males.	Females.	Males.	Females.	Males.	Females.	Males.	Females.	Males.	Females.	Males.	Females.	Males.	Females.	Males.	Females.
	189	190	191	192	193	194	195	196	197	198	199	200	201	202	203	204
1 Bangalore	...	...	...	...	...	...	...	...	424	409	35	53	27	20	362	336
2 Kolar	...	...	...	...	...	...	...	...	81	68	1	5	1	9	79	54
3 Tumkur	...	...	...	...	...	...	...	...	85	64	...	...	...	...	85	64
4 Mysore	...	...	...	...	...	...	...	...	159	151	7	12	22	16	130	123
5 Hassan	...	...	...	...	...	...	...	...	252	251	4	1	...	...	248	250
6 Shimoga...	...	...	...	...	...	...	...	...	17	6	...	...	...	...	17	6
7 Kadur	...	...	...	...	...	...	...	...	61	22	9	2	5	4	47	16
8 Chitaldurg	...	...	...	...	...	...	...	...	28	24	...	...	8	10	20	14
Total......	...	...	...	...	...	...	...	...	1,107	995	56	73	63	59	988	863
The Civil and Military Station, Bangalore......	...	1	...	...	...	...	...	1	26	24	17	16	6	5	3	3
GRAND TOTAL......	...	1	...	...	...	...	...	1	1,133	1,019	73	89	69	64	991	866

SUPPLEMENTARY TABLE A.

PART II.

CHRISTIANS BY RACE.

SUPPLEMENTARY TABLE A.

Christians by Race.

SUPPLEMENTARY TABLE A.

Christians by Race.

PART II.

Race.

	District.	Total Christians.			Distribution by Race. — Foreign (Europeans, &c.)																
					Total.			Roman Catholic.		Greek Church.		Church of England.		Church of Scotland.		Protestant.		Unsectarian.		Baptist.	
		Total.	Males.	Females.	Total.	Males.	Females.	Males.	Females.	Males.	Females.	Males.	Females.	Males.	Females.	Males.	Females.	Males.	Females.	Males.	Females.
	1	2	3	4	5	6	7	8	9	10	11	12	13	14	15	16	17	18	19	20	21
1	Bangalore	6,107	3,141	2,966	302	145	157	23	35	...	...	61	45	...	20	3	...	1	3	2	3
2	Kolar	2,996	1,712	1,284	302	264	38	80	13	23	...	66	8	1	...	24	6	2	...	...	...
3	Tumkur	713	401	312	27	16	11	...	...	...	...	10	8	...	...	4	...	...	...	...	...
4	Mysore	2,947	1,471	1,476	230	72	158	14	112	...	...	13	7	...	...	37	27	...	...	...	...
5	Hassan	3,296	1,710	1,586	132	97	35	20	...	...	...	25	13	4	...	32	20	1	...	...	...
6	Shimoga	1,651	1,034	617	32	17	15	5	3	...	...	5	2	...	...	...	...	...	...	...	...
7	Kadur	2,209	1,556	653	207	147	60	69	34	...	...	42	21	...	...	27	3	...	...	...	...
8	Chitaldurg	284	166	118	17	15	2	9	...	...	...	6	2	...	...	...	...	...	...	...	...
	Total......	20,233	11,101	9,042	1,249	773	476	220	187	23	...	228	106	5	20	127	56	4	3	2	3
	The Civil and Military Station, Bangalore......	17,902	9.115	8,787	5,022	3,273	1,749	601	411	...	..	2,145	1,007	14	7	25	29	26	39	23	27
	GRAND TOTAL......	38,135	20,306	17,829	6,271	4,046	2,225	821	598	23	...	2,373	1,113	19	27	152	85	30	42	25	30

SUPPLEMENTARY TABLE A. PART II—*Continued.*

	District.	Distribution by Race.																								
		Foreign (Europeans &c.)																								
		Wesleyan.		London Mission.		Presbyterian.		Lutheran.		Episcopalian.		Methodist.		Nonconformist.		Congregationalist.		Plymouth Brethren.		Open Brethren.		Theist.		Salvationist.		Not stated.	
		Males.	Females.	Males.	Females.	Males.	Females.	Males.	Females.	Males.	Females.	Males.	Females.	Males.	Females.	Males.	Females.	Males.	Females.	Males.	Females.	Males.	Females.	Males.	Females.	Males.	Females.
		22	23	24	25	26	27	28	29	30	31	32	33	34	35	36	37	38	39	40	41	42	43	44	45	46	
1	Bangalore	7	5	1	1	3	2	7	...	...	...	2	...	...	...	...	...	...	...	...	...	...	...	...	...	35	53
2	Kolar	53	2	...	...	...	...	1	...	7	4	6	...	...	...	...	...	...	...	...	...	...	...	...	...	1	5
3	Tumkur	2	3	...	...	...	...	...	...	...	...	...	...	...	...	...	...	...	...	...	...	...	...	...	...	...	...
4	Mysore	1	...	...	...	...	...	...	...	...	...	...	...	...	...	...	...	...	...	...	...	...	...	...	...	7	12
5	Hassan	3	1	...	...	8	...	...	...	...	...	...	...	...	...	...	...	...	...	...	...	...	...	...	...	4	1
6	Shimoga	7	10	...	...	...	...	...	...	...	...	...	...	...	...	...	...	...	...	...	...	...	...	...	...	...	...
7	Kadur	...	...	...	...	...	...	...	...	...	...	...	...	...	...	...	...	...	...	...	...	...	...	...	...	9	...
8	Chitaldurg	...	...	...	...	...	...	...	...	...	...	...	...	...	...	...	...	...	...	...	...	...	...	...	...	...	...
	Total......	73	21	1	1	11	2	8	...	7	4	8	...	...	...	...	...	...	...	...	...	...	...	...	...	56	73
	The Civil and Military Station, Bangalore......	186	94	...	...	183	52	1	5	36	41	8	7	2	2	2	6	1	1	...	1	1	...	2	4	17	16
	GRAND TOTAL......	259	115	1	1	194	54	9	5	43	45	16	7	2	2	2	6	1	1	...	1	1	...	2	4	73	89

SUPPLEMENTARY TABLE A. PART II.—*Continued.*

	District.	Total.			Distribution by Race. Eurasians											
					Roman Catholic.		Church of England.		Church of Scotland.		Saint Pauls' Church.		Protestant.		Methodist.	
		Total.	Males.	Females.	Males.	Females.	Males.	Females.	Males.	Females.	Males.	Females.	Males.	Females.	Males.	Females.
		47	48	49	50	51	52	53	54	55	56	57	58	59	60	61
1	Bangalore	401	199	202	49	54	62	72	...	23	1	1	10	13	4	3
2	Kolar	276	161	115	88	60	31	24	...	...	...	...	18	16	8	...
3	Tumkur	17	8	9	5	7	1	...	...	...	...	...	2	2	...	...
4	Mysore	208	118	90	70	46	14	16	...	...	...	...	8	9	...	...
5	Hassan	97	49	48	41	44	3	...	2	...	...	...	1	...	...	...
6	Shimoga	16	14	2	13	2	1	...	...	...	...	...	...	...	...	...
7	Kadur	229	134	95	82	28	28	23	...	...	...	...	16	35	...	...
8	Chitaldurg	38	23	15	3	5	12	...	...	...	...	...	...	...	...	...
	Total......	1,282	706	576	351	246	152	135	2	23	1	1	55	75	12	3
	The Civil and Military Station, Bangalore......	2,607	1,111	1,496	510	650	464	630	5	11	...	...	1	1	2	10
	GRAND TOTAL......	3,889	1,817	2,072	861	896	616	765	7	34	1	1	56	76	14	13

SUPPLEMENTARY TABLE A.—PART II.—*Continued.*

	District.	Distribution by Race. — Eurasians. — Baptist. Males.	Baptist. Females.	Wesleyan. Males.	Wesleyan. Females.	London Mission. Males.	London Mission. Females.	Lutheran. Males.	Lutheran. Females.	Episcopalian. Males.	Episcopalian. Females.	Unsectarian. Males.	Unsectarian. Females.	Presbyterian. Males.	Presbyterian. Females.	Congregationalist. Males.	Congregationalist. Females.	Not Stated. Males.	Not Stated. Females.
		62	63	64	65	66	67	68	69	70	71	72	73	74	75	76	77	78	79
1	Bangalore	5	5	10	1	6	4	25	...	...	...	...	6	...	...	...	...	27	20
2	Kolar	...	...	9	2	...	...	...	...	6	4	...	...	...	...	...	...	1	9
3	Tumkur	...	...	...	...	...	...	...	...	...	...	...	...	...	...	...	...	...	...
4	Mysore	...	...	4	3	...	...	...	...	...	...	...	...	...	...	...	...	22	16
5	Hassan	...	...	2	4	...	...	...	...	...	...	...	...	...	...	...	...	...	...
6	Shimoga	...	...	...	...	...	...	...	...	...	...	...	...	...	...	...	...	...	...
7	Kadur	...	...	3	5	...	...	...	...	...	...	...	...	...	...	...	...	5	4
8	Chitaldurg	...	...	...	...	...	...	...	...	...	...	...	...	...	...	...	...	8	10
	Total......	5	5	23	15	6	4	25	...	6	4	...	6	...	...	...	...	63	59
	The Civil and Military Station, Bangalore......	13	25	51	101	...	...	12	2	14	19	9	15	21	25	3	2	6	5
	GRAND TOTAL......	18	30	79	116	6	4	37	2	20	23	9	21	21	25	3	2	69	64

SUPPLEMENTARY TABLE A. PART II.—*Continued.*

	District.	Total.			Distribution by Race. Native Christians. Roman Catholic.		Church of England.		Church of Scotland.		Saint James' Church.		Protestant.		Methodist.		American Methodist.		Baptist.		Wesleyan.	
		Total.	Males.	Females.	Males.	Females.	Males.	Females.	Males.	Females.	Males.	Females.	Males.	Females.	Males.	Females.	Males.	Females.	Males.	Females.	Males.	Females.
		80	81	82	83	84	85	86	87	88	89	90	91	92	93	94	95	96	97	98	99	100
1	Bangalore	5,404	2,797	2,607	2,262	1,999	21	18	...	8	4	2	74	157	26	29	...	...	...	...	8	5
2	Kolar	2,418	1,287	1,131	969	835	7	7	...	...	...	...	71	61	48	23	27	37	3	...	17	10
3	Tumkur	690	377	332	106	132	1	...	...	...	...	...	133	75	...	...	...	...	...	...	52	51
4	Mysore	2,509	1,281	1,228	989	1,043	7	...	...	...	...	...	83	43	...	...	...	...	...	...	73	17
5	Hassan	3,067	1,564	1,503	1,276	1,223	4	1	...	...	...	...	23	25	...	...	...	...	...	...	...	1
6	Shimoga...	1,603	1,003	600	967	584	...	...	...	...	...	...	7	2	...	...	...	...	...	...	12	8
7	Kadur	1,773	1,275	498	1,096	430	59	19	...	...	...	...	73	33	...	...	...	...	...	...	...	...
8	Chitaldurg	290	128	101	86	74	...	...	...	...	...	...	17	13	...	...	...	...	...	...	5	...
	Total......	17,702	9,712	7,990	7,750	6,320	99	45	...	8	4	2	481	409	74	52	27	37	3	...	167	92
	The Civil and Military Station, Bangalore......	10,273	4,731	5,542	4,311	4,961	154	201	2	8	...	...	18	24	1	...	...	...	11	12	131	202
	GRAND TOTAL...	27,975	14,443	13,532	12,061	11,281	253	246	2	16	4	2	499	433	75	52	27	37	14	12	298	294

SUPPLEMENTARY TABLE A. PART II.—*Concluded.*

	District.	Distribution by Race.																					
		Native Christians.																					
		London Mission.		German Mission.		Presbyterian.		Congregationalist.		Lutheran.		Episcopalian.		Unsectarian.		Nonconformist.		Greek Church.		Heathen.		Not stated.	
		Males.	Females.	Males.	Females.	Males.	Females.	Males.	Females.	Males.	Females.	Males.	Females.	Males.	Females.	Males.	Females.	Males.	Females.	Males.	Females.	Males.	Females.
		101	102	103	104	105	106	107	108	109	110	111	112	113	114	115	116	117	118	119	120	121	122
1	Bangalore	2	6	...	...	5	4	32	42	1	1	...	...	...	...	...	...	...	...	...	...	362	336
2	Kolar	...	...	...	...	...	...	...	...	...	...	66	104	...	...	...	...	...	...	...	...	79	54
3	Tumkur	...	...	...	...	...	...	...	...	...	...	...	...	...	...	...	...	...	...	...	...	85	64
4	Mysore	...	...	...	...	...	2	...	...	...	...	...	...	...	...	...	...	...	...	...	...	130	123
5	Hassan	...	...	1	...	5	...	...	...	...	...	5	3	2	...	...	...	...	...	...	...	248	250
6	Shimoga	...	...	...	...	...	...	...	...	...	...	...	...	...	...	...	...	...	...	...	...	17	6
7	Kadur	...	...	...	...	...	...	...	...	...	...	...	...	...	...	...	...	...	...	...	...	47	16
8	Chitaldurg	...	...	...	...	...	...	...	...	...	...	...	...	...	...	...	...	...	...	...	...	20	14
	Total.....	*2*	*6*	*1*	...	*10*	*6*	*32*	*42*	*1*	*1*	*71*	*107*	*2*	...	...	...	...	...	...	...	*988*	*863*
	The Civil and Military Station Bangalore.....	...	...	...	...	8	9	27	37	47	64	7	3	2	...	8	14	1	3	...	1	3	3
	Grand Total.....	**2**	**6**	**1**	...	**18**	**15**	**59**	**79**	**48**	**65**	**78**	**110**	**4**	...	**8**	**14**	**1**	**3**	...	**1**	**991**	**866**

SUPPLEMENTARY TABLE B.

CHRISTIANS BY RACE AND AGE.

PART I.—BY DISTRICTS.

PART II.—BY TOWNS.

SUPPLEMENTARY TABLE B.
Christians by Race and Age.

PART I.

BY DISTRICTS

	District.	Total.			Non-Asiatics (Europeans, &c.)													
					All ages.			0–14.		15–34		35–49.		50 and over.		Age not stated.	
		Total.	Males.	Females.	Total.	Males.	Females.	Males.	Females.	Males.	Females.	Males.	Females.	Males.	Females.	Males.	Females.
	1	2	3	4	5	6	7	8	9	10	11	12	13	14	15	16	17
1	Bangalore	703	344	359	209	143	158	46	42	36	53	31	50	30	11	...	...
2	Kolar	578	425	153	302	264	38	41	6	128	19	74	10	21	3	...	...
3	Tumkur	44	24	20	27	16	11	8	4	4	5	4	2	...	..	...	...
4	Mysore...	438	190	248	230	72	158	26	67	20	58	16	31	10	2	...	...
5	Hassan	229	146	83	132	97	35	12	7	34	13	27	11	24	4	...	...
6	Shimoga	48	31	17	32	17	15	4	4	7	7	4	3	2	1	...	...
7	Kadur...	436	281	155	207	147	60	43	19	66	19	28	15	10	7	...	..
8	Chitaldurg	55	38	17	17	15	2	1	...	11	2	3	...	...	..	...	...
	Total......	2,531	1,479	1,052	1,240	771	475	181	149	306	176	187	122	97	28	...	...
	The Bangalore Civil Station	5,032	2,166	2,866	2,528	1,119	1,409	469	446	291	533	156	221	199	201	4	8
	" Military Do	2,597	2,218	379	2,488	2,151	337	300	161	1,779	147	69	24	2	5	1	...
	GRAND TOTAL......	10,160	5,863	4,297	6,262	4,041	2,221	950	756	2,376	856	412	367	298	234	5	8

SUPPLEMENTARY TABLE B. PART I.—*Continued.*

	District.	Eurasians.													Armenians.				
		All ages.			0—14		15—34.		35—49.		50 and over.		Age not stated.		All ages.			0—14.	
		Total.	Males.	Females.	Males.	Females.	Males.	Females.	Males.	Females.	Males.	Females.	Males.	Females.	Total.	Males.	Females.	Males.	Females.
		18	19	20	21	22	23	24	25	26	27	28	29	30	31	32	33	34	35
1	Bangalore	401	199	202	74	69	55	80	38	28	32	25	...	...	3	2	1	...	...
2	Kolar	276	161	115	47	54	65	43	20	10	29	8	...	...	...	...	...	...	...
3	Tumkur	17	8	9	2	2	3	5	2	1	1	1	...	...	...	...	...	...	...
4	Mysore	208	118	90	30	27	36	25	31	24	21	14	...	...	...	...	...	...	...
5	Hassan...	97	49	48	16	20	22	17	6	3	5	8	...	...	...	...	...	...	...
6	Shimoga	16	14	2	3	...	1	2	7	...	3	...	...	...	...	...	...	...	...
7	Kadur...	229	134	95	40	20	52	45	21	21	21	9	...	...	...	...	...	...	...
8	Chitaldurg	38	23	15	5	10	14	4	3	1	1	...	...	...	...	...	...	...	...
	Total...	1,282	706	576	217	202	248	221	128	88	113	65	...	...	3	2	1	...	...
	The Bangalore Civil Station.....	2,498	1,044	1,454	507	618	299	479	138	177	100	180	...	...	5	2	3	1	1
	" Military Do	109	67	42	19	14	34	22	4	4	10	2	...	...	...	...	...	...	...
	GRAND TOTAL.....	3,889	1,817	2,072	743	834	581	722	270	269	223	247	...	...	8	4	4	1	1

SUPPLEMENTARY TABLE B. PART I.—*Concluded.*

	District.	Armenians.—(*Continued*). 15—34.		35—49.		50 and over.		Age not stated.		Israelites. All ages.			0—14.		15—34.		35—49.		50 and over.		Age not stated.	
		Males.	Females.	Males.	Females.	Males.	Females.	Males.	Females.	Total.	Males.	Females.	Males.	Females.	Males.	Females.	Males.	Females.	Males.	Females.	Males.	Females.
		36	37	38	39	40	41	42	43	44	45	46	47	48	49	50	51	52	53	54	55	56
1	Bangalore	...	...	2	1	...	...	...	...	...	...	...	...	...	...	...	...	...	...	...	...	...
2	Kolar	...	...	...	...	...	...	...	...	...	...	...	...	...	...	...	...	...	...	...	...	...
3	Tumkur	...	...	...	...	...	...	...	...	...	...	...	...	...	...	...	...	...	...	...	...	...
4	Mysore	...	...	...	...	...	...	...	...	...	...	...	...	...	...	...	...	...	...	...	...	...
5	Hassan	...	...	...	...	...	...	...	...	...	...	...	...	...	...	...	...	...	...	...	...	...
6	Shimoga	...	...	...	...	...	...	...	...	...	...	...	...	...	...	...	...	...	...	...	...	...
7	Kadur	...	...	...	...	...	...	...	...	...	...	...	...	...	...	...	...	...	...	...	...	...
8	Chitaldurg	...	...	...	...	...	...	...	...	...	...	...	...	...	...	...	...	...	...	...	...	...
	Total......	...	...	2	1	...	...	...	...	...	...	...	...	...	...	...	...	...	...	...	...	...
	The Bangalore Civil Station......	...	...	1	2	...	...	...	...	1	1	...	...	...	1	...	...	...	...	...	...	...
	" Military Do	...	...	...	...	...	...	...	...	...	...	...	...	...	...	...	...	...	...	...	...	...
	GRAND TOTAL......	...	...	3	3	...	...	...	...	1	1	...	...	...	1	...	...	...	...	...	...	...

District.	Towns.	Total.			Non-Asiatics.						
					All Ages.			0—14.		15—34.	
		Total.	Males.	Females.	Total.	Males.	Females.	Males.	Females.	Males.	Females.
1	2	3	4	5	6	7	8	9	10	11	12
Bangalore	Bangalore City ...	491	220	265	211	93	118	39	36	20	41
	Devanhalli ...	2	2	...	...	...	...	...	...	...	...
	Yelahanka ...	2	2	...	1	1	...	...	...	...	...
Kolar	Kolar ...	32	20	12	12	8	4	2	2	3	1
Tumkur	Tumkur ...	23	13	10	23	13	10	8	4	2	4
	Maddagiri ...	4	2	2	...	...	...	...	...	...	...
	Chiknayakanhalli ...	4	3	1	4	3	1	...	...	2	1
	Gubbi ...	12	5	7	...	...	...	...	...	...	...
	Kunigal ...	1	1	...	...	...	...	...	...	...	...
Mysore	Mysore ...	324	129	195	194	53	141	18	64	17	50
	Seringapatam ...	13	4	9	13	4	9	4	1	...	5
	Hunsur ...	23	12	11	3	1	2	...	...	...	1
	Gundlupet ...	8	1	7	...	...	...	...	...	...	...
	Nanjangud ...	13	4	9	4	3	1	1	...	2	1
	Krishnarajpete ...	17	12	5	...	...	...	...	...	...	...
	Malavalli ...	5	1	4	...	...	...	...	...	...	...
Hassan	Hassan ...	20	14	6	20	14	6	...	...	3	1
	Belur ...	6	2	4	...	...	...	...	...	...	...
	Arsikere ...	3	2	1	...	...	...	...	...	...	...
Shimoga	Shimoga ...	23	11	12	17	7	10	4	2	2	6
	Chennagiri ...	1	1	...	1	1	...	...	...	...	...
	Shikarpur ...	2	2	...	...	...	...	...	...	...	...
	Sagar ...	1	1	...	...	...	...	...	...	...	...
Kadur	Chikmagalur ...	146	93	53	44	39	5	10	2	23	1
	Tarikere ...	11	5	6	...	...	...	...	...	...	...
	Kadur ...	8	4	4	...	...	...	...	...	...	...
	Yedahalli ...	1	1	...	...	...	...	...	...	...	...
Chitaldurg	Chitaldurg ...	18	13	5	7	7	...	...	...	6	...
	Challakere ...	1	...	1	...	...	...	...	...	...	...
	Davangere ...	21	19	2	9	7	2	1	...	4	2
	Total of Towns	1,239	608	631	563	254	309	87	111	84	114
	" Rural	1,292	871	421	683	517	166	94	38	222	62
	Total.....	2,531	1,479	1,052	1,246	771	475	181	149	306	176
	The Bangalore Civil Station...	5,032	2,166	2,866	2,528	1,119	1,409	469	446	291	333
	" Military Station...	2,597	2,218	379	2,488	2,151	337	300	161	1,779	147
	GRAND TOTAL.....	10,160	5,863	4,297	6,262	4,041	2,221	950	756	2,376	856

TABLE B.
and Age.
BY TOWNS·

(Europeans, &c.)						Eurasians.												
35—49.		50 and over.		Age not Stated.		All ages.			0—14.		15—34.		35—49.		50 and over.		Age not stated.	
Males.	Females.	Males.	Females.	Males.	Females.	Total.	Males.	Females.	Males.	Females.	Males.	Females.	Males.	Females.	Males.	Females.	Males.	Females.
13	14	15	16	17	18	19	20	21	22	23	24	25	26	27	28	29	30	31
21	31	13	10	...	...	280	134	146	43	45	42	60	27	23	22	18	...	...
...	...	...	...	...	...	2	2	...	...	...	2	...	...	...	...	...	...	...
...	...	1	...	...	...	1	1	...	...	...	...	...	1	...	...	...	...	...
2	1	1	...	...	...	20	12	8	4	2	6	5	2	1	...	...	...	...
3	2	...	...	...	...	...	...	...	...	...	...	...	...	...	...	...	...	...
...	...	...	...	...	...	4	2	2	1	...	...	2	...	...	1	...	...	...
1	...	...	...	...	...	...	...	...	...	...	...	...	...	...	...	...	...	...
...	...	...	...	...	...	12	5	7	1	2	3	3	1	1	...	1	...	...
...	...	...	...	...	...	1	1	...	...	...	...	...	1	...	...	...	...	...
10	25	8	2	...	...	130	78	54	18	13	26	15	16	14	16	12	...	...
...	3	...	...	...	...	...	...	...	...	...	...	...	...	...	...	...	...	...
1	1	...	...	...	...	20	11	9	6	4	3	3	2	2	...	...	...	...
...	...	...	...	...	...	8	1	7	...	3	...	...	1	4	...	...	...	...
...	...	...	...	...	...	9	1	8	...	3	...	2	1	2	...	1	...	...
...	...	...	...	...	...	17	12	5	2	1	1	2	4	1	5	1	...	...
...	...	...	...	...	...	5	1	4	...	1	...	2	1	1	...	...	...	...
8	4	3	1	...	...	...	...	...	...	...	...	...	...	...	...	...	...	...
...	...	...	...	...	...	6	2	4	...	3	...	1	1	...	1	...	...	...
...	...	...	...	...	...	3	2	1	1	...	...	1	1	...	...	...	...	...
1	2	...	...	...	...	6	4	2	2	...	...	2	2	...	...	...	...	...
1	...	...	...	...	...	...	...	...	...	...	...	...	...	...	...	...	...	...
..	...	...	...	...	...	2	2	...	...	...	...	...	...	...	2	...	...	...
...	...	...	...	...	...	1	1	...	...	...	...	...	1	...	...	...	...	...
6	2	...	...	...	...	102	54	48	22	6	17	29	15	11	...	2	...	...
...	...	...	...	...	...	11	5	6	...	1	5	3	...	...	...	2	...	...
...	...	...	...	...	...	8	4	4	1	2	3	1	...	1	...	...	...	...
...	...	...	...	...	...	1	1	...	...	...	1	...	...	...	...	...	...	...
1	...	...	...	...	...	11	6	5	3	2	2	2	...	1	1	...	...	...
...	...	...	...	...	...	1	...	1	...	...	...	1	...	...	...	...	...	...
2	...	...	...	...	...	12	12	...	...	...	11	...	1	...	...	...	...	...
57	71	26	13	...	...	673	352	321	104	88	122	134	78	62	48	37	...	...
130	51	71	15	...	...	609	354	255	113	114	126	87	50	26	65	26	..	...
187	122	97	28	...	...	1,282	706	576	217	202	248	221	128	88	113	65	...	...
156	221	199	201	4	8	2,498	1,044	1,454	507	618	299	470	138	177	100	180	...	...
69	24	2	5	1	...	109	67	42	19	14	34	22	4	4	10	2	...	...
412	367	298	234	5	8	3,889	1,817	2,072	743	834	581	722	270	269	223	247	...	...

District.	Towns.	Armenians.												
		All ages.			0—14.		15—34.		35—49.		50 and over.		Age not Stated.	
		Total.	Males.	Females.	Males.	Females.	Males.	Females.	Males.	Females.	Males.	Females.	Males.	Females.
		32	33	34	35	36	37	38	39	40	41	42	43	44
Bangalore	Bangalore City ...	3	2	1	...	...	...	...	2	1	...	...	...	...
	Devanhalli ...	...	...	...	...	...	...	...	...	...	...	...	...	...
	Yelahanka ...	...	...	...	...	...	...	...	...	...	...	...	...	...
Kolar	Kolar ...	...	...	...	...	...	...	...	...	...	...	...	...	...
Tumkur	Tumkur ...	...	...	...	...	...	...	...	...	...	...	...	...	...
	Maddagiri ...	...	...	...	...	...	...	...	...	...	...	...	...	...
	Chiknayakanhalli	...	...	...	...	...	...	...	...	...	...	...	...	...
	Gubbi ...	...	...	...	...	...	...	...	...	...	...	...	...	...
	Kunigal ...	...	...	...	...	...	...	...	...	...	...	...	...	...
Mysore	Mysore ...	...	...	...	...	...	...	...	...	...	...	...	...	...
	Seringapatam	...	...	...	...	...	...	...	...	...	...	...	...	...
	Hunsur ...	...	...	...	...	...	...	...	...	...	...	...	...	...
	Gundlupet ...	...	...	...	...	...	...	...	...	...	...	...	...	...
	Nanjangud ...	...	...	...	...	...	...	...	...	...	...	...	...	...
	Krishnarajpete	...	...	...	...	...	...	...	...	...	...	...	...	...
	Malavalli ...	...	...	...	...	...	...	...	...	...	...	...	...	...
Hassan	Hassan ...	...	...	...	...	...	...	...	...	...	...	...	...	...
	Belur ...	...	...	...	...	...	...	...	...	...	...	...	...	...
	Arisikere ...	...	...	...	...	...	...	...	...	...	...	...	...	...
Shimoga	Shimoga ...	...	...	...	...	...	...	...	...	...	...	...	...	...
	Channagiri ...	...	...	...	...	...	...	...	...	...	...	...	...	...
	Shikarpur ...	...	...	...	...	...	...	...	...	...	...	...	...	...
	Sagar ...	...	...	...	...	...	...	...	...	...	...	...	...	...
Kadur	Chikmagalur	...	...	...	...	...	...	...	...	...	...	...	...	...
	Tarikere ...	...	...	...	...	...	...	...	...	...	...	...	...	...
	Kadur ...	...	...	...	...	...	...	...	...	...	...	...	...	...
	Yedahalli ...	...	...	...	...	...	...	...	...	...	...	...	...	...
Chitaldurg	Chitaldurg ...	...	[illegible]	...	...	...	...	...	...	...	...	...	...	...
	Challakere ...	...	[illegible]	...	...	...	...	...	...	...	...	...	...	...
	Davangere ...	...	...	...	...	...	...	...	...	...	...	...	...	...
	Total of Towns...	3	2	1	...	...	...	...	2	1	...	...	...	...
	" Rural...	...	...	...	...	...	...	...	...	...	...	...	...	...
	Total...	3	2	1	...	...	...	...	2	1	...	...	...	...
	The Bangalore Civil Station.	5	2	3	1	1	...	...	1	2	...	...	...	...
	" Military Station...	...	...	...	...	...	...	...	...	...	...	...	...	...
	GRAND TOTAL...	8	4	4	1	1	...	...	3	3	...	...	...	...

Israelites.

All ages.			0—14.		15—34.		35—49.		50 and over		Age not Stated.	
Total.	Males.	Females.	Males.	Females.	Males.	Females.	Males.	Females.	Males.	Females.	Males.	Females.
45	46	47	48	49	50	51	52	53	54	55	56	57
...	...	...	...	...	...	...	...	...	...	...	...	...
...	...	...	...	...	...	...	...	...	...	...	...	...
...	...	...	...	...	...	...	...	...	...	...	...	...
...	...	...	...	...	...	...	...	...	...	...	...	...
...	...	...	...	...	...	...	...	...	...	...	...	...
...	...	...	...	...	...	...	...	...	...	...	...	...
...	...	...	...	...	...	...	...	...	...	...	...	...
...	...	...	...	...	...	...	...	...	...	...	...	...
...	...	...	...	...	...	...	...	...	...	...	...	...
...	...	...	...	...	...	...	...	...	...	...	...	...
...	...	...	...	...	...	...	...	...	...	...	...	...
...	...	...	...	...	...	...	...	...	...	...	...	...
...	...	...	...	...	...	...	...	...	...	...	...	...
...	...	...	...	...	...	...	...	...	...	...	...	...
...	...	...	...	...	...	...	...	...	...	...	...	...
...	...	...	...	...	...	...	...	...	...	...	...	...
...	...	...	...	...	...	...	...	...	...	...	...	...
...	...	...	...	...	...	...	...	...	...	...	...	...
...	...	...	...	...	...	...	...	...	...	...	...	...
...	...	...	...	...	...	...	...	...	...	...	...	...
...	...	...	...	...	...	...	...	...	...	...	...	...
...	...	...	...	...	...	...	...	...	...	...	...	...
...	...	...	...	...	...	...	...	...	...	...	...	...
...	...	...	...	...	...	...	...	...	...	...	...	...
...	...	...	...	...	...	...	...	...	...	...	...	...
...	...	...	...	...	...	...	...	...	...	...	...	...
...	...	...	...	...	...	...	...	...	...	...	...	...
...	...	...	...	...	...	...	...	...	...	...	...	...
...	...	...	...	...	...	...	...	...	...	...	...	...
...	...	...	...	...	...	...	...	...	...	...	...	...
...	...	...	...	...	...	...	...	...	...	...	...	...
...	...	...	...	...	...	...	...	...	...	...	...	...
...	...	...	...	...	...	...	...	...	...	...	...	...
...	...	...	...	...	...	...	...	...	...	...	...	...
1	1	...	...	...	1	...	...	...	...	...	...	...
1	1	...	...	...	1	...	...	...	...	...	...	...

SUPPLEMENTARY TABLE C.

LANGUAGE KNOWN BY THE LITERATE BY CASTE.

SUPPLEMENTARY
Language known by the

Caste and Religion.				Total Strength.					
				Males.			Females.		
					Literate.			Literate.	
Class.	Group.	Caste, &c. and sub-divisions.	Religion.	Total Males.	Total.	Knowing English.	Total Females.	Total.	Knowing English.
1	2	3	4	5	6	7	8	9	10
A.—Agricultural.	1. Military and Dominant.	Kshatriya ...	Hindu ...	**10,785**	**3,285**	**175**	10,382	183	4
		,, ...	Sikh ...	**13**	**3**	...	16	1	...
		Total ...	...	*10,798*	*3,288*	*175*	*10,398*	*184*	*4*
		Maráṭa ...	Hindu ...	**22,388**	**1,627**	**47**	20,914	30	...
		Ráchévár ...	,, ...	**1,745**	**403**	**10**	1,871	5	1
		Total ...	...	*34,931*	*5,318*	*232*	*33,183*	*219*	*5*
	2. Other Agricultural. (a) Cultivators.	Lingáyet, Gaudamané ...	Hindu ...	**28,710**	**1,970**	**8**	29,737	18	...
		,, Malava ...	,, ...	**402**	...	...	393	..	...
		,, Panchácháru ...	,, ...	**34,566**	**2,841**	**12**	34,320	35	...
		Náyar ...	,, ...	**3**	**3**	...	...	...	...
		Pille ...	,, ...	**311**	**45**	**20**	244	5	...
		Tigala ...	,, ...	**26,988**	**313**	**22**	26,409	2	...
		Vakkaliga ...	,, ...	**660,730**	**22,218**	**265**	671,423	274	2
		,, Sáda ...	Jain ...	**516**	**108**	**1**	493	4	...
		,, Tulu ...	Bramho ...	...	...	...	...	...	...
		Total ...	...	*752,226*	*27,498*	*328*	*763,039*	*338*	*2*
	4. Forest and Hill-tribes.	I'raliga ...	Hindu ...	**581**	...	...	551	...	...
		Koracha ...	,, ...	**5,462**	**47**	...	5,082	...	...
		Korama ...	,, ...	**6,771**	**109**	**1**	6,761	4	...
		Kuruba ...	,, ...	**1,136**	...	...	1,133	...	...
		Lambani ...	,, ...	**20,585**	**24**	...	18,552	...	...
		Uriya ...	,, ...	...	...	...	...	...	...
		Total ...	...	*34,535*	*180*	*1*	*32,079*	*4*	...
		Total Class A ...	...	**821,692**	**32,996**	**561**	**828,301**	**561**	**7**
B.—Professional.	5. Priests.	Brámhan ...	Hindu ...	**92,169**	**51,421**	**3,755**	89,063	2,169	45
		Dásari ...	,, ...	**576**	**48**	...	592	...	...
		Lingayet, A'rádhya ...	,, ...	**5,798**	**1,158**	**12**	5,820	27	...
		,, Gurust'hala ...	,, ...	**5,920**	**845**	**7**	6,209	16	...
		,, Junguma ...	,, ...	**19,157**	**298**	**1**	19,009	1	...
		Sátáni ...	,, ...	**9,982**	**1,865**	**16**	9,777	37	1
		Pítámbara ...	Jain ...	**5**	...	...	...	...	...
		Tírt'hankara ...	,, ...	**1,346**	**486**	**3**	1,218	16	...
		Total ...	...	*131,953*	*56,121*	*3,794*	*131,688*	*2,226*	*46*
	6. Devotees.	Bairágí ...	Hindu ...	**104**	...	...	118	...	...
		Baváji ...	Jain ...	...	...	...	...	...	...
		Digambara ...	...	**2,881**	**940**	**7**	2,581	37	...
		Gósáyi ...	Hindu ...	**208**	**48**	**2**	215	2	...
		Sanyási ...	,, ...	**357**	...	...	327	...	...
		S'vétámbara ...	Jain ...	**69**	**59**	...	10	...	...
		Lingáyet, Vadér ...	Hindu ...	**400**	**41**	**1**	545	2	...
		Total ...	...	*4,019*	*1,088*	*10*	*3,796*	*41*	...
	7. Temple Servants.	Brámhan ...	Hindu ...	**586**	...	...	568	...	...
	9. Writers.	Kanakkan ...	,, ...	...	...	...	...	...	...
		Káyasta ...	,, ...	...	...	...	...	...	...
		Total ...	...	...	...	...	...	...	...
	11. Musicians and Ballad reciters.	Bhat Ráju ...	Hindu ...	**722**	**93**	**3**	665	...	...
	12. Dancers and Singers.	Natuva ...	,, ...	**3,544**	**83**	**4**	3,895	90	...
	12 (a) Chittári, &c.	Ráchévár ...	,, ...	**2,407**	...	...	2,222	...	...
		Total Class B ...	...	**146,231**	**57,385**	**3,811**	**142,834**	**2,397**	**46**

TABLE C.

Literate by Caste.

Territorial Distribution.											
Bangalore.						Kólár.					
Males.			Females.			Males.			Females.		
Total.	Literate. Total.	Literate. Knowing English.	Total.	Literate. Total.	Literate. Knowing English.	Total.	Literate. Total.	Literate. Knowing English.	Total.	Literate. Total.	Literate. Knowing English.
11	12	13	14	15	16	17	18	19	20	21	22
1,892	695	60	1,823	16	2	928	391	32	879	...	...
1	1	...	1	...	...	...	...	...	...	...	...
1,893	*696*	*60*	*1,824*	*16*	*2*	*928*	*391*	*32*	*879*	...	...
4,857	475	24	4,615	11	...	2,319	223	4	2,321	...	...
391	114	3	399	3	...	214	21	...	198	...	...
7,141	*1,285*	*87*	*6,838*	*30*	*2*	*3,461*	*635*	*36*	*3,398*	...	...
4,998	240	1	5,011	4	...	216	8	...	205	...	...
...	...	...	...	...	...	...	...	...	...	...	...
1,595	95	...	1,570	2	...	519	9	...	481	...	...
...	...	...	...	...	...	3	3	...	...	...	...
51	18	14	63	1	...	115	2	1	61	2	...
13,081	205	8	12,798	1	...	5,097	39	11	5,059	...	...
105,619	3,417	101	109,290	50	1	81,085	2,448	40	82,073	32	...
456	89	1	426	4	...	2	...	...	...	...	...
...	...	...	...	...	...	...	...	...	...	...	...
125,800	*4,064*	*125*	*129,158*	*62*	*1*	*87,037*	*2,509*	*52*	*87,878*	*34*	...
534	...	...	508	...	...	12	...	...	10	...	...
1,011	20	...	1,015	...	...	1,686	9	...	1,635	...	...
1,373	28	...	1,429	...	...	47	8	...	46	...	...
104	...	...	115	...	...	64	...	...	83	...	...
1,777	1	...	1,538	...	...	412	...	...	339	...	...
...	...	...	...	...	...	...	...	...	...	...	...
4,799	*49*	...	*4,605*	...	...	*2,221*	*17*	...	*2,113*	...	...
137,740	**5,398**	**212**	**140,601**	**92**	**3**	**92,719**	**3,161**	**88**	**93,389**	**34**	...
14,584	9,022	1,234	13,865	452	13	11,693	7,075	425	11,632	198	...
91	...	...	67	...	...	80	10	...	85	...	...
606	198	1	533	4	...	63	21	...	63	...	...
345	49	1	834	3	...	187	23	1	225	...	...
1,705	38	1	1,845	...	...	1,428	14	...	1,381	...	...
1,768	493	10	1,746	8	1	962	303	3	975	6	...
1	...	...	...	...	...	...	...	...	...	...	...
173	74	2	163	5	...	157	73	...	135	...	...
19,273	*9,874*	*1,249*	*18,552*	*472*	*14*	*14,570*	*7,519*	*429*	*14,496*	*204*	...
43	...	...	67	...	...	7	...	...	6	...	...
...	...	...	...	...	...	...	...	...	...	...	...
39	14	...	49	...	...	304	103	...	280	...	...
37	22	1	14	1	...	17	9	...	22	...	...
34	...	...	18	...	...	200	...	...	212	...	...
7	5	...	...	...	...	...	...	...	...	...	...
24	4	...	22	...	...	...	...	...	...	...	...
184	*45*	*1*	*170*	*1*	...	*528*	*112*	...	*520*	...	...
136	...	...	142	...	...	298	...	...	207	...	...
...	...	...	...	...	...	...	...	...	...	...	...
...	...	...	...	...	...	...	...	...	...	...	...
...	...	...	...	...	...	...	...	...	...	...	...
255	23	...	212	...	...	196	22	...	192	...	...
107	19	2	194	21	...	340	41	1	428	28	...
59	...	...	65	...	...	29	...	...	35	...	...
20,014	**9,961**	**1,252**	**19,335**	**494**	**14**	**15,961**	**7,694**	**430**	**15,978**	**232**	...

SUPPLEMENTARY TABLE C.

Literate by Caste.

SUPPLEMENTARY

Caste and Religion.				Territorial					
				Tumkúr.					
				Males.			Females.		
					Literate			Literate.	
Class.	Group.	Caste, &c., and sub-divisions.	Religion.	Total.	Total.	Knowing English.	Total.	Total.	Knowing English.
				23	24	25	26	27	28
A.—Agricultural.	1. Military and Dominant.	Kshatriya	Hindu ...	996	277	1	984	16	...
		,, ...	Sikh ...	...	...	...	...	...	...
		Total......	...	*996*	*277*	*1*	*984*	*16*	...
		Maráṭa	Hindu ...	1,383	59	3	1,444	...	...
		Ráchevár	,, ...	188	32	1	213	...	...
		Total......	...	*2,567*	*368*	*5*	*2,641*	*16*	...
	2. Other Agricultural. (a) Cultivators.	Lingáyet, Gaudamané ...	Hindu ...	1,046	103	...	1,080	...	...
		,, Malava ...	,, ...	...	...	...	...	...	...
		,, Panchâchâra ...	,, ...	3,388	93	...	8,457	...	...
		Náyar	,, ...	...	...	...	...	...	...
		Pille	,, ...	15	2	...	9	...	...
		Tigala	,, ...	7,450	49	3	7,268	1	...
		Vakkaliga ...	,, ...	88,795	4,032	17	90,286	43	1
		,, Sáda ...	Jain ...	58	19	...	67	...	...
		,, Tulu ...	Bramho ...	...	...	...	...	...	...
		Total......	...	*100,753*	*4,298*	*20*	*102,167*	*44*	*1*
	4. Forest and Hill tribes.	Iraliga	Hindu ...	34	...	...	33	...	...
		Korucha	,, ...	487	1	...	485	...	...
		Korama	,, ...	779	11	1	719	...	...
		Kuruba	,, ...	725	...	...	725	...	...
		Lambáni	,, ...	1,563	1	...	1,414	...	...
		Uriya	,, ...	...	...	...	...	...	...
		Total......	...	*3,588*	*13*	*1*	*3,376*	...	...
		Total Class A......	...	**106,907**	**4,679**	**26**	**108,184**	**60**	**1**
B.—Professional.	5. Priests.	Brámhan	Hindu ...	8,570	4,840	174	8,437	200	6
		Dásari	,, ...	108	11	...	102	...	...
		Lingayet, A'rádhya ...	,, ...	1,038	297	2	1,081	3	...
		,, Gurust'hala ...	,, ...	757	173	1	774	2	...
		,, Jangama ...	,, ...	2,513	52	...	2,368	...	...
		Sátáni	,, ...	1,936	412	...	1,865	12	...
		Pítámbara	Jain ...	...	...	...	...	...	...
		Tírt'hankara ...	,, ...	233	89	...	174	2	...
		Total......	...	*15,155*	*5,874*	*177*	*14,709*	*219*	*6*
	6. Devotees.	Bairági	Hindu ...	12	...	...	6	...	...
		Báváji	Jain ...	...	...	...	...	...	...
		Digumbara	,, ...	567	235	...	548	5	...
		Gósáyi	Hindu ...	7	...	...	3	...	...
		Sanyási	,, ...	97	...	...	78	...	...
		S'vétámbara ...	Jain ...	3	2	...	1	...	...
		Lingáyet, Vadér ...	Hindu ...	7	...	...	8	...	...
		Total......	...	*693*	*237*	...	*644*	*5*	...
	7. Temple Servants.	Brámhan	Hindu ...	44	...	...	48	...	...
	9. Writers.	Karaṇikkan	,, ...	...	...	...	...	...	...
		Káyastha	,, ...	...	...	...	...	...	...
		Total...	...	...	...	...	...	...	...
	11. Musicians and Ballad reciters.	Bhaṭ Ráju	Hindu ...	65	30	3	69	...	...
	12. Dancers and Singers.	Naṭuva	,, ...	58	2	...	50	1	...
	12 (a) Chittári, &c.	Ráchevár ...	,, ...	132	...	...	110	...	...
		Total Class B......		**16,147**	**6,143**	**180**	**15,729**	**225**	**6**

TABLE C—(*Continued*).

Distribution.

Mysore.						Hassan.					
Males.			Females.			Males.			Females.		
Total.	Literate.		Total.	Literate.		Total.	Literate.		Total.	Literate.	
	Total.	Knowing English.		Total.	Knowing English.		Total.	Knowing English.		Total.	Knowing English.
29	30	31	32	33	34	35	36	37	38	39	40
3,391	1,107	35	3,450	120	1	822	150	4	889	4	...
12	2	...	15	1	...	...	...	...	...	...	...
3,403	*1,109*	*35*	*3,465*	*121*	*1*	*822*	*150*	*4*	*889*	*4*	...
3,893	317	9	3,927	14	...	1,116	46	2	1,055	...	...
613	203	4	700	1	1	227	11	...	259	...	...
7,909	*1,629*	*48*	*8,002*	*136*	*2*	*2,465*	*207*	*6*	*2,203*	*4*	...
18,276	1,325	6	19,369	10	...	3,086	196	...	3,017	1	...
...	...	...	...	...	...	6	...	...	4	...	...
7,096	896	4	7,523	7	...	6,517	257	1	6,630	2	...
...	...	...	...	...	...	...	...	...	...	...	...
78	7	2	76	...	...	8	2	1	11	1	...
589	13	...	633	...	...	374	...	...	340	...	...
158,168	4,588	54	167,389	94	...	83,436	2,642	19	87,887	17	...
...	...	...	...	...	...	...	...	...	...	...	...
...	...	...	...	...	...	...	...	...	...	...	...
181,207	*6,829*	*66*	*191,990*	*111*	...	*93,427*	*3,097*	*21*	*97,889*	*21*	...
...	...	...	...	...	...	1	...	...	...	...	...
171	4	...	164	...	...	103	2	...	102	...	...
1,880	17	...	1,954	...	...	618	15	...	614	...	...
209	...	...	191	...	...	26	...	...	19	...	...
528	1	...	556	...	...	1,451	...	...	1,395	...	...
...	...	...	...	...	...	...	...	...	...	...	...
2,788	*22*	...	*2,865*	...	...	*2,199*	*17*	...	*2,130*	...	...
194,904	**8,480**	**114**	**205,947**	**247**	**2**	**97,791**	**3,321**	**27**	**102,222**	**25**	...
21,223	12,106	883	21,775	440	17	8,499	4,808	204	8,561	72	3
69	10	...	83	...	...	22	10	...	19	...	...
1,859	259	3	1,888	8	...	496	119	1	497	2	...
1,961	247	1	2,068	6	...	577	89	...	541	...	...
1,943	23	...	1,944	...	...	3,429	52	...	3,425	...	...
2,223	370	3	2,257	8	...	1,797	147	...	1,863	...	...
...	...	...	...	...	...	...	...	...	...	...	...
310	76	1	320	3	...	246	93	...	226	6	...
29,588	*13,091*	*891*	*30,335*	*465*	*17*	*15,066*	*5,318*	*205*	*15,134*	*80*	*3*
12	...	...	4	...	...	...	...	...	...	...	...
...	...	...	...	...	...	...	...	...	...	...	...
687	207	3	611	8	...	368	174	2	404	22	...
72	6	1	58	1	...	27	...	...	99	...	...
4	...	...	...	...	...	...	...	...	...	...	...
...	...	...	...	...	...	...	...	...	...	...	...
163	16	...	164	2	...	...	...	...	...	...	...
938	*229*	*4*	*837*	*11*	...	*395*	*174*	*2*	*503*	*22*	...
8	...	...	7	...	...	52	...	...	39	...	...
...	...	...	...	...	...	...	...	...	...	...	...
...	...	...	...	...	...	...	...	...	...	...	...
...	...	...	...	...	...	...	...	...	...	...	...
113	...	...	96	...	...	45	...	...	54	...	...
2,907	21	1	3,080	39	...	48	...	...	73	...	...
169	...	...	174	...	...	4	...	...	8	...	...
33,723	**13,341**	**896**	**34,529**	**515**	**17**	**15,610**	**5,492**	**207**	**15,806**	**102**	**3**

SUPPLEMENTARY TABLE C:
Literate by Caste.

SUPPLEMENTARY

Caste and Religion.				Territorial.					
				Shimoga.					
				Males.			Females.		
					Literate.			Literate.	
Class.	Group.	Caste, &c., and sub-divisions.	Religion.	Total.	Total.	Knowing English.	Total.	Total.	Knowing English.
				41	42	43	44	45	46
A.—Agricultural.	1. Military and Dominant.	Kshatriya ...	Hindu	1,510	354	13	1,387	14	1
		„ ...	Sikh	...	...	...	...	...	...
		Total	...	*1,510*	*354*	*13*	*1,387*	*14*	*1*
		Maráta ...	Hindu	5,705	273	3	4,940	5	...
		Ráchévár ...	„	5	2	...	5	...	...
		Total	...	*7,220*	*629*	*16*	*6,332*	*19*	*1*
	2. Other Agricultural. (a) Cultivators.	Lingáyet, Gandamáné ...	Hindu	213	16	...	187	...	...
		„ Malava ...	„	...	...	...	...	...	...
		„ Panchácbára ...	„	7,051	347	2	6,507	6	...
		Náyar ...	„	...	...	...	...	...	...
		Pilli ...	„	9	...	...	7	...	...
		Tigala ...	„	127	6	...	70	...	...
		Vakkaliga ...	„	70,684	2,353	16	64,385	22	...
		„ Sáda ...	Jain	...	...	...	...	...	...
		„ Tulu ...	Brumho	...	...	...	...	...	...
		Total	...	*78,084*	*2,722*	*18*	*71,156*	*28*	...
	4. Forest and Hill tribes.	Praliga ...	Hindu	...	...	...	...	...	...
		Koracha ...	„	1,193	4	...	914	...	...
		Korama ...	„	1,162	5	...	1,129	...	...
		Kuruba ...	„	...	...	...	...	...	...
		Lambáni ...	„	7,256	6	...	6,871	...	...
		Uriya ...	„	...	...	...	...	...	...
		Total	...	*9,611*	*15*	...	*8,914*	...	...
		Total Class A	...	**94,915**	**3,366**	**34**	**86,402**	**47**	**1**
B.—Professional.	5. Priests	Brámhan ...	Hindu	15,728	7,064	253	13,616	112	5
		Dásari ...	„	84	1	...	135	...	...
		Lingáyet, A'rádhya ...	„	364	65	1	363	2	...
		„ Gurust'hala ...	„	401	59	...	370	...	...
		„ Jangama ...	„	3,947	45	...	4,664	...	...
		Sátáni ...	„	372	52	...	409	2	...
		Pitámbara ...	Jain	...	...	...	...	...	...
		Tírt'hankara ...	„	65	33	...	35	...	...
		Total	...	*20,962*	*7,319*	*254*	*18,922*	*116*	*5*
	6. Devotees	Bairági ...	Hindu	...	...	...	...	...	...
		Bávaji ...	Jain	...	...	...	...	...	...
		Digambara ...	„	188	57	1	124	...	...
		Gosáyi ...	Hindu	...	...	...	...	...	...
		Sanyási ...	„	19	...	...	3	...	...
		S'vétámbara ...	Jain	...	...	...	...	...	...
		Lingáyet, Vadér ...	Hindu	56	9	1	55	...	...
		Total	...	*264*	*66*	*2*	*182*	...	...
	7. Temple-Servants.	Brámhan ...	Hindu	2	...	...	3	...	...
	9. Writers	Kanakkan ...	„	...	...	...	...	...	...
		Káyastu ...	„	...	...	...	...	...	...
		Total	...	*2*	...	...	*3*	...	...
	11. Musicians and Ballad reciters.	Bhat Ráju ...	Hindu	...	...	...	...	...	...
	12. Dancers and Singers.	Natuva ...	„	71	...	...	44	1	...
	12 (a) Chittári, &ca.	Ráchávár ...	„	1,895	...	...	1,743	...	...
		Total Class B	...	**23,194**	**7,385**	**256**	**20,894**	**117**	**5**

SUPPLEMENTARY TABLE C.

Literate by Caste.

TABLE C.—(*Continued.*)

Distribution.

Kadúr.						Chitaldurg.					
Males.			Females.			Males.			Females.		
Total.	Literate.		Total.	Literate.		Total.	Literate.		Total.	Literate.	
	Total.	Knowing English.		Total.	Knowing English.		Total.	Knowing English.		Total.	Knowing English.
47	48	49	50	51	52	53	54	55	56	57	58
992	**209**	**28**	722	12	...	**254**	**102**	**2**	248	1	...
...	...	...	...	...	...	...	...	...	...	...	...
992	*209*	*28*	*722*	*12*	...	*254*	*102*	*2*	*248*	*1*	...
1,830	**110**	**1**	1,304	...	...	**1,285**	**124**	**1**	1,308	...	...
97	**20**	**2**	92	1	...	**10**	...	...	5	...	...
2,919	*339*	*31*	*2,118*	*13*	...	*1,549*	*226*	*3*	*1,561*	*1*	...
821	**82**	**1**	835	3	...	**54**	...	...	53	...	...
396	...	...	389	...	...	...	...	...	...	...	...
3,663	**305**	**2**	3,830	14	...	**4,737**	**839**	**3**	4,313	4	...
...	...	...	...	...	...	...	...	...	...	...	...
33	**13**	**1**	18	1	...	**2**	**1**	**1**	...	...	...
258	**1**	...	233	...	...	**12**	...	...	8	...	...
37,869	**1,313**	**5**	35,627	12	...	**35,074**	**1,425**	**13**	34,186	4	...
...	...		...	...	...	...	...	...	...	...	...
...	...		...	...	...	...	...	...	...	...	...
43,040	*1,714*	*9*	*40,941*	*30*	...	*39,879*	*2,265*	*17*	*38,560*	*8*	...
...	...	...	...	...	...	...	...	...	...	...	...
368	**1**	...	357	...	...	**443**	**6**	...	410	...	...
668	**19**	...	666	...	...	**244**	**6**	...	204	4	...
8	...	...	...	...	...	...	...	...	...	...	...
4,880	**5**	...	3,914	...	...	**2,718**	**10**	...	2,525	...	...
...	...		...	...	...	...	...	...	...	...	...
5,924	*25*	...	*4,937*	...	...	*3,405*	*22*	...	*3,139*	*4*	...
51,883	**2,078**	**40**	**47,996**	**43**	...	**44,833**	**2,513**	**20**	**43,560**	**13**	...
8,795	**4,643**	**408**	8,231	634	1	**3,077**	**1,863**	**174**	2,916	61	...
73	**4**	...	63	...	...	**49**	**2**	...	38	...	...
994	**112**	**2**	1,021	6	...	**378**	**87**	**2**	374	2	...
826	**103**	**2**	971	4	...	**866**	**102**	**1**	927	1	...
1,420	**17**	...	1,390	...	...	**2,772**	**57**	...	2,554	1	...
581	**30**	...	498	1	...	**342**	**58**	...	354	...	...
4	...	...	...	...	...	...	...	...	...	...	...
93	**19**	...	90	...	...	**69**	**29**	...	73	...	...
12,786	*4,928*	*412*	*12,264*	*645*	*1*	*7,553*	*2,198*	*177*	*7,236*	*65*	...
28	...	...	34	...	...	**2**	...	...	1	...	...
...	...	...	...	...	...	...	...	...	...	...	...
555	**67**	...	454	...	...	**163**	**83**	**1**	111	2	...
1	...	...	...	...	...	**47**	**11**	...	19	...	...
9	...	...	12	...	...	**3**	...	...	4	...	...
59	**52**	...	9	...	...	...	...	...	...	...	...
140	**10**	...	292	...	...	**10**	**2**	...	4	...	...
792	*129*	...	*801*	...	...	*225*	*96*	*1*	*139*	*2*	...
33	...	...	13	...	...	**13**	...	...	9	...	...
...	...	...	...	...	...	...	...	...	...	...	...
33	...	...	*13*	...	...	*13*	...	...	*9*	...	...
23	**2**	...	17	...	...	**25**	**16**	...	25	...	...
1	...		6	...	...	**12**	...	...	11	...	...
18	...	...	14	...	...	**101**	...	...	78	...	...
13,653	**5,059**	**412**	**13,065**	**645**	**1**	**7,929**	**2,310**	**178**	**7,498**	**67**	...

SUPPLEMENTARY TABLE C.
Literate by Caste.

SUPPLEMENTARY

Caste and Religion.				Territorial.		
				The Civil and Military Station,		
				Males.		
					Literate.	
Class.	Group.	Caste, &c., and sub-divisions.	Religion.	Total.	Total.	Knowing English.
				59	60	61
A.—Agricultural.	1. Military and Dominant.	Kshatriya	Hindu	350	170	42
		,,	Sikh	...	...	...
		Total		*350*	*170*	*42*
		Maráta	Hindu	573	186	28
		Ráchévár	,,	40	19	...
		Total		*963*	*375*	*70*
	2. Other Agricultural (a) Cultivators	Lingáyet, Gaudamané	Hindu	12	7	1
		,, Malava	,,	...	...	...
		,, Panchácbára	,,	...	...	...
		Náyar	,,	64	30	5
		Pillé	,,	3	12	...
		Tigaḷa	,,	1,672	189	51
		Vakkaliga	,,	4,786	1,553	561
		,, Sáda	Jain	...	...	...
		,, Tuḷu	Bramho	10	5	...
		Total		*6,547*	*1,786*	*618*
	4. Forest and Hill tribes.	Iraliga	Hindu	...	...	...
		Koracha	,,	116	1	...
		Korama	,,	94	6	...
		Kuruba	,,	...	...	...
		Lambáṇi	,,	...	...	...
		Uriya	,,	5	...	...
		Total		*215*	*7*	...
		Total Class A		**7,725**	**2,168**	**688**
B.—Professional.	5. Priests	Brámhan	Hindu	662	403	120
		Dásari	,,	7	2	...
		Lingayet, A'rádhya	,,	...	...	...
		,, Gurust'hala	,,	...	...	...
		,, Jangama	,,	21	4	...
		Sátáni	,,	112	46	4
		Pítámbara	Jain	...	...	...
		Tírt'hankara	,,	...	...	...
		Total		*802*	*455*	*124*
	6. Devotees	Bairági	Hindu	...	...	...
		Báváji	Jain	1	1	...
		Digambara	,,	10	8	...
		Gósáyi	Hindu	1	...	...
		Sanyási	,,	...	...	...
		S'vétámbara	Jain	6	6	2
		Lingáyet, Vadér	Hindu	6	1	...
		Total		*24*	*16*	*2*
	7. Temple Servant	Brámhan	Hindu	2	2	...
	9. Writers	Kaṇakan	,,	57	27	14
		Káyasta	,,	5	2	...
		Total		*62*	*29*	*14*
	11. Musicians and Ballad-reciters.	Bhaṭ Rája	Hindu	1	...	...
	12. Dancers and Singers	Naṭuva	,,	21	9	2
	12. (a). Chittári, &c.	Ráchévár	,,	6	2	...
		Total Class B		**918**	**513**	**142**

SUPPLEMENTARY TABLE C.
Literate by Caste.

TABLE C—(Continued.)

Distribution.

Bangalore.			Total strength including the Civil and Military Station, Bangalore.					
Females.			Males.			Females.		
Total.	Literate. Total.	Literate. Knowing English.	Total.	Literate. Total.	Literate. Knowing English.	Total.	Literate. Total.	Literate. Knowing English.
62	63	64	65	66	67	68	69	70
278	4	...	11,135	3,455	217	10,660	187	4
...	...	...	13	3	...	16	1	...
278	*4*	...	*11,148*	*3,458*	*217*	*10,676*	*188*	*4*
571	16	...	22,961	1,813	75	21,485	46	...
40	2	...	1,785	422	10	1,911	7	1
889	*22*	...	*35,894*	*5,083*	*202*	*31,072*	*241*	*5*
8	...	...	28,722	1,977	9	29,765	18	...
...	...	...	403	...	...	402	...	...
...	...	...	34,566	2,841	12	34,320	35	...
50	...	...	67	33	5	50	...	...
1	...	...	314	47	20	245	5	...
1641	18	...	28,660	502	73	28,050	20	...
4910	367	6	665,516	23,771	826	676,333	641	8
1	...	...	516	108	1	494	4	...
13	3	...	10	5	...	13	3	...
6,621	*388*	*6*	*758,773*	*29,284*	*946*	*769,672*	*726*	*8*
...	...	...	581	...	...	581	...	...
110	...	...	5,578	48	...	5,192	...	...
98	...	...	6,865	115	1	6,859	4	...
...	...	...	1,136	...	...	1,133	...	...
...	...	...	20,585	24	...	18,552	...	...
3	...	...	5	...	...	3	...	...
211	...	...	*34,750*	*187*	*1*	*32,290*	*4*	...
7,724	**410**	**6**	**829,417**	**35,164**	**1,249**	**836,025**	**971**	**13**
491	31	2	92,831	51,824	3,675	89,558	2,200	47
3	...	...	533	50	...	595	...	...
...	...	...	5,798	1,150	12	5,820	27	...
...	...	...	5,920	845	7	6,209	16	...
28	...	...	19,178	302	1	19,037	1	...
116	3	...	10,094	1,911	20	9,893	40	1
...	...	...	5	...	...	...	...	...
...	...	...	1,346	420	3	1,218	16	...
638	*34*	*2*	*135,705*	*56,576*	*3,918*	*132,326*	*2,300*	*48*
...	...	...	104	...	...	118	...	...
5	...	...	1	1	...	...	...	...
...	...	...	2,891	948	7	2,586	37	...
...	...	...	209	48	2	215	2	...
...	...	...	357	...	...	327	...	...
...	...	...	75	65	2	10	...	...
5	...	...	406	42	1	550	2	...
10	...	...	*4,043*	*1,104*	*12*	*3,806*	*41*	...
...	...	...	588	2	...	568	...	...
51	12	...	57	27	14	51	12	...
1	...	...	5	2	...	1	...	...
52	*12*	...	*62*	*29*	*14*	*52*	*12*	...
...	...	...	723	33	3	665	...	...
16	...	...	3,565	92	6	3,911	90	...
5	...	...	2,413	2	...	2,227	...	...
721	**46**	**2**	**147,149**	**57,898**	**3,953**	**143,555**	**2,443**	**48**

SUPPLEMENTARY TABLE C.

Literate by Caste.

SUPPLEMENTARY

Caste and Religion.				Total strength.					
				Males.			Females.		
					Literate.			Literate.	
Class.	Group.	Caste, &c. and sub-divisions.	Religion.	Total Males.	Total.	Knowing English.	Total Females.	Total.	Knowing English.
1	2	3	4	5	6	7	8	9	10
C.—Commercial.	14. Traders.	Baniya ...	Hindu ...	...	...	...	...	...	...
		" ...	Jain ...	...	...	...	...	...	...
		Banajiga ...	Hindu ...	53,529	7,107	300	52,864	494	11
		Guzarâti ...	" ...	31	25	...	20	4	...
		Jât ...	" ...	...	...	...	...	...	...
		Kômaṭi ...	" ...	15,157	8,831	185	13,843	101	3
		Lâdar ...	" ...	1,014	117	3	1,032	...	...
		Lingâyet ...	" ...	145,974	20,361	230	145,103	398	1
		Mudali ...	" ...	2,954	964	252	2,457	117	3
		Multâni ...	" ...	...	...	...	...	...	...
		Nagarta ...	" ...	11,902	2,839	12	10,842	7	...
		S'râvaka ...	Jain ...	1,038	95	...	924	...	...
		Jain (Sub-division or caste not returned) ...	" ...	1,090	286	5	871	10	...
		Mârvâdi ...	Buddhist ...	...	...	...	...	...	...
		Do ...	Hindu ...	...	...	...	...	...	...
		Do ...	Jain ...	55	...	...	5	...	...
		Total Class C ...		232,744	49,625	987	227,961	1,131	18
D—Artisan and Village Menial.	17. Goldsmiths ...	Panchâḷa ...	Hindu ...	49,596	8,677	71	47,494	153	...
	18. Barbers ...	Nâyinda ...	" ...	18,411	493	...	17,742	2	...
	19. Blacksmiths ...	Kammâra (Pâñchâḷa) ...	" ...	3,122	62	...	3,019	...	...
	20. Carpenters, &c.	Badagi (Pâñchâḷa) ...	" ...	4,409	40	...	4,225	...	...
		Gaunder ...	" ...	...	...	...	...	...	...
		Total ...		*4,409*	*40*	...	*4,225*	...	...
	21. Brass and Coppersmiths ...	Gejjegâra and Kanchugâra ...	" ...	111		...	119	...	...
	22. Tailors ...	Darzi ...	" ...	4,529	576	15	4,232	22	1
	23. Weavers ...	Góniga ...	" ...	743	13	...	668	...	...
		Gâdiya ...	Jain ...	...	...	...	...	...	...
		Néyigé ...	Hindu ...	43,313	5,157	50	43,500	112	6
		Total ...		*44,066*	*5,170*	*50*	*44,168*	*112*	*6*
	24. Washermen ...	Agasa ...	Hindu ...	42,376	306	1	42,288	2	...
	26. Shepherds and Wool-weavers.	Kuruba ...	" ...	172,014	2,456	8	173,960	33	1
	26(a) Cowherds ...	Golla ...	" ...	64,580	1,280	36	63,107	17	...
	27. Oil-pressers	Gâniga ...	" ...	17,645	1,402	7	18,030	9	...
	28. Potters ...	Kumbâra ...	" ...	21,026	708	1	19,432	4	...
	30. Salt workers ...	Uppâra ...	" ...	44,845	612	7	44,259	7	...
	32. Goldsmith's refuse collectors ...	Jalagâra ...	" ...	129	...	...	125	...	...
	33(a) Gold-lace makers ...	Râchévâr Sirigé ...	" ...	8	...	...	7	...	...
	35. Fishermen ...	Bésta ...	" ...	49,620	846	4	50,038	10	...
	36. Toddy-drawers.	Idiga ...	" ...	20,533	398	2	19,385	...	...
	38. Leather workers ...	Mâdiga ...	" ...	118,457	121	3	118,234	3	...
		Môchi ...	" ...	308	7	...	334	...	...
		Total ...		*118,765*	*128*	*3*	*118,568*	*3*	...
	38(a) Village watchmen ...	Holaya ...	" ...	251,188	862	35	250,821	15	2
		Total Class D ...		926,972	24,022	240	921,019	389	10

TABLE C.—(*Continued.*)

Territorial Distribution.											
Bangalore.	Bangalore.	Bangalore.	Bangalore.	Bangalore.	Bangalore.	Kólár.	Kólár.	Kólár.	Kólár.	Kólár.	Kólár.
Males.	Males.	Males.	Females.	Females.	Females.	Males.	Males.	Males.	Females.	Females.	Females.
Total.	Literate. Total.	Literate. Knowing English.	Total.	Literate. Total.	Literate. Knowing English.	Total.	Literate. Total.	Literate. Knowing English.	Total.	Literate. Total.	Literate. Knowing English.
11	12	13	14	15	16	17	18	19	20	21	22
	...	...	...	...	...	...	...	...	...	...	...
	...	...	...	...	...	...	...	...	...	...	...
9.753	1,900	136	10,342	196	1	18,190	1,651	33	18,106	74	...
3	3	...	3	1	...	...	...	...	...	...	...
	...	...	...	...	...	...	...	...	...	...	...
2.455	1,801	38	2,257	24	1	4.571	2,687	42	4,319	36	...
36	14	...	17	...	...	8	7	...	10	...	...
9.378	3.336	31	9.326	52	1	3.138	1,167	5	3,001	16	...
835	417	138	764	68	2	430	63	11	284	10	...
	...	...	...	...	...	...	...	...	...	...	...
2 504	1.646	6	2,565	2	...	1,446	383	5	1,558	1	...
...	...	...	...	...	...	...	...	...	...	...	...
56	18	1	32	...	...	16	8	...	2	...	...
	...	...	...	...	...	...	...	...	...	...	...
...	...	...	...	...	...	...	...	...	...	...	...
...	...	...	...	...	...	...	...	...	...	...	...
25,020	**8.529**	**350**	**25,306**	**343**	**5**	**27,799**	**5.966**	**96**	**27,280**	**137**	...
6.131	1.461	13	5,949	14	...	4.483	1.306	11	4,490	13	...
3.435	151	...	3,393	...	...	4.401	119	...	4,158	...	...
257	15	...	281	...	...	323	17	...	336	...	...
...	...	...	...	...	...	19	...	...	23	...	...
...	...	...		...	...		...	...	...	...	...
...	...	...	...	...	...	*19*	...	...	*23*	...	...
21	...	...	20	...	...	...	...	...	...	...	...
864	97	...	901	1	...	300	35	...	274	1	...
341	13	...	278	...	...	39	...	...	36	...	...
11.827	2.422	35	11,867	60	2	4.284	473	3	4,337	24	...
12,168	*2,435*	*35*	*12,115*	*60*	*2*	*4,323*	*473*	*3*	*4,373*	*24*	...
5.179	42	...	5,261	...	...	5.228	26	...	5,099	...	...
19.618	317	2	20,995	1	...	17.511	171	...	17,793	6	1
9,461	342	30	9,061	8	...	10.038	244	...	9,984	2	...
2.907	237	2	2,869	1		2.874	387	...	2,916	...	...
1.976	93	...	1,977	4	...	2.073	147	...	1,889	...	...
723	53	5	769	...	...	1.673	21	...	1,454	...	...
27	...	...	28	...	...	7	...	...	7	...	...
5	...	...	5	...	...	3	...	...	2	...	...
3.981	169	...	4,137		...	1.981	87	...	1,929	...	...
1.272	72	...	1,277		...	876	23	...	832	...	...
21.591	41	...	21,653	3	...	20.005	14	...	19,602	...	...
52	5	...	45	...	...	31	...	...	23	...	...
21,643	*46*	...	*21,698*	*3*	...	*20,036*	*14*	...	*19,625*	...	...
31.028	354	25	31,857	10	1	28.762	22	...	28,903	...	...
120.703	**5.324**	**112**	**123,232**	**105**	**3**	**104,911**	**3,092**	**14**	**104,087**	**46**	**1**

SUPPLEMENTARY TABLE C.
Literate by Caste.

Class.	Group.	Caste, &c. and sub-divisions.	Religion.	Territorial — Tumkúr, Males: Total.	Males: Literate. Total.	Males: Literate. Knowing English.	Females: Total.	Females: Literate. Total.	Females: Literate. Knowing English.
				23	24	25	26	27	28
C—Commercial.	14. Traders.	Baniya ...	Hindu ...	...	...	...	...	...	...
		Do ...	Jain ...	...	...	...	...	...	...
		Banajiga ...	Hindu ...	6,310	1,040	30	6,068	41	1
		Guzaráti ...	„ ...	...	...	...	...	...	...
		Ját ...	„ ...	...	...	...	...	...	...
		Kómaṭi ...	„ ...	2,891	1,775	8	2,413	8	...
		Ládar ...	„ ...	70	43	...	64	...	...
		Lingáyet ...	„ ...	10,781	5,671	19	10,508	68	...
		Mudali ...	„ ...	207	59	18	173	12	...
		Multáni ...	„ ...	...	...	...	...	...	...
		Nagartha ...	„ ...	163	19	...	152	...	...
		S'rávaka ...	Jain ...	...	...	...	...	...	...
		Jain (Sub-division or caste not returned) ...	...	182	63	...	123	2	...
		Márvádi ...	Buddhist ...	...	...	...	...	...	...
		Do ...	Hindu ...	...	...	...	...	...	...
		Do ...	Jain ...	...	...	...	...	...	...
		Total Class C ...		20,034	8,670	75	19,501	131	1
D—Artisan and Village menial.	17. Goldsmith ...	Pánchála ...	Hindu ...	4,266	1,091	12	1,221	66	...
	18. Barbers ...	Náyinda ...	„ ...	1,963	69	...	1,844	...	...
	19. Blacksmiths ...	Kammára (Pánchála) ...	„ ...	612	11		551	...	...
	20. Carpenters, &c.	Badagi (Pánchála) ...	„ ...	11		...	16	...	...
		Gaunder ...	„ ...	...	...	...	...	...	...
		Total ...		*11*	...	...	*16*	...	...
	21. Brass and Coppersmiths ...	Gejjégára and Kanchugárá ...	„ ...				...		...
	22. Tailors ...	Darzi ...	„ ...	465	64	2	443	...	...
	23. Weavers. ...	Góniga ...	...	222	...		200	...	...
		Gadiya ...	Jain ...	...			...	...	...
		Néyigé ...	Hindu ...	3,806	452	2	3,881	...	...
		Total ...		*4,028*	*452*	*2*	*4,081*	...	...
	24. Washermen ...	Agasa ...	Hindu ...	5,041	44	...	5,282	1	...
	26. Shepherds and Wool-weavers.	Kuruba ...	„	19,165	453	...	19,021	2	...
	26(a). Cowherds ...	Golla ...	„ ...	19,636	168	...	18,601	1	...
	27. Oil-pressers ...	Gániga ...	„ ...	1,599	112	...	1,706	1	...
	28. Potters ...	Kumbára ...	„ ...	1,618	159	...	1,565	...	...
	30. Salt workers ...	Uppara ...	„ ...	5,798	144	...	5,770	1	...
	32. Goldsmith's refuse collectors ...	Jalagára ...	„ ...	3	...		2	...	...
	33(a). Gold-lace makers. ...	Ráchévár, Sirigé ...	„ ...	...		...	...	...	...
	35. Fishermen ...	Besta ...	„ ...	2,215	92	2	1,986	4	...
	36. Toddy-drawers.	Idiga ...	„ ...	2,604	78	...	2,744	...	...
	38. Leather workers ...	Mádiga ...	„ ...	23,693	5	...	24,590	...	...
		Móchi ...	„ ...	17	2	...	24	...	...
		Total ...		*23,710*	*7*	...	*24,614*	...	...
	38(a). Village watchmen ...	Holaya ...	„ ...	11,723	55	2	11,893	..	...
		Total Class D ...		104,457	2,999	20	104,343	76	...

TABLE C.—(Continued.)

Distribution.

Mysore.						Hassan.					
Males.			Females.			Males.			Females.		
Total.	Literate.		Total.	Literate.		Total.	Literate.		Total.	Literate.	
	Total.	Knowing English.		Total.	Knowing English.		Total.	Knowing English.		Total.	Knowing English.
29	30	31	32	33	34	35	36	37	38	39	40
...	...	...	...	...	...	...	...	...	...	...	...
8,649	1,217	40	9,162	100	9	1,977	336	8	1,755	9	...
26	22	...	15	3	...	2	...	...	2	...	...
...	...	...	...	...	...	...	...	...	...	...	...
1,644	758	43	1,566	18	2	838	487	4	878	2	...
574	45	3	614	...	...	47	6	...	14	...	...
44,793	3,217	67	46,461	112		19,164	3,276	22	19,842	16	...
368	296	59	737	49	...	82	37	7	85	4	...
...	...	...		...		...			...		...
230	33	1	209		...	30	3	...	47	...	...
...	...	...	...	...	...	...			...	...	...
111	71	3	119	3	...	36	17	1	29	2	...
...	...		...	...	...	...	...	...	...	...	...
...	...	...		...	...			...	...	...	...
...	...	...	...	...	...	10	...	...	...	...	...
56,895	5,659	216	58,883	255	11	22,236	4,162	42	22,685	33	...
16,176	1,797	11	16,049	30	...	5,740	844	4	5,393	2	...
4,226	71	...	1,175	...		1,471	15	...	1,508	1	...
892	12	...	916	...	...	426	3	...	403		...
1,501	12	...	1,567	...	...	809	5	...	868	...	...
1,501	*12*	...	*1,567*	...	...	*809*	*5*	...	*868*	...	...
90	...	...	90		...	...	...	...	...	...	...
721	97	13	736	20	1	255	43	...	256		...
139	...	...	112	...	...	...	...	...	...	...	...
4,917	518	2	5,026	15	1	6,386	370	1	6,422	12	...
5,056	*518*	*2*	*5,138*	*15*	*1*	*6,386*	*370*	*1*	*6,422*	*12*	...
9,541	55	1	9,801	...	...	5,135	19	...	5,321	...	...
57,633	501	4	58,172	11	...	19,912	175	1	20,818	5	...
2,657	185	5	2,788	6	...	2,608	55	...	2,514	...	...
7,635	425	5	7,900	7	...	1,029	78	...	1,160	...	...
8,300	103	...	7,836	...	...	1,668	84	1	1,645	...	...
16,922	130	...	17,795	1	...	4,206	37	...	4,360	...	...
86	...	...	85	...	...	6	...	...	3	...	...
...	...	...			...	...	...	...	...	...	...
29,377	281	2	30,173	4	...	3,764	31	...	3,864	2	...
4,140	87	2	4,310	...	...	1,299	56	...	1,358	...	...
11,731	18	3	12,085	...		5,520	4	...	5,670	...	...
170	...	...	193	...	...	...	...	...	...	...	...
11,901	*18*	*3*	*12,278*	...	...	*5,520*	*4*	...	*5,670*	...	...
84,369	272	4	88,631	5	1	45,596	58	3	43,462	...	...
261,223	4,571	52	268,661	99	6	104,060	1,877	10	104,995	22	...

SUPPLEMENTARY TABLE C.

Literate by Caste.

SUPPLEMENTARY

Caste and Religion.				Territorial — Shimoga.					
				Males.			Females.		
					Literate.			Literate.	
Class.	Group.	Caste, &c. and sub-divisions.	Religion.	Total.	Total.	Knowing English.	Total.	Total.	Knowing English.
				41	42	43	44	45	46
C—Commercial.	14. Traders.	Baniya ...	Hindu ...	...	...	...	...	...	...
		Do ...	Jain ...	...	...	...	...	...	...
		Banajiga ...	Hindu ...	3.763	326	36	2,913	9	...
		Guzaráti ...	" ...	...	...	...	...	...	...
		Ját ...	" ...	...	...	...	...	...	...
		Kómati ...	" ...	617	304	13	558	4	...
		Ladar ...	" ...	10	...	...	1	...	...
		Lingâyet ...	" ...	25.333	4.514	51	24,000	22	...
		Madali ...	" ...	149	19	5	80	3	1
		Multáni ...	" ...	...	...	...	...	...	...
		Nagarta ...	" ...	4.203	1,302	...	3,758	4	...
		S'ravaka ...	Jain ...	1.038	95	...	924	...	...
		Jain (Sub-division or caste not returned) ...	...	535	10	...	177	...	...
		Márváli ...	Buddhist ...	...	...	...	...	...	...
		Do ...	Hindu ...	...	...	...	...	...	...
		Do ...	Jain ...	21	...	...	...	...	...
		Total Class C......		**35,677**	**6,639**	**105**	**32,746**	**42**	**1**
D—Artisan and Village menial.	17. Goldsmith ...	Pánchála ...	Hindu ...	5.532	820	16	4,882	20	...
	18. Barbers ...	Náyinda ...	" ...	1.460	17	...	1,368	1	...
	19. Blacksmiths ...	Kammára (Pánchála) ...	" ...	96	...	...	84	...	...
	20. Carpenters &c.	Badagi (Pánchála) ...	" ...	856	13	...	601	...	...
		Gounder ...	" ...	...	...	...	...	...	...
		Total......		*856*	*13*	...	*601*	...	...
	21. Brass and Coppersmiths ...	Gojjégára and Kanchugára ...	...	...	...	...	...	...	...
	22. Tailors ...	Darzi ...	...	1.097	93	...	983	...	...
	23. Weavers ...	Gániga ...	...	...	...	...	...	...	...
		Gadiya ...	Jain ...	...	...	...	...	...	...
		Néyigé ...	Hindu ...	3.394	178	...	3,280	...	...
		Total......		*3,394*	*178*	...	*3,280*	...	...
	24. Washermen ...	Agasa ...	Hindu ...	6,836	63	...	6,267	...	...
	26. Shepherds and Wool-weavers.	Kuruba ...	" ...	11,924	184	1	11,759	...	...
	26(a). Cowherds ...	Golla ...	" ...	2,101	52	...	1,894	...	...
	27. Oil-pressers ...	Gániga ...	" ...	377	33	...	370	...	...
	28. Potters ...	Kumbára ...	" ...	1.885	16	...	1,396	...	...
	30. Salt workers ...	Uppára ...	" ...	6.091	63	1	4,865	2	...
	32. Goldsmith's refuse collectors	Jalagára ...	" ...	...	...	...	...	...	...
	33(a). Gold-lace makers ...	Káchévár, Sirigé ...	" ...	...	...	...	...	...	...
	35. Fishermen ...	Besta ...	" ...	3,759	93	...	3,531	...	...
	36. Toddy-drawers.	Idiga ...	" ...	5.941	3	...	5,003	...	...
	38. Leather workers ...	Mádiga ...	" ...	11,948	13	...	11,069	...	...
		Móchi ...	" ...	12	...	...	14	...	...
		Total......		*11,960*	*13*	...	*11,083*	...	...
	38(a). Village watchmen ...	Holaya ...	" ...	19.342	40	...	18,658	...	...
		Total Class D......		**82.707**	**1,689**	**18**	**75,834**	**23**	...

SUPPLEMENTARY TABLE C.

Literate by Caste.

TABLE C.—(Continued.)

Distribution.

Kadúr.						Chitaldurg.					
Males.			Females.			Males.			Females.		
Total.	Literate. Total.	Literate. Knowing English.	Total.	Literate. Total.	Literate. Knowing English.	Total.	Literate. Total.	Literate. Knowing English.	Total.	Literate. Total.	Literate. Knowing English.
47	48	49	50	51	52	53	54	55	56	57	58
...	...	...	...	...	...	...	...	...	...	...	...
2,700	191	...	2,165	51	...	2,154	376	17	2,070	14	...
...	...	...	...	...	...	...	...	...	...	...	...
731	317	14	697	7	...	1,360	702	23	1,215	2	...
155	2	...	183	...	...	114	...	...	102	...	...
10,716	3,077	14	10,[illegible]	84	...	32,671	5,103	21	21,626	28	...
133	48	7	92	1	...	250	26	7	242	...	...
2,989	56	...	2,234	...		332	3	...	319	...	...
...	...	...	...	...	...	...	...	...	...	...	...
26	15	...	17	...	...	2,128	84	...	72	3	...
...	...	...	...	...	...	...	...	...	...	...	...
1	...	...	...	...	...	23	...	...	...	...	...
17,451	3,706	35	15,884	143	...	27,032	6,294	68	25,676	47	...
4,110	527	4	3,131	...	...	3,093	831	...	3,133	6	...
520	17	...	505	...	...	935	34	...	898	...	...
90	...	...	87	...	...	426	3	...	363	...	...
559	8	...	158	...	...	654	2	...	696	...	...
5[illegible]	*8*	...	*253*	...	...	*657*	*2*	...	*696*	...	...
...	...	...	...	...	...	...	...	...	...	...	...
409	42	...	325	...	...	418	102	...	704	...	...
7	...	...	12	...	...	...	...	...	...	...	...
5,106	368	...	5,113	...	...	3,593	376	7	3,576	1	...
5,177	*368*	...	*5,127*	...	...	*3,608*	*376*	*7*	*3,576*	*1*	...
2,199	23	...	1,987	1	...	3,217	30	...	3,177	...	...
13,246	333	...	13,069	3	...	13,005	393	...	12,393	2	...
2,127	46	...	2,022	...	...	15,892	188	1	15,613	...	...
550	28	...	512	...	...	694	103	...	668	...	...
2,153	32	...	1,866	...	...	1,352	74	...	1,258	...	...
5,115	105	1	4,885	...	...	4,312	59	...	4,361	3	...
...	...	...	...	...	...	...	...	...	...	...	...
...	...	...	...	...	...	...	...	...	...	...	...
2,064	32	...	2,038	...	...	2,479	61	...	2,359	...	...
2,167	10	...	1,715	...	...	2,133	60	...	2,146	...	...
5,490	7	...	4,958	...	...	18,479	19	...	18,607	...	...
4	...	...	1	...	...	22	...	...	31	...	...
5,491	*7*	...	*4,959*	...	...	*18,501*	*19*	...	*18,611*	...	...
28,161	16	...	25,130	...	...	4,207	39	1	4,284	...	...
74,085	1,594	5	65,981	6	...	74,836	2,316	8	73,836	12	...

SUPPLEMENTARY TABLE C.

Literate by Caste.

SUPPLEMENTARY

Class.	Group.	Caste, &c. and sub-divisions.	Religion.	Territorial — The Civil and Military Station, Males. Total.	Literate. Total.	Literate. Knowing English.
				59	60	61
C—Commercial.	14. Traders ...	Baniya	Hindu	23	22	...
		Do	Jain	77	53	2
		Baṇajiga	Hindu	4,124	1,623	299
		Guzaráti	,, ...	10	...	...
		Ját	,, ...	1	...	...
		Kómaṭi	,, ...	24	19	3
		Laḍar	,, ...	...	...	...
		Lingáyet	,, ...	518	140	7
		Mudali	,, ...	15	7	3
		Multáni	,, ...	1	...	...
		Nagarta	,, ...	113	35	1
		S'rávaka	Jain	...	...	...
		Jain (Sub-division or caste not returned)	... ...	...	...	...
		Márvádi	Buddhist ...	2	...	...
		Do.	Hindu	17	8	...
		Do.	Jain	11	9	...
		Total Class C.....		**4.941**	**1.916**	**315**
D—Artisan and Village menial.	17. Goldsmith	Pánchála	Hindu	556	187	6
	18. Barbers	Náyinda	,, ...	586	100	2
	19. Blacksmiths ...	Kaminára (Pánchaḷa)	,, ...	50	13	1
	20. Carpenters, &c. ...	Badage (Pánchaḷa)	,, ...	5	3	...
		Gounder	,, ...	2	...	...
		Total......		*7*	*3*	...
	21. Brass and Copper-smiths	Gejjégára and Kanchugára ...	,, ...	78	41	2
	22. Tailors	Darzi	,, ...	998	116	1
	23. Weavers... ...	Góṇiga	,, ...	6	1	...
		Gádiya	Jain	1	1	...
		Néyigé	Hindu	81	24	3
		Total......		*88*	*26*	*3*
	24. Washermen ...	Agasa	Hindu	503	21	1
	26. Shepherds and Wool-weavers... ...	Kuruba	,, ...	386	30	...
	26(a). Cowherds ...	Golla	,, ...	653	171	28
	27. Oil-pressers ...	Gáṇiga	,, ...	63	23	...
	28. Potters ...	Kumbára	,, ...	184	16	...
	30. Salt workers ...	Uppára	,, ...	9	1	...
	32. Gold-smith's refuse collectors ...	Jalagára	,, ...	2	...	...
	33(a). Gold-lace makers ...	Ráchévár, Sarigé	,, ...	...	...	...
	35. Fishermen ...	Besta	,, ...	115	15	5
	36. Toddy drawers ...	Idiga	,, ...	8	...	...
	38. Leather workers ...	Mádiga	,, ...	1,449	32	4
		Móchi	,, ...	53	8	...
		Total......		*1,502*	*40*	*4*
	38(a) Village watch men...	Holaya	,, ...	3.811	1,259	203
		Total Class D......		**14.599**	**2,062**	**256**

SUPPLEMENTARY TABLE C

Literate by Caste.

TABLE C.—(Continued.)

Distribution.

Bangalore.			Total strength including the Civil and Military Station, Bangalore.					
Females.			Males.			Females.		
Total.	Literate.		Total.	Literate.		Total.	Literate.	
	Total.	Knowing English.		Total.	Knowing English.		Total.	Knowing English.
62	63	64	65	66	67	68	69	70
13	...	...	28	22	...	13	...	...
43	...	...	77	53	2	43	...	...
4,218	110	2	57,653	8,730	599	57,082	631	13
40	...	...	41	25	...	30	4	...
...	...	...	1	...	...	...	...	...
30	...	...	15.181	88.50	188	13,873	101	3
...	...	...	1.014	117	3	1,032	...	...
478	...	...	146.492	29.501	237	145,581	398	1
11	...	...	2.969	971	255	2,468	117	3
1	...	...	1	...	...	1	...	...
107	...	...	12.015	2.874	13	10,949	7	...
...	...	...	1.038	95	...	924	...	...
...	...	...	1,090	286	5	871	10	...
...	...	...	2	...	...	...	...	...
4	1	...	17	8	...	4	1	...
9	1	...	66	9	...	14	1	...
4.924	**142**	**2**	**237.685**	**51.541**	**1.302**	**232.885**	**1.273**	**20**
535	12	...	50.152	8.864	77	48,029	165	...
557	5	...	18.997	593	2	18,299	7	...
59	2	...	3.172	75	1	3,078	2	...
4	...	...	4.414	43	...	4,229	...	...
1	...	...	2	...	...	1	...	...
5	...	...	*4.416*	*43*	...	*4,230*		
88	1	...	189	41	2	207	1	...
905	4	...	5.527	692	16	5,137	26	1
4	...	...	754	14	...	672	...	...
...	...	...	1	1	...	...	...	...
87	1	...	43.399	5,181	53	43,587	113	6
91	*1*	...	44.154	*5,196*	*53*	*44,259*	*113*	*6*
504	1	...	42,879	327	2	42,792	3	...
408	...	...	172.400	2.486	8	174,368	33	1
655	7	...	65.233	1.451	64	63,762	24	...
70	...	...	17.708	1.431	7	18,100	9	...
167	...	...	21.210	724	1	19,599	4	...
10	...	...	44,854	613	7	44,269	7	...
2	...	...	131	...	...	127	...	...
...	...	...	8	...	...	7	...	...
124	...	...	49.735	861	9	50,162	10	...
12	...	...	20,540	398	2	19,397	...	...
1,435	1	...	119.906	153	7	119,669	4	...
51	...	...	361	15	...	385	...	...
1,486	*1*	...	*120,267*	*168*	7	*120,054*	*4*	...
9,673	59	6	259.999	2.121	238	260,491	74	S
15.351	**93**	**6**	**941.571**	**26.084**	**496**	**936,370**	**482**	**16**

SUPPLEMENTARY TABLE C

Literate by Caste

SUPPLEMENTARY

Class.	Group.	Caste, &c., and sub-divisions.	Religion.	Total strength: Males: Total Males.	Males: Literate: Total.	Males: Literate: Knowing English.	Females: Total Females.	Females: Literate: Total.	Females: Literate: Knowing English.
1	2	3	4	5	6	7	8	9	10
E.—Vagrant Minor Artisans and Performers, &c.	41. Earthworkers and stone dressers.	Vaddar	Hindu	54,446	168	8	51,952	2	...
	43. Mat-makers.	Mēda	,,	2,318	16	...	1,912	...	...
	44. Hunters.	Bēda	,,	103,731	1,484	26	108,138	44	...
	45. Miscellaneous and disreputable livers.	Budubudiké	,,	553	...	...	539	...	...
		[illegible]	,,	461	36	...	464	3	...
		Sillekyāta	,,	55	...	...	38	...	...
		[illegible]	,,	...	...	...	...	...	...
		Sadarudasidde	,,	25	...	...	21	...	...
		Jōgi	,,	4,318	68	7	4,165	6	3
		Gondaliga	,,	16	...	...	13	...	...
		Mondara	,,	127	...	...	62	...	...
		Karnam	,,	...	...	...	...	...	...
		Sāniyar	,,	...	...	...	...	...	...
		Total Group 45		*5,555*	*104*	*7*	*5,302*	9	3
	46. Tumblers and Acrobats, &c.	Dombar	Hindu	1,217	3	...	1,283	...	...
		Ráchévár (Jatti)	,,	592	...	...	610	...	...
		Total Group 46		*1,809*	*3*	...	*1,893*	...	...
	47. Jugglers, snake-charmers and animal exhibiters.	Gardige	Hindu	411	...	...	465	...	...
		Total Class E		**173,270**	**1,775**	**41**	**169,662**	**55**	**3**
F.—Races and Nationalities.	48. Asiatic Races of reputed Foreign Origin.	Musalmán	Musalman	433	...	...	355	...	...
		Israelites	Christian	...	...	...	...	...	...
		Beluchi	Musalman	...	...	...	...	...	...
		Burmese	Christian	...	...	...	...	...	...
		Chinese		...	...	...	...	...	...
		Arab	Musalman	17	7	...	11	...	...
		Armenian	Christian	2	2	2	1	1	1
		Dáyaré	Musalman	1,081	44	...	1,419	...	...
		Hanafi		584	39	...	481	2	...
		Singhali	Buddhist	...	...	...	...	...	...
		Jew	Jew	9	4	...	11	5	...
		Jew	Christian	...	...	...	...	...	...
		Mogal	Musalman	4,527	430	25	4,245	146	...
		Khádri	,,	2	...	...	...	...	...
		Kandhári	,,	...	...	...	...	...	...
		Pársi	Pársi	15	7	4	14	8	...
		Páthan	Musalman	18,127	2,158	64	16,929	289	1
		Sharif	,,	431	19	...	421	7	...
		Syad	,,	18,616	3,831	127	16,958	552	4
		Shékh	,,	71,193	10,062	340	66,053	1,000	12
		Total Group 48		*115,037*	*16,603*	*562*	*106,898*	*2,010*	*18*
	49. Mixed Asiatic Races.	Jám	Musalman	...	...	...	...	...	...
		Laibbé	,,	1,859	114	3	961	12	...
		Māplé	,,	130	26	...	20	...	...
		Pinjári	,,	1,199	30	...	951	4	...
		Pindári (Kákar)	,,	1,064	43	...	984	3	...
		Mémon	,,	...	...	...	...	...	...
		Total Group 49		*4,252*	*213*	*3*	*2,916*	*19*	...
	50. Non-Asiatic Races.	European	Christian	771	579	579	475	265	265
		Australasian	,,	...	...	...	...	...	...
		Total Group 50		*771*	*579*	*579*	*475*	*265*	*265*
	51. Eurasians.	Eurasian	Christian	706	434	434	576	294	292
	52. Christian Converts.	Native Christian	,,	9,712	2,004	315	7,990	557	86
		Total Class F		**130,478**	**19,833**	**1,893**	**118,885**	**3,145**	**661**
	Caste not stated		Hindu	1,875	100	2	1,509	11	...
			Jain	...	...	...	...	...	...
	Provincial Total			**2,433,262**	**185,736**	**7,535**	**2,410,261**	**7,689**	**745**

SUPPLEMENTARY TABLE C.

Literate by Caste.

TABLE C.—(*Continued.*)

Territorial Distribution.

Bangalore.						Kolar.					
Males.			Females.			Males.			Females.		
Total.	Literate.		Total.	Literate.		Total.	Literate.		Total.	Literate.	
	Total.	Knowing English.		Total.	Knowing English.		Total.	Knowing English.		Total.	Knowing English.
11	12	13	14	15	16	17	18	19	20	21	22
10,062	32	2	9,979	...	...	11,768	16	...	11,322	1	...
202	2	...	221	...	...	102	...	...	98		...
7,303	136	4	7,477	7	...	23,923	152	4	23,406	3	...
76	...	...	68	...	...	55	...	...	45	...	...
215	17	...	226	1	...	23	...	...	29	...	...
...	...	...	...	...	...	...	...	...	...	...	...
...	...	...	...	...	...	...	...	...	...	...	...
...	...	...	...	...	...	...	...	...	...	...	...
995	6	3	1,038	2	...	766	22	...	739	...	...
7	...	...	8	...	...	4	...	...	2	...	...
...	...	...	...	...	...	62	...	...	52	...	...
...	...	...	...	...	...	...	...	...	...	...	...
...	...	...	...	...	...	...	...	...	...	...	...
1,293	*23*	*5*	*1,310*	*3*	..	*910*	*22*	...	*867*	...	...
194	...	..	225	..	...	283	1	...	317	...	...
97	...	..	112	...	...	21	...	...	17	...	...
291	...	...	*337*	...	...	*301*	*1*	...	*364*	...	...
136	...	...	149	...	...	55	...	...	51	...	...
19,237	**193**	**9**	**19,806**	**10**	...	**37,062**	**191**	**4**	**36,111**	**4**	...
305	...	...	256	...	...	91	...	...	78	...	...
...	...	...	...	...	...	...	...	...	...	...	...
...	...	...	...	...	...	...	...	...	...	...	...
...	...	...	...	...	...	...	...	...	...	...	...
10	4	...	5	...	...	...	...	...	...	...	...
2	2	2	1	1	1	...	...	...	...	...	...
1,034	40	...	1,385	...	...	...	...	...	...	...	...
...	...	...	...	...	...	3	2	...	3	...	...
...	...	...	...	...	...	...	...	...	...	...	...
...	...	...	...	...	...	...	...	...	...	...	...
694	98	2	660	27	...	631	56	1	603	6	...
...	...	...	...	...	...	...	...	...	...	...	...
...	...	...	...	...	...	...	...	...	...	...	...
3	2	2	2	2	...	1	1	...	...	...	...
4,369	436	12	4,165	97	...	2,638	315	3	2,299	10	...
9	...	...	8	...	...	5	...	...	6	...	...
4,307	897	48	4,091	176	1	3,500	820	9	3,911	85	1
12,131	2,046	60	11,491	233	2	9,993	1,308	27	8,868	122	2
22,861	*2,525*	*126*	*21,971*	*536*	*4*	*16,892*	*2,502*	*40*	*14,868*	*227*	*3*
...	...	...	...	...	...	...	...	...	...	...	...
158	21	1	43	4	...	181	10	...	18	...	...
...	...	...	...	...	...	...	...	...	...	...	...
82	9	...	42	2	...	240	10	...	207	1	...
32	10	...	98	2	...	...	...	...	...	...	...
...	...	...	...	...	...	...	...	...	...	...	...
222	*40*	*1*	*183*	*8*	...	*421*	*20*	...	*225*	*1*	...
143	98	98	156	114	114	264	225	225	38	32	32
...	...	...	...	...	...	...	...	...	...	...	...
143	*98*	*98*	*156*	*114*	*114*	*264*	*225*	*225*	*38*	*32*	*32*
199	125	125	209	123	121	161	94	94	115	61	61
2,797	551	126	2,607	179	42	1,287	392	10	1,131	91	9
26,325	**4,339**	**476**	**25,122**	**960**	**281**	**19,025**	**3,233**	**369**	**16,377**	**403**	**105**
208	20	1	214	10	..	173	4	...	153	...	...
...	...	...	...	...	...	...	...	...	...	...	...
349,297	**34,324**	**2,412**	**353,616**	**2,014**	**306**	**297,655**	**23,341**	**1,001**	**293,375**	**861**	**106**

SUPPLEMENTARY

Caste and Religion.				Territorial — Tumkúr.					
				Males.			Females.		
					Literate.			Literate	
Class.	Group.	Caste, &c., and sub-divisions.	Religion.	Total.	Total.	Knowing English.	Total.	Total.	Knowing English.
				23	24	25	26	27	28
E.—Vagrant Minor Artisans and Performers &c.	41. Earthworkers and stone dressers.	Vaddar ...	Hindu	6,908	30	...	6,478	1	...
	43. Mat-makers.	Méda ...	,,	186	6	...	183	...	...
	44. Hunters.	Béda ...	,,	21,762	348	10	21,608	12	...
	45. Miscellaneous and disreputable livers.	Budubudiké ...	,,	112	...	...	121	...	...
		Jangáliga ...	,,	37	1	...	26	...	...
		Sillekyáta ...	,,	...	...	...	...	...	...
		Pandáram ...	,,	...	...	...	...	...	...
		Sudagádusidda ...	,,	401	2	...	383	...	...
		Jógi ...	,,	...	...	...	...	...	...
		Gondaliga ...	,,	...	...	...	...	...	...
		Mondaru ...	,,	...	...	...	...	...	...
		Karman ...	,,	...	...	...	...	...	...
		Sapiyár ...	,,	...	...	...	...	...	...
		Total Group 45		*550*	*3*	...	*530*	...	...
	46. Tumblers and Acrobats, &c.	Dombar ...	Hindu	147	1	...	147	...	...
		Ráchévár (Jatti)	,,	37	...	...	30	...	...
		Total Group 46		*184*	*1*	...	*177*	...	...
	47. Jugglers, Snake-charmers and animal exhibiters.	Gárdiga ...	Hindu	63	...	...	57	...	...
		Total Class E		**29,653**	**388**	**10**	**29,033**	**13**	...
F.—Races and Nationalities.	48. Asiatic Races of reputed Foreign Origin.	Musalmán ...	Musalman	21	...	...	9	...	...
		Israelites ...	Christian	...	...	...	...	...	...
		Belúchi ...	Musalman	...	...	...	...	...	...
		Burmese ...	Christian	...	...	...	...	...	...
		Chinese ...	,,	...	...	...	...	...	...
		Arab ...	Musalman	...	...	...	...	...	...
		Armenian ...	Christian	...	...	...	...	...	...
		Dáyaré ...	Musalman	...	...	...	1	...	...
		Hanafi ...	,,	68	4	...	59	1	...
		Singháli ...	Buddhist	...	...	...	...	...	...
		Jew ...	Jew	...	...	...	...	...	...
		Jew ...	Christian	...	...	...	...	...	...
		Mogal ...	Musalman	522	11	1	510	5	...
		Khádri ...	,,	...	...	...	...	...	...
		Kandhári ...	,,	...	...	...	...	...	...
		Párse ...	Pársi	...	...	...	...	...	...
		Pathán ...	Musalman	2,205	52	2	2,257	17	...
		Sharif ...	,,	403	19	...	403	7	...
		Saiyad ...	,,	1,663	352	5	1,346	37	...
		Shékh ...	,,	7,140	1,083	13	7,107	127	...
		Total Group 48		*12,032*	*1,521*	*21*	*11,692*	*198*	...
	49. Mixed Asiatic Races.	Jám ...	Musalman	...	...	...	...	...	...
		Labbé ...	,,	74	8	...	18	...	...
		Máplé ...	,,	...	...	...	...	...	...
		Pinjári ...	,,	331	6	...	286	...	...
		Pindári (Kákar)	,,	400	7	...	408	1	...
		Mémon ...	,,	...	...	...	...	...	...
		Total Group 49		*805*	*21*	...	*712*	*1*	...
	50. Non-Asiatic Races.	European ...	Christian	16	10	10	11	7	7
		Australasian ...	,,	...	...	...	...	...	...
		Total Group 50		*16*	*10*	*10*	*11*	*7*	*7*
	51. Eurasians.	Eurasian ...	Christian	8	8	8	9	7	7
	52. Christian Converts.	Native Christian ...	,,	377	111	8	322	76	5
		Total Class F		**13,238**	**1,671**	**47**	**12,746**	**289**	**19**
Caste not stated			Hindu	97	5	...	117	...	...
			Jain	...	...	...	...	...	...
Provincial Total				**291,133**	**14,558**	**358**	**289,653**	**794**	**27**

TABLE C.—*Continued.*

Distribution.

Mysore						Hassan.					
Males.			Females.			Males.			Females.		
Total.	Literate.		Total.	Literate.		Total.	Literate.		Total.	Literate.	
	Total.	Knowing English.		Total.	Knowing English.		Total.	Knowing English.		Total.	Knowing English.
29	30	31	32	33	34	35	36	37	38	39	40
4,077	36	6	3,981	...	...	2,496	1	...	2,282	...	...
323	2	...	329	...	...	265	2	...	255	...	...
1,564	84	1	1,565	3	...	2,774	61	6	2,807	1	...
126	...	...	112	...	...	84	...	...	115	...	...
11	1	...	22	...	...	75	8	...	83	1	...
...	...	...	...	...	...	...	...	...	...	...	...
...	...	...	...	...	...	...	...	...	...	...	...
...	...	...	...	...	...	...	...	...	...	...	...
646	10	...	717	...	...	219	20	4	187	4	3
5	...	...	3	...	...	...	...	...	...	...	...
...	...	...	...	...	...	...	...	...	...	...	...
...	...	...	...	...	...	...	...	...	...	...	...
...	...	...	...	...	...	...	...	...	...	...	...
788	*11*	...	*854*	...	...	*378*	*28*	*4*	*385*	*5*	*3*
167	...	...	146	...	...	173	...	...	169	...	...
280	...	...	303	...	...	73	...	...	73	...	...
447	...	...	*451*	...	...	*246*	...	...	*242*	...	...
23	...	...	37	...	...	...	...	...	...	...	...
7,222	**133**	**7**	**7,217**	**3**	...	**6,159**	**92**	**10**	**5,971**	**6**	**3**
...	...	...	...	...	...	8	...	...	6	...	...
...	...	...	...	...	...	...	...	...	...	...	...
...	...	...	...	...	...	...	...	...	...	...	...
...	...	...	...	...	...	...	...	...	...	...	...
...	...	...	...	...	...	...	...	...	...	...	...
...	...	...	...	...	...	...	...	...	...	...	...
...	...	...	...	...	...	...	...	...	...	...	...
47	4	...	33	...	...	...	...	...	...	...	...
227	18	...	206	...	...	104	5	...	35	1	...
...	...	...	...	...	...	...	...	...	...	...	...
2	1	...	2	1	...	6	2	...	9	4	...
...	...	...	...	...	...	...	...	...	...	...	...
734	165	15	679	91	...	239	28	3	212	2	...
2	...	...	...	...	...	...	...	...	...	...	...
...	...	...	...	...	...	...	...	...	...	...	...
9	3	2	8	3	...	...	...	...	...	...	...
3,874	870	32	3,712	102	...	961	32	8	867	12	...
4	...	...	4	...	...	...	...	...	...	...	...
3,730	826	25	3,597	169	...	892	206	11	813	25	1
14,368	2,316	96	14,266	285	2	4,851	839	19	4,473	69	2
22,097	*4,203*	*170*	*22,507*	*651*	*2*	*7,061*	*1,112*	*51*	*6,445*	*113*	*3*
...	...	...	...	...	...	...	...	...	...	...	...
1,147	35	2	826	6	...	58	8	...	9	...	...
18	9	...	...	...	...	71	11	...	...	...	...
...	...	...	...	...	...	20	2	...	6	...	...
556	26	...	471	...	...	...	...	...	...	...	...
...	...	...	...	...	...	...	...	...	...	...	...
1,721	*70*	*2*	*1,297*	*6*	...	*149*	*21*	...	*15*	...	...
72	41	41	158	39	39	97	85	85	35	28	28
...	...	...	...	...	...	...	...	...	...	...	...
72	*41*	*41*	*158*	*39*	*39*	*97*	*85*	*85*	*35*	*28*	*28*
118	60	60	90	30	30	49	33	33	48	28	28
1,281	349	11	1,228	79	4	1,564	227	24	1,503	50	5
26,189	**4,723**	**284**	**25,280**	**805**	**75**	**8,920**	**1,478**	**193**	**8,046**	**228**	**64**
581	17	1	560	...	...	268	30	...	183	1	...
...	...	...	...	...	...	...	...	...	...	...	...
580,737	**36,924**	**1,570**	**601,077**	**1,924**	**111**	**255,044**	**16,425**	**489**	**259,809**	**417**	**70**

SUPPLEMENTARY TABLE C.

Literate by Caste.

SUPPLEMENTARY

Caste and Religion.				Territorial — Shimoga.					
				Males.			Females.		
					Literate.			Literate.	
Class.	Group.	Caste, &c., and sub-divisions.	Religion.	Total.	Total.	Knowing English.	Total.	Total.	Knowing English.
				41	42	43	44	45	46
E.—Vagrant Minor Artisans and Performers, &c.	41. Earthworkers and stone dressers.	Vaddar	Hindu ...	**7,775**	**26**	...	7,143	...	...
	43. Mat-makers.	Méda	" ...	**709**	**4**	...	351	...	...
	44. Hunters.	Béda	" ...	**12,949**	**121**	...	12,729	11	...
	45. Miscellaneous and disreputable livers.	Budabudikè	" ...	**45**	...	...	36	...	...
		Jangáliga	" ...	...	...	...	...	...	...
		Sillékyáta	" ...	**48**	...	...	31	...	...
		Pandarama	" ...	...	...	...	...	...	...
		Sudagádusidda ...	" ...	**25**	...	...	21	...	...
		Jógi	" ...	**561**	**1**	...	437	...	...
		Gondaliga	" ...	...	...	...	...	...	...
		Mondaru	" ...	...	...	...	...	...	...
		Karnan	" ...	...	...	...	...	...	...
		Saniyar	" ...	...	...	...	...	...	...
		Total Group 45......		*679*	*1*	...	*525*	...	...
	46. Tumblers and Acrobats, &c.	Dombar	Hindu ...	**53**	**1**	...	75	...	...
		Ráchévár (Jatti) ...	" ...	**76**	...	...	65	...	...
		Total Group 46......		*129*	...	...	*140*	...	...
	47. Jugglers, snake-charmers and animal exhibiters.	Gárdiga	Hindu ...	**134**	...	...	168	...	...
		Total Class E......		**22,375**	**153**	...	**21,056**	**11**	..
F.—Races and Nationalities.	48. Asiatic Races of reputed Foreign Origin	Musalmán	Musalman ...	...	...	...	...	...	...
		Isrælites	Christian ...	...	...	...	...	...	...
		Belúchi	Musalman ...	...	...	...	...	...	...
		Burmese	Christian ...	...	...	...	...	...	...
		Chinese	" ...	...	...	...	...	...	...
		A'rab	Musalman ...	...	...	...	...	...	...
		A'rminian	Christian ...	...	...	...	...	...	...
		Dáyaré	Musalman ...	...	...	...	...	...	...
		Hanaff	" ...	**167**	**5**	...	176	...	...
		Singháli	Budhist ...	...	...	...	...	...	...
		Jew	Jew ...	...	...	...	...	...	...
		Jew	Christian ...	...	...	...	...	...	...
		Mogal	Musalman ...	**1,356**	**35**	**1**	1,259	3	...
		Khádri	" ...	...	...	...	...	...	...
		Kandhári	" ...	...	...	...	...	...	...
		Pársi	Pársi ...	...	...	...	...	...	...
		Pat'hán	Musalman ...	**1,969**	**146**	**3**	1,784	19	1
		Sharíf	" ...	...	...	...	...	...	...
		Sayad	" ...	**2,267**	**325**	**18**	2,203	21	1
		Shékh	" ...	**9,888**	**823**	**91**	8,946	58	4
		Total Group 48......		*15,647*	*1,334*	*114*	*14,368*	*101*	*6*
	49. Mixed Asiatic Races.	Jám	Musalman ...	...	...	...	...	...	...
		Labbé	" ...	**89**	**12**	...	30	1	...
		Máplé	" ...	**1**	**1**	...	19	...	...
		Pinjári	" ...	**7**	...	...	3	...	...
		Pindári (Kakar) ...	" ...	**26**	...	...	7	...	...
		Mémon	" ...	...	...	...	...	...	...
		Total Group 49......		*123*	*13*	...	*59*	*1*	...
	50. Non-Asiatic Races.	European	Christian ...	**17**	**13**	**13**	15	11	11
		Australasian	" ...	...	...	...	...	...	...
		Total Group 50......		*17*	*13*	*13*	[illegible]	*11*	*11*
	51. Eurasians.	Eurasian	Christian ...	**14**	**11**	**11**	2	2	2
	52. Christian Converts.	Native Christian ...	" ...	**1,003**	**179**	**107**	600	25	12
		Total Class F......		**16,804**	**1,550**	**245**	**15,044**	**140**	**31**
		Caste not stated	Hindu ...	**212**	**3**	...	121	...	...
			Jain ...	...	...	...	...	...	...
		Provincial Total......		**275,884**	**20,785**	**658**	**252,097**	**380**	**38**

SUPPLEMENTARY TABLE C
Literate by Caste.

TABLE C—(Continued)

Distribution.

Kaḍūr.						Chitaldurg.					
Males.			Females.			Males.			Females.		
Total.	Literate.		Total.	Literate.		Total.	Literate.		Total.	Literate.	
	Total.	Knowing English.		Total.	Knowing English.		Total.	Knowing English.		Total.	Knowing English.
47	48	49	50	51	52	53	54	55	56	57	58
2,816	**5**	...	2,383	...	...	**8,544**	**22**	...	8,384	...	...
343	...	...	287	...	...	**188**	...	...	185	...	...
2,563	**83**	...	2,532	3	...	**35,893**	**499**	**1**	35,714	3	...
28	...	...	20	...	...	**27**	...	...	22	...	...
...	...	...	...	...	...	**100**	**9**	...	78	1	...
...	...	...	...	...	...	**7**	...	...	7	...	...
...	...	...	...	...	...	...	...	...	...	...	...
...	...	...	...	...	...	...	...	...	...	...	...
288	**7**	...	237	...	...	**442**	...	...	427	...	...
...	...	...	...	...	...	...	...	...	...	...	...
65	...	...	10	...	...	...	...	...	...	...	...
...	...	...	...	...	...	...	...	...	...	...	...
...	...	...	...	...	...	...	...	...	...	...	...
381	*7*	...	*257*	...	...	*576*	*9*	...	*534*	*1*	...
146	...	...	114	...	...	**54**	...	...	60	...	...
...	...	...	...	...	...	**8**	...	...	8	...	...
146	...	...	*114*	...	...	*62*	...	...	*58*	...	...
...	...	...	...	...	...	[illegible]	...	...	56	...	...
6,249	**95**	...	**5,583**	**3**	...	**45,203**	**530**	**1**	**44,885**	**5**	...
...	...	...	...	...	...	**8**	...	...	6	...	...
...	...	...	...	...	...	...	...	...	...	...	...
...	...	...	...	...	...	...	...	...	...	...	...
...	...	...	...	...	...	...	...	...	...	...	...
...	...	...	...	...	...	...	...	...	...	...	...
...	...	...	...	...	...	**7**	**3**	—	6	...	...
...	...	...	...	...	...	...	...	...	...	...	...
14	**4**	...	...	...	...	**1**	**1**	...	2	...	...
...	...	...	...	...	...	...	...	...	...	...	...
...	...	...	...	...	...	**1**	**1**	...	...	...	...
[illegible]	**25**	**1**	174	7	...	**119**	**12**	**1**	118	1	...
...	...	...	...	...	...	...	...	...	...	...	...
...	...	...	...	...	...	**2**	**1**	...	4	3	...
1,147	**208**	**1**	970	15	...	**964**	**99**	**3**	875	8	...
1,071	**223**	**1**	872	21	...	**1,186**	**182**	**10**	1,085	18	...
6,162	**1,020**	**2**	4,750	69	...	**6,660**	**627**	**21**	6,182	46	...
8,596	*1,480*	*5*	*6,766*	*112*	...	*8,048*	*929*	*35*	*8,278*	*76*	...
...	...	...	...	...	...	...	...	...	...	...	...
144	**15**	...	17	1	...	**8**	**5**	...	...	...	...
40	**5**	...	1	...	...	...	...	...	...	...	...
1	...	...	...	...	...	**518**	**3**	...	437	1	...
...	...	...	...	...	...	...	...	...	...	...	...
...	...	...	...	...	...	...	...	...	...	...	...
185	*20*	...	*18*	*1*	...	*526*	*8*	...	*437*	*1*	...
147	**94**	**94**	60	32	32	**15**	**13**	**13**	2	2	2
...	...	...	...	...	...	...	...	...	...	...	...
147	*94*	*94*	*60*	*32*	*32*	*15*	*13*	*13*	*2*	*2*	*2*
134	**84**	**84**	95	38	38	**23**	**19**	**19**	15	5	5
1,275	**150**	**17**	408	28	2	**128**	**45**	**12**	101	20	7
10,387	**1,828**	**200**	**7,437**	**211**	**72**	**9,640**	**1,011**	**79**	**8,833**	**104**	**41**
264	...	...	195	...	...	**67**	**21**	...	56	...	...
...	...	...	...	...	...	...	...	...	...	...	...
173,922	**14,360**	**692**	**156,141**	**1051**	**73**	**209,590**	**14,995**	**355**	**204,394**	**248**	**14**

SUPPLEMENTARY TABLE C.
Literate by Caste.

SUPPLEMENTARY

Caste and Religion.				Territorial. The Civil and Military Station, Males.		
Class.	Group.	Caste, &c., and sub-divisions.	Religion.	Total.	Literate. Total.	Literate. Knowing English.
				59	60	61
E.—Vagrant Minor Artisans and Performers, &c	41. Earthworkers and stone dressers.	Vaddar	Hindu	375	6	2
	43. Mat-makers.	Méda	,,	17	...	...
	44. Hunters.	Bedar	,,	121	9	1
	45. Miscellaneous and disreputable livers.	Budabudike	,,	1	...	...
		Jangáliga	,,	...	...	...
		Sillekyáta	,,	...	...	...
		Pandáram	,,	6	3	...
		Sudugádusidda	,,	...	...	...
		Jógi	,,	...	...	...
		Gondaliga	,,	...	...	...
		Mondaru	,,	...	...	...
		Karman	,,	3	3	...
		Sániyár	,,	1	...	...
		Total Group 45		*11*	*6*	...
	46. Tumblers and Acrobats, &c.	Dombar	Hindu	...	...	...
		Ráchévár (Jatti)	,,	1	1	...
		Total Group 46		*1*	*1*	...
	47. Jugglers, snake-charmers and animal exhibiters.	Gárdiga	Hindu	...	...	...
		Total Class E		**525**	**22**	**3**
F.—Races and Nationalities.	48. Asiatic Races of reputed Foreign Origin.	Musalmán	Musalman	45	18	...
		Isralites	Christian	1	1	1
		Belúchi	Musalman	2	...	...
		Burmese	Christian	2	1	...
		Chinese	,,	4	4	...
		A'rab	Musalman	...	...	...
		A'rmenian	Christian	2	1	1
		Dáyaré	Musalman	...	...	...
		Hanifí	,,	13	6	...
		Singhálí	Budhist	3	2	1
		Jew	Jew	1	1	...
		Jew	Christian	3	3	3
		Mogul	Musalman	327	115	23
		Khádri	,,	...	...	...
		Kandhári	,,	...	...	...
		Pársi	Pársi	3	2	2
		Pat'hán	Musalman	1,825	486	43
		Sharif	,,	22	11	1
		Sayad	,,	1,585	441	56
		Shekh	,,	7,737	2,019	184
		Total Group 47		*11,575*	*3,111*	*315*
	49. Mixed Asiatic Races.	Jám	Musalman	5	3	...
		Labbé	,,	500	236	9
		Máplo	,,	21	7	...
		Pinjári	,,	...	...	...
		Pindári (Kákar)	,,	...	...	...
		Memon	,,	128	62	4
		Total Group 48		*654*	*308*	*13*
	50. Non-Asiatic Races.	European	Christian	3,261	2,647	2,572
		Australasian	,,	1	1	1
		Total Group 49		*3,262*	*2,648*	*2,578*
	51. Eurasians.	Eurasian	Christian	1,127	556	514
	52. Christian Converts.	Native Christian	,,	4,715	1,363	398
		Total Class F		**21,333**	**7,986**	**3,813**
		Caste not stated	Jáin	138	48	11
			Hindu	101	4	...
		Provincial Total		**50,189**	**14,719**	**5,228**

SUPPLEMENTARY TABLE C.
Literate by Caste

TABLE C—(Concluded).

Distribution.

Bangalore.			Total strength including the Civil and Military Station, Bangalore.					
Females.			Males.			Females.		
Total.	Literate.		Total.	Literate.		Total.	Literate.	
	Total.	Knowing English.		Total.	Knowing English.		Total.	Knowing English.
62	63	64	65	66	67	68	69	70
430	1	...	54,821	174	10	52,383	3	...
14	...	...	2,335	16	...	1,926	...	...
138	3	...	108,852	1,493	27	108,276	47	...
...	...	...	553	...	...	539	...	...
1	...	...	462	36	...	465	3	...
...	...	...	55	...	...	38	...	...
9	...	...	6	3	...	9	...	...
...	...	...	258	...	...	21	...	...
...	...	...	4,318	68	7	4,165	6	3
...	...	...	16	...	...	13	...	...
...	...	...	127	...	...	62	...	...
4	...	...	3	3	...	4	...	...
2	...	...	1	...	...	2	...	...
16	...	...	*5,799*	*110*	*7*	*5,318*	*9*	*3*
...	...	...	1,217	3	...	1,283	...	...
...	...	...	593	1	...	610	...	...
...	...	...	*1,810*	*4*	...	*1,893*	...	...
...	...	...	411	...	...	465	...	...
598	**4**	...	**173,795**	**1,797**	**44**	**170,260**	**59**	**3**
28	1	...	478	18	...	383	1	...
...	...	...	1	1	1	...	...	...
...	...	...	2	...	...	...	...	...
2	1	...	2	1	...	2	1	...
...	...	...	4	4	...	...	...	...
...	...	...	17	7	...	11	...	...
3	2	2	4	3	3	4	3	3
...	...	...	1,081	44	...	1,419	...	...
20	2	...	507	45	...	501	4	...
...	...	...	3	2	1	...	...	...
...	...	...	10	5	...	11	5	...
...	...	...	3	3	3	...	...	...
318	32	1	4,354	545	48	4,563	178	1
...	...	...	...	...	...	...	...	...
2	...	...	...	...	...	2	...	...
3	2	2	18	9	6	17	10	2
1,698	63	1	19,952	2,644	107	18,627	343	2
18	2	...	453	30	1	439	9	...
1,514	88	...	20,201	4,272	183	18,472	640	4
7,564	431	6	78,930	12,081	524	73,617	1,410	18
11,170	*624*	*12*	*126,612*	*19,744*	*877*	*118,068*	*2,634*	*30*
...	...	...	5	3	...	...	...	...
397	33	...	2,359	350	12	1,358	45	...
7	...	...	151	33	...	27	...	...
...	...	...	1,199	30	...	981	4	...
...	...	—	1,064	43	...	984	3	...
116	16	1	128	62	4	116	16	1
520	*49*	*1*	*4,906*	*521*	*16*	*3,466*	*68*	*1*
1,723	1,153	1,112	4,032	3,226	3,151	2,198	1,418	1,377
...	...	...	1	1	1	...	...	...
1,723	*1,153*	...	*4,033*	*3,227*	*3,152*	*2,198*	*1,418*	*1,377*
1,522	831	787	1,833	990	948	2,098	1,125	1,079
5,537	439	105	14,427	3,367	713	13,527	996	191
20,472	**3,096**	**2,017**	**151,811**	**27,819**	**5,706**	**139,357**	**6,241**	**2,678**
100	2	...	2,013	148	13	1,699	13	...
2	...	...	10	4	...	2	...	...
49,892	**3,793**	**2,033**	**2,483,451**	**200,455**	**12,763**	**2,460,153**	**11,482**	**2,778**

SUPPLEMENTARY TABLE D.

EDUCATION BY CASTE.

SUPPLEMENTARY TABLE D.

Education by Caste.

Class.	Group.	Caste, &c., and Sub-division.	Religion.	Total Strength. Males. Total.	Pupils.	Literate.	Illiterate.	Education not stated.	Females. Total.	Pupils.	Literate.	Illiterate.	Education not stated.	Territorial Distribution. Bangalore. Males. Total.	Pupils.	Literate.	Illiterate.	Not stated.	Females. Total.	Pupils.	Literate.	Illiterate.	Not stated.
A.—Agricultural.	1 Military and Dominant.	Kshatriya ...	Hindu	10,785	855	3,285	6,645	...	10,282	68	183	10,131	...	1,892	135	695	1,062	...	1,823	6	16	1,801	...
		" ...	Sikh	13	2	3	8	...	16	...	1	15	...	1	......	1	......	...	1	...	...	1	...
		Total	...	10,798	857	3,288	6,653	...	10,298	68	184	10,146	...	1,893	135	696	1,062	...	1,824	6	16	1,802	...
		Maráta ...	Hindu	22,388	913	1,627	19,848	...	20,914	47	30	20,837	...	4,857	374	475	4,008	...	4,635	40	11	4,584	...
		Bachevár ...	"	1,745	129	403	1,213	...	1,871	17	5	1,849	...	391	52	114	225	...	399	15	3	381	...
		Total Group 1......	...	34,931	1,899	5,318	27,714	...	33,183	132	219	32,832	...	7,141	561	1,285	5,295	...	6,838	61	30	6,747	...
	2 Other Agricultural.	Lingáyet, Gaudmane	Hindu	28,710	618	1,970	26,122	...	29,757	13	18	29,726	...	4,998	238	240	4,520	...	5,011	...	4	5,007	...
		" Maláva ...	"	4.02	....	...	402	...	393	...	...	393	...	...	...	...	......	...	......	...	...	......	...
		" Panchácháru.	"	34,566	697	2,841	31,028	...	31,320	5	35	31,280	...	1,595	92	95	1,408	...	1,570	...	2	1,568	...
		Total......	...	63,678	1,315	4,811	57,552	...	61,470	18	53	61,399	...	6,593	330	335	5,928	...	6,581	...	6	6,575	...
	(a) Cultivators.	Nayar ...	"	3	......	3	...	...	......	...	...	......	...	......	...	...	......	...	......	...	...	......	...
		Gille ...	"	311	34	45	232	...	244	...	5	239	...	51	10	18	23	...	63	...	1	62	...
		Tigala ...	"	26,988	317	313	26,358	...	26,409	21	2	26,386	...	13,081	159	205	12,717	...	12,798	21	1	12,776	...
		Vokkaliga ...	"	660,730	8,670	22,218	629,842	...	671,393	506	274	670,613	...	105,619	1,583	3,417	100,619	...	100,290	185	50	100,055	...
		" Sáda ...	Jain	516	32	108	376	...	193	...	4	489	...	456	30	39	337	...	426	...	4	422	...
		" Tulu ...	Brahmo	......	......	......	......	...	......	...	...	......	...	......	...	...	......	...	......	...	...	......	...
		Total......	...	661,246	8,702	22,326	630,218	...	671,916	506	278	671,132	...	106,075	1,613	3,506	100,956	...	109,716	185	54	109,477	...
		Total Group 3 (a)...	...	752,226	10,368	27,498	714,360	...	763,039	545	338	762,156	...	125,800	2,112	4,031	119,621	...	129,158	206	62	128,890	
	4 Forest and Hilltribes.	Uraliga...	Hindu	581	......	...	581	...	551	...	...	551	...	534	...	...	534	...	508	...	...	508	...
		Koracha ...	"	5,462	36	47	5,379	...	5,082	...	...	5,082	...	1,011	17	20	974	...	1,015	...	...	1,015	...
		Korama...	"	6,771	47	109	6,615	...	6,761	...	4	6,757	...	1,373	29	28	1,316	...	1,129	...	...	1,129	...
		Kuruba...	"	1,136	......	...	1,136	...	1,133	...	...	1,133	...	104	...	...	104	...	115	...	...	115	...
		Lambáni ...	"	20,585	6	24	20,555	...	18,552	...	...	18,552	...	1,777	...	1	1,776	...	1,538	...	...	1,538	...
		Uriya ...	"	......	......	...	......	...	......	...	...	......	...	......	...	...	......	...	......	...		......	...
		Total Group 4	...	34,535	89	180	34,266	...	32,079		4	32,075	...	4,799	46	49	4,704	...	4,305	...	...	4,305	
		Total Class A....		**831,692**	**12,356**	**32,996**	**76,340**	...	**828,301**	**677**	**561**	**827,063**	...	**137,740**	**2,719**	**5,398**	**129,623**	...	**140,201**	**267**	**52**	**140,342**	

Class.	Group.	Caste, &c. and Sub-division.	Religion.	Kólár, Males. Total.	Pupils.	Literate.	Illiterate.	Not stated.	Kólár, Females. Total.	Pupils.	Literate.	Illiterate.	Not stated.	Tumkúr, Males. Total.	Pupils.	Literate.	Illiterate.	Not stated.	Tumkúr, Females. Total.	Pupils.	Literate.	Illiterate.	Not stated.
A.—Agricultural.—(Continued.)	1 Military and Dominant.	Kshatriya	Hindu	928	148	391	389	...	879	12	...	867	...	996	47	277	672	...	984	...	16	968	...
		,, ,,	Sikh	...	...	...	...	...	...	...	...	...	...	...	...	...	...	...	...	...	...	...	...
		Total	...	*928*	*148*	*391*	*389*	...	*879*	*12*	...	*867*	...	*996*	*47*	*277*	*672*	...	*984*	...	*16*	*968*	...
		Maráta	Hindu	2,319	229	223	1,867	...	2,321	...	...	2,321	...	1383	42	59	1,282	...	1,444	...	...	1,444	...
		Ráchévár	,,	214	34	21	159	...	198	...	...	198	...	188	14	32	142	...	213	...	...	213	...
		Total Group 1	...	*3,461*	*411*	*635*	*2,415*	...	*3,398*	*12*	...	*3,386*	...	*2,567*	*103*	*368*	*2,096*	...	*2,641*	...	*16*	*2,625*	...
	2 Other Agricultural.	Lingáyet, Gandamané	Hindu	216	23	8	185	...	205	...	...	205	...	1,046	79	103	864	...	1,080	5	...	1,075	...
		,, Malava	,,	...	...	...	...	...	...	...	...	...	...	...	...	...	...	...	...	...	...	...	...
		,, Panchácháras	,,	519	46	9	464	...	481	...	...	481	...	3,388	160	93	3,135	...	3,457	...	...	3,457	...
		Total	...	*735*	*69*	*17*	*649*	...	*686*	...	...	*686*	...	*4,434*	*239*	*196*	*3,999*	...	*4,537*	*5*	...	*4,532*	...
	(a) Cultivators	Náyar	,,	3	...	3	...	...	...	...	...	...	...	...	...	...	...	...	...	...	...	...	...
		Pillé	,,	115	16	2	97	...	(9)	...	2	58	...	15	3	2	10	...	9	...	...	9	...
		Tigala	,,	5,097	90	39	4,968	...	5,059	...	...	5,059	...	7,450	43	49	7,358	...	7,268	...	1	7,267	...
		Vakkaliga	,,	81,085	592	2,448	78,045	...	82,073	10	32	82,031	...	88,795	1,427	4,032	83,336	...	90,286	80	43	90,163	...
		,, Sáda	Jain	2	...	...	2	...	...	...	...	...	...	58	2	19	37	...	67	...	...	67	...
		,, Tulu	Bramho	...	...	...	...	...	...	...	...	...	...	...	...	...	...	...	...	...	...	...	...
		Total	...	*81,087*	*592*	*2,448*	*78,047*	...	*82,073*	*10*	*32*	*82,031*	...	*88,853*	*1,429*	*4,051*	*83,373*	...	*90,353*	*80*	*43*	*90,230*	...
		Total Group 2(a)	...	*87,037*	*707*	*2,509*	*83,761*	...	*87,878*	*10*	*34*	*87,834*	...	*100,752*	*1,714*	*4,298*	*94,710*	...	*102,167*	*85*	*44*	*102,038*	...
	4 Forest and Hill tribes.	Páliga	Hindu	12	...	...	12	...	10	...	...	10	...	34	...	...	34	...	33	...	...	33	...
		Koracha	,,	1,686	10	9	1,667	...	1,635	...	...	1,635	...	487	2	1	487	...	485	...	...	485	...
		Korama	,,	47	...	8	39	...	46	...	...	46	...	779	6	11	762	...	719	...	...	719	...
		Kurubа	,,	64	...	...	64	...	83	...	...	83	...	725	...	...	725	...	725	...	...	725	...
		Lambáni	,,	412	...	...	412	...	339	...	...	339	...	1,563	2	1	1,560	...	1,411	...	...	1,414	...
		Uriya	,,	...	...	...	...	...	...	...	...	...	...	...	...	...	...	...	...	...	...	...	...
		Total Group 4	...	*2,221*	*10*	*17*	*2,194*	...	*2,113*	...	...	*2,113*	...	*3,588*	*10*	*13*	*3,565*	...	*3,376*	...	...	*3,376*	...
		Total Class A		**92,719**	**1,188**	**3,161**	**88,370**	...	**93,389**	**22**	**34**	**93,333**	...	**106,907**	**1,827**	**4,679**	**100,401**	...	**108,184**	**85**	**60**	**108,039**	...

SUPPLEMENTARY TABLE D.—(Continued.)

Caste and Religion.				Territorial Distribution.—(Continued.)																			
				Mysore.										Hassan.									
				Males.					Females.					Males.					Females.				
Class.	Group.	Caste, &c. and Sub-division.	Religion.	Total.	Pupils.	Literate.	Illiterate.	Not stated.	Total.	Pupils.	Literate.	Illiterate.	Not stated.	Total.	Pupils.	Literate.	Illiterate.	Not stated.	Total.	Pupils.	Literate.	Illiterate.	Not stated.
A.—Agricultural.—(Continued.)	1 Military and Dominant.	Kshatriya	Hindu	3,391	324	1,107	1,960	...	3,450	38	120	3,292	...	822	60	150	612	...	889	3	4	882	...
		"	Sikh	12	2	2	8	...	15	...	1	14	...	...	...	...	...	...	...	...	...	...	...
		Total	....	3,403	326	1,109	1,968	...	3,465	38	121	3,306	...	822	60	150	612	...	889	3	4	882	...
		Marâtha	Hindu	3,893	141	317	3,435	...	3,927	5	14	3,908	...	1,116	12	46	1,058	...	1,055	...	...	1,055	...
		Lâchevâr	"	613	25	203	385	...	700	2	1	697	...	227	...	11	216	...	259	...	...	259	...
		Total Group 1	....	7,909	492	1,629	5,788	...	8,092	45	136	7,911	...	2,165	72	207	1,886	...	2,203	3	4	2,196	...
	2 Other Agricultural. (a) Cultivators.	Lingâyet, Gandamané	Hindu	18,276	203	1,325	16,748	...	19,369	6	10	19,353	...	3,086	52	196	2,838	...	3,017	...	1	3,016	...
		" Malava	"	......	...	...	...	...	...	...	...	...	...	6	...	...	6	...	4	...	...	4	...
		" Panchâchâra	"	7,096	114	896	6,086	...	7,523	4	7	7,512	...	6,517	48	257	6,214	...	6,630	...	2	6,628	...
		Total	....	25,372	317	2,221	22,834	...	26,892	10	17	26,865	...	9,609	98	453	9,058	...	9,651	...	3	9,648	...
		Nâyar	"	...	...	...	......	...	...	...	...	...	...	...	...	...	...	...	...	...	...	...	...
		Pille	"	78	2	7	69	...	76	...	...	76	...	8	...	2	6	...	11	...	1	10	...
		Tigala	"	589	19	13	557	...	633		...	633	...	374	...	...	374	...	340	...	...	340	...
		Vakkaliga	"	158,168	2,604	4,588	150,976	...	167,389	154	91	167,141	...	83,436	982	2,642	79,812	...	87,887	27	17	87,843	
		" Sâda	Jain	...	...	...	......	...	...	...	...	...	...	...	...	...	...	...	...	...	...	...	...
		" Tulu	Brâmho	...	...	...	...	...	...	...	...	2	...	...	...	...	...	...	...	...	...	...	...
		Total	....	158,168	2,604	4,588	150,976	...	167,389	154	94	167,141	...	83,436	982	2,642	79,812	...	87,887	27	17	87,843	...
		Total Group 2 (a)	....	184,207	2,942	6,829	174,436	...	191,990	164	111	191,715	...	93,427	1,080	3,096	89,250	...	97,889	27	21	97,841	...
	4 Forest and Hill tribes.	Pâligâr	Hindu	...	...	...	...	...	...	...	...	...	...	1	...	...	1	...	...	...	...	...	...
		Koracha	"	171	...	4	167	...	161	...	...	161	...	103	...	2	101	...	102	...	...	102	...
		Korama	"	1,830	4	17	1,859	...	1,954	...	...	1,954	...	618	2	15	601	...	614	...	...	614	...
		Kurubas	"	209	...	...	209	...	191	...	...	191	...	26	...	...	26	...	19	...	...	19	...
		Lambâni	"	528	...	1	527	...	556	...	...	556	...	1,451	...	...	1,451	...	1,395	...	...	1,395	...
		Uriya	"	...	...	...	......	...	...	...	...	...	...	...	...	...	...	...	...	...	...	...	...
		Total Group 4	....	2,788	4	22	2,762	...	2,865	...	...	2,865	...	2,199	2	17	2,180	...	2,130	...	...	2,130	...
		Total Class A	....	194,904	3,438	8,480	182,986	...	205,947	209	247	205,491	...	97,791	1,154	3,321	93,316	...	102,222	30	25	102,167	...

SUPPLEMENTARY TABLE D.—(Continued.)

V

Class	Group	Caste, &c. and Sub-division	Religion	Shimoga Males Total	Shimoga Males Pupils	Shimoga Males Literate	Shimoga Males Illiterate	Shimoga Males Not stated	Shimoga Females Total	Shimoga Females Pupils	Shimoga Females Literate	Shimoga Females Illiterate	Shimoga Females Not stated	Kadur Males Total	Kadur Males Pupils	Kadur Males Literate	Kadur Males Illiterate	Kadur Males Not stated	Kadur Females Total	Kadur Females Pupils	Kadur Females Literate	Kadur Females Illiterate	Kadur Females Not stated
A.—Agricultural.—(Continued.)	1 Military and Dominant.	Kshatriya	Hindu	1,510	85	354	1,071	...	1,387	8	11	1,365	..	992	38	209	745	...	722	...	12	710	...
		„	Sikh	...	...	...	...	...	...	...	...	...	..	...	...	...	...	..	...	...	...	...	...
		Total	...	1,510	85	354	1,071	...	1,387	8	11	1,365	..	992	38	209	745	..	722	...	12	710	
		Maráta	Hindu	5,705	54	273	5,378	...	1,940	2	5	1,933	..	830	49	110	1,671	...	1,304	...	...	1,304	...
		Ráchévár	„	5	...	2	3	...	5	..	...	5	..	97	4	20	73	...	92	...	1	91	...
		Total Group 1	...	7,220	139	629	6,452	...	3,332	10	19	3,303	..	2,919	91	339	2,489	...	2,118	...	13	2,105	...
	2 Other Agricultural.	Lingáyat, Gaudaman	„	213	...	16	197	...	187	...	...	187	...	821	18	83	721	...	835	2	3	830	...
		„ Malava	„	...	...	...	...	...	...	...	...	...	...	396	...	...	396	...	389	...	...	389	...
		„ Panchácháru	„	7,051	126	347	6,578	...	6,507	...	6	6,501	...	3,663	61	305	3,297	...	3,839	...	14	3,825	...
		Total	...	7,264	126	363	6,775	...	6,694	...	6	6,688	..	4,880	79	357	4,414	...	5,063	2	17	5,044	...
	(a) Cultivators	Náyar	„	...	...	...	...	...	...	...	...	...	...	...	...	...	...	...	...	...	...	...	...
		Pillai	„	9	...	...	9	...	7	...	...	7	...	33	3	13	17	...	18	...	1	17	...
		Tigala	„	127	2	6	119	...	70	...	...	70	...	258	4	1	253	...	233	...	...	233	...
		Vakkaliga	„	70,684	598	2,353	67,733	...	64,385	30	22	64,333	..	37,869	439	1,313	36,117	...	35,627	8	12	35,607	...
		„ Sála	Jain	...	...	...	...	...	...	...	...	...	...	...	...	...	...	...	...	...	...	...	...
		„ Tulu	Brahmo	...	...	...	...	...	...	...	...	...	...	...	...	...	...	...	...	...	...	...	...
		Total	...	70,681	598	2,353	67,733	...	64,285	30	22	64,333	..	37,869	439	1,313	36,117	...	35,627	8	12	35,607	...
		Total Group 2	...	78,081	726	2,722	71,636	...	71,156	30	28	71,098	...	43,040	525	1,714	40,801		40,941	10	30	40,901	
	4 Forest and Hill tribes.	Iruliga	Hindu	...	...	...	...	...	...	...	...	...	...	...	...	...	...	...	...	...	...	...	...
		Koracha	„	1,193	7	4	1,182	...	914	...	...	914	..	368	...	1	367	...	357	...	...	357	...
		Korama	„	1,162	5	5	1,152	...	1,129	...	..	1,129	...	668		19	649	...	666	...	...	666	...
		Kuruba	„	...	...	...	...	...	...	...	...	...	.	8	...	...	8	...	...	...	...	...	...
		Lambáni	„	7,256	4	6	7,246	...	6,871	...	...	6,871	...	4,880	..	5	4,875	...	3,914	...	...	3,914	...
		Uriya	„	...	...	...	...	...	...	...	..	...	...	..	...	..	...	...	...	...	...	...	...
		Total Group 4	...	9,611	16	15	9,580	...	8,914	...	...	8,941	...	5,924	...	25	5,899	...	4,937	...	...	4,937	...
		Total Class A		94,915	881	3,366	90,668	...	86,402	40	47	86,315	...	51,883	616	2,078	49,189	...	47,996	10	43	47,943	...

SUPPLEMENTARY TABLE D.—(Continued.)

Class.	Group.	Caste, &c. and Sub-division.	Religion.	Chitaldrug. Males. Total.	Pupils.	Literate.	Illiterate.	Not stated.	Chitaldrug. Females. Total.	Pupils.	Literate.	Illiterate.	Not stated.	The Civil and Military Station, Bangalore. Males. Total.	Pupils.	Literate.	Illiterate.	Not stated.	The Civil and Military Station, Bangalore. Females. Total.	Pupils.	Literate.	Illiterate.	Not stated.
A.—Agricultural.—(Continued.)	1 Military and Dominant.	Kshatriya	Hindu	254	18	102	134	...	218	1	1	216	...	350	46	170	132	2	278	6	4	268	...
		"	Sikh	...	...	...	...	...	...	...	...	...	...	...	...	...	...	...	...	...	...	...	...
		Total		254	18	102	134	...	218	1	1	216	...	350	46	170	132	2	278	6	4	268	...
		Marata	Hindu	1,285	12	124	1,149	...	1,508	...	...	1,508	...	573	64	136	323	...	571	37	16	518	...
		Rachevar	"	10	...	...	10	...	5	...	...	5	...	40	7	19	14	...	40	...	2	[illegible]	...
		Total Group 1		1,549	30	226	1,293	...	1,561	1	1	1,559	...	963	117	325	469	2	889	43	22	[illegible]	...
	2 Other Agricultural.	Lingayet Gandaganee	"	54	5	...	49	...	53	...	...	53	...	12	1	7	2	2	8	...	...	8	...
		" Malava	"	...	...	...	...	...	...	...	...	...	...	...	...	...	...	...	...	...	...	...	...
		" Panchachara	"	4,737	52	839	3,846	...	4,313	1	1	[illegible]	...	...	...	...	...	...	...	...	...	...	...
		Total		4,791	57	839	3,895	...	4,366	1	4	4,361	...	12	1	7	2	2	8	...	...	8	...
	(a) Cultivators	Nayar	"	...	...	...	...	...	...	...	...	...	...	64	15	30	19	...	50	1	...	49	...
		Pille	"	2	...	1	1	...	...	...	...	...	...	3	...	2	1	...	1	...	...	1	...
		Tigala	"	12	...	...	12	...	8	...	...	...	...	1,672	98	189	1,384	1	1,641	18	18	1,600	5
		Vakkaliga	"	35,074	445	1,425	33,204	...	31,186	12	4	31,170	...	4,786	719	1,523	2,452	22	4,910	230	367	1,285	28
		" Sida	Jain	...	...	...	...	...	...	...	...	...	...	...	...	...	...	...	1	...	...	1	...
		" Tulu	Brahmo	...	...	...	...	...	...	...	...	...	...	10	3	5	2	...	13	3	3	7	...
		Total		35,0[illegible]	445	1,425	33,2[illegible]	...	31,1[illegible]	12	4	31,1[illegible]	...	[illegible]	722	[illegible]	[illegible]	22	[illegible]	233	370	[illegible]	28
		Total Group 2 (a)		39,879	502	2,265	37,112	...	38,806	13	8	38,829	...	[illegible]	836	[illegible]	[illegible]	25	[illegible]	[illegible]	[illegible]	5,951	33
	4 Forest and Hill tribes.	Iraliga	Hindu	...	...	...	...	...	...	...	...	...	...	...	...	...	...	...	...	...	...	...	...
		Koracha	"	443	...	6	437	...	110	...	...	110	...	116	...	1	113	2	110	1	...	107	2
		Korama	"	244	1	6	237	...	201	...	1	200	...	94	1	6	67	...	98	...	...	98	...
		Kuruba	"	...	...	...	...	...	...	...	...	...	...	...	...	...	...	...	...	...	...	...	...
		Lambani	"	2,718	...	10	2,708	...	2,525	...	...	2,525	...	...	...	...	...	...	...	...	...	...	...
		Uriya	"	...	...	...	...	...	...	...	...	...	...	5	...	...	5	...	3	...	...	3	...
		Total Group 4		3,405	1	22	3,382	...	3,139	...	4	3,135	...	215	1	7	205	2	211	1	...	208	2
		Total Class A		44,833	533	2,513	41,787	...	43,560	14	13	43,533	...	7,725	954	2,168	4,574	29	7,724	266	410	7,013	35

SUPPLEMENTARY TABLE D.—(Continued.)

Total including the Civil and Military Station, Bangalore.

Class.	Group.	Caste, &c. and Sub-division.	Religion.	Males: Total.	Males: Pupils.	Males: Literate.	Males: Illiterate.	Males: Not stated.	Females: Total.	Females: Pupils.	Females: Literate.	Females: Illiterate.	Females: Not stated.
A.—Agricultural.—(Concluded.)	1 Military and Dominant.	Kshatriya	Hindu	11,135	901	3,455	6,777	2	10,660	71	157	10,332	...
		"	Sikh	13	2	3	8	...	16	...	1	15	...
		Total		*11,148*	*903*	*3,458*	*6,785*	*2*	*10,676*	*71*	*158*	*10,411*	...
		Maráta	Hindu	22,961	977	1,813	20,171	...	21,885	54	16	21,815	...
		Ráchevár	"	1,785	136	422	1,227	...	1,921	17	7	1,897	...
		Total Group 1		*35,894*	*2,016*	*5,693*	*28,183*	*2*	*34,482*	*142*	*211*	*34,086*	...
	2 Other Agricultural. (a) Cultivators	Lingáyet Gaudamané	"	28,722	610	1,977	26,124	2	29,765	13	18	29,734	...
		" Malava	"	403	...	...	402	...	393	...	...	393	...
		" Panchachára	"	34,563	697	2,041	21,023	...	31,320	5	35	31,280	...
		Total		*63,688*	*1,306*	*4,018*	*57,554*	*2*	*61,478*	*18*	*53*	*61,407*	...
		Náyar	"	67	15	33	19	...	50	1	...	49	...
		Pillé	"	314	34	47	233	...	215	...	5	210	...
		Tigala	"	28,660	415	502	27,742	1	28,029	39	20	27,986	5
		Vakkaliga	"	665,516	9,380	23,771	632,384	22	676,333	736	611	671,928	25
		" Sádu	Jain	518	32	103	3	...	494	...	4	490	...
		" Túlu	Brahmo	10	3	5	376	...	15	3	5	7	...
		Total		*666,012*	*9,421*	*23,581*	*632,711*	*22*	*676,810*	*779*	*648*	*675,425*	*28*
		Total Group 2 (a)		*758,773*	*11,291*	*29,281*	*718,230*	*25*	*738,963*	*796*	*736*	*738,167*	*33*
	4 Forest and Hill tribes.	Prdiga	Hindu	581	...	...	581	...	551	...	...	551	...
		Koracha	"	5,578	33	48	5,492	2	5,792	1	...	5,789	2
		Korama	"	6,865	48	115	6,702	...	6,539	...	4	6,535	...
		Karuba	"	1,136	...	...	1,136	...	1,133	...	...	1,133	...
		Lambáni	"	20,585	6	24	20,555	...	18,352	...	...	18,352	...
		Uriya	"	5	...	...	5	...	3	...	...	3	...
		Total Group 4		*34,750*	*89*	*187*	*34,471*	*2*	*32,290*	*1*	*4*	*32,283*	*2*
		Total Class A		**829,417**	**13,310**	**35,164**	**780,914**	**29**	**836,025**	**943**	**971**	**834,076**	**35**

SUPPLEMENTARY TABLE D.—(Continued).

Class.	Group.	Caste, &c., and sub-divisions.	Religion.	Total Strength — Males — Total.	Pupils.	Literate.	Illiterate.	Not stated.	Females — Total.	Pupils.	Literate.	Illiterate.	Not stated.	Territorial Distribution — Bangalore — Males — Total.	Pupils.	Literate.	Illiterate.	Not stated.	Females — Total.	Pupils.	Literate.	Illiterate.	Not stated.
B—Professional.	5. Priests.	Brâhman ...	Hindu ...	92,169	11.117	51 421	29.631	...	89,063	1,247	2,169	85,647	...	14.584	2.628	9,022	2,934	...	13,865	349	432	13,084	...
		Dásari ...	"	578	6	48	522	...	591	...	...	592	...	91	...	...	91	...	67	...	...	67	...
		Lingáyet, Arâdhya	"	5.798	289	1.158	4,351	...	5,824	16	37	5,777	...	606	57	198	351	...	533	...	4	529	...
		Do. Guru Chita	"	5.920	294	845	4.781	...	6,219	8	16	6,190	...	345	57	49	239	...	333	...	3	330	...
		Do. Jangam ...	"	19.157	575	298	18,284	...	19,009	3	1	19,005	...	1.705	113	38	1,554	...	1,845		...	1,845	...
		Total ...	...	*30,875*	*1,158*	*2,301*	*27,416*	...	*31,038*	*22*	*41*	*30,972*	...	*2,656*	*227*	*285*	*2,144*	...	*2,711*	...	*7*	*2,704*	...
		Sátâni ...	Hindu ...	9,982	889	1.865	7.223	...	9,777	49	37	9,691	...	1,768	234	493	1,041	...	1,746	...	6	1,738	...
		Pitámbara ...	Jain ...	5	...	...	5	...	...	...	...	...	...	1	...	...	1	...	...	...	...	...	...
		Tirthankara ...	" ...	1.346	106	486	754	...	1,218	5	16	1,197	...	173	18	74	81	...	163	...	5	158	...
		Total Group 5 ...		*131,953*	*13,276*	*56,121*	*65,556*	...	*131,088*	*1,323*	*2,266*	*128,000*		*19,273*	*3,107*	*9,874*	*6,292*	...	*18,552*	*349*	*472*	*17,731*	...
	6. Devotees.	Bairâgi ...	Hindu ...	104	...	...	104	...	118	...	...	118	...	43	...	...	43	...	67	...		67	...
		Bávâji ...	Jain ...	...	...	...	...			...	...	...	...	...	...	...	...	...	...	...	...	...	...
		Digambara ...	" ...	2,881	178	940	1 763	...	2,581	24	37	2,520	...	39	10	14	15	...	49	...	...	49	...
		Gósâvi ...	Hindu ...	203	5	48	155	...	215	...	2	213	...	37	3	22	12		14		1	13	...
		Sanyâsi ...	" ...	337	...	...	337	...	327		...	327	...	34	...	...	84		18	...	...	18	...
		Svetâmbara ...	Jain ...	69		59	10	...	10	...	...	10	...	7	...	5	2	...	...		...	...	...
		Lingáyet Valer ...	Hindu ...	400	15	41	344	...	345	...	2	343		24	...	4	20	...	22	...	...	22	...
		Total Group 6 ...		*4,010*	*198*	*1,088*	*2,733*	...	*3,796*	*24*	*41*	*3,731*	...	*181*	*13*	*45*	*126*	...	*170*	...	*1*	*169*	...
	7. Temple servants.	Brámhan ...	Hindu ...	583	27	...	559	...	568	...	...	568		136	3	...	133	...	142	...	..	142	...
		Kanakan ...	" ...	...	...	...	...		...	...		..	...		...	...	...	...	...	...	...	..	...
	9. Writers.	Káyastha ...	" ...	..	...		...	...	...	...	...		...	..	...	..	...	...	...	...	...	...	...
		Total Group 9 ...		..	...	...	...	...	...	...	...	...	...	...	...	...	...	...	...	...	...	...	...
	11. Musicians and Ballad-reciters.	Bhat Râju ...	Hindu ...	722	97	93	532	...	665	..	...	665	...	255	47	23	185	...	212	...	...	212	...
	12. Dancers and Singers.	Natva ...	" ...	3,544	72	83	3.389	...	3,895	94	90	3,711	...	107	..	19	88	...	194	26	21	147	
	12 (a). Chittâri, &c.	Râchêvâr ...	" ...	2.407	17	...	2.390		2,222	1		2,221	...	59	...	...	59	...	65	...	...	65	...
		Total Class B. ...		**146,231**	**13,687**	**57.385**	**75,159**	...	**142,834**	**1.442**	**2.397**	**138.995**	...	**20.014**	**3,170**	**9.961**	**6.883**	..	**19,335**	**375**	**494**	**18,466**	...

SUPPLEMENTARY TABLE.-D.-(Continued.)

B—Professional—(Continued.)

Group	Caste, &c. and sub-division	Religion	Kólár Males Total	Kólár Males Pupils	Kólár Males Literate	Kólár Males Illiterate	Kólár Males Not stated	Kólár Females Total	Kólár Females Pupils	Kólár Females Literate	Kólár Females Illiterate	Kólár Females Not stated	Tumkúr Males Total	Tumkúr Males Pupils	Tumkúr Males Literate	Tumkúr Males Illiterate	Tumkúr Males Not stated	Tumkúr Females Total	Tumkúr Females Pupils	Tumkúr Females Literate	Tumkúr Females Illiterate	Tumkúr Females Not stated
5. Priests.	Brámhan	Hindu	11,693	640	7,075	3,978	...	11,632	60	198	11,374	...	8,570	1,622	4,840	2,108	...	8,437	227	200	8,010	...
	Dásari	"	80	3	10	67	...	85	...	...	85	...	103	1	11	96	...	102	...	...	102	...
	Lingáyet A'rá'hya	"	63	12	21	23	...	61	...	...	61	...	1,038	114	297	627	...	1,081	15	3	1,063	...
	Do Gurust'hala	"	187	20	23	144	...	225	...	...	225	...	757	80	173	504	...	771	2	2	770	...
	Do Jangam	"	1,428	129	14	1,265	...	1,381	...	...	1,381	...	2,513	138	52	2,323	...	2,366	2	...	2,361	...
	Total		1,678	161	58	1,457	...	1,667	...	...	1,667	...	4,308	282	522	3,454	...	4,221	19	5	4,197	...
	Sátáni	Hindu	962	229	303	430	...	975	18	6	951	...	1,936	280	412	1,244	...	1,865	17	12	1,836	...
	Pitámbara	Jain	...	...	...	...	...	...	...	...	...	...	...	...	...	...	...	...	...	...	...	...
	Tírt'hankara	"	157	8	73	76	...	135	...	...	135	...	233	27	89	117	...	174	1	2	171	...
	Total Group 5		*14,570*	*1,042*	*7,519*	*6,008*	...	*14,496*	*98*	*204*	*14,194*	...	*15,155*	*2,212*	*5,874*	*7,019*	...	*14,799*	*264*	*219*	*14,316*	...
6. Devotees.	Bairági	Hindu	7	...	...	7	...	6	...	...	6	...	12	...	...	12	...	6	...	...	6	...
	Báráji	Jain	...	...	...	...	...	...	...	...	...	...	...	...	...	...	...	...	...	...	...	...
	Digambara		304	36	103	165	...	280	...	...	280	...	567	30	235	302	...	548	3	5	540	...
	Gósáyi	Hindu	17	...	9	8	...	22	...	...	22	...	7	...	...	7	...	3	...	...	3	...
	Sanyási	"	200	...	...	200	...	212	...	...	212	...	97	...	...	97	...	78	...	...	78	...
	Svétámbara	Jain	...	...	...	...	...	...	...	...	...	...	3	...	2	1	...	1	...	...	1	...
	Lingáyet Vadér	Hindu	...	...	...	...	...	...	...	...	...	...	7	...	...	7	...	8	...	...	8	...
	Total Group 6		*528*	*36*	*112*	*380*	...	*520*	...	...	*520*	...	*693*	*30*	*237*	*426*	...	*644*	*3*	*5*	*636*	...
7. Temple servants.	Brámhan	Hindu	298	24	...	274	...	307	...	...	307	...	44	...	...	44	...	48	...	...	48	...
9. Writers.	Kanakan	"	...	...	...	...	...	...	...	...	...	...	...	...	...	...	...	...	...	...	...	...
	Káyastha	"	...	...	...	...	...	...	...	...	...	...	...	...	...	...	...	...	...	...	...	...
	Total Group 9		...	...	...	...	...	...	...	...	...	...	...	...	...	...	...	...	...	...	...	...
11. Musicians and Ballad-reciters.	Bhat Ráju	Hindu	196	43	22	131	...	193	...	...	192	...	65	5	30	30	...	69	...	...	69	...
12. Dancers and Singers.	Natva	"	340	64	41	235	...	428	56	28	344	...	58	4	2	52	...	59	5	1	53	...
12 (a). Chittári, &c.	Ráchévár	"	29	4	...	25	...	35	...	...	35	...	132	...	...	132	...	110	...	...	110	...
	Total Class B		**15,961**	**1,214**	**7,694**	**7,053**	...	**15,978**	**154**	**232**	**15,592**	...	**16,147**	**2,301**	**6,143**	**7,703**	...	**15,729**	**272**	**225**	**15,232**	...

SUPPLEMENTARY TABLE D.—(*Continued*).

Class.	Caste and Religion.			Territorial Distribution—(*Continued*).																			
				Mysore.										Hassan.									
				Males.					Females.					Males.					Females.				
	Group.	Caste, &c. and sub-division.	Religion.	Total.	Pupils.	Literate.	Illiterate.	Not stated.	Total.	Pupils.	Literate.	Illiterate.	Not stated.	Total.	Pupils.	Literate.	Illiterate.	Not stated.	Total.	Pupils.	Literate.	Illiterate.	Not stated.
B—Professional—(*Continued*).	5. Priests.	Brámhan	Hindu	21,223	3,230	12,106	5,887	...	21,775	396	440	20,939	...	8,499	1,086	4,808	2,605	...	8,561	57	72	8,432	...
		Dásari	"	69	...	10	59	...	88	...	...	83	...	22	...	10	12	...	19	...	...	19	...
		Lingáyét Árádhya	"	1,859	21	259	1,579	...	1,888	...	8	1,880	...	496	18	119	359	...	497	...	2	495	...
		Do Gurusthala	"	1,961	53	247	1,661	...	2,068	1	6	2,061	...	577	23	89	465	...	541	...	...	541	...
		Do Jangam	"	1,943	20	23	1,900	...	1,944	...	...	1,944	...	3,429	64	52	3,313	...	3,425	...	...	3,425	...
		Total		*5,763*	*94*	*529*	*5,140*	...	*5,900*	*1*	*14*	*5,885*	...	*4,502*	*105*	*260*	*4,137*	...	*4,463*	...	*2*	*4,461*	...
		Sátáni	Hindu	2,223	83	370	1,770	...	2,257	10	8	2,239	...	1,797	28	147	1,622	...	1,863	2	...	1,861	...
		Pitámbara	Jain	...	...	...	...	...	...	...	...	...	...	...	...	...	...	...	...	...	...	...	...
		Tirthankara	"	310	33	76	201	...	320	...	3	317	...	246	16	93	137	...	228	4	6	218	...
		Total Group 5		*29,588*	*3,440*	*13,091*	*13,057*	...	*30,335*	*407*	*465*	*29,463*	...	*15,066*	*1,235*	*5,318*	*8,513*	...	*15,134*	*63*	*80*	*14,991*	...
	6. Devotees.	Bairági	Hindu	12	...	...	12	...	4	...	...	4	...	...	...	...	...	...	...	...	...	...	...
		Sávaji	Jain	...	...	...	...	...	...	...	...	...	...	...	...	...	...	...	...	...	...	...	...
		Digambara	"	687	44	207	436	...	611	7	8	596	...	368	33	174	161	...	404	3	22	379	...
		Gosáyi	Hindu	72	2	6	64	...	58	...	1	57	...	27	...	...	27	...	99	...	...	99	...
		Sanyási	"	4	...	...	4	...	...	...	...	...	...	...	...	...	...	...	...	...	...	...	...
		Svétámbara	Jain	...	...	...	...	...	...	...	...	...	...	...	...	...	...	...	...	...	...	...	...
		Lingáyét Vadér	Hindu	163	...	16	147	...	164	...	2	162	...	...	...	...	...	...	...	...	...	...	...
		Total Group 6		*938*	*46*	*229*	*663*	...	*837*	*7*	*11*	*819*	...	*395*	*33*	*174*	*188*	...	*503*	*3*	*22*	*478*	...
	7. Temple servants.	Brámhan	Hindu	8	...	...	8	...	7	...		7	...	52	...	...	52	...	39	...	...	39	...
	9. Writers.	Karakan	"	...	...	...	...	...	...	...	...	...	...	...	...	...	...	...	...	...	...	...	...
		Káyastha	"	...	...	...	...	...	...	...	...	...	...	...	...	...	...	...	...	...	...	...	...
		Total Group 9		...	...	...	...	...	...	...	...	...	...	...	...	...	...	...	...	...	...	...	...
	11. Musicians and Ballad-reciters.	Bhat Rája	Hindu	118	...	...	113	...	96	...	...	96	...	45	...	...	45	...	54	...	...	54	...
	12. Dancers and Singers.	Natva	"	2,907	4	21	2,882	...	3,080	7	39	3,034	...	48	...	...	48	...	73	...	...	73	...
	12 (a). Chittári, &c.	Báhérár	"	169	7	...	162	...	174	1	...	173	...	4	...	...	4	...	3	...	...	3	...
		Total Class B		**33,723**	**3,497**	**13,341**	**16,885**	...	**34,529**	**422**	**515**	**33,592**	...	**15,610**	**1,268**	**5,492**	**8,850**	...	**15,806**	**66**	**102**	**15,698**	...

SUPPLEMENTARY TABLE D.—(Continued).

Territorial Distribution—(Continued).

Class: B—Professional.—(Continued.)

Group	Caste &c. and sub-division	Religion	Shimoga. Males. Total.	Pupils.	Literate.	Illiterate.	Not stated.	Shimoga. Females. Total.	Pupils.	Literate.	Illiterate.	Not stated.	Kadúr. Males. Total.	Pupils.	Literate.	Illiterate.	Not stated.	Kadúr. Females. Total.	Pupils.	Literate.	Illiterate.	Not stated.
5. Priests.	Brámhan	Hindu	15,728	946	7,064	7,718	...	13,646	64	112	13,470	..	8,795	648	4,643	3,504	...	8,231	40	834	7,557	...
	Dásai	,,	84	...	1	83	...	135	...	...	135	...	73	2	4	67	...	63	...	...	63	...
	Lingáyet Arád'hya	,,	364	8	65	291	...	363	...	2	361	...	994	54	112	828	...	1,021	...	6	1,015	...
	Do Gurust'hala	,,	401	8	59	334	...	370	...	...	370	...	826	38	103	685	...	971	...	4	967	...
	Do Jangam	,,	3,947	73	45	3,826	...	4,064	1	...	4,063	...	1,420	12	17	1,391	..	1,430	...	...	1,430	...
	Total		*4,712*	*12*	*169*	*4,151*	...	*4,796*	*1*	*2*	*4,794*	...	*3,240*	*104*	*232*	*2,904*	...	*3,422*	...	*10*	*3,412*	...
	Sátáni	Hindu	373	15	52	306	...	309	...	2	307	...	581	14	30	537	...	408	...	1	407	...
	Pitámbara	Jain	...	...	...	...	...	...	...	...	...	...	4	...	...	4	...	...	...	...	...	...
	Tirt'hankara	,,	65	...	33	32	...	35	...	...	35	...	93	4	19	70	...	90	...	...	90	...
	Total Group 5		*20,962*	*1,053*	*7,319*	*12,590*	...	*18,922*	*65*	*116*	*18,741*	...	*12,786*	*772*	*4,928*	*7,086*	...	*12,211*	*40*	*645*	*11,529*	...
6. Devotees.	Bairági	Hindu	...	...	...	...	...	...	...	...	...	...	28	...	...	28	...	34	...	...	34	...
	Bávaji	Jain	...	...	...	...	...	...	...	...	...	...	...	...	...	...	...	...	...	...	...	...
	Digambara	,,	198	8	57	133	...	124	...	...	124	...	555	2	67	486	...	454	...	...	454	...
	Gósáyi	Hindu	...	...	...	...	...	...	...	...	...	...	1	...	...	1	...	...	...	...	...	...
	Sanyási	,,	10	...	...	10	...	3	...	...	3	...	9	...	...	9	...	12	...	...	12	...
	Svetámbara	Jain	...	...	...	...	...	...	...	...	...	...	59	...	52	7	...	9	...	...	9	...
	Lingáyet Vaddar	Hindu	56	...	9	47	...	55	...	...	55	...	140	15	10	115	...	292	...	...	292	...
	Total Group 6		*264*	*8*	*66*	*190*	...	*182*	...	...	*182*	...	*792*	*17*	*129*	*646*	...	*801*	...	...	*801*	...
7. Temple servants.	Brámhan	Hindu	2	...	...	2	...	3	...	...	3	...	33	...	...	33	...	13	...	...	13	...
9. Writers.	Kanakan	,,	...	...	...	...	...	...	...	...	...	...	...	...	...	...	...	...	...	...	...	...
	Káyastha	,,	...	...	...	...	...	...	...	...	...	...	...	...	...	...	...	...	...	...	...	...
	Total Group 9		...	...	...	...	...	...	...	...	...	...	...	...	...	...	...	...	...	...	...	...
11. Musicians and Ballad-reciters.	Bhat Ráju	Hindu	...	...	...	...	...	...	...	...	...	...	23	2	2	19	...	17	...	...	17	...
12. Dancers and Singers.	Natva	,,	71	...	...	71	...	44	...	1	43	...	1	...	...	1	...	6	...	...	6	...
(12 a). Chittari, &c.	Ráchévár	,,	1,895	4	...	1,891	...	1,743	...	...	1,743	...	18	...	...	18	...	14	...	...	14	...
	Total Class B		**23,194**	**1,065**	**7,385**	**14,744**	...	**20,894**	**65**	**117**	**20,712**	...	**13,653**	**791**	**5,059**	**7,803**	...	**13,065**	**40**	**645**	**12,380**	...

SUPPLEMENTARY TABLE-D—(Continued).

Class.	Group.	Caste, &c. and sub-division.	Religion.	Chitaldurg. Males. Total.	Pupils.	Literate.	Illiterate.	Not stated.	Chitaldurg. Females. Total.	Pupils.	Literate.	Illiterate.	Not stated.	The Civil and Military Station, Bangalore. Males. Total.	Pupils.	Literate.	Illiterate.	Not stated.	The Civil and Military Station, Bangalore. Females. Total.	Pupils.	Literate.	Illiterate.	Not stated.
B.—Professional—(Continued).	5. Priests.	Brámban	Hindu	3,077	317	1,863	897	...	2,916	34	61	2,821	...	662	123	403	134	2	491	5	31	454	1
		Dásari	"	49	...	2	47	...	38	...	...	38	...	7	...	2	5	...	3	...	...	3	...
		Lingáyet Arád'hya	"	378	3	87	288	...	374	1	2	371	...	...	...	...	...	...	...	...	...	...	...
		Do Gurust hala	"	866	15	102	749	...	927	...	1	926	...	...	...	...	...	...	...	...	...	...	...
		Do Jungam	"	2,772	23	57	2,692	...	2,554	...	1	2,553	...	21	7	4	10	...	28	...	...	28	...
		Total		*a* *4,016*	*41*	*246*	*3,729*	...	*3,855*	*1*	*4*	*3,850*	...	*21*	*7*	*4*	*10*	...	*28*	...	...	*28*	...
		Sátáni	Hindu	342	6	58	278	...	354	2	...	352	...	112	13	46	53	...	116	3	3	110	...
		Pírámbara	Jain	...	...	...	...	...	...	...	...	...	...	...	...	...	...	...	...	...	...	...	...
		Tirt'hankara	"	69	...	29	40	...	73	...	...	73	...	...	...	...	...	...	...	...	...	...	...
		Total Group 5		*7,553*	*364*	*2,198*	*4,991*	...	*7,236*	*37*	*65*	*7,134*	...	*802*	*143*	*455*	*202*	*2*	*638*	*8*	*34*	*595*	*1*
	6. Devotees.	Bairági	Hindu	2	...	...	2	...	1	...	...	1	...	...	...	...	...	...	...	...	...	...	...
		Háváji	Jain	...	...	...	...	...	...	...	...	...	...	1	...	1	...	...	...	...	...	...	...
		Digambara	"	163	15	83	65	...	111	11	2	98	...	10	...	8	2	...	5	...	...	5	...
		Gósáyi	Hindu	47	...	11	36	...	19	...	...	19	...	1	...	...	1	...	...	...	...	...	...
		Sanyási	"	3	...	...	3	...	4	...	...	4	...	...	...	...	...	...	...	...	...	...	...
		Svétámbara	Jain	...	...	...	...	...	...	...	...	...	...	6	...	6	...	...	...	...	...	...	...
		Lingáyet Vadér	Hindu	10	...	2	8	...	4	...	...	4	...	6	...	1	5	...	5	...	...	5	...
		Total Group 6		*225*	*15*	*96*	*114*	...	*139*	*11*	*2*	*126*	...	*24*	...	*16*	*8*	...	*10*	...	...	*10*	...
	7. Temple servants.	Brámhan	Hindu	13	...	...	13	...	9	...	...	9	...	2	...	2	...	...	...	...	...	...	...
	9. Writers.	Kanakan	"	...	...	...	...	...	...	...	...	...	...	57	21	27	9	...	51	6	12	33	...
		Káyastha	"	...	...	...	...	...	...	...	...	...	...	5	1	2	2	...	1	...	...	1	...
		Total Group 9		...	...	...	...	...	...	...	...	...	...	*62*	*22*	*29*	*11*	...	*52*	*6*	*12*	*34*	...
	11. Musicians and Ballad-reciters.	Bhat Ráju	Hindu	25	...	16	9	...	25	...	...	25	...	1	...	...	1	...	...	...	...	...	...
	12. Dancers and Singers.	Natra	"	12	...	...	12	...	11	...	...	11	...	21	5	9	7	...	16	1	...	15	...
	12 (a). Cihttari, &c.	Ráchèvár	"	101	2	...	99	...	78	...	...	78	...	6	1	2	3	...	5	...	...	5	...
		Total Class B		**7,029**	**381**	**2,310**	**5,238**	..	**7,498**	**48**	**67**	**7,385**	...	**918**	**171**	**513**	**232**	**2**	**721**	**15**	**46**	**659**	**1**

SUPPLEMENTARY TABLE D.—(Continued).

Total strength including the Civil and Military Station, Bangalore.

Class.	Group.	Caste, &c. and sub-division.	Religion.	Males. Total.	Males. Pupils.	Males. Literate.	Males. Illiterate.	Males. Not stated.	Females. Total.	Females. Pupils.	Females. Literate.	Females. Illiterate.	Females. Not stated.
B—Professional—(Concluded).	5. Priests.	Brámhan	Hindu	92,831	11,240	51,824	29,765	2	[illegible]	1,[illegible]	2,200	86,1[illegible]1	1
		Dásari	"	583	6	50	527	...	[illegible]	...	...	5[illegible]5	...
		Lingáyet A'rádhya	"	5,798	239	1,153	4,351	...	[illegible]	16	27	[illegible]	...
		Do Gurust'hala	"	5,920	294	845	4,781	...	[illegible]	3	16	6,190	...
		Do Jangam	"	19,173	522	302	18,294	...	[illegible]	3	1	19,033	...
		Total		30,896	1,165	2,395	27,[illegible]	...	31,[illegible]	22	144	31,[illegible]	...
		Sátáni	Hindu	10,094	902	1,911	7,281	...	9,893	51	40	9,801	...
		Pitámbara	Jain	5	...	...	5	...	...	...	...	...	...
		Tirt'hankara	"	1,346	106	486	754	...	1,21[illegible]	[illegible]	16	1,197	...
		Total Group 5		135,755	13,419	56,576	[illegible]	2	[illegible]	1,321	2,304	[illegible]	1
	6. Devotees.	Bairági	Hindu	104	...	...	104	...	115	...	...	115	...
		Báváji	Jain	1	...	1	...	...	...	...	...	...	...
		Digambara	"	2,891	178	948	1,765	...	[illegible]	24	37	[illegible]	...
		Gosáyi	Hindu	200	6	48	156	...	215	...	2	213	...
		Sanyási	"	357	...	...	357	...	327	...	...	327	...
		Svétámbara	Jain	75	...	65	10	...	10	...	...	10	...
		Lingáyat Vadér	Hindu	406	15	42	349	...	55[illegible]	...	2	[illegible]	...
		Total Group 6		4,013	198	1,104	2,741	...	3,[illegible]	21	41	3,7[illegible]	...
	7. Temple servants.	Brámhan	Hindu	588	27	2	559	...	563	...	...	563	...
	9. Writers.	Kanakan	"	57	21	27	9	...	51	6	12	33	...
		Káyashta	"	5	1	2	2	...	1	...	...	1	...
		Total Group 9		62	22	29	11	...	[illegible]	6	12	34	...
	11. Musicians and Ballad-reciters.	Bhat Ráju	Hindu	723	97	93	533	...	665	...	...	665	...
	12. Dancers and Singers.	Natva	"	3,565	77	92	3,396	...	3,911	95	90	3,725	...
	12 a. Chittári, &c.	Rachbérár	"	2,413	18	2	2,393	...	2,227	1	...	2,226	...
		Total Class B		147,149	13,858	57,898	75,391	2	143,555	1,457	2,443	139,654	1

SUPPLEMENTARY TABLE D.—(Continued.)

Class.	Group.	Caste, &c. and sub-division.	Religion.	Total Strength: Males: Total Males.	Pupils.	Literate.	Illiterate.	Education not stated.	Females: Total Females.	Pupils.	Literate.	Illiterate.	Education not stated.	Territorial Distribution: Bangalore: Males: Total.	Pupils.	Literate.	Illiterate.	Not stated.	Females: Total.	Pupils.	Literate.	Illiterate.	Not stated.
C—Commercial.	(14) Traders ...	Banya ...	Hindu ...	...	...	...	...	...	...	...	...	...	...	...	...	...	...	...	...	...	...	...	...
		" ...	Jain ...	...	...	...	...	...	...	...	...	...	...	...	...	...	...	...	...	...	...	...	...
		Banajiga ...	Hindu ...	53,529	2,330	7,107	44,092	...	52,864	242	494	52,128	...	9,753	614	1,900	7239	...	10,342	76	196	10,070	...
		Guzaráti ...	" ...	31	...	25	6	...	20	...	4	16	...	3	...	3	...	...	3	...	1	2	...
		Ját ...	" ...	...	...	...	...	...	...	...	...	...	...	...	...	...	...	...	...	...	...	...	...
		Kómati ...	" ...	15,157	1,239	8,831	5,087	...	13,843	68	101	13,674	...	2,455	326	1,801	328	...	2,257	31	24	2,202	...
		Láder ...	" ...	1,014	22	117	875	...	1,032	...	...	1,032	...	36	...	14	22	...	17	...	...	17	...
		Lingáyet ...	" ...	145,974	8,324	29,361	108,289	...	145,103	328	398	144,377	...	9,378	1,190	3,336	4,852	...	9,326	64	52	9,210	...
		Mudali ...	" ...	2,954	275	964	1,715	...	2,457	95	117	2,245	...	835	150	417	268	...	764	66	68	630	...
		Multáni ...	" ...	...	...	...	...	...	...	...	...	...	...	...	...	...	...	...	...	...	...	...	...
		Nagarta ...	" ...	11,902	525	2,839	3,538	...	10,842	...	7	10,835	...	2,504	274	1,040	1,190	...	2,565	...	2	2,563	...
		Jain ...	Jain ...	1,090	65	286	739	...	871	9	10	852	...	56	18	18	20	...	32	6	...	26	...
		Márvádi ...	" ...	55	...	...	55	...	5	...	...	5	...	...	...	...	...	...	...	...	...	...	...
		" ...	Hindu ...	...	...	...	...	...	...	...	...	...	...	...	...	...	...	...	...	...	...	...	...
		" ...	Buddhist ...	...	...	...	...	...	...	...	...	...	...	...	...	...	...	...	...	...	...	...	...
		S'rávaka ...	Jain ...	1,038	16	95	927	...	924	...	...	924	...	...	...	...	...	...	...	...	...	...	...
		Total Group 14...	...	*232,744*	*12,796*	*49,625*	*170,323*	...	*227,961*	*742*	*1,131*	*226,088*	...	*25,020*	*2,572*	*8,529*	*13,919*	...	*25,306*	*213*	*343*	*24,720*	...
		Total Class C...		**232,744**	**12,796**	**49,625**	**170,323**	...	**227,961**	**742**	**1,131**	**226,088**	...	**25,020**	**2,572**	**8,529**	**13,919**	...	**25,306**	**243**	**343**	**24,720**	...

SUPPLEMENTARY TABLE D.—(Continued.)

Class.	Group.	Caste, &c. and sub-division.	Religion.	Kólár Males Total.	Kólár Males Pupils.	Kólár Males Literate.	Kólár Males Illiterate.	Kólár Males Not stated.	Kólár Females Total.	Kólár Females Pupils.	Kólár Females Literate.	Kólár Females Illiterate.	Kólár Females Not stated.	Tumkur Males Total.	Tumkur Males Pupils.	Tumkur Males Literate.	Tumkur Males Illiterate.	Tumkur Males Not stated.	Tumkur Females Total.	Tumkur Females Pupils.	Tumkur Females Literate.	Tumkur Females Illiterate.	Tumkur Females Not stated.
C—Commercial.—(Continued.)	14 Traders...	Banya ...	... Hindu	...	...	...	...	...	...	...	...	...	...	...	...	...	...	...	...	...	...	...	...
		" ...	... Jain	...	...	...	...	...	...	...	...	...	...	...	...	...	...	...	...	...	...	...	...
		Banajiga	... Hindu	18,190	351	1,631	16,188	...	18,106	41	71	17,988	...	6,340	657	1,040	4,643	...	6,008	40	41	5,978	...
		Guzaráti	... "	...	...	...	...	...	...	...	...	...	...	...	...	...	...	...	...	...	...	...	...
		Ját ...	... "	...	...	...	...	...	...	...	...	...	...	...	...	...	...	...	...	...	...	...	...
		Kómaṭi	... "	4,571	277	2,687	1,607	...	4,319	17	36	4,266	...	2,891	238	1,775	878	...	2,113	4	8	2,401	...
		Láder ...	... "	8	...	7	1	...	10	...	...	10	...	70	...	43	27	...	64	...	...	64	...
		Lingáyet	... "	3,138	236	1,167	1,735	...	3,001	12	16	2,973	...	10,781	763	5,671	4,347	...	10,508	88	68	10,352	...
		Mudali	... "	430	47	63	320	...	281	15	10	259	...	207	22	59	126	...	173	8	12	153	...
		Multáni	... "	...	...	...	...	...	...	...	...	...	...	...	...	...	...	...	...	...	...	...	...
		Nagarta	... "	1,446	21	383	862	...	1,558	...	1	1,557	...	163	13	19	131	...	152	...	...	152	...
		Jain ...	... Jain	16	...	8	8	...	2	...	...	2	...	182	14	63	105	...	123	1	2	120	...
		Márvádi	... "	...	...	...	...	...	...	...	...	...	...	...	...	...	...	...	...	...	...	...	...
		" ...	... Hindu	...	...	...	...	...	...	...	...	...	...	...	...	...	...	...	...	...	...	...	...
		" ...	... Buddhist	...	...	...	...	...	...	...	...	...	...	...	...	...	...	...	...	...	...	...	...
		S'rávaka	... Jain	...	...	...	...	...	...	...	...	...	...	...	...	...	...	...	...	...	...	...	...
		Total Group 14 ...	...	*27,799*	*1,112*	*5,966*	*20,721*	...	*27,280*	*88*	*137*	*27,055*	...	*20,634*	*1,707*	*8,670*	*10,257*	...	*19,501*	*150*	*131*	*19,220*	...
		Total Class C ...		**27,799**	**1,112**	**5,966**	**20,721**	...	**27,280**	**88**	**137**	**27,055**	...	**20,634**	**1,707**	**8,670**	**10,257**	...	**19,501**	**150**	**131**	**19,220**	...

SUPPLEMENTARY TABLE D.—(Continued.)

Class.	Group.	Caste, &c. and sub-division.	Religion.	Mysore. Males. Total.	Pupils.	Literate.	Illiterate.	Not stated.	Mysore. Females. Total.	Pupils.	Literate.	Illiterate.	Not stated.	Hassan. Males. Total.	Pupils.	Literate.	Illiterate.	Not stated.	Hassan. Females. Total.	Pupils.	Literate.	Illiterate.	Not stated.
C—Commercial.—(Continued.)	14 Traders.	Banya ...	Hindu ...	...	...	...	...	...	...	...	...	...	...	...	...	...	...	...	...	...	...	...	...
		" ...	Jain ...	...	...	...	...	...	...	...	...	...	...	...	...	...	...	...	...	...	...	...	...
		Banajiga ...	Hindu ...	8,649	406	1,217	7,026	—	9,162	55	100	9,007	...	1,977	73	336	1,568	...	1,758	1	9	1,748	...
		Guzaráti ...	" ...	26	...	22	4	...	15	...	3	12	...	2	...	...	2	...	2	...	...	2	...
		Ját ...	" ...	...	...	...	...	...	...	...	...	...	...	...	...	...	...	...	...	...	...	...	...
		Kómati ...	" ...	1,644	147	753	739	...	1,566	6	18	1,530	...	888	57	487	344	...	878	1	2	575	...
		Láder ...	" ...	574	14	45	515	...	611	...	...	611	...	47	6	6	35	...	41	...	...	41	...
		Lingáyet ...	" ...	44,793	2,027	3,217	39,549	...	46,464	116	112	46,236	...	19,164	774	3,276	15,114	...	19,842	13	16	19,813	...
		Mudali ...	" ...	868	40	296	532	...	737	5	19	713	...	82	1	37	44	...	55	1	4	50	...
		Multáni ...	" ...	...	...	...	...	...	...	...	...	...	...	...	...	...	...	...	...	...	...	...	...
		Nagarta ...	" ...	230	...	23	197	...	209	...	...	209	...	30	...	3	27	...	47	...	...	47	...
		Jain ...	Jain ...	111	10	71	30	...	119	1	3	115	...	36	...	17	19	...	29	1	2	26	...
		Márvádi ...	" ...	...	...	...	...	...	...	...	...	...	...	10	...	...	10	...	...	...	...	...	...
		" ...	Hindu ...	...	...	...	...	...	...	...	...	...	...	...	...	...	...	...	...	...	...	...	...
		" ...	Buddhist ...	...	...	...	...	...	...	...	...	...	...	...	...	...	...	...	...	...	...	...	...
		Srávaka ...	Jain ...	...	...	...	...	...	...	...	...	...	...	...	...	...	...	...	...	...	...	...	...
		Total Group 14 ...	...	56,895	2,611	5,659	48,592	...	58,883	185	255	58,443	...	22,239	911	1,162	17,163	...	22,685	17	33	22,635	...
		Total Class C ...		**56,895**	**2,644**	**5,659**	**48,592**	...	**58,883**	**185**	**255**	**58,443**	...	**22,239**	**911**	**4,162**	**17,163**	...	**22,685**	**17**	**38**	**22,635**	...

SUPPLEMENTARY TABLE D.—(Continued.)

Class.	Group.	Caste, &c., and sub-division.	Religion.	Shimoga. Males. Total.	Shimoga. Males. Pupils.	Shimoga. Males. Literate.	Shimoga. Males. Illiterate.	Shimoga. Males. Not stated.	Shimoga. Females. Total.	Shimoga. Females. Pupils.	Shimoga. Females. Literate.	Shimoga. Females. Illiterate.	Shimoga. Females. Not stated.	Kadur. Males. Total.	Kadur. Males. Pupils.	Kadur. Males. Literate.	Kadur. Males. Illiterate.	Kadur. Males. Not stated.	Kadur. Females. Total.	Kadur. Females. Pupils.	Kadur. Females. Literate.	Kadur. Females. Illiterate.	Kadur. Females. Not stated.
C—Commercial—(Continued)	14 Traders	Banya ...	Hindu	...	...	...	...	...	...	...	...	...	...	...	...	...	...	...	...	...	...	...	...
		" ...	Jain	...	...	...	...	...	...	...	...	...	...	...	...	...	...	...	...	...	...	...	...
		Banajiga ...	Hindu	3,766	94	396	3,276	...	2,913	7	9	2,897	...	2,700	68	191	2,441	...	2,415	8	51	2,356	...
		Guzarâti ...	"	...	...	...	...	...	...	...	...	...	...	...	...	...	...	...	...	...	...	...	...
		Jat ...	"	...	...	...	...	...	...	...	...	...	...	...	...	...	...	...	...	...	...	...	...
		Komati ...	"	617	56	304	257	...	558	1	1	556	...	731	71	317	343	...	607	...	7	600	...
		Lâder ...	"	10	...	...	10	...	1	...	...	1	...	155	...	2	153	...	183	...	...	183	...
		Lingâyet ...	"	25,333	1,355	4,514	19,464	...	24,060	17	22	23,961	...	10,716	737	3,077	6,902	...	10,336	7	84	10,245	...
		Mudali ...	"	149	3	18	128	...	80	...	3	77	...	133	11	48	74	...	92	...	1	91	...
		Multâni ...	"	...	...	...	...	...	...	...	...	...	...	...	...	...	...	...	...	...	...	...	...
		Nagarta ...	"	4,208	27	1,302	2,879	...	3,758	...	1	3,751	...	2,939	10	56	2,923	...	2,234	...	...	2,234	...
		Jain ...	Jain	535	9	10	516	...	477	...	...	477	...	26	...	15	11	...	17	...	...	17	...
		Mârvâdi ...	"	21	...	...	21	...	5	...	...	5	...	1	...	...	1	...	...	...	...	...	...
		" ...	Hindu	...	...	...	...	...	...	...	...	...	...	...	...	...	...	...	...	...	...	...	...
		" ...	Buddhist	...	...	...	...	...	...	...	...	...	...	...	...	...	...	...	...	...	...	...	...
		S'râvaka ...	Jain	1,038	16	95	927	...	921	...	...	921	...	...	...	...	...	...	...	...	...	...	...
		Total Group 14 ...	...	*35,677*	*1,560*	*6,639*	*27,478*	...	*32,746*	*25*	*42*	*32,679*	...	*17,451*	*897*	*3,706*	*12,848*	...	*15,884*	*15*	*143*	*15,726*	...
		Total Class C ...		**35,677**	**1,560**	**6,639**	**27,473**	...	**32,746**	**25**	**42**	**32,679**	...	**17,451**	**897**	**3,706**	**12,848**	...	**15,884**	**15**	**143**	**15,726**	...

SUPPLEMENTARY TABLE D.—(Continued.)

Class.	Group.	Caste, &c. and sub-division.	Religion.	Chitaldurg. Males. Total.	Pupils.	Literate.	Illiterate.	Not stated.	Chitaldurg. Females. Total.	Pupils.	Literate.	Illiterate.	Not stated.	The Civil and Military Station, Bangalore. Males. Total.	Pupils.	Literate.	Illiterate.	Not stated.	The Civil and Military Station, Bangalore. Females. Total.	Pupils.	Literate.	Illiterate.	Not stated.
C—Commercial.—(Continued.)	14 Traders.	Banya ...	Hindu ...	...	...	...	...	...	...	...	...	...	...	28	2	22	4	...	13	...	...	13	...
		" ...	Jain ...	...	...	...	...	...	...	...	...	...	...	77	9	53	15	...	43	...	...	43	...
		Banajiga ...	Hindu ...	2,154	67	376	1,711	...	2,070	2	14	2,054	...	4,124	627	1,623	1,866	8	4,218	104	140	3,942	32
		Guzaráti ...	" ...	...	...	...	...	...	...	...	...	...	...	20	...	...	10	...	10	...	...	10	...
		Ját ...	" ...	...	...	...	...	...	...	...	...	...	...	1	...	...	1	...	...	...	...	...	...
		Kómati ...	" ...	1,360	67	702	591	...	1,245	3	2	1,240	...	24	2	19	3	...	30	...	...	30	...
		Láder ...	" ...	114	2	...	112	...	102	...	...	102	...	...	...	...	...	...	...	...	...	...	...
		Lingáyet ...	" ...	22,671	1,242	5,103	16,326	...	21,626	14	28	21,584	...	518	59	140	319	...	478	...	...	478	...
		Mudali... ...	" ...	250	1	26	223	...	242	...	...	242	...	15	...	7	7	1	11	3	...	8	...
		Multáni ...	" ...	...	...	...	...	...	...	...	...	...	...	1	...	...	1	...		...	...	1	...
		Nagarta ...	" ...	332	...	3	329	...	319	...	...	319	...	113	7	35	71	...	107	...	...	107	...
		Jain ...	Jain ...	128	14	84	30	...	72	...	3	69	...	...	...	...	...	...	...	...	...	...	...
		Marvádi ...	" ...	23	...	...	23	...	...	...	...	...	...	11	...	9	2	...	9	...	1	8	...
		" ...	Hindu ...	...	...	...	...	...	...	...	...	...	...	17	1	8	8	...	4	...	1	3	...
		" ...	Buddhist ...	...	...	...	...	...	...	...	...	...	...	2	...	...	2	...	...	...	...	...	...
		S'rávaka	Jain ...	...	...	...	...	...	...	...	...	...	...	...	...	...	...	...	...	...	...	...	...
		Total Group 14 ...	... ...	*27,032*	*1,393*	*6,294*	*19,345*	...	*25,676*	*19*	*47*	*25,610*	...	*4,941*	*707*	*1,916*	*2,309*	*9*	*4,924*	*107*	*142*	*4,643*	*32*
		Total Class C ...		**27,032**	**1,393**	**6,294**	**19,345**	...	**25,676**	**19**	**47**	**25,610**	...	**4,941**	**707**	**1,916**	**2,309**	**9**	**4,924**	**107**	**142**	**4,643**	**32**

SUPPLEMENTARY TABLE D.—(Continued.)

Total including the Civil and Military Station, Bangalore.

Class.	Group.	Caste, &c. and sub-division.	Religion.	Males. Total.	Males. Pupils.	Males. Literate.	Males. Illiterate.	Males. Not stated.	Females. Total.	Females. Pupils.	Females. Literate.	Females. Illiterate.	Females. Not stated.
C.—Commercial—(Concluded.)	14 Traders.	Banya ...	Hindu ...	28	2	22	4		13	...	...	13	...
		" ...	Jain ...	77	9	53	15	..	43		...	43	...
		Banajiga ...	Hindu ...	57,653	2,957	8,730	45,958	8	57,082	316	634	56,070	32
		Guzarāti ...	" ...	41	...	25	16	...	30	...	4	26	...
		Jāṭ ...	" ...	1	...	...	1	...		...	...	...	...
		Kōmaṭi ...	" ...	15,181	1,241	8,850	5,090	...	13,873	68	101	13,704	...
		Láḍer ...	" ...	1,014	22	117	875	...	1,032	...	...	1,032	...
		Lingáyet ...	" ...	146,492	8,383	2,9501	108,608	...	115,581	328	398	114,855	...
		Mudali ...	" ...	2,969	275	971	1,722	1	2,468	98	117	2,253	...
		Multáni ...	" ...	1	...	...	1	...	1	...	...	1	...
		Nagarta ...	" ...	12,015	532	2,874	8,609	...	10,949	...	7	10,912	...
		Jain ...	Jain ...	1,090	65	286	739	...	871	9	10	852	...
		Márváḍi ...	" ...	66	...	9	57	...	14	..	1	13	...
		" ...	Hindu ...	17	1	8	8	...	4	...	1	3	...
		" ...	Buddhist ...	2	...	...	2	...	...	...	...	...	...
		S'rávaka ...	Jain ...	1,038	16	95	927	...	924	...	...	924	...
		Total Group 14 ...	...	237,685	13,503	51,541	172,632	9	232,885	849	1,273	230,731	32
		Total Class C		**237,685**	**13,503**	**51,541**	**172,632**	**9**	**232,885**	**849**	**1 273**	**230,731**	**32**

SUPPLEMENTARY TABLE-D.—(Continued).

Class.	Group.	Caste, &c. and sub-division.	Religion.	Total Strength. Males. Total males.	Males. Pupils.	Males. Literate.	Males. Illiterate.	Males. Education not stated.	Females. Total Females.	Females. Pupils.	Females. Literate.	Females. Illiterate.	Females. Education not stated.	Territorial Distribution. Bangalore. Males. Total.	Males. Pupils.	Males. Literate.	Males. Illiterate.	Males. Not stated.	Females. Total.	Females. Pupils.	Females. Literate.	Females. Illiterate.	Females. Not stated.
D.—Artisan and Village Menial.	17 Gold-smiths	Pánchála	Hindu	49,596	2462.	8.677	38.457	...	47,494	93	153	47,248	...	6,131	665	1.461	4,005	...	5,919	30	14	5,905	...
	18 Barbers	Náyinda	"	18,411	331	493	17,587	...	17,742	...	2	17,740	...	3,435	42	151	3,242	...	3,393	...	...	3,393	...
	19 Black-smiths	Pánchála (Kammára)	"	3.122	55	62	3.005	...	3,019	...	...	3,019	...	257	32	15	210	...	281	...	...	281	...
	20 Carpenters &c.	Pánchála (Badagi)	"	4,409	13	40	4,356	...	4,225	...	...	4,225	...	...	...	...	...	...	...	...	...	...	...
		Gounder	"	...	...	...	...	...	...	...	...	...	...	...	...	...	...	...		...	...	...	...
		Total Group 20.		*4,409*	*13*	*40*	*4,356*	...	*4,225*	...	...	*4,225*	...	...	...	...	...	...	...	...	...	...	...
	21 Brass and Copper-smiths	Gejjégára and Kanchugára	Hindu	111	...	...	111	...	119	...	...	119	...	21	...	...	21	.	29	...	...	29	...
	22 Tailors	Darzi	"	4.529	202	576	3,751	...	4,232	21	22	4.189	...	864	65	97	702	..	901	4	1	896	
	23 Weavers, Calenderers and Dyers	Gónga	"	748	10	13	725	...	668	...	...	668	...	341	10	13	318	...	278	...	...	278	...
		Gádiya	Jain	...	...	...	...	...	...	...	...	...	...	...	...	...	...	...	...	...	...	...	...
		Néyige	Hindu	43.318	1,928	5.157	36 233	...	43,500	127	112	43,261	...	11.227	768	2,422	8.647	...	11,867	64	60	11,743	...
		Total Group 23		*41,006*	*1,933*	*5,170*	*36,958*	...	*44,168*	*127*	*112*	*43,920*	...	*12,168*	*768*	*2.435*	*8,965*	.	*12,145*	*64*	*60*	*12,021*	...
	24 Washermen	Agasa	Hindu	42,376	361	306	44.700	...	42,288	2	2	42,284	...	5.179	50	42	5.087	...	5,261	...	...	5,261	...
	26 Shepherds & woolweavers	Kuruba	"	172,014	1,223	2,456	138,335	...	173,960	55	33	173,872	...	19.618	178	317	19.123	...	20,995	19	4	20,972	...
	26(a) Cowherds, &c.	Golla	"	64.580	973	1 320	62 327	...	63,107	40	17	61,059	...	9,461	330	342	8.789	...	9,661	34	8	9,619	...
	27 Oil pressers	Gániga	"	17.645	665	1.408	15 571	1	18,040	14	9	18,007	...	2,007	139	237	2.501	...	2,869	7	1	2,861	...
	28 Potters	Kumbára	"	21,026	496	708	19.822	...	19,432	11	4	19,417	...	1.978	125	93	1.760	.	1,977	11	4	1,962	...
	30 Salt, &c., workers	Uppára	"	44.845	350	612	43.853	...	44,259	1	7	44,251	..	723	92	53	583	...	769	...	...	769	...
	32 Goldsmiths' refuse collectors	Jalagára	"	129	...	...	129	...	125	...	...	125	...	27	...	...	27	...	28	...	...	28	...
	33(a) Gold lace makers	Rachévár (Sarige)	"	8	...	...	8	...	7	...	...	7	...	5	...	...	5	...	5	...	...	5	...
	35 Fishermen, Boatmen and Pálakhi Bearers	Besta	"	49,620	543	846	48.231	..	50,038	12	10	50,016	...	3,981	91	169	3.721	...	4,137	7	...	4,130	...
	36 Distillers and Toddy drawers	Idiga	"	20,532	133	398	20,001	..	19,385	...	...	10,385	...	1 272	13	72	1.187	...	1,277	...	...	1,277	...
	38 Leather workers	Mádiga	"	118,457	88	121	118 241	7	118,234	4	3	118,213	14	21,591	60	41	21,490	..	21,653	4	3	21,646	...
		Móchi	"	308	1	7	300	...	331	...	...	314	...	52	..	5	47	..	45	...	...	45	...
		Total Group 38		*118,765*	*89*	*128*	*118,511*	*7*	*118,568*	*4*	*3*	*118,517*	*14*	*21,643*	*60*	*46*	*21,537*	...	*21,698*	*4*	*3*	*21,601*	..
	39(a) Village watchmen, &c.	Holaya	Hindu	251.188	181	862	250.139	6	250,821	19	15	250,775	12	31.023	48	354	30,626	..	31,857	19	10	31,828	...
	Total Class D			**926,972**	**10,045**	**24.022**	**862,891**	**14**	**921.019**	**399**	**389**	**920,205**	**28**	**120 703**	**2.728**	**5.884**	**112,091**	...	**123,232**	**199**	**105**	**122,928**	...

SUPPLEMENTARY TABLE D.—(*Continued.*)

Class: D.—Artisan and Village Menial—(*Continued*).

Caste and Religion			Territorial Distribution—(*Continued.*)																			
			Kólár.										Tumkúr.									
			Males.					Females.					Males.					Females.				
Group.	Caste, &c., and sub-division.	Religion.	Total.	Pupils.	Literate.	Illiterate.	Not stated.	Total.	Pupils.	Literate.	Illiterate.	Not stated.	Total.	Pupils.	Literate.	Illiterate.	Not Stated.	Total.	Pupils.	Literate.	Illiterate.	Not Stated.
17. Gold-smiths ...	Pánchála ...	Hindu ...	4,483	194	1,308	2,983	...	4,490	5	13	4,472	...	4,266	305	1,031	2,870	...	4,274	20	61	4,133	...
18. Barbers ...	Náyinda ...	" ...	4,401	213	119	4,064	...	4,158	...	...	4,153	...	1,903	20	69	1,874	...	1,844	...	...	1,844	...
19. Blacksmiths ...	Pánchála (Kammára) ...	" ...	323	...	17	306	...	336	...	...	336	...	612	2	11	599	...	551	...	...	551	...
20. Carpenters, &c. ...	Pánchála (Badagi)	" ...	19		...	19	...	23	...	...	23	...	11	...		11	...	16	...	...	16	...
	Gounder ...	" ...	...	...	...	...	...	...	...	...	...	...	...	...	...	...	...	...	...	...	...	...
	Total Group 20.		*19*	...	...	*19*	...	*23*	...	...	*23*	...	*11*	...	...	*11*	...	*16*	...	...	*16*	...
21. Brass and Copper-smiths ...	Gejjégára and Kanchugára ...	Hindu ...	...	...	...	...	...	...	...	...	...	...	...	...	...	...	...	...	...	...	...	...
22. Tailors ...	Darzi ...	" ...	300	64	35	201	...	274	8	1	265	...	465	9	64	392	...	443	...	...	443	...
23. Weavers, Calenderers and Dyers ...	Góniga ...	" ...	39	...	...	39	...	36	...	...	36	...	222	...	...	222	...	290	...	...	290	...
	Gadiya ...	Jain ...	...	...	...	...	...	...	...	...	...	...	...	...	...	...	...	...	...	...	...	...
	Néyigé ...	Hindu ...	4,284	303	473	3,508	...	4,317	17	21	[illegible]	...	3,808	242	452	3,112	...	3,881	20	...	3,861	...
	Total Group 23.		*4,323*	*303*	*473*	*3,547*	...	*4,373*	*17*	*21*	[illegible]	...	*4,028*	*212*	*452*	[illegible]	...	*4,031*	*20*	...	[illegible]	...
24. Washermen ...	Agasa ...	Hindu ...	5,228	134	26	5,068	...	5,099	...	...	5,099	...	5,041	70	44	4,927	...	5,282	2	1	5,279	...
25. Shepherds & wool-weavers	Kurnba ...	" ...	17,511	349	171	16,991	...	17,793	21	6	17,766	...	19,165	147	453	18,565	...	19,021	2	2	19,017	...
26.(a) Cowherds, &c. ...	Golla ...	" ...	10,038	386	244	9,408	...	9,984	...	2	9,982	...	19,636	128	138	19,340	...	18,601	2	1	18,598	...
27. Oil pressers ...	Gániga ...	" ...	2,874	293	387	2,193	1	2,916	...	...	2,916	...	1,599	28	112	1,459	...	1,706	...	1	1,705	...
28. Potters ...	Kumbára ...	" ...	2,073	222	147	1,704	...	1,889	...	...	1,889	...	1,618	46	159	1,413	...	1,565	...	...	1,565	...
30. Salt, &c., workers ...	Uppára ...	" ...	1,673	42	21	1,610	...	1,454	...	...	1,454	...	5,798	63	144	5,591	...	5,770	...	1	5,769	...
32. Gold-smiths' refuse collectors ...	Jalagára ...	" ...	7	...	...	7	...	7	...	...	7	...	3	...	...	3	...	2	...	...	2	...
33(a). Gold lace makers ...	Ráchévár (Sarige)	" ...	3	...	...	3	...	2	...	...	2	...	...	...	...	...	...	...	...	...	...	...
35. Fishermen, Boatmen and Palakhi bearers ...	Besta ...	" ...	1,981	206	87	1,688	...	1,929	...	...	1,929	...	2,215	44	92	2,079	...	1,986	2	4	1,980	...
36. Distillers and Toddy drawers ...	Idiga ...	" ...	876	44	23	809	...	832	...	...	832	...	2,604	18	78	2,508	...	2,744	...	...	2,744	...
38. Leather workers ...	Mádiga ...	" ...	20,005	13	14	19,978	...	19,602	...	...	19,602	...	23,693	2	5	23,679	7	24,590	...	...	24,578	14
	Móchi ...	" ...	31	...	...	31	...	23	...	...	23	...	17	1	2	14	...	24	...	...	24	...
	Total Group 38.		*20,036*	*13*	*14*	*20,009*	...	*19,625*	...	...	*19,625*	...	*23,710*	*3*	*7*	*23,693*	...	*24,614*	...	...	*24,600*	*14*
38(a). Village watchmen, &c. ...	Holaya ...	Hindu ...	28,762	7	22	28,733	...	28,903	...	...	28,903	...	11,723	26	55	11,636	6	11,893	...	...	11,881	12
	Total Class D		**104,911**	**2,475**	**3,092**	**99,343**	**1**	**104,087**	**51**	**46**	*103,990*	...	**104,457**	**1,151**	**2,999**	**100,294**	**13**	**104,343**	**48**	**76**	**104,193**	**26**

SUPPLEMENTARY TABLE D.—(*Continued.*)

Class.	Caste and Religion.			Territorial Distribution.—(*Continued.*)																			
				Mysore.										Hassan.									
				Males.					Females.					Males.					Females.				
	Group.	Caste, &c. and sub-division.	Religion.	Total.	Pupils.	Literate.	Illiterate.	Not Stated.	Total.	Pupils.	Literate.	Illiterate.	Not Stated.	Total.	Pupils.	Literate.	Illiterate.	Not Stated.	Total.	Pupils.	Literate.	Illiterate.	Not Stated.
D.—Artisan and Village Menial.—(*Continued.*)	17 Gold-smiths ...	Pánchála ...	Hindu ...	16,176	620	1,797	13,759	...	16,049	25	30	15,991	...	5740	217	844	4,679	...	5,333	4	2	5,327	...
	18 Barbers ...	Nayinda ...	" ...	4,226	26	71	4,123	...	4,175	...	...	4,175	...	1,471	15	15	1,441	...	1,308	...	1	1,307	...
	19 Black-smiths ...	Pánchála (Kammára) ...	" ...	892	5	13	874	...	916	...	...	916	...	426	3	3	420	...	403	...	...	403	...
	20 Carpenters, &c. ...	Pánchála(Badagi)	" ...	1,501	7	12	1,482	...	1,563	...	...	1,563	...	809	2	5	802	...	868	...	...	868	...
		Gounder ...	" ...	...	...	...	...	...	...	...	...	...	...	...	...	...	...	...	...	...	...	...	...
		Total Group 20.		*1,501*	7	*12*	*1,482*	...	*1,563*	...	...	*1,563*	...	*800*	2	*5*	*802*	...	*868*	...	...	868	...
	21 Brass and Copper-smiths ...	Gejjegára and Kanchugára ...	Hindu ...	90	...	...	90	...	90	...	...	90	...	...	...	...	...	...	...	...	...	...	...
	22 Tailors ...	Darzi ...	" ...	721	28	97	596	...	736	9	20	707	...	255	5	43	207	...	258	...	...	253	...
	23 Weavers, Calenderers and Dyers ...	Goniga ...	" ...	139	...	...	139	...	142	...	...	142	...	...	...	...	...	...	...	...	...	...	...
		Gadiya ...	Jain ...	...	...	...	...	...	...	...	...	...	...	...	...	...	...	...	...	...	...	...	...
		Néyige ...	Hindu ...	4,917	225	518	4,174	...	5,026	20	15	4,991	...	6,386	141	370	5,875	...	427	5	12	6,405	...
		Total Group 23.		*5,056*	*225*	*518*	*4,313*	...	*5,168*	*20*	*15*	*5,133*	...	*6,386*	*141*	*370*	*5,875*	...	*6,422*	5	*12*	*6,405*	...
	24 Washermen ...	Agasa ...	Hindu ...	9,541	35	55	9,451	...	9,894	...	...	9,894	...	5,135	23	19	5,093	...	5,321	...	...	5,321	...
	26 Shepherds & wool weavers ...	Kuruba ...	" ...	57,633	198	501	56,934	...	58,172	8	11	58,153	...	19,912	53	175	19,678	...	20,818	...	5	20,813	...
	26(*a*) Cowherds, &c. ...	Golla ...	" ...	2,657	41	185	2,431	...	2,785	2	6	2,780	...	2,668	13	55	2,600	...	2,544	2	...	2,542	...
	27 Oil pressers ...	Gániga ...	" ...	7,635	98	425	7,112	...	7,999	6	7	7,986	...	1,099	36	78	985	...	1,160	1	...	1,159	...
	28 Potters ...	Kumbára ...	" ...	8,300	51	103	8,146	...	7,834	...	...	7,846	...	1,668	19	84	1,565	...	1,645	...	...	1,645	...
	30 Salt, &c., workers ...	Uppára ...	" ...	16,922	48	130	16,744	...	17,795	...	1	17,794	...	4,206	26	37	4,143	...	4,360	...	...	4,360	...
	32 Gold-smiths refuse collectors ...	Jalagára ...	" ...	86	...	...	86	...	85	...	...	85	...	6	...	...	6	...	3	...	...	3	...
	33(*a*) Gold lace makers ...	Sáchevár(Sarige)	" ...	...	...	...	...	...	...	...	...	...	...	...	...	...	...	...	...	...	...	...	...
	35 Fishermen, Boatmen & Pálakhi bearers ...	Besta ...	" ...	28,377	116	281	28,980	...	30,173	1	4	30,168	...	3,764	22	31	3,711	...	3,864	...	2	3,862	...
	36 Distillers and Toddy drawers ...	I'diga ...	" ...	4,140	32	87	4,021	...	4,310	...	...	4,310	...	1,399	7	56	1,336	...	1,358	...	...	1,358	...
	38 Leather workers	Mádiga ...	" ...	11,731	4	18	11,709	...	12,085	...	...	12,085	...	5,520	2	4	5,514	...	5,670	...	...	5,670	...
		Móchi ...	" ...	170	...	...	170	...	193	...	...	193	...	...	...	...	...	...	...	...	...	...	...
		Total Group 38.		*11,901*	4	*18*	*11,879*	...	*12,278*	...	...	*12,278*	...	*5,520*	2	4	*5,514*	...	*5,670*	...	...	*5,670*	...
	39(*a*) Village Watchmen &c. ...	Holaya ...	Hindu ...	84,369	79	278	84,012	...	83,634	...	5	83,629	...	43,596	1	58	43,537	...	43,462	...	...	43,462	...
		Total Class D.		**261,223**	**1,613**	**4,571**	**255,039**	...	**268,661**	**71**	**99**	**268,491**	...	**104,060**	**591**	**1,877**	**101,592**	...	**104,995**	**12**	**22**	**104,961**	...

SUPPLEMENTARY TABLE D.—(Continued.)

Class: D.—Artisan and Village Menial.—(Continued).

Caste and Religion.			Territorial Distribution.—(Continued.)																			
			Shimoga.										Kadúr.									
			Males.					Females.					Males.					Females.				
Group.	Caste, &c. and sub-division.	Religion.	Total.	Pupils.	Literate.	Illiterate.	Not Stated.	Total.	Pupils.	Literate.	Illiterate.	Not Stated.	Total.	Pupils.	Literate.	Illiterate.	Not Stated.	Total.	Pupils.	Literate.	Illiterate.	Not Stated.
17 Gold-smiths ...	Pánchála ...	Hindu ...	5,588	175	820	4,593	...	4,832	4	20	4,858	...	4,119	165	527	3,427	...	3,434	3	2	3,429	...
18 Barbers ...	Náyinda ...	" ...	1,460	2	17	1,441	...	1,363	...	1	1,367	...	520	...	17	503	...	403	...	...	403	...
19 Black-smiths ...	Pánchála (Kammára)	" ...	96	1	...	95	...	84	...	...	84	...	90	...	...	90	...	85	...	...	85	...
	Pánchála (Badagi)	" ...	856	2	13	841	...	601	...	...	601	...	559	...	8	551	...	458	...	...	458	...
20 Carpenters, &c.	Gounder	" ...	...	...	...	...	...	...	...	...	...	...	...	...	...	...	...	...	...	...	...	...
	Total Group 20.	....	*856*	*2*	*13*	*841*	...	*601*	...	...	*601*	...	*559*	...	*8*	*551*	...	*458*	...	...	*458*	...
21 Brass and Copper-smiths ...	Gejjégára and Kanchugára ...	Hindu ...	...	...	...	...	...	...	...	...	...	...	...	...	...	...	...	...	...	...	...	...
22 Tailors ...	Darzi ...	" ...	1,097	7	96	994	...	993	...	...	993	...	409	15	42	352	...	325	...	...	325	...
23 Weavers, Calenderers and Dyers ...	Góniga ...	" ...	...	...	...	...	...	...	...	...	...	...	7	...	...	7	...	12	...	...	12	...
	Gadiya ...	Jain ...	...	...	...	...	...	...	...	...	...	...	...	...	...	...	...	...	...	...	...	...
	Neyige ...	Hindu ...	3,394	48	178	3,168	...	3,280	...	...	3,280	...	5,106	148	368	4,590	...	5,111	...	...	5,111	...
	Total Group 23.	....	*3,394*	*48*	*178*	*3,168*	...	*3,280*	...	...	*3,280*	...	*5,113*	*148*	*368*	*4,597*	...	*5,123*	...	...	*5,123*	...
24 Washermen ...	Agasa ...	Hindu ...	6,836	25	68	6,743	...	6,267	...	...	6,267	...	2,199	11	23	2,165	...	1,987	...	1	1,986	...
26 Shepherds & wool weavers ...	Kuruba ...	" ...	11,924	113	184	11,627	...	11,759	1	...	11,758	...	13,246	85	333	12,828	...	13,009	...	3	13,006	...
26(a) Cowherds, &c. ...	Golla ...	" ...	2,101	17	52	2,032	...	1,894	...	...	1,894	...	2,127	6	46	2,075	...	2,022	...	...	2,022	...
27 Oilpressers ...	Gániga ...	" ...	377	6	33	338	...	170	...	...	170	...	550	17	28	505	...	542	...	...	542	...
29 Potters ...	Kumbára ...	" ...	1,885	9	16	1,860	...	1,396	...	...	1,396	...	2,152	17	32	2,103	...	1,866	...	...	1,866	...
30 Salt, &c., workers	Uppára ...	" ...	6,091	29	63	5,999	...	4,865	1	2	4,862	...	5,115	52	105	4,958	...	4,885	...	...	4,885	...
32 Gold-smiths refuse collectors ...	Jalagára ...	" ...	...	...	...	...	...	...	...	...	...	...	...	...	...	...	...	...	...	...	...	...
33(a) Gold lace makers ...	Ráchéra (Jarige)	" ...	...	...	...	...	...	...	...	...	...	...	...	...	...	...	...	...	...	...	...	...
35 Fishermen, Boatmen and Palakhi bearers ...	Besta ...	" ...	3,759	29	93	3,637	...	3,531	1	...	3,530	...	2,064	17	32	2,015	...	2,038	...	...	2,038	...
36 Distillers and Toddy drawers ...	Idiga ...	" ...	5,941	1	3	5,937	...	5,003	...	...	5,003	...	2,167	5	10	2,152	...	1,715	...	...	1,715	...
38 Leather workers	Mádiga ...	" ...	11,948	3	13	11,932	...	11,069	...	...	11,069	...	5,490	...	7	5,483	...	4,958	...	...	4,958	...
	Mochi ...	" ...	12	...	...	12	...	14	...	...	14	...	4	...	...	4	...	1	...	...	1	...
	Total Group 38	....	*11,960*	*3*	*13*	*11,944*	...	*11,083*	...	...	*11,083*	...	*5,494*	...	*7*	*5,487*	...	*4,959*	...	...	*4,959*	...
38 (a) Village watchmen, &c....	Holaya ...	Hindu ...	19,342	15	40	19,287	...	18,658	...	...	18,658	...	28,161	1	16	28,144	...	23,130	...	...	23,130	...
	Total Class D.	......	**82,707**	**482**	**1,689**	**80,536**	...	**75,834**	**7**	**23**	**75,804**	...	**74,085**	**539**	**1,594**	**71,952**	...	**65,981**	**3**	**6**	**65,972**	...

SUPPLEMENTARY TABLE D.—(Continued.)

Class.	Caste and Religion.			Territorial Distribution—(Concluded.)																			
				Chitaldurg.										The Civil and Military Station Bangalore.									
				Males.					Females.					Males.					Females.				
	Group.	Caste, &c., and sub-division	Religion.	Total.	Pupils.	Literate.	Illiterate.	Not Stated.	Total.	Pupils.	Literate.	Illiterate.	Not Stated.	Total.	Pupils.	Literate.	Illiterate.	Not Stated.	Total.	Pupils.	Literate.	Illiterate.	Not Stated.
D.—Artisan and Village Menial.—(Continued.)	17 Gold-smiths	Pánchála	Hindu	3,093	121	831	2,141	...	3,133	2	6	3,125	..	556	61	187	306	2	535	18	12	504	1
	18 Barbers	Náyinda	"	935	8	34	893	..	893	...	..	893	..	583	45	100	436	5	557	6	5	538	8
	19 Black-smiths	Pánchála (Kammára)	"	426	12	3	411	..	303	...	...	303	...	50	5	13	32	...	59	4	2	53	...
	20 Carpenters, &c.	Pánchála (Badagi)	"	654	2	2	650	..	696	...	...	696	...	5	..	3	2	...	4	•	...	4	...
		Gounder	"	...	...	...	..	...	...	...	...	.	...	2	1	...	1	...	1	...	...	1	...
		Total Group 20.		654	2	2	650	...	696	...	...	696	...	7	1	3	3	...	5	...	...	5	...
	21 Brass and Copper-smiths	Gejjegára and Kanchugára	Hindu	...	...	...	...	...	...	...	...	...	...	78	16	41	21	...	88	2	1	85	...
	22 Tailors	Darzi	"	418	9	102	307	...	304	...	...	304	..	908	32	116	845	5	905	2	4	895	4
	23 Weavers, Calenderers and Dyers	Gániga	"	...	...	...	...	..	...	...	...	...	..	6	1	1	4	...	4	...	...	4	...
		Gidiya	Jain	...	...	...	...	...	...	...	...	...	...	1	...	1	...	...	...	...	...	...	...
		Néyige	Hindu	3,598	63	376	3,159	..	3,576	1	1	3,574	...	81	6	24	51	...	87	...	1	86	...
		Total Group 23.		3,598	63	376	3159	..	3,576	1	1	3,574	...	[illegible]	7	[illegible]	55	...	91	...	1	90	...
	24 Washermen	Agasa	Hindu	3,217	13	29	3,175	...	3,177	...	...	3,177	..	503	12	21	470	...	504	1	1	502	...
	26 Shepherds & woolweavers.	Kuruba	"	13,005	94	322	12,589	...	12,393	4	2	12,387	...	386	10	30	345	1	498	1	...	497	...
	26(a) Cowherds, &c.	Golla	"	15,892	52	188	15,652	..	15,613	...	...	15,613	..	653	49	171	433	...	655	12	7	636	...
	27 Oil pressers	Gániga	"	604	18	108	478	...	608	...	...	608	...	63	5	23	35	...	70	...	...	70	...
	28 Potters	Kumbára	"	1,352	7	74	1,271	...	1,258	5	...	1,253	..	284	1	16	266	1	167	...	...	167	...
	30 Salt, &c., workers.	Uppára	"	4,312	28	59	4,225	..	4,361	...	3	4,358	...	9	...	1	3	...	10	...	...	10	...
	32 Gold-smiths' refuse collectors	Jalagára	"	...	...	...	...	..	...	...	...	...	..	2	2	...	...	...	2	...	...	2	...
	33(a) Gold lace makers	Báchevár (Sarige)	"	...	...	...	...	..	...	...	...	...	...	...	...	...	...	...	...	...	...	...	...
	35 Fishermen, Boatmen and Pálakhi Bearers	Besta	"	2,479	18	61	2,400	...	2,380	10	...	2,370	...	115	9	15	91	...	121	...	...	121	...
	36 Distillers and Toddy drawers	I'diga	"	2,133	13	69	2,051	..	2,116	...	...	2,116	...	8	2	...	6	...	12	...	...	12	...
	38 Leather workers	Mádiga	"	18,479	4	19	18,456	...	18,607	...	...	18,607	..	1,449	13	32	1,401	3	1,445	...	1	1,444	...
		Móchi	"	22	...	..	22	...	34	...	...	34	...	53	1	8	44	...	51	...	...	51	...
		Total Group 38.		18,501	4	19	18,478	...	18,641	...	...	18,641	..	1,502	11	40	1,445	3	1,496	...	1	1,465	...
	38(a) Village watchmen, &c.	Holaya	Hindu	4,207	4	39	4,164	...	4,284	...	...	4,284	...	8,811	509	1,259	7,003	40	9,673	128	59	9,438	48
		Total Class D.		74,828	466	2,316	72,044	...	73,886	8	12	73,866	...	14,599	780	2,062	11,700	57	15,351	174	93	15,023	61

SUPPLEMENTARY TABLE D.—(Continued.)

Caste and Religion.				Total strength including the Civil and Military Station, Bangalore.									
				Males.					Females.				
Class.	Group.	Caste, &c. and sub-division.	Religion.	Total.	Pupils.	Literate.	Illiterate.	Not stated.	Total.	Pupils.	Literate.	Illiterate.	Not stated.
D. Artisan and Village Menial—(Concluded)	17. Gold-smiths	Pánchála	Hindu	50,152	2,523	8 864	38 763	2	48,029	111	165	47,752	1
	18. Barbers	Náyinda	"	18,997	376	593	18,023	5	18,299	6	7	18,278	8
	19. Black-smiths	Pánchála (Kammára)	"	3,172	60	75	3,037	...	3,078	4	2	3,072	...
	20. Carpenters, &c.	Pánchála (Badagi)	"	4,414	13	43	4,358	...	4,229	...	...	4,229	...
		Gounder	"	2	1	...	1	...	1	...	...	1	...
		Total Group 20		*4,416*	*14*	*43*	*4,359*	...	*4,230*	...	...	*4,230*	...
	21. Brass and Copper-smiths	Gejjégára and Kánchugára	"	189	16	41	132	...	207	2	1	204	...
	22. Tailors	Darzi	"	5,527	234	692	4,596	5	5,137	23	26	5,084	4
	23. Weavers, Calenderers and Dyers	Góniga	"	754	11	14	729	...	672	...	...	672	...
		Gádiya	Jain	1	...	1	...	...	...	...	...	...	...
		Néyige	Hindu	43,399	1,934	5,181	36,284	...	43,587	127	113	43,347	...
		Total Group 23		*44,154*	*1,945*	*5,196*	*37,013*	...	*44,259*	*127*	*113*	*44,019*	...
	24. Washermen	Agasa	"	42,879	373	327	42,179	...	42,792	3	3	42,786	...
	26. Shepherds and Wool-weavers	Kuruba	"	172,400	1,233	2,486	168,680	1	174,368	56	33	174,279	...
	26 (a). Cowherds, &c.	Golla	"	65,233	1,022	1,451	62,760	...	63,762	52	24	63,686	...
	27. Oil-pressers	Gániga	"	17,708	670	1,431	15,606	1	18,100	14	9	18,077	...
	28. Potters	Kumbára	"	21,210	497	724	19,988	1	19,599	11	4	19,584	...
	30. Salt, &c., workers	Uppára	"	44,854	380	613	43,861	...	44,269	1	7	44,261	...
	32. Gold-smiths' refuse collectors	Jalagára	"	131	2	...	129	...	127	...	...	127	...
	33 (a). Gold lace makers	Ráchévár (Sarigé)	"	8	...	...	8	...	7	...	...	7	...
	35. Fishermen, Boatmen and Palakhi bearers	Besta	"	49,735	552	861	48,322	...	50,162	12	10	50,140	...
	36. Distillers and Toddy drawers	I'diga	"	20,540	135	398	20,007	...	19,397	...	...	19,397	...
	38. Leather workers	Mádiga	"	119,906	101	153	119,642	10	119,669	4	4	119,647	14
		Móchi	"	361	2	15	344	...	385	...	...	385	...
		Total Group 38		*120,267*	*103*	*168*	*119,986*	*10*	*120,054*	*4*	*4*	*120,032*	*14*
	38 (a). Village watchmen, &c.	Holaya	"	259,999	690	2,121	257,142	46	260,494	147	74	260,213	60
		Total Class D		**941,571**	**10,825**	**26,084**	**904,591**	**71**	**936,370**	**573**	**482**	**935,228**	**87**

SUPPLEMENTARY TABLE D.—(Continued.)

Casto and Religion.				Total Strength.										Territorial Distribution.									
				Males.					Females.					Bangalore.									
														Males.					Females.				
Class.	Group.	Caste, &c. and Sub-division.	Religion.	Total.	Pupils.	Literate.	Illiterate.	Education not stated.	Total.	Pupils.	Literate.	Illiterate.	Education not stated.	Total.	Pupils.	Literate.	Illiterate.	Not stated.	Total.	Pupils.	Literate.	Illiterate.	Not stated.
E.—Vagrant Minor Artisans and performers.	41 Earth-workers & Stone-dressers.	Vadda ...	Hindu..	54,446	67	168	54,211	...	51,952	5	2	51,945	...	10,062	16	32	10,014	...	9,979	...	...	9,979	...
	43 Mat-makers & Cane-splitters ..	Méda ...	"	2,318	7	16	2,295	...	1,912	...	...	1,912	...	202	...	2	200	...	224	...	...	224	...
	44 Hunters, Fowlers, &c.	Béda ...	"	108,731	819	1,484	106,428	...	108,138	9	44	108,085	...	7,303	84	136	7,083	...	7,777	...	7	7,770	...
	45 Miscellaneous & Disreputable livers.	Budabudiké	"	553	1	...	552	...	539	...	...	539	...	76	...	...	76	...	68	...	...	68	...
		Sillékyáta	"	55	...	...	55	...	38	...	...	38	...	...	...	...	...	...	...	...	...	...	...
		Sudugádusidda..	"	25	...	...	25	...	21	...	...	21	...	...	...	...	...	...	...	...	...	...	...
		Gondaliga	"	16	...	...	16	...	13	...	...	13	...	7	...	...	7	...	8	...	...	8	...
		Jógi ...	"	4,318	41	68	4,209	...	4,165	...	6	4,159	...	895	...	6	889	...	1,038	...	2	1,036	...
		Jangáliga	"	461	3	36	422	...	464	...	3	461	...	215	3	17	195	...	226	...	1	225	...
		Karaman	"	...	...	...	...	...	...	...	...	...	...	...	...	...	...	...	...	...	...	...	...
		Mondaru	"	127	...	...	127	...	62	...	...	62	...	...	...	...	...	...	...	...	...	...	...
		Pandáram	"	...	...	...	...	...	...	...	...	...	...	...	...	...	...	...	...	...	...	...	...
		Sániyar	"	...	...	...	...	...	...	...	...	...	...	...	...	...	...	...	...	...	...	...	...
		Total Group 45......	...	*5,555*	*45*	*104*	*5,406*	...	*5,302*	...	*9*	*5,293*	...	*1,293*	*3*	*23*	*1,267*	...	*1,340*	...	*3*	*1,337*	...
	46 Tumblers and Acrobats.	Dombar	"	1,217	3	3	1,211	...	1,283	...	...	1,283	...	194	...	...	194	...	225	...	...	225	...
		Rá:lévár (Jatti)	"	592	19	...	573	...	610	...	...	610	...	97	...	...	97	...	112	...	...	112	...
		Total Group 46......	...	*1,809*	*22*	*3*	*1,784*	...	*1,893*	...	...	*1,893*	...	*291*	...	...	*291*	...	*337*	...	...	*337*	...
	47 Jugglers, Snake-charmers & Animal Exhibitors.	Gáradiga	"	411	...	...	411	...	465	...	...	465	...	136	...	...	136	...	149	...	...	149	...
		Total Class E......		**173,270**	**960**	**1,775**	**170,535**	...	**169,662**	**14**	**55**	**169,593**	...	**19,287**	**103**	**193**	**18,991**	...	**19,803**	...	**10**	**19,736**	...

SUPPLEMENTARY TABLE D.—(Continued.)

Class.	Caste and Religion.			Territorial Distribution.—(Continued.)																			
				Kólár.										Tumkúr.									
				Males.					Females.					Males.					Females.				
	Group.	Caste, &c. and Sub-division.	Religion.	Total.	Pupils.	Literate.	Illiterate.	Not stated.	Total.	Pupils.	Literate.	Illiterate.	Not stated.	Total.	Pupils.	Literate.	Illiterate.	Not stated.	Total.	Pupils.	Literate.	Illiterate.	Not stated.
E.—Vagrant Minor Artisans and Performers.—(Continued.)	41 Earth-workers & Stone dressers.	Vadda ...	Hindu	11,768	11	16	11,741	...	11,322	...	1	11,321	...	6,908	5	30	6,873	...	6,478	5	1	6,472	...
	43 Mat-makers and Cane-splitters ...	Méda ...	"	102	...	...	102	...	98	...	...	98	...	186	5	6	175	...	183	...	...	183	...
	44 Hunters, Fowlers, &c ...	Béda ...	"	23,923	299	152	23,472	...	23,406	...	3	23,403	...	21,762	158	348	21,256	...	21,608	9	12	21,587	...
	45 Miscellaneous & Disreputable livers ...	Budabudike ...	"	55	...	...	55	...	45	...	...	45	...	112	...	...	112	...	121	...	...	121	...
		Sillékyata ...	"	...	...	...	...	...	...	...	...	...	...	...	...	...	...	...	...	...	...	...	...
		Sudagádusidda ...	"	...	...	...	...	...	...	...	...	...	...	...	...	...	...	...	...	...	...	...	...
		Góndaliga ...	"	4	...	...	4	...	2	...	...	2	...	...	...	...	...	...	...	...	...	...	...
		Jógi ...	"	766	17	22	727	...	739	...	...	739	...	401	3	2	396	...	383	...	...	383	...
		Jangáliga ...	"	23	...	...	23	...	29	...	...	29	...	37	...	1	36	...	26	...	...	26	...
		Karaman ...	"	...	...	...	...	...	...	...	...	...	...	...	...	...	...	...	...	...	...	...	...
		Mondaru ...	"	62	...	...	62	...	52	...	...	52	...	...	...	...	...	...	...	...	...	...	...
		Pandáram ...	"	...	...	...	...	...	...	...	...	...	...	...	...	...	...	...	...	...	...	...	...
		Sániyar ...	"	...	...	...	...	...	...	...	...	...	...	...	...	...	...	...	...	...	...	...	...
		Total Group 45 ...	...	*910*	*17*	*22*	*871*	...	*867*	...	...	*867*	...	*550*	*3*	*3*	*544*	...	*530*	...	...	*530*	...
	46 Tumblers and Acrobats.	Dombar ...	"	283	3	1	279	...	347	...	...	347	...	147	...	1	146	...	117	...	...	117	...
		Kéchévár (Jatti) ...	"	21	...	...	21	...	17	...	...	17	...	37	...	...	37	...	60	...	...	30	...
		Total Group 46 ...	...	*304*	*3*	*1*	*300*	...	*364*	...	...	*364*	...	*184*	...	*1*	*183*	...	*177*	...	...	*177*	...
	47 Jugglers, snake-charmers & Animal Exhibitors.	Gáradiga ...	"	55	...	...	55	...	54	...	...	54	...	63	...	...	63	...	57	...	...	57	...
		Total Class E ...		**37,062**	**330**	**191**	**36,541**	...	**36,111**	...	**4**	**36,107**	...	**29,653**	**171**	**388**	**29,094**	...	**29,033**	**14**	**13**	**29,006**	...

SUPPLEMENTARY TABLE D.—(Continued.)

Class.	Group.	Caste, &c. and Sub-division.	Religion.	Mysore. Males. Total.	Pupils.	Literate.	Illiterate.	Not stated.	Mysore. Females. Total.	Pupils.	Literate.	Illiterate.	Not stated.	Hássan. Males. Total.	Pupils.	Literate.	Illiterate.	Not stated.	Hássan. Females. Total.	Pupils.	Literate.	Illiterate.	Not stated.
E.—Vagrant Minor Artisans and Performers.—(Continued.)	41 Earth-workers & Stone-dressers.	Vadda ...	Hindu..	4,077	8	36	4,033	...	3,981	...	...	3,981	...	2,496	5	1	2,490	...	2,282	...	...	2,282	...
	43 Mat-makers & Cane-splitters...	Méda ...	" ...	323	2	2	319	...	320	...	...	320	...	265	...	2	263	...	255	...	...	255	...
	44 Hunters, Fowlers, &c.	Béda ...	" ...	1,564	25	84	1,455	...	1,565	...	3	1,562	...	2,774	16	61	2,697	...	2,807	...	1	2,806	...
	45 Miscellaneous & Disreputable livers.	Budabudike ...	" ...	126	...	...	126	...	112	...	...	112	...	84	...	...	84	...	115	...	...	115	...
		Sillékyáta ...	" ...	...	...	...	...	...	...	...	...	...	...	...	...	...	...	...	...	...	...	...	...
		Sudugádusidda ...	" ...	...	...	...	...	...	...	...	...	...	...	...	...	...	...	...	...	...	...	...	...
		Gondaliga ...	" ...	5	...	...	5	...	3	...	...	3	...	...	...	...	...	...	...	...	...	...	...
		Jógi ...	" ...	646	9	10	627	...	717	...	...	717	...	219	3	20	196	...	187	...	1	183	...
		Jangáliga ...	" ...	11	...	1	10	...	22	...	...	22	...	75	...	8	67	...	83	...	1	82	...
		Karaman ...	" ...	...	...	...	...	...	...	...	...	...	...	...	...	...	...	...	...	...	...	...	...
		Mondaru ...	" ...	...	...	...	...	...	...	...	...	...	...	...	...	...	...	...	...	...	...	...	...
		Pandáram ...	" ...	...	...	...	...	...	...	...	...	...	...	...	...	...	...	...	...	...	...	...	...
		Sániyar... ...	" ...	...	...	...	...	...	...	...	...	...	...	...	...	...	...	...	...	...	...	...	...
		Total Group 45...	... ...	*786*	*9*	*11*	*768*	...	*854*	...	...	*854*	...	*378*	*3*	*28*	*347*	...	*385*	...	*5*	*380*	...
	46 Tumblers and Acrobats.	Dombar ...	" ...	167	...	...	167	...	146	...	...	146	...	173	...	...	173	...	169	...	...	169	...
		Ráchévár (Jatti) ...	" ...	280	19	...	261	...	305	...	...	305	...	73	...	...	73	...	73	...	...	73	...
		Total Group 46...	... ...	*447*	*19*	...	*428*	...	*451*	...	...	*451*	...	*246*	...	...	*246*	...	*242*	...	...	*242*	...
	47 Jugglers, Snake-charmers & Animal Exhibitors...	Gáradiga ...	" ...	23	...	...	23	...	37	...	...	37	...	...	...	...	...	...	...	...	...	...	...
		Total Class E.....		**7,222**	**63**	**133**	**7,026**	...	**7,217**	...	**3**	**7,214**	...	**6,159**	**24**	**92**	**6,043**	...	**5,971**	...	**6**	**5,965**	...

SUPPLEMENTARY TABLE D.—(Continued.)

Caste and Religion.				Territorial Distribution.—(Continued.)																			
				Shimoga.										Kadúr.									
				Males.					Females.					Males.					Females.				
Class.	Group.	Caste, &c. and Sub-division.	Religion.	Total.	Pupils.	Literate.	Illiterate.	Not stated.	Total.	Pupils.	Literate.	Illiterate.	Not stated.	Total.	Pupils.	Literate.	Illiterate.	Not stated.	Total.	Pupils.	Literate.	Illiterate.	Not stated.
E—Vagrant Minor Artisans and Performers.—(Continued.)	41 Earth-workers & Stone-dressers.	Vadda ...	Hindu.	7,775	16	26	7,733	...	7,143	...	...	7,143	...	2,816	...	5	2,811	...	2,383	...	...	2,383	...
	43 Mat-makers & Cane-splitters ...	Méda ...	"	709	...	4	705	...	351	...	...	351	...	343	...	...	343	...	287	...	...	287	...
	44 Hunters, Fowlers, &c. ...	Béda ...	"	12,949	43	121	2,785	...	12,729	...	11	12,718	...	2,563	22	83	2,458	...	2,532	...	3	2,529	...
	45 Miscellaneous & Disreputable livers ...	Budabudiké	"	45	1	...	44	...	36	...	...	36	...	28	...	...	28	...	20	...	...	20	...
		Silléyata	"	48	...	...	48	...	31	...	...	31	...	...	...	...	...	...	...	...	...	...	...
		Sudagádusiddu	"	25	...	...	25	...	21	...	...	21	...	...	...	...	...	...	...	...	...	...	...
		Gondaliga	"	...	...	...	...	...	...	...	...	...	...	...	...	...	...	...	...	...	...	...	...
		Jógi ...	"	581	1	1	559	...	437	...	...	437	...	288	8	7	273	...	237	...	...	237	...
		Jangáliga	"	...	...	...	...	...	...	...	...	...	...	...	...	...	...	...	...	...	...	...	...
		Karaman	"	...	...	...	...	...	...	...	...	...	...	...	...	...	...	...	...	...	...	...	...
		Mondaru	"	...	...	...	...	...	...	...	...	...	...	65	...	...	65	...	10	...	...	10	...
		Pandáram	"	...	...	...	...	...	...	...	...	...	...	...	...	...	...	...	...	...	...	...	...
		Sániyar...	"	...	...	...	...	...	...	...	...	...	...	...	...	...	...	...	...	...	...	...	...
		Total Group 45......	...	*679*	2	*1*	*676*	...	*525*	...	...	*525*	...	*381*	*8*	7	*366*	...	*267*	...	...	*267*	...
	46 Tumblers and Acrobats ...	Dombar...	"	53	...	1	52	...	75	...	...	75	...	146	...	...	146	...	114	...	...	114	...
		Háchévar (Jatti)	"	76	...	...	76	...	65	...	...	65	...	...	...	...	...	...	...	...	...	...	...
		Total Group 46......	...	*129*	...	*1*	*128*	...	*140*	...	...	*140*	...	*146*	...	...	*146*	...	*114*	...	...	*114*	...
	47 Jugglers, Snake-charmers & Animal Exhibitors.	Gárudiga	"	134	...	...	134	...	168	...	...	168	...	...	...	...	...	...	...	...	...	...	...
		Total Class E		22,375	61	153	22,161	..	21,056	...	11	21,045	...	6,249	30	95	6,124	...	5,583	...	3	5,580	...

SUPPLEMENTARY TABLE D.—(*Continued.*)

E.—Vagrant Minor Artisans and Performers.—(*Concluded.*)

Caste and Religion.			Territorial Distribution.—(*Concluded.*)																			
			Chitaldoorg										The Civil and Military Station, Bangalore.									
			Males.					Females.					Males.					Females.				
Group.	Caste, &c. and Sub-division.	Religion.	Total.	Pupils.	Literate.	Illiterate.	Not stated.	Total.	Pupils.	Literate.	Illiterate.	Not stated.	Total.	Pupils.	Literate.	Illiterate.	Not stated.	Total.	Pupils.	Literate.	Illiterate.	Not stated.
41 Earth-workers & Stone-dressers	Vadda ...	Hindu	8,544	6	22	8,516	...	8,384	...	...	8,384	...	375	4	6	365	...	430	...	1	425	4
43 Mat-makers & Cane-splitters ...	Méda ...	„	188	...	...	188	...	185	...	...	185	...	17	...	...	17	...	11	...	...	14	...
44 Hunters, Fowlers, &c. ..	Béda ...	„	35,893	172	499	35,222	...	35,714	..	4	35,710	...	121	8	9	103	1	138	...	3	135	..
45 Miscellaneous and Disreputable livers ...	Budabudike ...	„	27	...	...	27	...	22	...	...	22	...	...	...	...	...	...	...	...	...	...	...
	Sillékyata ...	„	7	...	...	7	...	7	...	...	7	...	...	...	...	...	...	...	...	...	...	...
	Sudagádusidda ...	„	...	...	...	...	...	...	...	...	...	...	...	...	...	...	...	...	...	...	...	...
	Gondaliga ...	„	...	...	...	...	...	...	...	...	...	...	...	...	...	...	...	...	...	...	...	...
	Jógi ...	„	442	...	...	442	...	427	...	...	427	...	...	...	...	...	...	...	...	...	...	...
	Jangáliga ...	„	100	...	9	91	...	78	...	1	77	...	1	...	...	1	...	1	...	...	1	...
	Karaman	„	...	...	...	...	...	...	...	...	...	...	3	...	3	...	...	4	...	...	4	...
	Mondaru ...	„	...	...	...	...	...	...	...	...	...	...	...	...	...	...	...	...	...	...	...	...
	Pandáram ...	„	...	...	...	...	...	...	...	...	...	...	6	1	3	2	...	9	...	...	9	...
	Sániyar... ...	„	...	...	...	...	...	...	...	...	...	...	1	...	...	1	...	2	...	...	2	...
	Total Group 45		*576*	..	*9*	*567*	...	*534*	...	*1*	*533*	...	*11*	*1*	*6*	*4*	...	*16*	...	...	*16*	...
46 Tumblers and Acrobats ...	Dombar ...	„	54	...	...	54	...	60	...	...	60	...	...	...	...	...	...	...	...	...	...	...
	Rachévár (Jatti) ...	„	8	...	...	8	...	8	...	...	8	...	1	...	1	...	...	...	...	...	...	..
	Total Group 46		*62*	...	...	*62*	...	*68*	...	...	*68*	...	*1*	...	*1*	...	...	...	...	...	...	...
47 Jugglers, Snake-charmers & Animal Exhibitors...	Gáradiga ...	„	...	...	...	...	...	...	...	...	...	...	...	...	...	...	...	...	...	...	...	...
Total Class E			45,263	178	530	44,555	...	44,885	...	5	44,880	...	525	13	22	489	1	593		4	590	4

SUPPLEMENTARY TABLE D.—(*Continued.*)

E.—Vagrant Minor Artisans and Performers.—(*Concluded.*)

Class. Group.	Caste, &c. and Sub-division.	Religion.	Males: Total.	Males: Pupils.	Males: Literate.	Males: Illiterate.	Males: Not stated.	Females: Total.	Females: Pupils.	Females: Literate.	Females: Illiterate.	Females: Not stated.
41 Earth-workers & Stone-dressers.	Vadda ...	Hindu.	54,821	71	174	54,576	...	52,382	5	3	52,370	4
43 Mat-makers & Cane-splitters ..	Méda ...	,,	2,335	7	16	2,312	...	1,926	...	...	1,926	...
44 Hunters, Fowlers, &c. ...	Béda ...	,,	108,852	527	1,493	106,531	1	108,276	9	47	108,220	...
45 Miscellaneous and Disreputable livers ...	Budabudiké ...	,,	553	1	...	552	...	539	...	...	539	...
	Sillékyâta ...	,,	55	...	...	55	...	38	...	...	38	...
	Sudugâdusidda ...	,,	25	...	...	25	...	21	...	...	21	...
	Gondaliga ...	,,	16	...	...	16	...	13	...	...	13	...
	Jógi ...	,,	4,318	41	68	4,209	...	4,165	...	6	4,159	...
	Jangâliga ...	,,	462	3	36	423	...	465	...	3	462	...
	Karaman ...	,,	3	...	3	...	...	4	...	...	4	...
	Mondaru ...	,,	127	...	...	127	...	62	...	...	62	...
	Pandâram ...	,,	6	1	3	2	...	9	...	...	9	...
	Sâniyar... ...	,,	1	...	...	1	...	2	...	...	2	...
	Total Group 45......		*5,566*	*46*	*110*	*5,410*	...	*5,318*	...	*9*	*5,309*	...
46 Tumblers and Acrobats.	Dombar	,,	1,217	3	3	1,211	...	1,283	...	...	1,283	...
	Râchévâr (Jatti) ...	,,	593	19	1	573	...	610	...	...	610	...
	Total Group 46......		*1,810*	*22*	*4*	*1,784*	...	*1,893*	...	...	*1,893*	...
47 Jugglers, Snake-charmers & Animal Exhibitors...	Gârudiga ...	,,	411	...	...	411	...	465	...	...	465	...
	Total Class E.....		**173,795**	**973**	**1,797**	**171,021**	**1**	**170,260**	**14**	**59**	**170,183**	**4**

Total including the Civil and Military Station, Bangalore.

SUPPLEMENTARY TABLE D. — Education by Caste

SUPPLEMENTARY TABLE D.—(*Continued.*)

Class.	Group.	Caste, &c. and Sub-division.	Religion.	Total Strength. Males. Total Males.	Pupils.	Literate.	Illiterate.	Education not stated.	Females. Total Females.	Pupils.	Literate.	Illiterate.	Education not stated.	Territorial Distribution. Bangalore. Males. Total.	Pupils.	Literate.	Illiterate.	Not stated.	Females. Total.	Pupils.	Literate.	Illiterate.	Not stated.
F.—Races and Nationalities.	48 Asiatic Races of reputed foreign origion.	A'rab	Musalmán	17	...	7	10	...	11	...	...	11	...	10	...	4	6	...	5	...	...	5	...
		A'rminian	Christian	2	...	2	...	...	1	...	1	...	...	2	...	2	...	...	1	...	1	...	...
		Belúchi	Musalmán	...	...	...	...	...	...	...	...	...	...	...	...	...	...	...	...	...	...	...	...
		Burmese	Christians	...	...	...	...	...	...	...	...	...	...	...	...	...	...	...	...	...	...	...	...
		Chinese	"	...	...	...	...	...	...	...	...	...	...	...	...	...	...	...	...	...	...	...	...
		Dáyare	Musalmán	1,081	20	44	1,017	...	1,419	...	...	1,419	...	1,034	20	40	974	...	1,385	...	...	1,385	...
		Hanifi	"	534	18	39	527	...	481	2	2	477	...	...	...	...	...	...	...	...	...	...	...
		Jews	Jew	9	5	4	...	...	11	2	5	4	...	...	...	...	...	...	...	...	...	...	...
		Jews	Christian	...	...	...	...	...	...	...	...	...	...	...	...	...	...	...	...	...	...	...	...
		Israelite	"	...	...	...	...	...	...	...	...	...	...	...	...	...	...	...	...	...	...	...	...
		Khádri	Musalmán	2	...	...	2	...	...	...	...	...	...	...	...	...	...	...	...	...	...	...	...
		Kandhári	"	...	...	...	...	...	...	...	...	...	...	...	...	...	...	...	...	...	...	...	...
		Mogal	"	4,527	252	430	3,845	...	4,245	33	146	4,066	...	694	31	98	565	...	660	3	27	630	...
		Musalmán	"	433	...	...	433	...	355	...	...	355	...	305	...	...	305	...	256	...	...	256	...
		Pársi	Pársi	15	1	7	7	...	14	...	8	6	...	3	...	2	1	...	2	...	2	...	...
		Patbán	Musalmán	18,127	966	2,158	15,003	...	16,929	127	280	16,522	...	4,369	313	436	3,620	...	4,165	36	97	4,032	...
		Shariff	"	431	5	19	407	...	421	9	7	405	...	9	...	...	9	...	8	...	...	8	...
		Sayad	"	18,616	1,152	3,831	13,633	...	16,958	176	552	16,230	...	4,307	303	897	3,107	...	4,001	30	176	3,775	...
		Shékh	"	71,193	2,811	10,062	58,320	...	66,053	482	1,009	61,562	...	12,131	824	2,046	9,261	...	11,491	152	253	11,166	...
		Singáleso	Buddhist	...	...	...	...	...	...	...	...	...	...	...	...	...	...	...	...	...	...	...	...
		Total Group 48	...	*115,037*	*5,230*	*16,603*	*93,204*	...	*106,898*	*831*	*2,010*	*104,057*	...	*22,864*	*1,491*	*3,525*	*17,848*	...	*21,574*	*241*	*536*	*21,197*	...

SUPPLEMENTARY TABLE D.—(*Continued.*)

Class.	Group.	Caste, &c. and Sub-division.	Religion.	Territorial Distribution.—(*Continued.*) Kólár. Males. Total.	Pupils.	Literate.	Illiterate.	Not stated.	Kólár. Females. Total.	Pupils.	Literate.	Illiterate.	Not stated.	Tumkúr. Males. Total.	Pupils.	Literate.	Illiterate.	Not stated.	Tumkúr. Females. Total.	Pupils.	Literate.	Illiterate.	Not stated.
F.—Races and Nationalities.—(*Continued.*)	48 Asiatic Races of Reputed Foreign Origin.	A'rab	Musalmán	...	...	...	...	...	...	...	...	...	...	...	...	...	...	...	...	...	...	...	...
		A'rmínian	Christian	...	...	...	...	...	...	...	...	...	...	...	...	...	...	...	...	...	...	...	...
		Belúchi	Musalmán	...	...	...	...	...	...	...	...	...	...	...	...	...	...	...	...	...	...	...	...
		Burmese	Christians	...	...	...	...	...	...	...	...	...	...	...	...	...	...	...	...	...	...	...	...
		Chinese	"	...	...	...	...	...	...	...	...	...	...	...	...	...	...	...	...	...	...	...	...
		Dáyare	Musalmán	...	...	...	...	...	...	...	...	...	...	...	...	...	...	...	1	...	...	1	...
		Hanifi	"	3	...	2	1	...	3	...	...	3	...	68	2	4	62	...	59	2	1	56	...
		Jews	Jew	...	...	...	...	...	...	...	...	...	...	...	...	...	...	...	...	...	...	...	...
		Jews	Christian	...	...	...	...	...	...	...	...	...	...	...	...	...	...	...	...	...	...	...	...
		Israelite	"	...	...	...	...	...	...	...	...	...	...	...	...	...	...	...	...	...	...	...	...
		Khádre	Musalmán	...	...	...	...	...	...	...	...	...	...	...	...	...	...	...	...	...	...	...	...
		Kandhári	"	...	...	...	...	...	...	...	...	...	...	...	...	...	...	...	...	...	...	...	...
		Mogal	"	661	43	56	562	...	603	6	6	591	...	522	10	11	501	...	510	9	9	492	...
		Musalmán	"	91	...	...	91	...	78	...	...	78	...	21	...	...	21	...	9	...	...	9	...
		Pársi	Parsi	1	...	1	...	...	...	...	...	...	...	...	...	...	...	...	...	...	...	...	...
		Pathán	Musalmán	2638	161	315	2,162	...	2,299	12	10	2,277	...	2,205	37	52	2,116	...	2,257	11	17	2,229	...
		Shariff	"	5	...	...	5	...	6	...	...	6	...	413	5	19	389	...	403	9	7	387	...
		Sayad	"	3,500	209	820	2,471	...	3,041	18	85	2,938	...	1,663	216	352	1,095	...	1,346	14	37	1,295	...
		Shékh	"	9,993	385	1,308	8,300	...	8,838	67	122	8,649	...	7,140	382	1,083	5.675	...	7,107	61	127	6,919	...
		Singháleso	Buddhist	...	...	...	...	...	...	...	...	...	...	...	...	...	...	...	...	...	...	...	...
		Total Group 48.	...	*16,892*	*798*	*2,502*	*13,592*	...	*14,868*	*103*	*223*	*14,542*	...	*12,032*	*652*	*1,521*	*9,859*	...	*11,662*	*106*	*168*	*11,388*	...

SUPPLEMENTARY TABLE D.—(Continued).

Class.	Group.	Caste, &c. and sub-division.	Religion.	Territorial Distribution.—(Continued.) Mysore. Males. Total.	Pupils.	Literate.	Illiterate.	Not stated.	Mysore. Females. Total.	Pupils.	Literate.	Illiterate.	Not stated.	Hassan. Males. Total.	Pupils.	Literate.	Illiterate.	Not stated.	Hassan. Females. Total.	Pupils.	Literate.	Illiterate.	Not stated.
F.—Races and Nationalities.—(Continued.)	48 Asiatic Races of Reputed Foreign Origion.	A'rab	Musalmán	...	...	...	...	...	...	...	...	...	...	...	...	...	...	...	...	...	...	...	...
		A'rminian	Christian	...	...	...	...	...	...	...	...	...	...	...	...	...	...	...	...	...	...	...	...
		Belúchi	Musalmán	...	...	...	...	...	...	...	...	...	...	...	...	...	...	...	...	...	...	...	...
		Burmese	Christians	...	...	...	...	...	...	...	...	...	...	...	...	...	...	...	...	...	...	...	...
		Chinese	,,	...	...	...	...	...	...	...	...	...	...	...	...	...	...	...	...	...	...	...	...
		Dáyare	Musalmán	47	...	4	43	...	33	...	...	33	...	...	...	...	...	...	...	...	...	...	...
		Hanifi	,,	227	7	18	202	...	206	...	...	206	...	104	6	5	93	...	35	...	1	34	...
		Jews	Jew	2	1	1	...	...	2	1	1	...	...	6	4	2	...	...	9	1	4	4	...
		Jews	Christian	...	...	...	...	...	...	...	...	...	...	...	...	...	...	...	...	...	...	...	...
		Israelite	,,	...	...	...	...	...	...	...	...	...	...	...	...	...	...	...	...	...	...	...	...
		Khádri	Musalmán	2	...	...	2	...	...	...	...	...	...	...	...	...	...	...	...	...	...	...	...
		Kandhári	,,	...	...	...	...	...	...	...	...	...	...	...	...	...	...	...	...	...	...	...	...
		Mogal	,,	734	54	165	515	...	679	8	91	580	...	239	37	28	174	...	242	...	2	240	...
		Musalmán	,,	...	...	...	...	...	...	...	...	...	...	8	...	...	8	...	6	...	...	6	...
		Pársi	Pársi	9	1	3	5	...	8	...	3	5	...	...	...	...	...	...	...	...	...	...	...
		Patháu	Buddhist	3,874	229	870	2,775	...	3,712	38	102	3,572	...	961	60	32	869	...	867	9	12	846	...
		Shariff	,,	4	...	...	4	...	4	...	...	4	...	...	...	...	...	...	...	...	...	...	...
		Sayad	,,	3,730	215	826	2,689	...	3,597	38	169	3,390	...	892	28	236	642	...	813	23	25	765	...
		Shékh	,,	14,368	643	2,316	11,409	...	14,266	107	285	13,874	...	4,851	95	839	3,917	...	4,473	43	69	4,361	...
		Singhalese	Buddhist	...	...	...	...	...	...	...	...	...	...	...	...	...	...	...	...	...	...	...	...
		Total Group 48.	...	*22,997*	*1,150*	*4,203*	*17,644*	...	*22,507*	*192*	*651*	*21,664*	...	*7,061*	*240*	*1,112*	*5,703*	...	*6,145*	*76*	*115*	*6,256*	...

SUPPLEMENTARY TABLE D.—(Continued.)

F.—Races and Nationalities.—(Continued.)

Class.	Group.	Caste, &c., and Sub-division.	Religion.	Shimoga. Males. Total.	Pupils.	Literate.	Illiterate.	Not stated.	Shimoga. Females. Total.	Pupils.	Literate.	Illiterate.	Not stated.	Kadúr. Males. Total.	Pupils.	Literate.	Illiterate.	Not stated.	Kadúr. Females. Total.	Pupils.	Literate.	Illiterate.	Not stated.
	(48) Asiatic Races of Reputed Foreign Origion.	A'rab	Musalmán	...	...	...	...	...	...	...	...	...	...	...	...	...	...	...	...	...	...	...	...
		A'rmínian	Christian	...	...	...	...	...	...	...	...	...	...	...	...	...	...	...	...	...	...	...	...
		Belúchi	Musalmán	...	...	...	...	...	...	...	...	...	...	...	...	...	...	...	...	...	...	...	...
		Burmese	Christian	...	...	...	...	...	...	...	...	...	...	...	...	...	...	...	...	...	...	...	...
		Chinese	"	...	...	...	...	...	...	...	...	...	...	...	...	...	...	...	...	...	...	...	...
		Dáyare	Musalmán	...	...	...	...	...	...	...	...	...	...	...	...	...	...	...	...	...	...	...	...
		Hanifi	"	167	3	5	159	...	176	...	...	176	...	14	...	4	10	...	...	...	...	...	...
		Jews	Jew	...	...	...	...	...	...	...	...	...	...	...	...	...	...	...	...	...	...	...	...
		Jews	Christian	...	...	...	...	...	...	...	...	...	...	...	...	...	...	...	...	...	...	...	...
		Isráelite	"	...	...	...	...	...	...	...	...	...	...	...	...	...	...	...	...	...	...	...	...
		Khádri	Musalmán	...	...	...	...	...	...	...	...	...	...	...	...	...	...	...	...	...	...	...	...
		Kandhári	"	...	...	...	...	...	...	...	...	...	...	...	...	...	...	...	...	...	...	...	...
		Mogal	"	1,356	36	35	1,285	...	1,259	3	3	1,253	...	202	31	25	143	...	174	4	7	163	...
		Musalmán	"	...	...	...	...	...	...	...	...	...	...	...	...	...	...	...	...	...	...	...	...
		Pársi	Parsi	...	...	...	...	...	...	...	...	...	...	...	...	...	...	...	...	...	...	...	...
		Patháu	Musalmán	1,969	81	146	1,742	...	1,784	9	19	1,756	...	1,147	58	208	831	...	970	5	15	950	...
		Shariff	"	...	...	...	...	...	...	...	...	...	...	...	...	...	...	...	...	...	...	...	...
		Sayad	"	2,267	94	325	1,848	...	2,203	13	21	2,169	...	1,071	33	223	815	...	872	62	21	845	...
		Shékh	"	9,888	174	823	8,891	...	8,946	18	58	8,870	...	6,162	132	1,020	5,010	...	4,750	14	69	4,667	...
		Singhálese	Buddhist	...	...	...	...	...	...	...	...	...	...	...	...	...	...	...	...	...	...	...	...
		Total Group 48	...	15,647	388	1,334	13,925	...	14,368	43	101	14,224	...	8,596	257	1,480	6,859	...	6,766	20	112	6,625	...

SUPPLEMENTARY TABLE D.—(Continued.)

Caste and Religion.				Territorial Distribution—(Concluded.)																			
				Chitaldurg.										The Civil and Military Station, Bangalore.									
				Males.					Females.					Males.					Females.				
Class.	Group.	Caste, &c., and Sub-divisions.	Religion.	Total.	Pupils.	Literate.	Illiterate.	Not stated.	Total.	Pupils.	Literate.	Illiterate.	Not stated.	Total.	Pupils.	Literate.	Illiterate.	Not stated.	Total.	Pupils.	Literate.	Illiterate.	Not stated.
F.—Races and Nationalities.—(Continued.)	48 Asiatic Races of Reputed Foreign Origin.	A'rab	Musalmán	7		3	4		6			6											
		Arminion	Christian	...										2		1	1		3		2	1	
		Belúchi	Musalmán	...										2			2						
		Burmese	Christian	...										2		1	1		2	1	1		
		Chinese	"	...										4		4							
		Dáyare	Musalmán	...																			
		Hanifi	"	1		1	...		2			2		13		6	7		20		2	18	
		Jews	Jew	1		1								1		1							
		Jews	Christian	...										3		3			...				
		Israelite	"	...										1		1							
		Khádri	Musalmán	...					...														
		Kaudhári	"																2			2	
		Mogal	"	119	7	12	100		118		1	117		327	45	115	167		315	20	32	266	
		Musalmán	"	8			8		6			6		45	3	18	24		28		1	27	
		Pársi	Parsi	2		1	1		4		3	1		3	1	2			3	1	2		
		Pathán	Musalmán	964	27	99	838		875	7	8	860		1,825	169	496	1 169	1	1,698	51	63	1,580	1
		Shariff	"											22	5	11	6		18	2	2	14	
		Sayad	"	1,186	44	182	960		1,08[illegible]	11	18	1,053		1,585	104	441	951	9	1,5[illegible]	36	88	1,361	12
		Sheikh	"	6,660	176	627	5,857		6,182	29	16	6,118		7,727	799	2,019	4,594	25	7,[illegible]	284	151	6,817	32
		Singhlese	Buddhist											3		2	1	..					
		Total Group 48.		8,948	251	926	7,768		8,278	11	76	8,161		11,[illegible]	[illegible]	2,111	7,223	[illegible]	11,176	412	621	10,3[illegible]	45

SUPPLEMENTARY TABLE D.—(*Continued.*)

Class.	Group.	Caste, &c. and Sub-division.	Religion.	Total including the Civil and Military Station, Bangalore. Males: Total.	Males: Pupils.	Males: Literate.	Males: Illiterate.	Males: Not stated.	Females: Total.	Females: Pupils.	Females: Literate.	Females: Illiterate.	Females: Not stated.
F.—Races and Nationalities.—(*Continued.*)	Asiatic Races of Reputed Foreign Origin.	A'rab	Musalmán	17		7	10		11			11	...
		A'rmenian	Christian	4		3	1		4		3	1	...
		Belúchi	Musalmán	2			2						...
		Burmese	Christian	2		1	1		2	1	1	...	...
		Chinese	...	4		4						...	...
		Dayare	Musalmán	1,081	20	44	1,017		1,419			1,419	
		Hanifi	„	597	18	45	534		501	2	4	495	
		Jews	Jew	10	5	5			11	2	5	4	
		Jews	Christian	3		3							
		Israelite	„	1		1							
		Khádri	Musalmán	2			2						
		Kandhári	„						2			2	
		Moghal	„	4,654	297	545	4,012		[illegible]	51	178	4,3[illegible]2	...
		Musalmán	„	478	3	18	457		383		1	382	
		Pársi	Pársi	18	2	9	7		17	1	10	6	
		Pathán	Musalmán	19,952	1,135	2,644	16,172	1	18,627	181	343	18,102	1
		Sharif	„	453	10	30	413		439	11	9	419	
		Sayad	„	20,201	1,336	4,272	14,584	9	18,472	226	640	17,594	12
		Shekh	„	76,930	3,610	12,081	63,214	25	73,017	706	1,[illegible]	71,379	32
		Singhalese	Buddhist	3		2	1						
		Total Group 43	...	*126,612*	*6,[illegible]36*	*19,741*	*100,[illegible]27*	*35*	*118,[illegible]*	*1,2[illegible]*	*2,[illegible]*	*114,146*	*15*

SUPPLEMENTARY TABLE D—(Continued.)

F—Races and Nationalities.—(Continued.)

Class. Group.	Caste, &c., and Sub-division.	Religion.	Total Strength. Males. Total Males.	Pupils.	Literate.	Illiterate.	Education not stated.	Females. Total Females.	Pupils.	Literate.	Illiterate.	Education not stated.	Territorial Distribution. Bangalore. Males. Total.	Pupils.	Literate.	Illiterate.	Not stated.	Females. Total.	Pupils.	Literate.	Illiterate.	Not stated.
49 Muslim Asiatic Races	Jám	Musalmán	...	...	...	...	...	...	...	...	...	...	...	...	...	...	...	...	...	...	...	...
	Labbe	...	1,859	52	114	1,693	...	961	1	12	948	...	168	1	21	146	...	43	...	4	39	...
	Maplá	...	130	2	26	102	...	20	...	...	20	...	...	...	...	...	...	...	...	...	...	...
	Memán	...	...	...	...	...	...	...	...	...	...	...	...	...	...	...	...	...	...	...	...	...
	Pindári	...	1,064	11	43	1,010	...	184	...	3	181	...	82	...	10	72	...	98	...	2	96	...
	Pinjári	...	1,199	17	30	1,152	...	981	5	4	972	...	82	...	9	73	...	42	...	2	40	...
	Total Group 49	...	*4,272*	*82*	*213*	*3,957*	...	*2,946*	*6*	*19*	*2,921*	...	*332*	*1*	*40*	*291*	...	*183*	...	*8*	*175*	...
50 Non-Asiatic Races	European	Christian	771	63	579	129	...	475	77	265	133	...	143	35	98	20	...	156	37	111	5	...
	Australasian	...	...	...	...	...	...	...	...	...	...	...	...	...	...	...	...	...	...	...	...	...
	Total Group 50	...	*771*	*63*	*579*	*129*	...	*475*	*77*	*265*	*133*	...	*143*	*25*	*98*	*20*	...	*156*	*37*	*111*	*5*	...
51 Eurasian / Christian	Eurasian	...	706	84	434	188	...	576	73	234	269	...	199	52	125	22	...	202	31	123	48	...
	Native Christian	...	9,712	445	2,004	7,263	...	7,950	158	527	7,265	...	2,737	212	551	2,105	...	2,587	31	179	2,387	...
Total Class F		...	130,476	5,904	19,830	104,742	...	118,885	1,155	3,145	114,585	...	26,[illegible]	[illegible]	[illegible]	20,273	...	25,122	310	990	23,822	...
Caste not stated	Hindu	...	1,875	8	100	1,767	...	1,599	...	11	1,588	...	208	...	20	188	...	21	...	10	20	...
	Jain	...	...	...	...	...	...	...	...	...	...	...	...	...	...	...	...	...	...	...	...	...
Provincial Total			2,433,262	65,736	185,735	2,181,756	[illegible]	2,410,231	4,429	7,683	2,398,127	26	349,297	13,002	34,324	301,971	...	353,620	1,424	2,014	350,178	...

F.—Races and Nationalities.—(Continued.)

Group	Caste, &c., and Subdivision	Religion	Kolár Males Total	Kolár Males Pupils	Kolár Males Literate	Kolár Males Illiterate	Kolár Males Not stated	Kolár Females Total	Kolár Females Pupils	Kolár Females Literate	Kolár Females Illiterate	Kolár Females Not stated	Tumkur Males Total	Tumkur Males Pupils	Tumkur Males Literate	Tumkur Males Illiterate	Tumkur Males Not stated	Tumkur Females Total	Tumkur Females Pupils	Tumkur Females Literate	Tumkur Females Illiterate	Tumkur Females Not stated
49 Mixed Asiatic Races	Jáva	Musalmán	...	...	...	...	...	...	...	...	...	...	...	...	...	...	...	...	...	...	...	...
	Labbe	"	181	11	10	160	...	18	...	...	18	...	74	2	8	64	...	18	...	...	18	...
	Máplé	"	...	...	...	...	...	...	...	...	...	...	...	...	...	...	...	...	...	...	...	...
	Memon	"	...	...	...	...	...	...	...	...	...	...	...	...	...	...	...	...	...	...	...	...
	Pindári	"	...	...	...	...	...	...	...	...	...	...	400	3	7	390	...	408	...	1	407	...
	Pinjári	"	240	8	10	222	...	207	...	1	206	...	331	3	6	322	...	286	...	...	286	...
	Total Group 49		*421*	*19*	*20*	*382*	...	*225*	...	*1*	*224*	...	*805*	*8*	*21*	*776*	...	*712*	...	*1*	*711*	...
50 Non-Asiatic Races	European	Christian	264	13	225	26	...	38	1	32	5	...	16	6	10	...	...	11	3	7	1	...
	Australasian	"	...	...	...	...	...	...	...	...	...	...	...	...	...	...	...	...	...	...	...	...
	Total Group 50		*264*	*13*	*225*	*26*	...	*38*	*1*	*32*	*5*	...	*16*	*6*	*10*	...	...	*11*	*3*	*7*	*1*	
51 Eurasians	Eurasian	"	161	13	94	51	...	115	15	61	39	...	8	...	8	...		9	1	7	1	...
52 Christian converts	Native Christian	"	1,287	60	392	835	...	1,131	23	91	1,017	...	377	103	111	163	...	322	13	76	233	...
Total Class F			19,025	803	3,233	11,989	...	16,377	142	408	15,827	...	13,238	760	[illegible]	10,728	...	12,746	123	289	12,334	...
Caste not stated	Hindu		178	...	4	274	...	153	...	...	153	...	97	...	5	92	...	117	...	...	117	...
	Jain		...	...	...	...	...	...	...	...	...	...	...	...	...	...	...	...	...	...	...	...
Provincial Total			297,655	7,222	23,241	267,0[illegible]	[illegible]	285,375	457	861	284,057	[illegible]	291,133	7,926	24,555	258,639	13	289,653	692	781	288,141	26

SUPPLEMENTARY TABLE D.—(Continued.)

Class.	Group.	Caste, &c. and subdivision.	Religion.	Mysore. Males. Total.	Pupils.	Literate.	Illiterate.	Not stated.	Mysore. Females. Total.	Pupils.	Literate.	Illiterate.	Not stated.	Hassan. Males. Total.	Pupils.	Literate.	Illiterate.	Not stated.	Hassan. Females. Total.	Pupils.	Literate.	Illiterate.	Not stated.
F.—Races and Nationalities.—(Continued.)	(49) Mixed Asiatic Races.	[illegible]	Musalman	...	...	...	...	...	...	...	...	...	...	...	...	...	...	...	...	...	...	...	...
		[illegible]	"	1,147	23	35	1,089	...	826	...	6	820	...	58	2	8	48	...	9	...	...	9	...
		Moghal	"	18	...	9	9	...		...	...	...		71	...	11	60	...	...	...	...	...	...
		Memon	"	...	...	...	...								...		...		...	...	...	...	...
		Pathan	"	556	8	26	522	...	471			471		...	...	...	...		...	...	...	...	...
		Punjabi	"	...	...	...	...		...	..		...		20	...	2	18		6	...	...	6	...
		Total Group 49	...	*1,721*	*31*	*70*	*1,620*	...	*1,297*	..	*6*	*1,291*		*149*	*2*	*21*	*126*		*15*	..	...	*15*	
	(50) Non-Asiatic Races.	European	Christian	72	13	41	18	...	158	25	39	94		97	3	85	9		35	...	28	7	...
		Australasian	...	...	...	...	...				...			...	...	...	...		...				...
		Total Group 50	...	*72*	*13*	*41*	*18*		*158*	*25*	*39*	*91*		*97*	*3*	*85*	*9*		*35*		*28*	*7*	...
	(51) Eurasians.	Eurasians	..	118	15	60	43		99	20	30	49		49	1	33	15	...	48	...	28	20	...
	(52) Christian Converts.	Native Christian	...	1,281	47	349	885		1,228	5	79	1,149		1,574	41	227	1,296	..	1,703	76	59	1,368	
Total Class F ...				**26,189**	**1,256**	**4,723**	**20,210**		**25,280**	**242**	**805**	**24,233**		**8,920**	**287**	**1,478**	**7,155**		**8,046**	**152**	**228**	**7,666**	
Caste not stated...			Hindu	581	8	17	556		559		...	559		268	..	30	238		183	...	1	182	
			Jain	...	...	...	...					...			...	...	..		..	..	...	...	
Provincial Total ...				**580,737**	**12,519**	**36,924**	**531,294**		**601,077**	**1,129**	**1,924**	**598,024**		**255,044**	**4,235**	**16,452**	**234,357**		**259,908**	**277**	**417**	**259,214**	...

SUPPLEMENTARY TABLE D.—(Continued.)

Caste and Religion.				Territorial Distribution.—(Continued.)																			
				Shimoga.										Kadúr.									
				Males.					Females.					Males.					Females.				
Class.	Group.	Caste, &c. and Sub-division.	Religion.	Total.	Pupils.	Literate.	Illiterate.	Not stated.	Total.	Pupils.	Literate.	Illiterate.	Not stated.	Total.	Pupils.	Literate.	Illiterate.	Not stated.	Total.	Pupils.	Literate.	Illiterate.	Not stated.
F.—Races and Nationalities.—(Continued.)	(49) Mixed Asiatic Races.	Jám	Musalmán	...	...	...	...	...	...	...	...	...	...	...	...	...	...	...	...	...	...	...	...
		Labbe	"	89	2	12	75	...	29	1	1	28	...	144	11	15	118	...	17	...	1	16	...
		Máppla	"	1	...	1	...	...	19	...	...	19	...	40	2	5	33	...	1	...	...	1	...
		Meman	"	...	...	...	...	...	...	[illegible]	...	...	...	...	...	...	...	...	...	...	...	...	...
		Pindári	"	26	...	...	26	...	7	...	...	7	...	...	...	...	...	...	...	...	...	...	...
		Pinjári	"	7	...	...	7	...	3	...	...	3	...	1	...	...	1	...	...	...	...	...	...
		Total Group 49.	...	*123*	*2*	*13*	*108*	...	*[illegible]*	*1*	*1*	*57*	...	*185*	*13*	*20*	*152*	...	*18*	...	*1*	*17*	...
	(50) Non-Asiatic Races.	European	Christian	17	2	13	2	...	15	2	11	2	...	147	...	94	53	...	60	9	32	19	...
		Australasian	"	...	...	...	...	...	...	...	...	[illegible]	...	...	...	...	...	...	...	...	...	...	...
		Total Group 50.	...	*17*	*2*	*13*	*2*	...	*15*	*2*	*11*	*2*	...	*147*	...	*94*	*53*	...	*60*	*9*	*32*	*19*	...
	(51) Eurasians.	Eurasian	"	14	2	11	1	...	2	...	2	...	...	134	[illegible]	84	50	...	95	4	38	53	...
	(52) Christian Converts.	Native Christian	"	1,003	24	173	806	...	620	26	25	569	...	1,275	19	150	1,106	...	498	11	28	479	...
	Total Class F.		...	26,801	418	1,550	24,836	...	15,01[illegible]	52	110	14,852	...	10,337	289	1,828	8,220	...	7,437	53	211	7,173	...
	Caste not stated.	Hindu		212	...	2	209	...	121	...	...	121	...	264	...	...	264	...	195	...	...	195	...
		Jain		...	...	...	...	...	...	...	...	...	...	...	...	...	...	...	...	...	...	...	...
	Provincial Total		...	275,88[illegible]	4,457	20,785	250,[illegible]	...	252,027	189	380	251,528	...	173,022	3,262	14,360	156,400	...	156,141	121	1,051	154,969	...

SUPPLEMENTARY TABLE D.—(Continued.)

Class.	Group.	Caste, &c. and Sub-division.	Religion.	Chitaldrug. Males. Total.	Pupils.	Literate.	Illiterate.	Not stated.	Chitaldrug. Females. Total.	Pupils.	Literate.	Illiterate.	Not stated.	The Civil and Military Station, Bangalore. Males. Total.	Pupils.	Literate.	Illiterate.	Not stated.	Females. Total.	Pupils.	Literate.	Illiterate.	Not stated.
F.—Races and Nationalities.—(Continued.)	49 Mixed Asiatic Races.	Jám ...	Musalmán ...	...	...	...	...	...	...	...	...	...	...	5	...	3	2	...	...	...	...	...	...
		Labbé ...	" ...	8	...	5	3	...	...	...	...	...	...	500	60	236	203	1	397	14	33	350	...
		Máplé ...	" ...	...	...	...	...	...	...	...	...	...	...	21	...	7	14	...	7	...	...	7	...
		Memán ...	" ...	...	...	...	...	...	...	...	...	...	...	128	31	62	35	...	116	14	16	86	...
		Pindári ...	" ...	...	...	...	...	...	...	...	...	...	...	...	...	...	...	...	...	...	...	...	...
		Pinjári ...	" ...	518	6	3	509	...	437	5	1	431	...	...	...	...	...	...	...	...	...	...	...
		Total Group 49 ...	...	*526*	*6*	*8*	*512*	...	*437*	*5*	*1*	*431*	...	*654*	*91*	*308*	*254*	*1*	*520*	*28*	*49*	*443*	...
	50 Non-Asiatic Races.	European ...	Christian ...	15	1	13	1	...	2	...	2	...	...	3,261	336	2,647	267	11	1,723	353	1,153	204	13
		Australasian ...	" ...	...	...	...	...	...	...	...	...	...	...	1	...	1	...	...	...	...	...	...	...
		Total Group 50 ...	...	*15*	*1*	*13*	*1*	...	*2*	...	*2*	...	...	*3,262*	*336*	*2,648*	*267*	*11*	*1,723*	*353*	*1,153*	*204*	*13*
	51 Eurasians...	Eurasian ...	" ...	23	1	19	3	...	15	2	5	8	...	1,127	367	556	200	4	1,522	350	831	339	2
	52 Christian Converts...	Native Christian	" ...	128	10	45	73	...	101	3	20	78	...	4,715	650	1,363	2,686	16	5,637	208	439	4,798	32
	Total Class F. ...		...	9,640	272	1,011	8,357	...	8,833	51	104	5,678	...	21,333	2,650	7,286	10,630	67	20,472	1,411	3,096	15,873	92
	Caste not stated.	Hindu ...		67	...	21	46	...	56	...	...	56	...	138	19	48	71	...	10	1	2	97	...
		Jain ...		...	...	...	...	...	...	...	...	...	...	10	3	4	3	...	2	...	...	2	...
	Provincial Total.....			209,590	3,223	14,995	191,372	...	204,394	140	248	204,006	...	50,189	5,297	14,719	30,008	165	49,892	1,974	3,793	43,900	225

SUPPLEMENTARY TABLE D.—(Concluded.)

Total including the Civil and Military Station, Bangalore.

Class.	Group.	Caste, &c. and Sub-division.	Religion.	Males. Total.	Males. Pupils.	Males. Literate.	Males. Illiterate.	Males. Not stated.	Females. Total.	Females. Pupils.	Females. Literate.	Females. Illiterate.	Females. Not stated.
F.—Races and Nationalities.—(Concluded.)	49 Mixed Asiatic Races.	Jám	Musalmán	5	...	3	2	...	...	...	...	...	...
		Labbe	"	2,359	112	350	1,896	1	1,358	15	45	1,298	...
		Maplé	"	151	2	33	116	...	27	...	...	27	...
		Meman	"	128	31	62	35	...	116	14	16	86	...
		Pindári	"	1,064	11	43	110	...	984	...	3	981	...
		Pinjári	"	1,199	17	30	1,152	...	981	5	4	972	...
		Total Group 49.	...	*4,906*	*173*	*521*	*4,211*	*1*	*3,466*	*34*	*68*	*3,364*	...
	50 Non-Asiatic Races.	European	Christian	4,022	399	3,226	396	11	2,198	430	1,418	337	13
		Australasian	"	1	...	1	...	...	...	...	...	...	...
		Total Group 50.	...	*4,033*	*399*	*3,227*	*396*	*11*	*2,198*	*430*	*1,418*	*337*	*13*
	51 Eurasians...	Eurasian	"	1,833	451	990	388	4	2,098	423	1,125	548	2
	52 Christian Converts..	Native Christian	"	14,427	1,095	3,367	9,949	16	13,527	430	996	12,063	38
	Total Class F.		...	**151,811**	**8,554**	**27,819**	**115,371**	**67**	**139,357**	**2,566**	**6,241**	**130,458**	**92**
	Caste not stated.		Hindu	2,013	27	148	1,838	..	1,699	1	13	1,685	...
			Jain	10	3	4	3	...	2	...	...	2	...
	Provincial Total......			**2,483,451**	**61,053**	**200,455**	**2,221,764**	**179**	**2,460,153**	**6,403**	**11,482**	**2,442,017**	**251**

SUPPLEMENTARY TABLE E.

CASTE, &c.,

BY CIVIL CONDITION AND AGE.

SUPPLEMENTARY

Caste, &c., by

Provin

Class.	Group.	Caste, &c. and sub-division.	Religion.	All ages. Total.	All ages. Single.	All ages. Married.	All ages. Widowed.	All ages. Civil condition not stated.
A.—Agricultural.	1. Military and Dominant.	Kshatriya. — Kshatriya ...	Hindu	6,203	3,301	2,502	400	...
		Kshatriya. — do. ...	Sikh	13	6	6	1	...
		Kshatriya. — Kumárapatta ...	Hindu	...	...	...	...	...
		Kshatriya. — Rájapindé ...	,,	794	439	316	39	...
		Kshatriya. — Kodagu (Coorgs) ...	,,	6	3	2	1	...
		Kshatriya. — Rájpút ...	,,	3,782	2,027	1,507	248	...
		Maráta.	,,	22,388	11,748	9,175	1,465	...
		Ráchévár & Ranngára ...	,,	1,745	927	710	108	...
		Total Group 1.......	... ...	*31,931*	*18,[illegible]51*	*11,218*	*2,262*	...
	2. Other Agricultural (a) Cultivators.	Lingáyet (Gaudamané, &c.) ...	,,	63,678	33,796	26,042	3,840	...
		Náyar	,,	3	1	2	...	...
		Pillé	,,	311	157	137	17	...
		Tigala	,,	26,988	14,266	11,476	1,246	...
		Vakkaliga. — Vakkaliga ...	,,	660,730	363,109	275,884	21,675	62
		Vakkaliga. — Sáda	Jain	516	294	134	38	...
		Vakkaliga. — Tulu	Bramho	...	...	...	...	...
		Total Group 2(a).......	... ...	*752,226*	*411,623*	*313,725*	*26,816*	*62*
	4. Forest and Hill Tribes.	I'raliga	Hindu	581	282	263	36	...
		Koracha	,,	5,462	2,806	2,297	359	...
		Korama	,,	6,771	3,631	2,793	347	...
		Kuruba	,,	1,136	532	524	80	...
		Lambáni	,,	20,585	11,937	7,792	856	...
		Uriya	,,	...	...	...	...	...
		Total Group 4.......	... ...	*34,535*	*19,188*	*13,669*	*1,678*	...
		Total Class A......	... ...	**821,692**	**449,262**	**341,612**	**30,756**	**62**
B.—Professional.	5. Priests.	Bráhman. — A'ruvélu ...	Hindu	2,220	1,116	931	173	...
		Bráhman. — A'ruvélu Niyógi ...	,,	10	6	4	...	...
		Bráhman. — Aravattu Vakkalu...	,,	2,447	1,215	1,056	176	...
		Bráhman. — Babbúr Kammé ...	,,	3,322	1,709	1,365	248	...
		Bráhman. — Badaga Nádu ...	,,	11,679	5,839	4,901	939	...
		Bráhman. — Brihacheharana ...	,,	62	304	265	52	...
		Bráhman. — Chitapávan ...	,,	1,537	774	592	171	...
		Bráhman. — Désasth	,,	8,448	4,056	3,623	769	...
		Bráhman. — Drávida ...	,,	4,088	1,979	1,694	415	...
		Bráhman. — Guzaráti ...	,,	2	...	2	...	...
		Bráhman. — Gauda	,,	1,066	563	402	101	...
		Bráhman. — Halé Kannadiga ...	,,	3,780	1,943	1,634	203	...
		Bráhman. — Havika	,,	1,602	833	613	156	...

Civil condition and Age.

cial.

Males.

0 to 9.					10 to 14.				
Total.	Single.	Married.	Widowed.	Civil condition not stated.	Total.	Single.	Married.	Widowed.	Civil condition not stated.
1,649	1,649	...	...	...	589	562	27	...	...
3	3	...	...	...	2	2	...	...	...
...	...	...	...	...	...	...	...	...	...
227	227	...	...	...	67	67	...	...	...
2	2	...	...	...	1	1	...	...	...
1,038	1,038	...	...	...	356	355	1	...	...
6,083	6,081	2	...	...	2,536	2,424	110	2	...
488	488	...	...	...	169	169	...	...	...
9,490	*9,488*	*2*	...	...	*3,720*	*3,580*	*138*	*2*	...
16,755	16,722	33	...	...	7,093	6,890	203	...	...
...	...	...	...	...	1	1	...	...	...
72	...	...	...	...	27	27	...	...	...
8,032	8,032	...	...	...	2,850	2,833	17	...	...
175,252	175,071	175	6	...	52,056	50,500	1,531	22	3
147	...	...	...	...	46	46	...	...	...
...	...	...	...	...	...	...	...	...	...
200,253	*200,011*	*208*	*6*	...	*62,073*	*60,297*	*1,751*	*22*	*3*
190	190	...	...	...	46	46	...	...	...
1,648	1,648	...	...	...	477	477	...	...	...
2,125	2,125	...	...	...	639	631	8	...	...
245	245	...	...	...	80	80	...	...	...
6,507	6,507	...	...	...	2,127	2,094	33	...	...
...	...	...	...	...	...	...	...	...	...
10,715	*10,715*	...	...	...	*3,369*	*3,328*	*41*	...	...
220,247	**220,247**	**210**	**6**	...	**69,162**	**67,205**	**1,930**	**24**	**3**
592	586	6	...	...	260	210	50	...	...
4	4	...	...	...	1	1	...	...	...
700	699	1	...	...	201	183	18	...	...
1,100	1,093	7	...	...	303	253	49	1	...
3,269	3,254	14	1	...	1,034	915	113	6	...
153	153	...	...	...	62	57	5	...	...
437	437	...	...	...	213	213	...	...	...
2,194	2,169	23	2	...	821	698	121	2	...
1,056	1,050	6	...	...	437	366	70	1	...
...	...	...	...	...	...	...	...	...	...
305	305	...	...	...	78	77	1	...	...
1,096	1,077	18	1	...	429	356	70	3	...
335	331	4	...	...	170	163	7	...	...

Provin

Class.	Group.	Caste, &c. and sub-division.	Religion.	15 to 3[illegible] Total.	Single.	Married.	Widowed.	Civil condition not stated.
A.—Agricultural—(Continued).	1. Military and Dominant.	Kshatriya. — Kshatriya	Hindu	2,721	1,026	1,5[illegible]	100	...
		Kshatriya. — Do.	Sikh	5	1	4	...	...
		Kshatriya. — Kumárapatta	Hindu	...	...	...	...	...
		Kshatriya. — Rájapindé	,,	354	142	205	9	...
		Kshatriya. — Kodaga (Coorgs)	,,	2	...	2	...	...
		Kshatriya. — Rájput	,,	1,563	594	912	57	...
		Maráṭa	,,	9,020	3,084	5,547	389	...
		Ráchévár & Rangárí	,,	715	253	4[illegible]	26	...
		Total Group 1.	...	14,[illegible]	5,11[illegible]	8,[illegible]	582	...
	2. Other Agricultural. (a) Cultivators.	Lingáyet (Gaudamané, &c.)	,,	26,163	9,776	15,424	963	...
		Náyar	,,	1	...	1	...	...
		Pillé	,,	15[illegible]	56	95	5	...
		Tigala	,,	10,164	3,243	6,698	223	...
		Vakkaliga. — Vakkaliga	,,	281,818	132,918	145,306	3,583	11
		Vakkaliga. — Sáda	Jain	201	97	97	7	...
		Vakkaliga. — Tulu	Brahmo	...	...	...	...	...
		Total Group 2(a).	...	318,[illegible]	[illegible]	[illegible]	[illegible]	11
	4. Forest and Hill Tribes.	Iruliga	Hindu	209	12	189	8	...
		Koracha	,,	2,151	637	1,420	94	...
		Korama	,,	2,704	830	1,779	95	...
		Kuruba	,,	542	190	333	19	...
		Lambáṇi	,,	8,074	3,204	4,638	232	...
		Uriya	,,	...	...	...	...	...
		Total Group 4.	...	13,680	4,[illegible]	8,[illegible]	418	...
		Total Class A		**346,569**	**156,103**	**184,645**	**5,810**	**11**
B.—Professional—(Continued).	5. Priests.	Bráhman. — A'ruvélu	Hindu	863	297	533	33	...
		Bráhman. — A'ruvélu Niyógi	,,	2	...	2	...	...
		Bráhman. — Aravattu Vakkalu	,,	1,021	312	670	39	...
		Bráhman. — Babbúr Kammé	,,	1,267	341	862	64	...
		Bráhman. — Badaga Nádu	,,	4,78[illegible]	1,550	3,001	236	...
		Bráhman. — Brihachcharaṇa	,,	268	91	168	9	...
		Bráhman. — Chitapávan	,,	591	119	425	47	...
		Bráhman. — Dés'asth	,,	3,570	1,117	2,238	215	...
		Bráhman. — Drávida	,,	1,662	528	1,022	112	...
		Bráhman. — Guzaráti	,,	2	...	2	...	...
		Bráhman. — Gauda	,,	448	168	253	27	...
		Bráhman. — Halé Kannadiga	,,	1,511	499	971	41	...
		Bráhman. — Havika	,,	692	311	350	31	...

TABLE E.—(Continued.)

cial.

Males.

10 and over.					Age not stated.				
Total.	Single.	Married.	Widowed.	Civil condition not stated.	Total.	Single.	Married.	Widowed.	Civil condition not stated.
1,244	54	890	300	...	...	...	...	...	...
3	...	2	1	...	...	...	...	...	...
...	...	...	...	...	...	...	...	...	...
144	3	111	30	...	...	...	...	...	...
	...	...	1		...	...	...	...	...
825	40	594	191	...	...	...	...	...	...
4,749	159	3,516	1,074	...	...	...	...	...	...
369	17	270	82	...	...	...	...	...	...
7,335	*273*	*5,383*	*1,679*	...	...	...	...	...	...
13,667	408	10,382	2,877	...	...	...	...	...	...
1	...	1	...	...	...	...	...	...	...
56	2	42	12	...	...	...	...	...	...
5,942	158	4,761	1,023	...	...	...	...	...	...
151,249	4,447	128,776	18,020	6	355	173	96	44	42
122	4	87	31	...	...	...	...	...	...
...	...	...	...	...	...	...	...	...	...
171,037	*5,019*	*144,049*	*21,963*	*6*	*355*	*173*	*96*	*44*	*42*
136	4	104	28	...	...	...	...	...	...
1,186	44	877	265	...	...	...	...	...	...
1,303	15	1,006	282	...	...	...	...	...	...
269	17	191	61	...	...	...	...	...	...
3,877	132	3,121	624	...	...	...	...	...	...
...	...	...	...	...	...	...	...	...	...
6,771	*212*	*5,299*	*1,260*	...	...	...	...	...	...
185,143	**5,534**	**154,731**	**24,872**	**6**	**355**	**173**	**96**	**44**	**42**
505	23	342	140	...	...	...	...	...	...
3	1	2	...	...	...	...	...	...	...
525	21	367	137	...	...	...	...	...	...
652	22	447	183	...	...	...	...	...	...
2,589	120	1,773	696	...	...	...	...	...	...
138	3	92	43	...	...	...	...	...	...
296	5	167	124	...	...	...	...	...	...
1,863	72	1,241	550	...	...	...	...	...	...
933	35	596	302	...	...	...	...	...	...
...	...	...	...	...	...	...	...	...	...
235	13	148	74	...	...	...	...	...	...
744	11	575	158	...	...	...	...	...	...
405	28	252	125	...	...	...	...	...	...

Class.	Group.	Caste, &c. and sub-division.	Religion.	All Ages. Total.	Single.	Married.	Widowed.	Civil condition not stated.
A.—Agricultural—(Continued.)	1. Military and Dominant.	Kshatriya { Kshatriya	Hindu	5,916	2,070	2,665	1,181	...
		Do	Sikh	16	3	7	6	...
		Kumárapatta	Hindu	...	...	...	...	...
		Rájapindi	,,	833	301	368	161	...
		Kodaga (Coorge)	,,	3	1	2	...	...
		Rájpút	,,	3,610	1,290	1,582	738	...
		Maráta	,,	20,914	7,438	9,160	1,316	...
		Ráchévár & Ranagára	,,	1,871	730	793	318	...
		Total Group 1	...	33,183	11,856	11,577	6,750	...
	2. Other Agricultural (a) Cultivators.	Lingáyet (Gaudamané, &c.)	,,	64,470	23,625	27,712	13.133	...
		Náyar	,,	...	...	...	...	...
		Pillé	,,	241	87	111	43	...
		Tigala	,,	26,409	10,206	11,676	1,527	...
		Vakkaliga { Vakkaliga	,,	671,423	226,601	385,121	159,326	75
		Sáda	Jain	493	157	214	122	...
		Tulu	Bramho	...	...	...	...	...
		Total Group 2(a)	...	763,039	260,676	325,137	177,151	75
	4. Forest and Hill Tribes.	Uraliga	Hindu	551	225	254	72	...
		Koracha	,,	5,082	1,901	2,352	829	...
		Korama	,,	6,761	2,534	2,974	1,253	...
		Kuruba	,,	1,133	331	484	318	...
		Lambáni	,,	18,552	7,753	8,315	2,484	...
		Uriya	,,	...	...	...	...	...
		Total Group 4	...	32,079	12,741	11,379	4,956	...
		Total Class A		**828,301**	**285,276**	**354,093**	**138,837**	**75**
B.—Professional—(Continued.)	5. Priests. a	Brámhan { A'ruvélu	Hindu	2,174	634	988	552	...
		A'ruvélu Niyógi	,,	9	2	6	1	...
		Aruvattu Vakkalu	,,	2,547	744	1,182	621	...
		Babbúr Kammé	,,	3,403	1,068	1,529	806	...
		Badaga Nádu	,,	11,225	3,326	5,141	2,758	...
		Brihachcharanam	,,	600	176	282	142	...
		Chitapávan	,,	808	213	383	212	...
		Dés'asth	,,	8,622	2,736	3,789	2,166	...
		Drávida	,,	4,747	1,030	1,778	939	...
		Guzaráti	,,	...	...	...	...	...
		Gauda	,,	957	312	410	235	...
		Halé Kannadiga	,,	3,766	1,222	1,723	821	...
		Havika	,,	1,644	385	774	485	...

TABLE E.—*Continued.*

cial.

Females.

0 to 9.					10 to 14.				
Total.	Single.	Married.	Widowed.	Civil condition not stated.	Total.	Single.	Married.	Widowed.	Civil condition not stated.
1,555	1,522	33	...	...	653	427	222	4	...
3	3	...	...	...	...	...	...	...	...
...	...	...	...	...	...	...	...	...	...
201	199	2	...	...	104	82	22	...	...
1	1	...	...	...	...	...	...	...	...
1,002	996	6	...	...	298	224	73	1	...
5,895	5,767	128	...	...	1,898	1,281	615	2	...
561	559	2	...	...	175	127	48	...	...
9,218	*9,047*	*171*	...	...	*3,128*	*2,111*	*980*	*7*	...
17,311	17,007	302	2	...	6,480	4,793	1,666	21	...
...	...	...	...	...	...	...	...	...	...
61	61	...	...	...	25	19	6	...	...
8,215	8,208	37	...	...	2,012	1,510	501	1	...
193,306	184,272	8,930	103	1	46,672	26,641	19,379	650	2
148	144	4	...	...	30	10	19	1	...
...	...	...	...	...	...	...	...	...	...
219,071	*209,692*	*9,273*	*105*	*1*	*55,219*	*32,973*	*21,571*	*673*	*2*
183	182	1	...	...	32	29	3	...	...
1,392	1,383	9	...	...	400	365	35	...	...
2,009	1,986	23	...	...	542	403	139	...	...
238	236	2	...	...	77	57	20	...	...
5,715	5,701	14	...	...	1,590	1,358	232	...	...
...	...	...	...	...	...	...	...	...	...
9,537	*9,488*	*49*	...	...	*2,641*	*2,222*	*419*	...	...
237,826	**228,227**	**9,493**	**105**	**1**	**60,988**	**37,336**	**22,970**	**680**	**2**
583	550	33	...	...	210	84	126	4	...
1	1	...	...	...	3	1	2	...	...
682	654	28	...	...	242	90	151	1	...
977	932	40	5	...	357	136	195	26	...
3,006	2,870	132	4	...	1,192	456	686	50	...
165	158	7	...	...	63	18	44	1	...
171	167	4	...	...	116	46	69	1	...
2,471	2,332	133	6	...	963	404	494	65	...
925	857	67	1	...	453	173	276	4	...
...	...	...	...	...	...	...	...	...	...
266	256	10	...	...	95	56	37	2	...
1,072	1,021	45	6	...	340	201	132	23	...
275	259	16	...	...	246	126	138	2	...

Class.	Group.	Caste and Religion: Caste, &c. and sub-division.	Religion.	15 to 39: Total.	Single.	Married.	Widowed.	Civil condition not stated.
A.—Agricultural—(Continued.)	1. Military and Dominant.	Kshatriya. — Kshatriya ...	Hindu	2,322	139	1,828	355	...
		Kshatriya. — Do. ...	Sikh	6	...	6	...	...
		Kshatriya. — Kumárapatta ...	Hindu	...	...	...	...	...
		Kshatriya. — Rájapindé ...	,,	334	23	263	48	...
		Kshatriya. — Kodaga (Coorgs) ...	,,	2	...	2	...	...
		Kshatriya. — Rájpút ...	,,	1,488	69	1,191	228	...
		Maráta ...	,,	8,241	379	6,536	1,326	...
		Ráchévár & Rayagára ...	,,	680	44	549	87	...
		Total Group 1.	...	*13,073*	*651*	*10,375*	*2,041*	...
	2. Other Agricultural. (a) Cultivators.	Lingáyet (Gaudamané, &c.) ...	,,	25,497	1,713	20,123	3,661	...
		Náyar ...	,,	...	...	...	...	...
		Piļļé ...	,,	99	7	82	10	...
		Tigaļa ...	,,	10,712	432	9,046	1,214	...
		Vakkaliga. — Vakkaliga ...	,,	284,923	12,971	224,058	47,890	4
		Vakkaliga. — Sáda ...	Jain	212	3	166	43	...
		Vakkaliga. — Tuļu ...	Bramho	...	...	...	...	...
		Total Group 2(a).	...	*321,413*	*15,146*	*253,475*	*52,818*	*4*
	4. Forest and Hill Tribes.	Uraliga ...	Hindu	241	13	207	21	...
		Koracha ...	,,	2,203	145	1,845	213	...
		Koráma ...	,,	2,620	142	2,159	319	...
		Kuruba ...	,,	498	36	357	105	...
		Lambáņi ...	,,	7,897	652	6,668	577	...
		Uriya ...	,,	...	...	...	...	...
		Total Group 4.	...	*13,459*	*988*	*11,236*	*1,235*	...
		Total Class A		**347,975**	**16,788**	**275,086**	**56,097**	**4**
B.—Professional—(Continued).	5. Priests.	Bráhmaņ. — A'ruvélu ...	Hindu	791	...	638	153	...
		Bráhmaņ. — A'ruvélu Niyógi ...	,,	3	...	3	...	...
		Bráhmaņ. — Aravattu Vakkalu ...	,,	1,000	...	816	184	...
		Bráhmaņ. — Babbúr Kammé ...	,,	1,294	...	1,057	237	...
		Bráhmaņ. — Baḍaga Náḍu ...	,,	4,420	...	3,508	912	...
		Bráhmaņ. — Brihachcharaņa ...	,,	220	...	184	36	...
		Bráhmaņ. — Chitupávan ...	,,	299	...	232	67	...
		Bráhmaņ. — Dés'asth ...	,,	3,227	...	2,529	698	...
		Bráhmaņ. — Dráviḍa ...	,,	1,468	...	1,164	304	...
		Bráhmaņ. — Guzaráti ...	,,	...	...	...	...	...
		Bráhmaņ. — Gauḍa ...	,,	364	...	292	72	...
		Bráhmaņ. — Haļé Kannaḍiga ...	,,	1,400	...	1,165	235	...
		Bráhmaņ. — Havíka ...	,,	697	...	522	175	...

TABLE E.—(Continued.)

cial.

Females.

40 and over.					Age not stated.				
Total.	Single.	Married.	Widowed.	Civil condition not stated.	Total.	Single.	Married.	Widowed.	Civil condition not stated.
1,406	2	582	822	...	...	...	...	...	...
7	...	1	6	...	...	...	...	...	...
...	...	...	...	...	...	...	...	...	...
194	...	81	113	...	...	...	...	...	...
...	...	...	...	...	...	...	...	...	...
822	1	312	509	...	...	...	...	...	...
4,880	11	1,881	2,988	...	...	...	...	...	...
455	...	194	261	...	...	...	...	...	...
7,761	*11*	*3,051*	*4,699*	...	...	...	...	...	...
15,182	112	5,621	9,449	...	...	...	...	...	...
...	...	...	...	...	...	...	...	...	...
59	...	26	33	...	...	...	...	...	...
5,440	36	2,092	3,312	...	...	...	...	...	...
146,177	2,570	32,977	110,617	13	345	147	77	66	55
103	...	25	78	...	...	...	...	...	...
...	...	...	...	...	...	...	...	...	...
166,961	*2,718*	*40,741*	*123,489*	*13*	*345*	*147*	*77*	*66*	*55*
95	1	43	51	...	...	...	...	...	...
1,087	8	463	616	...	...	...	...	...	...
1,590	3	653	934	...	...	...	...	...	...
320	2	105	213	...	...	...	...	...	...
3,350	32	1,411	1,907	...	...	...	...	...	...
...	...	...	...	...	...	...	...	...	...
6,442	*46*	*2,675*	*3,721*	...	...	...	...	...	...
181,167	**2,778**	**46,467**	**131,909**	**13**	**345**	**147**	**77**	**66**	**55**
564	...	169	395	...	...	...	...	...	...
2	...	1	1	...	...	...	...	...	...
623	...	187	436	...	...	...	...	...	...
775	...	237	538	...	...	...	...	...	...
2,607	...	815	1,792	...	...	...	...	...	...
152	...	47	105	...	...	...	...	...	...
222	...	78	144	...	...	...	...	...	...
1,961	...	624	1,337	...	...	...	...	...	...
901	...	271	630	...	...	...	...	...	...
...	...	...	...	...	...	...	...	...	...
232	...	71	161	...	...	...	...	...	...
948	...	391	557	...	...	...	...	...	...
406	...	98	308	...	...	...	...	...	...

Class.	Group.	Caste and Religion.			All Ages.				
		Caste, &c. and sub-division.		Religion.	Total.	Single.	Married.	Widowed.	Civil condition not stated.
A. Agricultural.—(Continued.)	1. Military and Dominant.	Kshatriya.	Kshatriya ...	Hindu.	1,200	652	443	103	...
			do ...	Sikh.	1	...	1	...	...
			Kumárapatta	Hindu.	...	...	...	...	...
			Rájapindé	,,	12	6	4	2	...
			Kodagu (Coorgs)	,,	...	...	...	...	...
			Rájpút	,,	680	373	260	47	...
		Maráta ...		,,	4,857	2,534	1,975	348	...
		Ráchévár and Raungára		,,	391	205	149	37	...
		Total Group 1		...	*7,141*	*3,772*	*2,832*	*537*	...
	2. Other Agriculturists. (a) Cultivators.	Lingáyet (Gandaganné, &c.)		Hindu.	6,593	3,339	2,748	506	...
		Náyar ...		,,	...	...	...	...	...
		Pillé ...		,,	51	24	22	5	...
		Tigala ...		,,	13,081	6,831	5,624	626	...
		Vakkaliga.	Vakkaliga	,,	105,619	54,798	47,195	3,607	19
			Sáda ...	Jain.	456	254	167	35	...
			Tulu ...	Bramho.	...	..	...	...	...
		Total Group 2(a)		...	*125,800*	*65,246*	*55,756*	*4,779*	*19*
	4. Forest and Hill Tribes.	I'ruliga ...		Hindu.	534	261	245	28	...
		Koracha ...		,,	1,011	538	412	61	...
		Koruma ...		,,	1,373	670	631	72	...
		Kuruba ...		,,	104	61	36	7	...
		Lambáni ...		,,	1,777	937	751	89	...
		Uriya ...		,,	...	...	...	...	...
		Total Group 4		...	*4,799*	*2,467*	*2,075*	*257*	...
		Total Class A			**137,740**	**71,485**	**60,663**	**5,573**	**19**
B. Professional.—(Continued.)	5. Priests.	Bráhman.	A'ruvélu ...	Hindu.	585	316	257	32	...
			A'ruvélu Niyógi	,,	10	6	4	...	...
			Aravattu Vakkalu	,,	479	223	222	34	...
			Babbúr kammé	,,	145	78	55	12	...
			Badaganádu ...	,,	2,655	1,402	1,060	193	...
			Brihachcharana	,,	356	168	159	29	...
			Chitpávan	,,	1	1	...	...	...
			Dés'ast'h	,,	1,689	816	737	136	...
			Drávida	,,	292	148	113	31	...
			Guzaráti	,,	2	...	2	...	...
			Gauda ...	,,	82	49	29	4	...
			Halé kannadiga	,,	117	60	50	7	...
			Hávíka ..	,,	...	...	...	...	...

TABLE E.—(*Continued.*)

District.

Males.									
0 to 9					10 to 14				
Total.	Single.	Married.	Widowed.	Civil condition not stated.	Total.	Single.	Married.	Widowed.	Civil condition not stated.
315	315	...	...	...	131	121	10	...	...
	...	...	...	...	...	...		...	...
		...	...	...	...	...	...	...	...
3	3	...	...	...	2	2	...	...	...
...	...	...	...	...	...	...	...	...	...
183	183	...	...	...	70	70	...	...	...
1,266	1,265	1	...	...	679	645	34	...	...
110	110	...	...	...	39	39	...		...
1,877	*1,876*	*1*	...		*921*	*877*	*44*	...	
1,712	1,685	27	...	...	683	574	109	...	...
...	...	...	...	...	...	...	...	...	...
12	12	...	...	...	6	6	...	...	...
3,884	3,884	...	...	...	1,193	1,181	12	...	...
31,404	31,384	19	1	...	6,336	6,264	61	8	3
123	123	...	...	...	44	44	...	...	...
...	...	...	...	...	...	...	...	...	...
37,135	*37,088*	*46*	*1*	...	*8,262*	*8,069*	*182*	*8*	*3*
176	176	...	...	...	45	45	...	...	...
340	340	...	...	...	107	107	...	...	...
467	467	...	...	...	108	104	4	...	...
34	34	...	...	...	11	11	...	...	...
542	542	...	...	...	243	241	2	...	...
...	...	...	...	...		...		...	...
1,559	*1,559*	...	...	...	*514*	*508*	*6*	...	...
40,571	**40,523**	**47**	**1**	...	**9,697**	**9,454**	**232**	**8**	**3**
166	166	...	...	...	72	62	10	...	...
4	4	...	...	...	1	1	...	...	...
130	130	...	...	...	39	34	5	...	...
49	49	...	...	...	16	13	3	...	...
761	761	...	...	...	204	195	9	...	...
76	76	...	...	...	42	38	4	...	...
...	...	...	...	...	...	...	...	...	...
398	387	11	...	...	226	198	28	...	...
84	84	...	...	...	25	21	4	...	...
...	...	...	...	...	...	...	...	...	...
25	25	...	...	...	1	1	...	...	...
34	34	...	...	...	28	23	5	...	...
...	...	...	...	...	...		...	...	...

Bangalore

Class.	Group.	Caste, &c. and sub-division.	Religion.	15 to 39 Total.	Single.	Married.	Widowed.	Civil condition not stated.
A.—Agricultural.—(Continued.)	1. Military and Dominant.	Kshatriya. — Kshatriya ...	Hindu.	485	209	250	26	
		do ...	Sikh	1	...	1	...	...
		Kumárapatta ...	Hindu.				...	...
		Rájapindé	,,	4	1	3	...	...
		Kodagu (Coorgs)	,,	...	...	...	...	...
		Rájpút	,,	272	111	146	15	
		Maráta	,,	1,813	590	1,145	78	...
		Ráchévár and Rajagára.	,,	143	50	81	12	...
		Total Group 1...	... ...	*2,718*	*961*	*1,626*	*131*	...
	2. Other Agricultural. (a) Cultivators.	Lingáyet, (Gaudumané, &c.) ...	,,	2,611	1,023	1,510	78	78
		Náyar	,,	...	...	...	...	
		Pillé	,,	23	6	15	2	...
		Tigala	,,	4,928	1,683	3,156	89	...
		Vakkaliga. — Vakkaliga ...	,,	41,209	16,548	23,952	698	11
		Sáda ...	Jain	177	83	88	6	...
		Tuḷu ...	Brambo.		...	...	...	...
		Total Group 2(a)...	... ...	*48,948*	*19,343*	*28,721*	*873*	*11*
	4. Forest and Hill tribes.	Praliga	Hindu.	190	36	149	5	
		Koracha	,,	354	87	250	17	...
		Korama	,,	518	91	410	17	...
		Kuruba	,,	40	16	23	1	
		Lambáni	,,	611	146	438	27	
		Uriya	,,	...	...	...	...	...
		Total Group 4...	... ...	*1,713*	*376*	*1,270*	*67*	...
		Total Class A......		**53,379**	**20,680**	**31,617**	**1,071**	**11**
B.—Professional.—(Continued.)	5. Priests.	Bráhman. — A'ruvélu ...	Hindu	214	83	127	4	
		A'ruvélu Niyógi ...	,,	2	...	2	...	...
		Aravattu Vakkalu...	,,	194	56	132	6	...
		Babbur kammé ...	,,	54	16	34	4	—
		Badaganádu ...	,,	1,124	420	658	46	...
		Brihacharana ...	,,	157	52	101	4	...
		Chitpávan ...	,,	...	...	...	...	...
		Dés'ast'h ...	,,	704	221	451	32	...
		Drávida ...	,,	122	42	72	8	...
		Guzaráti ...	,,	2	...	2	...	...
		Gauḍa	,,	35	23	12	...	...
		Halé Karnadiga ...	,,	37	3	30	4	...
		Havíka	,,	...	...		...	...

TABLE E.—(*Continued.*)

District.

Males. 40 and over. Total.	Single.	Married.	Widowed.	Civil condition not stated.	Age not stated. Total.	Single.	Married.	Widowed.	Civil condition not stated.
269	9	183	77	...	...	...	...	...	...
...	...	...	...	...	...	...	...	...	...
...	...	...	...	...	...	...	...	...	...
3	...	1	2	...	...	...	...	...	...
...	...	...	...		...	...	...	...	...
155	9	111	35	...	...	...	...	...	...
1,029	34	725	270	...	...	...	...	...	...
99	6	68	25	...	...	...	...	...	...
1,625	*58*	*1,161*	*406*	...	...	...	...	...	...
1,587	57	1,102	428	...	...	...	...	...	...
		...	...	...	...	...	...	...	...
10	...	7	3	...	...	...	...	...	...
3,076	83	2,456	537	...	...	...	...	...	...
26,621	579	23,157	2,880	5	49	23	6	20	...
112	4	79	29	...	...	...	...	...	...
...	...	...	...	...	...	...	...	...	...
31,406	*723*	*26,801*	*3,877*	*5*	*49*	*23*	*6*	*20*	...
123	4	96	23	...	...	...	...	...	...
210	4	162	44		...	...	...	...	...
280	8	217	55	...	...	...	...	...	...
19	...	13	6	...	...	...	...	...	...
381	8	311	62	...	...	...	...	...	...
...	...	...	...	...	...	...	...	...	...
1,013	*24*	*799*	*190*	...	...	...		...	...
34,024	**805**	**23,761**	**4,473**	**5**	**49**	**23**	**6**	**20**	...
133	5	100	28	...	...		...	...	...
3	1	2	...	.			...	...	...
116	3	85	28		...		...	...	...
26	...	18	8	...		...	...	...	...
566	26	393	147			...	...	...	...
81	2	54	25	...		...	...	...	...
1	1	...	...		...	...	...	...	...
361	10	247	104	...			...	...	...
61	1	37	23	...		...	...	...	...
...	...	...	...			...	...	...	...
21	...	17	4	...		...	...	...	...
18	...	15	3	...		...	...	...	...
...	...	...	...	...		...	...	...	...

Bangalore

Class.	Group.	Caste, &c. and sub-division.	Religion.	All Ages. Total.	Single.	Married.	Widowed.	Civil condition not stated.
A Agricultural.—(Continued.)	1. Military and Dominant.	Kshatriya. { Kshatriya ...	Hindu	1,131	446	497	188	...
		do ...	Sikh	1	...	1	...	...
		Kumárapatta ...	Hindu	...	...	...	...	...
		Rájapindé ...	,,	18	9	6	3	...
		Kodaga (Coorgs) ...	,,	...	...	...	...	...
		Rájpút ...	,,	671	252	260	162	...
		Maráta ...	,,	4,615	1,588	1,975	1,052	...
		Ráchéwár and Rayagára ...	,,	399	140	168	91	...
		Total Group 1...	...	6,838	2,135	2,907	1,496	...
	2. Other Agricultural. (a) Cultivators.	Lingáyet (Gaudamaná, &c.) ...	Hindu	6,581	2,142	3,006	1,433	...
		Náyar ...	,,	...	...	...	...	...
		Pillé ...	,,	63	22	27	14	...
		Tigala ...	,,	12,798	4,971	5,752	2,075	...
		Vakkaliga. { Vakkaliga ...	,,	109,290	33,916	52,115	23,235	24
		Sáda ...	Jain	426	141	173	112	...
		Tulu ...	Bramho	...	...	...	...	...
		Total Group 2(a)...	...	129,158	41,192	61,073	26,869	24
	4. Forest and Hill tribes.	Iraliga ...	Hindu	508	214	236	58	...
		Korachu ...	,,	1,015	419	425	171	...
		Koracha ...	,,	1,429	514	644	271	...
		Kúruba ...	,,	115	44	49	22	...
		Lambáni ...	,,	1,538	585	750	203	...
		Uriya ...	,,	...	...	...	...	...
		Total Group 4...	...	4,605	1,776	2,104	725	...
		Total Class A......		**140,601**	**45,403**	**66,084**	**29,090**	**24**
B.—Professional.—(Continued.)	5. Priests.	Brámhan. { A'ruvélu ...	Hindu	557	194	232	131	...
		A'ruvélu Niyógi ...	,,	9	2	6	1	...
		Aravattu Vakkalu ...	,,	499	138	238	123	...
		Babbúru kammé ...	,,	106	31	52	23	...
		Badaganádu ...	,,	2,541	769	1,104	668	...
		Brihachcharana ...	,,	335	91	160	84	...
		Chitpávan ...	,,	1	...	...	1	...
		Dés'ast'h ...	,,	1,664	503	743	418	...
		Drávida ...	,,	275	85	109	81	...
		Guzaráti ...	,,	...	...	...	...	...
		Gauda ...	,,	73	23	35	15	...
		Halé kannadiga ...	,,	110	38	61	11	...
		Havíka ...	,,	...	...	...	...	...

TABLE E.—(*Continued.*)

District.

Females.

0 to 9					10 to 14.				
Total.	Single.	Married.	Widowed	Civil condition not stated.	Total.	Single.	Married.	Widowed.	Civil condition not stated.
313	311	2	...	...	132	95	37	...	...
...	...	...	...	...	...	...	...	...	...
...	...	...	...	...	...	...	...	...	...
6	6	...	...	...	4	2	2	...	...
...	...	...	...	...	...	...	...	...	...
188	186	2	...	...	80	51	29	...	...
1,303	1,282	21	...	...	395	251	144	...	...
112	111	1	...	...	38	20	18	...	...
1,022	*1,896*	*26*	...	...	*649*	*419*	*230*	...	...
1,645	1,607	38	...	...	690	388	299	3	...
...	...	...	...	...	...	...	...	...	...
18	18	...	...	...	3	3	...	...	...
4,044	4,027	17	...	...	929	681	248	...	...
30,281	29,119	1,144	17	1	6,346	3,393	2,895	56	2
132	129	3	...	...	23	9	13	1	...
...	...	...	...	...	...	...	...	...	...
36,120	*34,960*	*1,202*	*17*	*1*	*7,991*	*4,471*	*3,455*	*60*	*2*
178	177	1	...	...	30	27	3	...	...
281	281	...	...	...	106	104	2	...	...
427	426	1	...	...	95	64	31	...	...
32	31	1	...	...	15	9	6	...	...
501	500	1	...	...	109	73	36	...	...
...	...	...	...	...	...	...	...	...	...
1,419	*1,415*	*4*	...	...	*355*	*277*	*78*	...	...
39,431	**38,211**	**1,232**	**17**	**1**	**8,995**	**5,170**	**3,763**	**60**	**2**
184	173	11	...	...	49	21	27	1	...
1	1	...	...	...	3	1	2	...	...
133	127	6	...	...	45	11	34	...	...
26	24	2	...	...	24	7	16	1	...
705	677	28	...	...	283	92	184	7	...
86	83	3	...	...	33	8	25	...	...
...	...	...	...	...	...	...	...	...	...
441	418	23	...	...	235	85	120	30	...
73	68	5	...	...	35	17	17	1	...
...	...	...	...	...	...	...	...	...	...
20	20	...	...	...	7	3	4	...	...
33	22	11	...	...	26	16	10	...	...
...	...	...	...	...	...	...	...	...	...

Bangalore

Class.	Group.	Caste, &c., and sub-division.	Religion.	15 to 39 Total.	Single.	Married.	Widowed.	Civil condition not stated.
A. Agricultural.—(Continued).	1. Military and Dominant.	Kshatriya. — Kshatriya	Hindu.	443	39	353	51	...
		Kshatriya. — do	Sikh.	1	...	1	...	...
		Kshatriya. — Kumárapatta	Hindu.	...	...	...	...	...
		Kshatriya. — Rajapindé	,,	6	1	4	1	...
		Kshatriya. — Kodagu (Coorgs)	,,	...	...	...	...	...
		Kshatriya. — Rájpút	,,	235	15	179	41	...
		Maráta	,,	1,738	54	1,384	300	...
		Ráchévár and Rangáre.	,,	146	9	121	16	...
		Total Group 1		*2,569*	*118*	*2,042*	*409*	...
	2. Other Agricultural (a) Cultivators.	Lingáyet (Gaudamané, &c.)	Hindu.	2,650	139	2,134	377	...
		Náyar	,,	...	...	...	...	...
		Pillé	,,	22	1	17	4	...
		Tigala	,,	5,024	237	4,284	503	...
		Vakkaliga — Vakkaliga	,,	47,752	1,126	40,666	5,956	4
		Vakkaliga — Sáda	Jain.	180	3	137	40	...
		Vakkaliga — Tulu	Brámho.	...	...	...	...	...
		Total Group 2(a)		*55,628*	*1,506*	*47,238*	*6,880*	*4*
	4. Forest and Hill Tribes.	Uraliga	Hindu.	222	10	194	18	...
		Koracha	,,	390	33	325	32	...
		Korama	,,	564	23	476	65	...
		Kuruba	,,	43	4	33	6	...
		Lambani	,,	639	12	593	34	...
		Uriya	,,	...	...	...	...	...
		Total Group 4		*1,858*	*82*	*1,621*	*155*	...
		Total Class A		**60,055**	**1,706**	**50,901**	**7,444**	**4**
B. Professional.—(Continued).	5. Priests.	Brámhan. — Á'ruvélu	Hindu.	190	...	147	43	...
		Brámhan. — Á'ruvélu Niyógi	,,	3	...	3	...	...
		Brámhan. — Aravattu-Vakkalu	,,	197	...	159	38	...
		Brámhan. — Babbúru Kammé	,,	33	...	27	6	...
		Brámhan. — Badaganádu	,,	930	...	719	211	...
		Brámhan. — Brihacharana	,,	122	...	105	17	...
		Brámhan. — Chitpávan	,,	...	...	...	...	...
		Brámhan. — Dés'ast'h	,,	577	...	452	125	...
		Brámhan. — Drávida	,,	82	...	68	14	...
		Brámhan. — Gazaráti	,,	...	...	...	...	...
		Brámhan. — Ganda	,,	28	...	24	4	...
		Brámhan. — Halé kannadiga	,,	26	...	24	2	...
		Brámhan. — Havíka	,,	...	...	...	...	...

TABLE E.—*(Continued.)*

District.

Females.									
40 and over.					Age not stated.				
Total.	Single.	Married.	Widowed.	Civil condition not stated.	Total.	Single.	Married.	Widowed.	Civil condition not stated.
243	1	105	137	...	...	...	...	...	...
...	...	...	...	...	...	...	...	...	...
...	...	...	...	...	...	...	...	...	...
2	...	...	2	...	...	...	...	...	...
...	...	...	...	...	...	...	...	...	...
171	...	50	121	...	...	...	...	...	...
1,179	1	426	752	...	...	...	...	...	...
103	...	28	75	...	...	...	...	...	...
1,698	*2*	*609*	*1,087*	...	...	...	...	...	...
1,593	8	532	1,053	...	...	...	...	...	...
...	...	...	...	...	...	...	...	...	...
20	...	10	10	...	...	...	...	...	...
2,801	26	1,203	1,572	...	...	...	...	...	...
24,866	256	7,396	17,201	13	45	22	14	5	4
91	...	20	71	...	...	...	...	...	...
...	...	...	...	...	...	...	...	...	...
29,371	*290*	*9,161*	*19,907*	*13*	*45*	*22*	*14*	*5*	*4*
78	...	38	40	...	...	...	...	...	...
238	1	98	139	...	...	...	...	...	...
343	1	136	206	...	...	...	...	...	...
25	...	9	16	...	...	...	...	...	...
289	...	120	169	...	...	...	...	...	...
	...	...	...	...	...	...	...	...	...
973	*2*	*401*	*570*	...	...	...	...	*4*	*4*
32,045	**294**	**10,174**	**21,564**	**13**	**45**	**22**	**14**	**5**	**4**
134	...	47	87	...	...	...	...	...	...
2	...	1	1	...	...	...	...	...	...
124	...	39	85	...	...	...	...	...	...
23	...	7	16	...	...	...	...	...	...
603	...	173	430	...	...	...	...	...	...
94	...	27	67	...	...	...	...	...	...
1	...	...	1	...	...	...	...	...	...
411	...	148	263	...	...	...	...	...	...
85	...	19	66	...	...	...	...	...	...
...	...	...	...	...	...	...	...	...	...
18	...	7	11	...	...	...	...	...	...
25	...	16	9	...	...	...	...	...	...
...	...	...	...	...	...	...	...	...	...

Kolar

Class.	Group.	Caste, &c. and sub-division.	Religion.	All Ages. Total.	Single.	Married.	Widowed.	Civil condition not stated.
A. Agricultural.—(Continued.)	1. Military and Dominant.	Kshatriya. — Kshatriya	Hindu	416	219	169	28	...
		do	Sikh	...	...	...	...	...
		Kumârapatta	Hindu	...	...	...	...	...
		Râjapinde	,,	31	16	12	3	...
		Kodagu (Coorgs)	,,	6	3	2	1	...
		Rajpût	,,	475	243	197	35	...
		Marâta ...	,,	2,319	1,239	945	135	...
		Râchêvâr and Ranagâra	,,	214	114	87	13	...
		Total Group 1 ...		*3,461*	*1,834*	*1,412*	*215*	...
	2. Other Agricultural. (a) Cultivators.	Lingâyet (Gaudamané, &c.)	Hindu	735	363	329	43	...
		Nâyar ...	,,	3	1	2	...	...
		Pillê ...	,,	115	46	63	6	...
		Tigala ...	,,	5,097	2,564	2,325	208	...
		Vakkaliga — Vakkaliga	,,	81,025	41,788	35,348	3,948	...
		Sâda	Jain	2	...	...	2	...
		Tulu	Brâmhô	...	...	...	...	...
		Total Group 2(a) ...		*87,037*	*44,762*	*38,067*	*4,207*	...
	4. Forest and Hill Tribes.	Uraliga ...	Hindu	12	8	4	...	...
		Koracha ...	,,	1,686	857	725	104	...
		Koranna ...	,,	47	22	23	2	...
		Kuruba ...	,,	64	33	24	7	...
		Lambâni ...	,,	412	235	163	14	...
		Uriya ...	,,	...	...	...	...	...
		Total Group 4 ...		*2,221*	*1,155*	*939*	*127*	...
		Total Class A ...		**92,719**	**47,751**	**40,418**	**4,549**	**1**
B. Professional.—(Continued.)	2. Priests.	Brâmhan. — A'ruvêlu	Hindu	384	201	148	35	...
		A'ruvêlu Niyôgi	,,	...	...	...	...	...
		Aravattu-Vakkalu	,,	750	388	323	39	...
		Babbûr kammé	,,	30	17	13	...	...
		Badaganâdu	,,	1,424	655	663	106	...
		Brihachcharana	,,	59	25	29	5	...
		Chitpâvan	,,	...	...	...	...	...
		Dêsasth	,,	1,270	574	587	109	...
		Drâvida	,,	760	345	352	63	...
		Gûzarâti	,,	...	...	...	...	...
		Gauda ...	,,	52	27	23	2	...
		Halê kannadiga	,,	2	...	2	...	...
		Havika ...	,,	...	...	...	...	...

TABLE E.—(*Continued.*)

District.

Males.									
0 to 9					10 to 14				
Total.	Single.	Married.	Widowed.	Civil condition not stated.	Total.	Single.	Married.	Widowed.	Civil condition not stated.
110	110	...	...	...	35	35	...	...	...
...	...	...		...	...	...	...	...	...
...	...	...			...	...	...	...	...
7	7	...	...	...	2	2	...	...	...
2	2	...	...	...	1	1	...	...	...
131	131	...			28	28	[illegible]	...	...
681	681	...	...	...	199	195	4	...	...
59	59	...	...	...	17	17	...	...	...
990	*990*	...	...	...	*282*	*278*	*4*	...	...
176	176	...	...	...	54	53	1	...	...
...	...	...	...	...	1	1	...	...	...
20	20		...	...	5	5	...	...	...
1,466	1,466	...	...		331	381	...	...	...
17,610	17,576	32	2	...	6,278	6,218	56	4	...
...	...	...	...	...	...	...	...	...	...
	...		...	...	...	...	...	...	...
19,272	*19,238*	*32*	*2*	...	*6,669*	*6,608*	*57*	*4*	...
5	5	...	...	...	1	1	...	...	...
536	526	...	...	...	113	113	...	...	...
12	12	...	...	...	4	4	...	...	...
16	16	...	...	...	5	5	...	...	...
144	144	...	...	...	36	36	...	...	...
...	...	...	...	...	...	...	...	...	...
703	*703*	...	...	...	*159*	*159*	...	...	...
20,985	**20,931**	**32**	**2**		**7,110**	**7,045**	**61**	**4**	...
92	92	...	...	...	33	30	3	...	...
...	...	...	...	...	...	...	...	...	...
212	212	...	...	...	74	68	6	...	...
8	8	...	...	...	2	2	...	...	...
341	341		...	...	100	91	9	...	...
14	14	...	...		6	5	1	...	...
...	...	...	...		...	...	...	...	...
325	325	...	...	...	93	81	12	...	...
188	188	...	...	...	56	50	6	...	...
...	...	...	...	...	...	...	...	...	...
13	13	...	...	...	5	5	...	...	...
...	...	...	...	...	...	...	...	...	...
...	...	...	...	...	...	...	...	...	...

Kolar

Class.	Group.	Caste, &c., and sub-division.	Religion.	15 to 39 Total.	Single.	Married.	Widowed.	Civil condition not stated.
A. Agricultural.—(Continued.)	1. Military and Dominant.	Kshatriya. — Kshatriya	Hindu	174	69	100	5	...
		do	Sikh	...	...	...	...	...
		Kumárapatta	Hindu	...	...	...	...	...
		Rájapindé	,,	16	7	8	1	...
		Kodaga (Coorgs)	,,	2	...	2	...	...
		Rájpút	,,	211	76	128	7	...
		Maráṭa	,,	879	340	510	29	...
		Ráchévár and Ranagára.	,,	95	34	58	3	...
		Total Group 1	...	*1,377*	*526*	*806*	*45*	...
	2. Other Agricultural (a) Cultivators.	Lingáyet (Gandamané, &c.)	Hindu	313	122	184	7	...
		Náyar	,,	1	...	1	...	...
		Pillé	,,	67	21	45	1	...
		Tigaḷa	,,	2,156	736	1,381	39	...
		Vakkaliga. — Vakkaliga	,,	34,476	17,169	16,876	431	...
		Sáda	Jain	...	...	...	...	...
		Tuḷu	Brahmo	...	...	...	...	...
		Total Group 2(a)	...	*37,013*	*18,048*	*18,187*	*478*	...
	4. Forest and Hill Tribes.	Iruliga	Hindu	6	2	4	...	...
		Koracha	,,	643	208	415	20	...
		Korama	,,	22	5	16	1	...
		Kuruba	,,	29	12	15	2	...
		Lambáṇi	,,	143	49	91	3	...
		Uriya	,,	...	...	...	...	...
		Total Group 4	...	*843*	*276*	*541*	*26*	...
		Total Class A		**39,233**	**18,850**	**19,834**	**549**	..
B. Professional.—(Continued.)	5. Priests.	Bráhman. — A'ruvélu	Hindu.	161	71	81	9	...
		A'ruvélu Niyógi	,,	...	...	...	...	...
		Aruvattu-Vakkalu	,,	303	99	196	8	...
		Babbúru kammé	,,	14	6	8	...	...
		Badaganáḍu	,,	587	203	363	21	...
		Brihachcharaṇa	,,	27	5	21	1	...
		Chitpávan	,,	...	...	...	...	...
		Dés'ast'h	,,	532	152	342	38	...
		Drávida	,,	311	93	205	13	...
		Guzaráti	,,	...	...	...	...	...
		Gauḍa	,,	20	8	12	...	...
		Haḷé kannaḍiga	,,	1	...	1	...	...
		Havíka	,,	...	...	...	...	...

TABLE E.—(*Continued.*)

District.

Males.									
40 and over.					Age not stated.				
Total.	Single.	Married.	Widowed.	Civil condition not stated.	Total.	Single.	Married.	Widowed.	Civil condition not stated.
97	5	69	23	...	...	...	...	...	...
...	...	...	...	...	...	...	...	...	...
...	...	...	...	...	...	...	...	...	...
6	...	4	2	...	...	...	...	...	...
1	...	...	1	...	...	...	...	...	...
105	8	69	28	...	...	...	...	...	...
560	23	431	106	...	...	...	...	...	...
43	4	29	10	...	...	...	...	...	...
812	*40*	*602*	*170*	...	...	...	...	...	...
192	12	144	36	...	...	...	...	...	...
1	...	1	...	...	...	...	...	...	...
23	...	18	5	...	...	...	...	...	...
1,144	31	944	169	...	...	...	...	...	...
22,626	792	18,329	3,504	1	95	33	55	7	...
2	...	...	2	...	...	...	...	...	...
...	...	...	...	...	...	...	...	...	...
23,988	*835*	*19,436*	*3,716*	*1*	*95*	*33*	*55*	*7*	...
...	...	...	...	...	...	...	...	...	...
404	10	310	84	...	...	...	...	...	...
9	1	7	1	...	...	...	...	...	...
14	...	9	5	...	...	...	...	...	...
89	6	72	11	...	...	...	...	...	...
...	...	...	...	...	...	...	...	...	...
516	*17*	*398*	*101*	...	...	...	...	...	...
25,316	**892**	**20,436**	**3,987**	**1**	**95**	**33**	**55**	**7**	...
98	8	64	26	...	...	...	...	...	...
...	...	...	...	...	...	...	...	...	...
161	9	121	31	...	...	...	...	...	...
6	1	5	...	...	...	...	...	...	...
396	20	291	85	...	...	...	...	...	...
12	1	7	4	...	...	...	...	...	...
...	...	...	...	...	...	...	...	...	...
320	16	233	71	...	...	...	...	...	...
205	14	141	50	...	...	...	...	...	...
...	...	...	...	...	...	...	...	...	...
14	1	11	2	...	...	...	...	...	...
1	...	1	...	...	...	...	...	...	...
...	...	...	...	...	...	...	...	...	...

Kolar

Class.	Group.	Caste, &c. and sub-division.	Religion.	All Ages. Total.	Single.	Married.	Widowed.	Civil condition not stated.
A. Agricultural.—(Continued.)	1. Military and Dominant.	Kshatriya.—Kshatriya ...	Hindu	367	110	178	79	...
		do	Sikh	...	...	...	...	...
		Kumarápatta ...	Hindu	...	...	...	...	...
		Rájapindé ...	,,	37	9	16	12	...
		Kodaga (Coorgs) ...	,,	3	1	2	...	...
		Rájpút ...	,,	472	140	219	113	...
		Maráta	,,	2,321	750	1,033	538	...
		Ráchévár and Rangára ...	,,	198	56	95	47	...
		Total Group 1...	... ...	3,398	1,066	1,543	789	...
	2. Other Agricultural. (a) Cultivators.	Lingáyet, (Gaudamané, &c.) ..	Hindu	686	238	322	126	...
		Náyar ...	,,	[illegible]	...	...	...	...
		Pillé ...	,,	60	21	32	7	...
		Tigala ...	,,	5,059	1,769	2,382	908	...
		Vakkaliga.—Vakkaliga ...	,,	82,073	24,628	35,661	21,784	...
		Sáda ...	Jain	...	...	...	...	...
		Tulu ...	Bramho	...	...	...	...	...
		Total Group 2(a)...	... ...	87,878	26,656	38,397	22,825	...
	4. Forest and Hill Tribes.	I'galiga ...	Hindu	10	2	4	4	...
		Koracha ...	,,	1,635	573	771	291	...
		Koranna ...	,,	46	18	20	8	...
		Kuruba ...	,,	83	30	37	16	...
		Lambáni ...	,,	339	132	164	43	...
		Uriya ...	,,	...	...	...	...	...
		Total Group 4...	... ...	2,113	755	996	362	...
		Total Class A.....		**93,389**	**28,477**	**40,936**	**23,976**	...
B. Professional.—(Continued)	5. Priests.	Brámhan.—A'ruvélu ...	Hindu	374	82	171	121	...
		A'ruvélu Niyógi ...	,,	...	...	...	...	...
		Aruvattu Vakkalu ...	,,	787	226	365	196	...
		Bábbúr kammé ...	,,	25	10	14	1	...
		Badaganádu ...	,,	1,347	357	647	313	...
		Brihachcharana ...	,,	67	18	35	14	...
		Chitpávan ...	,,	...	...	...	...	...
		Dés'asth ...	,,	1,233	289	607	337	...
		Drávida ...	,,	883	216	408	259	...
		Guzaráti ...	,,	...	...	...	...	...
		Gauda ...	,,	59	22	24	13	...
		Halé kannadiga ...	,,	2	...	2	...	...
		Havíka ...	,,	...	...	...	...	...

TABLE E.—(*Continued.*)

District.

Females.

0 to 9					10 to 14				
Total.	Single.	Married.	Widowed.	Civil condition not stated.	Total.	Single.	Married.	Widowed.	Civil condition not stated.
97	96	1	...	...	24	12	12	...	...
...	...	...	...	...	...	...	...	...	...
...	...	...	...	...	...	...	...	...	...
6	6	...	...	...	4	2	2	...	...
1	1	...	...	...	...	...	...	...	...
121	120	1	...	...	35	19	15	1	...
653	638	15	...	...	161	90	71	...	...
42	42	...	...	...	15	11	4	...	...
920	*903*	*17*	...	...	*239*	*134*	*104*	*1*	...
213	207	6	...	...	37	23	14	...	...
...	...	...	...	...	...	...	...	...	...
16	16	...	...	...	5	4	1	...	...
1,469	1,419	20	...	...	358	244	114	...	...
22,076	20,173	1,874	29	...	5,979	3,349	2,498	132	...
...	...	...	...	...	...	...	...	...	...
...	...	...	...	...	...	...	...	...	...
23,774	*21,845*	*1,900*	*29*	...	*6,379*	*3,620*	*2,627*	*132*	...
...	...	...	...	...	1	1	...	...	...
467	467	...	...	...	84	73	11	...	...
14	14	...	...	...	4	3	1	...	...
23	23	...	...	...	6	4	2	...	...
115	115	...	...	...	18	12	6	...	...
...	...	...	...	...	...	...	...	...	...
619	*619*	...	...	...	*113*	*93*	*20*	...	...
25,313	**23,367**	**1,917**	**29**	...	**6,731**	**3,847**	**2,751**	**133**	...
79	68	11	...	...	41	14	26	1	...
...	...	...	...	...	...	...	...	...	...
224	210	14	...	...	67	16	51	...	...
9	9	...	...	...	6	1	4	...	...
358	332	26	...	...	117	25	89	3	...
17	16	1	...	...	11	2	8	1	...
...	...	...	...	...	...	...	...	...	...
304	271	33	...	...	107	18	85	4	...
222	196	25	1	...	69	20	48	1	...
...	...	...	...	...	...	...	...	...	...
19	19	...	...	...	4	3	1	...	...
...	...	...	...	...	...	...	...	...	...
...	...	...	...	...	...	...	...	...	...

- Kolar

Class.	Group.	Caste, &c. and sub-division.	Religion.	15 to 39 Total.	15 to 39 Single.	15 to 39 Married.	15 to 39 Widowed.	15 to 39 Civil condition not stated.
A. Agricultural.—(Continued.)	1. Military and Dominant.	Kshatriya. — Kshatriya ...	Hindu	153	2	120	22	...
		Kshatriya. — do ...	Sikh	...	...	...	...	...
		Kshatriya. — Kumárapatta	Hindu	...	...	...	...	...
		Kshatriya. — Rájapindé	,,	16	1	12	3	...
		Kshatriya. — Kodaga (Coorge)	,,	2	...	2	...	...
		Kshatriya. — Rájpút	,,	202	1	164	37	...
		Maráta	,,	936	21	753	162	...
		Ráchévár and Rangáru.	,,	86	3	65	18	...
		Total Group 1......	... ...	*1,395*	*28*	*1,125*	242	...
	2. Other Agricultural. (a) Cultivators.	Lingáyet, (Gaudamané, &c.)	Hindu	291	7	258	26	...
		Náyar	,,	...	...	...	...	...
		Pillé	,,	26	1	23	2	...
		Tigala ...	,,	2,172	71	1,873	228	...
		Vakkaliga — Vakkaliga	,,	31,090	993	26,951	6,146	
		Vakkaliga — Sáda ...	Jain	...	...	...	..	...
		Vakkaliga — Tulu ...	Bramho	...	...	...	...	...
		Total Group 2(a)...	... ...	*36,579*	*1,072*	*29,105*	*6,402*	...
	4. Forest and Hill Tribes.	I'raliga	Hindu	5	...	4	1	...
		Korachu	,,	702	29	597	76	...
		Korama	,,	19	1	17	1	...
		Kuruba	,,	33	3	28	2	...
		Lambáni	,,	137	3	128	6	...
		Uriya	,,	...	...	...	...	...
		Total Group 4......	... ...	*890*	*36*	*774*	*86*	...
		Total Class A......		**38,870**	**1,136**	**31,004**	**6,730**	...
B. Professional.—(Continued.)	5. Priests.	Brámhan. — A'ruvélu	Hindu	130	...	98	32	...
		Brámhan. — A'ruvélu Niyógi...	,,	...	...	...	...	...
		Brámhan. — Aruvattu Vakkalu...	,,	284	...	233	51	...
		Brámhan. — Babbúr kammé	,,	7	...	7	...	...
		Brámhan. — Badaganádu	,,	504	...	411	93	...
		Brámhan. — Brihachcharana	,,	26	...	21	5	...
		Brámhan. — Chitpávan	,,	...	...	...	...	...
		Brámhan. — Dés'ast'h	,,	489	...	373	116	...
		Brámhan. — Drávida	,,	335	...	266	69	...
		Brámhan. — Guzaráti	,,	...	...	...	...	...
		Brámhan. — Gauda ...	,,	21	...	18	3	...
		Brámhan. — Halé kannadiga	,,	2	...	2	...	...
		Brámhan. — Havika ...	,,	...	...	...	...	...

TABLE E.—(*Continued.*)

District.

Females.

40 and over.					Age not stated.				
Total.	Single.	Married.	Widowed.	Civil condition not stated.	Total.	Single.	Married.	Widowed.	Civil condition not stated.
93	...	36	57	...	...	...	...	...	...
...	...	...	...	...	...	...	...	..	..
...	...	...	...	...	...	...	...	...	...
11	...	2	9	...	...	...	...	...	...
...	...	...	...	...	...	...	...	...	...
114	...	39	75	...		...	...	...	...
571	1	194	376	...	...		...	...	...
55		26	29	...		...	...		...
844	*1*	*297*	*546*		...	...	...	...	...
145	1	44	100		...		...		...
...	...	...	...	...	...	...		...	...
13	...	8	5	...	..	...	...	...	...
1,060	5	375	690	...	...	...	...	...	...
19,858	84	4,326	15,418	...	70	29	12	29	...
...	...	...	...	..	...	...	...	...	...
...	...	...	...	...	...	...	...	...	...
21,076	*90*	*4,753*	*16,233*	...	*70*	*29*	*12*	*29*	...
4	1	...	3		...			...	...
382	4	163	215	...	...	...	...	...	...
9	...	2	7	...	...	...	...	...	...
21		7	14	...	...	...	...	...	...
69	2	30	37			...	...	...	...
...		...	...	...		...	...	...	...
485	*7*	*202*	*276*	...		...	...	...	...
22,405	**98**	**5,252**	**17,055**		**70**	**29**	**12**	**29**	...
124	...	36	88	...	...	...		...	...
...	...	...	...	...	...	...	...	...	...
212		67	145	...	...	...	...	...	...
4	...	3	1	...	...	...	...	...	...
338		121	247			...		...	...
13	...	5	8	...	...	...		...	...
...	..	...	...	...	...	...	...	...	...
333	...	116	217	...	...	...	...	...	...
257	..	69	188		...	...	...	...	...
...	...	...	...		...	...	...	...	...
15		5	10	...	...	...	...	...	...
...	...	...	...		...	...	...	...	...
...	...	...	...	...	...	...	...	...	...

Tumkur

Class.	Group.	Caste, &c. and sub-division.	Religion.	All Ages. Total.	Single.	Married.	Widowed.	Civil condition not stated.
A.—Agricultural.—(*Continued*)	1. Military and Dominant.	Kshatriya.—Kshatriya	Hindu.	445	199	213	33	...
		do	Sikh.	...	...	...	...	...
		Kumárapatta	Hindu.	...	...	...	...	...
		Rájapindé	,,	49	26	20	3	...
		Kodaga (Coorgs)	,,	...	...	...	...	...
		Rájpút	,,	502	256	197	49	...
		Maráta	,,	1,383	718	583	82	...
		Káchévár and Rangagára	,,	182	94	80	14	...
		Total Group 1	...	*2,567*	*1,293*	*1,093*	*181*	...
	2. Other Agricultural (*a*) Cultivators.	Lingáyet, (Gaudamané, &c.)	Hindu.	4,434	2,278	1,726	430	...
		Náyar	,,	...			...	...
		Pillé	,,	15	10	5	...	...
		Tigala	,,	7,450	4,104	3,004	342	...
		Vakkaliga.—Vakkaliga	,,	88,795	50,414	35,214	3,154	13
		Sáda	Jain.	58	40	17	1	...
		Túlu	Bramho.	...	...	...	...	...
		Total Group 2(a)	...	*100,752*	*56,846*	*39,966*	*3,927*	*13*
	4. Forest and Hill Tribes.	Uraliga	Hindu.	34	12	14	8	...
		Koracha	,,	487	200	244	43	...
		Korama	,,	779	471	285	23	...
		Kuruba	,,	725	306	364	55	...
		Lambáni	,,	1,563	927	602	34	...
		Uriya	,,	...	...		...	...
		Total Group 4	...	*3,588*	*1,916*	*1,509*	*163*	...
		Total Class A		**106,907**	**60,055**	**42,568**	**4,271**	**13**
B.—Professional.—(*Continued.*)	5. Priests.	Bráhman.—A'ruvélu	Hindu.	217	91	113	13	...
		A'ruvélu Niyógi	,,	...	...	...	...	...
		Aravattu Vakkalu	,,	259	108	130	21	...
		Babbúru kammé	,,	237	99	122	16	...
		Badaganádu	,,	1,989	924	904	161	...
		Brihachcharana	,,	10	3	6	1	...
		Chitpávan	,,	...	...	...	...	...
		Dés'ast'h	,,	538	187	299	52	...
		Drávida	,,	129	45	76	8	...
		Guzaráti	,,	...	...	...	...	...
		Gauda	,,	34	22	8	4	...
		Halé kannadiga	,,	229	107	106	16	...
		Hevíka	,,	...	...	...	...	...

TABLE E.—(*Continued.*)

District.

Males.

0 to 9					10 to 14				
Total.	Single.	Married.	Widowed.	Civil condition not stated.	Total.	Single.	Married.	Widowed.	Civil condition not stated.
101	101	...	...	...	26	26	...	...	...
...	...	...	...	...	...	...	...	...	...
...	...	...	...		...	...	...	...	...
17	17	...	...	...	2	2	...	...	...
...	...	...	...	...	...	...	...	...	...
138	138	...	...	...	28	28	...	...	...
425	425	...	...	...	153	123	30	...	...
50	50		...	...	27	27	...	...	...
731	*731*	...	...	...	*236*	*206*	*30*	...	...
1,232	1,232	...	..	...	424	401	23	...	...
...	...	...	...	..	...	...	...	...	...
3	3		...	..	4	4	...	...	...
2,319	2,319	..	...	...	1,188	1,185	3	...	...
23,271	23,254	14	3	...	1,486	1,486	...	..	...
24	24		...	...	2	2	..	...	...
...	...	...	...	..	..	...	...	...	...
26,849	*26,832*	*14*	*3*	...	*3,104*	*3,078*	*26*	...	
9	9	...	...	...	...	...	...	...	...
126	126	...	...	...	27	27	...	...	...
295	295	...	...	...	65	64	1	..	...
134	134	...	...	...	42	42	...	...	...
551	551	...	...	...	181	175	6	...	...
...	...	...	...	...	...	...	...	...	...
1,115	*1,115*	...	...	...	*315*	*308*	*7*	...	...
28,695	**28,678**	**14**	**3**	...	**3,655**	**3,592**	**63**	...	...
52	52	...	...	...	20	16	4	...	...
...	...	...	...	...	...	...	...	...	...
51	51	...	...	...	14	12	2	...	...
52	52	...	...	...	25	21	4	...	...
470	470		...	...	163	158	5	...	...
3	3	...	...	...		...	...	...	...
...	...	...	...	...	...	...	...	...	...
97	97	..	...	...	34	31	3	...	...
25	25	...	...	...	8	7	1	...	...
...	...	...	...	...	...	...	...	...	...
6	6	...	...	...	2	2	...	...	...
69	69	...	...	...	21	20	1	...	...
...	...	...	...	...	...	...	...	...	...

Tumkur

Class.	Group.	Caste, &c. and sub-division.	Religion.	15 to 39 Total.	Single.	Married.	Widowed.	Civil condition not stated.
A.—Agricultural.—(Continued.)	1. Military and Dominant.	Kshatriya. — Kshatriya	Hindu	223	70	147	6	...
		do ...	Sikh.	...	...	...	...	...
		Kumárapatta	Hindu.	...	...	...	...	...
		Rájpindé	,,	22	7	14	1	...
		Kodaga (Coorgs)	,,	...	...	...	...	...
		Rájpút	,,	214	83	121	10	...
		Maráta ...	,,	505	160	332	13	...
		Rácbévár and Rangára	,,	73	16	55	2	...
		Total Group 1	... ...	*1,037*	*336*	*669*	*32*	...
	2. Other Agricultural (a) Cultivators.	Lingáyet, (Gaudamané, &c.)	Hindu.	1,746	620	1,011	115	...
		Náyar ...	,,	...	...	...	...	...
		Pillé ...	,,	7	3	4	...	...
		Tigala ...	,,	2,499	568	1,844	87	...
		Vakkaliga. — Vakkaliga	,,	44,896	25,056	19,333	507	...
		Sáda ...	Jain	24	14	9	1	...
		Túlu ...	Brahmo.	...	..	...	...	...
		Total Group 2(a)	... ...	*49,172*	*26,261*	*22,201*	*710*	...
	4. Forest and Hill Tribes.	Uraliga ...	Hindu.	12	3	6	3	...
		Koracha	,,	216	39	164	13	...
		Korama	,,	271	110	157	4	...
		Kuruba ...	,,	368	121	232	15	...
		Lambáni	,,	557	198	348	11	...
		Uriya ...	,,	...	...	...	...	...
		Total Group 4	... ...	*1,424*	*471*	*907*	*46*	...
		Total Class A		**51,633**	**27,068**	**23,777**	**788**	...
B.—Professional.—(Continued.)	5. Priests.	Bramhan. — A'ruvélu	Hindu.	102	22	78	2	...
		A'ruvélu Niyógi	,,	...	...	...	...	...
		Aravattu Vakkalu	,,	143	44	92	7	...
		Babbúru kammé	,,	102	23	72	7	...
		Badaganádu	,,	837	255	536	46	...
		Brihatcharana	,,	4	...	4	...	...
		Chitpávan	,,	...	...	...	...	...
		Désasth	,,	280	51	207	22	...
		Drávida	,,	61	10	48	3	...
		Guzaráti	,,	...	...	...	...	...
		Gauda	,,	13	9	4	...	...
		Halé kannadiga	,,	95	17	75	3	...
		Havika	,,	...	...	...	...	...

TABLE E.—(Continued.)

District.

Males.									
40 and over.					Age not stated.				
Total.	Single.	Married.	Widowed.	Civil condition not stated.	Total.	Single.	Married.	Widowed.	Civil condition not stated.
95	2	66	27	...	...	...	...	...	...
...	...	...	...	...	...	...	...	...	...
...	...	...	...	...	...	...	...	...	...
8	...	6	2	...	...	...	...	...	...
...	...	...	...	...	...	...	...	...	...
122	7	76	39	...	...	...	...	...	...
300	10	221	69	...	...	...	...	...	...
38	1	25	12	...	...	...	...	...	...
563	*20*	*394*	*149*	...	...	...	...	...	...
1,032	25	692	315	...	...	...	...	...	...
...	...	...	...	...	...	...	...	...	...
1	1	...	...	...	...	...	...	...	...
1,444	32	1,157	255	...	...	...	...	...	...
19,045	564	15,845	2,636	...	97	54	22	8	13
8	...	8	...	...	...	...	...	...	...
...	...	...	...	...	...	...	...	...	...
21,530	*621*	*17,703*	*3,206*	...	*97*	*54*	*22*	*8*	*13*
13	...	8	5	...	...	...	...	...	...
118	8	80	30	...	...	...	...	...	...
148	2	127	19	...	...	...	...	...	...
181	9	132	40	...	...	...	...	...	...
274	3	248	23	...	...	...	...	...	...
...	...	...	...	...	...	...	...	...	...
731	*22*	*595*	*117*	...	...	...	...	...	...
22,837	**663**	**18,692**	**3,472**	...	**97**	**54**	**22**	**8**	**13**
43	1	31	11	...	...	...	...	...	...
...	...	...	...	...	...	...	...	...	...
51	1	36	14	...	...	...	...	...	...
58	3	46	9	...	...	...	...	...	...
519	41	363	115	...	...	...	...	...	...
3	...	2	1	...	...	...	...	...	...
...	...	...	...	...	...	...	...	...	...
127	8	89	30	...	...	...	...	...	...
35	3	27	5	...	...	...	...	...	...
...	...	...	...	...	...	...	...	...	...
13	5	4	4	...	...	...	...	...	...
44	1	30	13	...	...	...	...	...	...
...	...	...	...	...	...	...	...	...	...

Tumkur

Class.	Group.	Caste, &c. and sub-division.	Religion.	All Ages. Total.	Single.	Married.	Widowed.	Civil condition not stated.
A.—Agricultural.—(Continued.)	1. Military and Dominant.	Kshatriya. — Kshatriya ...	Hindu.	453	163	228	62	...
		do	Sikh.	...	...	...	...	...
		Kumárapatta ...	Hindu.	...	...	...	...	...
		Rájapinde ...	,,	43	8	26	9	...
		Kodagu (Coorgs) ...	,,	...	...	...	...	...
		Rájpút ...	,,	488	171	220	97	...
		Marúṭa	,,	1,444	539	604	301	...
		Rachévár and Ranagara ...	,,	213	83	91	39	...
		Total Group 1......	... ...	2,641	964	1,169	508	...
	2. Other Agricultural. (a) Cultivators.	Lingáyet, (Gaudamane, &c.) ...	Hindu.	4,537	1,440	2,200	897	...
		Náyar	,,	...	...	...	...	...
		Pille	,,	9	4	4	1	...
		Tigaḷa	,,	7,268	2,959	3,011	1,298	...
		Vakkaliga. — Vakkaliga ...	,,	90,286	26,833	37,980	25,447	26
		Sáda	Jain.	67	16	41	10	...
		Túlu	Bramho.	[illegible]	...	...	...	...
		Total Group 2(a)...	... ...	102,167	31,252	43,236	27,653	26
	4. Forest and Hill Tribes.	I'ruliga	Hindu.	33	9	14	10	...
		Koracha	,,	485	178	253	54	...
		Koruma	,,	719	319	307	93	...
		Kuruba	,,	725	190	304	231	...
		Lambáṇi	,,	1,414	632	675	107	...
		Uriya	,,	...	...	...	...	...
		Total Group 4......	... ...	3,376	1,328	1,553	495	...
		Total Class A......		**108,184**	**33,544**	**45,958**	**28,656**	**26**
B.—Professional.—(Continued.)	5. Priests.	Brámhan. — A'ruvélu ...	Hindu.	207	44	130	33	...
		A'ruvélu Niyógi ...	,,	...	...	...	...	...
		Aravattu Vakkalu ...	,,	306	94	146	66	...
		Babburu Kammé ...	,,	259	72	120	67	...
		Badaganáḍu ...	,,	1,999	572	956	471	...
		Brihachcharaṇa ...	,,	17	2	11	4	...
		Chitpávan ...	,,	...	...	...	...	...
		Dés'ast'h ...	,,	544	133	288	123	...
		Drāviḍa ...	,,	131	20	87	24	...
		Guzaráti ...	,,	...	...	...	...	...
		Gauḍa ...	,,	20	5	6	9	...
		Halékannaḍiga ...	,,	193	42	132	10	...
		Havíka ...	,,	...	...	...	...	...

TABLE E.—*(Continued.)*

District

Females.

0 to 9					10 to 14				
Total.	Single.	Married.	Widowed.	Civil condition not stated.	Total.	Single.	Married.	Widowed.	Civil condition not stated.
117	117	...	...	...	37	31	6	...	...
...	...	...	...	...	...	...	...	...	...
...	...	...	...	...	...	...	...	...	...
8	8	...	...	...	...	...	...	...	...
...	...	...	...	...	...	...	...	...	...
140	140	...	...	...	28	23	5	...	...
452	450	2	...	...	116	72	44	...	...
62	62	...	...	...	22	18	4	...	...
779	*777*	*2*	...	...	*203*	*144*	*59*	...	...
1,089	1,088	1	...	...	408	283	125	...	...
...	...	...	...	...	...	...	...	...	...
3	3	...	...	...	1	1	...	...	...
2,385	2,385	...	...	...	584	459	125	...	...
26,846	24,825	2,012	9	...	4,776	1,324	3,390	62	...
16	15	1	...	...	7	1	6	...	...
...	...	...	...	...	...	...	...	...	...
30,339	*28,316*	*2,014*	*9*	...	*5,776*	*2,068*	*3,646*	*62*	...
5	5	...	...	...	1	1	...	...	...
143	143	...	...	...	18	18	...	...	...
277	275	2	...	...	39	29	10	...	...
136	135	1	...	...	36	31	5	...	...
540	540	...	...	...	104	79	25	...	...
...	...	...	...	...	...	...	...	...	...
1,101	*1,098*	*3*	...	...	*198*	*158*	*40*	...	...
32,219	**30,191**	**2,019**	**9**	...	**6,177**	**2,370**	**3,745**	**62**	...
42	41	1	...	...	18	3	15	...	...
...	...	...	...	...	...	...	...	...	...
69	67	2	...	...	37	27	10	...	...
64	61	3	...	...	31	11	20	...	...
543	518	25	...	...	155	54	101	...	...
2	2	...	...	...	...	...	...	...	...
...	...	...	...	...	...	...	...	...	...
127	123	4	...	...	39	10	26	3	...
23	19	4	...	...	18	1	17	...	...
...	...	...	...	...	...	...	...	...	...
3	3	...	...	...	2	2	...	...	...
42	42	...	...	...	3	...	3	...	...
...	...	...	...	...	...	...	...	...	...

Class.	Group.	Caste, &c. and sub-division.	Religion.	15 to 39 Total.	15 to 39 Single.	15 to 39 Married.	15 to 39 Widowed.	15 to 39 Civil condition not stated.
A.—Agricultural.—(Continued).	1. Military and Dominant.	Kshatriya. — Kshatriya ...	Hindu.	187	15	151	21	...
		do	Sikh	...	...	...	...	...
		Kumárapatta ...	Hindu.	...	...	...	...	...
		Rájapindé ...	"	26	...	23	3	...
		Kodaga (Coorgs) ...	"	...	...	...	...	...
		Rájpút ...	"	213	8	173	32	...
		Maráta	"	540	17	437	86	...
		Ráchévár and Rajagara ...	"	86	3	73	10	...
		Total Group 1......	... ...	*1,052*	*43*	*857*	*152*	...
	2. Other Agricultural. (a) Cultivators.	Lingáyet. (Gandamané, &c.) ...	"	1,855	66	1,489	300	...
		Náyar	"	...	...	...	...	...
		Pille	"	3	...	3	...	...
		Tigala	"	3,014	111	2,494	409	...
		Vakkaliga. — Vakkaliga ...	"	37,609	520	29,168	7,921	...
		Sádu	Jain.	32	...	29	3	...
		Túlu	Brahmo.	...	...	...	...	...
		Total Group 2(a)...	... ...	*42,513*	*697*	*33,183*	*8,633*	...
	4. Forest and Hill Tribes.	Uraliga	Hindu	14	3	9	2	...
		Koracha	"	238	16	209	13	...
		Korama	"	273	15	239	19	...
		Kuruba	"	338	22	231	[illegible]	...
		Lambáni	"	530	13	500	17	...
		Uriya	"	...	...	...	...	...
		Total Group 4	... ...	*1,393*	*69*	*1,188*	*136*	...
		Total Class A...		**44,958**	**809**	**35,228**	**8,921**	...
B.—Professional.—(Continued).	5. Priests.	Bráhman. — A'ruvélu ...	Hindu.	102	...	92	10	...
		A'ruvélu Niyógi ...	"	...	...	...	...	...
		Aravattu Vakkalu ...	"	142	...	117	25	...
		Babbúr Kammé ...	"	97	...	72	25	...
		Badaganádu ...	"	848	...	674	174	...
		Brihacharana ...	"	10	...	9	1	...
		Chitpávan ...	"	...	...	...	...	...
		Dés'ast'h ...	"	270	...	223	47	...
		Drávida ...	"	69	...	59	10	...
		Guzaráti ...	"	...	...	...	...	...
		Gauda ...	"	8	...	5	3	...
		Halé Kannadiga ...	"	115	...	111	4	...
		Havika ...	"	...	...	...	...	...

TABLE E.—(*Continued.*)

District.

Females.

40 and over.					Age not stated.				
Total.	Single.	Married.	Widowed.	Civil condition not stated.	Total.	Single.	Married.	Widowed.	Civil condition not stated.
112	...	71	41	...	...	...	...	...	...
...	...	...	...	...	...	...	...	...	...
...	...	...	...	...	...	...	...	...	...
9	...	3	6	...	...	...	...	...	...
...	...	...	...	...	...	...	...	...	...
107	...	42	65	...	...	...	...	...	...
336	...	121	215	...	...	...	...	...	...
43	...	14	29	...	...	...	...	...	...
607	...	*251*	*356*	...	...	...	...	...	...
1,185	3	585	597	...	...	...	...	...	...
...	...	...	...	...	...	...	...	...	...
2	...	1	1	...	...	...	...	...	...
1,285	4	392	889	...	...	...	...	...	...
20,951	136	3,377	17,438	...	104	28	33	17	26
12	...	5	7	...	...	...	...	...	...
...	...	...	...	...	...	...	...	...	...
23,435	*143*	*4,360*	*18,932*	...	*104*	*28*	*33*	*17*	*26*
13	...	5	8	...	...	...	...	...	...
86	1	44	41	...	...	...	...	...	...
130	...	56	74	...	...	...	...	...	...
215	2	67	146	...	...	...	...	...	...
240	...	150	90	...	...	...	...	...	...
...	...	...	...	...	...	...	...	...	...
684	*3*	*322*	*359*	...	...	...	...	...	...
24,726	**146**	**4,933**	**19,647**	...	**104**	**28**	**33**	**17**	**26**
45	...	22	23	...	...	...	...	...	...
...	...	...	...	...	...	...	...	...	...
58	...	17	41	...	...	...	...	...	...
67	...	25	42	...	...	...	...	...	...
453	...	156	297	...	...	...	...	...	...
5	...	2	3	...	...	...	...	...	...
...	...	...	...	...	...	...	...	...	...
108	...	35	73	...	...	...	...	...	...
21	...	7	14	...	...	...	...	...	...
...	...	...	...	...	...	...	...	...	...
7	...	1	6	...	...	...	...	...	...
33	...	18	15	...	...	...	...	...	...
...	...	...	...	...	...	...	...	...	...

Mysore

Class.	Group.	Caste, &c. and sub-divisions.	Religion.	All Ages. Total.	Single.	Married.	Widowed.	Civil condition not stated.
A.—Agricultural.—(Continued.)	1. Military and Dominant.	Kshatriya. — Kshatriya	Hindu.	1,827	984	768	75	...
		Kshatriya. — do	Sikh.	12	6	5	1	...
		Kshatriya. — Kumárapatta	Hindu.	...	...	...	...	...
		Kshatriya. — Rájapindé	,,	634	357	255	22	...
		Kshatriya. — Kodagı (Coorgs)	,,	...	...	...	...	...
		Kshatriya. — Rájpút	,,	930	498	395	37	...
		Maráta	,,	3,893	2,039	1,701	153	...
		Ráchévár & Raṇagára	,,	613	327	269	17	...
		Total Group 1		*7,909*	*4,211*	*3,393*	*305*	...
	2. Other Agricultural. (a) Cultivators.	Lingâyet (Gandamané, &c.)	Hindu.	25,372	13,510	10,844	1,018	...
		Náyar	,,	...	...	...	...	...
		Pálé	,,	78	46	29	3	...
		Tigaḷa	,,	583	310	250	23	...
		Vakkaliga. — Vakkaliga	,,	158,168	82,518	71,811	3,838	1
		Vakkaliga. — Sáda	Jain.	...	...	...	...	...
		Vakkaliga. — Tuḷu	Bramho.	...	...	...	...	...
		Total Group 2(a)		*184,207*	*96,384*	*82,910*	*4,882*	*1*
	4. Forest and Hill Tribes.	I'raliga	Hindu.	...	...	...	...	...
		Koracha	,,	171	97	69	5	...
		Korama	,,	1,880	989	804	87	...
		Kuruba	,,	209	111	91	7	...
		Lambâṇi	,,	528	262	245	21	...
		Uriya	,,	...	...	...	...	...
		Total Group 4		*2,788*	*1,459*	*1,209*	*120*	...
		Total Class A		**194,904**	**102,054**	**87,542**	**5,307**	**1**
B.—Professional.—(Continued.)	5. Priests.	Bramhaṇ. — A'ruvélu	Hindu.	859	412	371	76	...
		Bramhaṇ. — A'ruvélu Niyógi	,,	...	...	...	...	...
		Bramhaṇ. — Aravattu Vakkalu	,,	442	244	167	31	...
		Bramhaṇ. — Babbúr Kammé	,,	951	507	365	79	...
		Bramhaṇ. — Baḍaga Náḍu	,,	1,660	891	654	115	...
		Bramhaṇ. — Brihachcharaṇa	,,	185	102	67	16	...
		Bramhaṇ. — Chitpávan	,,	...	...	...	...	...
		Bramhaṇ. — Dés'ast'h	,,	1,748	948	687	113	...
		Bramhaṇ. — Dráviḍa	,,	738	398	276	64	...
		Bramhaṇ. — Guzaráti	,,	...	...	...	...	...
		Bramhaṇ. — Gauḍa		600	314	224	62	...
		Bramhaṇ. — Haḷé Kannaḍiga		2,762	1,439	1,199	124	...
		Bramhaṇ. — Havika	,,	...	...	...	...	...

TABLE E.—(*Continued.*)

District.

Males.

0 to 9.					10 to 14.				
Total.	Single.	Married.	Widowed.	Civil condition not stated.	Total.	Single.	Married.	Widowed.	Civil condition not stated.
518	518	...	...	...	144	144	...	...	...
3	3	...	...	...	2	2	...	...	...
...		...	...	...	..	...	...	...	...
182	182	...	...	...	57	57	...	...	...
...		...	..	...	...	...	...	...	...
257	257	...	...	...	77	77	...	...	...
1,117	1,117	...	...	...	314	311	3	...	...
186	186	...	...	...	52	52	...	...	...
2,263	*2,263*	...	...	...	*646*	*643*	*3*	...	...
6,854	6,854	...	...	...	2,908	2,900	8	...	...
...	...	...	...	...	...	...	...	...	...
24	24	...	...	...	6	6	...	...	...
165	165	...	...	...	49	49	...	...	...
44,983	44,915	68	...	...	17,439	16,145	1,294	...	...
...	...	...	...	...	...	...		...	...
...	...		...	...	...	...	...	...	...
52,240	*51,958*	*68*	...	...	*20,402*	*19,100*	*1,302*	...	...
...	...	...	...	...	...	...	...	...	...
50	50	...	...	...	15	15	...	...	...
523	523	...	...	...	156	156		...	...
55	55	...	...	...	17	17	...	...	...
136	136	...	...	...	44	44	...	...	...
		...	...	...	...	...	...	...	...
761	*761*	...	...	...	*232*	*232*	...	...	...
55,053	**54,985**	**63**	...	...	**21,280**	**19,975**	**1,305**	...	...
228	222	6	...	...	113	80	33	...	...
...	...	...	..	...	...	...	...	...	...
161	160	1	...	...	33	31	2	...	...
343	335	7	...	...	98	61	37	1	...
647	634	12	1		233	83	18	1	...
58	58	...	...	...	13	13	...	...	...
...	...		...	...	...	...	...	...	...
564	552	11	1	...	169	115	52	2	...
248	242	6	...	...	78	50	28	...	...
...	...	...	...	...	...	...	...	...	...
192	192	...	...	...	38	38	...	...	...
802	784	18	1	...	300	236	61	3	...
...	...	...	...	...	...	...	..	...	...

Mysore

Class.	Group.	Caste, &c. and sub-division.	Religion.	15 to 39. Total.	Single.	Married.	Widowed.	Civil condition not stated.
A.—Agricultural.—(Continued.)	1. Military and Dominant.	Kshatriya.—Kshatriya	Hindu.	819	305	497	17	...
		do	Sikh.	4	1	3	...	...
		Kumárapaṭṭa	Hindú.	...	...	...	...	...
		Rájapiṇḍé	,,	282	115	163	4	...
		Koḍaga (Coorgs)	,,	...	...	...	...	...
		Rájput	,,	405	156	242	7	...
		Maráṭa	,,	1,708	593	1,079	36	...
		Ráchévár & Raṇgára	,,	253	85	165	3	...
		Total Group 1		*3,471*	*1,255*	*2,149*	*67*	...
	2. Agricultural. (a) Cultivators.	Lingáyet (Gandamané, &c.)	Hindu.	10,255	3,668	6,364	223	...
		Náyar	,,	...	...	...	...	...
		Piḷḷé	,,	33	15	18	...	...
		Tigaḷa	,,	249	95	151	3	...
		Vakkaligá.—Vakkaliga	,,	56,894	20,327	36,258	309	...
		Sáda	Jain.	...	...	...	...	...
		Tuḷu	Brumho.	...	...	...	...	...
		Total Group 2(a)		*67,431*	*24,105*	*42,791*	*535*	...
	4. Forest and Hill Tribes.	U'rliga	Hindu.	...	...	...	...	...
		Koracha	,,	75	31	43	1	...
		Korama	,,	860	303	538	19	...
		Kuruba	,,	89	33	56	...	...
		Lambáṇi	,,	233	79	150	4	...
		Uriya	,,	...	...	...	...	...
		Total Group 4		*1,257*	*446*	*787*	*24*	...
		Total Class A		**72,159**	**25,806**	**45,727**	**626**	...
B.—Professional.—(Continued).	5. Priests.	Brahmo.—A'ruvélu	Hindu.	319	102	204	13	...
		A'ruvélu Niyógi	,,	...	...	...	...	...
		Aravattu Vakkalu	,,	166	48	113	5	...
		Babbúr Kammé	,,	320	101	197	22	...
		Baḍaga Náḍu	,,	561	162	366	33	...
		Brihachcharaṇa	,,	77	31	42	4	...
		Chitpávan	,,	...	...	...	...	...
		Dés'ast'h	,,	698	276	390	32	...
		Dráviḍa	,,	268	99	148	21	...
		Guzaráti	,,	...	...	...	...	...
		Gauḍa	,,	237	79	138	20	...
		Haḷé Kannaḍiga	,,	1,111	416	672	23	...
		Havíka	,,	...	...	...	...	...

TABLE E.—(*Continued.*)

District.

Males.

40 and over.					Age not stated.				
Total	Single.	Married.	Widowed.	Civil condition not stated.	Total.	Single.	Married.	Widowed.	Civil condition not stated.
346	17	271	58	...	...	...	...	...	...
6	...	2	1	...	...	...	...	...	...
...	...	...	...	...	...	...	...	...	...
113	3	92	18	...	...	...	...	...	...
...	...	...	...	...	...	...	...	...	...
191	8	153	30	...	...	...	...	...	...
754	18	619	117	...	...	...	...	...	...
122	4	104	14	...	...	...	...	...	...
1,529	*50*	*1,241*	*238*	...	...	...	...	...	...
5,355	88	4,472	795	...	...	...	...	...	...
...	...	...	...	...	...	...	...	...	...
15	1	11	3	...	...	...	...	...	...
126	1	105	20	...	...	...	...	...	...
38,812	1,104	34,184	3,524	...	40	27	7	5	1
...	...	...	...	...	...	...	...	...	...
...	...	...	...	...	...	...	...	...	...
44,308	*1,194*	*38,772*	*4,342*	...	*40*	*27*	*7*	*5*	*1*
...	...	...	...	...	...	...	...	...	...
31	1	26	4	...	...	...	...	...	...
341	7	266	68	...	...	...	...	...	...
48	6	35	7	...	...	...	...	...	...
115	3	95	17	...	...	...	...	...	...
...	...	...	...	...	...	...	...	...	...
535	*17*	*422*	*96*	...	...	...	...	...	...
46,372	**1,261**	**40,435**	**4,676**	...	**40**	**27**	**7**	**5**	**1**
199	8	128	63	...	...	...	...	...	...
...	...	...	...	...	...	...	...	...	...
82	5	51	26	...	...	...	...	...	...
190	9	125	56	...	...	...	...	...	...
320	12	228	80	...	...	...	...	...	...
37	...	25	12	...	...	...	...	...	...
...	...	...	...	...	...	...	...	...	...
317	5	234	78	...	...	...	...	...	...
144	7	94	43	...	...	...	...	...	...
...	...	...	...	...	...	...	...	...	...
133	5	86	42	...	...	...	...	...	...
549	7	445	97	...	...	...	...	...	...
...	...	...	...	...	...	...	...	...	...

Mysore

Class.	Group.	Caste, &c. and sub-division.	Religion.	All Ages. Total.	Single.	Married.	Widowed.	Civil condition not stated.
A.—Agricultural.—(*Continued.*)	1. Military and Dominant.	Kshatriya. — Kshatriya ...	Hindu.	*1,888	704	799	385	...
		Kshatriya. — do. ...	Sikh.	15	3	6	6	...
		Kshatriya. — Kumárapatta ...	Hindu.	...	...	...	...	...
		Kshatriya. — Rájapindé ...	,,	681	261	294	126	...
		Kshatriya. — Kodaga (Coorgs) ...	,,	...	...	...	...	...
		Kshatriya. — Rájpút ...	,,	881	313	387	181	...
		Maráta ...	,,	3,927	1,407	1,724	796	...
		Ráchévár & Ravagira ...	,,	700	299	293	108	...
		Total Group 1		8,092	2,987	3,503	1,602	...
	2. Other Agricultural. (*a*) Cultivators.	Lingáyet (Gandamane, &c.) ...	Hindu	26,892	9,884	11,259	5,749	...
		Náyar ...	,,	...	...	...	...	...
		Pille ...	,,	76	25	34	17	...
		Tigala ...	,,	633	227	227	120	...
		Vakkaliga. — Vakkaliga ...	,,	167,359	50,746	81,514	35,127	2
		Vakkaliga. — Sáda ...	Jain.	...	...	...	...	...
		Vakkaliga. — Tulu ...	Brahmo.	...	...	...	...	...
		Total Group 2(a)		194,990	60,882	93,084	41,022	2
	4. Forest and Hill tribes.	Iraliga ...	Hindu.	...	...	...	...	...
		Koracha ...	,,	104	52	77	35	...
		Korama ...	,,	1,954	695	823	436	...
		Kuruba ...	,,	191	61	88	42	...
		Lambáni ...	,,	556	207	253	96	...
		Uriya ...	,,	...	...	...	...	...
		Total Group 4		2,865	1,015	1,241	609	...
		Total Class A		**205,947**	**64,084**	**97,828**	**43,233**	**2**
B.—Professional.—(*Continued.*)	5. Priests.	Bráhman. — A'ruvelu ...	Hindu.	888	273	387	228	...
		Bráhman. — A'ruvélu Niyógi ...	,,	...	...	...	...	...
		Bráhman. — Aravattu Vakkalu ...	,,	445	150	183	112	...
		Bráhman. — Babbúr Kámmé ...	,,	1,036	342	427	267	...
		Bráhman. — Badaga Nádu ...	,,	1,638	566	685	387	...
		Bráhman. — Brihachcharana ...	,,	164	60	67	37	...
		Bráhman. — Chitpávan ...	,,	...	...	...	...	...
		Bráhman. — Dés'ast'h ...	,,	1,860	708	719	433	...
		Bráhman. — Drávida ...	,,	741	267	289	185	...
		Bráhman. — Gúzaráti ...	,,	...	...	...	...	...
		Bráhman. — Gauda ...	,,	582	198	227	157	...
		Bráhman. — Halé Kannadiga ...	,,	2,818	917	1,220	681	...
		Bráhman. — Havika ...	,,	...	...	...	...	...

TABLE E.—(Continued.)

District.

Females.

0 to 9. Total.	Single.	Married.	Widowed.	Civil condition not stated.	10 to 14. Total.	Single.	Married.	Widowed.	Civil condition not stated.
538	529	9	...	...	192	138	54	...	...
3	3	...	...	...	...	...	...	...	...
...	...	...	...	...	...	...	...	...	...
167	165	2	...	...	92	76	16	...	...
...	...	...	...	...	...	...	...	...	...
236	233	3	...	...	67	54	13	...	...
1,147	1,127	20	..	...	335	211	124	...	...
250	249	1	...	...	57	38	19	...	...
2,341	*2,306*	*35*	...	..	*743*	*517*	*226*	...	...
7,462	7,321	141	...	...	2,185	1,710	475	...	...
...	...	...	...	...	...	...	...	...	...
14	14	...	...	...	9	6	3	...	...
168	168	...	...	...	60	51	9	...	...
44,619	41,981	2,613	25	...	12,715	5,462	6,990	263	...
...	...	...	...	...	...	...	...	...	...
...	...	...	...	...	...	...	...	...	...
52,263	*49,484*	*2,754*	*25*	...	*14,960*	*7,229*	*7,477*	*263*	...
...	...	...	...	...	...	...	...	...	...
36	36	...	...	...	14	12	2	...	...
549	543	6	...	...	182	117	65	...	...
45	45	...	...	...	19	12	7	...	...
162	162	...	...	...	43	38	5	...	...
...	...	...	...	..	...	...	...	...	...
792	*786*	*6*	...	...	*258*	*179*	*79*	...	...
55,396	**52,576**	**2,795**	**25**	...	**15,970**	**7,925**	**7,782**	**263**	...
242	232	10	...	...	87	41	45	1	...
...	...	..	...	...	...	...	...	..	...
139	135	4	...	...	44	15	29	...	...
310	295	11	4	...	110	47	51	12	...
505	490	12	3	...	151	76	61	14	...
55	52	3	...	...	18	8	10	...	...
...	...	...	...	...	...	...	...	...	...
656	617	33	6	...	206	91	97	18	...
239	219	20	...	...	84	48	34	2	...
...	...	...	...	...	...	..	...	...	...
171	163	8	...	...	59	33	22	2	...
847	809	32	6	...	234	108	103	23	...
...	...	...	...	...	...	...	...	...	...

Class.	Group.	Caste and Religion.			15 to 39.				
			Caste, &c. and sub-division.	Religion.	Total.	Single.	Married.	Widowed.	Civil condition not stated.
A.—Agricultural—(Continued.)	1. Military and Dominant.	Kshatriya.	Kshatriya	Hindu.	723	37	576	110	...
			do	Sikh.	5	..	5	...	...
			Komárapatta	Hindu.	...	...	...	...	...
			Rájapindé	,,	261	20	204	37	...
			Kodaga (Coorgs)	,,	...	...	...	...	...
			Rájpút	,,	317	26	271	50	...
		Maráta		,,	1,459	64	1,112	283	...
		Ráchévár & Rayagára		,,	223	12	180	31	...
		Total Group 1			*3,018*	*159*	*2,348*	*511*	...
	2. Other Agricultural. (a) Cultivators.	Lingáyet (Gaudamané, &c.)		,,	10,328	798	8,129	1,410	...
		Náyar		,,	...	...	...	...	...
		Pille		,,	34	5	25	4	...
		Tigala		,,	235	8	188	39	...
		Vakkaliga.	Vakkaliga	,,	73,572	2,481	62,282	8,809	...
			Sáda	Jain.	..	...	...	...	...
			Tulu	Bramho.	...	...	...	...	...
		Total Group 2(a)			*84,169*	*3,292*	*70,615*	*10,262*	...
	4. Forest and Hill Tribes.	Uraliga		,,	...	...	...	...	...
		Koracha		,,	67	4	54	9	..
		Korama		,,	723	35	584	104	...
		Kuruba		,,	73	4	59	10	...
		Lambáni		,,	213	2	180	29	...
		Uriya		,,	...	...	...	...	...
		Total Group 4			*1,076*	*50*	*877*	*149*	...
		Total Class A			**88,263**	**3,501**	**73,840**	**10,922**	...
B.—Professional—(Continued.)	5. Priests.	Bráhman.	A'ruvelu	,,	317	...	259	58	...
			A'ruvélu Niyógi	,,	...	...	...	...	...
			Aravatta Vakkalu	,,	166	...	127	39	...
			Babbúr Kamme	,,	377	...	295	82	...
			Badaga Nádu	,,	629	...	495	134	...
			Brihachcharana	,,	54	...	42	12	...
			Chitpaván	,,	...	...	...	...	...
			Desást'h	,,	622	...	461	161	...
			Drávida	,,	261	...	191	70	...
			Guzaráti	,,	...	...	...	...	...
			Gauda	,,	209	...	157	52	...
			Hale Kannadiga	,,	994	...	794	200	...
			Havika	,,	...	...	...	...	...

TABLE E.—(*Continued.*)

District.

Females.

45 and over. Total.	Single.	Married.	Widowed.	Civil condition not stated.	Age not stated. Total.	Single.	Married.	Widowed.	Civil condition not stated.
435	...	160	275	...	...	...	...	...	...
7	...	1	6	...	...	...	...	...	...
...	...	...	...	...	...	...	...	...	...
161	...	72	89	...	...	...	...	...	...
...	...	...	...	...	...	...	...	...	...
231	...	100	131	...	...	...	...	...	...
986	5	468	513	...	...	...	...	...	...
170	...	93	77	...	...	...	...	...	...
1,990	*5*	*894*	*1,091*	...	...	...	...	...	...
6,917	55	2,523	4,339	...	...	...	...	...	...
...	...	...	...	...	...	...	...	...	...
19	...	6	13	...	...	...	...	...	...
170	...	80	90	...	...	...	...	...	...
36,432	791	9,622	26,019	...	51	31	7	11	2
...	...	...	...	...	...	...	...	...	...
...	...	...	...	...	...	...	...	...	...
43,538	*846*	*12,231*	*30,461*	...	*51*	*31*	*7*	*11*	*2*
...	...	...	...	...	...	...	...	...	...
47	...	21	26	...	...	...	...	...	...
500	...	168	332	...	...	...	...	...	...
54	...	22	32	...	...	...	...	...	...
138	...	68	70	...	...	...	...	...	...
...	...	...	...	...	...	...	...	...	...
739	...	*279*	*460*	...	...	...	...	...	...
46,267	**851**	**13,404**	**32,012**	...	**51**	**31**	**7**	**11**	**2**
242	...	73	169	...	...	...	...	...	...
...	...	...	...	...	...	...	...	...	...
96	...	23	73	...	...	...	...	...	...
239	...	70	169	...	...	...	...	...	...
353	...	117	236	...	...	...	...	...	...
37	...	12	25	...	...	...	...	...	...
...	...	...	...	...	...	...	...	...	...
376	...	128	248	...	...	...	...	...	...
187	...	41	113	...	...	...	...	...	...
...	...	...	...	...	...	...	...	...	...
143	...	40	103	...	...	...	...	...	...
743	...	291	452	...	...	...	...	...	...
...	...	...	...	...	...	...	...	...	...

Hassan

Class.	Group.	Caste, &c. and sub-division.	Religion.	All Ages. Total.	Single.	Married.	Widowed.	Civil condition not stated.
A.—Agricultural.—(*Continued.*)	1. Military and Dominant.	Kshatriya. — Kshatriya	Hindu.	644	352	239	53	...
		do.	Sikh.	...	...	...	...	...
		Kumārapatta	Hindu.	...	...	...	...	...
		Rājapindé	,,	...	...	...	...	...
		Kodaga (Coorgs)	,,	...	...	...	...	...
		Rājapūt	,,	178	100	72	6	...
		Marāṭa	,,	1,116	573	451	92	...
		Rāchēvār and Rāṇagāra	,,	227	123	89	15	...
		Total Group 1	...	*2,165*	*1,148*	*851*	*166*	...
	2. Other Agricultural. (*a*) Cultivators.	Lingāyet, (Gaudmané, &c.)	,,	9,609	5,268	3,839	442	...
		Nāyar	,,	...	...	...	...	...
		Pillé	,,	8	4	4	...	...
		Tigaḷa	,,	374	228	123	23	...
		Vakkaliga. — Vakkaliga	,,	83,436	50,216	31,313	1,853	24
		Sāda	Jain.	...	...	...	...	...
		Tuḷu	Bramho.	...	...	...	...	...
		Total Group 2 (a)	...	*93,427*	*55,716*	*35,279*	*2,318*	*24*
	4. Forest and Hill Tribes.	U'raliga	Hindu.	1	1	...	...	...
		Koracha	,,	103	57	37	9	...
		Korama	,,	618	347	221	50	...
		Kuruba	,,	26	16	6	4	...
		Lambāṇi	,,	1,451	816	569	66	...
		Uriya	,,	...	...	...	...	...
		Total Group 4	...	*2,199*	*1,237*	*833*	*129*	...
		Total Class A		**97,791**	**58,131**	**37,023**	**2,613**	**24**
B.—Professional.—(*Continued.*)	E.? Priests.	Brāhman. — A'ruvēlu	Hindu	49	22	22	5	...
		A'ruvēlu Niyōgi	,,	...	...	...	...	...
		Aravattu Vakkalu	,,	63	32	27	4	...
		Babbūr Kammé	,,	1,168	597	476	95	...
		Baḍaga Nāḍu	,,	450	219	194	37	...
		Brāhmacharaṇa	,,	10	6	4	...	...
		Chitapāvan	,,	...	...	...	...	...
		Dēśast'h	,,	216	96	103	17	...
		Drāviḍa	,,	310	127	157	26	...
		Guzarāti	,,	...	...	...	...	...
		Gauḍa	,,	33	13	15	5	...
		Haḷé Karnāḍiga	,,	362	175	148	39	...
		Havika	,,	...	...	...	...	...

TABLE E.—(*Continued.*)

District.

Males.

0 to 9					10 to 14				
Total.	Single.	Married.	Widowed.	Civil condition not stated.	Total.	Single.	Married.	Widowed.	Civil condition not stated.
175	175	...	...	...	95	88	7	...	...
...	...	...	...	...	...	...	...	...	...
...	...	...	...	...	...	...	...	...	...
...	...	...	...	...	...	...	...	...	...
...	...	...	...	...	...	...	...	...	...
54	54	...	...	...	16	16	...	...	...
302	302	...	...	...	141	132	7	2	...
55	55	...	...	...	24	24	...	...	...
586	*586*	...	...	...	*270*	*260*	*14*	2	...
2,375	2,373	2	...	...	1,356	1,350	6	...	...
...	...	...	...	...	...	...	...	...	...
2	2	...	...	...	1	1	...	...	...
99	99	...	...	...	42	42	...	...	...
25,831	25,823	8	...	...	7,646	7,599	45	2	...
...	...	...	...	...	...	...	...	...	...
...	...	...	...	...	...	...	...	...	...
28,307	*28,297*	*10*	...	...	*9,045*	*8,992*	*51*	2	...
...	...	...	...	...	...	...	...	...	...
26	26	...	...	...	14	14	...	...	...
206	206	...	...	...	63	63	...	...	...
6	6	...	...	...	4	4	...	...	...
484	484	...	...	...	115	114	1	...	...
	...	...	...	...	...	...	...	...	...
722	*722*	...	...	...	*196*	*195*	*1*	...	...
29,695	**29,605**	**10**	...	...	**9,517**	**9,447**	**66**	**4**	...
14	14	...	...	...	6	6	...	...	...
...	...	...	...	...	...	...	...	...	...
18	18	...	...	...	6	5	1	...	...
423	423	...	...	...	86	81	5	...	...
140	140	...	...	...	48	42	6	...	...
2	2	...	...	...	1	1	...	...	...
...	...	...	...	...	...	...	...	...	...
58	58	...	...	...	15	15	...	...	...
80	80	...	...	...	34	30	4	...	...
...	...	...	...	...	...	...	...	...	...
9	9	...	...	...	2	1	1	...	...
96	96	...	...	...	49	49	...	...	...
...	...	...	...	...	...	...	...	...	...

Hassan

Class.	Group.	Caste, &c. and sub-division.	Religion.	15 to 39 Total.	Single.	Married.	Widowed.	Civil condition not stated.
A.—Agricultural.—(Continued.)	1. Military and Dominant.	Kshatriya. { Kshatriya ...	Hindu.	264	85	159	20	...
		do ...	Sikh.	...	...	...	...	...
		Kumárapatta ...	Hindu.	...	...	...	...	...
		Rájpindé ...	,,	...	...	...	...	...
		Kodaga (Coorgs) ...	,,	...	...	...	...	...
		Rájput ...	,,	71	30	41	...	
		Maráta ...	,,	436	131	284	21	...
		Ráchevar and Ráṇagara ...	,,	103	43	57	3	...
		Total Group 1...	... ...	*871*	*289*	*541*	*41*	...
	2. Other Agricultural. (a) Cultivators.	Lingáyet (Gaudamané, &c.) ...	,,	3,826	1,483	2,238	105	...
		Nayar ...	,,		...	...	...	...
		Pillai ...	,,	5	1	4		...
		Tigala ...	,,	157	84	72	1	...
		Vakkaliga { Vakkaliga ...	,,	33,891	16,428	16,978	485	...
		[illegible] ...	Jain.	...	...	...	...	...
		Tulu ...	Brahmo.	...	...	...	...	...
		Total Group 2 (a)...	... ...	*37,882*	*17,996*	*19,292*	*594*	...
	4. Forest and Hill Tribes.	Iruliga ...	Hindu.	1	1	...	...	...
		Koracha ...	,,	40	16	21	3	...
		Korama ...	,,	222	66	138	18	...
		Kuruba ...	,,	12	6	5	1	
		Lambâni ...	,,	529	207	305	17	...
		Uriya ...	,,	...	...	...	...	...
		Total Group 4...	... ...	*804*	*296*	*469*	*39*	...
		Total Class A...		**39,560**	**18,581**	**20,302**	**677**	...
B.—Professional.—(Continued.)	5. Priests.	Bráhman. { A'rádhya ...	Hindu.	18	2	15	1	...
		A'ruvela Niyógi ...	,,	...	...	...	...	...
		Aravattu Vakkalu ...	,,	27	9	18	...	...
		Babbúr Kamme ...	,,	441	91	330	20	...
		Badaga Nádu ...	,,	180	36	138	6	...
		Brihachcharaṇa ...	,,	3	3	...	...	...
		Chitapávan ...	,,	...	...	...	...	...
		Dés'asth ...	,,	90	22	63	5	...
		Drávida ...	,,	118	17	95	6	...
		Guzaráti ...	,,	...	...	...	...	...
		Gauda ...	,,	12	3	8	1	...
		Halé Karnátaka ...	,,	143	30	108	5	...
		Hoysala ...	,,	...	...	...	...	...

TABLE E.—(Continued.)

District.

Males.

40 and over.					Age not stated.				
Total.	Single.	Married.	Widowed.	Civil condition not stated.	Total.	Single.	Married.	Widowed.	Civil condition not stated.
110	4	73	33	...	...	...	...	...	...
...	..	...	..	...	...	..	...	...	...
.	...	...	...	...	...	.	...	...	...
...	...	...	...	...	...	...	...	...	...
...	...	..	.	...	...	.	...	...	...
37	...	31	6	...	...	...	...	...	...
237	8	160	69	...	...	...	...	...	...
45	1	32	12	...	...	...	...	...	...
429	*13*	*296*	*120*		...		...		...
2,052	62	1,653	337	...	...	...	...	...	...
...	...	...	...	...	...	...	...	...	...
...	...	...		...	...	...	...	...	...
76	3	51	22	...	...	..	...	...	...
16,014	376	14,276	1,362	...	51	20	6	1	24
...	...	...	...	...	...	...	...	...	...
...	...	...	...	.	...	...	...	...	...
18,142	*441*	*15,980*	*1,721*	...	*51*	*20*	*6*	*1*	*24*
...		...	...	...	...	...	...	...	...
23	1	16	6	..		...	...	...	.
127	12	83	32	...	...	...	...	...	...
4	...	1	3	...	...	...	...	...	...
323	11	263	49	...	...	...	...	...	...
...	...	.	...	...	...	...	...	...	...
477	*24*	*363*	*90*	...	...	...	...	...	...
19,048	**478**	**16,639**	**1,931**	...	**51**	**20**	**6**	**1**	**24**
11	...	7	4	...	...	...	...	...	...
...	..	...	..	...	...	...	...	...	...
12	...	8	4	...	...	...	...	...	...
218	2	141	75	...	...	...	...	...	...
82	1	50	31	...	...	...	...	...	...
4	...	4	...	...	...	...	...	...	...
...	...	...	...	...	...	...	...	...	...
53	1	40	12	...	...	...	...	...	...
78	...	58	20	...	...	...	...	...	...
...	...	...	...	...	...	...	...	...	...
10	...	6	4	...	...	...	...	...	...
74	...	40	34	...	...	...	...	...	...
...	...	...	...	...	...	...	...	...	...

Hassan

Class.	Group.	Caste, &c. and sub-division.	Religion.	All Ages. Total.	Single.	Married.	Widowed.	Civil condition not stated.
A.—Agricultural.—(Continued.)	1. Military and Dominant.	Kshatriya. — Kshatriya ...	Hindu.	703	242	308	153	...
		Kshatriya. — Do ...	Sikh	...	...	...	...	...
		Kshatriya. — Kumárapatta ...	Hindu.	...	...	...	...	...
		Kshatriya. — Rájpindé ...	,,	...	...	...	...	...
		Kshatriya. — Kodaga (Coorgs) ...	,,	...	...	...	...	...
		Kshatriya. — Rájpút ...	,,	186	81	76	29	...
		Maráṭa	,,	1,055	390	431	234	...
		Ráchévár and Ranagára ...	,,	259	113	102	44	...
		Total Group 1 ...	... ...	2,203	826	917	460	...
	2. Other Agricultural. (a) Cultivators.	Lingáyet (Gaudamané, &c.) ...	,,	9,651	4,119	3,879	1,653	...
		Ṇáyar	,,	...	...	...	...	...
		Pillé	,,	11	4	5	2	...
		Tigaḷa	,,	340	153	131	56	...
		Vakkaliga. — Vakkaliga ...	,,	87,887	34,662	32,956	20,265	4
		Vakkaliga. — Sádu	Jain	...	...	...	...	...
		Vakkaliga. — Túlu	Brahmo.	...	...	...	...	...
		Total Group 2 (a) ...	... ...	97,889	38,938	36,971	21,976	4
	4. Forest and Hill Tribes.	I'ruliga	Hindu	...	...	...	...	...
		Koracha	,,	102	40	45	17	...
		Korama	,,	614	262	258	94	...
		Kuruba	,,	19	6	6	7	...
		Lambáṇi	,,	1,395	651	598	146	...
		Uriya	,,	...	...	...	...	...
		Total Group 4 ...	... ...	2,130	959	907	264	...
		Total Class A ...		**102,222**	**40,723**	**38,795**	**22,700**	**4**
B.—Professional.—(Continued.)	5. Priests.	Brámhaṇ. — A'ruvélu	Hindu.	52	15	25	12	...
		Brámhaṇ. — A'ruvélu Niyógi ...	,,	...	...	...	...	...
		Brámhaṇ. — Aruvattu Vakkalu ...	,,	76	15	41	20	...
		Brámhaṇ. — Babbúr Kammé ...	,,	1,200	404	546	250	...
		Brámhaṇ. — Badaga Nádu ...	,,	413	120	212	81	...
		Brámhaṇ. — Brihachcharaṇa ...	,,	17	5	9	3	...
		Brámhaṇ. — Chitapávan ...	,,	...	...	...	...	...
		Brámhaṇ. — Dés'ast'h ...	,,	225	57	120	48	...
		Brámhaṇ. — Drávida ...	,,	305	81	158	66	...
		Brámhaṇ. — Guzaráti ...	,,	...	...	...	...	...
		Brámhaṇ. — Gauda	,,	29	11	14	4	...
		Brámhaṇ. — Haḷé Kannaḍiga ...	,,	379	131	173	75	...
		Brámhaṇ. — Havika	,,	...	...	...	...	...

TABLE E.—(*Continued.*)

District.

Females.

0 to 9					10 to 14				
Total.	Single.	Married.	Widowed.	Civil condition not stated.	Total.	Single.	Married.	Widowed.	Civil condition not stated.
159	157	2	...	...	107	62	41	4	...
...	...	...	...	...	...	...	...	...	...
...	...	...	...	...	...	...	...	...	...
...	...	...	...	...	...	...	...	...	...
...	...	...	...	...	...	...	...	...	...
60	60	...	...	...	21	16	5	...	...
277	274	3	...	...	140	99	41	...	...
69	69	...	...	...	36	33	3	...	...
565	*560*	*5*	...	...	*304*	*210*	*90*	*4*	...
2,856	2,840	16	...	...	1,144	963	171	10	...
...	...	...	...	...	...	...	...	...	...
3	3	...	...	...	1	1	...	...	...
94	94	...	...	...	44	42	1	1	...
25,618	25,461	152	5	...	7,224	6,155	1,045	24	...
...	...	...	...	...	...	...	...	...	...
...	...	...	...	...	...	...	...	...	...
28,571	*28,398*	*168*	*5*	...	*8,413*	*7,161*	*1,217*	*35*	...
...	...	...	...	...	...	...	...	...	...
24	24	...	...	...	12	12	...	...	...
102	102	...	...	...	55	53	2	...	...
2	2	...	...	...	1	1	...	...	...
496	496	...	...	...	124	114	10	...	...
...	...	...	...	...	...	...	...	...	...
714	*714*	...	...	...	*192*	*180*	*12*	...	...
29,850	**29,672**	**173**	**5**	...	**8,909**	**7,551**	**6**	**1**	**4**
15	15	...	...	...	3	...	3	...	...
...	...	...	...	...	...	...	...	...	...
14	13	1	...	...	6	2	4	...	...
377	367	10	...	...	101	37	60	4	...
103	100	3	...	...	39	20	18	1	...
5	5	...	...	...	1	...	1	...	...
...	...	...	...	...	...	...	...	...	...
51	49	2	...	...	30	8	21	1	...
82	74	8	...	...	31	7	24	...	...
...	...	...	...	...	...	...	...	...	...
10	10	...	...	...	3	1	2	...	...
85	85	...	...	...	46	46	...	...	...
...	...	...	...	...	...	...	...	...	...

Hassan

Class.	Group.	Caste, &c. and sub-division.	Religion.	15 to 39 Total.	Single.	Married.	Widowed.	Civil condition not stated.
A.—Agricultural—(Continued.)	1. Military and Dominant.	Kshatriya. Kshatriya ...	Hindu.	276	22	201	53	...
		do ...	Sikh.	...	...	...	...	...
		Kumárapatta	Hindu.	...	...	...	...	...
		Rájapindé	,,	...	...	...	...	...
		Kodaga (Coorgs)	,,	...	...	...	...	...
		Rájput ...	,,	65	5	53	7	...
		Maráta	,,	394	16	310	68	...
		Rácbévár and Ranagára	,,	97	11	79	7	...
		Total Group 1...	...	*832*	*54*	*643*	*135*	...
	2. Other Agricultural (a) Cultivators.	Lingáyet. (Gaudamané, &c.)	Hindu.	3,481	308	2,723	450	...
		Náyar	,,	...	...	...	...	...
		Pille	,,	5	...	5	...	...
		Tigala	,,	144	16	110	18	...
		Vakkaliga. Vakkaliga	,,	36,110	2,849	27,737	5,524	...
		Sáda ...	Jain.	...	...	...	...	...
		Tulu ...	Bramho.	...	...	...	...	...
		Total Group 2 (a)......	...	*39,740*	*3,173*	*30,575*	*5,992*	...
	4. Forest and Hill Tribes.	Uraliga	Hindu.	...	...	...	...	...
		Koracha	,,	39	3	32	4	...
		Korama	,,	240	17	202	21	...
		Kuruba	,,	11	3	6	2	...
		Lambáni	,,	546	41	473	32	...
		Uriya	,,	...	...	...	...	...
		Total Group 4...	...	*836*	*64*	*713*	*59*	...
		Total Class A...		**41,408**	**3,291**	**31,931**	**6,186**	...
B.—Professional.—(Continued.)	Priests.	Brámhan. A'ruvélu ...	Hindu.	20	...	17	3	...
		A'ruvélu Niyógi ...	,,	...	...	...	...	...
		Aravattu Vakkalu...	,,	37	...	31	6	...
		Babbúru Kammé ...	,,	477	...	408	69	...
		Badaganádu ...	,,	168	...	152	16	...
		Brihachcharana ...	,,	8	...	7	1	...
		Chitpávan ...	,,	...	...	...	...	...
		Dés'ast'h ...	,,	87	...	71	16	...
		Drávida ...	,,	130	...	104	26	...
		Guzaráti ...	,,	...	...	...	...	...
		Gauda	,,	10	...	10	...	...
		Halé Kannadiga ...	,,	161	...	144	17	...
		Hávika	,,	...	...	...	...	...

TABLE E.—(Continued.)

District.

Females.

40 and over. Total.	Single.	Married.	Widowed.	Civil condition not stated.	Age not stated. Total.	Single.	Married.	Widowed.	Civil condition not stated.
161	1	64	96	...	...	...	...	...	...
	...	...	...	...	...	...	...	...	...
...	...	...	...	...	...	...	...	...	...
...	...	...	...	...	...	...	...	...	...
...	...	...	...	...	...	...	...	...	...
40	...	18	22	...	...	...	...	...	...
244	1	77	166	...	...	...	...	...	...
57	...	20	37	...	...	...	...	...	...
502	*2*	*179*	*321*	...	...	...	...	...	...
2,170	8	969	1,193	...	...	...	...	...	...
...		...	...	...	...	...	...	...	...
2	...	...	2	...	...	...	...	...	...
58	1	20	37	...	...	...	...	...	...
18,905	178	4,016	14,711	...	30	19	6	1	4
...	...	...	...	...	...	...	...	...	...
...	...		...	...	...	...	...	...	...
21,135	*187*	*5,005*	*15,943*	...	*30*	*19*	*6*	*1*	*4*
...	...	...	...	...	...	...	...	...	...
27	1	13	13	...	...	...	...	...	...
127	...	54	73	...	...	...	...	...	...
5	...	..	5	...	...	...	...	...	...
229	...	115	114	...	...	...	...	...	...
	...	...	...	...	...	...	...	...	...
388	*1*	*182*	*205*	...	...	...	...	...	...
22,025	**190**	**5,366**	**16,469**	...	**30**	**19**	**6**	**1**	**4**
14	...	5	9	...	...	...	...	...	...
...	...	...	...	...	...	...	...	...	...
19	...	5	14	...	...	...	...	...	...
245	...	68	177	...	...	...	...	...	...
105	...	39	64	...	...	...	...	...	...
3	...	1	2	...	...	...	...	...	...
...		...	...	...	...	...	...	...	...
57	...	26	31	...	...	...	...	...	...
62	...	22	40	...	...	...	...	...	...
...	...	...	...	...	...	...	...	...	...
6	...	2	4	...	...	...	...	...	...
87	...	29	58	...	...	...	...	...	...
...	...	...	...	...	...	...	...	...	...

Class.	Group.	Caste, &c. and sub-division.	Religion.	All ages. Total.	Single.	Married.	Widowed.	Civil condition not stated.
A.—Agricultural.—(Continued.)	1. Military and Dominant.	Kshatriya.—Kshatriya	Hindu	659	377	253	29	...
		do.	Sikh	...	...	...	...	...
		Kumárapatta	Hindu	...	...	...	...	...
		Rájapindé	,,	10	5	4	1	...
		Kodaga (Coorgs)	,,	...	...	...	...	...
		Rájpút	,,	841	458	324	59	...
		Maráta	,,	5,705	2,941	2,289	475	...
		Rácheváar & Ranagára	,,	5	3	2	...	...
		Total Group 1	...	7,220	3,784	2,872	564	...
	2. Other Agricultural (a) Cultivators.	Lingáyet (Gandamané, &c.)	,,	7,264	3,807	2,721	736	...
		Náyar	,,	...	...	...	...	...
		Pillé	,,	9	6	3	...	...
		Tigala	,,	127	69	51	7	...
		Vakkaliga.—Vakkaliga	,,	70,684	44,188	24,500	1996	...
		Sáda	Jain	...	...	...	...	...
		Tulu	Brahmo	...	...	...	...	...
		Total Group 2(a)	...	78,084	48,070	27,275	2,739	...
	4. Forest and Hill Tribes.	Paraliga	Hindu	...	...	...	...	...
		Koracha	,,	1,193	645	457	91	...
		Korama	,,	1,162	636	448	78	...
		Kuruba	,,	...	...	...	...	...
		Lambáni	,,	7,256	4,352	2,567	337	...
		Uriya	,,	...	...	...	...	...
		Total Group 4	...	9,611	5,633	3,472	506	...
		Total Class A		94,915	57,487	33,619	3,809	...
B.—Professional.—(Continued.)	5. Priests.	Bráhman.—A'ruvélu	Hindu	83	51	23	9	...
		A'ruvélu Niyógi	,,	...	...	...	...	...
		Aravattu Vakkalu	,,	172	89	68	15	...
		Babbúr Kammé	,,	249	125	112	12	...
		Badaga Nádu	,,	1,855	925	707	223	...
		Brihachcharana	,,	...	...	...	...	...
		Chitapávan	,,	1,397	702	537	158	...
		Désasth	,,	1,823	869	725	229	...
		Drávida	,,	1,720	841	666	213	...
		Guzaráti	,,	...	...	...	...	...
		Gauda	,,	136	67	54	15	...
		Halé Kannadiga	,,	192	109	77	6	...
		Havika	,,	1,595	828	612	155	...

TABLE E.—(*Continued.*)

District.

Males.

0 to 9.					10 to 14.				
Total.	Single.	Married.	Widowed.	Civil condition not stated.	Total.	Single.	Married.	Widowed.	Civil condition not stated.
182	182	...	...	...	69	69	...	...	...
...	...	...	...	...	...	...	...	...	...
...	...	...	...	...	...	...	...	...	...
3	3	...	...	...	...	...	...	...	...
...	...	...	...	...	...	...	...	...	...
232	232	...	...	...	116	115	1	...	...
1,167	1,167	...	...	...	702	689	13	...	...
2	2	...	...	...	1	1	...	...	...
1,886	*1,886*	...	...	...	*888*	*874*	*14*	...	...
1,677	1,677	...	...	...	847	812	35	...	...
...	...	...	...	...	...	...	...	...	...
3	3	...	...	...	2	2	...	...	...
31	31	...	...	...	18	18	...	...	...
16,640	16,620	20	...	...	7,276	7,221	52	3	...
...	...	...	...	...	...	...	...	...	...
...	...	...	...	...	...	...	...	...	...
18,351	*18,331*	*20*	...	...	*8,143*	*8,053*	*87*	*3*	...
...	...	...	...	...	...	...	...	...	...
374	374	...	...	...	132	132	...	...	...
324	324	...	...	...	148	145	3	...	...
...	...	...	...	...	...	...	...	...	...
2,305	2,305	...	...	...	859	839	20	...	...
...	...	...	...	...	...	...	...	...	...
3,003	*3,003*	...	...	...	*1,139*	*1,116*	*23*	...	...
23,240	**23,220**	**20**	...	...	**10,170**	**10,043**	**124**	**3**	...
27	27	...	...	...	10	10	...	...	...
...	...	...	...	...	...	...	...	...	...
57	57	...	...	...	17	15	2	...	...
77	77	...	...	...	23	22	1	...	...
503	503	...	...	...	225	201	22	2	...
...	...	...	...	...	...	...	...	...	...
400	400	...	...	...	203	203	...	...	...
491	491	...	...	...	173	151	22	...	...
386	386	...	...	...	224	197	28	1	...
...	...	...	...	...	...	...	...	...	...
26	26	...	...	...	14	14	...	...	...
69	69	...	...	...	23	23	...	...	...
333	329	4	...	...	169	162	7	...	...

Shimoga

Class.	Group.	Caste, &c. and sub-division.	Religion.	15 to 39. Total.	Single.	Married.	Widowed.	Civil condition not stated.
A.—Agricultural.—(Continued.)	1. Military and Dominant.	Kshatriya — Kshatriya ...	Hindu	273	121	146	6	...
		Kshatriya — do ...	Sikh	...	...	...	...	...
		Kshatriya — Kumáraputta ...	Hindu	...	...	...	...	...
		Kshatriya — Rájapindé ...	,,	5	2	3	...	...
		Kshatriya — Kodaga (Coorgs) ...	,,	...	...	...	...	...
		Kshatriya — Rájpút ...	,,	309	104	191	14	...
		Maráṭa	,,	2,366	755	1,452	159	...
		Ráchévár & Ranagára ...	,,	2	...	2	...	...
		Total Group 1.......	... ...	*2,955*	*982*	*1,794*	*179*	...
	2. Other Agricultural. (a) Cultivators.	Lingáyet (Gandamáné, &c.) ...	,,	3,078	1,221	1,628	229	...
		Náyar	,,	...	...	...	...	...
		Pillé	,,	2	1	1	...	...
		Tigaḷa	,,	50	14	36	...	...
		Vakkaliga — Vakkaliga ...	,,	34,468	19,495	14,664	309	...
		Vakkaliga — Sáda	Jain	...	...	...	...	...
		Vakkaliga — Tuḷu	Bramho	...	...	...	...	...
		Total Group 2(a).......	... ...	*37,598*	*20,731*	*16,329*	*538*	...
	4. Forest and Hill Tribes.	I'raliga	Hindu	...	...	...	...	...
		Koracha	,,	438	131	285	22	...
		Korama	,,	450	158	266	26	...
		Kuruba	,,	...	...	...	...	...
		Lambáṇi	,,	2,780	1,158	1,526	96	...
		Uriya	,,	...	...	...	...	...
		Total Group 4.......	... ...	*3,668*	*1,447*	*2,077*	*144*	...
		Total Class A.......		**44,221**	**23,160**	**20,200**	**861**	...
B.—Professional.—(Continued.)	5. Priests.	Brámhan — A'ruvélu ...	Hindu	33	13	17	3	...
		Brámhan — A'ruvélu Niyógi ...	,,	...	...	...	...	...
		Brámhan — Aravattu Vakkalu...	,,	63	17	43	3	...
		Brámhan — Babbúr Kammé ...	,,	100	23	75	2	...
		Brámhan — Baḍaga Náḍu ...	,,	753	216	468	69	...
		Brámhan — Brihachcharaṇa ...	,,	...	...	...	...	...
		Brámhan — Chitupávan ...	,,	530	97	387	46	...
		Brámhan — Dés'ast'h ...	,,	775	221	492	62	...
		Brámhan — Dráviḍa ...	,,	719	248	412	59	...
		Brámhan — Guzaráti ...	,,	...	...	...	...	...
		Brámhan — Gauḍa	,,	69	25	41	3	...
		Brámhan — Haḷé Kannaḍiga ...	,,	68	17	49	2	...
		Brámhan — Havíka ...	,,	690	309	350	31	...

TABLE E.—(*Continued.*)

District.

Males.

40 and over.					Age not stated.				
Total.	Single.	Married.	Widowed.	Civil condition not stated.	Total.	Single.	Married.	Widowed.	Civil condition not stated.
135	5	107	23	...	...	...	...	...	...
...	...	...	...	...	...	...	...	...	...
...	...	...	...	...	...	...	...	...	...
2	...	1	1	...	...	...	...	...	...
...	...	...	...	...	...	...	...	...	...
184	7	132	45	...	...	...	...	...	...
1,170	30	824	316	...	...	...	...	...	...
...	...	...	...	...	...	...	...	...	...
1,491	*42*	*1,064*	*385*	...	...	...	...	...	...
1,662	97	1,058	507	...	...	...	...	...	...
...	...	...	...	...	...	...	...	...	...
2	...	2	...	...	...	...	...	...	...
28	6	15	7	...	...	...	...	...	...
12,293	846	9,764	1,683	...	7	6	...	1	...
...	...	...	...	...	...	...	...	...	...
...	...	...	...	...	...	...	...	...	...
13,985	*949*	*10,839*	*2,197*	...	*7*	*6*	...	*1*	...
...	...	...	...	...	...	...	...	...	...
249	8	172	69	...	...	...	...	...	...
240	9	179	52	...	...	...	...	...	...
...	...	...	...	...	...	...	...	...	...
1,312	50	1,021	241	...	...	...	...	...	...
...	...	...	...	...	...	...	...	...	...
1,801	*67*	*1,372*	*362*	...	...	...	...	...	...
17,277	**1,058**	**13,275**	**2,944**	...	**7**	**6**	...	**1**	...
13	1	6	6	...	...	...	...	...	...
...	...	...	...	...	...	...	...	...	...
35	...	23	12	...	...	...	...	...	...
49	3	36	10	...	...	...	...	...	...
374	5	217	152	...	...	...	...	...	...
...	...	...	...	...	...	...	...	...	...
264	2	150	112	...	...	...	...	...	...
384	6	211	167	...	...	...	...	...	...
391	10	228	153	...	...	...	...	...	...
...	...	...	...	...	...	...	...	...	...
27	2	13	12	...	...	...	...	...	...
32	...	28	4	...	...	...	...	...	...
403	28	251	124	...	...	...	...	...	...

Class.	Group.	Caste, &c. and sub-division.	Religion.	All Ages. Total.	Single.	Married.	Widowed.	Civil condition not stated.
A.—Agricultural.—(Continued.)	1. Military and Dominant.	Kshatriya — Kshatriya	Hindu	546	216	236	94	...
		Kshatriya — do	Sikh	...	...	...	...	...
		Kshatriya — Kumárapatta	Hindu	...	...	...	...	...
		Kshatriya — Rájapindé	,,	14	6	5	3	...
		Kshatriya — Kodaga (Coorgs)	,,	...	...	...	...	...
		Kshatriya — Rájpút	,,	827	310	371	146	...
		Maráṭa	,,	4,910	1,826	2,201	910	...
		Ráchévár & Raṇagára	,,	5	2	3	...	...
		Total Group 1	...	6,332	2,360	2,819	1,153	...
	2. Other Agricultural (a) Cultivators.	Lingáyet (Gaudamané, &c.)	,,	6,694	2,334	3,078	1,282	...
		Náyar	,,	...	...	...	...	...
		Piḷḷé	,,	7	4	3	...	...
		Tigaḷa	,,	70	24	41	5	...
		Vakkaliga — Vakkaliga	,,	61,385	28,181	18,638	17,566	...
		Vakkaliga — Sáda	Jain	...	...	...	...	...
		Vakkaliga — Tuḷu	Bramho	...	...	...	...	...
		Total Group 2(a)	...	71,156	30,543	21,760	18,853	...
	4. Forest and Hill Tribes.	I'raliga	Hindu	...	...	...	...	...
		Koracha	,,	914	354	433	127	...
		Korama	,,	1,129	404	525	200	...
		Kuruba	,,	...	...	...	...	...
		Lambáṇi	,,	6,871	2,867	2,946	1,058	...
		Uriya	,,	...	...	...	...	...
		Total Group 4	...	8,914	3,625	3,904	1,385	...
		Total Class A		**86,402**	**36,528**	**28,483**	**21,391**	...
B.—Professional.—(Continued.)	5. Priests.	Brámhaṇ — A'ruvélu	Hindu	47	14	22	11	...
		Brámhaṇ — A'ruvélu Niyógi	,,	...	...	...	...	...
		Brámhaṇ — Aravattu Vakkalu	,,	181	64	86	31	...
		Brámhaṇ — Babbúr Kammé	,,	228	72	107	49	...
		Brámhaṇ — Baḍaga Náḍu	,,	1,667	535	791	341	...
		Brámhaṇ — Brihachcharaṇa	,,	...	...	...	...	...
		Brámhaṇ — Chitapávan	,,	684	181	330	173	...
		Brámhaṇ — Dés'ast'h	,,	1,981	774	820	3,087	...
		Brámhaṇ — Dráviḍa	,,	1,276	329	656	291	...
		Brámhaṇ — Guzaráti	,,	...	...	...	...	...
		Brámhaṇ — Gauḍa	,,	116	35	57	24	...
		Brámhaṇ — Haḷé Kannaḍiga	,,	159	65	85	9	...
		Brámhaṇ — Havika	,,	1,640	382	773	485	...

TABLE E.—(Continued.)

District.

Females.

0 to 9					10 to 14				
Total.	Single.	Married.	Widowed.	Civil condition not stated.	Total.	Single.	Married.	Widowed.	Civil condition not stated.
141	141	...	...	...	71	55	16	...	...
...	...	...	...	...	...	...	...	...	...
...	...	...	...	...	...	...	...	...	...
5	5	...	...	...	1	1	...	...	...
...	...	...	...	...	...	...	...	...	...
238	238	...	...	...	60	57	3	...	...
1,305	1,294	11	...	...	508	381	126	1	...
2	2	...	...	...	...	...	...	...	...
1,691	*1,680*	*11*	...	...	*640*	*494*	*115*	*1*	...
1,647	1,629	18	...	...	937	592	341	4	...
...	...	...	...	...	...	...	...	...	...
3	3	...	...	...	1	1	...	...	...
15	15	...	...	...	9	9	...	...	...
20,516	20,062	448	6	...	5,412	4,024	1,327	61	...
...	...	...	...	...	...	...	...	...	...
...	...	...	...	...	...	...	...	...	...
2,181	*21,709*	*466*	*6*	...	*6,359*	*4,626*	*1,668*	*65*	...
...	...	...	...	...	...	...	...	...	...
225	225	...	...	...	103	90	13	...	...
292	292	...	...	...	102	85	17	...	...
...	...	...	...	...	...	...	...	...	...
1,956	1,943	13	...	...	694	609	85	...	...
...	..	...	...	...	...	...	...	...	...
2,473	*2,460*	*13*	...	...	*899*	*784*	*115*	...	...
26,345	**25,849**	**490**	**6**	...	**7,898**	**5,904**	**1,904**	**1,928**	**66**
11	11	...	...	...	8	3	5	...	...
...	...	...	...	...	...	...	...	...	...
51	51	...	...	...	25	13	12	...	...
58	58	...	...	...	23	14	9	...	...
399	386	13	...	...	283	149	127	7	...
...	...	...	...	...	...	...	...	...	...
138	138	...	...	...	106	43	63	...	...
627	615	12	...	...	229	159	69	1	...
253	251	2	...	...	204	78	126	...	...
...	...	...	...	...	...	...	...	...	...
26	26	...	...	...	11	9	2	...	...
37	37	...	...	...	28	28	...	...	...
273	257	16	...	...	265	125	138	2	...

Class.	Group.	Caste, &c. and sub-division.	Religion.	15 to 39. Total.	Single.	Married.	Widowed.	Civil condition not stated.
A.—Agricultural—(Continued.)	1. Military and Dominant.	Kshatriya. Kshatriya ...	Hindu	212	20	162	30	...
		do ...	Sikh	...	...	...	...	...
		Kumárapatta ...	Hindu	...	...	...	...	...
		Rájapindé ...	,,	5	...	4	1	...
		Kodagu (Coorgs) ...	,,	...	...	...	...	...
		Rájput ...	,,	389	14	318	57	...
		Maráta	,,	2,134	149	1,716	269	...
		Báchévár & Ranagára ...	,,	3	...	3	...	...
		Total Group 1	... ...	2,743	183	2,203	357	...
	2. Other Agricultural. (a) Cultivators.	Lingáyet (Gaudamané, &c.) ...	,,	2,845	102	2,282	461	...
		Náyar	,,	...	...	...	...	...
		Pillé	,,	3	...	3	...	...
		Tigala	,,	29	...	29	...	...
		Vakkaliga. Vakkaliga ...	,,	24,989	3,225	14,589	7,175	...
		Sáda ...	Jain	...	...	...	...	...
		Tulu ...	Brahmo	...	...	...	...	...
		Total Group 2(a)	... ...	27,866	3,327	16,903	7,636	...
	4. Forest and Hill Tribes.	Uraliga	Hindu	...	...	...	...	...
		Koracha	,,	411	39	338	34	...
		Korama	,,	435	25	348	62	...
		Kuruba	,,	...	...	...	...	...
		Lambáni	,,	3,019	303	2,447	269	...
		Uriya	,,	...	...	...	...	...
		Total Group 4	... ...	3,895	367	3,163	365	...
		Total Class A		**34,504**	**3,877**	**22,269**	**8,358**	...
B.—Professional—(Continued).	5. Priests.	Bráhman. A'ruvélu ...	Hindu	17	...	14	3	...
		A'ruvélu Niyógi ...	,,	...	...	...	...	...
		Aravattu Vakkalu ...	,,	66	...	58	8	...
		Babbúr Kammé ...	,,	95	...	77	18	...
		Badaga Nádu ...	,,	655*	...	543	112	...
		Brihachcharana ...	,,	...	...	...	...	...
		Chitapávan ...	,,	252	...	198	54	...
		Dés'ast'h ...	,,	764	...	644	120	...
		Drávida ...	,,	526	...	424	103	...
		Guzaráti ...	,,	...	...	...	...	...
		Gauda ...	,,	51	...	45	6	...
		Halé Kannadiga ...	,,	59	...	56	3	...
		Havika ...	,,	696	...	521	175	...

TABLE E.—(*Continued.*)

District.

Females.

40 and over.					Age not stated.				
Total.	Single.	Married.	Widowed.	Civil condition not stated.	Total.	Single.	Married.	Widowed.	Civil condition not stated.
122	...	58	64	...	...	...	...	...	...
...	...	...	...	...	...	...	...	...	...
...	...	...	...	...	...	...	...	...	...
3	...	1	2	...	...	...	...	...	...
...	...	...	...	...	...	...	...	...	...
140	1	50	89	...	...	...	...	...	...
993	2	351	640	...	...	...	...	...	...
...	...	...	...	...	...	...	...	...	...
1,258	*3*	*460*	*795*	...	...	...	...	...	...
1,265	11	437	817	...	...	...	...	...	...
...	...	...	...	...	...	...	...	...	...
...	...	...	...	...	...	...	...	...	...
17	...	12	5	...	...	...	...	...	...
13,456	862	2,270	10,324	...	12	8	4	...	...
...	...	...	...	...	...	...	...	...	...
...	...	...	...	...	...	...	...	...	...
14,738	*873*	*2,719*	*11,146*	...	*12*	*8*	*4*	...	...
...	...	...	...	...	...	...	...	...	...
145	...	52	93	...	...	...	...	...	...
300	2	160	138	...	...	...	...	...	...
...	...	...	...	...	...	...	...	...	...
1,202	12	401	789	...	...	...	...	...	...
...	...	...	...	...	...	...	...	...	...
1,649	*14*	*613*	*1,020*	...	...	...	...	...	...
17,643	**890**	**3,792**	**12,961**	...	**12**	**8**	**4**	...	...
11	...	3	8	...	...	...	...	...	...
...	...	...	...	...	...	...	...	...	...
39	...	16	23	...	...	...	...	...	...
52	...	21	31	...	...	...	...	...	...
330	...	108	222	...	...	...	...	...	...
...	...	...	...	...	...	...	...	...	...
188	...	69	119	...	...	...	...	...	...
361	...	95	266	...	...	...	...	...	...
293	...	104	189	...	...	...	...	...	...
...	...	...	...	...	...	...	...	...	...
28	...	10	18	...	...	...	...	...	...
35	...	29	6	...	...	...	...	...	...
406	...	98	308	...	...	...	...	...	...

Kadur

Class.	Group.	Caste, &c. and sub-division.	Religion.	All Ages. Total.	Single.	Married.	Widowed.	Civil condition not stated.
A.—Agricultural.—(Continued.)	1. Military and Dominant.	Kshatriya.—Kshatriya	Hindu.	809	423	320	66	...
		do	Sikh.	...	...	...	...	...
		Kumárapatta ...	Hindu.	...	...	...	...	...
		Rájapindé ...	,,	58	29	21	8	...
		Kodagu (Coorgs) ...	,,	...	...	...	...	...
		Rájpút ...	,,	125	72	41	12	...
		Maráta	,,	1,830	956	763	111	...
		Ráchévár and Ranagára ...	,,	97	56	31	10	...
		Total Group 1...	... ...	*2,919*	*1,536*	*1,176*	*207*	...
	2. Other Agricultural. (a) Cultivators.	Lingáyet (Gaudamané, &c.) ...	Hindu.	4,830	2,714	1,872	294	...
		Náyar	,,	...	...	...	...	...
		Pillé	,,	33	19	11	3	...
		Tigala	,,	258	156	87	15	...
		Vakkaliga.—Vakkaliga ...	,,	37,869	19,036	16,886	1,943	4
		Sáda	Jain.	...	...	...	...	...
		Tulu	Bramho.	...	...	...	...	...
		Total Group 2(a)...	... ...	*43,013*	*21,925*	*18,856*	*2,255*	*4*
	4. Forest and Hill Tribes.	I'raliga	Hindu.	...	...	...	...	...
		Koracha	,,	368	189	158	21	...
		Korama	,,	668	358	279	31	...
		Kuruba	,,	8	5	3	...	...
		Lambáni	,,	4,880	2,805	1,899	176	...
		Uriya	,,	...	...	...	...	...
		Total Group 4...	... ...	*5,924*	*3,357*	*2,339*	*228*	...
		Total Class A		**51,883**	**26,818**	**22,371**	**2,690**	**4**
B.—Professional.—(Continued.)	5. Priests.	Brámhan.—A'ruvélu ...	Hindu.	23	13	8	2	...
		A'ruvélu Niyógi ...	,,	...	...	...	...	...
		Aravattu Vakkalu...	,,	47	26	17	4	...
		Babbúr Kammé ...	,,	484	252	202	30	...
		Badaganáda... ...	,,	1049	527	460	62	...
		Brihachchárana ...	,,	1	...	...	1	...
		Chitpávan ...	,,	139	71	55	13	...
		Dés'ast'h ...	,,	470	244	198	28	...
		Drávida ...	,,	129	70	49	10	...
		Guzaráti ...	,,	...	...	...	...	...
		Gauda	,,	113	64	42	7	...
		Halé Kannadiga ...	,,	103	48	45	10	...
		Havika	,,	7	5	1	1	...

TABLE E.—(Continued.)

District.

Males.

0 to 9					10 to 14				
Total.	Single.	Married.	Widowed.	Civil condition not stated.	Total.	Single.	Married.	Widowed.	Civil condition not stated.
186	186	...	...	...	78	68	10	...	...
...	...	...	...	...	...	...	...	...	...
...	...	...	...	...	...	...	...	...	...
15	15	...	...	...	4	4	...	...	...
...	...	...	...	...	...	...	...	...	...
28	28	...	...	...	15	15	...	...	...
377	377	...	...	...	204	193	11	...	...
24	24	...	...	...	9	9	...	...	...
630	*630*	...	...	...	*310*	*289*	*21*	...	...
1,213	1,212	1	...	...	472	451	21	...	...
...	...	...	...	...	...	...	...	...	...
8	8	...	...	...	3	3	...	...	...
66	66	...	...	...	25	25	...	...	...
6,685	6,685	...	...	...	3,684	3,684	...	...	...
...	...	...	...	...	...	...	...	...	...
...	...	...	...	...	...	...	...	...	...
7,972	*7,971*	*1*	...	...	*4,184*	*4,163*	*21*	...	...
...	...	...	...	...	...	...	...	...	...
79	79	...	...	...	34	34	...	...	...
211	211	...	...	...	68	68	...	...	...
...	...	...	...	...	1	1	...	...	...
1,344	1,344	...	...	...	421	421	...	...	...
...	...	...	...	...	...	...	...	...	...
1,634	*1,634*	...	...	...	*524*	*524*	...	...	...
10,236	**10,235**	**1**	...	...	**5,018**	**4,976**	**42**	...	...
7	7	...	...	...	4	4	...	...	...
...	...	...	...	...	...	...	...	...	...
13	13	...	...	...	4	4	...	...	...
123	123	...	...	...	49	49	...	...	...
266	264	2	...	...	103	87	13	3	...
...	...	...	...	...	...	...	...	...	...
37	37	...	...	...	10	10	...	...	...
102	101	1	...	...	54	52	2	...	...
40	40	...	...	...	12	11	1	...	...
...	...	...	...	...	...	...	...	...	...
29	29	...	...	...	14	14	...	...	...
22	22	...	...	...	7	7	...	...	...
2	2	...	...	...	1	1	...	...	...

Kadur

Class.	Group.	Caste, &c. and sub-division.	Religion.	15 to 39 Total.	Single.	Married.	Widowed.	Civil condition not stated.
A.—Agricultural.—(Continued.)	1. Military and Dominant.	Kshatriya. — Kshatriya	Hindu.	397	157	223	17	...
		Kshatriya. — do	Sikh	...	...	...	...	...
		Kshatriya. — Kumárapatta	Hindu.	...	...	...	...	...
		Kshatriya. — Rájapindé	,,	27	10	14	3	...
		Kshatriya. — Kodagu (Coorgs)	,,	...	...	...	...	...
		Kshatriya. — Rájpút	,,	61	28	29	4	...
		Maráta ...	,,	868	361	469	38	...
		Ráchévár and Ranagára.	,,	45	23	19	3	...
		Total Group 1...	...	*1,398*	*579*	*754*	*65*	...
	2. Other Agricultural. (a) Cultivators.	Lingáyet, (Gaudamané, &c.)	,,	2,312	1,009	1,212	91	...
		Náyar	,,	...	...	...	...	...
		Pillé	,,	17	7	8	2	...
		Tigala	,,	121	63	55	3	...
		Vakkaliga. — Vakkaliga	,,	19,469	8,512	10,309	643	...
		Vakkaliga. — Sáda	Jain	...	...	...	...	...
		Vakkaliga. — Tulu	Bramho.	...	...	...	...	...
		Total Group 2(a)...	...	*21,919*	*9,591*	*11,584*	*744*	...
	4. Forest and Hill Tribes.	I'ralíga	Hindu.	...	...	...	...	...
		Koracha	,,	189	70	109	10	...
		Korama	,,	274	75	189	10	...
		Kuruba	,,	4	2	2	...	...
		Lambáni	,,	2,245	996	1,198	51	...
		Uriya	,,	...	...	...	...	...
		Total Group 4...	...	*2,712*	*1,143*	*1,498*	*71*	...
		Total Class A......		**26,029**	**11,313**	**13,836**	**880**	...
B.—Professional.—(Continued.)	5. Priests.	Bráhman. — A'ruvélu	Hindu	7	2	5	...	...
		Bráhman. — A'ruvélu Niyógi	,,	...	...	...	...	...
		Bráhman. — Aravattu Vakkalu	,,	20	7	12	1	...
		Bráhman. — Babbúr Kammé	,,	217	76	133	8	...
		Bráhman. — Badaganádu	,,	490	168	313	9	...
		Bráhman. — Brihacharana	,,	...	...	...	...	...
		Bráhman. — Chitpávan	,,	61	22	38	1	...
		Bráhman. — Dés'ast'h	,,	207	83	117	7	...
		Bráhman. — Drávida	,,	59	19	38	2	...
		Bráhman. — Guzaráti	,,	...	...	...	...	...
		Bráhman. — Gauda	,,	56	21	33	2	...
		Bráhman. — Halé Kannadiga	,,	51	16	31	4	...
		Bráhman. — Havíka	,,	2	2	...	...	...

TABLE E.—(Continued.)

District.

Males.

40 and over.					Age not stated.				
Total.	Single.	Married.	Widowed.	Civil condition not stated.	Total.	Single.	Married.	Widowed.	Civil condition not stated.
148	12	87	49	...	...	...	...	...	...
...	...	...	...	...	...	...	...	...	...
...	...	...	...	...	...	...	...	...	...
12	...	7	5	...	...	...	...	...	...
...	...	...	...	...	...	...	...	...	...
21	1	12	8	...	...	...	...	...	...
381	25	283	73	...	...	...	...	...	...
19	...	12	7	...	...	...	...	...	...
581	*38*	*401*	*142*	...	...	...	...	...	...
883	42	638	203	...	...	...	...	...	...
...	...	...	...	...	...	...	...	...	...
5	1	3	1	...	...	...	...	...	...
46	2	32	12	...	...	...	...	...	...
8,027	135	657	1,295	...	4	...	...	...	4
...	...	...	...	...	...	...	...	...	...
...	...	...	...	...	...	...	...	...	...
8,961	*200*	*7,250*	*1,511*	...	*4*	...	...	...	*4*
...	...	...	...	...	...	...	...	...	...
66	6	49	11	...	...	...	...	...	...
115	4	90	21	...	...	...	...	...	...
3	2	1	...	...	...	...	...	...	...
870	41	701	125	...	...	...	...	...	...
...	...	...	...	...	...	...	...	...	...
1,054	*56*	*841*	*157*	...	...	...	...	...	...
10,596	**294**	**8,492**	**1,810**	...	**4**	...	...	...	**4**
5	...	3	2	...	...	...	...	...	...
...	...	...	...	...	...	...	...	...	...
10	2	5	3	...	...	...	...	...	...
95	4	69	22	...	...	...	...	...	...
190	8	132	50	...	...	...	...	...	...
1	...	...	1	...	...	...	...	...	...
31	2	17	12	...	...	...	...	...	...
107	8	78	21	...	...	...	...	...	...
18	...	10	8	...	...	...	...	...	...
...	...	...	...	...	...	...	...	...	...
14	...	9	5	...	...	...	...	...	...
23	3	14	6	...	...	...	...	...	...
2	...	1	1	...	...	...	...	...	...

Kadur

Class.	Group.	Caste, &c. and sub-division.	Religion.	All Ages. Total.	Single.	Married.	Widowed.	Civil condition not stated.
A.—Agricultural—(Continued.)	1. Military and Dominant.	Kshatriya. Kshatriya ...	Hindu	641	140	318	183	...
		do	Sikh	...	...		...	...
		Kumárapaṭṭa ...	Hindu	...	...	...	...	...
		Rájapinḍé ...	,,	40	11	21	8	...
		Koḍaga (Coorgs) ...	,,		...	...	...	...
		Rájpút ...	,,	41	10	26	5	...
		Maráṭa	,,	1,501	441	602	258	...
		Ráchévár and Raṇagára	,,	92	35	38	19	...
		Total Group 1...	... ...	2,118	640	1,005	473	...
	2. Other Agricultural. (a) Cultivators.	Lingáyet, (Gauḍamané, &c.) ...	Hindu	5,063	1,954	1,925	1,181	...
		Náyar ...	,,	...	...	...	...	...
		Pillé ...	,,	18	7	9	2	...
		Tigaḷa ...	,,	233	101	78	58	...
		Vakkaliga. Vakkaliga ...	,,	35,627	16,134	13,820	5,654	19
		Sáda ...	Jain	...	...	...	...	...
		Tuḷu ...	Brahmo	...	...	...	...	...
		Total Group 2(a)...	... ...	40,941	18,196	15,832	6,894	19
	4. Forest and Hill Tribes.	Uraliga ...	Hindu	...	...	...	...	...
		Koracha ...	,,	357	110	172	75	...
		Koraṃa ...	,,	666	239	306	121	...
		Kuruba ...	,,	...	...	...	...	...
		Lambáṇi ...	,,	3,914	1,541	1,845	528	...
		Uriya ...	,,	...	...	...	...	...
		Total Group 4...	... ...	4,937	1,890	2,323	724	...
		Total Class A......		**47,996**	**20,726**	**19,160**	**8,091**	**19**
B.—Professional—(Continued)	5. Priests.	Bráhmaṇ. A'ruvéḷu ...	Hindu	27	7	11	9	...
		A'ruvéḷu Niyógi ...	,,	...	...	...	...	...
		Aravattu Vakkalu...	,,	43	9	24	10	...
		Babbúr Kammé ...	,,	487	116	230	141	...
		Baḍagaṇáḍu ..	,,	1,024	268	454	302	...
		Brihachcharaṇa ..	,,	...	...	...	...	...
		Chitpávan ...	,,	123	32	53	38	...
		Dés'ast'h ...	,,	397	98	179	120	...
		Dráviḍa ...	,,	128	29	67	32	...
		Guzaráti ...	,,	...	...	...	...	...
		Gauḍa ...	,,	64	12	39	13	...
		Haḷé Kannaḍiga ...	,,	92	26	42	24	...
		Havíka ...	,,	4	3	1	...	...

TABLE E.—(*Continued.*)

District.

Females.

0 to 9					10 to 14				
Total.	Single.	Married.	Widowed.	Civil condition not stated.	Total.	Single.	Married.	Widowed.	Civil condition not stated.
133	114	19	...	...	70	22	48	...	...
...	...	...	...	...	...	...	...	...	...
...	...	...	...	...	...	...	...	...	...
9	9	...	...	...	3	1	2	...	...
...	...	...	...	...	...	...	...	...	...
8	8	...	...	...	5	2	3	...	...
374	318	56	...	...	123	90	33	...	...
22	22	...	...	...	7	7	...	...	...
546	*471*	*75*	...	...	*208*	*122*	*86*	...	...
1,390	1,240	60	...	...	548	458	90	...	...
...	...	...	...	...	...	...	...	...	...
4	4	...	...	...	5	3	2	...	...
68	68	...	...	...	28	24	4	...	...
12,328	12,083	245	...	...	2,993	,9	299	...	...
...	...	...	...	...	...	...	...	...	...
...	...	...	...	...	...	...	...	...	...
13,700	*13,395*	*305*	...	...	*3,574*	*3,179*	*395*	...	...
...	...	...	...	...	...	...	...	...	...
79	70	9	...	...	30	23	7	...	...
194	180	14	...	...	51	38	13	...	...
...	...	...	...	...	...	...	...	...	...
1,042	1,042	...	...	...	301	269	32	...	...
...	...	...	...	...	...	...	...	...	...
1,315	*1,292*	*23*	...	...	*382*	*330*	*52*	...	...
15,561	**15,158**	**403**	...	...	**4, 64**	**3,631**	**533**	...	...
5	5	...	...	...	7	2	4	1	...
...	...	...	...	...	...	...	...	...	...
9	8	1	...	...	6	1	5	...	...
114	99	14	1	...	59	17	33	9	...
261	239	21	1	...	122	21	75	18	...
...	...	...	...	...	...	...	...	...	...
33	29	4	...	...	10	3	6	1	...
92	86	6	...	...	43	12	25	6	...
30	27	3	...	...	11	2	9	...	...
...	...	...	...	...	...	...	...	...	...
11	9	2	...	...	7	3	4	...	...
25	23	2	...	...	9	3	6	...	...
2	2	...	...	...	1	1	...	...	...

Kadur

Class.	Group.	Caste, &c. and sub-division.	Religion.	15 to 39: Total.	Single.	Married.	Widowed.	Civil condition not stated.
A.—Agricultural.—(Continued.)	1. Military and Dominant.	Kshatriya. — Kshatriya	Hindu	253	4	192	57	...
		Kshatriya. — do	Sikh	...	...	...	...	...
		Kshatriya. — Kumáraputtu	Hindu	...	...	...	...	...
		Kshatriya. — Rájapinde	,,	20	1	16	3	...
		Kshatriya. — Kodaga (Coorgs)	,,	...	...	...	...	...
		Kshatriya. — Rájpút	,,	19	...	17	2	...
		Maráta	,,	501	36	380	85	...
		Ráchévár and Ranagára.	,,	36	6	25	5	...
		Total Group 1	...	*820*	*47*	*630*	*152*	...
	2. Other Agricultural. (a) Cultivators.	Lingáyet, (Gaudanamé, &c.)	Hindu	2,602	231	1,388	383	...
		Náyar	,,	...	...	...	...	...
		Pillé	,,	6	...	6	...	...
		Tigala	,,	91	9	65	17	...
		Vakkaliga — Vakkaliga	,,	15,907	1,234	12,310	2,310	...
		Vakkaliga — Sáda	Jain	...	...	...	...	...
		Vakkaliga — Tulu	Bramho	...	...	...	...	...
		Total Group 2(a)	...	*18,006*	*1,474*	*13,769*	*2,703*	...
	4. Forest and Hill Tribes.	I'raliga	Hindu	...	...	...	...	...
		Koracha	,,	161	16	122	23	...
		Korama	,,	283	21	220	42	...
		Kuruba	,,	...	...	...	...	...
		Lambáni	,,	1,836	222	1,492	122	...
		Uriya	,,	...	...	...	...	...
		Total Group 4	...	*2,280*	*259*	*1,834*	*187*	...
		Total Class A		**21,115**	**1,780**	**16,233**	**3,102**	...
B.—Professional.—(Continued.)	5. Priests.	Brámhan. — A'ruvélu	Hindu	9	...	6	3	...
		Brámhan. — A'ruvélu Niyógi	,,	...	...	...	...	...
		Brámhan. — Aravattu Vakkalu	,,	18	...	15	3	...
		Brámhan. — Babbúr Kammé	,,	183	...	149	34	...
		Brámhan. — Badaganádu	,,	413	...	307	106	...
		Brámhan. — Brihachcharana	,,	...	...	...	...	...
		Brámhan. — Chitpávan	,,	47	...	34	13	...
		Brámhan. — Dés'ast'h	,,	151	...	113	38	...
		Brámhan. — Drávida	,,	63	...	50	13	...
		Brámhan. — Guzaráti	,,	...	...	...	...	...
		Brámhan. — Gauda	,,	33	...	29	4	...
		Brámhan. — Halé Kannadiga	,,	36	...	27	9	...
		Brámhan. — Havika	,,	1	...	1	...	...

TABLE E.—(*Continued.*)

District.

Females.

40 and over.					Age not stated.				
Total.	Single.	Married.	Widowed.	Civil condition not stated.	Total.	Single.	Married.	Widowed.	Civil condition not stated.
185	...	59	126	...	...	...	...	...	...
...	...	...	...	...	...	...	...	...	...
...	...	...	...	...	...	...	...	...	...
8	...	3	5	...	...	...	...	...	...
...	...	...	...	...	...	...	...	...	...
9	...	6	3	...	...	...	...	...	...
306	...	133	173	...	...	...	...	...	...
27	...	13	14	...	...	...	...	...	...
535	...	*214*	*321*	...	...	...	...	...	...
1,213	25	387	801	...	...	...	...	...	...
...	...	...	...	...	...	...	...	...	...
3	...	1	2	...	...	...	...	...	...
46	...	9	37	...	...	...	...	...	...
4,360	123	966	3,291	...	19	...	...	...	19
...	...	...	...	...	...	...	...	...	...
...	...	...	...	...	...	...	...	...	...
5,612	*148*	*1,363*	*4,181*	...	*19*	...	...	...	*19*
...	...	...	...	...	...	...	...	...	...
87	1	34	52	...	...	...	...	...	...
138	...	59	79	...	...	...	...	...	...
...	...	...	...	...	...	...	...	...	...
735	8	321	406	...	...	...	...	...	...
...	...	...	...	...	...	...	...	...	...
960	*9*	*414*	*537*	...	...	...	...	...	...
7,137	**157**	**1,991**	**4,989**	...	**19**	...	...	...	**19**
6	...	1	5	...	...	...	...	...	...
...	...	...	...	...	...	...	...	...	...
10	...	3	7	...	...	...	...	...	...
131	...	34	97	...	...	...	...	...	...
228	...	51	177	...	...	...	...	...	...
...	...	...	...	...	...	...	...	...	...
33	...	9	24	...	...	...	...	...	...
111	...	35	76	...	...	...	...	...	...
24	...	5	19	...	...	...	...	...	...
...	...	...	...	...	...	...	...	...	...
13	...	4	9	...	...	...	...	...	...
22	...	7	15	...	...	...	...	...	...
...	...	...	...	...	...	...	...	...	...

Chitaldurg

Class.	Group.	Caste, &c. and sub-division.	Religion.	All Ages. Total.	Single.	Married.	Widowed.	Civil condition not stated.
A.—Agricultural.—(Continued.)	1. Military and Dominant.	Kshatriya. — Kshatriya	Hindu	203	93	97	13	...
		do	Sikh	...	...	...	...	...
		Kumârapatta	Hindu	...	...	...	...	...
		Râjapindé	,,	...	...	...	...	...
		Kodaga (Coorgs)	,,	...	...	...	...	...
		Râjpût	,,	51	27	21	3	...
		Marâta	,,	1,285	748	468	69	...
		Râchévâr and Ranagâra	,,	10	5	3	2	...
		Total Group 1	...	*1,549*	*873*	*589*	*87*	...
	2. Other Agricultural. (a) Cultivators.	Lingâyet (Gaudamané, &c.)	Hindu	4,791	2,517	1,803	371	...
		Nâyar	,,	...	...	...	...	...
		Pillé	,,	2	2	...	...	...
		Tigala	,,	12	4	6	2	...
		Vakkaliga. — Vakkaliga	,,	35,074	20,121	13,617	1,336	...
		Sâda	Jain	...	...	...	...	...
		Tulu	Brumho	...	...	...	...	...
		Total Group 2(a)	...	*39,879*	*22,614*	*15,526*	*1,709*	...
	4. Forest and Hill Tribes.	Iraliga	Hindu	...	...	...	...	...
		Koracha	,,	443	223	195	25	...
		Korama	,,	244	138	102	4	...
		Kuruba	,,	...	...	...	...	...
		Lambâni	,,	2,718	1,603	996	119	...
		Uriya	,,	...	...	...	...	...
		Total Group 4	...	*3,405*	*1,964*	*1,293*	*148*	...
		Total Class A		**44,833**	**25,481**	**17,408**	**1,944**	...
B.—Professional.—(Continued.)	5. Priests.	Brâhman. — A'ruvélu	Hindu	20	10	9	1	...
		A'ruvélu Niyógi	,,	...	...	...	...	...
		Aruvattu-Vakkalu	,,	235	105	102	28	...
		Babbûr Kammé	,,	58	34	20	4	...
		Badaganâdu	,,	597	296	259	42	...
		Brihacharana	,,	...	...	...	...	...
		Chitpâvan	,,	...	...	...	...	...
		Dés'ast'h	,,	694	322	287	85	...
		Drâvida	,,	10	5	5	...	...
		Guzarâti	,,	...	...	...	...	...
		Gauda	,,	16	7	7	2	...
		Halé Kannadiga	,,	13	5	7	1	...
		Havika	,,	...	...	...	...	...

TABLE E.—(Continued.)

District.

Males.

0 to 9					10 to 14				
Total.	Single.	Married.	Widowed.	Civil condition not stated.	Total.	Single.	Married.	Widowed.	Civil condition not stated.
62	62	...	...	...	11	11	...	...	...
...	...	...	...	...	...	...	...	...	...
...	...	...	...	...	...	...	...	...	...
...	...	...	...	...	...	...	...	...	...
...	...	...	...	...	...	...	...	...	...
15	15	...	...	...	6	6	...	...	...
448	447	1	...	...	144	136	8	...	...
2	2	...	...	...	...	...	...	...	...
527	*526*	*1*	...	...	*161*	*153*	*8*	...	...
1,516	1,513	3	...	...	319	319	...	...	...
...	...	...	...	...	...	...	...	...	...
...	...	...	...	...	...	...	...	...	...
2	2	...	...	...	4	2	2	...	...
8,828	8,814	14	...	...	1,911	1,883	23	5	...
...	...	...	...	...	...	...	...	...	...
...	...	...	...	...	...	...	...	...	...
10,346	*10,329*	*17*	...	...	*2,264*	*2,234*	*25*	*5*	...
...	...	...	...	...	...	...	...	...	...
127	127	...	...	...	35	35	...	...	...
87	87	...	...	...	27	27	...	...	...
...	...	...	...	...	...	...	...	...	...
1,001	1,001	...	...	...	228	224	4	...	...
		...	...	...	...	...	...	...	...
1,215	*1,215*	...	...	...	*290*	*286*	*4*	...	...
12,088	**12,070**	**18**	...	...	**2,715**	**2,673**	**37**	**5**	...
6	6	...	...	...	2	2	...	...	...
...	...	...	...	...	...	...	...	...	...
58	58	...	...	...	14	14	...	...	...
25	25	...	...	...	4	4	...	...	...
141	141	...	...	...	59	58	1	...	...
...	...	...	...	...	...	...	...	...	...
...	...	...	...	...	...	...	...	...	...
159	158	...	1	...	57	55	2	...	...
5	5	...	...	...	...	...	...	...	...
...	...	...	...	...	...	...	...	...	...
5	5	...	...	...	2	2	...	...	...
4	4	...	...	...	1	1	...	...	...
...	...	...	...	...	...	...	...	...	...

Chitaldurg

Class.	Group.	Caste, &c. and sub-division.	Religion.	15 to 39 Total.	Single.	Married.	Widowed.	Civil condition not stated.
A.—Agricultural.—(Continued.)	1. Military and Dominant.	Kshatriya. — Kshatriya	Hindu	86	20	63	3	...
		Kshatriya. — do	Sikh	...	...	...	...	...
		Kshatriya. — Kumárapaṭṭa	Hindu	...	...	...	...	...
		Kshatriya. — Rájapinḍé	,,	...	...	...	...	...
		Kshatriya. — Koḍaga (Coorgs)	,,	...	...	...	...	...
		Kshatriya. — Rájpút	,,	20	6	14	...	...
		Maráṭa	,,	445	154	276	15	...
		Ráchévár and Raṇagára.	,,	5	2	3	...	...
		Total Group 1	...	*556*	*182*	*356*	*18*	...
	2. Other Agricultural (a) Cultivators.	Lingáyet. (Gauḍamané, &c.)	Hindu	2,022	630	1,277	115	...
		Náyar	,,	...	...	...	...	...
		Piḷḷé	,,	2	2	...	...	...
		Tigaḷa	,,	4	...	3	1	...
		Vakkaliga. — Vakkaliga	,,	16,512	9,383	6,936	193	...
		Vakkaliga. — Sáda	Jain	...	...	...	...	...
		Vakkaliga. — Tuḷu	Bramho	...	...	...	...	...
		Total Group 2(a)	...	*18,540*	*10,015*	*8,216*	*309*	...
	4. Forest and Hill Tribes.	I'ruliga	Hindu	...	...	...	...	...
		Koracha	,,	196	55	133	8	...
		Korama	,,	87	22	65	...	...
		Kuruba	,,	...	...	...	...	...
		Lambáṇi	,,	976	371	582	23	...
		Uriya	,,	...	...	...	...	...
		Total Group 4	...	*1,259*	*448*	*780*	*31*	...
		Total Class A		**20,355**	**10,645**	**9.352**	**358**	...
B.—Professional.—(Continued.)	5. Priests.	Brámhaṇ. — A'ruvélu	Hindu.	9	2	6	1	...
		Brámhaṇ. — A'ruvélu Niyógi	,,	...	...	...	...	...
		Brámhaṇ. — Aruvattu-Vakkalu	,,	105	32	64	9	...
		Brámhaṇ. — Babbúru Kammé	,,	19	5	13	1	...
		Brámhaṇ. — Baḍaganáḍu	,,	255	90	159	6	...
		Brámhaṇ. — Brihachcharaṇa	,,	...	...	...	...	...
		Brámhaṇ. — Chitpávan	,,	...	...	...	...	...
		Brámhaṇ. — Dés'ast'h	,,	284	91	176	17	...
		Brámhaṇ. — Dráviḍa	,,	4	...	4	...	...
		Brámhaṇ. — Guzaráti	,,	...	...	...	...	...
		Brámhaṇ. — Gauḍa	,,	6	...	5	1	...
		Brámhaṇ. — Haḷé Kannaḍiga	,,	5	...	5	...	...
		Brámhaṇ. — Havika	,,	...	...	...	...	...

TABLE E.—(Continued)

District.

Males.

40 and over.					Age not stated.				
Total.	Single.	Married.	Widowed.	Civil condition not stated.	Total.	Single.	Married.	Widowed.	Civil condition not stated.
44	...	34	10	...	...	...	...	...	...
...	...	...	...	...	...	...	...	...	...
...	...	...	...	...	...	...	...	...	...
...	...	...	...	...	...	...	...	...	...
...	...	...	...	...	...	...	...	...	...
10	...	7	3	...	...	...	...	...	...
248	11	183	54	...	...	...	...	...	...
3	1	...	2	...	...	...	...	...	...
305	*12*	*224*	*69*	...	...	...	...	...	...
904	25	623	256	...	...	...	...	...	...
...	...	...	...	...	...	...	...	...	...
...	...	...	...	...	...	...	...	...	...
2	...	1	1	...	...	...	...	...	...
7,811	31	6,644	1,136	...	12	10	...	2	...
...	...	...	...	...	...	...	...	...	...
...	...	...	...	...	...	...	...	...	...
8,717	*56*	*7,268*	*1,393*	...	*12*	*10*	...	*2*	...
...	...	...	...	...	...	...	...	...	...
85	6	62	17	...	...	...	...	...	...
43	2	37	4	...	...	...	...	...	...
...	...	...	...	...	...	...	...	...	...
513	7	410	96	...	...	...	...	...	...
...	...	...	...	...	...	...	...	...	...
641	*15*	*509*	*117*	...	...	...	...	...	...
9,663	**83**	**8,001**	**1,579**	...	**12**	**10**	...	**2**	...
3	...	3	...	...	...	...	...	...	...
...	...	...	...	...	...	...	...	...	...
58	1	38	19	...	...	...	...	...	...
10	...	7	3	...	...	...	...	...	...
142	7	99	36	...	...	...	...	...	...
...	...	...	...	...	...	...	...	...	...
...	...	...	...	...	...	...	...	...	...
194	18	109	67	...	...	...	...	...	...
1	...	1	...	...	...	...	...	...	...
...	...	...	...	...	...	...	...	...	...
3	...	2	1	...	...	...	...	...	...
3	...	2	1	...	...	...	...	...	...
...	...	...	...	...	...	...	...	...	...

Chitaldurg

Class.	Group.	Caste, &c. and sub-division.		Religion.	All Ages. Total.	Single.	Married.	Widowed.	Civil condition not stated.
A–Agricultural.–(*Continued.*)	1. Military and Dominant.	Kshatriya.	Kshatriya	Hindu	*207*	*69*	*101*	*37*	...
			do	Sikh	...	...	...	...	...
			Kumárapatta	Hindu	...	...	...	...	...
			Rájapindé	,,	...	...	...	...	...
			Kodagu (Coorgs)	,,	...	...	...	...	...
			Rájpút	,,	*41*	*13*	*23*	*5*	...
		Maráta		,,	*1,308*	*494*	*587*	*227*	...
		Ráchévár and Ranagára		,,	*5*	*2*	*3*	...	...
		Total Group 1...		...	*1,561*	*578*	*714*	*269*	...
	2. Other Agricultural. (a) Cultivators.	Lingáyat (Gaudamané, &c.)		Hindu	*4,366*	*1,514*	*2,043*	*809*	...
		Náyar		,,	...	...	...	...	...
		Pillé		,,	...	...	...	...	...
		Tigala		,,	*8*	*2*	*4*	*2*	...
		Vakkaliga.	Vakkaliga	,,	*34,486*	*11,501*	*12,737*	*10,248*	...
			Sáda	Jain	...	...	...	...	...
			Tulu	Bramho	...	...	...	...	...
		Total Group 2(a)...		...	*38,860*	*13,017*	*14,784*	*11,059*	...
	4. Forest and Hill Tribes.	Paliga		Hindu	...	...	...	...	...
		Koracha		,,	*410*	*175*	*176*	*59*	...
		Korama		,,	*201*	*82*	[illegible]	*30*	...
		Kuruba		,,	...	...	...	...	...
		Lambáni		,,	*2,525*	*1,138*	*1,084*	*303*	...
		Uriya		,,	...	...	...	...	...
		Total Group 4...		...	*3,139*	*1,396*	*1,351*	*392*	...
		Total Class A...			**43,560**	**14,991**	**16,849**	**11,720**	...
B.–Professional.–(*Continued.*)	5. Priests.	Brámhan.	A'ruvélu	Hindu	*22*	*5*	*10*	*7*	...
			A'rvélu Niyógi	,,	...	...	...	...	...
			Arávattu Vakkalu	,,	*210*	*48*	*99*	*63*	...
			Babbúru Kammé	,,	*62*	*21*	*33*	*8*	...
			Badaganádu	,,	*596*	*139*	*292*	*165*	...
			Brihachcharana	,,	...	...	...	...	...
			Chitpávan	,,	...	...	...	...	...
			Dés'ast'h	,,	*718*	*174*	*304*	*240*	...
			Drávida	,,	*8*	*3*	*4*	*1*	...
			Guzaráti	,,	...	...	...	...	...
			Gauda	,,	*14*	*6*	*8*	...	...
			Halé Kannadiga	,,	*13*	*3*	*8*	*2*	...
			Havíka	,,	...	...	...	...	...

TABLE E.—(*Continued.*)

District.

Females.

0 to 9					10 to 14.				
Total.	Single.	Married.	Widowed.	Civil condition not stated.	Total.	Single.	Married.	Widowed.	Civil condition not stated.
57	57	...	...	...	20	12	8	...	...
...	...	...	...	...	...	...	...	...	...
...	...	...	...	...	...	...	...	...	...
...	...	...	...	...	...	...	...	...	...
...	...	...	...	...	...	...	...	...	...
11	11	...	...	...	2	2	...	...	...
384	384	...	...	...	120	87	32	1	...
2	2	...	...	...	...	...	...	...	...
454	*454*	...	...	...	*142*	*101*	*40*	*1*	...
1,099	1,075	22	2	...	531	376	151	4	...
...	...	...	...	...	...	...	...	...	...
...	...	...	...	...	...	...	...	...	...
2	2	...	...	...	...	...	...	...	...
11,022	10,568	442	12	...	1,227	240	935	52	...
...	...	...	...	...	...	...	...	...	...
...	...	...	...	...	...	...	...	...	...
12,123	*11,645*	*464*	*14*	...	*1,758*	*616*	*1,086*	*56*	...
...	...	...	...	...	...	...	...	...	...
137	137	...	...	...	33	33	...	...	...
64	64	...	...	...	14	14	...	...	...
...	...	...	...	...	...	...	...	...	...
903	903	...	...	...	197	174	23	...	...
...	...	...	...	...	...	...	...	...	...
1,104	*1,104*	...	...	...	*244*	*221*	*23*	...	...
13,681	**13,203**	**464**	**14**	...	**2,144**	**938**	**1,149**	**57**	...
5	5	...	...	...	3	...	3	...	...
...	...	...	...	...	...	...	...	...	...
43	43	...	...	...	12	5	6	1	...
19	19	...	...	...	4	2	2	...	...
132	128	4	...	...	42	11	31	...	...
...	...	...	...	...	...	...	...	...	...
...	...	26	...	...	...	...	...	...	...
173	153	20	...	...	74	21	51	2	...
3	3	...	...	...	1	...	1	...	...
...	...	...	...	...	...	...	...	...	...
6	6	...	...	...	2	...	2	...	...
3	3	...	...	...	...	...	...	...	...
...	...	...	...	...	...	...	...	...	...

Chitaldurg

Class.	Group.	Caste, &c. and sub-division.	Religion.	15 to 39 Total.	15 to 39 Single.	15 to 39 Married.	15 to 39 Widowed.	15 to 39 Civil condition not stated.
A.—Agricultural.—(Continued).	1. Military and Dominant.	Kshatriya.—Kshatriya	Hindu.	75	...	64	11	...
		Kshatriya.—do	Sikh.	...	...	...	...	...
		Kshatriya.—Kumárapatta	Hindu.	...	...	...	...	...
		Kshatriya.—Rájapindé	,,	...	...	...	...	...
		Kshatriya.—Kodaga (Coorg.)	,,	...	...	...	...	...
		Kshatriya.—Rájpút	,,	18	...	16	2	...
		Maráta	,,	539	22	444	73	...
		Ráchévár and Rayagára	,,	3	...	3	...	...
		Total Group 1	...	*635*	*22*	*527*	*86*	...
	2. Other Agricultural. (a) Cultivators.	Lingáyet (Gandamané, &c.)	Hindu.	2,045	62	1,729	254	...
		Náyar	,,	...	...	...	...	...
		Pillé	,,	...	...	...	...	...
		Tigala	,,	3	...	3	...	...
		Vakkaliga—Vakkaliga	,,	14,894	543	10,355	3,996	...
		Vakkaliga—Sáda	Jain.	...	...	...	...	...
		Vakkaliga—Tulu	Brahmo.	...	...	...	...	...
		Total Group 2(a)	...	*16,942*	*605*	*12,087*	*4,250*	...
	4. Forest and Hill Tribes.	Uraliga	Hindu.	...	...	...	...	...
		Koracha	,,	165	5	138	22	...
		Korama	,,	83	5	73	5	...
		Kuruba	,,	...	...	...	...	...
		Lambáni	,,	977	51	855	71	...
		Uriya	,,	...	...	...	...	...
		Total Group 4	...	*1,225*	*61*	*1,066*	*98*	...
		Total Class A		**18,802**	**688**	**13,680**	**4,434**	...
B.—Professional.—(Continued.)	5. Priests.	Bráhman.—A'ravélu	Hindu.	6	...	5	1	...
		Bráhman.—A'ravélu Niyógi	,,	...	...	...	...	...
		Bráhman.—Aravattu Vakkalu	,,	90	...	76	14	...
		Bráhman.—Babbúru Kammé	,,	25	...	22	3	...
		Bráhman.—Badaganádu	,,	253	...	207	46	...
		Bráhman.—Brihachcharana	,,	...	...	...	...	...
		Bráhman.—Chitpávan	,,	...	...	...	...	...
		Bráhman.—Dés'ast'h	,,	267	...	192	75	...
		Bráhman.—Drávida	,,	2	...	2	...	...
		Bráhman.—Guzaráti	,,	...	...	...	...	...
		Bráhman.—Gauda	,,	4	...	4	...	...
		Bráhman.—Halé Kannadiga	,,	7	...	7	...	...
		Bráhman.—Havika	,,	...	...	...	...	...

TABLE E.—(*Continued.*)

District.

Females.

40 and over.					Age not stated.				
Total.	Single.	Married.	Widowed.	Civil condition not stated.	Total.	Single.	Married.	Widowed.	Civil condition not stated.
55	...	29	26	...	...	...	...	...	...
...	...	...	...	...	...	...	...	...	...
...	...	...	...	...	...	...	...	...	...
...	...	...	...	...	...	...	...	...	...
...	...	...	...	...	...	...	...	...	...
10	...	7	3	...	...	...	...	...	...
265	1	111	153	...	...	...	...	...	...
...	...	...	...	...	...	...	...	...	...
330	*1*	*147*	*182*	...	...	...	...	...	...
691	1	141	549	...	...	...	...	...	...
...	...	...	...	...	...	...	...	...	...
...	...	...	...	...	...	...	...	...	...
3	...	1	2	...	...	...	...	...	...
7,329	140	1,004	6,185	...	14	10	1	3	...
...	...	...	...	...	...	...	...	...	...
...	...	...	...	...	...	...	...	...	...
8,023	*141*	*1,146*	*6,736*	...	*14*	*10*	*1*	*3*	...
...	...	...	...	...	...	...	...	...	...
75	...	38	37	...	...	...	...	...	...
43	...	18	25	...	...	...	...	...	...
...	...	...	...	...	...	...	...	...	...
448	10	206	232	...	...	...	...	...	...
...	...	...	...	...	...	...	...	...	...
566	*10*	*262*	*294*	...	...	...	...	...	...
8,919	**152**	**1,555**	**7,212**	...	**14**	**10**	**1**	**3**	...
8	...	2	6	...	...	...	...	...	...
...	...	...	...	...	...	...	...	...	...
65	...	17	48	...	...	...	...	...	...
14	...	9	5	...	...	...	...	...	...
169	...	50	119	...	...	...	...	...	...
...	...	...	...	...	...	...	...	...	...
...	...	...	...	...	...	...	...	...	...
204	...	41	163	...	...	...	...	...	...
2	...	1	1	...	...	...	...	...	...
...	...	...	...	...	...	...	...	...	...
2	...	2	...	...	...	...	...	...	...
3	...	1	2	...	...	...	...	...	...
...	...	...	...	...	...	...	...	...	...

SUPPLEMENTARY TABLE E.

Caste, &c., by Civil condition and Age.

SUPPLEMENTARY

The Civil and Military

Class.	Group.	Caste, &c. and sub-division.		Religion.	All Ages. Total.	Single.	Married.	Widowed.	Civil condition not stated.
A.—Agricultural.—(Continued.)	1. Military and Dominant.	Kshatriya.	Kshatriya ...	Hindu.	68	29	36	3	...
			do	Sikh.	...	...	...	...	...
			Kumárapatta ...	Hindu.	...	...	...	...	...
			Rájapindé ...	,,	...	...	...	...	...
			Kodaga (Coorgs) ...	,,	2	1	1	...	...
			Rájpút ...	,,	280	164	103	13	...
		Maráta		,,	573	298	247	28	...
		Ráchévár and Ranagara ...		,,	40	19	20	1	...
		Total Group 1......		... ...	*963*	*511*	*407*	*45*	...
	2. Other Agricultural. (a) Cultivators.	Lingáyet, (Gaudamané, &c.)		Hindu.	12	4	7	1	...
		Náyar		,,	64	39	25	...	...
		Pillo		,,	3	1	1	1	...
		Tigála		,,	1,672	885	716	68	3
		Vakkaliga.	Vakkaliga ...	,,	4,786	2,537	2,042	207	...
			Sáda	Jain.	...	...	...	...	...
			Tulu	Bramho.	10	6	4	...	...
		Total Group 2(a)...		... ...	*6,547*	*3,472*	*2,705*	*277*	3
	4. Forest and Hill Tribes.	I'raliga		Hindu.	...	...	...	...	...
		Koracha		,,	116	58	54	4	...
		Korama		,,	94	41	49	4	...
		Kuruba		,,	...	...	...	...	...
		Lambáni		,,	...	...	...	...	...
		Uriya		,,	5	4	1	...	...
		Total Group 4......		... ...	*215*	*103*	*104*	*8*	...
		Total Class A......			**7,725**	**4,086**	**3,306**	**330**	**3**
B.—Professional.—(Continued.)	5. Priests.	Bráhman.	A'ruvélu ...	Hindu.	41	23	16	2	...
			A'ruvélu Niyógi ...	,,	...	...	...	...	...
			Aravattu Vakkalu ...	,,	2	1	1	...	...
			Babbúru Kammé ...	,,	...	...	...	...	...
			Badaganádu ...	,,	60	32	25	3	...
			Brihachcharana ...	,,	36	13	21	2	...
			Chitpávan ...	,,	...	...	...	...	...
			Dés'ast'h ...	,,	39	13	22	4	...
			Drávida ...	,,	11	3	7	1	...
			Guzaráti ...	,,	...	...	...	...	...
			Gauda ...	,,	18	7	6	5	...
			Haló Kannadiga ...	,,	...	...	...	...	...
			Havíka ...	,,	...	...	...	...	...

TABLE E.—*(Continued.)*

Station, Bangalore.

Males.

0 to 9					10 to 14				
Total.	Single.	Married.	Widowed.	Civil condition not stated.	Total.	Single.	Married.	Widowed.	Civil condition not stated.
8	8	...	...	...	5	5	...	...	...
...	...	...	...	...	...	...	...	...	...
...	...	...	...	...	...	...	...	...	...
...	...	...	...	...	...	...	...	...	...
1	1	...	...	...	...	...	...	...	...
61	61	...	...	...	24	24	...	...	...
126	126	...	...	...	58	58	...	...	...
15	15	...	...	...	3	3	...	...	...
211	*211*	...	...	...	*90*	*90*	...	...	...
1	1	...	...	...	1	1	...	...	...
16	16	...	...	...	7	7	...	...	...
...	...	...	...	...	...	...	...	...	...
470	466	2	1	1	170	169	1	...	...
1,213	1,209	2	1	...	500	494	5	1	...
...	...	...	...	...	...	...	...	...	...
4	4	...	...	...	...	...	...	...	...
1,703	*1,696*	*4*	*2*	*1*	*678*	*671*	*6*	*1*	...
...	...	...	...	...	...	...	...	...	...
35	35	...	...	...	6	6	...	...	...
22	22	...	...	...	13	12	1	...	...
...	...	...	...	...	...	...	...	...	...
...	...	...	...	...	...	...	...	...	...
3	3	...	...	...	1	1	...	...	...
60	*60*	...	...	...	*20*	*19*	*1*	...	...
1,974	**1,967**	**4**	**2**	**1**	**788**	**780**	**7**	**1**	...
10	10	...	...	...	6	6	...	...	...
...	...	...	...	...	...	...	...	...	...
...	...	...	...	...	...	...	...	...	...
...	...	...	...	...	...	...	...	...	...
15	15	...	...	...	7	7	...	...	...
5	5	...	...	...	3	3	...	...	...
...	...	...	...	...	...	...	...	...	...
3	3	...	...	...	3	3	...	...	...
2	2	...	...	...	...	...	...	...	...
...	...	...	...	...	...	...	...	...	...
1	1	...	...	...	...	...	...	...	...
...	...	...	...	...	...	...	...	...	...
...	...	...	...	...	...	...	...	...	...

The Civil and Military

Class.	Group.	Caste, &c. and sub-division.	Religion.	15 to 39 Total.	Single.	Married.	Widowed.	Civil condition not stated.
A.—Agricultural.—(Continued).	1. Military and Dominant.	Kshatriya.—Kshatriya ...	Hindu.	35	14	20	1	...
		do ...	Sikh	...	...	...	...	...
		Kumárapatta ...	Hindu.	...	...	...	...	...
		Rájapindé ...	,,	...	...	...	...	...
		Kodagi (Coorgs) ...	,,	1	...	1	...	...
		Rájpút ...	,,	153	77	71	5	...
		Maráta	,,	260	108	145	7	...
		Ráchévár and Ranagára ...	,,	15	1	14	...	...
		Total Group 1	... ...	*464*	*200*	*251*	*13*	...
	2. Other Agricultural. (a) Cultivators.	Lingáyet, (Gaudamané, &c.) ...	,,	7	2	5	...	...
		Náyar	,,	32	15	17	...	...
		Pillo	,,	2	1	...	1	...
		Tigala	,,	663	243	403	16	1
		Vakkaliga.—Vakkaliga ...	,,	2,003	810	1,159	34	...
		Sáda	Jain.	...	...	...	...	...
		Tulu	Brahmo.	4	2	2	...	...
		Total Group 2(a) ...	... ...	*2,711*	*1,073*	*1,586*	*51*	*1*
	4. Forest and Hill Tribes.	I'raliga	Hindu	...	...	...	...	...
		Koracha	,,	48	17	30	1	...
		Korama	,,	34	7	25	2	...
		Kuruba	,,	...	...	...	...	...
		Lambáni	,,	...	...	...	...	...
		Uriya	,,	...	...	...	...	...
		Total Group 4	... ...	*82*	*24*	*55*	*3*	...
		Total Class A		**3,557**	**1,297**	**1,892**	**67**	**1**
B.—Professional.—(Continued).	5. Priests.	Brámhan.—A'ruvélu ...	Hindu.	16	7	9	...	...
		A'ruvélu Niyógi ...	,,	...	...	...	...	...
		Aruvattu Vakkalu ...	,,	2	1	1	...	...
		Babbúr Kammé ...	,,	...	...	...	...	...
		Badaganádu ...	,,	27	10	17	...	...
		Brihachcharana ...	,,	19	5	14	...	...
		Chitpávan ...	,,	...	...	...	...	...
		Dés'ast'h ...	,,	24	6	18	...	...
		Drávida ...	,,	4	1	3	...	...
		Guzaráti ...	,,	...	...	...	...	...
		Gauda ...	,,	10	4	4	2	...
		Halé Kannadiga ...	,,	...	...	...	...	...
		Havíká ...	,,	...	...	...	...	...

TABLE E.—(*Continued.*)

Station, Bangalore.

Males.

40 and over.					Age not stated.				
Total.	Single.	Married.	Widowed.	Civil condition not stated.	Total.	Single.	Married.	Widowed.	Civil condition not stated.
20	2	16	2	...	...	...	...	...	...
...	...	...	...	...	...	...	...	...	...
...	...	...	...	...	...	...	...	...	...
...	...	...	...	...	...	...	...	...	...
...	...	...	...	...	...	...	...	...	...
42	2	33	8	...	...	...	...	...	...
129	6	102	21	...	...	...	...	...	...
7	...	6	1	...	...	...	...	...	...
198	*10*	*156*	*32*	...	...	...	...	...	...
3		2	1	...	...	...	...	...	...
9		8	...	...	...	...	...	...	...
1	...	1	...	...	...	...	...	...	...
360	7	310	31	1	...	...	...	...	...
1,071	24	876	171	...	...	...	...	...	...
...	...	...	...	...	...	...	...	...	...
2	...	2	...	...	...	...	...	...	...
1,455	*32*	*1,190*	*233*	*1*	...	...	...	...	...
...	...	...	...	...	...	...	...	...	...
27	...	24	3	...	...	...	...	...	...
25	...	23	2	...	...	...	...	...	...
...	...	...	...	...	...	...	...	...	...
...	...	...	...	...	...	...	...	...	...
1	...	1	...	...	...	...	...	...	...
53	...	*48*	*5*	...	...	...	...	...	...
1,706	**42**	**1,403**	**260**	**1**	...	...	...	...	...
9	...	7	2	...	...	...	...	...	...
...	...	...	...	...	...	...	...	...	...
...	...	...	...	...	...	...	...	...	...
...	...	...	...	...	...	...	...	...	...
11	...	8	3	...	...	...	...	...	...
9	...	7	2	...	...	...	...	...	...
...	...	...	...	...	...	...	...	...	...
9	1	4	4	...	...	...	...	...	...
5	...	4	1	...	...	...	...	...	...
...	...	...	...	...	...	...	...	...	...
7	2	2	3	...	...	...	...	...	...
...	...	...	...	...	...	...	...	...	...
...	...	...	...	...	...	...	...	...	...

The Civil and Military

Class.	Group.	Caste, &c. and sub-division.	Religion.	All Ages. Total.	Single.	Married.	Widowed.	Civil condition not stated.
A.—Agricultural.—(Continued)	1. Military and Dominant.	Kshatriya. — Kshatriya	Hindu.	54	18	22	14	...
		do ...	Sikh.	...	...	...	...	...
		Kumárapatta	Hindu.	...	...	...	...	...
		Rájapindé	,,	...	...	...	...	...
		Kodaga (Coorgs)	,,	1	...	1	...	...
		Rájpút ...	,,	223	63	105	55	...
		Maráta ...	,,	571	166	256	149	...
		Káchévár and Rangára	,,	40	16	16	8	...
		Total Group 1	...	889	263	400	226	...
	2. Other Agricultural (a) Cultivators.	Lingáyet, (Gaudamané, &c.)	Hindu.	8	1	5	2	...
		Náyar ...	,,	50	13	28	9	...
		Pillé ...	,,	1	...	...	1	...
		Tigala ...	,,	1,641	595	769	275	2
		Vakkaliga. — Vakkaliga	,,	4,910	1,661	2,096	1,153	...
		Sáda	Jain.	1	...	...	1	...
		Tulu ...	Bramho.	13	6	3	4	...
		Total Group 2(a)	...	6,624	2,276	2,901	1,445	2
	4. Forest and Hill Tribes.	Uraliga ...	Hindu.	...	...	...	...	...
		Koracha ...	,,	110	34	56	20	...
		Korama ...	,,	98	34	51	13	...
		Kuruba ...	,,	...	...	...	...	...
		Lambáni ...	,,	...	...	...	...	...
		Uriya ...	,,	3	1	2	...	...
		Total Group 4	...	211	69	109	33	...
		Total Class A		**7,724**	**2,608**	**3,410**	**1,704**	**2**
B.—Professional.—(Continued.)	5. Priests.	Brámhan. — A'ruvélu	Hindu.	32	4	20	8	...
		A'ruvélu Niyógi	,,	...	...	...	...	...
		Aravattu Vakkalu	,,	1	...	...	1	...
		Babbúru Kammé	,,	...	...	...	...	...
		Badaganádu	,,	55	8	33	14	...
		Brihachcharana	,,	36	8	20	8	...
		Chitpávan	,,	...	...	...	...	...
		Désast'h	,,	18	4	7	7	...
		Drávida	,,	10	2	6	2	...
		Guzaráti	,,	...	...	...	...	...
		Gauda	,,	4	...	2	2	...
		Halé Karnádiga	,,	...	...	...	...	...
		Havíka	,,	...	...	...	...	...

TABLE E.—(Continued.)

Station, Bangalore.

Females.

0 to 9					10 to 14				
Total.	Single.	Married.	Widowed.	Civil condition not stated.	Total.	Single.	Married.	Widowed.	Civil condition not stated.
13	13	...	...	...	6	4	2	...	...
...	...	...	...	...	...	...	...	...	...
...	...	...	...	...	...	...	...	...	...
...	...	...	...	...	...	...	...	...	...
...	...	...	...	...	...	...	...	...	...
54	52	2	...	...	20	11	9	...	...
131	130	1	...	...	53	29	24	...	...
14	14	...	...	...	3	2	1	...	...
212	*209*	*3*	...	...	*82*	*46*	*36*	...	...
...	...	...	...	...	1	1	...	...	...
10	10	...	...	...	3	2	1	...	...
...	...	...	...	...	...	...	...	...	...
449	443	5	...	1	152	110	42	...	...
1,192	1,179	13	...	...	508	377	129	2	...
...	...	...	...	...	...	...	...	...	...
5	5	...	...	...	1	1	...	...	...
1,656	*1,637*	*18*	...	*1*	*665*	*491*	*172*	*2*	...
...	...	...	...	...	...	...	...	...	...
28	28	...	...	...	7	5	2	...	...
31	31	...	...	...	4	3	1	...	...
...	...	...	...	...	...	...	...	...	...
...	...	...	...	...	...	...	...	...	...
1	1	...	...	...	...	...	...	...	...
60	*60*	...	...	...	*11*	*8*	*3*	...	...
1,928	**1,906**	**21**	...	**1**	**758**	**545**	**211**	**2**	...
4	4	...	...	...	1	...	1	...	...
...	...	...	...	...	...	...	...	...	...
...	...	...	...	...	...	...	...	...	...
...	...	...	...	...	...	...	...	...	...
10	8	2	...	...	6	...	6	...	...
6	6	...	...	...	5	2	3	...	...
...	...	...	...	...	...	...	...	...	...
4	4	...	...	...	...	...	...	...	...
3	2	1	...	...	1	...	1	...	...
...	...	...	...	...	...	...	...	...	...
...	...	...	...	...	...	...	...	...	...
...	...	...	...	...	...	...	...	...	...
...	...	...	...	...	...	...	...	...	...

The Civil and Military

Class.	Group.	Caste, &c. and sub-division.		Religion.	15 to 39 Total.	Single.	Married.	Widowed.	Civil condition not stated.
A.—Agricultural.—(*Continued.*)	1. Military and Dominant.	Kshatriya.	Kshatriya	Hindu.	20	1	14	5	...
			do	Sikh.	...	...	...	...	...
			Kumárajatta	Hindu.	...	...	...	...	...
			Rájpindé	,,	...	...	...	...	...
			Kodagu (Coorgs)	,,	1	...	1	...	...
			Rájpút	,,	95	...	80	15	...
		Maráta		,,	246	6	192	48	...
		Ráchévár and Rayagára		,,	18	...	15	3	...
		Total Group 1		...	*380*	*7*	*302*	*71*	...
	2. Other Agricultural (*a*) Cultivators.	Lingáyet, (Gaudamané, &c.)		Hindu.	5	...	5	...	...
		Náyar		,,	26	1	23	2	...
		Pillé		,,	...	...	...	...	...
		Tigala		,,	685	40	586	59	...
		Vakkaliga.	Vakkaliga	,,	1,960	95	1,574	291	...
			Sáda	Jain	...	...	...	...	...
			Tulu	Brahmo.	4	...	2	2	...
		Total Group 2(a)		...	*2,680*	*136*	*2,190*	*354*	...
	4. Forest and Hill Tribes.	I'raliga		Hindu.	...	...	...	...	...
		Koracha		,,	42	1	38	3	...
		Korama		,,	43	...	38	5	...
		Kuruba		,,	...	...	...	...	...
		Lambáni		,,	...	...	...	...	...
		Uriya		,,	1	...	1	...	...
		Total Group 4		...	*86*	*1*	*77*	*8*	...
		Total Class A			**3,146**	**144**	**2,569**	**433**	...
B.—Professional.—(*Continued.*)	5. Priests.	Bráhman.	A'ruvélu	Hindu.	17	...	15	2	...
			A'ruvélu Niyógi	,,	...	...	...	...	...
			Aruvatta Vakkalu	,,	...	...	...	...	...
			Babbúru Kammé	,,	...	...	...	...	...
			Badaganádu	,,	23	...	19	4	...
			Brihacharana	,,	16	...	13	3	...
			Chitpávan	,,	...	...	...	...	...
			Dés'ast'h	,,	9	...	6	3	...
			Dráviḍa	,,	4	...	4	...	...
			Guzaráti	,,	...	...	...	...	...
			Gauda	,,	2	...	2	...	...
			Halé Kannadiga	,,	...	...	...	...	...
			Havika	,,	...	...	...	...	...

TABLE E.—(Continued.)

Military Station, Bangalore.

Females.

40 and over.					Age not stated.				
Total.	Single.	Married.	Widowed.	Civil condition not stated.	Total.	Single.	Married.	Widowed.	Civil condition not stated.
15	...	6	9	...	...	...	...	...	...
...	...	...	...	...	...	...	...	...	...
...	...	...	...	...	...	...	...	...	...
...	...	...	...	...	...	...	...	...	...
...	...	...	...	...	...	...	...	...	...
54	...	14	40	...	...	...	...	...	...
141	1	39	101	...	...	...	...	...	...
5	...	...	5	...	...	...	...	...	...
215	*1*	*59*	*155*	...	...	...	...	...	...
2	...	...	2	...	...	...	...	...	...
11	...	4	7	...	...	...	...	...	...
1	...	...	1	...	...	...	...	...	...
355	2	136	216	1	...	...	...	...	...
1,250	10	380	860	...	...	...	...	...	...
1	...	...	1	...	...	...	...	...	...
3	...	1	2	...	...	...	...	...	...
1,623	*12*	*521*	*1,089*	*1*	...	...	...	...	...
...	...	...	...	...	...	...	...	...	...
33	...	16	17	...	...	...	...	...	...
20	...	12	8	...	...	...	...	...	...
...	...	...	...	...	...	...	...	...	...
...	...	...	...	...	...	...	...	...	...
1	...	1	...	...	...	...	...	...	...
54	...	*29*	*25*	...	...	...	...	...	...
1,892	**13**	**609**	**1,269**	**1**	...	...	...	...	...
10	...	4	6	...	...	...	...	...	...
...	...	...	...	...	...	...	...	...	...
1	...	...	1	...	...	...	...	...	...
...	...	...	...	...	...	...	...	...	...
16	...	6	10	...	...	...	...	...	...
9	...	4	5	...	...	...	...	...	...
...	...	...	...	...	...	...	...	...	...
5	...	1	4	...	...	...	...	...	...
2	...	...	2	...	...	...	...	...	...
...	...	...	...	...	...	...	...	...	...
2	...	...	2	...	...	...	...	...	...
...	...	...	...	...	...	...	...	...	...
...	...	...	...	...	...	...	...	...	...

Total including the Civil and

Class.	Group.	Caste, &c. and sub-divisions.		Religion.	All Ages. Total.	Single.	Married.	Widowed.	Civil condition not stated.
A.—Agricultural.—(Continued.)	1. Military and Dominant.	Kshatriya.	Kshatriya ...	Hindu.	6,271	3,330	2,538	403	...
			do ...	Sikh.	13	6	6	1	...
			Kumárapaṭṭa ..	Hindu.	...	...	...	...	...
			Rájapiṇḍé ...	,,	794	439	316	39	...
			Koḍaga (Coorgs) ...	,,	8	4	3	1	...
			Rájpút ...	,,	4,062	2,191	1,610	261	...
		Maráṭa		,,	22,961	12,016	9,422	1,493	...
		Ráchévár & Raṇagára		,,	1,785	946	730	109	...
		Total Group 1			35,894	18,962	14,625	2,307	...
	2. Other Agricultural. (a) Cultivators.	Lingáyet (Gauḍamané, &c.)		Hindu.	63,690	33,800	26,049	3,841	...
		Náyar		,,	67	40	27	...	...
		Piḷḷé		,,	314	158	138	18	
		Tigaḷa		,,	28,660	15,151	12,192	1,314	3
		Vakkaliga.	Vakkaliga ...	,,	665,516	365,646	277,926	21,882	62
			Sáda ...	Jain	516	294	184	38	...
			Tuḷu ..	Bramho.	10	6	4		..
		Total Group 2(a)			758,773	415,095	316,520	27,093	65
	4. Forest and Hill Tribes.	Iraliga		Hindu.	581	282	263	36	...
		Koracha		,,	5,578	2,864	2,351	363	..
		Korama		,,	6,865	3,672	2,842	351	..
		Kuruba		,,	1,136	532	524	80	.
		Lambáṇi		,,	20,585	11,937	7,792	856	...
		Uriya		,,	5	4	1	...	
		Total Group 4			34,750	19,291	13,773	1,686	...
		Total Class A			829,417	453,348	344,918	31,086	65
B.—Professional.—(Continued.)	5. Priests.	Bramhaṇ.	A'ruvélu ...	Hindu.	2,261	1,139	947	175	...
			A'ruvélu Niyógi ...	,,	10	6	4	...	...
			Aravattu Vakkalu ..	,,	2,449	1,216	1,057	176	...
			Babbúr Kammé ...	,,	3,322	1,709	1,365	248	...
			Baḍaga Náḍu ...	,,	11,739	5,871	4,926	942	...
			Brihachcharaṇa	,,	657	317	286	54	...
			Chitpávan ...	,,	1,537	774	592	171	
			Dés'ast'h ...	,,	8,487	4,069	3,645	773	
			Dráviḍa ...	,,	4,099	1,982	1,701	416	...
			Guzaráti ...	,,	2	...	2	...	...
			Gauḍa ...	,,	1,084	570	408	106	...
			Haḷé Kannaḍiga ...	,,	3,780	1,943	1,634	203	...
			Havika ...	,,	1,602	833	613	156	...

TABLE E.—(*Continued.*)

Military Station, Bangalore.

Males.

0 to 9.					10 to 14.				
Total.	Single.	Married.	Widowed.	Civil condition not stated.	Total.	Single.	Married.	Widowed.	Civil condition not stated.
1,657	1,657	...	...	...	594	567	27	...	...
3	3	...	...	...	2	2	...	...	...
...	...	...	...	...	...	...	...	...	...
227	227	...	...	...	67	67	...	...	...
3	3	...	...	...	1	1	...	...	...
1,099	1,099	...	...	...	380	379	1	...	...
6,209	6,207	2	...	...	2,594	2,482	110	2	...
503	503	...	...	...	172	172	...	...	...
9,701	*9,699*	*2*	...	...	*3,810*	*3,670*	*138*	*2*	...
16,756	16,723	33	...	...	7,094	6,891	203	...	...
16	16	...	...	...	8	8	...	...	...
72	72	...	...	...	27	27	...	...	...
8,502	8,498	2	1	1	3,020	3,002	18	...	...
176,464	176,280	177	7	...	52,556	50,994	1,536	23	3
147	147	...	...	...	46	46	...	...	...
4	4	...	...	...	...	...	...	...	...
201,961	*201,740*	*212*	*8*	*1*	*62,751*	*60,968*	*1,757*	*23*	*3*
190	190	...	...	...	46	46	...	...	...
1,683	1,683	...	...	...	483	483	...	...	...
2,147	2,147	...	...	...	652	643	9	...	...
245	245	...	...	...	80	80	...	...	...
6,507	6,507	...	...	...	2,127	2,094	33	...	...
3	3	...	...	...	1	1	...	...	...
10,775	*10,775*	...	...	...	*3,389*	*3,347*	*42*	...	...
222,437	**222,214**	**214**	**8**	**1**	**69,950**	**67,985**	**1,937**	**25**	**3**
602	596	6	...	...	268	216	50	...	...
4	4	...	...	...	1	1	...	...	...
700	699	1	...	...	201	183	18	...	...
1,100	1,093	7	...	...	301	253	49	4	...
3,281	3,266	14	1	...	1,041	922	113	6	...
158	158	...	...	...	65	60	5	...	...
437	437	...	...	...	213	213	...	...	...
2,197	2,172	23	2	...	824	701	121	2	...
1,058	1,052	6	...	...	437	366	70	1	...
...	...	...	...	...	...	...	...	...	...
306	306	...	...	...	73	72	1	...	...
1,096	1,077	18	1	...	429	356	70	3	...
335	331	4	...	...	170	163	7	...	...

Total including the Civil and

Class.	Group.	Caste, &c. and subdivision.	Religion.	15 to 39. Total.	Single.	Married.	Widowed.	Civil condition not stated.
A.—Agricultural—(Continued.)	1. Military and Dominant.	Kshatriya. { Kshatriya	Hindu.	2,758	1,050	1,605	101	...
		do	Sikh.	5	1	4	...	...
		Kombrapatta	Hindu.	...	...	...	...	...
		Rájapinde	,,	356	142	205	9	...
		Kodaga (Coorgs)	,,	8	...	3	...	...
		Rájpút	,,	1,716	671	933	62	...
		Maráta	,,	9,280	3,192	5,692	396	...
		Báchévár & Rayagára	,,	734	254	454	26	...
		Total Group 1		*14,850*	*5,310*	*8,946*	*594*	...
	2. Other Agricultural. (a) Cultivators.	Lingáyet (Gandamané, &c.)	,,	26,170	9,778	15,429	963	...
		Náyar	,,	33	15	18	...	...
		Pille	,,	158	57	95	6	...
		Tigála	,,	16,827	8,486	7,101	239	1
		Vakkaliga. { Vakkaliga	,,	283,821	133,728	146,465	3,617	11
		Sáda	Jain.	201	97	97	7	...
		Tulu	Bramho.	4	2	2	...	...
		Total Group 2(a)		*321,214*	*147,163*	*169,207*	*4,832*	*12*
	4. Forest and Hill Tribes.	I'raliga	,,	209	42	159	8	...
		Koracha	,,	2,199	654	1,459	95	...
		Korama	,,	2,738	837	1,804	97	...
		Kuruba	,,	542	190	333	19	...
		Lambáni	,,	8,074	3,204	4,638	232	...
		Uriya	,,	...	...	...	...	...
		Total Group 4		*13,762*	*4,927*	*8,384*	*451*	...
		Total Class A		**349,826**	**157,400**	**186,537**	**5,877**	**12**
B.—Professional—(Continued.)	5. Priests.	Bráhman. { A'ruvelu	,,	879	304	542	33	...
		A'ruvélu Niyógi	,,	2	...	2	...	...
		Aravatta Vakkalu	,,	1,023	313	671	39	...
		Babbúr Kammo	,,	1,267	341	862	64	...
		Badaga Nádu	,,	4,814	1,560	3,018	236	...
		Brihachcharana	,,	287	96	182	9	...
		Chitpaván	,,	591	119	425	47	...
		Desást'h	,,	3,594	1,123	2,256	215	...
		Drávida	,,	1,666	529	1,025	112	...
		Guzaráti	,,	2	...	2	...	...
		Gauda	,,	458	172	257	29	...
		Hale Karnádiga	,,	1,511	499	971	41	...
		Havika	,,	692	311	350	31	...

TABLE E.—(Continued.)

Military Station, Bangalore.

Males.

40 and over. Total.	Single.	Married.	Widowed.	Civil condition not stated.	Age not stated. Total.	Single.	Married.	Widowed.	Civil condition not stated.
1,264	56	906	302	...	...	...	...	...	...
3	...	2	1	...	...	...	...	...	...
...	...	...	...	...	...	...	...	...	...
144	3	111	30	...	...	...	...	...	...
1	...	...	1	...	...	...	...	...	...
867	42	626	199	...	...	...	...	...	...
4,878	165	3,618	1,095	...	...	...	...	...	...
376	17	276	83	...	...	...	...	...	...
7,533	*283*	*5,539*	*1,711*	...	...	...	...	...	...
13,760	498	10,384	2,878	...	...	...	...	...	...
10	1	9	...	...	...	...	...	...	...
57	2	43	12	...	...	...	...	...	...
6,311	165	5,071	1,074	1	...	...	...	...	...
152,320	4,471	129,652	18,191	6	355	173	96	44	42
122	4	87	31	...	...	...	...	...	...
2	...	2	...	...	...	...	...	...	...
172,493	*5,051*	*145,248*	*22,186*	*7*	*355*	*173*	*96*	*44*	*42*
136	4	104	28	...	...	...	...	...	...
1,213	44	901	268	...	...	...	...	...	...
1,328	45	1,029	254	...	...	...	...	...	...
269	17	191	61	...	...	...	...	...	...
3,877	132	3,121	624	...	...	...	...	...	...
1	...	1	...	...	...	...	...	...	...
6,824	*242*	*5,347*	*1,235*	...	...	...	...	...	...
186,849	**5,576**	**156,134**	**25,132**	**7**	**355**	**173**	**96**	**44**	**42**
514	23	349	142	...	...	...	...	...	...
3	1	2	...	...	...	...	...	...	...
525	21	367	137	...	...	...	...	...	...
652	22	447	183	...	...	...	...	...	...
2,600	120	1,781	699	...	...	...	...	...	...
147	3	99	45	...	...	...	...	...	...
296	5	167	124	...	...	...	...	...	...
1,872	73	1,245	554	...	...	...	...	...	...
938	33	600	305	...	...	...	...	...	...
...	...	...	...	...	...	...	...	...	...
242	15	150	77	...	...	...	...	...	...
744	11	575	158	...	...	...	...	...	...
405	28	252	125	...	...	...	...	...	...

Total including the Civil and

Class.	Group.	Caste, &c. and sub-division.	Religion.	All Ages. Total.	Single.	Married.	Widowed.	Civil condition not stated.
A.—Agricultural.—(Continued.)	1. Military and Dominant.	Kshatriya.— Kshatriya	Hindu.	5,990	2,108	2,687	1,195	...
		do	Sikh.	16	3	7	6	...
		Kumárapatta	Hindu.	...	...	...	...	...
		Rájapindé	,,	833	304	368	161	...
		Kodaga (Coorgs)	,,	4	1	3	...	...
		Rájpút	,,	3,833	1,353	1,687	793	...
		Maráta	,,	21,185	7,604	9,416	4,165	...
		Ráchévár & Ranagára	,,	1,881	716	809	356	...
		Total Group 1		34,072	12,119	14,977	6,976	...
	2. Other Agricultural. (a) Cultivators.	Lingáyet (Gandamané, &c.)	Hindu	64,478	23,620	27,717	13,135	...
		Náyar	,,	50	13	28	9	...
		Pille	,,	245	87	114	44	...
		Tigala	,,	28,050	10,801	12,445	4,802	2
		Vakkaliga.— Vakkaliga	,,	676,333	228,262	287,517	160,479	75
		Sáda	Jain.	494	157	214	123	...
		Tulu	Brahmo.	13	6	3	4	...
		Total Group 2(a)		769,663	262,952	328,038	178,596	77
	4. Forest and Hill Tribes.	Eraliga	Hindu.	551	225	254	72	...
		Koracha	,,	5,192	1,935	2,408	849	...
		Korama	,,	6,859	2,568	3,025	1,266	...
		Kuruba	,,	1,133	334	481	318	...
		Lambáni	,,	18,552	7,753	8,315	2,484	...
		Uriya	,,	3	1	2	...	...
		Total Group 4		32,290	12,813	14,488	4,989	...
		Total Class A		**836,025**	**287,884**	**357,503**	**190,561**	**77**
B.—Professional.—(Continued.)	5. Priests.	Bráhman.— A'ruvelu	Hindu.	2,206	638	1,008	560	...
		A'ruvélu Niyógi	,,	9	2	6	1	...
		Aravattu Vakkalu	,,	2,548	744	1,182	622	...
		Babbúr Kammé	,,	3,403	1,068	1,529	806	...
		Badaga Nádu	,,	11,280	3,334	5,174	2,772	...
		Brihachcharana	,,	636	184	302	150	...
		Chitpávan	,,	808	213	383	212	...
		Dés'ast'h	,,	8,640	2,740	3,787	2,113	...
		Drávida	,,	3,757	1,032	1,784	941	...
		Guzaráti	,,	...	...	...	...	...
		Gauda	,,	961	312	412	237	...
		Halé Kannadiga	,,	3,760	1,222	1,723	821	...
		Havika	,,	1,644	385	774	485	...

TABLE E.—(*Continued.*)

Military Station, Bangalore.

Females.

0 to 9: Total.	Single.	Married.	Widowed.	Civil condition not stated.	10 to 14: Total.	Single.	Married.	Widowed.	Civil condition not stated.
1,568	1,535	33	...	...	659	431	224	4	...
3	3	...	...	...	...	...	...	...	...
...	...	...	...	...	...	...	...	...	...
201	199	2	...	...	104	82	22	...	...
1	1	...	...	...	...	...	...	...	...
1,056	1,048	8	...	...	318	235	82	1	...
6,026	5,897	129	...	...	1,951	1,310	639	2	...
575	573	2	...	...	173	129	43	...	...
9,430	*9,256*	*174*	...	...	*3,210*	*2,187*	*1,016*	*7*	...
17,311	17,007	302	2	...	6,481	4,794	1,663	21	...
10	10	...	...	...	3	2	1	...	...
61	61	...	...	...	25	19	6	...	...
8,694	8,651	42	...	1	2,164	1,620	543	1	...
194,168	185,151	8,913	103	1	47,180	27,018	19,508	652	2
148	144	4	...	...	30	10	19	1	...
5	5	...	...	...	1	1	...	...	...
220,727	*211,329*	*9,291*	*105*	*2*	*55,884*	*33,464*	*21,743*	*675*	*2*
183	182	1	...	...	32	29	3	...	...
1,420	1,411	9	...	...	407	370	37	...	...
2,041	2,017	23	...	...	548	408	140	...	...
238	236	2	...	...	77	57	20	...	...
5,715	5,701	14	...	...	1,560	1,338	222	...	...
1	1	...	...	...	...	...	...	...	...
9,597	*9,548*	*49*	...	...	*2,652*	*2,230*	*422*	...	...
239,754	**230,133**	**9,514**	**105**	**2**	**61,746**	**37,881**	**23,181**	**682**	**2**
587	554	33	...	...	217	84	129	4	...
1	1	...	...	...	3	1	2	...	...
682	654	28	...	...	242	90	151	1	...
977	932	40	5	...	357	136	195	26	...
3,016	2,878	134	4	...	1,198	456	692	50	...
171	164	7	...	...	68	20	47	1	...
171	167	4	...	...	116	46	69	1	...
2,475	2,336	133	6	...	963	404	494	65	...
928	859	68	1	...	454	173	277	4	...
...	...	...	...	...	...	...	...	...	...
266	253	10	...	...	95	56	37	2	...
1,072	1,031	45	6	...	341	201	122	23	...
275	259	16	...	...	266	126	138	2	...

Total including the Civil and

Class.	Group.	Caste, &c. and sub-division.	Religion.	15 to 39. Total.	Single.	Married.	Widowed.	Civil condition not stated.
A.—Agricultural.—(Continued.)	1. Military and Dominant.	Kshatriya. — Kshatriya	Hindu.	2,342	140	1,842	360	...
		do	Sikh.	6	..	6	...	...
		Kumárapaṭṭa	Hindu.	...	...	...	..	...
		Rájapindé	,,	334	23	263	48	...
		Kodagu (Coorgs)	,,	3	...	3	...	...
		Rájput	,,	1,583	69	1,271	243	...
		Maráṭa ...	,,	8,487	385	6,728	1,374	...
		Ráchévár & Raṇagára	,,	698	44	564	90	...
		Total Group 1		*13,453*	*661*	*10,677*	*2,115*	...
	2. Agricultural, (a) Cultivators.	Lingáyet (Gaṇḍamané, &c.)	Hindu.	25,502	1,713	20,128	3,661	...
		Náyar	,,	26	1	23	2	...
		Piḷḷé	,,	99	7	82	10	...
		Tigaḷa	,,	11,397	492	9,632	1,273	...
		Vakkaliga. — Vakkaliga	,,	286,883	13,066	225,632	48,181	4
		Sáda	Jain.	212	3	166	43	...
		Tuḷu	Bramho.	4	..	2	2	...
		Total Group 2(a)		*324,123*	*15,282*	*255,665*	*53,172*	*4*
	4. Forest and Hill Tribes.	Urliga	Hindu.	241	13	207	21	...
		Koracha	,,	2,245	146	1,883	216	...
		Korama	,,	2,633	142	2,167	324	...
		Kuruba	,,	498	36	357	105	...
		Lambáṇi	,,	7,897	652	6,668	577	...
		Uriya	,,	1	...	1	...	...
		Total Group 4		*13,515*	*989*	*11,313*	*1,213*	...
		Total Class A		**351,121**	**16,932**	**277,655**	**56,530**	**4**
B.—Professional.—(Continued).	5. Priests.	Bráhmaṇ. — A'ruvélu	Hindu.	808	...	653	155	...
		A'ruvélu Niyógi	,,	3	...	3	...	...
		Aravattu Vakkalu	,,	1,000	...	816	184	...
		Babbúr Kammé	,,	1,294	...	1,057	237	...
		Badaga Náḍu	,,	4,443	...	3,527	916	...
		Brihachcharaṇa	,,	236	...	197	39	...
		Chitpávan	,,	299	...	232	67	...
		Dés'ast'h	,,	3,236	...	2,535	701	...
		Dráviḍa	,,	1,472	...	1,168	304	...
		Guzaráti	,,	...	...	...	...	...
		Gauḍa	,,	366	...	294	72	...
		Haḷé Kannaḍiga	,,	1,400	...	1,165	235	...
		Havika	,,	697	...	522	175	...

TABLE E.—(Continued.)

Military Station, Bangalore.

Females.

40 and over.					Age not stated.				
Total.	Single.	Married.	Widowed.	Civil condition not stated.	Total.	Single.	Married.	Widowed.	Civil condition not stated.
1,421	2	588	831	...	...	...	...	...	...
7	...	1	6	...	...	...	...	...	...
...			...	...	...	...	...	...	...
194	...	81	113	...	...	...	...	...	...
...	...	...	...	...	...	...	...	...	...
876	1	326	549	...	...	...	...	...	...
5,021	12	1,920	3,089	...	...	...	...	...	...
460	...	194	266	...	...	...	...	...	...
7,979	*15*	*3,110*	*4,854*	...	...	...	...	...	...
15,184	112	5,621	9,451	...	...	...	...	...	...
11	...	4	7	...	...	...	...	...	...
60	...	26	34	...	...	...	...	...	...
5,795	38	2,228	3,528	1	...	...	...	...	...
147,427	2,580	33,357	111,477	13	345	147	77	66	55
104	...	25	79	...	...	...	...	...	...
3	...	1	2	...	...	...	...	...	...
168,584	*2,730*	*41,262*	*124,578*	*14*	*345*	*147*	*77*	*66*	*55*
95	1	43	51	...	...	...	...	...	...
1,120	8	479	633	...	...	...	...	...	...
1,610	3	665	942	...	...	...	...	...	...
320	2	105	213	...	...	...	...	...	...
3,350	32	1,411	1,907	...	...	...	...	...	...
1	...	1	...	...	...	...	...	...	...
6,496	*46*	*2,704*	*3,746*	...	...	...	...	...	...
183,059	**2,791**	**47,076**	**133,178**	**14**	**345**	**147**	**77**	**66**	**55**
594	...	193	401	...	...	...	...	...	...
2	...	1	1	...	...	...	...	...	...
624	...	187	437	...	...	...	...	...	...
775	...	237	538	...	...	...	...	...	...
2,623	...	821	1,802	...	...	...	...	...	...
161	...	51	110	...	...	...	...	...	...
222	...	78	144	...	...	...	...	...	...
1,966	...	625	1,341	...	...	...	...	...	...
903	...	271	632	...	...	...	...	...	...
	...	...	...	...	...	...	...	...	...
234	...	71	163	...	...	...	...	...	...
948	...	391	557	...	...	...	...	...	...
406	...	98	308	...	...	...	...	...	...

Class.	Group.	Caste, &c., and sub-division.	Religion.	All Ages. Total.	Single.	Married.	Widowed.	Civil condition not stated.
B.—Professional.—(Continued.)	5. Priests.—(Continued.)	Brámhan.—(Concluded.)						
		Hois'aniga ...	Hindu.	4,141	1,916	1,858	367	...
		Karnáṭaka ...	,,	462	240	174	48	...
		Kumbálu or Tóṭada Tigala.	,,	62	28	25	9	...
		Kandávaru ...	,,	106	57	39	10	...
		Kannada Kammé ...	,,	1,330	666	550	114	...
		Karáḍe	,,	133	54	62	17	...
		Kásalnáḍ ...	,,	17	10	6	1	...
		Kavargri	,,	5	3	1	1	...
		Kóṭa	,,	10	5	3	2	...
		Kánakubja or Kanyákubja.	,,	9	4	4	1	...
		Konkaṇast'h ...	,,	150	81	57	12	...
		Kandáḍe ...	,,	6	2	3	1	...
		Kátyáyana ...	,,	67	35	27	5	...
		Mulikináḍu or Murikináḍu.	,,	5,586	2,739	2,344	503	...
		Mandyáttár ...	,,	312	146	130	36	...
		Nambúri ...	,,	8	4	3	1	...
		Nandavaidíka ...	,,	639	319	255	65	...
		Prat'hamas'ákhe ...	,,	2,541	1,202	1,132	207	...
		Prativádi Bhayankaruttár.	,,	1	...	1		...
		Panchagráma ...	,,	184	85	77	22	...
		Sankéti	,,	1,255	610	527	118	...
		Sárasvata ...	,,	77	39	33	5	...
		S'irnáḍu ...	,,	1,798	867	764	167	...
		S'is'uvarga ...	,,	64	33	28	3	...
		Sivaḷḷi	,,	1,220	618	512	90	...
		Smárta	,,	12,091	5,791	5,537	763	...
		Srívaishṇava ...	,,	8,287	4,279	3,519	489	...
		Kaḍámbiyár ...	,,	2	1	1	...	...
		Srívaishṇava, Hebbár.	,,	851	448	343	60	...
		Telaghánya ...	,,	980	524	388	68	...
		Tuḷuva	,,	2	1	1	...	...
		Tirumaleyár ...	,,	130	58	63	9	...
		Ulachakammé ...	,,	2,395	1,213	1,007	175	...
		Utráji (Uttrádi) ...	,,	237	119	103	15	...
		Vadama ...	,,	709	347	308	54	...
		Vangípuram ...	,,	96	41	46	9	...
		Velnáḍu	,,	1,648	795	712	141	...
		Vijápurada kammé ...	,,	20	10	8	2	...
		Véginádu ...	,,	1	...	1	...	...
		Vaishṇava (Mádhva) ...	,,	3,715	1,819	1,635	261	...
		Total Brámhan ...		92,169	45,546	39,369	7,254	...

TABLE E.—(Continued)

cial.

Males.

0 to 9					10 to 14				
Total.	Single.	Married.	Widowed.	Civil condition not stated.	Total.	Single.	Married.	Widowed.	Civil condition not stated.
1,100	1,089	10	1	...	318	268	49	1	...
125	125	...	...	...	35	35	...	...	...
14	14	...	...	...	10	10	...	...	...
38	38	...	...	...	9	9	...	...	...
428	428	...	...	...	95	87	8	...	...
29	29	...	...	...	11	11	...	...	...
5	5	...	...	...	3	2	1	...	...
1	1	...	...	...	1	1	...	...	...
3	3	...	...	...	1	1	...	...	...
1	1	...	...	...	2	2	...	...	...
48	48	...	...	...	14	14	...	...	...
2	2	...	...	...	...	...	...	...	...
16	16	...	...	...	14	14	...	...	...
1,465	1,465	...	...	...	521	485	36	...	...
95	88	7	...	...	46	29	16	1	...
3	3	...	...	...	1	1	...	...	...
131	131	...	...	...	45	44	1	...	...
667	667	...	...	...	207	195	11	1	...
...	...	...	...	...	...	...	...	...	...
45	45	...	...	...	18	18	...	...	...
375	370	5	...	...	116	96	20	...	...
20	20	...	...	...	10	10	...	...	...
455	453	2	...	...	151	133	13	...	...
21	21	...	...	...	8	7	1	...	...
263	260	3	...	...	136	122	14	...	...
2,831	2,798	30	3	...	1,021	924	93	4	...
2,379	2,348	29	2	...	910	799	107	4	...
1	1	...	...	...	...	...	...	...	...
263	263	...	...	...	88	84	4	...	...
246	245	1	...	...	106	99	7	...	...
1	1	...	...	...	...	...	...	...	...
43	43	...	...	...	12	10	2	...	...
674	674	...	...	...	203	197	6	...	...
59	59	...	...	...	38	38	...	...	...
192	190	2	...	...	64	61	3	...	...
26	26	...	...	...	7	7	...	...	...
417	417	...	...	...	142	141	1	...	...
6	6	...	...	...	3	3	...	...	...
...	...	...	...	...	...	...	...	...	...
883	868	14	1	...	394	334	56	4	...
24,631	*24,438*	*182*	*11*	...	*8,709*	*7,758*	*953*	*28*	...

Provin

Class.	Group.	Caste, &c., and sub-division.		Religion.	15 to 30. Total.	Single.	Married.	Widowed	Civil condition not stated.
B.—Professional.—(Continued.)	5. Priests.—(Concluded.)	Bráhman.—(Continued.)	Hois'aṇiga ...	Hindu.	1,782	512	1,157	113	...
			Karṇáṭika ...	,,	211	71	124	16	..
			Kambalúr or Tóṭada Tigaḷa.	,,	23	4	17	2	...
			Kandávara ...	,,	42	10	31	1	..
			Kannaḍa Kammé ...	,,	547	141	369	37	..
			Karádé ...	,,	61	14	65	2	..
			Kásalnáḍ ...	,,	5	3	2		..
			Kavarga... ...	,,	2	1	1		..
			Kóṭa	,,	4	1	2	1	..
			Káṇakubja or Kanyákubja.	,,	4	1	3	...	..
			Konkaṇásth ...	,,	58	19	36	3	..
			Kandáḍé ..	,,	1	...	1	...	..
			Kátyáyana ...	,,	23	4	19	...	..
			Mulikinádu or Murikinádu.	,,	2,233	711	1,423	99	..
			Mandyáttar ...	,,	106	23	78	5	..
			Nambúri ...	,,	2	...	2	...	...
			Nandavaidika ...	,,	290	121	153	16	...
			Prat'hamas'ákhe ...	,,	1,027	311	680	36	...
			Prativádi Bhayankarattár.	,,	1	...	1	...	...
			Panchagráma ...	,,	78	21	49	8	...
			Sankéti	,,	491	144	320	27	...
			Sárasvata ...	,,	29	8	19	2	...
			S'irnáḍu... ...	,,	757	250	471	36	...
			S'is'uvarga ...	,,	24	5	18	1	...
			Sivaḷḷi	,,	578	224	340	14	...
			Smárta	,,	5,682	1,996	3,511	175	...
			Srivaishṇava ...	,,	3,267	1,083	2,078	106	...
			Kaḍámbiyár ...	,,	1	...	1	...	...
			Śrivaishṇava, Hebbár	,,	338	96	227	15	...
			Telaghánya ...	,,	416	169	231	16	...
			Tuḷuva	,,	1	...	1	...	...
			Tirumaleyár ...	,,	46	5	39	2	...
			Uḷachakammé ...	,,	958	314	606	38	...
			Utráji (Uttrádi) ...	,,	93	20	71	2	...
			Vaḍama ...	,,	319	92	214	13	...
			Vangípuram ...	,,	43	7	34	2	...
			Velnáḍu... ...	,,	666	212	425	29	...
			Vijápurada kammé ...	,,	8	1	7	...	...
			Véginádu ...	,,	...	...	...	...	...
			Vaishṇava (Mádhva)..	,,	1,706	586	1,044	76	...
			Total Bráhman......		*38,607*	*12,513*	*24,347*	*1,747*	...

TABLE E.—(Continued.)

cial.

Males.

40 and over.					Age not stated.				
Total.	Single.	Married.	Widowed.	Civil condition not stated.	Total.	Single.	Married.	Widowed.	Civil condition not stated.
932	38	642	252	...	...	...	...	...	...
91	9	50	32	...	...	...	...	...	...
15	...	8	7	...	...	...	...	...	...
17	...	8	9	...	...	...	...	...	...
260	10	173	77	...	...	...	...	...	...
32	...	17	15	...	...	...	...	...	...
4	...	3	1	...	...	...	...	...	...
1	...	...	1	...	...	...	...	...	...
2	...	1	1	...	...	...	...	...	...
2	...	1	1	...	...	...	...	...	...
30	...	21	9	...	...	...	...	...	...
3	...	2	1	...	...	...	...	...	...
14	1	8	5	...	...	...	...	...	...
1,367	78	885	404	...	...	...	...	...	...
65	6	29	30	...	...	...	...	...	...
2	...	1	1	...	...	...	...	...	...
173	23	101	49	...	...	...	...	...	...
640	29	441	170	...	...	...	...	...	...
...	...	...	...	...	...	...	...	...	...
43	1	28	14	...	...	...	...	...	...
273	...	182	91	...	...	...	...	...	...
18	1	14	3	...	...	...	...	...	...
435	26	278	131	...	...	...	...	...	...
11	...	9	2	...	...	...	...	...	...
243	12	155	76	...	...	...	...	...	...
2,557	73	1,903	581	...	...	...	...	...	...
1,731	49	1,305	377	...	...	...	...	...	...
...	...	...	...	...	...	...	...	...	...
162	5	112	45	...	...	...	...	...	...
212	11	149	52	...	...	...	...	...	...
...	...	...	...	...	...	...	...	...	...
29	...	22	7	...	...	...	...	...	...
560	28	395	137	...	...	...	...	...	...
47	2	32	13	...	...	...	...	...	...
134	4	89	41	...	...	...	...	...	...
20	1	12	7	...	...	...	...	...	...
423	25	286	112	...	...	...	...	...	...
3	...	1	2	...	...	...	...	...	...
1	...	1	...	...	...	...	...	...	...
732	31	521	180	...	...	...	...	...	...
20,172	*817*	*13,887*	*5,468*	...	...	...	...	...	...

Class.	Caste and Religion.			All Ages.				
	Group.	Caste, &c., and sub-division.	Religion.	Total.	Single.	Married.	Widowed.	Civil condition not stated.
B.—Professional.—(Continued.)	5. Priests.—(Continued.)	Brámhan.—(Concluded.) Hois'aniga ...	Hindu.	4,187	1,255	1,880	1,052	...
		Karnátaka ...	,,	414	94	175	145	...
		Kumbálúr or Tótada Tigala.	,,	51	16	27	8	...
		Kandávara ...	,,	107	24	49	34	...
		Kannada Kammé ...	,,	1,389	498	592	299	...
		Karádé	,,	120	33	68	10	...
		Kásalnád ...	,,	13	6	6	1	...
		Kavarga ...	,,	2	1	1	...	...
		Kóta	,,	15	3	4	8	...
		Kánnakubja or Kanyákubja.	,,	3	...	3	...	...
		Konkanast'h ...	,,	137	42	66	29	...
		Kandádé ...	,,	3	1	2	...	...
		Kátyáyana ...	,,	72	21	30	21	...
		Mulikinádu or Murikinádu.	,,	5,422	1,579	2,515	1,328	...
		Mandyáttár ...	,,	254	88	111	65	...
		Nambúri ...	,,	6	1	3	2	...
		Nandavaidika ...	,,	587	167	250	170	...
		Prat'hamas'ákhe ...	,,	2,469	659	1,233	577	...
		Prativádi Bhayankarattár.	,,	1	...	1	...	...
		Panchagráma ...	,,	174	50	77	47	...
		Sankéti ...	,,	1,267	434	542	291	...
		Sárasvata ...	,,	47	15	26	6	...
		S'irnádu ...	,,	1,691	464	797	430	...
		S'is'uvarga ...	,,	75	20	29	26	...
		Sivalli ...	,,	1,177	278	556	343	...
		Smárta ...	,,	11,153	3,271	5,236	2,646	...
		Srívaishnava ...	,,	8,415	2,586	3,790	2,039	...
		Kadámbiyár ...	,,	1	...	1	...	...
		Srivaishnava, Hebbár	,,	873	281	397	195	...
		Telagbánya ...	,,	925	272	401	252	...
		Tuluva	,,	2	1	1	...	...
		Tirumaleyár ...	,,	232	46	55	31	...
		Ulachakammé ...	,,	2,349	645	1,101	603	...
		Utráji (Uttrádi) ...	,,	188	74	87	27	...
		Vadama ...	,,	710	226	341	143	...
		Vangipuram ...	,,	97	28	51	18	...
		Velnádu ...	,,	1,467	367	700	400	...
		Vijápurada kammé.	,,	17	4	10	3	...
		Véginádu ...	,,	...	...	...	...	...
		Vaishnava (Mádhva).	,,	3,549	1,086	1,701	762	...
		Total Brámhan...	....	89,063	20,484	40,891	21,688	...

TABLE E.—(*Continued.*)

cial.

Females.

0 to 9					10 to 14				
Total.	Single.	Married.	Widowed.	Civil condition not stated.	Total.	Single.	Married.	Widowed.	Civil condition not stated.
1,126	1,069	51	6	...	434	186	220	28	...
91	91	...	...	...	28	3	21	4	...
11	10	1	...	...	6	6	...	...	...
21	20	1	...	...	8	4	4	...	...
447	435	12	...	...	122	63	56	3	...
26	26	...	...	...	11	7	4	...	...
6	6	...	...	...	1	...	1	...	...
1	1	...	...	...	...	...	...	...	...
3	3	...	...	...	1	...	1	...	...
...	...	...	...	...	...	...	...	...	...
36	33	3	...	...	16	9	7	...	...
1	1	...	...	...	...	...	...	...	...
20	19	1	...	...	7	2	5	...	...
1,498	1,415	81	2	...	512	164	332	16	...
90	77	13	...	...	46	11	33	2	...
1	1	...	...	...	1	...	1	...	...
153	146	7	...	...	58	21	36	1	...
643	603	40	...	...	201	56	142	3	...
...	...	...	...	...	...	...	...	...	...
42	40	2	...	...	22	10	10	2	...
413	391	20	2	...	124	43	74	7	...
14	14	...	...	...	4	1	3	...	...
439	418	21	...	...	154	46	107	1	...
18	16	2	...	...	8	4	4	...	...
292	256	33	3	...	157	22	121	14	...
2,883	2,679	176	28	...	1,345	592	646	107	...
2,365	2,227	126	12	...	928	359	518	51	...
...	...	...	...	...	...	...	...	...	...
246	236	10	...	...	91	45	46	...	...
254	236	18	...	...	123	36	83	4	...
1	1	...	...	...	...	...	...	...	...
44	44	...	...	...	8	2	6	...	...
646	606	40	...	...	192	39	152	1	...
60	60	...	...	...	26	14	12	...	...
211	195	16	...	...	85	31	53	1	...
29	27	2	...	...	9	1	8	...	...
363	336	27	...	...	131	31	97	3	...
4	4	...	...	...	3	...	3	...	...
...	...	...	...	...	...	...	...	...	...
943	879	51	13	...	431	207	193	31	...
24,035	*22,678*	*1,269*	*88*	...	*9,605*	*3,806*	*5,341*	*458*	...

Class.	Group.	Caste, &c. and sub-division.	Religion.	15 to 39. Total.	Single.	Married.	Widowed.	Civil condition not stated.
B.—Professional—(Continued.)	5. Priests.—(Continued.)	Brámhan.—(Concluded.) Hois'aṇiga	Hindu.	1,583	...	1,250	333	...
		Karṇáṭaka	,,	160	...	122	47	...
		Kumbálúr or Tóṭada Tigala.	,,	20	...	18	2	...
		Kandávara	,,	46	...	37	9	...
		Kaṇṇaḍa Kammé	,,	530	...	423	107	...
		Karáḍe	,,	55	...	50	5	...
		Kásalnád	,,	4	...	4	...	...
		Kavarga	,,	1	...	1	...	...
		Kóṭa	,,	6	...	3	3	...
		Káṇakubja or Kanyákubja.	,,	3	...	3	...	...
		Konkaṇast'h	,,	54	...	45	9	...
		Kandáḍé	,,	1	...	1	...	...
		Kátyáyana	,,	28	...	19	9	...
		Mulikináḍu or Murikináḍu.	,,	2,018	...	1,636	382	...
		Maṇḍyáttár	,,	65	...	46	19	...
		Nambúri	,,	2	...	2	...	...
		Nandavaidíka	,,	204	...	153	51	...
		Prat'hamas'ákho	,,	1,021	...	834	187	...
		Partivádi Bhayankaruttár.	,,	1	...	1	...	...
		Panchagráma	,,	60	...	45	15	...
		Sankéti	,,	446	...	359	87	...
		Sárasvata	,,	22	...	21	1	...
		S'írnáḍu	,,	656	...	521	135	...
		S'is'uvarga	,,	30	...	19	11	...
		Sivaḷḷi	,,	444	...	328	116	...
		Smárta	,,	3,993	...	3,327	666	...
		Srívaishṇava	,,	2,911	...	2,385	526	...
		Kaḍámbiyár	,,	1	...	1	...	...
		Srívaishṇava, Hebbár	,,	319	...	267	52	...
		Telaghánya	,,	349	...	247	102	...
		Tuḷuva	,,	1	...	1	...	...
		Tirumaleyár	,,	44	...	35	9	...
		Ulachakammé	,,	935	...	733	202	...
		Utráji (Uttrádi)	,,	65	...	58	7	...
		Vaḍama	,,	266	...	221	45	...
		Vangípuram	,,	39	...	37	2	...
		Velnáḍu	,,	589	...	455	134	...
		Vijápurada kammé	,,	7	...	7	...	...
		Végináḍu	,,	...	...	...	...	...
		Vaishṇava (Mádhva)	,,	1,249	...	1,079	170	...
		Total Brámhaṇ		33,420	...	26,904	6,516	...

TABLE E.—(*Continued.*)

cial.

Females.

40 and over.					Age not stated.				
Total.	Single.	Married.	Widowed.	Civil condition not stated.	Total.	Single.	Married.	Widowed.	Civil condition not stated.
1,044	...	359	685	...	...	...	...	...	...
126	...	32	94	...	...	...	...	...	...
14	...	8	6	...	...	...	...	...	...
32	...	7	25	...	...	...	...	...	...
290	...	101	189	...	...	...	...	...	...
28	...	14	14	...	...	...	...	...	...
2	...	1	1	...	...	...	...	...	...
...	...	...	...	...	...	...	...	...	...
5	...	...	5	...	...	...	...	...	...
...	...	...	...	...	...	...	...	...	...
31	...	11	20	...	...	...	...	...	...
1	...	1	...	...	...	...	...	...	...
17	...	5	12	...	...	...	...	...	...
1,394	...	466	928	...	...	...	...	...	...
53	...	19	34	...	...	...	...	...	...
2	...	...	2	...	...	...	...	...	...
172	...	54	118	...	...	...	...	...	...
604	...	217	387	...	...	...	...	...	...
...	...	...	...	...	...	...	...	...	...
50	...	20	30	...	...	...	...	...	...
284	...	89	195	...	...	...	...	...	...
7	...	2	5	...	...	...	...	...	...
412	...	118	294	...	...	...	...	...	...
19	...	4	15	...	...	...	...	...	...
284	...	74	210	...	...	...	...	...	...
2,932	...	1,087	1,845	...	...	...	...	...	...
2,211	...	761	1,450	...	...	...	...	...	...
...	...	...	...	...	...	...	...	...	...
217	...	74	143	...	...	...	...	...	...
199	...	53	146	...	...	...	...	...	...
...	...	...	...	...	...	...	...	...	...
36	...	14	22	...	...	...	...	...	...
576	...	176	400	...	...	...	...	...	...
37	...	17	20	...	...	...	...	...	...
148	...	51	97	...	...	...	...	...	...
20	...	4	16	...	...	...	...	...	...
384	...	121	263	...	...	...	...	...	...
3	...	...	3	...	...	...	...	...	...
...	...	...	...	...	...	...	...	...	...
926	...	378	548	...	...	...	...	...	...
22,003	...	*7,377*	*14,626*	...	...	...	...	...	...

Bangalore

Class.	Group.	Caste, &c. and sub-division.	Religion.	All Ages. Total.	All Ages. Single.	All Ages. Married.	All Ages. Widowed.	All Ages. Civil condition not stated.
B.—Professional.—(Continued.)	5. Priests.—(Continued.)	Brámhan.—(Concluded.) Hois'aniga ...	Hindu.	481	238	201	45	...
		Karṇáṭaka ...	,,	...	...	...	...	...
		Kumbálár or Tóṭada Tigaḷa.	,,	7	4	2	1	...
		Kandávara ...	,,	1	1	...	...	...
		Kannaḍa Kammé ...	,,	161	82	63	16	...
		Karáḍe ...	,,	4	2	1	1	...
		Kásalnáḍ ...	,,	13	7	5	1	...
		Kavarga	,,	...	...	...	...	...
		Kóṭa ...	,,	...	...	...	...	...
		Káṇakubja or Kanyákubja.	,,	4	1	2	1	...
		Konkaṇasth ...	,,	18	8	10	...	...
		Kandáḍé ...	,,	...	...	...	...	...
		Kátyáyana ...	,,	...	...	...	...	...
		Mulikináḍu or Murikináḍu.	,,	1,833	883	822	128	...
		Mandyáttár ...	,,	275	125	116	34	...
		Nambúri ...	,,	...	...	...	...	...
		Nandavaidíka ...	,,	101	47	47	7	...
		Prathamas'ákhe ...	,,	836	404	277	55	...
		Prativádi Bhayankarattár.	,,	...	...	...	...	...
		Panchagráma ...	,,	...	...	...	...	...
		Sankéti ...	,,	10	4	4	2	...
		Sárasvata ...	,,	5	2	3	...	...
		S'irnáḍu ...	,,	428	200	183	45	...
		S'is'uvarga ...	,,	...	...	...	...	...
		Sivaḷḷi ...	,,	3	1	2	...	...
		Smárta ...	,,	806	365	385	56	...
		Srívaishṇava ...	,,	1,155	589	509	57	...
		Kaḍámbiyár ...	,,	2	1	1	...	...
		Srívaishṇava, Hebbár	,,	66	34	24	8	...
		Telaghánya ...	,,	154	79	59	16	...
		Tuḷuva ...	,,	2	1	1	...	...
		Tirumaleyár ...	,,	123	55	60	8	...
		Ulachakammé ...	,,	94	201	166	27	...
		Utráji (Uttrádi) ...	,,	61	27	28	6	...
		Vaḍama ...	,,	194	85	98	11	...
		Vangipuram ...	,,	9	3	5	1	...
		Velnáḍu ...	,,	543	242	256	45	...
		Vijápurada kammé ...	,,	6	3	2	1	...
		Véginádu ...	,,	...	...	...	...	...
		Vaishṇava (Mádhva) ...	,,	473	229	211	33	...
		Total Brámhan		*14,584*	*7,190*	*6,311*	*1,083*	...

TABLE E.—(Continued.)

District.

Males.

0 to 9					10 to 14				
Total.	Single.	Married.	Widowed.	Civil condition not stated.	Total.	Single.	Married.	Widowed.	Civil condition not stated.
146	114	2	...	...	36	27	9	...	...
...	...	...	...	...	...	...	...	...	...
2	2	...	...	...	1	1	...	...	...
...	...	...	...	...	...	...	...	...	...
47	47	...	...	...	15	14	1	...	...
1	1	...	...	...	1	1	...	...	...
3	3	...	...	...	3	2	1	...	...
...	...	...	...	...	...	...	...	...	...
...	...	...	...	...	...	...	...	...	...
...	...	...	...	...	1	1	...	...	...
7	7	...	...	...	1	1	...	...	...
...	...	...	...	...	...	...	...	...	...
...	...	...	...	...	...	...	...	...	...
469	469	...	...	...	206	190	16	...	...
82	75	7	...	...	43	26	16	...	...
...	...	...	...	...	...	...	...	...	...
18	18	...	...	...	8	8	...	...	...
228	228	...	...	...	70	65	5	...	...
...	...	...	...	...	...	...	...	...	...
...	...	...	...	...	...	...	...	...	...
3	3	...	...	...	1	1	...	...	...
1	1	...	...	...	1	1	...	...	...
110	108	2	...	...	42	36	6	...	...
...	...	...	...	...	...	...	...	...	...
1	1	...	...	...	...	...	...	...	...
174	173	1	...	...	77	73	4	...	...
319	319	...	...	...	118	110	8	...	...
1	1	...	...	...	...	...	...	...	...
20	20	...	...	...	5	5	...	...	...
46	46	...	...	...	19	15	4	...	...
1	1	...	...	...	...	...	...	...	...
43	43	...	...	...	10	8	2	...	...
97	97	...	...	...	34	32	2	...	...
11	11	...	...	...	9	9	...	...	...
39	39	...	...	...	25	23	2	...	...
3	3	...	...	...	...	...	...	...	...
119	119	...	...	...	55	55	...	...	...
2	2	...	...	...	1	1	...	...	...
...	...	...	...	...	...	...	...	...	...
103	103	...	...	...	49	41	8	...	...
3,823	*3,799*	*23*	...	...	*1,485*	*1,332*	*152*	*1*	...

Caste and Religion.				15 to 39				
Class.	Group.	Caste, &c. and sub-division.	Religion.	Total.	Single.	Married.	Widowed.	Civil condition not stated.
B.—Professional.—(Continued.)	5. Priests.—(Continued.)	Brámhan.—(Concluded.) Hois'aniga	Hindu.	203	63	128	12	...
		Karnâṭaka	,,	...	...	...	...	...
		Kumbálúr or Tóṭada Tigaḷa.	,,	3	1	1	1	...
		Kandâvara	,,	1	1	...	...	...
		Kannaḍa Kammé	,,	69	19	46	4	...
		Karáde	,,	1	...	1	...	...
		Kasalnâḍ	,,	3	2	1	...	...
		Kavarga	,,	...	...	...	...	...
		Kōṭa	,,	...	...	...	...	...
		Káṇakubja or Kanyákubja.	,,	1	...	1	...	...
		Konkaṇast'h	,,	7	...	7	...	...
		Kandâḍé	,,	...	...	...	...	...
		Kâtyâyana	,,	...	...	...	...	...
		Mulikináḍu or Murikináḍu.	,,	702	207	472	23	...
		Manḍyáttár	,,	91	18	68	5	...
		Nambúri	,,	...	...	...	...	...
		Nandavaidíka	,,	53	21	31	1	...
		Prat'hamas'âkha	,,	325	106	212	7	...
		Prativadi Bhayankarattár.	,,	...	...	...	...	...
		Panchagrâma	,,	...	...	...	...	...
		Sankéti	,,	4	...	3	1	...
		Sárasvata	,,	2	...	2	1	...
		S'irnâḍu	,,	171	50	113	8	...
		S'is'u varga	,,	...	...	...	...	...
		Sivaḷḷi	,,	1	...	1	...	...
		Smárta	,,	321	109	203	9	...
		Srivaishṇava	,,	488	147	326	15	...
		Kaḍâmbiyár	,,	1	...	1	...	...
		Srivaishṇava, Hebbár	,,	29	9	17	3	...
		Telaghâṇya	,,	53	18	33	2	...
		Tuḷuva	,,	1	...	1	...	...
		Tirumalêyár	,,	43	5	36	2	...
		Uluchakammé	,,	163	64	94	5	...
		Utrâji (Uttrâḍi)	,,	26	7	18	1	...
		Vaḍama	,,	89	20	68	1	...
		Vangipuram	,,	4	...	4	...	...
		Velnaḍu	,,	198	60	134	4	...
		Vijapurada kammé	,,	2	...	2	...	...
		Véginâḍu	,,	...	...	...	...	...
		Vaishṇava (Mádhva)	,,	206	80	120	6	...
		Total Brámhan	....	*5,906*	*1,923*	*3,765*	*218*	...

TABLE E.—(*Continued.*)

District.

Males.

40 and over.					Age not stated.				
Total.	Single.	Married.	Widowed.	Civil condition not stated.	Total.	Single.	Married.	Widowed.	Civil condition not stated.
99	4	62	33	...	...	...	...	...	...
...	...	...	...	...	...	...	...	...	...
1	...	1	...	...	...	...	...	...	...
...	...	...	...	...	...	...	...	...	...
30	2	16	12	...	...	...	...	...	...
1	...	...	1	...	...	...	...	...	...
4	...	3	1	...	...	...	...	...	...
...	...	...	...	...	...	...	...	...	...
...	...	...	...	...	...	...	...	...	...
2	...	1	1	...	...	...	...	...	...
3	...	3	...	...	...	...	...	...	...
...	...	...	...	...	...	...	...	...	...
...	...	...	...	...	...	...	...	...	...
456	17	334	105	...	...	...	...	...	...
59	6	25	28	...	...	...	...	...	...
...	...	...	...	...	...	...	...	...	...
22	...	16	6	...	...	...	...	...	...
213	5	160	48	...	...	...	...	...	...
...	...	...	...	...	...	...	...	...	...
...	...	...	...	...	...	...	...	...	...
2	...	1	1	...	...	...	...	...	...
1	...	...	...	...	...	...	...	...	...
105	6	62	37	...	...	...	...	...	...
...	...	...	...	...	...	...	...	...	...
1	...	1	...	...	...	...	...	...	...
234	10	177	47	...	...	...	...	...	...
230	13	175	42	...	...	...	...	...	...
...	...	...	...	...	...	...	...	...	...
12	...	7	5	...	...	...	...	...	...
36	...	22	14	...	...	...	...	...	...
...	...	...	...	...	...	...	...	...	...
28	...	22	6	...	...	...	...	...	...
100	8	70	22	...	...	...	...	...	...
15	...	10	5	...	...	...	...	...	...
41	3	28	10	...	...	...	...	...	...
2	...	1	1	...	...	...	...	...	...
171	8	122	41	...	...	...	...	...	...
1	...	...	1	...	...	...	...	...	...
...	...	...	...	...	...	...	...	...	...
115	5	83	27	...	...	...	...	...	...
3,371	*136*	*2,371*	*864*	...	...	...	...	...	...

Class.	Group.	Caste and Religion. Caste, &c. and sub-division.		Religion.	All Ages. Total.	Single.	Married.	Widowed.	Civil condition not stated.
B.—Professional.—(Continued.)	5. Priests.—(Continued.)	Bramhan.—(Concluded.)	Hois'aniga ...	Hindu.	439	116	213	110	...
			Karnáṭaka ...	,,	...	...	...	...	...
			Kumbálúr or Tóṭadu Tigula.	,,	2	...	2	...	...
			Kandávara ...	,,	...	...	...	...	...
			Kannaḍa Kammé ...	,,	138	35	65	38	...
			Karáḍe	,,	4	2	1	1	...
			Kásalnád ...	,,	11	5	5	1	...
			Kavarga ...	,,	...	...	...	...	...
			Kóṭa	,,	...	...	...	...	...
			Kuṇakubja or Kanyákubja.	,,	1	...	1	...	...
			Konkaṇast'h ...	,,	21	5	10	6	...
			Kandáḍé ...	,,	...	...	...	...	...
			Kátyáyana ...	,,	...	...	...	...	...
			Mulikináḍu or Murikináḍu.	,,	1,803	505	879	419	...
			Maṇḍyáttár ...	,,	210	71	93	46	...
			Nambúri ...	,,	...	...	...	...	...
			Nandavaidika ...	,,	89	25	46	18	...
			Prat'hamas'ákhe ...	,,	781	207	393	181	...
			Prativádi Bhayankarattár.	,,	...	...	...	...	...
			Panchagráma ...	,,	...	...	...	...	...
			Sankéti	,,	10	3	5	2	...
			Sárasvata ...	,,	3	1	2	...	...
			S'irnáḍu	,,	413	103	205	105	...
			S'is'uvarga ...	,,	...	...	...	...	...
			Sivaḷḷi	,,	3	...	3	...	...
			Smárta	,,	768	290	340	138	...
			Srivaishṇava ...	,,	1,114	323	516	275	...
			Kuḍámbiyár ...	,,	1	...	1	...	...
			Srivaishṇava, Hebbár.	,,	66	21	27	18	...
			Telaghâṇya ...	,,	131	37	61	33	...
			Tuḷuva	,,	2	1	1	...	...
			Tirumaleyár ...	,,	125	45	51	29	...
			Ulachakammé ...	,,	412	121	185	106	...
			Utráji (Uttrádi) ...	,,	49	13	28	8	...
			Vaḍama	,,	138	34	72	32	...
			Vangípuram ...	,,	10	3	4	3	...
			Velnáḍu ...	,,	480	108	245	127	...
			Vijapuraḍa kammé ...	,,	4	1	2	1	...
			Végináḍu ...	,,	...	...	...	...	...
			Vaishṇava (Mádhva) ..	,,	467	160	205	102	...
			Total Brámhan		13,865	4,109	6,401	3,355	...

TABLE E.—(*Continued.*)

District.

Females.

0 to 9					10 to 14				
Total.	Single.	Married.	Widowed.	Civil condition not stated.	Total.	Single.	Married.	Widowed.	Civil condition not stated.
104	102	2	...	...	45	14	31	...	...
...	...	...	...	...	...	...	...	...	...
...	...	...	...	...	...	...	...	...	...
...	...	...	...	...	...	...	...	...	...
31	29	2	...	...	15	6	9	...	...
2	2	...	...	...	...	...	...	...	...
5	5	...	...	...	1	...	1	...	...
...	...	...	...	...	...	...	...	...	...
...	...	...	...	...	...	...	...	...	...
...	...	...	...	...	...	...	...	...	...
5	5	...	...	...	1	...	1	...	...
...	...	...	...	...	...	...	...	...	...
...	...	...	...	...	...	...	...	...	...
474	452	22	...	...	168	53	114	1	...
75	63	12	...	...	38	8	28	2	...
...	...	...	...	...	...	...	...	...	...
24	22	2	...	...	11	3	8	...	...
208	197	11	...	...	44	10	33	1	...
...	...	...	...	...	...	...	...	...	...
...	...	...	...	...	...	...	...	...	...
3	3	...	...	...	...	...	...	...	...
1	1	...	...	...	...	...	...	...	...
100	99	1	...	...	35	4	31	...	...
...	...	...	...	...	...	...	...	...	...
...	...	...	...	...	1	...	1	...	...
242	220	20	2	...	110	70	40	...	...
318	300	17	1	...	105	23	80	2	...
...	...	...	...	...	...	...	...	...	...
15	14	1	...	...	14	7	7	...	...
31	31	...	...	...	14	6	8	...	...
1	1	...	...	...	...	...	...	...	...
43	43	...	...	...	6	2	4	...	...
120	113	7	...	...	39	8	31	...	...
12	12	...	...	...	4	1	3	...	...
35	32	3	...	...	8	2	6	...	...
3	3	...	...	...	...	...	...	...	...
110	102	8	...	...	42	6	35	1	...
1	1	...	...	...	...	...	...	...	...
...	...	...	...	...	...	...	...	...	...
160	150	10	...	...	47	10	35	2	...
3,825	*3,615*	*207*	*3*	...	*1,488*	*494*	*945*	*49*	...

Class.	Group.	Caste, &c. and sub-division.		Religion.	15 to 39. Total.	Single.	Married.	Widowed.	Civil condition not stated.
B.—Professional.—(Continued.)	5. Priests.—(Continued.)	Bráhman.—(Concluded.)	Hois'aṇiga ...	Hindu.	175	...	140	35	...
			Karṇáṭaka ...	,,	...	...	..	...	...
			Kumbálúr or Tóṭada Tigaḷa	,,	2	..	2	...	...
			Kandávara ...	,,	...	...	...	...	...
			Kannaḍa Kammé ...	,,	57	...	44	13	...
			Karáde ...	,,	1	...	1	...	...
			Kásalnád ...	,,	3	...	3	...	...
			Kavarga ...	,,	...	...	...	...	...
			Kóṭa	,,	...	...	...	...	...
			Kanyakubja or Kanyákubja.	,,	1	...	1	...	...
			Konkaṇast'h ...	,,	9	...	8	1	...
			Kandáḍé ...	,,	...	...	...	...	...
			Kátyáyana ...	,,	...	...	...	...	...
			Mulikináḍu or Murikináḍu.	,,	646	...	547	99	...
			Mandyáttár ...	,,	53	...	35	18	...
			Nambúri ..	,,	...	...	...	...	...
			Nandavaidika ...	,,	30	...	27	3	...
			Prat'hamas'ákhe ...	,,	323	...	267	56	...
			Prativádi Bhayankarattár.	,,	...	...	..	...	...
			Panchagráma ...	,,	...	...	...	...	...
			Sankéti ...	,,	4	...	4	...	...
			Sárasvata ...	,,	2	...	2	...	...
			S'irnáḍu ...	,,	157	...	127	30	...
			S'is'uvarga ..	,,	...	...	...	...	...
			Sivaḷḷi	,,	2	...	2	...	...
			Smárta... ...	,,	254	...	210	44	...
			Srivaishṇava ...	,,	423	...	349	74	...
			Kaḍámbiyár ...	,,	1	...	1	...	...
			Srivaishṇava, Hebbár.	,,	25	...	14	11	...
			Tolaghánya ...	,,	49	...	39	10	...
			Tuḷuva	,,	1	...	1	...	...
			Tirumaleyár ...	,,	41	...	33	8	...
			Ulachakammé ...	,,	145	...	110	35	...
			Utráji (Uttrádi) ...	,,	22	...	19	3	...
			Vadama ...	,,	60	...	50	10	...
			Vangipuram ...	,,	5	...	4	1	...
			Veḷnáḍu ...	,,	195	...	155	40	...
			Vijápurada kammé..	,,	2	...	2	...	...
			Véginádu ...	,,	...	...	...	...	...
			Vaishṇava (Mádhva)..	,,	140	...	120	20	...
			Total Bráhman........		5,036	...	4,045	991	...

TABLE E.—(*Continued.*)

District.

Females.

40 and over.					Age not stated.				
Total.	Single.	Married.	Widowed.	Civil condition not stated.	Total.	Single.	Married.	Widowed.	Civil condition not stated.
115	...	40	75	...	...	...	...	...	...
...	...	...	...	...	...	...	...	...	...
...	...	...	...	...	...	...	...	...	...
...	...	...	...	...	...	...	...	...	...
35	...	10	25	...	...	...	...	...	...
1	...	...	1	...	...	...	...	...	...
2	...	1	1	...	...	...	...	...	...
...	...	...	...	...	...	...	...	...	...
...	...	...	...	...	...	...	...	...	...
...	...	...	...	...	...	...	...	...	...
6	...	1	5	...	...	...	...	...	...
...	...	...	...	...	...	...	...	...	...
...	...	...	...	...	...	...	...	...	...
515	...	196	319	...	...	...	...	...	...
41	...	18	20	...	...	...	...	...	...
...	...	...	...	...	...	...	...	...	...
24	...	9	15	...	...	...	...	...	...
206	...	82	124	...	...	...	...	...	...
...	...	...	...	...	...	...	...	...	...
...	...	...	...	...	...	...	...	...	...
3	...	1	2	...	...	...	...	...	...
...	...	...	...	...	...	...	...	...	...
121	...	46	75	...	...	...	...	...	...
...	...	...	...	...	...	...	...	...	...
...	...	...	...	...	...	...	...	...	...
162	...	70	92	...	...	...	...	...	...
266	...	70	196	...	...	...	...	...	...
...	...	...	...	...	...	...	...	...	...
13	...	5	7	...	...	...	...	...	...
37	...	14	23	...	...	...	...	...	...
...	...	...	...	...	...	...	...	...	...
35	...	14	21	...	...	...	...	...	...
108	...	37	71	...	...	...	...	...	...
11	...	6	5	...	...	...	...	...	...
35	...	13	22	...	...	...	...	...	...
2	...	...	2	...	...	...	...	...	...
133	...	47	86	...	...	...	...	...	...
1	...	...	1	...	...	...	...	...	...
...	...	...	...	...	...	...	...	...	...
120	...	40	80	...	...	...	...	...	...
3,516	...	*1,204*	*2,312*	...	...	...	...	...	...

Kolar

Class.	Group.	Caste, &c. and sub-division.	Religion.	All ages. Total.	Single.	Married.	Widowed.	Civil condition not stated.
B.—Professional.—(Continued.)	5. Priests.—(Continued).	Brámhan.—(Concluded.) Hoisániga	Hindu.	33	14	15	4	...
		Karnáṭaka	,,	...	...	...	...	...
		Kumbálúr or Toṭada Tigaḷa.	,,	5	2	2	1	...
		Kandavara	,,	...	...	...	...	...
		Kannaḍa kammé	,,	43	22	16	5	...
		Karáḍe	,,	...	...	...	...	...
		Kásalnáḍ	,,	4	3	1	...	...
		Kavarga	,,	...	...	...	...	...
		Kúṭa	,,	...	...	...	...	...
		Kaṇṇakubja or Kanyákubja	,,	...	...	...	...	...
		Konkaṇasth	,,	...	...	...	...	...
		Kandáḍe	,,	6	2	3	1	...
		Kátyáyana	,,	...	...	...	...	...
		Mulikiṇáḍu or Murikináḍu.	,,	1,508	726	637	145	...
		Manḍyáttár	,,	...	...	...	...	...
		Nambúri	,,	...	...	...	...	...
		Nandavaidika	,,	367	186	137	44	...
		Prathamas'ákhe	,,	879	413	386	80	...
		Prativádi Bhayankarattár.	,,	1	...	1	...	...
		Panchagráma	,,	...	...	...	...	...
		Sankéti	,,	4	1	3	...	...
		Sárasvata	,,	...	...	...	...	...
		S'irnáḍu	,,	535	264	233	38	...
		S'is'avarga	,,	...	...	...	...	...
		Sivaḷḷi	,,	...	...	...	...	...
		Smárta	,,	514	226	243	45	...
		Srivishṇava	,,	930	460	394	76	...
		Kaḍámbiyár	,,	...	...	...	...	...
		Srivaishṇava, Hebbár	,,	43	20	20	3	...
		Telughánya	,,	46	21	20	5	...
		Tuḷuva	,,	...	...	...	...	...
		Tirumaleyár	,,	7	3	3	1	...
		Ulachakammé	,,	1,024	514	443	67	...
		Utráji (Uttrádi)	,,	12	6	5	1	...
		Vaḍama	,,	245	120	109	16	...
		Vangipuram	,,	22	7	13	2	...
		Velnáḍu	,,	343	148	159	36	...
		Vyápurada kammé	,,	14	7	6	1	...
		Véginádu	,,	1	...	1	...	...
		Vaishṇava (Mádhva)	,,	376	201	129	46	...
		Total Brámhan		*11,693*	*5,598*	*5,119*	*976*	...

TABLE E.—(*Continued.*)

District.

Males.

0 to 9.					10 to 14.				
Total.	Single.	Married.	Widowed.	Civil condition not stated.	Total.	Single.	Married.	Widowed.	Civil condition not stated.
6	6	...	...	...	6	6	...	...	...
...	...	...	...	...	...	...	...	...	...
...	...	...	...	...	1	1	...	...	...
...	...	...	...	...	...	...	...	...	...
10	10	...	...	...	8	8	...	...	...
...	...	...	...	...	...	...	...	...	...
2	2	...	...	...	...	...	...	...	...
...	...	...	...	...	...	...	...	...	...
...	...	...	...	...	...	...	...	...	...
...	...	...	...	...	...	...	...	...	...
...	...	...	...	...	...	...	...	...	...
2	2	...	...	...	...	...	...	...	...
...	...	...	...	...	...	...	...	...	...
378	378	...	...	...	118	116	2	...	...
...	...	...	...	...	...	...	...	...	...
...	...	...	...	...	...	...	...	...	...
74	74	...	...	...	27	27	...	...	...
212	212	...	...	...	69	67	2	...	...
...	...	...	...	...	...	...	...	...	...
...	...	...	...	...	...	...	...	...	...
1	1	...	...	...	...	...	...	...	...
...	...	...	...	...	...	...	...	...	...
127	127	...	...	...	38	36	2	...	...
...	...	...	...	...	...	...	...	...	...
...	...	...	...	...	...	...	...	...	...
109	109	...	...	...	33	31	2	...	...
264	264	...	...	...	89	87	2	...	...
...	...	...	...	...	...	...	...	...	...
9	9	...	...	...	5	5	...	...	...
10	10	...	...	...	3	3	...	...	...
...	...	...	...	...	...	...	...	...	...
1	1	...	...	...	2	2	...	...	...
278	278	...	...	...	93	90	3	...	...
4	4	...	...	...	2	2	...	...	...
62	62	...	...	...	20	20	...	...	...
3	3	...	...	...	1	1	...	...	...
74	74	...	...	...	22	22	...	...	...
4	4	...	...	...	2	2	...	...	...
...	...	...	...	...	...	...	...	...	...
127	127	...	...	...	34	31	3	...	...
2,950	*2,950*	...	...	...	*937*	*884*	*53*	...	...

Kolar

Class.	Group.	Caste, &c. and sub-division.	Religion.	15 to 39. Total.	Single.	Married.	Widowed.	Civil condition not stated.
B.—Professional.—(Continued.)	5. Priests.—(Continued.)	Brámhan.—(Concluded.) Hois'aniga ...	Hendu.	14	2	11	1	...
		Karnataka ...	,,	...	...	...	...	...
		Kumbálúr or Toṭada Tigaḷa.	,,	3	1	2	...	...
		Kandávara ...	,,	...	...	...	...	...
		Kannaḍa Kammé ...	,,	22	9	11	2	...
		Karáḍe ...	,,	...	...	...	...	...
		Kásalnád ...	,,	2	1	1	...	...
		Kavarga ...	,,	...	...	...	...	...
		Kóṭa	,,	...	...	...	...	...
		Káṇakubja or Kanyákubja.	,,	...	...	...	...	...
		Konkaṇast'h ...	,,	...	...	...	...	...
		Kandadé ...	,,	1	...	1	...	...
		Katyáyana ...	,,	...	...	...	...	...
		Mulikináḍu or Murikináḍu.	,,	597	198	372	27	...
		Mandyattár ...	,,	...	...	...	...	...
		Nambúri ...	,,	...	...	...	...	...
		Nandavaidika ...	,,	162	71	79	12	...
		Prat'hamas'ákhe ...	,,	352	117	223	12	...
		Prativádi Bhayankarattar.	,,	1	...	1	...	...
		Panchagráma ...	,,	...	...	...	...	...
		Sankéti ...	,,	3	...	3	...	...
		Sárasvata ...	,,	...	...	...	...	...
		S'irnáḍu ...	,,	245	96	141	8	...
		S'is'uvarga ...	,,	...	...	...	...	...
		Sivaḷḷi ...	,,	...	...	...	...	...
		Smárta ...	,,	247	83	153	8	...
		Srivaishṇava ...	,,	360	98	245	17	...
		Kaḍámbiyár ...	,,	...	...	...	...	...
		Srivaishṇava, Hebbar.	,,	18	4	14	...	...
		Telaghánya ...	,,	22	7	14	1	...
		Tuḷuva ...	,,	...	...	...	...	...
		Tirumaleyár ...	,,	3	...	3	...	...
		Uchchakammé ...	,,	417	132	270	15	...
		Utráji (Uttradi) ...	,,	4	...	4	...	...
		Vadama ...	,,	122	37	80	5	...
		Vangipuram ...	,,	13	2	10	1	...
		Velnáḍu ...	,,	147	45	91	11	...
		Vijápurada kammé.	,,	6	1	5	...	...
		Végináḍu ...	,,	...	...	...	...	...
		Vaishṇava (Mádhva).	,,	146	32	91	23	...
		Total Brámhan	......	*4,863*	*1,573*	*3,057*	*233*	...

TABLE E.—(*Continued.*)

District.

Males.

40 and over.					Age not stated.				
Total.	Single.	Married.	Widowed.	Civil condition not stated.	Total.	Single.	Married.	Widowed.	Civil condition not stated.
7	...	4	3	...	...	...	...	...	...
...	...	...	...	...	...	...	...	...	...
1	...	...	1	...	...	...	...	...	...
...	...	...	...	...	...	...	...	...	...
8	...	5	3	...	...	...	...	...	...
...	...	...	...	...	...	...	...	...	...
...	...	...	...	...	...	...	...	...	...
...	...	...	...	...	...	...	...	...	...
...	...	...	...	...	...	...	...	...	...
...	...	...	...	...	...	...	...	...	...
...	...	...	...	...	...	...	...	...	...
3	...	2	1	...	...	...	...	...	...
...	...	...	...	...	...	...	...	...	...
415	34	263	118	...	...	...	...	...	...
...	...	...	...	...	...	...	...	...	...
...	...	...	...	...	...	...	...	...	...
104	14	58	32	...	...	...	...	...	...
246	17	161	68	...	...	...	...	...	...
...	...	...	...	...	...	...	...	...	...
...	...	...	...	...	...	...	...	...	...
...	...	...	...	...	...	...	...	...	...
...	...	...	...	...	...	...	...	...	...
125	5	90	30	...	...	...	...	...	...
...	...	...	...	...	...	...	...	...	...
...	...	...	...	...	...	...	...	...	...
125	3	85	37	...	...	...	...	...	...
217	11	147	59	...	...	...	...	...	...
...	...	...	...	...	...	...	...	...	...
11	2	6	3	...	...	...	...	...	...
11	1	6	4	...	...	...	...	...	...
...	...	...	...	...	...	...	...	...	...
1	...	...	1	...	...	...	...	...	...
236	14	170	52	...	...	...	...	...	...
2	...	1	1	...	...	...	...	...	...
41	1	29	11	...	...	...	...	...	...
5	1	3	1	...	...	...	...	...	...
100	7	68	25	...	...	...	...	...	...
2	...	1	1	...	...	...	...	...	...
1	...	1	...	...	...	...	...	...	...
69	11	35	23	...	...	...	...	...	...
2,043	*191*	*2,009*	*743*	...	...	...	...	...	...

Kolar

Class.	Group.	Caste and Religion.	Caste, &c. and sub-division.	Religion.	All Ages. Total.	Single.	Married.	Widowed.	Civil condition not stated.
B.—Professional.—(Continued.)	5. Priests.—(Continued.)	Brámhan.—(Concluded.)	Hois'aṇiga ...	Hindu.	46	15	21	10	...
			Karṇâṭaka ...	,,	...	...	...	...	...
			Kumbálûr or Toṭada Tigaḷa.	,,	4	1	3	...	...
			Kandaváru ...	,,	...	...	...	...	...
			Kannaḍa Kummê ...	,,	50	13	22	15	...
			Karáḍe ...	,,	...	...	...	...	...
			Kásalnád ...	,,	2	1	1	...	...
			Kávarga ...	,,	...	...	...	...	...
			Kôṭa ...	,,	...	...	...	...	...
			Kâṇakubja or Kanyâkubja.	,,	...	...	...	...	...
			Konkaṇast'h ...	,,	...	...	...	...	...
			Kandâḍê ...	,,	3	1	2	...	...
			Kátyáyana ...	,,	...	...	...	...	...
			Muḷikinâḍu or Murikinâḍu.	,,	1,478	373	691	414	...
			Manḍyáttár ...	,,	...	...	...	...	...
			Nambúri ...	,,	...	...	...	...	...
			Nandavaidika ...	,,	355	100	147	108	...
			Prat'hamas'ákha ...	,,	885	215	429	241	...
			Prativâdi Bhayankarattár	,,	1	...	1	...	...
			Panchagráma ...	,,	...	...	...	...	...
			Sankéti ...	,,	6	2	3	1	...
			Sârasvata ...	,,	...	...	...	...	...
			S'irnâḍu ...	,,	510	130	241	139	...
			S'is'uvarga ...	,,	...	...	...	...	...
			Sivaḷḷi ...	,,	...	...	...	...	...
			Smárta ...	,,	438	141	219	78	...
			Srivaishṇava ...	,,	940	232	453	255	...
			Kaḍâmbiyár ...	,,	...	...	...	...	...
			Srivaishṇava, Hebbar	,,	41	11	20	10	...
			Telaghaṇya ...	,,	45	15	21	9	...
			Tuḷuva ...	,,	...	...	...	...	...
			Tirumaleyár ...	,,	7	1	4	2	...
			Uchchakamme ...	,,	1,006	267	484	255	...
			Utrâji (Uttradi) ...	,,	13	3	7	3	...
			Vaḍama ...	,,	290	95	143	52	...
			Vangipuram ...	,,	16	4	9	3	...
			Velnáḍu ...	,,	313	74	160	79	...
			Vijâpuraḍa kammé ...	,,	13	3	8	2	...
			Véginâḍu ...	,,	...	...	...	...	...
			Vishṇava (Mádhva) ...	,,	393	67	188	138	...
			Total Brámhan	....	11,632	2,984	5,550	3,098	...

TABLE E.—(Continued.)

District.

Females.

0 to 9					10 to 14				
Total.	Single.	Married.	Widowed.	Civil condition not stated.	Total.	Single.	Married.	Widowed.	Civil condition not stated.
13	13	...	...	...	4	2	2	...	...
...	...	...	...	...	...	...	...	...	...
2	1	1	...	...	...	...	...	...	...
...	...	...	...	...	...	...	...	...	...
11	11	...	...	...	6	2	4	...	...
...	...	...	...	...	...	...	...	...	...
1	1	...	...	...	...	...	...	...	...
...	...	...	...	...	...	...	...	...	...
...	...	...	...	...	...	...	...	...	...
...	...	...	...	...	...	...	...	...	...
...	...	...	...	...	...	...	...	...	...
1	1	...	...	...	...	...	...	...	...
...	...	...	...	...	...	...	...	...	...
354	340	14	...	...	129	33	90	6	...
...	...	...	...	...	...	...	...	...	...
...	...	...	...	...	...	...	...	...	...
92	88	4	...	...	35	12	22	1	...
226	204	22	...	...	73	11	60	2	...
...	...	...	...	...	...	...	...	...	...
...	...	...	...	...	...	...	...	...	...
2	2	...	...	...	1	...	1	...	...
...	...	...	...	...	...	...	...	...	...
128	121	7	...	...	46	9	36	1	...
...	...	...	...	...	...	...	...	...	...
...	...	...	...	...	...	...	...	...	...
140	129	11	...	...	55	12	42	1	...
227	206	21	...	...	101	26	73	2	...
...	...	...	...	...	...	...	...	...	...
12	10	2	...	...	5	1	4	...	...
15	13	2	...	...	6	2	4	...	...
...	...	...	...	...	...	...	...	...	...
1	1	...	...	...	2	...	2	...	...
268	250	18	...	...	87	17	69	1	...
3	3	...	...	...	1	...	1	...	...
92	85	7	...	...	37	10	27	...	...
5	4	1	...	...	2	...	2	...	...
69	65	4	...	...	33	9	23	1	...
3	3	...	...	...	3	...	3	...	...
...	...	...	...	...	...	...	...	...	...
55	54	1	...	...	36	13	21	2	...
2,952	*2,726*	*225*	...	...	*1,083*	*258*	*798*	*27*	...

Kolar

Class.	Group.	Caste, &c. and sub-division.		Religion.	15 to 39. Total.	Single.	Married.	Widowed.	Civil condition not stated.
B.—Professional—(Continued).	5. Priests.—(Continued.)	Brâmhan.—(Concluded.)	Hois'anigа	Hindu.	18	...	14	4	...
			Karṇâṭaka	,,	...	...	...	...	...
			Kumbâlúr or Toṭada Tigaḷa.	,,	2	...	2	...	...
			Kandávara	,,	...	...	...	...	...
			Kannaḍa Kummé	,,	18	...	13	5	...
			Karâḍe ...	,,	...	...	...	...	...
			Kásalnád	,,	1	...	1	...	...
			Kavarga...	,,	...	...	...	...	...
			Kôṭa ...	,,	...	...	...	...	...
			Káṇakubja or Kanyá-kubja.	,,	...	...	...	...	...
			Konkaṇast'h	,,	...	...	...	...	...
			Kandâdê	,,	1	...	1	...	...
			Kâtyâyana	,,	...	...	...	...	...
			Mulikiṇâḍu or Muri-kinâḍu.	,,	583	...	467	116	...
			Manḍyâṭṭár	,,	...	...	...	...	...
			Nambúri	,,	...	...	...	...	...
			Nandavaidika	,,	117	...	84	33	...
			Prat'hamasâkhe	,,	349	...	272	77	...
			Prativâdi Bhayan-karattár.	,,	1	...	1	...	...
			Panchagráma	,,	...	...	...	...	...
			Sankéti ...	,,	2	...	2	...	...
			Sârasvata	,,	...	...	...	...	...
			S'irnâḍu ...	,,	201	...	151	50	...
			S'is'uvarga	,,	...	...	...	...	...
			Sivaḷḷi ...	,,	...	...	...	...	...
			Smârta ...	,,	176	...	127	49	...
			Srivaishṇava	,,	368	...	278	90	...
			Kaḍâmbiyár	,,	...	...	...	...	...
			Srivaishṇava, Hebbár	,,	14	...	11	3	...
			Telaghâṇya	,,	15	...	12	3	...
			Tuḷuva ...	,,	...	...	...	...	...
			Tirumaleyár	,,	3	...	2	1	...
			Ulachakamme	,,	399	...	316	83	...
			Utrâji (Uttrádi)	,,	6	...	5	1	...
			Vaḍama ...	,,	102	...	84	18	...
			Vangipuram	,,	6	...	6	...	...
			Velnâḍu ...	,,	132	...	106	26	...
			Vijâpuraḍa kammé ...	,,	5	...	5	...	...
			Véginâḍu	,,	...	...	...	...	...
			Vaishṇava (Mádhva)	,,	140	...	128	12	...
		Total–Brâmhan			*4,457*	...	*3,517*	*940*	...

TABLE E.—(Continued.)

District.

Females.

40 and over.					Age not stated.				
Total.	Single.	Married.	Widowed.	Civil condition not stated.	Total.	Single.	Married.	Widowed.	Civil condition not stated.
11	...	5	6	...	...	...	...	...	...
...	...	...	...	...	...	...	...	...	...
...	...	...	...	...	...	...	...	...	...
...	...	...	...	...	...	...	...	...	...
15	...	5	10	...	...	...	...	...	...
...	...	...	...	...	...	...	...	...	...
...	...	...	...	...	...	...	...	...	...
...	...	...	...	...	...	...	...	...	...
...	...	...	...	...	...	...	...	...	...
...	...	...	...	...	...	...	...	...	...
...	...	...	...	...	...	...	...	...	...
1	...	1	...	...	...	...	...	...	...
...	...	...	...	...	...	...	...	...	...
412	...	120	292	...	...	...	...	...	...
...	...	...	...	...	...	...	...	...	...
...	...	...	...	...	...	...	...	...	...
111	...	37	74	...	...	...	...	...	...
237	...	75	162	...	...	...	...	...	...
...	...	...	...	...	...	...	...	...	...
...	...	...	...	...	...	...	...	...	...
1	...	...	1	...	...	...	...	...	...
...	...	...	...	...	...	...	...	...	...
135	...	47	88	...	...	...	...	...	...
...	...	...	...	...	...	...	...	...	...
...	...	...	...	...	...	...	...	...	...
67	...	39	28	...	...	...	...	...	...
244	...	81	163	...	...	...	...	...	...
...	...	...	...	...	...	...	...	...	...
10	...	3	7	...	...	...	...	...	...
9	...	3	6	...	...	...	...	...	...
...	...	...	...	...	...	...	...	...	...
1	...	...	1	...	...	...	...	...	...
252	...	81	171	...	...	...	...	...	...
3	...	1	2	...	...	...	...	...	...
59	...	25	34	...	...	...	...	...	...
3	...	...	3	...	...	...	...	...	...
79	...	27	52	...	...	...	...	...	...
2	...	...	2	...	...	...	...	...	...
...	...	...	...	...	...	...	...	...	...
162	...	38	124	...	...	...	...	...	...
3,140	...	*1,010*	*2,130*	...	...	...	...	...	...

Tumkur

Class.	Group.	Caste, &c. and sub-division.	Religion.	All Ages. Total.	Single.	Married.	Widowed.	Civil condition not stated.
B—Professional.—(Continued.)	5. Priests.—(Continued.)	Brâmhan.—(Concluded.) Hoyis'aniga ...	Hindu	720	226	434	60	...
		Karnâtaka	,,	...	...	...	...	...
		Kumbâtâr or Tôtada Tigala.	,,	3	...	3	...	...
		Kandâvara ...	,,	...	...	...	...	...
		Kannada Kammé ...	,,	220	97	115	8	...
		Karâde	,,	...	...	...	...	...
		Kâsalnâd	,,	...	...	...	...	...
		Kavarga ...	,,	...	...	...	...	...
		Kôta	,,	...	...	...	...	...
		Kânakubja or Kanyâkubja.	,,	...	...	...	...	...
		Konkanast'h ...	,,	...	...	...	...	...
		Kandâdé ...	,,	...	...	...	...	...
		Kâtyâyana ...	,,	...	...	...	...	...
		Mulikinâdu or Murikinâdu.	,,	619	308	229	82	...
		Mandyâttâr ...	,,	...	...	...	...	...
		Nambûri ...	,,	...	...	...	...	...
		Nandavaidîka ...	,,	76	40	28	8	...
		Prat'hamas'âkhe ...	,,	293	113	150	30	...
		Prativâdi Bhayankarattâr.	,,	...	...	...	...	...
		Panchagrâma ...	,,	...	...	...	...	...
		Sankéti ...	,,	2	1	1	...	...
		Sârasvata ...	,,	...	...	...	...	...
		S'irnâdu ...	,,	648	307	278	63	...
		S'is'uvarga ...	,,	...	...	...	...	...
		S'ivalli ...	,,	...	...	...	...	...
		Smârta ...	,,	443	227	197	19	...
		S'rîvaishnava ...	,,	494	234	202	58	...
		Kadâmbiyâr	,,	...	...	...	...	...
		S'rîvaishnava, Hebbâr	,,	242	122	97	23	...
		Telaghânya ...	,,	72	44	22	6	...
		Tuluva ...	,,	...	...	...	...	...
		Tirumaleyâr ...	,,	...	...	...	...	...
		Uchchakammé ...	,,	545	281	222	42	...
		Utrâji (Uttrâdi) ...	,,	7	3	4	...	...
		Vadama ...	,,	28	14	12	2	...
		Vangîpuram ...	,,	38	18	18	2	...
		Velnâdu ...	,,	275	131	116	28	...
		Vijâpurada kammé.	,,	...	...	...	...	...
		Véginâdu ...	,,	...	...	...	...	...
		Vaishnava (Mâdhva).	,,	203	80	95	28	...
		Total Brâmhan ...	...	*8,570*	*3,832*	*3,987*	*751*	...

TABLE E.—(*Continued.*)

District.

Males.

0 to 9					10 to 14				
Total.	Single.	Married.	Widowed.	Civil condition not stated.	Total.	Single.	Married.	Widowed.	Civil condition not stated.
107	107	...	...	...	42	36	6	...	...
...	...	...	...	...	...	...	...	...	...
...	...	...	...	...	...	...	...	...	...
...	...	...	...	...	...	...	...	...	...
61	61	...	...	...	21	16	5	...	...
...	...	...	...	...	...	...	...	...	...
...	...	...	...	...	...	...	...	...	...
...	...	...	...	...	...	...	...	...	...
...	...	...	...	...	...	...	...	...	...
...	...	...	...	...	...	...	...	...	...
...	...	...	...	...	...	...	...	...	...
...	...	...	...	...	...	...	...	...	...
...	...	...	...	...	...	...	...	...	...
147	147	...	...	...	48	41	7	...	...
...	...	...	...	...	...	...	...	...	...
...	...	...	...	...	...	...	...	...	...
13	13	...	...	...	2	2	...	...	...
62	63	...	...	...	17	15	1	1	...
...	...	...	...	...	...	...	...	...	...
...	...	...	...	...	...	...	...	...	...
...	...	...	...	...	...	...	...	...	...
...	...	...	...	...	...	...	...	...	...
166	168	...	...	...	59	54	5	...	...
...	...	...	...	...	...	...	...	...	...
...	...	...	...	...	...	...	...	...	...
155	139	16	...	...	67	23	44	...	...
135	135	...	...	...	40	38	2	...	...
...	...	...	...	...	...	...	...	...	...
83	83	...	...	...	22	22	...	...	...
25	25	...	...	...	10	9	1	...	...
...	...	...	...	...	...	...	...	...	...
...	...	...	...	...	...	...	...	...	...
183	183	...	...	...	33	83	...	...	...
2	2	...	...	...	1	1	...	...	...
13	13	...	...	...	2	2	...	...	...
13	13	...	...	...	2	2	...	...	...
70	70	...	...	...	28	27	1	...	...
...	...	...	...	...	...	...	...	...	...
...	...	...	...	...	...	...	...	...	...
47	47	...	...	...	57	23	32	2	...
2,106	*2,090*	*16*	...	...	*738*	*611*	*124*	*3*	...

Class.	Group.	Caste, &c. and sub-division.	Religion.	15 to 39 Total.	Single.	Married.	Widowed.	Civil condition not stated.
B.—Professional.—(Continued.)	5. Priests.—(Continued.)	Brâmhan.—(Concluded.) Hoyis'âniga	Hindu	380	76	273	31	...
		Karnâṭaka	,,	...	...	...	...	...
		Kumbâlúr or Tótada Tigaḷa	,,	2	...	2	...	...
		Kandâvara	,,	...	...	...	...	...
		Kannaḍa Kammé	,,	100	16	82	2	...
		Karâḍe	,,	...	...	...	...	...
		Kásalnâḍ	,,	...	...	...	...	...
		Kavarga	,,	...	...	...	...	...
		Kóṭa	,,	...	...	...	...	...
		Kânyakubja or Kanyâkubja	,,	...	...	...	...	...
		Konkaṇast'h	,,	...	...	...	...	...
		Kandâḍe	,,	...	...	...	...	...
		Kâtyâyana	,,	...	...	...	...	...
		Mulikinâḍu or Murikinâḍu	,,	262	108	134	20	...
		Mandyâttâr	,,	...	...	...	...	...
		Nambûri	,,	...	...	...	...	...
		Nandavaidika	,,	33	16	15	2	...
		Prat'hamas'âkhe	,,	131	30	91	10	...
		Prativâdi Bhayankarattâr	,,	...	...	...	...	...
		Panchagrâma	,,	...	...	...	...	...
		Sankéti	,,	2	1	1	...	...
		Sârasvata	,,	...	...	...	...	...
		S'irnâḍu	,,	259	73	171	15	...
		S'is'uvarga	,,	...	...	...	...	...
		S'ivaḷḷi	,,	...	3	...	...	...
		Smârta	,,	169	57	106	6	...
		S'rívaishṇava	,,	219	58	141	20	...
		Kaḷâmbiyâr	,,	...	...	...	...	...
		S'rívaishṇava, Hebbâr	,,	92	16	70	6	...
		Telaghâṇya	,,	23	10	10	3	...
		Tuḷuva	,,	...	...	...	...	...
		Tirumaleyâr	,,	...	...	...	...	...
		Ulachakammé	,,	197	63	124	10	...
		Utrâji (Uttrâdi)	,,	3	...	3	...	...
		Vaḍama	,,	10	...	9	1	...
		Vangípuram	,,	17	3	13	1	...
		Velnâḍu	,,	115	31	76	8	...
		Vijâpuraḍa kammé	,,	...	...	...	...	...
		Véginâḍu	,,	...	...	...	...	...
		Vaishṇava (Mâdhva)	,,	50	10	33	7	...
		Total Brâmhan	...	3,701	999	2,470	232	...

TABLE E.—(*Continued.*)

District.

Males.

40 and over.					Age not stated.				
Total.	Single.	Married.	Widowed.	Civil condition not stated.	Total.	Single.	Married.	Widowed.	Civil condition not stated.
191	7	135	29	...	...	...	...	...	...
...	...	...	...	...	...	...	...	...	...
1	...	1	...	...	...	...	...	...	...
...	...	...	...	...	...	...	...	...	...
33	[illegible]	28	6	...	...	...	...	...	...
...	...	...	...	...	...	...	...	...	...
...	...	...	...	...	...	...	...	...	...
...	...	...	...	...	...	...	...	...	...
...	...	...	...	...	...	...	...	...	...
...	...	...	...	...	...	...	...	...	...
...	...	...	...	...	...	...	...	...	...
...	...	...	...	...	...	...	...	...	...
...	...	...	...	...	...	...	...	...	...
162	12	88	62	...	...	...	...	...	...
...	...	...	...	...	...	...	...	...	...
...	...	...	...	...	...	...	...	...	...
28	9	13	6	...	...	...	...	...	...
83	6	53	19	...	...	...	...	...	...
...	...	...	...	...	...	...	...	...	...
...	...	...	...	...	...	...	...	...	...
...	...	...	...	...	...	...	...	...	...
...	...	...	...	...	...	...	...	...	...
164	14	102	48	...	...	...	...	...	...
...	...	...	...	...	...	...	...	...	...
...	...	...	...	...	...	...	...	...	...
52	8	31	13	...	...	...	...	...	...
100	3	59	38	...	...	...	...	...	...
...	...	...	...	...	...	...	...	...	...
45	1	27	17	...	...	...	...	...	...
14	...	11	3	...	...	...	...	...	...
...	...	...	...	...	...	...	...	...	...
...	...	...	...	...	...	...	...	...	...
132	2	98	32	...	...	...	...	...	...
1	...	1	...	...	...	...	...	...	...
4	...	3	1	...	...	...	...	...	...
6	...	5	1	...	...	...	...	...	...
62	3	39	20	...	...	...	...	...	...
...	...	...	...	...	...	...	...	...	...
...	...	...	...	...	...	...	...	...	...
49	...	30	19	...	...	...	...	...	...
2,025	132	1,377	516	...	...	...	...	...	...

Tumkur

Class.	Group.	Caste and Religion. Caste, &c. and sub-division.	Religion.	All Ages. Total.	Single.	Married.	Widowed.	Civil condition not stated.
B.—Professional.—(Continued.)	5. Priests.—(Continued.)	Brámhan.—(Concluded.) Hoyis'anige ...	Hindu	746	193	393	160	...
		Karṇáṭaka ...	,,	...	...	...	...	...
		Kumbálúr or Tóṭada Tigala.	,,	2	...	2	...	...
		Kandávara ...	,,	...	...	...	...	...
		Kannaḍa Kammé ...	,,	249	106	118	25	...
		Karáḍe ...	,,	...	...	...	...	...
		Kás'alnád ...	,,	...	...	...	...	...
		Kavarga ...	,,	...	...	...	...	...
		Kóṭa ...	,,	...	...	...	...	...
		Káṇakubja or Kanyákubja.	,,	...	...	...	...	...
		Konkaṇast'h ...	,,	...	...	...	...	...
		Kandáḍé ...	,,	...	...	...	...	...
		Katyáyana ...	,,	...	...	...	...	...
		Mulikináḍu or Murikináḍu.	,,	538	141	237	160	...
		Manḍyattár ...	,,	...	...	...	...	...
		Namburi ...	,,	...	...	...	...	...
		Nandavaidika ...	,,	67	20	21	26	...
		Prat'hamas'ákhe ...	,,	284	73	165	46	...
		Prativádi Bhayankarattár.	,,	...	...	...	...	...
		Panchagráma ...	,,	...	...	...	...	...
		Sankéti ...	,,	...	...	...	...	...
		Sárasvata ...	,,	...	...	...	...	...
		S'irnaḍu ...	,,	594	173	283	138	...
		S'is'uvarga ...	,,	...	...	...	...	...
		S'ivaḷḷi ...	,,	...	...	...	...	...
		Smárta ...	,,	425	136	190	99	...
		S'rívaishṇava ...	,,	463	129	207	127	...
		Kaḍámbiyár ...	,,	...	...	...	...	...
		S'rívaishṇava, Hobbar	,,	264	83	131	50	...
		Telaghánya ...	,,	67	15	35	17	...
		Tuḷuva ...	,,	...	...	...	...	...
		Tirumaleyár ...	,,	...	...	...	...	...
		Ulachakammé ...	,,	499	117	241	141	...
		Utráji (Uttr[illegible]) ...	,,	3	...	3	...	...
		Vaḍama ...	,,	25	3	21	1	...
		Vangipuram ...	,,	39	10	24	5	...
		Velnáḍu ...	,,	276	50	123	97	...
		Vijápurada kammé.	,,	...	...	...	...	...
		Végináḍu ...	,,	...	...	...	...	...
		Vaishṇava (Mádhva)	,,	220	23	115	82	...
		Total Brámhan ...	...	8,437	2,262	4,185	1,990	...

TABLE E.—(Continued)

District.

Females.

0 to 9					10 to 14				
Total.	Single.	Married.	Widowed.	Civil condition not stated.	Total.	Single.	Married.	Widowed.	Civil condition not stated.
164	163	3	...	...	74	31	43	...	...
...	...	...	...	...	...	...	...	...	...
...	...	...	...	...	...	...	...	...	...
...	...	...	...	...	...	...	...	...	...
91	90	1	...	...	21	16	5	...	...
...	...	...	...	...	...	...	...	...	...
...	...	...	...	...	...	...	...	...	...
...	...	...	...	...	...	...	...	...	...
...	...	...	...	...	...	...	...	...	...
...	...	...	...	...	...	...	...	...	...
...	...	...	...	...	...	...	...	...	...
...	...	...	...	...	...	...	...	...	...
...	...	...	...	...	...	...	...	...	...
139	132	7	...	...	35	9	26	...	...
...	...	...	...	...	...	...	...	...	...
...	...	...	...	...	...	...	...	...	...
18	18	...	...	...	3	2	1	...	...
62	60	2	...	...	31	13	18	...	...
...	...	...	...	...	...	...	...	...	...
...	...	...	...	...	...	...	...	...	...
...	...	...	...	...	...	...	...	...	...
...	...	...	...	...	...	...	...	...	...
161	149	12	...	...	54	24	30	...	...
...	...	...	...	...	...	...	...	...	...
...	...	...	...	...	...	...	...	...	...
163	132	21	10	...	93	4	61	28	...
121	116	5	...	...	36	13	23	...	...
...	...	...	...	...	...	...	...	...	...
84	83	1	...	...	3	...	3	...	...
14	14	...	...	...	7	1	6	...	...
...	...	...	...	...	...	...	...	...	...
...	...	...	...	...	...	...	...	...	...
119	115	4	...	...	32	2	30	...	...
...	...	...	...	...	...	...	...	...	...
3	3	...	...	...	4	...	4	...	...
10	10	...	...	...	4	...	4	...	...
63	56	6	...	...	20	...	19	1	...
...	...	...	...	...	...	...	...	...	...
...	...	...	...	...	...	...	...	...	...
31	21	1	9	...	18	2	6	10	...
2,157	*2,037*	*101*	*19*	...	*738*	*225*	*471*	*42*	...

Tumkur

Class.	Group.	Caste, &c. and sub-division.	Religion.	15 to 39 Total.	Single.	Married.	Widowed.	Civil condition not stated.
B.—Professional.—(Continued.)	5. Priests.—(Continued.)	Brâhman.—(Concluded.) Hoyis'aniga	Hindu.	339	...	275	55	...
		Karnâṭaka	,,	...	...	...	...	...
		Kumbâtâr or Toṭṭada Tigala	,,	1	...	1	...	...
		Kandâvara	,,	...	...	...	...	...
		Kannada Kammé	,,	97	...	90	7	...
		Karâḍe ...	,,	...	...	...	...	...
		Kâsalnâḍ	,,	...	...	...	...	...
		Kavarga...	,,	...	...	...	...	...
		Kôṭa ...	,,	...	...	...	...	...
		Kânyakubja or Kanyâkubja.	,,	...	...	...	...	...
		Konkaṇast'h	,,	...	...	...	...	...
		Kandâḍe	,,	...	...	...	...	...
		Kâtyâyana	,,	...	...	...	...	...
		Mulikinâḍu or Murikinâḍu.	,,	224	...	163	61	...
		Mandyâttâr	,,	...	...	...	...	...
		Nambûri	,,	...	...	...	...	...
		Nandavaidika	,,	25	...	16	9	...
		Prat'hamas'âkhe	,,	135	...	119	16	...
		Prativâdi Bhayankarattâr.	,,	...	...	...	...	...
		Panchagrâma	,,	...	...	...	...	...
		Sankêti ...	,,	...	...	...	...	...
		Sârasvata	,,	...	...	...	...	...
		S'irnâḍu...	,,	235	...	197	38	...
		S'is'uvarga	,,	...	...	...	...	...
		S'ivaḷḷi ...	,,	...	...	...	...	...
		Smârta ...	,,	102	...	62	40	...
		S'rîvaishṇava	,,	186	...	144	42	...
		Kaḍâmbiyâr	,,	...	...	...	...	...
		S'rîvaishṇava, Hebbâr	,,	111	...	102	9	...
		Telaghâṇya	,,	31	...	22	9	...
		Tuḷuva ...	,,	...	...	...	...	...
		Tirumaleyâr	,,	...	...	...	...	...
		Uchchakammé	,,	222	...	178	44	...
		Utrâji (Uttrâdi)	,,	3	...	3	...	...
		Vaḍama	,,	16	...	16	...	...
		Vangipuram	,,	17	...	17	...	...
		Velnâḍu...	,,	110	...	79	31	...
		Vijâpurada kammé.	,,	...	...	...	...	...
		Vêgnâḍu	,,	...	...	...	...	...
		Vaishṇava (Mâdhva).	,,	90	...	87	3	...
		Total Brâhman...	...	3,596	...	2,933	663	...

TABLE E.—(*Continued.*)

District.

Females.

40 and over.					Age not stated.				
Total.	Single.	Married.	Widowed.	Civil condition not stated.	Total.	Single.	Married.	Widowed.	Civil condition not stated.
178	...	73	105	...	...	...	...	...	...
...	...	...	...	...	...	...	...	...	...
1	...	1	...	...	...	...	...	...	...
...	...	...	...	...	...	...	...	...	...
40	...	22	18	...	...	...	...	...	...
...	...	...	...	...	...	...	...	...	...
...	...	...	...	...	...	...	...	...	...
...	...	...	...	...	...	...	...	...	...
...	...	...	...	...	...	...	...	...	...
...	...	...	...	...	...	...	...	...	...
...	...	...	...	...	...	...	...	...	...
...	...	...	...	...	...	...	...	...	...
...	...	...	...	...	...	...	...	...	...
140	...	41	99	...	...	...	...	...	...
...	...	...	...	...	...	...	...	...	...
...	...	...	...	...	...	...	...	...	...
21	...	4	17	...	...	...	...	...	...
56	...	26	30	...	...	...	...	...	...
...	...	...	...	...	...	...	...	...	...
...	...	...	...	...	...	...	...	...	...
...	...	...	...	...	...	...	...	...	...
[illegible]	...	...	...	...	...	...	...	...	...
144	...	41	100	...	...	...	...	...	...
...	...	...	...	...	...	...	...	...	...
...	...	...	...	...	...	...	...	...	...
67	...	46	21	...	...	...	...	...	...
120	...	35	85	...	...	...	...	...	...
...	...	...	...	...	...	...	...	...	...
66	...	25	41	...	...	...	...	...	...
15	...	7	8	...	...	...	...	...	...
...	...	...	...	...	...	...	...	...	...
...	...	...	...	...	...	...	...	...	...
126	...	29	97	...	...	...	...	...	...
...	...	...	...	...	...	...	...	...	...
2	...	1	1	...	...	...	...	...	...
8	...	6	5	...	...	...	...	...	...
84	...	19	65	...	...	...	...	...	...
...	...	...	...	...	...	...	...	...	...
...	...	...	...	...	...	...	...	...	...
81	...	21	60	...	...	...	...	...	...
1,946	...	*680*	*1,266*	...	...	...	...	...	...

Class.	Group.	Caste, &c. and sub-division.	Religion.	All Ages. Total.	Single.	Married.	Widowed.	Civil condition not stated.
B.—Professional.—(Continued.)	5. Priests.—(Continued.)	Brâmhan.—(Concluded).						
		Hois'aniga ...	Hindu.	1,408	713	553	142	...
		Karnâtaka ...	"	...	...	...	...	...
		Kumbálúr or Totada Tigala.	"	...	...	...	...	...
		Kandávara ...	"	...	...	...	...	...
		Kannada Kammé ...	"	690	360	271	59	...
		Karâde ...	"	5	3	1	1	...
		Kâsalnâd ...	"	...	...	...	...	...
		Kavarga ...	"	...	...	...	...	...
		Kôta ...	"	...	...	...	...	...
		Kânakubja or Kanyâkubja.	"	...	...	...	...	...
		Konkanast'h ...	"	21	14	6	1	...
		Kandâdé ...	"	...	...	...	...	...
		Kâtyâyana ...	"	...	...	...	...	...
		Mulikinâdu or Murikinâdu.	"	970	505	384	81	...
		Mandyattâr ...	"	36	21	13	2	...
		Nambûri ...	"	...	...	...	...	...
		Nandavaidika ...	"	79	39	35	5	...
		Prat'hamas'âkhe ...	"	114	60	45	9	...
		Prativâdi Bhayankaruttâr.	"	...	...	...	...	...
		Panchagrâma ...	"	...	...	...	...	...
		Sankâti ...	"	687	352	269	66	...
		Sârasvata ...	"	2	1	1	...	...
		S'irnâdu ...	"	156	81	56	19	...
		S'is'uvarga ...	"	...	...	...	...	...
		S'ivalli ...	"	...	...	...	...	...
		Smârta ...	"	1,927	1,001	852	74	...
		S'rivaishnava ...	"	3,085	1,761	1,206	118	...
		Kadâmbiyâr ...	"	...	...	...	...	...
		S'rivaishnava, Hebbâr	"	269	157	102	10	...
		Telaghânya ...	"	105	57	38	10	...
		Tuluva ...	"	...	...	...	...	...
		Tirumaloyâr ...	"	...	...	...	...	...
		Ulachakammé ...	"	341	177	134	30	...
		Utrâji (Uttrâdi) ...	"	2	1	1	...	...
		Vadama ...	"	209	110	76	23	...
		Vanginuram ...	"	25	13	9	3	...
		Velnâdu ...	"	333	188	123	22	...
		Vijâpurada kammé ...	"	...	...	...	...	...
		Vêginâdu ...	"	...	...	...	...	...
		Vaishnava (Mâdhva).	"	814	421	362	31	...
		Total Brâmhan ...	...	21,223	11,290	8,517	1,380	...

TABLE. E.—(*Continued.*)

District.

Males.

0 to 9					10 to 14				
Total.	Single.	Married.	Widowed.	Civil condition not stated.	Total.	Single.	Married.	Widowed.	Civil condition not stated.
438	429	8	1	...	98	73	24	1	...
...	...	...	...	...	...	...	...	...	...
...	...	...	...	...	...	...	...	...	...
...	...	...	...	...	...	...	...	...	...
225	225	...	...	...	38	36	2	...	...
1	1	...	...	...	1	1	...	...	...
...	...	...	...	...	...	...	...	...	...
...	...	...	...	...	...	...	...	...	...
...	...	...	...	...	...	...	...	...	...
...	...	...	...	...	...	...	...	...	...
8	8	...	...	...	2	2	...	...	...
...	...	...	...	...	...	...	...	...	...
...	...	...	...	...	...	...	...	...	...
297	297	...	...	...	72	65	7	...	...
13	13	...	...	...	3	3	...	...	...
...	...	...	...	...	...	...	...	...	...
23	23	...	...	...	7	6	1	...	...
38	38	...	...	...	10	9	1	...	...
...	...	...	...	...	...	...	...	...	...
...	...	...	...	...	...	...	...	...	...
219	214	5	...	...	57	45	12	...	...
1	1	...	...	...	...	...	...	...	...
47	47	...	...	...	9	9	...	...	...
...	...	...	...	...	...	...	...	...	...
...	...	...	...	...	...	...	...	...	...
509	502	5	2	...	162	143	16	3	...
975	949	24	2	...	379	301	74	4	...
...	...	...	...	...	...	...	...	...	...
84	84	...	...	...	28	28	...	...	...
33	33	...	...	...	7	7	...	...	...
...	...	...	...	...	...	...	...	...	...
...	...	...	...	...	...	...	...	...	...
96	96	...	...	...	30	29	1	...	...
1	1	...	...	...	...	...	...	...	...
69	69	...	...	...	14	13	1	...	...
7	7	...	...	...	4	4	...	...	...
115	115	...	...	...	23	22	...	...	...
...	...	...	...	...	...	...	...	...	...
...	...	...	...	...	...	...	...	...	...
215	213	2	...	...	69	61	6	2	...
6,657	*6,544*	*105*	*8*	...	*1,986*	*1,561*	*408*	*17*	...

Mysore

Class.	Group.	Caste, &c.	Caste, &c. and subdivision.	Religion.	15 to 39 Total.	15 to 39 Single.	15 to 39 Married.	15 to 39 Widowed.	15 to 39 Civil condition not stated.
B.—Professional.—(Continued.)	5. Priests.—(Continued.)	Bráhman.—(Concluded.)	Hoys'aṇige	Hindu.	560	197	318	45	...
			Karṇáṭaka	,,	...	...	...	...	...
			Kumbáḷár or Toṭada Tigaḷa	,,	...	...	...	...	...
			Kandávara	,,	...	...	...	...	...
			Kannaḍa Kammé	,,	296	95	180	21	...
			Karáḍe ...	,,	2	1	1	...	...
			Kásalnád	,,	...	...	...	...	...
			Kavarga...	,,	...	...	...	...	...
			Kóṭa ...	,,	...	...	...	...	...
			Káṇakubja or Kanyákubja.	,,	...	...	...	...	...
			Konkaṇast'h	,,	8	4	4	...	...
			Kandáḍé...	,,	...	...	...	...	...
			Kutyáyana	,,	...	...	...	...	...
			Mulikináḍu or Murikináḍu	,,	411	132	261	18	...
			Manḍyattár	,,	14	5	9	...	...
			Nambúri	,,	...	...	...	...	...
			Nandavaidika	,,	32	10	21	1	...
			Prat hamas'ákhe	,,	45	13	30	2	...
			Prativádi Bhayankarattár.	,,	...	...	...	...	...
			Panchagráma		...	...	...	...	...
			Sankéti ...	,,	258	93	150	15	...
			Sárasvata	,,	1	...	1	...	...
			S'irnáḍu	,,	66	25	36	5	...
			S'is'uvarga	,,	...	...	...	...	...
			S'ivaḷḷi ...	,,	...	...	...	...	...
			Smárta ...	,,	885	348	513	24	...
			S'rívaishṇava,	,,	1,143	501	627	15	...
			Kaḍámbiyár	,,	...	...	...	...	...
			S'rívaishṇava, Hebbár	,,	105	45	59	1	...
			Telughánya	,,	44	17	24	3	...
			Tuḷuva ...	,,	...	...	...	...	...
			Tirumaleyár	,,	...	...	...	...	...
			Ulachakamme	,,	141	49	87	5	...
			Utráji (Uttrádi)	,,	1	...	1	...	...
			Vaḍama ...	,,	83	28	49	6	...
			Vangipuram	,,	8	2	6	...	...
			Velnáḍu	,,	131	47	80	4	...
			Vijápurada Kammé...	,,	...	...	...	...	...
			Véginádu	,,	...	...	...	...	...
			Vaishṇava (Madhva.)	,,	385	143	231	11	...
			Total Bráhman		*8,370*	*3,069*	*4,958*	*349*	...

TABLE E.—(Continued)

District.

Males.

40 and over.					Age not stated.				
Total.	Single.	Married.	Widowed.	Civil condition not stated.	Total.	Single.	Married.	Widowed.	Civil condition not stated.
312	14	203	95	...	...	...	...	...	...
...	...	...	...	...	...	...	...	...	...
...	...	...	...	...	...	...	...	...	...
...	...	...	...	...	...	...	...	...	...
131	4	89	38	...	...	...	...	...	...
1	...	...	1	...	...	...	...	...	...
...	...	...	...	...	...	...	...	...	...
...	...	...	...	...	...	...	...	...	...
...	...	...	...	...	...	...	...	...	...
...	...	...	...	...	...	...	...	...	...
3	...	2	1	...	...	...	...	...	...
...	...	...	...	...	...	...	...	...	...
...	...	...	...	...	...	...	...	...	...
190	11	116	63	...	...	...	...	...	...
6	...	4	2	...	...	...	...	...	...
...	...	...	...	...	...	...	...	...	...
17	...	13	[illegible]	...	...	...	...	...	...
21	...	14	7	...	...	...	...	...	...
...	...	...	...	...	...	...	...	...	...
...	...	...	...	...	...	...	...	...	...
153	...	102	51	...	...	...	...	...	...
...	...	...	...	...	...	...	...	...	...
34	...	20	14	...	...	...	...	...	...
...	...	...	...	...	...	...	...	...	...
...	...	...	...	...	...	...	...	...	...
371	8	318	45	...	...	...	...	...	...
688	10	481	97	...	...	...	...	...	...
...	...	...	...	...	...	...	...	...	...
52	...	43	9	...	...	...	...	...	...
21	...	14	7	...	...	...	...	...	...
...	...	...	...	...	...	...	...	...	...
...	...	...	...	...	...	...	...	...	...
74	3	46	25	...	...	...	...	...	...
...	...	...	...	...	...	...	...	...	...
43	...	26	17	...	...	...	...	...	...
6	...	3	3	...	...	...	...	...	...
65	4	43	18	...	...	...	...	...	...
...	...	...	...	...	...	...	...	...	...
...	...	...	...	...	...	...	...	...	...
145	4	123	18	...	...	...	...	...	...
4,204	*116*	*3,076*	*1,012*	...	...	...	...	...	...

Class.	Group.	Caste, &c. and sub-division.	Religion.	All Ages. Total.	Single.	Married.	Widowed.	Civil condition not stated.
B.—Professional.—(Continued.)	5. Priests.—(Continued).	Brámhan.—(Concluded.) Hois'aniga ...	Hindu.	1,458	522	563	373	...
		Karnátaka ...	,,	...	...	...	...	...
		Kumbálúr or Tótada Tigala.	,,	...	...	...	...	...
		Kandávara ...	,,	...	...	...	...	...
		Kannada Kammé ...	,,	731	273	278	180	...
		Karáde... ...	,,	2	...	1	1	...
		Kásalnád ...	,,	...	...	...	...	...
		Kavarga... ...	,,	...	...	...	...	...
		Kóta	,,	...	...	...	...	...
		Kánakubja or Kanyákubja.	,,	...	...	...	...	...
		Konkanast'h ...	,,	37	17	13	7	...
		Kandádé... ...	,,	...	...	...	...	...
		Kátyáyana ...	,,	...	...	...	...	...
		Mulikinádu or Murikinádu.	,,	1,008	375	414	219	...
		Mandyattár ...	,,	44	17	18	9	...
		Nambúri ...	,,	...	...	...	...	...
		Nandavaidika ...	,,	62	19	29	14	...
		Part'hamas'ákhe ...	,,	112	37	49	26	...
		Prativádi Bhayankarrattár.	,,	...	...	...	...	...
		Panchagráma ...	,,	...	...	...	...	...
		Sankéti	,,	705	300	280	185	...
		Sárasvata ...	,,	3	1	1	1	...
		S'irnádu... ...	,,	148	49	58	41	...
		S'is'uvarga ...	,,	...	...	...	...	...
		S'ivalli	,,	...	...	...	...	...
		Smárta	,,	1,977	665	878	434	...
		S'rívaishnava ...	,,	3,204	1,143	1,285	776	...
		Kadámbiyár ...	,,	...	...	...	...	...
		S'rívaishnava, Hebbár	,,	282	98	113	71	...
		Telaghánya ...	,,	115	42	43	30	...
		Tuluva	,,	...	...	...	...	...
		Tirumaleyár ...	,,	...	...	...	...	...
		Úlachakamme ...	,,	342	113	143	86	...
		Utráji (Uttrádi) ...	,,	1	...	...	1	...
		Vadama	,,	225	83	89	53	...
		Vangipuram ...	,,	30	10	13	7	...
		Velnádu... ...	,,	298	93	124	81	...
		Vijápurada kammé...	,,	...	...	...	...	...
		Véginádu ...	,,	...	...	...	...	...
		Vaishnava (Mádhva.)	,,	759	244	352	163	...
		Total Brámhan......		21,775	7,583	8,948	5,345	...

TABLE E.—(*Continued.*)

District.

Females.

0 to 9					10 to 14				
Total.	Single.	Married.	Widowed.	Civil condition not stated.	Total.	Single.	Married.	Widowed.	Civil condition not stated.
467	434	28	5	...	166	88	65	13	...
...	...	...	...	...	...	...	...	...	...
...	...	...	...	...	...	...	...	...	...
...	...	...	...	...	...	...	...	...	...
246	237		...	...	61	36	23	2	...
...	...	...	...	...	...	...	...	...	...
...	...		...	...	...	...	...	...	...
...	...	...	...	...	...	...	...	...	...
...	...	...	...	...	...	...	...	...	...
...	...	...	...	...	...	...	...	...	...
16	13	3	...	...	8	4	4	...	...
...	...		...	...	...	...	...	...	...
	...	...	...	...	...	...	...	...	...
356	332	22	2	...	105	43	56	6	...
15	14	1	...	...	8	3	5	...	...
...	...	...	...	...	...	...	...	...	...
16	15	1	...	...	8	4	4	...	...
32	30	2	...	...	15	7	8	...	...
...	...	...	...	...	...	...	...	...	...
...	...	...	...	...	...	...	...	...	...
279	266	11	2	...	72	34	33	5	...
1	1	...	...	...	...	...	...	...	...
41	40	1	...	...	17	9	8	...	...
...	...	...	...	...	...	...	...	...	...
...	...	...	...	...	...	...	...	...	...
501	486	12	6	...	229	179	39	11	...
980	927	42	11	...	388	216	134	38	...
...	...	...	...	...	...	...	...	...	...
78	75	3	...	...	38	23	15	...	...
35	32	3	...	...	17	10	7	...	...
...	...	...	...	...	...	...	...	...	...
...	...	...	...	...	...	...	...	...	...
107	101	6	...	...	28	12	16	...	...
...	...	...	...	...	...	...	...	...	...
73	67	6	...	...	30	16	13	1	...
10	9	1	...	...	3	1	2	...	...
83	77	6	...	...	28	16	12	...	...
...	...	...	...	...	...	...	...	...	...
...	...	...	...	...	...	...	...	...	...
200	193	6	1	...	73	51	19	3	...
6,703	*6,361*	*296*	*40*	...	*2,287*	*1,221*	*915*	*151*	...

Class.	Group.	Caste, &c. and sub-division.	Religion.	15 to 39 Total.	Single.	Married.	Widowed.	Civil condition not stated.
B.—Professional.—(Continued.)	5. Priests.—(Continued.)	Brámhan.—(Concluded.) Hoisʼaṇiga ...	Hindu	503	...	3[illegible]9	134	...
		Karṇáṭaka ...	,,	...	...	...	...	...
		Kumbálúr or Toṭuda Tigaḷa. ...	,,	...	...	...	...	...
		Kandávara ...	,,	...	...	...	...	...
		Kannaḍa Kammé ...	,,	265	...	198	67	...
		Karáḍe ...	,,	1	...	1	...	...
		Kásalnáḍ ...	,,	...	...	...	...	...
		Kavarga ...	,,	...	...	...	...	...
		Kóṭa ...	,,	...	...	...	...	...
		Káṇakubja or Kanyákubja.	,,	...	...	...	...	...
		Konkaṇastʼh ...	,,	7	...	5	2	...
		Kandáḍé ...	,,	...	...	...	...	...
		Kátyáyana ...	,,	...	...	...	...	...
		Mulikináḍu or Murikináḍu.	,,	344	...	265	79	...
		Manḍyattár ...	,,	12	...	11	1	...
		Nambúri ...	,,	...	...	...	...	...
		Nandavaidika ...	,,	25	...	20	5	...
		Prathamasʼákhe ...	,,	43	...	34	9	..
		Prativáḍi Bhayankarattár.	,,	...	...	...	...	...
		Panchagráma ...	,,	...	...	...	...	...
		Sankéti ...	,,	245	...	182	63	...
		Sárasvata ...	,,	1	...	1	...	...
		Sʼirnáḍu ...	,,	56	...	39	17	...
		Sʼisʼuvarga ...	,,	...	...	...	...	...
		Sʼivaḷḷi ...	,,	...	...	...	...	...
		Smárta ...	,,	603	...	511	92	...
		Sʼrivaishṇava ...	,,	984	...	807	177	...
		Kaḍámbiyár ...	,,	...	...	...	...	...
		Sʼrivaishṇava, Hebbár	,,	86	...	69	17	...
		Telaghányа ...	,,	38	...	27	11	...
		Tuḷuva ...	,,	...	...	...	...	...
		Tirumaleyár ...	,,	...	...	...	...	...
		Ulachakamme ...	,,	132	...	96	36	...
		Utráji (Uttrádi) ...	,,	...	...	...	...	...
		Vaḍama ...	,,	75	...	60	15	...
		Vangipuram ...	,,	10	...	9	1	...
		Veḷnáḍu ...	,,	119	...	85	33	...
		Vijápuraḍa kammé ...	,,	...	...	...	...	...
		Végináḍu ...	,,	...	...	...	...	...
		Vaishṇava (Mádhva).	,,	245	...	195	50	...
		Total Brámhan ...		*7,423*	...	*5,806*	*1,617*	...

TABLE E.—(Continued.)

District.

Females.

40 and over.					Age not stated.				
Total.	Single.	Married.	Widowed.	Civil condition not stated.	Total.	Single.	Married.	Widowed.	Civil condition not stated.
322	...	101	221	...	...	...	...	...	...
...	...	...	...	...	...	...	...	...	...
...	...	...	...	...	...	...	...	...	...
...	...	...	...	...	...	...	...	...	...
159	...	48	111	...	...	...	...	...	...
1	...	...	1	...	...	...	...	...	...
...	...	...	...	...	...	...	...	...	...
...	...	...	...	...	...	...	...	...	...
...	...	...	...	...	...	...	...	...	...
...	...	...	...	...	...	...	...	...	...
6	...	1	5	...	...	...	...	...	...
...	...	...	...	...	...	...	...	...	...
...	...	...	...	...	...	...	...	...	...
203	...	71	132	...	...	...	...	...	...
9	...	1	8	...	...	...	...	...	...
...	...	...	...	...	...	...	...	...	...
13	...	4	9	...	...	...	...	...	...
22	...	5	17	...	...	...	...	...	...
...	...	...	...	...	...	...	...	...	...
...	...	...	...	...	...	...	...	...	...
169	...	54	115	...	...	...	...	...	...
1	...	...	1	...	...	...	...	...	...
34	...	10	24	...	...	...	...	...	...
...	...	...	...	...	...	...	...	...	...
...	...	...	...	...	...	...	...	...	...
641	...	316	325	...	...	...	...	...	...
852	...	302	550	...	...	...	...	...	...
...	...	...	...	...	...	...	...	...	...
80	...	26	54	...	...	...	...	...	...
25	...	6	19	...	...	...	...	...	...
...	...	...	...	...	...	...	...	...	...
...	...	...	...	...	...	...	...	...	...
75	...	25	50	...	...	...	...	...	...
1	...	...	1	...	...	...	...	...	...
47	...	10	37	...	...	...	...	...	...
7	...	1	6	...	...	...	...	...	...
68	...	20	48	...	...	...	...	...	...
...	...	...	...	...	...	...	...	...	...
...	...	...	...	...	...	...	...	...	...
241	...	132	109	...	...	...	...	...	...
5,363	...	*1,931*	*3,432*	...	...	...	...	...	...

Hassan

Class.	Group.	Caste, &c. and sub-division.	Religion.	All Ages. Total.	Single.	Married.	Widowed.	Civil condition not stated.
B.—Professional.—(*Continued.*)	5. Priests.—(*Continued.*)	Bráhman.—(*Concluded.*) Hois'aniga ...	Hindu.	950	458	415	77	...
		Karnátaka ...	,,	...	...	...	...	...
		Kumbálúr or Tótada Tigalu.	,,	...	...	...	...	...
		Kandávara ...	,,	...	...	...	...	...
		Kannada Kammé ...	,,	216	105	85	26	...
		Karádé	,,	4	2	1	1	...
		Kásalnád ...	,,	...	...	...	...	...
		Kavarga ...	,,	...	...	...	...	...
		Kóta	,,	...	...	...	...	...
		Kánakubja or Kanyákubja.	,,	...	...	...	...	...
		Konkanast'h ...	,,	16	7	7	2	...
		Kandádé ...	,,	...	...	...	...	...
		Kátyáyana ...	,,	...	...	...	...	...
		Mulikinádu or Murikinádu.	,,	254	123	112	19	...
		Mandyattár ...	,,	1	...	1	...	...
		Nambúri ...	,,	...	...	...	...	...
		Nandavaidika ...	,,	7	2	5	...	...
		Prat'hamas'ákhe ...	,,	185	91	78	16	...
		Prativádi Bhayankarattár.	,,	...	...	...	...	...
		Panchagráma ...	,,	...	...	...	...	...
		Sankéti ...	,,	415	183	193	39	...
		Sárasvata ...	,,	...	...	...	...	...
		S'irnádu ...	,,	3	2	1	...	...
		S'is'uvarga ...	,,	...	...	...	...	...
		Sivalli	,,	4	1	2	1	...
		Smárta	,,	1,565	761	672	132	...
		S'rívaishnava ...	,,	1,839	874	892	123	...
		Kadámbiyár ...	,,	...	...	...	...	...
		S'rívaishnava, Hebbár	,,	83	43	33	7	...
		Telaghánya ...	,,	18	9	7	2	...
		Tuluva	,,	...	...	...	...	...
		Tirumaleyár ...	,,	...	...	...	...	...
		Ulachakammé ...	,,	18	10	7	1	...
		Útráji (Uttrádi) ...	,,	1	...	1	...	...
		Vadama ...	,,	...	...	...	...	...
		Vangipuram ...	,,	2	...	1	1	...
		Velnádu ...	,,	19	9	8	2	...
		Vijápurada kammé ...	,,	...	...	...	...	...
		Véginádu ...	,,	...	...	...	...	...
		Vaishnava (Mádhva) ..	,,	188	107	68	13	...
		Total Brámhan ...		*8,499*	*4,074*	*3,735*	*690*	...

TABLE E.—(Continued.)

District.

Males.

0 to 9					10 to 14				
Total.	Single.	Married.	Widowed.	Civil condition not stated.	Total.	Single.	Married.	Widowed.	Civil condition not stated.
260	239	...	...	...	91	86	5	...	...
...	...	...	...	...	...	...	...	...	...
...	...	...	...	...	...	...	...	...	...
...	...	...	...	...	...	...	...	...	...
83	83	...	...	...	18	18	...	...	...
2	2	...	...	...	...	...	...	...	...
...	...	...	...	...	...	...	...	...	...
...	...	...	...	...	...	...	...	...	...
...	...	...	...	...	...	...	...	...	...
...	...	...	...	...	...	...	...	...	...
...	...	...	...	...	...	...	...	...	...
...	...	...	...	...	...	...	...	...	...
...	...	...	...	...	...	...	...	...	...
65	65	...	...	...	39	36	3	...	...
...	...	...	...	...	...	...	...	...	...
...	...	...	...	...	...	...	...	...	...
2	2	...	...	...	...	...	...	...	...
59	59	...	...	...	20	18	2	...	...
...	...	...	...	...	...	...	...	...	...
...	...	...	...	...	...	...	...	...	...
115	115	...	...	...	45	37	8	...	...
...	...	...	...	...	...	...	...	...	...
...	...	...	...	...	...	...	...	...	...
...	...	...	...	...	...	...	...	...	...
1	1	...	...	...	...	...	...	...	...
473	473	...	...	...	188	182	6	...	...
603	498	5	...	...	202	190	12	...	...
...	...	...	...	...	...	...	...	...	...
27	27	...	...	...	14	10	4	...	...
6	6	...	...	...	1	1	...	...	...
...	...	...	...	...	...	...	...	...	...
...	...	...	...	...	...	...	...	...	...
6	6	...	...	...	2	2	...	...	...
...	...	...	...	...	...	...	...	...	...
...	...	...	...	...	...	...	...	...	...
...	...	...	...	...	...	...	...	...	...
7	7	...	...	...	...	...	...	...	...
...	...	...	...	...	...	...	...	...	...
...	...	...	...	...	...	...	...	...	...
56	56	...	...	...	28	26	2	...	...
2,516	*2,511*	*5*	...	...	*895*	*836*	*59*	...	...

Hassan

Class.	Group.	Caste, &c. and sub-division.	Religion.	15 to 39 Total.	Single.	Married.	Widowed.	Civil condition not stated.
B.—Professional.—(Continued.)	5. Priests.—(Continued.)	Brâmhan.—(Concluded.) Hois'aniga	Hindu.	372	97	262	13	...
		Karnâtaka	,,	...	...	...	...	...
		Kumbâlár or Tótada Tigala.	,,	...	...	...	...	...
		Kandâvara	,,	...	...	...	...	...
		Kannada Kammé	,,	60	2	50	8	...
		Karáde ...	,,	1	...	1	...	...
		Kasalnâd ...	,,	...	...	...	...	...
		Kavarga...	,,	...	...	...	...	...
		Kóta	,,	...	...	...	...	...
		Kânakubja or Kanyâkubja.	,,	...	...	...	...	...
		Konkanast'h	,,	13	7	5	1	...
		Kandâdé	,,	...	...	...	...	...
		Kâtyâyana	,,	...	...	...	...	...
		Mulikinâdu or Murikinâdu.	,,	95	21	71	3	...
		Mandyattâr	,,	1	...	1	...	...
		Nambúri	,,	...	...	...	...	...
		Nandavaidíka	,,	5	...	5	...	...
		Prat'hamas'âkhe	,,	77	14	60	3	...
		Prativadi-Bhayankarattâr.	,,	...	...	...	...	...
		Panchagrâma	,,	...	...	...	...	...
		Sankéti	,,	166	31	128	7	...
		Sârasvata	,,	...	...	...	...	...
		S'irnâdu...	,,	3	2	1	...	...
		S'is'uvarga	,,	...	...	...	...	...
		Sivalli ...	,,	2	...	2	...	...
		Smârta ...	,,	612	99	479	34	...
		S'rivaishnava	,,	743	176	538	29	...
		Kadâmbiyâr	,,	...	...	...	...	...
		S'rivaishnava, Hebbâr	,,	32	6	24	2	...
		Telaghânya	,,	6	2	4	...	...
		Tuluva ...	,,	...	...	...	...	...
		Tirumaleyâr	,,	...	...	...	...	...
		Ulachakammé	,,	6	2	4	...	...
		Utrâji (Uttrâdi)	,,	1	...	1	...	...
		Vadama ...	,,	...	...	...	...	...
		Vangípuram	,,	1	...	1	...	...
		Velnadu	,,	9	2	6	1	...
		Vijâpurudakammé	,,	...	...	...	...	...
		Véginâdu	,,	...	...	...	...	...
		Vaishnava (Mâdhva)..	,,	76	24	49	3	...
		Total Brâmhan		3,313	698	2,467	148	...

TABLE E.—(*Continued.*)

District.

Males.

40 and over.					Age not stated.				
Total.	Single.	Married.	Widowed.	Civil condition not stated.	Total.	Single.	Married.	Widowed.	Civil condition not stated.
218	6	148	64	...	...	...	...	...	...
...	...	...	...	...	...	...	...	...	...
...	...	...	...	...	...	...	...	...	...
...	...	...	...	...	...	...	...	...	...
51	...	35	16	...	...	...	...	...	...
1	...	...	1	...	...	...	...	...	...
...	...	...	...	...	...	...	...	...	...
...	...	...	...	...	...	...	...	...	...
...	...	...	...	...	...	...	...	...	...
...	...	...	...	...	...	...	...	...	...
3	...	2	1	...	...	...	...	...	...
...	...	...	...	...	...	...	...	...	...
...	...	...	...	...	...	...	...	...	...
55	1	38	16	...	...	...	...	...	...
...	...	...	...	...	...	...	...	...	...
...	...	...	...	...	...	...	...	...	...
...	...	...	...	...	...	...	...	...	...
29	...	16	13	...	...	...	...	...	...
...	...	...	...	...	...	...	...	...	...
...	...	...	...	...	...	...	...	...	...
89	...	57	32	...	...	...	...	...	...
...	...	...	...	...	...	...	...	...	...
...	...	...	...	...	...	...	...	...	...
...	...	...	...	...	...	...	...	...	...
1	...	...	1	...	...	...	...	...	...
292	7	187	98	...	...	...	...	...	...
441	10	337	94	...	...	...	...	...	...
...	...	...	...	...	...	...	...	...	...
10	...	5	5	...	...	...	...	...	...
5	...	3	2	...	...	...	...	...	...
...	...	...	...	...	...	...	...	...	...
...	...	...	...	...	...	...	...	...	...
4	...	3	1	...	...	...	...	...	...
...	...	...	...	...	...	...	...	...	...
...	...	...	...	...	...	...	...	...	...
1	...	...	1	...	...	...	...	...	...
3	...	2	1	...	...	...	...	...	...
...	...	...	...	...	...	...	...	...	...
...	...	...	...	...	...	...	...	...	...
28	1	17	10	...	...	...	...	...	...
1,775	*20*	*1,204*	*542*	...	...	...	...	...	...

Hassan

Class.	Group.	Caste, &c. and sub-division.	Religion.	All Ages. Total.	All Ages. Single.	All Ages. Married.	All Ages. Widowed.	All Ages. Civil condition not stated.
B.—Professional.—(Continued.)	5. Priests.—(Continued.)	Brámhan.—(Concluded.) Hoys'aniga	Hindu.	917	256	431	230	...
		Karṇáṭaka	,,	...	...		...	...
		Kumbálúr or Tóṭada Tigaḷá.	,,	...	...		...	...
		Kandávara	,,	...	...	...		
		Kannada Kammé	,,	221	71	109	41	...
		Karáḍé	,,	2	1	1	...	...
		Kásalnáḍ	,,	...	...	...	...	...
		Kavargá	,,	...	...	...	...	...
		Kóṭa	,,	...	...	...	...	...
		Káṇakubja or Kanyá-kubja.	,,	...	...	...	...	...
		Konkaṇast'h	,,	3	...	3	...	...
		Kandáḍé	,,	...	...	...	...	...
		Kátyáyana	,,	...	...	...	...	...
		Mulikináḍu or Murki-náḍu.	,,	255	73	130	52	...
		Mandyattár	,,	...	...	...	...	...
		Nambúri	,,	...	...	...	...	...
		Nandavaidika	,,	11	3	5	3	...
		Prat'hamas'ákhe	,,	186	63	95	28	...
		Prativádi Bhayan-karattár.	,,	...	...	...	...	...
		Panchagráma	,,	...	...	...	...	...
		Sankéti	,,	409	112	215	82	...
		Sárasvata	,,	...	...	...	...	...
		S'írnáḍu	,,	2	...	1	1	...
		S'is'uvarga	,,	...	...	...	...	...
		Sivaḷḷi	,,	3	...	3	...	...
		Smárta	,,	1,545	552	720	273	...
		S'rívaishṇava	,,	2,002	540	1,009	453	...
		Kaḍámbiyár	,,	...	...	...	...	...
		S'rívaishṇava, Hebbár	,,	89	33	44	12	...
		Telaghánya	,,	13	3	7	3	...
		Tuḷuva	,,	...	...	...	...	...
		Tirumaléyár	,,	...	...	...	...	...
		Ulachakammé	,,	8	2	5	1	...
		Utráji (Uttrádi)	,,	4	1	2	1	...
		Vaḍama	,,	...	...	...	...	...
		Vangipuram	,,	2	1	1	...	...
		Velnáḍu	,,	18	7	4	7	...
		Vijápurada kammé.	,,	...	...	...	...	...
		Végináḍu	,,	...	...	...	...	...
		Vaishṇava (Mádhva).	,,	175	72	74	29	...
		Total Brámhan		8,561	2,629	4,157	1,775	...

TABLE E.—(*Continued.*)

District.

Females.

0 to 9					10 to 14				
Total.	Single.	Married.	Widowed.	Civil condition not stated.	Total.	Single.	Married.	Widowed.	Civil condition not stated.
232	226	5	1	...	78	30	48	...	...
...	...	...	...	...	...	...	...	...	...
...	...	...	...	...	...	...	...	...	...
...	...	...	...	...	...	...	...	...	...
68	68	...	...	...	19	8	15	1	...
...	...	...	...	...	1	1	...	...	...
...	...	...	...	...	...	...	...	...	...
...	...	...	...	...	...	...	...	...	...
...	...	...	...	...	...	...	...	...	...
...	...	...	...	...	...	...	...	...	...
...	...	...	...	...	...	...	...	...	...
...	...	...	...	...	...	...	...	...	...
...	...	...	...	...	...	...	...	...	...
62	61	1	...	...	32	12	20	...	...
...	...	...	...	...	...	...	...	...	...
...	...	...	...	...	...	...	...	...	...
3	3	...	...	...	1	...	1	...	...
56	56	...	...	...	22	7	15	...	...
...	...	...	...	...	...	...	...	...	...
...	...	...	...	...	...	...	...	...	...
113	105	8	...	...	39	7	32	...	...
...	...	...	...	...	...	...	...	...	...
...	...	...	...	...	...	...	...	...	...
...	...	...	...	...	...	...	...	...	...
...	...	...	...	...	...	...	...	...	...
496	485	11	...	...	125	67	55	3	...
616	602	14	...	...	184	38	143	3	...
...	...	...	...	...	...	...	...	...	...
25	23	2	...	...	19	10	9	...	...
3	3	...	...	...	2	...	2	...	...
...	...	...	...	...	...	...	...	...	...
...	...	...	...	...	...	...	...	...	...
2	2	...	...	...	...	...	...	...	...
1	1	...	...	...	1	...	1	...	...
...	...	...	...	...	...	...	...	...	...
1	1	...	...	...	...	...	...	...	...
7	7	...	...	...	...	...	...	...	...
...	...	...	...	...	...	...	...	...	...
...	...	...	...	...	...	...	...	...	...
61	59	2	...	...	24	13	11	...	...
2,388	*2,320*	*67*	*1*	...	*807*	*309*	*485*	*13*	...

Hassan

Class.	Group.	Caste, &c. and sub-division.	Religion.	15 to 39. Total.	Single.	Married.	Widowed.	Civil condition not stated
B.—Professional—(Continued.)	5. Priests.—(Continued.)	Brâhman.—(Concluded.) Hoisanige	Hindu.	314	...	284	60	...
		Karnâṭaka	,,	...	...	...	...	...
		Kumbâlâr or Tôṭada Tigaḷ	,,	...	...	...	...	...
		Kandâvara	,,	...	...	...	...	...
		Kannada Kammê	,,	93	...	78	15	...
		Karâḍe	,,	1	...	1	...	...
		Kâsalnâḍ	,,	...	...	...	...	...
		Kavarga	,,	...	...	...	...	...
		Kôṭa	,,	...	...	...	...	...
		Kânakubja or Kanyâkubja	,,	...	...	...	...	...
		Konkanast'h	,,	2	...	2	...	...
		Kandâḍê	,,	...	...	...	...	...
		Kâtyâyana	,,	...	...	...	...	...
		Mulikinâḍu or Murikinâḍu	,,	105	...	90	15	...
		Mandyattâr	,,	...	...	...	...	...
		Nambûri	,,	...	...	...	...	...
		Nandavaidika	,,	4	...	4	...	...
		Prat'hamas'âkha	,,	76	...	68	8	...
		Partivâdi Bhayankarattâr	,,	...	...	...	...	...
		Panchagrâma	,,	...	...	...	...	...
		Sankêti	,,	167	...	147	20	...
		Sârasvata	,,	...	...	...	...	...
		S'îrnâḍu	,,	1	...	1	...	...
		S'is'nvarga	,,	...	...	...	...	...
		Sivaḷḷi	,,	3	...	3	...	...
		Smârta	,,	591	...	506	85	...
		S'rîvaishṇava	,,	748	...	642	106	...
		Kaḍâmbiyâr	,,	...	...	...	...	...
		S'rîvaishṇâva. Hebbâr	,,	33	...	30	3	...
		Telaghâṇya	,,	5	...	4	1	...
		Tuḷuva	,,	...	...	...	...	...
		Tirumaleyâr	,,	...	...	...	...	...
		Ulachakammê	,,	4	...	4	...	...
		Utrâji (Úttrâdi)	,,	1	...	1	...	...
		Vaḍama	,,	...	...	...	...	...
		Vangipuram	,,	1	...	1	...	...
		Vêlnâḍu	,,	7	...	4	3	...
		Vijâpurada kammê	,,	...	...	...	...	...
		Vêginâḍu	,,	...	...	...	...	...
		Vaishṇava (Mâdhva)	,,	59	...	52	7	...
		Total Brâhman		3,313	...	2,866	477	...

TABLE E.—(*Continued.*)

District.

Females.

40 and over.					Age not stated.				
Total.	Single.	Married.	Widowed	Civil condition not stated.	Total.	Single.	Married.	Widowed	Civil condition not stated.
263	...	94	169	...	...	...	...	...	...
...	...	...	...	...	...	...	...	...	...
...	...	...	...	...	...	...	...	...	...
...	...	...	...	...	...	...	...	...	...
41	...	16	25	...	...	...	...	...	...
...	...	...	...	...	...	...	...	...	...
...	...	...	...	...	...	...	...	...	...
...	...	...	...	...	...	...	...	...	...
...	...	...	...	...	...	...	...	...	...
...	...	...	...	...	...	...	...	...	...
1	...	1	...	...	...	...	...	...	...
...	...	...	...	...	...	...	...	...	...
...	...	...	...	...	...	...	...	...	...
56	...	19	37	...	...	...	...	...	...
...	...	...	...	...	...	...	...	...	...
...	...	...	...	...	...	...	...	...	...
3	...	...	3	...	...	...	...	...	...
32	...	12	20	...	...	...	...	...	...
...	...	...	...	...	...	...	...	...	...
...	...	...	...	...	...	...	...	...	...
90	...	28	62	...	...	...	...	...	...
...	...	...	...	...	...	...	...	...	...
1	...	...	1	...	...	...	...	...	...
...	...	...	...	...	...	...	...	...	...
...	...	...	...	...	...	...	...	...	...
333	...	148	185	...	...	...	...	...	...
554	...	210	344	...	...	...	...	...	...
...	...	...	...	...	...	...	...	...	...
12	...	3	9	...	...	...	...	...	...
3	...	1	2	...	...	...	...	...	...
...	...	...	...	...	...	...	...	...	...
...	...	...	...	...	...	...	...	...	...
2	...	1	1	...	...	...	...	...	...
1	...	...	1	...	...	...	...	...	...
...	...	...	...	...	...	...	...	...	...
...	...	...	...	...	...	...	...	...	...
4	...	...	4	...	...	...	...	...	...
...	...	...	...	...	...	...	...	...	...
...	...	...	...	...	...	...	...	...	...
31	...	9	22	...	...	...	...	...	...
2,023	...	739	1,284	...	...	...	...	...	...

Shimoga

Class.	Group.	Caste, &c. and sub-division.	Religion.	All ages. Total.	All ages. Single.	All ages. Married.	All ages. Widowed.	All ages. Civil condition not stated.
B.—Professional.—(Continued.)	5. Priests.—(Continued.)	Brámhan.—(Concluded.) Hois'aniga ...	Hindu.	74	39	31	4	...
		Karnátaka ...	,,	272	147	108	17	...
		Kumbálár or Totada Tigala.	,,	47	22	18	7	...
		Kandávara ...	,,	14	6	6	2	...
		Kannada kammé ...	,,	...	...	...	...	...
		Karádo ...	,,	104	40	51	13	...
		Kásalnád	,,	...	...	...	...	...
		Kavarga ...	,,	...	...	...	...	...
		Kóta	,,	...	...	...	...	...
		Kánakubja or Kanyákubja.	,,	5	3	2	...	...
		Konkanast'h ...	,,	86	47	30	9	...
		Kandádé ...	,,	...	...	...	...	...
		Kátyáyana ...	,,	...	...	...	...	...
		Mulikinadu or Murikinádu.	,,	116	64	43	9	...
		Mandyattár ...	,,	...	...	...	...	...
		Nambúri ...	,,	...	...	...	...	...
		Nandavaidika ...	,,	...	...	...	...	...
		Prat'hamas'ákhe ...	,,	91	49	36	6	...
		Prativádi Bhayankarattár.	,,	...	...	...	...	...
		Panchagráma ...	,,	101	46	41	14	...
		Sankéti ...	,,	3	1	1	1	...
		Sárasvata ...	,,	56	27	26	3	...
		S'irnádu ...	,,	...	...	...	...	...
		S'is'uvarga ...	,,	...	...	...	...	...
		Sivalli	,,	...	...	...	...	...
		Smárta	,,	3,746	1,706	1,820	220	...
		S'rivishnava ...	,,	292	146	128	18	...
		Kadámbiyár ...	,,	...	...	...	...	...
		S'rivaishnava, Hobbár	,,	80	39	37	4	...
		Tolaghánya ...	,,	13	7	5	1	...
		Tuluva	,,	...	...	...	...	...
		Tirumaleyár ...	,,	...	...	...	...	...
		Ulachakammé ...	,,	...	...	...	...	...
		Utráji (Uttrádi) ...	,,	154	82	64	8	...
		Vadama ...	,,	32	17	13	2	...
		Vangipuram ...	,,	...	...	...	...	...
		Velnádu ...	,,	...	...	...	...	...
		Vijápurada kammé.	,,	...	...	...	...	...
		Véginádu ...	,,	...	...	...	...	...
		Vaishnava (Mádhva)	,,	1,220	549	592	79	...
		Total Brámhan......	... ...	*15,728*	*7,643*	*6,633*	*1,452*	...

TABLE E.—(*Continued.*)

District.

Males.

0 to 9.					10 to 14.				
Total.	Single.	Married.	Widowed.	Civil condition not stated.	Total.	Single.	Married.	Widowed.	Civil condition not stated.
17	17	...	...	...	4	4	...	...	...
60	60	...	...	...	26	26	...	...	...
12	12	...	...	...	8	8	...	...	...
8	3	...	...	...	2	2	...	...	...
...	...	...	...	...	...	...	...	...	...
22	22	...	...	...	8	8	...	...	...
...	...	...	...	...	...	...	...	...	...
...	...	...	...	...	...	...	...	...	...
...	...	...	...	...	...	...	...	...	...
1	1	...	...	...	1	1	...	...	...
30	30	...	...	...	9	9	...	...	...
...	...	...	...	...	...	...	...	...	...
...	...	...	...	...	...	...	...	...	...
37	37	...	...	...	11	11	...	...	...
...	...	...	...	...	...	...	...	...	...
...	...	...	...	...	...	...	...	...	...
...	...	...	...	...	...	...	...	...	...
31	31	...	...	...	9	9	...	...	...
...	...	...	...	...	...	...	...	...	...
28	28	...	...	...	10	10	...	...	...
...	...	...	...	...	...	...	...	...	...
13	13	...	...	...	7	7	...	...	...
...	...	...	...	...	...	...	...	...	...
...	...	...	...	...	...	...	...	...	...
...	...	...	...	...	...	...	...	...	...
626	621	5	...	...	263	263	...	...	...
79	79	...	...	...	42	38	4	...	...
...	...	...	...	...	...	...	...	...	...
24	21	...	...	...	8	8	...	...	...
3	3	...	...	...	3	3	...	...	...
...	...	...	...	...	...	...	...	...	...
...	...	...	...	...	...	...	...	...	...
...	...	...	...	...	...	...	...	...	...
41	41	...	...	...	26	26	...	...	...
10	8	2	...	...	3	3	...	...	...
...	...	...	...	...	...	...	...	...	...
...	...	...	...	...	...	...	...	...	...
...	...	...	...	...	...	...	...	...	...
...	...	...	...	...	...	...	...	...	...
223	211	11	...	...	96	96	...	...	...
3,628	*3,606*	22	...	...	*1,617*	*1,530*	84	3	...

Shimoga

Class.	Group.	Caste, &c. and sub-division.	Religion.	15 to 39. Total.	Single.	Married.	Widowed.	Civil condition not stated.
B.—Professional.—(Continued.)	5. Priests.—(Continued.)	Brâmhan.—(Concluded.) Hoisʼaniga	Hindu.	41	17	23	1	...
		Karnataka	,,	135	55	77	3	...
		Kumbhâlûr or Toṭada Tigala.	,,	15	2	12	1	...
		Kandâvara	,,	5	1	4	...	...
		Kannaḍa Kammé	,,	...	...	...	...	...
		Karâḍe	,,	48	10	36	2	...
		Kâsalnâḍ	,,	...	...	...	...	...
		Kavarga	,,	...	...	...	...	...
		Kôṭa	,,	...	...	...	...	...
		Kânakubja or Kanyâkubja.	,,	3	1	2	...	...
		Konkaṇast'h	,,	27	8	17	2	...
		Kandaḍé	,,	...	...	...	...	...
		Kâtyâyana	,,	...	...	...	...	...
		Mulikinâḍu or Murikinâḍu.	,,	50	16	32	2	...
		Manḍyatiâr	,,	...	...	...	...	...
		Nambûri	,,	...	...	...	...	...
		Nandavaidika	,,	...	...	...	...	...
		Prat'hamas'âkho	,,	34	9	24	1	...
		Prativâdi Bhayankarattâr.	,,	...	...	...	...	...
		Panchagrâma	,,	35	8	24	3	...
		Sankéti	,,	2	1	1	...	...
		Sârasvata	,,	22	6	14	2	...
		S'irnâḍu	,,	...	...	...	...	...
		S'is'uvarga	,,	...	...	...	...	...
		Sivaḷḷi	,,	...	...	...	...	...
		Smârta	,,	1,974	821	1,119	34	...
		S'rîvaishṇava	,,	118	29	85	4	...
		Kaḍâmbiyâr	,,	...	...	...	...	...
		S'rîvaishṇava, Hebbâr	,,	31	6	24	1	...
		Telaghâṇya	,,	4	1	3	...	...
		Tuḷava	,,	...	...	...	...	...
		Tirumaleyâr	,,	...	...	...	...	...
		Ulachakammé	,,	...	...	...	...	...
		Utrâji (Uttradi)	,,	58	13	44	1	...
		Vaḍama	,,	14	6	8	...	...
		Vangîpuram	,,	...	...	...	...	...
		Velnâḍu	,,	...	...	...	...	...
		Vijâpurada kammé.	,,	...	...	...	...	...
		Vêginâḍu	,,	...	...	...	...	...
		Vaishṇava (Mâdhva).	,,	652	242	391	19	...
		Total Brâmhan	... ...	7,068	2,438	4,274	356	...

TABLE E.—(*Continued.*)

District.

Males.

40 and over.					Age not stated.				
Total.	Single.	Married.	Widowed.	Civil condition not stated.	Total.	Single.	Married.	Widowed.	Civil condition not stated.
12	1	6	3	...	...	...	...	...	...
51	6	31	14	...	...	...	...	...	...
12	...	6	6	...	...	...	...	...	...
4	...	2	2	...	...	...	...	...	...
...	...	...	...	...	...	...	...	...	...
26	...	15	11	...	...	...	...	...	...
...	...	...	...	...	...	...	...	...	...
...	...	...	...	...	...	...	...	...	...
...	...	...	...	...	...	...	...	...	...
...	...	...	...	...	...	...	...	...	...
20	...	13	7	...	...	...	...	...	...
...	...	...	...	...	...	...	...	...	...
...	...	...	...	...	...	...	...	...	...
18	...	11	7	...	...	...	...	...	...
...	...	...	...	...	...	...	...	...	...
...	...	...	...	...	...	...	...	...	...
...	...	...	...	...	...	...	...	...	...
17	...	12	5	...	...	...	...	...	...
...	...	...	...	...	...	...	...	...	...
28	...	17	11	...	...	...	...	...	...
1	...	...	1	...	...	...	...	...	...
14	1	12	1	...	...	...	...	...	...
...	...	...	...	...	...	...	...	...	...
...	...	...	...	...	...	...	...	...	...
...	...	...	...	...	...	...	...	...	...
883	1	696	186	...	...	...	...	...	...
53	...	39	14	...	...	...	...	...	...
...	...	...	...	...	...	...	...	...	...
17	1	13	3	...	...	...	...	...	...
3	...	2	1	...	...	...	...	...	...
...	...	...	...	...	...	...	...	...	...
...	...	...	...	...	...	...	...	...	...
...	...	...	...	...	...	...	...	...	...
29	2	20	7	...	...	...	...	...	...
5	...	3	2	...	...	...	...	...	...
...	...	...	...	...	...	...	...	...	...
...	...	...	...	...	...	...	...	...	...
...	...	...	...	...	...	...	...	...	...
...	...	...	...	...	...	...	...	...	...
250	...	190	60	...	...	...	...	...	...
3,415	*69*	*2,253*	*1,093*	...	...	...	...	...	...

Shimoga

Class.	Group.	Caste, &c. and subdivision.	Religion.	All Ages. Total.	Single.	Married.	Widowed.	Civil condition not stated.
B.—Professional.—(Continued.)	5. Priests.—(Continued.)	Bráhman.—(Concluded.) Hoisʼaniga ...	Hindu.	48	15	25	8	...
		Karnátaka ...	,,	257	72	100	85	...
		Kumbhálúr or Tótada Tigala.	,,	43	15	20	8	...
		Kandávara ...	,,	8	2	5	1	...
		Kannada Kammé ...	,,	...	...	...	...	...
		Karáde	,,	92	23	57	12	...
		Kásalnáḍ ...	,,	...	...	...	...	...
		Kavarga ...	,,	...	...	...	...	...
		Kóṭa	,,	...	...	...	...	...
		Kánakubja or Kanyákubja.	,,	2	...	2	...	...
		Konkanasthʼ ...	,,	62	16	33	13	...
		Kandádé ...	,,	...	...	...	...	...
		Katyáyana ...	,,	...	...	...	...	...
		Mulikináḍu or Murikináḍu.	,,	105	40	48	17	...
		Mandyattár ...	,,	...	...	...	...	...
		Nambúri ...	,,	...	...	...	...	...
		Nandavaidika ...	,,	...	...	...	...	...
		Prathamasʼákhe ...	,,	97	30	45	22	...
		Prativádi Bhayankaráttár.	,,	...	...	...	...	...
		Panchagráma ...	,,	94	37	45	12	...
		Sankéti	,,	...	...	...	...	...
		Sárasvata ...	,,	38	13	20	5	...
		Sʼirnáḍu... ...	,,	...	...	...	...	...
		Sʼisʼuvarga ...	,,	...	...	...	...	...
		Sivaḷḷi	,,	...	...	...	...	...
		Smárta	,,	3,305	1,015	1,508	782	...
		Sʼrivaishṇava ...	,,	233	81	104	48	...
		Kaḍámbiyár ...	,,	...	...	...	...	...
		Sʼrivaishṇava, Hebbár.	,,	78	20	37	21	...
		Telaghánya ...	,,	8	1	5	2	...
		Tuḷuva	,,	...	...	...	...	...
		Tirumaleyár ...	,,	...	...	...	...	...
		Ulachakammé ...	,,	...	...	...	...	...
		Utráji (Uttrádi) ...	,,	118	57	47	14	...
		Vadama	,,	32	11	16	5	...
		Vangipuram ...	,,	...	...	...	...	...
		Velnáḍu ...	,,	...	...	...	...	...
		Viápurada kammé ...	,,	...	...	...	...	...
		Véginádu ...	,,	...	...	...	...	...
		Vaishṇava (Mádhva)..	,,	1,017	410	512	125	...
		Total Bráhman......	... ...	13,640	4,309	6,350	2,981	...

TABLE E.—(Continued.)

District.

Females.

0 to 9					10 to 14				
Total.	Single.	Married.	Widowed.	Civil condition not stated.	Total.	Single.	Married.	Widowed.	Civil condition not stated.
10	10	...	...	...	6	5	1	...	...
69	69	...	...	...	14	3	11	...	...
9	9	...	...	...	6	6	...	...	...
2	2	...	...	...	...	...	...	...	...
	...	...	...	...	...	...	...	...	...
18	18	...	...	...	8	5	3	...	...
...	...	...	...	...	...	...	...	...	...
...	...	...	...	...	...	...	...	...	...
...	...	...	...	...	...	...	...	...	...
...	...	...	...	...	...	...	...	...	...
12	12	...	...	...	5	4	1	...	...
...	...	...	...	...	...	...	...	...	...
...	...	...	...	...	...	...	...	...	...
34	33	1	...	...	13	7	5	...	...
...	...	...	...	...	...	...	...	...	...
...	...	...	...	...	...	...	...	...	...
...	...	...	...	...	...	...	...	...	...
24	24	...	...	...	10	6	4	...	...
...	...	...	...	...	...	...	...	...	...
29	29	...	...	...	11	8	3	...	...
...	...	...	...	...	...	...	...	...	...
12	12	...	...	...	3	1	2	...	...
...	...	...	...	...	...	...	...	...	...
...	...	...	...	...	...	...	...	...	...
...	...	...	...	...	...	...	...	...	...
868	809	51	8	...	488	206	232	50	...
62	62	...	...	...	30	19	11	...	...
...	...	...	...	...	...	...	...	...	...
18	18	...	...	...	7	2	5	...	...
1	1	...	...	...	...	...	...	...	...
...	...	...	...	...	...	...	...	...	...
...	...	...	...	...	...	...	...	...	...
...	...	...	...	...	...	...	...	...	...
44	44	...	...	...	20	13	7	...	...
8	8	...	...	...	6	3	3	...	...
...	...	...	...	...	...	...	...	...	...
...	...	...	...	...	...	...	...	...	...
...	...	...	...	...	...	...	...	...	...
...	...	...	...	...	...	...	...	...	...
328	305	20	3	...	178	105	63	10	...
3,421	*3,295*	*115*	*11*	...	*1,986*	*1,014*	*902*	*70*	...

Class.	Group.	Caste, &c. and sub-division.	Religion.	15 to 39 Total.	15 to 39 Single.	15 to 39 Married.	15 to 39 Widowed.	15 to 39 Civil condition not stated.
B.—Professional.—(Continued.)	5. Priests.—(Continued.)	Brámhan.—(Concluded.) Hois'aṇiga ...	Hindu.	22	...	19	3	...
		Karṇáṭaka ...	,,	106	...	77	29	...
		Kumbálúr or Tóṭada Tigaḷa	,,	15	...	13	2	...
		Kandávara ...	,,	4	...	3	1	...
		Kannaḍa Kammé ...	,,		...	...	...	...
		Karáḍe ...	,,	44	...	41	3	...
		Kásalnád ...	,,	...	...	...	...	...
		Kavarga ...	,,	...	...	...	...	...
		Kóṭa	,,	...	...	...	...	...
		Káṇakubja or Kanyákubja.	,,	2	...	2	...	...
		Konkaṇast'h ...	,,	30	...	25	5	...
		Kandáḍé ...	,,	...	...	...	...	...
		Kátyáyana ..	,,	...	...	...	...	...
		Mulikináḍu or Murikináḍu.	,,	36	...	33	3	...
		Mandyattár ...	,,	...	...	...	...	...
		Nambúri ..	,,	...	...	...	...	...
		Nandavaidíka ...	,,	...	...	...	...	...
		Prat'hamas'ákhe ...	,,	43	...	32	11	...
		Prativádi Bhayankaruttár.	,,	...	...	...	...	...
		Panchagráma ...	,,	30	...	27	3	...
		Sankéti ...	,,	...	...	...	...	...
		Sárasvata ...	,,	17	...	16	1	...
		S'irnáḍu ...	,,	...	...	...	...	...
		S'is'uvarga ..	,,	...	...	...	...	...
		Sivaḷḷi	,,	...	...	...	...	...
		Smárta... ...	,,	1,096	...	994	102	...
		S'rivaishṇava ...	,,	75	...	65	10	...
		Kaḍámbiyár ...	,,	...	...	...	...	...
		S'rivaishṇava, Hobbár	,,	32	...	25	7	...
		Telaghâṇya ...	,,	5	...	5	...	...
		Tuḷuva	,,	...	...	...	...	...
		Tirumaleyár ...	,,	...	...	...	...	...
		Ulachakammé ...	,,	...	...	...	...	...
		Utráji (Uttrádi) ...	,,	33	...	30	3	...
		Vaḍama ...	,,	13	...	11	2	...
		Vangipuram ...	,,	...	...	...	...	...
		Veḷnáḍu ...	,,	...	...	...	...	...
		Vijápurada kammé..	,,	...	...	...	...	...
		Véginádu ...	,,	...	...	...	...	...
		Vaishṇava (Mádhva)..	,,	372	...	332	40	...
		Total Brámhaṇ......	....	*5,156*	...	*4,330*	*826*	...

TABLE E.—(*Continued.*)

District.

Females.

40 and over.					Age not stated.				
Total.	Single.	Married.	Widowed.	Civil condition not stated.	Total.	Single.	Married.	Widowed.	Civil condition not stated.
10	...	5	5	...	...	...	...	...	...
68	...	12	56	...	...	...	...	...	...
13	...	7	6	...	...	...	...	...	...
2	...	2	...	...	...	...	...	...	...
...	...	...	...	...	...	...	...	...	...
22	...	13	9	...	...	...	...	...	...
...	...	...	...	...	...	...	...	...	...
...	...	...	...	...	...	...	...	...	...
...	...	...	...	...	...	...	...	...	...
...	...	...	...	...	...	...	...	...	...
15	...	7	8	...	...	...	...	...	...
...	...	...	...	...	...	...	...	...	...
...	...	...	...	...	...	...	...	...	...
23	...	9	14	...	...	...	...	...	...
...	...	...	...	...	...	...	...	...	...
...	...	...	...	...	...	...	...	...	...
...	...	...	...	...	...	...	...	...	...
20	...	9	11	...	...	...	...	...	...
...	...	...	...	...	...	...	...	...	...
24	...	15	9	...	...	...	...	...	...
...	...	...	...	...	...	...	...	...	...
6	...	2	4	...	...	...	...	...	...
...	...	...	...	...	...	...	...	...	...
...	...	...	...	...	...	...	...	...	...
...	...	...	...	...	...	...	...	...	...
853	...	231	623	...	...	...	...	...	...
66	...	28	38	...	...	...	...	...	...
...	...	...	...	...	...	...	...	...	...
21	...	7	14	...	...	...	...	...	...
2	...	...	2	...	...	...	...	...	...
...	...	...	...	...	...	...	...	...	...
...	...	...	...	...	...	...	...	...	...
...	...	...	...	...	...	...	...	...	...
21	...	10	11	...	...	...	...	...	...
5	...	2	3	...	...	...	...	...	...
...	...	...	...	...	...	...	...	...	...
...	...	...	...	...	...	...	...	...	...
...	...	...	...	...	...	...	...	...	...
...	...	...	...	...	...	...	...	...	...
169	...	97	72	...	...	...	...	...	...
3,083	...	*1,009*	*2,074*	...	...	...	...	...	...

Class.	Group.	Caste, &c. and sub-division.		Religion.	All Ages. Total.	Single.	Married.	Widowed.	Civil condition not stated.
B—Professional.—(Continued.)	5. Priests.—(Continued.)	Brâmhan.—(Concluded.)	Hoyisaṇiga	Hindu	460	223	203	34	...
			Karṇâṭaka	,,	140	79	45	16	...
			Kumbâlár or Tóṭada Tigaḷa.	,,	...	...	...	...	...
			Kandavara	,,	91	59	33	2	...
			Kannaḍa Kammé	,,	...	...	...	...	...
			Karâḍe	,,	16	7	8	1	...
			Kâsalnâḍ	,,	...	...	...	...	...
			Kavarga	,,	5	3	1	1	...
			Kôṭa	,,	10	5	3	2	...
			Kâṇakubja or Kanyâkubja.	,,	...	...	...	...	...
			Konkaṇastʻh	,,	9	5	4	...	...
			Kaṇḍâḍé	,,	...	...	...	...	...
			Kâtyâyana	,,	67	35	27	5	...
			Mulikinâḍu or Murikinaḍu.	,,	121	60	52	9	...
			Mâṇḍyattâr	,,	...	...	...	...	...
			Nambûri	,,	8	4	3	1	...
			Nandavaidíka	,,	3	1	1	1	...
			Pratʻhamasʻakhe	,,	90	42	40	8	...
			Prativâdi Bhayankarattâr.	,,	...	...	...	...	...
			Panchagrâma	,,	83	39	35	9	...
			Sankéti	,,	134	68	56	10	...
			Sarasvata	,,	14	9	3	2	...
			S'irnâḍu	,,	...	...	...	...	...
			S'is'uvarga	,,	64	33	28	3	...
			S'ivaḷḷi	,,	1,213	618	506	89	...
			Smârta	,,	2,463	1,229	1,072	162	...
			S'rîvaishṇava	,,	333	169	140	24	...
			Kaḍâmbiyâr	,,	...	...	...	...	...
			S'rîvaishṇava, Hebbar	,,	45	23	18	4	...
			Tôlaghâṇya	,,	568	306	235	27	...
			Tuḷuva	,,	...	...	...	...	...
			Tirumaleyâr	,,	...	...	...	...	...
			Ulachakammé	,,	16	7	9	...	...
			Utrâji (Uttrâdi)	,,	...	...	...	...	...
			Vaḍama	,,	1	1	...	...	...
			Vangipuram	,,	...	...	...	...	...
			Velnâḍu	,,	101	61	34	6	...
			Vijâpurada kammé.	,,	...	...	...	...	...
			Vêginâḍu	,,	...	...	...	...	...
			Vaishṇava (Mâdhva).	,,	175	85	79	11	...
			Total Brâmhan	... ...	*8,795*	*4,480*	*3,715*	*600*	...

TABLE E.—(*Continued*)

District.

Males.

0 to 9					10 to 14				
Total.	Single.	Married.	Widowed.	Civil condition not stated.	Total.	Single.	Married.	Widowed.	Civil condition not stated.
122	122	...	...	...	40	35	5	...	...
57	57	...	...	...	9	9	...	...	...
...	...	...	...	...	...	...	...	...	...
35	35	...	...	...	7	7	...	...	...
...	...	...	...	...	...	...	...	...	...
3	3	...	...	...	1	1	...	...	...
...	...	...	...	...	...	...	...	...	...
1	1	...	...	...	1	1	...	...	...
3	3	...	...	...	1	1	...	...	...
...	...	...	...	...	...	...	...	...	...
3	3	...	...	...	2	2	...	...	...
...	...	...	...	...	...	...	...	...	...
16	16	...	...	...	14	14	...	...	...
36	36	...	...	...	10	9	1	...	...
...	...	...	...	...	...	...	...	...	...
3	3	...	...	...	1	1	...	...	...
...	...	...	...	...	...	...	...	...	...
20	20	...	...	...	7	7	...	...	...
...	...	...	...	...	...	...	...	...	...
17	17	...	...	...	8	8	...	...	...
37	37	...	...	...	13	13	...	...	...
5	5	...	...	...	2	2	...	...	...
...	...	...	...	...	...	...	...	...	...
21	21	...	...	...	8	7	1	...	...
261	258	3	...	...	136	122	14	...	...
606	602	3	1	...	190	172	17	1	...
81	81	...	...	...	29	24	5	...	...
...	...	...	...	...	...	...	...	...	...
11	11	...	...	...	2	2	...	...	...
122	121	1	...	...	63	61	2	...	...
...	...	...	...	...	...	...	...	...	...
...	...	...	...	...	...	...	...	...	...
3	3	...	...	...	2	2	...	...	...
...	...	...	...	...	...	...	...	...	...
...	...	...	...	...	...	...	...	...	...
...	...	...	...	...	...	...	...	...	...
25	25	...	...	...	11	11	...	...	...
...	...	...	...	...	...	...	...	...	...
...	...	...	...	...	...	...	2	...	...
46	44	1	1	...	22	17	5	...	...
2,175	2,163	11	2	...	837	787	66	4	...

Kadur

Class.	Group.	Caste, &c. and sub-division.	Religion.	15 to 39 Total.	Single.	Married.	Widowed.	Civil condition not stated.
B.—Professional.—(Continued.)	5 Priests.—(Continued.)	Bráhman.—(Concluded.) Hoyis'aniga ...	Hindu	208	60	138	10	...
		Karnátaka ...	,,	52	11	34	7	...
		Kumbálúr or Tótada Tigala.	,,	...	...	...	...	...
		Kandávara	,,	36	8	27	1	...
		Kannada Kammé ...	,,	...	...	...	...	...
		Karáde ...	,,	9	3	6	...	...
		Kásalnád	,,	...	...	...	...	...
		Kavarga ...	,,	2	1	1	...	...
		Kóta ...	,,	4	1	2	1	...
		Kánakubja or Kanyákubja	,,	...	...	...	...	...
		Konkanast'h ...	,,	3	...	3	...	...
		Kandálé ...	,,	...	...	...	...	...
		Kátyáyana ...	,,	23	4	19	...	...
		Mulikinádu or Murikinádu.	,,	54	15	37	2	...
		Mandyattar ...	,,	...	...	...	...	...
		Nambúri ...	,,	2	...	2	...	...
		Nandavaidika ...	,,	2	1	1	...	...
		Prat'hamas'ákhe ...	,,	43	14	28	1	...
		Prativádi Bhayankarattár	,,	...	...	...	...	...
		Panchagráma ...	,,	43	13	25	5	...
		Sankéti ...	,,	56	18	34	4	...
		Sárasvata ...	,,	4	2	2	...	...
		S'irnádu ...	,,	...	...	...	...	...
		S'is'uvarga ...	,,	24	5	18	1	...
		S'ivalli ...	,,	575	224	337	14	...
		Smárta ...	,,	1,209	428	736	45	...
		S'rivaishnava ...	,,	144	62	80	2	...
		Kadámbiyár ...	,,	...	...	...	...	...
		S'rivaishnava, Hebbár	,,	22	9	11	2	...
		Telagháñya ...	,,	263	114	142	7	...
		Tulava ...	,,	...	...	...	...	...
		Tirumaleyár ...	,,	...	...	...	...	...
		Ulachakammé ...	,,	8	2	6	...	...
		Utráji (Uttrádi) ...	,,	...	...	...	...	...
		Vadama ...	,,	1	1	...	...	...
		Vangipuram ...	,,	...	...	...	...	...
		Velnádu ...	,,	49	23	25	1	...
		Vijápurada kammé ...	,,	...	...	...	...	...
		Véginádu ...	,,	...	...	...	...	...
		Vaishnava (Mádhva)	,,	80	19	59	2	...
		Total Bráhman ...	...	*4,086*	*1,454*	*2,493*	*139*	...

TABLE E.—(*Continued.*)

District.

Males.

40 and over.					Age not stated.				
Total.	Single.	Married.	Widowed.	Civil condition not stated.	Total.	Single.	Married.	Widowed.	Civil condition not stated.
90	6	60	24	...	...	...	...	...	...
22	2	11	9	...	...	...	...	...	...
...	...	...	...	...	...	...	...	...	...
13	...	6	7	...	...	...	...	...	...
...	...	...	...	...	...	...	...	...	...
3	...	2	1	...	...	...	...	...	...
...	...	...	...	...	...	...	...	...	...
1	...	...	1	...	...	...	...	...	...
2	...	1	1	...	...	...	...	...	...
...	...	...	...	...	...	...	...	...	...
1	...	1	...	...	...	...	...	...	...
...	...	...	...	...	...	...	...	...	...
14	1	8	5	...	...	...	...	...	...
21	...	14	7	...	...	...	...	...	...
...	...	...	...	...	...	...	...	...	...
2	...	1	1	...	...	...	...	...	...
1	...	...	1	...	...	...	...	...	...
20	1	12	7	...	...	...	...	...	...
...	...	...	...	...	...	...	...	...	...
15	1	11	3	...	...	...	...	...	...
28	...	22	6	...	...	...	...	...	...
3	...	1	2	...	...	...	...	...	...
...	...	...	...	...	...	...	...	...	...
11	...	9	2	...	...	...	...	...	...
241	12	154	75	...	...	...	...	...	...
458	27	316	115	...	...	...	...	...	...
79	2	55	22	...	...	...	...	...	...
...	...	...	...	...	...	...	...	...	...
10	1	7	2	...	...	...	...	...	...
120	10	90	20	...	...	...	...	...	...
...	...	...	...	...	...	...	...	...	...
...	...	...	...	...	...	...	...	...	...
3	...	3	...	...	...	...	...	...	...
...	...	...	...	...	...	...	...	...	...
...	...	...	...	...	...	...	...	...	...
...	...	...	...	...	...	...	...	...	...
16	2	9	5	...	...	...	...	...	...
...	...	...	...	...	...	...	...	...	...
...	...	...	...	...	...	...	...	...	...
27	5	14	8	...	...	...	...	...	...
1,697	*97*	*1,145*	*455*	...	...	...	...	...	...

Class.	Group.	Caste, &c. and sub-division.	Religion.	All Ages. Total.	Single.	Married.	Widowed.	Civil condition not stated.
B.—Professional.—(Continued.)	5. Priests.—(Continued.)	Brámhan.—(Concluded.)						
		Hoyis'aṇiga ...	Hindu	522	134	228	160	...
		Karṇáṭaka ...	,,	105	13	50	42	...
		Kumbálúr or Tóṭada Tigaḷa.	,,	...	...	...	...	...
		Kandávara ...	,,	99	22	44	33	...
		Kannada Kammé ...	,,	...	...	...	...	...
		Karáḍe ...	,,	20	7	8	5	...
		Kásalinád ...	,,	...	...	...	...	...
		Kavarga ...	,,	2	1	1	...	...
		Kóṭa ...	,,	15	3	4	8	...
		Káṇakubja or Kanyákubja.	,,	...	...	...	...	...
		Konkaṇast'h ...	,,	14	4	7	3	...
		Kandáḍe ...	,,	...	...	...	...	...
		Katyáyana ...	,,	72	21	30	21	...
		Mulikináḍu or Murikináḍu.	,,	79	16	46	17	...
		Manḍyattár ...	,,	...	...	...	...	...
		Nambúri ...	,,	6	1	3	2	...
		Nandava dika ...	,,	...	...	...	...	...
		Prat'hamas'ákha ...	,,	60	12	27	21	...
		Prativádi Bhayankarattár.	,,	...	...	...	...	...
		Panchagráma ...	,,	80	13	32	35	...
		Sankéti ...	,,	77	17	39	21	...
		Sárasvata ...	,,	3	...	3	...	...
		S'irnaḍu ...	,,	...	...	...	...	...
		S'is'uvarga ...	,,	75	20	29	26	...
		S'ivaḷḷi ...	,,	1,171	278	550	343	...
		Smárta ...	,,	2,207	356	1,093	758	...
		S'rívaishṇava ...	,,	354	103	160	91	...
		Kaḍámbiyár ...	,,	...	...	...	...	...
		S'rívaishṇava, Hebbar		30	10	13	7	...
		Telagháṇya ...	,,	540	157	227	156	...
		Tuḷuva ...	,,	...	...	...	...	...
		Tirumaleyár ...	,,	...	...	...	...	...
		Ulachakammé ...	,,	13	2	8	3	...
		Utráji (Uttrádi) ...	,,	...	...	...	...	...
		Vaḍama ...	,,	...	...	...	...	...
		Vangíparam ...	,,	...	...	...	...	...
		Velnáḍu ...	,,	44	13	25	6	...
		Vijápurada kammé ...	,,	...	...	...	...	...
		Véginaḍu ...	,,	...	...	...	...	...
		Vaishṇava (Mádhva)	,,	254	60	139	55	...
		Total Brámhan......	... ...	8,231	1,863	3,866	2,502	...

TABLE. E.—(*Continued.*)

District.

Females.

0 to 9					10 to 14				
Total.	Single.	Married.	Widowed.	Civil condition not stated.	Total.	Single.	Married.	Widowed.	Civil condition not stated.
132	118	14	...	...	60	16	29	15	...
13	13	...	...	...	9	...	5	4	...
...	...	...	...	...	...	...	...	...	...
19	18	1	...	...	8	4	4	...	...
...	...	...	...	...	...	...	...	...	...
6	6	...	...	...	2	1	1	...	...
...	...	...	...	...	...	...	...	...	...
1	1	...	...	...	...	...	...	...	...
3	3	...	...	...	1	...	1	...	...
...	...	...	...	...	...	...	...	...	...
3	3	...	...	...	2	1	1	...	...
...	...	...	...	...	...	...	...	...	...
20	19	1	...	...	7	2	5	...	...
15	12	3	...	...	16	4	9	3	...
...	...	...	...	...	...	...	...	...	...
1	1	...	...	...	1	...	1	...	...
...	...	...	...	...	...	...	...	...	...
14	11	3	...	...	4	1	3	...	...
...	...	...	...	...	...	...	...	...	...
13	11	2	...	...	11	2	7	2	...
16	15	1	...	...	12	2	8	2	...
...	...	...	...	...	1	...	1	...	...
...	...	...	...	...	...	...	...	...	...
18	16	2	...	...	8	4	4	...	...
293	256	33	8	...	156	22	120	14	...
358	308	48	2	...	223	48	161	14	...
96	80	16	...	...	72	23	43	6	...
...	...	...	...	...	...	...	...	...	...
10	9	1	...	...	4	1	3	...	...
154	141	13	...	...	76	16	56	4	...
...	...	...	...	...	...	...	...	...	...
...	...	...	...	...	...	...	...	...	...
2	2	...	...	...	2	...	2	...	...
...	...	...	...	...	...	...	...	...	...
...	...	...	...	...	...	...	...	...	...
...	...	...	...	...	...	...	...	...	...
14	13	1	...	...	4	...	4	...	...
...	...	...	...	...	...	...	...	...	...
...	...	...	...	...	...	...	...	...	...
62	53	9	...	...	32	7	21	4	...
1,844	*1,636*	*201*	*7*	...	*986*	*227*	*656*	*103*	...

Kadur

Class.	Group.	Caste and Religion. Caste, &c. and sub-division.	Religion.	15 to 39 Total.	Single.	Married.	Widowed.	Civil condition not stated.
B.—Professional.—(Continued.)	5. Priests.—(Continued.)	Brámhan.—(Concluded.) Hoyis'anige ...	Hindu.	187		145	42	...
		Karnátaka ...	,,	43	...	33	10	...
		Kumbálúr or Tòtada Tigala	,,	...	...	...	...	...
		Kandávara ...	,,	42	...	34	8	...
		Kannada Kammé ...	,,	...	...	...	...	...
		Karáde	,,	8	...	6	2	...
		Kásalnád ...	,,	...	...	...	...	...
		Kayarga... ...	,,	1	...	1	...	...
		Kóta	,,	6	...	3	3	...
		Kánakubja or Kanyákubja.	,,	...	...	...	...	...
		Konkanast'h ...	,,	6	...	5	1	...
		Kandádó ...	,,	...	...	...	...	...
		Kátyáyana ...	,,	28	...	19	9	...
		Mulikinádu or Murikinádu.	,,	32	...	28	4	...
		Mandyattár ...	,,	...	...	...	...	...
		Nambúri ...	,,	2	...	2	...	...
		Nandavaidika ...	,,	...	...	...	...	...
		Prat'hamas'ákhe ...	,,	23	...	17	6	...
		Prativádi Bhayankarattár.	,,	...	...	...	...	...
		Panchagráma ...	,,	30	...	18	12	...
		Sankéti	,,	28	...	24	4	...
		Sárasvata ...	,,	2	...	2	...	...
		S'irnádu... ...	,,	...	...	...	...	...
		S'is'uvarga ...	,,	30	...	19	11	...
		S'ivalli	,,	439	...	323	116	...
		Smárta	,,	943	...	713	230	...
		S'rívaishnava ...	,,	97	...	[illegible]	23	...
		Kadámbiyár ...	,,	...	...	...	...	...
		S'rívaishnava, Hebbár	,,	9	...	7	2	...
		Telagháṇya ...	,,	203	...	136	67	...
		Tuḷuva	,,	...	...	...	...	...
		Tirumaleyár ...	,,	...	...	...	...	...
		Uchchakammé ...	,,	7	...	6	1	...
		Utráji (Uttrádi) ...	,,	...	...	...	...	...
		Vaḍama ...	,,	...	...	...	...	...
		Vangipuram ...	,,	...	...	...	...	...
		Velnádu... ...	,,	15	...	14	1	...
		Vijñaparada kammé.	,,	...	...	...	...	...
		Véginádu ...	,,	...	...	...	...	...
		Vaishṇava (Mádhva).	,,	109	...	94	15	...
		Total Brámhan...	... ...	*3,241*	...	*2,451*	*790*	...

TABLE E.—(Continued.)

District.

Females,

40 and over.					Age not stated.				
Total.	Single.	Married.	Widowed.	Civil condition not stated.	Total.	Single.	Married.	Widowed.	Civil condition not stated.
113	...	10	103	...	...	...	...	...	...
40		12	29	...	...	...	...	...	...
...	...	...	...	...	...	...	...	...	...
30	...	5	25	...	...	...	...	...	...
...	...	...	...	...	...	...	...	...	...
4	...	1	3	...	...	...	...	...	...
...	...	...	...	...	...	...	...	...	...
...	...	...	...	...	...	...	...	...	...
5	...	...	5	...	...	...	...	...	...
...	...	...	...	...	...	...	...	...	...
3	...	1	2	...	...	...	...	...	...
...	...	...	...	...	...	...	...	...	...
17	...	5	12	...	...	...	...	...	...
16	...	6	10	...	...	...	...	...	...
...	...	...	...	...	...	...	...	...	...
2	...	...	2	...	...	...	...	...	...
...	...	...	...	...	...	...	...	...	...
19	...	4	15	...	...	...	...	...	...
...	...	...	...	...	...	...	...	...	...
26	...	5	21	...	...	...	...	...	...
21	...	6	15	...	...	...	...	...	...
...	...	...	...	...	...	...	...	...	...
...	...	...	...	...	...	...	...	...	...
19	...	4	15	...	...	...	...	...	...
281	...	74	210	...	...	...	...	...	...
683	...	171	512	...	...	...	...	...	...
89	...	27	62	...	...	...	...	...	...
...	...	...	...	...	...	...	...	...	...
7	...	2	5	...	...	...	...	...	...
107	...	22	85	...	...	...	...	...	...
...	...	...	...	...	...	...	...	...	...
...	...	...	...	...	...	...	...	...	...
2	...	...	2	...	...	...	...	...	...
...	...	...	...	...	...	...	...	...	...
...	...	...	...	...	...	...	...	...	...
...	...	...	...	...	...	...	...	...	...
11	...	6	5	...	...	...	...	...	...
...	...	...	...	...	...	...	...	...	...
...	...	...	...	...	...	...	...	...	...
31	...	15	36	...	...	...	...	...	...
2,157	...	555	1,603	...	...	...	...	...	...

Chitaldurg

Class.	Group.	Caste, &c.	Caste, &c. and sub-division.	Religion.	All Ages. Total.	Single.	Married.	Widowed.	Civil condition not stated.
B.—Professional.—(Continued.)	5. Priests.—(Continued.)	Brâmhan.—(Concluded.)	Hosʼaniga ...	Hindu.	12	5	6	1	...
			Karnataka ...	,,	50	14	21	15	...
			Kumbálúr or Totada Tigala ...	,,	...	...	...	...	...
			Kandávara ...	,,	...	...	...	...	...
			Kannada Kammé ...	,,	...	...	...	...	...
			Karádo	,,	...	...	...	...	...
			Kásalnad ...	,,	...	...	...	...	...
			Kavarga... ...	,,	...	...	...	...	...
			Kóta	,,	...	...	...	...	...
			Kányakubja or Kanyákubja.	,,	...	...	...	...	...
			Konkanast'h ...	,,	...	...	...	...	...
			Kándadé	,,	...	...	...	...	...
			Kátyáyana ...	,,	...	...	...	...	...
			Mulikinádu or Murikinádu ...	,,	165	70	65	30	...
			Mandyattár ...	,,	...	...	...	...	...
			Nambúri ...	,,	...	...	...	...	...
			Nandavaidika ...	,,	6	4	2	...	...
			Prat'hamas'ákhe ...	,,	53	30	20	3	...
			Prativádi Bhayankaratár.	,,	...	...	...	...	...
			Panchagráma ...	,,	...	...	...	...	...
			Sankéti	,,	...	...	...	...	...
			Sárasvata ...	,,	...	...	...	...	...
			S'írnadu ...	,,	28	13	13	2	...
			S'is'uvarga ...	,,	...	...	...	...	...
			S'ivalli	,,	...	...	...	...	...
			Smárta	,,	627	276	296	55	...
			S'rivaishṇava, ...	,,	109	46	48	15	...
			Kudámbiyár ...	,,	...	...	...	...	...
			S'rivaishṇava, Hebbár	,,	23	10	12	1	...
			Telaghánya ...	,,	4	1	2	1	...
			Tuluva	,,	...	...	...	...	...
			Tirumaleyár ...	,,	...	...	...	...	...
			Ulachukammo ...	,,	57	23	26	8	...
			Utráji (Uttrádi) ...	,,	...	...	...	...	...
			Vadama	,,	...	...	...	...	...
			Vangipuram ...	,,	...	...	...	...	...
			Velnádu ...	,,	34	16	16	2	...
			Vijápuradi kammé...	,,	...	...	...	...	...
			Véginadu ...	,,	...	...	...	...	...
			Vaishṇava (Mádhva.)	,,	266	147	99	20	...
		Total Brâmhan			*3,077*	*1,439*	*1,322*	*316*	...

TABLE E.—(Continued.)

District.

Males.

0 to 9					10 to 14				
Total.	Single.	Married.	Widowed.	Civil condition not stated.	Total.	Single.	Married.	Widowed.	Civil condition not stated.
4	4	...	...	...	1	1	...	...	...
8	8	...	...	...	...	...	...	...	...
...	...	...	...	...	...	...	...	...	...
...	...	...	...	...	...	...	...	...	...
...	...	...	...	...	...	...	...	...	...
...	...	...	...	...	...	...	...	...	...
...	...	...	...	...	...	...	...	...	...
...	...	...	...	...	...	...	...	...	...
...	...	...	...	...	...	...	...	...	...
...	...	...	...	...	...	...	...	...	...
...	...	...	...	...	...	...	...	...	...
...	...	...	...	...	...	...	...	...	...
...	...	...	...	...	...	...	...	...	...
36	36	...	...	...	17	17	...	...	...
...	...	...	...	...	...	...	...	...	...
...	...	...	...	...	...	...	...	...	...
1	1	...	...	...	1	1	...	...	...
17	17	...	...	...	5	5	...	...	...
...	...	...	...	...	...	...	...	...	...
...	...	...	...	...	...	...	...	...	...
...	...	...	...	...	...	...	...	...	...
...	...	...	...	...	...	...	...	...	...
5	5	...	...	...	3	3	...	...	...
...	...	...	...	...	...	...	...	...	...
...	...	...	...	...	...	...	...	...	...
179	179	...	...	...	41	37	4	...	...
23	23	...	...	...	11	11	...	...	...
...	...	...	...	...	...	...	...	...	...
5	5	...	...	...	4	4	...	...	...
1	1	...	...	...	...	...	...	...	...
...	...	...	...	...	...	...	...	...	...
...	...	...	...	...	...	...	...	...	...
11	11	...	...	...	9	9	...	...	...
...	...	...	...	...	...	...	...	...	...
...	...	...	...	...	...	...	...	...	...
...	...	...	...	...	...	...	...	...	...
7	7	...	...	...	4	4	...	...	...
...	...	...	...	...	...	...	...	...	...
...	...	...	...	...	...	...	...	...	...
67	67	...	...	...	39	39	...	...	...
767	*766*	...	*1*	...	*274*	*267*	*7*	...	...

Class.	Group.	Caste, Sect and Sub-division.	Religion.	Total.	[illegible]	[illegible]	[illegible]	[illegible]
B.—Professional.—(Continued.)	5. Priests.—(Continued.)	Brâhman.—(Concluded.) Hoi'sagara	Hindu	4	...	3	...	...
		Karnâtaka	"	24	5	13	6	...
		Kambâlûr or Totada Tigala	"	...	...	...	...	...
		Kamlâsara	"	...	...	...	...	...
		Kannada Kamme	"	...	...	...	...	...
		Karâde	"	...	...	...	...	...
		Kôsalnâd	"	...	...	...	...	...
		Kavarga	"	...	...	...	...	...
		Kôta	"	...	...	...	...	...
		Kâsakuhja or Kanyakubja	"	...	...	...	...	...
		Konkanastha	"	...	...	...	...	...
		Kandâde	"	...	...	...	...	...
		Kâtyâyana	"	...	...	...	2	...
		Mulikinâdu or Murikinadu	"	62	11	34	1	...
		Mandyattâr	"	...	...	...	...	...
		Nambûri	"	...	...	...	...	...
		Nandavaidika	"	3	2	1	...	...
		Prathamasâkhe	"	29	8	12	...	...
		Prativâdi Bhayankarattâr	"	...	...	...	...	...
		Pombhagâra	"	...	...	...	...	...
		Sankâti	"	...	...	...	...	...
		Sârasvata	"	...	...	...	...	...
		S'irnâdu	"	13	4	9	...	...
		S'is'ntorga	"	...	...	...	...	...
		S'ivalli	"	...	...	...	...	...
		Smârta	"	265	51	199	15	...
		S'rîvaishnava	"	52	12	36	4	...
		Kadâmbiyâr	"	...	...	...	...	...
		S'rîvaishnava, Hebbâr	"	9	1	8	...	...
		Telaghânya	"	1	...	1	...	...
		Tuluva	"	...	...	...	...	...
		Tirumaleyâr	"	...	...	...	...	...
		Ulachakamme	"	26	2	21	3	...
		Utrâji (Uttrâdi)	"	...	...	...	...	...
		Vadama	"	...	...	...	...	...
		Varagapuram	"	...	...	...	...	...
		Velnâdu	"	17	4	13	...	...
		Vijâporada Vamme		...	...	...	...	...
		Vêginâdu		...	...	...	...	...
		Vaishnava (Mâdhva)		111	36	70	5	...
		Total Brâhman		1,294	319	883	72	...

TABLE E.—(Continued)

District.

Males.

40 and over.					Age not stated.				
Total.	Single.	Married.	Widowed.	Civil condition not stated.	Total.	Single.	Married.	Widowed.	Civil condition not stated.
3	...	2	1	...	...	...	...	...	...
18	1	8	9	...	...	...	...	...	...
...	...	...	...	...	...	...	...	...	...
...	...	...	...	...	...	...	...	...	...
...	...	...	...	...	...	...	...	...	...
...	...	...	...	...	...	...	...	...	...
...	...	...	...	...	...	...	...	...	...
...	...	...	...	...	...	...	...	...	...
...	...	...	...	...	...	...	...	...	...
...	...	...	...	...	...	...	...	...	...
...	...	...	...	...	...	...	...	...	...
...	...	...	...	...	...	...	...	...	...
...	...	...	...	...	...	...	...	...	...
50	3	21	26	...	...	...	...	...	...
...	...	...	...	...	...	...	...	...	...
...	...	...	...	...	...	...	...	...	...
1	...	1	...	...	...	...	...	...	...
11	...	8	3	...	...	...	...	...	...
...	...	...	...	...	...	...	...	...	...
...	...	...	...	...	...	...	...	...	...
...	...	...	...	...	...	...	...	...	...
...	...	...	...	...	...	...	...	...	...
7	1	4	2	...	...	...	...	...	...
...	...	...	...	...	...	...	...	...	...
...	...	...	...	...	...	...	...	...	...
142	9	93	40	...	...	...	...	...	...
23	...	12	11	...	...	...	...	...	...
...	...	...	...	...	...	...	...	...	...
5	...	4	1	...	...	...	...	...	...
2	...	1	1	...	...	...	...	...	...
...	...	...	...	...	...	...	...	...	...
...	...	...	...	...	...	...	...	...	...
11	1	5	5	...	...	...	...	...	...
...	...	...	...	...	...	...	...	...	...
...	...	...	...	...	...	...	...	...	...
...	...	...	...	...	...	...	...	...	...
6	1	3	2	...	...	...	...	...	...
...	...	...	...	...	...	...	...	...	...
...	...	...	...	...	...	...	...	...	...
49	5	29	15	...	...	...	...	...	...
742	47	452	243	...	...	...	...	...	...

Chitaldurg

Class.	Group.	Caste, &c. and sub-division.	Religion.	All Ages. Total.	Single.	Married.	Widowed.	Civil condition not stated.
B.—Professional.—(Continued.)	5. Priests.—(Continued.)	Brâmhan.—(Concluded.) Hois'aniga	Hindu.	11	4	6	1	...
		Karnâṭaka	,,	52	9	25	18	...
		Kumbâlâr or Tóṭada Tigaḷa.	,,	...	...	...	...	...
		Kandâvara	,,	...	...	...	...	...
		Kannaḍa Kammé	,,	...	...	...	...	...
		Karâḍe...	,,	...	...	...	...	...
		Kâsalnâḍ	,,	...	...	...	...	...
		Kavargm...	,,	...	...	...	...	...
		Kóṭa ...	,,	...	...	...	...	...
		Kânakubja or Kanyâkubja.	,,	...	...	...	...	...
		Konkanast'h	,,	...	...	...	...	...
		Kanḍâḍé...	,,	...	...	...	...	...
		Kâtyâyana	,,	...	...	...	...	...
		Mulikinâḍu or Murikinâḍu.	,,	156	56	70	30	...
		Mandyattâr	,,	...	...	...	...	...
		Nambûri	,,	...	...	...	...	...
		Nandavaidika	,,	3	...	2	1	...
		Part'hamas'âkhe	,,	64	22	30	12	...
		Prativâdi Bhayankarrattâr.	,,	...	...	...	...	...
		Panchagrâma	,,	...	...	...	...	...
		Sankéti ...	,,	...	...	...	...	...
		Sârasvata	,,	...	...	...	...	...
		S'irnâḍu...	,,	24	9	9	6	...
		S'is'uvarga	,,	...	...	...	...	...
		S'ivaḷḷi ...	,,	...	...	...	...	...
		Smârta ...	,,	458	136	238	84	...
		S'rivaishṇava	,,	105	35	56	14	...
		Kaḍâmbiyâr	,,	...	...	...	...	...
		S'rivaishṇava, Hebbâr	,,	23	5	12	6	...
		Telaghâṇya	,,	6	2	2	2	...
		Tuḷuva ...	,,	...	...	...	...	...
		Tirumâleyâr	,,	...	...	...	...	...
		Ulachakamme	,,	69	23	35	11	...
		Utrâji (Uttrâdi)	,,	...	...	...	...	...
		Vaḍama...	,,	...	...	...	...	...
		Vangipuram	,,	...	...	...	...	...
		Velnâḍu...	,,	38	16	19	3	...
		Vijâpurada kammé...	,,	...	...	...	...	...
		Véginâḍu	,,	...	...	...	...	...
		Vaishṇava (Mâdhva.)	,,	234	50	116	68	...
		Total Brâmhan......	....	2,916	746	1,428	742	...

TABLE E.—(Continued.)

District.

Females.

0 to 9					10 to 14				
Total.	Single.	Married.	Widowed.	Civil condition not stated.	Total.	Single.	Married.	Widowed.	Civil condition not stated.
4	4	...	...	...	1	...	1	...	...
9	9	...	...	...	5	...	5	...	...
...	...	...	...	...	...	...	...	...	...
...	...	...	...	...	...	...	...	...	...
...	...	...	...	...	...	...	...	...	...
...	...	...	...	...	...	...	...	...	...
...	...	...	...	...	...	...	...	...	...
...	...	...	...	...	...	...	...	...	...
...	...	...	...	...	...	...	...	...	...
...	...	...	...	...	...	...	...	...	...
...	...	...	...	...	...	...	...	...	...
...	...	...	...	...	...	...	...	...	...
...	...	...	...	...	...	...	...	...	...
64	53	11	...	...	15	3	12	...	...
...	...	...	...	...	...	...	...	...	...
...	...	...	...	...	...	...	...	...	...
...	...	...	...	...	...	...	...	...	...
21	21	...	...	...	2	1	1	...	...
...	...	...	...	...	...	...	...	...	...
...	...	...	...	...	...	...	...	...	...
...	...	...	...	...	...	...	...	...	...
...	...	...	...	...	...	...	...	...	...
9	9	...	...	...	2	...	2	...	...
...	...	...	...	...	...	...	...	...	...
...	...	...	...	...	...	...	...	...	...
112	110	2	...	...	23	6	16	...	...
45	34	11	...	...	12	1	11	...	...
...	...	...	...	...	...	...	...	...	...
4	4	...	...	...	1	1	...	...	...
1	1	...	...	...	1	1	...	...	...
...	...	...	...	...	...	...	...	...	...
...	...	...	...	...	...	...	...	...	...
28	23	5	...	...	4	...	4	...	...
...	...	...	...	...	...	...	...	...	...
...	...	...	...	...	...	...	...	...	...
...	...	...	...	...	...	...	...	...	...
18	16	2	...	...	4	...	4	...	...
...	...	...	...	...	...	...	...	...	...
...	...	...	...	...	...	...	...	...	...
46	44	2	...	...	23	6	17	...	...
745	688	57	...	...	230	58	169	3	...

Chitaldurg

Class.	Group.	Caste, &c. and sub-division.	Religion.	15 to 39 Total.	Single.	Married.	Widowed.	Civil condition not stated.
B.—Professional.—(Continued.)	5. Priests.—(Continued.)	Brâmhan.—(Concluded.) Hois'aniga ...	Hindu	4	...	4	...	...
		Karnâtaka ...	,,	20	...	12	8	...
		Kumbâlúr or Totada Tigala. ...	,,	...	...	...	...	...
		Kandávara ...	,,	...	...	...	...	...
		Kannada Kammé ...	,,	...	...	...	...	...
		Karâde... ...	,,	...	...	...	...	...
		Kásalnâd ...	,,	...	...	...	...	...
		Kavarga... ...	,,	...	...	...	...	...
		Kóta	,,	...	...	...	...	...
		Kânakubja or Kanyâkubja.	,,	...	...	...	...	...
		Konkanast'h ...	,,	...	...	...	...	...
		Kandâde... ...	,,	...	...	...	...	...
		Kâtyâyana ...	,,	...	...	...	...	...
		Mulikinâdu or Murikinâdu.	,,	48	...	43	5	...
		Mandyattâr ...	,,	...	...	...	...	...
		Nambúri ...	,,	...	...	...	...	...
		Nandavaidika ...	,,	3	...	2	1	...
		Prat'hamas'âkhe ...	,,	29	...	25	4	...
		Prativâdi Bhayankarattâr.	,,	...	...	...	...	...
		Panchagráma ...	,,	...	...	...	...	...
		Sankéti... ...	,,	...	...	...	...	...
		Sârasvata ...	,,	...	...	...	...	...
		S'irnâdu... ...	,,	6	...	6	...	...
		S'is'uvarga ...	,,	...	...	...	...	...
		S'ivalli	,,	...	...	...	...	...
		Smârta	,,	228	...	204	24	...
		S'rivaishnava ...	,,	30	...	26	4	...
		Kadâmbiyâr ...	,,	...	...	...	...	...
		S'rivaishnava, Hobbâr	,,	9	...	9	...	...
		Telaghânya ...	,,	3	...	2	1	...
		Tuluva	,,	...	...	...	...	...
		Tirumaloyár ...	,,	...	...	...	...	...
		Ulachakamme ...	,,	26	...	23	3	...
		Utrâji (Uttrâdi) ...	,,	...	...	...	...	...
		Vadama	,,	...	...	...	...	...
		Vangipuram ...	,,	...	...	...	...	...
		Velnâdu	,,	11	...	11	...	...
		Vijápurada kammé ...	,,	...	...	...	...	...
		Véginâdu ...	,,	...	...	...	...	...
		Vaishnava (Mâdhva).	,,	94	...	71	23	...
		Total Brâmhan ...	...	1,165	...	953	212	...

TABLE E.—(Continued.)

District.

Females.

40 and over.					Age not stated.				
Total.	Single.	Married.	Widowed.	Civil condition not stated.	Total.	Single.	Married.	Widowed.	Civil condition not stated.
2	...	1	1	...	...	...	...	...	...
18	...	8	10	...	...	...	...	...	...
...	...	...	...	...	...	...	...	...	...
...	...	...	...	...	...	...	...	...	...
...	...	...	...	...	...	...	...	...	...
...	...	...	...	...	...	...	...	...	...
...	...	...	...	...	...	...	...	...	...
...	...	...	...	...	...	...	...	...	...
...	...	...	...	...	...	...	...	...	...
...	...	...	...	...	...	...	...	...	...
...	...	...	...	...	...	...	...	...	...
...	...	...	...	...	...	...	...	...	...
...	...	...	...	...	...	...	...	...	...
29	...	4	25	...	...	...	...	...	...
...	...	...	...	...	...	...	...	...	...
...	...	...	...	...	...	...	...	...	...
...	...	...	...	...	...	...	...	...	...
12	...	4	8	...	...	...	...	...	...
...	...	...	...	...	...	...	...	...	...
...	...	...	...	...	...	...	...	...	...
...	...	...	...	...	...	...	...	...	...
...	...	...	...	...	...	...	...	...	...
7	...	1	6	...	...	...	...	...	...
...	...	...	...	...	...	...	...	...	...
...	...	...	...	...	...	...	...	...	...
126	...	66	60	...	...	...	...	...	...
18	...	8	10	...	...	...	...	...	...
...	...	...	...	...	...	...	...	...	...
	...	3	6	...	...	...	...	...	...
1	...	...	1	...	...	...	...	...	...
...	...	...	...	...	...	...	...	...	...
...	...	...	...	...	...	...	...	...	...
11	...	3	8	...	...	...	...	...	...
...	...	...	...	...	...	...	...	...	...
...	...	...	...	...	...	...	...	...	...
...	...	...	...	...	...	...	...	...	...
5	...	2	3	...	...	...	...	...	...
...	...	...	...	...	...	...	...	...	...
...	...	...	...	...	...	...	...	...	...
71	...	26	45	...	...	...	...	...	...
776	...	249	527	...	...	...	...	...	...

Class.	Group.	Caste, &c. and sub-divisions.	Religion.	All Ages. Total.	Single.	Married.	Widowed.	Civil condition not stated.
B.—Professional—(Continued.)	5. Priests.—(Continued.)	Bráhman.—(Concluded.) Hois'aṇiga	Hindu.	...	...	...	...	...
		Karṇáṭaka	,,	21	7	13	1	...
		Kumbálúr or Tóṭada Tigaḷa.	,,	...	...	...	...	...
		Kandávara	,,	...	...	...	...	...
		Kannaḍa Kammé	,,	...	...	...	...	...
		Karáḍe	,,	...	...	...	...	...
		Kásalnáḍ	,,	...	...	...	...	...
		Kavarga	,,	...	...	...	...	...
		Kóṭa	,,	...	...	...	...	...
		Káṇakubja or Kanyákubja.	,,	6	3	2	1	...
		Konkaṇast'h	,,	7	2	4	1	...
		Kandáḍé	,,	...	...	...	...	...
		Kátyáyana	,,	...	...	...	...	...
		Mulikináḍu or Murikináḍu.	,,	92	41	48	3	...
		Mandyattár	,,	...	...	...	...	...
		Nambúri	,,	...	...	...	...	...
		Nandavaidíka	,,	16	8	7	1	...
		Prat'hamas'ákhe	,,	10	3	6	1	...
		Partiváḍi Bhayankarattár.	,,	...	...	...	...	...
		Panchagráma	,,	...	...	...	...	...
		Sankéti	,,	...	...	...	...	...
		Sárasvata	,,	7	4	2	1	...
		S'írnáḍu	,,	1	...	1	...	...
		S'is'uvarga	,,	...	...	...	...	...
		Sivaḷḷi	,,	...	...	...	...	...
		Smárta	,,	69	27	38	4	...
		S'rívaishṇava	,,	70	26	39	5	...
		Kaḍámbiyár	,,	...	...	...	...	...
		S'rívaishṇava, Hebbár	,,	...	...	...	...	...
		Telagháṇya	,,	...	...	...	...	...
		Tuḷuva	,,	1	1	...	...	...
		Tirumaleyár	,,	...	...	...	...	...
		Uchchakammé	,,	20	11	9	...	...
		Utráji (Uttrádi)	,,	...	...	...	...	...
		Vaḍama	,,	18	6	12	...	...
		Vangípuram	,,	...	...	...	...	...
		Velnáḍu	,,	37	15	22	...	...
		Vijápuradá kammé	,,	...	...	...	...	...
		Véginádu	,,	...	...	...	...	...
		Vaishṇava (Mádhva)	,,	11	...	8	3	...
				69	29	38	2	...
		Total Bráhman		*662*	*275*	*347*	*40*	...

TABLE E.—(Continued.)

Station, Bangalore.

Males.

0 to 9.					10 to 14.				
Total.	Single.	Married.	Widowed.	Civil condition not stated.	Total.	Single.	Married.	Widowed.	Civil condition not stated.
...	...	...	...	...	...	...	...	...	...
1	1	...	...	...	2	2	...	...	...
...	...	...	...	...	...	...	...	...	...
...	...	...	...	...	...	...	...	...	...
...	...	...	...	...	...	...	...	...	...
...	...	...	...	...	...	...	...	...	...
...	...	...	...	...	...	...	...	...	...
...	...	...	...	...	...	...	...	...	...
...	...	...	...	...	...	...	...	...	...
...	...	...	...	...	...	...	...	...	...
2	2	...	...	...	...	...	...	...	...
...	...	...	...	...	...	...	...	...	...
...	...	...	...	...	...	...	...	...	...
25	25	...	...	...	10	9	1	...	...
...	...	...	...	...	...	...	...	...	...
...	...	...	...	...	...	...	...	...	...
6	6	...	...	...	...	...	...	...	...
...	...	...	...	...	...	...	...	...	...
...	...	...	...	...	...	...	...	...	...
...	...	...	...	...	...	...	...	...	...
...	...	...	...	...	...	...	...	...	...
...	...	...	...	...	...	...	...	...	...
...	...	...	...	...	...	...	...	...	...
...	...	...	...	...	...	...	...	...	...
...	...	...	...	...	...	...	...	...	...
15	15	...	...	...	3	3	...	...	...
6	6	...	...	...	10	10	...	...	...
...	...	...	...	...	...	...	...	...	...
...	...	...	...	...	...	...	...	...	...
...	...	...	...	...	...	...	...	...	...
...	...	...	...	...	...	...	...	...	...
...	...	...	...	...	...	...	...	...	...
8	8	...	...	...	1	1	...	...	...
...	...	...	...	...	...	...	...	...	...
6	6	...	...	...	...	...	...	...	...
...	...	...	...	...	...	...	...	...	...
7	7	...	...	...	3	3	...	...	...
...	...	...	...	...	...	...	...	...	...
...	...	...	...	...	...	...	...	...	...
...	...	...	...	...	...	...	...	...	...
8	8	...	...	...	3	3	...	...	...
120	*120*	...	...	...	*51*	*50*	*1*	...	...

Class.	Group.	Caste, &c. and sub-division.	Religion.	15 to 39. Total.	Single.	Married.	Widowed.	Civil condition not stated.
B.—Professional.—(Continued.)	5. Priests.—(Continued.) Brâmhan.—(Concluded.)	Hois'aniga ...	Hindu.	...	...	...	...	—
		Karnâtaka ...	,,	13	3	10	...	—
		Kumbâlúr or Tóṭada Tigala.	,,	...	...	...	...	—
		Kaṇḍávara ...	,,	...	...	...	...	—
		Kannaḍa Kammé ...	,,	...	...	...	...	—
		Karâḍé	,,	...	...	...	...	—
		Kásalnâḍ ...	,,	...	...	...	...	...
		Kavarga ...	,,	...	...	...	...	...
		Kóṭa	,,	...	...	...	...	...
		Káṇakubja or Kanyâkubja.	,,	6	3	2	1	...
		Konkaṇast'h ...	,,	2	...	2	...	...
		Kandâḍé ...	,,	...	...	...	...	...
		Kátyâyana ...	,,	...	...	...	...	...
		Mulikinâḍu or Murikinâḍu.	,,	35	7	27	1	...
		Maṇḍyattár ...	,,	...	...	...	...	...
		Nambúri ...	,,	...	...	...	...	...
		Nandavaidika ...	,,	8	2	5	1	...
		Prat'hamas'âkhe ...	,,	8	3	5	...	...
		Prativâdi Bhayankarattár.	,,	...	...	...	...	...
		Panchagráma ...	,,	...	...	...	...	...
		Sankéti ...	,,	...	...	...	...	...
		Sârasvata ...	,,	5	4	1	...	...
		S'írnâḍu ...	,,	1	...	1	...	...
		S'is'uvarga ...	,,	...	...	...	...	...
		Sivaḷḷi ...	,,	...	...	...	—	...
		Smárta ...	,,	34	9	25	...	...
		S'rívaishṇava ...	,,	33	8	23	2	...
		Kadâmbiyár ...	,,	...	...	...	...	...
		S'rivaishṇava, Hebbâr	,,	...	...	...	...	...
		Telaghâṇya ...	,,	...	...	...	...	...
		Tuḷuva ...	,,	1	1	...	...	...
		Tirumâleyár ...	,,	...	...	...	...	...
		Ulachakammé ...	,,	9	2	7	...	...
		Utrâji (Uttrâdi) ...	,,	...	...	...	...	...
		Vaḍama ...	,,	16	...	16	...	...
		Vangipuram ...	,,	...	...	...	...	...
		Velnâḍu ...	,,	18	5	13	...	...
		Vijâpuraḍa kammé.	,,	...	...	...	...	...
		Véginâḍu ...	,,	...	...	...	...	...
		Vaishṇava (Mâdhva).	,,	7	...	7	...	...
				42	17	25	...	...
		Total Brâmhan.....	....	*334*	*98*	*229*	*7*	...

TABLE E.—(*Continued.*)

Station, Bangalore.

Males.

40 and over.					Age not stated.				
Total.	Single.	Married.	Widowed.	Civil condition not stated.	Total.	Single.	Married.	Widowed.	Civil condition not stated.
...			...	...	...	...	...	...	...
5	1	3	1	...	...	...	...	...	...
...	...	...	...	...	...	...	...	...	...
...	...	...	...	...	...	...	...	...	...
...	...	...	...	...	...	...	...	...	...
...	...	...	...	...	...	...	...	...	...
...	...	...	...	...	...	...	...	...	...
...	...	...	...	...	...	...	...	...	...
..	...	...	...	...	...	...	...	...	...
...	...	...	...	...	...	...	...	...	...
3	...	2	1	...	...	...	...	...	...
...	...	...	...	...	...	...	...	...	...
...	...	...	...	...	...	...	...	...	...
22	...	20	2	...	...	...	...	...	...
...	...	...	...	...	...	...	...	...	...
...	...	...	...	...	...	...	...	...	...
2	...	2	...	...	...	...	...	...	...
2	...	1	1	...	...	...	...	...	...
...	...	...	..	...	...	...	...	...	...
...	...	...	...	...	...	...	...	...	...
...	...	...	...	...	...	...	...	...	...
2	...	1	1	...	...	...	...	...	...
...	...	...	...	...	...	...	...	...	...
...	...	...	...	...	...	...	...	...	...
...	...	...	...	...	...	...	...	...	...
17	...	13	4	...	...	...	...	...	...
21	2	16	3	...	...	...	...	...	...
...	...	...	...	...	...	...	...	...	...
...	...	...	...	...	...	...	...	...	...
...	...	...	...	...	...	...	...	...	...
...	...	...	...	...	...	...	...	...	...
...	...	...	..	...	...	...	...	...	...
2	...	2	...	...	...	...	...	...	...
...	...	...	...	...	...	...	...	...	...
2	...	2	...	...	...	...	...	...	...
...	...	...	...	...	...	...	...	...	...
9	...	9	...	...	...	...	...	...	...
...	...	...	...	...	...	...	...	...	...
...	...	...	...	...	...	...	...	...	...
4	...	1	3	...	...	...	...	...	...
16	1	18	2	...	...	...	...	...	...
157	*7*	*117*	*33*	...	...	...	...	...	...

Class.	Group.	Caste, &c. and sub-division.	Religion.	All Ages. Total.	Single.	Married.	Widowed.	Civil condition not stated.
B.—Professional.—(Continued.)	5. Priests.—(Continued.)	Brámhan.—(Concluded.) Hoisʼanigu	Hindu.	...	...	...	...	...
		Karnátaka	,,	9	2	6	1	...
		Kumbálur or Tótada Tigalu	,,	...	...	...	...	...
		Kandávara	,,	...	...	...	...	...
		Kannada Kammé	,,	...	...	...	...	...
		Karáde	,,	...	...	...	...	...
		Kásalnád	,,	...	...	...	...	...
		Kavarga	,,	...	...	...	...	...
		Kóta	,,	...	...	...	...	...
		Kánakubja or Kanyákubja	,,	2	...	1	1	...
		Konkanasth	,,	2	...	2	...	...
		Kandáde	,,	...	...	...	...	...
		Kátyáyana	,,	...	...	...	...	...
		Mulikinádu or Murikinádu	,,	88	35	44	9	...
		Mandyattár	,,	...	...	...	...	...
		Nambúri	,,	...	...	...	...	...
		Nandavaidika	,,	15	3	10	2	...
		Prathamasʼákhe	,,	7	...	4	3	...
		Prativádi Bhayankarattár	,,	...	...	...	...	...
		Panchagráma	,,	...	...	...	...	...
		Sankéti	,,	...	...	...	...	...
		Sárasvata	,,	2	1	...	1	...
		Sʼirnádu	,,	...	...	...	...	...
		Sʼisʼuvarga	,,	...	...	...	...	...
		Sivalli	,,	...	...	...	...	...
		Smárta	,,	61	19	33	9	...
		Sʼrivaishnava	,,	42	14	19	9	...
		Kadámbiyár	,,	...	...	...	...	...
		Sʼrívaishnava, Hebbár	,,	...	...	...	...	...
		Telaghánya	,,	...	...	...	...	...
		Tuluva	,,	...	...	...	...	...
		Tirumaleyár	,,	...	...	...	...	...
		Ulachakammé	,,	20	6	10	4	...
		Utráji (Uttrádi)	,,	...	...	...	...	...
		Vadama	,,	17	5	8	4	...
		Vangípuram	,,	...	...	...	...	...
		Vetnádu	,,	29	3	18	8	...
		Vijápurada kammé	,,	...	...	...	...	...
		Véginádu	,,	...	...	...	...	...
		Vaishnava (Mádhva)	,,	5	1	2	2	...
				36	12	19	5	...
		Total Brámhan		491	127	264	100	...

TABLE E.—(Continued.)

Station, Bangalore.

Females.

0 to 9. Total.	Single.	Married.	Widowed.	Civil condition not stated.	10 to 14. Total.	Single.	Married.	Widowed.	Civil condition not stated.
...	...	...	...	...	...	...	...	...	...
2	2	...	...	...	...	...	...	...	...
...	...	...	...	...	...	...	...	...	...
...	...	...	...	...	...	...	...	...	...
...	...	...	...	...	...	...	...	...	...
...	...	...	...	...	...	...	...	...	...
...	...	...	...	...	...	...	...	...	...
...	...	...	...	...	...	...	...	...	...
...	...	...	...	...	...	...	...	...	...
...	...	...	...	...	...	...	...	...	...
...	...	...	...	...	...	...	...	...	...
...	...	...	...	...	...	...	...	...	...
...	...	...	...	...	...	...	...	...	...
34	33	1	...	...	6	2	4	...	...
...	...	...	...	...	...	...	...	...	...
...	...	...	...	...	...	...	...	...	...
3	3	...	...	...	3	...	3	...	...
...	...	...	...	...	1	...	1	...	...
...	...	...	...	...	...	...	...	...	...
...	...	...	...	...	...	...	...	...	...
...	...	...	...	...	...	...	...	...	...
1	1	...	...	...	...	...	...	...	...
...	...	...	...	...	...	...	...	...	...
...	...	...	...	...	...	...	...	...	...
...	...	...	...	...	...	...	...	...	...
20	19	1	...	...	4	...	3	1	...
13	13	...	...	...	4	1	3	...	...
...	...	...	...	...	...	...	...	...	...
...	...	...	...	...	...	...	...	...	...
...	...	...	...	...	...	...	...	...	...
...	...	...	...	...	...	...	...	...	...
...	...	...	...	...	...	...	...	...	...
5	5	...	...	...	1	1	...	...	...
...	...	...	...	...	...	...	...	...	...
6	5	1	...	...	1	...	1	...	...
...	...	...	...	...	...	...	...	...	...
2	2	...	...	...	3	1	2	...	...
...	...	...	...	...	...	...	...	...	...
...	...	...	...	...	...	...	...	...	...
1	1	...	...	...	...	...	...	...	...
12	12	...	...	...	3	...	2	[illegible]	...
126	120	[illegible]	...	...	39	7	30	2	...

The Civil and Military

Class.	Group.	Caste, &c. and sub-division.	Religion.	15 to 39. Total.	Single.	Married.	Widowed.	Civil condition not stated.
B.—Professional.—(Continued.)	5. Priests.—(Continued.)	Brámhan.—(Concluded.) Hois'anigu ...	Hindu.	...	...	...	...	...
		Karnátaka	,,	4	...	4	...	...
		Kumbálúr or Tótada Tigula.	,,	...	...	...	...	...
		Kandávara ...	,,	...	...	...	...	...
		Kannada Kammé ...	,,	...	...	...	...	...
		Karáde	,,	...	...	...	...	...
		Kasalnád	,,	...	...	...	...	...
		Kavarga... ...	,,	...	...	...	...	...
		Kóta	,,	...	...	...	...	...
		Kánakubja or Kanyákubja.	,,	...	...	...	...	...
		Konkanast'h ...	,,	2	...	2	...	...
		Kandáde ...	,,	...	...	...	...	...
		Kátyáyana ...	,,	...	...	...	...	...
		Mulikinádu or Murikinádu.	,,	33	...	29	4	...
		Mandyattár ...	,,	...	...	...	...	...
		Nambúri ...	,,	...	...	...	...	...
		Nandavaidíka ...	,,	5	...	5	...	...
		Prat'hamas'ákhe ...	,,	4	...	3	1	...
		Prativádi Bhayankarattár.	,,	...	...	...	...	...
		Panchagráma ...	,,	...	...	...	...	...
		Sankéti	,,	...	...	...	...	...
		Sárasvata ...	,,	...	...	...	...	...
		S'irnádu... ...	,,	...	...	...	...	...
		S'is'uvarga ...	,,	...	...	...	...	...
		Sivalli	,,	...	...	...	...	...
		Smárta	,,	31	...	25	6	...
		S'rivaishnava ...	,,	16	...	14	2	...
		Kadámbiyár ...	,,	...	...	...	...	...
		S'rivaishnava, Hobbár	,,	...	...	...	...	...
		Telaghánya ...	,,	...	...	...	...	...
		Tuluva	,,	...	...	...	...	...
		Tirumaleyár ...	,,	...	...	...	...	...
		Ulachakammé ...	,,	8	...	8	...	...
		Utráji (Uttrádi) ...	,,	...	...	...	...	...
		Vadama	,,	8	...	5	3	...
		Vangípuram ...	,,	...	...	...	...	...
		Velnadu ...	,,	15	...	11	4	...
		Vijápuradakammé ...	,,	...	...	...	...	...
		Véginádu ...	,,	...	...	...	...	...
		Vais'nava (Mádhva)..	,,	3	...	2	1	...
				15	...	14	1	...
		Total Brámhan........		*215*	...	*181*	*34*	...

TABLE E.—(Continued.)

Station, Bangalore.

Females.

40 and over.					Age not stated.				
Total.	Single.	Married.	Widowed.	Civil condition not stated.	Total.	Single.	Married.	Widowed.	Civil condition not stated.
...	...	...	...	...	...	...	...	...	...
3	...	2	1	...	...	...	...	...	...
...	...	...	...	...	...	...	...	...	...
...	...	...	...	...	...	...	...	...	...
...	...	...	...	...	...	...	...	...	...
...	...	...	...	...	...	...	...	...	...
...	...	...	...	...	...	...	...	...	...
...	...	...	...	...	...	...	...	...	...
...	...	...	...	...	...	...	...	...	...
2	...	1	1	...	...	...	...	...	...
...	...	...	...	...	...	...	...	...	...
...	...	...	...	...	...	...	...	...	...
...	...	...	...	...	...	...	...	...	...
15	...	10	5	...	...	...	...	...	...
...	...	...	...	...	...	...	...	...	...
...	...	...	...	...	...	...	...	...	...
4	...	2	2	...	...	...	...	...	...
2	...	...	2	...	...	...	...	...	...
...	...	...	...	...	...	...	...	...	...
...	...	...	...	...	...	...	...	...	...
...	...	...	...	...	...	...	...	...	...
1	...	...	1	...	...	...	...	...	...
...	...	...	...	...	...	...	...	...	...
...	...	...	...	...	...	...	...	...	...
...	...	...	...	...	...	...	...	...	...
6	...	4	2	...	...	...	...	...	...
9	...	2	7	...	...	...	...	...	...
...	...	...	...	...	...	...	...	...	...
...	...	...	...	...	...	...	...	...	...
...	...	...	...	...	...	...	...	...	...
...	...	...	...	...	...	...	...	...	...
...	...	...	...	...	...	...	...	...	...
6	...	2	4	...	...	...	...	...	...
...	...	...	...	...	...	...	...	...	...
2	...	1	1	...	...	...	...	...	...
...	...	...	...	...	...	...	...	...	...
9	...	5	4	...	...	...	...	...	...
...	...	...	...	...	...	...	...	...	...
...	...	...	...	...	...	...	...	...	...
1	...	...	1	...	...	...	...	...	...
6	...	3	3	...	...	...	...	...	...
111	...	*47*	*64*	...	...	...	...	...	...

Total including the Civil and

Class.	Group.	Caste, &c. and sub-division.	Religion.	All Ages. Total.	Single.	Married.	Widowed.	Civil condition not stated.
B.—Professional.—(Continued.)	5. Priests.—(Continued.)	Brâhman.—(Concluded.) Hoisʼaniga ...	Hindu.	4,141	1,916	1,858	367	...
		Karnâṭaka ...	,,	483	247	187	49	...
		Kumbâlûr or Toṭada Tigaḷa.	,,	62	28	25	9	...
		Kandâvara		106	57	39	10	...
		Kannada Kummé ...		1,330	666	550	114	...
		Karâḍe ...		133	54	62	17	...
		Kâsalnâd ...	,,	17	10	6	1	...
		Kavarga ...	,,	5	3	1	1	...
		Kôṭa ...	,,	10	5	3	2	...
		Kânyakubja or Kanyakubja.	,,	15	7	6	2	
		Koṅkaṇast'h ...	,,	157	83	61	13	...
		Kundâḍe ...	,,	6	2	3	1	...
		Kâtyâyana ...	,,	67	35	27	5	...
		Mulikinâḍu or Murikinâḍu.	,,	5,678	2,780	2,392	506	...
		Mandyattâr ...	,,	312	146	130	36	...
		Namburi ...	,,	8	4	3	1	...
		Nandavaidika ...	,,	655	327	262	66	
		Prathamasʼâkhe ...	,,	2,551	1,205	1,138	208	
		Prativâdi Bhayankarattâr	,,	1	...	1	...	...
		Panchagrâma ...	,,	184	85	77	22	...
		Sankéti ...	,,	1,255	610	527	118	...
		Sârasvata ...	,,	84	43	35	6	...
		Sʼirnâḍu ...	,,	1,799	867	765	167	...
		Sʼisʼuvarga ...	,,	64	33	28	3	...
		Sivaḷḷi ...	,,	1,220	618	512	90	...
		Smârta ...	,,	12,160	5,818	5,575	767	...
		Srîvaishṇava ...	,,	8,357	4,305	3,558	494	...
		Kaḍâmbiyâr ...	,,	2	1	1	...	...
		Srîvaishṇava, Hebbâr	,,	851	448	343	60	...
		Telaghaṇya ...	,,	980	524	388	68	...
		Tuḷuva ...	,,	3	2	1	...	...
		Tirumaleyâr ...	,,	130	58	63	9	...
		Uchchakamme ...	,,	2,415	1,224	1,016	175	...
		Utrâji (Uttradi) ...	,,	237	119	103	15	...
		Vaḍama ...	,,	727	353	320	54	...
		Vangipuram ...	,,	96	41	46	9	...
		Velnâḍu ...	,,	1,685	810	734	141	...
		Vijâpurada kammé...	,,	20	10	8	2	...
		Vêginâḍu ...	,,	1	...	1	...	...
		Vaishṇava (Mâdhva)...	,,	3,726	1,819	1,643	264	...
				69	29	38	2	
		Total Brâhman......	....	*92,831*	*45,821*	*39,716*	*7,294*	...

TABLE E.—(*Continued.*)

Military Station, Bangalore.

Males.

0 to 9.					10 to 14.				
Total.	Single.	Married.	Widowed.	Civil condition not stated.	Total.	Single.	Married.	Widowed.	Civil condition not stated.
1,109	1,098	10	1	...	318	268	49	1	...
126	126	...	...	...	37	37	...	...	...
14	14	...	...	...	10	10	...	...	...
38	38	...	...	...	9	9	...	...	...
428	428	...	...	...	95	87	8	...	...
29	29	...	...	...	11	11	...	...	...
5	5	...	...	...	3	2	1	...	...
1	1	...	...	...	1	1	...	...	...
3	3	...	...	...	1	1	...	...	...
1	1	...	...	...	2	2	...	...	...
50	50	...	...	...	14	14	...	...	...
2	2	...	...	...	...	...	...	...	...
16	16	...	...	...	14	14	...	...	...
1,490	1,490	...	...	...	531	494	37	...	...
95	88	7	...	...	46	29	16	1	...
3	3	...	...	...	1	1	...	...	...
137	137	...	...	...	45	44	1	...	...
667	667	...	...	...	207	195	11	1	...
...	...	...	...	...	...	...	...	...	...
45	45	...	...	...	18	18	...	...	...
375	370	5	...	...	116	96	20	...	...
20	20	...	...	...	10	10	...	...	...
455	453	2	...	...	151	138	13	...	...
21	21	...	...	...	8	7	1	...	...
263	260	3	...	...	136	122	14	...	...
2,846	2,813	30	3	...	1,024	927	93	4	...
2,385	2,354	29	2	...	920	809	107	4	...
1	1	...	...	...	...	...	...	...	...
263	263	...	...	...	88	84	4	...	...
246	245	1	...	...	106	99	7	...	...
1	1	...	...	...	...	...	...	...	...
43	43	...	...	...	12	10	2	...	...
682	682	...	...	...	204	198	6	...	...
59	59	...	...	...	38	38	...	...	...
198	196	2	...	...	64	61	3	...	...
26	26	...	...	...	7	7	...	...	...
424	424	...	...	...	145	144	1	...	...
6	6	...	...	...	3	3	...	...	...
...	...	...	...	...	...	...	...	...	...
883	868	14	1	...	394	334	56	4	...
8	8	...	...	...	3	3	...	...	...
24,741	*24,548*	*182*	*11*	...	*8,820*	*7,838*	*954*	*28*	...

Total including the Civil and

Class.	Group.	Caste, &c. and sub-division.	Religion.	15 to 39 Total.	15 to 39 Single.	15 to 39 Married.	15 to 39 Widowed.	15 to 39 Civil condition not stated.
B.—Professional.—(Continued.)	5. Priests.—(Continued.)	Brámhan.—(Concluded.)						
		Hois'aṇiga ...	Hindu.	1,782	512	1,157	113	...
		Karṇáṭaka ...	,,	224	74	134	16	...
		Kumbálúr or Tóṭada Tigaḷa.	...	23	4	17	2	...
		Kandávara ...	,,	42	10	31	1	..
		Kannaḍa Kammé ...	,,	547	141	369	37	
		Karáḍé ...	,,	61	14	45	2	..
		Kásalnáḍ ...	,,	5	3	2	...	..
		Kavarga ...	,,	2	1	1	...	..
		Kóṭa ...	,,	1	1	2	1	..
		Káṇakubja or Kanyákubja.	,,	10	4	5	1	..
		Konkaṇást'h ...	,,	60	19	38	3	..
		Kandáḍé ..	,,	1	...	1	...	..
		Kátyáyana ...	,,	23	14	9	...	..
		Mulikináḍu or Murikináḍu.	,,	2,268	718	1,450	100	.
		Mandyattár ...	,,	106	23	78	5	..
		Nambúri ...	,,	2	...	2	...	..
		Nandavajdika ...	,,	298	123	158	17	..
		Prat'hamas'ákhe ...	,,	1,035	314	685	36	...
		Prativádi Bhayankarattár.	,,	1	...	1	...	
		Panchagráma ...	,,	78	21	49	8	...
		Sankéti	,,	491	144	320	27	...
		Sarasvata ...	,,	34	12	20	2	...
		S'irnáḍu... ...	,,	758	250	472	36	...
		S'is'uvarga ...	,,	24	5	18	1	...
		Sivaḷḷi	,,	578	224	340	14	...
		Smárta	,,	5,746	2,005	3,536	175	...
		Srivaishṇava ...	,,	3,300	1,091	2,101	108	...
		Kaḍámbiyár ...	,,	1	...	1	...	...
		Srívaishṇava, Hebbár	,,	338	96	227	15	...
		Telaghánya ...	,,	416	169	231	16	...
		Tuḷuva	,,	2	1	1	...	...
		Tirumaleyár ...	,,	46	5	39	2	...
		Ulachakammé ...	,,	9 7	316	613	28	...
		Utráji (Uttráḍi) ...	,,	93	20	71	2	...
		Vaḍama ...	,,	329	92	224	13	...
		Vangípuram ...	,,	43	7	34	2	...
		Volnáḍu... ...	,,	681	217	438	29	...
		Vijápurada kammé ...	,,	8	1	7	...	...
		Véginádu ...	,,	...	...	...	...	...
		Vaishṇava (Mádhva)..	,,	1,713	586	1051	76	...
				42	17	25	...	...
		Total Brámhan.....	....	*38,941*	*12,611*	*24,576*	*1,754*	...

TABLE E.—(Continued.)

Military Station, Bangalore.

Males.

40 and over.					Age not stated.				
Total.	Single.	Married.	Widowed.	Civil condition not stated.	Total.	Single.	Married.	Widowed.	Civil condition not stated.
932	38	612	252	...	...	...	...	...	...
96	10	53	33	...	...	...	...	...	...
15	...	8	7	...	...	...	...	...	...
17	...	8	9	...	...	...	...	...	...
260	10	173	77	...	...	...	...	...	...
32	...	17	15	...	...	...	...	...	...
4	...	3	1	...	...	...	...	...	...
1	...	...	1	...	...	...	...	...	...
2	...	1	1	...	...	...	...	...	...
2	...	1	1	...	...	...	...	...	...
33	...	23	10	...	...	...	...	...	...
3	...	2	1	...	...	...	...	...	...
14	1	8	5	...	...	...	...	...	...
1,389	78	905	406	...	...	...	...	...	...
65	6	29	30	...	...	...	...	...	...
2	...	1	1	...	...	...	...	...	...
175	23	103	49	...	...	...	...	...	...
612	29	412	171	...	...	...	...	...	...
...	...	...	...	...	...	...	...	...	...
43	1	28	14	...	...	...	...	...	...
273	...	182	91	...	...	...	...	...	...
20	1	15	4	...	...	...	...	...	...
435	26	278	131	...	...	...	...	...	...
11	...	9	2	...	...	...	...	...	...
243	12	155	76	...	...	...	...	...	...
2,574	73	,916	385	...	...	...	...	...	...
1,752	51	,321	380	...	...	...	...	...	...
...	...	...	...	...	...	...	...	...	...
162	5	112	45	...	...	...	...	...	...
212	11	149	52	...	...	...	...	...	...
...	...	...	...	...	...	...	...	...	...
29	...	22	7	...	...	...	...	...	...
562	28	397	137	...	...	...	...	...	...
47	2	32	13	...	...	...	...	...	...
136	4	91	41	...	...	...	...	...	...
20	1	12	7	...	...	...	...	...	...
432	25	295	112	...	...	...	...	...	...
3	...	1	2	...	...	...	...	...	...
1	...	1	...	...	...	...	...	...	...
736	31	522	183	...	...	...	...	...	...
16	1	13	2	...	...	...	...	...	...
20,329	*824*	*14,004*	*5,501*	...	...	...	...	...	...

Total including the Civil and

Class.	Group.	Caste, &c. and sub-division.	Religion.	All Ages. Total.	Single.	Married.	Widowed.	Civil condition not stated.
B.—Professional.—(Continued.)	5. Priests.—(Continued.)	Bráhman.—(Concluded.) Hois'anigu ...	Hindu.	4,187	1,255	1,880	1,052	...
		Karnátaka ...	,,	423	96	181	146	...
		Kumbálúr or Tótuda Tigala.	,,	51	16	27	8	...
		Kandávaru ...	,,	107	24	49	34	...
		Kannada Kammé ...	,,	1,389	498	592	299	...
		Karádo	,,	120	33	68	19	...
		Kásalnád ...	,,	13	6	6	1	...
		Kavargu	,,	2	1	1	...	...
		Kóta	,,	15	3	4	8	...
		Kánakubja or Kanyákubja.	,,	5	...	4	1	...
		Konkanast'h ...	,,	139	42	68	29	...
		Kandáde ...	,,	3	1	2	...	...
		Kátyáyana ...	,,	72	21	30	21	...
		Mulikinádu or Murikinádu.	,,	5,510	1,614	2,559	1,337	...
		Mandyattár ...	,,	254	88	111	55	...
		Nambúri ...	,,	6	1	3	2	...
		Nandavaidika ...	,,	602	170	260	172	...
		Prat'hamas'ákhe ...	,,	2,476	659	1,237	580	...
		Prativádi Bhayankarattár.	,,	1	...	1	...	...
		Panchagráma ...	,,	174	50	77	47	...
		Sankéti	,,	1,267	434	542	291	...
		Sárasvata ...	,,	49	16	26	7	...
		S'irnádu ...	,,	1,691	464	797	430	...
		S'is'uvargu ...	,,	75	20	29	26	...
		Sivalli	,,	1,177	278	556	343	...
		Smárta	,,	11,214	3,290	5,269	2,655	...
		Srivaishnava ...	,,	8,457	2,600	3,809	2,048	...
		Kadámbiyár ...	,,	1	...	1	...	...
		Srívaishnava, Hebbár.	,,	873	281	397	195	...
		Telagháṇya ...	,,	925	272	401	252	...
		Tuluvá	,,	2	1	1	...	...
		Tirumaleyár ...	,,	132	46	55	31	...
		Ulachakammé ...	,,	2,369	651	1,111	607	...
		Utráji (Uttarádi) ...	,,	188	74	87	27	...
		Vaduma ...	,,	727	231	349	147	...
		Vangipuram ...	,,	97	28	51	18	...
		Velnádu	,,	1,496	370	718	408	...
		Vijápurada kammé ...	,,	17	4	10	3	...
		Véginádu ...	,,	...	...	...	...	...
		Vaishnava (Mádhva) ...	,,	3,554	1,087	1,703	764	...
				36	12	19	5	...
		Total Bráhman ...		89,554	26,611	41,155	21,788	...

TABLE E.—(*Continued.*)

Military Station, Bangalore.

Females.

0 to 9					10 to 14				
Total.	Single.	Married.	Widowed.	Civil condition not stated.	Total.	Single.	Married.	Widowed.	Civil condition not stated.
1,126	1,069	51	6	...	434	186	220	28	...
93	93	...	...	...	28	3	21	4	...
11	10	1	...	...	6	6	...	...	...
21	20	1	...	...	8	4	4	...	...
447	435	12	...	...	122	63	56	3	...
26	26	...	...	...	11	7	4	...	...
6	6	...	...	...	1	...	1	...	...
1	1	...	...	...	...	...	...	...	...
3	3	...	...	...	1	...	1	...	...
...	...	...	...	...	...	...	...	...	...
36	33	3	...	...	16	9	7	...	...
1	1	...	...	...	...	...	...	...	...
20	19	1	...	...	7	2	5	...	...
1,532	1,448	82	2	...	518	166	336	16	...
90	77	13	...	...	46	11	33	2	...
1	1	...	...	...	1	...	1	...	...
156	149	7	...	...	61	21	39	1	...
643	603	40	...	...	202	56	143	3	...
...	...	...	...	...	...	...	...	...	...
42	40	2	...	...	22	10	10	2	...
413	391	20	2	...	124	43	74	7	...
15	15	...	...	...	4	1	3	...	...
439	418	21	...	...	154	46	107	1	...
18	16	2	...	...	8	4	4	...	...
292	256	33	3	...	157	22	121	14	...
2,903	2,698	177	28	...	1,349	592	649	108	...
2,378	2,240	126	12	...	932	360	521	51	...
...	...	...	...	...	...	...	...	...	...
246	236	10	...	...	91	45	46	...	...
254	236	18	...	...	123	36	83	4	...
1	1	...	...	...	...	...	...	...	...
44	44	...	...	...	8	2	6	...	...
651	611	40	...	...	193	40	152	1	...
60	60	...	...	...	26	14	12	...	...
217	200	17	...	...	86	31	54	1	...
29	27	2	...	...	9	1	8	...	...
365	338	27	...	...	134	32	99	3	...
4	4	...	...	...	3	...	3	...	...
...	...	...	...	...	...	...	...	...	...
944	880	51	13	...	431	207	193	31	...
12	12	...	...	...	3	...	2	1	...
24,161	*22,798*	*1,275*	*88*	...	*9,644*	*3,813*	*5,371*	*460*	...

Total including the Civil and

Class.	Group.	Caste, &c. and sub-division.	Religion.	15 to 39 Total.	Single.	Married.	Widowed.	Civil condition not stated.
B.—Professional—(Continued).	5. Priests.—(Continued.)	Brámhan.—(Concluded.) Hois'anigu	Hindu.	1,583	...	1,250	333	...
		Karnátaka	,,	173	...	126	47	...
		Kumbálúr or Totada Tigala.	,,	20	...	18	2	...
		Kandávara	,,	46	...	37	9	...
		Kannada Kammé	,,	530	...	423	107	...
		Karáde	,,	55	...	50	5	...
		Kásalnád	,,	4	...	4	...	...
		Kavarga	,,	1	...	1	...	...
		Kóta	,,	6	...	3	3	...
		Kánakubja or Kanyákubja.	,,	3	...	3	...	...
		Konkanast'h	,,	56	...	47	9	...
		Kandádé	,,	1	...	1	...	...
		Kátyáyana	,,	28	...	19	9	...
		Mulikinádu or Murikinádu.	,,	2,051	...	1,665	386	...
		Mandyáttar	,,	65	...	46	19	...
		Nambúri	,,	2	...	2	...	...
		Nandavaidika	,,	209	...	158	51	...
		Prat'hamasákhe	,,	1,025	...	837	188	...
		Prátivádi Bhayankarattár.	,,	1	...	1	...	...
		Panchagráma	,,	60	...	45	15	...
		Sankéti	,,	446	...	359	87	...
		Sárasvata	,,	22	...	21	1	...
		S'irnádu	,,	656	...	521	135	...
		S'is'uvarga	,,	30	...	19	11	...
		Sivalli	,,	444	...	328	116	...
		Smárta	,,	4,024	...	3,352	672	...
		Srivaishnava	,,	2,927	...	2,399	528	...
		Kadámbiyár	,,	1	...	1	...	...
		Srivaishnava, Hebbár	,,	319	...	267	52	...
		Telaghánya	,,	349	...	247	103	...
		Tuluva	,,	1	...	1	...	...
		Tirumaleyár	,,	44	...	35	9	...
		Ulachakamme	,,	943	...	741	202	...
		Utráji (Uttrádi)	,,	65	...	58	7	...
		Vaduma	,,	274	...	226	48	...
		Vangipuram	,,	39	...	37	2	...
		Velnádu	,,	604	...	466	138	...
		Vijápurada kammé	,,	7	...	7	...	...
		Véginádu	,,	...	...	...	...	—
		Vaishnava (Mádhva)	,,	1,252	...	1,081	171	...
				15	...	14	1	...
		Total Brámhan		33,635	...	27,085	6,550	...

TABLE E.—(*Continued.*)

Military Station, Bangalore.

Females.

40 and over. Total.	Single.	Married.	Widowed.	Civil condition not stated.	Age not stated. Total.	Single.	Married.	Widowed.	Civil condition not stated.
1,044	...	361	683	...	...	...	...	...	...
129	...	34	96	...	...	...	...	...	...
14	...	8	6	...	...	...	...	...	...
32	...	7	25	...	...	...	...	...	...
281	...	101	180	...	...	...	...	...	...
28	...	14	14	...	...	...	...	...	...
2	...	1	1	...	...	...	...	...	...
...	...	...	...	...	...	...	...	...	...
5	...	...	5	...	...	...	...	...	...
2	...	1	1	...	...	...	...	...	...
31	...	11	20	...	...	...	...	...	...
1	...	1	...	...	...	...	...	...	...
17	...	5	12	...	...	...	...	...	...
1,409	...	476	933	...	...	...	...	...	...
53	...	19	34	...	...	...	...	...	...
2	...	...	2	...	...	...	...	...	...
176	...	56	120	...	...	...	...	...	...
606	...	217	389	...	...	...	...	...	...
...	...	...	...	...	...	...	...	...	...
50	...	20	30	...	...	...	...	...	...
284	...	89	195	...	...	...	...	...	...
8	...	2	6	...	...	...	...	...	...
442	...	148	294	...	...	...	...	...	...
19	...	4	15	...	...	...	...	...	...
284	...	74	210	...	...	...	...	...	...
2,938	...	1,091	1,847	...	...	...	...	...	...
2,220	...	763	1,457	...	...	...	...	...	...
...	...	...	...	...	...	...	...	...	...
217	...	74	143	...	...	...	...	...	...
199	...	53	146	...	...	...	...	...	...
...	...	...	...	...	...	...	...	...	...
36	...	14	22	...	...	...	...	...	...
582	...	178	404	...	...	...	...	...	...
37	...	17	20	...	...	...	...	...	...
150	...	52	98	...	...	...	...	...	...
20	...	4	16	...	...	...	...	...	...
393	...	126	267	...	...	...	...	...	...
3	...	...	3	...	...	...	...	...	...
...	...	...	...	...	...	...	...	...	...
927	...	378	549	...	...	...	...	...	...
6	...	3	3	...	...	...	...	...	...
22,114	...	*7,434*	*14,680*	...	...	...	...	...	...

Class.	Group.	Caste, &c. and sub-division.	Religion.	All Ages. Total.	Single.	Married.	Widowed.	Civil condition not stated.
B.—Professional.—(Concluded.)	5. Priests.—(Concluded.)	Dásari	Hindu.	576	272	264	40	...
		Lingáyet	,,	30,875	16,471	12,512	1,892	...
		Tirt'hankara	Jain.	1,346	714	521	111	...
		Pitámbara	,,	5	3	1	1	...
		Sátáni	Hindu.	9,982	5,167	4,133	682	...
		Total Group 5		*134,953*	*68,173*	*56,800*	*9,980*	...
	6. Devotees.	Bairági	,,	104	55	44	5	...
		Bávâji	Jain.	...	...	...	...	...
		Digambara	,,	2,881	1,582	1,097	202	...
		Gósáyi	Hindu.	208	128	66	14	...
		Sanyâsi	,,	357	190	134	33	...
		S'vétámbara	Jain.	69	33	25	11	...
		Lingáyet—Vadér	Hindu.	400	219	158	23	...
		Total Group 6		*4,019*	*2,207*	*1,524*	*288*	...
	7. Temple Servants.	Brâmhan—Páncharátra ...	,,	66	29	32	5	...
		Brâmhan—S'ivadvija ...	,,	310	142	130	38	...
		Brâmhan—Tamballa	,,	...	...	...	...	...
		Brâmhan—Vaikhánasa ...	,,	210	100	86	24	...
		Total Group 7		*586*	*271*	*248*	*67*	...
	9. Writers.	Kanakkan	,,	...	...	...	...	...
		Káyast'ha	,,	...	...	...	...	...
		Total Group 9		...	...	...	...	...
	11. Musicians and Ballad-reciters. ...	Bhat Ráju	,,	722	374	296	52	...
	12. Dancers & Singers.	Natuva	,,	3,544	2,174	1,208	162	...
	12. (a) Chittári, &c.	Ráchóvár—Chitragára ...	,,	2,407	1,255	985	167	...
		Total Class B		**146,231**	**74,454**	**61,061**	**10,716**	...
C.—Commercial.—(Continued.)	14. Traders.	Baniya	Hindu.	...	...	...	...	...
		Do.	Jain.	...	...	...	...	...
		Banajiga	Hindu.	53,529	27,998	22,302	3,229	...
		Guzaráti	,,	31	16	13	2	...
		Ját	,,	...	...	...	...	...
		Kômati	,,	15,157	7,427	6,546	1,184	...
		Lingáyet	,,	145,974	79,598	58,235	8,141	...
		Ládar	,,	1,014	509	440	65	...
		Mudali	,,	2,954	1,549	1,211	194	...

TABLE E.—(*Continued.*)

cial.

Males.

0 to 9					10 to 14				
Total.	Single.	Married.	Widowed.	Civil condition not stated.	Total.	Single.	Married.	Widowed.	Civil condition not stated.
158	156	2	...	...	47	47	...	...	...
8,449	8,449	...	...	...	3,066	3,008	58	...	...
326	326	...	...	...	100	97	3	...	...
...	...	...	...	...	1	1	...	...	...
2,727	2,727	...	...	...	929	913	16	...	...
36,281	*36,086*	*184*	*11*	...	*12,912*	*11,854*	*1,030*	*28*	...
19	19	...	...	...	12	11	1	...	...
...	...	...	...	...	...	...	...	...	...
629	627	2	...	...	272	263	9	...	...
27	27	...	...	...	15	15	...	...	...
100	100	...	...	...	27	27	...	...	...
4	4	...	...	...	8	8	...	...	...
116	116	...	...	...	35	35	...	...	...
895	*893*	2	...	...	*369*	*359*	*10*	...	...
17	17	...	...	...	9	8	1	...	...
74	74	...	...	...	30	28	2	...	...
...	...	...	...	...	...	...	...	...	...
53	53	...	...	...	21	19	2	...	...
144	*144*	...	...	...	*60*	55	5	...	...
...	...	...	...	...	...	...	...	...	...
...	...	...	...	...	...	...	...	...	...
...	...	...	...	...	...	...	...	...	...
168	168	...	...	...	64	63	1	...	...
1,085	1,085	...	...	...	316	316	...	...	...
636	633	...	...	...	255	251	4	...	...
39,209	**39,012**	**186**	**11**	...	**13,976**	**12,898**	**1,050**	**28**	...
...	...	...	...	...	...	...	...	...	...
...	...	...	...	...	...	...	...	...	...
13,619	13,614	5	...	...	4,967	4,873	94	...	...
5	5	...	...	...	3	3	...	...	...
...	...	...	...	...	...	...	...	...	...
3,895	3,894	1	...	...	1,467	1,374	93	...	...
39,703	39,671	32	...	...	17,066	16,917	147	2	...
253	253	...	...	...	80	80	...	...	...
754	754	...	...	...	294	292	2	...	...

Class.	Group.	Caste, &c. and sub-division.	Religion.	15 to 39. Total.	Single.	Married.	Widowed.	Civil condition not stated.
B.—Professional.—(Concluded.)	5. Priests.—(Concluded.)	Dásari	Hindu.	243	68	166	9	...
		Lingáyet	,,	12,765	4,751	7,597	417	...
		Tírt'hankara	Jain.	574	264	286	24	...
		Pítámbara	,,	2	2	...	...	...
		Sátáni	Hindu.	4,085	1,430	2,493	162	...
		Total Group 5		*50,276*	*19,078*	*28,839*	*2,359*	...
	6. Devotees.	Bairági	,,	49	22	27	...	...
		Báváji	Jain.	...	...	...	...	...
		Digambara	,,	1,281	633	600	48	...
		Gósáyi	Hindu.	94	52	41	1	...
		Sanyási	,,	144	46	90	8	...
		S'vétámbara	Jain.	45	21	20	4	...
		Lingáyet—Vadér	Hindu.	163	62	99	2	...
		Total Group 6		*1,776*	*836*	*877*	*63*	...
	7. Temple Servants.	Bráhman. Páncharátra ...	,,	23	4	21	1	...
		Bráhman. Sivadvija ...	,,	127	36	84	7	...
		Bráhman. Tambalia ...	,,	...	...	...	...	...
		Bráhman. Vaikhánasa ...	,,	95	28	61	6	...
		Total Group 7		*248*	*68*	*166*	*14*	...
	9. Writers.	Kanakkan	,,	...	...	...	...	...
		Káyast'ha	,,	...	...	...	...	...
		Total Group 9		...	...	...	...	...
	11. Musicians and Ballad-reciters. ...	Bhat Ráju	,,	321	134	178	9	...
	12. Dancers & Singers.	Natuva	,,	1,521	740	728	53	...
	12. (a) Chittári, &c.	Ráchévár—Chitragára ...	,,	1,009	347	626	36	...
		Total Class B		**61,151**	**21,153**	**37,464**	**2,534**	...
C.—Commercial.—(Continued.)	14. Traders.	Baniya	Hindu.	...	...	...	...	...
		Do.	Jain.	...	...	...	...	...
		Banajiga	Hindu.	22,839	8,886	13,214	729	...
		Guzaráti	,,	18	7	11	...	...
		Ját	,,	...	...	...	...	...
		Kómati	,,	6,234	2,009	3,964	261	...
		Lingáyet	,,	59,010	21,874	35,195	1,941	...
		Ládar	,,	459	168	274	17	...
		Mudali	,,	1,273	465	771	37	...

TABLE E.—(*Continued.*)

cial.

Males.

40 and over.					Age not stated.				
Total.	Single.	Married.	Widowed.	Civil condition not stated.	Total.	Single.	Married.	Widowed.	Civil condition not stated.
128	1	96	31	...	...	...	...	...	...
6,595	263	4,857	1,475	...	...	...	...	...	...
316	27	232	87	...	...	...	...	...	...
2	...	1	1	...	...	...	...	...	...
2,241	97	1,624	520	...	...	...	...	...	...
29,484	*1,205*	*20,697*	*7,582*	...	...	...	...	...	...
24	3	16	5	...	...	...	...	...	...
...	...	...	...	...	...	...	...	...	...
695	59	486	150	...	4	...	...	4	...
72	34	25	13	...	...	...	...	...	...
86	17	44	25	...	...	...	...	...	...
12	...	5	7	...	...	...	...	...	...
86	6	59	21	...	...	...	...	...	...
975	*119*	*635*	*221*	...	4	...	...	4	...
14	...	10	4	...	...	...	...	...	...
79	4	44	31	...	...	...	...	...	...
...	...	...	...	...	...	...	...	...	...
41	...	23	18	...	...	...	...	...	...
134	*4*	*77*	*53*	...	...	...	...	...	...
...	...	...	...	...	...	...	...	...	...
...	...	...	...	...	...	...	...	...	...
...	...	...	...	...	...	...	...	...	...
169	9	117	43	...	...	...	...	...	...
632	33	480	119	...	...	...	...	...	...
507	21	355	131	...	...	...	...	...	...
31,891	**1,391**	**22,361**	**8,139**	...	**4**	...	...	**4**	...
...	...	...	...	...	...	...	...	...	...
...	...	...	...	...	...	...	...	...	...
12,084	625	8,959	2,500	...	...	...	...	...	...
5	1	2	2	...	...	...	...	...	...
...	...	...	...	...	...	...	...	...	...
3,561	150	2,488	923	...	...	...	...	...	...
30,195	1,136	22,861	6,198	...	...	...	...	...	...
222	8	166	48	...	...	...	...	...	...
633	38	438	157	...	...	...	...	...	...

Provin

Class.	Group.	Caste, &c. and sub-division.	Religion.	All Ages. Total.	Single.	Married.	Widowed.	Civil condition not stated.
B.—Professional.—(Concluded.)	5. Priests.—(Concluded.)	Dásari	Hindu.	592	200	289	103	...
		Lingáyet	„	31,038	11,740	13,360	5,938	...
		Tírt'hankara	Jain.	1,218	392	517	309	...
		Pítámbara	„	...	...	...	...	...
		Sátáni	Hindu.	9,777	3,227	4,401	2149	...
		Total Group 5		131,688	42,043	59,458	30,187	...
	6. Devotees.	Bairági	„	118	50	48	20	...
		Báváji	Jain.	...	...	...	...	...
		Digambara	„	2,581	850	1,027	704	...
		Gósáyi	Hindu.	215	108	64	43	...
		Sanyási	„	327	127	148	52	...
		S'vétámbara	Jain.	10	4	4	2	...
		Lingáyet—Vadér ...	Hindu.	545	199	223	123	...
		Total Group 6		3,796	1,358	1,514	944	...
	7. Temple Servants.	Brámhan. Pánchar[illegible]tral ...	„	76	27	29	11	...
		Brámhan. Sivadvija ...	„	295	58	146	91	...
		Brámhan. Tamballa ...	„	...	...	...	...	...
		Brámhan. Vaikhánasa ...	„	197	47	105	45	...
		Total Group 7		568	128	290	150	...
	9. Writers.	Kanakkan	„	...	...	...	...	...
		Káyast'ha	„	...	...	...	...	...
		Total Group 9		...	...	...	...	...
	11. Musicians and Ballad-reciters.	Bhaṭ Ráju		665	213	309	143	...
	12. Dancers & Singers.	Naṭuva	„	3,895	2,645	1,151	96	...
	12. (a) Chittári, &c.	Ráchévár—Chitragára ...	„	2,222	753	1,082	387	...
		Total Class B		142,834	47,120	63,807	31,907	..
C.—Commercial.—(Continued.)	14. Traders.	Baniya	Hindu.	...	...	...	...	...
		Do.	Jain.	...	...	...	...	...
		Banajiga	Hindu.	52,864	17,947	23,258	11,659	...
		Guzaráti	„	20	9	9	2	...
		Ját	„	...	...	...	...	...
		Kómaṭi	„	13,843	4,230	6,467	3,146	..
		Lingáyet	„	145,103	54,449	60,343	30,311	...
		Láḍer	„	1,032	356	439	237	...
		Mudali	„	2,457	866	1,148	443	...

TABLE E.—(*Continued.*)

cial.

Females.

0 to 9					10 to 14				
Total.	Single.	Married.	Widowed.	Civil condition not stated.	Total.	Single.	Married.	Widowed.	Civil condition not stated.
142	142	...	...	...	61	39	22	...	...
8,805	8,720	85	...	...	3,206	2,350	851	5	...
319	313	6	...	...	109	66	43	...	...
...	...	...	...	...	...	...	...	...	...
2,681	2,613	68	...	...	915	537	378	...	...
35,982	*34,466*	*1,428*	*88*	...	*13,896*	*6,798*	*6,635*	*463*	...
25	25	...	...	...	10	8	2	...	...
...	...	...	...	...	...	...	...	...	...
677	660	16	1	...	224	139	80	5	...
65	65	...	...	...	31	31	...	...	...
101	101	...	...	...	29	23	6	...	...
3	3	...	...	...	2	1	1	...	...
152	115	3	...	...	54	37	17	...	...
1,023	[illegible]	*23*	*1*	...	*350*	*239*	*106*	*5*	...
22	19	3	...	...	10	4	5	1	...
54	48	6	...	...	20	10	10	...	...
...	...	...	...	...	...	...	...	...	...
45	41	4	...	...	20	6	14	...	...
121	*108*	*13*	...	...	*50*	*20*	*29*	*1*	...
...	...	...	...	...	...	...	...	...	...
...	...	...	...	...	...	...	...	...	...
...	...	...	...	...	...	...	...	...	...
151	151	...	...	...	69	41	25	...	...
509	501	8	...	...	333	301	32	...	...
558	557	1	...	...	232	165	67	...	...
38,346	**36,784**	**1,473**	**89**	...	**14,930**	**7,567**	**6,894**	**469**	...
...	...	...	...	...	...	...	...	...	...
...	...	...	...	...	...	...	...	...	...
14,021	13,637	380	4	...	4,394	2,868	1,507	19	...
5	5	...	...	...	2	2	...	...	...
...	...	...	...	...	...	...	...	...	...
3,968	3,742	226	...	...	1,422	484	906	32	...
40,315	39,609	704	2	...	15,620	11,061	4,525	34	...
282	272	10	...	...	117	80	35	2	...
630	624	6	...	...	242	180	62	...	...

Class.	Group.	Caste, &c. and sub-division.	Religion.	15 to 39 Total.	15 to 39 Single.	15 to 39 Married.	15 to 39 Widowed.	15 to 39 Civil condition not stated.
B.—Professional.—(Concluded.)	5. Priests.—(Concluded.)	Dásari	Hindu.	245	18	201	26	...
		Lingáyet ...	,,	12,455	630	10,084	1,741	...
		Tírt'hankara	Jain.	478	12	387	79	...
		Pitámbara	,,	...	...	...	...	...
		Sátáni	Hindu.	3,714	73	3,013	628	...
		Total Group 5		*50,312*	*733*	*40,589*	*8,990*	...
	6. Devotees.	Bairági	,,	51	16	32	3	...
		Báváji	Jain.	...	...	...	...	...
		Digambara	,,	1,002	41	755	205	...
		Gósáyi	Hindu.	62	9	45	8	...
		Sanyási	,,	131	3	111	17	...
		S'vétámbara	Jain.	3	...	3	...	...
		Lingáyet—Vader	Hindu.	210	17	153	40	
		Total Group 6		*1,459*	*89*	*1,099*	*271*	...
	7. Temple Servants.	Brámhan.—Páncharátra	,,	27	...	24	3	...
		Brámhan.—Sivadvija	,,	136	...	106	30	...
		Brámhan.—Tamballa	,,	...	...	...	...	...
		Brámhan.—Vaikhánasa	,,	87	...	74	13	...
		Total Group 7		*250*	...	*204*	*46*	...
	9. Writers.	Kaṇakkan	,,		...	...	...	...
		Káyast'ha	,,	...	...	...	...	...
		Total Group 9		...	...	...	...	...
	11. Musicians and Ballad-reciters.	Bhaṭ Ráju	,,	277	16	210	42	...
	12. Dancers & Singers.	Naṭuva	,,	2,484	1,602	862	20	...
	12. (a) Chittári, &c.	Ráchévár—Chitragára	,,	981	29	833	119	...
		Total Class B		**55,763**	**2,469**	**43,806**	**9,488**	...
C.—Commercial.—(Continued.)	14. Traders.	Baṇiya	Hindu.	...	...	...	...	...
		Do.	Jain.	...	...	...	...	...
		Baṇajiga	Hindu.	21,687	1,162	17,047	3,478	...
		Guzaráti	,,	10	2	7	1	...
		Ját	,,	...	...	...	...	...
		Kómaṭi	,,	5,159	4	4,160	995	...
		Lingáyet	,,	57,360	3,514	45,038	8,808	...
		Láder	,,	370	4	288	78	...
		Muduli	,,	961	60	790	111	...

TABLE E.—(Continued.)

cial.

Females.

40 and over.					Age not stated.				
Total.	Single.	Married.	Widowed.	Civil condition not stated.	Total.	Single.	Married.	Widowed.	Civil condition not stated.
144	1	63	77	...	...	...	...	...	...
6,572	40	2,340	4,192	...	...	...	...	...	...
312	1	81	230	...	...	...	...	...	...
...	...	...	...	...	...	...	...	...	...
2,467	4	942	1,521	...	...	...	...	...	...
31,498	*46*	*10,806*	*20,646*	...	...	...	...	...	...
32	1	14	17	...	...	...	...	...	...
...	...	...	...	...	...	...	...	...	...
678	7	176	495	...	...	...	...	...	...
57	3	19	35	...	...	...	...	...	...
66	...	31	35	...	...	...	...	...	...
2	...	...	2	...	...	...	...	...	...
129	...	46	83	...	...	...	...	...	...
964	*11*	*286*	*667*	...	...	...	...	...	...
17	...	7	10	...	...	...	...	...	...
85	...	24	61	...	...	...	...	...	...
...	...	...	...	...	...	...	...	...	...
45	...	13	32	...	...	...	...	...	...
147	...	*44*	*103*	...	...	...	...	...	...
...	...	...	...	...	...	...	...	...	...
...	...	...	...	...	...	...	...	...	...
...	...	...	...	...	...	...	...	...	...
166	...	65	101	...	...	...	...	...	...
569	241	252	76	...	...	...	...	...	...
451	2	181	268	...	...	...	...	...	...
33,795	**300**	**11,634**	**21,861**	...	...	...	...	...	...
...	...	...	...	...	...	...	...	...	...
...	...	...	...	...	...	...	...	...	...
12,762	280	4,324	8,158	...	...	...	...	...	...
3	...	2	1	...	...	...	...	...	...
...	...	...	...	...	...	...	...	...	...
3,294	...	1,175	2,119	...	...	...	...	...	...
31,808	265	10,076	21,467	...	...	...	...	...	...
263	...	106	157	...	...	...	...	...	...
624	2	290	332	...	...	...	...	...	...

Class.	Group.	Caste, &c. and sub-division.	Religion.	All Ages. Total.	Single.	Married.	Widowed.	Civil condition not stated.
B.—Professional.—(Concluded.)	5. Priests.—(Concluded.)	Dásari	Hindu.	91	37	40	14	...
		Lingáyet	,,	2,656	1,394	1,071	191	...
		Tírt'hankara	Jain.	173	82	78	13	...
		Pítámbara	,,	1	...	...	1	...
		Sátáni	Hindu.	1,768	866	753	144	
		Total Group 5	....	*19,273*	*9,569*	*8,258*	*1,446*	...
	6. Devotees.	Bairágí	,,	43	21	21	1	...
		Báváji	Jain.	...	...	...	...	...
		Digambara	,,	39	18	16	5	...
		Gósáyi	Hindu.	37	28	7	2	...
		Sanyási	,,	34	21	9	4	...
		S'vétámbara	Jain.	7	5	1	1	...
		Lingáyet—Vader	Hindu.	24	15	7	2	...
		Total Group 6	....	*184*	*108*	*61*	*15*	...
	7. Temple Servants.	Bráhman.—Páncharátráí	,,	43	20	20	3	...
		Bráhman.—Sivadvija	,,	67	25	32	10	...
		Bráhman.—Tamballa		...	...	...	...	...
		Bráhman.—Vaikhánasa	,,	26	14	9	3	...
		Total Group 7	....	*136*	*59*	*61*	*16*	
	9. Writers.	Kanakkan	,,	...	...	..	...	...
		Káyast'ha	,,	...	..	...	...	...
		Total Group 9	....	..	...		..	...
	11. Musicians and ballad reciters	Bhat Ráju	,,	255	136	102	17	...
	12. Dancers & Singers	Natuva	,,	107	68	36	3	...
	12. (a) Chitári, &c.	Rácbévár—Chitragára	,,	59	29	24	6	...
		Total Class B	....	**20,014**	**9,969**	**8,542**	**1,503**	...
C.—Commercial.—(Continued.)	14. Traders.	Baniya	Hindu.	...	...	...	...	...
		Do.	Jain	...	...	...	...	...
		Baṇajiga	Hindu.	9,753	5,389	4,024	340	...
		Guzaráti	,,	3	2	1	...	...
		Ját	,,	...	...	...	...	...
		Kómaṭi	,,	2,455	1,167	1,110	178	...
		Lingáyet	,,	9,373	4,850	3,846	682	...
		Láḍar	,,	36	17	15	4	...
		Mudali	,,	835	429	333	73	...

TABLE E.—(Continued.)

District.

Males.

0 to 9.					10 to 14.				
Total.	Single.	Married.	Widowed.	Civil condition not stated.	Total.	Single.	Married.	Widowed.	Civil condition not stated.
19	19	...	...	...	8	8	...	...	...
782	782	...	...	...	259	241	18	...	...
40	10	...	...	...	10	10	...	...	...
...	...	...	...	...	...	...	...	...	...
445	415	...	...	...	143	140	3	...	...
5,108	*5,085*	*23*	...	...	*1,905*	*1,731*	*173*	*1*	...
7	7	...	...	...	5	4	1	...	...
...	...	...	...	...	...	...	...	...	...
8	8	...	...	...	4	4	...	...	...
2	2	...	...	...	2	2	...	...	...
3	3	...	...	...	2	2	...	...	...
2	2	...	...	...	1	1	...	...	...
9	9	...	...	...	4	4	...	...	...
31	*31*	...	...	...	*18*	*17*	*1*	...	...
11	11	...	...	...	7	6	1	...	...
14	14	...	...	...	8	8	...	...	...
...	...	...	...	...	...	...	...	...	...
8	8	...	...	...	2	2	...	...	...
33	*33*	...	...	...	*17*	*16*	*1*	...	...
...	...	...	...	...	...	...	...	...	...
...	...	...	...	...	...	...	...	...	...
...	...	...	...	...	...	...	...	...	...
60	60	...	...	...	20	19	1	...	...
26	26	...	...	...	8	8	...	...	...
12	12	...	...	...	6	6	...	...	...
5,27[illegible]	**5,247**	**23**	...	...	**1,974**	**1,787**	**176**	**1**	...
...	...	...	...	...	...	...	...	...	...
...	...	...	...	...	...	...	...	...	...
2,270	2,270	...	...	...	1,250	1,246	4	...	...
...	...	...	...	...	...	...	...	...	...
...	...	...	...	...	...	...	...	...	...
673	672	1	...	...	278	264	14	...	...
2,473	2,473	...	...	...	786	760	26	...	...
4	4	...	...	...	2	2	...	...	...
208	208	...	...	...	102	101	1	...	...

Bangalore

Class.	Group.	Caste, &c. and sub-division.	Religion.	15 to 39. Total.	Single.	Married.	Widowed.	Civil condition not stated.
B.—Professional.—(Concluded.)	5. Priests.—(Concluded.)	Dásari	Hindu.	35	10	19	6	...
		Lingáyet	,,	991	347	614	30	...
		Tírt'hankara	Jain.	80	30	48	2	...
		Pítámbara	,,	...	...	...	...	...
		Sátáni	Hindu.	722	2[illegible]4	425	33	...
		Total Group 5	....	*7,734*	*2,574*	*4,871*	*289*	...
	6. Devotees.	Bairági	,,	20	8	12	...	...
		Báváji	Jain.	...	...	...	...	...
		Digambara	,,	18	6	11	1	...
		Gósáyi	Hindu.	16	9	7	...	...
		Sanyási	,,	12	7	4	1	...
		S'vétámbara	Jain.	3	2	1	...	...
		Lingáyet—Vadér	Hindu.	7	2	5	...	...
		Total Group 6	....	*76*	*34*	*40*	*2*	...
	7. Temple Servants.	Bráhman.—Páncharátra	,,	15	3	11	1	...
		Bráhman.—Sivadvija	,,	23	3	20	...	...
		Bráhman.—Tambaḷḷa	,,	...	...	...	...	...
		Bráhman.—Vaikánasa	,,	13	4	7	1	...
		Total Group 7	....	*50*	*10*	*38*	*2*	...
	9. Writers.	Kaṇakkan	,,	...	...	...	...	...
		Káyast'ha	,,	...	...	...	...	...
		Total Group 9	....	...	...	...	...	...
	11. Musicians and ballad-reciters	Bhaṭ Ráju	,,	119	55	60	4	...
	12. Dancers & Singers	Naṭuva	,,	53	29	23	1	...
	12. (a) Chitári, &c.	Ráchévár—Chitragára	,,	28	11	15	2	...
		Total Class B	....	**8,060**	**2,713**	**5,047**	**300**	...
C.—Commercial.—(Continued.)	14. Traders.	Baniya	Hindu	...	...	...	...	...
		Do	Jain	...	...	...	...	...
		Baṇajiga	Hindu	4,279	1,793	2,419	67	...
		Guzaráti	,,	3	2	1	...	...
		Ját	,,	...	...	...	...	...
		Kómaṭi	,,	871	207	639	25	...
		Lingáyet	,,	3,902	1,502	2,271	129	...
		Láḍar	,,	19	11	7	1	...
		Mudali	,,	339	115	213	11	...

TABLE E.—*(Continued.)*

District.

Males.

40 and over.					Age not stated.				
Total.	Single.	Married.	Widowed.	Civil condition not stated.	Total.	Single.	Married.	Widowed.	Civil condition not stated.
29	...	21	8	...	...	...	...	...	...
624	24	439	161	...	...	...	...	...	...
43	2	30	11	...	...	...	...	...	...
1	...	...	1	...	...	...	...	...	...
458	17	330	111	...	...	...	...	...	...
4,526	*179*	*3,191*	*1,156*	...	...	...	...	...	...
11	2	8	1	...	...	...	...	...	...
...	...	...	...	...	...	...	...	...	...
9	...	5	4	...	...	...	...	...	...
17	15	...	2	...	...	...	...	...	...
17	9	5	3	...	...	...	...	...	...
1	...	...	1	...	...	...	...	...	...
4	...	2	2	...	...	...	...	...	...
59	*26*	*20*	*13*	...	...	...	...	...	...
10	...	8	2	...	...	...	...	...	...
22	...	12	10	...	...	...	...	...	...
...	...	...	...	...	...	...	...	...	...
4	...	2	2	...	...	...	...	...	...
36	...	*22*	*14*	...	...	...	...	...	...
...	...	...	...	...	...	...	...	...	...
...	...	...	...	...	...	...	...	...	...
...	...	...	...	...	...	...	...	...	...
54	2	41	13	...	...	...	...	...	...
20	5	13	2	...	...	...	...	...	...
13	...	9	4	...	...	...	...	...	...
4,710	**212**	**3,296**	**1,202**	...	...	...	...	...	...
...	...	...	...	...	...	...	...	...	...
...	...	...	...	...	...	...	...	...	...
1,954	80	1,601	273	...	...	...	...	...	...
...	...	...	...	...	...	...	...	...	...
...	...	...	...	...	...	...	...	...	...
633	24	456	153	...	...	...	...	...	...
2,217	115	1,549	553	...	...	...	...	...	...
11	...	8	3	...	...	...	...	...	...
186	5	119	62	...	...	...	...	...	...

Bangalore

Class.	Group.	Caste, &c. and sub-division.	Religion.	All Ages. Total.	Single.	Married.	Widowed.	Civil condition not stated.
B.—Professional.—(Concluded.)	5. Priests.—(Concluded.)	Dásari	Hindu.	67	22	35	10	...
		Lingáyat	,,	2,711	1,011	1,101	596	...
		Tirt'hankára	Jain.	163	53	70	40	...
		Pitámbara	,,	...	...	...	...	...
		Sátáni	Hindu.	1,746	503	797	446	...
		Total Group 5	....	18,552	5,701	8,404	4,447	...
	6. Devotees.	Bairági	,,	67	32	23	12	...
		Báváji	Jain.	...	...	...	...	...
		Digambara	,,	49	12	20	17	...
		Gósáyi	Hindu.	14	1	7	6	...
		Sanyási	,,	18	7	8	3	...
		S'vétámbara	Jain.	...	...	...	...	...
		Lingáyat—Vadér	Hindu.	22	10	9	3	...
		Total Group 6	....	170	62	67	41	...
	7. Temple Servants.	Bráhman.—Páncharátral	,,	52	16	27	9	...
		Bráhman.—Sivadvija	,,	66	11	36	16	...
		Bráhman.—Tamballa	,,	...	...	...	...	...
		Bráhman.—Vaikhánasa	,,	24	5	13	6	...
		Total Group 7	....	142	35	76	31	...
	9. Writers.	Kanakkan	,,	...	...	...	...	...
		Káyast'ha	,,	...	...	...	...	...
		Total Group 9	....	...	...	...	...	...
	11. Musicians and ballad-reciters	Bhat Ráju	,,	212	60	94	58	...
	12. Dancers & Singers	Natuva	,,	194	158	29	7	...
	12. (a) Chitári, &c.	Ráchévár—Chitragára	,,	65	27	24	14	...
		Total Class B	....	**19,335**	**6,043**	**8,694**	**4,598**	...
C.—Commercial.—(Continued).	14. Traders.	Baniya	Hindu.	...	...	...	...	...
		Do	Jain.	...	...	...	...	...
		Banajiga	Hindu.	10,342	3,518	4,780	2,044	...
		Guzaráti	,,	3	2	1	...	...
		Ját	,,	...	...	...	...	...
		Kómati	,,	2,257	754	977	526	...
		Lingáyat	,,	9,326	3,299	3,905	2,122	...
		Ládar	,,	17	3	10	4	...
		Mudali	,,	764	248	357	159	...

TABLE E.—(Continued.)

District.

Females.

0 to 9					10 to 14				
Total.	Single.	Married.	Widowed.	Civil condition not stated.	Total.	Single.	Married.	Widowed.	Civil condition not stated.
16	16	...	...	...	6	4	2	...	...
823	810	13	...	...	258	160	98	...	...
43	43	...	...	...	12	10	2	...	...
...	...	...	...	...	...	...	...	...	...
442	419	23	...	...	151	69	82	...	...
5,149	*4,903*	*243*	*3*	...	*1,015*	*737*	*1,129*	*49*	...
17	17	...	...	...	7	7	...	...	...
...	...	...	...	...	...	...	...	...	...
11	11	...	...	...	2	1	1	...	...
1	1	...	...	...	...	...	...	...	...
3	3	...	...	...	3	3	...	...	...
...	...	...	...	...	...	...	...	...	...
7	7	...	...	...	4	3	1	...	...
39	*39*	...	...	...	*16*	*14*	*2*	...	...
17	14	3	...	...	8	2	5	1	...
15	14	1	...	...	1	...	1	...	...
...	...	...	...	...	...	...	...	...	...
5	4	1	...	...	3	1	2	...	...
37	*32*	*5*	...	...	*12*	*3*	*8*	*1*	...
...	...	...	...	...	...	...	...	...	...
...	...	...	...	...	...	...	...	...	...
...	...	...	...	...	...	...	...	...	...
40	40	...	...	...	29	16	13	...	...
45	45	...	...	...	21	21	...	...	...
18	18	...	...	...	9	7	2	...	...
5,328	**5,077**	**248**	**3**	...	**2,002**	**798**	**1,154**	**50**	...
...	...	...	...	...	...	...	...	...	...
...	...	...	...	...	...	...	...	...	...
2,922	2,780	140	2	...	903	573	323	6	...
1	1	...	...	...	1	1	...	...	...
...	...	...	...	...	...	...	...	...	...
687	657	30	...	...	233	97	130	6	...
2,701	3,656	45	...	...	827	492	335	...	...
2	2	...	...	...	1	1	...	...	...
160	162	4	...	...	70	53	17	...	...

Bangalore

Class.	Group.	Caste, &c. and sub-division.	Religion.	15 to 39. Total.	Single.	Married.	Widowed.	Civil condition not stated
B.—Professional.—(Concluded.)	5. Priests.—(Concluded.)	Dámri	Hindu.	26	2	24	...	...
		Lingáyet	,,	929	40	743	146	...
		Tirt'hankara	Jain.	70	...	60	10	...
		Pitámbara	,,	...	...	...	...	...
		Sátáni	Hindu.	674	15	538	121	...
		Total Group 5	....	*6,735*	*57*	*5,410*	*1,268*	...
	6. Devotees.	Bairági	,,	24	8	14	2	...
		Báváji	Jain.	...	...	...	...	...
		Digambara	,,	18	...	15	3	...
		Gósáyi	Hindu.	5	...	5	...	...
		Sanyási	,,	6	1	4	1	...
		S'vétámbara	Jain.	...	...	...	...	...
		Lingáyet—Vadér	Hindu.	7	...	6	1	...
		Total Group 6	....	*60*	*9*	*44*	*7*	...
	7. Temple Servants.	Brámhan. Páncharátra	,,	16	...	14	2	...
		Brámhan. Sivadvija	,,	31	...	29	5	...
		Brámhan. Tambalia	,,	...	...	...	...	...
		Brámhan. Vaikhánasa	,,	10	...	9	1	...
		Total Group 7	....	*60*	...	*52*	*8*	...
	9. Writers.	Kaṇakkan	,,	...	...	...	...	...
		Káyast'ha	,,	...	...	...	...	...
		Total Group 9	....	...	...	...	...	...
	11. Musicians and ballad-reciters	Bhaṭ Ráju	,,	88	4	68	16	...
	12. Dancers & Singers	Naṭuva	,,	94	72	22	...	...
	12. (a) Chitári, &c.	Ráchérár—Chitragára	,,	23	2	18	2	...
		Total Class B	....	**7,059**	**144**	**5,614**	**1,301**	...
C.—Commercial.—(Continued.)	14. Traders.	Baniya	Hindu.	...	...	...	...	...
		Do	Jain	...	...	...	...	...
		Baṇajiga	Hindu	4,073	130	3,315	628	...
		Guzaráti	,,	1	...	1	...	...
		Ját	,,	...	...	...	...	...
		Kómaṭi	,,	796	...	654	142	...
		Lingáyet	,,	3,375	135	2,669	571	...
		Láḍar	,,	8	...	8	...	...
		Mudali	,,	308	33	249	26	...

TABLE E.—(*Continued.*)

District.

Females.

40 and over.					Age not stated.				
Total.	Single.	Married.	Widowed.	Civil condition not stated.	Total.	Single.	Married.	Widowed.	Civil condition not stated.
19	...	9	10	...	...	...	...	...	...
701	4	247	450	...	...	...	...	...	...
38	...	8	30	...	...	...	...	...	...
...	...	...	...	...	...	...	...	...	...
479	...	154	325	...	...	...	...	...	...
4,753	*4*	*1,622*	*3,127*	...	...	...	...	...	...
19	...	9	10	...	...	...	...	...	...
...	...	...	...	...	...	...	...	...	...
18	...	4	14	...	...	...	...	...	...
8	...	2	6	...	...	...	...	...	...
6	...	4	2	...	...	...	...	...	...
...	...	...	...	...	...	...	...	...	...
4	...	2	2	...	...	...	...	...	...
55	...	*21*	*34*	...	...	...	...	...	...
11	...	5	6	...	...	...	...	...	...
16	...	5	11	...	...	...	...	...	...
...	...	...	...	...	...	...	...	...	...
6	...	1	5	...	...	...	...	...	...
33	...	*11*	*22*	...	...	...	...	...	...
...	...	...	...	...	...	...	...	...	...
...	...	...	...	...	...	...	...	...	...
...	...	...	...	...	...	...	...	...	...
55	...	13	42	...	...	...	...	...	...
34	20	7	7	...	...	...	...	...	...
16	...	4	12	...	...	...	...	...	...
4,946	**24**	**1,673**	**3,244**	...	...	...	...	...	...
...	...	...	...	...	...	...	...	...	...
...	...	...	...	...	...	...	...	...	...
2,445	35	1,002	1,408	...	...	...	...	...	...
...	...	...	...	...	...	...	...	...	...
...	...	...	...	...	...	...	...	...	...
541	...	163	378	...	...	...	...	...	...
2,423	16	856	1,551	...	...	...	...	...	...
6	...	2	4	...	...	...	...	...	...
220	...	87	133	...	...	...	...	...	...

Class.	Group.	Caste, &c. and sub-division.	Religion.	All Ages. Total.	All Ages. Single.	All Ages. Married.	All Ages. Widowed.	Civil condition not stated.
B.—Professional—(Concluded.)	5. Priests.—(Concluded.)	Dâsari	Hindu.	80	41	34	5	...
		Lingâyet	"	1,678	812	737	129	...
		Tirt'hankara	Jain.	157	89	55	13	
		Pitâmbara	...	...	...	...	...	
		Sâtani	Hindu	962	453	413	96	
		Total Group 5 ...	......	[illegible]	[illegible]	[illegible]	[illegible]	...
	6. Devotees.	Bairâgi	...	7	3	3	1	
		Bâvâji	Jain.	...	...	...	...	...
		Digambara ...	"	304	164	110	30	...
		Gôsâyi	Hindu.	17	5	9	3	
		Sanyâsi	"	209	107	75	18	
		S'vêtâmbara ...	Jain.	...	...	...	...	
		Lingâyet—Vader ...	Hindu.	...	...	...	...	...
		Total Group 6 ...	... .	[illegible]	[illegible]	[illegible]	52	...
	7. Temple Servants.	Brâhman. Pâncharâtrâ ...	"	8	2	5	1	...
		Brâhman. Sivadvija ...	"	159	72	67	20	...
		Brâhman. Tamballa ...	"	...	...	...	...	...
		Brâhman. Vaikhânasa ...	"	131	59	56	16	...
		Total Group 7 ...	... ...	298	133	128	37	...
	9. Writers.	Kanakkan ...	"	...	...	...	...	...
		Kâyast'ha ...	"	...	...	...	...	...
		Total Group 9 ...	......	...	...	...	...	...
	11. Musicians and ballad-reciters ...	Bhat Râju ...	"	196	108	75	13	...
	12. Dancers & Singers ...	Natuva	"	340	194	116	30	...
	12. (a) Chitâri, &c.	Râchêvâr—Chitragâra	"	29	13	13	3	...
		Total Class B ...	....	15,961	7,720	6,887	1,354	...
C.—Commercial.—(Continued.)	14. Traders.	Baniyâ	Hindu.	...	...	...	...	...
		Do	Jain.	...	...	...	...	...
		Banajiga ...	Hindu.	18,190	9,278	7,791	1,121	...
		Guzarâti	...	...	...	...	...	...
		Jât	—	...	...	...	...	...
		Kômati	"	4,571	2,239	1,968	364	...
		Lingâyat	"	3,138	1,599	1,293	246	...
		Mârvâr	"	8	4	3	1	...
		Mudali	"	430	238	173	19	...

TABLE E.—(*Continued.*)

District.

Males.

Total	Single	Married	Widowed	Civil condition not stated	10 to 14 Total	Single	Married	Widowed	Civil condition not stated
26	26	...	...	...	8	8	...	...	...
355	355	...	...	...	151	145	6	...	...
43	43	...	...	...	5	3	2	...	...
...		...	...	...	...	...	...	...	...
249	239	..	...	...	64	62	2	...	...
3,613	*3,613*	...	...	...	*1,165*	*1,102*	*63*	...	...
2	2	...	...	...	...	...	...	...	...
	...	...	...	...	...	...	...	...	...
66	65	1	...	...	36	34	2	...	...
1	1	...	...	...	1	1	...	...	...
63	63	...	...	...	15	15	...	...	...
	...	...	...	...	...	...	...	...	...
	...	...	...	...	...	...	...	...	...
132	*131*	*1*	...	...	*52*	*50*	*2*	...	...
1	1	...	...	...	...	...	...	...	...
32	32	...	...	...	16	14	2	...	...
...	...	...	...	...	...	...	...	...	...
29	29	...	...	...	12	11	1	...	...
62	*62*	...	...	...	*28*	*25*	*3*	...	...
...	...	...	...	...	...	...	...	...	...
...	...	...	...	...	...	...	...	...	...
...	...	...	...	...	...	...	...	...	...
45	45	...	...	...	20	20	...	...	...
110	110	...	...	...	26	26	...	...	...
7	7	...	...	...	2	2	...	...	...
3,969	**3,968**	**1**	...	...	**1,293**	**1,225**	**68**	...	...
...	...	...	...	...	...	...	...	...	...
...	...	...	...	...	...	...	...	...	...
4,458	4,458	...	...	...	1,454	1,443	11	...	...
...	...	...	...	...	...	...	...	...	...
...	...	...	...	...	...	...	...	...	...
1,125	1,125	...	...	...	409	391	18	...	...
738	738	...	...	...	240	235	5	...	...
3	3	...	...	...	1	1	...	...	...
86	86	...	...	...	35	35	..	...	...

Class.	Group.	Caste, &c. and sub-division.	Religion.	15 to 39 Total.	Single.	Married.	Widowed.	Civil condition not stated.
B.—Professional.—(Concluded.)	5. Priests.—(Concluded.)	Dásari	Hindu.	27	7	20	...	...
		Lingáyet	,,	680	284	370	26	...
		Tirt'hankára	Jain.	70	40	29	1	...
		Pitámbara	,,	...	...	...	...	...
		Sátáni	Hindu.	404	143	245	16	...
		Total Group 5	....	*6,044*	*2,047*	*3,721*	*276*	...
	6. Devotees.	Bairági	,,	3	1	2	...	...
		Báváji	Jain.	...	...	...	...	...
		Digambara	,,	113	53	53	7	...
		Gosáyi	Hindu.	6	2	4	...	...
		Sanyási	,,	77	25	47	5	...
		S'vétámbara	Jain.	...	...	...	...	...
		Lingáyet—Vadér	Hindu.	...	...	...	...	...
		Total Group 6	....	*199*	*81*	*106*	*12*	...
	7. Temple Servants.	Bráhman.—Pánchárátra	,,	5	1	4	...	...
		Bráhman.—Sivadvija	,,	70	22	42	6	...
		Bráhman.—Tambalia	,,	...	...	...	...	...
		Bráhman.—Vaikhánasa	,,	61	19	38	4	...
		Total Group 7	....	*136*	*42*	*84*	*10*	...
	9. Writers.	Kanakkan	,,	...	...	...	...	...
		Káyast'ha	,,	...	...	...	...	...
		Total Group 9	....	...	...	...	...	...
	11. Musicians and ballad-reciters	Bhat Ráju	,,	87	40	46	1	...
	12. Dancers & Singers	Naṭuva	,,	132	47	77	8	...
	12. (a) Chitári, &c.	Ráchévár—Chitragára	,,	12	3	9	...	...
		Total Class B.	....	**6,610**	**2,260**	**4,043**	**307**	...
C.—Commercial.—(Contd.)	14. Traders.	Baniya	Hindu.	[illegible]	...	...	...	...
		Do.	Jain.	...	...	...	...	...
		Banajiga	Hindu.	7,588	3,139	4,238	211	...
		Guzaráti	,,	...	...	...	...	...
		Ját	,,	...	...	...	...	...
		Kómati	,,	1,889	665	1,154	70	...
		Lingáyet	,,	1,312	571	692	49	...
		Ládar	,,	1	...	1	...	...
		Mudali	,,	220	111	103	6	...

TABLE E.—(*Continued.*)

District.

Males.

40 and over.					Age not stated.				
Total.	Single.	Married.	Widowed.	Civil condition not stated.	Total.	Single.	Married.	Widowed.	Civil condition not stated.
19	...	14	5	...	...	...	...	...	...
492	28	361	103	...	...	...	...	...	...
39	3	24	12	...	...	...	...	...	...
...	...	...	...	...	...	...	...	...	...
255	9	166	80	...	...	...	...	...	...
3,748	*231*	*2,574*	*943*	...	...	...	...	...	...
2	...	1	1	...	...	...	...	...	...
...	...	...	...	...	...	...	...	...	...
85	12	54	19	...	4	...	...	4	...
9	1	5	3	...	...	...	...	...	...
45	4	28	13	...	...	...	...	...	...
...	...	...	...	...	...	...	...	...	...
...	...	...	...	...	...	...	...	...	...
141	*17*	*88*	*36*	...	*4*	...	...	*4*	...
2	...	1	1	...	...	...	...	...	...
41	4	23	14	...	...	...	...	...	...
...	...	...	...	...	...	...	...	...	...
29	...	17	12	...	...	...	...	...	...
72	*4*	*41*	*27*	...	...	...	...	...	...
...	...	...	...	...	...	...	...	...	...
...	...	...	...	...	...	...	...	...	...
...	...	...	...	...	...	...	...	...	...
44	3	29	12	...	...	...	...	...	...
72	11	39	23	...	...	...	...	...	...
8	1	4	3	...	...	...	...	...	...
4,085	**267**	**2,775**	**1,043**	...	**4**	...	...	**4**	...
...	...	...	...	...	...	...	...	...	...
...	...	...	...	...	...	...	...	...	...
4,690	238	3,542	910	...	...	...	...	...	...
...	...	...	...	...	...	...	...	...	...
...	...	...	...	...	...	...	...	...	...
1,148	58	796	294	...	...	...	...	...	...
848	55	596	197	...	...	...	...	...	...
3	...	2	1	...	...	...	...	...	...
89	6	70	13	...	...	...	...	...	...

Kolar

Class.	Group.	Caste, &c. and sub-division.	Religion.	All Ages. Total.	Single.	Married.	Widowed.	Civil condition not stated.
B.—Professional.—(Concluded.)	5. Priests.—(Concluded.)	Dâsari	Hindu.	85	30	43	12	...
		Lingâyet	..	1,669	501	744	424	...
		Tîrt'hankara	Jain.	75	19	18	38	...
		Pîtâmbara	..	...	...	...	...	...
		Sâtâni	Hindu.	675	229	172	274	...
		Total Group 5......	....	14,406	3,703	6,857	3,846	...
	6. Devotees.	Bairâgi	..	6	2	3	1	...
		Bâvâji	Jain.	...	...	...	...	...
		Digambara	..	280	78	122	80	...
		Gôsayi	Hindu.	22	5	13	4	...
		Sanyâsi	..	212	83	93	36	...
		S'vêtâmbara	Jain.	...	...	...	...	...
		Lingâyet Vader	Hindu.	...	...	...	...	...
		Total Group 6......	....	520	168	231	121	...
	7. Temple Servants.	Brâhman.—Pâñcharâtra ...	..	7	...	4	3	...
		Brâhman.—Sivadvija ...	..	163	31	74	58	...
		Brâhman.—Tamballa ...	..	...	...	...	...	...
		Brâhman.—Vaikhânasa ...	..	137	36	69	32	...
		Total Group 7......	....	307	67	147	93	...
	9. Writers.	Kaṇakkan	..	...	...	...	...	...
		Kâyast'ha	..	...	...	...	...	...
		Total Group 9......	....	...	...	...	...	...
	11. Musicians and ballad-reciters ...	Bhaṭ Râju	..	192	60	92	40	...
	12. Dancers & Singers...	Naṭuva	..	428	302	89	37	...
	12. (a) Chitâri, &c.	Râchêvâr—Chitragâra ...	..	35	18	14	3	...
		Total Class B......	....	**15,978**	**4,408**	**7,430**	**4,140**	...
C.—Commercial.—(Continued.)	14. Traders.	Baniya	Hindu.	...	...	...	...	...
		Do.	Jain.	...	...	...	...	...
		Baṇajiga	Hindu.	18,106	5,634	8,010	4,462	...
		Guzarâti	..	...	...	...	...	...
		Jât	..	...	...	...	...	...
		Kômaṭi	..	4,319	1,216	2,049	1,054	...
		Lingâyet	..	3,001	889	1,284	828	...
		Lâḍar	..	10	3	6	1	...
		Mudali	..	284	93	141	50	...

TABLE E.—(*Continued.*)

District.

Females.

0 to 9					10 to 14				
Total.	Single.	Married.	Widowed.	Civil condition not stated.	Total.	Single.	Married.	Widowed.	Civil condition not stated.
24	24	...	...	...	11	4	7	...	...
421	415	6	...	...	140	70	70	...	...
40	40	...	...	...	13	9	4	...	...
...	...	...	...	...	...	...	...	...	...
211	202	9	...	...	69	14	55	...	...
3,648	*3,407*	*240*	*1*	...	*1,316*	*355*	*934*	*27*	...
2	2	...	...	...	...	...	...	...	...
...	...	...	...	...	...	...	...	...	...
67	63	4	...	...	20	13	7	1	...
2	2	...	...	...	3	3	...	...	...
69	69	...	...	...	14	12	2	...	...
...	...	...	...	...	...	...	...	...	...
...	...	...	...	...	...	...	...	...	...
140	*136*	*4*	...	...	*37*	*27*	*9*	*1*	...
...	...	...	...	...	...	...	...	...	...
27	22	5	...	...	16	9	7	...	...
...	...	...	...	...	...	...	...	...	...
35	33	2	...	...	12	3	9	...	...
62	*55*	*7*	...	...	*28*	*12*	*16*	...	...
...	...	...	...	...	...	...	...	...	...
...	...	...	...	...	...	...	...	...	...
...	...	...	...	...	...	...	...	...	...
42	42	...	...	...	20	15	5	...	...
110	110	...	...	...	31	29	2	...	...
14	14	...	...	...	3	3	...	...	...
4,016	**3,764**	**251**	**1**	...	**1,435**	**441**	**966**	**28**	...
...	...	...	...	...	...	...	...	...	...
...	...	...	...	...	...	...	...	...	...
4,579	4,530	49	...	...	1,218	742	476	...	...
...	...	...	...	...	...	...	...	...	...
...	...	...	...	...	...	...	...	...	...
1,209	1,140	69	...	...	421	76	335	10	...
736	722	14	...	...	228	124	104	...	...
2	2	...	...	...	1	1	...	...	...
71	71	...	...	...	26	16	10	...	...

Kolar

Class.	Group.	Caste, &c., and sub-division.	Religion.	15 to 39 Total.	Single.	Married.	Widowed.	Civil condition not stated.
B.—Professional.—(Concluded.)	5. Priests.—(Concluded.)	Dásari ...	Hindu.	31	2	27	2	...
		Lingáyet ...	,,	658	14	542	102	...
		Tirt'hankara ...	Jain.	50	...	41	9	...
		Pithámbara ...	,,	...	...	...	...	...
		Sátáni ...	Hindu.	407	11	324	72	...
		Total Group 5......	....	*5,603*	*27*	*4,451*	*1,125*	...
	6. Devotees.	Bairági ...	,,	3	...	3	..	...
		Bávájí ...	Jain.	...	...	...	...	...
		Digambara ...	,,	117	3	89	25	...
		Gósáyi ...	Hindu.	12	..	11	1	...
		Sanyási ...	,,	82	2	68	12	...
		S'vétámbara ...	Jain.	...	...	...	...	...
		Lingáyet—Vader ...	Hindu.	...	...	...	...	...
		Total Group 6.....	....	*211*	*5*	*171*	*38*	...
	7. Temple Servants.	Bráhman.—Páncharátráf ...	,,	4	...	3	1	...
		Bráhman.—Sivadvija ...	,,	70	...	49	21	...
		Bráhman.—Tambulla ...	,,	..	...	...	...	...
		Bráhman.—Vaikhánasa ...	,,	57	...	47	10	...
		Total Group 7......	....	*131*	...	*99*	*32*	...
	9. Writers.	Kanakkan ...	,,	...	...	...	...	...
		Káyast'ha ...	,,	...	...	...	...	...
		Total Group 9......	....	...	...	...	...	...
	11. Musicians and ballad-reciters ...	Bhaṭ Ráju ...	,,	80	3	67	10	...
	12. Dancers & Singers...	Naṭuva ...	,,	196	116	74	6	...
	12. (a) Chitári, &c...	Rachévár—Chitragára ...	,,	13	...	11	2	...
		Total Class B......	....	**6,237**	**151**	**4,873**	**1,213**	...
C.—Commercial.—(Continued.)	14. Traders.	Baniya ...	Hindu.	...	...	...	...	...
		Do. ...	Jain.	...	...	...	...	...
		Banajiga ...	Hindu.	7,546	280	6,050	1,216	...
		Guzaráti ...	,,	...	...	...	...	...
		Ját ...	,,	...	...	...	...	...
		Kómaṭi ...	,,	1,647	...	1,326	321	...
		Lingáyet ...	,,	1,212	36	944	232	...
		Ládar ...	,,	2	...	2	...	...
		Mudali ...	,,	125	5	106	14	...

TABLE E.—(*Continued.*)

District.

Females.

40 and over.					Age not stated.				
Total.	Single.	Married.	Widowed.	Civil condition not stated.	Total.	Single.	Married.	Widowed.	Civil condition not stated.
19	...	9	10	...	...	...	...	...	...
450	2	126	322	...	...	...	...	...	...
32	...	3	29	...	...	...	...	...	...
...	...	...	...	...	...	...	...	...	...
288	2	84	202	...	...	...	...	...	...
3,929	*4*	*1,232*	*2,693*	...	...	...	...	...	...
1	...	...	1	...	...	...	...	...	...
...	...	...	...	...	...	...	...	...	...
76	...	22	54	...	...	...	...	...	...
5	...	2	3	...	...	...	...	...	...
47	...	23	24	...	...	...	...	...	...
...	...	...	...	...	...	...	...	...	...
...	...	...	...	...	...	...	...	...	...
129	...	*47*	*82*	...	...	...	...	...	...
3	...	1	2	...	...	...	...	...	...
50	...	13	37	...	...	...	...	...	...
...	...	...	...	...	...	...	...	...	...
33	...	11	22	...	...	...	...	...	...
86	...	*25*	*61*	...	...	...	...	...	...
...	...	...	...	...	...	...	...	...	...
...	...	...	...	...	...	...	...	...	...
...	...	...	...	...	...	...	...	...	...
50	...	20	30	...	...	...	...	...	...
91	47	13	31	...	...	...	...	...	...
5	1	3	1	...	...	...	...	...	...
4,290	**52**	**1,340**	**2,898**	...	...	...	...	...	...
...	...	...	...	...	...	...	...	...	...
...	...	...	...	...	...	...	...	...	...
4,763	82	1,435	3,246	...	...	...	...	...	...
...	...	...	...	...	...	...	...	...	...
...	...	...	...	...	...	...	...	...	...
1,042	...	319	723	...	...	...	...	...	...
825	7	222	596	...	...	...	...	...	...
5	...	4	1	...	...	...	...	...	...
62	1	25	36	...	...	...	...	...	...

Class.	Group.	Caste, &c. and sub-division.	Religion.	All Ages. Total.	Single.	Married.	Widowed.	Civil condition not stated.
B.—Professional.—(Concluded.)	5. Priests.—(Concluded.)	Dásari	Hindu.	108	40	63	5	...
		Lingáyet	,,	4,308	2,070	1,908	330	...
		Tirt'hankara	Jain.	233	126	84	23	...
		Pítámbara	,,	...	...	...	...	...
		Sátáni	Hindu.	1,936	998	802	136	...
		Total Group 5	....	*15,155*	*7,066*	*6,844*	*1,245*	...
	6. Devotees.	Bairági	,,	12	9	3	...	...
		Báváji	Jain.	...	...	...	...	...
		Digambara	,,	567	291	232	44	...
		Gosáyi	Hindu.	7	3	4	...	...
		Sanyási	,,	97	46	42	9	...
		S'vétámbara	Jain.	3	1	1	1	...
		Lingáyet—Vadêr	Hindu.	7	4	2	1	...
		Total Group 6	....	*693*	*354*	*284*	*55*	...
	7. Temple Servants.	Bráhman—Páncharátrá]	,,	7	4	3	...	...
		Bráhman—S'ivadvija	,,	37	20	13	4	...
		Bráhman—Tamballa	,,	...	...	...	...	...
		Bráhman—Vaikhánasa	,,	...	...	...	...	...
		Total Group 7	....	*44*	*24*	*16*	*4*	...
	9. Writers.	Kanakkan	,,	...	...	...	...	...
		Káyast'ha	,,	...	...	...	...	...
		Total Group 9	....	...	...	...	...	...
	11. Musicians and ballad-reciters	Bhat Ráju	,,	65	23	34	8	
	12. Dancers & Singers	Natuva	,,	58	22	34	2	...
	12. (a) Chitári, &c.	Ráchévár—Chitragára	,,	132	56	61	15	...
		Total Class B	....	**16,147**	**7,545**	**7,273**	**1,329**	...
C.—Commercial.—(Continued.)	14. Traders.	Baniya	Hindu.	...	...	...	...	...
		Do.	,,	...	...	...	...	...
		Banajiga	,,	6,340	3,044	2,642	654	...
		Guzaráti	,,	...	...	...	...	...
		Ját	,,	...	...	...	...	...
		Kómati	,,	2,891	1,347	1,270	274	...
		Lingáyet	,,	10,781	5,288	4,859	634	...
		Ládar	,,	70	39	23	8	...
		Mudali	,,	207	94	99	14	...

TABLE E.—(*Continued*)

District.

Males.

0 to 9					10 to 14				
Total.	Single.	Married.	Widowed.	Civil condition not stated.	Total.	Single.	Married.	Widowed.	Civil condition not stated.
26	26	...	...	...	3	3	...	...	...
1,223	1,223	...	...	...	242	242	...	...	...
50	50	...	...	...	16	16	...	...	...
...	...	...	...	...	...	...	...	...	...
551	551	...	...	...	235	233	2	...	...
3,956	*3,940*	*16*	...	...	*1,234*	*1,105*	*126*	*3*	...
3	3	...	...	...	1	1	...	...	...
...	...	...	...	...	...	...	...	...	...
113	113	...	...	...	42	41	1	...	...
...	...	...	...	...	...	...	...	...	...
29	29	...	...	...	8	8	...	...	...
...	...	...	...	...	1	1	...	...	...
2	2	...	...	...	...	...	...	...	...
147	*147*	...	...	...	*52*	*51*	*1*	...	...
3	3	...	...	...	1	1	...	...	...
13	13	...	...	...	3	3	...	...	...
...	...	...	...	...	...	...	...	...	...
...	...	...	...	...	...	...	...	...	...
16	*16*	...	...	...	*4*	*4*	...	...	...
...	...	...	...	...	...	...	...	...	...
...	...	...	...	...	...	...	...	...	...
...	...	...	...	...	...	...	...	...	...
12	12	...	...	...	5	5	...	...	...
12	12	...	...	...	6	6	...	...	...
24	24	...	...	...	13	13	...	...	...
4,167	**4,151**	**16**	...	...	**1,314**	**1,184**	**127**	**3**	...
...	...	...	...	...	...	...	...	...	...
...	...	...	...	...	...	...	...	...	...
1,514	1,514	...	...	...	473	456	17	...	...
...	...	...	...	...	...	...	...	...	...
...	...	...	...	...	...	...	...	...	...
641	641	...	...	...	252	230	13	...	...
2,687	2,687	...	...	...	1,323	1,323	...	...	...
14	14	...	...	...	7	7	...	...	...
52	52	...	...	...	21	20	1	...	...

Class.	Group.	Caste, &c. and sub-division.	Religion.	15 to 39 Total.	Single.	Married.	Widowed.	Civil condition not stated.
B.—Professional.—(Concluded.)	5. Priests.—(Concluded.)	Dásari	Hindu.	51	11	41	2	...
		Lingáyet	,,	1,709	542	1,110	57	...
		Tírt'hankara	Jain.	92	51	32	9	...
		Pitámbara	,,	...	...	...	...	...
		Sátáni	Hindu.	680	181	466	33	...
		Total Group 5......	....	*6,236*	*1,784*	*4,119*	*333*	...
	6. Devotees.	Bairági	,,	6	5	1	...	...
		Báváji	Jain.	...	...	...	...	...
		Digambara	,,	240	121	112	7	...
		Gósáyi	Hindu.	5	2	3	...	...
		Sanyási	,,	40	7	31	2	...
		Svétámbara	Jain.	2	...	1	1	...
		Lingáyet—Vader	Hindu.	2	1	1	...	...
		Total Group 6......	....	*295*	*136*	*149*	*10*	...
	7. Temple Servants.	Brámhan—Pancharátra	,,	8	...	3	...	...
		Brámhan—S'ivadvija	,,	14	4	9	1	...
		Brámhan—Tamballa	,,	...	...	...	...	...
		Brámhan—Vaikhánasa	,,	...	...	...	...	...
		Total Group 7......	....	*17*	*4*	*12*	*1*	...
	9. Writers.	Kanakkan	,,	...	...	...	...	...
		Káyast'ha	,,	...	...	...	...	...
		Total Group 9......	....	...	...	...	...	...
	11. Musicians and Ballad reciters	Bhat Ráju	,,	22	3	18	1	...
	12. Dancers & Singers...	Natuva	,,	26	4	22	...	...
	12. (a) Chitári, &c..	Káchévár—Chitragára	,,	58	18	36	4	...
		Total Class B......	....	**6,654**	**1,949**	**4,356**	**349**	...
C.—Commercial.—(Continued.)	14. Traders.	Baniya	Hindu.	...	...	...	...	...
		Do.	Jain.	...	...	...	...	...
		Banajiga	Hindu.	2,747	967	1,636	144	...
		Guzaráti	,,	...	...	...	...	...
		Ját	,,	...	...	...	...	...
		Kómati	,,	1,206	442	781	73	...
		Lingáyet	,,	4,206	1,141	2,966	189	...
		Ládar	,,	35	18	14	3	...
		Mudali	,,	89	21	63	5	...

TABLE E.—(*Continued.*)

District.

Males.

40 and over.					Age not stated.				
Total.	Single.	Married.	Widowed.	Civil condition not stated.	Total.	Single.	Married.	Widowed.	Civil condition not stated.
25	...	22	3	...	...	...	...	...	...
1,134	63	798	273	...	...	...	...	...	...
75	9	52	14	...	...	...	...	...	...
...	...	...	...	...	...	...	...	...	...
470	33	334	103	...	...	...	...	...	...
3,729	*237*	*2,583*	*900*	...	...	...	...	...	...
2	...	2	...	...	...	...	...	...	...
...	...	...	...	...	...	...	...	...	...
172	16	119	37	...	...	...	...	...	...
2	1	1	...	...	...	...	...	...	...
20	2	11	7	...	...	...	...	...	...
...	...	...	...	...	...	...	...	...	...
3	1	1	1	...	...	...	...	...	...
199	*20*	*134*	*45*	...	...	...	...	...	...
...	...	...	...	...	...	...	...	...	...
7	...	4	3	...	...	...	...	...	...
...	...	...	...	...	...	...	...	...	...
...	...	...	...	...	...	...	...	...	...
7	...	*4*	*3*	...	...	...	...	...	...
...	...	...	...	...	...	...	...	...	...
...	...	...	...	...	...	...	...	...	...
...	...	...	...	...	...	...	...	...	...
26	3	16	7	...	...	...	...	...	...
14	...	12	2	...	...	...	...	...	...
37	1	25	11	...	...	...	...	...	...
4,012	**261**	**2,774**	**977**	...	...	...	...	...	...
...	...	...	...	...	...	...	...	...	...
...	...	...	...	...	...	...	...	...	...
1,606	107	989	510	...	...	...	...	...	...
...	...	...	...	...	...	...	...	...	...
...	...	...	...	...	...	...	...	...	...
702	25	476	201	...	...	...	...	...	...
2,475	137	1,893	445	...	...	...	...	...	...
14	...	9	5	...	...	...	...	...	...
45	1	35	9	...	...	...	...	...	...

Tumkur

Class.	Group.	Caste, &c. and sub-division.	Religion.	All Ages. Total.	Single.	Married.	Widowed.	Civil condition not stated.
B.—Professional.—(Concluded.)	5. Priests.—(Concluded.)	Dásari	Hindu.	102	31	57	14	...
		Lingáyet	,,	4,221	1,639	2,053	529	...
		Tírt'hankara	Jain.	174	40	78	56	...
		Pítámbara	,,	...	...	...	...	...
		Sátáni	Hindu.	1,865	667	809	389	...
		Total Group 5	....	14,790	4,630	7,182	2,978	...
	6. Devotees.	Bairági	,,	6	2	3	1	...
		Báváji	Jain.	...	...	...	...	...
		Digambara	,,	548	176	230	142	...
		Gósáyi	Hindu.	3	2	1	...	...
		Sanyási	,,	78	31	39	8	...
		S'vétámbara	Jain.	1	...	...	1	...
		Lingáyet—Vaḍér	Hindu.	8	4	3	1	...
		Total Group 6	....	644	215	276	153	...
	7. Temple Servants.	Brámhaṇ.—Páncharátrál	,,	9	3	5	1	...
		Brámhaṇ.—S'ivadvija	,,	39	5	22	12	...
		Brámhaṇ.—Tamballa	,,	...	...	...		...
		Brámhaṇ.—Vaikhánasa	,,	..	...	...		...
		Total Group 7	....	48	8	27	13	...
	9. Writers.	Kaṇakkan	,,	...	...	...	...	...
		Káyast'ha	,,	...	...	...	...	...
		Total Group 9	... .	...	...	...	...	...
	11. Musicians and Ballad-reciters	Bhaṭ Ráju	,,	69	27	33	9	...
	12. Dancers & Singers	Naṭuva	,,	59	27	29	3	...
	12. (a) Chitári, &c.	Ráchévár—Chitragára		110	39	54	17	...
		Total Class B	....	**15,729**	**4,955**	**7,601**	**3,173**	...
C.—Commercial.—(Continued.)	14. Traders.	Baniya	Hindu.	...	...	...	...	...
		Do.	Jain.	...	...	...	...	...
		Baṇajiga	Hindu.	6,068	1,966	2,638	1,464	...
		Guzaráṭi	,,	...	...	...	...	...
		Jáṭ	,,	...	...	...	...	...
		Kómaṭi	,,	2,413	675	1,153	585	...
		Lingáyet	,,	10,508	3,795	4,181	2,532	...
		Láḍar	,,	64	24	25	15	...
		Mudali	,,	173	76	81	16	...

TABLE E.—(*Continued.*)

District.

Females.

0 to 9					10 to 14				
Total.	Single.	Married.	Widowed.	Civil condition not stated.	Total.	Single.	Married.	Widowed.	Civil condition not stated.
24	24	...	...	...	3	3	...	...	...
1,411	1,408	3	...	...	339	198	141	...	...
40	38	2	...	...	6	2	4	...	...
...	...	...	...	...	...	...	...	...	...
530	515	5	...	...	218	115	103	...	...
4,182	*4,052*	*111*	*19*	...	*1,304*	*543*	*719*	*42*	...
1	1	...	...	...	1	...	1	...	...
...	...	...	...	...	...	...	...	...	...
148	144	4	...	...	32	19	12	1	...
1	1	...	...	...	...	...	...	...	...
24	24	...	...	...	11	7	4	...	...
...	...	...	...	...	...	...	...	...	...
3	3	...	...	...	1	1	...	...	...
177	*173*	*4*	...	...	*45*	*27*	*17*	*1*	...
2	2	...	...	...	1	1	...	...	...
4	4	...	...	...	1	1	...	...	...
...	...	...	...	...	...	...	...	...	...
...	...	...	...	...	...	...	...	...	...
6	*6*	...	...	...	2	2	...	...	...
...	...	...	...	...	...	...	...	...	...
...	...	...	...	...	...	...	...	...	...
...	...	...	...	...	...	...	...	...	...
19	19	...	...	...	3	1	2	...	...
7	7	...	...	...	4	4	...	...	...
30	30	...	...	...	11	8	3	...	...
4,421	**4,287**	**115**	**19**	...	**1,369**	**585**	**741**	**43**	...
...	...	...	...	...	...	...	...	...	...
...	...	...	...	...	...	...	...	...	...
1,524	1,457	65	2	...	470	293	171	7	...
...	...	...	...	...	...	...	...	...	...
...	...	...	...	...	...	...	...	...	...
693	642	51	...	...	163	29	134	...	...
2,682	2,670	12	...	...	1,426	955	460	2	...
21	21	...	...	...	4	2	2	...	...
49	49	...	...	...	26	25	1	...	...

Tumkur

Class.	Group.	Caste, &c. and sub-division.	Religion.	15 to 39 Total.	Single.	Married.	Widowed.	Civil condition not stated.
B.—Professional.—(Concluded).	5. Priests.—(Concluded.)	Dásari	Hindu.	47	3	39	5	...
		Lingáyet	,,	1,730	32	1,535	163	...
		Tírt'hankara	Jain.	63	...	52	11	...
		Pitámbara	,,	...	...	...	...	...
		Sátáni	Hindu.	690	7	547	136	...
		Total Group 5	....	*6,126*	*42*	*5,106*	*978*	...
	6. Devotees.	Bairági	...	3	1	2	...	...
		Báváji	Jain.	...	...	...	...	...
		Digambara	,,	212	12	159	41	...
		Gósáyi	Hindu.	2	1	1	...	...
		Sanyási	,,	35	...	31	4	...
		S'vétámbara	Jain.	...	...	...	...	...
		Lingáyet—Vader	Hindu.	3	...	8	...	...
		Total Group 6	....	*255*	*14*	*196*	*45*	...
	7. Temple Servants.	Bráhman. Páncharátrul	,,	4	...	4	...	...
		Bráhman. S'ivadvija	,,	22	...	18	4	...
		Bráhman. Tambalhi	,,	...	...		...	...
		Bráhman. Vaikhánasa	,,	...	...	...	...	...
		Total Group 7	....	*26*	...	*22*	*4*	...
	9. Writers.	Kanakkan	,,	...	...	...	...	...
		Káyast'ha	,,	...	...	...	...	...
		Total Group 9	....	...	...	...	...	...
	11. Musicians and Ballad-reciters	Bhat Ráju	,,	38	7	25	6	...
	12. Dancers & Singers	Natuva	,,	40	12	27	1	...
	12. (a) Chitári, &c.	Ráchévár—Chitragára	,,	44	1	39	4	...
		Total Class B	....	**6,529**	**76**	**5,415**	**1,038**	...
C.—Commercial.—(Continued.)	11. Traders.	Baniya	Hindu.	...	...	...	...	...
		Do.	Jain.	...	...	...	...	...
		Banajiga	Hindu.	2,649	163	1,926	560	...
		Guzaráti	,,	...	...	...	...	...
		Ját	,,	...	...	...	...	...
		Kómati	,,	1,006	4	791	211	...
		Lingáyet	,,	3,729	164	2,812	753	...
		Ládar	,,	25	1	20	4	...
		Mudali	,,	68	2	63	3	...

TABLE E.—(*Continued.*)

District.

Females.

40 and over.					Age not stated.				
Total.	Single.	Married.	Widowed.	Civil condition not stated.	Total.	Single.	Married.	Widowed.	Civil condition not stated.
28	1	18	9	...	...	...	...	...	...
741	1	374	366	...	...	...	...	...	...
65	...	20	45	...	...	...	...	...	...
...	...	...	...	...	...	...	...	...	...
407	...	154	253	...	...	...	...	...	...
3,187	*2*	*1,246*	*1,939*	...	...	...	...	...	...
1	...	...	1	...	...	...	...	...	...
...	...	...	...	...	...	...	...	...	...
156	1	55	100	...	...	...	...	...	...
...	...	...	...	...	...	...	...	...	...
8	...	4	4	...	...	...	...	...	...
1	...	...	1	...	...	...	...	...	...
1	...	...	1	...	...	...	...	...	...
167	*1*	*59*	*107*	...	...	...	...	...	...
2	...	1	1	...	...	...	...	...	...
12	...	4	8	...	...	...	...	...	...
...	...	...	...	...	...	...	...	...	...
...	...	...	...	...	...	...	...	...	...
14	...	*5*	*9*	...	...	...	...	...	...
...	...	...	...	...	...	...	...	...	...
...	...	...	...	...	...	...	...	...	...
...	...	...	...	...	...	...	...	...	...
9	...	6	3	...	...	...	...	...	...
8	4	2	2	...	...	...	...	...	...
25	...	12	13	...	...	...	...	...	...
3,410	**7**	**1,330**	**2,073**	...	...	...	...	...	...
...	...	...	...	...	...	...	...	...	...
...	...	...	...	...	...	...	...	...	...
1,425	54	476	895	...	...	...	...	...	...
...	...	...	...	...	...	...	...	...	...
...	...	...	...	...	...	...	...	...	...
...	...	...	...	...	...	...	...	...	...
551	...	177	374	...	...	...	...	...	...
2,071	6	888	1,177	...	...	...	...	...	...
14	...	3	11	...	...	...	...	...	...
30	...	17	13	...	...	...	...	...	...

Class.	Group.	Caste, &c. and sub-division.	Religion.	All Ages. Total.	Single.	Married.	Widowed.	Civil condition not stated.
B.—Professional.—(Concluded.)	5. Priests.—(Concluded.)	Dásari	Hindu.	69	36	30	3	...
		Lingáyet	,,	5,763	3,024	2,513	226	...
		Tírt'hankara	Jain.	310	163	132	15	...
		Pítámbara	,,	...	...	...	...	...
		Sátáni	Hindu.	2,223	1,182	938	103	...
		Total Group 5	....	*29,588*	*15,695*	*12,160*	*1,733*	...
	6. Devotees.	Bairági	,,	12	10	...	2	...
		Báváji	Jain.	...	...	...	...	...
		Digambara	,,	687	366	271	50	...
		Gósáyi	Hindu.	72	48	19	5	...
		Sanyási	,,	4	2	...	2	...
		S'vétámbara	Jain.	...	...	...	...	...
		Lingáyet—Vadēr	Hindu.	163	86	71	6	...
		Total Group 6	....	*938*	*512*	*361*	*65*	...
	7. Temple Servants.	Brámhan.—Páncharátral	,,	...	...	...	...	...
		S'ivadvija	,,	7	4	3	...	...
		Tamballa	,,	...	...	...	...	...
		Vaikhánasa	,,	1	...	1	...	...
		Total Group 7	....	*8*	*4*	*4*	...	...
	9. Writers.	Kaṇakkan	,,	...	...	...	...	...
		Káyast'ha	,,	...	...	...	...	...
		Total Group 9	....	...	...	...	...	...
	11. Musicians and Ballad reciters	Bhaṭ Ráju	,,	113	56	52	5	...
	12. Dancers & Singers	Naṭuva	,,	2,907	1,821	969	117	...
	12. (a) Chitári, &c.	Ráchévár—Chitragára	,,	169	90	72	7	...
		Total Class B	....	**33,723**	**18,178**	**13,618**	**1,927**	...
C.—Commercial.—(Continued.)	14. Traders.	Baniya	Hindu.	...	...	...	...	...
		Do.	Jain.	...	...	...	...	...
		Baṇajiga	Hindu.	8,649	4,563	3,688	398	...
		Guzaráṭi	,,	26	14	10	2	...
		Jáṭ	,,	...	...	...	...	...
		Kómaṭi	,,	1,644	889	682	73	...
		Lingáyet	,,	44,793	23,913	19,233	1,647	...
		Ládar	,,	574	296	253	25	...
		Mudali	,,	868	465	361	42	...

TABLE E.—(*Continued.*)

District.

Males.

0 to 9					10 to 14				
Total.	Single.	Married.	Widowed.	Civil condition not stated.	Total.	Single.	Married.	Widowed.	Civil condition not stated.
21	21	...	...	...	6	6	...	...	...
1,555	1,555	...	...	...	483	483	...	...	...
78	78	...	...	...	27	27	...	...	...
...	...	...	...	...	...	...	...	...	...
626	626	...	...	...	191	187	4	...	...
8,937	*8,821*	*105*	*8*	...	*2,693*	*2,264*	*412*	*17*	...
3	3	...	...	...	5	5	...	...	...
...	...	...	...	...	...	...	...	...	...
175	174	1	...	...	67	65	2	...	...
12	12	...	...	...	6	6	...	...	...
...	...	...	...	...	...	...	...	...	...
...	...	...	...	...	...	...	...	...	...
44	44	...	...	...	12	12	...	...	...
234	*233*	*1*	...	...	*90*	*88*	*2*	...	...
...	...	...	...	...	...	...	...	...	...
3	3	...	...	...	1	1	...	...	...
...	...	...	...	...	...	...	...	...	...
...	...	...	...	...	...	...	...	...	...
3	*3*	...	...	...	*1*	*1*	...	...	...
...	...	...	...	...	...	...	...	...	...
...	...	...	...	...	...	...	...	...	...
...	...	...	...	...	...	...	...	...	...
29	29	...	...	...	8	8	...	...	...
911	911	...	...	...	259	259	...	...	...
53	53	...	...	...	12	12	...	...	...
10,167	**10,053**	**106**	**8**	...	**3,063**	**2,632**	**414**	**17**	...
...	...	...	...	...	...	...	...	...	...
...	...	...	...	...	...	...	...	...	...
2,499	2,495		...	...	710	694	16	...	...
75	5	...	...	...	3	3	...	...	...
...	...	...	...	...	...	...	...	...	...
480	480	...	...	...	146	186	10	...	...
12,666	12,661	5	...	...	5,088	5,072	16	...	...
150	150	...	...	...	47	47	...	...	...
242	242	...	...	...	73	73	...	...	...

Class.	Group.	Caste, &c. and sub-division.	Religion.	15 to 39. Total.	Single.	Married.	Widowed.	Civil condition not stated.
B.—Professional.—(Concluded.)	5. Priests.—(Concluded.)	Dásari	Hindú.	29	9	20	...	...
		Lingáyet	,,	2,537	945	1,532	60	...
		Tirt'hankara	Jain.	123	51	69	3	...
		Pítámbara	,,	...	...	...	...	...
		Sátáni	Hindu.	989	355	608	26	...
		Total Group 5......	....	*12,054*	*4,429*	*7,187*	*438*	...
	6. Devotees.	Bairági	,,	2	2	...	...	...
		Bávāji	Jain.	...	...	...	...	...
		Digambara	,,	271	115	144	12	...
		Gósáyi	Hindu.	28	17	10	1	...
		Sanyási	,,	2	2	...	...	...
		S'vétámbara	Jain.	...	...	...	...	...
		Lingáyet—Vadér	Hindu.	71	27	33	1	...
		Total Group 6......	....	*374*	*163*	*107*	*14*	...
	7. Temple Servants.	Brámhan.—Páncharátra ...	,,	...	...	...	...	...
		Brámhan.—S'ivadvija ...	,,	3	...	3	...	...
		Brámhan.—Tamballa ...	,,	...	...	...	...	...
		Brámhan.—Vaikhánasa ...	,,	1	...	1	...	...
		Total Group 7......	....	4	...	4	...	...
	9. Writers.	Kaṇakkan	,,	...	...	...	...	...
		Káyast'ha	,,	...	...	...	...	...
		Total Group 9......	....	...	...	...	...	...
	11. Musicians and Ballad-reciters ...	Bhaṭ Rája	,,	50	19	30	1	...
	12. Dancers & Singers...	Naṭuva	,,	1,250	635	572	43	...
	12. (a) Chitári, &c..	Ráchévár—Chitragára ...	,,	72	24	47	1	...
		Total Class B......	....	**13,804**	**5,270**	**8,037**	**497**	...
C.—Commercial.—(Continued.)	14. Traders.	Baniya	Hindu.	...	...	...	...	...
		Do.	Jain.	...	...	...	...	...
		Baṇajiga	Hinud.	3,631	1,259	2,307	65	...
		Guzaráti	,,	13	5	8	...	...
		Jáṭ	,,	...	...	...	...	...
		Kómaṭi	,,	715	259	442	14	...
		Lingáyet	,,	17,702	6,008	11,314	380	...
		Láḍar	,,	260	95	159	6	...
		Mudali	,,	381	112	234	8	...

TABLE E.—(*Continued.*)

District.

Males.

40 and over.					Age not stated.				
Total.	Single.	Married.	Widowed.	Civil condition not stated.	Total.	Single.	Married.	Widowed.	Civil condition not stated.
13	...	10	3	...	...	...	...	...	...
1,188	41	981	166	...	...	...	...	...	...
82	7	63	12	...	...	...	...	...	...
...	...	...	...	...	...	...	...	...	...
417	14	326	77	...	...	...	...	...	...
5,001	*178*	*4,456*	*1,270*	...	...	...	...	...	...
2	...	...	2	...	...	...	...	...	...
...	...	...	...	...	...	...	...	...	...
174	12	124	38	...	...	...	...	...	...
26	13	9	4	...	...	...	...	...	...
2	...	...	2	...	...	...	...	...	...
...	...	...	...	...	...	...	...	...	...
36	3	28	5	...	...	...	...	...	...
240	*28*	*161*	*51*	...	...	...	...	...	...
...	...	...	...	...	...	...	...	...	...
...	...	...	...	...	...	...	...	...	...
...	...	...	...	...	...	...	...	...	...
...	...	...	...	...	...	...	...	...	...
...	...	...	...	...	...	...	...	...	...
...	...	...	...	...	...	...	...	...	...
...	...	...	...	...	...	...	...	...	...
...	...	...	...	...	...	...	...	...	...
26	...	22	4	...	...	...	...	...	...
487	16	397	74	...	...	...	...	...	...
32	1	25	6	...	...	...	...	...	...
6,689	**223**	**5,061**	**1,405**	...	...	...	...	...	...
...	...	...	...	...	...	...	...	...	...
...	...	...	...	...	...	...	...	...	...
1,809	115	1,361	333	...	...	...	...	...	...
5	1	2	2	...	...	...	...	...	...
...	...	...	...	...	...	...	...	...	...
303	14	230	59	...	...	...	...	...	...
9,337	172	7,898	1,267	...	...	...	...	...	...
117	4	94	19	...	...	...	...	...	...
169	8	127	34	...	...	...	...	...	...

Mysore

Class.	Group.	Caste, &c. and sub-division.	Religion.	All Ages. Total.	Single.	Married.	Widowed.	Civil condition not stated.
B.—Professional.—(Concluded.)	5. Priests.—(Concluded.)	Dásari	Hindu.	83	29	40	14	...
		Lingáyet	"	5,900	2,100	2,538	1,262	...
		Tirt'hankara	Jain.	320	115	136	69	...
		Pítámbara	"	...	...	...	...	...
		Sátáni	Hindu.	2,257	786	968	503	...
		Total Group 5......	....	30,335	10,612	12,630	7,093	...
	6. Devotees.	Bairági	"	4	2	...	2	...
		Báváji	Jain.	...	...	...	...	...
		Digumbara	"	611	192	264	155	...
		Gósáyi	Hindu.	58	29	19	10	...
		Sanyási	"	...	...	...	...	...
		S'vétámbara	Jain.	...	...	...	...	...
		Lingáyet—Vadêr	Hindu.	164	58	71	35	...
		Total Group 6......	....	837	281	354	202	...
	7. Temple Servants.	Brâmhan. Páncharátra ...	"	...	...	...	...	...
		Brâmhan. S'ivadvija ...	"	7	2	3	2	...
		Brâmhan. Tamballa ...	"	...	...	...	...	...
		Brâmhan. Vaikhânasa ...	"	...	...	...	...	...
		Total Group 7......	....	7	2	3	2	...
	9. Writers.	Kaṇakkan	"	...	...	...	...	...
		Káyast'ha	"	...	...	...	...	...
		Total Group 9......	....	...	...	...	...	...
	11. Musicians and Ballad-reciters ...	Bhaṭ Ráju	"	96	29	49	18	...
	12. Dancers & Singers...	Naṭuva	"	3,080	2,080	968	32	...
	12. (a) Chitári, &c..	Ráchévár—Chitragára ...	"	174	61	80	33	...
		Total Class B......	....	**34,529**	**13,065**	**14,084**	**7,330**	...
C.—Commercial.—(Continued.)	14. Traders.	Banyia	Hindu.	...	...	...	...	...
		Do.	Jain.	...	...	...	...	...
		Banajiga	Hindu.	9,162	3,302	3,857	2,003	...
		Guzaráti	"	15	6	7	2	...
		Jáṭ	"	...	...	...	...	...
		Kómaṭi	"	1,560	538	667	301	...
		Lingáyet	"	46,464	6,914	19,577	9,973	...
		Láḍer	"	611	233	246	133	...
		Mudali	"	737	272	310	155	...

TABLE E.—(Continued.)

District.

Females.

0 to 9.					10 to 14.				
Total.	Single.	Married.	Widowed.	Civil condition not stated.	Total.	Single.	Married.	Widowed.	Civil condition not stated.
23	23	...	...	...	12	4	8	...	...
1,561	1,531	30	...	...	608	451	157	...	...
97	95	2	...	...	32	16	16	...	...
...	...	...	...	...	...	...	...	...	...
669	648	21	...	...	192	134	58	...	...
9,053	*8,658*	*349*	*46*	...	*3,131*	*1,826*	*1,154*	*151*	...
...	...	...	...	...	...	...	...	...	...
...	...	...	...	...	...	...	...	...	...
154	150	3	1	...	62	34	27	1	...
15	15	...	...	...	8	8	...	...	...
...	...	...	...	...	...	...	...	...	...
...	...	...	...	...	...	...	...	...	...
43	42	1	...	...	22	14	8	...	...
212	*207*	*4*	*1*	...	*92*	*56*	*35*	*1*	...
...	...	...	...	...	...	...	...	...	...
2	2	...	...	...	...	...	...	...	...
...	...	...	...	...	...	...	...	...	...
...	...	...	...	...	...	...	...	...	...
2	*2*	...	...	...	...	...	...	...	...
...	...	...	...	...	...	...	...	...	...
...	...	...	...	...	...	...	...	...	...
...	...	...	...	...	...	...	...	...	...
24	24	...	...	...	8	5	3	...	...
329	321	8	...	...	266	238	28	...	...
49	49	...	...	...	21	11	10	...	...
9,669	**9,261**	**361**	**47**	...	**3,518**	**2,136**	**1,230**	**152**	...
...	...	...	...	...	...	...	...	...	...
...	...	...	...	...	...	...	...	...	...
2,547	2,484	63	...	...	838	561	273	4	...
3	3	...	...	...	1	1	...	...	...
...	...	...	...	...	...	...	...	...	...
461	438	23	...	...	197	100	86	11	...
12,845	12,538	307	...	...	4,894	2,888	2,006	...	...
177	177	...	...	...	58	52	6	...	...
210	208	2	...	...	79	50	29	...	...

Mysore

Class.	Group.	Caste, &c. and sub-division.	Religion.	15 to 39 Total.	Single.	Married.	Widowed.	Civil condition not stated.
B.—Professional.—(Concluded.)	5. Priests.—(Concluded.)	Dásari	Hindu.	29	2	25	2	...
		Lingáyot	,,	2,117	109	1,693	315	...
		Tírt'hankara	Jain.	117	3	100	14	...
		Pítámbara	,,	...	...	...	...	...
		Sátani	Hindu.	824	4	678	142	...
		Total Group 5	....	*10,540*	*118*	*8,302*	*2,090*	...
	6. Devotees.	Bairági	,,	1	1	...	...	...
		Báváji	Jain.	...	...	...	...	...
		Digambara	,,	224	6	185	33	...
		Gósáyi	Hindu.	20	3	13	4	...
		Sanyási	,,	...	...	...	...	...
		S'vétámbara	Jain.	...	...	...	...	...
		Lingáyot—Vader	Hindu.	59	2	46	11	...
		Total Group 6	....	*304*	*12*	*244*	*48*	...
	7. Temple Servants.	Bráhman—Páncharátra ...	,,	...	...	...	...	...
		Bráhman—S'ivadvija ...	,,	3	...	3	...	...
		Bráhman—Tamballa ...	,,	...	...	...	...	...
		Bráhman—Vaikánasa ...	,,	...	...	...	...	...
		Total Group 7	....	*3*	...	*3*	...	...
	9. Writers.	Kanakkan	,,	...	...	...	...	...
		Káyast'ha	,,	...	...	...	...	...
		Total Group 9	....	...	...	...	...	...
	11. Musicians and ballad-reciters ...	Bhat Ráju ...	,,	35	...	30	5	...
	12. Dancers & Singers...	Natuva	,,	2,076	1,359	709	8	...
	12. (a) Chitári, &c..	Ráchévár—Chitragára ...	,,	65	1	57	7	...
		Total Class B	....	**12,993**	**1,490**	**9,345**	**2,158**	...
C.—Commercial.—(Continued.)	14. Traders.	Baniya	Hindu.	...	...	...	...	...
		Do.	Jain.	...	...	...	...	...
		Banajiga	Hindu.	3,593	221	2,846	531	...
		Guzaráti	,,	8	2	5	1	...
		Ját	,,	...	...	...	...	...
		Kómati	,,	527	...	414	113	...
		Lingáyot	,,	18,128	1,412	13,964	2,752	...
		Ládar	,,	211	3	166	42	...
		Mudali	,,	268	13	200	55	...

TABLE E.—(*Continued.*)

District.

Females.

40 and over.					Age not stated.				
Total.	Single.	Married.	Widowed.	Civil condition not stated.	Total.	Single.	Married.	Widowed.	Civil condition not stated.
19	...	7	12	...	...	...	...	...	...
1,614	9	658	947	...	...	...	...	...	...
74	1	18	55	...	...	...	...	...	...
...	...	...	...	...	...	...	...	...	...
572	...	211	361	...	...	...	...	...	...
7,641	*10*	*2,825*	*4,306*	...	...	...	...	...	...
3	1	...	2	...	...	...	...	...	...
...	...	...	...	...	...	...	...	...	...
171	2	49	120	...	...	...	...	...	...
15	3	6	6	...	...	...	...	...	...
...	...	...	...	...	...	...	...	...	...
...	...	...	...	...	...	...	...	...	...
40	...	16	24	...	...	...	...	...	...
229	*6*	*71*	*152*	...	...	...	...	...	...
...	...	...	...	...	...	...	...	...	...
2	...	...	2	...	...	...	...	...	...
...	...	...	...	...	...	...	...	...	...
...	...	...	...	...	...	...	...	...	...
2	...	...	2	...	...	...	...	...	...
...	...	...	...	...	...	...	...	...	...
...	...	...	...	...	...	...	...	...	...
...	...	...	...	...	...	...	...	...	...
29	...	16	13	...	...	...	...	...	...
409	162	223	24	...	...	...	...	...	...
39	...	13	26	...	...	...	...	...	...
8,349	**178**	**3,148**	**5,023**	...	...	...	...	...	...
...	...	...	...	...	...	...	...	...	...
...	...	...	...	...	...	...	...	...	...
2,179	36	675	1,468	...	...	...	...	...	...
3	...	2	1	...	...	...	...	...	...
...	...	...	...	...	...	...	...	...	...
381	...	144	237	...	...	...	...	...	...
10,597	76	3,300	7,221	...	...	...	...	...	...
165	...	74	91	...	...	...	...	...	...
180	1	79	100	...	...	...	...	...	...

Class.	Group.	Caste, &c. and sub-division.	Religion.	All Ages. Total.	Single.	Married.	Widowed.	Civil condition not stated.
B.—Professional.—(Concluded.)	5. Priests.—(Concluded.)	Dásari	Hindu.	22	10	12	...	...
		Lingáyet	,,	4,502	2,489	1,757	256	...
		Tirt'hankara	Jain.	246	133	89	24	...
		Pitámbara	,,	...	...	...	...	...
		Sátáni	Hindu.	1,797	960	726	111	...
		Total Group 5......	....	*15,006*	*7,666*	*6,319*	*1,081*	...
	6. Devotees.	Bairági	,,	...	...	...	...	...
		Báváji	Jain.	...	...	...	...	...
		Digambara	,,	368	219	130	19	...
		Gósáyi	Hindu.	27	18	8	1	...
		Sanyási	,,	...	...	...	...	...
		S'vétámbara	Jain.	...	...	...	...	...
		Lingáyet—Vadér	Hindu.	...	...	...	...	...
		Total Group 6......	....	*395*	*237*	*138*	*20*	...
	7. Temple Servants.	Brámhan.—Páncharátrál ...	,,	6	3	2	1	...
		Brámhan.—S'ivadvija ...	,,	...	...	...	...	...
		Brámhan.—Tamballa ...	,,	...	...	...	...	...
		Brámhan.—Vaikhánasa ...	,,	46	24	17	5	...
		Total Group 7......	....	*52*	*27*	*19*	*6*	...
	9. Writers.	Kanakkan	,,	...	...	...	...	
		Káyast'ha ...	,,	...	...	...	...	
		Total Group 9......	....	...	...	...	...	...
	11. Musicians and Ballad-reciters ...	Bhat Ráju	,,	45	23	15	7	...
	12. Dancers & Singers...	Natuva	,,	48	21	25	2	...
	12. (a) Chitári, &c..	Ráchévár—Chitragára ...	,,	4	2	2	...	...
		Total Class B......	....	**15,610**	**7,976**	**6,518**	**1,116**	...
C.—Commercial.—(Continued.)	14. Traders.	Banija	Hindu.	...	...	...	...	...
		Do.	Jain.	...	...	...	...	...
		Banajiga	Hindu.	1,977	1,053	793	131	...
		Guzaráti	,,	2	...	2	...	...
		Ját	,,	...	...	...	...	...
		Kómaṭi	,,	888	442	390	56	...
		Lingáyet	,,	19,164	10,628	7,224	1,312	...
		Ládar	,,	47	21	19	7	...
		Mudali	,,	82	42	35	5	...

TABLE E.—(*Continued.*)

District.

Males.

0 to 9					10 to 14				
Total.	Single.	Married.	Widowed.	Civil condition not stated.	Total.	Single.	Married.	Widowed.	Civil condition not stated.
2	2	...	...	...	4	4	...	...	...
1,129	1,129	...	...	...	528	522	6	...	...
57	57	...	...	...	23	22	...	...	...
...	...	...	...	...	...	...	...	...	...
477	477	...	...	...	173	168	5	...	...
4,181	*4,176*	5	...	...	*1,632*	*1,562*	70	...	...
...	...	...	...	...	...	...	...	...	...
...	...	...	...	...	...	...	...	...	...
87	87	...	...	...	38	38	...	...	...
8	8	...	...	...	5	5	...	...	...
...	...	...	...	...	...	...	...	...	...
...	...	...	...	...	...	...	...	...	...
...	...	...	...	...	...	...	...	...	...
95	*95*	...	...	...	*43*	*43*	...	...	...
2	2	...	...	...	1	1	...	...	...
...	...	...	...	...	...	...	...	...	...
...	...	...	...	...	...	...	...	...	...
15	15	...	...	...	7	6	1	...	...
17	*17*	...	...	...	*8*	*7*	*1*	...	...
...	...	...	...	...	...	...	...	...	...
...	...	...	...	...	...	...	...	...	...
...	...	...	...	...	...	...	...	...	...
9	9	...	...	...	5	5	...	...	...
9	9	...	...	...	6	6	...	...	...
2	2	...	...	...	...	...	...	...	...
4,313	**4,308**	**5**	...	...	**1,684**	**1,613**	**71**	...	...
...	...	...	...	...	...	...	...	...	...
...	...	...	...	...	...	...	...	...	...
529	528	1	...	...	224	217	7	...	...
...	...	...	...	...	...	...	...	...	...
...	...	...	...	...	...	...	...	...	...
257	257	...	...	...	118	106	13	...	...
4,913	4,913	...	...	...	2,353	2,333	20	...	...
15	15	...	...	...	2	2	...	...	...
34	34	...	...	...	6	6	...	...	...

Hassan

Class.	Group.	Caste, &c. and sub-division.	Religion.	15 to 39 Total.	Single.	Married.	Widowed.	Civil condition not stated.
B.—Professional.—(Concluded.)	5. Priests.—(Concluded.)	Dásari	Hindu.	12	4	8	...	...
		Lingáyet	,,	1,957	812	1,086	59	...
		Tirt'hankara	Jain.	109	50	56	3	...
		Pitámbara	,,	...	...	...	...	...
		Sátáni	Hindu.	750	305	413	32	...
		Total Group 5	....	*6,141*	*1,869*	*4,030*	*242*	...
	6. Devotees.	Bairági	,,	...	...	...	...	...
		Báváji	Jain.	...	...	...	...	...
		Digambara	,,	169	87	77	5	...
		Gósáyi	Hindu.	10	5	5	...	...
		Sanyási	,,	...	...	...	...	...
		Svêtámbara	Jain.	...	...	...	...	...
		Lingáyet—Vadêr	Hindu.	...	...	...	...	...
		Total Group 6	....	*179*	*92*	*82*	*5*	...
	7. Temple Servants.	Brámhan.—Páncharátrá	,,	1	...	1	...	...
		Brámhan.—S'ivadvija	,,	...	...	...	...	...
		Brámhan.—Tamballa	,,	...	...	...	...	...
		Brámhan.—Vaikhánasa	,,	16	3	12	1	...
		Total Group 7	....	*17*	*3*	*13*	*1*	...
	9. Writers.	Kaṇakkan	,,	...	...	...	...	...
		Káyast'ha	,,	...	...	...	...	...
		Total Group 9	....	...	...	...	...	...
	11. Musicians and Ballad-reciters	Bhaṭ Ráju	,,	21	9	10	2	...
	12. Dancers & Singers	Naṭuva	,,	23	6	17	...	...
	12. (a) Chitári, &c.	Ráchêvár—Chitragára	,,	2	...	2	...	...
		Total Class B	....	**6,383**	**1,979**	**4,154**	**250**	...
C.—Commercial.—(Continued.)	14. Traders.	Baniya	Hindu.	...	...	...	...	...
		Do.	Jain.	...	...	...	...	...
		Banajiga	Hindu.	792	295	462	35	...
		Guzaráti	,,	2	...	2	...	...
		Jáṭ	,,	...	...	...	...	...
		Kómaṭi	,,	335	71	253	11	...
		Lingáyet	,,	8,199	3,298	4,533	368	...
		Ládar	,,	22	4	16	2	...
		Muduli	,,	28	2	26	...	...

TABLE E.—(Continued.)

District.

Males.

40 and over.					Age not stated.				
Total.	Single.	Married.	Widowed.	Civil condition not stated.	Total.	Single.	Married.	Widowed.	Civil condition not stated.
4	...	4	...	...	...	...	...	...	...
888	26	665	197	...	...	...	...	...	...
55	1	33	21	...	...	...	...	...	...
		...	...	...	...	...	...	...	...
397	10	308	79	...	...		...	...	...
3,129	*60*	*2,214*	*[illegible]*	...		...	...	...	
...	...	...	...	...	...	...	...	...	...
...	...	...	...	...	...	...	...	...	...
74	7	53	14	...	...	...	...	...	...
4	...	3	1	...	...	...	...	...	...
...	...	...	...	...	...	...	...	...	...
...		...	...		...	...	...	...	...
...	...	...	...	...	...	...	...	...	...
78	7	*58*	*13*	...	...	...	...	...	...
2	...	1	1	...	...	...	...	...	...
...	...	...	...	...	...	...	...	...	...
...	...	...	...	...	...	...	...	...	...
8	...	4	4	...	...	...	...	...	...
10	...	5	5	...	...	...	...	...	...
...	...	...	...	...	...	...	...	...	...
...	...	...	...	...	...	...	...	...	...
...	...	...	...	...	...	...	...	...	...
10	...	5	5	...	...	...	...	...	...
10	...	8	2	...	...	...	...	...	...
...	...	...		...	...	...	...	...	...
3,290	**76**	**[illegible]**	**[illegible]**	...	...	...	...	...	...
...	...	...	...	...	...	...	...	...	...
...	...	...	...	...	...	...	...	...	...
432	13	323	96	...	...	...	...	...	...
...	...	...	...	...	...	...	...	...	...
...	...	...	...	...	...	...	...	...	...
	8	125	45	...	...	...	...	...	...
[illegible]	[illegible]	2,671	914	...	...	...	...	...	...
8	...	3	5	...	...	...	...	...	...
14	...	9	5	...	...	...	...	...	...

Hassan

Class.	Group.	Caste, &c. and sub-division.	Religion.	All Ages. Total.	Single.	Married.	Widowed	Civil condition not stated.
B.—Professional.—(Concluded.)	5. Priests.—(Concluded.)	Dásari	Hindu.	19	7	9	3	...
		Lingáyet	,,	4,463	1,985	1,645	833	...
		Tirt'hankara	Jain.	228	81	81	66	...
		Pitámbara	,,	...	...	...	...	...
		Sátáni	Hindu.	1,863	675	827	361	...
		Total Group 5......	....	15,134	5,377	6,719	3,038	...
	6. Devotees.	Bairági	,,	...	...	...	...	...
		Báváji	Jain.	...	...	...	...	...
		Digambara	,,	404	135	145	124	...
		Gósáyi	Hindu.	99	61	17	21	...
		Sanyási	,,	...	...	...	...	...
		S'vétámbara	Jain.	...	...	...	...	...
		Lingáyet—Vadér	Hindu.	...	...	...	...	...
		Total Group 6......	....	503	196	162	145	...
	7. Temple Servants.	Brámhan.—Pánchrátra ...	,,	5	3	1	1	...
		Brámhan.—S'ivadvija ...	,,	...	...	...	...	...
		Brámhan.—Tamballa ...	,,	...	...	...	...	...
		Brámhan.—Vaikhánasa ...	,,	34	6	21	7	...
		Total Group 7......	....	39	9	22	8	...
	9. Writers.	Kaṇakkan	,,	...	...	...	...	...
		Káyast'ha	,,	...	...	...	...	...
		Total Group 9......	....	...	...	...	...	...
	11. Musicians and ballad-reciters ...	Bhat Ráju	,,	54	25	20	9	...
	12. Dancers & Singers...	Naṭuva	,,	73	48	20	5	...
	12. (a) Chitári, &c...	Ráchévár—Chitragára ...	,,	3	1	2	...	...
		Total Class B......	....	**15,806**	**5,656**	**6,945**	**3,205**	
C.—Commercial.—(Continued.)	14. Traders.	Baniya	Hindu.	...	...	...	...	...
		Do.	Jain.	...	...	...	...	...
		Baṇajiga	Hindu.	1,758	636	828	294	...
		Guzaráti	,,	2	1	1	...	...
		Jáṭ	,,	...	...	...	...	...
		Kómaṭi	,,	878	324	409	145	...
		Lingáyet	,,	19,842	8,574	7,941	3,327	...
		Láḍar	,,	44	16	17	11	...
		Muḍali	,,	85	37	38	10	

TABLE E.—(Continued.)

District

Females.

0 to 9					10 to 14				
Total.	Single.	Married.	Widowed.	Civil condition not stated.	Total.	Single.	Married.	Widowed.	Civil condition not stated.
5	5	...	...	...	2	2	...	...	...
1,413	1,411	2	...	...	546	462	79	5	...
58	58	...	...	...	22	18	4	...	...
...	...	...	...	...	...	...	...	...	...
536	533	3	...	...	165	117	48	...	...
4,400	*4,327*	*72*	*1*	...	*1,542*	*908*	*616*	*18*	...
...	...	...	...	...	...	...	...	...	...
...	...	...	...	...	...	...	...	...	...
84	83	1	...	...	59	40	18	1	...
40	40	...	...	...	19	19	...	...	...
...	...	...	...	...	...	...	...	...	...
...	...	...	...	...	...	...	...	...	...
...	...	...	...	...	...	...	...	...	...
124	*123*	*1*	...	...	*78*	*59*	*18*	*1*	...
2	2	...	...	...	1	1	...	...	...
...	...	...	...	...	...	...	...	...	...
...	...	...	...	...	...	...	...	...	...
4	4	...	...	...	5	2	3	...	...
6	*6*	...	...	...	*6*	*3*	*3*	...	...
...	...	...	...	...	...	...	...	...	...
...	...	...	...	...	...	...	...	...	...
...	...	...	...	...	...	...	...	...	...
20	20	...	...	...	5	4	1	...	...
5	5	...	...	...	6	5	1	...	...
1	1	...	...	...	...	...	...	...	...
4,556	**4,482**	**73**	**1**	...	**1,637**	**979**	**639**	**19**	...
...	...	...	...	...	...	...	...	...	...
...	...	...	...	...	...	...	...	...	...
428	425	3	...	...	178	149	29	...	...
1	1	...	...	...	...	...	...	...	...
...	...	...	...	...	...	...	...	...	...
266	260	6	...	...	122	64	56	2	...
5,895	5,876	19	...	...	2,353	2,079	265	9	...
10	10	...	...	...	7	6	1	...	...
29	29	...	...	...	11	8	3	...	...

Hassan

Class.	Group.	Caste, &c. and sub-division.	Religion.	15 to 39. Total.	Single.	Married.	Widowed.	Civil condition not stated.
B.—Professional—(Concluded.)	5. Priests.—(Concluded.)	Dásari	Hindu.	8	...	8	...	...
		Lingáyet	"	1,670	109	1,310	251	...
		Tírt'hankara	Jain.	94	5	64	25	...
		Pítámbara	"	...	...	...	...	...
		Sátáni	Hindu.	691	25	567	99	...
		Total Group 5	....	*5,806*	*139*	*4,815*	852	...
	6. Devotees.	Bairági	"	...	...	...	...	...
		Báváji	Jain.	...	...	...	...	...
		Digambara	"	163	10	107	46	...
		Gósáyi	Hindu.	15	2	10	3	...
		Sanyási	"	...	...	...	...	...
		S'vétámbara	Jain.	...	...	...	...	...
		Lingáyet—Vadér	Hindu.	...	...	...	...	...
		Total Group 6	....	*178*	*12*	*117*	*49*	...
	7. Temple Servants.	Brámhan—Pâncharâtra	"	1	...	1	...	...
		Brámhan—Sívadvija	"	...	...	...	...	...
		Brámhan—Tamalla	"	...	...	...	...	...
		Brámhan—Vaikhánasa	"	19	...	17	2	...
		Total Group 7	....	20	...	*18*	2	...
	9. Writers.	Kanakkan	"	...	...	...	...	...
		Káyast'ha	"	...	...	...	...	...
		Total Group 9	....	...	...	...	...	...
	11. Musicians and ballad-reciters	Bhat Ráju	"	17	1	13	3	...
	12. Dancers & Singers	Natuva	"	53	33	18	2	...
	12. (a) Chitári, &c.	Ráchévár—Chitragára	"	2	...	2	...	...
		Total Class B	....	**6,076**	**185**	**4,983**	**908**	...
C.—Commercial.—(Continued.)	14. Traders.	Baniya	Hindu.	...	...	...	...	...
		Do.	Jain.	...	...	...	...	...
		Banajiga	Hindu.	743	55	601	86	...
		Guzaráti	"	1	...	1	...	...
		Ját	"	...	...	...	...	...
		Kómati	"	324	...	277	47	...
		Lingáyet	"	7,384	593	5,777	1,014	...
		Láder	"	16	...	13	3	...
		Mudali	"	34	...	32	2	...

TABLE E.—(*Continued.*)

District

Females.

40 and over.					Age not stated.				
Total	Single.	Married.	Widowed.	Civil condition not stated.	Total.	Single.	Married.	Widowed.	Civil condition not stated.
4	...	1	3	...	...	...	...	...	...
834	3	254	577	...	...	...	...	...	...
54	...	13	41	...	...	...	...	...	...
...	...	...	...	...	...	...	...	...	...
471	...	209	262	...	...	...	...	...	...
3,386	*3*	*1,216*	*2,167*	...	...	...	...	...	...
...	...	...	...	...	...	...	...	...	...
...	...	...	...	...	...	...	...	...	...
98	2	19	77	...	...	...	...	...	...
25	...	7	18	...	...	...	...	...	...
...	...	...	...	...	...	...	...	...	...
...	...	...	...	...	...	...	...	...	...
...	...	...	...	...	...	...	...	...	...
123	*2*	*26*	*95*	...	...	...	...	...	...
1	...	...	1	...	...	...	...	...	...
...	...	...	...	...	...	...	...	...	...
...	...	...	...	...	...	...	...	...	...
6	...	1	5	...	...	...	...	...	...
7	...	*1*	*6*	...	...	...	...	...	...
...	...	...	...	...	...	...	...	...	...
...	...	...	...	...	...	...	...	...	...
...	...	...	...	...	...	...	...	...	...
12	...	6	6	...	...	...	...	...	...
9	5	1	3	...	...	...	...	...	...
...	...	...	...	...	...	...	...	...	...
3,537	**10**	**1,250**	**2,277**	...	...	...	...	...	...
...	...	...	...	...	...	...	...	...	...
...	...	...	...	...	...	...	...	...	...
407	7	192	208	...	...	...	...	...	...
...	...	...	...	...	...	...	...	...	...
...	...	...	...	...	...	...	...	...	...
166	...	70	96	...	...	...	...	...	...
4,210	26	1,880	2,304	...	...	...	...	...	...
11	...	3	8	...	...	...	...	...	...
11	...	3	8	...	...	...	...	...	...

Class.	Group.	Caste, &c. and sub-division.	Religion.	All Ages. Total.	All Ages. Single.	All Ages. Married.	All Ages. Widowed.	All Ages. Civil condition not stated.
B.—Professional.—(Concluded.)	5. Priests.—(Concluded.)	Dásari	Hindu.	84	42	36	6	...
		Lingâyet	,,	4,712	2,566	1,801	345	...
		Tirt'hankara	Jain.	65	33	27	5	...
		Pitámbara	,,	...	...	...	...	...
		Sátáni	Hindu.	373	202	141	30	...
		Total Group 5.		*20,962*	*10,486*	*8,638*	*1,838*	...
	6. Devotees.	Bairâgi	,,	...	...	...	...	...
		Bâvâji	Jain.	...	...	...	...	...
		Digambara	,,	198	112	73	13	...
		Gósâyi	Hindu.	...	...	...	...	...
		Sanyâsi	,,	10	8	2	...	...
		S'vêtâmbara	Jain.	...	...	...	...	...
		Lingâyet—Vadér	Hindu.	56	35	17	4	...
		Total Group 6.		*264*	*155*	*92*	*17*	...
	7. Temple Servants.	Brâmhan—Páncharátral ...	,,	2	...	2	...	...
		Brâmhan—S'ivadvija ...	,,	...	...	...	...	...
		Brâmhan—Tamballa ...	,,	...	...	...	...	...
		Brâmhan—Vaikhânasa ...	,,	...	...	...	...	...
		Total Group 7.		*2*	...	*2*	...	...
	9. Writers.	Kanakkan	,,	...	...	...	...	...
		Káyast'ha	,,	...	...	...	...	...
		Total Group 9.		...	...	...	...	...
	11. Musicians and Ballad-reciters. ...	Bhat Râju	,,	...	...	...	...	...
	12. Dancers & Singers.	Natuva	,,	71	36	27	8	...
	12. (a) Chitári, &c.	Ráchêvár—Chitragâra ...	,,	1,895	996	769	130	...
		Total Class B.		**23,194**	**11,673**	**9,528**	**1,993**	.
C.—Commercial.—(Continued.)	11. Traders.	Baniya	Hindu.	...	...	...	...	...
		Do.	Jain.	...	...	...	...	...
		Banajiga	Hindu.	3,766	1,974	1,480	312	...
		Guzaráti	,,	...	...	...	...	...
		Ját	,,	...	...	...	...	...
		Kómati	,,	617	289	262	66	...
		Lingâyet	,,	25,333	13,978	9,610	1,745	...
		Ládar	,,	10	4	5	1	...
		Mudali	,,	149	77	62	10	...

TABLE E.—(*Continued.*)

District.

Males.

0 to 9					10 to 14				
Total.	Single.	Married.	Widowed.	Civil condition not stated.	Total.	Single.	Married.	Widowed.	Civil condition not stated.
22	22	...	...	...	9	9	...	...	...
1,206	1,206	...	...	...	608	580	28	...	...
19	19	...	...	...	8	7	1	...	...
...	...	...	...	...	...	...	...	...	...
108	108	...	...	...	43	43	...	...	...
4 983	*4,961*	*22*	...	...	*2,285*	*2,169*	*113*	*3*	...
...	...	...	...	...	...	...	...	...	...
...	...	...	...	...	...	...	...	...	...
46	46	...	...	...	12	11	1	...	...
...	...	...	...	...	...	...	...	...	...
2	2	...	...	...	1	1	...	...	...
...	...	...	...	...	...	...	...	...	...
20	20	...	...	...	5	5	...	...	...
68	*68*	...	...	...	*18*	*17*	*1*	...	...
...	...	...	...	...	...	...	...	...	...
...	...	...	...	...	...	...	...	...	...
...	...	...	...	...	...	...	...	...	...
...	...	...	...	...	...	...	...	...	...
...	...	...	...	...	...	...	...	...	...
...	...	...	...	...	...	...	...	...	...
...	...	...	...	...	...	...	...	...	...
...	...	...	...	...	...	...	...	...	...
...	...	...	...	...	...	...	...	...	...
17	17	...	...	...	9	9	...	...	...
492	493	...	...	...	213	209	4	...	...
5,560	**5,538**	**22**	...	...	**2,525**	**2,404**	**118**	**3**	...
...	...	...	...	...	...	...	...	...	...
...	...	...	...	...	...	...	...	...	...
915	915	...	...	...	434	396	38	...	...
...	...	...	...	...	...	...	...	...	...
...	...	...	...	...	...	...	...	...	...
151	151	...	...	...	57	52	5	...	...
6,516	6,515	1	...	...	3,167	3,121	44	2	...
2	2	...	...	...	1	1	...	...	...
40	40	...	...	...	19	19	...	...	...

Shimoga

Class.	Group.	Caste, &c., and subdivision.	Religion.	15 to 39. Total.	Single.	Married.	Widowed.	Civil condition not stated.
B.—Professional.—(Concluded.)	5. Priests.—(Concluded.)	Dásari	Hindu.	36	11	25	...	...
		Lingáyet	..	1,929	731	1,122	76	...
		Tírthankara	Jain.	26	7	16	3	...
		Pítámbara	..	...	...	...	...	...
		Sátáni	Hindu.	146	46	93	7	...
		Total Group 5	....	*9205*	*3,233*	*5,560*	*412*	...
	6. Devotees.	Bairági	..	...	...	...	...	...
		Báváji	Jain.	...	...	...	...	...
		Digambara	..	105	55	48	2	...
		Gósáyi	Hindu.	...	...	...	...	...
		Sanyási	..	6	4	2	...	...
		S'vétámbara	Jain.	...	...	...	...	...
		Lingáyet—Vadèr	Hindu.	21	9	12	...	...
		Total Group 6	....	*132*	*68*	*62*	2	...
	7. Temple Servants.	Bráhman.—Páncharátral	..	2	...	2	...	...
		Bráhman.—S'ivadvija	..	...	...	...	...	...
		Bráhman.—Tambalila	..	...	...	...	...	...
		Bráhman.—Vaikánasa	..	...	...	...	...	...
		Total Group 7	....	2	...	2	...	...
	9. Writers.	Kaṇakkan	..	...	...	...	...	...
		Káyast'ha	..	...	...	...	...	...
		Total Group 9	....	...	...	...	...	...
	11. Musicians and Ballad-reciters	Bhat Ráju	..	...	...	...	...	...
	12. Dancers & Singers	Natuva	..	27	10	16	1	...
	12. (a) Chitári, &c.	Ráchévár—Chitragára	..	792	277	486	29	...
		Total Class B	....	**10,158**	**3,588**	**6,096**	**474**	...
C.—Commercial.[4]—(Continued.)	11. Traders.	Baniya	Hindu	...	...	...	...	...
		Do	Jain	...	...	...	...	...
		Baṇajiga	Hindu	1,746	614	997	135	...
		Guzaráti	..	...	...	...	...	...
		Ját	..	...	...	...	...	...
		Kómaṭi	..	261	83	165	13	...
		Lingáyet	..	10,152	3,973	5,737	442	...
		Ládar	..	4	1	3	...	...
		Mudali	..	62	17	44	1	...

TABLE E.—(Continued.)

District.

Males.

40 and over.					Age not stated.				
Total.	Single.	Married.	Widowed.	Civil condition not stated.	Total.	Single.	Married.	Widowed.	Civil condition not stated.
17	...	11	6	...	...	...	...	...	...
960	49	651	260	...	...	...	...	...	...
12	...	10	2	...	...	...	...	...	...
...	...	...	...	...	...	...	...	...	...
76	5	48	23	...	...	...	...	...	...
4,489	*123*	*2,973*	*1,393*	...	...	...	...	...	...
...	...	...	...	...	...	...	...	...	...
...	...	...	...	...	...	...	...	...	...
35	...	24	11	...	...	...	...	...	...
...	...	...	...	...	...	...	...	...	...
1	1	...	...	...	...	...	...	...	...
...	...	...	...	...	...	...	...	...	...
10	1	5	4	...	...	...	...	...	...
46	*2*	*29*	*15*	...	...	...	...	...	...
...	...	...	...	...	...	...	...	...	...
...	...	...	...	...	...	...	...	...	...
...	...	...	...	...	...	...	...	...	...
...	...	...	...	...	...	...	...	...	...
...	...	...	...	...	...	...	...	...	...
...	...	...	...	...	...	...	...	...	...
...	...	...	...	...	...	...	...	...	...
...	...	...	...	...	...	...	...	...	...
...	...	...	...	...	...	...	...	...	...
18	...	11	7	...	...	...	...	...	...
398	18	279	101	...	...	...	...	...	...
4,951	**143**	**3,292**	**1,516**	...	...	...	...	...	...
...	...	...	...	...	...	...	...	...	...
...	...	...	...	...	...	...	...	...	...
671	49	445	177	...	...	...	...	...	...
...	...	...	...	...	...	...	...	...	...
...	...	...	...	...	...	...	...	...	...
148	3	92	53	...	...	...	...	...	...
5,498	369	3,828	1,301	...	...	...	...	...	...
3	...	2	1	...	...	...	...	...	...
28	1	18	9	...	...	...	...	...	...

Shimoga

Class.	Group.	Caste, &c. and sub-division.	Religion.	All Ages. Total.	Single.	Married.	Widowed.	Civil condition not stated.
B.—Professional.—(Concluded.)	5. Priests.—(Concluded.)	Dásari	Hindu.	135	46	57	32	...
		Lingáyet	,,	4,797	1,572	2,294	931	...
		Tírt'hankara	Jain.	35	7	21	7	...
		Pítámbara	,,	...	...	...	...	...
		Sátáni	Hindu.	309	116	144	49	...
		Total Group 5		18,922	6,050	8,872	4,000	...
	6. Devotees.	Bairági	,,	...	...	...	...	...
		Báváji	Jain.	...	...	...	...	...
		Digambara	,,	124	36	61	27	...
		Gósáyi	Hindu.	...	...	...	...	...
		Sanyási	,,	3	...	2	1	...
		S'vétámbara	Jain.	...	...	...	...	...
		Lingáyet—Vadér	Hindu.	55	16	25	14	...
		Total Group 6		182	52	88	42	...
	7. Temple Servants.	Bráhman.—Páncharátral ...	,,	3	1	2	...	...
		Bráhman.—S'ivadvija ...	,,	...	...	...	...	...
		Bráhman.—Tamballa ...	,,	...	...	...	...	...
		Bráhman.—Vaikhánasa ...	,,	...	...	...	...	...
		Total Group 7		3	1	2	...	...
	9. Writers.	Kanakkan	,,	...	...	...	...	...
		Káyast'ha	,,	...	...	...	...	...
		Total Group 9		...	...	...	...	...
	11. Musicians and Ballad-reciters. ...	Bhat Ráju	,,	...	...	...	...	...
	12. Dancers & Singers.	Naṭuva	,,	44	14	18	12	...
	12. (a) Chitári, &c..	Ráchévár—Chitragára ...	,,	1,743	577	860	306	...
		Total Class B		**20,894**	**6,694**	**9,840**	**4,360**	...
C.—Commercial.—(Continued.)	14. Traders.	Baniya	Hindu.	...	...	...	...	...
		Do.	Jain.	...	...	...	...	...
		Baṇajiga	Hindu.	2,943	1,056	1,331	556	...
		Guzaráti	,,	...	...	...	...	...
		Ját	,,	...	...	...	...	...
		Kómaṭi	,,	558	181	261	116	..
		Lingáyet	,,	24,000	8,689	10,760	4,551	...
		Láder	,,	1	...	1	...	...
		Mudali	,,	80	20	52	8	...

TABLE E.—(Continued.)

District.

Females.

0 to 9 Total.	0 to 9 Single.	0 to 9 Married.	0 to 9 Widowed.	0 to 9 Civil condition not stated.	10 to 14 Total.	10 to 14 Single.	10 to 14 Married.	10 to 14 Widowed.	10 to 14 Civil condition not stated.
27	27	...	...	...	17	13	4	...	...
1,057	1,051	6	...	...	[illegible]	123	266	...	...
5	5	...	...	...	2	2	...	...	...
...	...	...	...	...	...	...	...	...	...
80	80	...	...	...	29	25	4	...	...
4,590	*4,158*	*121*	*11*	...	*2,723*	*1,177*	*1,176*	*70*	...
...	...	...	...	...	...	...	...	...	...
...	...	...	...	...	...	...	...	...	...
29	29	...	...	...	15	7	8	...	...
...	...	...	...	...	...	...	...	...	...
...	...	...	...	...	...	...	...	...	...
...	...	...	...	...	...	...	...	...	...
11	11	...	...	...	5	4	1	...	...
40	*40*	...	...	...	*20*	*11*	*9*	...	...
1	1	...	...	...	...	...	...	...	...
...	...	...	...	...	...	...	...	...	...
...	...	...	...	...	...	...	...	...	...
...	...	...	...	...	...	...	...	...	...
1	*1*	...	...	...	...	...	...	...	...
...	...	...	...	...	...	...	...	...	...
...	...	...	...	...	...	...	...	...	...
...	...	...	...	...	...	...	...	...	...
...	...	...	...	...	...	...	...	...	...
11	11	...	...	...	3	2	1	...	...
425	425	...	...	...	178	127	51	...	...
5,067	**4,935**	**121**	**11**	...	**2,924**	**1,617**	**1,237**	**70**	...
...	...	...	...	...	...	...	...	...	...
...	...	...	...	...	...	...	...	...	...
570	567	3	...	...	423	274	143	2	...
...	...	...	...	...	...	...	...	...	...
...	...	...	...	...	...	...	...	...	...
152	144	8	...	...	70	37	33	...	...
5,929	5,846	83	...	...	2,991	2,136	744	21	...
...	...	...	...	...	...	...	...	...	...
13	13	...	...	...	5	5	...	...	...

Shimoga.

Class.	Group.	Caste, &c. and sub-division.	Religion.	15 to 39 Total.	Single.	Married.	Widowed.	Civil condition not stated.
B.—Professional.—(Concluded.)	5. Priests.—(Concluded.)	Dásari	Hindu.	56	6	40	10	...
		Lingáyet	"	2,255	94	1,820	341	...
		Tirt'hankara	Jain.	16	...	14	2	...
		Pitámbara	"	...	...	...	...	...
		Sátáni	Hindu.	126	9	100	17	...
		Total Group 5		7,606	109	6,301	1,196	...
	6. Devotees.	Bairági	"	...	...	...	...	...
		Báváji	Jain.	...	...	...	...	...
		Digambara	"	48	...	42	6	...
		Gósáyi	Hindu.	...	...	...	...	...
		Sanyási	"	2	...	2	...	...
		S'vétámbara	Jain.	...	...	...	...	...
		Lingáyet—Vadér	Hindu.	20	1	16	3	...
		Total Group 6		70	1	60	9	...
	7. Temple Servants.	Brámhan.—Páncharátra ...	"	2	...	2	...	...
		Brámhan.—S'ivadvija ...	"	...	...	...	...	...
		Brámhan.—Tamballa ...	"	...	...	...	...	...
		Brámhan.—Vaikhánasa ...	"	...	...	...	...	...
		Total Group 7		2	...	2	...	...
	9. Writers.	Kanakkan	"	...	...	...	...	...
		Káyast'ha	"	...	...	...	...	...
		Total Group 9		...	...	...	...	...
	11. Musicians and Ballad-reciters. ...	Bhat Rája	"	...	...	...	...	...
	12. Dancers & Singers.	Natuva	"	15	1	11	3	...
	12. (a) Chitári, &c.	Ráchévár—Chitragára ...	"	797	24	672	101	...
		Total Class B		**8,493**	**135**	**7,049**	**1,309**	...
C.—Commercial.—(Continued.)	14. Traders.	Banya	Hindu.	...	...	...	...	...
		Do.	Jain.	...	...	...	...	...
		Banajiga	Hindu.	1,367	172	988	207	...
		Guzaráti	"	...	...	...	...	...
		Ját	"	...	...	...	...	...
		Kómati	"	189	...	148	41	...
		Lingáyet	"	10,725	627	8,652	1,446	...
		Ládar	"	1	...	1	...	...
		Mudali	"	41	2	38	1	...

TABLE E.—(Continued.)

District.

Females.

10 and over.					Age not stated.				
Total	Single.	Married.	Widowed.	Civil condition not stated.	Total.	Single.	Married.	Widowed.	Civil condition not stated.
35	...	13	22	...	...	...	...	...	...
7,06[illegible]	4	202	[illegible]	...	...	...	...	...	...
12	...	7	5	...	...	...	...	...	...
...	...	...	...	...	...	...	...	...	...
74	2	40	32	...	...	...	...	...	...
1,000	*6*	*1,271*	*[illegible]*	...	...	...	...	...	...
...		...	...	...	...	...	...	...	...
...	...	...	...	...	...	...	...	...	...
32	...	11	21	...	...	...	...	...	...
...	...	...		...	...	...	...	...	...
1	...		1	...	...	...	...	...	...
...	...	...		...	...	...	...	...	...
19	...	8	11	...	...	...	...	...	...
53	...	*19*	*33*	...	...	...	...	...	...
...	...	...		...	...	...	...	...	...
...	...	...	...	...	...	...	...	...	...
...	...	...	...	...	...	...	...	...	...
...	...	...		...	...	...	...	...	...
...	...	...	...	...	...	...	...	...	...
...	...	...	...	...	...	...	...	...	...
...	...	...	...	...	...	...	...	...	...
...	...	...	...	...	...	...	...	...	...
...	...	...	...	...	...	...	...	...	...
15	...	6	9	...	...	...	...	...	...
343	1	137	205	...	...	...	...	...	...
4,410	**7**	**1,433**	**2,970**	...	...	...	...	...	...
...	...	...	...	...	...	...	...	...	...
...	...	...	...	...	...	...	...	...	...
583	39	197	347	...	...	...	...	...	...
...	...	...	...	...	...	...	...	...	...
...	...	...	...	...	...	...	...	...	...
147	...	72	75	...	...	...	...	...	...
4,445	80	1,281	3,084	...	...	...	...	...	...
...	...	...	...	...	...	...	...	...	...
21	...	14	7	...	...	...	...	...	...

Kadur

Class.	Group.	Caste, &c. and sub-division.	Religion.	All Ages. Total.	All Ages. Single.	All Ages. Married.	All Ages. Widowed.	All Ages. Civil condition not stated.
B.—Professional.—(Concluded.)	5. Priests.—(Concluded.)	Dásari ...	Hindu.	73	45	23	5	...
		Lingáyet ...	,,	3,240	1,912	1,170	158	...
		Tirt'hankara	Jain.	93	50	34	9	...
		Pítámbara	,,	4	3	1	...	...
		Sátani ...	Hindu	581	321	212	48	...
		Total Group 5	....	*12,756*	*6,811*	*5,155*	*820*	...
	6. Devotees.	Bairági ...	,,	28	11	16	1	...
		Báváji ...	Jain.	...	...	...	...	...
		Digambara	,,	555	324	197	34	...
		Gósáyi ...	Hindu.	1	1	...	...	...
		Sanyási ...	,,	9	4	5	...	...
		S'vétámbara	Jain.	59	27	23	9	...
		Lingáyet—Vader ...	Hindu.	140	75	56	9	...
		Total Group 6	....	*792*	*112*	*297*	*53*	...
	7. Temple Servants.	Brámhan. Pánchárátrá	,,	...	...	...	...	...
		Brámhan. S'ivadvija	,,	27	13	10	4	...
		Brámhan. Tambalá	,,	...	...	...	...	...
		Brámhan. Vaikhánasa	,,	6	3	3	...	...
		Total Group 7	....	*33*	*16*	*13*	*4*	...
	9. Writers.	Kanakkan ...	,,	...	...	...	...	...
		Káyast'ha ...	,,	...	...	...	...	...
		Total Group 9	....	...	...	...	...	...
	11. Musicians and Ballad-reciters ...	Bhat Ráju	,,	23	13	9	1	...
	12. Dancers & Singers ...	Natuva ...	,,	1	1	...	...	...
	12. (a) Chitári, &c.	Ráchévár—Chitragára	,,	18	11	6	1	...
		Total Class B	....	**13,653**	**7,294**	**5,480**	**879**	...
C.—Commercial.—(Continued.)	14. Traders.	Baniya	Hindu.	...	...	...	...	...
		Do ...	Jain.	...	...	...	...	...
		Banajiga ...	Hindu.	2,700	1,525	1,027	148	...
		Guzaráti ...	,,	...	...	...	...	...
		Ját ...	,,	...	...	...	...	...
		Kómati ...	,,	731	375	325	31	...
		Lingáyet ...	,,	10,716	6,072	4,094	550	...
		Ládar ...	,,	155	75	69	11	...
		Mudali ...	,,	133	66	56	11	...

TABLE E.—(*Continued.*)

District.

Males.

0 to 9					10 to 14				
Total.	Single.	Married.	Widowed.	Civil condition not stated.	Total.	Single.	Married.	Widowed.	Civil condition not stated.
26	26	...	...	...	6	6	...	...	...
902	902	...	...	...	384	384	...	...	...
24	24	...	...	...	6	6	...	...	...
...		...	...	...	1	1	...	...	...
162	163	...	...	...	53	53	...	...	...
3,289	*3,276*	*11*	*2*	...	*1,287*	*1,217*	*66*	*4*	...
3	3	...	...	...	1	1	...	...	...
...	...	...	...	...	...	...	...	...	...
118	118	...	...	...	52	52	...	...	...
...	...	...	...	...	...	...	...	...	...
2	2	...	...	...	1	1	...	...	...
2	2	...	...	...	6	6	...	...	...
39	39	...	...	...	12	12	...	...	...
164	*164*	...	...	...	*72*	*72*	...	...	...
...	...	...	...	...	...	...	...	...	...
8	8	...	...	...	1	1	...	...	...
...	...	...	...	...	...	...	...	...	...
1	1	...	...	...	...	...	...	...	...
9	*9*	...	...	...	*1*	*1*	...	...	...
...	...	...	...	...	...	...	...	...	...
...	...	...	...	...	...	...	...	...	...
...	...	...	...	...	...	...	...	...	...
3	3	...	...	...	2	2	...	...	...
...	...	...	...	...	...	...	...	...	...
6	6	...	...	...	1	1	...	...	...
3,471	**3,458**	**11**	**2**	...	**1,363**	**1,293**	**66**	**4**	...
...	...	...	...	...	...	...	...	...	...
...	...	...	...	...	...	...	...	...	...
713	713	...	...	...	291	291	...	...	...
...	...	...	...	...	...	...	...	...	...
...	...	...	...	...	...	...	...	...	...
178	178	...	...	...	77	72	5	...	...
2,772	2,772	...	...	...	1,113	1,085	28	...	...
34	34	...	...	...	12	12	...	...	...
28	28	...	...	...	14	14	...	...	...

Kadur

Class.	Group.	Caste, &c. and sub-division.	Religion.	15 to 39. Total.	Single.	Married.	Widowed.	Civil condition not stated.
B.—Professional.—(*Concluded.*)	5. Priests.—(*Concluded.*)	Dásari	Hindu.	29	12	16	1	...
		Lingáyet	"	1,393	617	720	56	...
		Tírt'hankara	Jain.	46	19	24	3	...
		Pitámbara	"	2	2	...	...	...
		Sátáni	Hindu.	258	99	148	11	...
		Total Group 5		*5,814*	*2,203*	*3,401*	*210*	...
	6. Devotees.	Bairági	"	17	6	11	...	...
		Báváji	Jain.	...	...	...	...	...
		Digambara	"	265	146	108	11	...
		Gôsáyi	Hindu.	...	...	...	...	...
		Sanyási	"	6	1	5	...	...
		S'vétámbara	Jain.	40	19	18	3	...
		Lingáyet—Vadér	Hindu.	59	23	35	1	...
		Total Group 6		*387*	*195*	*177*	*15*	...
	7. Temple Servants.	Brámhan—Páncharátra	"	...	...	...	...	...
		Brámhan—S'ivadvija	"	10	4	6	...	...
		Brámhan—Tamballa	"	...	...	...	...	...
		Brámhan—Vaikhánasa	"	5	2	3	...	...
		Total Group 7		*15*	*6*	*9*	...	...
	9. Writers.	Kanakkan	"	...	...	...	...	...
		Káyast'ha	"	...	...	...	...	...
		Total Group 9		...	...	...	...	...
	11. Musicians and Ballad-reciters.	Bhat Ráju	"	14	7	7	...	...
	12. Dancers & Singers.	Natuva	"	1	1	...	...	...
	12. (*a*) Chitári, &c.	Ráchévár—Chitragára	"	8	4	4	...	...
		Total Class B		**6,239**	**2,416**	**3,598**	**225**	...
C.—Commercial.—(*Continued.*)	14. Traders.	Baniya	Hindu.	...	...	...	...	...
		Do.	Jain.	...	...	...	...	...
		Banajiga	Hindu.	1,176	507	631	38	...
		Guzaráti	"	...	...	...	...	...
		Ját	"	...	...	...	...	...
		Kómati	"	318	119	189	10	...
		Lingáyet	"	4,849	2,156	2,544	149	...
		Láder	"	71	25	43	3	...
		Mudali	"	59	20	36	3	...

TABLE E.—(Continued.)

District.

Males.

40 and over.					Age not stated.				
Total.	Single.	Married.	Widowed.	Civil condition not stated.	Total.	Single.	Married.	Widowed.	Civil condition not stated.
12	1	7	4	...	...	...	...	...	...
561	9	450	102	...	...	...	...	...	...
17	1	10	6	...	...	...	...	...	...
1	...	1	...	...	...	...	...	...	...
108	7	64	37	...	...	...	...	...	...
2,396	*115*	*1,677*	*601*	...	...	...	...	...	...
7	1	5	1	...	...	...	...	...	...
...	...	...	...	...	...	...	...	...	...
120	8	89	23	...	...	...	...	...	...
1	1	...	...	...	...	...	...	...	...
...	...	...	...	...	...	...	...	...	...
11	...	5	6	...	...	...	...	...	...
30	1	21	8	...	...	...	...	...	...
169	*11*	*120*	*38*	...	...	...	...	...	...
...	...	...	...	...	...	...	...	...	...
8	...	4	4	...	...	...	...	...	...
...	...	...	...	...	...	...	...	...	...
...	...	...	...	...	...	...	...	...	...
8	...	*4*	*4*	...	...	...	...	...	...
...	...	...	...	...	...	...	...	...	...
...	...	...	...	...	...	...	...	...	...
...	...	...	...	...	...	...	...	...	...
4	1	2	1	...	...	...	...	...	...
...	...	...	...	...	...	...	...	...	...
3	...	2	1	...	...	...	...	...	...
2,580	**127**	**1,805**	**648**	...	...	...	...	...	...
...	...	...	...	...	...	...	...	...	...
...	...	...	...	...	...	...	...	...	...
520	14	396	110	...	...	...	...	...	...
...	...	...	...	...	...	...	...	...	...
...	...	...	...	...	...	...	...	...	...
158	6	131	21	...	...	...	...	...	...
1,983	59	1,523	401	...	...	...	...	...	...
38	4	26	8	...	...	...	...	...	...
32	4	20	8	...	...	...	...	...	...

Kadur

Class.	Group.	Caste, &c. and sub-division.	Religion.	All Ages. Total.	Single.	Married.	Widowed.	Civil condition not stated.
B.—Professional.—(Concluded.)	5. Priests.—(Concluded.)	Dásari	Hindu.	65	17	29	17	...
		Lingáyat	[illegible]	3,422	1,421	1,278	723	...
		Tirt'hankara	Jain.	90	21	41	28	...
		Pitámbara	[illegible]	...	...	...	...	...
		Sátáni	Hindu.	408	130	203	75	...
		Total Group 5	....	12,214	3,452	5,417	3,345	...
	6. Devotees.	Bairági	..	34	12	18	4	[illegible]
		Báváji	Jain.	...	...	...	...	...
		Digambara	..	454	192	147	115	...
		Gósayi	Hindu.	...	...	...	...	...
		Sanyási	..	12	4	5	3	...
		S'vêtámbara	Jain.	9	4	4	1	...
		Lingáyat—Vadér	Hindu.	292	110	113	69	...
		Total Group 6	....	801	322	287	192	...
	7. Temple-Servants.	Bráhman—Páncharátra	..	...		...	...	...
		Bráhman—Sivadvija	..	11	3	7	1	...
		Bráhman—Tamballa	..	...	...	...	...	...
		Bráhman—Vaikhánasa	..	2	...	2	...	...
		Total Group 7	....	13	3	9	1	...
	9. Writers.	Kaṇakkan	..	...	...	...	...	...
		Káyast'ha	..	...	...	...	...	...
		Total Group 9	....	...	...	...	...	...
	11. Musicians and Ballad-reciters	Bhat Ráju	..	17	5	9	3	...
	12. Dancers & Singers	Natuva	..	6	6	...	...	...
	12. (a) Chitári, &c.	Ráchévár—Chitragára	..	14	4	6	4	...
		Total Class B	....	**13,065**	**3,792**	**5,728**	**3,545**	...
C.—Commercial.—(Continued.)	14. Traders.	Baniya	Hindu.	...	...	...	...	...
		Do.	Jain.	...	...	...	...	...
		Baṇajiga	Hindu.	2,415	954	986	475	...
		Guzaráti	..	...	...	...	...	...
		Ját	..	...	...	...	...	...
		Kómaṭi	..	607	169	305	133	...
		Lingáyat	..	10,336	4,076	3,933	2,327	...
		Ládar	..	183	49	85	49	...
		Mudali	..	92	27	45	20	...

TABLE E.—(*Continued.*)

District.

Females.

0 to 9					10 to 14				
Total.	Single.	Married.	Widowed.	Civil condition not stated.	Total.	Single.	Married.	Widowed.	Civil condition not stated.
11	11	...	...	...	6	5	1	...	...
956	931	25	...	...	321	284	37	...	...
17	17	...	...	...	9	4	5	...	...
...	...	...	...	...	...	...	...	...	...
99	95	4	...	...	50	35	15	...	...
2,927	*2,690*	*230*	*7*	...	*1,372*	*555*	*714*	*103*	...
5	5	...	...	...	2	1	1	...	...
...	...	...	...	...	...	...	...	...	...
157	154	3	...	...	28	23	5	...	...
...	...	...	...	...	...	...	...	...	...
4	4	...	...	...	...	...	...	...	...
3	3	...	...	...	2	1	1	...	...
87	81	6	...	...	22	15	7	...	...
256	*247*	*9*	...	...	*51*	*40*	*11*	...	...
...	...	...	...	...	...	...	...	...	...
3	3	...	...	...	2	...	2	...	...
...	...	...	...	...	...	...	...	...	...
1	...	1	...	...	...	...	...	...	...
4	*3*	*1*	...	...	*2*	...	*2*	...	...
...	...	...	...	...	...	...	...	...	...
...	...	...	...	...	...	...	...	...	...
...	...	...	...	...	...	...	...	...	...
3	3	...	...	...	2	2	...	...	...
2	2	...	...	...	...	...	...	...	...
2	2	...	...	...	1	1	...	...	...
3,194	**2,947**	**240**	**7**	...	**1,431**	**598**	**730**	**103**	...
...	...	...	...	...	...	...	...	...	...
...	...	...	...	...	...	...	...	...	...
714	659	55	...	...	244	171	73	...	...
...	...	...	...	...	...	...	...	...	...
...	...	...	...	...	...	...	...	...	...
179	153	24	...	...	91	16	72	3	...
2,974	2,810	163	1	...	1,113	924	189	...	...
50	40	10	...	...	36	9	26	1	...
16	16	...	...	...	8	6	2	...	...

Class.	Group.	Caste, &c. and sub-division.	Religion.	15 to 39 Total.	Single.	Married.	Widowed.	Civil condition not stated.
B.—Professional.—(Concluded.)	5. Priests.—(Concluded.)	Dásari	Hindu.	31	1	23	7	...
		Lingáyet	,,	1,455	190	1,036	229	...
		Tirthankára	Jain.	34	...	27	7	...
		Pitámbara	,,	...	...	...	...	...
		Sátáni	Hindu.	160	...	141	19	...
		Total Group 5	...	*4,921*	*191*	*3,681*	*1,052*	...
	6. Devotees.	Bairági	,,	19	6	12	1	...
		Báváji	Jain.	...	...	...	...	...
		Digambara	,,	180	13	127	40	...
		Gósáyi	Hindu.	...	...	...	...	...
		Sanyási	,,	5	...	5	...	...
		S'vêtámbara	Jain.	3	...	3	...	...
		Lingáyet—Vadér	Hindu.	120	14	81	25	...
		Total Group 6	...	*327*	*33*	*228*	*66*	...
	7. Temple Servants.	Bráhman—Páncharátrál	,,	...	...	...	...	...
		Bráhman—S'ivadvija	,,	4	...	4	...	...
		Bráhman—Tamballa	,,	...	...	...	...	...
		Bráhman—Vaikhánasa	,,	1	...	1	...	...
		Total Group 7	...	*5*	...	*5*	...	...
	9. Writers.	Kanakkan	,,	...	...	...	...	...
		Káyastha	,,	...	...	...	...	...
		Total Group 9	...	...	...	...	...	...
	11. Musicians and Ballad-reciters	Bhat Ráju	,,	8	...	7	1	...
	12. Dancers & Singers	Natuva	,,	3	3	...	...	...
	12. (a) Chitári, &c.	Ráchêyár—Chitragára	,,	6	1	5	...	...
		Total Class B	...	**5,273**	**228**	**3,926**	**1,119**	...
C.—Commercial.—(Continued.)	14. Traders.	Baniya	Hindu	...	...	...	...	...
		Do.	Jain.	...	...	...	...	...
		Banajiga	Hindu.	926	103	691	132	...
		Guzaráti	,,	...	...	...	...	...
		Jât	,,	...	...	...	...	...
		Kómati	,,	203	...	158	45	...
		Lingáyet	,,	4,016	310	2,966	740	...
		Ládar	,,	61	...	41	20	...
		Mudali	,,	42	5	32	5	...

TABLE E.—(*Continued.*)

District.

Females.

60 and over.					Age not stated.				
Total.	Single.	Married.	Widowed.	Civil condition not stated.	Total.	Single.	Married.	Widowed.	Civil condition not stated.
15	...	5	10	...	...	...	...	...	...
630	16	[illegible]	[illegible]	...	...	...	...	...	...
30	...	9	21	...	...	...	...	...	...
...	...	...	...	...	...	...	...	...	...
69	...	13	56	...	...	...	...	...	...
[illegible]	[illegible]	[illegible]	[illegible]	...	...	...	...	...	...
8	...	5	3	...	...	...	...	...	...
...	...	...	...	...	...	...	...	...	...
89	2	12	75	...	...	...	...	...	...
...	...	...	...	...	...	...	...	...	...
3	...	...	3	...	...	...	...	...	...
1	...	...	1	...	...	...	...	...	...
63		19	44	...	...	...	...	...	...
161	*2*	[illegible]	[illegible]	...	...	...	...	...	...
...	...	...	...	...	...	...	...	...	...
2	...	1	1	...	...	...	...	...	...
...	...	...	...	...	...	...	...	...	...
...	...	...	...	...	...	...	...	...	...
2	...	*1*	*1*	...	...	...	...	...	...
...	...	...	...	...	...	...	...	...	...
...	...	...	...	...	...	...	...	...	...
...	...	...	...	...	...	...	...	...	...
4	...	2	2	...	...	...	...	...	...
1	1	...	...	...	...	...	...	...	...
5	...	1	4	...	...	...	...	...	...
3,167	**19**	**832**	**2,316**	...	...	...	...	...	...
...	...	...	...	...	...	...	...	...	...
...	...	...	...	...	...	...	...	...	...
531	21	167	343	...	...	...	...	...	...
...	...	...	...	...	...	...	...	...	...
...	...	...	...	...	...	...	...	...	...
134	...	49	85	...	...	...	...	...	...
2,233	32	615	1,586	...	...	...	...	...	...
36	...	8	28	...	...	...	...	...	...
26	...	11	15	...	...	...	...	...	...

Class.	Group.	Caste, &c. and sub-division.	Religion.	All Ages. Total.	Single.	Married.	Widowed.	Civil condition not stated.
B.—Professional.—(Concluded.)	5. Priests.—(Concluded.)	Dásari	Hindu.	49	21	26	2	...
		Lingáyet	,,	4,016	2,204	1,555	257	...
		Tirt'hankara	Jain.	69	38	22	9	...
		Pítámbara	,,	...	...	...	...	...
		Sátáni	Hindu.	343	185	143	14	...
		Total Group 5	....	*7,553*	*3,887*	*3,068*	*598*	...
	6. Devotees.	Bairági	,,	2	1	1	...	...
		Báváji	Jain.	...	...	...	...	...
		Digambara	,,	163	88	68	7	...
		Gósáyi	Hindu.	47	25	19	3	...
		Sanyási	,,	3	2	1	...	...
		S'vétámbara	Jain.	...	...	...	...	...
		Lingáyet—Vadér	Hindu.	10	4	5	1	...
		Total Group 6	....	*225*	*120*	*94*	*11*	...
	7. Temple Servants.	Bráhman. Páncharátrál	,,	...	...	...	...	...
		Bráhman. S'ivadvija	,,	13	8	5	...	...
		Bráhman. Tamballa	,,	...	...	...	...	...
		Bráhman. Vaikhánasa	,,	...	...	...	...	...
		Total Group 7	....	*13*	*8*	*5*	...	...
	9. Writers.	Kanakkan	,,	...	...	...	...	...
		Káyast'ha	,,	...	...	...	...	...
		Total Group 9	....	...	...	...	...	...
	11. Musicians and Ballad reciters	Bhat Ráju	,,	25	15	9	1	...
	12. Dancers & Singers	Natuva	,,	12	11	1	...	...
	12. (a) Chitari, &c.	Ráchévár—Chitrugára	,,	101	58	38	5	...
		Total Class B	....	**7,929**	**4,099**	**3,215**	**615**	...
C.—Commercial.—(Continued.)	14. Traders.	Baniya	Hindu.	...	...	...	...	...
		Do.	Jain	...	...	...	...	...
		Banajiga	Hindu.	2,154	1,172	857	125	...
		Guzaráti	,,	...	...	...	...	...
		Ját	,,	...	...	...	...	...
		Kómati	,,	1,360	679	539	142	...
		Lingáyet	,,	22,671	13,270	8,076	1,325	...
		Ládar	,,	114	53	53	8	...
		Mudali	,,	250	138	92	20	...

TABLE E.—(Continued)

District.

Males.

0 to 9					10 to 14				
Total.	Single.	Married.	Widowed.	Civil condition not stated.	Total.	Single.	Married.	Widowed.	Civil condition not stated.
16	14	2	...	...	3	3	...	...	...
1,297	1,297	...	...	...	411	411	...	...	...
15	15	...	...	...	6	6	...	...	...
...	...	...	...	...	...	...	...	...	...
119	119	...	...	...	27	27	...	...	...
2,214	*2,211*	*2*	*1*	...	*721*	*714*	*7*	...	...
1	1	...	...	...	...	...	...	...	...
...	...	...	...	...	...	...	...	...	...
16	16	...	...	...	21	18	3	...	...
4	4	...	...	...	1	1	...	...	...
1	1	...	...	...	...	...	...	...	...
...	...	...	...	...	...	...	...	...	...
2	2	...	...	...	2	3	...	...	...
24	*21*	...	...	...	*21*	*21*	*3*	...	...
...	...	...	...	...	...	...	...	...	...
4	4	...	...	...	1	1	...	...	...
...	...	...	...	...	...	...	...	...	...
...	...	...	...	...	...	...	...	...	...
4	*4*	...	...	...	*1*	*1*	...	...	...
...	...	...	...	...	...	...	...	...	...
...	...	...	...	...	...	...	...	...	...
...	...	...	...	...	...	...	...	...	...
10	10	...	...	...	4	4	...	...	...
...	...	...	...	...	2	2	...	...	...
40	40	...	...	...	8	8	...	...	...
2,292	**2,289**	**2**	**1**	...	**760**	**750**	**20**	...	...
...	...	...	...	...	...	...	...	...	...
...	...	...	...	...	...	...	...	...	...
721	721	...	...	...	131	130	1	...	...
...	...	...	...	...	...	...	...	...	...
...	...	...	...	...	...	...	...	...	...
300	300	...	...	...	130	114	16	...	...
6,936	6,910	26	...	...	2,996	2,958	8	...	...
31	31	...	...	...	8	8	...	...	...
64	64	...	...	...	21	21	...	...	...

Chitaldurg

Class	Group	Caste, &c. and sub-division	Religion	15 to 39. Total	Single	Married	Widowed	Civil condition not stated
B.—Professional.—(Concluded.)	5. Priests.—(Concluded.)	Dásari	Hindu.	21	4	17	...	...
		Lingáyet	,,	1,269	173	1,043	53	...
		Tirt'hankara	Jain.	28	16	12	...	...
		Pitámbara	,,	...	...	...	...	...
		Sátáni	Hindu	136	37	95	4	...
		Total Group 5	....	*3,048*	*889*	*2,030*	*129*	...
	6. Devotees.	Bairági	,,	1	...	1	...	...
		Báváji	Jain.	...	...	...	...	...
		Digambara	,,	100	50	47	3	...
		Gósáyi	Hindu.	29	17	12	...	...
		Sanyási	,,	1	...	1	...	...
		S'vêtámbara	Jain.	...	...	...	...	...
		Lingáyet—Vadér	Hindu.	3	...	3	...	...
		Total Group 6	....	*134*	*67*	*64*	3	...
	7. Temple Servants.	Bráhman—Páncharátrál		...	...	...	...	...
		Bráhman—S'ivadvija		7	3	4	...	...
		Bráhman—Tamballa		...	...	...	...	...
		Bráhman—Vaikhánasa		...	...	...	...	...
		Total Group 7	....	7	3	4	...	...
	9. Writers.	Kanakkan	,,	...	...	...	...	...
		Káyast'ha	,,	...	...	...	...	...
		Total Group 9	....	...	...	...	...	...
	11. Musicians and Ballad-reciters ...	Bhat Ráju	,,	8	1	7	...	...
	12. Dancers & Singers...	Natuva	,,	9	8	1	...	...
	12. (a) Chitári, &c..	Rachévár—Chitragára	,,	37	10	27	...	...
		Total Class B	....	**3,243**	**973**	**2,133**	**132**	...
C.—Commercial.—(Continued.)	14. Traders.	Baniya	Hindu.	...	...	...	...	...
		Do.	Jain.	...	...	...	...	...
		Banajiga	Hindu.	900	312	554	34	...
		Guzaráti	,,	...	...	...	...	...
		Ját	,,	...	...	...	...	...
		Kómati	,,	549	163	341	45	...
		Lingáyet	,,	8,598	3,225	5,138	235	...
		Ládar	,,	47	14	31	2	...
		Mudali	,,	92	37	52	3	...

TABLE E.—(*Continued.*)

District.

Males.

40 and over.					Age not stated.				
Total.	Single.	Married.	Widowed.	Civil condition not stated.	Total.	Single.	Married.	Widowed.	Civil condition not stated.
9	...	7	2	...	...	...	...	...	...
739	23	512	204	...	...	...	...	...	...
20	1	10	9	...	...	...	...	...	...
...	...	...	...	...	...	...	...	...	...
60	2	48	10	...	...	...	...	...	...
1,570	*73*	*1,029*	*468*	...	...	...	...	...	...
...	...	...	...	...	...	...	...	...	...
...	...	...	...	...	...	...	...	...	...
26	4	18	4	...	4	...	...	4	...
13	3	7	3	...	...	...	...	...	...
1	1	...	...	...	...	...	...	...	...
...	...	...	...	...	...	...	...	...	...
3	...	2	1	...	...	...	...	...	...
43	*8*	*27*	*8*	...	...	...	...	...	...
...	...	...	...	...	...	...	...	...	...
1	...	1	...	...	...	...	...	...	...
...	...	...	...	...	...	...	...	...	...
...	...	...	...	...	...	...	...	...	...
1	...	*1*	...	...	...	...	...	...	...
...	...	...	...	...	...	...	...	...	...
...	...	...	...	...	...	...	...	...	...
...	...	...	...	...	...	...	...	...	...
3	...	2	1	...	...	...	...	...	...
1	1	...	...	...	...	...	...	...	...
16	...	11	5	...	...	...	...	...	...
1,634	**82**	**1,070**	**482**	...	...	...	...	...	...
...	...	...	...	...	...	...	...	...	...
...	...	...	...	...	...	...	...	...	...
402	9	302	91	...	...	...	...	...	...
...	...	...	...	...	...	...	...	...	...
...	...	...	...	...	...	...	...	...	...
291	12	182	97	...	...	...	...	...	...
4,141	147	2,904	1,090	...	...	...	...	...	...
28	...	22	6	...	...	...	...	...	...
70	13	40	17	...	...	...	...	...	...

Chitaldurg

Class.	Group.	Caste, &c. and sub-division.	Religion.	All Ages. Total.	Single.	Married.	Widowed.	Civil condition not stated.
B.—Professional.—(Concluded.)	5. Priests.—(Concluded.)	Dásari	Hindu.	38	18	19	1	...
		Lingáyet	,,	3,855	1,508	1,707	640	...
		Tirt'hankára	Jain.	73	26	42	5	...
		Pítámbara	,,	...	...	...	...	...
		Sátáni	Hindu.	354	121	181	52	...
		Total Group 5......	....	7,236	2,419	3,377	1,440	...
	6. Devotees.	Bairági	,,	1	...	1	...	...
		Báváji	Jain.	...	...	...	...	...
		Digambara	,,	111	29	38	44	...
		Gósáyi	Hindu.	19	10	7	2	...
		Sanyási	,,	4	2	1	1	...
		S'vétámbara	Jain.	...	...	...	...	...
		Lingáyet—Vadér	Hindu.	4	1	2	1	...
		Total Group 6......	....	139	42	49	48	...
	7. Temple Servants.	Brámhan. { Pánchirátral ...	,,	...	...	...	...	...
		Brámhan. { S'ivadvija ...	,,	9	3	4	2	...
		Brámhan. { Tamballa ...	,,	...	...	...	...	...
		Brámhan. { Vaikhánasa ...	,,	...	...	...	...	...
		Total Group 7......	....	9	3	4	2	...
	9. Writers.	Kanakkan	,,	...	...	...	...	...
		Káyast'ha	,,	...	...	...	...	...
		Total Group 9......	....	...	...	...	...	...
	11. Musicians and Ballad-reciters ...	Bhat Ráju	,,	25	7	12	6	...
	12. Dancers & Singers...	Natuva	,,	11	10	1	...	...
	12. (a) Chitári, &c.	Ráchévár—Chitragára ...	,,	78	26	42	10	...
		Total Class B......	....	7,498	2,507	3,485	1,506	...
C.—Commercial.—(Continued).	14. Traders.	Baniya	Hindu.	...	...	...	...	...
		Do	Jain.	...	...	...	...	...
		Banajiga	Hindu.	2,070	881	828	361	...
		Guzaráti	,,	...	...	...	...	...
		Ját	,,	...	...	...	...	...
		Kómati	,,	1,245	373	646	226	...
		Lingáyet	,,	21,626	8,213	8,762	4,651	...
		Ládar	,,	102	29	49	24	...
		Mudali	,,	342	93	124	25	...

TABLE E.—(Continued.)

District.

Females.

0 to 9					10 to 14				
Total.	Single.	Married.	Widowed.	Civil condition not stated.	Total.	Single.	Married.	Widowed.	Civil condition not stated.
12	12	...	...	...	4	4	...	...	...
1,163	1,163	..	...	...	305	302	3	...	...
19	17	2	...	...	13	5	8	...	...
...	...	...	...	...	...	...	...	...	...
94	91	3	...	...	41	28	13	...	...
2,033	*1,971*	*62*	...	...	*593*	*397*	*193*	*3*	...
..	...	...	...	...	...	...	...	...	...
..	...	...	...	...	...	...	...	...	...
27	26	1	...	...	6	3	2	1	...
6	6	...	..	...	1	1	...	...	...
1	1	...	...	...	1	1	...	...	...
...	...	...	...	...	...	...	...	...	...
1	1	...	...	...	...	...	...	...	...
35	*34*	*1*	...	...	*8*	*5*	*2*	*1*	...
—	...	...	...	...	...	...	...	...	...
3	3	...	...	...	...	...	...	...	...
...	...	...	...	...	...	...	...	...	...
...	...	...	...	...	...	...	...	...	...
3	*3*	...	...	...	...	...	...	...	...
...	...	...	...	...	...	...	...	...	...
...	...	...	...	...	...	...	...	...	...
...	...	...	...	...	...	...	...	...	...
5	5	...	...	...	2	1	1	...	...
...	...	...	...	...	2	2	...	...	...
19	18	1	...	...	9	8	1	...	...
2,096	**2,031**	**64**	...	...	**614**	**413**	**197**	**4**	..
...	...	...	...	...	...	...	...	...	...
...	...	...	...	...	...	...	...	...	...
737	735	2	...	...	121	102	19	...	...
...	...	...	...	...	...	...	...	...	...
..	...	...	...	...	...	...	...	...	...
321	308	13	...	...	125	65	60	...	...
4,553	6,491	61	1	...	1,578	1,463	413	2	...
20	20	...	...	...	10	9	...	1	...
76	76	...	...	...	17	17	...	...	...

Class.	Group.	Caste, &c. and sub-division.	Religion.	15 to 39 Total.	15 to 39 Single.	15 to 39 Married.	15 to 39 Widowed.	15 to 39 Civil condition not stated.
B.—Professional.—(Concluded.)	5. Priests.—(Concluded.)	Dásari	Hindu.	17	2	15	...	...
		Lingáyat	"	1,641	42	1,405	194	...
		Tirthankara	Jain.	34	4	29	1	...
		Pitámbara	"	...	...	...	...	...
		Sátáni	Hindu.	142	2	118	22	...
		Total Group 5......	....	*2,999*	*50*	*2,520*	*429*	...
	6. Devotees.	Bairági	"	1	...	1	...	...
		Báváji	Jain.	...	...	...	...	...
		Digambara	"	40	...	31	9	...
		Gósáyi	Hindu.	8	3	5	...	...
		Sanyási	"	1	...	1	...	...
		S'vétámbara	Jain.	...	...	...	...	...
		Lingáyat—Vadér	Hindu.	1	...	1	...	...
		Total Group 6......	....	*51*	3	*39*	*9*	...
	7. Temple Servants.	Bráhman.—Páncharátral ...	"	...	...	...	...	...
		Bráhman.—S'ivadvija ...	"	3	...	3	...	...
		Bráhman.—Tamballa ...	"	...	...	...	...	...
		Bráhman.—Vaikhánasa ...	"	...	...	...	...	...
		Total Group 7......	....	*3*	...	*3*	...	...
	9. Writers.	Kanakkan	"	...	...	...	...	...
		Káyast'ha	"	...	...	...	...	...
		Total Group 9......	....	...	...	...	...	...
	11. Musicians and Ballad-reciters ...	Bhat Ráju	"	*11*	1	9	1	...
	12. Dancers & Singers...	Natuva	"	7	6	1	...	...
	12. (a) Chitári, &c.	Ráchévár—Chitragára ...	"	32	...	29	3	...
		Total Class B......	....	**3,103**	**60**	**2,601**	**442**	...
C.—Commercial.—(Continued.)	13. Traders.	Baniya	Hindu.	...	...	...	...	...
		Do	Jain	...	...	...	...	...
		Banajiga	Hindu	783	38	627	118	...
		Guzaráti	"	...	...	...	...	...
		Ját	"	...	...	...	...	...
		Kómati	"	467	...	392	75	...
		Lingáyat	"	8,791	237	7,254	1,800	...
		Ládar	"	46	...	37	9	...
		Mudali	"	75	...	70	5	...

TABLE E.—(*Continued.*)

District.

Females.

40 and over.					Age not stated.				
Total.	Single.	Married.	Widowed.	Civil condition not stated.	Total.	Single.	Married.	Widowed.	Civil condition not stated.
5	...	4	1	...	...	...	...	...	...
716	1	299	446	...	...	...	...	...	...
7	...	3	4	...	...	...	...	...	...
...	...	...	...	...	...	...	...	...	...
77	...	47	30	...	...	...	...	...	...
1,611	*1*	*602*	*1,008*	...	...	...	...	...	...
...	...	...	...	...	...	...	...	...	...
...	...	...	...	...	...	...	...	...	...
38	...	4	34	...	...	...	...	...	...
4	...	2	2	...	...	...	...	...	...
1	...	...	1	...	...	...	...	...	...
...	...	...	...	...	...	...	...	...	...
2	...	1	1	...	...	...	...	...	...
45	...	*7*	*38*	...	...	...	...	...	...
...	...	...	...	...	...	...	...	...	...
3	...	1	2	...	...	...	...	...	...
...	...	...	...	...	...	...	...	...	...
...	...	...	...	...	...	...	...	...	...
3	...	*1*	*2*	...	...	...	...	...	...
...	...	...	...	...	...	...	...	...	...
...	...	...	...	...	...	...	...	...	...
...	...	...	...	...	...	...	...	...	...
7	...	2	5	...	...	...	...	...	...
2	2	...	...	...	...	...	...	...	...
18	...	11	7	...	...	...	...	...	...
1,686	**3**	**623**	**1,060**	...	...	...	...	...	...
...	...	...	...	...	...	...	...	...	...
...	...	...	...	...	...	...	...	...	...
429	6	180	243	...	...	...	...	...	...
...	...	...	...	...	...	...	...	...	...
...	...	...	...	...	...	...	...	...	...
332	...	181	151	...	...	...	...	...	...
4,404	22	1,034	3,318	...	...	...	...	...	...
26	...	12	14	...	...	...	...	...	...
74	...	54	20	...	...	...	...	...	...

Class.	Group.	Caste, &c. and sub-division.	Religion.	All Ages. Total.	Single.	Married.	Widowed.	Civil condition not stated.
B.—Professional.—(Concluded.)	5. Priests.—(Concluded.)	Dásari	Hindu.	7	4	2	1	...
		Lingáyet	"	21	14	7	...	...
		Tirt'hankara	Jain.	...	...	...	...	...
		Pítámbara	"	...	...	...	...	...
		Sátáni	Hindu.	112	49	58	5	...
		Total Group 5	....	*802*	*342*	*414*	*46*	...
	6. Devotees.	Bairági	"	...	...	...	...	...
		Báváji	Jain.	1	...	1	...	...
		Digambara	"	10	6	4	...	...
		Gósáyi	Hindu.	1	...	1	...	...
		Sanyási	"	...	...	...	...	...
		S'vetámbara	Jain.	6	5	...	1	...
		Lingáyet—Vader	Hindu.	6	4	2	...	...
		Total Group 6	....	*24*	*15*	*8*	*1*	...
	7. Temple Servants.	Brámhan—Páncharátrá	"	...	[illegible]	...	...	...
		Brámhan—S'ivadvija	"	...	...	...	...	...
		Brámhan—Tamballa	"	2	...	2	...	...
		Brámhan—Vaikhánasa	"	...	...	...	...	...
		Total Group 7	....	*2*	...	*2*	...	...
	9. Writers.	Kanakkan	"	57	32	23	2	...
		Káyast'ha	"	5	3	2	...	...
		Total Group 9	....	*62*	*35*	*25*	*2*	...
	11. Musicians and Ballad-reciters	Bhat Ráju	"	1	...	1	...	...
	12. Dancers & Singers	Natuva	"	21	14	7	...	...
	12. (a) Chitári, &c.	Róchévár—Chitragára	"	6	1	5	...	...
		Total Class B	....	**918**	**407**	**462**	**49**	...
C.—Commercial.—(Continued.)	14. Traders.	Baniya	Hindu.	28	2	25	1	...
		Do.	Jain.	77	36	39	2	...
		Banajiga	Hindu.	4,124	2,113	1,803	208	...
		Guzaráti	"	10	5	3	2	...
		Ját	"	1	1	...	...	...
		Kómati	"	24	8	14	2	...
		Lingáyet	"	518	264	232	22	...
		Ládar	"	...	...	...	...	...
		Mudali	"	15	9	6	...	...

TABLE E.—(Continued.)

Station, Bangalore.

Males

0 to 9					10 to 14				
Total.	Single.	Married.	Widowed.	Civil condition not stated.	Total.	Single.	Married.	Widowed.	Civil condition not stated.
1	1	...	...	...	...	...	...	...	...
7	7	...	...	...	4	4	...	...	...
...	...	...	...	...	...	...	...	...	...
...	...	...	...	...	...	...	...	...	...
23	22	...	...	...	12	12	...	...	...
150	*150*	...	...	...	*67*	*66*	*1*	...	...
...	...	...	...	...	...	...	...	...	...
...	...	...	...	...	...	...	...	...	...
...	...	...	...	...	2	2	...	...	...
...	...	...	...	...	...	...	...	...	...
...	...	...	...	...	...	...	...	...	...
1	1	...	...	...	2	2	...	...	...
1	1	...	...	...	...	...	...	...	...
2	*2*	...	...	...	*4*	*4*	...	...	...
...	...	...	...	...	...	...	...	...	...
...	...	...	...	...	...	...	...	...	...
...	...	...	...	...	...	...	...	...	...
...	...	...	...	...	...	...	...	...	...
...	...	...	...	...	...	...	...	...	...
9	8	1	...	...	6	6	...	...	...
3	3	...	...	...	...	...	...	...	...
12	*11*	*1*	...	...	*6*	*6*	...	...	...
...	...	...	...	...	...	...	...	...	...
4	4	...	...	...	2	2	...	...	...
...	...	...	...	...	...	...	...	...	...
168	**167**	**1**	...	...	**79**	**78**	**1**	...	...
...	...	...	...	...	...	...	...	...	...
14	14	...	...	...	5	5	...	...	...
1,026	1,026	...	...	...	415	411	3	1	...
2	2	...	...	...	2	2	...	...	...
...	...	...	...	...	...	...	...	...	...
3	3	...	...	...	...	...	...	...	...
132	132	...	...	...	60	56	4	...	...
...	...	...	...	...	...	...	...	...	...
5	5	...	...	...	...	...	...	...	...

Class.	Group.	Caste, &c. and sub-division.	Religion.	15 to 39. Total.	Single.	Married.	Widowed.	Civil condition not stated.
B.—Professional.—(Concluded.)	5. Priests.—(Concluded.)	Dásari	Hindu.	5	3	2	...	...
		Lingáyet	,,	5	2	3	...	...
		Tírt'hankara	Jain.	...	...	...	...	...
		Pitámbara	,,	...	...	...	...	...
		Sátáni	Hindu.	41	14	25	2	...
		Total Group 5	....	385	117	259	9	...
	6. Devotees.	Bairági	,,	...	...	...	...	...
		Báváji	Jain.	...	...	...	...	...
		Digambara	,,	7	4	3	...	...
		Gósáyi	Hindu.	...	...	...	...	...
		Sanyási	,,	...	...	...	...	...
		S'vetámbara	Jain.	2	2	...	...	...
		Lingáyet—Vader	Hindu.	4	3	1	...	...
		Total Group 6	....	13	9	4	...	...
	7. Temple Servants.	Brámhan. Pánchárátrál	,,	...	...	...	...	...
		Brámhan. S'ivadvija	,,	...	...	...	...	...
		Brámhan. Tamballa	,,	2	...	2	...	...
		Brámhan. Vaikhánasa	,,	...	...	...	...	...
		Total Group 7	....	2	...	2	...	...
	9. Writers.	Kaṇakkan	,,	27	14	13	...	...
		Káyast'ha	,,	2	...	2	...	...
		Total Group 9	....	29	14	15	...	...
	11. Musicians and Ballad reciters ...	Bhaṭ Ráju	,,	1	...	1	...	...
	12. Dancers & Singers...	Naṭuva	,,	13	8	5	...	...
	12. (a) Chitári, &c..	Ráchévár—Chitragára	,,	1	...	1	...	...
	Total Class B		....	**444**	**148**	**287**	**9**	...
C.—Commercial.—(Continued.)	14. Traders.	Baniya	Hindu.	18	1	17	...	...
		Do.	Jain.	47	16	30	1	...
		Baṇajiga	Hindu.	1,787	657	1,081	49	...
		Guzaráti	,,	3	1	2	...	...
		Jáṭ	,,	1	1	...	...	...
		Kómaṭi	,,	15	5	10	...	...
		Lingáyet	,,	210	72	132	6	...
		Láḍar	,,	...	...	...	...	...
		Mudáli	,,	7	4	3	...	...

TABLE E.—(*Continued.*)

Station, Bangalore.

Males.

40 and over.					Age not stated.				
Total.	Single.	Married.	Widowed.	Civil condition not stated.	Total.	Single.	Married.	Widowed.	Civil condition not stated.
1	...	...	1	...	...	...	...	...	...
5	1	4	...	...	...	...	...	...	...
...	...	...	...	...	...	...	...	...	...
...	...	...	...	...	...	...	...	...	...
37	1	33	3	...	...	...	...	...	...
200	*9*	*154*	*37*	...	...	...	...	...	...
...	...	...	...	...	...	...	...	...	...
1	...	1	...	...	...	...	...	...	...
1	...	1	...	...	...	...	...	...	...
1	...	1	...	...	...	...	...	...	...
...	...	...	...	...	...	...	...	...	...
1	...	...	1	...	...	...	...	...	...
1	...	1	...	...	...	...	...	...	...
5	...	*4*	*1*	...	...	...	...	...	...
...	...	...	...	...	...	...	...	...	...
...	...	...	...	...	...	...	...	...	...
...	...	...	...	...	...	...	...	...	...
...	...	...	...	...	...	...	...	...	...
...	...	...	...	...	...	...	...	...	...
15	4	9	2	...	...	...	...	...	...
...	...	...	...	...	...	...	...	...	...
15	*4*	*9*	*2*	...	...	...	...	...	...
...	...	...	...	...	...	...	...	...	...
2	...	2	...	...	...	...	...	...	...
5	1	4	...	...	...	...	...	...	...
227	**14**	**173**	**40**	...	...	...	...	...	...
10	1	8	1	...	...	...	...	...	...
11	1	9	1	...	...	...	...	...	...
896	19	719	158	...	...	...	...	...	...
3	...	1	2	...	...	...	...	...	...
...	...	...	...	...	...	...	...	...	...
6	...	4	2	...	...	...	...	...	...
116	4	96	16	...	...	...	...	...	...
...	...	...	...	...	...	...	...	...	...
3	...	3	...	...	...	...	...	...	...

The Civil and Military

Class.	Group.	Caste, &c. and sub-division.	Religion.	All Ages. Total.	Single.	Married.	Widowed.	Civil condition not stated.
B.—Professional.—(Concluded.)	5. Priests.—(Concluded.)	Dásari	Hindu.	3	...	3	...	...
		Lingáyat	,,	28	11	12	5	...
		Tírt'hankara	Jain.	...	...	...	...	...
		Pítámbara	,,	...	...	...	...	...
		Sátáni	Hindu.	110	46	52	18	...
		Total Group 5	....	638	184	331	123	...
	6. Devotees.	Bairági	,,	...	...	...	...	...
		Báváji	Jain.	...	...	...	...	...
		Digambara	,,	5	2	3	...	...
		Gósáyi	Hindu.	...	...	...	...	...
		Sanyási	,,	...	...	...	...	...
		S'vétámbara	Jain.	...	...	...	...	...
		Lingáyat—Vaḍér	Hindu.	5	1	2	2	...
		Total Group 6	....	10	3	5	2	...
	7. Temple Servants.	Brámhan.—Páncharátrál ...	,,	...	...	...	...	...
		Brámhan.—S'ivadvija ...	,,	...	...	...	...	...
		Brámhan.—Tamballa ...	,,	...	...	...	...	...
		Brámhan.—Vaikhánasa ...	,,	...	...	...	...	...
		Total Group 7	....	...	...	...	...	...
	9. Writers.	Kaṇakkan	,,	51	29	13	9	...
		Káyast'ha	,,	1	...	1	...	...
		Total Group 9	....	52	29	14	9	...
	11. Musicians and Ballad-reciters ...	Bhaṭ Ráju	,,	...	...	...	...	...
	12. Dancers & Singers ...	Naṭuva	,,	16	5	7	4	...
	12. (a) Chitári, &c..	Ráchévár—Chitragára ...	,,	5	3	2	...	...
		Total Class B	....	**781**	**224**	**359**	**138**	...
C.—Commercial.—(Continued.)	14. Traders.	Baniya	Hindu.	13	5	8	...	...
		Do.	Jain.	43	12	25	6	...
		Baṇajiga	Hindu.	4,218	1,350	1,935	933	...
		Guzaráṭi	,,	10	3	4	3	...
		Ját	,,	...	...	...	...	...
		Kómaṭi	,,	30	8	17	5	...
		Lingáyat	,,	478	151	241	86	...
		Láḍar	,,	...	...	...	...	...
		Mudali	,,	11	6	5	...	...

TABLE E.—*(Continued.)*

Station, Bangalore.

Females.

0 to 9					10 to 14				
Total.	Single.	Married.	Widowed.	Civil condition not stated.	Total.	Single.	Married.	Widowed.	Civil condition not stated.
...	...	...	...	...	...	...	...	...	...
8	8	...	...	...	3	3	...	...	...
...	...	...	...	...	...	...	...	...	...
...	...	...	...	...	...	...	...	...	...
37	37	...	...	...	8	5	3	...	...
171	*165*	*6*	...	...	*60*	*15*	*33*	*2*	...
...	...	...	...	...	...	...	...	...	...
...	...	...	...	...	...	...	...	...	...
2	2	...	...	...	...	...	...	...	...
...	...	...	...	...	...	...	...	...	...
...	...	...	...	...	...	...	...	...	...
...	...	...	...	...	...	...	...	...	...
1	1	...	...	...	...	...	...	...	...
3	*3*	...	...	...	...	...	...	...	...
...	...	...	...	...	...	...	...	...	...
...	...	...	...	...	...	...	...	...	...
...	...	...	...	...	...	...	...	...	...
...	...	...	...	...	...	...	...	...	...
...	...	...	...	...	...	...	...	...	...
11	11	...	...	...	8	7	1	...	...
...	...	...	...	...	...	...	...	...	...
11	*11*	...	...	...	*8*	*7*	*1*	...	...
...	...	...	...	...	...	...	...	...	...
4	4	...	...	...	3	1	2	...	...
2	2	...	...	...	...	...	...	...	...
191	**185**	**6**	...	...	**61**	**23**	**36**	**2**	...
4	4	...	...	...	...	...	...	...	...
10	10	...	...	...	2	2	...	...	...
1,068	1,037	10	1	...	414	231	181	2	...
2	2	...	...	...	2	1	1	...	...
...	...	...	...	...	...	...	...	...	...
8	7	1	...	...	5	1	4	...	...
129	125	4	...	...	33	15	18	...	...
...	...	...	...	...	...	...	...	...	...
5	5	...	...	...	1	1	...	...	...

The Civil and Military

Class.	Group.	Caste, &c. and sub-division.	Religion.	15 to 39. Total.	Single.	Married.	Widowed.	Civil condition not stated.
B.—Professional.—(Concluded.)	5. Priests.—(Concluded.)	Dásari	Hindu.	3	...	3	...	...
		Lingáyet	,,	8	...	8	...	...
		Tírt'hankara	Jain.	...	...	...	...	...
		Pítámbara	,,	...	...	...	...	...
		Sátáni	Hindu.	46	3	38	5	...
		Total Group 5	....	*272*	*3*	*230*	*39*	...
	6. Devotees.	Bairági	,,	...	...	...	...	...
		Báváji	Jain.	...	...	...	...	...
		Digambara	,,	3	...	3	...	...
		Gósáyi	Hindu.	...	...	...	...	...
		Sanyási	,,	...	...	...	...	...
		S'vétámbara	Jain.	...	...	...	...	...
		Lingáyet—Vadêr	Hindu.	1	...	1	...	...
		Total Group 6	....	*4*	...	*4*	...	...
	7. Temple Servants.	Brámhan.—Pánchharátrá ...	,,	...	...	...	...	...
		Brámhan.—S'ivadvija ...	,,	...	...	...	...	...
		Brámhan.—Tamballa ...	,,	...	...	...	...	...
		Brámhan.—Vaikhánasa ...	,,	...	...	...	...	...
		Total Group 7	....	...	...	...	...	...
	9. Writers.	Kanakkan	,,	12	3	8	1	...
		Káyast'ha	,,	1	...	1	...	...
		Total Group 9	....	*13*	*3*	*9*	*1*	...
	11. Musicians and Ballad-reciters ...	Bhat Ráju ...	,,	...	...	...	...	...
	12. Dancers & Singers ...	Natuva	,,	5	...	5	...	...
	12. (a) Chitári, &c..	Ráchévár—Chitragára ...	,,	1	...	1	...	...
		Total Class B	....	**295**	**6**	**249**	**40**	...
C.—Commercial.—(Continued.)	14. Traders.	Baniya	Hindu.	7	...	7	...	...
		Do.	Jain.	25	...	24	1	...
		Banajiga	Hindu.	1,689	57	1,401	231	...
		Guzaráti	,,	3	...	2	1	...
		Ját	,,	...	...	...	...	...
		Kómati	,,	12	...	9	3	...
		Lingáyet	,,	205	8	179	18	...
		Ládar	,,	...	...	...	...	...
		Mudali	,,	3	...	3	...	...

TABLE E.—(Continued.)

Station, Bangalore.

Females.

40 and over.					Age not stated.				
Total.	Single.	Married.	Widowed.	Civil condition not stated.	Total.	Single.	Married.	Widowed.	Civil condition not stated.
...	...	...	...	...	...	...	...	...	...
9	...	4	5	...	...	...	...	...	...
...	...	...	...	...	...	...	...	...	...
...	...	...	...	...	...	...	...	...	...
25	1	11	13	...	...	...	...	...	...
145	*1*	*62*	*82*	...	...	...	...	...	...
...	...	...	...	...	...	...	...	...	...
...	...	...	...	...	...	...	...	...	...
...	...	...	...	...	...	...	...	...	...
...	...	...	...	...	...	...	...	...	...
...	...	...	...	...	...	...	...	...	...
...	...	...	...	...	...	...	...	...	...
3	...	1	2	...	...	...	...	...	...
3	...	*1*	*2*	...	...	...	...	...	...
...	...	...	...	...	...	...	...	...	...
...	...	...	...	...	...	...	...	...	...
...	...	...	...	...	...	...	...	...	...
...	...	...	...	...	...	...	...	...	...
...	...	...	...	...	...	...	...	...	...
20	8	4	8	...	...	...	...	...	...
...	...	...	...	...	...	...	...	...	...
20	*8*	*4*	*8*	...	...	...	...	...	...
...	...	...	...	...	...	...	...	...	...
4	...	...	4	...	...	...	...	...	...
2	1	1	...	...	...	...	...	...	...
174	**10**	**68**	**96**	...	...	...	...	...	...
2	1	1	...	...	...	...	...	...	...
6	...	1	5	...	...	...	...	...	...
1,047	5	343	699	...	...	...	...	...	...
3	...	1	2	...	...	...	...	...	...
...	...	...	...	...	...	...	...	...	...
5	...	3	2	...	...	...	...	...	...
111	3	40	68	...	...	...	...	...	...
...	...	...	...	...	...	...	...	...	...
2	...	2	...	...	...	...	...	...	...

Total including the Civil and

Class.	Group.	Caste, &c. and sub-division.	Religion.	All Ages. Total.	Single.	Married.	Widowed.	Civil condition not stated.
B.—Professional—(Concluded.)	5. Priests.—(Concluded.)	Dásari	Hindu.	583	276	266	41	...
		Lingáyet	"	30,896	16,485	12,519	1,892	...
		Tírt'hankara	Jain.	1,346	714	521	111	...
		Pítámbara	"	5	3	1	1	...
		Sátáni	Hindu.	10,094	5,216	4,191	687	...
		Total Group 5......	....	135,755	68,515	57,214	10,026	...
	6. Devotees.	Bairági	"	104	55	44	5	...
		Báváji	Jain.	1	...	1	...	...
		Digambara	"	2,891	1,588	1,101	202	...
		Gósáyi	Hindu.	209	123	67	14	...
		Sanyási	"	357	190	134	33	...
		S'vêtámbara	Jain.	75	33	25	12	...
		Lingáyet—Vadêr	Hindu.	406	223	160	23	...
		Total Group 6......	....	3,686	2,032	1,308	250	...
	7. Temple Servants.	Bráhman. Páncharátrál ...	"	66	29	32	5	...
		Bráhman. S'ivadvija ...	"	310	142	130	38	...
		Bráhman. Tamballa ...	"	2	...	2	...	...
		Bráhman. Vaikhánasa ...	"	210	100	86	24	...
		Total Group 7......	....	588	271	250	67	...
	9. Writers.	Kaṇakkan	"	57	32	23	2	...
		Káyast'ha...	"	5	3	2	...	...
		Total Group 9......	....	62	35	25	2	...
	11. Musicians and Ballad reciters ...	Bhaṭ Ráju	"	723	374	297	52	...
	12. Dancers & Singers...	Naṭuva	"	3,565	2,188	1,215	162	...
	12. (a) Chitári, &c..	Ráchévár—Chitragára ...	"	2,413	1,256	990	167	...
		Total Class B......	....	147,149	74,861	61,523	10,765	...
C.—Commercial.—(Continued.)	14. Traders.	Baniya	Hindu.	28	2	25	1	...
		Do.	Jain.	77	36	39	2	...
		Baṇajiga	Hindu.	57,653	30,111	24,105	3,437	...
		Guzaráṭi	"	41	21	16	4	...
		Jáṭ	"	1	1	...	...	...
		Kómaṭi	"	15,181	7,435	6,560	1,186	...
		Lingáyet	"	146,492	79,862	58,467	8,163	...
		Láḍar	"	1,014	509	440	65	...
		Mudali	"	2,969	1,558	1,217	194	...

TABLE E.—*(Continued.)*

Military Station, Bangalore.

Males.

0 to 9.					10 to 14.				
Total.	Single.	Married.	Widowed.	Civil condition not stated.	Total.	Single.	Married.	Widowed.	Civil condition not stated.
159	157	2	...	...	47	47	...	...	...
8,456	8,456	...	...	...	3,070	3,012	58	...	...
326	326	...	...	...	100	97	3	...	...
...	...	...	...	...	1	1	...	...	...
2,749	2,749	...	...	...	941	925	16	...	...
36,431	*36,286*	*134*	*11*	...	*12,979*	*11,920*	*1,031*	*28*	...
19	19	...	...	...	12	11	1	...	...
...	...	...	...	...	...	...	...	...	...
629	627	2	...	...	274	265	9	...	...
27	27	...	...	...	15	15	...	...	...
100	100	...	...	...	27	27	...	...	...
5	5	...	...	...	10	10	...	...	...
117	117	...	...	...	35	35	...	...	...
797	*795*	*2*	...	...	*346*	*336*	*10*	...	...
17	17	...	...	...	9	8	1	...	...
74	74	...	...	...	30	28	2	...	...
...	...	...	...	...	...	...	...	...	...
53	53	...	...	...	21	19	2	...	...
144	*144*	...	...	...	*60*	*55*	*5*	...	...
9	8	1	...	...	6	6	...	...	...
3	3	...	...	...	...	...	...	...	...
12	*11*	*1*	...	...	*6*	*6*	...	...	...
168	168		...	...	64	63	1	...	...
1,089	1,089	...	...	...	318	318	...	...	...
636	636	...	...	...	255	251	4	...	...
39,377	**39,179**	**187**	**11**	...	**14,055**	**12 976**	**1,051**	**28**	...
...	...	...	...	...	...	...	...	...	...
14	14	...	...	...	5	5	...	...	...
14,645	14,640	5	...	...	5,382	5,284	97	1	...
7	7	...	...	...	5	5	...	...	...
...	...	...	...	...	...	...	...	...	...
3,898	3,897	1	...	...	1,467	1,374	93	...	...
39,835	39,803	32	...	...	17,126	16,973	151	2	...
253	253	...	...		80	80	...	...	...
759	759	...	...	...	294	292	2	...	...

Total including the Civil and

Class.	Group.	Caste, &c. and sub-division.	Religion.	15 to 39. Total.	Single.	Married.	Widowed.	Civil condition not stated.
B.—Professional.—(Concluded)	5. Priests.—(Concluded.)	Dásari	Hindu.	248	71	168	9	...
		Lingáyet	,,	12,770	4,753	7,600	417	...
		Tirt'hankara	Jain.	574	264	286	24	...
		Pítámbara	,,	2	2	...	...	...
		Sátáni	Hinglu.	4,126	1,444	2,518	164	...
		Total Group 5.	....	*56,661*	*19,145*	*35,148*	*2,368*	...
	6. Devotees.	Bairági	,,	49	22	27	...	...
		Báváji	Jain.	...	...	...	...	...
		Digambara	,,	1,288	637	603	48	...
		Gósay[illegible]	Hindu.	94	52	41	1	...
		Sanyási	,,	144	46	99	8	...
		S'vétámbara	Jain.	47	23	20	4	...
		Lingáyet—Vadér	Hindu.	167	65	100	2	...
		Total Group 6.	....	*1,645*	*7,999*	*791*	*55*	...
	7. Temple Servants.	Bráhman.—Páncharátrá ...	,,	26	4	21	1	...
		Bráhman.—S'ivadvija ...	,,	127	36	84	7	...
		Bráhman.—Tamballa ...	,,	2	...	2	...	...
		Bráhman.—Vaikhánasa ...	,,	93	28	61	6	...
		Total Group 7.	....	*250*	*68*	*168*	*14*	...
	9. Writers.	Kaṇakkan	,,	27	14	13	...	...
		Káyast'ha	,,	2	...	2	...	...
		Total Group 9.	....	*29*	*14*	*15*	...	...
	11. Musicians and Ballad-reciters ...	Bhaṭ Ráju. ...	,,	322	134	179	9	...
	12. Dancers & Singers...	Naṭuva	,,	1,534	748	733	53	...
	12. (a) Chitári, &c..	Ráchévár—Chitragára ...	,,	1,010	347	627	36	...
		Total Class B	....	**61,595**	**21,301**	**37,751**	**2,543**	...
C.—Commercial.—(Continued.)	14. Traders.	Baniya	Hindu.	18	1	17	...	...
		Do.	Jain.	47	16	30	1	...
		Bannjiga	Hinud.	24,646	9,543	14,325	778	...
		Guzaráti	,,	21	8	13	...	...
		Jáṭ	,,	1	1	...	...	...
		Kómaṭi	,,	6,249	2,014	3,974	261	...
		Lingáyet	,,	59,220	21,946	35,327	1,947	...
		Láḍar	,,	459	168	274	17	...
		Múdali	,,	1,280	469	774	37	...

TABLE E.—(*Continued.*)

Military Station, Bangalore.

Males.

40 and over.					Age not stated.				
Total.	Single.	Married.	Widowed.	Civil condition not stated.	Total.	Single.	Married.	Widowed.	Civil condition not stated.
129	1	96	32	...	...	...	...	...	...
6,600	264	4,861	1,475	...	...	...	...	...	...
346	27	232	87	...	...	...	...	...	...
2	...	1	1	...	...	...	...	...	...
2,278	98	1,657	523	...	...	...	...	...	...
29,684	*1,214*	*20,851*	*7,619*	...	...	...	...	...	...
24	3	16	5	...	...	...	...	...	...
1	...	1	...	...	...	...	...	...	...
606	50	407	150	...	4	...	...	4	...
73	34	26	13	...	...	...	...	...	...
86	17	44	25	...	...	...	...	...	...
13	...	5	8	...	...	...	...	...	...
87	6	60	21	...	...	...	...	...	...
894	*102*	*595*	*197*	...	*4*	...	...	*4*	...
14	...	10	4	...	...	...	...	...	...
79	4	44	31	...	...	...	...	...	...
...	...	...	...	...	...	...	...	...	...
41	...	23	18	...	...	...	...	...	...
134	*4*	*77*	*53*	...	...	...	...	...	...
15	4	9	2	...	...	...	...	...	...
...	...	...	...	...	...	...	...	...	...
15	*4*	*9*	*2*	...	...	...	...	...	...
169	9	117	43	...	...	...	...	...	...
624	33	483	100	...	...	...	...	...	...
512	22	359	131	...	...	...	...	...	...
32,118	**1,405**	**22,534**	**8,179**	...		...	...		...
10	1	8	1	...	...	...	...	...	...
11	1	9	1	...	...	...	...	...	...
12,980	644	9,678	2,658	...	...	...	...	...	...
8	1	3	4	...	...	...	...	...	...
...	...	...	...	...	...	...	...	...	...
3,567	150	3,492	925	...	...	...	...	...	...
30,311	1,140	23,957	6,214	...	...	...	...	...	...
223	8	166	48	...	...	...	...	...	...
636	38	441	157	...	...	...	...	...	...

Total including the Civil and

Class.	Group.	Caste, &c. and sub-division.	Religion.	All Ages. Total.	Single.	Married.	Widowed.	Civil condition not stated.
B.—Professional.—(Concluded.)	5. Priests.—(Concluded.)	Dásari	Hindu.	595	200	292	103	...
		Lingáyet	,,	31,066	11,751	13,372	5,943	...
		Tírt'hankara	Jain.	1,213	392	517	309	...
		Pítámbara	,,	...	...	...	...	...
		Sátáni	Hindu.	9,893	3,273	4,453	2,167	...
		Total Group 5	....	132,326	42,227	59,789	30,310	...
	6. Devotees.	Bairági	,,	118	50	48	20	...
		Báváji	Jain.	...	...	...	...	...
		Digambara	,,	2,586	852	1,030	704	...
		Gósáyi	Hindu.	215	108	64	43	...
		Sanyási	,,	327	127	148	52	...
		S'vétámbara	Jain.	10	4	4	2	...
		Lingáyet—Vadér	Hindu.	550	200	225	125	...
		Total Group 6	....	3,479	1,214	1,371	894	...
	7. Temple Servants.	Bráhman—Pancharátral	,,	76	23	39	14	...
		Bráhman—S'ivadvija	,,	295	58	146	91	...
		Bráhman—Tamballa	,,	...	...	...	...	...
		Bráhman—Vaikhánasa	,,	197	47	105	45	...
		Total Group 7	....	568	128	290	150	...
	9. Writers.	Kanakkan	,,	51	29	13	9	...
		Káyast'ha	,,	1	...	1	...	...
		Total Group 9	....	52	29	14	9	...
	11. Musicians and Ballad-reciters ...	Bhat Ráju	,,	665	213	309	143	...
	12. Dancers & Singers...	Natuva	,,	3,911	2,650	1,161	100	...
	12. (a) Chitári, &c..	Ráchévár—Chitragára	,,	2,227	756	1,084	387	...
		Total Class B	....	**143,555**	**47,344**	**64,166**	**32,045**	...
C.—Commercial.—(Continued.)	14. Traders.	Baniya	Hindu.	13	5	8	...	...
		Do.	Jain.	43	12	25	6	...
		Banajiga	Hindu.	57,082	19,297	25,193	12,592	...
		Guzaráti	,,	30	12	13	5	...
		Ját	,,	...	...	...	...	...
		Kómati	,,	13,873	4,238	6,484	3,151	...
		Lingáyet	,,	145,581	54,600	60,584	30,397	...
		Ládar	,,	1,032	356	439	237	...
		Mudali	,,	2,468	862	1,153	443	...

TABLE E.—(*Continued.*)

Military Station. Bangalore.

Females.

0 to 9.					10 to 14.				
Total.	Single.	Married.	Widowed.	Civil condition not stated.	Total.	Single.	Married.	Widowed.	Civil condition not stated.
142	142	...	...	...	61	39	22	...	...
8,813	8,728	85	...	...	3,200	2,353	831	5	...
319	313	6	...	...	109	66	43	...	...
...	...	...	...	...	...	...	...	...	...
2,718	2,650	68	...	...	923	542	381	...	...
36,153	*34,631*	*1,434*	*88*	...	*13,946*	*6,813*	*6,668*	*465*	...
25	25	...	...	...	10	8	2	...	...
...	...	...	...	...	...	...	...	...	...
679	662	16	1	...	224	139	80	5	...
65	65	...	...	...	31	31	...	...	...
101	101	...	...	...	29	23	6	...	...
3	3	...	...	...	2	1	1	...	...
153	146	7	...	...	54	37	17	...	...
925	*901*	*23*	*1*	...	*321*	*216*	*100*	*5*	...
23	19	3	...	...	10	4	5	1	...
54	48	6	...	...	20	10	10	...	...
...	...	...	...	...	...	...	...	...	...
45	41	4	...	...	20	6	14	...	...
121	*108*	*13*	...	...	*50*	*20*	*29*	*1*	...
11	11	...	...	...	8	7	1	...	...
...	...	...	...	...	...	...	...	...	...
11	*11*	...	...	...	*8*	*7*	*1*	...	...
158	158	...	...	...	69	44	25	...	...
513	505	8	...	...	336	303	34	...	...
560	559	1	...	...	232	165	67	...	...
38,537	**36,969**	**1,479**	**89**	...	**14,991**	**7,590**	**6,930**	**471**	...
4	4	...	...	...	...	...	...	...	...
10	10	...	...	...	2	2	...	...	...
15,089	14,694	390	5	...	4,806	3,099	1,688	21	...
7	7	...	...	...	4	3	1	...	...
...	...	...	...	...	...	...	...	...	...
3,976	3,749	227	...	...	1,427	485	910	32	...
40,444	39,734	708	2	...	15,653	11,076	4,543	34	...
282	272	10	...	...	117	80	35	2	...
635	629	6	...	...	243	181	62	...	...

Total including the Civil and

Class.	Group.	Caste, &c. and sub-division.	Religion.	15 to 39 Total.	Single.	Married.	Widowed.	Civil condition not stated.
B.—Professional.—(Concluded.)	5. Priests.—(Concluded.)	Dásari	Hindu.	248	18	204	26	...
		Lingáyot	,,	12,463	630	10,092	1,741	...
		Tírt'hankara	Jain.	478	12	387	79	...
		Pítámbara	,,	...	...	...	...	...
		Sátani	Hindu.	3,760	76	3,031	633	...
		Total Group 5......	....	*50,584*	*736*	*40,819*	*9,029*	...
	6. Devotees.	Bairági	,,	51	16	32	3	...
		Báváji	Jain.	...	...	...	...	...
		Digambara	,,	1,005	44	758	203	...
		Gósáyi	Hindu.	62	9	45	8	...
		Sanyási	,,	131	3	111	17	...
		S'vétámbara	Jain.	3	...	3	...	...
		Lingáyot—Vadér	Hindu.	211	17	154	40	...
		Total Group 6......	....	*1,332*	*86*	*992*	*254*	...
	7. Temple Servants.	Brámhan—Páncharátrál ...	,,	27	...	24	3	...
		Brámhan—S'ivadvija ...	,,	136	...	106	30	...
		Brámhan—Tamballa ...	,,	...	...	...	...	...
		Brámhan—Vaikánasa ...	,,	87	...	74	13	...
		Total Group 7......	....	*250*	...	*204*	*46*	...
	9. Writers.	Kanakkan	,,	12	3	8	1	...
		Káyast'ha	,,	1	...	1	...	...
		Total Group 9......	....	*13*	*3*	*9*	*1*	...
	11. Musicians and Ballad-reciters ...	Bhat Ráju	,,	277	16	219	42	...
	12. Dancers & Singers...	Natuva	,,	2,489	1,602	867	20	...
	12. (a) Chitári, &c..	Ráchévár—Chitragára ...	,,	982	29	834	119	..
		Total Class B......	....	**56,058**	**2,475**	**44,055**	**9,528**	...
C.—Commercial.—(Continued.)	14. Traders.	Baniya	Hindu.	7	...	7	...	...
		Do.	Jain.	25	...	24	1	...
		Banajiga	Hindu.	23,376	1,219	18,448	3,709	...
		Guzaráti	,,	13	2	9	2	...
		Ját	,,	...	...	...	...	...
		Kómati	,,	5,171	4	4,169	998	...
		Lingáyot	,,	57,565	3,522	45,217	8,826	...
		Ládar	,,	370	4	288	78	...
		Mudali	,,	964	60	793	111	...

TABLE E.—(*Continued.*)

Military Station, Bangalore.

Females.

40 and over.					Age not stated.				
Total.	Single.	Married.	Widowed.	Civil condition not stated.	Total.	Single.	Married.	Widowed.	Civil condition not stated.
144	1	66	77	...	...	...	...	...	...
6,561	40	2,344	4,197	...	...	...	...	...	...
312	1	81	230	...	...	...	...	...	...
...	...	...	...	...	...	...	...	...	...
2,492	5	953	1,534	...	...	...	...	...	...
31,643	*47*	*10,868*	*20,728*	...	...	...	...	...	...
83	1	14	17	...	...	...	...	...	...
...	...	...	...	...	...	...	...	...	...
678	7	176	495	...	...	...	...	...	...
57	3	19	35	...	...	...	...	...	...
66	...	31	35	...	...	...	...	...	...
2	...	...	2	...	...	...	...	...	...
132	...	47	85	...	...	...	...	...	...
901	*11*	*256*	*634*	...	...	...	...	...	...
17	...	7	10	...	...	...	...	...	...
85	...	24	61	...	...	...	...	...	...
...	...	...	...	...	...	...	...	...	...
45	...	13	32	...	...	...	...	...	...
147	...	*44*	*103*	...	...	...	...	...	...
20	8	4	8	...	...	...	...	...	...
...	...	...	...	...	...	...	...	...	...
20	*8*	*4*	*8*	...	...	...	...	...	...
166	...	65	101	...	...	...	...	...	...
573	241	253	80	...	...	...	...	...	...
453	3	182	268	...	...	...	...	...	...
33,969	**310**	**1,170**	**21,957**	...	...	...	...	...	...
2	1	1	...	...	...	...	...	...	...
6	...	1	5	...	...	...	...	...	...
13,809	285	4,667	8,857	...	...	...	...	...	...
6	...	3	3	...	...	...	...	...	...
...	...	...	...	...	...	...	...	...	...
3,299	...	1,178	2,121	...	...	...	...	...	...
31,919	268	10,116	21,535	...	...	...	...	...	...
263	...	106	157	...	...	...	...	...	...
626	2	292	332	...	...	...	...	...	...

Class.	Group.	Caste, &c. and sub-division.	Religion.	All Ages. Total.	Single.	Married.	Widowed.	Civil condition not stated.
C.—Commercial.—(Concluded.)	14. Traders.—(Concluded.)	Multáni ...	Hindu.	...	...	...	...	...
		Nagarta ...	,,	11,902	6,317	4,704	881	...
		Jain ...	Jain.	1,090	591	410	89	...
		Marvádi ...	,,	55	30	22	3	...
		Do. ...	Hindu.	...	...	...	...	...
		Do. ...	Buddhist.	...	...	...	...	...
		S'rávaka ...	Jain.	1,038	659	303	76	...
		Total Group 14	....	*232,744*	*124,694*	*94,186*	*13,864*	...
		Total Class C	....	**232,744**	**124,694**	**94,186**	**13,864**	...
D.—Artisan and Village menial.—(Continued.)	17. Gold smiths.	Pánchála ...	Hindu.	49,596	26,246	20,371	2,979	...
	18. Barbers ...	Náyinda ...	,,	18,411	9,655	7,739	1,017	...
	19. Black smiths	Pánchála.—Kammára	,,	3,122	1,627	1,238	207	...
	20. Carpenters, &c.	Pánchála. { Badagi ...	,,	4,409	2,325	1,830	254	...
		Pánchála. { Gaunder ...	,,	...	...	...	...	...
		Total Group 20	....	*4,409*	*2,325*	*1,830*	*254*	...
	21. Brass & Copper-smiths ...	Pánchála.—Gojjégára	,,	111	62	44	5	...
	22. Tailors ...	Darzi ...	,,	4,529	2,302	1,956	271	...
	23. Weavers, Calenderers and Dyers.	Góniga ...	,,	748	337	364	47	...
		Gádiya ...	Jain.	...	...	...	...	...
		Néyigé ...	Hindu.	43,318	21,916	18,816	2,586	...
		Total Group 23	....	*44,066*	*22,253*	*19,180*	*2,633*	...
	24. Washermen.	Agasa ...	Hindu.	42,370	22,218	17,691	2,467	...
	25 (a). Cowherds, &c. ...	Golla ...	,,	64,530	34,459	26,354	3,767	...
	26. Shepherds and Wool-weavers. ...	Kuruba ...	,,	172,014	91,111	72,567	8,336	...
	27. Oil-pressers.	Gániga ...	,,	17,645	8,273	7,765	903	...
	28. Potters ...	Kumbára ...	,,	21,026	10,838	9,001	1,187	...
	30. Salt, &c., workers ...	Uppára ...	,,	44,845	24,119	18,628	2,098	...
	32. Gold-smith's refuse collectors. ...	Pánchála.—Jalagára ...	,,	129	67	53	9	...
	33 (a). Gold-lace makers ...	Rachévár.—Sarigé ...	,,	8	3	5	...	...

TABLE E.—(Continued.)

cial.

Males.

0 to 9					10 to 14				
Total.	Single.	Married.	Widowed.	Civil condition not stated.	Total.	Single.	Married.	Widowed.	Civil condition not stated.
...	...	...	...	...	...	...	...	...	...
3,125	3,125	...	...	...	1,394	1,361	28	2	...
229	227	1	1	...	119	118	1	...	...
9	9	...	...	...	5	5	...	...	...
...	...	...	...	...		...	...	...	...
...	...	...	...	...	...	...	...	...	...
213	213	...	...	...	115	112	3	...	...
61,805	*61,765*	*39*	*1*	...	*25,510*	*25,138*	*368*	*4*	...
61,805	**61,765**	**39**	**1**	...	**25,510**	**25,138**	**333**	**4**	...
13,368	13,359	9	...	...	5,529	5,359	169	1	
5,251	5,251	...	...	...	1,085	1,055	30	...	...
855	855	...	...	...	359	337	22	...	...
1,165	1,165		...	...	425	419	6	...	
...		...	...	...	...	...		...	...
1,165	*1,165*	...	...		*425*	*419*	*6*	...	...
32	32		...	...	12	12	...	...	...
1,249	1,248	1	...	...	451	439	15	...	...
201	201	...	...	...	72	71	1	...	
...	...		...	...	...		...	...	...
11,746	11,723	24	...	...	4,263	4,117	144	2	...
11,947	*11,923*	*24*	...	...	*4,[illegible]*	*4,188*	*155*	*2*	...
12,051	12,045	6	...	...	3,774	3,690	84	...	...
17,589	17,588	1	...		5,738	5,574	164	...	...
49,470	49,437	33	...	...	17,157	16,921	234	2	...
4,796	4,793	3	...	...	1,428	1,407	21	...	...
5,658	5,656	2	...	...	1,966	1,931	35	...	...
12,687	12,686	1	...		4,[illegible]45	4,854	61	...	...
36	36	...	...	...	12	12	...	...	...
2	2	...		...	1	1	...	...	...

Class.	Group.	Caste, &c. and sub-division.	Religion.	15 to 39. Total.	Single.	Married.	Widowed.	Civil condition not stated.
C.—Commercial.—(Concluded.)	14. Traders.—(Concluded.)	Multáni ...	Hindu.	...	...	...	...	...
		Nagarta ...	"	4,914	1,677	2,969	268	...
		Jain ...	Jain.	495	225	257	13	...
		Márvádi ...	"	32	16	15	1	...
		Do. ...	Hindu.	...	...	...	...	...
		Do. ...	Buddhist.	...	...	...	...	...
		S'rávaka ...	Jain.	497	311	161	25	...
		Total Group 14	....	*95,791*	*35,638*	*56,861*	*3,292*	...
		Total Class C	....	**95,791**	**35,638**	**56,861**	**3,292**	...
D.—Artisan and Village menial.—(Continued.)	17. Gold smiths.	Pánchála ...	Hindu.	19,815	6,864	12,206	745	...
	18. Barbers ...	Náyinda ...	"	7,449	2,617	4,616	216	...
	19. Black smiths	Pánchála.—Kammárá	"	1,268	411	807	50	...
	20. Carpenters, &c.	Pánchála. Badagi ...	"	1,914	707	1,148	59	...
		Pánchála. Gaundor ...	"	...	...	...	...	...
		Total Group 20	....	*1,914*	*707*	*1,148*	*59*	...
	21. Brass & Copper-smiths...	Pánchála.—Gójjégára	"	44	17	27	...	...
	22. Tailors ...	Darzi ...	"	1,865	580	1,215	70	...
	23. Weavers, Calenderers and Dyers.	Góniga ...	"	308	64	231	13	...
		Gádiya ...	Jain.	...	...	...	...	...
		Néyigé ...	Hindu.	17,811	5,790	11,423	598	....
		Total Group 23	....	*18,119*	*5,854*	*11,654*	*611*	...
	24. Washermen.	Agasa ...	"	17,252	6,149	10,643	560	...
	25 (a). Cowherds, &c ...	Golla ...	"	26,893	10,709	15,296	888	...
	26. Shepherds and Wool-weavers. ...	Kuruba ...	"	69,832	23,925	43,807	2,100	...
	27. Oil-pressers.	Gániga ...	"	7,602	2,645	4,749	208	...
	28. Potters ...	Kumbára ...	"	8,959	3,113	5,526	320	...
	30. Salt, &c., workers ...	Uppára ...	"	18,170	6,282	11,369	519	...
	32. Gold-smith's refuse collectors ...	Pánchála.—Jalagára ...	"	56	18	36	2	
	33 (a). Gold-lace makers ...	Ráchévár.—Sarigé ...	"	2	...	2	...	...

TABLE E.—(Continued.)

cial.

Males.

40 and over.					Age not stated.				
Total.	Single.	Married.	Widowed.	Civil condition not stated.	Total.	Single.	Married.	Widowed.	Civil condition not stated.
...	...	...	...	...	...	...	...	...	...
2,469	151	1,707	611	...	...	...	...	...	...
247	21	151	75	...		...	...	...	...
9	...	7	2	...	...	...	...	...	...
...	...	...		...	...	...	...	...	...
	...	...		...	...	...	...	...	...
213	23	139	51	...	...	...	...	...	...
49,638	*2,153*	*36,918*	*10,567*	...	...	...	...	...	...
49,638	**3,153**	**36,918**	**10,507**	...	...	...	...	...	...
10,683	354	7,987	2,342	...	...	...	...	...	...
4,026	133	3,093	800	...	...	...	...	...	...
640	24	459	157	...	...	...	...		...
905	34	676	195	...	...	...	...	...	...
...	...	...	...	..	...	...	...	...	...
905	*34*	*676*	*195*	...		...	...	...	...
23	1	17	5	...	...		...	...	...
961	35	725	201	...	...	...	...	...	...
167	1	132	34	...	...	...	..	...	...
...		...	...	...	...	...	...	...	...
9,498	287	7,225	1,986	...	...	...	...	...	...
9,665	*288*	*7,357*	*2,020*	...	...	...	...	...	...
9,199	334	6,958	1,907	...	...	...	...	...	...
14,360	588	10,893	2,879	...	...	...	...	...	..
35,555	828	28,493	6,234	...	...	...	...	...	...
3,819	128	2,996	695	...	...	...	...	...	...
4,413	138	3,438	837	...	...	...	...	...	...
9,043	267	7,197	1,579	...		...	...	...	..
25	1	17	7	...	...	...	...	...	...
3	...	3		...	...	...	...	...	...

Class.	Group.	Caste, &c., and sub-division.	Religion.	All Ages. Total.	Single.	Married.	Widowed.	Civil condition not stated.
C.—Commercial.—(Concluded.)	14. Traders.—(Concluded.)	Multáni	Hindu.	...		..	...	...
		Nagarta	"	10,612	[illegible]	4,779	2,151	...
		Jain	Jain.	871	269	327	275	..
		Marvádi	..	5	2	3	...	...
		Do	Hindu.	...	...	...	...	...
		Do	Buddhist.	...	...	...	...	...
		S'rávaka	Jain.	924	373	305	246	...
		Total Group 14......	....	227,961	82,113	97,078	48,470	
		Total Class C......	....	**227,961**	**82,413**	**97,078**	**48,470**	...
D.—Artisan and Village menial.—(Continued.)	17. Gold smiths.	Pánchála	Hindu.	47,694	17,072	20,758	9,864	...
	18. Barbers ...	Náyinda	..	17,742	6,191	7,941	3,610	...
	19. Black smiths	Pánchála.—Kammára ...	..	3,019	1,155	1,328	536	...
	20. Carpenters, &c.	Pánchála { Badagi	..	4,225	1,505	1,815	905	...
		Pánchála { Gaunder	..	...	...	...	...	...
		Total Group 20...	....	4,225	1,505	1,815	905	...
	21. Brass & Copper-smiths...	Pánchála.—Gejjégára ...	..	119	43	50	26	...
	22. Tailors ...	Darzi	..	4,232	1,430	2,046	756	...
	23. Weavers, Calenderers and Dyers.	Gópiga	..	668	216	327	125	...
		Gádiya	Jain.	...	...	...	...	...
		Néyigé	Hindu.	43,500	15,347	19,810	8,343	...
		Total Group 23......	....	44,168	15,563	20,137	8,468	...
	24. Washermen.	Agasa	Hindu.	42,268	15,378	18,316	8,594	...
	25 (a). Cowherds, &c. ..	Golla	..	63,107	22,168	27,056	13,883	...
	26. Shepherds and wool weavers ...	Kuruba	..	173,960	63,347	74,518	36,095	...
	27. Oil-pressers.	Gániga	..	18,030	6,423	7,918	3,689	...
	28. Potters ..	Kumbára...	..	19,432	6,790	8,832	3,810	...
	30. Salt, &c., workers....	Uppára	..	44,250	16,968	18,558	8,733	...
	32. Gold-smith's refuse collectors. ..	Pánchála.—Jalagára... ...	"	125	43	57	25	...
	33 (a). Gold-lace makers ...	Ráchévár.—Sarigé	..	7	1	5	1	...

TABLE E.—(Continued.)

cial.

Females.

0 to 9					10 to 14				
Total.	Single.	Married.	Widowed.	Civil condition not stated.	Total.	Single.	Married.	Widowed.	Civil condition not stated.
...	...	...	...	...	...	...	...	...	...
2,932	2,860	72	...	...	1,162	822	338	2	...
196	194	2	...	...	92	61	30	1	...
2	2	...	...	...	...	...	...	...	...
...	...	...	...	...	...	...	...	...	...
...	...	...	...	...	...	...	...	...	...
250	242	7	1	...	141	104	35	2	...
62,601	*61,187*	*1,407*	*7*	...	*23,192*	*15,662*	*7,438*	*92*	...
62,601	**61,187**	**1,407**	**7**	...	**23,192**	**15,662**	**7,438**	**92**	...
13,414	13,150	262	2	...	4,661	3,219	1,419	23	...
4,925	4,867	58	...	...	1,518	1,039	479	...	...
875	864	11	...	...	339	246	93	...	...
1,133	1,108	25	...	...	460	322	137	1	...
...	...	...	...	...	...	...	...	...	...
1,133	*1,108*	25	...	...	*460*	*322*	*137*	*1*	...
30	28	2	...	...	21	14	7	...	...
1,208	1,176	32	...	...	367	234	132	1	...
179	179	...	...	...	39	25	14	...	...
...	...	...	...	...	...	...	...	...	...
12,368	12,018	350	...	...	4,275	2,601	1,660	14	...
12,547	*12,197*	*350*	...	...	*4,314*	*2,626*	*1,674*	*14*	...
11,941	11,718	222	1	...	3,600	2,587	1,002	11	...
17,973	17,752	221	...	...	4,522	3,158	1,355	9	...
49,092	48,503	575	15	...	15,136	10,228	4,876	32	...
5,035	4,979	56	...	...	4,599	4,159	439	1	...
5,289	5,200	89	...	...	1,603	1,151	449	3	...
12,762	12,610	152	...	...	3,817	2,990	815	12	...
30	30	...	...	...	19	10	9	...	...
1	1	...	...	...	...	...	...	...	...

Class.	Group.	Caste, &c., and sub-division.	Religion.	15 to 39 Total.	Single	Married.	Widowed.	Civil condition not stated.
C.—Commercial.—(Concluded.)	14. Traders.—(Concluded.)	Multáni	Hindu.	...	.	...	...	...
		Nagarta	,,	4,506	224	3,586	696	...
		Jain	Jain.	354	14	238	102	...
		Marvádi	,,	3	...	3	...	...
		Do	Hindu.	...	...	...	...	...
		Do	Buddhist.	...	...	...	...	...
		S'rávaka	Jain.	366	22	243	101	...
		Total Group 14......	....	*90,776*	*5,006*	*71,400*	*14,370*	...
		Total Class C......	... ...	**90,776**	**5,006**	**71,400**	**14,370**	...
D.—Artisan and Village menial.—(Continued.)	17. Gold smiths.	Pánchála	Hindu.	18,187	656	14,710	2,821	...
	18. Barbers ...	Nayinda	,,	7,251	268	5,900	1,083	...
	19. Black smiths	Pánchála.—Kammára ...	,,	1,131	41	933	157	...
	20. Carpenters, &c.	Pánchála. { Badagi	,,	1,566	75	1,234	254	...
		Pánchála. { Gaunder	,,	...	...	...	...	...
		Total Group 20......	....	*1,566*	75	*1,234*	257	...
	21. Brass & Copper-smiths.	Pánchála.—Gejjégára ...	,,	35	1	30	4	...
	22. Tailors ...	Darzi	,,	1,710	20	1,505	185	...
	23. Weavers, Calenderers and Dyers.	Gôniga	,,	283	12	243	28	...
		Gádiya	Jain.	...	..	...	...	...
		Nêyigé	Hindu.	17,098	657	14,081	2,360	...
		Total Group 23......	....	*17,381*	*669*	*14,324*	2,388	...
	24. Washermen	Agasa	Hindu.	17,442	997	13,899	2,555	...
	25 (a). Cowherds, &c.	Golla	,,	25,796	1,184	20,240	4,372	...
	26. Shepherds and Wool-weavers.	Kuruba	,,	70,369	4,307	56,037	10,025	...
	27. Oil-pressers	Gániga	,,	6,896	240	5,600	1,056	...
	28. Potters ...	Kumbára	,,	7,818	413	6,346	1,059	...
	30. Salt, &c., workers....	Uppára	,,	17,748	1,283	13,884	2,581	...
	32. Gold-smith's refuse collectors.	Pánchála.—Jalagára... ...	,,	47	3	38	6	...
	33 (a). Gold-lace makers ...	Ráchévár.—Sarigé	,,	5	...	5	...	...

TABLE E.—(Continued.)

cial.

Females.

40 and over.					Age not stated.				
Total.	Single.	Married.	Widowed.	Civil condition not stated.	Total.	Single.	Married.	Widowed.	Civil condition not stated.
...			...	...	...	...	...	...	
2,242	6	783	1,453	...	...	...	...	...	...
229	...	57	172	...	...	...		...	...
...	...	...	...	...	...	...		...	...
...	...	...		...		...	...	...	...
...	...	...		...	...	...	...	...	...
167	5	20	142	...	...	...	...	...	...
51,392	*558*	*16,833*	*34,001*	...		...	...	...	...
51,392	**558**	**16,833**	**34,001**	...	...	...	...	...	...
11,202	47	[illegible]	6,818	...	...			...	...
4,048	17	1,504	2,527	...	...	...		...	...
671	1	291	379	...	...	...	...	...	...
1,066	...	419	647	...	...			...	...
...	...	...	...	...	...	...	...	...	
1,066	...	*419*	*647*	...	...	...	...	...	...
33		11	22	...	...	...	...	...	...
947	...	377	570	...			...	...	...
167	...	70	97	...			...	...	...
...	...	...		...			...	...	...
9,759	71	3,719	5,969	...	...	...	...	...	...
9,926	*71*	*3,789*	*6,066*	...	...	...	...	...	...
9,305	76	3,203	6,026	...		...	...		...
14,816	74	5,240	9,502	...	...	...		...	...
39,363	310	13,027	26,026	...	...	...	...	...	...
4,500	15	1,853	2,632	...	...	...		...	...
[illegible]	[illegible]	1,948	2,718	...	...	...	...	...	...
9,932	85	3,707	6,140	...	...	...	...	...	...
29	...	10	19	...	...	...		...	...
1	...	...	1	...	...	...		...	...

Bangalore

Class.	Group.	Caste, &c. and sub-division.	Religion.	All Ages. Total.	Single.	Married.	Widowed.	Civil condition not stated.
C.—Commercial.—(Concluded.)	11. Traders.—(Concluded.)	Multáni	Hindu.	...	...	...	...	..
		Nagarta	..	2,504	1,226	1,099	179	...
		Jain	Jain.	56	27	26	3	...
		Marvádi	..	...	...	...	...	...
		Do.	Hindu.		...	...	...	...
		Do.	Buddhist.		...	...	...	...
		S'rávaka	Jain.	...	...	...	...	...
		Total Group 11......	....	*25,020*	*13,107*	*10,454*	*1,459*	...
	Total Class C...		....	**25,020**	**13,107**	**10,454**	**1,459**	...
D.—Artisan and Village menial.—(Continued.)	17. Gold smiths.	Pánchála	Hindu.	6,131	3,077	2,657	397	...
	18. Barbers ...	Náyinda	..	3,435	1,703	1,547	185	...
	19. Black smiths	Pánchála.—Kammára ..	..	257	120	113	24	...
	20. Carpenters, &c.	Pánchála. { Badagi ...	..	...	...	...	...	...
		Pánchála. { Gaundar ...	..	...	...	...	...	...
		Total Group 20......	....	...	...	...	...	...
	21. Brass & Copper-smiths ...	Pánchála.—Gojjégára	..	21	9	11	1	...
	22. Tailors...	Darzi	..	864	417	407	40	...
	23. Weavers, Calenderers and Dyers.	Góniga	..	341	182	160	19	...
		Gadiya	Jain.	...	...	...	...	...
		Néyigé	Hindu.	11,827	5,326	5,748	753	...
		Total Group 23......	....	*12,168*	*5,488*	*5,908*	*772*	...
	24. Washermen .	Agasa	..	5,179	2,557	2,295	327	...
	26 (a). Cowherds, &c. ...	Golla	..	9,461	4,749	4,096	616	...
	26. Shepherds and Wool-weavers.	Kuruba	..	19,618	9,426	8,934	1,258	...
	27. Oil-pressers .	Gániga	..	2,907	1,431	1,324	152	...
	28. Potters ...	Kumbára	..	1,978	956	919	103	...
	31. Salt, &c., workers. ..	Uppára	..	728	358	312	58	...
	32. Gold-smith's refuse collectors. ...	Pánchála.—Jalagára	..	27	17	8	2	...
	33 (a). Gold-lace makers ...	Ráchévár—Sarigé	..	5	2	3	...	...

TABLE E.—(*Continued.*)

District

Males.

0 to 9					10 to 14				
Total.	Single.	Married.	Widowed.	Civil condition not stated.	Total.	Single.	Married.	Widowed.	Civil condition not stated.
...	...	...	...	...	...	...	...	...	...
623	623	...	...	...	263	254	8	1	...
7	7	...	...	...	5	5	...	...	...
...	...	...	...	...	...	...	...	...	...
...	...	...	...	...	...	...	...	...	...
...	...	...	...	...	...	...	...	...	...
...	...	...	...	...	...	...	...	...	...
6,258	*6,257*	*1*	...	...	*2,686*	*2,632*	*53*	*1*	...
6,258	**6,257**	**1**	...	...	**2,686**	**2,632**	**53**	**1**	...
1,635	1,633	2	...	...	648	626	22	...	...
989	989	...	...	...	276	270	6	...	...
71	71		...	...	23	23	...	...	...
...	...	...	...	...	...	...	...	...	...
...	...	...	...	...	...	...	...	...	...
...	...	...	...	...	...	...	...	...	...
5	5	...	...	...	2	2	...	...	...
236	235	1	...	...	102	95	7	...	...
97	97	...	...	...	42	42	...	...	...
...	...	...	...	...	...	...	...	...	...
3,020	2,999	21	...	...	1,096	999	96	1	...
3,117	*3,096*	*21*	...	...	*1,138*	*1,041*	*96*	*1*	...
1,484	1,480	4	...	...	128	111	17	...	...
2,536	2,536	...	...	...	882	849	33	...	...
5,186	5,186	...	...	...	1,673	1,627	46	...	...
834	834	...	...	...	260	253	7	...	...
593	592	...	...	...	175	168	7	...	...
176	176	...	...	...	63	63	...	...	...
9	9	...	...	...	4	4	...	...	...
2	2	...	...	...	...	...	...	...	...

Class.	Group.	Caste, &c. and sub-division.	Religion.	15 to 39. Total.	Single.	Married.	Widowed.	Civil condition not stated.
C.—Commercial.—(Concluded.)	14. Traders.—(Concluded.)	Multáni	Hindu.	...	...	...	...	...
		Nagarta	,,	987	316	641	30	...
		Jain	Jain.	31	14	16	1	...
		Marvádi	,,	...		...	...	...
		Do.	Hindu.	...	...	...	...	...
		Do.	Buddhist.	...	...	...	...	...
		S'rávaka	Jain.	...	...	...	...	...
		Total Group 14	....	*10,431*	*3,960*	*6,207*	*264*	...
		Total Class C	....	**10,431**	**3,960**	**6,207**	**264**	...
D.—Artisan and Village menial.—(Continued.)	17. Gold smiths.	Pánchála	Hindu.	2,438	776	1,583	79	...
	18. Barbers	Náyinda	,,	1,342	428	878	36	...
	19. Black smiths	Pánchála.—Kammára	,,	101	23	75	3	...
	20. Carpenters, &c.	Pánchála. Badagi	,,	...	...	...	...	...
		Pánchála. Gaunder	,,	...	...	...	...	...
		Total Group 20	....	...	...	...	...	...
	21. Brass & Copper-smiths	Pánchála.—Gejjégára	,,	10	2	8	...	...
	22. Tailors	Darzi	,,	321	86	228	7	...
	23. Weavers, Calenderers and Dyers.	Góniga	,,	119	22	91	6	...
		Gádiya	Jain.	...	...	...	...	...
		Néyigé	Hindu.	4,736	1,245	3,321	167	...
		Total Group 23	....	*4,855*	*1,267*	*3,415*	*173*	...
	24. Washermen	Agasa	,,	1,962	644	1,251	67	...
	26 (a). Cowherds, &c.	Golla	,,	3,668	1,296	2,246	126	...
	26. Shepherds and Wool-weavers.	Kuruba	,,	7,931	2,534	5,106	291	...
	27. Oil-pressers.	Gániga	,,	1,111	325	759	27	...
	28. Potters.	Kumbára	,,	753	184	546	23	...
	30. Salt, &c. workers.	Uppára	,,	303	115	175	13	...
	32. Gold-smith's refuse collectors.	Pánchála.—Julagára	,,	9	3	6	...	...
	33 (a). Gold-lace makers.	Náchévár—Sarigé	,,	2	...	2	...	...

TABLE E.—(Continued.)

District.

Males.

40 and over. Total.	Single.	Married.	Widowed.	Civil condition not stated.	Age not stated. Total.	Single.	Married.	Widowed.	Civil condition not stated.
...	...	...	...	...	...	...	...	...	...
631	33	450	148	...			...	...	...
13	1	10	2	...	...	...	...	...	...
...	...	...	...	...	...	...	...	...	...
...	...	...	...	...	...	...	...	...	...
...	...	...	...	...	...	...	...	...	...
...	...	...	...	...	...	...	...	...	...
5,645	*258*	*4,193*	*1,194*	...	...	...	...	...	...
5,645	**258**	**4,193**	**1,194**	...	...	...	...	...	...
1,410	42	1,050	318	...	...	...	...	...	...
828	16	663	149	...	...	...	...	...	...
62	3	38	21	...	...	...	...	...	...
...	...	...	...	...	...	...	...	...	...
...	...	...	...	...	...	...	...	...	...
...	...	...	...	...	...	...	...	...	...
4	...	3	1	...	...	...	...	...	...
205	1	171	33	...	...	...	...	...	...
83	1	69	13	...	...	...	...	...	...
...	...	...	...	...	...	...	...	...	...
2,975	83	2,307	585	...	...	...	...	...	...
3,058	*84*	*2,376*	*598*	...	...	...	...	...	...
1,305	22	1,023	260	...	...	...	...	...	...
2,375	68	1,817	490	...	...	...	...	...	...
4,828	79	3,782	967	...	...	...	...	...	...
702	19	558	125	...	...	...	...	...	...
458	12	366	80	...	...	...	...	...	...
186	4	137	45	...	...	...	...	...	...
5	1	2	2	...	...	...	...	...	...
1	...	1	...	...	...	...	...	...	...

Bangalore

Class.	Group.	Caste, &c. and sub-division.	Religion.	All Ages. Total.	Single.	Married.	Widowed.	Civil condition not stated.
C.—Commercial.—(*Concluded.*)	14. Traders.—(*Concluded.*)	Múltani	Hindu.	...	...	...	...	...
		Nagarta	,,	2,565	887	1,088	590	...
		Jain	Jain.	32	10	11	8	...
		Marvádi	,,	...	...	...	...	...
		Do.	Hindu.	...	...	...	...	...
		Do.	Buddhist.	...	...	...	...	...
		S'rávaka	Jain.	...	...	...	...	...
		Total Group 14......	....	25,306	8,721	11,132	5,453	...
		Total Class C......	....	**25,306**	**8.721**	**11,132**	**5,453**	...
D.—Artisan and Village menial.—(*Continued.*)	17. Gold smiths.	Pánchála	Hindu.	5,949	1,955	2,805	1,189	...
	18. Barbers	Náyinda	,,	3,393	1,128	1,551	714	...
	19. Black smiths	Pánchála.—Kammára ...	,,	281	106	132	43	...
	20. Carpenters, &c.	Pánchála. { Badagi ...	,,	...	...	...	...	...
		Pánchála. { Gáunder ...	,,	...	...	...	...	...
		Total Group 20......	....	...	...	...	...	...
	21. Brass & Copper-smiths...	Pánchála.—Gejjégára ...	,,	29	9	14	6	...
	22. Tailors ...	Darzi	,,	901	325	420	156	...
	23. Weavers, Calenderers and Dyers.	Góniga	,,	278	98	136	44	...
		Gádiya	Jain.	...	...	...	...	...
		Néyigé	Hindu.	11,867	3,772	5,895	2,200	...
		Total Group 23......	....	12,145	3,870	6,034	2,244	...
	24. Washermen.	Agasa	,,	5,261	1,832	2,403	1,026	...
	26 (*a*). Cowherds, &c. ...	Golla ...	,,	9,661	3,042	4,256	2,363	...
	26. Shepherds and Wool-weavers.	Kuruba	,,	20,995	6,561	9,595	4,839	...
	27. Oil-pressers.	Gániga	,,	2,869	975	1,335	559	...
	28. Potters ...	Kumbára	,,	1,977	609	946	422	...
	30. Salt, &c. workers.	Uppára	,,	769	245	332	192	...
	32. Gold-smith's refuse collectors. ...	Pánchála.—Jalagára ...	,,	28	12	10	6	...
	33 (*a*). Gold-lace makers	Rachévar.—Sarigé	,,	5	1	3	1	...

TABLE E.—(*Continued.*)

District.

Females.

0 to 9					10 to 14				
Total.	Single.	Married.	Widowed.	Civil condition not stated.	Total.	Single.	Married.	Widowed.	Civil condition not stated.
...	...	...		...	...	...	...	...	...
674	66[illegible]	[illegible]	..	.	21[illegible]	15[illegible]	59	...	...
10	9	1	...	..	3	1	2	...	...
...	...	...	...		...		...	...	...
...	...	...	...	...			...	...	...
...	...		...	...	...	...	...	...	...
...	...	...	...		...	...	...	...	...
7,163	*6,933*	*228*	*2*	...	*2,2[illegible]1*	*1,[illegible]73*	*866*	*12*	...
7,163	**6,933**	**228**	**2**	..	**2 251**	**1 573**	**866**	**12**	...
1,591	1,545	47	[illegible]	.	5[illegible]	318	2[illegible]5	[illegible]3	...
962	939	23	..	.	250	154	96	...	...
79	78	1	..	.	[illegible]	12	11	...	...
...	...	...		...	...		...	...	...
...		...	...		..	...	...	...	...
...	...	...	..	...	..	...	...	...	...
5	5	...	...	...	4	3	1	...	...
283	272	11	...	...	87	53	34	...	...
84	84	...	...	...	22	11	11	...	...
...	...	...	...		...	...	...	..	...
3,357	3,217	140	...	...	1,080	445	630	5	...
3,441	*3,301*	*140*	...	...	*1,102*	*456*	*641*	5	...
1,541	1,488	52	1	..	379	248	127	4	...
2,531	2,487	44	...	...	797	441	355	...	...
5,352	5,260	92	...	...	1,703	1,027	676	...	...
847	830	17	...	...	224	123	101	...	...
528	511	17	...	...	131	73	58	...	...
198	195	3	...	...	67	44	23	...	...
7	7	...	...	...	7	3	4	...	...
1	1	...	...	...	...		...	...	...

Bangalore

Class.	Group.	Caste, &c. and sub-division.	Religion.	15 to 39 Total.	Single.	Married.	Widowed.	Civil condition not stated.
C.—Commercial.—(Concluded.)	14. Traders.—(Concluded.)	Multani	Hindu.	...	...	...	...	...
		Nagarta	,,	985	61	773	151	...
		Jain	Jain.	7	...	6	1	...
		Marvádi	,,	...	...	...	...	...
		Do.	Hindu.	...	...	...	...	...
		Do.	Buddhist.	...	...	...	...	...
		S'rávaka	Jain.	...	...	...	...	...
		Total Group 14......	....	*9,553*	*359*	*7,675*	*1,519*	...
		Total Class C......	....	**9,553**	**359**	**7,675**	**1,519**	...
D.—Artisan and Village menial.—(Continued.)	17. Gold smiths.	Pánchála	Hindu.	2,387	58	2,016	313	...
	18. Barbers ...	Náyinda	,,	1,331	31	1,164	186	...
	19. Black smiths	Pánchála.—Kammára ...	,,	110	6	90	14	...
	20. Carpenters, &c.	Pánchála. { Badagi	,,	...	...	...	...	...
		Pánchála. { Gaunder... ...	,,	...	...	...	...	...
		Total Group 20......	....	...	...	...	...	...
	21. Brass & Copper-smiths...	Pánchála.—Gejjégára ...	,,	10	1	9	..	...
	22. Tailors ...	Darzi	,,	308	...	283	25	...
	23. Weavers, Calenderers and Dyers.	Góniga	,,	109	3	100	6	...
		Gádiya	Jain.	...	...	...	...	...
		Néyigé	Hindu.	4,585	100	3,987	498	...
		Total Group 23......	....	4,694	*103*	*4,087*	504	...
	24. Washermen.	Agasa	,,	2,074	84	1,771	219	...
	26 (a). Cowherds, &c. ...	Golla	,,	3,723	99	2,983	641	...
	26. Shepherds and Wool-weavers. ...	Kuruba	,,	8,474	236	6,893	1,345	...
	27. Oil-pressers.	Gániga	,,	1,076	20	912	144	...
	28. Potters.	Kumbára...	,,	801	20	675	106	...
	30. Salt, &c. workers....	Uppára	,,	283	5	240	38	...
	32. Gold-smith's refuse collectors ...	Pánchála.—Jalagára... ...	..	9	2	5	2	..
	33 (a). Gold-lace makers ...	Ráchévár.—Sarigé	,,	3	...	3	...	...

TABLE E.—(*Continued.*)

District.

Females.

40 and over.					Age not stated.				
Total.	Single.	Married.	Widowed.	Civil condition not stated.	Total.	Single.	Married.	Widowed.	Civil condition not stated.
...	...	...	...	...	...	...	...	...	...
692	5	248	439	...	...	...	...	...	...
12	...	5	7	...	...	...	...	...	...
...	...	...	...	...	...	...	...	...	...
...	...	...	...	...	...	...	...	...	...
...	...	...	...	...	...	...	...	...	...
...	...	...	...	...	...	...	...	...	...
6,339	*56*	*2,363*	*3,924*	...	...	...	...	...	...
6,339	**56**	**2,363**	**3,924**	...	...	...	...	...	...
1,404	4	529	871	...	...	...	...	...	...
800	4	268	528	...	...	...	...	...	...
59	...	30	29	...	...	...	...	...	...
...	...	...	...	...	...	...	...	...	...
...	...	...	...	...	...	...	...	...	...
...	...	...	...	...	...	...	...	...	...
10	...	4	6	...	...	...	...	...	...
223	...	92	131	...	...	...	...	...	...
63	...	25	38	...	...	...	...	...	...
...	...	...	...	...	...	...	...	...	...
2,845	10	1,138	1,697	...	...	...	...	...	...
2,908	*10*	*1,163*	*1,735*	...	...	...	...	...	...
1,267	12	453	802	...	...	...	...	...	...
2,610	12	876	1,722	...	...	...	...	...	...
5,466	38	1,944	3,484	...	...	...	...	...	...
722	2	305	415	...	...	...	...	...	...
517	5	196	316	...	...	...	...	...	...
221	1	66	154	...	...	...	...	...	...
5	...	1	4	...	...	...	...	...	...
1	...	...	1	...	...	...	...	...	...

Kolar

Class.	Group.	Caste, &c. and subdivision.	Religion.	All Ages. Total.	Single.	Married.	Widowed.	Civil condition not stated.
C.—Commercial.—(*Concluded.*)	14. Traders.—(*Concluded.*)	Multáni	Hindu.	...	...	...	...	...
		Nagarta	"	1,426	737	603	107	...
		Jain	Jain.	13	9	5	2	...
		Marvádi	"	...	...	...	...	...
		Do.	Hindu.	...	...	...	...	...
		Do.	Buddhist.	...	...	...	...	...
		S'rávaka	Jain.	...	...	...	...	...
		Total Group 14	....	*27,739*	*14,104*	*11,835*	*1,860*	...
		Total Class C	....	**27,739**	**14,104**	**11,835**	**1,860**	...
D.—Artisan and Village menial.—(*Continued.*)	17. Gold smiths.	Pánchála	Hindu.	4,483	2,224	1,947	312	...
	18. Barbers ...	Náyinda	"	4,401	2,174	1,937	290	...
	19. Black smiths	Pánchála.—Kammára	"	323	165	137	21	...
	20. Carpenters, &c.	Pánchála. { Badagi	"	19	7	11	1	...
		Pánchála. { Gaundar... ...	"	...	...	...	...	...
		Total Group 20	....	*19*	*7*	*11*	*1*	...
	21. Brass & Copper-smiths ...	Pánchála.—Gejjégára ...	"	...	...	...	...	...
	22. Tailors ...	Darzi	"	300	153	140	7	...
	23. Weavers, Calenderers and Dyers.	Gópiga	"	39	24	13	2	...
		Gádiya	Jain.	...	...	...	...	...
		Néyigé	Hindu.	4,284	2,041	1,957	286	...
		Total Group 23	....	*4,323*	*2,065*	*1,970*	*288*	...
	24. Washermen ...	Agasa	"	5,228	2,619	2,245	364	...
	26 (*a*). Cowherds, &c. ...	Golla	"	10,038	5,111	4,243	684	...
	26. Shepherds and Wool weavers.	Kuruba	"	17,511	9,347	7,151	1,013	...
	27. Oil-pressers...	Gániga	"	2,874	1,363	1,309	202	...
	28. Potters ...	Kumbára...	"	2,073	1,005	906	162	...
	30. Salt, &c., workers ...	Uppára	"	1,673	831	761	81	...
	32. Gold-smith's refuse collectors. ...	Pánchála.—Jalagára... ...	"	7	3	3	1	...
	33 (*a*). Gold-lace makers ...	Rácbévár.—Sarigé	"	3	1	2	...	...

TABLE E.—(*Continued.*)

District.

Males.

0 to 9					10 to 14.				
Total.	Single.	Married.	Widowed.	Civil condition not stated.	Total.	Single.	Married.	Widowed.	Civil condition not stated.
...	...	...	...	...	...	...	...	...	...
317	317	...	...	...	129	127	2	...	...
1	1	...	...	...	2	2	...	...	...
...	...	...	...	...	...	...	...	...	...
...	...	...	...	...	...	...	...	...	...
...	...	...	...	...	...	...	...	...	...
...	...	...	...	...	...	...	...	...	...
6,728	*6,728*	...	...	...	*2,270*	*2,234*	*36*	...	...
6,728	**6,728**	...	...	...	**2,270**	**2,234**	**36**	...	...
1,070	1,070	...	...	...	356	348	8	...	...
1,170	1,170	...	...	...	284	279	5	...	...
72	72	...	...	...	29	28	1	...	...
3	3	...	...	...	2	2	...	...	...
...	...	...	...	...	...	...	...	...	...
3	*3*	...	...	...	2	2	...	*4*	...
...	...	...	...	...	...	...	...	...	...
91	91	...	...	...	19	19	...	...	...
16	16	...	...	...	5	5	...	...	...
...	...	...	...	...	...	...	...	...	...
1,065	1,065	...	...	...	310	301	9	...	...
1,081	*1,081*	...	...	...	*315*	*306*	*9*	...	...
1,370	1,370	...	...	...	381	379	2	...	...
2,466	2,466	...	...	...	722	714	8	...	...
5,809	5,799	10	...	...	1,284	1,272	12	...	...
714	714	...	...	...	205	202	3	...	...
554	554	...	...	...	149	149	...	...	...
390	390	...	...	...	111	111	...	...	...
1	1	...	...	...	2	2	...	...	...
...	...	...	...	...	1	1	...	...	...

Class.	Group.	Caste, &c. and sub-division.	Religion.	15 to 30. Total.	15 to 30. Single.	15 to 30. Married.	15 to 30. Widowed.	15 to 30. Civil condition not stated.
C.—Commercial.—(Concluded.)	14. Traders.—(Concluded.)	Multâni	Hindu.	...	...	...	...	...
		Nagarta	,,	635	273	343	19	...
		Jain	Jain.	7	4	3	...	...
		Marvâḍi	,,	...	...	...	...	...
		Do.	Hindu.	...	...	...	...	...
		Do.	Buddhist.	...	...	...	...	...
		S'râvaka	Jain.	...	...	...	...	...
		Total Group 14......	....	*11,652*	*4,763*	*6,531*	*355*	...
		Total Class C......	....	**11,652**	**4,763**	**6,534**	**355**	...
D.—Artisan and Village menial.—(Continued.)	17. Gold smiths.	Pânchâḷa	Hindu.	1,919	741	1,097	81	...
	18. Barbers ...	Nâyindâ	,,	1,825	682	1,091	52	...
	19. Black smiths	Pânchâḷa.—Kammâra ...	,,	152	61	88	3	...
	20. Carpenters, &c.	Pânchâḷa. { Baḍagi ...	,,	10	2	7	1	...
		Pânchâḷa. { Gaunḍêr... ...	,,	...	...	...	...	...
		Total Group 20......	....	*10*	*2*	*7*	*1*	...
	21. Brass & Copper-smiths...	Pânchâḷa.—Gejjêgâra ...	,,	...	...	...	...	...
	22. Tailors ...	Darzi	,,	130	43	86	1	...
	23. Weavers, Calenderers and Dyers.	Gôṇiga	,,	11	3	8	...	...
		Gadiya	Jain.	...	...	...	...	...
		Nêyigê	Hindu.	1,809	629	1,124	56	...
		Total Group 23......	....	*1,820*	*632*	*1,132*	*56*	...
	24. Washermen.	Agasa	,,	2,121	799	1,253	69	...
	26 (a). Cowherds, &c. ...	Golla	,,	4,344	1,812	2,407	125	...
	26. Shepherds and Wool-weavers.	Kuruba	,,	6,782	2,130	4,354	298	...
	27. Oil-pressers .	Gâṇiga	,,	1,173	408	729	36	...
	28. Potters ...	Kumbâra...	,,	829	287	505	37	...
	30. Salt, &c., workers ...	Uppâra	,,	780	312	450	18	...
	32. Gold-smith's refuse collectors. ...	Pânchâḷa.—Jalagâra... ...	,,	3	..	3	...	...
	33 (a). Gold-lace makers ...	Râchêvâr.—Surigê	,,	...	...	...	...	...

TABLE E.—(*Continued.*)

District.

Males.

10 and over.					Age not stated.				
Total.	Single.	Married.	Widowed.	Civil condition not stated.	Total.	Single.	Married.	Widowed.	Civil condition not stated.
...	...	...	...	...	...	...	...	...	...
365	20	257	88	...	...	...	...	...	...
6	2	2	2	...	...	...	...	...	...
...	...	...	...	...	...	...	...	...	...
...	...	...	...	...	...	...	...	...	...
...	...	...	...	...	...	...	...	...	...
...	...	...	...	...	...	...	...	...	...
7,149	*379*	*5,265*	*1,505*	...	...	...	...	...	...
7,149	**379**	**5,265**	**1,505**	...	...	...	...	...	...
1,138	65	842	231	...	...	...	...	...	...
1,122	43	841	238	...	...	...	...	...	...
70	4	48	18	...	...	...	...	...	...
4	...	4	...	...	...	...	...	...	...
...	...	...	...	...	...	...	...	...	...
4	...	*4*	...	...	...	...	...	...	...
...	...	...	...	...	...	...	...	...	...
60	...	54	6	...	...	...	...	...	...
7	...	5	2	...	...	...	...	...	...
...	...	...	...	...	...	...	...	...	...
1,100	46	824	230	...	...	...	...	...	...
1,107	*46*	*829*	*232*	...	...	...	...	...	...
1,356	71	990	295	...	...	...	...	...	...
2,506	119	1,828	559	...	...	...	...	...	...
3,636	146	2,775	715	...	...	...	...	...	...
782	39	577	166	...	...	...	...	...	...
541	15	401	125	...	...	...	...	...	...
392	18	311	63	...	...	...	...	...	...
1	...	...	1	...	...	...	...	...	...
2		2	...	...	...	...	...	...	...

Kolar

Class.	Group.	Caste, &c. and sub-division.	Religion.	All Ages. Total.	Single.	Married.	Widowed.	Civil condition not stated.
C.—Commercial.—(Concluded.)	14. Traders.—(Concluded).	Multáni ...	Hindu.	...	...	...	...	...
		Nagarta ...	,,	1,558	473	663	423	...
		Jain ...	Jain.	2	...	2	...	...
		Marvádi ...	,,	...	...	...	...	...
		Do. ...	Hindu.	...	...	...	...	...
		Do. ...	Budhist.	...	...	...	...	...
		S'rávaka ...	Jain.	...	...	...	...	...
		Total Group 14	....	2,7280	8,308	12,154	6,818	...
		Total Class C	....	**27,280**	**8,308**	**12,154**	**6,818**	...
D.—Artisan and Village monial.—(Continued.)	17. Gold smiths.	Pánchála ...	Hindu.	4,490	1,314	2,030	1,146	...
	18. Barbers ...	Náyinda ...	,,	4,158	1,297	1,896	965	...
	19. Black-smiths	Pánchála.—Kammára ...	,,	336	111	130	95	...
	20. Carpenters, &c.	Pánchála. { Badagi ...	,,	23	8	12	3	...
		Pánchála. { Gaunder ...	,,	...	...	...	...	...
		Total Group 20	....	23	8	12	3	...
	21. Brass & Copper-smiths ...	Pánchála.—Gejjégára ...	,,	...	...	...	...	...
	22. Tailors ...	Darzi ...	,,	274	90	142	42	...
	23. Weavers, Calenderers and Dyers.	Góniga ...	,,	36	17	12	7	...
		Gádiya ...	Jain.	...	...	...	...	...
		Néyigé ...	Hindu.	4,337	1,252	2,035	1,050	...
		Total Group 23	....	4,373	1,269	2,047	1,057	...
	24. Washermen.	Agasa ...	,,	5,099	1,571	2,285	1,243	...
	26 (a). Cowherds, &c.	Golla ...	,,	9,984	3,122	4,250	2,612	...
	26. Shepherds and Wool-weavers.	Kuruba ...	,,	17,793	5,740	7,784	4,269	...
	27. Oil-pressers.	Gániga ...	,,	2,916	861	1,329	726	...
	28. Potters ...	Kumbára ...	,,	1,889	586	873	430	...
	30. Salt, &c., workers. ...	Uppára ...	,,	1,454	470	647	337	...
	32. Golp smith's refuse collectors.	Pánchála.—Jalagára ...	,,	7	1	5	1	...
	33 (a). Gold-lace makers. ...	Rachóvar.—Sarigé ...	,,	2	...	2	...	...

TABLE E.—(*Continued*.)

District.

Females.

0 to 9					10 to 14				
Total.	Single.	Married.	Widowed.	Civil condition not stated.	Total.	Single.	Married.	Widowed.	Civil condition not stated.
...	...	...	...	...	...	...	...	...	...
364	360	4	...	...	111	75	36	...	...
...	...	...	...	...	...	...	...	...	...
...		...	...	...	...	...	...	...	...
...	...	...	...	...	...	...	...	...	...
...	...	...	...	...	...	...	...	...	...
...	...	...	...	...	...	...	...	...	...
6,961	*6,825*	*136*	...	...	*2,005*	*1,034*	*961*	*10*	...
6,961	**6,825**	**136**	...	...	**2,005**	**1,034**	**961**	**10**	...
1,145	1,117	28	...	...	315	161	150	4	...
1,159	1,144	15	...	...	275	120	155	...	...
97	95	2	...		26	12	14	...	...
7	7	...	...	...	2	1	1	...	...
...	...	...	...	...	...	...	...	...	...
7	*7*	...	...	...	*2*	*1*	*1*	...	...
...	...	...	...	...	...	...	...		
81	78	3	...	...	20	12	8	...	...
13	13	...	...	...	5	4	1	...	...
...	...	...	...	...	...	...	...	...	...
1,107	1,077	30	...	...	303	137	162	4	...
1,120	*1,090*	*30*	...	...	*308*	*141*	*163*	*4*	...
1,328	1,328	...	...	...	271	173	98	...	...
2,556	2,546	10	...	...	687	422	264	1	...
4,589	4,490	84	15	...	1,494	939	542	13	...
697	697	...	...	...	201	131	69	1	...
495	495	...	...	...	114	69	45	...	...
388	383	5	...	...	105	58	47	...	
1	1	...	...	...	2	...	2	...	...
...	...	...	...	...	...	...		...	...

Class.	Group.	Caste, &c. and sub-division.	Religion.	15 to 39 Total.	15 to 39 Single.	15 to 39 Married.	15 to 39 Widowed.	15 to 39 Civil condition not stated.
C.—Commercial.—(Concluded.)	14. Traders.—(Concluded.)	Multáni ...	Hindu.	...	...	...	...	...
		Nagarta ...	,,	642	37	486	119	...
		Jain ...	Jain.	2	...	2	...	...
		Marvâḍi ...	,,	...	...	...	...	...
		Do. ...	Hindu.	...	...	...	...	...
		Do. ...	Buddhist.	...	...	...	...	...
		S'rávaka ...	Jain.	...	...	...	...	...
		Total Group 14	....	*11,176*	*358*	*8,916*	*1,902*	...
		Total Class C	....	**11,176**	**358**	**8,916**	**1,902**	...
D.—Artisan and Village menial.—(Continued.)	17. Gold smiths.	Pánchála ...	Hindu.	1,832	33	1,475	325	...
	18. Barbers	Náyinda ...		1,718	31	1,399	288	...
	19. Black smiths	Pánchála.—Kammára		134	1	92	38	...
	20. Carpenters, &c.	Pánchála—Badagi ...		8	...	7	1	...
		Pánchála—Gaunder ...		...	...	...	...	...
		Total Group 20	....	*8*	...	*7*	*1*	...
	21. Brass & Copper-smiths ...	Pánchála.—Gejjégára	,,	...	...	...	...	...
	22. Tailors ...	Darzi ...	,,	110	...	102	8	...
	23. Weavers, Calenderers and Dyers.	Góniga ...	,,	12	...	10	2	...
		Gádiya ...	Jain.	...	...	...	...	...
		Néyigé ...	Hindu.	1,772	37	1,445	290	...
		Total Group 23	....	*1,784*	*37*	*1,455*	*290*	...
	24. Washermen	Agasa ...	,,	2,226	67	1,787	372	...
	26 (a). Cowherds, &c.	Golla ...	,,	4,242	143	3,259	840	...
	26. Shepherds and Wool weavers.	Kuruba ...	,,	6,930	302	5,390	1,238	...
	27. Oil-pressers	Gániga ...	,,	1,246	30	1,013	203	...
	28. Potters ...	Kumbára ...	,,	808	20	667	121	...
	30. Salt, &c., workers.	Uppára ...	,,	608	24	489	95	...
	32. Gold smith's refuse collectors.	Pánchála.—Jalagára ...	,,	3	...	3	...	...
	33 (a). Gold-lace makers ...	Ráchévár.—Sarigé ...	,,	2	...	2	...	...

TABLE E.—(*Continued.*)

District.

Females.

40 and over.					Age not stated.				
Total.	Single.	Married.	Widowed.	Civil condition not stated.	Total.	Single.	Married.	Widowed.	Civil condition not stated.
...	...	...	...	...	...	...	...	...	...
441	1	136	304	...	...	...	...	...	...
...	...	...	...	...	...	...	...	...	...
...	...	...	...	...	...	...	...	...	...
...	...	...	...	...	...	...	...	...	...
...	...	...	...	...	...	...	...	...	...
...	...	...	...	...	...	...	...	...	...
7,138	*91*	*2,141*	*4,906*	...	...	...	...	...	...
7,138	**91**	**2,141**	**4,906**	...	...	...	...	...	...
1,198	4	377	817	...	...	...	...	...	...
1,006	2	327	677	...	...	...	...	...	...
79	...	22	57	...	...	...	...	...	...
6	...	4	2	...	...	...	...	...	...
...	...	...	...	...	...	...	...	...	...
6	...	*4*	*2*	...	...	...	...	...	...
...	...	...	...	...	...	...	...	...	...
63	...	29	34	...	...	...	...	...	...
6	...	1	5	...	...	...	...	...	...
...	...	...	...	...	...	...	...	...	...
1,155	1	398	756	...	...	...	...	...	...
1,161	*1*	*399*	*761*	...	...	...	...	...	...
1,274	3	400	871	...	...	...	...	...	...
2,499	11	717	1,771	...	...	...	...	...	...
4,780	9	1,768	3,003	...	...	...	...	...	...
772	3	247	522	...	...	...	...	...	...
472	2	161	309	...	...	...	...	...	...
353	5	106	242	...	...	...	...	...	...
1	...	...	1	...	...	...	...	...	...
...	...	...	...	...	...	...	...	...	...

Class.	Group.	Caste, &c. and sub-division.	Religion.	All Ages. Total.	Single.	Married.	Widowed.	Civil condition not stated.
C.—Commercial—(Concluded.)	14. Traders—(Concluded.)	Multáni	Hindu.	...	...	...	...	...
		Nagarta	,,	163	92	61	10	...
		Jain	Jain.	182	98	69	15	...
		Márváḍi	,,	...	...	...	...	...
		Do.	Hindu.	...	...	...	...	...
		Do.	Buddhist.	...	...	...	...	...
		S'rávaka	Jain.	...	...	...	...	...
		Total Group 14......	....	*20,634*	*10,002*	*9,023*	*1,609*	...
		Total Class C......	....	**20,634**	**10,002**	**9,023**	**1,609**	...
D.—Artisan and Village menial—(Continued.)	17. Gold smiths.	Pánchála	Hindu.	4,266	2,212	1,771	283	...
	18. Barbers ...	Náyinda	,,	1,963	1,026	812	125	...
	19. Black smiths	Pánchála.—Kammára ...	,,	612	303	265	44	...
	20. Carpenters, &c.	Pánchála.—Badagi	,,	11	5	6	...	...
		Pánchála.—Gaunder ...	,,	...	...	...	...	...
		Total Group 20......	....	*11*	*5*	*6*	...	...
	21. Brass & Copper-smiths ...	Pánchála.—Gejjégára ...	,,	...	...	...	...	...
	22. Tailors ...	Darzi	,,	465	209	229	27	...
	23. Weavers, Calenderers and Dyers.	Góniga	,,	222	74	130	18	...
		Gádiyá	Jain.	...	...	...	...	...
		Néyigé	Hindu.	3,806	1,912	1,633	261	...
		Total Group 23......	....	*4,028*	*1,986*	*1,763*	*279*	...
	24. Washermen.	Agasa	,,	5,041	2,454	2,220	367	...
	26 (a). Cowherds, &c. ...	Golla	,,	19,636	10,907	7,596	1,133	...
	26. Shepherds and Wool-weavers.	Kuruba	,,	19,165	9,780	8,331	1,054	...
	27. Oil-pressers.	Gániga	,,	1,599	792	728	79	...
	28. Potters ...	Kumbára...	,,	1,618	766	732	120	...
	30. Salt, &c., workers ...	Uppára	,,	5,798	3,204	2,274	320	...
	32. Gold-smith's refuse collectors.	Pánchála.—Julagára... ...	,,	3	1	2	...	...
	33 (a). Gold-lace makers. ...	Ráchévár.—Sarigé	,,	...	...	...	...	...

TABLE E.—*(Continued.)*

District.

Males.

0 to 9					10 to 14				
Total.	Single.	Married.	Widowed.	Civil condition not stated.	Total.	Single.	Married.	Widowed.	Civil condition not stated.
...	...	...	...	...	...	...	...	...	...
44	44	...	...	...	23	23	...	...	...
34	34	...	...	...	14	14	...	...	...
...	...	...	...	...	...	...	...	...	...
...	...	...	...	...	...	...	...	...	...
...	...	...	...	...	...	...	...	...	...
...	...	...	...	...	...	...	...	...	...
4,986	*4,986*	...	...	...	*2,113*	*2,082*	*31*	...	...
4,986	**4,986**	...	...	...	**2,113**	**2,082**	**31**	...	...
1,282	1,282	...	...	...	686	653	33	...	...
569	569	...	...	...	297	287	10	...	...
172	172	...	...	...	106	93	13	...	...
4	4	...	...	...	1	1	...	...	...
...	...	...	...	...	...	...	...	...	...
4	*4*	...	...	...	*1*	*1*	...	...	...
...	...	...	...	...	...	...	...	...	...
120	120	...	...	...	31	30	1	...	...
41	41	...	...	...	13	12	1	...	...
...	...	...	...	...	...	...	...	...	...
1,085	1,085	...	...	...	521	513	8	...	...
1,126	*1,126*	...	...	...	*534*	*525*	*9*	...	...
1,363	1,362	1	...	...	345	331	14	...	...
4,994	4,993	1	...	...	1,453	1,423	30	...	...
5,547	5,547	...	...	...	1,439	1,414	25	...	...
468	466	2	...	...	102	98	4	...	...
385	384	1	...	...	132	123	9	...	...
1,720	1,720	...	...	...	875	871	4	...	...
1	1	...	...	...	...	...	...	...	...
...	...	...	...	...	...	...	...	...	...

Class.	Group.	Caste, &c. and sub-division.	Religion.	15 to 39. Total.	Single.	Married.	Widowed.	Civil condition not stated.
C.—Commercial.—(Concluded.)	14. Traders.—(Concluded.)	Multáni	Hindu.	...	...	...	...	...
		Nagarta	,,	70	21	47	2	...
		Jain	Jain.	95	46	46	3	...
		Marvâdi	,,	...	...	...	...	...
		Do.	Hindu.	...	...	...	...	...
		Do.	Buddhist.	...	...	...	...	...
		S'râvaka	Jain.	...	...	...	...	...
		Total Group 14...	....	*8,628*	*2,656*	*5,553*	*419*	...
		Total Class C......	....	**8,628**	**2,656**	**5,553**	**419**	...
D.—Artisan and Village menial.—(Continued.)	17. Gold smiths.	Pánchâla	Hindu.	1,350	235	1,044	71	...
	18. Barbers ...	Nâyinda	,,	664	146	494	24	...
	19. Black smiths	Pánchâla.—Kammâra ...	,,	194	31	155	8	...
	20. Carpenters, &c.	Pánchâla. { Badagi ...	,,	5	...	5	...	...
		Pánchâla. { Gaunder...	,,	...	...	...	...	...
		Total Group 20......	....	*5*	...	*5*	...	...
	21. Brass & Copper-smiths ...	Pánchâla.—Gejjégâra ...	,,	...	...	...	...	...
	22. Tailors ...	Darzi	,,	220	55	157	8	...
	23. Weavers, Calenderers and Dyers.	Gôniga	,,	112	21	86	5	...
		Gádiya	Jain.	...	...	...	...	...
		Nêyigê	Hindu.	1,357	293	1,000	64	...
		Total Group 23......	....	*1,469*	*314*	*1,086*	69	...
	24. Washermen.	Agasa	,,	2,175	723	1,355	97	...
	26 (a). Cowherds, &c. ...	Golla	,,	8,815	4,325	4,213	277	...
	26. Shepherds and Wool weavers.	Kuruba	,,	8,251	2,703	5,262	286	...
	27. Oil-pressers...	Gâniga	,,	682	213	450	19	...
	28. Potters ...	Kumbára...	,,	686	238	423	25	...
	30. Salt, &c., workers ...	Uppára	,,	2,079	579	1,422	78	...
	32. Gold-smith's refuse collectors ...	Pánchâla.—Jalagára	,,	1	...	1	...	...
	33 (a). Gold-lace makers ...	Ráchêvár.—Sarigé	,,	...	...	...	...	...

TABLE E.—(*Continued.*)

District.

Males.

40 and over.					Age not stated.				
Total.	Single.	Married.	Widowed.	Civil condition not stated.	Total.	Single.	Married.	Widowed.	Civil condition not stated.
...	...	...	...	...	...	...	...	...	...
26	4	14	8	...	...	...	...	...	...
39	4	23	12	...	...	...	...	...	...
...	...	...	...	...	...	...	...	...	...
...	...	...	...	...	...	...	...	...	...
...	...	...	...	...	...	...	...	...	...
...	...	...	...	...	...	...	...	...	...
4,907	*278*	*3,439*	*1,190*	...	...	...	...	...	...
4,907	**278**	**3,439**	**1,190**	...	...	...	...	...	...
948	42	694	212	...	...	...	...	...	...
433	24	308	101	...	...	...	...	...	...
140	7	97	36	...	...	...	...	...	...
1	...	1	...	...	...	...	...	...	...
...	...	...	...	...	...	...	...	...	...
1	...	*1*	...	...	...	...	...	...	...
...	...	...	...	...	...	...	...	...	...
94	4	71	19	...	...	...	...	...	...
56	...	43	13	...	...	...	...	...	...
...	...	...	...	...	...	...	...	...	...
843	21	625	197	...	...	...	...	...	...
899	*21*	*668*	*210*	...	...	...	...	...	...
1,158	38	850	270	...	...	...	...	...	...
4,374	166	3,352	856	...	...	...	...	...	...
3,928	116	3,044	768	...	...	...	...	...	...
347	15	272	60	...	...	...	...	...	...
415	21	299	95	...	...	...	...	...	...
1,124	34	848	242	...	...	...	...	...	...
1	...	1	...	...	...	...	...	...	...
...	...	...	...	...	...	...	...	...	...

Class.	Group.	Caste, &c. and sub-division.	Religion.	All Ages. Total.	Single.	Married.	Widowed.	Civil condition not stated.
C.—Commercial.—(Concluded.)	14. Traders.—(Concluded.)	Multâni	Hindu.	...	...	...	...	...
		Nagarta	,,	152	58	75	19	...
		Jain	Jain.	123	34	54	35	...
		Marvâḍi	,,	...	...	...	...	...
		Do.	Hindu.	...	...	...	...	...
		Do.	Buddhist.	...	...	...	...	...
		S'râvaka	Jain.	...	...	...	...	...
		Total Group 14......	....	19,501	6,628	8,207	4,666	...
		Total Class C......	....	**19,501**	**6,628**	**8,207**	**4,666**	...
D.—Artisan and Village menial.—(Continued.)	17. Gold smiths.	Pánchâḷa	Hindu.	4,224	1,607	1,773	844	...
	18. Barbers ...	Nâyinda	,,	1,844	646	826	372	...
	19. Black smiths	Pânchâḷa—Kammâra ...	,,	551	219	267	65	...
	20. Carpenters, &c.	Pânchâḷa. { Baḍagi	,,	16	8	8	...	...
		Pânchâḷa. { Gaunḍer ...	,,	...	...	...	...	...
		Total Group 20......	....	16	8	8	...	...
	21. Brass & Copper-smiths ...	Pânchâḷa.—Gejjégâra ...	,,	...	...	...	...	...
	22. Tailors ...	Darzi	,,	443	145	222	76	...
	23. Weavers, Calenderers and Dyers.	Góṇiga	,,	200	49	120	31	...
		Gâdiya	Jain.	...	...	...	...	...
		Nêyigé	Hindu.	3,881	1,352	1,854	675	...
		Total Group 23......	....	4,081	1,401	1,974	706	...
	24. Washermen .	Agasa	,,	5,282	1,825	2,203	1,254	...
	26 (a). Cowherds, &c. ...	Golla	,,	18,601	6,133	7,759	4,709	...
	26. Shepherds and Wool-weavers.	Kuruba	,,	19,021	6,737	8,027	4,257	...
	27. Oil-pressers .	Gâṇiga	,,	1,706	565	744	397	...
	28. Potters ...	Kumbâra...	,,	1,565	480	746	339	...
	30. Salt, &c., workers ...	Uppâra	,,	5,770	2,297	2,265	1,208	...
	32. Gold-smith's refuse collectors.	Pânchaḷa.—Jalagâra... ...	,,	2	...	2	...	...
	33 (a). Gold-lace makers ...	Râchévâr.—Sarigé	,,	...	...	...	...	...

TABLE E.—(*Continued.*)

District.

Females.

0 to 9					10 to 14				
Total.	Single.	Married.	Widowed.	Civil condition not stated.	Total.	Single.	Married.	Widowed.	Civil condition not stated.
...	...	...	...	...	...	...	...	...	...
41	41	...	...	...	17	15	2	...	...
24	24	...	...	...	16	5	11	...	...
...	...	...	...	...	...	...	...	...	...
...	...	...	...	...	...	...	...	...	...
...	...	...	...	...	...	...	...	...	...
...	...	...	...	...	...	...	...	...	...
5,034	*4,904*	*128*	*2*	...	*2,122*	*1,323*	*790*	*9*	...
5,034	**4,904**	**128**	**2**	...	**2,122**	**1,323**	**790**	**9**	...
1,340	1,340	...	...	...	377	235	142	...	...
522	521	1	...	...	147	104	43	...	...
160	160	...	...	...	66	56	10	...	...
7	7	...	...	...	1	1	...	...	...
...	...	...	...	...	...	...	...	...	...
7	7	...	...	...	1	1	...	...	...
...	...	...	...	...	...	...	...	...	...
137	134	3	...	...	21	11	10	...	...
37	37	...	...	...	5	5	...	...	...
...	...	...	...	...	...	...	...	...	...
1,129	1,129	...	...	...	306	181	125	...	...
1,166	*1,166*	...	...	...	*311*	*186*	*125*	...	...
1,600	1,534	66	...	...	320	181	134	5	...
5,184	5,068	116	...	...	1,128	769	354	5	...
5,595	5,573	22	...	...	1,035	808	225	2	...
491	484	7	...	...	96	61	35	...	...
391	376	15	...	...	94	65	28	1	...
1,768	1,768	...	...	...	506	453	52	1	...
...	...	...	...	...	...	...	...	...	...
...	...	...	...	...	...	...	...	...	...

Class.	Group.	Caste, &c. and sub-division.	Religion.	15 to 30: Total.	Single.	Married.	Widowed.	Civil condition not stated.
C.—Commercial.—(Concluded.)	14. Traders.—(Concluded.)	Multáni	Hindu.	...	...	...	...	...
		Nagarta	,,	63	2	56	5	...
		Jain	Jain.	48	5	35	8	...
		Márvádi	,,	...	...	...	...	...
		Do.	Hindu.	...	...	...	...	...
		Do.	Buddhist.	...	...	...	...	...
		S'rávrka	Jain.	...	...	...	...	...
		Total Group 14	....	*7,588*	*341*	*5,703*	*1,544*	..
		Total Class C	....	**7,588**	**341**	**5,703**	**1,544**	..
D.—Artisan and Village menial.—(Continued.)	17. Gold smiths.	Pánchála	Hindu.	657	32	1,346	279	...
	18. Barbers	Náyinda	,,	812	21	674	117	...
	19. Black smiths	Pánchála.—Kammára	,,	227	3	212	12	...
	20. Carpenters, &c.	Pánchála. Badagi	,,	6	...	6	...	...
		Pánchála. Gaunder	,,	...	...	...	...	...
		Total Group 20	....	*6*	...	*6*	...	...
	21. Brass & Copper-smiths	Pánchála.—Gejjégára	,,	...	...	...	...	...
	22. Tailors	Darzi	...	203	...	182	21	...
	23. Weavers, Calenderers and Dyers.	Góniga	,,	102	7	86	9	...
		Gádiya	Jain.	...	...	...	...	...
		Nóyigé	Hindu.	1,691	38	1,436	217	...
		Total Group 23	....	*1,793*	*45*	*1,522*	*226*	...
	24. Washermen	Agasa	,,	2,258	106	1,712	440	...
	25 (a). Cowherds, &c.	Golla	,,	7,978	273	6,082	1,623	...
	26. Shepherds and Wool-weavers.	Kuruba	,,	8,489	332	6,075	1,482	...
	27. Oil-pressers	Gániga	,,	754	19	593	142	...
	28. Potters	Kumbára	,,	721	35	587	102	...
	30. Salt, &c., workers	Uppára	,,	2,420	72	1,936	412	...
	32. Gold-smith's refuse collectors.	Pánchála.—Jalagára	,,	2	...	2	...	...
	33 (a). Gold-lace makers	Ráchévár.—Sarigé	,,	...	...	...	...	...

TABLE E.—*(Continued.)*

District.

Females.

40 and over.					Age not stated.				
Total.	Single.	Married.	Widowed.	Civil condition not stated.	Total.	Single.	Married.	Widowed.	Civil condition not stated.
...	...	...	...	...	...	...	...	...	...
31	...	17	14	...	...	...	...	...	...
35	...	8	27	...	...	...	...	...	...
...	...	...	...	...	...	...	...	...	...
...	...	...	...	...	...	...	...	...	...
...	...	...	...	...	...	...	...	...	...
...	...	...	...	...	...	...	...	...	...
4,757	*60*	*1,586*	*3,111*	...	...	...	...	...	...
4,757	**60**	**1,586**	**3,111**	...	...	...	...	...	...
830	...	285	565	...	...	...	...	...	...
363	...	108	255	...	...	...	...	...	...
98	...	35	63	...	...	...	...	...	...
2		2	...	...	...	...	...	...	...
...	...	...	...	...	...	...	...	...	...
2	...	2	...	...	...	...	...	...	...
...	...	...	...	...	...	...	...	...	...
82		27	55	...	...	...	...	...	...
56	...	31	22	...	...	...	...	...	...
...	...	...	...	...	...	...	...	...	...
755	4	293	458	...	...	...	...	...	...
811	*4*	*327*	*480*	...	...	...	...	...	...
1,101	4	291	806	...	...	...	...	...	...
4,311	23	1,207	3,081	...	...	...	...	...	...
3,902	24	1,105	2,773	...	...	...	...	...	...
365	1	105	259	...	...	...	...	...	...
356	4	116	236	...	...	...	...	...	...
1,076	4	277	795	...	...	...	...	...	...
...	...	...	...	...	...	...	...	...	...
...	...	...	...	...	...	...	...	...	...

Class.	Group.	Caste, &c. and sub-division.	Religion.	All Ages. Total.	Single.	Married.	Widowed.	Civil condition not stated.
C.—Commercial.—(Concluded.)	14. Traders.—(Concluded.)	Multáni ...	Hindu.	...	...	...	...	...
		Nagarta ...	,,	230	132	92	6	...
		Jain ...	Jain.	111	62	44	5	...
		Marvádi ...	,,	...	...	...	...	...
		Do ...	Hindu	...	...	...	...	...
		Do ...	Buddhist.	...	...	...	...	...
		S'rávaka ...	Jain.	...	...	...	...	...
		Total Group 14	......	*56,895*	*30,334*	*24,363*	*2,198*	...
		Total Class C	......	**56,895**	**30,334**	**24,363**	**2,198**	...
D.—Artisan and Village menial.—(Continued.)	17. Gold smiths.	Pánchála ...	Hindu.	16,176	8,574	6,965	637	...
	18. Barbers ...	Náyinda ...	,,	4,226	2,310	1,756	160	...
	19. Black smiths	Pánchála.—Kammára	,,	892	476	380	36	...
	20. Carpenters, &c.	Pánchála. Badagi ...	,,	1,501	794	646	61	...
		Pánchála. Gaunder	,,	...	...	...	...	...
		Total Group 20	......	*1,501*	*794*	*646*	*61*	...
	21. Brass & Copper smiths...	Gejjégára...	,,	90	53	33	4	...
	22. Tailors ...	Darzi ...	,,	721	392	297	32	...
	23. Weavers, Calendarers and Dyers.	Góniga ...	,,	139	73	58	8	...
		Gádiya ...	Jain.	...	...	...	...	...
		Néyigé ...	Hindu.	4,917	2,551	2,156	210	...
		Total Group 23	......	*5,056*	*2,624*	*2,214*	*218*	...
	24. Washermen.	Agasa ...	,,	9,541	5,028	4,130	383	...
	26 (a). Cowherds, &c.	Golla ...	,,	2,657	1,397	1,156	104	...
	26. Shepherds and Wool-weavers.	Kuruba ...	,,	57,033	30,737	24,324	2,072	...
	27. Oil-pressers.	Gániga ...	,,	7,633	3,985	3,363	284	...
	28. Potters ...	Kumbára...	,,	8,300	4,284	3,705	311	...
	30. Salt, &c., workers	Uppára ...	,,	16,922	8,997	7,326	599	...
	32. Gold-smith's refuse collectors.	Pánchála.—Julagára	,,	86	43	38	5	...
	33 (a). Gold-lace makers ...	Ráchóvár.—Sarigé ...	,,	...	...	...	...	...

TABLE E.—(Continued.)

District.

Males.

0 to 9.					10 to 14.				
Total.	Single.	Married.	Widowed.	Civil condition not stated.	Total.	Single.	Married.	Widowed.	Civil condition not stated.
...	...	...	...	...	...	...	...	...	...
70	70	...	...	...	23	23	...	...	...
31	31	...	...	...	10	10	...	...	...
...	...	...	...	...	...	...	...	...	...
...	...	...	...	...	...	...	...	...	...
...	...	...	...	...	...	...	...	...	...
...	...	...	...	...	...	...	...	...	...
16,143	*16,134*	*9*	...	...	*6,100*	*6,058*	*42*	...	...
16,143	**16,134**	**9**	...	...	**6,100**	**6,058**	**42**	...	...
4,518	4,512	6	...	...	1,860	1,795	65	...	...
1,249	1,249	...	...	...	320	320	...	...	...
242	242	...	...	...	74	74	...	...	...
403	403	...	...	...	119	117	2	...	...
...	...	...	...	...	...	...	...	...	...
403	*403*	...	...	...	*119*	*117*	*2*	...	...
27	27	...	...	...	10	10	...	...	...
209	209	...	...	...	65	65	...	...	...
45	45	...	...	...	11	11	...	...	...
...	...	...	...	...	...	...	...	...	...
1,360	1,360	...	...	...	399	399	...	...	...
1,405	*1,405*	...	...	...	*410*	*410*	...	...	...
2,866	2,866	...	...	...	711	708	3	...	...
750	750	...	...	...	213	213	...	...	...
16,293	*16,279*	*14*	...	...	*6,830*	*6,768*	*62*	...	...
2,072	2,071	1	...	...	593	588	5	...	...
2,250	2,249	1	...	...	643	639	4	...	...
4,910	4,909	1	...	...	1,722	1,711	11	...	...
24	24	...	...	...	6	6	...	...	...
...	...	...	...	...	...	...	...	...	...

Class.	Group.	Caste, &c. and sub-division.	Religion.	15 to 30. Total.	Single.	Married.	Widowed.	Civil condition not stated.
C.—Commercial.—(Concluded.)	14. Traders.—(Concluded.)	Multáni	Hindu.	...	...	...	...	...
		Nagarta	,,	95	37	56	2	...
		Jain	Jain.	44	18	26	...	...
		Márvádi	,,	...	...	...	...	...
		Do.	Hindu.	...	...	...	...	...
		Do.	Buddhist.	...	...	...	...	...
		S'rávaka	Jain.	...	...	...	...	...
		Total Group 14	....	*22,844*	*7,823*	*14,546*	*475*	...
	Total Class C		....	**22,844**	**7,823**	**14,546**	**475**	...
D.—Artisan and Village menial.—(Continued.)	17. Gold smiths.	Pánchála	Hindu.	6,548	2,198	4,214	136	...
	18. Barbers	Náyinda	,,	1,877	715	1,119	43	...
	19. Black smiths	Pánchála.—Kammára	,,	405	154	242	9	...
	20. Carpenters, &c.	Pánchála. Badagi	,,	676	261	401	14	...
		Pánchála. Gaunder	,,	...	...	...	...	...
		Total Group 20	....	*676*	*261*	*401*	*14*	...
	21. Brass & Copper-smiths	Pánchála.—Gejjégára	,,	34	15	19	...	...
	22. Tailors	Darzi	,,	311	116	186	9	...
	23. Weavers, Calendarers and Dyers.	Góyiga	,,	63	17	44	2	...
		Gádiya	Jain.	...	...	...	...	...
		Nêyigé	Hindu.	2,266	775	1,446	45	...
		Total Group 23	....	*2,329*	*792*	*1,490*	*47*	...
	24. Washermen	Agasa	,,	4,018	1,397	2,549	72	...
	26 (a). Cowherds, &c.	Golla	,,	1,222	425	770	27	...
	26. Shepherds and Wool-weavers	Kuruba	,,	22,737	7,551	14,749	437	...
	27. Oil-pressers	Gániga	,,	3,491	1,290	2,127	74	...
	28. Potters	Kumbára	,,	3,728	1,353	2,295	80	...
	30. Salt, &c., workers	Uppára	,,	6,829	2,305	4,403	121	...
	32. Gold-smith's refuse collectors	Pánchála.—Jalagára	,,	40	13	25	2	...
	33 (a). Gold-lace makers	Ráchévár.—Sarigé	,,	...	...	...	...	...

TABLE E.—(*Continued.*)

District.

Females.

40 and over.					Age not stated.				
Total.	Single.	Married.	Widowed.	Civil condition not stated.	Total.	Single.	Married.	Widowed.	Civil condition not stated.
...	...	...	...	...	...	...	...	...	...
42	2	36	4	...	...	...	...	...	...
26	3	16	5	...	...	...	...	...	...
...	...	...	...	...	...	...	...	...	...
...	...	...	...	...	...	...	...	...	...
...	...	...	...	...	...	...	...	...	...
...	...	...	...	...	...	...	...	...	...
11,808	*319*	*9,766*	*1,723*	...	...	...	...	...	...
11,808	**319**	**9,766**	**1,723**	...	...	...	...	...	...
3,250	69	2,680	501	...	...	...	...	...	...
780	26	637	117	...	...	...	...	...	...
171	6	138	27	...	...	...	...	...	...
303	13	243	47	...	...	...	...	...	...
...	...	...	...	...	...	...	...	...	...
303	*13*	*243*	*47*	...	...	...	...	...	...
19	1	14	4	...	...	...	...	...	...
136	2	111	23	...	...	...	...	...	...
20	...	14	6	...	...	...	...	...	...
...	...	...	...	...	...	...	...	...	...
892	17	710	165	...	...	...	...	...	...
912	*17*	*724*	*171*	...	...	...	...	...	...
1,946	57	1,578	311	...	...	...	...	...	...
472	9	386	77	...	...	...	...	...	...
11,773	139	9,999	1,635	...	...	...	...	...	...
1,479	36	1,233	210	...	...	...	...	...	...
1,679	43	1,405	231	...	...	...	...	...	...
3,461	72	2,911	478	...	...	...	...	...	...
16	...	13	3	...	...	...	...	...	...
...	...	...	...	...	...	...	...	...	...

Class.	Group.	Caste, &c. and sub-division.	Religion.	All Ages. Total.	Single.	Married.	Widowed.	Civil condition not stated.
C.—Commercial.—(Concluded.)	14. Traders.—(Concluded.)	Multáni	Hindu.	...	...	...	...	...
		Nagarta	,,	209	87	90	32	...
		Jain	Jain.	119	45	48	26	...
		Marvádi	,,	...	...	...	...	...
		Do	Hindu.	...	...	...	...	...
		Do	Buddhist.	...	...	...	...	...
		S'rávaka	Jain	...	...	...	...	...
		Total Group 14......	....	58,883	21,396	24,802	12,685	...
		Total Class C......	....	**58,883**	**21,396**	**24,802**	**12,685**	...
D.—Artisan and Village menial.—(Continued.)	17. Gold smiths.	Pánchála	Hindu.	16,049	5,724	7,001	3,324	...
	18. Barbers ...	Náyinda	,,	4,175	1,467	1,791	917	...
	19. Black smiths	Pánchála.—Kammára ...	,,	916	350	384	182	...
	20. Carpenters, &c.	Pánchála.—Badagi ...	,,	1,563	533	679	351	...
		Pánchála.—Gaundor...	,,	...	...	...	...	...
		Total Group 20......	....	1,563	533	679	351	...
	21. Brass & Copper smiths ...	Pánchála.—Gejjégára ...	,,	90	34	36	20	...
	22. Tailors ...	Darzi	,,	736	287	306	143	...
	23. Weavers, Calenderers and Dyers.	Góniga	,,	142	46	55	41	...
		Gádiya	Jain.	...	...	...	...	...
		Néyigé	Hindu.	5,026	1,777	2,162	1,087	...
		Total Group 23......	....	6,168	1,823	2,217	1,128	...
	24. Washermen.	Agasa	Hindu.	9,894	3,661	4,303	1,930	...
	26 (a). Cowherds, &c. ...	Golla	,,	2,788	1,068	1,178	542	...
	26. Shepherds and Wool-weavers ...	Kuruba	,,	58,172	21,178	24,838	12,156	...
	27. Oil-pressers.	Gániga	,,	7,999	3,062	3,458	1,479	...
	28. Potters ...	Kumbára... ...	,,	7,836	2,771	3,517	1,548	...
	30. Salt, &c., workers ...	Uppára	,,	17,795	6,727	7,418	3,626	...
	32. Gold-smith's refuse collectors ...	Pánchála.—Jalagára ...	,,	85	29	38	18	...
	33 (a). Gold-lace makers ...	Ráchévár.—Sarigé ...	,,	...	...	...	...	...

TABLE E.—(*Continued.*)

District.

Females.

0 to 9.					10 to 14.				
Total.	Single.	Married.	Widowed.	Civil condition not stated.	Total.	Single.	Married.	Widowed.	Civil condition not stated.
...	...	...	...	...	...	...	...	...	...
64	63	1	...	...	35	24	11	...	...
34	34	...	...	...	12	9	3	...	...
...	...	...	...	...	...	...	...	...	...
...	...	...	...	...	...	...	...	...	...
...	...	...	...	...	...	...	...	...	...
...	...	...	...	...	...	...	...	...	...
16,341	*15,945*	*396*	...	...	*6,114*	*3,685*	*2,414*	*15*	...
16,341	**15,945**	**396**	...	...	**6,114**	**3,685**	**2,414**	**15**	...
4,501	4,414	87	...	...	1,543	1,086	457	...	...
1,138	1,119	19	...	...	395	275	120	...	...
273	267	6	...	...	97	68	29	...	...
416	408	8	...	...	155	107	48	...	...
...	...	...	...	...	...	...	...	...	...
416	*408*	*8*	...	...	*155*	*107*	*48*	...	...
25	23	2	...	...	17	11	6	...	...
219	213	6	...	...	104	70	34	...	...
43	43	...	...	...	5	4	1	...	...
...	...	...	...	...	...	...	...	...	...
1,327	1,287	40	...	...	571	430	141	...	...
1,369	*1,329*	*40*	...	...	*576*	*434*	*142*	...	...
2,783	2,710	73	...	...	967	637	330	...	...
851	842	9	...	...	251	193	58	...	...
16,222	15,953	269	...	...	5,740	3,362	2,378	...	...
3,321	3,299	22	...	...	849	682	167	...	...
2,175	2,133	42	...	...	679	478	199	2	...
4,948	4,870	78	...	...	1,488	1,159	329	...	...
21	21	...	...	...	10	7	3	...	...
...	...	...	...	...	...	...	...	...	...

Class.	Group.	Caste, &c. and sub-division.	Religion.	15 to 39 Total.	15 to 39 Single.	15 to 39 Married.	15 to 39 Widowed.	15 to 39 Civil condition not stated.
C.—Commercial.—(Concluded.)	14. Traders.—(Concluded.)	Multáni	Hindu.	...	...	...	...	...
		Nagarta	,,	68	...	58	10	...
		Jain	Jain.	46	2	38	6	...
		Márvádi	,,	...	...	...	...	...
		Do.	Hindu.	...	...	...	...	...
		Do.	Buddhist.	...	...	...	...	...
		S'rávaka	Jain.	...	...	...	...	...
		Total Group 14......	....	*22,854*	*1,653*	*17,691*	*3,510*	...
		Total Class C......	....	**22,854**	**1,653**	**17,691**	**3,510**	...
D.—Artisan and Village menial.—(Continued.)	17. Gold smiths.	Pánchála	Hindu.	5,691	201	4,611	879	...
	18. Barbers ...	Náyinda	,,	1,578	64	1,232	282	...
	19. Black smiths.	Pánchála.—Kammára ...	,,	325	14	262	49	...
	20. Carpenters, &c.	Pánchála. { Badagi	,,	570	18	469	83	...
		Pánchála. { Gaunder... ...	,,	...	...	...	...	...
		Total Group 20......	....	*570*	*18*	*469*	*83*	...
	21. Brass & Copper-smiths ...	Pánchála.—Gejjégára ...	,,	25	...	21	4	...
	22. Tailors ...	Darzi	,,	233	4	189	40	...
	23. Weavers, Calenderers and Dyers.	Góniga	,,	56	...	45	11	...
		Gádiya	Jain.	...	...	...	...	...
		Néyigé	Hindu.	1,867	54	1,539	274	...
		Total Group 23......	....	*1,923*	*54*	*1,584*	*285*	...
	24. Washermen.	Agasa	,,	3,894	293	3,110	491	...
	26 (a). Cowherds, &c. ...	Golla	,,	125	30	846	149	...
	26. Shepherds and Wool-weavers.	Kuruba	,,	22,756	1,766	18,045	2,945	...
	27. Oil-pressers.	Gániga	,,	2,779	74	2,300	405	...
	28. Potters ...	Kumbára	,,	2,890	149	2,346	395	...
	30. Salt, &c., workers ...	Uppára	,,	6,759	647	5,236	876	...
	32. Gold smith's refuse collectors ...	Pánchála.—Jálagára ...	,,	31	1	26	4	...
	33 (a). Gold-lace makers ...	Ráchévár.—Sarigé ...	,,	...	...	...	...	...

TABLE E.—*(Continued.)*

District.

Females.

40 and over.					Age not stated.				
Total.	Single.	Married.	Widowed.	Civil condition not stated.	Total.	Single.	Married.	Widowed.	Civil condition not stated.
...	...	...	...	...	...	...	...	...	...
42	...	20	22	...	...	...	...	...	...
27	...	7	20	...	...	...	...	...	...
...	...	...	...	...	...	...	...	...	...
...	...	...	...	...	...	...	...	...	...
...	...	...	...	...	...	...	...	...	...
...	...	...	...	...	...	...	...	...	...
13,574	*113*	*4,301*	*9,160*	...	...	...	...	...	...
13,574	**113**	**4,301**	**9,160**	...	...	...	...	...	...
4,314	23	1,846	2,445	...	...	...	...	...	...
1,064	9	420	635	...	...	...	...	...	...
221	1	87	133	...	...	...	...	...	...
422	...	154	268	...	...	...	...	...	...
...	...	...	...	...	...	...	...	...	...
422	...	*154*	*268*	...	...	...	...	...	...
23	...	7	16	...	...	...	...	...	...
180	...	77	103	...	...	...	...	...	...
39	...	9	30	...	...	...	...	...	...
...	...	...	...	...	...	...	...	...	...
1,261	6	442	813	...	...	...	...	...	...
1,300	*6*	*451*	*843*	...	...	...	...	...	...
2,251	21	791	1,439	...	...	...	...	...	...
661	3	265	393	...	...	...	...	...	...
13,454	97	4,146	9,211	...	...	...	...	...	...
2,050	7	969	1,074	...	...	...	...	...	...
2,092	11	930	1,151	...	...	...	...	...	...
4,600	51	1,799	2,750	...	...	...	...	...	...
23	...	9	14	...	...	...	...	...	...
...	...	...	...	...	...	...	...	...	...

Class.	Group.	Caste, &c. and sub-division.	Religion.	All Ages. Total.	Single.	Married.	Widowed	Civil condition not stated.
C.—Commercial.—(Concluded.)	14. Traders.—(Concluded.)	Multáni	Hindu.	...	...	...	...	...
		Nagarta	,,	30	14	14	2	...
		Jain	Jain.	36	18	17	1	...
		Marvádi	,,	10	7	3	...	...
		Do.	Hindu.	...	...	...	...	...
		Do.	Buddhist.	...	...	...	...	...
		S'rávaka	Jain.	...	...	...	...	...
		Total Group 14......	....	*22,236*	*12,225*	*8,497*	*1,514*	...
		Total Class C......	....	**22,236**	**12,225**	**8,497**	**1,514**	...
D.—Artisan and Village menial.—(Continued.)	17. Gold smiths.	Pánchála	Hindu.	5,740	3,187	2,192	316	...
	18. Barbers ...	Náyinda	,,	1,471	788	619	64	...
	19. Black smiths	Pánchála.—Kammárá ...	,,	426	240	153	33	...
	20. Carpenters, &c.	Pánchála.—Badagi ...	,,	809	450	307	52	...
		Pánchála.—Gaunder ...	,,	...	...	...	...	...
		Total Group 20......	....	*809*	*450*	*307*	*52*	...
	21. Brass & Copper-smiths...	Pánchála.—Gejjégára ...	,,	...	...	...	...	...
	22. Tailors ...	Darzi	,,	255	116	123	16	...
	23. Weavers, Calénderers and Dyers.	Gónigá	,,	...	...	...	...	...
		Gádiya	Jain.	...	...	...	...	...
		Néyigé	Hindu.	6,386	3,533	2,509	344	...
		Total Group 23......	....	*6,386*	*3,533*	*2,509*	*344*	...
	24. Washermen.	Agasa	Hindu.	5,135	2,717	2,061	357	...
	25 (a). Cowherds, &c. ...	Golla	,,	2,668	1,411	1,010	247	...
	26. Shepherds and Wool-weavers. ...	Kuruba	,,	19,912	10,837	8,261	814	...
	27. Oil-pressers.	Gániga	,,	1,099	583	448	68	...
	28. Potters ...	Kumbára	,,	1,668	876	691	101	...
	30. Salt, &c., workers...	Uppára	,,	4,206	2,229	1,780	197	...
	32. Gold-smith's refuse collectors. ...	Pánchála.—Jalagára...	,,	6	3	2	[illegible]	...
	33 (a). Gold-lace makers ...	Rachévár.—Sarigé ...	,,	...	...	...	...	...

TABLE E.—(*Continued.*)

District.

Males.

0 to 9					10 to 14				
Total.	Single.	Married.	Widowed.	Civil condition not stated.	Total.	Single.	Married.	Widowed.	Civil condition not stated.
...	...	...	...	...	...	...	...	...	...
7	7	...	...	...	3	3	...	...	...
[illegible]	11	...	...	...	3	3	...	...	...
...	...	...	...	...	1	1	...	...	...
...	...	...	...	...	...	...	...	...	...
...	...	...	...	...	...	...	...	...	...
...	...	...	...	...	...	...	...	...	...
5,768	*5,767*	*1*	...	...	*2,710*	*2,671*	*39*	...	...
5,768	**5,767**	**1**	...	...	**2,710**	**2,671**	**39**	...	...
1,493	1,493	...	...	...	751	733	17	1	...
409	409	...	...	...	166	157	9	...	...
110	110	...	...	...	66	58	8	...	...
241	241	...	...	...	86	86	...	...	...
...	...	...	...	...	...	...	...	...	...
241	*241*	...	...	...	*86*	*86*	...	...	...
...	...	...	...	...	...	...	...	...	...
61	61	...	...	...	30	29	1	...	...
...	...	...	...	...	...	...	...	...	...
...	...	...	...	...	...	...	...	...	...
1,840	1,840	...	...	...	638	634	3	1	...
1,840	*1,840*	...	...	...	*638*	*634*	*3*	*1*	...
1,403	1,403	...	...	...	607	587	20	...	...
649	649	...	...	...	393	391	2	...	...
5,503	5,499	3	...	...	2,017	1,997	19	1	...
328	328	...	...	...	104	103	1	...	...
450	450	...	...	...	230	225	5	...	...
1,149	1,149	...	...	...	431	426	5	...	...
1	1	...	...	...	...	...	...	...	...
...	...	...	...	...	...	...	...	...	...

H..ssan

Class	Group	Caste, &c. and sub-division	Religion	15 to 39. Total	Single	Married	Widowed	Civil condition not stated
C.—Commercial.—(Concluded.)	14. Traders.—(Concluded.)	Multáni	Hindu.	...	...	...	...	...
		Nagarta	,,	13	4	9	...	...
		Jain	Jain.	15	4	11	...	...
		Márvádi	,,	9	6	3	...	...
		Do.	Hindu.	...	...	...	...	...
		Do.	Buddhist.	...	...	...	...	...
		S'rávaka	Jain.	...	...	...	...	...
		Total Group 14	....	*9,415*	*3,684*	*5,315*	*416*	...
		Total Class C	....	**9,415**	**3,684**	**5,315**	**416**	...
D.—Artisan and Village menial.—(Continued.)	17. Gold smiths.	Pánchála	Hindu.	2,323	918	1,343	62	...
	18. Barbers ...	Náyinda	,,	580	214	355	11	...
	19. Black smiths	Pánchála.—Kammára ...	,,	173	71	93	9	...
	20. Carpenters, &c.	Pánchála. { Badagi ...	,,	331	119	201	11	...
		Pánchála. { Gaunder ...	,,	...	...	...	...	...
		Total Group 20	...	*331*	*119*	*201*	*11*	...
	21. Brass & Copper-smiths ...	Pánchála.—Gojjégára	...	...	...	...	...	...
	22. Tailors ...	Darzi ...	,,	106	25	80	1	...
	23. Weavers, Calenderers and Dyers.	Ganiga	,,	...	...	...	...	...
		Gádiya	Jain.	...	...	...	...	...
		Néyigé	Hindu.	2,682	1,019	1,577	86	...
		Total Group 23	....	*2,682*	*1,019*	*1,577*	*86*	...
	24. Washermen.	Agasa	,,	2,098	711	1,300	87	...
	26 (a). Cowherds, &c ...	Golla	,,	1,012	362	619	31	...
	26. Shepherds and Wool-weavers. ...	Kuruba ...	,,	8,320	3,272	4,885	163	...
	27. Oil-pressers.	Ganiga ...	,,	463	143	306	14	...
	28. Potters ...	Kumbára	,,	660	191	444	25	...
	30. Salt, &c. workers ...	Uppára ...	,,	1,843	644	1,158	41	...
	32. Gold-smith's refuse collectors ...	Pánchála.—Jalagára ...	,,	3	2	1	...	...
	33 (a). Gold-lace makers ...	Ráchévár.—Sarigé ...	,,	...	...	...	...	...

TABLE E.—(*Continued.*)

District.

Males.

40 and over.					Age not stated.				
Total.	Single.	Married.	Widowed.	Civil condition not stated.	Total.	Single.	Married.	Widowed.	Civil condition not stated.
...	...	...	...	...	...	...	...	...	...
7	...	5	2	...	...	...	...	...	...
7	...	6	1	...	...	...	...	...	...
...	...	...	...	...	...	...	...	...	...
...	...	...	...	...	...	...	...	...	...
...	...	...	...	...	...	...	...	...	...
...	...	...	...	...	...	...	...	...	...
4,343	*103*	3,142	*1,098*	...	...	...	...	...	...
4,343	**103**	**3,142**	**1,098**	...	...	...	...	...	...
1,173	13	832	298	...	...	...	...	...	...
316	8	255	53	...	...	...	...	...	...
77	1	52	24	...	...	...	...	...	...
151	4	106	41	...	...	...	...	...	...
...	...	...	...	...	...	...	...	...	...
151	*4*	*106*	*41*	...	...	...	...	...	...
...	...	...	...	...	...	...	...	...	...
58	1	42	15	...	...	...	...	...	...
...	...	...	...	...	...	...	...	...	...
...	...	...	...	...	...	...	...	...	...
1,226	40	929	257	...	...	...	...	...	...
1,226	*40*	*929*	*257*	...	...	...	...	...	...
1,027	16	741	270	...	...	...	...	...	...
614	9	389	216	...	...	...	...	...	...
4,073	69	3,354	650	...	...	...	...	...	...
201	9	141	51	...	...	...	...	...	...
328	10	242	76	...	...	...	...	...	...
783	10	617	156	...	...	...	...	...	...
2	...	1	1	...	...	...	...	...	...
...	...	...	...	...	...	...	...	...	...

Hassan

Class.	Group.	Caste, &c., and sub-division.	Religion.	All Ages. Total.	Single.	Married.	Widowed.	Civil condition not stated.
C.—Commercial.—(Concluded.)	14. Traders.—(Concluded.)	Multáni	Hindu.	...	...	...	...	...
		Nagarta	,,	47	15	20	12	...
		Jain	Jain.	29	11	15	3	...
		Marvâdi	,,	...	...	...	...	...
		Do	Hindu.	...	...	...	...	...
		Do	Buddhist.	...	...	...	...	...
		S'rávaka	Jain.	...	...	...	...	...
		Total Group 14	....	22,685	9,614	9,269	3,802	...
	Total Class C		....	**22,685**	**9,614**	**9,269**	**3,802**	...
D.—Artisan and Village menial.—(Continued.)	17. Gold smiths.	Páncháḷa	Hindu.	5,333	2,152	2,225	956	...
	18. Barbers	Náyinda	,,	1,508	599	703	206	...
	19. Black smiths	Páncháḷa.—Kammára	,,	403	144	183	76	...
	20. Carpenters, &c.	Páncháḷa { Badagi	,,	868	348	366	154	...
		Páncháḷa { Gaundor	,,	...	...	...	...	...
		Total Group 20	....	868	348	366	154	...
	21. Brass & Copper-smiths	Páncháḷa.—Gejjégára	,,	...	...	...	...	...
	22. Tailors	Darzi	,,	256	93	125	38	...
	23. Weavers, Calenderers and Dyers.	Góṇiga	,,	...	...	...	...	...
		Gádiya	Jain.	...	...	...	...	...
		Néyigé	Hindu.	6,422	2,417	2,871	1,134	...
		Total Group 23	....	6,422	2,417	2,871	1,134	...
	24. Washermen	Agasa	Hindu.	5,321	2,099	2,217	1,005	...
	26 (a). Cowherds, &c.	Golla	,,	2,544	1,063	1,026	455	...
	26. Shepherds and wool weavers	Kuruba	,,	20,818	8,248	9,014	3,526	...
	27. Oil-pressers	Gáṇiga	,,	1,160	420	496	244	...
	28. Potters	Kumbára	,,	1,645	637	715	293	...
	30. Salt, &c., workers	Uppára	,,	4,360	1,681	1,894	785	...
	32. Gold-smith's refuse collectors.	Páncháḷa.—Jalagára	,,	3	1	2	...	...
	33 (a). Gold-lace makers	Ráchéwár.—Sarigé	,,	...	...	...	...	...

TABLE E.—(*Continued.*)

District.

Females.

0 to 9					10 to 14				
Total.	Single.	Married.	Widowed.	Civil condition not stated.	Total.	Single.	Married.	Widowed.	Civil condition not stated.
...	...	...	...	...	...	...	...	...	...
13	13	...	...	...	4	2	2	...	...
10	10	...	...	...	1	1	...	...	...
...	...	...	...	...	...	...	...	...	...
...	...	...	...	...	...	...	...	...	...
...	...	...	...	...	...	...	...	...	...
...	...	...	...	...	...	...	...	...	...
6,652	*6,624*	*28*	...	...	*2,676*	*2,309*	*356*	*11*	...
6,652	**6,624**	**28**	...	...	**2,676**	**2,309**	**356**	**11**	...
1,631	1,620	11	...	...	515	405	110	...	...
418	418	...	...	...	157	130	27	...	...
104	104	...	...	...	47	29	18	...	...
242	241	1	...	...	105	78	27	...	...
...	...	...	...	...	...	...	...	...	...
242	*241*	*1*	...	...	*105*	*78*	*27*	...	...
...	...	...	...	...	...	...	...	...	...
70	70	...	...	...	26	23	3	...	...
...	...	...	...	...	...	...	...	...	...
...	...	...	...	...	...	...	...	...	...
1,881	1,866	15	...	...	662	418	240	4	...
1,881	*1,866*	*15*	...	...	*662*	*418*	*240*	*4*	...
1,419	1,419	...	...	...	624	503	121	...	...
787	787	...	...	...	230	190	39	1	...
6,208	6,173	35	...	...	1,732	1,396	330	6	...
300	300	...	...	...	98	86	12	...	...
462	460	2	...	...	151	119	32	...	...
1,221	1,218	3	...	...	440	340	94	6	...
1	1	...	...	...	...	...	...	...	...
...	...	...	...	...	...	...	...	...	...

Hassan

Class.	Group.	Caste, &c., and sub-division.	Religion.	15 to 39 Total	Single	Married	Widowed	Civil condition not stated
C.—Commercial.—(Concluded.)	14. Traders.—(Concluded.)	Multáni	Hindu.	...	...	...	...	...
		Nagarta	,,	19	...	16	3	...
		Jain	Jain.	11	...	10	1	...
		Marvádi	,,	...	...	...	...	...
		Do	Hindu.	...	...	...	...	...
		Do	Buddhist.	...	...	...	...	...
		S'rávaka	Jain.	...	...	...	...	...
		Total Group 14	....	8,534	648	6,730	1,156	...
		Total Class C	....	**8,534**	**648**	**6,730**	**1,156**	...
D.—Artisan and Village menial.—(Continued.)	17. Gold smiths.	Pánchála	Hindu.	2,048	125	1,648	275	...
	18. Barbers ...	Náyinda	,,	605	50	495	60	...
	19. Black smiths	Pánchála.—Kammára ...	,,	163	11	131	21	...
	20. Carpenters, &c.	Pánchála. { Badagi ...	,,	333	29	257	47	...
		Pánchála. { Gaunder ...	,,	...	...	...	..	...
		Total Group 20	....	333	29	257	47	...
	21. Brass & Copper-smiths...	Pánchála.—Gejjégára ...	,,	...	...	...	...	...
	22. Tailors ...	Darzi	,,	99	...	90	9	...
	23. Weavers, Calenderers and Dyers.	Góniga	,,	...	...	...	...	...
		Gádiya	Jain.	...	...	...	...	...
		Néyigé	Hindu.	2,603	122	2,086	395	...
		Total Group 23	....	2,603	122	2,086	395	...
	24. Washermen.	Agasa	Hindu.	2,034	166	1,694	274	...
	25 (a). Cowherds, &c. ..	Golla	,,	948	80	707	161	...
	26. Shepherds and Wool-weavers. ...	Kuruba	,,	8,486	641	7,001	844	...
	27. Oil-pressers.	Gániga	,,	486	32	393	61	...
	28. Potters ...	Kumbára	,,	647	56	524	67	...
	30. Salt, &c., workers...	Uppára	,,	1,763	117	1,417	229	...
	32. Gold-smith's refuse collectors. ...	Pánchála.—Jalagára... ...	,,	2	...	2	...	...
	33 (a). Gold-lace makers ...	Ráchévár.—Sarigé	,,	...	...	...	...	...

TABLE E.—(*Continued*)

District.

Females.

40 and over.					Age not stated.				
Total.	Single.	Married.	Widowed.	Civil condition not stated.	Total.	Single.	Married.	Widowed.	Civil condition not stated.
...	...	...	...	...	...	...	...	...	...
11	...	2	9	...	...	...	...	...	...
7	...	5	2	...	...	...	...	...	...
...	...	...	...	...	...	...	...	...	...
...	...	...	...	...	...	...	...	...	...
...	...	...	...	...	...	...	...	...	...
...	...	...	...	...	...	...	...	...	...
4,823	*33*	*2,155*	*2,635*	...	...	...	...	...	...
4,823	**33**	**2,155**	**2,635**	...	...	...	...	...	...
1,139	2	456	681	...	...	...	...	...	...
328	1	181	146	...	...	...	...	...	...
89	...	34	55	...	...	...	...	...	...
188	...	81	107	...	...	...	...	...	...
...	...	...	...	...	...	...	...	...	...
188	...	*81*	*107*	...	...	...	...	...	...
...	...	...	...	...	...	...	...	...	...
61	...	32	29	...	...	...	...	...	...
...	...	...	...	...	...	...	...	...	...
...	...	...	...	...	...	...	...	...	...
1,276	11	530	735	...	...	...	...	...	...
1,276	*11*	*530*	*735*	...	...	...	...	...	...
1,244	11	502	731	...	...	...	...	...	...
579	6	280	293	...	...	...	...	...	...
4,392	38	1,678	2,676	...	...	...	...	...	...
276	2	91	183	...	...	...	...	...	...
385	2	157	226	...	...	...	...	...	...
936	6	380	550	...	...	...	...	...	...
...	...	...	...	...	...	...	...	...	...
...	...	...	...	...	...	...	...	...	...

Class.	Group.	Caste, &c. and sub-division.	Religion.	All Ages. Total.	Single.	Married.	Widowed.	Civil condition not stated.
C.—Commercial.—(Concluded.)	14. Traders.—(Concluded.)	Multâni	Hindu.	...	...	...	...	...
		Nagarta	,,	4,208	2,197	1,611	400	...
		Jain	Jain.	535	281	204	50	...
		Mârvâdi	,,	21	12	9	...	...
		Do.	Hindu.	...	...	...	...	...
		Do.	Buddhist.	...	...	...	...	...
		S'râvaka	Jain.	1,038	659	303	76	...
		Total Group 14	....	*35,677*	*19,471*	*13,546*	*2,660*	...
		Total Class C	....	**35,677**	**19,471**	**13,546**	**2,660**	...
D.—Artisan and Village menial.—(Continued.)	17. Gold smiths.	Pánchâla	Hindu.	5,588	2,880	2,160	548	...
	18. Barbers	Nâyinda	,,	1,460	814	553	93	...
	19. Black smiths	Pánchâla.—Kammâra	,,	96	50	36	10	...
	20. Carpenters, &c.	Pánchâla. Badagi	,,	856	446	355	55	...
		Pánchâla. Gaunder	,,	...	...	...	...	...
		Total Group 20	....	*856*	*446*	*355*	*55*	...
	21. Brass & Copper-smiths	Pánchâla.—Gejjegâra	,,	...	...	...	...	...
	22. Tailors	Darzi	,,	1,097	570	431	96	...
	23. Weavers, Calenderers and Dyers.	Gónîga	,,	...	...	...	...	...
		Gádiya	Jain.	...	...	...	...	...
		Néyigé	Hindu.	3,394	1,893	1,286	215	...
		Total Group 23	....	*3,394*	*1,893*	*1,286*	*215*	...
	24. Washermen	Agasa	,,	6,836	3,858	2,588	390	...
	25 (a). Cowherds, &c.	Golla	,,	2,101	1,134	851	116	...
	26. Shepherds and Wool weavers.	Kuruba	,,	11,924	6,579	4,515	830	...
	27. Oil-pressers	Gániga	,,	377	190	157	30	...
	28. Potters	Kumbâra	,,	1,885	1,001	726	158	...
	30. Salt, &c., workers	Uppâra	,,	6,091	3,213	2,499	379	...
	32. Gold-smith's refuse collectors.	Pánchâla.—Julagâra	,,	...	...	...	...	...
	33 (a). Gold-lace makers	Ráchévâr.—Sarigé	,,	...	...	...	...	...

TABLE E.—(*Continued.*)

District.

Males.

0 to 9					10 to 14				
Total.	Single.	Married.	Widowed.	Civil condition not stated.	Total.	Single.	Married.	Widowed.	Civil condition not stated.
...	...	...	...	...	...	...	...	...	...
1,193	1,193	...	...	...	565	549	15	1	...
99	97	1	1	...	72	71	1	...	...
3	3	...	...	...	2	2	...	...	...
...	...	...	...	...	...	...	...	...	...
...	...	...	...	...	...	...	...	...	...
213	213	...	...	...	115	112	3	...	...
9,132	*9,129*	*2*	*1*	...	*4,432*	*4,323*	*106*	*3*	...
9,132	**9,129**	**2**	**1**	...	**4,432**	**4,323**	**106**	**3**	...
1,418	1,418	...	...	...	748	739	9	...	...
396	396	...	...	...	192	192	...	...	...
24	24	...	...	...	11	11	...	...	...
213	213	...	...	...	100	96	4	...	...
...	...	...	...	...	...	...	...	...	...
213	*213*	...	...	...	*100*	*96*	*4*	...	...
...	...	...	...	...	...	...	...	...	...
286	286	...	...	...	150	147	3	...	...
...	...	...	...	...	...	...	...	...	...
...	...	...	...	...	...	...	...	...	...
921	918	3	...	...	473	470	3	...	...
921	*918*	*3*	...	...	*473*	*470*	*3*	...	...
1,843	1,843	...	...	...	925	915	10	...	...
554	554	...	...	...	337	332	5	...	...
3,253	3,251	2	...	...	1,460	1,421	38	1	...
70	70	...	...	...	41	40	1	...	...
489	489	...	...	...	253	243	10	...	...
1,501	1,501	...	...	...	867	836	31	...	...
...	...	...	...	...	...	...	...	...	...
...	...	...	...	...	...	...	...	...	...

Class.	Group.	Caste, &c. and sub-division.	Religion.	15 to 30. Total.	Single.	Married.	Widowed.	Civil condition not stated.
C.—Commercial—(Concluded.)	14. Traders.—(Concluded.)	Multāni ...	Hindu.	...	...	...	...	...
		Nagarta ...	,,	1,595	388	1,065	142	...
		Jain ...	Jain.	237	104	126	7	...
		Mārvādi ...	,,	12	7	5	...	...
		Do. ...	Hindu.	...	...	...	...	...
		Do. ...	Buddhist.	...	...	...	...	...
		S'rāvaka ...	Jain.	497	311	161	25	...
		Total Group 14	....	*14,566*	*5,498*	*8,303*	*765*	...
		Total Class C	....	**14,566**	**5,498**	**8,303**	**765**	...
D.—Artisan and Village menial.—(Continued.)	17. Gold smiths.	Pānchāla ...	Hindu.	2,104	681	1,235	188	...
	18. Barbers ...	Nāyinda ...	,,	574	221	333	20	...
	19. Black smiths	Pānchāla.—Kammāra	,,	40	15	23	2	...
	20. Carpenters, &c.	Pānchāla.—Badagi ...	,,	367	130	225	12	...
		Pānchāla.—Gaunder ...	,,	...	...	...	...	...
		Total Group 20	....	*367*	*130*	*225*	*12*	...
	21. Brass & Copper-smiths...	Pānchāla.—Gejjēgāra	,,	...	...	...	...	...
	22. Tailors ...	Darzi ...	,,	419	126	262	31	...
	23. Weavers, Calenderers and Dyers.	Gōniga ...	,,	...	...	...	...	...
		Gādiya ...	Jain.	...	...	...	...	...
		Nēyigē ...	Hindu.	1,283	486	747	50	...
		Total Group 23	....	*1,283*	*486*	*747*	*50*	...
	24. Washermen.	Agasa ...	,,	2,634	1,010	1,529	95	...
	26 (a). Cowherds, &c. ...	Golla ...	,,	782	237	496	49	...
	26. Shepherds and Wool-weavers.	Kuruba ...	,,	4,844	1,835	2,758	251	...
	27. Oil-pressers.	Gāniga ...	,,	193	78	106	9	...
	28. Potters ...	Kumbāra ...	,,	756	261	445	50	...
	30. Salt, &c., workers ...	Uppāra ...	,,	2,418	796	1,504	118	...
	32. Gold-smith's refuse collectors. ...	Pānchāla.—Jalagāra...	,,	...	...	...	...	...
	33 (a). Gold-lace makers. ...	Rāchēvār.—Sarigē ...	,,	...	...	...	...	...

TABLE E.—(*Continued.*)

District.

Males.

40 and over.					Age not stated.				
Total.	Single.	Married.	Widowed.	Civil condition not stated.	Total.	Single.	Married.	Widowed.	Civil condition not stated.
...	...	...	...	...	...	...	...	...	...
855	67	531	257	...	...	...	...	...	...
127	9	76	42	...	...	...	...	...	...
4	...	4	...	...	...	...	...	...	...
...	...	...	...	...	...	...	...	...	...
...	...	...	...	...	...	...	...	...	...
213	23	139	51	...	...	...	...	...	...
7,547	*521*	*5,135*	*1,891*	...	...	...	...	...	...
7,547	**531**	**5,135**	**1,891**	...	...	...	...	...	...
1,318	43	916	360	...	...	...	...	...	...
298	5	220	73	...	...	...	...	...	...
21	...	13	8	...	...	...	...	...	...
176	7	126	43	...	...	...	...	...	...
...	...	...	...	...	...	...	...	...	...
176	*7*	*126*	*43*	...	...	...	...	...	...
...	...	...	...	...	...	...	...	...	...
242	11	166	65	...	...	...	...	...	...
...	...	...	...	...	...	...	...	...	...
...	...	...	...	...	...	...	...	...	...
717	19	533	165	...	...	...	...	...	...
717	*19*	*533*	*165*	...	...	...	...	...	...
1,434	90	1,049	295	...	...	...	...	...	...
428	11	350	67	...	...	...	...	...	...
2,367	72	1,717	578	...	...	...	...	...	...
73	2	50	21	...	...	...	...	...	...
387	8	271	103	...	...	...	...	...	...
1,305	80	964	201	...	...	...	...	...	...
...	...	...	...	...	...	...	...	...	...
...	...	...	...	...	...	...	...	...	...

Shimoga

Class	Group	Caste, &c. and sub-division	Religion	All Ages. Total	Single	Married	Widowed	Civil condition not stated
C.—Commercial.—(Concluded.)	14. Traders.—(Concluded).	Multáni ...	Hindu.	...	...	...	...	...
		Nagarta ...	,,	3,758	1,390	1,770	598	...
		Jain ...	Jain.	477	147	153	177	...
		Márvádi ...	,,	5	2	3	...	...
		Do. ...	Hindu.	...	...	...	...	...
		Do. ...	Buddhist.	...	...	...	...	...
		S'rávaka ...	Jain.	924	373	305	246	...
		Total Group 14	....	32,746	11,858	14,636	6,252	...
		Total Class C	....	**32,746**	**11,858**	**14,636**	**6,252**	...
D.—Artisan and Village menial.—(Continued.)	17. Gold smiths.	Pánchála ...	Hindu.	4,882	1,605	3,261	1,016	...
	18. Barbers ...	Náyindu ...	,,	1,368	514	621	233	...
	19. Black smiths	Pánchála.—Kammára	,,	84	30	38	16	...
	20. Carpenters, &c.	Pánchála. { Badagi ...	,,	601	165	283	153	...
		Pánchála. { Gaunder ...	,,	...	...	...	...	...
		Total Group 20	....	601	165	283	153	...
	21. Brass & Copper-smiths ...	Pánchála.—Gejjégára	,,	...	...	...	...	...
	22. Tailors ...	Darzi ...	,,	993	316	509	168	...
	23. Weavers, Calenderers and Dyers.	Góniga ...	,,	...	...	...	...	...
		Gádiya ...	Jain.	...	...	...	...	...
		Néyigé ...	Hindu.	3,280	1,281	1,420	579	...
		Total Group 23	....	3,280	1,281	1,420	579	...
	24. Washermen.	Agasa ...	,,	6,267	2,355	2,759	1,153	...
	26 (a). Cowherds, &c. ...	Golla ...	,,	1,894	675	937	283	...
	26. Shepherds and Wool-weavers.	Kuruba ...	,,	11,759	4,622	5,059	2,078	...
	27. Oil-pressors.	Gániga ...	,,	170	47	91	32	...
	28. Potters ...	Kumbára ...	,,	1,396	457	724	215	...
	30. Salt, &c., workers....	Uppára ...	,,	4,866	1,758	2,226	881	...
	32. Gold smith's refuse collectors.	Pánchála.—Julagára ...	,,	...	...	...	...	...
	33 (a). Gold-lace makers. ...	Bachévar.—Sarigé ...	,,	...	...	...	...	...

TABLE E.—(*Continued.*)

District.

Females.

0 to 9					10 to 14				
Total.	Single.	Married.	Widowed.	Civil condition not stated.	Total.	Single.	Married.	Widowed.	Civil condition not stated.
...	...	...	...	...	...	...	...	...	...
943	942	1	...	...	478	358	119	1	...
101	100	1	...	...	55	40	14	1	...
2	2	...	...	...	...	...	...	...	...
...	...	...	...	...	...	...	...	...	...
...	...	...	...	...	...	...	...	...	...
250	242	7	1	...	141	104	35	2	...
7,960	*7,856*	*103*	*1*	...	*4,073*	*2,958*	*1,088*	*27*	...
7,960	**7,856**	**103**	**1**	...	**4,073**	**2,958**	**1,088**	**27**	...
1,147	1,129	18	...	...	515	363	147	5	...
327	327	...	...	...	162	138	24	...	...
19	19	...	...	...	12	9	3	...	...
123	120	3	...	...	57	40	16	1	...
...	...	...	...	...	...	...	...	...	...
123	*120*	*3*	...	...	*57*	*40*	*16*	*1*	...
...	...	...	...	...	...	...	...	...	...
261	255	6	...	...	67	45	22	...	...
...	...	...	...	...	...	...	...	...	...
...	...	...	...	...	...	...	...	...	...
924	914	10	...	...	359	281	78	...	...
924	*914*	*10*	...	...	*359*	*281*	*78*	...	...
1,652	1,642	10	...	...	658	546	111	1	...
470	470	...	...	...	188	165	23	...	...
3,401	3,346	55	...	...	1,250	964	275	11	...
39	36	3	...	...	16	7	9	...	...
320	310	1	...	...	135	96	39	...	...
1,244	1,233	11	...	...	465	387	75	3	...
...	...	...	...	...	...	...	...	...	...
...	...	...	...	...	...	...	...	...	...

Class.	Group.	Caste, &c. and sub-division.	Religion.	15 to 39 Total.	15 to 39 Single.	15 to 39 Married.	15 to 39 Widowed.	15 to 39 Civil condition not stated.
C.—Commercial.—(Concluded.)	14. Traders.—(Concluded.)	Multáni	Hindu.	...	...	...	...	...
		Nagarta	,,	1,753	90	1,446	217	...
		Jain	Jain.	193	7	113	73	...
		Márvádi	,,	3	...	3	...	...
		Do.	Hindu.	...	...	...	...	...
		Do.	Buddhist.	...	...	...	...	...
		S'rávaka	Jain.	366	22	243	101	...
		Total Group 14......	....	*14,638*	*920*	*11,632*	*2,086*	...
		Total Class C.......	....	**14,638**	**920**	**11,632**	**2,086**	...
D.—Artisan and Village menial.—(Continued.)	17. Gold smiths.	Páncháḷa	Hindu.	2,176	100	1,733	343	...
	18. Barbers ...	Náyinda	,,	667	49	527	91	...
	19. Black smiths	Páncháḷa.—Kammára ...	,,	33	2	27	4	...
	20. Carpenters, &c.	Páncháḷa. { Baḍagi	,,	241	5	194	42	...
		Páncháḷa. { Gaunder	,,	...	...	...	...	...
		Total Group 20......	....	*241*	*5*	*194*	*42*	...
	21. Brass & Copper-smiths ...	Páncháḷa.—Gejjégára ...	,,	...	...	...	...	...
	22. Tailors ...	Darzi	,,	481	16	423	42	...
	23. Weavers, Calenderers and Dyers.	Góniga	,,	...	...	...	...	...
		Gádiya	Jain.	...	...	...	...	...
		Nëyigé	Hindu.	1,345	77	1,121	147	...
		Total Group 23......	....	*1,345*	*77*	*1,121*	*147*	...
	24. Washermen .	Agasa	,,	2,786	148	2,210	428	...
	26 (a): Cowherds, &c.	Golla	,,	953	39	808	106	...
	26. Shepherds and Wool weavers.	Kuruba	,,	5,059	273	4,035	751	...
	27. Oil-pressers .	Gániga	,,	81	4	65	12	...
	28. Potters ...	Kumbára... ...	,,	667	41	557	69	...
	30. Salt, &c., workers. ..	Uppára	,,	2,212	128	1,754	330	...
	32. Gold smith's refuse collectors.	Páncháḷa.—Jalagára	,,	...	...	...	...	...
	33 (a). Gold-lace makers ...	Ráchévár.—Sarigé	,,	...	...	...	...	...

TABLE E.—(Continued.)

District.

Females.

40 and over.					Age not stated.				
Total.	Single.	Married.	Widowed.	Civil condition not stated.	Total.	Single.	Married.	Widowed.	Civil condition not stated.
...	...	...	...	...	...	...	...	...	...
584	...	204	380	...	...	...	...	...	...
128	...	25	103	...	...	...	...	...	...
...	...	...	...	...	...	...	...	...	...
...	...	...	...	...	...	...	...	...	...
...	...	...	...	...	...	...	...	...	...
167	5	20	142	...	...	...	...	...	...
6,075	*124*	*1,813*	*4,138*	...	...	...	...	...	...
6,075	**124**	**1,813**	**4,138**	...	...	...	...	...	...
1,044	13	363	668	...	...	...	...	...	...
212	...	70	142	...	...	...	...	...	...
20	...	8	12	...	...	...	...	...	...
180	...	70	110	...	...	...	...	...	...
...	...	...	...	...	...	...	...	...	...
180	...	*70*	*110*	...	...	...	...	...	...
...	...	...	...	...	...	...	...	...	...
184	...	58	126	...	...	...	...	...	...
...	...	...	...	...	...	...	...	...	...
...	...	...	...	...	...	...	...	...	...
652	9	211	432	...	...	...	...	...	...
652	*9*	*211*	*432*	...	...	...	...	...	...
1,171	19	428	724	...	...	...	...	...	...
283	1	106	176	...	...	...	...	...	...
2,049	39	694	1,316	...	...	...	...	...	...
34	...	14	20	...	...	...	...	...	...
274	1	127	146	...	...	...	...	...	...
944	10	383	548	...	...	...	...	...	...
...	...	...	...	...	...	...	...	...	...
...	...	...	...	...	...	...	...	...	...

Class.	Group.	Caste, &c. and sub-division.	Religion.	All Ages. Total.	All Ages. Single.	All Ages. Married.	All Ages. Widowed.	All Ages. Civil condition not stated.
C.—Commercial.—(Concluded.)	14. Traders.—(Concluded.)	Multáni ...	Hindu.	...	...	...	...	..
		Nagartu ...	"	2,989	1,752	1,097	140	...
		Jain ...	Jain.	26	13	10	3	...
		Márvádi ...	"	1	1	...	...	...
		Do. ...	Hindu.	...	...	...	...	...
		Do. ...	Buddhist.	...	...	...	...	...
		S'rávaka ...	Jain.	...	...	...	...	...
		Total Group 14	....	*17,451*	*9,879*	*6,678*	*894*	...
		Total Class C	....	**17,451**	**9,879**	**6,678**	**894**	...
D.—Artisan and Village menial.—(Continued.)	17. Gold-smiths.	Pánchála ...	Hindu.	4,119	2,375	1,551	193	...
	18. Barbers ...	Náyinda ...	"	520	320	173	27	...
	19. Black smiths	Pánchála.—Kammára ...	"	90	49	31	10	...
	20. Carpenters, &c.	Pánchála. Badagi ...	"	559	296	232	31	...
		Pánchála. Gaunder ...	"	...	...	...	...	...
		Total Group 20	....	*559*	*296*	*232*	*31*	...
	21. Brass & Copper-smiths ...	Pánchála.—Gejjégára ...	"	...	...	...	...	...
	22. Tailors ...	Darzi ...	"	409	230	158	21	...
	23. Weavers, Calenderers and Dyers.	Gónigé ...	"	7	4	3	...	...
		Gádiya ...	Jain.	...	...	...	...	...
		Néyigé ...	Hindu.	5,106	2,810	2,032	264	...
		Total Group 23	....	*5,113*	*2,814*	*2,035*	*264*	...
	24. Washermen .	Agasa ...	"	2,199	1,205	876	118	...
	26 (a). Cowherds, &c. ...	Golla ...	"	2,127	1,231	771	125	...
	26. Shepherds and Wool-weavers.	Kuruba ...	"	13,246	7,305	5,366	575	...
	27. Oil-pressers .	Gániga ...	"	550	304	216	30	...
	28. Potters ...	Kumbára ...	"	2,152	1,202	816	134	...
	30. Salt, &c., workers ...	Uppára ...	"	5,115	2,830	2,061	224	...
	32. Gold-smith's refuse collectors. ...	Pánchála.—Jalagára ...	"	...	...	...	...	...
	33 (a). Gold-lace makers ...	Ráchévár.—Sarigé ...	"	...	...	...	...	...

TABLE E.—(*Continued.*)

District

Males,

0 to 9					10 to 14				
Total.	Single.	Married.	Widowed.	Civil condition not stated.	Total.	Single.	Married.	Widowed.	Civil condition not stated.
...	...	...	...	...	...	...	...	...	...
755	755	...	...	...	350	348	2	...	...
6	6	...	...	...	2	2	...	...	...
...	...	...	...	...	...	...	...	...	...
...	...	...	...	...	...	...	...	...	...
...	...	...	...	...	...	...	...	...	...
...	...	...	...	...	...	...	...	...	...
4,486	*4,486*	...	...	...	*1,859*	*1,824*	35	...	...
4,486	**4,486**	...	...	...	**1,859**	**1,824**	**35**	...	...
1,081	1,081	...	...	...	423	423	...	...	...
157	157	...	...	...	61	61	...	...	...
23	23	...	...	...	9	9	...	...	...
148	148	...	...	...	52	52	...	...	...
...	...	...	...	...	...	...	...	...	...
148	*148*	...	...	...	*52*	*52*	...	...	...
...	...	...	...	...	...	...	...	...	...
90	90	...	...	...	35	32	3	...	...
2	2	...	...	...	1	1	...	...	...
...	...	...	...	...	...	...	...	...	...
1,377	1,377	...	...	...	513	513	...	...	...
1,370	*1,370*	...	...	...	*514*	*514*	...	...	...
569	569	...	...	...	189	188	1	...	...
552	552	...	...	...	216	216	...	...	...
3,646	3,646	...	...	...	1,410	1,378	32	...	...
137	137	...	...	...	50	50	...	...	...
510	510	...	...	...	236	236	...	...	...
1,441	1,441	...	...	...	483	481	2	...	...
...	...	...	...	...	...	...	...	...	...
...	...	...	...	...	...	...	...	...	...

Kadur

Class.	Group.	Caste, &c. and sub-division.	Religion.	15 to 39 Total.	15 to 39 Single.	15 to 39 Married.	15 to 39 Widowed.	15 to 39 Civil condition not stated.
C.—Commercial.—(Concluded.)	14. Traders.—(Concluded.)	Multáni	Hindu.	...	...	...	...	...
		Nagarta	,,	1,406	624	722	60	...
		Jain	Jain.	13	5	7	1	...
		Márvádi	,,	1	1	...	...	...
		Do.	Hindu.	...	...	...	...	...
		Do.	Buddhist.	...	...	...	...	...
		S'rávaka	Jain.	...	...	...	...	...
		Total Group 14	....	*7,893*	*3,457*	*4,172*	*264*	...
		Total Class C	....	**7,893**	**3,457**	**4.172**	**264**	...
D.—Artisan and Village menial.—(Continued.)	17. Gold smiths.	Pánchála	Hindu.	1,902	838	1,014	50	...
	18. Barbers	Náyinda	,,	225	96	122	7	...
	19. Black smiths	Pánchála.—Kammára	,,	40	16	21	3	...
	20. Carpenters, &c.	Pánchála.—Badagi	,,	254	90	151	13	...
		Pánchála.—Gaunder	,,	...	...	...	...	...
		Total Group 20	....	*254*	*90*	*151*	*13*	...
	21. Brass & Copper-smiths	Pánchála.—Gejjégára	,,	...	...	...	...	...
	22. Tailors	Darzi	,,	208	96	102	10	...
	23. Weavers, Calenderers and Dyers.	Góniga	,,	3	1	2	...	...
		Gádiya	Jain.	...	...	...	...	...
		Néyigé	Hindu.	2,241	881	1,293	67	...
		Total Group 23	....	*2,244*	*882*	*1,295*	*67*	...
	24. Washermen.	Agasa	,,	1,010	424	581	35	...
	26 (a). Cowherds, &c.	Golla	,,	952	444	479	29	...
	26. Shepherds and Wool-weavers.	Kuruba	,,	5,691	2,172	3,358	161	...
	27. Oil-pressers.	Gániga	,,	256	113	131	12	...
	28. Potters.	Kumbára	,,	1,035	433	552	50	...
	30. Salt, &c. workers.	Uppára	,,	2,223	878	1,282	63	...
	32. Gold-smith's refuse collectors	Pánchála.—Jalagára	,,	...	...	...	...	..
	33 (a). Gold-lace makers	Ráchévár.—Sarigé	,,	...	...	...	...	...

TABLE E.—*(Continued.)*

District.

Males.

40 and over.					Age not stated.				
Total.	Single.	Married.	Widowed.	Civil condition not stated.	Total.	Single.	Married.	Widowed.	Civil condition not stated.
...	...	...	...	...	...	...	...	...	...
478	25	373	80	...	...	...	...	...	...
5	...	3	2	...	...	...	...	...	...
...	...	...	...	...	...	...	...	...	...
...	...	...	...	...	...	...	...	...	...
...	...	...	...	...	...	...	...	...	...
...	...	...	...	...	...	...	...	...	...
3,213	*112*	*2,471*	*630*	...	...	...	...	...	...
3,213	**112**	**2,471**	**630**	...	...	...	...	...	...
713	33	537	143	...	...	...	...	...	...
77	6	51	20	...	...	...	...	...	...
18	1	10	7	...	...	...	...	...	...
105	6	81	18	...	...	...	...	...	...
...	...	...	...	...	...	...	...	...	...
105	*6*	*81*	*18*	...	...	...	...	...	...
...	...	...	...	...	...	...	...	...	...
76	13	53	11	...	...	...	...	...	...
1	...	1	...	...	...	...	...	...	...
...	...	...	...	...	...	...	...	...	...
975	39	739	197	...	...	...	...	...	...
976	*39*	*740*	*197*	...	...	...	...	...	...
401	24	294	83	...	...	...	...	...	...
407	19	292	96	...	...	...	...	...	...
2,499	109	1,976	414	...	...	...	...	...	...
107	4	85	18	...	...	...	...	...	...
371	23	264	84	...	...	...	...	...	...
968	30	777	161	...	...	...	...	...	...
...	...	...	...	...	...	...	...	...	...
...	...	...	...	...	...	...	...	...	...

Kadur

Class.	Group.	Caste, &c. and sub-division.	Religion.	All Ages. Total.	Single.	Married.	Widowed.	Civil condition not stated.
C.—Commercial.—(Concluded.)	14. Traders.—(Concluded.)	Múltáni	Hindu.	...	...	...	...	...
		Nagarta	,,	2,234	873	934	427	...
		Jain	Jain.	17	3	11	3	...
		Márvádi	,,	...	...	...	...	...
		Do.	Hindu.	...	...	...	...	...
		Do.	Buddhist.	...	...	...	...	...
		S'rávaka	Jain.	...	...	...	...	...
		Total Group 14......	....	*15,884*	*6,151*	*6,299*	*3,434*	...
		Total Class C......	....	**15,884**	**6,151**	**6,299**	**3,434**	...
D.—Artisan and Village menial.—(Continued.)	17. Gold smiths.	Pánchála	Hindu.	3,434	1,278	1,412	744	...
	18. Barbers ...	Náyinda	,,	403	147	164	92	...
	19. Black smiths	Pánchála.—Kammára ...	,,	85	23	40	22	...
	20. Carpenters, &c.	Pánchála. { Badagi	,,	458	136	210	112	...
		Pánchála. { Gáunder	,,	...	...	...	...	...
		Total Group 20......	....	*458*	*136*	*210*	*112*	...
	21. Brass & Copper-smiths ...	Pánchála.—Gejjégára ...	,,	...	...	...	...	...
	22. Tailors ...	Darzi	,,	325	91	171	63	...
	23. Weavers, Calenderers and Dyers.	Góniga	,,	12	6	4	2	...
		Gádiya	Jain.	...	...	...	...	...
		Néyigé	Hindu.	5,111	1,962	2,050	1,099	...
		Total Group 23......	....	*5,123*	*1,968*	*2,054*	*1,101*	...
	24. Washermen.	Agasa	,,	1,987	745	863	379	...
	25 (a). Cowherds, &c. ...	Golla	,,	2,022	776	788	458	...
	26. Shepherds and Wool-weavers.	Kuruba	,,	13,009	5,047	5,326	2,636	...
	27. Oil-pressers.	Gániga	,,	542	191	230	121	...
	28. Potters ...	Kumbára	,,	1,866	724	771	371	...
	30. Salt, &c. workers.	Uppára	,,	4,885	1,965	1,998	922	...
	32. Gold-smith's refuse collectors. ...	Pánchála.—Jalagára ...	,,	...	...	...	...	...
	33 (a). Gold-lace makers ...	Rachévar.—Sarigé	,,	...	...	3	...	...

TABLE E.—(*Continued.*)

District.

Females.

0 to 9					10 to 14				
Total.	Single.	Married.	Widowed.	Civil condition not stated.	Total.	Single.	Married.	Widowed.	Civil condition not stated.
...	...	...	...	...	...	...	...	...	...
730	672	58	...	...	274	167	106	1	...
2	2	...	...	...	1	1	...	...	...
...	...	...	...	...	...	...	...	...	...
...	...	...	...	...	...	...	...	...	...
...	...	...	...	...	...	...	...	...	...
...	...	...	...	...	...	...	...	...	...
4,665	*4,352*	*312*	*1*	...	*1,767*	*1,294*	*468*	*5*	...
4,665	**4,352**	**312**	**1**	...	**1,767**	**1,294**	**468**	**5**	...
1,063	992	71	...	...	419	283	131	5	...
94	94	...	...	...	40	35	5	...	...
19	19	...	...	...	8	4	4	...	...
106	93	13	...	...	79	41	38	...	...
...	...	...	...	...	...	...	...	...	...
106	*93*	*13*	...	...	*79*	*41*	*38*	...	...
...	...	...	...	...	...	...	...	...	...
79	76	3	...	...	32	15	16	1	...
3	3	...	...	...	2	1	1	...	...
...	...	...	...	...	...	...	...	...	...
1,503	1,400	103	...	...	601	426	174	1	...
1,506	*1,403*	*103*	...	...	*603*	*427*	*175*	*1*	...
565	545	20	...	...	203	142	61	...	...
570	555	15	...	...	187	146	41	...	...
3,648	3,634	14	...	...	1,153	972	181	...	...
129	122	7	...	...	51	39	12	...	...
524	512	12	...	...	186	156	30	...	...
1,523	1,472	51	...	...	449	342	107	...	...
...	...	...	...	...	...	...	...	...	...
...	...	...	...	...	...	...	...	...	...

Kadur

Class.	Group.	Caste, &c. and sub-division.	Religion.	15 to 39. Total.	Single.	Married.	Widowed.	Civil condition not stated.
C.—Commercial.—(Concluded.)	14. Traders.—(Concluded.)	Multáni ...	Hindu.	...	...	...	...	...
		Nagarta ...	,,	847	34	641	172	...
		Jain ...	Jain.	10	...	9	1	...
		Márváḍi ...	,,	...	...	...	...	...
		Do. ...	Hindu.	...	...	...	...	...
		Do. ...	Buddhist.	...	...	...	...	...
		S'rávaka ...	Jain.	...	...	...	...	...
		Total Group 14......	....	*6,105*	*452*	*4,538*	*1,115*	...
		Total Class C......	... .	**6,105**	**452**	**4,538**	**1,115**	...
D.—Artisan and Village menial.—(Continued.)	17. Gold smiths.	Pánchála ...	Hindu.	1,271	3	1,000	268	...
	18. Barbers ...	Náyinda ...	,,	174	17	128	29	...
	19. Black smiths	Pánchála.—Kammára	,,	33	...	26	7	...
	20. Carpenters, &c.	Pánchála. { Badagi ...	,,	155	2	118	35	...
		Pánchála. { Gaunḍer...	,,	...	...	...	...	...
		Total Gorup 20......	....	*155*	*2*	*118*	*35*	...
	21. Brass & Copper-smiths ...	Pánchála—Gejjégára	,,	...	...	...	...	...
	22. Tailors ...	Darzi ...	,,	137	...	117	20	...
	23. Weavers, Calenderers and Dyers.	Góṇiga ...	,,	4	2	2	...	...
		Gádiya ...	Jain.	...	...	...	...	...
		Néyigé ...	Hindu.	1,956	136	1,442	378	...
		Total Group 23......	... .	*1,960*	*138*	*1,444*	*378*	...
	24. Washermen.	Agasa ...	,,	847	56	667	124	...
	26 (a). Cowherds, &c. ...	Golla ...	,,	813	71	591	151	...
	26. Shepherds and Wool-weavers.	Kuruba ...		5,344	408	4,191	745	...
	27. Oil-pressers.	Gániga ...		231	30	163	38	...
	28. Potters. ...	Kumbára...	,,	778	55	593	130	...
	30. Salt, &c. workers.	Uppára ...	,,	1,958	148	1,481	329	...
	32. Gold-smith's refuse collectors.	Pánchála—Jalagára...	,,	...	...	...	...	...
	33 (a). Gold-lace makers. ...	Ráchévár—Sarigé ...	,,	...	...	...	...	...

TABLE E.—(*Continued.*)

District.

Females.

40 and over.					Age not stated.				
Total	Single.	Married.	Widowed.	Civil condition not stated.	Total.	Single.	Married.	Widowed.	Civil condition not stated.
...	...	...	...	...	...	...	...	...	...
383	...	129	254	...	...	...	...	...	...
4	...	2	2	...	...	...	...	...	...
...	...	...	...	...	...	...	...	...	...
...	...	...	...	...	...	...	...	...	...
...	...	...	...	...	...	...	...	...	...
3,347	53	981	2,313	...	...	...	...	...	...
3,347	*53*	*981*	*2,313*	...	...	...	...	...	...
3,347	**53**	**981**	**2,313**	...	...	...	...	...	...
681	...	210	471	...	...	...	...	...	...
95	1	31	63	...	...	...	...	...	...
25	...	10	15	...	...	...	...	...	...
118	...	41	77	...	...	...	...	...	...
...	...	...	...	...	...	...	...	...	...
118	...	*41*	*77*	...	...	...	...	...	...
...	...	...	...	...	...	...	...	...	...
77	...	35	42	...	...	...	...	...	...
3	...	1	2	...	...	...	...	...	...
...	...	...	...	...	...	...	...	...	...
1,051	...	331	720	...	...	...	...	...	...
1,054	...	*332*	*722*	...	...	...	...	...	...
372	2	115	255	...	...	...	...	...	...
452	4	141	307	...	...	...	...	...	...
2,864	33	940	1,891	...	...	...	...	...	...
131	...	48	83	...	...	...	...	...	...
378	1	137	241	...	...	...	...	...	...
955	3	359	593	...	...	...	...	...	...
...	...	...	...	...	...	...	...	...	...
...	...	...	...	...	...	...	...	...	...

Chitaldurg

Class.	Group.	Caste and Religion: Caste, &c. and sub-division.	Caste and Religion: Religion.	All Ages: Total.	All Ages: Single.	All Ages: Married.	All Ages: Widowed.	All Ages: Civil condition not stated.
C.—Commercial.—(Concluded.)	14. Traders.—(Concluded.)	Multáni	Hindu.	...	...	...	...	...
		Nagarta	,,	332	167	128	37	...
		Jain	Jain.	128	83	35	10	...
		Márváḍi	,,	23	10	10	3	...
		Do	Hindu	...	...	...	...	...
		Do	Buddhist.	...	...	...	...	...
		S'rávaka	Jain.	...	...	...	...	...
		Total Group 14	....	*27,032*	*15,572*	*9,790*	*1,670*	...
	Total Class C		....	**27,032**	**15,572**	**9,790**	**1,670**	...
D.—Artisan and Village menial.—(Continued.)	17. Gold smiths.	Pánchála	Hindu.	3,093	1,717	1,128	248	...
	18. Barbers ..	Náyinda	,,	935	520	342	73	...
	19. Black smiths	Pánchála.—Kammára ...	,,	426	224	173	29	...
	20. Carpenters, &c.	Pánchála. { Baḍagi	,,	654	327	273	54	...
		Pánchála. { Gaunḍer ...	,,	...	...	...	...	...
		Total Group 20	... .	*654*	*327*	*273*	*54*	...
	21. Brass & Copper smiths...	Gejjégára...	,,	...	...	...	...	...
	22. Tailors ...	Darzi	,,	418	215	171	32	...
	23. Weavers, Calendarers and Dyers.	Góṇiga	,,	...	...	...	...	...
		Gádiya	Jain.	...	...	...	...	...
		Náyigé	Hindu.	3,598	1,850	1,495	253	...
		Total Group 23	....	*3,598*	*1,850*	*1,495*	*253*	...
	24. Washermen .	Agasa	,,	3,217	1,780	1,276	161	...
	26 (a). Cowherds, &c. ...	Golla	,,	15,892	8,519	6,631	742	...
	23. Shepherds and Wool-weavers.	Kuruba	,,	13,005	7,100	5,185	720	...
	27. Oil-pressers .	Gáṇiga	,,	604	325	221	58	...
	28. Potters ...	Kumbára	,,	1,352	743	506	98	...
	30. Salt, &c., workers ...	Uppára	,,	4,312	2,457	4,615	240	...
	32. Gold-smith's refuse collectors.	Pánchála.—Jalagára ...	,,	...	...	...	...	...
	33 (a) Gold-lace makers ...	Ráchévár.—Sarigé	,,	...	...	...	...	...

TABLE E.—(*Continued.*)

District.

Males.

0 to 9					10 to 14				
Total.	Single.	Married.	Widowed.	Civil condition not stated.	Total.	Single.	Married.	Widowed.	Civil condition not stated.
...	...	...	...	...	...	...	...	...	...
116	116	...	...	...	38	37	1	...	...
40	40	...	...	...	11	11	2	...	...
6	6	...	...	...	2	2	...	...	...
...	...	...	...	...	...	...	...	...	...
...	...	...	...	...	...	...	...	...	...
...	...	...	...	...	...	...	...	...	...
8,304	*8,278*	*26*	...	...	*3,340*	*3,314*	*26*	...	...
8,304	**8,278**	**26**	...	...	**3,340**	**3,314**	**26**	...	...
871	870	1	...	...	357	343	15	...	...
312	312	...	...	...	89	89	...	...	...
141	141	...	...	...	41	41	...	...	...
153	153	...	...	...	65	65	...	...	...
...	...	...	...	...	...	...	...	...	...
153	*153*	...	...	...	*65*	*65*	...	...	...
...	...	...	...	...	...	...	...	...	...
156	156	...	...	...	23	23	...	...	...
...	...	...	...	...	...	...	...	...	...
...	...	...	...	...	...	...	...	...	...
1,078	1,078	...	...	...	313	288	25	...	...
1,078	*1,078*	...	...	...	*313*	*288*	*25*	...	...
1,153	1,152	1	...	...	188	171	17	...	...
5,088	5,088	...	...	...	1,522	1,436	86	...	...
4,234	4,230	4	...	...	1,044	1,044	...	...	...
173	173	...	...	...	73	73	...	...	...
428	428	...	...	...	448	418	...	...	...
1,400	1,400	...	...	...	303	383	8	...	...
...	...	...	...	...	...	...	...	...	...
...	...	...	...	...	...	...	...	...	...

Chitald

Class.	Group.	Caste, &c. and sub-division.	Religion.	15 to 39. Total.	Single.	Married.	Widowed.
C.—Commercial.—(Concluded.)	14. Traders.—(Concluded.)	Multáni	Hindu.	...	...	...	...
		Nagarta	,,	113	14	86	13
		Jain	Jain.	53	30	22	1
		Márvádi	,,	10	2	7	1
		Do.	Hindu.	...	...	...	...
		Do.	Buddhist.	...	...	...	...
		S'rávaka	Jain.	...	...	...	...
		Total Group 14......	....	*10,362*	*3,797*	*6,231*	*334*
		Total Class C......	....	**10,362**	**4,797**	**6,231**	**334**
D.—Artisan and Village menial.—(Continued.)	17. Gold smiths.	Pánchála	Hindu.	1,231	477	676	78
	18. Barbers ...	Náyinda	,,	362	115	224	23
	19. Black smiths	Pánchála.—Kammára	,,	163	40	110	13
	20. Carpenters, &c.	Pánchála. { Badagi	,,	271	105	158	8
		Pánchála. { Gaunder... ...	,,	...	...	...	...
		Total Group 20......	....	*271*	*105*	*158*	*8*
	21. Brass & Copper-smiths ...	Pánchála.—Gojjégára	,,	...	...	...	...
	22. Tailors ...	Darzi	,,	150	33	114	3
	23. Weavers, Calendarers and Dyers.	Góniga	,,	...	...	...	...
		Gádiya	Jain.	...	...	...	...
		Néyigé	Hindu.	1,437	462	912	63
		Total Group 23......	....	*1,437*	*462*	*912*	*63*
	24. Washermen.	Agasa	,,	1,304	441	825	38
	25 (a). Cowherds, &c. ...	Golla	,,	6,098	1,808	4,066	244
	26. Shepherds and Wool-weavers ...	Kuruba	,,	5,276	1,728	3,335	213
	27. Oil-pressers.	Gániga	,,	233	75	141	17
	28. Potters ...	Kumbára	,,	512	166	316	30
	30. Salt &c., workers ...	Uppára	,,	1,695	653	975	67
	32. Gold-smith's refuse collectors ...	Pánchála.—Jalagára... ...	,,	...	...	...	...
	33 (a). Gold-lace makers ...	Ráchévár.—Sarigé	,,	...	...	...	...

TABLE E.—(Continued.)

District.

Males.

40 and over.					Age not stated.				
Total.	Single.	Married.	Widowed.	Civil condition not stated.	Total.	Single.	Married.	Widowed.	Civil condition not stated.
...	...	...	...	...	...	...	...	...	...
65	...	41	24	...	...	...	...	...	...
24	2	13	9	...	...	...	...	...	...
5	...	3	2	...	...	...	...	...	...
...	...	...	...	...	...	...	...	...	...
...	...	...	...	...	...	...	...	...	...
...	...	...	...	...	...	...	...	...	...
5,026	*183*	*3,507*	*1,336*	...	...	...	...	...	...
5,026	**183**	**3,507**	**1,336**	...	...	...	...	...	...
634	28	436	170	...	...	...	...	...	...
172	4	118	50	...	...	...	...	...	...
81	2	63	16	...	...	...	...	...	...
165	4	115	46	...	...	...	...	...	...
...	...	...	...	...	...	...	...	...	...
165	*4*	*115*	*46*	...	...	...	...	...	...
...	...	...	...	...	...	...	...	...	...
90	4	57	29	...	...	...	...	...	...
...	...	...	...	...	...	...	...	...	...
...	...	...	...	...	...	...	...	...	...
770	22	558	190	...	...	...	...	...	...
770	*22*	*558*	*190*	...	...	...	...	...	...
572	16	433	123	...	...	...	...	...	...
3,184	187	2,479	518	...	...	...	...	...	...
2,451	98	1,846	507	...	...	...	...	...	...
125	4	80	41	...	...	...	...	...	...
264	6	190	68	...	...	...	...	...	...
824	19	632	173	...	...	...	...	...	...
...	...	...	...	...	...	...	...	...	...
...	...	...	...	...	...	...	...	...	...

Class.	Group.	Caste, &c. and sub-division.	Religion.	All Ages. Total.	Single.	Married.	Widowed.	Civil condition not stated.
C.—Commercial.—(Concluded.)	14. Traders.—(Concluded.)	Multáni	Hindu.	...	...	...	...	...
		Nagarta	,,	319	129	140	50	...
		Jain	Jain.	72	19	30	23	...
		Márvádi	,,	...	...	...	...	...
		Do.	Hindu.	...	...	...	...	...
		Do.	Buddhist.	...	...	...	...	...
		S'rávaka	Jain.	...	...	...	...	...
		Total Group 14......	....	25,676	9,737	10,579	5,360	...
	Total Class C......		....	**25,676**	**9,737**	**10,579**	**5,360**	...
D.—Artisan and Village menial.—(Continued.)	17. Gold smiths.	Pánchála	Hindu.	3,133	1,437	1,251	445	...
	18. Barbers ...	Náyinda	,,	803	303	389	111	...
	19. Black smiths	Pánchála.—Kammára ...	,,	363	172	154	37	...
	20. Car penters, &c.	Pánchála. { Badagi	,,	696	307	257	132	...
		Pánchála. { Gaunder ...	,,	...	...	...	...	...
		Total Group 20......	....	696	307	257	132	...
	21. Brass & Copper-smiths ...	Pánchála.—Gejjégára ...	,,	...	...	...	...	...
	22. Tailors ...	Darzi	,,	304	83	151	70	...
	23. Weavers, Calenderers and Dyers.	Góniga	,,	...	...	...	...	...
		Gádiya	Jain.	...	...	...	...	...
		Néyigé	Hindu.	3,576	1,534	1,523	519	...
		Total Group 23......	....	3,576	1,534	1,523	519	...
	24. Washermen ...	Agasa	,,	3,177	1,200	1,283	604	...
	26 (a). Cowherds, &c. ...	Golla	,,	15,613	6,289	6,862	2,462	...
	26. Shepherds and Wool-weavers.	Kuruba	,,	12,393	5,214	4,842	2,337	...
	27. Oil-pressers .	Gániga	,,	668	302	235	131	...
	28. Potters ...	Kumbára...	,,	1,258	526	540	192	...
	30. Salt, &c., workers ...	Uppára	,,	4,361	1,825	1,754	782	...
	32. Gold-smith's refuse collectors.	Pánchála.—Jalagára ...	,,	...	...	...	...	...
	33 (a). Gold-lace makers ...	Ráchévár.—Sarigé	,,	...	...	...	...	...

TABLE E.—*(Continued.)*

District.

Females.

0 to 9					10 to 14.				
Total.	Single.	Married.	Widowed	Civil condition not stated.	Total.	Single.	Married.	Widowed.	Civil condition not stated.
...	...	...	...	...	...	...	...	...	...
103	103	...	...	...	29	26	3	...	...
15	15	...	...	...	4	4	...	...	...
...	...	...	...	...	...	...	...	...	...
...	...	...	...	...	...	...	...	...	...
...	...	...	...	...	...	...	...	...	...
...	...	...	...	...	...	...	...	...	...
7,825	*7,748*	*76*	*1*	...	*2,184*	*1,686*	*495*	*3*	...
7,825	**7,748**	**76**	**1**	...	**2,184**	**1,686**	**495**	**3**	...
993	993	...	...	...	443	338	99	6	...
305	305	...	...	...	92	83	9	...	...
127	125	2	...	...	50	46	4	...	...
232	232	...	...	...	61	54	7	...	...
...	...	...	...	...	...	...	...	...	...
232	*232*	...	...	...	*61*	*54*	*7*	...	...
...	...	...	...	...	...	...	...	...	...
78	78	...	...	...	10	5	5	...	...
...	...	...	...	...	...	...	...	...	...
...	...	...	...	...	...	...	...	...	...
1,140	1,128	12	...	...	393	283	110	...	...
1,140	*1,128*	*12*	...	...	*393*	*283*	*110*	...	...
1,054	1,052	2	...	...	178	157	20	1	...
5,024	4,997	27	...	...	1,054	829	223	2	...
4,077	4,073	4	...	...	1,029	760	269	...	...
211	211	...	...	...	64	60	4	...	...
394	394	...	...	...	113	95	18	...	...
1,472	1,471	1	...	...	297	207	88	2	...
...	...	...	...	...	...	...	...	...	...
...	...	...	...	...	...	...	...	...	...

Class.	Group.	Caste, &c. and sub-division.	Religion.	15 to 39. Total.	Single.	Married.	Widowed.	Civil condition not stated.
C.—Commercial.—(Concluded.)	14. Traders.—(Concluded.)	Multáni	Hindu.	...	...	...	...	...
		Nagarta	,,	129	...	110	19	...
		Jain	Jain.	37	...	25	12	...
		Márvádi	,,	...	...	...	...	...
		Do.	Hindu.	...	...	...	...	...
		Do.	Buddhist.	...	...	...	...	...
		S'rávaka	Jain.	...	...	...	...	...
		Total Group 14	....	*10,328*	*275*	*8,515*	*1,538*	...
		Total Class C	....	**10,328**	**275**	**8,515**	**1,538**	...
D.—Artisan and Village menial.—(Continued.)	17. Gold smiths.	Pánchála	Hindu.	1,125	1[illegible]	881	139	...
	18. Barbers ...	Náyinda	,,	316	5	281	30	...
	19. Black smiths	Pánchála—Kammára ...	,,	106	1	93	12	...
	20. Carpenters, &c.	Pánchála, Badagi ...	,,	253	21	183	49	...
		Pánchála, Gaunder ...	,,	...	...	...	...	...
		Total Group 20	....	*253*	*21*	*183*	*49*	...
	21. Brass & Copper-smiths ...	Pánchála.—Gejjégára	,,	...	...	...	...	...
	22. Tailors ...	Darzi	,,	139	...	119	20	...
	23. Weavers, Calenderers and Dyers.	Góniga	,,	...	...	...	...	...
		Gádiya	Jain.	...	...	...	...	...
		Néyigé	Hindu.	1,279	93	1,025	161	...
		Total Group 23	....	*1,279*	*93*	*1,025*	*161*	...
	24. Washermen .	Agasa	,,	1,323	77	138	208	...
	26 (a). Cowherds, &c. ...	Golla	,,	6,114	419	4,964	701	...
	26. Shepherds and Wool-weavers.	Kuruba	,,	4,831	349	3,807	675	...
	27. Oil-pressers .	Gániga	,,	243	31	161	51	...
	28. Potters ...	Kumbára	,,	503	37	397	69	...
	30. Salt, &c. workers ...	Uppára	,,	1,745	142	1,331	272	...
	32. Gold-smith's refuse collectors.	Pánchala.—Julagára...	,,	...	...	...	...	...
	31 (a). Gold-lace makers ...	Ráchévár.—Sarigé ...	,,	...	...	...	...	...

TABLE E.—*(Continued.)*

District.

Females.

40 and over.					Age not stated.				
Total.	Single.	Married.	Widowed.	Civil condition not stated.	Total.	Single.	Married.	Widowed.	Civil condition not stated.
...	...	...	...	...	...	...	...	...	...
58	...	27	31	...	...	...	...	...	...
16	...	5	11	...	...	...	...	...	...
...	...	...	...	...	...	...	...	...	...
...	...	...	...	...	...	...	...	...	...
...	...	...	...	...	...	...	...	...	...
...	...	...	...	...	...	...	...	...	...
5,339	*28*	*1,493*	*3,818*	...	...	...	...	...	...
5,339	**28**	**1,493**	**3,818**	...		...	...	...	...
572	1	271	300	...		...	...	...	...
180	...	99	81	...	...	...	...	...	...
80	...	55	25	...	...	...	...	...	...
150	...	67	83	...	...	...	...	...	...
...	...	...	...	...	...	...	...	...	...
150	...	*67*	*83*	...	...	...	...	...	...
...	...	...	...	...	...	...	...	...	...
77	...	*27*	*50*	...	...	...	...	...	...
...	...	...	...	...	...	...	...	...	...
...	...	...	...	...	...	...	...	...	...
764	30	376	358	...	...	...	...	...	...
764	*30*	*376*	*358*	...	...	...	...	...	...
622	4	223	395	...	...	...	...	...	...
3,421	14	1,648	1,759	...	...	...	...	...	...
2,456	32	762	1,662	...	...	...	...	...	...
150	...	70	80	...	...	...	...	...	...
248	...	125	123	...	...	...	...	...	...
847	5	334	508	...	...	...	...	...	...
...	...	...	...	...	...	...	...	...	...
...	...	...	...	...	...	...	...	...	...

The Civil and Military

Class.	Group.	Caste, &c., and sub-division.	Religion.	All Ages. Total.	Single.	Married.	Widowed.	Civil condition not stated.
C.—Commercial.—(Concluded.)	14. Traders.—(Concluded.)	Multáni	Hindu.	1	...	1	...	...
		Nagarta	,,	113	46	65	2	...
		Jain	Jain.	...	...	...	...	...
		Márváḍi	,,	17	4	12	1	...
		Do.	Hindu.	11	4	7	...	...
		Do.	Buddhist.	2	1	1	...	...
		S'rávaka	Jain.	...	...	...	...	...
		Total Group 14	....	*4,941*	*2,493*	*2,208*	*240*	...
		Total Class C	....	**4,941**	**2,493**	**2,208**	**240**	...
D.—Artisan and Village menial.—(Continued.)	17. Goldsmiths.	Pánchâḷa	Hindu.	556	296	228	32	...
	18. Barbers ...	Náyinda	,,	586	302	254	30	...
	19. Blacksmiths	Pánchâḷa.—Kammára ...	,,	50	23	22	5	...
	20. Carpenters, &c.	Pánchâḷa. { Baḍagi ...	,,	5	2	3	...	...
		Pánchâḷa. { Gaunḍar ...	,,	2	1	1	...	...
		Total Group 20	....	*7*	*3*	*4*	...	...
	21. Brass & Copper smiths ...	Pánchâḷa.—Gojjégára	,,	78	45	31	2	...
	22. Tailors ...	Darzi	,,	998	517	449	32	...
	23. Weavers, Calenderers and Dyers.	Góṇiga	,,	6	2	3	1	...
		Gádiya	Jain.	1	1	...	...	...
		Néyigé	Hindu.	81	36	40	5	...
		Total Group 23	....	*88*	*39*	*43*	*6*	...
	24. Washermen.	Agasa	,,	503	283	198	22	...
	25 (a). Cowherds, &c. ...	Golla	,,	653	324	298	31	...
	26. Shepherds and Wool-weavers.	Kuruba	,,	386	174	196	16	...
	27. Oil-pressers.	Gáṇiga	,,	63	32	29	2	...
	28. Potters ...	Kumbára...	,,	184	83	84	17	...
	30. Salt, &c., workers ...	Uppára	,,	9	2	6	1	...
	33. Goldsmith's refuse collectors.	Pánchâḷa.—Jaḷagára... ...	,,	2	2	...	...	...
	33 (a). Gold-lace makers. ...	Ráchévár.—Sarigé	,,	...	...	...	...	...

TABLE E.—(*Continued.*)

Station, Bangalore.

Males.

0 to 9					10 to 14				
Total.	Single.	Married.	Widowed.	Civil condition not stated.	Total.	Single.	Married.	Widowed.	Civil condition not stated.
...	...	...	...	...	...	...	...	...	...
20	19	1	...	...	9	7	2	...	...
...	...	...	...	...	...	...	...	...	...
3	2	...	...	...	1	1	...	...	...
2	2	...	...	...	1	1	...	...	...
...	...	...	...	...	...	...	...	...	...
...	...	...	...	...	...	...	...	...	...
1,206	*1,205*	*1*	...	...	*493*	*483*	*9*	*1*	...
1,206	**1,205**	**1**	...	...	**493**	**483**	**9**	**1**	...
151	151	...	...	...	49	49	...	...	...
170	169	1	...	...	54	52	2	...	...
8	8	...	...	...	7	7	...	...	...
1	1	...	...	...	1	1	...	...	...
...	...	...	...	...	...	...	...	...	...
1	*1*	...	...	...	*1*	*1*	...	...	...
21	20	1	...	...	11	11	...	...	...
314	313	...	1	...	106	101	5	...	...
1	1	...	...	...	1	1	...	...	...
...	...	...	...	...	...	...	...	...	...
15	15	...	...	...	3	2	1	...	...
16	*16*	...	...	...	*4*	*3*	*1*	...	...
164	164	...	...	...	43	43	...	...	...
160	160	...	...	...	58	57	1	...	...
95	95	...	...	...	37	34	3	...	...
23	23	...	...	...	1	1	...	...	...
53	53	...	...	...	15	12	3	...	...
2	2	...	...	...	...	...	...	...	...
1	1	...	...	...	1	1	...	...	...
...	...	...	...	...	...	...	...	...	...

Class	Group	Caste, &c., and sub-division	Religion	15 to 39. Total	Single	Married	Widowed	Civil condition not stated
C.—Commercial.—(Concluded.)	14. Traders.—(Concluded.)	Multáni	Hindu.	...	...	...	...	...
		Nagartá	,,	43	9	32	2	...
		Jain	Jain.	...	...	...	...	...
		Márvádi	,,	8	...	8	...	...
		Do.	Hindu.	7	1	6	...	...
		Do.	Buddhist.	2	1	1	...	...
		S'rávaka	Jain.	...	...	...	...	...
		Total Group 14	....	*2,148*	*768*	*1,322*	*58*	...
		Total Class C	....	**2,148**	**768**	**1,322**	**58**	..
D.—Artisan and Village menial.—(Continued.)	17. Goldsmiths.	Pánchála	Hindu.	216	86	123	7	...
	18. Barbers	Náyinda	,,	219	76	133	10	...
	19. Blacksmiths	Pánchála.—Kammára	,,	23	7	13	3	...
	20. Carpenters, &c.	Pánchála.—Badagi	,,	3	...	3	...	...
		Pánchála.—Gaundar	,,	1	1	...	...	...
		Total Group 20	....	*4*	*1*	*3*	...	...
	21. Brass & Copper smiths	Pánchála.—Gejjégára	,,	33	14	19	...	...
	22. Tailors	Darzi	,,	359	101	250	8	...
	23. Weavers, Calenderers and Dyers.	Gániga	,,	2	...	2	...	...
		Gádiya	Jain.	1	1	...	...	...
		Néyigé	Hindu.	51	19	30	2	...
		Total Group 23	....	*54*	*20*	*32*	*2*	...
	24. Washermen	Agasa	,,	196	75	114	7	...
	25 (a). Cowherds, &c.	Golla	,,	287	106	172	9	...
	26. Shepherds and Wool-weavers.	Kuruba	,,	164	43	117	4	...
	27. Oil-pressers	Gániga	,,	27	8	18	1	...
	28. Potters	Kumbára	,,	70	17	50	3	...
	30. Salt, &c., workers	Uppára	,,	3	...	3	...	...
	32. Goldsmith's refuse collectors	Pánchála.—Jalagára	,,	...	...	...	...	...
	33 (a). Gold-lace makers	Ráchévár.—Sarigé	,,	...	...	...	...	...

TABLE E.—(*Continued.*)

Station, Bangalore.

Males.

40 and over.					Age not stated.				
Total.	Single.	Married.	Widowed.	Civil condition not stated.	Total.	Single.	Married.	Widowed.	Civil condition not stated.
1		1	...	...	...	...	...	...	...
41	11	30	...	...	...	...	...	...	...
...	...	...	...	...	...	...	...	...	...
6	1	4	1	...	...	...	...	...	...
1	...	1	...	...	...	...	...	...	...
...	...	...	...	...	...	...	...	...	...
...	...	...	...	...	...	...	...	...	...
1,094	*37*	*876*	*181*	...	...	...	...	...	...
1,094	**37**	**876**	**181**	...	...	...	...	...	...
140	10	105	25	...	...	...	...	...	...
143	5	118	20	...	...	...	...	...	...
12	1	9	2	...	...	...	...	...	...
...	...	...	...	...	...	...	...	...	...
1	...	1	...	...	...	...	...	...	...
1	...	*1*	...	...	...	...	...	...	...
13	...	11	2	...	...	...	...	...	...
219	2	194	23	...	...	...	...	...	...
2	...	1	1	...	...	...	...	...	...
...	...	...	...	...	...	...	...	...	...
12	...	9	3	...	...	...	...	...	...
14	...	*10*	4	...	...	...	...	...	...
100	1	84	15	...	...	...	...	...	...
148	1	125	22	...	...	...	...	...	...
90	2	76	12	...	...	...	...	...	...
12	...	11	1	...	...	...	...	...	...
46	1	31	14	...	...	...	...	...	...
4	...	3	1	...	...	...	...	...	...
...	...	...	...	...	...	...	...	...	...
...	...	...	...	...	...	...	...	...	...

The Civil and Military

Class.	Group.	Caste, &c., and sub-division.	Religion.	All Ages. Total.	Single.	Married.	Widowed.	Civil condition not stated.
C.—Commercial.—(Concluded.)	14. Traders.—(Concluded.)	Multáni	Hindu.	1	...	1	...	...
		Nagarta	"	107	35	63	9	...
		Jain	Jain.	...	...	...	...	...
		Márvádi	"	4	2	1	1	...
		Do.	Hindu.	9	3	3	3	...
		Do.	Buddhist.	...	...	...	...	...
		S'rávaka	Jain.	...	...	...	...	...
		Total Group 14......	....	4,924	1,575	,303	1,046	...
		Total Class C......	....	**4,924**	**1,575**	**2,303**	**1,046**	...
D.—Artisan and Village menial.—(Continued.)	17. Goldsmiths.	Pánchála	Hindu.	535	185	249	101	...
	18. Barbers ...	Náyinda	"	557	200	267	90	...
	19. Blacksmiths	Pánchála.—Kammára ...	"	59	28	19	12	...
	20. Carpenters, &c.	Pánchála. { Badagi	"	4	2	2	...	...
		Pánchála. { Gaundar... ...	"	1	...	...	1	...
		Total Group 20......	....	5	2	2	1	...
	21. Brass & Copper smiths...	Pánchála.—Gejjégára	"	88	31	33	24	...
	22. Tailors ...	Darzi	"	905	338	457	110	...
	23. Weavers, Calenderers and Dyers.	Gániga	"	4	1	2	1	...
		Gádiya	Jain.	...	...	...	...	...
		Néyigé	Hindu.	87	29	44	14	...
		Total Group 23......	....	91	30	46	15	...
	24. Washermen.	Agasa	"	504	205	200	99	...
	26 (a). Cowherds, &c. ...	Golla	"	655	209	304	142	...
	26. Shepherds and Wool-weavers. ...	Kuruba	"	408	145	198	65	...
	27. Oil-pressers.	Gániga	"	70	26	30	14	...
	28. Potters ...	Kumbára...	"	167	60	79	28	...
	30. Salt, &c., workers ...	Uppára	"	10	5	5	...	...
	32. Goldsmith's refuse collectors ...	Pánchála.—Jalagára	"	2	1	1	...	...
	33 (a). Gold-lace makers ...	Ráchévár.—Sarigé	"	...	...	...	...	...

TABLE E.—(*Continued.*)

Station, Bangalore.

Females.

0 to 9					10 to 14				
Total.	Single.	Married.	Widowed.	Civil condition not stated.	Total.	Single.	Married.	Widowed.	Civil condition not stated.
...	...	...	...	...	...	...	...	...	...
15	12	3	...	...	13	5	8	...	...
...	...	...	...	...	...	...	...	...	...
...	...	...	...	...	1	1	...	...	...
3	3	...	...	...	...	...	...	...	...
...	...	...	...	...	...	...	...	...	...
...	...	...	...	...	...	...	...	...	...
1,244	*1,225*	*18*	*1*	...	*471*	*257*	*212*	*2*	...
1,244	**1,225**	**18**	**1**	...	**471**	**257**	**212**	**2**	...
150	145	4	1	...	43	29	13	1	...
150	147	3	...	...	47	26	20	1	...
24	24	...	...	...	5	4	1	...	...
2	2	...	...	...	...	...	...	...	...
...	...	...	...	...	...	...	...	...	...
2	2	...	...	...	...	...	...	...	...
26	26	...	...	...	6	4	2	...	...
282	275	7	...	...	98	56	41	1	...
1	1	...	...	...	...	...	...	...	...
...	...	...	...	...	...	...	...	...	...
24	24	...	...	...	11	2	9	...	...
25	25	...	...	...	*11*	2	*9*	...	...
152	149	3	...	...	52	40	12	...	...
169	165	4	...	...	59	37	22	...	...
107	105	2	...	...	36	27	9	...	...
24	24	...	...	...	6	2	4	...	...
52	51	1	...	...	15	8	7	...	...
3	3	...	...	...	1	1	...	...	...
1	1	...	...	...	...	...	...	...	...
...	...	...	...	...	...	...	...	...	...

The Civil and Military

Class.	Group.	Caste, &c., and sub-division.	Religion.	15 to 39 Total.	Single.	Married.	Widowed.	Civil condition not stated.
C.—Commercial.—(Concluded.)	14. Traders.—(Concluded.)	Multáni	Hindu.	1	...	1	...	...
		Nagarta	,,	47	16	30	1	...
		Jain	Jain.	...	...	...	...	...
		Márvádi	,,	2	1	1	...	...
		Do.	Hindu.	3	...	3	...	...
		Do.	Buddhist.	...	...	...	...	...
		S'rávaka	Jain.	...	...	...	...	...
		Total Group 14	....	*1,997*	*82*	*1,660*	*255*	...
		Total Class C	....	**1,997**	**82**	**1,660**	**255**	...
D.—Artisan and Village menial.—(Continued.)	17. Goldsmiths.	Pánchála	Hindu.	231	11	194	26	...
	18. Barbers ...	Náyinda	,,	232	27	185	20	...
	19. Blacksmiths	Pánchála.—Kammára ...	,,	21	...	16	5	...
	20. Carpenters, &c.	Pánchála.—Badagi	,,	2	...	2	...	...
		Pánchála.—Gaundar	,,	...	...	...	...	...
		Total Group 20	....	2	...	2	...	...
	21. Brass & Copper smiths ...	Pánchála.—Gejjégára ...	,,	32	1	26	5	...
	22. Tailors ...	Darzi	,,	344	7	320	17	...
	23. Weavers, Calenderers and Dyers.	Góniga	,,	2	...	2	...	...
		Gádiya	Jain.	...	...	...	...	...
		Néyigé	Hindu.	34	1	29	4	...
		Total Group 23	....	*36*	*1*	*31*	*4*	...
	24. Washermen.	Agasa	Hindu.	189	16	145	28	...
	25 (a). Cowherds, &c. ...	Golla	,,	264	7	224	33	...
	26. Shepherds and Wool-weavers. ...	Kuruba	,,	173	10	153	10	...
	27. Oil-pressers.	Gániga	,,	26	...	24	2	...
	28. Potters ...	Kumbára ...	,,	65	1	55	9	...
	30. Salt, &c., workers. ...	Uppára	,,	3	...	3	...	...
	32. Gold-smith's refuse collectors. ...	Pánchála.—Jalagára	,,	...	...	...	...	...
	33 (a). Gold-lace makers ...	Ráchévár.—Sarigé	,,	...	...	...	...	...

TABLE E.—(*Continued.*)

Station, Bangalore.

Females.

40 and over.					Age not stated.				
Total.	Single.	Married.	Widowed.	Civil condition not stated.	Total.	Single.	Married.	Widowed.	Civil condition not stated.
...	...	...	...	...	...	...	...	...	...
32	2	22	8	...	...	...	...	...	...
...	...	...	...	...	...	...	...	...	...
1	...	...	1	...	...	...	...	...	...
3	...	...	3	...	...	...	...	...	...
...	...	...	...	...	...	...	...	...	...
...	...	...	...	...	...	...	...	...	...
1,212	*11*	*413*	*788*	...	...	...	...	...	...
1,212	**11**	**413**	**788**	...	...	...	...	...	...
111	...	38	73	...	...	...	...	...	...
128	...	59	69	...	...	...	...	...	...
9	...	2	7	...	...	...	...	...	...
...	...	...	...	...	...	...	...	...	...
1	...	...	1	...	...	...	...	...	...
1	...	...	*1*	...	...	...	...	...	...
24	...	5	19	...	...	...	...	...	...
181	...	89	92	...	...	...	...	...	...
1	...	...	1	...	...	...	...	...	...
...	...	...	...	...	...	...	...	...	...
18	2	6	10	...	...	...	...	...	...
19	*2*	*6*	*11*	...	...	...	...	...	...
111	...	40	71	...	...	...	...	...	...
163	...	54	109	...	...	...	...	...	...
93	3	34	56	...	...	...	...	...	...
14	...	2	12	...	...	...	...	...	...
35	...	16	19	...	...	...	...	...	...
3	1	2	...	...	...	...	...	...	...
1	...	1	...	...	...	...	...	...	...
...	...	...	...	...	...	...	...	...	...

Total including the Civil and

Class.	Group.	Caste, &c. and sub-division.	Religion.	All Ages. Total.	Single.	Married.	Widowed.	Civil condition not stated.
C.—Commercial.—(Concluded.)	14. Traders.—(Concluded.)	Multáni	Hindu.	1	...	1	...	...
		Nagarta	,,	12,015	6,363	4,769	883	...
		Jain	Jain.	1,090	591	410	89	...
		Márvádi	,,	66	34	29	3	...
		Do	Hindu.	17	4	12	1	...
		Do.	Buddhist.	2	1	1	...	...
		S'rávaka	Jain.	1,038	659	303	76	...
		Total Group 14	....	*237,685*	*127,187*	*96,394*	*14,104*	...
		Total Class C	....	**237,683**	**127,187**	**96,394**	**14,104**	...
D.—Artisan and Village menial.—(Continued.)	17. Gold smiths.	Pánchála	Hindu.	50,152	26,542	20,599	3,011	...
	18. Barbers	Náyinda	,,	18,997	9,957	7,993	1,047	...
	19. Black smiths	Páncháḷa.—Kammára	,,	3,172	1,650	1,310	212	...
	20. Carpenters, &c.	Pánchála { Badagi	,,	4,414	2,327	1,833	254	...
		Pánchála { Gaundor	,,	2	1	1	...	...
		Total Group 20	....	*4,416*	*2,328*	*1,834*	*254*	...
	21. Brass & Copper-smiths	Páncháḷa.—Gejjégára		189	107	75	7	...
	22. Tailors	Darzi		5,527	2,819	2,405	303	...
	23. Weavers, Calenderers and Dyers.	Góniga	,,	754	339	367	48	...
		Gádiya	Jain.	1	1	...	...	...
		Néyigé	Hindu.	43,399	21,952	18,856	2,591	...
		Total Group 23	....	*44,154*	*22,292*	*19,223*	*2,639*	...
	24. Washermen	Agasa	Hindu.	42,879	22,501	17,889	2,489	...
	25 (a). Cowherds, &c.	Golla	,,	65,233	34,783	26,652	3,798	...
	26. Shepherds and wool-weavers	Kuruba	,,	172,400	91,285	72,763	8,352	...
	27. Oil-pressers	[illegible]	,,	17,708	9,005	7,798	905	...
	28. Potters	Kumbára		21,210	10,921	9,085	1,204	...
	30. Salt, &c., workers	Uppára	,,	44,854	24,121	18,634	2,099	...
	32. Gold-smith's refuse collectors	Páncháḷa.—Jalagára	,,	131	69	53	9	...
	33 (d). Gold-lace makers	Ráchévár.—Sarigé	,,	8	3	5	...	...

TABLE E.—(Continued.)

Military Station, Bangalore.

Males.

0 to 9					10 to 14				
Total.	Single.	Married.	Widowed.	Civil condition not stated.	Total.	Single.	Married.	Widowed.	Civil condition not stated.
...	...	...	...	...	...	...	...	...	...
3,145	3,144	1	...	...	1,103	1,371	30	2	...
229	227	1	1	...	119	118	1	...	...
11	11	...	...	...	6	6	...	...	...
2	2	...	...	...	1	1	...	...	...
...	...	...	...	...	...	...	...	...	...
213	213	...	...	...	115	112	3	...	...
63,011	*62,970*	*40*	*1*	...	*26,003*	*25,621*	*377*	*5*	...
63.011	**62,970**	**40**	**1**	...	**26,003**	**25,621**	**377**	**5**	...
13,519	13,510	9	...	...	5,878	5,708	169	1	...
5,421	5,420	1	...	...	1,739	1,707	32	...	...
863	863	...	...	...	366	344	22	...	...
1,166	1,166	...	...	...	426	420	6	...	...
...	...	...	...	...	...	...	...	...	...
1,166	*1,166*	...	...	...	*426*	*420*	*6*	...	...
53	52	1	...	...	23	23	...	...	...
1,563	1,561	1	1	...	560	540	20	...	...
202	202	...	...	...	73	72	1	...	...
...	...	...	...	...	...	...	...	...	...
11,761	11,737	24	...	...	4,266	4,119	145	2	...
11,963	*11,939*	*24*	...	...	*4,339*	*4,191*	*146*	*2*	...
12,215	12,209	6	...	...	3,817	3,733	84	...	...
17,749	17,748	1	...	...	5,796	5,631	165	...	...
49,565	49,532	33	...	...	17,194	16,955	237	2	...
4,819	4,816	3	...	...	1,429	1,408	21	...	...
5,711	5,709	2	...	...	1,981	1,943	38	...	...
12,689	12,688	1	...	...	4,945	4,854	61	...	...
37	37		...	...	13	13	...	...	...
2	2	...	...	...	1	1	...	...	...

Total including the Civil and

Class.	Group.	Caste, &c. and sub-division.	Religion.	15 to 39 Total.	15 to 39 Single.	15 to 39 Married.	15 to 39 Widowed.	15 to 39 Civil condition not stated.
C.—Commercial.—(Concluded.)	14. Traders.—(Concluded.)	Multáni ...	Hindu.	...	...	...	...	...
		Nagarta ...	,,	4,057	1,886	3,001	270	...
		Jain ...	Jain.	495	225	257	13	...
		Márvádi ...	,,	39	17	21	1	...
		Do. ...	Hindu.	8	...	8	...	...
		Do. ...	Buddhist.	2	1	1	...	...
		S'rávaka ...	Jain.	497	311	161	25	...
		Total Group 14	....	*97,939*	*36,406*	*58,183*	*3,350*	...
		Total Class C	....	**97,939**	**36,406**	**58,183**	**3,350**	...
D.—Artisan and Village menial.—(Continued.)	17. Gold smiths.	Pánchála ...	Hindu.	20,031	6,950	12,329	752	...
	18. Barbers ..	Náyinda ...	,,	7,668	2,693	4,749	226	...
	19. Black smiths.	Pánchála.—Kammára	,,	1,291	418	820	53	...
	20. Carpenters, &c.	Pánchála. { Badagi ...	,,	1,917	707	1,151	59	...
		Pánchála. { Gaunder ...	,,	1	1	...	...	...
		Total Group 20	....	*1,918*	*708*	*1,151*	*59*	...
	21. Brass & Copper-smiths ...	Pánchála.—Gejjégára	,,	77	31	46	...	...
	22. Tailors ...	Darzi ...	,,	2,224	681	1,465	78	...
	23. Weavers, Calenderers and Dyers.	Gúniga ...	,,	310	64	233	13	...
		Gádiya ...	Jain.	1	1	...	...	...
		Néyigé ...	Hindu.	17,862	5,809	11,453	600	...
		Total Group 23	....	*18,173*	*5,874*	*11,686*	*613*	...
	24. Washermen .	Agasa ...	,,	17,548	6,224	10,757	567	...
	25 (a). Cowherds, &c. ...	Golla ...	,,	27,180	10,815	15,468	897	...
	26. Shepherds and Wool-weavers.	Kuruba ...	,,	69,996	23,968	43,924	2,104	...
	27. Oil-pressers.	Gániga ...	,,	7,629	2,658	4,767	209	...
	28. Potters ...	Kumbára ...	,,	9,029	3,130	5,576	323	...
	30. Salt, &c., workers ...	Uppára ...	,,	18,173	6,282	11,372	519	...
	32. Gold smith's refuse collectors ...	Pánchála.—Jálagára ...	,,	56	18	36	2	...
	33 (a). Gold-lace makers ...	Ráchévár.—Sarigé ...	,,	2	...	2	...	...

TABLE E.—(*Continued.*)

Military Station, Bangalore.

Males.

40 and over.					Age not stated.				
Total.	Single.	Married.	Widowed.	Civil condition not stated.	Total.	Single.	Married.	Widowed.	Civil condition not stated.
1	...	1	...	...	...	...	...	...	...
2,510	162	1,737	611	...	...	...	...	...	...
247	21	151	75	...	...	...	...	...	...
10	...	8	2	...	...	...	...	...	...
6	1	4	1	...	...	...	...	...	...
...	...	...	...	...	...	...	...	...	...
213	23	139	51	...	...	...	...	...	...
50,732	*2,190*	*37,794*	*10,748*	...	...	...	...	...	...
50,732	**2,190**	**37,794**	**10,748**	...	...	...	...	...	...
10,724	374	8,093	2,253	...	...	...	...	...	...
4,169	137	3,211	821	...	...	...	...	...	...
652	25	468	159	...	...	...	...	...	...
905	34	676	195	...	...	...	...	...	...
1	...	1	...	...	...	...	...	...	...
906	*34*	*677*	*195*	...	...	...	...	...	...
36	1	28	7	...	...	...	...	...	...
1,180	37	919	224	...	...	...	...	...	...
169	1	133	35	...	...	...	...	...	...
...	...	...	...	...	...	...	...	...	...
9,510	287	7,234	1,989	...	...	...	...	...	...
9,679	*288*	*7,367*	*2,024*	...	...	...	...	...	...
9,299	335	7,042	1,922	...	...	...	...	...	...
14,508	589	11,018	2,901	...	...	...	...	...	...
35,615	830	28,569	6,216	...	...	...	...	...	...
3,831	128	3,007	696	...	...	...	...	...	...
4,480	139	3,460	881	...	...	...	...	...	...
9,047	267	7,200	1,580	...	...	...	...	...	...
25	1	17	7	...	...	...	...	...	...
3	...	3	...	...	...	...	...	...	...

Total including the Civil and

Class.	Group.	Caste, &c. and sub-division.	Religion.	All Ages. Total.	Single.	Married.	Widowed.	Civil condition not stated.
C.—Commercial.—(Concluded.)	14. Traders.—(Concluded.)	Multáni	Hindu.	1	...	1	...	...
		Nagarta	,,	10,949	3,947	4,842	2,160	...
		Jain	Jain.	871	269	327	275	...
		Márvádi	,,	14	5	6	3	...
		Do	Hindu.	4	2	1	1	...
		Do	Buddhist.	...	...	...	...	...
		S'rávaka	Jain	924	373	305	246	...
		Total Group 14......	....	232,885	83,088	99,381	49,516	...
		Total Class C......	....	**232,885**	**83,288**	**99,381**	**49,516**	...
D.—Artisan and Village menial.—(Continued.)	17. Gold smiths.	Pánchála	Hindu.	48,029	17,257	21,007	9,765	...
	18. Barbers ...	Náyinda	,,	18,299	6,391	8,208	3,700	...
	19. Black smiths	Pánchála.—Kammára ...	,,	3,078	1,183	1,347	548	...
	20. Carpenters, &c.	Pánchála. { Badagi ...	,,	4,229	1,507	1,817	905	...
		Pánchála. { Gaunder...	,,	1	...	...	1	...
		Total Group 20......	....	4,230	1,507	1,817	906	...
	21. Brass & Copper smiths ...	Pánchála.—Gejjégára ...	,,	207	74	83	50	...
	22. Tailors ...	Darzi	,,	5,137	1,768	2,503	866	...
	23. Weavers, Calenderers and Dyers.	Gániga	,,	672	217	329	126	...
		Gádiya	Jain.	...	...	...	...	...
		Néyigé	Hindu.	43,587	15,376	19,854	8,357	...
		Total Group 23......	....	44,259	15,593	20,183	8,483	...
	24. Washermen.	Agasa	Hindu	42,792	15,583	18,516	8,693	...
	25 (a). Cowherds, &c. ...	Golla	,,	63,762	22,377	27,360	14,025	...
	26. Shepherds and Wool-weavers ...	Kuruba	,,	174,368	63,492	74,713	36,163	...
	27. Oil-pressers.	Gániga	,,	18,100	6,449	7,948	3,703	...
	28. Potters ...	Kumbára...	,,	19,599	6,850	8,911	3,838	...
	30. Salt, &c., workers ...	Uppára	,,	44,269	16,973	18,563	8,733	...
	32. Gold-smith's refuse collectors	Pánchála.— Jalagára ...	,,	127	44	58	25	...
	33 (a). Gold-lace makers ...	Ráchévár.—Sarigé ...	,,	7	1	5	1	...

TABLE E.—(*Continued.*)

Military Station, Bangalore.

Females.

0 to 9.					10 to 14.				
Total.	Single.	Married.	Widowed.	Civil condition not stated.	Total.	Single.	Married.	Widowed.	Civil condition not stated.
...	...	...	...	...	...	...	...	...	...
2,947	2,873	75	...	...	1,175	827	346	2	...
196	194	2	...	...	92	61	30	1	...
5	5	...	...	...	...	...	...	...	...
...	...	...	...	...	1	1	...	...	...
...	...	...	...	...	...	...	...	...	...
250	242	7	1	...	141	104	35	2	...
63,845	*62,412*	*1,425*	*8*	...	*23,663*	*15,919*	*7,650*	*94*	...
63,845	**62,412**	**1,425**	**8**	...	**23,663**	**15,919**	**7,650**	**94**	...
13,564	13,293	268	3	...	4,734	3,248	1,462	24	...
5,075	5,014	61	...	...	1,545	1,035	409	1	...
902	891	11	...	...	344	250	94	...	...
1,135	1,110	25	...	...	460	322	137	1	...
...	...	...	...	...	...	...	...	...	...
1,135	*1,110*	*25*	...	...	*460*	*322*	*137*	*1*	...
56	54	2	...	...	27	18	9	...	...
1,490	1,451	39	...	...	465	290	173	2	...
180	180	...	...	...	39	25	14	...	...
...	...	...	...	...	...	...	...	...	...
12,392	12,042	350	...	...	4,286	2,603	1,669	14	...
12,572	*12,222*	*350*	...	...	*4,325*	*2,628*	*1,683*	*14*	...
12,093	11,867	225	1	...	3,652	2,627	1,014	11	...
18,142	17,917	225	...	...	4,581	3,195	1,377	9	...
49,199	48,607	577	15	...	15,172	10,255	4,885	32	...
5,059	5,003	56	...	...	1,605	1,191	413	1	...
5,341	5,251	90	...	...	1,618	1,159	456	3	...
12,765	12,613	152	...	...	3,818	2,991	815	12	...
31	31	...	...	...	19	10	9	...	...
1	1	...	...	...	...	...	...	...	...

Total including the Civil and

Class.	Group.	Caste, &c. and sub-division.	Religion.	15 to 39. Total.	Single.	Married.	Widowed.	Civil condition not stated.
C.—Commercial.—(Concluded.)	14. Traders.—(Concluded.)	Multáni ...	Hindu.	1	...	1	...	...
		Nagarta ...	,,	4,553	240	3,616	697	...
		Jain ...	Jain.	354	14	238	102	...
		Márvádi ...	,,	6	...	6	...	...
		Do ...	Hindu.	2	1	1	...	...
		Do ...	Buddhist.	...	...	...	...	...
		S'rávaka ...	Jain.	366	22	243	101	...
		Total Group 14......	....	*92,773*	*5,088*	*73,060*	*14,625*	...
		Total Class C......	...	**92,773**	**5,088**	**73,060**	**14,625**	...
D.—Artisan and Village menial.—(Continued.)	17. Gold smiths.	Pánchála ...	Hindu.	18,418	667	14,904	2,847	...
	18. Barbers ...	Náyinda ...	,,	7,483	205	6,085	1,103	...
	19. Black smiths	Pánchála.—Kammára	,,	1,152	41	919	162	...
	20. Carpenters, &c.	Pánchála. { Badagi ...	,,	1,568	75	1,236	257	...
		Pánchála. { Gaunder ...	,,	...	...	...	...	...
		Total Group 20......	....	*1,568*	*75*	*1,236*	*257*	...
	21. Brass & Copper-smiths...	Pánchála.—Gejjégára	,,	67	2	56	9	...
	22. Tailors ...	Darzi ...	,,	2,054	27	1,825	202	...
	23. Weavers, Calenderers and Dyers.	Góniga ...	,,	285	12	245	28	...
		Gániya ...	Jain.	...	...	...	...	...
		Néyigé ...	Hindu.	17,132	658	14,110	2,364	...
		Total Group 23......	....	*17,417*	*670*	*14,355*	*2,392*	...
	24. Washermen.	Agasa ...	Hindu.	17,631	1,013	14,034	2,584	...
	25 (a). Cowherds, &c. ...	Golla ...	,,	26,060	1,191	20,464	4,405	...
	26. Shepherds and Wool-weavers. ...	Kuruba ...	,,	70,542	4,317	56,190	10,035	...
	27. Oil-pressors.	Gániga ...	,,	6,922	240	5,624	1,058	...
	28. Potters ...	Kumbára...	,,	7,883	414	6,401	1,068	...
	30. Salt, &c., workers...	Uppára ...	,,	17,751	1,283	13,887	2,581	...
	33. Gold-smith's refuse collectors.	Pánchála.—Jalagára...	,,	47	3	38	6	...
	33 (a). Gold-lace makers ...	Ráchévár.—Surigé ...	,,	5	...	5	...	...

TABLE E.—(*Continued.*)

Military Station, Bangalore.

Males.

40 and over.					Age not stated.				
Total.	Single.	Married.	Widowed.	Civil condition not stated.	Total.	Single.	Married.	Widowed.	Civil condition not stated.
...	...	...	...	...	...	...	...	...	...
2,274	8	805	1,461	...	...	...	...	...	...
229	...	57	172	...	...	...	...	...	...
3	...	...	3	...	...	...	...	...	...
1	...	...	1	...	...	...	...	...	...
...	...	...	...	...	...	...	...	...	...
167	5	20	142	...	...	...	...	...	...
52,601	*569*	*17,246*	*31,789*	...	...	...	...	...	...
52,604	**569**	**17,246**	**34,789**	...	...	...	...	...	...
11,313	47	4,375	6,801	...	...	...	...	...	...
4,176	17	1,563	2,596	...	...	...	...	...	...
680	1	293	386	...	...	...	...	...	...
1,066	...	419	647	...	...	...	...	...	...
1	...	...	1	...	...	...	...	...	...
1,067	...	419	648	...	...	...	...	...	...
57	...	16	41	...	...	...	...	...	...
1,128	...	463	662	...	...	...	...	...	...
168	...	70	98	...	...	...	...	...	...
...	...	...	...	...	...	...	...	...	...
9,777	73	3,725	5,979	...	...	...	...	...	...
9,945	*73*	*3,795*	*6,077*	...	...	...	...	...	...
9,416	76	3,243	6,097	...	...	...	...	...	...
14,979	74	5,294	9,611	...	...	...	...	...	...
39,455	313	13,061	26,081	...	...	...	...	...	...
4,514	15	1,855	2,644	...	...	...	...	...	...
4,757	26	1,964	2,767	...	...	...	...	...	...
9,935	86	3,709	6,140	...	...	...	...	...	...
30	...	11	19	...	...	...	...	...	...
1	...	...	1	...	...	...	...	...	...

Class.	Group.	Caste, &c. and sub-division.	Religion.	All Ages. Total.	Single.	Married.	Widowed.	Civil condition not stated.
D.—Artisan & Village menial.—(*Concluded.*)	35. Fishermen, Boatmen and Palakhi bearers.	Besta	Hindu.	49,620	26,256	21,115	2,249	...
	36. Distilers and Toddy drawers ...	I'diga	,,	20,532	10,713	8,663	1,156	...
	38. Leather Workers.	Mádiga	,,	118,457	62,591	49,526	6,340	...
		Móchi	,,	308	155	134	19	...
		Total Group 38......	....	*118,765*	*62,746*	*49,660*	*6,359*	...
	38 (*a*). Village Watchmen, &c...	Holaya	,,	251,188	136,432	104,318	10,438	...
		Total Class D......	....	926,972	492,405	388,232	46,335	...
E.—Vagrant, Minor Artisans and Performers.	41. Earth Workers and stone dressers ...	Vaddar	Hindu.	54,446	29,339	22,336	2,771	...
	43. Mat makers and cane splitters...	Méda	,,	2,318	1,236	946	136	...
	44. Hunters, Fowlers, &c.	Béda	,,	108,731	60,597	42,048	6,086	...
	45. Miscellaneous and disreputable livers.	Budabudiké	,,	553	283	228	42	...
		S'illékyáta	,,	55	24	30	1	...
		Sudagádusidda	,,	25	14	10	1	...
		Gondaliga	,,	16	7	8	1	...
		Jógi	,,	4,779	2,503	1,969	307	...
		Karma	,,	...	...	...	...	...
		Mondaru	,,	127	67	48	12	...
		Pandáram	,,	...	...	...	...	...
		S'ápiyár	,,	...	...	...	...	...
		Total Group 45......	....	*5,555*	*2,898*	*2,293*	*364*	...
	46. Tumblers and Acrobats.	Dombar	,,	1,217	641	494	82	...
		Ráchévár—Jatti ...	,,	592	309	248	35	...
		Total Group 46......	....	*1,809*	*950*	*742*	*117*	...
	47. Jugglers, snake charmers & animal exhibiters ...	Gárdiga	,,	411	198	190	23	...
		Total Class E......	....	173,270	95,218	68,555	9,497	...

TABLE E.—(*Continued.*)

cial.

Males.

0 to 9					10 to 14				
Total.	Single.	Married.	Widowed.	Civil condition not stated.	Total.	Single.	Married.	Widowed.	Civil condition not stated.
13,599	13,596	3	...	...	4,582	4,502	80	...	...
5,196	5,196			...	2,019	1,990	29	...	...
33,365	33,310	52	3	...	11,363	11,140	217	6	...
82	82	...	...	...	25	24	1	...	...
33,447	*33,392*	*52*	*3*	...	*11,388*	*11,164*	*218*	*6*	...
71,569	71,508	60	1	...	22,714	22,313	398	3	...
259,967	**259,768**	**195**	**4**	...	**88,823**	**87,098**	**1,711**	**14**	...
16,419	16,419	...	...	...	4,687	4,627	60	...	...
670	670	...	...	...	220	219	1	...	...
31,204	31,189	15	...	...	7,693	7,618	71	4	...
145	145	...	...	...	61	60	1	...	...
10	10	...	...	...	8	7	1	...	...
9	9	...	...	...	1	1	...	...	...
5	5	...	...	...	1	1	...	...	...
1,456	1,456	...	...	...	422	420	2	...	...
...	...	...	...	...	...	...	...	...	...
34	34	...	...	...	9	9	...	...	...
...	...	...	...	...	...	...	...	...	...
...	...	...	...	...	...	...	...	...	...
1,659	*1,659*	...	...	...	*502*	*498*	*4*	...	...
365	364	1	...	...	93	93	...	...	...
161	161	...	...	...	62	61	1	...	...
526	*525*	*1*	...	...	*155*	*154*	*1*	...	...
104	104	...	...	...	50	50	...	...	...
50,582	**50,566**	**16**	...	...	**13,307**	**13,166**	**137**	**4**	...

Class.	Group.	Caste, &c. and sub-division.	Religion.	15 to 39 Total.	Single.	Married.	Widowed.	Civil condition not stated.
D.—Artisan & Village menial.—(Concluded.)	35. Fishermen, Boatmen and Palakhi bearers.	Besta ...	Hindu.	21,353	7,862	12,916	575	...
	36. Distilers and Toddy drawers ...	I'diga ...	,,	9,266	3,336	5,594	336	...
	38. Leather workers.	Mádiga ...	,,	47,749	16,375	29,756	1,618	...
		Móchi ...	,,	137	49	85	3	...
		Total Group 38	....	*47,886*	*16,424*	*29,841*	*1,621*	...
	38 (a). Village Watchmen, &c ...	Holaya ...	,,	101,938	40,666	59,152	2,120	...
		Tota Class D	....	**379,783**	**138,179**	**230,604**	**1,100**	...
E.—Vagrant, Minor Artisans and Performers.	41. Earth workers and stone dressers ...	Vaddar ...	Hindu.	21,336	7,978	12,670	688	...
	43. Mat makers and cane splitters ...	Méda ...	,,	970	330	615	25	...
	44. Hunters, Fowlers, &c.	Béda ...	,,	46,242	20,401	24,678	1,165	...
	45. Miscellaneous and disreputable livers.	Budabudiké ...	,,	203	72	125	6	...
		S'illékyáta ...	,,	27	7	20	...	...
		Sudagádusidda ...	,,	10	3	7	...	...
		Gondaliga ...	,,	8	1	7	...	...
		Jógi ...	,,	1,859	588	1,215	56	...
		Karma ...	,,	...	...	...	...	...
		Mondaru ...	,,	55	22	29	4	...
		Pandáram ...	,,	...	...	...	...	...
		S'ániyár ...	,,	...	...	...	...	...
		Total Group 45	....	*2,162*	*693*	*1,403*	*66*	...
	46. Tumblers and Acrobats ...	Dombar ...	,,	459	165	278	16	...
		Ráchévár—Jatti ...	,,	242	82	156	4	...
		Total Group 46	....	*701*	*247*	*434*	*20*	...
	47. Jugglers, snake charmers, & animal exhibitors ...	Gárdiga ...	,,	161	35	118	8	...
		Total Class E	....	**71,572**	**29,684**	**39,916**	**1,972**	...

TABLE E.—(*Continued.*)

cial.

Females.

40 and over.					Age not stated.				
Total.	Single.	Married.	Widowed.	Civil condition not stated.	Total.	Single.	Married.	Widowed.	Civil condition not stated.
10,086	296	8,116	1,674	...	...	...	...	...	...
4,051	191	3,040	820	...	...	...	...	...	...
25,969	1,757	19,500	4,712	...	11	9	1	1	...
64	...	48	16	...	...	...	...	...	...
26,033	*1,757*	*19,548*	*4,728*	...	*11*	*9*	*1*	*1*	...
54,906	1,912	44,702	8,292	...	61	33	6	22	...
198,327	**7,318**	**155,715**	**35,294**	...	**72**	**42**	**7**	**23**	...
12,004	315	9,606	2,083	...	...	...	...	...	...
458	17	330	111	...	...	...	...	...	...
23,592	1,389	17,286	4,917	...	...	...	...	...	...
144	6	102	36	...	...	...	...	...	...
10	...	9	1	...	...	...	...	...	...
5	1	3	1	...	...	...	...	...	...
2	...	1	1	...	...	...	...	...	...
1,042	39	752	251	...	...	...	...	...	...
...	...	...	...	...	...	...	...	...	...
29	2	19	8	...	...	...	...	...	...
...	...	...	...	...	...	...	...	...	...
...	...	...	...	...	...	...	...	...	...
1,232	*48*	*886*	*298*	...	...	...	...	...	...
300	19	215	66	...	...	...	...	...	...
127	5	91	31	...	...	...	...	...	...
427	*24*	*306*	*97*	...	...	...	...	...	...
96	9	92	15	...	...	...	...	...	...
37,809	**1,802**	**28,486**	**7,521**	...	...	...	...	...	...

Caste and Religion.				All Ages.				
Class.	Group.	Caste, &c., and sub-division.	Religion.	Total.	Single.	Married.	Widowed.	Civil condition not stated.
D.—Artisan & Village menial.—(Concluded.)	35. Fishermen, Boatmen and Palakhi bearers.	Besta	Hindu.	50,038	18,518	21,898	9,622	...
	36. Distilers and Toddy drawers ...	I'ḍiga	,,	19,385	7,126	8,508	3,751	...
	38. Leather Workers.	Mádiga	,,	118,234	48,195	46,548	23,491	...
		Móchi	,,	334	126	144	64	...
		Total Group 38......	....	118,568	48,321	46,692	23,555	...
	38 (a). Village Watchmen, &c...	Holaya	,,	250,821	97,887	100,996	51,938	...
		Total Class D......	....	**921,019**	**345,929**	**387,426**	**187,664**	...
E.—Vagrant, Minor Artisans and Performers.	41. Earth Workers and stone dressers ...	Vaḍḍar	Hindu.	51,952	20,333	22,912	8,707	...
	43. Mat makers and cane splitters...	Méda	,,	1,912	690	860	353	...
	44. Hunters, Fowlers, &c.	Béḍa	,,	108,138	42,271	43,596	22,271	...
	45. Miscellaneous and disreputable livers.	Buḍabuḍiké	,,	539	227	243	69	...
		S'iḷḷékyáta	,,	38	12	23	3	...
		Suḍagáḍusidda	,,	21	7	11	3	...
		Gondaliga	,,	13	5	6	2	...
		Jógi	,,	4,629	1,693	2,113	823	...
		Karma	,,	...	...	...	...	...
		Monḍáru	,,	62	10	38	14	...
		Panḍáram	,,	...	...	...	...	...
		S'áṇiyár	,,	...	...	...		...
		Total Group 45......	....	5,302	1,960	2,428	914	...
	46. Tumblers and Acrobats.	Dombar	,,	1,283	616	515	152	...
		Ráchévár—Jaṭṭi	,,	610	228	271	111	...
		Total Group 46......	....	1,893	844	786	263	...
	47. Jugglers, snake charmers & animal exhibiters ...	Gárdiga	,,	465	167	221	77	...
		Total Class E......	,,	**169,662**	**66,274**	**70,803**	**32,585**	...

TABLE E.—(*Continued.*)

cial.

Females.

0 to 9					10 to 14				
Total.	Single.	Married.	Widowed.	Civil condition not stated.	Total.	Single.	Married.	Widowed.	Civil condition not stated.
13,871	13,509		1	...	4,637	3,241	1,393	3	...
5333	5,219	14	...	...	1,752	1,262	483	7	...
36,752	36,007	739	6	...	9,259	6,720	2,477	63	...
100	99	1	..	...	34	23	11	...	...
36,852	*36,106*	*740*	*6*	...	*9,293*	*6,743*	*2,488*	*62*	..
76,846	75,299	1,530	17	...	20,775	14,773	5,885	117	...
269,160	**264,318**	**4,800**	**42**	...	**78,463**	**55,032**	**23,135**	**296**	...
16,239	16,155	84	...	...	3,954	3,078	876	...	..
476	474	2	...	...	196	158	38	...	...
32,254	31,810	441	3	...	7,863	5,444	2,379	40	...
173	172	1	...	...	45	39	6	...	...
9	9	...	...	...	3	3	...	...	...
5	5	...	...	...	2	2	...	...	...
5	5	...	...	...	...	...	...	...	...
1,292	1,283	10	...	...	357	297	60	...	...
...	...	...	...	..	...	...	...	...	...
13	13	...	...	...	3	3	...	...	...
...	...	...	...	...	...	...	...	...	...
...	...	...	...	...	...	...	...	...	...
1,497	*1,486*	*11*	...	...	*410*	*344*	*66*	...	...
359	356	3	...	...	110	101	9	...	...
185	185	...	...	...	44	36	8	...	...
544	*541*	*3*	...	...	*154*	*137*	*17*	...	...
108	108	...	...	...	46	43	4	...	...
51,118	**50,574**	**541**	**3**	...	**12,623**	**9,203**	**3,380**	**40**	...

Class.	Group.	Caste, &c., and sub-division.	Religion.	15 to 39 Total.	Single.	Married.	Widowed.	Civil condition not stated.
D.—Artisan & Village menial.—(Concluded.)	35. Fishermen, Boatmen and Palakhi bearers.	Besta	Hindu.	20,303	1,575	16,190	2,628	...
	36. Distlers and Toddy drawers ...	I'diga	,,	8,263	501	6,514	1,163	...
	38. Leather workers ...	Mádiga	,,	48,522	4,513	36,250	7,759	...
		Móchi	,,	124	4	102	18	...
		Total Group 38......	....	48,646	4,517	36,352	7,777	...
	38 (a) Village Watchmen, &c...	Holaya	,,	99,359	6,248	78,346	14,765	...
		Total Class D......	....	**370,048**	**23,088**	**292,077**	**54,883**	...
E.—Vagrant, Minor Artisans and Performers.	41. Earth workers and stone dressers ...	Vaddar	Hindu.	20,855	1,020	17,679	2,156	...
	43. Mat makers and cane splitters ...	Méda	,,	803	65	646	92	...
	44. Hunters, Fowlers, &c.	Béda	,,	46,263	3,879	34,910	7,474	...
	45. Miscellaneous and disreputable livers.	Budabudiké	,,	203	13	174	16	...
		S'illékyáta	,,	18	...	18	...	...
		Sudagádusidda	,,	10	...	9	1	...
		Gondaliga	,,	5	...	5	...	...
		Jógi	,,	1,912	108	1,590	214	...
		Karma	,,	...	...	...	...	...
		Mondaru	,,	31	...	26	5	...
		Pandárum	,,	...	...	...	...	...
		S'ániyár	,,	...	...	...	...	...
		Total Group 45......	....	2,179	121	1,822	236	...
	46. Tumblers and Acrobats ...	Dombar	,,	529	119	378	32	...
		Ráchévár—Jatti	,,	229	6	192	31	...
		Total Group 46......	....	758	125	570	63	...
	47. Jugglers, snake charmers & animal exhibiters ...	Gárdiga	,,	223	17	179	27	...
		Total Class E......	....	**71,081**	**5,227**	**56,806**	**10,048**	...

TABLE E.—(*Continued.*)

cial.

Females.

40 and over.					Age not stated.				
Total.	Single.	Married.	Widowed.	Civil condition not stated.	Total.	Single.	Married.	Widowed.	Civil condition not stated.
11,137	193	3,954	6,990	...	...	...	...	...	...
4,032	54	1,397	2,581	...	...	...	...	...	...
23,686	944	7,080	15,662	...	15	11	2	2	...
76	...	30	46	...	...	...	..	...	...
23,762	*944*	*7,110*	*15,708*	...	*15*	*11*	*2*	*2*	...
53,786	1,539	15,220	37,027	...	55	28	15	12	..
203,278	**3,452**	**6,7397**	**132,429**	...	**70**	**39**	**17**	**14**	...
10,904	80	4,273	6,551	...	...	...	...	...	...
437	2	174	261	...	...	...	...	...	...
21,758	1,138	5,866	14,754	...	...	...	...	...	...
118	3	62	53	...	...	...	...	...	...
8	...	5	3	...	...	...	...	...	...
4	...	2	2	...	...	..	...	...	...
3	...	1	2	...	...	...	...	...	...
1,068	6	453	609	...	...	...	...	...	...
...	...	...	...	...	...	...	...	...	...
15	...	6	9	...	...	...	...	...	...
...	...	...	...	...	...	...	...	...	...
...	...	...	...	...	..	...	...	...	...
1,216	*9*	*529*	*678*	...	...	...	...	...	...
285	40	125	120	...	...	...	...	...	...
152	1	71	80	...	...	...	...	...	...
437	*41*	*196*	*200*	...	...	...	...	...	...
88	...	38	50	...	...	...	...	..	...
34,840	**1,270**	**11,076**	**22,494**	...	..	...	...	...	...

Class.	Group.	Caste, &c., and sub-division.	Religion.	All Ages. Total.	Single.	Married.	Widowed.	Civil condition not stated.
D.—Artisan & Village menial.—(Concluded.)	35. Fishermen, Boatmen and Palakhi bearers.	Besta	Hindu.	3,981	1,948	1,785	248	...
	36. Distillers & Toddy drawers ...	I'diga	,,	1,272	629	575	68	...
	38 Leather workers.	Mádiga ...	,,	21,591	10,544	10,222	825	...
		Móchi ...	,,	52	24	25	3	...
		Total Group 38......	....	21,643	10,568	10,247	828	...
	38 (a). Village Watchmen &c...	Holaya	,,	31,028	15,205	14,128	1,695	...
		Total Class D......	....	120,703	58,660	55,239	6,774	...
E.—Vagrant, Minor Artisans and Performers	41. Earth workers and stone dressers ...	Vaddar	Hindu.	10,0 2	5,084	4,454	524	...
	43. Mat makers and cane splitters...	Méda	,,	202	94	98	10	...
	44. Hunters, Fowlers, &c.	Béda	,,	7,303	3,617	3,226	460	...
	45. Miscellaneous and disreputable livers.	Budabudikó	,,	76	47	26	3	...
		S'illékyáta	,,	...	...	...	...	...
		Sudagádusidda	,,	...	...	...	...	...
		Gondaliga	,,	7	2	5	...	...
		Jógi	,,	1,210	596	535	79	...
		Karma	,,	...	...	...	...	...
		Mondaru	,,	...	...	...	...	...
		Pandáram	,,	...	...	...	...	...
		S'ániyár	,,	...	...	...	...	...
		Total Group 45......	....	1,293	645	566	82	...
	46. Tumblers and Acrobats...	Dombar	,,	194	95	91	8	...
		Ráchévár—Jatti		97	48	41	8	...
		Total Group 46	....	291	143	132	16	...
	47. Jugglers, snake charmers & animal exhibitors ...	Gárdiga	,,	136	63	67	6	...
		Total Class E......	....	19,287	9,646	8,543	1,098	...

TABLE E.—(*Continued.*)

District

Males.

0 to 9					10 to 14				
Total.	Single.	Married.	Widowed.	Civil condition not stated.	Total.	Single.	Married.	Widowed.	Civil condition not stated.
1,101	1,101	...	...	...	322	307	15	...	...
382	382	...	...	...	100	96	4	...	...
4,527	4,524	3	...	...	2,425	2,422	12	1	...
16	16		...	...	2	2	...	...	...
4,543	*4,540*	*3*	...	...	*2,437*	*2,424*	*12*	*1*	...
8,308	8,302	5	1	...	2,421	2,403	16	2	...
31,206	**31,169**	**36**	**1**	...	**10,954**	**10,662**	**288**	**4**	...
2,961	2,961		...	...	771	763	8	...	...
53	53	...	...	...	18	18	...	...	...
2,123	2,123	...	..	...	510	498	12	...	...
27	27	...	...	...	10	10	...	...	...
...	...	...	...	...	...	...	..	...	...
...	...	...	...	...	...	...	...	...	...
2	2	...	..	...	...	...	...	...	...
386	386	...	...	...	87	86	1	...	...
...	...	...	...	...	...	...	...	...	...
...	...	...	...	...	...	...	...	...	...
...	...	...	...	...	...	...	...	...	...
...	...	...	...	...	...	...	...	...	...
415	*415*	...	...	...	*97*	*96*	*1*	...	...
64	64	...	...	...	12	12	...	...	...
22	22	...	...	...	12	12	...	..	...
86	*86*	...	...	...	*24*	*24*	...	...	...
40	40	...	...	...	13	13	...	...	...
5,678	**5,678**	...	...	...	**1,423**	**1,412**	**21**	...	...

Class.	Group.	Caste, &c., and sub-division.	Religion.	15 to 39 Total.	Single.	Married.	Widowed.	Civil condition not stated.
D.—Artisan & Village menial.—(*Concluded.*)	35. Fishermen, Boatmen and Palakhi bearers.	Besta	Hindu.	1,639	517	1,076	46	...
	36. Distillers & Toddy drawers ...	I'diga	,,	503	145	337	21	...
	38. Leather workers ...	Mádiga	,,	9,527	3,421	5,963	143	...
		Móchi	,,	23	6	16	1	...
		Total Group 38 ...	....	*9,550*	*3,427*	*5,979*	*144*	...
	38 (a). Village watchmen, &c....	Holaya	,,	12,527	4,207	8,091	229	...
		Total Class D ...	....	**49,025**	**15,979**	**31,761**	**1,285**	...
E.—Vagrant, Minor Artisans and Performers.	41. Earth workers and stone dressers ...	Vaddar	Hindu.	3,783	1,313	2,330	140	...
	43. Mat makers and cane splitters ...	Méda	,,	76	22	53	1	...
	44. Hunters; Fowlers, &c.	Béda	,,	3,010	920	1,996	94	...
	45. Miscellaneous and disreputable livers.	Budabudiké	,,	20	8	12	...	...
		S'iḷḷékyáta	,,	...	...	...	...	...
		Sudagáḍusidda	,,	...	...	...	...	...
		Gondaliga	,,	4	...	4	...	...
		Jógi	,,	442	120	316	6	...
		Karma	,,	...	...	...	...	...
		Mondaru	,,	...	...	...	...	...
		Pandáram	,,	...	...	...	...	...
		S'áṇiyár	,,	...	...	...	...	...
		Total Group 45 ...	....	*466*	*128*	*332*	*6*	...
	46. Tumblers and Acrobats ...	Dombar	,,	66	19	45	2	...
		Ráchévár.—Jatti	,,	37	12	24	1	...
		Total Group 46 ...	....	*103*	*31*	*69*	*3*	...
	47. Jugglers, snake charmers & animal exhibitors ...	Gárḍigu	,,	53	10	43	...	...
		Total Class E ...	....	**7,491**	**2,424**	**4,823**	**244**	...

TABLE E.—(*Continued*)

District.

Males.

40 and over.					Age not stated.				
Total.	Single.	Married.	Widowed.	Civil condition not stated.	Total.	Single.	Married.	Widowed.	Civil condition not stated.
919	23	694	202	...	...	...	...	...	...
287	6	234	47	...	...	...	...	...	...
5,102	177	4,244	681	...	...	...	...	...	...
11	...	9	2	...	...	...	...	...	...
5,113	*177*	*4,253*	*683*	..	...	...	...	...	...
7,732	273	6,014	1,445	...	40	20	2	18	...
29,478	**830**	**23,182**	**5,466**	...	**40**	**20**	**2**	**18**	...
2,547	47	2,116	384	...	...	...	...	...	...
55	1	45	9	...	...	...	...	...	...
1,660	76	1,218	366	...	...	...	...	...	...
19	2	14	3	...	...	...	...	...	...
...	...	...	...	...	...	...	...	...	...
...	...	...	...	...	...	...	...	...	...
1	...	1	...	...	...	...	...	..	...
295	4	218	73	...	...	...	...	...	...
...	...	...	...	...	...	...	...	...	...
...	...	...	...	...	...	...	..	...	...
...	...	...	...	...	...	...	...	...	...
...	...	...	...	...	...	...	...	...	...
315	6	233	*76*	...	...	...	...	...	...
52	...	46	6	...	...	...	...	...	...
26	3	17	7	...	...	...	...	...	...
78	2	*63*	*13*	...	...	...	..	...	...
30	...	24	6	...	...	...	...	...	..
4,685	**132**	**3,699**	**854**	...	...	...	...	...	...

Bangalore

Class.	Group.	Caste, &c. and sub-division.	Religion.	All Ages. Total.	Single.	Married.	Widowed.	Civil condition not stated.
D.—Artisan & Village menial.—(Concluded.)	35. Fishermen, Boatmen and Palakhi bearers.	Besta	Hindu.	4,137	1,454	1,825	858	...
	36. Distillers & Toddy drawers ...	I'ḍiga	,,	1,277	472	566	239	...
	38. Leather workers ...	Mádiga	,,	21,653	6,907	10,009	4,737	...
		Mōchi	,,	45	14	25	6	...
		Total Group 38...	....	21,698	6,921	10,034	4,743	...
	38 (a). Village watchmen &c..	Holaya	,,	31,857	11,103	13,026	7,728	...
		Total Class D......	....	**123,232**	**40,620**	**55,284**	**2,7328**	...
E.—Vagrant, Minor Artisans and Performers.	41. Earth workers and stone dressers ...	Vaḍḍar	Hindu.	9,979	3,722	4,485	1,772	...
	43. Mat makers and cane splitters ...	Méda	,,	224	84	103	37	...
	44. Hunters, Fowlers, &c.	Bēḍa	,,	7,777	2,744	3,329	1,704	...
	45. Miscellaneous and disreputable livers.	Buḍabuḍiké	,,	68	35	26	7	...
		S'iḷḷékyáta	,,	...	...	...	...	...
		Suḍagáḍusidda	,,	...	...	...	...	...
		Gondaliga	,,	8	3	4	1	...
		Jōgi	,,	1,264	451	564	249	...
		Karma	,,	...	...	...	...	...
		Mondaru	,,	...	...	...	...	...
		Panḍáram	,,	...	...	...	...	...
		S'áṇiyár	,,	...	...	...	...	...
		Total Group 45......	....	1,340	489	594	257	...
	46. Tumblers and Acrobats ...	Dombar	,,	225	105	92	28	...
		Ráchévár—Jaṭṭi	,,	112	31	47	34	...
		Total Group 46......	....	337	136	139	62	...
	47. Jugglers, snake charmers, & animal exhibitors ...	Gárḍiga	,,	149	45	75	29	...
		Total Class E	....	**19,806**	**7,220**	**8,725**	**3,861**	...

TABLE E.—(Continued.)

District.

Females.

0 to 9					10 to 14				
Total.	Single.	Married.	Widowed.	Civil condition not stated.	Total.	Single.	Married.	Widowed.	Civil condition not stated.
1,221	1,181	40	...	...	321	187	134	...	...
400	393	7	...	...	91	63	28	...	...
6,129	5,892	234	3	...	1,347	733	602	12	...
14	13	1	...	...	4	1	3	...	...
6,143	*5,905*	*235*	*3*	...	*1,351*	*734*	*605*	*12*	...
9,891	9,511	374	6	...	2,099	1,139	940	20	...
35,024	**33,909**	**1,103**	**12**	...	**9,210**	**5,121**	**4,045**	**44**	...
3,094	3,079	15	...	...	667	516	151	...	...
66	66	...	...	...	17	15	2	...	...
2,335	2,272	63	...	...	517	340	173	4	...
34	33	1	...	...	2	2	...	...	...
...	...	...	...	...	...	...	...	...	...
...	...	...	...	...	...	...	...	...	...
3	3	...	...	...	...	...	...	...	...
352	345	7	...	...	113	87	26	...	...
...	...	...	...	...	...	...	...	...	...
...	...	...	...	...	...	...	...	...	...
...	...	...	...	...	...	...	...	...	...
...	...	...	...	...	...	...	...	...	...
389	*381*	*8*	...	...	*115*	*89*	*26*	...	...
65	63	2	...	...	17	15	2	...	...
27	27	...	...	...	7	4	3	...	...
92	*90*	*2*	...	...	*24*	*19*	*5*	...	...
25	25	...	...	...	12	11	1	...	...
6,001	**5,913**	**88**	...	...	**1,352**	**990**	**358**	**4**	...

Bangalore

Class.	Caste and Religion.			15 to 39				
	Group.	Caste, &c. and sub-division.	Religion.	Total.	Single.	Married.	Widowed.	Civil condition not stated.
D.—Artisan & Village menial.—(*Concluded.*)	35. Fishermen, Boatmen and Palakhi bearers.	Besta	Hindu.	1,648	79	1,344	225	...
	36. Distillers & Toddy drawers ...	I'diga	,,	493	12	432	49	...
	33. Leather Workers.	Mádiga	,,	9,085	230	7,601	1,254	...
		Móchi	,,	21	...	20	1	...
		Total Group 33......	....	*9,106*	*230*	*7,621*	*1,255*	...
	38 (*a*). Village Watchmen, &c ..	Holaya	,,	11,677	360	9,143	2,174	...
		Total Class D... ..	....	**48,257**	**1,346**	**39,671**	**7,240**	...
E.—Vagrant, Minor Artisans and Performers.	41. Earth Workers and stone dressers ...	Vaddar	Hindu.	3,903	121	3,367	395	...
	43. Mat makers and cane splitters...	Méda	,,	97	3	85	9	...
	44. Hunters, Fowlers, &c.	Béda	,,	2,982	105	2,427	450	...
	45. Miscellaneous and disreputable livers.	Budabudiké	,,	21	...	20	1	...
		S'illékyáta...	,,	...	...	...	...	...
		Sudagádusidda	,,	...	...	...	...	...
		Gondaliga	,,	3	...	3	...	...
		Jógi	,,	496	17	419	60	...
		Karma	,,	...	...	...	...	...
		Mondaru	,,	...	...	...	...	...
		Pandáram	,,	...	...	...	...	...
		S'ányiár	,,	...	...	...	...	...
		Total Group 45......	....	*520*	*17*	*442*	*61*	...
	46. Tumblers and Acrobats	Dombar	,,	96	19	68	9	...
		Ráchévár.—Jatti	,,	40	...	31	9	...
		Total Group 46......	....	*136*	*19*	*99*	*18*	...
	47. Jugglers, snake charmers & animal exhibitors ...	Gárdiga	,,	90	9	63	18	...
		Total Class E....	....	**7,728**	**274**	**6,503**	**951**	...

TABLE E.—(*Continued.*)

District.

Females.

40 and over.					Age not stated.				
Total.	Single.	Married.	Widowed.	Civil condition not stated.	Total.	Single.	Married.	Widowed.	Civil condition not stated.
947	7	307	633	...	...	...		...	...
293	4	99	190	...	...	...	...	...	...
5,092	52	1,572	3,468	...	...	...	...	...	...
6	...	1	5	...	...	...	...	...	...
5,098	*53*	*1,573*	*3,473*	...	...	...	...	...	...
8,169	83	2,559	5,527	...	21	10	10	1	...
30,720	**234**	**10,455**	**20,031**	...	**21**	**10**	**10**	**1**	...
2,315	6	932	1,377	...	...	...	...	...	...
44	...	16	28	...	...	...	...	...	...
1,943	27	666	1,250	...	...	...	...	...	...
11	...	5	6	...	...	...	...	...	...
...	...	...	...	...	...	...	...	...	...
...	...	...	...	...	...	...	...	...	...
2	...	1	1	...	...	...	...	...	...
303	2	112	189	...	...	...	...	...	...
...	...	...	...	...	...	...	...	...	...
...	...	...	...	...	...	...	...	...	...
...	...	...	...	...	...	...	...	...	...
...	...	...	...	...	...	...	...	...	...
316	*2*	*118*	*196*	...	...	...	...	...	...
47	8	20	19	...	...		...	...	...
38	...	13	25	...	...	...	...	...	...
85	*8*	*33*	*44*	...	...	...	...	...	...
22	...	11	11	...	...	...		...	...
4,725	**43**	**1,776**	**2,906**	...	...	...	...	...	...

Kola

Class.	Group.	Caste, &c. and sub-division.	Religion.	All Ages. Total.	Single.	Married.	Widowed.	Civil condition not stated.
D.—Artisan & Village menial—(*Concluded.*)	35. Fishermen, Boatmen and Palakhi bearers.	Besta	Hindu.	1,981	1,026	801	154	...
	36. Distillers & Toddy Drawers ...	I'diga	,,	876	474	341	61	...
	38. Leather Workers.	Mádiga	,,	20,005	10,677	8,005	1,323	...
		Móchi	,,	31	17	11	3	...
		Total Group 38......	....	*20,036*	*10,694*	*8,016*	*1,326*	...
	38 (*a*). Village Watchmen, &c...	Holaya	,,	28,762	14,609	12,474	1,679	...
		Total Class D......	....	**104,911**	**53,871**	**44,394**	**6,646**	...
E.—Vagrant, Minor Artisans and Performers.	41. Earth Workers and stone dressers ...	Vaddar	Hindu.	11,768	6,261	5,000	507	...
	43. Mat makers and cane splitters...	Méda	,,	102	45	48	9	...
	44. Hunters, Fowlers, &c.	Béda	,,	23,923	12,845	9,511	1,567	...
	45. Miscellaneous and disreputable livers.	Budabudiké	,,	55	28	25	2	...
		S'illékyáta	,,	...	...	...	...	...
		Sudagádusidda	,,	...	...	...	...	...
		Gondaliga	,,	4	2	1	1	...
		Jógi	,,	789	403	328	58	...
		Karma	,,	...	...	...	...	...
		Mondaru	,,	62	31	25	6	...
		Pandáram	,,	...	...	...	...	...
		S'ániyár	,,	...	...	...	...	...
		Total Group 45......	....	*910*	*464*	*379*	*67*	...
	46. Tumblers, and Acrobats...	Dombar	,,	283	160	112	11	...
		Ráchévár—Jatti	,,	21	11	7	3	...
		Total Group 46......	....	*304*	*171*	*119*	*14*	...
	47. Jugglers, snake charmers & animal exhibitors ...	Gárdiga	,,	55	30	23	2	...
		Total Class E......	....	**37,062**	**19,816**	**15,080**	**2,166**	...

TABLE E.—*(Continued.)*

District.

Males.

0 to 9					10 to 14				
Total.	Single.	Married.	Widowed.	Civil condition not stated.	Total.	Single.	Married.	Widowed.	Civil condition not stated.
465	465	...	...	...	139	139	...	...	...
258	258	...	...	...	48	48	...	...	...
6,787	6,750	34	3	...	1,302	1,187	111	4	...
8	8	...	...	...	4	4	...	...	...
6,795	*6,758*	*34*	*3*	...	*1,306*	*1,191*	*111*	*4*	...
8,376	8,350	26	...	...	1,900	1,660	240	...	...
30,685	**30,612**	**70**	**3**	...	**7,253**	**6,850**	**399**	**4**	...
3,535	3,535	...	...	...	823	815	8	...	...
25	25	...	...	...	6	6	...	...	...
6,720	6,720	...	...	...	1,555	1,555	...	...	...
13	13	...	...	...	7	7	...	...	...
...	...	...	...	...	...	...	...	...	...
...	...	...	...	...	...	...	...	...	...
1	1	...	...	...	...	...	...	...	...
207	207	...	...	...	83	83	...	...	...
...	...	...	...	...	...	...	...	...	...
19	19	...	...	...	3	3	...	...	...
...	...	...	...	...	...	...	...	...	...
...	...	...	...	...	...	...	...	...	...
240	*240*	...	...	...	*93*	*93*	...	...	...
95	95	...	...	...	22	22	...	...	...
4	4	...	...	...	2	2	...	...	...
99	*99*	...	...	...	*24*	*24*	...	...	...
16	16	...	...	...	5	5	...	...	...
10,635	**10,635**	...	...	...	**2,506**	**2,498**	**8**	...	...

Class.	Group.	Caste, &c. and sub-division.	Religion.	15 to 39. Total.	Single.	Married.	Widowed.	Civil condition not stated.
D.—Artisan & Village menial.—(Concluded.)	35. Fishermen, Boatmen and Palakhi bearers.	Besta	Hindu.	866	377	459	30	...
	36. Distillers & Toddy drawers ...	I'diga	,,	352	154	189	9	...
	38. Leather Workers.	Mádiga	,,	7,559	2,479	4,743	337	...
		Móchi	,,	12	5	7	...	...
		Total Group 38	....	*7,571*	*2,484*	*4,750*	*337*	...
	38 (a). Village Watchmen, &c...	Holaya	,,	11,613	4,328	6,911	374	...
		Total Class D	....	**42,290**	**15,252**	**25,511**	**1,527**	...
E.—Vagrant, Minor Artisans and Performers.	41. Earth Workers and stone dressers ...	Vaddar	Hindu.	4,743	1,799	2,848	96	...
	43. Mat makers and cane splitters. ...	Méda	,,	41	13	28	...	...
	44. Hunters, Fowlers, &c.	Béda	,,	9,743	4,147	5,253	343	...
	45. Miscellaneous and disreputable livers.	Budabudiké	,,	25	8	17	...	...
		S'illekyáta	,,	...	...	...	...	...
		Sudagádusidda	,,	...	...	...	...	...
		Gondaligu	,,	2	1	1	...	...
		Jógi	,,	315	[illegible]	202	14	...
		Karma	,,	...	...	...	...	...
		Mondaru	,,	25	8	15	2	...
		Pandáram	,,	...	...	...	...	...
		S'ániyár	,,	...	...	...	...	...
		Total Group 45	....	*367*	*116*	*235*	*16*	...
	46. Tumblers and Acrobats...	Dombar	,,	105	41	63	1	...
		Ráchévár—Jatti	,,	9	5	4	...	...
		Total Group 46	....	*114*	*46*	*67*	*1*	...
	47. Jugglers, snake charmers & animal exhibiters ...	Gárdiga	,,	24	9	14	1	...
		Total Class E	....	**15,032**	**6,130**	**8,445**	**457**	...

TABLE E.—(Continued.)

District.

Males.

40 and over.					Age not stated.				
Total.	Single.	Married.	Widowed.	Civil condition not stated.	Total.	Single.	Married.	Widowed.	Civil condition not stated.
511	45	342	124	...	...	...	...	...	...
218	14	152	52	...	...	...	...	...	...
4,357	261	3,117	979	...	...	...	...	...	...
7	...	4	3	...	...	...	...	...	...
4,364	261	3,121	982	...	...	...	...	...	...
6,873	271	5,297	1,305	...	...	...	...	...	...
24,683	**1,157**	**18,414**	**5,112**	...	...	...	...	...	...
2,667	112	2,144	411	...	...	...	...	...	...
30	1	20	9	...	...	...	...	...	...
5,905	423	4,258	1,224	...	...	...	...	...	...
10	...	8	2	...	...	...	...	...	...
...	...	...	...	...	...	...	...	...	...
...	...	...	...	...	...	...	...	...	...
1	...	...	1	...	...	...	...	...	...
184	14	126	44	...	...	...	...	...	...
...	...	...	...	...	...	...	...	...	...
15	1	10	4	...	...	...	...	...	...
...	...	...	...	...	...	...	...	...	...
...	...	...	...	...	...	...	...	...	...
210	15	144	51	...	...	...	...	...	...
61	2	49	10	...	...	...	...	...	...
6	...	3	3	...	...	...	...	...	...
67	2	52	13	...	...	...	...	...	...
10	...	9	1	...	...	...	...	...	...
8,889	**553**	**6,627**	**1,709**	...	...	...	...	...	...

Kolar

Class.	Group.	Caste, &c. and sub-division.	Religion.	All Ages. Total.	Single.	Married.	Widowed.	Civil condition not stated.
D.—Artisan & Village menial.—(Concluded.)	35. Fishermen, Boatmen and Palakhi bearers.	Besta	Hindu.	1,920	549	850	521	...
	36. Distillers & Toddy drawers ...	I'diga	,,	832	260	359	213	...
	38. Leather workers...	Mádiga	,,	19,602	7,424	7,985	4,193	...
		Móchi	,,	23	8	13	2	...
		Total Group 38	....	19,625	7,432	7,998	4,195	...
	38 (a). Village watchmen, &c...	Holaya	,,	28,903	10,593	12,099	6,211	...
		Total Class D. ...	....	**104,087**	**3[illegible]274**	**44,747**	**24,066**	...
E.—Vagrant, Minor Artisans and Performers.	41. Earth workers and stone dressers ...	Vaddar	Hindu.	11,322	4,373	5,135	1,814	...
	41. Mat makers and cane splitters...	Méda	,,	98	33	46	19	...
	44. Hunters, Fowlers, &c.	Béda	,,	23,406	8,086	9,878	5,442	...
	45. Miscellaneous and disreputable livers.	Budabudiké	,,	45	17	25	3	...
		S'illékyata	,,	...	...	...	...	...
		Sudagádusidda ...	,,	...	...	...	...	...
		Gondaliga	,,	2	1	1	...	...
		Jógi	,,	768	256	362	150	...
		Karma	,,	...	...	...	...	...
		Mondaru	,,	52	14	25	13	...
		Pandáram	,,	...	...	...	...	...
		S'ániyár	,,	...	...	...	...	...
		Total Group 45	....	867	288	413	166	...
	46. Tumblers and Acrobats ...	Dombar	,,	347	180	134	33	...
		Ráchévár.—Jatti	,,	17	4	10	3	...
		Total Group 46 ...	....	364	184	144	36	...
	47. Jugglers, snake charmers & animal exhibitors ...	Gárdiga	,,	54	19	25	10	...
		Total Class E. ...	....	**36,111**	**12,983**	**15,641**	**7,487**	...

TABLE E.—(*Continued.*)

District.

Females.

0 to 9					10 to 14				
Total.	Single.	Married.	Widowed.	Civil condition not stated.	Total.	Single.	Married.	Widowed.	Civil condition not stated.
448	445	3	...	...	115	73	42	...	...
207	206	1	...	...	53	30	23	...	...
7,005	6,655	348	2	...	961	395	549	17	...
5	5	...	...	...	2	2	...	...	...
7,010	*6,660*	*348*	*2*	...	*963*	*397*	*549*	*17*	...
9,138	8,918	210	...	...	1,479	1,031	437	11	...
30,486	**29,730**	**739**	**17**	...	**6,430**	**3,770**	**2,609**	**51**	...
3,704	3,666	38	...	...	728	502	226	...	...
32	32	...	...	...	4	1	3	...	...
6,768	6,730	38	...	...	1,383	831	552	...	...
14	14	...	...	...	3	3	...	...	...
...	...	...	...	...	...	...	...	...	...
...	...	...	...	...	...	...	...	...	...
1	1	...	...	...	...	...	...	...	...
201	201	...	...	...	42	35	7	...	...
...	...	...	...	...	...	...	...	...	...
12	12	...	...	...	2	2	...	...	...
...	...	...	...	...	...	...	...	...	...
...	...	...	...	...	...	...	...	...	...
228	*228*	...	...	...	*47*	*40*	*7*	...	...
103	103	...	...	...	27	25	2	...	...
3	3	...	...	...	1	1	...	...	...
106	*106*	...	...	...	*28*	*26*	*2*	...	...
12	12	...	...	...	6	6	...	...	...
10,850	**10,774**	**76**	...	...	**2,196**	**1,406**	**790**	...	...

Class.	Group.	Caste, &c., and sub-division.	Religion.	15 to 39. Total.	Single.	Married.	Widowed.	Civil condition not stated.
D.—Artisan & Village menial.—(Concluded)	35. Fishermen, Boatmen and Palakhi bearers.	Besta	Hindu.	833	25	657	151	...
	36. Distillers & Toddy drawers ...	I'diga	,,	366	21	278	67	...
	38. Leather Workers.	Mádiga	,,	7,919	320	6,003	1,596	...
		Móchi	,,	11	1	9	1	...
		Total Group 38......	....	7,930	321	6,012	1,597	...
	38 (a). Village Watchmen, &c...	Holaya	,,	11,620	448	9,360	1,812	...
		Total Class D......	....	**42,400**	**1,505**	**33,447**	**7,448**	...
E.—Vagrant, Minor Artisans and Performers.	41. Earth Workers and stone dressers. ...	Vaddar	Hindu.	4,573	190	3,975	408	...
	43. Mat makers and cane splitters...	Méda	,,	45	...	39	6	...
	44. Hunters, Fowlers, &c.	Béda	,,	9,976	446	7,715	1,815	...
	45. Miscellaneous and disreputable livers.	Budabudiké	,,	19	...	19	...	...
		S'illékyata	,,	...	...	...	...	...
		Sudagádusidda	,,	...	...	...	...	...
		Gondaliga	,,	1	...	1	...	...
		Jógi	,,	311	20	252	39	...
		Karma	,,	...	...	...	...	...
		Mondaru	,,	25	...	20	5	...
		Pandáram	,,	...	...	...	...	...
		Sáníyár	,,	...	...	...	...	...
		Total Group 45......	....	356	20	292	44	...
	46. Tumblers and Acrobats...	Dombar	,,	139	41	96	2	...
		Ráchévár.—Jatti	,,	7	...	7	...	...
		Total Group 46......	....	146	41	103	2	...
	47. Jugglers, snake charmers & animal exhibiters ...	Gárdiga	,,	23	1	20	2	...
		Total Class E......	....	**15,119**	**698**	**12,144**	**2,277**	...

TABLE E.—(Continued.)

District.

Females.

40 and over.					Age not stated.				
Total.	Single.	Married.	Widowed.	Civil condition not stated.	Total.	Single.	Married.	Widowed.	Civil condition not stated.
533	6	157	370	...	...	...	...	...	...
206	3	57	146	...	...	...	...	...	...
3,717	54	1,085	2,578	...	...	...	...	...	...
5	...	4	1	...	...	...	...	...	...
3,722	*51*	*1,05[illegible]*	*2,579*	...	...	...	...	...	...
6,646	166	2,092	4,388	...	...	...	...	...	...
24,771	**269**	**7,953**	**16,550**	...	...	...	...	...	...
2,317	15	896	1,406	...	...	...	...	...	...
17	...	4	13	...	...	...	...	...	...
5,279	79	1,573	3,627	...	...	...	...	...	...
9	...	6	3	...	...	...	...	...	...
...	...	...	...	...	...	...	...	...	...
...	...	...	...	...	...	...	...	...	...
...	...	...	...	...	...	...	...	...	...
214	...	103	111	...	...	...	...	...	...
...	...	...	...	...	...	...	...	...	...
13	...	5	8	...	...	...	...	...	...
...	...	...	...	...	...	...	...	...	...
...	...	...	...	...	...	...	...	...	...
230	...	*11[illegible]*	*122*	...	...	...	...	...	...
78	11	36	31	...	...	...	...	...	...
6	...	3	3	...	...	...	...	...	...
84	*11*	*39*	*34*	...	...	...	...	...	...
13	...	5	8	...	...	...	...	...	...
7,946	**105**	**2,631**	**5,210**	...	...	...	...	...	...

Class.	Group.	Caste, &c. and sub-division.	Religion.	All Ages. Total.	Single.	Married.	Widowed.	Civil condition not stated.
D.—Artisan & Village menial.—(Concluded.)	35. Fishermen, Boatmen and Palakhi bearers ...	Besta	Hindu.	2,215	1,023	1,053	129	...
	36. Distillers & Toddy drawers ...	Idiga	,,	2,604	1,336	1,116	152	...
	38. Leather Workers.	Mádiga	,,	23,693	13,254	9,377	1,062	...
		Móchi	,,	17	7	9	1	...
		Total Group 38	....	*23,710*	*13,261*	*9,386*	*1,063*	...
	38 (a). Village Watchmen, &c...	Holaya	,,	11,723	6,288	4,550	885	...
		Total Class D......	....	**104,457**	**55,558**	**42,839**	**6,060**	...
E.—Vagrant, Minor Artisans and Performers.	41. Earth Workers and stone dressers ...	Vaddar	Hindu.	6,908	3,872	2,742	294	...
	43. Mat makers and cane splitters...	Méda	,,	186	96	73	12	...
	44. Hunters, Fowlers, &c.	Béda	,,	21,762	12,634	7,723	1,405	...
	45. Miscellaneous and disreputable livers.	Budabudiké	,,	112	48	56	8	...
		S'illékyáta	,,	...	...	...	...	...
		Sudagádusidda	,,	...	...	...	...	...
		Gondaliga	,,	...	...	...	...	...
		Jógi	,,	438	119	205	34	...
		Karma	,,	...	...	...	...	...
		Mondaru	,,	...	...	...	...	...
		Pandáram	,,	...	...	...	...	...
		S'ániyár	,,	...	...	...	...	...
		Total Group 45......	....	*550*	*247*	*261*	*42*	...
	46. Tumblers and Acrobats	Dombar	,,	147	83	55	9	...
		Bácbévár,—Jatti	,,	37	18	17	2	...
		Total Group 46 ...	....	*184*	*101*	*72*	*11*	...
	67. Jugglers, snake charmers & animal exhibiters ...	Gardiga	,,	63	23	30	10	...
		Total Class E......	....	**29,653**	**16,973**	**10,906**	**1,774**	...

TABLE E.—(*Continued.*)

District.

Males.

0 to 9					10 to 14.				
Total.	Single.	Married.	Widowed.	Civil condition not stated.	Total.	Single.	Married.	Widowed.	Civil condition not stated.
545	545	...		...	143	140	3	...	...
715	715	...	...	...	177	174	3	...	...
8,183	8,183	...	...	...	3,102	3,062	40	...	...
5	5	...	...	...	1	1	...	...	...
8,188	*8,183*	...	...	...	*3,103*	*3,063*	*40*	...	...
3,731	3,731	...	...	...	808	736	72	...	...
30,930	**30,925**	**5**	...	...	**10,232**	**9,962**	**270**	...	...
2,296	2,296	...		...	612	611	1	...	
52	52	...	...	...	28	27	1	...	...
6,437	6,433	4	...	...	1,374	1,359	15	...	...
25	25	...	...	...	5	5	...	...	...
...	...	...	...	...	...	...	...	...	...
...	...	...	...	...	...	...	...	...	...
...	...	...	...	...	...	...	...	...	...
130	130	...	...	...	25	24	1	...	...
...	...	...	...	...	...	...	...	...	...
...	...	...	...	...	...	...	...	...	...
...	...	...	...	...	...	...	...	...	...
...	...	...	...	...	...	...	...	...	...
155	*155*	...	...	...	*30*	*29*	*1*	...	...
50	49	1	...	...	9	9	...	...	...
12	12	...	...	...	4	3	1	...	...
62	*61*	*1*	...	...	*13*	*12*	*1*	...	...
9	9	...	...	...	4	4	...		...
9,011	**9,006**	**5**	...	...	**2,061**	**2,042**	**19**	...	...

Class.	Group.	Caste, &c. and sub-division.	Religion.	15 to 39 Total.	Single.	Married.	Widowed.	Civil condition not stated.
D.—Artisan & Village menial.—(Concluded.)	35. Fishermen, Boatmen and Palakhi bearers.	Besta	Hindu.	1,036	321	676	39	...
	36. Distillers & Toddy drawers ...	I'diga	,,	1,136	417	683	36	...
	38. Leather Workers.	Mádiga	,,	7,575	1,757	5,601	217	...
		Móchi	,,	8	1	7	...	...
		Total Group 38......	....	*7,583*	*1,758*	*5,608*	*217*	...
	38 (a). Village Watchmen, &c...	Holaya	,,	4,248	1,735	2,389	124	...
		Total Class D......	....	**40,594**	**13,793**	**25,423**	**1,378**	...
E.—Vagrant, Minor Artisans and Performers.	41. Earth Workers and stone dressers ...	Vaddar	Hindu.	2,527	946	1,486	95	...
	43. Mat makers and cane splitters...	Méda	,,	70	17	52	1	...
	44. Hunters, Fowlers, &c	Béda	,,	9,551	4,570	4,597	384	...
	45. Miscellaneous and disreputable livers.	Budabudiké	,,	42	18	23	1	...
		S'illékyáta	,,	...	...	...	...	...
		Sudagádusidda	,,	...	...	...	...	...
		Gonduliga	,,	...	...	...	...	...
		Jógi	,,	177	42	127	8	...
		Karma	,,	...	...	...	...	...
		Mondáru	,,	...	...	...	...	...
		Pandáram	,,	...	...	...	...	...
		S'áuiyár	,,	...	...	...	...	...
		Total Group 45......	....	*219*	*60*	*150*	9	...
	46. Tumblers and Acrobats...	Dombar	,,	46	21	23	2	...
		Ráchévár.—Jatti ...	,,	15	3	12	...	...
		Total Group 46......	....	*61*	*24*	*35*	2	...
	47. Jugglers, snake charmers & animal exhibiters ..	Gárdiga	,,	28	2	20	6	...
		Total Class E......	....	**12,456**	**5,619**	**6,340**	**497**	...

TABLE E.—(Continued.)

District.

Males.

40 and over.					Age not stated.				
Total.	Single.	Married.	Widowed.	Civil condition not stated.	Total.	Single.	Married.	Widowed.	Civil condition not stated.
491	22	379	90	...	...	...	...	...	...
576	30	430	116	...	...	...	...	...	...
4,833	252	3,736	845	...	...	...	...	...	...
3	...	2	1	...	...	...	...	...	...
4,836	*252*	*3,738*	*846*	...	...	...	...	...	...
2,936	86	2,059	791	...	...	...	...	...	...
22,701	**878**	**17,141**	**4,682**	...	...	...	...	...	...
1,473	19	1,255	199	...	...	...	...	...	...
36	...	25	11	...	...	...	...	...	...
4,400	272	3,107	*1,021*	...	...	...	...	...	...
40	...	33	7	...	...	...	...	...	...
...	...	...	...	...	...	...	...	...	...
...	...	...	...	...	...	...	...	...	...
...	...	...	...	...	...	...	...	...	...
106	3	77	26	...	...	...	...	...	...
...	...	...	...	...	...	...	...	...	...
...	...	...	...	...	...	...	...	...	...
...	...	...	...	...	...	...	...	...	...
...	...	...	...	...	...	...	...	...	...
146	*3*	*110*	*33*	...	...	...	...	...	...
42	4	31	7	...	...	...	...	...	...
6	...	4	2	...	...	...	...	...	...
48	*4*	*35*	*9*	...	...	...	...	...	...
22	8	10	4	...	...	...	...	...	...
6,125	**306**	**4,542**	**1,277**	...	...	...	...	...	...

Class.	Group.	Caste, &c. and sub-division.	Religion.	All Ages. Total.	Single.	Married.	Widowed.	Civil condition not stated.
D.—Artisan & Village menial.—(Concluded.)	35. Fishermen, Boatmen and Palakhi bearers.	Besta	Hindu.	1,986	644	971	371	...
	36. Distillers & Toddy drawers ...	I'ḍiga	,,	2,744	988	1,218	538	...
	38. Leather Workers.	Mádiga	,,	24,590	11,276	9,446	3,868	...
		Móchi	,,	24	9	9	6	...
		Total Group 38......	....	24,614	11,285	9,455	3,874	...
	38 (a). Village Watchmen, &c ...	Holaya	,,	11,893	4,530	4,904	2,459	...
		Total Class D......	....	**104,343**	**39,510**	**43,364**	**21,469**	...
E.—Vagrant, Minor Artisans and Performers.	41. Earth Workers and stone dressers ...	Vaḍḍar	Hindu.	6,478	2,728	2,789	961	...
	43. Mat makers and cane splitters...	Méda	,,	183	59	87	37	...
	44. Hunters, Fowlers, &c.	Béḍa	,,	21,608	8,712	7,799	5,097	...
	45. Miscellaneous and disreputable livers.	Buḍabuḍiké	,,	121	46	57	18	...
		S'iḷḷékyáta	,,	...	...	...	...	...
		Suḍugáḍusidda	,,	...	...	...	...	...
		Gondaliga	,,	...	...	...	...	...
		Jógi	,,	409	164	196	49	...
		Karma	,,	...	...	...	...	...
		Monḍaru	,,	...	...	...	...	...
		Panḍáram	,,	...	...	...	...	...
		S'áṇiyár	,,	...	...	...	...	...
		Total Group 45......	....	530	210	253	67	...
	46. Tumblers and Acrobats	Dombar	,,	147	81	55	11	...
		Ráchévár—Jaṭṭi	,,	30	18	12	...	...
		Total Group 46......	....	177	99	67	11	...
	47. Jugglers, snake charmers & animal exhibiters ...	Gárḍiga	,,	57	22	24	11	...
		Total Class E......	....	**29,033**	**11,830**	**11,019**	**6,184**	...

TABLE E.—(Continued.)

District.

Females.

0 to 9					10 to 14				
Total.	Single.	Married.	Widowed.	Civil condition not stated.	Total.	Single.	Married.	Widowed.	Civil condition not stated.
466	438	28	...	...	110	61	49	...	...
860	857	3	...	...	106	83	22	1	...
8,185	8,185	...	...	...	1,884	1,575	308	1	...
8	8	...	...	...	1	1	...	...	...
8,193	*8,193*	...	...	...	*1,885*	*1,576*	*308*	*1*	...
3,763	3,715	48	...	...	749	502	247	...	...
31,643	**31,334**	**309**	...	...	**6,952**	**5,152**	**1,784**	**16**	...
2,209	2,209	...	...	...	386	307	79	...	...
41	41	...	...	...	16	14	2	...	...
6,491	6,320	168	3	...	1,180	818	355	7	...
34	34	...	...	...	7	6	1	...	...
...	...	...	...	...	...	...	...	...	...
...	...	...	...	...	...	...	...	...	...
...	...	...	...	...	...	...	...	...	...
130	130	...	...	...	21	21	...	...	...
...	...	...	...	...	...	...	...	...	...
...	...	...	...	...	...	...	...	...	...
...	...	...	...	...	...	...	...	...	...
...	...	...	...	...	...	...	...	...	...
164	*164*	...	...	...	28	27	*1*	...	...
52	52	...	...	...	4	4	...	...	...
13	13	...	...	...	4	4	...	...	...
65	*65*	...	...	...	*8*	*8*	...	...	...
10	10	...	...	...	8	8	...	...	...
9,070	**8,899**	**168**	**3**	...	**1,626**	**1,182**	**437**	**7**	...

Class.	Group.	Caste, &c. and sub-division.	Religion.	15 to 39. Total.	Single.	Married.	Widowed.	Civil condition not stated.
D.—Artisan & Village menial.—(Concluded).	35. Fishermen, Boatmen and Palakhi bearers ...	Besta	Hindu.	919	107	699	113	...
	36. Distillers & Toddy drawers ...	I'diga	,,	1,295	45	1,035	215	...
	38 Leather Workers.	Mádiga	,,	10,196	1,221	7,647	1,328	...
		Móchi	,,	9	...	8	1	...
		Total Group 38......	....	*10,205*	*1,221*	*7,655*	*1,329*	...
	38 (a). Village Watchmen, &c...	Holaya	,,	5,043	277	3,920	846	...
		Total Class D......	....	**44,785**	**2,588**	**34,838**	**7,359**	...
E.—Vagrant, Minor Artisans and Performers.	41. Earth Workers and stone dressers ...	Vaddar	Hindu.	2,596	117	2,250	229	...
	43. Mat makers and cane splitters...	Méda	,,	83	4	73	6	...
	44. Hunters, Fowlers, &c.	Béda	,,	9,417	1,226	6,244	1,947	...
	45. Miscellaneous and disreputable livers.	Budabudiké	,,	45	3	34	8	...
		S'illékyáta	,,	...	...	...	...	...
		Sudagádusidda	,,	...	...	...	...	...
		Gondaliga	,,	...	...	...	...	...
		Jógi	,,	183	12	160	11	...
		Karma	,,	...	...	...	...	...
		Mondáru	,,	...	...	...	...	...
		Pandáram	,,	...	...	...	...	...
		S'ániyár	,,	...	...	...	...	...
		Total Group 45......	....	*228*	*15*	*194*	*19*	...
	46. Tumblers and Acrobats.	Dombar	,,	54	15	36	3	...
		S'illékyátar—Jatti	,,	12	1	11	...	...
		Total Group 46......	....	*66*	*16*	*47*	*3*	...
	47. Jugglers, snake charmers & animal exhibitors ...	Gárdiga ...	,,	20	4	14	2	...
		Total Class E......	....	**12,410**	**1,382**	**8,822**	**2,206**	...

TABLE E.—(*Continued.*)

District.

Females.

40 and over.					Age not stated.				
Total.	Single.	Married.	Widowed.	Civil condition not stated.	Total.	Single.	Married.	Widowed.	Civil condition not stated.
491	38	195	258	...	...	...	...	...	...
483	3	158	322	...	...	...	...	...	...
4,325	295	1,491	2,539	...	...	...	...	...	...
6	...	1	5	...	...	...	...	...	...
4,331	*295*	*1,492*	*2,544*	...	...	...	...	...	...
2,338	36	689	1,613	...	...	...	...	...	...
20,963	**436**	**6,433**	**14,094**	...	...	...	...	...	...
1,197	5	460	732	...	...	...	...	...	...
43	...	12	31	...	...	...	...	...	...
4,520	348	1,032	3,140	...	...	...	...	...	...
35	3	22	10	...	...	...	...	...	...
...	...	...	...	...	...	...	...	...	...
...	...	...	...	...	...	...	...	...	...
...	...	...	...	...	...	...	...	...	...
75	1	36	38	...	...	...	...	...	...
...	...	...	...	...	...	...	...	...	...
...	...	...	...	...	...	...	...	...	...
...	...	...	...	...	...	...	...	...	...
...	...	...	...	...	...	...	...	...	...
110	*4*	*58*	*48*	...	...	...	...	...	...
37	10	19	8	...	...	...	...	...	...
1	...	1	...	...	...	...	...	...	...
38	*10*	*20*	*8*	...	...	...	...	...	...
19	...	10	9	...	...	...	...	...	...
5,927	**367**	**1,592**	**3,968**	...	...	...	...	...	...

Mysore

Class.	Group.	Caste, &c. and sub-division.	Religion.	All Ages. Total.	Single.	Married.	Widowed.	Civil condition not stated.
D.—Artisan & Village menial.—(Concluded.)	35. Fishermen, boatmen and Palakhi bearers.	Besta	Hindu.	29,377	15,587	12,822	968	...
	36. Distillers & Toddy drawers ...	I'diga	,,	4,140	2,236	1,731	173	...
	38. Leather Workers.	Mádiga	,,	11,731	6,342	5,013	376	...
		Móchi	,,	170	88	74	8	...
		Total Group 38......	....	*11,901*	*6,430*	*5,087*	*384*	...
	38 (a). Village Watchmen, &c....	Holaya ...	,,	84,369	43,622	38,032	2,715	...
		Total Class D......	....	**261,223**	**137,569**	**114,508**	**9,146**	...
E.—Vagrant, Minor Artisans and Performers.	41. Earth Workers and stone dressers ...	Vaddar	Hindu.	4,077	2,152	1,783	142	...
	43. Mat makers and cane splitters...	Méda	,,	323	181	130	12	...
	44. Hunters, Fowlers, &c.	Beda	,,	1,564	880	611	73	...
	45. Miscellaneous and disreputable livers.	Budabudiké	,,	126	66	49	11	...
		S'illékyáta	,,	...	...	...	...	...
		Sudagádusidda	,,	...	...	...	...	...
		Gondaliga	,,	5	3	2	...	...
		Jógi	,,	657	371	255	31	...
		Karma	,,	...	...	...	...	...
		Mondaru	,,	...	...	...	...	...
		Pandáram	,,	...	...	...	...	...
		S'áníyár	,,	...	...	...	...	...
		Total Group 45......	....	*788*	*440*	*306*	*42*	...
	46. Tumblers, and Acrobats...	Dombar	,,	167	86	69	12	...
		Ráchévár.—Jatti	,,	280	147	124	9	...
		Total Group 46......	....	*447*	*233*	*193*	*21*	...
	47. Jugglers, snake charmers & animal exhibitors ...	Gárdiga	,,	23	13	9	1	...
		Total Class E......	....	**7,222**	**3,899**	**3,032**	**291**	...

TABLE E.—(Continued.)

District.

Males.

0 to 9.					10 to 14.				
Total.	Single.	Married.	Widowed.	Civil condition not stated.	Total.	Single.	Married.	Widowed.	Civil condition not stated.
8,110	8,108	2	...	...	2,594	2,552	42	...	...
1,258	1,258	...	...	...	363	363	...	...	...
3,289	3,289	...	...	...	1,011	1,011	...	...	...
46	46	...	...	...	13	13	...	...	...
3,335	*3,335*	...	...	...	*1,024*	*1,024*	...	...	...
23,326	23,326	...	...	...	9,098	9,080	18	...	...
73,247	**73,222**	**25**	...	...	**26,655**	**26,443**	**212**	...	...
1,180	1,180	...	...	...	333	333	...	...	...
99	99	...	...	...	28	28	...	...	...
486	486	...	...	...	140	138	2	...	...
36	36	...	...	...	14	14	...	...	...
...	...	...	...	...	...	...	...	...	...
...	...	...	...	...	...	...	...	...	...
2	2	...	...	...	1	1	...	...	...
202	202	...	...	...	59	59	...	...	...
...	...	...	...	...	...	...	...	...	...
...	...	...	...	...	...	...	...	...	...
...	...	...	...	...	...	...	...	...	...
...	...	...	...	...	...	...	...	...	...
240	240	...	...	...	74	74	...	...	...
44	44	...	...	...	15	15	...	...	...
78	78	...	...	...	25	25	...	...	...
122	*122*	...	...	...	40	40	...	...	...
7	7	...	...	...	2	2	...	...	...
2,134	**2,134**	...	...	...	**617**	**615**	**2**	...	...

Class.	Group.	Caste, &c., and sub-division.	Religion.	15 to 39 Total.	15 to 39 Single.	15 to 39 Married.	15 to 39 Widowed.	15 to 39 Civil condition not stated.
D.—Artisan & Village menial.—(Concluded.)	35. Fishermen, Boatmen and Palakhi bearers.	Besta	Hindu.	12,636	4,825	7,778	2,033	...
	36. Distillers & Toddy drawers ...	I'diga	"	1,801	595	1,164	42	...
	38. Leather Workers.	Mádiga	"	5,118	1,996	3,034	88	...
		Móchi	"	75	29	45	1	...
		Total Group 38	....	5,193	2,025	3,079	89	...
	38 (a). Village Watchmen, &c. ...	Holaya	"	33,958	10,839	22,481	638	...
		Total Class D	....	**108,033**	**36,869**	**69,091**	**2,073**	...
E.—Vagrant, Minor Artisans and Performers.	41. Earth Workers and stone dressers ...	Vaddar	Hindu.	1,746	613	1,105	28	...
	43. Mat makers and cane splitters...	Méda	"	130	53	76	1	...
	44. Hunters, Fowlers, &c.	Béda	"	656	243	395	18	...
	45. Miscellaneous and disreputable livers.	Budabudiké	"	45	15	29	1	...
		S'illékyáta	"	...	...	...	...	...
		Sudagádusidda	"	...	...	...	...	...
		Gondaliga	"	2	...	2	...	...
		Jógi	"	281	105	172	4	...
		Karma	"	...	...	...	...	...
		Mondaru	"	...	...	...	...	...
		Pandáram	"	...	...	...	...	...
		S'águyár	"	...	...	...	...	...
		Total Group 45	....	*328*	*120*	*203*	*5*	...
	46. Tumblers, and Acrobats.	Dombar	"	71	24	45	2	...
		Báchévár—Jatti	"	117	41	75	1	...
		Total Group 46	....	*188*	*65*	*120*	*3*	...
	47. Jugglers, snake charmers & animal exhibitors ...	Gárdiga	"	10	4	6	...	...
		Total Class E	....	**3,056**	**1,098**	**1,905**	**55**	...

TABLE E.—*(Continued.)*

District,

Males.

40 and over.					Age not stated.				
Total.	Single.	Married.	Widowed.	Civil condition not stated.	Total.	Single.	Married.	Widowed.	Civil condition not stated.
5,837	102	5,000	735	..	...	...	...	..	...
718	20	567	131	..	...	...	...	...	...
2,302	37	1,978	287	...	11	9	1	1	..
36	...	29	7	...	...	...	...	...	...
2,338	*37*	*2,007*	*294*	...	*11*	*9*	*1*	*1*	...
17,963	361	15,530	2,071	...	19	13	3	3	...
53,258	**1,013**	**45,176**	**7,069**	...	**30**	**22**	**4**	**4**	...
818	26	678	114	...	...	...	...	...	...
66	1	54	11	...	...	...	...	...	...
282	13	214	55	...	...	...	...	...	...
31	1	20	10	...	...	...	...	...	...
...	...	...	...	...	...	...	...	...	...
...	...	...	...	...	...	...	...	...	...
...	...	...	...	...	...	...	...	...	...
115	5	83	27	...	...	...	...	...	...
...	...	...	...	...	...	...	...	...	...
...	...	...	...	...	...	...	...	...	...
...	...	...	...	...	...	...	...	...	...
...	...	...	...	...	...	...	...	...	...
146	*6*	*103*	*37*	...	...	...	...	...	...
37	3	24	10	...	...	...	...	...	...
60	3	49	8	...	...	...	...	...	...
97	*6*	*73*	*18*	...	...	...	...	...	...
4	...	3	1	...	...	...	...	...	...
1,413	**52**	**1,125**	**236**	...	...	...	...	...	...

Class.	Group.	Caste, &c. and sub-division.	Religion.	All Ages. Total.	Single.	Married.	Widowed.	Civil condition not stated.
D.—Artisan & Village menial.—(Concluded.)	35. Fishermen, Boatmen and Palakhi bearers ...	Besta	Hindu.	30,173	11,195	13,275	5,703	...
	33. Distillers & Toddy drawers ...	Idiga	"	4,310	1,497	1,840	973	...
	38. Leather Workers.	Mádiga	"	12,085	4,624	5,315	2,146	...
		Móchi	"	193	72	82	39	...
		Total Group 38......	....	12,278	4,696	5,397	2,185	...
	38 (a). Village Watchmen, &c...	Holaya	"	88,634	33,802	38,545	16,287	...
		Total Class D......	....	**268,661**	**99,904**	**116,245**	**52,512**	...
E.—Vagrant, Minor Artisans and Performers.	41. Earth Workers and stone dressers ...	Vaddar	Hindu.	3,981	1,470	1,716	795	...
	43. Mat makers and cane splitters...	Méda	"	329	106	143	80	...
	44. Hunters, Fowlers, &c.	Bédar	"	1,565	542	630	393	...
	45. Miscellaneous and disreputable livers.	Budabudiké	"	112	43	48	21	...
		S'illékyáta	"	...	...	...	...	...
		Sudagádusiddu	"	...	...	...	...	...
		Gondaliga	"	3	1	1	1	...
		Jogi	"	739	282	296	161	...
		Karma	"	...	...	...	...	...
		Mondaru	"	...	...	...	...	...
		Pandáram	"	...	...	...	...	...
		S'aniyár...	"	...	...	...	...	...
		Total Group 45......	....	854	326	345	183	...
	46. Tumblers and Acrobats.	Dombar	"	146	58	66	22	...
		Ráchévár.—Jatti	"	305	116	138	51	...
		Total Gorup 46......	....	451	174	204	73	...
	47. Jugglers, snake charmers & animal exhibiters ...	Gárdiga	"	37	15	14	8	...
		Total Class E......	....	**7,217**	**2,633**	**3,050**	**1,532**	...

TABLE E.—(Continued.)

District.

Females.

Total.	Single.	Married.	Widowed.	Civil condition not stated.	10 to 14 Total.	Single.	Married.	Widowed.	Civil condition not stated.
	...								
8,707	8,457	250	..	...	2,781	1,812	972	...	...
1,114	1,094	20	..	...	415	297	117	1	...
3,844	3,340	4	...	...	914	819	95	...	...
57	57	...	...	...	21	13	8	...	...
3,401	3,397	4	...	...	965	862	103	...	...
26,971	26,437	534	...	...	7,146	4,669	2,477	...	...
77,454	**75,986**	**1,468**	...	...	**24,481**	**16,509**	**7,969**	**3**	...
1,113	1,103	10	...	...	331	281	50	...	...
75	73	2	...	...	48	33	16	...	...
407	396	11	...	...	141	99	42	...	...
30	30	...	...	...	13	10	3	...	...
...	...	...	...	...	...	...	...	...	...
...	...	...	...	...	...	...	...	...	...
1	1	...	...	...	...	...	...	...	...
212	209	3	...	...	67	50	17	...	...
...	...	...	...	...	...	...	...	...	...
...	...	...	...	...	...	...	...	...	...
...	...	...	...	...	...	...	...	...	...
...	...	...	...	...	...	...	...	...	...
243	240	3	...	...	80	60	20	...	...
39	38	1	...	...	15	12	8	...	...
99	99	...	...	...	18	14	4	...	...
138	137	1	...	...	33	26	7	...	...
10	10	...	...	...	6	3	3	...	...
1,986	**1,959**	**27**	...	...	**639**	**501**	**138**	...	...

Mysore

Class.	Group.	Caste, &c. and sub-division.	Religion.	15 to 39. Total.	Single.	Married.	Widowed.	Civil condition not stated.
D.—Artisan & Village menial.—(Concluded.)	35. Fishermen, Boatmen and Palakhi bearers.	Besta	Hindu.	12,036	870	9,694	1,472	...
	36. Distillers & Toddy drawers ...	I'diga	,,	1,684	94	1,363	227	...
	38. Leather Workers.	Mádiga	,,	4,608	375	3,634	599	...
		Mōchi	,,	67	2	53	12	...
		Total Group 38......	....	*4,675*	*377*	*3,687*	*611*	...
	38 (a). Village Watchmen, &c...	Holaya	,,	35,013	2,157	29,393	3,463	...
		Total Class D......	....	**103,887**	**6,813**	**84,414**	**12,660**	...
E.—Vagrant, Minor Artisans and Performers.	41. Earth Workers and stone dressers ...	Vaddar	Hindu.	1,468	78	1,222	168	...
	43. Mat makers and cane splitters...	Méda	,,	116	1	94	21	...
	44. Hunters, Fowlers, &c.	Béda	,,	608	40	471	97	...
	45. Miscellaneous and disreputable livers.	Budabudiké	,,	39	3	33	3	...
		S'iḷḷékyáta	,,	...	...	...	...	...
		Sudagáḍusidda	,,	...	...	...	...	...
		Gondaliga	,,	1	...	1	...	...
		Jógi	,,	278	20	215	43	...
		Karma	,,	...	...	...	...	...
		Mondaru	,,	...	...	...	...	...
		Panḍáram	,,	...	...	...	...	...
		S'áṇiyár	,,	...	...	...	...	...
		Total Group 55......	....	*318*	*23*	*249*	*46*	...
	46. Tumblers and Acrobats	Dombar		62	6	52	4	...
		Ráchévár.—Jaṭṭi	,,	112	3	95	14	...
		Total Group 46......	....	*174*	*9*	*147*	*18*	...
	47. Jugglers, snake charmers & animal exhibiters ...	Gárḍiga	,,	13	2	9	2	...
		Total Class E......	....	**2,697**	**153**	**2,192**	**352**	...

TABLE E.—(*Continued.*)

District.

Females.

40 and over.					Age not stated.				
Total.	Single.	Married.	Widowed.	Civil condition not stated.	Total.	Single.	Married.	Widowed.	Civil condition not stated.
6,646	56	2,359	4,231	...	...	...	...	...	...
1,097	12	340	745	...	...	...	...	...	...
3,174	49	1,580	1,545	...	15	11	2	2	...
48	...	21	27	...	...	...	...	...	...
3,222	*49*	*1,601*	*1,572*	...	*15*	*11*	2	2	...
19,176	222	6,136	12,818	...	28	17	5	6	...
62,796	**568**	**22,387**	**39,841**	...	**43**	**28**	**7**	**8**	...
1,069	8	434	627	...	...	...	...	...	...
90	...	31	59	...	...	...	...	...	...
409	7	106	296	...	...	...	...	...	...
30	...	12	18	...	...	...	...	...	...
...	...	...	...	...	...	...	...	...	...
...	...	...	...	...	...	...	...	...	...
1	...	...	1	...	...	...	...	...	...
183	8	61	118	...	...	...	...	...	...
...	...	...	...	...	...	...	...	...	...
...	...	...	...	...	...	...	...	...	...
...	...	...	...	...	...	...	...	...	...
...	...	...	...	...	...	...	...	...	...
213	*3*	*73*	*137*	...	...	...	...	...	...
30	2	10	18	...	...	...	...	...	...
76	...	39	37	...	...	...	...	...	...
106	*2*	*49*	*55*	...	...	...	...	...	...
8	...	2	6	...	...	...	...	...	...
1,895	**20**	**695**	**1,180**	...	...	...	...	...	...

Class.	Group.	Caste, &c. and sub-division.	Religion.	All Ages. Total.	Single.	Married.	Widowed.	Civil condition not stated.
D.—Artisan & Village menial.—(*Concluded.*)	35. Fishermen, Boatmen and Palakhi bearers.	Besta	Hindu.	3,764	2,018	1,509	237	...
	36. Distillers & Toddy drawers ...	I'diga	,,	1,399	764	541	94	...
	38. Leather Workers.	Mádiga	,,	5,520	2,235	2,820	465	...
		Móchi	,,	...	...	...	...	...
		Total Group 38......	....	*5,520*	*2,235*	*2,820*	*465*	...
	38 (a). Village Watchmen, &c...	Holaya	,,	43,596	25,710	16,921	965	...
		Total Class D.....	....	**104,060**	**57,697**	**41,947**	**4,416**	...
E.—Vagrant, Minor Artisans and Performers.	41. Earth Workers and stone dressers ...	Vaddar	Hindu.	2,496	1,445	888	163	...
	43. Mat makers and cane splitters...	Méda	,,	265	140	104	21	...
	44. Hunters, Fowlers, &c.	Béda	,,	2,774	1,562	1,067	145	...
	45. Miscellaneous and disreputable livers.	Budabudiké	,,	84	42	33	9	...
		S'illékyáta	,,	...	...	...	...	...
		Sudagádusidda	,,	...	...	...	...	...
		Gondaliga	,,	...	...	...	...	...
		Jógi	,,	294	167	108	19	...
		Karma	,,	...	...	...	...	...
		Mondaru	,,	...	...	...	...	...
		Pandáram	,,	...	...	...	...	...
		S'áṇiyár	,,	...	...	...	...	...
		Total Group 45......	....	*378*	*209*	*141*	*28*	...
	46. Tumblers and Acrobats	Dombar	,,	173	91	69	13	...
		Ráchévár.—Jatti	,,	73	38	27	8	...
		Total Group 46......	....	*246*	*129*	*96*	*21*	...
	47. Jugglers, snake charmers & animal exhibitors ...	Gárdiga	,,	...	...	...	...	...
		Total Class E.....	....	**6,159**	**3,485**	**2,296**	**378**	...

TABLE E.—(*Continued.*)

District.

Males.

0 to 9.					10 to 14.				
Total.	Single.	Married.	Widowed.	Civil condition not stated.	Total.	Single.	Married.	Widowed.	Civil condition not stated.
1,047	1,047	...	...	...	454	441	13	...	...
400	400	...	...	...	193	189	4	...	...
1,021	1,015	6	...	...	520	510	10	...	...
...	...	...	...	...	...	...	...	...	...
1,021	*1,015*	*6*	...	...	*520*	*510*	*10*	...	...
12,838	12,830	8	...	...	3,949	3,923	25	1	...
28,942	**28,925**	**17**	...	...	**10,635**	**10,489**	**142**	**4**	...
773	773	...	...	...	229	221	8	...	...
74	74	...	...	...	21	21	...	...	...
716	716	...	...	...	327	325	2	...	...
20	20	...	...	...	11	11	...	...	...
...	...	...	...	...	...	...	...	...	...
...	...	...	...	...	...	...	...	...	...
...	...	...	...	...	...	...	...	...	...
86	86	...	...	...	36	36	...	...	...
...	...	...	...	...	...	...	...	...	...
...	...	...	...	...	...	...	...	...	...
...	...	...	...	...	...	...	...	...	...
...	...	...	...	...	...	...	...	...	...
106	*106*	...	...	...	*47*	*47*	...	...	...
41	41	...	...	...	21	21	...	...	...
14	14	...	...	...	9	9	...	...	...
55	*55*	...	...	...	*30*	*30*	...	...	...
...	...	...	...	...	...	...	...	...	...
1,724	**1,724**	...	...	...	**654**	**644**	**10**	...	...

Hassan

Class.	Group.	Caste, &c., and sub-division.	Religion.	15 to 39 Total.	Single.	Married.	Widowed.	Civil condition not stated.
D.—Artisan & Village menial.—(Concluded.)	35. Fishermen, Boatmen and Palakhi bearers.	Besta	Hindu.	1,504	523	919	62	...
	36. Distillers & Toddy drawers ...	I'diga	,,	549	164	362	23	...
	38. Leather workers ...	Mádiga	,,	2,794	620	2,010	164	...
		Móchi	,,	...	...	...	...	...
		Total Group 38	....	*2,794*	*620*	*2,010*	*164*	...
	38 (a). Village watchmen, &c. ...	Holaya	,,	18,036	8,820	9,009	207	...
		Total Class D	....	**43,477**	**17,818**	**24,662**	**997**	...
E.—Vagrant, Minor Artisans and Performers.	41. Earth workers and stone dressers ...	Vaddar	Hindu.	960	435	498	27	...
	43. Mat makers and cane splitters ...	Méda	,,	118	44	69	5	...
	44. Hunters, Fowlers, &c.	Béda	,,	1,210	498	674	38	...
	45. Miscellaneous and disreputable livers.	Budabudiké	,,	32	10	20	2	...
		S'illékyáta	,,	...	...	...	...	...
		Sudagádusidda	,,	...	...	...	...	...
		Gondaliga	,,	...	...	...	...	...
		Jógi	,,	114	42	70	2	...
		Karma	,,	...	...	...	...	...
		Mondaru	,,	...	...	...	...	...
		Pandáram	,,	...	...	...	...	...
		S'ániyár	,,	...	...	...	...	...
		Total Group 45	....	*146*	*52*	*90*	*4*	...
	46. Tumblers and Acrobats ...	Dombar	,,	63	21	39	3	...
		Ráchévár.—Jatti	,,	34	15	17	2	...
		Total Group 46	....	*97*	*36*	*56*	*5*	...
	47. Jugglers, snake charmers & animal exhibitors ...	Gárdiga	,,	...	...	...	...	...
		Total Class E	....	**2,831**	**1,065**	**1,387**	**79**	...

TABLE E.—(*Continued.*)

District.

Males.

40 and over.					Age not stated.				
Total.	Single.	Married.	Widowed.	Civil condition not stated.	Total.	Single.	Married.	Widowed.	Civil condition not stated.
759	7	577	175	...	...	...	...	...	...
257	11	175	71	...	...	...	...	...	...
1,185	90	791	301	...	...	...	...	...	...
—	...	...	...	...	...	...	...	...	...
1,185	*90*	*791*	*301*	...	...	...	...	...	...
8,773	137	7,879	757	...	...	...	...	...	...
21,006	**465**	**17,126**	**3,415**	...	...	...	...	...	...
531	16	383	136	...	...	...	...	...	...
52	1	35	16	...	...	...	...	...	...
521	23	391	107	...	...	...	...	...	...
21	1	13	7	...	...	...	...	...	...
...	...	...	...	...	...	...	...	...	...
...	...	...	...	...	...	...	...	...	...
...	...	...	...	...	...	...	...	...	...
58	3	38	17	...	...	...	...	...	...
...	...	...	...	...	...	...	...	...	...
...	...	...	...	...	...	...	...	...	...
...	...	...	...	...	...	...	...	...	...
...	...	...	...	...	...	...	...	...	...
79	*4*	*51*	*24*	...	...	...	...	...	...
48	8	30	10	...	...	...	...	...	...
16	...	10	6	...	...	...	...	...	...
64	*8*	*40*	*16*	...	...	...	...	...	...
...	...	...	...	...	...	...	...	...	...
1,230	**52**	**899**	**299**	...	...	...	...	...	...

Class.	Caste and Religion.			All Ages.				
	Group.	Caste, &c., and sub-division.	Religion.	Total.	Single.	Married.	Widowed.	Civil condition not stated.
D.—Artisan & Village menial.—(Concluded.)	35. Fishermen, Boatmen and Palakhi bearers.	Besta	Hindu.	3,864	1,471	1,665	728	...
	36. Distillers & Toddy drawers ...	I'diga	,,	1,358	514	586	258	...
	38 Leather workers.	Mádiga	,,	5,670	1,917	2,413	1,340	...
		Móchi	,,	...	...	...	...	...
		Total Group 38......	... .	5,670	1,917	2,413	1,340	...
	38 (a). Village Watchmen &c...	Holaya	,,	43,462	17,621	16,726	9,115	...
		Total Class D......	....	**104,995**	**41,425**	**43,257**	**20,313**	...
E.—Vagrant, Minor Artisans and Performers.	41. Earth workers and stone dressers ...	Vaddar	Hindu.	2,282	911	1,010	361	...
	43. Mat makers and cane splitters...	Méda	,,	255	99	113	43	...
	44. Hunters, Fowlers, &c.	Béda	,,	2,807	1,246	1,022	539	...
	45. Miscellaneous and disreputable livers.	Budabudiké	,,	115	52	48	15	...
		S'illékyáta	,,	...	...	...	...	...
		Sudagádusidda	,,	...	...	...	...	...
		Gondaliga	,,	...	...	...	...	...
		Jógi	,,	270	109	123	38	...
		Karma	,,	...	...	...	...	...
		Mondaru	,,	...	...	...	...	...
		Pandáram	,,	...	...	...	...	...
		S'ániyár	,,	...	...	...	...	...
		Total Group 45......	....	385	161	171	53	...
	46. Tumblers and Acrobats...	Dombar	,,	169	78	73	18	...
		Ráchévár—Jatti	,,	73	31	26	16	...
		Total Group 46......	... .	242	109	99	34	...
	47. Jugglers, snake charmers & animal exhibitors ...	Gárdiga	,,	...	...	...	...	...
		Total Class E......	....	**5,971**	**2,526**	**2,415**	**1,030**	...

TABLE E.—(*Continued.*)

District.

Females.

0 to 9					10 to 14				
Total.	Single.	Married.	Widowed.	Civil condition not stated.	Total.	Single.	Married.	Widowed.	Civil condition not stated.
902	899	2	1	...	417	362	52	3	...
341	340	1	...	...	132	115	16	1	...
1,050	1,027	23	...	...	1,019	710	309	...	...
...	...	...	...	...	...	...	...	...	...
1,050	*1,027*	*23*	...	...	*1,019*	*710*	*309*	...	...
13,100	13,007	91	2	...	3,721	3,209	498	14	...
30,137	**29,950**	**184**	**3**	...	**10,076**	**8,113**	**1,928**	**35**	...
669	669	...	...	...	208	155	53	...	...
71	71	...	...	...	22	21	1	...	...
765	765	...	...	...	269	258	11	...	...
38	38	...	...	...	11	9	2	...	...
...	...	...	...	...	...	...	...	...	...
...	...	...	...	...	...	...	...	...	...
...	...	...	...	...	...	...	...	...	...
77	77	...	...	...	22	22	...	...	...
...	...	...	...	...	...	...	...	...	...
...	...	...	...	...	...	...	...	...	...
...	...	...	...	...	...	...	...	...	...
...	...	...	...	...	...	...	...	...	...
115	*115*	...	...	...	*33*	*31*	2	...	...
37	37	...	...	...	15	15	...	...	...
21	21	...	...	...	8	8	...	...	...
58	*58*	...	...	...	*23*	*23*	...	...	...
...	...	...	...	...	...	...	...	...	...
1,678	**1,678**	...	...	...	**555**	**488**	**67**	...	...

Hassan

Class.	Group.	Caste, &c. and sub-division.	Religion.	15 to 39 Total.	Single.	Married.	Widowed.	Civil condition not stated.
D.—Artisan & Village menial.—(Concluded.)	35. Fishermen, Boatmen and Palakhi bearers.	Besta	Hindu.	1,609	187	1,226	196	...
	36. Distillers & Toddy drawers ...	I'diga	"	556	58	445	53	...
	38. Leather workers.	Mádiga	"	2,481	160	1,811	510	...
		Móchi	"	...	...	...	...	...
		Total Group 38	....	*2,481*	*160*	*1,811*	*510*	...
	38 (a). Village Watchmen, &c. ...	Holaya	"	18,503	1,281	14,292	2,930	...
		Total Class D	....	**43,366**	**3,115**	**34,119**	**6,132**	...
E.—Vagrant, Minor Artisans and Performers.	41. Earth workers and stone dressers ...	Vaddar	Hindu.	917	82	748	87	...
	43. Mat makers and cane splitters ...	Méda	"	114	7	97	10	...
	44. Hunters, Fowlers, &c.	Bêda	"	1,112	208	738	166	...
	45. Miscellaneous and disreputable livers.	Budabudiké	"	49	5	40	4	...
		S'illékyáta	"	...	...	...	...	...
		Sudagádusidda	"	...	...	...	...	...
		Gondaliga	"	...	...	...	...	...
		Jógi	"	110	10	91	9	...
		Karma	"	...	...	...	...	...
		Mondaru	"	...	...	...	...	...
		Pandáram	"	...	...	...	...	...
		S'ániyár	"	...	...	...	...	...
		Total Group 45	....	*150*	*15*	*131*	*13*	...
	46. Tumblers and Acrobats ...	Dombar	"	76	18	54	4	...
		Ráchévár—Jatti	"	27	1	20	6	...
		Total Group 46	....	*103*	*19*	*74*	*10*	...
	47. Jugglers, snake charmers, & animal exhibitors ...	Gárdiga	"	...	...	...	...	...
		Total Class E	....	**2,405**	**331**	**1,788**	**286**	...

TABLE E.—(*Continued.*)

District.

Females.

40 and over.					Age not stated.				
Total.	Single.	Married.	Widowed.	Civil condition not stated.	Total.	Single.	Married.	Widowed.	Civil condition not stated.
936	23	385	528	...	...	...	...	...	...
329	1	124	204	...	...	...	...	...	...
1,120	20	270	830	...	...	...	...	...	...
...	...	...	...	...	...	...	...	...	...
1,120	*20*	*270*	*830*	...	...	...	...	...	...
8,138	124	1,845	6,169	...	...	...	...	...	...
21,416	**247**	**7,026**	**14,143**	...	...	...	...	...	...
488	5	209	274	...	...	...	...	...	...
48	...	15	33	...	...	...	...	...	...
661	15	273	373	...	...	...	...	...	...
17	...	6	11	...	...	...	...	...	...
...	...	...	...	...	...	...	...	...	...
...	...	...	...	...	...	...	...	...	...
...	...	...	...	...	...	...	...	...	...
61	...	32	29	...	...	...	...	...	...
...	...	...	...	...	...	...	...	...	...
...	...	...	...	...	...	...	...	...	...
...	...	...	...	...	...	...	...	...	...
...	...	...	...	...	...	...	...	...	...
78	...	*38*	*40*	...	...	...	...	...	...
41	8	19	14	...	...	...	...	...	...
17	1	6	10	...	...	...	...	...	...
58	*9*	25	*24*	...	...	...	...	...	...
	...	...	...	...	...	...	...	...	...
1,333	**29**	**560**	**744**	...	...	...	...	...	...

Shimoga

Class.	Group.	Caste, &c. and sub-division.	Religion.	All Ages. Total.	All Ages. Single.	All Ages. Married.	All Ages. Widowed.	All Ages. Civil condition not stated.
D.—Artisan & Village menial.—(Concluded.)	35. Fishermen, Boatmen and Palaki bearers.	Besta	Hindu.	3,759	2,053	1,431	275	...
	36. Distillers & Toddy drawers	I'diga	,,	5,941	3,006	2,576	359	...
	38. Leather Workers.	Mádiga	,,	11,948	6,221	4,720	1,007	...
		Móchi	,,	12	6	5	1	...
		Total Group 38	....	*11,960*	*6,227*	*4,725*	*1,008*	...
	39 (a). Village Watchmen, &c.	Holaya	,,	19,342	10,243	7,920	1,179	...
		Total Class D	....	82,707	44,157	32,809	5,741	...
E.—Vagrant, Minor Artisans and Performers.	41. Earth Workers and stone dressers	Vaddar	Hindu.	7,775	4,096	3,080	599	...
	43. Mat makers and cane splitters	Méda	,,	709	388	285	36	...
	44. Hunters, Fowlers, &c.	Béda	,,	12,949	7,335	4,750	884	...
	45. Miscellaneous and disreputable livers.	Budabudikè	,,	45	25	18	2	...
		S'iḷḷèkyáta	,,	48	20	27	1	...
		Sudagáḍusidda	,,	25	14	10	1	...
		Gondaliga	,,	...	...	...	...	...
		Jógi	,,	561	311	219	31	...
		Karma	,,	...	...	...	...	...
		Mondaru	,,	...	...	...	...	...
		Pandáram	,,	...	...	...	...	...
		S'áṇiyár	,,	...	...	...	...	...
		Total Group 45	....	*679*	*370*	*274*	*35*	...
	46. Tumblers and Acrobats.	Dombar	,,	53	27	21	5	...
		Ráchèvár—Jaṭṭi	,,	76	43	29	4	...
		Total Group 46	....	*129*	*70*	*50*	*9*	...
	47. Jugglers, snake charmers & animal exhibitors	Gárḍiga	,,	134	69	61	4	...
		Total Class E	....	22,375	12,328	8,500	1,547	...

TABLE E.—(*Continued.*)

District.

Males.

0 to 9					10 to 14				
Total.	Single.	Married.	Widowed.	Civil condition not stated.	Total.	Single.	Married.	Widowed.	Civil condition not stated.
924	924	...	...	...	475	471	4	...	...
1,112	1,112	...	...	...	729	715	14	...	...
2,216	2,208	8	...	...	1,131	1,121	10	..	...
2	2	...	...	...	1	1	...	...	...
2,218	*2,210*	*8*	...	...	*1,132*	*1,122*	*10*	...	...
4,149	4,128	21	...	...	1,206	1,182	24	...	...
19,371	**19,337**	**34**	...	...	**9,099**	**8,932**	**166**	**1**	...
2,021	2,021	...	...	...	873	855	18	...	...
226	226	...	...	...	68	68	...	...	...
3,579	3,579	...	...	...	1,675	1,648	27	...	...
13	13	...	...	...	7	7	...	...	...
8	8	...	...	...	7	6	1	...	...
9	9	...	...	...	1	1	...	...	...
...	...	...	...	...	...	...	...	...	...
158	158	...	...	...	71	71	...	...	...
...	...	...	...	...	...	...	...	...	...
...	...	...	...	...	...	...	...	...	...
...	...	...	...	...	...	...	...	...	...
...	...	...	...	...	...	...	...	...	...
188	*188*	...	...	...	*86*	*85*	*1*	...	...
15	15	...	...	...	2	2	...	...	...
28	28	...	...	...	9	9	...	...	...
43	*43*	...	...	...	*11*	*11*	...	...	...
32	32	...	...	...	26	26	...	...	...
6,089	**6,089**	...	...	...	**2,739**	**2,693**	**46**	...	...

Class.	Group.	Caste, &c. and sub-division.	Religion.	15 to 39. Total.	Single	Married.	Widowed.	Civil condition not stated.
D.—Artisan & Village menial.—(Concluded.)	35. Fishermen, Boatmen and Palakhi bearers.	Besta	Hindu.	1,602	611	898	93	...
	36. Distillers & Toddy drawers ...	I'ḍiga	„	2,898	1,133	1,651	114	...
	38. Leather Workers.	Mádiga	„	5,348	2,303	2,822	223	...
		Móchi	„	7	3	4	...	...
		Total Group 38......	....	5,355	2,306	2,826	223	...
	38 (a). Village Watchmen, &c...	Holaya	„	8,808	4,319	4,215	274	...
		Total Class D......	....	**35,077**	**14,245**	**19,253**	**1,579**	...
E.—Vagrant, Minor Artisans and Performers.	41. Earth Workers and stone dressers ...	Vaddar	Hindu.	3,157	1,165	1,832	160	...
	43. Mat makers and cane splitters...	Méda	„	295	91	197	7	...
	44. Hunters, Fowlers, &c.	Béḍa	„	5,030	1,944	2,902	184	...
	45. Miscellaneous and disreputable livers.	Budabudiké	„	15	4	11	...	...
		S'iḷḷékyáta	„	24	6	18	...	...
		Suḍagáḍusidda	„	10	3	7	...	...
		Gondaliga	„	...	...	...	...	...
		Jógi	„	206	77	122	7	...
		Karma	„	...	...	...	...	...
		Monḍáru	„	...	...	...	...	...
		Panḍáram	„	...	...	...	...	...
		S'áṇiyár	„	...	...	...	...	...
		Total Group 45......	....	255	90	158	7	...
	46. Tumblers and Acrobats.	Dombar	„	24	10	14	...	...
		Ráchévár—Jaṭṭi	„	27	6	21	...	...
		Total Group 46......	....	51	16	35	...	...
	47. Jugglers, snake charmers & animal exhibiters ...	Gárḍiga	„	46	10	35	1	...
		Total Class E......	„	**8,834**	**3,316**	**5,159**	**359**	...

TABLE E.—(*Continued.*)

District.

Males.

40 and over.					Age not stated.				
Total.	Single.	Married.	Widowed.	Civil condition not stated.	Total.	Single.	Married.	Widowed.	Civil condition not stated.
758	47	529	182	...	...	...	...	...	...
1,202	46	911	245	...	...	...	...	...	...
3,253	589	1,880	784	...	...	...	...	...	...
2	...	1	1	...	...	...	...	...	...
3,255	*589*	*1,881*	*785*	...	...	...	...	...	...
5,179	614	3,660	905	...	...	...	...	...	...
19,160	**1,643**	**13,356**	**4,161**	...	...	...	...	...	...
1,724	55	1,230	439	...	...	...	...	...	...
120	3	88	29	...	...	...	...	...	...
2,665	164	1,821	680	...	...	...	...	...	...
10	1	7	2	...	...	...	...	...	...
9	...	8	1	...	...	...	...	...	...
5	1	3	1	...	...	...	...	...	...
...	...	...	...	...	...	...	...	...	...
126	5	97	24	...	...	...	...	...	...
...	...	...	...	...	...	...	...	...	...
...	...	...	...	...	...	...	...	...	...
...	...	...	...	...	...	...	...	...	...
...	...	...	...	...	...	...	...	...	...
150	*7*	*115*	*28*	...	...	...	...	...	...
12	...	7	5	...	...	...	...	...	...
12	...	8	4	...	...	...	...	...	...
24	...	*15*	*9*	...	...	...	...	...	...
30	1	26	3	...	...	...	...	...	...
4,713	**230**	**3295**	**1,188**	...	...	...	...	...	...

Class.	Group.	Caste, &c. and sub-division.	Religion.	All Ages. Total.	Single.	Married.	Widowed.	Civil condition not stated.
D.—Artisan & Village menial.—(*Concluded.*)	35. Fishermen, Boatmen and Palakhi bearers.	Besta	Hindu.	3,531	1,296	1,535	700	...
	36. Distillers & Toddy drawers ...	I'diga	,,	5,003	1,907	2,215	881	...
	38. Leather workers ...	Mádiga	,,	11,069	5,223	2,372	3,474	...
		Môchi	,,	14	5	6	3	...
		Total Group 38......	....	11,083	5,228	2,378	3,477	...
	38 (*a*). Village watchmen &c..	Holaya	,,	18,658	8,221	6,237	4,200	...
		Total Class D......	....	**75,834**	**30,477**	**29,293**	**16,064**	...
E.—Vagrant, Minor Artisans and Performers.	41. Earth workers and stone dressers	Vuddar	Hindu.	7,143	2,596	3,299	1,248	...
	43. Mat makers and cane splitters ...	Méda	,,	351	114	178	59	...
	44. Hunters, Fowlers, &c.	Béda	,,	12,729	5,576	5,193	1,960	...
	45. Miscellaneous and disreputable livers.	Budabudiké	,,	36	15	20	1	...
		S'iḷḷékyáta	,,	31	11	18	2	...
		Sudagádusidda	,,	21	7	11	3	...
		Gondaliga	,,	...	...	...	...	...
		Jógi	,,	437	176	213	48	...
		Karma	,,	...	...	...	...	...
		Mondaru	,,	...	...	...	...	...
		Pandáram	,,	...	...	...	...	...
		S'ániyár	,,	...	...	...	...	...
		Total Group 45......	....	525	209	262	54	...
	46. Tumblers and Acrobats ...	Dombar	,,	75	37	30	8	...
		Ráchévár—Jaṭṭi	,,	65	25	35	5	...
		Total Group 46......	....	140	62	65	13	...
	47. Jugglers, snake charmers, & animal exhibitors ...	Gárḍiga	,,	168	66	83	19	...
		Total Class E	....	**21,056**	**8,623**	**9,080**	**3,353**	...

TABLE E.—(*Continued.*)

District

Females.

0 to 9 Total.	Single.	Married.	Widowed.	Civil condition not stated.	10 to 14 Total.	Single.	Married.	Widowed.	Civil condition not stated.
818	813	5	...	...	391	321	70	...	...
1,354	1,334	20	...	...	528	366	158	4	...
3,148	3,121	26	1	...	1,337	1,034	275	28	...
2	2	...	...	...	2	2	...	...	...
3,150	*3,123*	*26*	*1*	...	*1,339*	*1,036*	*275*	*28*	...
5,432	5,192	231	9	...	2,628	1,428	1,128	72	...
20,681	**20,272**	**399**	**10**	...	**8,770**	**6,192**	**2,453**	**125**	...
1,881	1,881	...	...	...	679	495	184	...	...
75	75	...	...	...	34	28	6	...	...
3,321	3,314	7	...	...	1,524	1,247	277	...	...
10	10	...	...	...	5	5	...	...	...
8	8	...	...	...	3	3	...	...	...
5	5	...	...	...	2	2	...	...	...
...	...	...	...	...	...	...	...	...	...
127	127	...	...	...	39	37	2	...	...
...	...	...	...	...	...	...	...	...	...
...	...	...	...	...	...	...	...	...	...
...	...	...	...	...	...	...	...	...	...
...	...	...	...	...	...	...	...	...	...
150	*150*	...	...	...	*49*	*47*	*2*	...	...
17	17	...	...	...	10	9	1	...	...
19	19	...	...	...	6	5	1	...	...
36	*36*	...	...	...	*16*	*14*	*2*	...	...
51	51	...	...	...	14	14	...	...	...
5,514	**5,507**	**7**	...	...	**2,316**	**1,845**	**471**	...	...

Class.	Group.	Caste, &c. and sub-division.	Religion.	15 to 39 Total.	15 to 39 Single.	15 to 39 Married.	15 to 39 Widowed.	15 to 39 Civil condition not stated.
D.—Artisan & Village menial.—(*Concluded.*)	35. Fishermen, Boatmen and Palukhi bearers.	Besta	Hindu.	1,581	130	1,218	233	...
	36. Distillers & Toddy drawers ...	I'ḍiga	,,	2,278	178	1,786	314	...
	38. Leather workers ...	Mádiga	,,	3,775	911	1,741	1,123	...
		Móchi	,,	7	1	5	1	...
		Total Group 38......	....	*3,782*	*912*	*1,746*	*1,124*	...
	38 (*a*) Village Watchmen, &c...	Hólaya	,,	6,441	1,011	4,230	1,200	...
		Total Class D......	....	**30,783**	**3,113**	**22,434**	**5,236**	...
E.—Vagrant, Minor Artisans and Performers.	41. Earth workers and stone dressers ...	Vaddar	Hindu.	3,152	205	2,621	326	...
	43. Mat makers and cane splitters ...	Méda	,,	151	11	128	12	...
	44. Hunters, Fowlers, &c.	Béḍa	,,	5,787	778	4,344	665	...
	45. Miscellaneous and disreputable livers.	Buḍabuḍiké	,,	12	...	12	...	...
		S'iḷḷékyáta	,,	14	...	14	...	...
		Suḍagáḍusidda	,,	10	...	9	1	...
		Gondaliga	,,	...	...	...	...	...
		Jógi	,,	208	12	181	15	...
		Karma	,,	...	...	...	...	...
		Monḍaru	,,	...	...	...	...	...
		Pandárum	,,	...	...	...	...	...
		S'ániyár	,,	...	...	...	...	...
		Total Group 45......	....	*244*	*12*	*216*	*16*	...
	46. Tumblers and Acrobats ...	Dombar	,,	37	11	26	...	...
		Ráchévár—Jaṭṭi ...	,,	28	1	25	2	...
		Total Group 46......	....	*65*	*12*	*51*	*2*	...
	47. Jugglers, snake charmers & animal exhibiters ...	Gárḍiga	,,	77	1	73	3	...
		Total Class E......	....	**9,476**	**1,019**	**7,433**	**1,024**	...

TABLE E.—(*Continued*)

District.

Females.

40 and over.					Age not stated.				
Total.	Single.	Married.	Widowed.	Civil condition not stated.	Total.	Single.	Married.	Widowed.	Civil condition not stated.
741	32	242	467	...	...	...	...	...	...
843	29	251	563	...	...	...	...	...	...
2,809	151	330	2,322	...	...	...	...	...	...
3	...	1	2	...	...	...	...	...	...
2,812	*157*	*331*	*2,324*	...	...	...	...	...	...
4,157	590	648	2,919	...	...	...	...	...	...
15,600	**900**	**4,007**	**10,693**	...	...	...	...	...	...
1,431	15	494	922	...	...	...	...	...	...
91	...	44	47	...	...	...	...	...	...
2,097	237	565	1,295	...	...	...	...	...	...
9	...	8	1	...	...	...	...	...	...
6	...	4	2	...	...	...	...	...	...
4	...	2	2	...	...	...	...	...	...
...	...	...	...	...	...	...	...	...	...
63	...	30	33	...	...	...	...	...	...
...	...	...	...	...	...	...	...	...	...
...	...	...	...	...	...	...	...	...	...
...	...	...	...	...	...	...	...	...	...
...	...	...	...	...	...	...	...	...	...
82	...	*44*	*38*	...	...	...	...	...	...
11	...	3	8	...	...	...	...	...	...
12	...	9	3	...	...	...	...	...	...
23	...	*12*	*11*	...	...	...	...	...	...
26	...	10	16	...	...	...	...	...	...
3,750	**252**	**1,169**	**2,329**	...	...	...	...	...	...

Class.	Group.	Caste, &c. and sub-division.	Religion.	All Ages. Total.	Single.	Married.	Widowed.	Civil condition not stated.
D.—Artisan & Village menial—(Concluded.)	35. Fishermen, Boatmen and Palakhi bearers.	Besta ...	Hindu.	2,064	1,171	782	111	...
	36. Distillers & Toddy drawers ...	I'diga ...	,,	2,167	1,151	908	108	...
	38. Leather Workers.	Mádiga ...	,,	5,490	2,939	2,088	463	...
		Móchi ...	,,	4	2	2	...	...
		Total Group 38......	....	*5,494*	*2,941*	*2,090*	*463*	...
	38 (a). Village Watchmen, &c...	Holaya ...	,,	28,161	18,409	8,840	912	...
		Total Class D......	....	**74,085**	**43,833**	**26,906**	**3,346**	...
E.—Vagrant, Minor Artisans and Performers.	41. Earth Workers and stone dressers ...	Vaddar ...	Hindu.	2,816	1,593	1,116	107	...
	43. Mat makers and cane splitters...	Méda ...	,,	343	202	120	21	...
	44. Hunters, Fowlers, &c.	Béda ...	,,	2,563	1,460	1,006	97	...
	45. Miscellaneous and disreputable livers.	Budabudikó ...	,,	28	15	10	3	...
		S'illékyáta ...	,,	...	...	...	...	...
		Sudagádusidda ...	,,	...	...	...	...	...
		Gondaliga ...	,,	...	...	...	...	...
		Jógi ...	,,	288	161	105	22	...
		Karma ...	,,	...	...	...	...	...
		Mondaru ...	,,	65	36	23	6	...
		Pandáram ...	,,	...	...	...	...	...
		S'ániyár ...	,,	...	...	...	...	...
		Total Group 45......	....	*381*	*212*	*138*	*31*	...
	46. Tumblers, and Acrobats...	Dombar ...	,,	146	73	53	20	...
		Ráchévár—Jatti ...	,,	...	...	...	...	...
		Total Group 46......	....	*146*	*73*	*53*	*20*	...
	47. Jugglers, snake charmers & animal exhibitors ...	Gárdiga ...	,,	...	...	...	...	...
		Total Class E....	....	**6,249**	**3,540**	**2,433**	**276**	...

TABLE E.—(*Continued.*)

District.

Males.

0 to 9					10 to 14				
Total.	Single.	Married.	Widowed.	Civil condition not stated.	Total.	Single.	Married.	Widowed.	Civil condition not stated.
501	501	...	...	...	226	226	...	...	...
455	455	...	...	...	243	243	...	...	...
1,032	1,032	...	...	...	549	549	...	...	...
...	...	...	...	...	1	1	...	...	...
1,032	*1,032*	...	...	...	*550*	*550*	...	...	...
9,452	9,452	...	...	...	2,975	2,975	...	...	...
21,173	**21,173**	...	...	...	**7,672**	**7,634**	**38**	...	...
815	815	...	...	...	282	282	...	...	...
97	97	...	...	...	28	28	...	...	...
648	648	...	...	...	260	260	...	...	...
5	5	...	...	...	3	3	...	...	...
...	...	...	...	...	...	...	...	...	...
...	...	...	...	...	...	...	...	...	...
...	...	...	...	...	...	...	...	...	...
88	88	...	...	...	27	27	...	...	...
...	...	...	...	...	...	...	...	...	...
15	15	...	...	...	6	6	...	...	...
...	...	...	...	...	...	...	...	...	...
...	...	...	...	...	...	...	...	...	...
103	*108*	...	...	...	*30*	*30*	...	...	...
36	36	...	...	...	9	9	...	...	...
...	...	...	...	...	...	...	...	...	...
36	*36*	...	...	...	*9*	*9*	...	...	...
...	...	...	...	...	...	...	...	...	...
1,704	**1,704**	...	...	...	**615**	**615**	...	...	...

Class.	Group.	Caste, &c., and sub-division.	Religion.	15 to 39. Total.	Single.	Married.	Widowed.	Civil condition not stated.
D.—Artisan & Village menial.—(Concluded)	35. Fishermen, Boatmen and Palakhi bearers. ...	Besta	Hindu.	948	414	502	32	...
	36. Distillers & Toddy drawers, ...	I'diga	"	1,089	428	620	41	...
	38. Leather Workers.	Mádiga	"	2,672	1,256	1,233	183	...
		Móchi	"	2	1	1	...	...
		Total Group 38	....	*2,674*	*1,257*	*1,234*	*183*	...
	38 (a). Village Watchmen, &c...	Holaya	"	11,111	5,866	5,115	130	...
		Total Class D	....	**31,892**	**14,447**	**16,559**	**886**	...
E.—Vagrant, Minor Artisans and Performers.	41. Earth Workers and stone dressers. ...	Vaddar	Hindu.	1,208	481	694	33	...
	43. Mat makers and cane splitters...	Méda	"	160	71	84	5	...
	44. Hunters, Fowlers, &c.	Béda	"	1,229	515	694	20	...
	45. Miscellaneous and disreputable livers.	Budabudikó	"	13	6	6	1	...
		S'illékyata	"	...	...	...	...	...
		Sudagádusidda	"	...	...	...	...	...
		Gondaliga	"	...	...	...	...	...
		Jógi	"	115	44	64	7	...
		Karma	"	...	...	...	...	...
		Mondaru	"	30	14	14	2	...
		Pandáram	"	...	...	...	...	...
		Sániyár	"	...	...	...	...	...
		Total Group 45	....	*158*	*64*	*84*	*10*	...
	46. Tumblers and Acrobats...	Dombar	"	63	26	31	6	...
		Ráchévár.—Jatti	"	...	...	...	...	...
		Total Group 46	....	*63*	*26*	*31*	*6*	...
	47. Jugglers, snake charmers & animal exhibitors ...	Gárdiga	"	...	...	...	...	...
		Total Class E	....	**2,818**	**1,157**	**1,587**	**74**	...

TABLE E.—*(Continued.)*

District.

Males.

40 and over.					Age not stated.				
Total.	Single.	Married.	Widowed	Civil condition not stated.	Total.	Single.	Married.	Widowed	Civil condition not stated.
389	30	280	79	...	...	...	...	...	...
380	25	288	67	...	...	...	...	...	...
1,237	102	855	280	...	...	...	...	...	...
1	...	1	...	...	...	...	...	...	...
1,238	*102*	*856*	*280*	...	...	...	...	...	...
4,621	116	3,724	781	...	2	...	1	1	...
13,346	**579**	**10,308**	**2,459**	...	**2**	...	**1**	**1**	...
511	15	422	74	...	...	...	...	...	...
58	6	36	16	...	...	...	...	...	...
426	37	312	77	...	...	...	...	...	...
7	1	4	2	...	...	...	...	...	...
...	...	...	...	...	...	...	...	...	...
...	...	...	...	...	...	...	...	...	...
...	...	...	...	...	...	...	...	...	...
58	2	41	15	...	...	...	...	...	...
...	...	...	...	...	...	...	...	...	...
14	1	9	4	...	...	...	...	...	...
...	...	...	...	...	...	...	...	...	...
...	...	...	...	...	...	...	...	...	...
79	*4*	*54*	*21*	...	...	...	...	...	...
38	2	22	14	...	...	...	...	...	...
...	...	...	...	...	...	...	...	...	...
38	*2*	*22*	*14*	...	...	...	...	...	...
...	...	...	...	...	...	...	...	...	...
1,112	**64**	**846**	**202**	...	...	...	...	...	...

Kadur

Class.	Group.	Caste, &c. and sub-division.	Religion.	All Ages. Total.	Single.	Married.	Widowed.	Civil condition not stated.
D.—Artisan & Village menial.—(*Concluded.*)	35. Fishermen, Boatmen and Palakhi bearers.	Besta	Hindu.	2,038	829	798	411	...
	36. Distillers & Toddy drawers ...	I'diga	,,	1,715	612	796	307	...
	38. Leather Workers.	Mádiga	,,	4,958	2,146	1,939	873	...
		Móchi	,,	1	...	1	...	...
		Total Group 38......	....	4,959	2,146	1,940	873	...
	38 (a). Village Watchmen, &c...	Holaya	,,	23,130	9,921	7,949	5,260	...
		Total Class D......	....	**65,981**	**26,599**	**25,510**	**13,872**	...
E.—Vagrant, Minor Artisans and Performers.	41. Earth Workers and stone dressers ...	Vaddar	Hindu.	2,383	842	1,065	476	...
	43. Mat makers and cane splitters. ...	Méda	,,	287	110	111	66	...
	44. Hunters, Fowlers, &c.	Béda	,,	2,532	1,070	979	483	...
	45. Miscellaneous and disreputable livers.	Budabudiké	,,	20	8	9	3	...
		S'illekyáta	,,	...	...	...	...	...
		Sudagádusidda	,,	...	...	...	...	...
		Gondaliga	,,	...	...	...	...	...
		Jógi	,,	237	79	115	43	...
		Karma	,,	...	...	...	...	...
		Mondaru	,,	10	2	7	1	...
		Pandáram	,,	...	...	...	...	...
		S'ániyár	,,	...	...	...	...	...
		Total Group 45......	....	267	89	131	47	...
	46. Tumblers and Acrobats...	Dombar	,,	114	54	39	21	...
		Ráchévár—Jatti	,,	...	...	...	...	...
		Total Group 46	....	114	54	39	21	...
	47. Jugglers, snake charmers & animal exhibitrs ...	Gárdiga	,,	...	...	...	...	...
		Total Class E......	....	**5,583**	**2,165**	**2,325**	**1,093**	...

TABLE E.—(*Continued.*)

District.

Females.

0 to 9					10 to 14.				
Total.	Single.	Married.	Widowed.	Civil condition not stated.	Total.	Single.	Married.	Widowed.	Civil condition not stated.
561	531	30	...	...	197	140	57	...	...
451	395	56	...	...	228	148	80	...	...
1,038	1,006	32	...	...	697	656	41	...	...
...	...	...	...	...	...	...	...	...	...
1,038	*1,006*	*32*	...	...	*697*	*656*	*41*	...	...
7,052	7,010	43	...	...	2,026	1,965	61	...	...
18,928	**18,459**	**469**	...	...	**6,558**	**5,511**	**1,040**	**7**	...
628	614	14	...	...	211	157	54	...	...
62	62	...	...	...	37	29	8	...	...
609	680	10	...	...	239	203	36	...	...
4	4	...	...	...	2	2	...	...	...
...	...	...	...	...	...	...	...	...	...
...	...	...	...	...	...	...	...	...	...
...	...	...	...	...	...	...	...	...	...
52	52	...	...	...	23	17	6	...	...
...	...	...	...	...	...	...	...	...	...
1	1	...	...	...	1	1	...	...	...
...	...	...	...	...	...	...	...	...	...
...	...	...	...	...	...	...	...	...	...
57	*57*	...	...	...	*20*	*20*	*6*	...	...
31	31	...	...	...	15	15	...	...	...
...	...	...	...	...	...	...	...	...	...
31	*31*	...	...	...	*15*	*15*	...	...	...
...	...	...	...	...	...	...	...	...	...
1,477	**1,453**	**24**	...	...	**528**	**424**	**104**	...	...

Kadur

Class.	Group.	Caste, &c. and sub-division.	Religion.	15 to 30 Total.	Single.	Married.	Widowed.	Civil condition not stated.
D.—Artisan & Village menial.—(Concluded.)	35. Fishermen, Boatmen and Palakhi bearers.	Bosta	Hindu.	863	136	576	150	...
	36. Distillers & Toddy drawers ...	I'diga	,,	687	68	505	114	...
	38. Leather Workers.	Mådiga	,,	2,211	421	1,392	398	...
		Móchi	,,	1	...	1	...	...
		Total Group 38	....	*2, 12*	*421*	*1.393*	*398*	...
	38 (a). Village Watchmen, &c ...	Holaya	,,	9,775	631	7,030	2,114	...
		Total Class D	....	**27,237**	**2,184**	**20,023**	**5,030**	...
E.—Vagrant, Minor Artisans and Performers.	41. Earth Workers and stone dressers ...	Vaddar	Hindu.	1,038	68	820	150	...
	43. Mat makers and cane splitters ...	Méda	,,	124	17	83	24	...
	44. Hunters, Fowlers, &c.	Béda	,,	1,071	148	789	134	...
	45. Miscellaneous and disreputable livers.	Budabudikè	,,	9	2	7	...	...
		S'illékyáta	,,	...	...	...	...	...
		Sudagádusidda	,,	...	...	...	...	...
		Gondaliga	,,	...	...	...	...	...
		Jógi	,,	108	10	85	13	...
		Karma	,,	...	...	...	...	...
		Mondáru	,,	6	...	6	...	...
		Pandáram	,,	...	...	...	...	...
		S'ániyár	,,	...	...	...	...	...
		Total Group 45	....	*1[illegible]*	*12*	*98*	*13*	...
	46. Tumblers and Acrobats...	Dombar	,,	41	7	27	7	...
		Ráchévár.—Jatti	,,	...	...	...	...	...
		Total Group 46	....	*41*	*7*	*27*	*7*	...
	47. Jugglers, snake charmers & animal exhibitors ...	Gárdiga	,,	...	...	...	...	...
		Total Class E	....	**2,397**	**252**	**1,817**	**328**	...

TABLE E.—(*Continued.*)

District.

Females.

40 and over.					Age not stated.				
Total.	Single.	Married.	Widowed.	Civil condition not stated.	Total.	Single.	Married.	Widowed.	Civil condition not stated.
418	22	135	261	...	...	...	...	...	...
349	1	155	192	...	...	...	...	...	...
1,012	63	474	475	...	...	...	...	...	...
...	...	...	...	...	...	...	...	...	...
1,012	*63*	*474*	*475*	...	-	...	...	...	...
4,271	314	816	3,141	...	6	1	...	5	...
13,252	**444**	**3,978**	**8,830**	...	**6**	**1**	...	**5**	...
506	3	177	326	...	...	...	...	...	...
64	2	20	42	...	...	...	...	...	...
523	30	144	349	...	...	...	...	...	...
5	...	2	3	...	...	...	...	...	...
...	...	...	...	...	...	...	...	...	...
...	...	...	...	...	...	...	...	...	...
...	...	...	...	...	...	...	...	...	...
54	...	24	30	...	...	...	...	...	...
...	...	...	...	...	...	...	...	...	...
2	...	1	1	...	...	...	...	...	...
...	...	...	...	...	...	...	...	...	...
...	...	...	...	...	...	...	...	...	...
61	...	*27*	*34*	...	...	...	...	...	...
27	1	12	14	...	...	...	...	...	...
...	...	...	...	...	...	...	...	...	...
27	*1*	*12*	*14*	...	...	...	...	...	...
...	...	...	...	...	...	...	...	...	...
1,181	**36**	**380**	**765**	...	...	...	...	...	...

Chitaldurg

Class.	Group.	Caste, &c. and sub-division.	Religion.	All Ages. Total.	Single.	Married.	Widowed.	Civil condition not stated.
D.—Artisan & Village menial.—(Concluded.)	35. Fishermen, Boatmen and Palakhi bearers ...	Besta	Hindu.	2,479	1,425	927	127	...
	36. Distillers & Toddy drawers ...	I'diga	,,	2,133	1,117	875	141	...
	38. Leather workers.	Mádiga	,,	18,479	10,379	7,281	819	...
		Móchi	,,	22	11	8	3	...
		Total Group 38	....	*18,501*	*10,390*	*7,289*	*822*	...
	38 (a). Village watchmen, &c...	Holaya	,,	4,207	2,346	1,453	403	...
		Total Class D	....	**74,826**	**41,060**	**29,560**	**4,206**	...
E.—Vagrant, Minor Artisans and Performers.	41. Earth workers and stone dressers ...	Vaddar	Hindu.	8,544	4,836	3,273	435	...
	43. Mat makers and cane splitters...	Móda	,,	188	90	83	15	...
	44. Hunters, Fowlers, &c.	Bóda	,,	35,893	20,264	14,154	1,475	...
	45. Miscellaneous and disreputable livers.	Budabudiké	,,	27	12	11	4	...
		S'iḷḷékyáta	,,	7	4	3	...	...
		Sudagádusidda	,,	...	...	...	...	...
		Gondaliga	,,	...	...	...	...	...
		Jógi	,,	542	295	214	33	...
		Karma	,,	...	...	...	...	...
		Mondaru	,,	...	...	...	...	...
		Pandáram	,,	...	...	...	...	...
		S'áṇiyár	,,	...	...	...	...	...
		Total Group 45	....	*576*	*311*	*228*	*37*	...
	46. Tumblers and Acrobats	Dombar	,,	54	26	24	4	...
		Ráchévár.—Jatti	,,	8	4	3	1	...
		Total Group 46 ...	....	*62*	*30*	*27*	*5*	...
	67. Jugglers, snake charmers & animal exhibitors ...	Gárdiga	,,	...	...	...	...	...
		Total Class E	....	**45,263**	**25,531**	**17,765**	**1,967**	...

TABLE E.—(Continued.)

District.

Mmales.

0 to 9					10 to 14				
Total.	Single.	Married.	Widowed.	Civil condition not stated.	Total.	Single.	Married.	Widowed.	Civil condition not stated.
906	905	1	...	...	229	226	3	...	...
616	616	...	...	...	166	162	4	...	...
6,310	6,309	1	...	...	1,313	1,278	34	1	...
5	5	...	..	...	3	2	1	...	...
6,315	*6,314*	*1*	...	...	*1,316*	*1,280*	*35*	*1*	...
1,389	1,389	...	...	...	357	354	3	...	...
24,413	**24,405**	**8**	...	...	**6,323**	**6,126**	**196**	**1**	.
2,838	2,838	...	...	...	764	747	17	...	...
44	44	...	...	...	23	23	...	...	...
10,495	10,484	11	...	..	1,852	1,835	13	4	...
6	6	...	...	...	4	3	1	...	...
2	2	...	...	...	1	1	...	...	...
...	...	...	...	...	...	...	...	...	...
...	...	...	...	...	...	...	...	...	...
199	199	...	...	...	34	34	...	...	...
...	...	...	...	...	...	...	...	...	...
...	...	...	...	...	...	...	...	...	...
...	...	...	...	...	...	...	...	...	...
...	...	...	...	...	...	...	...	...	...
207	*207*	...	...	...	*39*	*38*	*1*	...	...
20	20	...	...	...	3	3	...	...	...
8	8	...	...	...	1	1	...	...	...
23	*23*	...	...	...	*4*	*4*	...	...	...
...	...	...	...	...	...	...	...	...	...
13,607	**13,596**	**11**	...	...	**2,682**	**2,647**	**31**	**4**	...

Class.	Group.	Caste, &c. and sub-division.	Religion.	15 to 39. Total.	Single.	Married.	Widowed.	Civil condition not stated.
D.—Artisan & Village menial.—(*Concluded.*)	35. Fishermen, Boatmen and Palakhi bearers ...	Besta	Hindu.	922	274	608	40	...
	36. Distillers & Toddy drawers ...	I'diga	,,	938	300	588	50	...
	38. Leather workers	Mádiga	,,	7,156	2,543	4,350	263	...
		Móchi	,,	10	4	5	1	...
		Total Group 38......	....	*7,166*	*2,547*	*4,355*	*264*	...
	38 (a). Village watchmen, &c...	Holaya	,,	1,637	552	941	144	...
		Total Class D......	....	**29,395**	**9,776**	**18,344**	**1,275**	...
E.—Vagrant, Minor Artisans and Performers.	41. Earth workers and stone dressers ...	Vaddar	Hindu.	3,212	1,226	1,877	109	...
	43. Mat makers and cane splitters...	Méda	,,	80	19	56	5	...
	44. Hunters, Fowlers, &c.	Béda	,,	15,813	7,564	8,165	84	...
	45. Miscellaneous and disreputable livers.	Budabudiké	,,	11	3	7	1	...
		S'illékyáta	,,	3	1	2	...	...
		Sudagádusidda	,,	...	...	...	...	...
		Gondaliga	,,	...	...	...	...	...
		Jógi	,,	209	59	142	8	...
		Karma	,,	...	...	...	...	...
		Mondáru	,,	...	...	...	...	...
		Pandáram	,,	...	...	...	...	...
		S'ániyár	,,	...	...	...	...	...
		Total Group 45......	....	*223*	*63*	*151*	*9*	...
	46. Tumblers and Acrobats.	Domba	,,	21	3	18	...	...
		Ráchévár—Jatti	,,	3	...	3	...	...
		Total Group 46......	....	*24*	*3*	*21*	...	...
	47. Jugglers, snake charmers & animal exhibitors ...	Gárdiga	,,	...	...	...	...	...
		Total Class E......	....	**19,352**	**8,875**	**10,270**	**207**	...

TABLE E.—*(Continued.)*

District.

Males.

40 and over.					Age not stated.				
Total.	Single.	Married.	Widowed.	Civil condition not stated.	Total.	Single.	Married.	Widowed.	Civil condition not stated.
437	20	330	87	...		...	...	...	...
413	39	283	91	...	...	...	...	...	...
3,700	249	2,896	555	...	...	...	...	...	...
4	...	2	2	...	...	...	...	...	...
3,704	*249*	*2,898*	*557*	...	...	...	...	...	...
824	51	508	264	...	...	...	...	...	...
14,695	**753**	**11,012**	**2,930**	...	...	...	...	...	...
1,730	25	1,379	326	...	...	...	...	...	...
41	4	27	10	...	...	...	...	...	...
7,733	381	5,965	1,387	...	...	...	...	...	...
6	...	3	3	...	...	...	...	...	...
1	...	1	...	...	...	...	...	...	...
...	...	...	...	...	...	...	...	...	...
...	...	...	...	...	...	...	...	...	...
100	3	72	25	...	...	...	...	...	...
...	...	...	...	...	...	...	...	...	...
...	...	...	...	...	...	...	...	...	...
...	...	...	...	...	...	...	...	...	...
...	...	...	...	...	...	...	...	...	...
107	*3*	*76*	*28*	...	...	...	...	...	...
10	...	6	4	...	...	...	...	...	...
1	...	...	1	...	...	...	...	...	...
11	...	6	5	...	...	...	...	...	...
...	...	...	...	...	...	...	...	...	...
9,622	**413**	**7,453**	**1,756**	...	...	...	...	...	...

Chitaldurg

Class.	Group.	Caste, &c. and sub-division.	Religion.	All Ages. Total.	Single.	Married.	Widowed.	Civil condition not stated.
D.—Artisan & Village menial—(Concluded.)	35. Fishermen, Boatmen and Palakhi bearers.	Besta	Hindu.	2,380	1,080	970	330	...
	36. Distillers & Toddy drawers ...	I'diga	"	2,146	876	928	342	...
	38. Leather workers...	Mádiga	"	18,607	8,678	7,069	2,860	...
		Móchi	"	34	18	8	8	...
		Total Group 38 ...	... ...	18,641	8,696	7,077	2,868	...
	38 (a). Village watchmen, &c...	Holaya	"	4,281	2,093	1,510	678	...
		Total Class D ...	... ...	**73,886**	**32,120**	**29,726**	**12,040**	...
E.—Vagrant, Minor Artisans and Performers.	41. Earth workers and stone dressers ...	Vaddar	Hindu.	8,384	3,691	3,413	1,280	...
	44. Mat makers and cane splitters...	Méda	"	185	94	79	12	...
	44. Hunters, Fowlers, &c.	Béda	"	35,714	14,295	14,766	6,653	...
	45. Miscellaneous and disreputable livers.	Budabudiké	"	23	11	10	2	...
		S'illékyata	"	7	1	5	1	...
		Sudagádusidda	"	...	...	...	...	...
		Gondaligu	"	...	...	...	...	...
		Jógi	"	505	176	244	85	...
		Karma	"	...	...	...	...	...
		Mondaru	"	...	...	...	...	...
		Bandáram	"	...	...	...	...	...
		S'ániyár	"	...	...	...	...	...
		Total Group 45 ...	... ...	534	188	259	87	...
	46. Tumblers and Acrobats ...	Dombar	"	60	23	26	11	...
		Dáchévár,—Jatti ...	"	8	3	3	2	...
		Total Group 46 ...	... ...	68	26	29	13	...
	47. Jugglers, snake charmers & animal exhibitors ...	Gárdiga	"	...	...	...	...	...
		Total Class E ...	... ...	**44,885**	**18,294**	**18,546**	**8,045**	...

TABLE E.—(*Continued.*)

District.

Females.

0 to 9					10 to 14				
Total.	Single.	Married.	Widowed.	Civil condition not stated.	Total.	Single.	Married.	Widowed.	Civil condition not stated.
748	745	3	...	...	302	285	17	...	...
606	600	6	...	...	199	160	39	...	...
6,853	6,781	72	...	...	1,070	768	298	4	...
14	14	...	...	...	4	4	...	...	...
6,867	*6,795*	*72*	...	...	*1,074*	*772*	*298*	*4*	...
1,479	1,479	...	...	...	627	590	97	...	...
24,807	**24,678**	**129**	...	...	**5,986**	**4,664**	**1,307**	**15**	...
2,851	2,844	7	...	...	744	665	79	...	...
54	54	...	...	...	18	18	...	...	...
11,468	11,324	144	...	...	2,610	1,648	933	29	...
9	9	...	...	...	2	2	...	...	...
1	1	...	...	...	...	...	...	...	...
...	...	...	...	...	...	...	...	...	...
...	...	...	...	...	...	...	...	...	...
141	141	...	...	...	30	28	2	...	...
...	...	...	...	...	...	...	...	...	...
...	...	...	...	...	...	...	...	...	...
...	...	...	...	...	...	...	...	...	...
...	...	...	...	...	...	...	...	...	...
151	*151*	...	...	...	*32*	*30*	*2*	...	...
15	15	...	...	...	7	6	1	...	...
3	3	...	...	...	...	...	...	...	...
18	*18*	...	...	...	*7*	*6*	*1*	...	...
...	...	...	...	...	...	...	...	...	...
14,542	**14,391**	**151**	...	...	**3,411**	**2,367**	**1,015**	**29**	...

Class.	Group.	Caste, &c. and sub-division.	Religion.	15 to 39. Total.	Single.	Married.	Widowed.	Civil condition not stated.
D.—Artisan & Village menial.—(Concluded.)	35. Fishermen, Boatmen and Palakhi bearers.	Besta	Hindu.	905	41	776	88	...
	36. Distillers & Toddy drawers ...	I'diga	,,	909	115	670	124	...
	38. Leather workers.	Mádiga	,,	8,247	875	6,421	951	...
		Móchi	,,	8	...	6	2	...
		Total Group 38......	....	8,255	875	6,427	953	...
	38 (a). Village watchmen, &c ...	Holaya	,,	1,287	83	978	226	...
		Total Class D......	....	29,333	2,424	23,131	3,778	...
E.—Vagrant, Minor Artisans and Performers.	41. Earth workers and stone dressers ...	Vaddar	Hindu.	3,208	159	2,656	393	...
	43. Mat makers and cane splitters...	Méda	,,	73	22	47	4	...
	44. Hunters, Fowlers, &c.	Béda	,,	15,310	928	12,182	2,200	...
	45. Miscellaneous and disreputable livers.	Budabudiké	,,	9	...	9	...	...
		S'iḷḷékyata	,,	4	—	4	...	...
		Sudágádusidda	,,	...	...	...	...	...
		Gondaliga	,,	...	...	...	...	...
		Jógi	,,	218	7	187	24	...
		Karma	,,	...	...	...	...	...
		Mondaru	,,	...	...	...	...	...
		Pandáram	,,	...	...	...	...	...
		S'áṇiyár	,,	...	...	...	...	...
		Total Group 45......	....	231	7	200	24	...
	46. Tumblers and Acrobats	Dombar	,,	24	2	19	3	...
		Ráchévár—Jatti	,,	3	...	3	...	...
		Total Group 46......	....	27	2	22	3	...
	47. Jugglers, snake charmers & animal exhibitors ...	Gárdiga	,,	...	...	...	...	...
		Total Class E......	....	18,849	1,118	15,107	2,624	...

TABLE E.—(*Continued.*)

District.

Females.

40 and over.					Age not stated.				
Total.	Single.	Married.	Widowed.	Civil condition not stated.	Total.	Single.	Married.	Widowed.	Civil condition not stated.
425	9	174	242	...	...	...	...	...	...
432	1	213	218	...	...	...	...	...	...
2,437	254	278	1,905	...	...	...	...	...	...
8	...	2	6	...	...	...	...	...	...
2,445	254	280	1,911	...	...	...	...	...	...
891	4	435	452	...	...	...	...	...	...
13,760	**354**	**5,159**	**8,247**	...	...	...	...	...	...
1,581	23	671	887	...	...	...	...	...	...
40	...	32	8	...	...	...	...	...	...
6,326	395	1,507	4,424	...	...	...	...	...	...
2	...	1	1	...	...	...	...	...	...
2	...	1	1	...	...	...	...	...	...
...	...	...	...	...	...	...	...	...	...
...	...	...	...	...	...	...	...	...	...
116	...	55	61	...	...	...	...	...	...
...	...	...	...	...	...	...	...	...	...
...	...	...	...	...	...	...	...	...	...
...	...	...	...	...	...	...	...	...	...
...	...	...	...	...	...	...	...	...	...
120	...	*57*	*63*	...	...	...	...	...	...
14	...	6	8	...	...	...	...	...	...
2	...	...	2	...	...	...	...	...	...
16	...	*6*	*10*	...	...	...	...	...	...
...	...	...	...	...	...	...	...	...	...
8,083	**418**	**2,273**	**5,392**	...			...	...	...

Class.	Group.	Caste, &c. and sub-division.	Religion.	All Ages. Total.	Single.	Married.	Widowed.	Civil condition not stated.
D.—Artisan & Village menial.—(Concluded.)	35. Fishermen, boatmen and Palakhi bearers.	Besta	Hindu.	115	56	53	6	...
	36. Distillers & Toddy drawers ...	Idiga	,,	8	5	3	...	...
	38. Leather workers.	Madiga	,,	1,449	740	662	46	1
		Móchi	,,	53	15	36	2	...
		Total Group 38	... ...	*1,502*	*755*	*698*	*48*	*1*
	38 (a). Village watchmen, &c....	Holaya	,,	8,811	5,092	3,415	304	...
		Total Class D	... ...	**14,599**	**8,033**	**6,011**	**554**	**1**
E.—Vagrant, Minor Artisans and Performers.	41. Earth workers and stone dressers ...	Vaddar	Hindu.	375	179	181	15	...
	43. Mat makers and cane splitters...	Méda	,,	17	3	13	1	...
	44. Hunters, Fowlers, &c.	Beda	,,	121	60	56	5	...
	45. Miscellaneous and disreputable livers.	Buḍabuḍiké	,,	...	...	...	...	...
		S'iḷḷékyáta	,,	...	...	...	...	...
		Sudugáḍusidda	,,	...	...	...	...	...
		Gondaliga ...	,,	...	...	...	...	...
		Jógi	,,	1	...	...	1	...
		Karma	,,	3	2	1	...	...
		Mondaru	,,	...	...	...	...	...
		Panḍáram	,,	6	3	...	...	...
		S'ániyár	,,	1	1	...	...	...
		Total Group 45	... ...	*11*	*6*	*4*	*1*	...
	46. Tumblers, and Acrobats...	Dombar	,,	...	...	...	...	...
		Kíláchévár,—Jatti	,,	1	...	...	1	...
		Total Group 46	... ...	*1*	...	...	*1*	...
	47. Jugglers, snake charmers & animal exhibitors ...	Sárḍiga	,,	...	...	...	...	...
		Total Class E	... ...	**525**	**248**	**254**	**23**	...

TABLE E.—*(Continued.)*

Station, Bangalore.

Males.

0 to 9					10 to 14				
Total.	Single.	Married.	Widowed.	Civil condition not stated.	Total.	Single.	Married.	Widowed.	Civil condition not stated.
30	30	...	...	...	5	5	...	...	...
2	2	...	...	...	...	...	...	...	...
476	476	...	...	...	113	110	3	...	...
8	8	...	...	...	3	3	...	...	...
484	*484*	...	...	...	*116*	*113*	*3*	...	...
2,709	2,705	1	3	...	892	888	2	2	...
4,404	**1,397**	**3**	**4**	...	**4,400**	**1,378**	**20**	**2**	...
118	118	...	...	...	28	28	...	...	...
...	...	...	...	...	2	...	2	...	...
31	31	...	...	...	10	10	...	...	...
...	...	...	...	...	...	...	...	...	...
...	...	...	...	...	...	...	...	...	...
...	...	...	...	...	...	...	...	...	...
...	...	...	...	...	...	...	...	...	...
...	...	...	...	...	...	...	...	...	...
2	2	...	...	...	...	...	...	...	...
...	...	...	...	...	...	...	...	...	...
2	2	...	...	...	...	...	...	...	...
1	1	...	...	...	...	...	...	...	...
5	*5*	...	...	...	...	...	...	...	...
...	...	...	...	...	...	...	...	...	...
...	...	...	...	...	...	...	...	...	...
...	...	...	...	...	...	...	...	...	...
...	...	...	...	...	...	...	...	...	...
152	**152**	...	...	...	**40**	**38**	**2**	...	...

Class.	Group.	Caste, &c., and sub-division.	Religion.	15 to 39 Total.	Single.	Married.	Widowed.	Civil condition not stated.
D.—Artisan & Village menial.—(Concluded.)	35. Fishermen, Boatmen and Palakhi bearers.	Besta	Hindu.	52	21	29	2	...
	36. Distillers & Toddy drawers ...	I'diga	,,	4	3	1	...	...
	38. Leather workers.	Mádiga	,,	494	149	337	7	1
		Móchi	,,	22	4	17	1	...
		Total Group 38......	....	*516*	*153*	*354*	*8*	*1*
	38 (a). Village watchmen, &c...	Holaya	,,	3,310	1,450	1,811	49	...
		Total Class D......	....	**5,537**	**2,181**	**3,242**	**113**	**1**
E.—Vagrant, Minor Artisans and Performers.	41. Earth workers and stone dressers ...	Vaddar	Hindu.	127	33	90	4	...
	43. Mat makers and cane splitters...	Méda	,,	5	...	5	...	...
	44. Hunters, Fowlers, &c.	Béda	,,	46	17	30	1	...
	45. Miscellaneous and disreputable livers.	Budabudiké	,,	...	...	...	...	...
		S'illékyáta	,,	...	...	...	...	...
		Sudagádusiddá	,,	...	...	...	...	...
		Gondaliga	,,	...	...	...	...	...
		Jógi	,,	...	...	...	...	...
		Karma	,,	1	...	1	...	...
		Mondaru	,,	...	...	...	...	...
		Pandáram	,,	4	1	3	...	...
		S'ániyár	,,	...	...	...	...	...
		Total Group 45......	....	*5*	*1*	*4*	...	...
	46. Tumblers, and Acrobats.	Dombar	,,	...	...	...	...	...
		Rácbévár—Jatti	,,	...	...	...	...	...
		Total Group 46......	....	...	...	...	...	...
	47. Jugglers, snake charmers & animal exhibitors ...	Gárdiga	,,	...	...	...	...	...
		Total Class E......	....	**185**	**51**	**129**	**5**	...

TABLE E.—(*Continued.*)

Station, Bangalore.

Males.

40 and over					Age not stated.				
Total.	Single.	Married.	Widowed.	Civil condition not stated.	Total.	Single.	Married.	Widowed.	Civil condition not stated.
28	...	24	4	...	...	...		...	...
2	...	2	...	...	...	...	...	...	...
366	5	322	39	...	...	...	...	...	...
20	...	19	1	...	...	...	...	...	...
386	*5*	*341*	*40*	...	...	...	...	...	...
1,900	49	1,601	250	...	...	...	...	...	...
3,258	**77**	**2,746**	**435**	...	...	...	...	...	...
102	...	91	11	...	...	...	...	...	...
10	3	6	1	...	...	...	...	...	...
32	2	26	4	...	...	...	...	...	...
...	...	...	...	...	...	...	...	...	...
...	...	...	...	...	...	...	...	...	...
...	...	...	...	...	...	...	...	...	...
...	...	...	...	...	...	...	...	...	...
1	...	...	1	...	...	...	...	...	...
...	...	...	...	...	...	...	...	...	...
...	...	...	...	...	...	...	...	...	...
...	...	...	...	...	...	...	...	...	...
...	...	...	...	...	...	...	...	...	...
1	...	...	*1*	...	...	...	...	...	...
...	...	...	...	...	...	...	...	...	...
1	...	...	1	...	...	...	...	...	...
1	...	...	*1*	...	...	...	...	...	...
...	...	...	...	...	...	...	...	...	...
146	**5**	**123**	**18**	...	...	...	...	...	...

Class.	Group.	Caste, &c. and sub-division.	Religion.	All Ages.— Total.	Single.	Married.	Widowed.	Civil condition not stated.
D.—Artisan & Village-menial.—(Concluded.)	35. Fishermen, Boatmen and Palakhi bearers.	Besta	Hindu.	124	43	60	21	...
	36. Distillers & Toddy drawers ...	I'diga	"	13	6	5	1	...
	38. Leather workers.	Mádiga	"	1,435	559	676	200	...
		Móchi	"	51	17	26	8	...
		Total Group 38......	....	1,486	576	702	208	...
	38 (a). Village watchmen, &c...	Holaya	"	9,673	4,059	3,791	1,823	...
		Total Class D......	....	15,351	6,149	6,448	2,754	...
E.—Vagrant, Minor Artisans and Performers.	41. Earth workers and stone dressers ...	Vaddar	Hindu.	430	146	213	71	...
	43. Mat makers and cane splitters...	Méda	"	14	1	10	3	...
	44. Hunters, Fowlers, &c.	Béda	"	138	43	68	27	...
	45. Miscellaneous and disreputable livers.	Búdabudiké	"	...	...	...	...	...
		S'illékyáta	"	...	...	...	...	...
		Sudagádusidda	"	...	...	...	...	...
		Gondaliga	"	...	...	...	...	...
		Jógi	"	1	...	...	1	...
		Karma	"	4	2	2	...	...
		Mondaru	"	...	...	...	...	...
		Pandáram	"	9	4	3	2	...
		S'ániyár	"	2	1	1	...	...
		Total Group 45......	....	16	7	6	3	...
	46. Tumblers and Acrobats.	Dombar	"	...	...	...	...	...
		Ráchévár.—Jatti ...	"	...	...	...	...	...
		Total Group 46......	....	...	...	...	...	...
	47. Jugglers, snake charmers & animal exhibiters ...	Gárdiga	"	...	...	...	...	...
		Total Class E......	....	598	197	297	104	...

TABLE E.—(*Continued.*)

Station, Bangalore.

Females.

0 to 9					10 to 14				
Total.	Single.	Married.	Widowed.	Civil condition not stated.	Total.	Single.	Married.	Widowed.	Civil condition not stated.
33	33	...	...	...	17	8	9	...	...
5	5	...	...	...	1	1	...	...	...
469	462	7	...	...	101	65	36	...	...
13	13	...	...	...	9	4	5	...	...
482	*475*	*7*	...	...	*110*	*69*	*41*	...	...
2,713	2,706	7	...	...	855	731	122	2	...
4,400	**4,361**	**38**	**1**	...	**1,262**	**1,045**	**312**	**5**	...
114	113	1	...	...	40	28	11	1	...
...	...	...	...	...	...	...	...	...	...
32	32	...	...	...	11	6	5	...	...
...	...	...	...	...	...	...	...	...	...
...	...	...	...	...	...	...	...	...	...
...	...	...	...	...	...	...	...	...	...
...	...	...	...	...	...	...	...	...	...
...	...	...	...	...	...	...	...	...	...
2	2	...	...	...	...	...	...	...	...
...	...	...	...	...	...	...	...	...	...
4	4	...	...	...	...	...	...	...	...
1	1	...	...	...	...	...	...	...	...
7	*7*	...	...	...	...	...	...	...	...
...	...	...	...	...	...	...	...	...	...
...	...	...	...	...	...	...	...	...	...
...	...	...	...	...	...	...	...	...	...
...	...	...	...	...	...	...	...	...	...
153	**152**	**1**	...	...	**51**	**34**	**16**	**1**	...

The Civil and Military

Class	Group	Caste, &c. and sub-division	Religion	15 to 39. Total	Single	Married	Widowed	Civil condition not stated
D.—Artisan & Village menial.—(Concluded.)	35. Fishermen, Boatmen and Palakhi bearers ...	Besta	Hindu.	43	2	36	5	...
	36. Distillers & Toddy drawers ...	I'diga	,,	4	...	4	...	...
	38. Leather workers.	Mádiga	,,	580	28	502	50	...
		Móchi	,,	18	...	15	3	...
		Total Group 38	....	598	28	517	53	...
	38 (a). Village watchmen, &c...	Holaya	,,	3,998	594	2,910	484	...
		Total Class D......	....	**6,251**	**705**	**4,845**	**701**	...
E.—Vagrant, Minor Artisans and Performers.	41. Earth workers and stone dressers ...	Vaddar	Hindu.	181	5	155	21	...
	43. Mat makers and cane splitters...	Méda	,,	9	1	7	1	...
	44. Hunters, Fowlers, &c,	Béda	,,	56	3	49	4	...
	45. Miscellaneous and disreputable livers.	Budabudiké	,,	...	...	...	...	...
		S'illékyáta	,,	...	...	...	...	...
		Sudagádusidda	,,	...	...	...	...	...
		Gondaliga	,,	...	...	...	...	...
		Jogi	,,	...	...	...	...	...
		Karma	,,	2	...	2	...	...
		Mondaru	,,	...	...	...	...	...
		Pandáram	,,	4	...	3	1	...
		S'ániyár... ...	,,	1	...	1	...	...
		Total Group 45......	....	7	...	6	1	...
	46. Tumblers and Acrobats.	Dombar	,,	...	...	...	...	...
		Ráchévár.—Jatti	,,	...	...	...	...	...
		Total Gorup 46......	....	...	...	...	...	...
	47. Jugglers, snake charmers & animal exhibitors ...	Gárudiga	,,	...	...	...	...	...
		Total Class E......	....	**253**	**9**	**217**	**27**	...

TABLE E.—(*Continued.*)

Station, Bangalore.

Females.

40 and over.					Age not stated.				
Total.	Single.	Married.	Widowed.	Civil condition not stated.	Total.	Single.	Married.	Widowed.	Civil condition not stated.
31	...	15	16	...	...	...	...	...	...
2	...	1	1	...	...	...	...	...	...
285	4	131	150	...	...	...	...	...	...
11	...	6	5	...	...	...	...	...	...
296	*4*	*137*	*155*	...	...	...	...	...	...
2,116	25	732	1,356	...	1	...	...	1	...
3,337	**38**	**1,253**	**2,046**	...	**1**	...	...	**1**	...
95	...	46	49	...	...	...	...	...	...
5	...	3	2	...	...	...	...	...	...
39	2	14	23	...	...	...	...	...	...
...	...	...	...	...	...	...	...	...	...
...	...	...	...	...	...	...	...	...	...
...	...	...	...	...	...	...	...	...	...
...	...	...	...	...	...	...	...	...	...
1	...	...	1	...	...	...	...	...	...
...	...	...	...	...	...	...	...	...	...
...	...	...	...	...	...	...	...	...	...
1	...	...	1	...	...	...	...	...	...
...	...	...	...	...	...	...	...	...	...
2	...	...	2	...	...	...	...	...	...
...	...	...	...	...	...	...	...	...	...
...	...	...	...	...	...	...	...	...	...
...	...	...	...	...	...	...	...	...	...
...	...	...	...	...	...	...	...	...	...
141	**2**	**63**	**76**	...	...	...	...	...	...

Total including the Civil and

Class	Group	Caste, &c., and sub-division	Religion	All Ages				
					Single.	Married.	Widowed.	Civil condition not stated.
D.—Artisan & Village menial.—(Concluded.)	35. Fishermen, Boatmen and Pálkhi bearers	Besta	Hindu.	49,735	26,312	21,168	2,255	...
	36. Distillers & Toddy drawers ..	Idiga	,,	20,540	10,718	8,666	1,156	...
	38. Leather workers.	Mádiga	,,	119,906	63,331	50,188	6,386	1
		Móchi	,,	361	170	170	21	...
		Total Group 38......	....	*120,267*	*63,501*	*50,358*	*6,407*	*1*
	38 (a). Village watchmen, &c ..	Holaya	,,	259,999	141,524	107,733	10,742	...
		Total Class D...	....	941,571	500,438	394,243	46,889	1
E.—Vagrant, Minor Artisans and Performers.	41. Earth workers and stone dressers ...	Vaddar	Hindu.	54,821	29,518	22,517	2,786	...
	43. Mat makers and cane splitters...	Méda	,,	2,335	1,239	959	137	...
	44. Hunters, Fowlers, &c.	Béda	,,	108,852	60,657	42,104	6,091	...
	45. Miscellaneous and disreputable livers.	Budabudiké	,,	553	283	228	42	...
		S'illékyáta	,,	55	24	30	1	...
		Sudagádusidda	,,	25	14	10	1	...
		Gondaliga	,,	16	7	8	...	1
		Jógi	,,	4,780	2,503	1,969	308	...
		Karma	,,	3	2	1	...	...
		Mondaru	,,	127	67	48	12	...
		Pandáram	,,	6	3	3	...	...
		S'ániyár	,,	1	1	...	...	...
		Total Group 45......	....	*5,566*	*2,904*	*2,297*	*364*	*1*
	46. Tumblers and Acrobats	Dombar	,,	1,217	641	494	82	...
		Ráchévár.—Jatti	,,	593	309	248	36	...
		Total Group 46......	....	*1,810*	*950*	*742*	*118*	...
	47. Juggler snake-charmers & animal exhibitors ...	Gárdiga	,,	411	198	190	23	...
		Total Class E....	....	173,795	95,466	809	9,520	1

TABLE E.—(*Continued.*)

Military Station, Bangalore.

Males.

0 to 9. Total.	Single.	Married.	Widowed.	Civil condition not stated.	10 to 14. Total.	Single.	Married.	Widowed.	Civil condition not stated.
13,629	13,626	3	...	...	4,587	4,507	80	...	...
5,198	5,198	...	...	...	2,019	1,990	29	...	...
33,841	33,786	52	3	...	11,476	11,250	220	6	...
90	90	...	...	...	28	27	1	...	...
33,931	*33,876*	*52*	*3*	...	*11,504*	*11,277*	*221*	*6*	...
74,278	74,213	61	4	...	23,60	23,201	400	5	...
264,371	**264,165**	**198**	**8**	...	**90,223**	**88,476**	**1,731**	**16**	...
16,537	16,537	...	...	...	4,715	4,655	60	...	...
670	670	...	..	...	222	219	3	...	...
31,235	31,220	15	...	...	7,703	7,628	71	4	...
145	145	...	...	...	61	60	1	...	...
10	10	...	...	...	8	7	1	...	...
9	9	...	...	...	1	1	...	...	...
5	5	...	...	...	1	1	...	...	...
1,456	1,456	...	...	...	422	420	2	...	...
2	2	...	...	...	...	...	...	...	...
34	34	...	...	...	9	9	...	...	...
2	2	...	...	...	...	...	...	...	...
1	1	...	...	...	...	...	...	...	...
1,664	*1,664*	...	...	...	*502*	*498*	*4*	...	...
365	364	1	...	...	93	93	...	...	...
161	161	...	...	...	62	61	1	...	...
526	*525*	*1*	...	...	*155*	*154*	*1*	...	...
104	104	...	...	...	50	50	...	...	...
50,736	**50,720**	**16**	...	...	**13,347**	**13,204**	**139**	**4**	...

Total including the Civil and

Class.	Group.	Caste, &c., and sub-division.	Religion.	15 to 39 Total.	15 to 39 Single.	15 to 39 Married.	15 to 39 Widowed.	15 to 39 Civil condition not stated.
D.—Artisan & Village menial.—(Concluded.)	35. Fishermen, Boatmen and Pálkhi bearers	Besta	Hindu.	21,405	7,883	12,945	577	...
	36. Distillers & Toddy drawers ...	I'diga	,,	9,270	3,339	5,595	336	...
	38. Leather workers ...	Mádiga	,,	48,243	16,524	30,093	1,625	1
		Móchi	,,	159	53	102	4	...
		Total Group 38 ...	....	*48,402*	*16,577*	*[illegible]95*	*1,629*	*1*
	38 (a). Village watchmen, &c. ...	Holaya	,,	105,248	42,116	60,963	2,169	...
		Total Class D ...	....	**385,320**	**140,360**	**233,816**	**11,113**	**1**
E.—Vagrant, Minor Artisans and Performers.	41. Earth workers and stone dressers ...	Vaddar	Hindu.	21,463	8,011	12,760	692	...
	43. Mat makers and cane splitters ...	Méda	,,	975	330	620	25	...
	44. Hunters, Fowlers, &c.	Béda	,,	46,290	20,418	24,706	1,166	...
	45. Miscellaneous and disreputable livers.	Budabudiké	,,	203	72	125	6	...
		S'illékyáta	,,	27	7	20	...	...
		Sudagádusidda	,,	10	3	7	...	...
		Gondaliga	,,	8	1	7	...	...
		Jógi	,,	1,859	588	1,215	56	...
		Karma	,,	1	...	1	...	...
		Mondaru	,,	55	22	29	4	...
		Pandáram	,,	4	1	3	...	...
		S'ápiyár	,,	...	...	...	...	...
		Total Group 45 ...	....	*2,167*	*694*	*1,407*	*66*	...
	46. Tumblers and Acrobats ...	Dombar	,,	459	165	278	16	...
		Ráchévár.—Jatti ...	,,	242	82	156	4	...
		Total Group 46 ...	....	*701*	*247*	*434*	*20*	...
	47. Jugglers, snake charmers & animal exhibitors ...	Gárdiga	,,	161	35	118	8	...
		Total Class E ...	....	**71,757**	**29,735**	**40,045**	**1,977**	...

TABLE E.—(*Continued.*)

Military Station, Bangalore.

Males.

40 and over.					Age not stated.				
Total.	Single.	Married.	Widowed.	Civil condition not stated.	Total.	Single.	Married.	Widowed.	Civil condition not stated.
10,114	296	8,140	1,678	...				...	...
4,053	191	3,012	820	...	...	...	...	...	...
26,335	1,762	19,822	4,751	...	11	9	1	1	...
84	...	67	17	...	...	...	...	...	...
26,41[illegible]	*1,762*	*19,889*	*4,768*	...	*11*	*9*	*1*	*1*	—
56,806	1,961	46,303	8,542	...	61	33	6	22	...
201,585	**7,395**	**158,461**	**35,729**	...	**72**	**42**	**7**	**23**	...
12,106	315	9,697	2,094	...	...	...	...	...	...
468	20	336	112	...	...	...	...	...	...
23,624	1,391	17,312	4,921	...	...	...	...	...	...
144	6	102	36	...	...	...	...	...	...
10	...	9	1	...	...	...	...	...	...
5	1	3	1	...	...	...	...	...	...
2	...	1	1	...	...	...	...	...	...
1,043	39	752	252	...	...	...	...	...	...
...	...	...	...	...		...	...	...	...
29	2	19	8	...	...	...	...	...	...
...	...	...	...	...	...	...	...	...	...
...	...	...	...	...	...	...	...	...	...
1,233	*48*	*886*	*299*	...	...	...	...	...	...
300	19	215	66	...	...	...	...	...	...
128	5	91	32	...	...	...	...	...	...
428	*24*	*306*	*98*	...	...	...	...	...	...
96	9	72	15	...	...	...	...	...	...
37,955	**1,807**	**28,609**	**7,539**	...	...	...	...	...	...

Total including the Civil and

Class.	Group.	Caste, &c., and sub-division.	Religion.	All Ages. Total.	Single.	Married.	Widowed.	Civil condition not stated.
D.—Artisan & Village menial.—(Concluded.)	35. Fishermen, Boatmen and Pálkhi bearers.	Besta	Hindu.	50,162	18,561	21,958	9,643	...
	36. Distillers & Toddy drawers ...	I'diga	,,	19,397	7,132	8,513	3,752	...
	38. Leather workers ...	Mádiga	,,	119,669	48,754	47,224	23,691	...
		Móchi	,,	385	143	170	72	...
		Total Group 38......	....	120,054	48,897	47,394	23,763	...
	38 (a) Village Watchmen, &c...	Holaya	,,	260,494	101,946	104,787	53,761	...
		Total Class D......	....	**936,370**	**352,078**	**393,874**	**190,418**	...
E.—Vagrant, Minor Artisans and Performers.	41. Earth workers and stone dressers ...	Vaddar	Hindu.	52,382	20,479	23,125	8,778	...
	43. Mat makers and cane splitters ...	Méda	,,	1,926	700	870	356	...
	44. Hunters, Fowlers, &c.	Béda	,,	108,276	42,314	43,664	22,298	...
	45. Miscellaneous and disreputable livers.	Budubudiké	,,	539	227	243	69	...
		S'illékyáta	,,	38	12	23	3	...
		Sudagádusidda	,,	21	7	11	3	...
		Gondaliga	,,	13	5	6	2	...
		Jógi	,,	4,630	1,693	2,113	824	...
		Karma	,,	4	2	2	...	...
		Mondaru	,,	62	16	32	14	...
		Pandárum	,,	9	4	3	2	...
		S'ániyár	,,	2	1	1	...	...
		Total Group 45......	....	5,318	1,967	2,434	917	...
	46. Tumblers and Acrobats ...	Dombar	,,	1,283	616	515	152	...
		Ráchévár—Jatti	,,	610	228	271	111	...
		Total Group 46......	....	1,893	844	786	263	...
	47. Jugglers, snake charmers & animal exhibitors ...	Gárdiga	,,	465	167	221	77	...
		Total Class E......	....	**170,260**	**66,471**	**71,100**	**32,689**	...

TABLE E.—(Continued.)

Military Station, Bangalore.

Females.

0 to 9					10 to 14				
Total	Single.	Married.	Widowed.	Civil condition not stated.	Total.	Single.	Married.	Widowed.	Civil condition not stated.
13,904	13,542	361	1	...	4,654	3,249	1,402	3	...
5,338	5,224	114	...	...	1,753	1,263	483	7	...
37,221	36,469	746	6	...	9,360	6,785	2,513	62	...
113	112	1	...	...	43	27	16	...	...
37,334	*36,581*	*747*	*6*	...	*9,403*	*6,812*	*2,529*	*62*	...
79,559	78,005	1,537	17	...	21,630	15,504	6,007	119	...
273,560	**268,679**	**4,838**	**43**	...	**79,825**	**56,077**	**23,447**	**301**	...
16,353	16,268	85	...	...	3,994	3,106	887	1	...
476	474	2	...	...	196	158	38	...	...
32,286	31,842	441	3	...	7,874	5,450	2,384	40	...
173	172	1	...	...	45	39	6	...	...
9	9	...	...	...	3	3	...	...	...
5	5	...	...	...	2	2	...	...	...
5	5	...	...	...	...	...	...	...	...
1,292	1,282	10	...	...	357	297	60	...	...
2	2	...	...	...	...	...	...	...	...
13	13	...	...	...	3	3	...	...	...
4	4	...	...	...	...	...	...	...	...
1	1	...	...	...	...	...	...	...	...
1,504	*1,493*	*11*	...	...	*410*	*344*	*66*	...	...
359	356	3	...	...	110	101	9	...	...
185	185	...	...	...	44	36	8	...	...
544	*541*	*3*	...	...	*154*	*137*	*17*	...	...
106	106	...	...	...	46	42	4	...	...
51,271	**50,726**	**542**	**3**	...	**12,674**	**9,237**	**3,396**	**41**	...

Total including the Civil and

Class.	Group.	Caste, &c., and sub-division.	Religion.	15 to 39 Total.	15 to 39 Single.	15 to 39 Married.	15 to 39 Widowed.	15 to 39 Civil condition not stated.
D.—Artisan & Village menial.—(Concluded.)	35. Fishermen, Boatmen and Pálkhi bearers.	Besta	Hindu.	20,436	1,577	16,226	2,633	...
	36. Distillers & Toddy drawers	I'digu	,,	8,272	591	6,518	1,163	...
	38. Leather workers.	Mádiga	,,	49,102	4,541	36,752	7,809	...
		Móchi	,,	142	4	117	21	...
		Total Group 38	....	*49,244*	*4,545*	*36,869*	*7,830*	...
	38 (a). Village watchmen, &c.	Holaya	,,	103,347	6,842	81,256	15,249	...
		Total Class D	....	**376,299**	**23,793**	**296,922**	**55,584**	...
E.—Vagrant, Minor Artisans and Performers.	41. Earth workers and stone dressers	Vaddar	Hindu.	21,036	1,025	17,834	2,177	...
	43. Mat makers and cane splitters	Méda	,,	812	66	653	93	...
	44. Hunters, Fowlers, &c.	Béda	,,	46,319	3,882	34,959	7,478	...
	45. Miscellaneous and disreputable livers.	Budabudiké	,,	203	13	174	16	...
		S'illékyáta	,,	18	...	18	...	...
		Sudagádusidda	,,	10	...	9	1	...
		Gondaliga	,,	5	...	5	...	...
		Jógi	,,	1,912	108	1,590	214	...
		Karma	,,	2	...	2	...	...
		Mondaru	,,	31	...	26	5	...
		Pandáram	,,	4	...	3	1	...
		S'ániyár	,,	1	...	1	...	...
		Total Group 45	....	*2,186*	*121*	*1,828*	*237*	...
	46. Tumblers, and Acrobats.	Dombar	,,	520	119	378	33	...
		Ráchévár—Jutti	,,	229	6	193	31	...
		Total Group 46	....	*758*	*125*	*570*	*63*	...
	47. Jugglers, snake charmers & animal exhibitors	Gárdiga	,,	223	17	179	27	...
		Total Class E	....	**71,334**	**5,236**	**56,023**	**10,075**	...

TABLE E.—(Continued)

Military Station, Bangalore.

Females.

40 and over.					Age not stated.				
Total.	Single.	Married.	Widowed.	Civil condition not stated.	Total.	Single.	Married.	Widowed.	Civil condition not stated.
11,168	193	3,969	7,006	...	...	...	...	...	...
4,034	54	1,393	2,583	...	...	...	...	...	...
23,971	948	7,211	15,812	...	15	11	2	2	...
87	...	36	51	...	...	...	...	...	...
24,058	*948*	*7,247*	*15,863*	...	*15*	*11*	*2*	*2*	...
55,903	1,567	15,972	38,363	...	56	28	15	13	...
206,615	**3,490**	**68,650**	**134,475**	...	**71**	**39**	**17**	**15**	...
10,999	80	4,319	6,600	...	...	...	...	...	...
442	2	177	263	...	...	...	...	...	...
2,1797	1,140	5,880	14,777	...	...	...	...	...	...
118	3	62	53	...	...	...	...	...	...
8	...	5	3	...	...	...	...	...	...
4	...	2	3	...	...	...	...	...	...
3	...	1	2	...	...	...	...	...	...
1,069	6	453	610	...	...	...	...	...	...
...	...	...	...	...	...	...	...	...	...
15	...	6	9	...	...	...	...	...	...
1	...	...	1	...	...	...	...	...	...
...	...	...	...	...	...	...	...	...	...
1,218	*9*	*529*	*680*	...	...	...	...	...	...
285	40	125	120	...	...	...	...	...	...
152	1	71	80	...	...	...	...	...	...
437	*41*	*196*	*200*	...	...	...	...	...	...
88		38	50	...	...	...	...	...	...
34,981	**1,272**	**11,139**	**22,570**	...	...	...		...	...

Class.	Group.	Caste, &c. and sub-division.	Religion.	All Ages. Total.	Single.	Married.	Widowed.	Civil condition not stated.
F.—Races and Nationalities.	48. Asiatic Races of reputed Foreign origin.	Arab	Musalmán.	17	6	8	3	...
		Belúchi	,,	...	...	...	...	...
		Dáyurê	,,	1,081	662	404	15	...
		Hanifi	,,	584	298	235	51	...
		Khádri	,,	2	2	...	...	...
		Kandhári...	,,	...	...	...	...	...
		Mogal	,,	4,527	2,488	1,819	220	...
		Musalmán	,,	433	237	174	22	...
		Paṭhán	,,	18,127	10,073	7,358	696	...
		Shékh	,,	71,193	40,286	29,086	1,819	2
		Sayad	,,	18,616	10,318	7,561	737	...
		Sharif	,,	431	221	177	33	...
		Armenian...	Christian.	2	1	1	...	...
		Burmese	,,	...	...	...	...	...
		Chinese	,,	...	...	...	...	...
		Jews	Jews.	9	5	3	1	...
		Jews	Christian.	...	...	...	...	...
		Jews.—Israelites	,,	...	...	...	...	...
		Pársi	Pársi.	15	8	7	...	...
		Singháli	Buddhist.	...	...	...	...	...
		Total Group 48......	....	*115,037*	*64,605*	*46,833*	*3,597*	3
	49. Mixed Asiatic Races.	Labbé	Musalmán.	1,859	1,012	783	64	...
		Jám	,,	...	...	...	...	...
		Mápḷé	,,	130	62	60	8	...
		Méman	,,	...	...	...	...	...
		Pindári	,,	1,064	600	422	42	...
		Pinjári	,,	1,199	617	498	84	...
		Total Group 49...	....	*4,252*	*2,291*	*1,763*	*198*	...
	50. Non-Asiatic races.	European...	Christian.	771	413	333	25	...
		Australasian		...	...	...	...	...
		Total Group 50......	....	*771*	*413*	*333*	*25*	...
	51. Eurasian ...	Eurasian	,,	706	379	300	27	...
	52. Christian converts...	Native Christian	,,	9,712	5,347	4,032	333	...
		Total Class F......	....	**130,478**	**73,035**	**53,261**	**4,180**	**2**
		Caste not stated......	....	*1,875*	*924*	*807*	*144*	...
		Grand Total......	....	**2,433,262**	**1,309,992**	**1,007,714**	**115,492**	**64**

TABLE E.—(*Continued.*)

cial.

Males.

0 to 9					10 to 14				
Total.	Single.	Married.	Widowed.	Civil condition not stated.	Total.	Single.	Married.	Widowed.	Civil condition not stated.
2	2	...	...	...	1	1	...	...	...
...	...	...	...	...	...	...	...	...	...
379	379	...	...	...	117	116	1	...	...
125	125	...	...	...	61	61	...	...	...
...	...	...	...	...	...	...	...	...	...
...	...	...	...	...	...	...	...	...	...
1,362	1,362	...	...	...	448	439	9	...	...
123	123	...	...	...	52	51	1	...	...
5,294	5,290	[illegible]	...	...	1,880	1,848	32	...	...
19,784	19,747	36	1	...	6,829	6,749	76	3	1
5,369	5,352	17	...	...	1,835	1,780	55	...	...
164	164	...	...	...	34	34	...	...	...
...	...	...	...	...	...	...	...	...	...
...	...	...	...	...	...	...	...	...	...
...	...	...	...	...	...	...	...	...	...
3	3	...	...	...	2	2	...	...	...
...	...	...	...	...	...	...	...	...	...
...	...	...	...	...	...	...	...	...	...
2	2	...	...	...	1	1	...	...	...
...	...	...	...	...	...	...	...	...	...
32,607	*32,540*	*57*	*1*	...	*11,260*	*11,082*	*174*	*3*	*1*
388	388	...	...	...	172	167	5	...	...
...	...	...	...	...	...	...	...	...	...
...	...	...	...	...	6	6	...	...	...
...	...	...	...	...	...	...	...	...	...
332	332	...	...	...	136	136	...	...	...
323	323	...	...	...	114	112	2	...	...
1,043	*1,043*	...	...	...	*428*	*421*	*7*	...	...
144	144	...	...	...	46	46	...	...	...
...	...	...	...	...	...	...	...	...	...
144	*144*	...	...	...	*46*	*46*	...	...	...
140	149	...	...	...	45	45	...	...	...
2,376	2,374	2	...	...	895	879	16	...	...
36,319	**36,259**	**59**	**1**	...	**12,674**	**12,473**	**197**	**3**	**1**
433	*433*	...	...	...	*163*	*168*	...	...	...
668,778	**668,050**	**705**	**23**	...	**223,620**	**218,146**	**5,393**	**77**	**4**

Class.	Group.	Caste, &c. and sub-division.	Religion.	15 to 39 Total.	Single.	Married.	Widowed.	Civil condition not stated.
F.—Races and Nationalities.	48. Asiatic Races of reputed Foreign origin.	Arab	Musalmán.	10	3	7	...	...
		Belúchi	,,	...	...	...	...	...
		Dáyaré	,,	346	163	182	1	...
		Hanifi	,,	276	107	158	11	...
		Khádri	,,	1	1	...	...	...
		Kandhári	,,	...	...	...	...	...
		Mogal	,,	1,798	653	1,094	51	...
		Musalmán	,,	160	59	97	4	...
		Paṭhán	,,	6,924	2,703	4,063	158	...
		Shékh	,,	28,633	13,208	5,008	416	1
		Sayad	,,	7,629	3,039	4,429	161	...
		Sharíf	,,	150	16	126	8	...
		Armenian	Christian.	2	1	1	...	...
		Burmese	,,	...	...	...	...	...
		Chinese	,,	...	...	...	...	...
		Jews	Jews.	3	...	2	1	...
		Jews	Christian.	...	...	...	...	...
		Jews.—Israelites ...	,,	...	...	...	...	...
		Pársi	Pársi.	9	5	4	...	...
		Singhálí	Buddhist.	...	...	...	...	...
		Total Group 48......	... ...	*45,911*	*19,958*	*25,171*	*811*	*1*
	49. Mixed Asiatic Races.	Labbé	Musalmán.	935	420	502	13	...
		Jám	,,	...	...	...	...	...
		Mápló	,,	103	54	48	1	...
		Méman	,,	...	...	...	...	...
		Pindári	,,	406	131	268	7	...
		Pinjári	,,	495	165	310	20	...
		Total Group 49......	....	*1,959*	*770*	*1,128*	*41*	...
	50. Non-Asiatic races.	European	Christian.	448	208	237	3	...
		Australasian	,,	...	...	...	...	...
		Total Group 50......	....	*448*	*208*	*237*	*3*	...
	51. Eurasian ...	Eurasian	,,	369	180	184	5	...
	52. Christian converts ...	Native Christian ...	,,	4,559	1,977	2,464	118	...
		Total Class F......	....	**53,256**	**23,093**	**29,184**	**978**	**1**
		Caste not stated......	....	*865*	*297*	*533*	*36*	...
		Grand Total......	....	**1,008,987**	**404,147**	**579,206**	**25,622**	**12**

TABLE E.—(Continued.)

cial.

Males.

40 and over.					Age not stated.				
Total.	Single.	Married.	Widowed.	Civil condition not stated.	Total.	Single.	Married.	Widowed.	Civil condition not stated.
4	...	1	3	...	...	...	...	...	...
...	...	...	...	...	...	...	...	...	...
239	4	221	14	...	...	...	...	...	...
122	5	77	40	...	...	...	...	...	...
1	1	...	...	...	...	...	...	...	...
...	...	...	...	...	...	...	...	...	...
919	34	716	169	...	...	...	...	...	...
98	4	76	18	...	...	...	...	...	...
4,029	232	3,259	538	...	...	...	...	...	...
15,936	573	13,964	1,399	...	11	9	2	...	...
3,783	147	3,060	576	...	...	...	...	...	...
83	7	51	25	...	...	...	...	...	...
...	...	...	...	...	...	...	...	...	...
...	...	...	...	...	...	...	...	...	...
...	...	...	...	...	...	...	...	...	...
1	...	1	...	...	...	...	...	...	...
...	...	...	...	...	...	...	...	...	...
...	...	...	...	...	...	...	...	...	...
3	...	3	...	...	...	...	...	...	...
...	...	...	...	...	...	...	...	...	...
25,218	*1,007*	*21,429*	*2,782*	...	*11*	*9*	*2*	...	...
364	37	276	51	...	...	...	...	...	...
...	...	...	...	...	...	...	...	...	...
21	2	12	7	...	...	...	...	...	...
...	...	...	...	...	...	...	...	...	...
190	1	154	35	...	...	...	...	...	...
267	17	186	64	...	...	...	...	...	...
842	*57*	*628*	*157*	...	...	...	...	...	...
133	15	96	22	...	...	...	...	...	...
...	...	...	...	...	...	...	...	...	...
133	*15*	*96*	*22*	...	...	...	...	...	...
143	5	116	22	...	...	...	...	...	...
1,880	116	1,550	214	...	2	1	...	1	...
28,216	**1,200**	**23,819**	**3,197**	...	**13**	**10**	**2**	**1**	...
409	*26*	*275*	*108*	...	...	...	...	...	...
531,433	**19,424**	**422,305**	**89,698**	**6**	**444**	**225**	**105**	**72**	**42**

Class.	Group.	Caste, &c., and sub-division.	Religion.	All Ages. Total.	Single.	Married.	Widowed.	Civil condition not stated.
F.—Races and Nationalities.	48. Asiatic Races of reputed Foreign origin.	Arab	Musalman.	11	4	6	1	...
		Belúchi	,,	...	...	...	...	...
		Dáyaró	,,	1,419	540	540	339	...
		Haniti	,,	481	157	229	95	...
		Khâdri	,,	...	...	...	...	...
		Kandhári	,,	...	...	...	...	...
		Mogal	,,	4,245	1,617	1,890	738	...
		Musalmán	,,	355	131	165	59	...
		Pat'hán	,,	16,929	6,524	7,344	3,061	...
		Shékh	,,	66,053	26,407	27,537	12,102	7
		Sayad	,,	16,958	6,385	7,567	3,006	...
		Sharif	,,	421	180	182	59	...
		Armenian	Christian.	1	...	1	...	...
		Burmese	,,	...	...	...	...	...
		Chinese	,,	...	...	...	...	...
		Jews	Jews.	11	6	5	...	...
		Jews	Christian.	...	...	...	...	...
		Jews.—Israelites ...	,,	...	...	...	...	...
		Pársi	Pársi	14	8	4	2	...
		Singhâli	Buddhist.	...	...	...	...	...
		Total Group 48......	....	106,808	41,959	45,470	19,462	7
	49. Mixed Asiatic Races.	Labbé	Musalmán.	961	351	449	161	...
		Jáin	,,	...	...	...	...	...
		Máplé	,,	20	7	10	3	...
		Méman	,,	...	...	...	...	...
		Pindári	,,	984	374	429	181	...
		Pinjári	,,	981	384	464	133	...
		Total Group 49......	... .	2,946	1,116	1,352	478	...
	50. Non-Asiatic Races.	European...	Christian.	475	213	213	49	...
		Australasian	,,	...	...	...	...	...
		Total Group 50......	....	475	213	313	49	...
	51. Eurasian ...	Eurasian	,,	570	253	267	56	...
	52. Christian converts.	Native Christian ...	,,	7,990	3,533	3,223	1,234	...
		Total Class F.....	....	**118,885**	**47,074**	**50,525**	**21,279**	**7**
		Caste not stated......	....	1,599	534	732	333	...
		Grand Total.....	....	**2,410,261**	**874,620**	**1,024,464**	**511,095**	**82**

TABLE E.—(*Continued.*)

cial.

Females.

0 to 9					10 to 14				
Total.	Single.	Married.	Widowed.	Civil condition not stated.	Total.	Single.	Married.	Widowed.	Civil condition not stated.
3	3	...	...	...	1	1	...	...	...
...	...	...	...	...	...	...	...	...	...
398	398	...	...	...	111	98	13	...	...
113	113	...	...	...	46	32	14	...	...
...	...	...	...	...	...	...	...	...	...
...	...	...	...	...	...	...	...	...	...
1,235	1,229	6	...	...	371	294	77	...	...
110	110	...	...	...	25	17	8	...	...
5,048	4,976	72	...	...	1,409	1,139	270	...	...
21,349	21,126	214	9	...	5,571	3,939	1,594	38	...
4,886	4,831	53	2	...	1,479	1,233	243	3	...
105	105	...	...	...	66	65	1	...	...
...	...	...	...	...	...	...	...	...	...
...	...	...	...	...	...	...	...	...	...
...	...	...	...	...	...	...	...	...	...
5	5	...	...	...	...	...	...	...	...
...	...	...	...	...	...	...	...	...	...
...	...	...	...	...	...	...	...	...	...
2	2	...	...	...	2	2	...	...	...
...	...	...	...	...	...	...	...	...	...
33,254	*32,898*	*345*	*11*	...	*9,081*	*6,820*	*2,220*	*41*	...
244	244	...	...	...	94	74	20	...	...
...	...	...	...	...	...	...	...	...	...
3	3	...	...	...	3	2	1	...	...
...	...	...	...	...	...	...	...	...	...
304	304	...	...	...	69	53	16	...	...
277	277	...	...	...	90	82	8	...	...
828	*828*	...	...	...	*256*	*211*	*45*	...	...
121	121	...	...	...	37	37	...	...	...
...	...	...	...	...	...	...	...	...	...
121	*121*	...	...	...	*37*	*37*	...	...	...
149	149	...	...	...	38	38	...	...	...
2,387	2,377	10	...	...	786	659	126	1	...
36,729	**36,373**	**355**	**11**	...	**10,198**	**7,765**	**2,391**	**42**	...
352	*349*	*3*	...	...	*153*	*136*	*17*	...	...
696,142	**677,812**	**18,072**	**257**	**1**	**200,547**	**132,701**	**66,225**	**1,619**	**2**

Provin

Class.	Group.	Caste, &c. and sub-division.	Religion.	15 to 39. Total.	Single.	Married.	Widowed.	Civil condition not stated.
F.—Races and Nationalities.	48. Asiatic Races of reputed Foreign origin.	Arab	Musalmán.	6	...	6	...	...
		Belúchi	,,	...	...	...	...	...
		Dáyaré	,,	527	44	413	70	...
		Hanifi	,,	205	12	159	34	...
		Khádri	,,	...	...	...	...	...
		Kandhári	,,	...	...	...	...	...
		Mogul	,,	1,655	91	1,383	181	...
		Musalmán	,,	143	4	124	15	...
		Paṭhán	,,	6,619	367	5,552	700	...
		Shékh	,,	25,614	1,163	21,608	2,842	1
		Sayad	,,	6,492	292	5,550	650	...
		Sharif	,,	187	10	158	19	...
		Armenian	Christian.	1	...	1	...	...
		Burmese	,,	...	...	...	...	...
		Chinese	,,	...	...	...	...	...
		Jews	Jews.	5	1	4	...	...
		Jews	Christian.	...	...	...	...	...
		Jews.—Israelites	,,	...	...	...	...	...
		Pársi	Pársi.	7	4	3	...	...
		Singháli	Buddhist.	...	...	...	...	...
		Total Group 48......	....	*41,461*	*1,988*	*34,961*	*4,511*	*1*
	49. Mixed Asiatic Races.	Labbé	Musalmán.	397	33	323	41	...
		Jám	,,	...	...	...	...	...
		Máplé	,,	8	2	6	...	...
		Méman	,,	...	...	...	...	...
		Pindári	,,	357	17	289	51	...
		Pinjári	,,	411	24	356	31	...
		Total Group 49......	....	*1,173*	*76*	*974*	*123*	...
	50. Non-Asiatic races.	European...	Christian.	247	52	175	20	...
		Australasian	,,	...	...	...	...	...
		Total Group 50......	....	*247*	*52*	*175*	*20*	...
	51. Eurasian ...	Eurasian	,,	290	64	208	18	...
	52. Christian converts ...	Native Christian	,,	3,405	458	2,574	373	...
		Total Class F......	....	**46,576**	**2,638**	**38,892**	**5,045**	**1**
		Caste not stated......	....	*661*	*40*	*547*	*74*	...
		Grand Total......	....	**982,880**	**55,256**	**777,614**	**150,005**	**5**

TABLE E.—(*Continued.*)

cial.

Females.

40 and over.					Age not stated.				
Total.	Single.	Married.	Widowed.	Civil condition not stated.	Total.	Single.	Married.	Widowed.	Civil condition not stated.
1	...	...	1	...	...	...	...	...	...
...	...	...	...	...	...	...	...	...	...
383	...	114	269	...	...	...	...	...	...
117	...	56	61	...	...	...	...	...	...
...	...	...	...	...	...	...	...	...	...
...	...	...	...	...	...	...	...	...	...
984	3	424	557	...	...	...	...	...	...
77	...	33	44	...	...	...	...	...	...
3,853	42	1,450	2,361	...	...	...	...	...	...
13,491	168	4,115	9,208	...	28	11	6	5	6
4,101	29	1,721	2,351	...	...	...	...	...	...
63	...	23	40	...	...	...	...	...	...
...	...	...	...	...	...	...	...	...	...
...	...	...	...	...	...	...	...	...	...
...	...	...	...	...	...	...	...	...	...
1	...	1	...	...	...	...	...	...	...
...	...	...	...	...	...	...	...	...	...
...	...	...	...	...	...	...	...	...	...
3	...	1	2	...	...	...	...	...	...
...	...	...	...	...	...	...	...	...	...
23,074	*242*	*7,938*	*14,894*	...	*28*	*14*	*6*	*5*	*6*
226	...	106	120	...	...	...	...	...	...
...	...	...	...	...	...	...	...	...	...
6	...	3	3	...	...	...	...	...	...
...	...	...	...	...	...	...	...	...	...
254	...	124	130	...	...	...	...	...	...
203	1	100	102	...	...	...	...	...	...
689	*1*	*333*	*355*	...	...	...	...	...	...
70	3	38	29	...	...	...	...	...	...
...	...	...	...	...	...	...	...	...	...
70	*3*	*38*	*29*	...	...	...	...	...	...
99	2	59	38	...	...	...	...	...	...
1,409	39	510	860	...	3	...	3	...	...
25,341	**287**	**8,878**	**16,176**	...	**31**	**11**	**9**	**5**	**6**
433	9	165	259	...	...	...	...	...	...
530,246	**8,654**	**162,450**	**359,129**	**18**	**446**	**197**	**103**	**85**	**61**

Bangalore

Class.	Group.	Caste, &c. and sub-division.	Religion.	All Ages. Total.	Single.	Married.	Widowed.	Civil condition not stated.
F.—Races and Nationalities.	48. Asiatic Races of reputed Foreign origin.	Arab	Musalmán.	10	3	4	3	...
		Belúchi	,,	...	...	...	...	...
		Dáyaré	,,	1,034	634	387	13	...
		Hanifi	,,	...	...	...	...	...
		Khádri	,,	...	...	...	...	...
		Kandhári	,,	...	...	...	...	...
		Mogal	,,	694	377	294	23	...
		Musalmán	,,	305	168	121	16	...
		Paṭ'hán	,,	4,369	2,415	1,792	162	...
		Shékh	,,	12,131	6,845	5,070	214	2
		Sayad	,,	4,307	2,368	1,748	191	..
		Sharif	,,	9	4	4	1	...
		Armenian	Christian.	2	1	1	...	...
		Burmese	,,	...	...	...	...	...
		Chinese	,,	...	...	...	...	...
		Jews	Jews.	...	...	...	...	...
		Jews	Christian.	...	...	...	...	...
		Jews.—Israelites	,,	...	...	...	...	...
		Pársi	Pársi.	3	2	1	...	...
		Singháli	Buddhist.	...	...	...	...	...
		Total Group 48......	....	*22,884*	*12,817*	*9,422*	*623*	*2*
	49. Mixed Asiatic Races.	Labbé	Musalmán.	158	82	74	2	...
		Jám	,,	...	...	...	...	...
		Máplé	,,	...	...	...	...	...
		Móman	,,	...	...	...	...	...
		Pindári	,,	82	43	31	8	...
		Pinjári	,,	82	41	31	10	...
		Total Group 49......	....	*322*	*166*	*136*	*20*	...
	50. Non-Asiatic races.	European	Christian.	143	75	64	4	...
		Australasian	,,	...	...	...	...	...
		Total Group 50......	....	*143*	*75*	*64*	*4*	...
	51. Eurasian ...	Eurasian	,,	199	106	88	5	...
	52. Christian converts ...	Native Christian	,,	2,797	1,632	1,067	98	...
		Total Class F......	....	**26,325**	**14,796**	**10,777**	**750**	**2**
		Caste not stated......	....	*208*	*92*	*98*	*18*	...
		Grand Total......	....	**349,297**	**177,755**	**154,346**	**17,175**	**21**

TABLE E.—(Continued.)

District.

Males.

0 to 9					10 to 14				
Total.	Single.	Married.	Widowed.	Civil condition not stated.	Total.	Single.	Married.	Widowed.	Civil condition not stated.
...	...	...	...	...	...	...	...	...	...
...	...	...	...	...	...	...	...	...	...
364	364	...	...	...	113	112	1	...	...
...	...	...	...	...	...	...	...	...	...
...	...	...	...	...	...	...	...	...	...
...	...	...	...	...	...	...	...	...	...
224	224	...	...	...	75	75	...	...	...
82	82	...	...	...	39	38	1	...	...
1,293	1,291	2	...	...	418	414	4	...	...
3,550	3,545	4	1	...	1,218	1,203	13	1	1
1,277	1,277	...	...	...	383	383	...	...	...
3	3	...	...	...	1	1	...	...	...
...	...	...	...	...	...	...	...	...	...
...	...	...	...	...	...	...	...	...	...
...	...	...	...	...	...	...	...	...	...
...	...	...	...	...	...	...	...	...	...
...	...	...	...	...	...	...	...	...	...
...	...	...	...	...	...	...	...	...	...
1	1	...	...	...	...	...	...	...	...
...	...	...	...	...	...	...	...	...	...
6,794	*6,787*	*6*	*1*	...	*2,247*	*2,226*	*19*	*1*	*1*
9	9	...	...	...	15	15	...	...	...
...	...	...	...	...	...	...	...	...	...
...	...	...	...	...	...	...	...	...	...
...	...	...	...	...	...	...	...	...	...
26	26	...	...	...	11	11	...	...	...
15	15	...	...	...	7	7	...	...	...
50	*50*	...	...	...	*33*	*33*	...	...	...
40	40	...	...	...	6	6	...	...	...
...	...	...	...	...	...	...	...	...	...
40	*40*	...	...	...	*6*	*6*	...	...	...
65	65	...	...	...	9	9	...	...	...
813	813	...	...	...	316	312	4	...	...
7,762	**7,755**	**6**	**1**	...	**2,611**	**2,586**	**23**	**1**	**1**
40	*40*	...	...	...	*11*	*11*	...	...	...
96,785	**96,689**	**113**	**3**	...	**29,366**	**28,554**	**793**	**15**	**4**

Bangalore

Class.	Group.	Caste, &c., and sub-division.	Religion.	15 to 39. Total.	Single.	Married.	Widowed.	Civil condition not stated.
F.—Races and Nationalities.	48. Asiatic Races of reputed Foreign origin.	Arab	Musalmán.	7	3	4	...	...
		Belúchi	,,	...	...	...	...	...
		Dáyaré	,,	329	155	173	1	...
		Hanifi	,,	...	...	...	...	...
		Khádri	,,	...	...	...	...	...
		Kandhári	,,	...	...	...	...	...
		Mogal	,,	237	74	162	1	...
		Musalmán	,,	115	45	66	4	...
		Paṭ'hán	,,	1,693	688	974	31	...
		Shékh	,,	4,432	1,964	2,404	63	1
		Sayad	,,	1,687	682	974	31	...
		Sharíf	,,	4	...	4	...	...
		Armenian	Christian.	2	1	1	...	...
		Burmese	,,	...	...	...	...	...
		Chinese	,,	...	...	...	...	...
		Jews	Jews.	...	...	...	...	...
		Jews	Christian.	...	...	...	...	...
		Jews.—Israelites	,,	...	...	...	...	...
		Pársi	Pársi.	2	1	1	...	...
		Singháli	Buddhist.	...	...	...	...	...
		Total Group 48......	....	*8,508*	*3,613*	*4,763*	*131*	*1*
	49. Mixed Asiatic Races.	Labbé	Musalmán.	105	56	49	...	...
		Jám	,,	...	...	...	...	...
		Máplé	,,	...	...	...	...	...
		Mêman	,,	...	...	...	...	...
		Pindári	,,	26	6	19	1	...
		Pinjári	,,	39	17	20	2	...
		Total Group 49......	....	*170*	*79*	*88*	*3*	...
	50. Non-Asiatic races.	European	Christian.	54	26	28	...	...
		Australasian	,,	...	...	...	...	...
		Total Group 50......		*54*	*26*	*28*	...	...
	51. Eurasian ...	Eurasian	,,	71	30	40	1	...
	52. Christian converts ...	Native Christian	,,	1,120	491	608	21	...
		Total Class D......	....	**9,983**	**4,239**	**5,527**	**186**	**1**
		Caste not stated......	....	*110*	*41*	*67*	*2*	...
		Grand Total......	....	**138,419**	**50,036**	**85,049**	**3,322**	**12**

TABLE E.—(*Continued*)

District.

Males.

40 and over.					Age not stated.				
Total.	Single.	Married.	Widowed.	Civil condition not stated.	Total.	Single.	Married.	Widowed.	Civil condition not stated.
3	...	...	3	...	...	...	...	...	...
...	...	...	...	...	...	...	...	...	...
228	3	213	12	...	...	...	...	...	...
...	...	...	...	...	...	...	...	...	...
...	...	...	...	...	...	...	...	...	...
...	...	...	...	...	...	...	...	...	...
158	4	132	22	...	...	...	...	...	...
69	3	54	12	...	...	...	...	...	...
965	22	812	131	...	...	...	...	...	...
2,923	127	2,647	149	...	8	6	2	...	...
960	26	774	160	...	...	...	...	...	...
1	...	...	1	...	...	...	...	...	...
...	...	...	...	...	...	...	...	...	...
...	...	...	...	...	...	...	...	...	...
...	...	...	...	...	...	...	...	...	...
...	...	...	...	...	...	...	...	...	...
...	...	...	...	...	...	...	...	...	...
...	...	...	...	...	...	...	...	...	...
...	...	...	...	...	...	...	...	...	...
...	...	...	...	...	...	...	...	...	...
5,307	*185*	*4,632*	*490*	...	*8*	*6*	*2*	...	...
29	2	25	2	...	...	...	...	...	...
...	...	...	...	...	...	...	...	...	...
...	...	...	...	...	...	...	...	...	...
...	...	...	...	...	...	...	...	...	...
19	...	12	7	...	...	...	...	...	...
21	2	11	8	...	...	...	...	...	...
69	*4*	*48*	*17*	...	...	...	...	...	...
43	3	36	4	...	...	...	...	...	...
...	...	...	...	...	...	...	...	...	...
43	*3*	*36*	*4*	...	...	...	...	...	...
51	2	48	4	...	...	...	...	...	...
518	16	455	77	...	...	...	...	...	...
6,021	**210**	**5,219**	**592**	...	**8**	**6**	**2**	...	...
47	...	*31*	*16*	...	...	...	...	...	...
84,630	**2,447**	**68,381**	**13,797**	**5**	**97**	**49**	**10**	**38**	...

Bangalore

Class.	Group.	Caste, &c. and sub-division.	Religion.	All Ages. Total.	Single.	Married.	Widowed.	Civil condition not stated.
F.—Races and Nationalities.	48. Asiatic Races of reputed Foreign origin.	Arab	Musalmán.	5	2	2	1	...
		Belúchi	,,	...	...	...	...	...
		Dáyaré	,,	1,385	529	525	331	...
		Hanifi	,,	...	...	...	...	...
		Khádri	,,	...	...	...	...	...
		Kandhári	,,	...	...	...	...	...
		Mogal	,,	660	257	295	108	...
		Musalmán	,,	256	95	115	46	...
		Paṭ'hán	,,	4,165	1,655	1,846	664	...
		Shékh	,,	11,491	4,517	5,072	1,901	1
		Sayad	,,	4,001	1,498	1,815	688	...
		Sharif	,,	8	3	5	...	...
		Armenian	Christian.	1	...	1	...	...
		Burmese	,,	...	...	...	...	...
		Chinese	,,	...	...	...	...	...
		Jews	Jews.	...	...	...	...	...
		Jews	Christian.	...	...	...	...	...
		Jews.—Israelites	,,	...	...	...	...	...
		Pársi	Pársi.	2	1	1	...	...
		Singháli	Buddhist.	...	...	...	...	...
		Total Group 48......	....	21,974	8,557	9,677	3,739	1
	49. Mixed Asiatic Races.	Labbé	Musalmán.	43	16	20	7	...
		Jám	,,	...	...	...	...	...
		Máple	,,	...	...	...	...	...
		Méman	,,	...	...	...	...	...
		Pindári	,,	98	36	44	18	...
		Pinjári	,,	43	13	21	8	...
		Total Group 49......	....	183	65	85	33	...
	50. Non-Asiatic races.	European	,,	156	68	77	11	...
		Australasian	,,	...	...	...	...	...
		Total Group 50......	....	156	68	77	11	...
	51. Eurasian ...	Eurasian	,,	202	96	87	19	...
	52. Christian converts ...	Native Christian	,,	2,607	1,105	1,085	417	...
		Total Class F......	....	**25,122**	**9,891**	**11,011**	**4,219**	**1**
		Caste not stated......	....	214	71	99	44	...
		Grand Total......	....	**353,616**	**117,969**	**161,029**	**74,593**	**25**

TABLE E.—(*Continued.*)

District.

Females.

0 to 9					10 to 14.				
Total.	Single.	Married.	Widowed.	Civil condition not stated.	Total.	Single.	Married.	Widowed.	Civil condition not stated.
1	1	...	...	...	1	1	...	...	...
...	...	...	...	...	...	...	...	...	...
392	392	...	...	...	107	95	12	...	...
...	...	...	...	...	...	...	...	...	...
...	...	...	...	...	...	...	...	...	...
...	...	...	1	...	...	...	...	...	...
207	207	...	...	...	52	40	12	...	...
78	78	...	...	...	15	13	2	...	...
1,333	1,323	10	...	...	346	274	72	...	...
3,693	3,677	15		...	932	627	296	9	...
1,200	1,196	4	...	...	306	246	60	...	...
2	2	...	...	...	1	1	...	...	...
...	...	...	...	...	...	...	...	...	...
...	...	...	...	...	...	...	...	...	...
...	...	...	...	...	...	...	...	...	...
...	...	...	...	...	...	...	...	...	...
...	...	...	...	...	...	...	...	...	...
...	...	...	...	...	...	...	...	...	...
1	1	...	...	...	...	...	...	...	...
...	...	...	...	...	...	...	...	...	...
6,907	*6,877*	*29*	*1*	...	*1,760*	*1,297*	*454*	*9*	...
10	10	...	...	...	6	6	...	...	...
...	...	...	...	...	...	...	...	...	...
...	...	...	...	...	...	...	...	...	...
...	...	...	...	...	...	...	...	...	...
25	25	...	...	...	9	8	1	...	...
10	10	...	...	...	2	2	...	...	...
45	*45*	...	...	...	*17*	*16*	*1*	...	...
35	35	...	...	...	7	7	...	...	...
...	...	...	...	...	...	...	...	...	...
35	*35*	...	...	...	*7*	*7*	...	...	...
59	59	...	...	...	10	10	...	...	...
775	775	...	...	...	230	200	30	...	...
7,821	**7,791**	**29**	**1**	...	**2,024**	**1,530**	**485**	**9**	...
52	*52*	...	...	...	*18*	*18*	...	...	...
100,850	**97,886**	**2,928**	**35**	**1**	**25,852**	**15,000**	**10,671**	**179**	**2**

Class.	Group.	Caste, &c. and sub-division.	Religion.	15 to 39: Total.	Single.	Married.	Widowed.	Civil condition not stated.
F.—Races and Nationalities.	48. Asiatic Races of reputed Foreign origin.	Arab	Musalmán.	2	...	2	...	...
		Belúchi	,,	...	...	...	...	...
		Dáyari	,,	513	42	403	68	...
		Hanifi	,,	...	...	...	...	...
		Khádri	,,	...	...	...	...	...
		Kandhári...	,,	...	...	...	...	...
		Mogal	,,	254	10	225	19	...
		Musalmán	,,	105	4	89	12	...
		Pat'han	,,	1,587	58	1,385	144	...
		Shékh	,,	4,430	193	3,852	384	1
		Sayad	,,	1,568	51	1,389	128	...
		Sharif	,,	4	...	4	...	...
		Armenian	Christian.	1	...	1	...	...
		Burmese	,,	...	...	...	...	...
		Chinese	,,	...	...	...	...	...
		Jews	Jews.	...	...	...	...	...
		Jews	Christian.	...	...	...	...	...
		Jews.—Israelites	,,	...	...	...	...	...
		Pársi	Pársi.	1	...	1	...	...
		Singháli	Buddhist.	...	...	...	...	...
		Total Group 48......	....	*8,465*	*358*	*7,351*	*755*	*1*
	49. Mixed Asiatic Races.	Labbé	Musalmán.	17	...	15	2	...
		Jám	,,	...	...	...	...	...
		Máplé	,,	...	...	...	...	...
		Méman	,,	...	...	...	...	...
		Pindári	,,	35	3	30	2	...
		Pinjári	,,	20	1	19	...	...
		Total Group 49......	....	72	*4*	*64*	*4*	...
	50. Non-Asiatic races...	European...	,,	91	23	64	4	...
		Australasian	,,	...	...	...	...	...
		Total Group 50......	....	*91*	*23*	*64*	*4*	...
	51. Eurasian ...	Eurasian	,,	101	26	68	7	...
	52. Christian converts ...	Native Christian ...	,,	1,076	118	845	113	...
		Total Class F......	....	**9,805**	**529**	**8,392**	**883**	**1**
		Caste not stated......	....	*93*	*1*	*78*	*14*	...
		Grand Total......	....	**142,550**	**4,359**	**118,834**	**19,352**	**5**

TABLE E.—*(Continued.)*

District.

Females.

40 and over.					Age not stated.				
Total.	Single.	Married.	Widowed.	Civil condition not stated.	Total.	Single.	Married.	Widowed.	Civil condition not stated.
1	...	...	1	...	...	...	...	...	...
...	...	...	...	...	...	...	...	...	...
373	...	110	263	...	...	...	...	...	...
...	...	...	...	...	...	...	...	...	...
...	...	...	...	...	...	...	...	...	...
...	...	...	...	...	...	...	...	...	...
147	...	58	89	...	...	...	...	...	...
58	...	24	34	...	...	...	...	...	...
899	...	379	520	...	...	...	...	...	...
2,427	16	905	1,506	...	9	4	4	1	...
927	5	362	560	...	...	...	...	...	...
1	...	1	...	...	...	...	...	...	...
...	...	...	...	...	...	...	...	...	...
...	...	...	...	...	...	...	...	...	...
...	...	...	...	...	...	...	...	...	...
...	...	...	...	...	...	...	...	...	...
...	...	...	...	...	...	...	...	...	...
...	...	...	...	...	...	...	...	...	...
...	...	...	...	...	...	...	...	...	...
...	...	...	...	...	...	...	...	...	...
4,833	*21*	*1,839*	*2,973*	...	*9*	*4*	*4*	*1*	...
10	...	5	5	...	...	...	...	...	...
...	...	...	...	...	...	...	...	...	...
...	...	...	...	...	...	...	...	...	...
...	...	...	...	...	...	...	...	...	...
29	...	13	16	...	...	...	...	...	...
10	...	2	8	...	...	...	...	...	...
49	...	*20*	*29*	...	...	...	...	...	...
23	3	13	7	...	...	...	...	...	...
...	...	...	...	...	...	...	...	...	...
23	*3*	*13*	*7*	...	...	...	...	...	...
32	1	19	12	...	...	...	...	...	...
523	12	207	304	...	3	...	3	...	...
5,460	**37**	**2,098**	**3,325**	...	**12**	**4**	**7**	**1**	...
51	...	*21*	*30*	...	...	...	...	...	...
84,286	**688**	**28,565**	**55,020**	**13**	**78**	**36**	**31**	**7**	**4**

Kolar

Class.	Group.	Caste, &c. and sub-division.	Religion.	Total.	Single.	Married.	Widowed.	Civil condition not stated.
		Caste and Religion.		**All Ages.**				
F.—Races and Nationalities.	48. Asiatic Races of reputed Foreign origin.	Arab	Musalmán.	...	...	...	...	...
		Belúchi	,,	...	...	...	...	...
		Dáyaré	,,	...	...	...	...	...
		Hanifi	,,	3	2	1	...	...
		Khádri	,,	...	...	...	...	...
		Kandhári	,,	...	...	...	...	...
		Mogal	,,	661	358	282	21	...
		Musalmán	,,	91	50	39	2	...
		Pat'hán	,,	2,638	1,454	1,103	81	...
		Shékh	,,	9,993	5,446	4,242	305	...
		Sayud	,,	3,500	1,892	1,504	104	...
		Sharif	,,	5	2	2	1	...
		Armenian...	Christian.	...	...	...	...	...
		Burmese	,,	...	...	...	...	...
		Chinese	,,	...	...	...	...	...
		Jews	Jews.	...	...	...	...	...
		Jews	Christian.	...	...	...	...	...
		Jews.—Israelites	,,	...	...	...	...	...
		Pársi	Pársi.	1	...	1	...	...
		Singháli	Buddhist.	...	...	...	...	...
		Total Group 48......	... ...	*16,892*	*9,204*	*7,174*	*514*	...
	49. Mixed Asiatic Races.	Labbé	Musalmán.	181	108	69	4	...
		Jám	,,	...	...	...	...	...
		Máplé	,,	...	...	...	...	...
		Méman	,,	...	...	...	...	...
		Pindári	,,	...	...	...	...	...
		Pinjári	,,	240	132	98	10	...
		Total Gorup 49......	....	*421*	*240*	*167*	*14*	...
	50. Non-Asiatic races.	European	Christian.	264	110	147	7	...
		Australasian	,,	...	...	...	...	...
		Total Group 50	....	*264*	*110*	*147*	*7*	...
	51. Eurasian ...	Eurasian		161	62	92	7	...
	52. Christian converts ...	Native Christian		1,287	662	588	37	...
		Total Class F......	... .	**19,025**	**10,278**	**8,168**	**579**	...
		Caste not stated......	....	*178*	*88*	*67*	*23*	...
		Grand Total......	... .	**297,655**	**153,628**	**126,849**	**17,177**	**1**

TABLE E.—(Continued.)

District.

Males.

0 to 9					10 to 14				
Total.	Single.	Married.	Widowed.	Civil condition not stated.	Total.	Single.	Married.	Widowed.	Civil condition not stated.
...	...	...	...	...	...	...	...	...	...
...	...	...	...	...	...	...	...	...	...
...	...	...	...	...	...	...	...	...	...
1	1	...	...	...	1	1	...	...	...
...	...	...	...	...	...	...	...	...	...
...	...	...	...	...	...	...	...	...	...
217	217	...	...	...	45	45	...	...	...
31	31	...	...	...	7	7	...	...	...
840	840	...	...	...	227	227	...	...	...
2,839	2,823	16	...	...	938	918	20	...	...
1,012	999	13	...	...	326	296	30	...	...
1	1	...	...	...	...	...	...	...	...
...	...	...	...	...	...	...	...	...	...
...	...	...	...	...	...	...	...	...	...
...	...	...	...	...	...	...	...	...	...
...	...	...	...	...	...	...	...	...	...
...	...	...	...	...	...	...	...	...	...
...	...	...	...	...	...	...	...	...	...
...	...	...	...	...	...	...	...	...	...
...	...	...	...	...	...	...	...	...	...
4,944	*4,915*	*29*	...	...	*1,544*	*1,494*	*50*	...	...
21	21	...	...	...	25	20	5	...	...
...	...	...	...	...	...	...	...	...	...
...	...	...	...	...	...	...	...	...	...
...	...	...	...	...	...	...	...	...	...
...	...	...	...	...	...	...	...	...	...
68	68	...	...	...	21	21	...	...	...
89	*89*	...	...	...	*46*	*41*	*5*	...	...
46	46	...	...	...	5	5	...	...	...
...	...	...	...	...	...	...	...	...	...
46	*46*	...	...	...	*5*	*5*	...	...	...
19	19	...	...	...	6	6	...	...	...
345	344	1	...	...	90	90	...	...	...
5,443	**5,413**	**30**	...	...	**1,691**	**1,636**	**55**	...	...
54	*54*	...	...	...	*27*	*27*	...	...	...
78,479	**78,341**	**133**	**5**	...	**22,150**	**21,515**	**627**	**8**	...

Class.	Group.	Caste, &c. and sub-division.	Religion.	15 to 39 Total.	Single.	Married.	Widowed.	Civil condition not stated.
F.—Races and Nationalities.	48. Asiatic races of Reputed Foreign origin.	Arab	Musalmán.	...	...	...	...	...
		Bolúchi	,,	...	...	...	...	...
		Dáyaré	,,	...	...	...	...	...
		Hanifi	,,	1	...	1	...	...
		Khâdri	,,	...	...	...	...	...
		Kandhâri	,,	...	...	...	...	...
		Mogal	,,	259	92	163	4	...
		Muselmán	,,	29	8	21	...	...
		Paṭ'han	,,	1,019	367	636	16	...
		Shékh	,,	3,952	1,587	2,273	92	...
		Sayad	,,	1,447	571	852	24	...
		Shariff	,,	3	1	2	...	...
		Armenian	Christian.	...	...	...	...	...
		Burmese	,,	...	...	...	...	...
		Chinese	,,	...	...	...	...	...
		Jews	Jews.	...	...	...	...	...
		Jews	Christian.	...	...	...	...	...
		Jews.—Israelites	,,	...	...	...	...	...
		Pársi	Pársi.	1	...	1	...	...
		Singhâli	Buddhist.	...	...	...	...	...
		Total Group 48	....	*6,711*	*2,626*	*3,949*	*136*	...
	49. Mixed Asiatic Races.	Labbé	Musalmán.	99	58	41	...	...
		Jám	,,	...	...	...	...	...
		Máplé	,,	...	...	...	...	...
		Móman	,,	...	...	...	...	...
		Pindári	,,	...	...	...	...	...
		Pinjári	,,	102	38	62	2	...
		Total Group 49	....	*201*	*96*	*103*	*2*	...
	50. Non-Asiatic races.	European ...	Christian.	177	59	117	1	...
		Australasian	,,	...	...	...	...	...
		Group 50		*177*	*59*	*117*	*1*	...
	51. Eurasian ...	Eurasian ...	,,	107	37	68	2	...
	52. Christian converts ...	Native Christian		603	217	373	13	...
		Total Class F.	....	**7,799**	**3,035**	**4,610**	**154**	...
		Caste not stated	....	*64*	*7*	*49*	*8*	...
		Grand Total	....	**122,680**	**50,297**	**69,026**	**3,357**	...

TABLE E.—*(Continued.)*

District.

Males:

40 and over.					Age not stated.				
Total.	Single.	Married.	Widowed.	Civil condition not stated.	Total.	Single.	Married.	Widowed.	Civil condition not stated.
...	...	...	...	...	...	...	...	...	...
...	...	...	...	...	...	...	...	...	...
...	...	...	...	...	...	...	...	...	...
...	...	...	...	...	...	...	...	...	...
...	...	...	...	...	...	...	...	...	...
...	...	...	...	...	...	...	...	...	...
140	4	119	17	...	...	...	...	...	...
21	1	18	2	...	...	...	...	...	...
552	20	467	65	...	...	...	...	...	...
2,264	118	1,933	213	...	...	...	...	...	...
715	26	609	80	...	...	...	...	...	...
1	...	...	1	...	...	...	...	...	...
...	...	...	...	...	...	...	...	...	...
...	...	...	...	...	...	...	...	...	...
...	...	...	...	...	...	...	...	...	...
...	...	...	...	...	...	...	...	...	...
...	...	...	...	...	...	...	...	...	...
...	...	...	...	...	...	...	...	...	...
...	...	...	...	...	...	...	...	...	...
...	...	...	...	...	...	...	...	...	...
3,693	*169*	*3,146*	*378*	...	...	...	...	...	...
36	9	23	4	...	...	...	...	...	...
...	...	...	...	...	...	...	...	...	...
...	...	...	...	...	...	...	...	...	...
...	...	...	...	...	...	...	...	...	...
...	...	...	...	...	...	...	...	...	...
49	5	36	8	...	...	...	...	...	...
85	*14*	*59*	*12*	...	...	...	...	...	...
36	...	30	6	...	...	...	...	...	...
...	...	...	...	...	...	...	...	...	...
36	...	*30*	*6*	...	...	...	...	...	...
29	...	24	5	...	...	...	...	...	...
249	11	214	24	...	...	...	...	...	...
4,092	**194**	**3,473**	**425**	...	...	...	...	...	...
33	...	*18*	*15*	...	...	...	...	...	...
74,247	**3,442**	**57,008**	**13,796**	**1**	**90**	**33**	**55**	**11**	...

Kolar

Class.	Group.	Caste, &c. and sub-division.	Religion.	All Ages: Total.	Single.	Married.	Widowed.	Civil condition not stated.
F.—Races and Nationalities.	48. Asiatic Races of reputed Foreign origin.	Arab	Musalmán.	...	...	...	...	...
		Belúchi	,,	...	...	...	...	...
		Dáyaré	,,	...	...	...	...	...
		Hanifii	,,	3	1	1	1	...
		Khádri	,,	...	...	...	...	...
		Kandhári	,,	...	...	...	...	...
		Mogal	,,	603	234	273	96	...
		Musalmán	,,	78	29	39	10	...
		Pat'hán	,,	2,290	863	1,092	344	...
		Shékh	,,	8,838	3,405	3,963	1,470	...
		Saynd	,,	3,041	1,165	1,372	504	...
		Shariff	,,	6	2	3	1	...
		Armenian...	Christian.	...	...	...	...	...
		Burmese	,,	...	...	...	...	...
		Chinese	,,	...	...	...	...	...
		Jews	Jews.	...	...	...	...	...
		Jews	,,	...	...	...	...	...
		Jews.—Israelites	Christian.	...	...	...	...	...
		Pársi	Pársi.	...	...	...	...	...
		Singháli	,,	...	...	...	...	...
		Total Group 48......	....	14,868	5,699	6,743	2,426	...
	49. Mixed Asiatic Races.	Labbé	Musalmán.	18	5	11	2	...
		Jám	,,	...	...	...	...	...
		Máplé	,,	...	...	...	...	...
		Móman	,,	...	...	...	...	...
		Pindári	,,	...	...	...	...	...
		Pinjári	,,	207	65	110	32	...
		Total Group 49......	....	225	70	121	34	...
	50. Non-Asiatic races.	European...	Christian.	38	15	20	3	...
		Australasian	,,	...	...	...	...	...
		Total Group 50......	....	38	15	20	3	...
	51. Eurasian ...	Eurasian	,,	115	47	58	10	...
	52. Christian converts ...	Native Christian	,,	1,134	495	519	117	...
		Total Class F......	....	**16,377**	**6,326**	**7,461**	**2,590**	...
		Caste not stated......	....	153	63	61	29	...
		Grand Total......	....	**293,375**	**95,839**	**128,430**	**69,106**	...

TABLE E.—(*Continued.*)

District.

Females.

0 to 9					10 to 14				
Total.	Single.	Married.	Widowed.	Civil condition not stated.	Total.	Single.	Married.	Widowed.	Civil condition not stated.
...	...	...	...	...	...	...	...	...	...
...	...	...	...	...	...	...	...	...	...
...	...	...	...	...	...	...	...	...	...
1	1	...	...	...	...	...	...	...	...
...	...	...	...	...	...	...	...	...	...
...	...	...	...	...	...	...	...	...	...
202	201	1	...	...	41	26	15	...	...
27	27	...	...	...	7	2	5	...	...
744	724	20	...	...	139	116	23	...	...
2,921	2,857	62	2	...	759	402	349	8	...
994	964	30	...	...	202	160	42	...	...
1	1	...	...	...	2	1	1	...	...
...	...	...	...	...	...	...	...	...	...
...	...	...	...	...	...	...	...	...	...
...	...	...	...	...	...	...	...	...	...
...	...	...	...	...	...	...	...	...	...
...	...	...	...	...	...	...	...	...	...
...	...	...	...	...	...	...	...	...	...
...	...	...	...	...	...	...	...	...	...
...	...	...	...	...	...	...	...	...	...
4,890	*4,775*	*113*	*2*	...	*1,150*	*707*	*435*	*8*	...
2	2	...	...	...	3	3	...	...	...
...	...	...	...	...	...	...	...	...	...
...	...	...	...	...	...	...	...	...	...
...	...	...	...	...	...	...	...	...	...
...	...	...	...	...	...	...	...	...	...
51	51	...	...	...	13	10	3	...	...
53	*53*	...	...	...	*16*	*13*	*3*	...	...
8	8	...	...	...	3	3	...	...	...
...	...	...	...	...	...	...	...	...	...
8	*8*	...	...	...	*3*	*3*	...	...	...
30	30	...	...	...	9	9	...	...	...
377	374	3	...	...	78	66	12	...	...
5,358	**5,240**	**116**	**2**	...	**1,256**	**798**	**450**	**8**	...
47	*47*	...	...	...	*18*	*16*	*2*	...	...
83,031	**79,747**	**3,235**	**49**	...	**20,071**	**11,312**	**8,529**	**230**	...

Class.	Group.	Caste, &c., and sub-division.	Religion.	15 to 30. Total.	Single.	Married.	Widowed.	Civil condition not stated.
F.—Races and Nationalities.	48. Asiatic Races of reputed Foreign origin.	Arab	Musalmán.	...	...	...	...	...
		Belúchi	„	...	...	...	...	...
		Dáyaré	„	...	...	...	...	...
		Hanifi	„	1	...	1	...	...
		Khádri	„	...	...	...	...	...
		Kandhári	„	...	...	...	...	...
		Mogal	„	235	6	200	29	...
		Musalmán	„	31	...	28	3	...
		Pat'hán	„	903	22	813	68	...
		Shékh	„	3,441	128	2,940	373	...
		Sayad	„	1,167	38	1,033	97	...
		Sharif	„	2	...	2	...	...
		Armenian	Christian.	...	...	...	...	...
		Burmese	„	...	...	...	...	...
		Chinese	„	...	...	...	...	...
		Jews	Jews.	...	...	...	...	...
		Jews	Christian.	...	...	...	...	...
		Jews.—Israelites	„	...	...	...	...	...
		Pársi	Pársi.	...	...	...	...	...
		Singháli	Buddhist.	...	...	...	...	...
		Total Group 48	....	*5,780*	*194*	*5,016*	*570*	...
	49. Mixed Asiatic Races.	Labbé	Musalmán.	8	...	8	...	...
		Jáno	„	...	...	...	...	...
		Máplé	„	...	...	...	...	...
		Meman	„	...	...	...	...	...
		Pindári	„	...	...	...	...	...
		Pinjári	„	87	4	74	9	...
		Total Group 49	....	*95*	*4*	*82*	*9*	...
	50. Non-Asiatic races.	European	Christian.	21	4	18	2	...
		Australasian	„	...	...	...	...	...
		Total Group 50	....	*21*	*4*	*18*	*2*	...
	51. Eurasian	Eurasian	„	55	7	43	5	...
	52. Christian converts	Native Christian	„	527	54	447	26	...
		Total Class F	....	**6,481**	**263**	**5,606**	**612**	...
		Caste not stated	....	*18*	...	*40*	*8*	...
		Grand Total	....	**120,331**	**4,111**	**96,030**	**20,190**	...

TABLE E.—(*Continued.*)

District.

Females.

40 and over.					Age not stated.				
Total.	Single.	Married.	Widowed.	Civil condition not stated.	Total.	Single.	Married.	Widowed.	Civil condition not stated.
...	...	...	...	...	...	...	...	...	...
...	...	...	...	...	...	...	...	...	...
...	...	...	...	...	...	...	...	...	...
	...	...	1	...	...	...	...	...	...
...	...	...	...	...	...	...	...	...	...
...	...	...	...	...	...	...	...	...	...
125	1	57	67	...	...	...	...	...	...
13	...	6	7	...	...	...	...	...	...
513	1	236	276	...	...	...	...	...	...
1,717	13	612	1,087	...	...	...	...	...	...
678	3	263	407	...	...	...	...	...	...
1	...	...	1	...	...	...	...	...	...
...	...	...	...	...	...	...	...	...	...
...	...	...	...	...	...	...	...	...	...
...	...	...	...	...	...	...	...	...	...
...	...	...	...	...	...	...	...	...	...
...	...	...	...	...	...	...	...	...	...
...	...	...	...	...	...	...	...	...	...
...	...	...	...	...	...	...	...	...	...
...	...	...	...	...	...	...	...	...	...
3,048	*23*	*1,179*	*1,846*	...	...	...	...	...	...
5	...	3	2	...	...	...	...	...	...
...	...	...	...	...	...	...	...	...	...
...	...	...	...	...	...	...	...	...	...
...	...	...	...	...	...	...	...	...	...
...	...	...	...	...	...	...	...	...	...
56	...	33	23	...	...	...	...	...	...
61	...	*36*	*25*	...	...	...	...	...	...
8	...	2	1	...	...	...	...	...	...
...	...	...	...	...	...	...	...	...	...
3	...	*2*	*1*	...	...	...	...	...	...
21	1	15	5	...	...	...	...	...	...
149	1	57	91	...	...	...	...	...	...
3,282	**25**	**1,289**	**1,968**	...	...	...	...	...	...
40	...	*19*	*21*	...	...	...	...	...	...
69,872	**640**	**20,624**	**48,608**	...	**70**	**29**	**12**	**29**	...

Tumkur

Class.	Group.	Caste, &c. and sub-division.	Religion.	All Ages. Total.	Single.	Married.	Widowed.	Civil condition not stated.
F.—Races and Nationalities.	48. Asiatic Races of reputed Foreign origin.	Arab	Musalmán.	...	...	...	...	...
		Belúchi	,,	...	...	...	...	...
		Dáyaré	,,	...	...	...	...	...
		Hanifi	,,	68	15	34	19	...
		Khádri	,,	...	...	...	...	...
		Kandhári...	,,	...	...	...	...	...
		Mogal	,,	522	305	197	20	...
		Musalmán	,,	21	9	9	3	...
		Pat'hán	,,	2,205	1,210	900	95	...
		Shékh	,,	7,140	4,135	2,857	148	...
		Sayad	,,	1,663	941	662	60	...
		Sharif	,,	413	213	169	31	...
		Armenian	Christian.	...	...	...	...	...
		Burmese	,,	...	...	...	...	...
		Chinese	,,	...	...	...	...	...
		Jews	Jews.	...	...	...	...	...
		Jews	Christian.	...	...	...	...	...
		Jews.—Israelites	,,	...	...	...	...	...
		Pársi	Pársi.	...	...	...	...	...
		Singhálí	Buddhist.	...	...	...	...	...
		Total Group 48......	....	12,032	6,828	4,828	376	...
	49. Mixed Asiatic Races.	Labbé	Musalmán.	74	42	29	3	...
		Jám	,,	...	...	...	...	...
		Máplé	,,	...	...	...	...	...
		Méman	,,	...	...	...	...	...
		Pindári	,,	400	244	140	16	...
		Pinjári	,,	331	172	140	19	...
		Total Group 49......	....	805	458	309	38	...
	50. Non-Asiatic races.	European	Christian.	16	12	4	...	...
		Australasian ...	,,	...	...	...	...	...
		Total Group 50......	....	16	12	4	...	...
	51. Eurasian ...	Eurasian	,,	8	5	3	...	...
	52. Christian converts ...	Native Christian ...	,,	377	234	131	12	...
		Total Class F......	....	13,238	7,537	5,275	426	...
		Caste not stated......	....	97	41	48	8	...
		Grand Total......	....	291,133	157,111	117,932	15,477	13

TABLE E.—(*Continued.*)

District.

Males.

0 to 9					10 to 14				
Total.	Single.	Married.	Widowed.	Civil condition not stated.	Total.	Single.	Married.	Widowed.	Civil condition not stated.
...	...	...	...	...	...	...	...	...	...
...	...	...	...	...	...	...	...	...	...
...	...	...	...	...	...	...	...	...	...
5	5	...	...	...	...	...	...	...	...
...	...	...	...	...	...	...	...	...	...
...	...	...	...	...	...	...	...	...	...
219	219	...	...	...	57	52	5	...	...
3	3	...	...	...	2	2	...	...	...
718	718	...	...	...	307	306	1	...	...
2,248	2,248	...	...	...	386	382	4	...	...
548	548	...	...	...	211	208	3	...	...
159	159	...	...	...	32	32	...	...	...
...	...	...	...	...	...	...	...	...	...
...	...	...	...	...	...	...	...	...	...
...	...	...	...	...	...	...	...	...	...
...	...	...	...	...	...	...	...	...	...
...	...	...	...	...	...	...	...	...	...
...	...	...	...	...	...	...	...	...	...
...	...	...	...	...	...	...	...	...	...
...	...	...	...	...	...	...	...	...	...
3,900	3,900	...	...	...	995	982	13	...	...
9	9	...	...	...	4	4	...	...	...
...	...	...	...	...	...	...	...	...	...
...	...	...	...	...	...	...	...	...	...
...	...	...	...	...	...	...	...	...	...
136	136	...	...	...	75	75	...	...	...
93	93	...	...	...	35	35	...	...	...
238	*238*	...	...	...	*114*	*114*	...	...	...
2	2	...	...	...	6	6	...	...	...
...	...	...	...	...	...	...	...	...	...
3	*2*	...	...	...	*6*	*6*	...	...	...
1	1	...	...	...	1	1	...	...	...
113	113	...	...	...	25	25	...	...	...
4,254	**4,254**	...	...	...	**1,141**	**1,128**	**13**	...	...
24	*24*	...	...	...	*5*	*5*	...	...	...
82,067	**82,021**	**40**	**3**	...	**20,521**	**19,995**	**523**	**3**	...

Class.	Group.	Caste, &c. and sub-division.	Religion.	15 to 39. Total.	Single.	Married.	Widowed.	Civil condition not stated.
F.—Races and Nationalities.	48. Asiatic Races of reputed Foreign origin.	Arab	Musalmán.	...	...	...	...	...
		Belúchi	,,	...	...	...	...	...
		Dáyaré	,,	...	...	...	...	...
		Hanifi	,,	39	10	25	4	...
		Khádri	,,	...	...	...	...	...
		Kandhári	,,	...	...	...	...	...
		Mogal	,,	167	32	131	4	...
		Musalmán	,,	10	4	6	...	...
		Paṭ'han	,,	675	166	493	16	...
		Shékh	,,	2,862	1,459	1,373	30	...
		Sayad	,,	562	171	379	12	...
		Sharif	,,	141	15	118	8	...
		Armenian	Christian.	...	...	...	...	...
		Burmese	,,	...	...	...	...	...
		Chinese	,,	...	...	...	...	...
		Jews	Jews.	...	...	...	...	...
		Jews	Christian.	...	...	...	...	...
		Jews.—Israelites	,,	...	...	...	...	...
		Pársi	Pársi.	...	...	...	...	...
		Singhâli	Buddhist.	...	...	...	...	...
		Total Group 48	....	*4,456*	*1,857*	*2,525*	74	...
	49. Mixed Asiatic Races.	Labbé	Musalmán.	50	28	22	...	...
		Jám	,,	...	...	...	...	...
		Máplé	,,	...	...	...	...	...
		Méman	,,	...	...	...	...	...
		Pinḍári	,,	126	32	92	2	...
		Pinjári	,,	141	38	100	3	...
		Total Group 49	....	*317*	*98*	*214*	5	...
	50. Non-Asiatic races.	European	Christian.	7	4	3	...	...
		Australasian	,,	...	...	...	...	...
		Total Group 50	....	*7*	*4*	*3*	...	...
	51. Eurasian	Eurasian	,,	5	3	2	...	...
	52. Christian converts	Native Christian	,,	189	94	91	4	...
		Total Class F	....	**4,974**	**2,056**	**2,835**	**83**	...
		Casto not stated	....	*43*	*12*	*29*	2	...
		Grand Total	....	**124,982**	**53,153**	**68,313**	**3,516**	...

TABLE E.—(*Continued.*)

District.

Males.

40 and over.					Age not stated.				
Total.	Single.	Married.	Widowed.	Civil condition not stated.	Total.	Single.	Married.	Widowed.	Civil condition not stated.
...	...	...	...	...	...	...	...	...	...
...	...	...	...	...	...	...	...	...	...
...	...	...	...	...	...	...	...	...	...
24	...	9	15	...	...	...	...	...	...
...	...	...	...	...	...	...	...	...	...
...	...	...	...	...	...	...	...	...	...
79	2	61	16	...	...	...	...	...	...
6	...	3	3	...	...	...	...	...	...
505	20	406	79	...	...	...	...	...	...
1,644	46	1,480	118	...	...	...	...	...	...
343	14	280	48	...	...	...	...	...	...
81	7	51	23	...	...	...	...	...	...
...	...	...	...	...	...	...	...	...	...
...	...	...	...	...	...	...	...	...	...
...	...	...	...	...	...	...	...	...	...
...	...	...	...	...	...	...	...	...	...
...	...	...	...	...	...	...	...	...	...
...	...	...	...	...	...	...	...	...	...
...	...	...	...	...	...	...	...	...	...
...	...	...	...	...	...	...	...	...	...
2,681	*89*	*2,290*	*303*	...	...	...	...	...	...
11	1	7	3	...	...	...	...	...	...
...	...	...	...	...	...	...	...	...	...
...	...	...	...	...	...	...	...	...	...
...	...	...	...	...	...	...	...	...	...
63	1	48	14	...	...	...	...	...	...
62	6	40	16	...	...	...	...	...	...
136	*8*	*95*	*33*	...	...	...	...	...	...
1	...	1	...	...	...	...	...	...	...
...	...	...	...	...	...	...	...	...	...
1	...	*1*	...	...	...	...	...	...	...
1	...	1	...	...	...	...	...	...	...
50	2	40	8	...	...	...	...	...	...
2,869	**99**	**2,427**	**343**	...	...	...	...	...	...
25	...	*19*	*6*	...	...	...	...	...	...
63,466	**2,485**	**49,034**	**11,947**	...	**97**	**54**	**22**	**8**	**13**

Class.	Group.	Caste, &c. and sub-division.	Religion.	All Ages. Total.	Single.	Married.	Widowed.	Civil condition not stated.
F.—Races and Nationalities.	48. Asiatic Races of reputed Foreign origin.	Arab	Musalmán.	...	...	...	...	...
		Belúchi	,,	...	...	...	...	...
		Dáyaré	,,	1	...	...	1	...
		Hanifi	,,	59	11	29	19	...
		Khádri	,,	...	...	...	...	...
		Kandhári	,,	...	...	...	...	...
		Mogal	,,	510	253	194	63	...
		Musalmán	,,	9	3	5	1	...
		Pat'hán	,,	2,257	917	939	401	...
		Shékh	,,	7,107	2,837	2,939	1,331	...
		Sayad	,,	1,346	517	649	180	...
		Shárif	,,	403	174	172	57	...
		Armenian	Christian.	...	...	...	...	...
		Burmese	,,	...	...	...	...	...
		Chinese	,,	...	...	...	...	...
		Jews	Jews.	...	...	...	...	...
		Jews	Christian.	...	...	...	...	...
		Jews.—Israelites	,,	...	...	...	...	...
		Pársi	Párai.	...	...	...	...	...
		Singháli	Buddhist.	...	...	...	...	...
		Total Group 48...	....	11,692	4,712	4,927	2,053	...
	49. Mixed Asiatic Races.	Labbé	Musalmán.	18	6	10	2	...
		Jám	,,	...	...	...	...	...
		Máplé	,,	...	...	...	...	...
		Méman	,,	...	...	...	...	...
		Pindári	,,	408	176	175	57	...
		Pinjári	,,	286	102	148	36	...
		Total Group 49......	....	712	234	333	95	...
	50. Non-Asiatic races.	European	,,	11	5	6	...	...
		Australasian	,,	...	...	...	...	...
		Total Group 50......	....	11	5	6	...	...
	51. Eurasian ...	Eurasian	,,	9	6	3	...	...
	52. Christian converts...	Native Christian	,,	322	155	129	38	...
		Total Class F...	...	**12,746**	**5,162**	**5,398**	**2,186**	...
		Caste not stated......	....	117	30	51	27	...
		Grand Total......	....	**289,653**	**101,668**	**121,598**	**66,361**	**26**

TABLE E.—(Continued.)

District.

Females.

0 to 9.					10 to 14.				
Total.	Single.	Married.	Widowed.	Civil condition not stated.	Total.	Single.	Married.	Widowed.	Civil condition not stated.
...	...	...	...	...	...	...	...	...	...
...	...	...	...	...	...	...	...	...	...
...	...	...	...	...	...	...	...	...	...
9	9	...	...	...	2	2	...	...	...
...	...	...	...	...	...	...	...	...	...
...	...	...	...	...	...	...	...	...	...
200	200	...	...	...	57	49	8	...	...
2	2	...	...	...	1	1	...	...	...
764	764	...	...	...	152	131	21	...	...
2,428	2,394	34	...	...	493	285	204	4	...
119	119	...	...	...	90	82	8	...	...
101	101	...	...	...	63	63	...	...	...
...	...	...	...	...	...	...	...	...	...
...	...	...	...	...	...	...	...	...	...
...	...	...	...	...	...	...	...	...	...
...	...	...	...	...	...	...	...	...	...
...	...	...	...	...	...	...	...	...	...
...	...	...	...	...	...	...	...	...	...
...	...	...	...	...	...	...	...	...	...
...	...	...	...	...	...	...	...	...	...
3,923	*3,889*	*34*	...	...	*858*	*613*	*241*	*4*	...
5	5	...	...	...	1	1	...	...	...
...	...	...	...	...	...	...	...	...	...
...	...	...	...	...	...	...	...	...	...
...	...	...	...	...	...	...	...	...	...
136	136	...	...	...	41	30	11	...	...
77	77	...	...	...	21	19	2	...	...
218	*218*	...	...	...	*63*	*50*	*13*	...	...
3	3	...	...	...	1	1	...	...	...
...	...	...	...	...	...	...	...	...	...
3	*3*	...	...	...	*1*	*1*	...	...	...
2	2	...	...	...	...	...	...	...	...
117	117	...	...	...	27	23	4	...	...
4,263	**4,229**	**34**	...	...	**949**	**687**	**258**	**4**	...
26	*26*	...	...	...	*9*	*9*	...	...	...
86,676	**83,870**	**2,773**	**33**	...	**19,203**	**11,208**	**7,785**	**141**	...

Class.	Group.	Caste, &c. and sub-division.	Religion.	15 to 39. Total.	Single.	Married.	Widowed.	Civil condition not stated.
F.—Races and Nationalities.	48. Asiatic Races of reputed Foreign origin.	Arab	Musalmán.	...	...	...	...	...
		Belúchi	,,	...	...	...	...	...
		Dáyaré	,,	...	...	...	...	...
		Hanifi	,,	28	...	20	8	...
		Khádri	,,	...	...	...	...	...
		Kandhári	,,	...	...	...	...	...
		Mogal	,,	160	4	143	13	...
		Musalmán	,,	3	...	3	...	...
		Pat'hán	,,	857	20	745	92	...
		Shékh	,,	2,694	119	2,261	314	...
		Sayad	,,	562	16	501	45	...
		Sharif	,,	179	10	150	19	...
		Armenian	Christian.	...	...	...	...	...
		Burmese	,,	...	...	...	...	...
		Chinese	,,	...	...	...	...	...
		Jews	Jews	...	...	...	...	...
		Jews	Christian.	...	...	...	...	...
		Jews—Israelites	,,	...	...	...	...	...
		Pársi	Pársi.	...	...	...	...	...
		Singháli	Buddhist.	...	...	...	...	...
		Total Group 48	....	*4,483*	*160*	*3,823*	*491*	...
	49. Mixed Asiatic Races.	Labbé	Musalmán.	9	...	9	...	...
		Jám	,,	...	...	...	...	...
		Máplé	,,	...	...	...	...	...
		Méman	,,	...	...	...	...	...
		Pindári	,,	145	10	122	13	...
		Pinjári	,,	138	6	123	9	...
		Total Group 49	....	*292*	*16*	*254*	*22*	...
	50. Non-Asiatic races.	European	Christian.	6	1	5	...	...
		Australasian	,,	...	...	...	...	...
		Total Group 50	....	*6*	*1*	*5*	...	...
	51. Eurasian	Eurasian	Christian.	6	4	2	...	...
	50. Non-Asiatic races.	Native Christian	,,	138	15	114	9	...
		Total Class F	....	**4,925**	**205**	**4,198**	**522**	...
		Caste not stated	....	*50*	*4*	*40*	*6*	...
		Grand Total	....	**121,245**	**5,405**	**94,244**	**21,596**	...

TABLE E.—*(Continued.)*

District.

Females.

40 and over. Total.	Single.	Married.	Widowed.	Civil condition not stated.	Age not stated. Total.	Single.	Married.	Widowed.	Civil condition not stated.
...	...	...	...	...	...	...	...	...	...
...	...	...	...	...	...	...	...	...	...
1	...	...	1	...	...	...	...	...	...
20	...	9	11	...	...	...	...	...	...
...	...	...	...	...	...	...	...	...	...
...	...	...	...	...	...	...	...	...	...
93	...	43	50	...	...	...	...	...	...
3	...	2	1	...	...	...	...	...	...
484	2	173	309	...	...	...	...	...	...
1,492	39	440	1,013	...	...	...	...	...	...
275	...	140	135	...	...	...	...	...	...
60	...	22	38	...	...	...	...	5	...
...	...	...	...	...	...	...	...	...	...
...	...	...	...	...	...	...	...	...	...
...	...	...	...	...	...	...	...	...	...
...	...	...	...	...	...	...	...	...	...
...	...	...	...	...	...	...	...	...	...
...	...	...	...	...	...	...	...	...	...
...	...	...	...	...	...	...	...	...	...
...	...	...	...	...	...	...	...	...	...
2,428	*41*	*829*	*1,558*	...	...	...	...	...	...
3	...	1	2	...	...	...	...	...	...
...	...	...	...	...	...	...	...	...	...
...	...	...	...	...	...	...	...	...	...
...	...	...	...	...	...	...	...	...	...
86	...	42	44	...	...	...	...	...	...
50	...	23	27	...	...	...	...	...	...
139	...	*66*	*73*	...	...	...	...	...	...
1	...	1	...	...	...	...	...	...	...
...	...	...	...	...	...	...	...	...	...
1	...	*1*	...	...	...	...	...	...	...
1	...	1	...	...	...	...	...	...	...
40	...	11	29	...	...	...	...	...	...
2,609	**41**	**908**	**1,660**	...	...	...	...	...	...
32	...	*11*	*21*	...	...	...	...	...	...
62,424	**1,057**	**16,793**	**44,574**	...	**104**	**28**	**33**	**17**	**26**

Mysore

Class.	Group.	Caste, &c., and sub-division.	Religion.	All Ages. Total.	Single.	Married.	Widowed.	Civil condition not stated.
F.—Races and Nationalities.	48. Asiatic Races of reputed Foreign origin.	Arab	Musalmán.	...	...	...	...	...
		Belúchi	,,	...	...	...	...	...
		Dáyaré	,,	47	28	17	2	...
		Hanifi	,,	227	120	98	9	...
		Khádri	,,	2	2	...	...	...
		Kandhári	,,	...	...	...	...	...
		Mogal	,,	734	388	317	29	...
		Musalmán	,,	...	...	...	...	...
		Pat'hán	,,	3,874	2,223	1,508	143	...
		Shékh	,,	14,368	8,066	5,941	361	...
		Sayad	,,	3,730	2,019	1,573	138	...
		Sharif	,,	4	2	2	...	...
		Armenian	Christian.	...	...	...	...	...
		Burmese	,,	...	...	...	...	...
		Chinese	,,	...	...	...	...	...
		Jews	Jews.	2	1	1	...	...
		Jews	Christian.	...	...	...	...	...
		Jews.—Israelites	,,	...	...	...	...	...
		Pársi	Pársi.	9	5	4	...	...
		Singháli	Buddhist.	...	...	...	...	...
		Total Group 48......	....	*22,997*	*12,854*	*9,461*	*682*	...
	49. Mixed Asiatic Races.	Labbé	Musalmán.	1,147	625	480	42	...
		Jám	,,	...	...	...	...	...
		Máplé	,,	18	6	10	2	...
		Méman	,,	...	...	...	...	...
		Pinjári	,,	556	298	241	17	...
		Pinjári	,,	...	...	...	...	...
		Total Group 49......	....	*1,721*	*929*	*731*	*61*	...
	50. Non-Asiatic races.	European	Christian.	72	42	25	5	...
		Australasian	,,	...	...	...	...	...
		Total Group 50......	....	*72*	*42*	*25*	*5*	...
	51. Eurasian ...	Eurasian	,,	118	68	41	9	...
	52. Christian converts ...	Native Christian	,,	1,281	748	459	74	...
		Total Class F.....	....	**26,189**	**14,641**	**10,717**	**831**	...
		Caste not stated......	....	*581*	*310*	*247*	*24*	...
		Grand Total.....	....	**580,737**	**306,985**	**254,027**	**19,724**	**1**

TABLE E.—(Continued.)

District.

Males.

0 to 9					10 to 14				
Total.	Single.	Married.	Widowed.	Civil condition not stated.	Total.	Single.	Married.	Widowed.	Civil condition not stated.
...	...	...	...	...	...	...	...	...	...
...	...	...	...	...	...	...	...	...	...
15	15	...	...	...	4	4	...	...	...
52	52	...	...	...	20	20	...	...	...
...	...	...	...	...	...	...	...	...	...
...	...	...	...	...	...	...	...	...	...
201	201	...	...	...	59	59	...	...	...
...	...	...	...	...	...	...	...	...	...
1,090	1,090	...	...	...	400	381	19	...	...
3,694	3,691	3	...	...	1,662	1,651	10	1	...
1,033	1,031	2	...	...	315	309	6	..	...
1	1	...	...	...	1	1	...	...	...
...	...	...	...	...	...	...	...	...	...
...	...	...	...	...	...	...	...	...	...
...	...	...	...	...	...	...	...	...	...
1	1	...	...	...	...	...	...	...	...
...	...	...	...	...	...	...	...	...	...
...	...	...	...	...	...	...	...	...	...
1	1	...	...	...	1	1	...	...	...
...	...	...	...	...	...	...	...	...	...
6,088	*6,083*	*5*	...	...	*2,462*	*2,426*	*35*	*1*	...
307	307	...	...	...	102	102	...	...	...
...	...	...	...	...	...	..	...	...	...
...	...	...	...	...	...	...	...	...	...
...	...	...	...	...	...	...	...	...	...
163	163	...	...	...	46	46	...	...	...
...	...	...	...	...	...	...	...	...	...
470	*470*	...	...	...	*148*	*148*	...	...	...
19	19	...	...	...	7	7	...	...	...
...	...	...	...	...	...	...	...	...	...
19	*19*	...	...	...	*7*	*7*	...	...	...
21	21	...	...	...	9	9	...	...	...
373	373	...	...	...	136	133	3	...	...
6,971	**6,966**	**5**	...	...	**2,762**	**2,723**	**38**	**1**	...
157	*157*	...	...	...	45	45	...	...	...
163,872	**163,651**	**213**	**8**	...	**60,522**	**58,491**	**2,013**	**18**	...

Mysore

Class.	Group.	Caste, &c., and sub-division.	Religion.	15 to 39 Total.	Single.	Married.	Widowed.	Civil condition not stated.
F.—Races and Nationalities.	48. Asiatic Races of repated Foreign origin.	Aráb	Musalmán.	...	...	...	...	...
		Belúch	,,	...	...	...	...	...
		Dáyaré	,,	17	8	9	...	...
		Hanifi	,,	107	44	62	1	...
		Khádri	,,	1	1	...	...	...
		Kandhári	,,	...	...	...	...	...
		Mogul	,,	315	122	190	3	...
		Musalmán	,,	...	...	...	...	...
		Paṭ'hán	,,	1,421	624	761	36	...
		Shékh	,,	5,558	2,666	2,843	49	...
		Sayad	,,	1,641	648	960	33	...
		Sharif	,,	2	...	2	...	...
		Armenian	Christian.	...	...	...	...	...
		Burmese	,,	...	...	...	...	...
		Chinese	,,	...	...	...	...	...
		Jews	Jews.	1	...	1	...	...
		Jews	Christian.	...	...	...	...	...
		Jews.—Israelites	,,	...	...	...	...	...
		Pársi	Pársi.	5	3	2	...	...
		Singháli	Buddhist.	...	...	...	...	...
		Total Group 48	....	*9,068*	*4,116*	*4,830*	*122*	...
	49. Mixed Asiatic Races.	Labbé	Musalmán.	513	204	300	9	...
		Jám	,,	...	...	...	...	...
		Máplé	,,	13	6	7	...	...
		Méman	,,	...	...	...	...	...
		Pindári	,,	243	89	150	4	...
		Pinjári	,,	...	...	...	...	...
		Total Group 49	....	*769*	*299*	*457*	*13*	...
	50. Non-Asiatic races.	European	Christian.	33	16	16	1	...
		Australasian	,,	...	...	...	...	...
		Total Group 50	....	*33*	*16*	*16*	*1*	...
	51. Eurasian	Eurasian	,,	62	38	22	2	...
	52. Christian converts	Native Christian	,,	513	223	258	32	...
		Total Class 1	....	**10,445**	**4,692**	**5,583**	**170**	...
		Caste not stated	....	*209*	*101*	*104*	*4*	...
		Grand Total	....	**230,612**	**81,659**	**145,053**	**3,900**	...

TABLE E.—(Continued.)

District.

Males.

40 and over.					Age not stated.				
Total.	Single.	Married.	Widowed.	Civil condition not stated.	Total.	Single.	Married.	Widowed.	Civil condition not stated.
...	...	...	...	...	...	...	...	...	...
...	...	...	...	...	...	...	...	...	...
11	1	8	2	...	...	...	...	...	...
48	4	36	8	...	...	...	...	...	...
1	1	...	...	...	...	...	...	...	...
...	...	...	...	...	...	...	...	...	...
159	6	127	26	...	...	...	...	...	...
...	...	...	...	...	...	...	...	...	...
963	128	728	107	...	...	...	...	...	...
3,451	55	3,085	311	...	3	3	...	...	...
741	31	605	105	...	...	...	...	...	...
...	...	...	...	...	...	...	...	...	...
...	...	...	...	...	...	...	...	...	...
...	...	...	...	...	...	...	...	...	...
...	...	...	...	...	...	...	...	...	...
...	...	...	...	...	...	...	...	...	...
...	...	...	...	...	...	...	...	...	...
...	...	...	...	...	...	...	...	...	...
2	...	2	...	...	...	...	...	...	...
...	...	...	...	...	...	...	...	...	...
5,376	*226*	*4,591*	*559*	...	*3*	*3*	...	...	...
225	12	180	33	...	...	...	...	...	...
...	...	...	...	...	...	...	...	...	...
5	...	3	2	...	...	...	...	...	...
...	...	...	...	...	...	...	...	...	...
104	...	91	13	...	...	...	...	...	...
...	...	...	...	...	...	...	...	...	...
334	*13*	*274*	*48*	...	...	...	...	...	...
13	...	9	4	...	...	...	...	...	...
...	...	...	...	...	...	...	...	...	...
13	...	*9*	*4*	...	...	...	...	...	...
26	...	19	7	...	...	...	...	...	...
257	18	198	41	...	2	1	...	1	...
6,006	**256**	**5,091**	**659**	...	**5**	**4**	...	**1**	...
110	*7*	*83*	*20*	...	...	...	...	...	...
125,656	**3,131**	**106,737**	**15,788**	...	**75**	**53**	**11**	**10**	**1**

Mysore

Class.	Group.	Caste, &c., and sub-division.	Religion.	All Ages. Total.	Single.	Married.	Widowed.	Civil condition not stated.
F.—Races and Nationalities.	48. Asiatic Races of reputed Foreign origin.	Arab	Musalmán.	...	...	...	...	...
		Belúchi	,,	...	...	...	...	...
		Dáyaré	,,	33	11	15	7	...
		Hanifi	,,	206	77	91	38	...
		Khádri	,,	...	...	...	...	...
		Kandhári	,,	...	...	...	...	...
		Mogal	,,	679	258	305	116	...
		Musalmán	,,	...	...	...	...	...
		Pat'hán	,,	3,712	1,293	1,535	884	...
		Shékh	,,	14,266	5,525	5,870	2,865	6
		Sayad	,,	3,597	1,249	1,563	785	...
		Sharíf	,,	4	1	2	1	...
		Armenian	Christian.	...	...	...	...	...
		Burmese	,,	...	...	...	...	...
		Chinese	,,	...	...	...	...	...
		Jews	Jews.	2	1	1	...	...
		Jews	Christian.	...	...	...	...	...
		Jews.—Israelites	,,	...	...	...	...	...
		Pársi	Pársi.	8	5	2	1	...
		Singháli	Buddhist.	...	...	...	...	...
		Total Group 48	....	22,507	8,420	9,384	4,607	6
	49. Mixed Asiatic Races.	Labbé	Musalmán.	826	309	369	148	...
		Jám	,,	...	...	...	...	...
		Máplé	,,	...	...	...	...	...
		Méman	,,	...	...	...	...	...
		Pindári	,,	471	159	206	106	...
		Pinjári	,,	...	...	...	...	...
		Total Group 49	....	1,297	468	575	254	...
	50. Non-Asiatic races.	European	Christian.	158	71	55	32	...
		Australasian	,,	...	...	...	...	...
		Total Group 50	....	158	71	55	32	...
	51. Eurasian ...	Eurasian	,,	90	39	33	18	...
	52. Christian converts ...	Native Christian	,,	1,[illegible]	540	433	246	...
		Total Class F......	....	**25,280**	**9,547**	**10,480**	**5,247**	**6**
		Caste not stated......	....	500	187	258	115	...
		Grand Total......	....	**601,077**	**211,616**	**266,749**	**122,704**	**8**

TABLE E.—(Continued.)

District.

Females.

0 to 9					10 to 14				
Total.	Single.	Married.	Widowed.	Civil condition not stated.	Total.	Single.	Married.	Widowed.	Civil condition not stated.
...	...	...	...	...	...	...	...	...	...
...	...	...	...	...	...	...	...	...	...
6	6	...	...	...	4	3	1	...	...
55	55	...	...	...	22	13	9	...	...
...	...	...	...	...	...	...	...	...	...
...	...	...	...	...	...	...	...	...	...
167	167	...	...	...	73	61	12	...	...
...	...	...	...	...	...	...	...	...	...
892	864	28	...	...	316	236	80	...	...
4,335	4,303	29	3	...	1,258	970	279	9	...
888	888	...	...	...	322	287	35	...	...
1	1	...	...	...	...	...	...	...	...
...	...	...	...	...	...	...	...	...	...
...	...	...	...	...	...	...	...	...	...
...	...	...	...	...	...	...	...	...	...
1	1	...	...	...	...	...	...	...	...
...	...	...	...	...	...	...	...	...	...
...	...	...	...	...	...	...	...	...	...
1	1	...	...	...	1	1	...	...	...
[illegible]	...	...	...	...	...	...	...	...	...
6,346	*6,296*	*57*	*3*	...	*1,996*	*1,571*	*416*	*9*	...
216	216	...	...	...	81	61	20	...	...
...	...	...	...	...	...	...	...	...	...
...	...	...	...	...	...	...	...	...	...
...	...	...	...	...	...	...	...	...	...
141	141	...	...	...	18	14	4	...	...
...	...	...	...	...	...	...	...	...	...
357	*357*	...	...	...	*99*	*75*	*24*	...	...
45	45	...	...	...	22	22	...	...	...
...	...	...	...	...	...	...	...	...	...
45	*45*	...	...	...	*22*	*22*	...	...	...
18	18	...	...	...	9	9	...	...	...
346	*346*	...	...	...	*125*	*101*	*23*	*1*	...
7,112	**7,052**	**57**	**3**	...	**2,251**	**1,778**	**463**	**10**	...
115	*115*	...	...	...	*57*	*52*	*5*	...	...
168,073	**162,894**	**5,104**	**75**	...	**53,030**	**32,586**	**20,001**	**443**	...

Mysore

Class.	Group.	Caste, &c., and sub-division.	Religion.	15 to 39 Total.	Single.	Married.	Widowed.	Civil condition not stated.
F.—Races and Nationalities.	48. Asiatic Races of reputed Foreign origin.	Arab	Musalmán.	...	...	...	...	...
		Belúchi	,,	...	...	...	...	...
		Dáyuré	,,	14	2	10	2	...
		Hanifi	,,	83	9	57	16	...
		Khádri	,,	...	...	...	...	...
		Kandhári	,,	...	...	...	...	...
		Mogal	,,	278	30	216	32	...
		Musalmán	,,	...	...	...	...	...
		Pat'hán	,,	1,536	158	1,181	197	...
		Shékh	,,	5,306	281	4,534	541	...
		Sayad	,,	1,321	69	1,083	169	...
		Sharíf	,,	2	...	2	...	...
		Armenian	Christian.	...	...	...	...	...
		Burmese	,,	...	...	...	...	...
		Chinese	,,	...	...	...	...	...
		Jews	Jews.	1	...	1	...	...
		Jews	Christian.	...	...	...	...	...
		Jews.—Israelites	,,	...	...	...	...	...
		Pársi	Pársi.	5	3	2	...	...
		Singháli	Buddhist.	...	...	...	...	...
		Total Group 48	....	*8,545*	*502*	*7,086*	*957*	...
	49. Mixed Asiatic Races.	Labbé	Musalmán.	333	33	262	39	...
		Jám	,,	...	...	...	...	...
		Máplé	,,	...	...	...	...	...
		Memun	,,	...	...	...	...	...
		Pindári	,,	174	4	134	36	...
		Pinjári	,,	...	...	...	...	...
		Total Group 49	....	*507*	*36*	*396*	*75*	...
	50. Non-Asiatic races.	European	Christian.	56	4	40	12	...
		Australasian	,,	...	...	...	...	...
		Total Group 50	....	*56*	*4*	*40*	*12*	...
	51. Eurasian	Eurasian	,,	41	12	24	5	...
	52. Christian converts	Native Christian	,,	511	90	323	98	...
		Total Class F	....	**9,660**	**644**	**7,869**	**1,147**	...
		Caste not stated	....	*213*	*18*	*177*	*18*	...
		Grand Total	....	**240,567**	**14,272**	**195,528**	**30,767**	...

TABLE E.—(*Continued.*)

District.

Females.

40 and over. Total.	Single.	Married.	Widowed.	Civil condition not stated.	Age not stated. Total.	Single.	Married.	Widowed.	Civil condition not stated.
...	...	...	...	...	...	...	...	...	...
...	...	...	...	...	...	...	...	...	...
9	...	4	5	...	...	...	...	...	...
47	...	25	22	...	...	...	...	...	...
...	...	...	...	...	...	...	...	...	...
...	...	...	...	...	...	...	...	...	...
161	...	77	84	...	...	...	...	...	...
...	...	...	...	...	...	...	...	...	...
963	35	246	687	...	...	...	...	...	...
3,352	15	1,026	2,311	...	15	6	[illegible]	1	6
1,066	5	445	616	...	...	...	...	...	...
1	...	...	1	...	...	...	...	...	...
...	...	...	...	...	...	...	...	...	...
...	...	...	...	...	...	...	...	...	...
...	...	...	...	...	...	...	...	...	...
...	...	...	...	...	...	...	...	...	...
...	...	...	...	...	...	...	...	...	...
...	...	...	...	...	...	...	...	...	...
1	...	...	1	...	...	...	...	...	...
...	...	...	...	...	...	...	...	...	...
5,605	*55*	*1,823*	*3,727*	...	*15*	*6*	*2*	*1*	*6*
196	...	87	109	...	...	...	...	...	...
...	...	...	...	...	...	...	...	...	...
...	...	...	...	...	...	...	...	...	...
...	...	...	...	...	...	...	...	...	...
188	...	68	70	...	...	...	...	...	...
...	...	...	...	...	...	...	...	...	...
334	...	*155*	*179*	...	...	...	...	...	...
35	...	15	20	...	...	...	...	...	...
...	...	...	...	...	...	...	...	...	...
35	...	*15*	*20*	...	...	...	...	...	...
22	...	*9*	*13*	...	...	...	...	...	...
246	12	87	147	...	...	...	...	...	...
6,242	**67**	**2,089**	**4,086**	...	**15**	**6**	**2**	**1**	**6**
175	2	*76*	*97*	...	...	...	...	...	...
139,298	**1,799**	**46,100**	**91,399**	...	**109**	**65**	**16**	**20**	**8**

Hassan

Class.	Group.	Caste, &c. and sub-division.	Religion.	All Ages. Total.	Single.	Married.	Widowed.	Civil condition not stated.
F.—Races and Nationalities.	48. Asiatic Races of reputed Foreign origin.	Arab	Musalmán.	...	...	...	...	...
		Belúchi	,,	...	...	...	...	...
		Dáyaré		...	...	...	...	...
		Hanifi	,,	104	61	36	7	...
		Khádri	,,	...	...	...	...	...
		Kandhári...	,,	...	...	...	...	...
		Mogal	,,	239	145	88	6	...
		Musalmán	,,	8	5	2	1	...
		Pat'hán	,,	961	545	374	42	...
		Shékh	,,	4,851	2,763	1,984	104	...
		Sayad	,,	892	473	374	45	...
		Sharif	,,	...	...	...	...	...
		Armenian...	Christian.	...	...	...	...	...
		Burmese	,,	...	...	...	...	...
		Chinese	,,	...	...	...	...	...
		Jews	Jews.	6	4	2	...	...
		Jews	Christian.	...	...	...	...	...
		Jews.—Israelites	,,	...	...	...	...	...
		Pársi	Pársi.	...	...	...	...	...
		Singháli	Buddhist.	...	...	...	...	...
		Total Group 48......	....	*7,061*	*3,996*	*2,860*	*205*	...
	49. Mixed Asiatic Races.	Labbé	Musalmán.	58	32	25	1	...
		Jám	,,	...	...	...	...	...
		Máplé	,,	71	39	32	...	...
		Méman	,,	...	...	...	...	...
		Pindári	,,	...	...	...	...	...
		Pinjári	,,	20	10	8	2	...
		Total Group 49......	....	*149*	*81*	*65*	*3*	...
	50. Non-Asiatic races.	European...	Christian.	97	58	34	5	...
		Australasian	,,	...	...	...	...	...
		Total Group 50......	....	*97*	*58*	*34*	*5*	...
	51. Eurasian ...	Eurasian	,,	49	31	17	1	...
	52. Christian converts...	Native Christian ...	,,	1,564	880	636	48	...
		Total Class F......	....	**8,920**	**5,046**	**3,612**	**262**	...
		Caste not stated......	....	*268*	*128*	*111*	*29*	...
		Grand Total......	....	**255,044**	**144,688**	**100,004**	**10,328**	**24**

TABLE E.—(*Continued.*)

District.

Males.

0 to 9					10 to 14				
Total.	Single.	Married.	Widowed.	Civil condition not stated.	Total.	Single.	Married.	Widowed.	Civil condition not stated.
...	...	...	...	...	...	...	...	...	...
...	...	...	...	...	...	...	...	...	...
...	...	...	...	...	...	...	...	...	...
18	18	...	...	...	9	9	...	...	...
...	...	...	...	...	...	...	...	...	...
...	...	...	...	...	...	...	...	...	...
74	74	...	...	...	29	20	...	...	...
1	1	...	...	...	2	2	...	...	...
247	246	1	...	...	100	98	2	...	...
1,368	1,365	3	...	...	466	463	3	...	...
253	231	2	...	...	69	69	...	...	...
...	...	...	...	...	...	...	...	...	...
...	...	...	...	...	...	...	...	...	...
...	...	...	...	...	...	...	...	...	...
...	...	...	...	...	...	...	...	...	...
2	2	...	...	...	2	2	...	...	...
...	...	...	...	...	...	...	...	...	...
...	...	...	...	...	...	...	...	...	...
...	...	...	...	...	...	...	...	...	...
...	...	...	...	...	...	...	...	...	...
1,943	*1,937*	*6*	...	...	*677*	*672*	*5*	...	...
3	3	...	...	...	5	5	...	...	...
...	...	...	...	...	...	...	...	...	...
...	...	...	...	...	...	...	...	...	...
...	...	...	...	...	...	...	...	...	...
...	...	...	...	...	...	...	...	...	...
3	3	...	...	...	2	2	...	...	...
6	*6*	...	...	...	*7*	*7*	...	...	...
8	8	...	...	...	4	4	...	...	...
...	...	...	...	...	...	...	...	...	...
8	*8*	...	...	...	*4*	*4*	...	...	...
11	11	...	...	...	5	5	...	...	...
402	401	1	...	...	156	154	2	...	...
2,370	**2,363**	**7**	...	...	**849**	**842**	**7**	...	**1**
50	*50*	...	...	...	*31*	*31*	...	...	...
72,782	**72,742**	**40**	...	...	**26,080**	**25,737**	**335**	**8**	...

Class.	Group.	Caste, &c. and sub-division.	Religion.	15 to 39. Total.	Single.	Married.	Widowed.	Civil condition not stated.
F.—Races and Nationalities.	48. Asiatic Races of reputed Foreign origin.	Arab	Musalmán.	...	...	...	...	...
		Belúchi	,,	...	...	...	...	...
		Dáyaré	,,	...	...	...	...	...
		Hanifi	,,	61	34	26	1	...
		Khádri	,,	...	...	...	...	...
		Kandhári	,,	...	...	...	...	...
		Mogal	,,	91	42	48	1	...
		Musalmán	,,	4	2	2	...	...
		Pat'hán	,,	413	195	206	12	...
		Shékh	,,	2,041	905	1,100	36	...
		Sayad	,,	373	162	203	8	...
		Sharíf	,,	...	...	...	...	...
		Armenian	Christian.	...	...	...	...	...
		Burmese	,,	...	...	...	...	...
		Chinese	,,	...	...	...	...	...
		Jews	Jews.	1	...	1	...	...
		Jews	Christian.	...	...	...	...	...
		Jews.—Israelites	,,	...	...	...	...	...
		Pársi	Pársi.	...	...	...	...	...
		Singháli	Buddhist.	...	...	...	...	...
		Total Group 48......	....	*2,984*	*1,340*	*1,586*	*58*	...
	49. Mixed Asiatic Races.	Labbé	Musalmán.	42	24	18	...	...
		Jám	,,	...	...	...	...	...
		Máplé	,,	67	39	28	...	...
		Méman	,,	...	...	...	...	...
		Pindári	,,	...	...	...	...	...
		Pinjári	,,	10	5	5	...	...
		Total Group 49......	....	*119*	*68*	*51*	...	...
	50. Non-Asiatic races.	European	Christian.	68	45	23	...	...
		Australasian	,,	...	...	...	...	...
		Total Group 50......		*68*	*45*	*23*	...	...
	51. Eurasian ...	Eurasian	,,	27	15	12	...	...
	52. Christian converts ...	Native Christian	,,	709	310	382	17	...
		Total Class F......	....	**3,907**	**1,778**	**2,054**	**75**	...
		Caste not stated......	....	*117*	*40*	*70*	*7*	...
		Grand Total.....	....	**105,309**	**44,945**	**57,944**	**2,501**	...

TABLE E.—(*Continued.*)

District.

Males.

40 and over.					Age not stated.				
Total.	Single.	Married.	Widowed.	Civil condition not stated.	Total.	Single.	Married.	Widowed.	Civil condition not stated.
...	...	...	...	...	...	...	...	...	...
...	...	...	...	...	...	...	...	...	...
...	...	...	...	...	...	...	...	...	...
16	...	10	6	...	...	...	...	...	...
...	...	...	...	...	...	...	...	...	...
...	...	...	...	...	...	...	...	...	...
45	...	40	5	...	...	...	...	...	...
1	...	...	1	...	...	...	...	...	...
201	6	165	30	...	...	...	...	...	...
976	30	878	68	...	...	...	...	...	...
217	11	169	37	...	...	...	...	...	...
...	...	...	...	...	...	...	...	...	...
...	...	...	...	...	...	...	...	...	...
...	...	...	...	...	...	...	...	...	...
...	...	...	...	...	...	...	...	...	...
1	...	1	...	...	...	...	...	...	...
...	...	...	...	...	...	...	...	...	...
...	...	...	...	...	...	...	...	...	...
...	...	...	...	...	...	...	...	...	...
...	...	...	...	...	...	...	...	...	...
1,457	*47*	*1,263*	*147*	...	...	...	...	...	...
8	...	7	1	...	...	...	...	...	...
...	...	...	...	...	...	...	...	...	...
4	...	4	...	...	...	...	...	...	...
...	...	...	...	...	...	...	...	...	...
...	...	...	...	...	...	...	...	...	...
5	...	3	2	...	...	...	...	...	...
17	...	*14*	*3*	...	...	...	...	...	...
17	1	11	5	...	...	...	...	...	...
...	...	...	...	...	...	...	...	...	...
17	*1*	*11*	*5*	...	...	...	...	...	...
6	...	5	1	...	...	...	...	...	...
297	15	251	31	...	...	...	...	...	...
1,764	**63**	**1,544**	**187**	...	...	...	...	...	...
70	*7*	*41*	*22*	...	...	...	...	...	...
50,741	**1,244**	**41,679**	**7,818**	...	**51**	**20**	**6**	**1**	**24**

Hassan

Class.	Group.	Caste, &c., and sub-division.	Religion.	All Ages. Total.	Single.	Married.	Widowed.	Civil condition not stated.
F.—Races and Nationalities.	48. Asiatic Races of reputed Foreign origin.	Arab	Musalman.	...	...	...	...	...
		Bolúchi	,,	...	...	...	...	...
		Dáyaré	,,	...	...	...	...	...
		Hanifi	,,	35	14	15	6	...
		Khádri	,,	...	...	...	...	...
		Kandhári	,,	...	...	...	...	...
		Mogal	,,	242	96	113	33	...
		Musalmán	,,	6	2	3	1	...
		Paṭ'hán	,,	867	336	375	156	...
		Shékh	,,	4,473	1,849	1,793	831	...
		Sayad	,,	813	324	340	149	...
		Sharíf	,,	...	...	...	...	...
		Armenian	Christian.	...	...	...	...	...
		Burmese	,,	...	...	...	...	...
		Chinese	,,	...	...	...	...	...
		Jews	Jews.	9	5	4	...	...
		Jews	Christian.	...	...	...	...	...
		Jews.—Israelites	,,	...	...	...	...	...
		Pársi	Pársi.	...	...	...	...	...
		Singháli	Buddhist.	...	...	...	...	...
		Total Group 48	....	6,445	2,626	2,643	1,176	...
	49. Mixed Asiatic Races.	Labbé	Musalmán.	9	2	6	1	...
		Jám	,,	...	...	...	...	...
		Máplé	,,	...	...	...	...	...
		Méman	,,	...	...	...	...	...
		Pindári	,,	...	...	...	...	...
		Pinjári	,,	6	...	6	...	...
		Total Group 49	....	15	2	12	1	...
	50. Non-Asiatic Races.	European	Christian.	35	17	17	1	...
		Australasian	,,	...	...	...	...	...
		Total Group 50	....	35	17	17	1	...
	51. Eurasian ...	Eurasian	,,	48	25	17	5	...
	52. Christian converts.	Native Christian	,,	1,503	700	561	242	...
		Total Class F	....	**8,046**	**3,371**	**3,250**	**1,425**	...
		Caste not stated	....	183	63	80	40	...
		Grand Total	....	**259,908**	**103,378**	**104,011**	**52,518**	**4**

TABLE E.—(*Continued.*)

District.

Females.

0 to 9					10 to 14				
Total.	Single.	Married.	Widowed.	Civil condition not stated.	Total.	Single.	Married.	Widowed.	Civil condition not stated.
...	...	...	...	...	...	...	...	...	...
...	...	...	...	...	...	...	...	...	...
...	...	...	...	...	...	...	...	...	...
10	10	...	...	...	2	2	...	...	...
...	...	...	...	...	...	...	...	...	...
...	...	...	...	...	...	...	...	...	...
70	70	...	...	...	28	21	7	...	...
1	1	...	...	...	2	1	1	...	...
247	244	3	...	...	80	66	14	...	...
1,406	1,400	6	...	...	390	301	89	...	...
249	248	1	...	...	71	58	13	...	...
...	...	...	...	...	...	...	...	...	...
...	...	...	...	...	...	...	...	...	...
...	...	...	...	...	...	...	...	...	...
...	...	...	...	...	...	...	...	...	...
4	4	...	...	...	...	...	...	...	...
...	...	...	...	...	...	...	...	...	...
...	...	...	...	...	...	...	...	...	...
...	...	...	...	...	...	...	...	...	...
...	...	...	...	...	...	...	...	...	...
1,987	*1,977*	*10*	...	...	*573*	*449*	*124*	...	...
2	2	...	...	...	...	...	...	...	...
...	...	...	...	...	...	...	...	...	...
...	...	...	...	...	...	...	...	...	...
...	...	...	...	...	...	...	...	...	...
...	...	...	...	...	...	...	...	...	...
...	...	...	...	...	...	...	...	...	...
2	2	...	...	...	...	...	...	...	...
5	5	...	...	...	2	2	...	...	...
...	...	...	...	...	...	...	...	...	...
5	5	...	...	...	3	3	...	...	...
16	16	...	...	...	4	4	...	...	...
441	441	...	...	...	165	141	24	...	...
2,451	**2,441**	**10**	...	...	**744**	**596**	**148**	...	...
41	*41*	...	...	...	*18*	*16*	*2*	...	...
75,365	**74,888**	**468**	**9**	...	**24,615**	**20,052**	**4,459**	**104**	...

Class.	Group.	Caste, &c. and sub-division.	Religion.	15 to 30 Total.	Single.	Married.	Widowed.	Civil condition not stated.
F.—Races and Nationalities.	48. Asiatic Races of reputed Foreign origin.	Arab	Musalmán.	...	...	...	...	...
		Bolúchi	,,	...	...	...	...	...
		Dáyari	,,	...	...	...	...	...
		Hanifi	,,	12	2	10	...	...
		Khádri	,,	...	...	...	...	...
		Kandhári...	,,	...	...	...	...	...
		Mogal	,,	99	5	84	10	...
		Musalmán	,,	2	...	2	...	...
		Paṭ'han	,,	357	26	299	32	...
		Shékh	,,	1,740	123	1,406	211	...
		Sayad	,,	324	18	275	31	...
		Sharif	,,	...	...	...	...	...
		Armenian	Christian.	...	...	...	...	...
		Burmese	,,	...	...	...	...	...
		Chinese	,,	...	...	...	...	...
		Jews	Jews.	4	1	3	...	...
		Jews	Christian.	...	...	...	...	...
		Jews.—Israelites	,,	...	...	...	...	...
		Pársi	Pársi.	...	...	...	...	...
		Singhâli	Buddhist.	...	...	...	...	...
		Total Group 48......	....	*2,538*	*175*	*2,079*	*284*	...
	49. Mixed Asiatic Races.	Labbé	Musalmán.	5	...	5	...	...
		Jâm	,,	...	...	...	...	...
		Máplé	,,	...	...	...	...	...
		Méman	,,	...	...	...	...	...
		Pinḍári	,,	...	...	...	...	...
		Pinjári	,,	5	...	5	...	...
		Total Group 49......	....	*10*	...	*10*	...	...
	50. Non-Asiatic races.	European...	,,	23	10	13	...	...
		Australasian	,,	...	...	...	...	...
		Total Group 50......	....	*23*	*10*	*13*	...	...
	51. Eurasian ...	Eurasian	,,	22	6	15	1	...
	52. Christian converts ...	Native Christian	,,	624	114	443	67	...
		Total Class F......	....	**3,217**	**305**	**2,560**	**352**	...
		Caste not stated......	....	*78*	*5*	*65*	*8*	...
		Grand Total......	....	**105,084**	**7,880**	**82,176**	**15,028**	...

TABLE E.—(Continued)

District.

Females.

40 and over.					Age not stated.				
Total.	Single.	Married.	Widowed.	Civil condition not stated.	Total.	Single.	Married.	Widowed.	Civil condition not stated.
...	...		...	...	...	...	...	...	...
...	...		...	...	...	...	...	...	...
...	...	...	...	...	...	...	...	...	...
11	...	5	6	...	...	...	...	...	...
...	...	...	...	...	...	...	...	...	...
...	...	...	...	...	...	...	...	...	...
45	...	22	23	...	...	...	...	...	...
1	...	...	1	...	...	...	...	...	...
183	...	59	124	...	...	...	...	...	...
937	25	293	620	...	...	...	...	...	...
169	...	51	118	...	...	...	...	...	...
...	...	...	...	...	...	...	...	...	...
...	...	...	...	...	...	...	...	...	...
...	...	...	...	...	...	...	...	...	...
...	...	...	...	...	...	...	...	...	...
1	...	1	...	...	...	...	...	...	...
...	...	...	...	...	...	...	...	...	...
...	...	...	...	...	...	...	...	...	...
...	...	...	...	...	...	...	...	...	...
...	...	...	...	...	...	...	...	...	...
1,347	*25*	*430*	*892*	...	...	...	[illegible]	...	...
2	...	1	1	...	...	...	...	...	...
...	...	...	...	...	...	...	...	...	...
...	...	...	...	...	...	...	...	...	...
...	...	...	...	...	...	...	...	...	...
...	...	...	...	...	...	...	...	...	...
1	...	1	...	...	...	...	...	...	...
3	...	*2*	*1*	...	...	...	...	...	...
5	...	4	1	...	...	...	...	...	...
...	...	...	...	...	...	...	...	...	...
5	...	*4*	*1*	...	...	...	...	...	...
6	...	2	4	...	...	...	...	...	...
273	4	94	175	...	...	...	...	...	...
1,634	**29**	**532**	**1,073**	...	...	...	...	...	...
46	*1*	*13*	*32*	...	...	...	...	...	...
54,814	**539**	**16,902**	**37,373**	...	**30**	**19**	**6**	**1**	**4**

Class.	Group.	Caste, &c. and sub-division.	Religion.	All Ages. Total.	Single.	Married.	Widowed.	Civil condition not stated.
F.—Races and Nationalities.	48. Asiatic Races of reputed Foreign origin.	Arab	Musalmán.	...	...	...	...	...
		Belúchi	,,	...	...	...	...	...
		Dáyaró	,,	...	...	...	...	...
		Hanifi	,,	167	93	60	14	...
		Khádri	,,	...	...	...	...	...
		Kandhári...	,,	...	...	...	...	...
		Mogal	,,	1,356	748	508	100	...
		Musalmán	,,	...	...	...	...	...
		Paṭ'hán	,,	1,969	1,072	801	96	...
		Shékh	,,	9,888	5,891	3,669	328	...
		Sayad	,,	2,267	1,306	858	103	...
		Sharif	,,	...	...	...	...	...
		Armenian	Christian.	...	...	...	...	...
		Burmese	,,	...	...	...	...	...
		Chinese	,,	...	...	...	...	...
		Jews	Jews.	...	...	...	...	...
		Jews	Christian.	...	...	...	...	...
		Jews.—Israelites	,,	...	...	...	...	...
		Pársi	Pársi.	...	...	...	...	...
		Singhálí	Buddhist.	...	...	...	...	...
		Total Group 48......	....	*15,647*	*9,110*	*5,896*	*641*	...
	49. Mixed Asiatic Races.	Labbé	Musalmán.	89	44	43	2	...
		Jám	,,	...	...	...	...	...
		Mápḷé	,,	1	1	...	...	...
		Méman	,,	...	...	...	...	...
		Pinḍári	,,	26	15	10	1	...
		Pinjári	,,	7	4	3	...	...
		Total Group 49......	....	*123*	*64*	*56*	*3*	...
	50. Non-Asiatic races.	European...	Christian.	17	11	6	...	...
		Australasian	,,	...	...	...	...	...
		Total Group 50......	....	*17*	*11*	6	...	...
	51. Eurasian ...	Eurasian	,,	14	11	2	1	...
	52. Christian converts...	Native Christian	,,	1,003	473	506	24	...
		Total Class F......	....	**16,804**	**9,669**	**6,466**	**669**	...
		Caste not stated......	....	*212*	*97*	*99*	*16*	...
		Grand Total......	....	**275,884**	**154,882**	**104,567**	**16,435**	...

TABLE E.—(*Continued.*)

District.

Males.

0 to 9					10 to 14				
Total.	Single.	Married.	Widowed.	Civil condition not stated.	Total.	Single.	Married.	Widowed.	Civil condition not stated.
...	...	...	...	...	...	...	...	...	...
...	...	...	...	...	...	...	...	...	...
...	...	...	...	...	...	...	...	...	...
45	45	...	...	...	30	30	...	...	...
...	...	...	...	...	...	...	...	...	...
...	...	...	...	...	...	...	...	...	...
341	341	...	...	...	154	150	4	...	...
...	...	...	...	...	...	...	...	...	...
567	566	1	...	...	217	211	6	...	...
2,620	2,619	1	...	...	1,066	1,054	11	1	...
624	624	...	...	...	328	321	7	...	...
...	...	...	...	...	...	...	...	...	...
...	...	...	...	...	...	...	...	...	...
...	...	...	...	...	...	...	...	...	...
...	...	...	...	...	...	...	...	...	...
...	...	...	...	...	...	...	...	...	...
...	...	...	...	...	...	...	...	...	...
...	...	...	...	...	...	...	...	...	...
...	...	...	...	...	...	...	...	...	...
...	...	...	...	...	...	...	...	...	...
4,197	*4,195*	*2*	...	...	*1,795*	*1,766*	*28*	*1*	...
9	9	...	...	...	12	12	...	...	...
...	...	...	...	...	...	...	...	...	...
...	...	...	...	...	...	...	...	...	...
...	...	...	...	...	...	...	...	...	...
7	7	...	...	...	4	4	...	...	...
2	2	...	...	...	1	1	...	...	...
18	*18*	...	...	...	*17*	*17*	...	...	...
3	3	...	...	...	1	1	...	...	...
...	...	...	...	...	...	...	...	...	...
3	*3*	...	...	...	*1*	*1*	...	...	...
1	1	...	...	...	1	1	...	...	...
168	168	...	...	...	91	86	5	...	...
4,386	**4,384**	**2**	...	...	**1,905**	**1,871**	**33**	**1**	...
40	*40*	...	...	...	*15*	*18*	...	...	...
67,818	**67,737**	**80**	**1**	...	**30,888**	**30,284**	**593**	**11**	...

Shimoga.

Class.	Group.	Caste, &c. and sub-division.	Religion.	15 to 39. Total.	Single.	Married.	Widowed.	Civil condition not stated.
F.—Races and Nationalities.	48. Asiatic Races of reputed Foreign origin.	Arab	Musalmán.	...	...	...	...	...
		Belúchi	,,	...	...	...	...	...
		Dáyaré	,,	...	...	...	...	...
		Hanifi		61	17	39	5	...
		Khádri	,,	...	...	...	...	...
		Kandhári	,,	...	...	...	...	...
		Mogal	,,	590	242	316	32	...
		Musalmán	,,	...	...	...	...	...
		Pat'hán	,,	769	282	461	26	...
		Shékh	,,	4,144	2,139	1,959	46	...
		Sayad	,,	910	341	543	26	...
		Sharif	,,	...	...	...	...	...
		Armenian	Christian.	...	...	...	...	...
		Burmese	,,	...	...	...	...	...
		Chinese	,,	...	...	...	...	...
		Jews	Jews.	...	...	...	...	...
		Jews	Christian.	...	...	...	...	...
		Jews.—Israelites	,,	...	...	...	...	...
		Pársi	Pársi.	...	...	...	...	...
		Singháli	Buddhist.	...	...	...	...	...
		Total Group 48......	....	*6,474*	*3,021*	*3,318*	*135*	...
	49. Mixed Asiatic Races.	Labbé	Musalmán.	56	23	33	...	...
		Jám	,,	...	...	...	...	...
		Máplé	,,	1	1	...	...	...
		Méman	,,	...	...	...	...	...
		Pindári	,,	11	4	7	...	...
		Pinjári	,,	3	1	2	...	...
		Total Group 49......	....	*71*	*29*	*42*	...	...
	50. Non-Asiatic races.	European	Christian.	11	6	5	...	...
		Australasian	,,	...	...	...	...	...
		Total Group 50......	....	*11*	*6*	*5*	...	...
	51. Eurasian ...	Eurasian	,,	11	9	2	...	...
	52. Christian converts ...	Native Christian	,,	532	208	314	10	...
		Total Class F......	....	**7,099**	**3,273**	**3,681**	**145**	...
		Caste not stated......	....	*104*	*39*	*61*	*4*	...
		Grand Total......	....	**120,059**	**53,119**	**62,753**	**4,187**	...

TABLE E.—(*Continued.*)

District.

Males.

40 and over.					Age not stated.				
Total.	Single.	Married.	Widowed.	Civil condition not stated.	Total.	Single.	Married.	Widowed.	Civil condition not stated.
...	...	...	...	...	...	...	...	...	...
—	...	...	...	...	...	...	...	...	...
...	...	...	...	...	...	...	...	...	...
31	1	21	9	...	...	...	...	...	...
...	...	...	...	...	...	...	...	...	...
...	...	...	...	...	...	...	...	...	...
271	15	188	68	...	...	...	...	...	...
...	...	...	...	...	...	...	...	...	...
416	13	333	70	...	...	...	...	...	...
2,058	79	1,698	281	...	...	...	...	...	...
405	20	308	77	...	...	...	...	...	...
...	...	...	...	...	...	...	...	...	...
...	...	...	...	...	...	...	...	...	...
...	...	...	...	...	...	...	...	...	...
...	...	...	...	...	...	...	...	...	...
...	...	...	...	...	...	...	...	...	...
...	...	...	...	...	...	...	...	...	...
...	...	...	...	...	...	...	...	...	...
...	...	...	...	...	...	...	...	...	...
...	...	...	...	...	...	...	...	...	...
3,181	*128*	*2,548*	*505*	...	...	...	...	...	...
12	...	10	2	...	...	...	...	...	...
...	...	...	...	...	...	...	...	...	...
...	...	...	...	...	...	...	...	...	...
...	...	...	...	...	...	...	...	...	...
4	...	3	1	...	...	...	...	...	...
1	...	1	...	...	...	...	...	...	...
17	...	*14*	*3*	...	...	...	...	...	...
3	2	1	...	...	...	...	...	...	...
...	...	...	...	...	...	...	...	...	...
3	*2*	*1*	...	...	...	...	...	...	...
1	...	...	1	...	...	...	...	...	...
212	11	187	14	...	...	...	...	...	...
3,414	**141**	**2,750**	**523**	...	...	...	...	...	...
50	...	*38*	*12*	...	...	...	...	...	...
57,112	**3,736**	**41,141**	**12,235**	...	**7**	**6**	...	**1**	...

Class.	Group.	Caste, &c. and sub-division.	Religion.	All Ages. Total.	Single.	Married.	Widowed.	Civil condition not stated.
F.—Races and Nationalities.	48. Asiatic Races of reputed Foreign origin.	Arab	Musalmán.	...	...	...	...	...
		Belúchi	"	...	...	[illegible]	...	...
		Dáyaré	"	...	...	...	...	...
		Hanifi	"	176	53	92	31	...
		Khádri	"	...	...	...	...	...
		Kandhári	"	...	...	...	...	...
		Mogal	"	1,259	417	580	262	...
		Musalmán	"	...	...	...	...	...
		Pat'hán	"	1,784	699	779	306	...
		Shékh	"	8,946	3,870	3,319	1,759	...
		Sayad	"	2,203	824	1,019	360	...
		Sharif	"	...	...	...	...	...
		Armenian	Christian.	...	...	...	...	...
		Burmese	"	...	...	...	...	...
		Chinese	"	...	...	...	...	...
		Jews	Jews-	...	...	...	...	...
		Jews	Christian.	...	...	...	...	...
		Jews.—Israelites ...	"	...	...	...	...	...
		Pársi	Pársi.	...	...	...	...	...
		Singháli	Buddhist.	...	...	...	...	...
		Total Group 48......	....	14,368	5,863	5,789	2,716	...
	49. Mixed Asiatic Races.	Labbé	Musalmán.	30	10	19	1	...
		Jám	"	...	...	...	...	...
		Máplé	"	19	7	9	3	...
		Méman	"	...	...	...	...	...
		Pindári	"	7	3	4	...	...
		Pinjári	"	3	1	2	...	...
		Total Group 49......	....	59	21	34	4	...
	50. Non-Asiatic races.	European...	"	15	12	3	...	...
		Australasian	"	...	...	...	...	...
		Total Group 50......	....	15	12	3	...	...
	51. Eurasian ...	Eurasian	"	2	...	2	...	...
	52. Christian converts ...	Native Christian	"	600	278	239	83	...
		Total Class F...	....	**15,044**	**6,174**	**6,067**	**2,803**	...
		Caste not stated.....	....	121	50	45	26	...
		Grand Total.....	....	**252,097**	**100,404**	**97,444**	**54,249**	...

TABLE E.—(*Continued.*)

District.

Females.

0 to 9					10 to 14.				
Total.	Single.	Married.	Widowed.	Civil condition not stated.	Total.	Single.	Married.	Widowed.	Civil condition not stated.
...	...	...	...	...	...	...	...	...	...
...	...	...	...	...	...	...	...	...	...
...	...	...	...	...	...	...	...	...	...
87	87	...	...	...	20	15	5	...	...
...	...	...	...	...	...	...	...	...	...
...	...	...	...	...	...	...	...	...	...
315	310	5	...	...	96	76	20	...	...
...	...	...	...	...	...	...	...	...	...
514	506	8	...	...	205	167	38	...	...
2,905	2,889	15	1	...	904	727	175	2	...
536	526	10	...	...	283	226	57	...	...
...	...	...	...	...	...	...	...	...	...
...	...	...	...	...	...	...	...	...	...
...	...	...	...	...	...	...	...	...	...
...	...	...	...	...	...	...	...	...	...
...	...	...	...	...	...	...	...	...	...
...	...	...	...	...	...	...	...	...	...
...	...	...	...	...	...	...	...	...	...
...	...	...	...	...	...	...	...	...	...
...	...	...	...	...	...	...	...	...	...
4,307	*4,268*	*38*	*1*	...	*1,508*	*1,211*	*205*	*2*	...
6	6	...	...	...	3	3	...	...	...
...	...	...	...	...	...	...	...	...	...
3	3	...	...	...	3	2	1	...	...
...	...	...	...	...	...	...	...	...	...
2	2	...	...	...	1	1	...	...	...
1	1	...	...	...	...	...	...	...	...
12	*12*	...	...	...	*7*	*6*	*1*	...	...
6	6	...	...	...	2	2	...	...	...
...	...	...	...	...	...	...	...	...	...
6	*6*	...	...	...	*2*	*2*	...	...	...
...	...	...	...	...	...	...	...	...	...
163	163	...	...	...	83	75	8	...	...
4,488	**4,449**	**38**	**1**	...	**1,600**	**1,294**	**304**	**2**	...
38	*38*	...	...	...	*10*	*10*	...	...	...
70,093	**68,906**	**1,158**	**29**	...	**27,591**	**19,820**	**7,481**	**270**	...

Class.	Group.	Caste, &c. and sub-division.	Religion.	15 to 39 Total.	Single.	Married.	Widowed.	Civil condition not stated.
F.—Races and Nationalities.	48. Asiatic Races of reputed Foreign origin.	Arab	Musalmán.	...	...	...	...	...
		Belúchi	,,	...	...	...	...	...
		Dáyaré	,,	...	...	...	...	...
		Hanifi	,,	81	1	70	10	...
		Khádri	,,	...	...	...	...	...
		Kandhári...	,,	...	...	...	...	...
		Mogal	,,	502	29	413	60	...
		Musalmán	,,	...	...	...	...	...
		Paṭhán	,,	655	25	550	80	...
		Shékh	,,	3,591	224	2,884	483	...
		Sayad	,,	813	56	666	91	...
		Sharif	,,	...	...	...	...	...
		Armenian...	Christian.	...	...	...	...	...
		Burmese	,,	...	...	...	...	...
		Chinese	,,	...	...	...	...	...
		Jews	Jews.	...	...	...	...	...
		Jews	Christian.	...	...	...	...	...
		Jews.—Israelites	,,	...	...	...	...	...
		Pársi	Pársi.	...	...	...	...	...
		Singháli	Buddhist.	...	...	...	...	...
		Total Group 48......	....	*5,642*	*335*	*4,583*	*724*	...
	49. Mixed Asiatic Races.	Labbé	Musalmán.	15	1	14	...	...
		Jám	,,	...	...	...	...	...
		Máplé	,,	7	2	5	...	...
		Méman	,,	...	...	...	...	...
		Pindári	,,	3	...	3	...	...
		Pinjári	,,	2	...	2	...	...
		Total Group 49......	....	*27*	*3*	*24*	...	...
	50. Non-Asiatic races.	European...	Christian.	7	4	3	...	...
		Australasian	,,	...	...	...	...	...
		Total Group 50......	....	*7*	*4*	*3*	...	...
	51. Eurasian ...	Eurasian	,,	2	...	2	...	...
	52. Christian converts ...	Native Christian	,,	261	34	204	23	...
		Total Class F......	....	**5,939**	**376**	**4,816**	**747**	...
		Caste not stated......	....	*47*	*2*	*39*	*6*	...
		Grand Total......	....	**103,880**	**9,442**	**75,672**	**18,766**	...

TABLE E.—(Continued.)

District.

Females.

40 and over.					Age not stated.				
Total.	Single.	Married.	Widowed.	Civil condition not stated.	Total.	Single.	Married.	Widowed.	Civil condition not stated.
...	...	...	...	...	...	...	...	...	...
...	...	...	...	...	...	...	...	...	...
...	...	...	...	...	...	...	...	...	...
38	...	17	21	...	...	...	...	...	...
...	...	...	...	...	...	...	...	...	...
...	...	...	...	...	...	...	...	...	...
346	2	142	202	...	...	...	...	...	...
...	...	...	...	...	...	...	...	...	...
410	1	183	226	...	...	...	...	...	...
1,545	30	245	1,270	...	1	...	...	1	...
571	16	286	269	...	...	...	...	...	...
...	...	...	...	...	...	...	...	...	...
...	...	...	...	...	...	...	...	...	...
...	...	...	...	...	...	...	...	...	...
...	...	...	...	...	...	...	...	...	...
...	...	...	...	...	...	...	...	...	...
...	...	...	...	...	...	...	...	...	...
...	...	...	...	...	...	...	...	...	...
...	...	...	...	...	...	...	...	...	...
...	...	...	...	...	...	...	...	...	...
2,910	*49*	*873*	*1,988*	...	*1*	...	...	*1*	...
6	...	5	1	...	...	...	...	...	...
...	...	...	...	...	...	...	...	...	...
6	...	3	3	...	...	...	...	...	...
...	...	...	...	...	...	...	...	...	...
1	...	1	...	...	...	...	...	...	...
...	...	...	...	...	...	...	...	...	...
13	...	*9*	*4*	...	...	...	...	...	...
...	...	...	...	...	...	...	...	...	...
...	...	...	...	...	...	...	...	...	...
...	...	...	...	...	...	...	...	...	...
...	...	...	...	...	...	...	...	...	...
93	*8*	*27*	*60*	...	...	...	...	...	...
3,016	**55**	**909**	**2,052**	...	**1**	...	...	**1**	...
26	...	*6*	*20*	...	...	...	...	...	...
50,520	**2,228**	**13,129**	**35,163**	...	**13**	**8**	**4**	**1**	...

Class.	Group.	Caste, &c. and sub-division.	Religion.	All Ages. Total.	Single.	Married.	Widowed.	Civil condition not stated.
F.—Races and Nationalities.	48. Asiatic Races of reputed Foreign origin.	Arab	Musalmán.	...	...	...	...	...
		Belúchi	"	...	...	...	...	...
		Dáyaré	"	...	...	...	...	...
		Hanifi	"	14	7	5	2	...
		Khádri	"	...	...	...	...	...
		Kandhári	"	...	...	...	...	...
		Mogal	"	202	101	89	12	...
		Musalmán	"	...	...	...	...	...
		Pat'hán	"	1,147	608	509	30	...
		Shékh	"	6,162	3,420	2,579	163	...
		Sayad	"	1,071	655	370	46	...
		Sharif	"	...	...	...	...	...
		Armenian	Christian.	...	...	...	...	...
		Burmese	"	...	...	...	...	...
		Chinese	"	...	...	...	...	...
		Jews	Jews.	...	...	...	...	...
		Jews	Christian.	...	...	...	...	...
		Jews.—Israelites	"	...	...	...	...	...
		Pársi	Pársi.	...	...	...	...	...
		Singháli	Buddhist.	...	...	...	...	...
		Total Group 48	....	*8,596*	*4,791*	*3,552*	*253*	...
	49. Mixed Asiatic Races.	Labbé	Musalmán.	144	73	61	10	...
		Jám	"	...	...	...	...	...
		Máplé	"	40	16	18	6	...
		Méman	"	...	...	...	...	...
		Pindári	"	...	...	...	...	...
		Pinjári	"	1	...	...	1	...
		Total Group 49	....	*185*	*89*	*79*	*17*	...
	50. Non-Asiatic races.	Europe and ...	Christian.	147	94	49	4	...
		Austr[illegible]lasian	"	...	...	...	...	...
		Total Group 50	....	*147*	*94*	*49*	*4*	...
	51. Eurasian	Eu[illegible]	"	134	83	48	3	...
	52. Christian converts	Native Christian	"	1,275	652	594	29	...
		Total Class F	....	**10,337**	**5,709**	**4,322**	**306**	...
		Caste not stated	....	*264*	*134*	*100*	*21*	...
		Grand Total	....	**173,922**	**97,207**	**68,299**	**8,412**	**4**

TABLE E.—(*Continued.*)

District.

Males.

0 to 9					10 to 14				
Total.	Single.	Married.	Widowed.	Civil condition not stated.	Total.	Single.	Married.	Widowed.	Civil condition not stated.
...	...	...	...	...	...	...	...	...	...
...	...	...	...	...	...	...	...	...	...
...	...	...	...	...	...	...	...	...	...
4	4	...	...	...	1	1	...	...	...
...	...	...	...	...	...	...	...	...	...
...	...	...	...	...	...	...	...	...	...
47	47	...	...	...	19	19	...	...	...
...	...	...	...	...	...	...	...	...	...
243	243	...	...	...	109	109	...	...	...
1,331	1,328	3	...	...	564	563	1	...	...
245	245	...	...	...	105	101	4	...	...
...	...	...	...	...	...	...	...	...	...
...	...	...	...	...	...	...	...	...	...
...	...	...	...	...	...	...	...	...	...
...	...	...	...	...	...	...	...	...	...
...	...	...	...	...	...	...	...	...	...
...	...	...	...	...	...	...	...	...	...
...	...	...	...	...	...	...	...	...	...
...	...	...	...	...	...	...	...	...	...
...	...	...	...	...	...	...	...	...	...
...	...	...	...	...	...	...	...	...	...
1,870	*1,867*	*3*	...	...	*798*	*793*	*5*	...	...
30	30	...	...	...	9	9	...	...	...
...	...	...	...	...	...	...	...	...	...
...	...	...	...	...	6	6	...	...	...
...	...	...	...	...	...	...	...	...	...
...	...	...	...	...	...	...	...	...	...
...	...	...	...	...	...	...	...	...	...
30	*30*	...	...	...	*15*	*15*	...	...	...
26	26	...	...	...	17	17	...	...	...
...	...	...	...	...	...	...	...	...	...
26	*26*	...	...	...	*17*	*17*	...	...	...
28	28	...	...	...	12	12	...	...	...
124	124	...	...	...	76	74	2	...	...
2,078	**2,075**	**3**	...	...	**918**	**911**	**7**	...	...
46	*46*	...	...	...	*27*	*27*	...	...	...
43,194	**43,177**	**15**	**2**	...	**17,472**	**17,280**	**188**	**4**	...

Kadur

Class.	Group.	Caste, &c., and sub-division.	Religion.	15 to 30. Total.	Single.	Married.	Widowed.	Civil condition not stated.
F.—Races and Nationalities	48. Asiatic Races of reputed Foreign origin.	Arab	Musalmán.	...	...	...	...	...
		Belûchi	,,	...	...	...	...	...
		Dâyaré	,,	6	2	4	...	...
		Hanifi	,,	...	...	...	...	...
		Khâdri	,,	...	...	...	...	...
		Kandhâri	,,	87	32	51	4	...
		Mogal	,,	...	...	...	...	...
		Musalmán	,,	546	237	300	9	...
		Pat'hân	,,	3,022	1,466	1,509	47	...
		Shêkh	,,	558	295	246	17	...
		Sayad	,,	...	...	...	...	...
		Sharif	,,	...	...	...	...	...
		Armenian	Christian.	...	...	...	...	...
		Burmese	,,	...	...	...	...	...
		Chinese	,,	...	...	...	...	...
		Jews	Jews.	...	...	...	...	...
		Jews	Christian.	...	...	...	...	...
		Jews.—Israelites	,,	...	...	...	...	...
		Pársi	Pársi.	...	...	...	...	...
		Singhâli	Buddhist.	...	...	...	...	...
		Total Group 48	....	*4,219*	*2,032*	*2,110*	*77*	...
	49. Mixed Asiatic Races.	Labbé	Musalmán.	66	24	38	4	...
		Jâm	,,	...	...	...	...	...
		Mâplé	,,	22	8	13	1	...
		Méman	,,	...	...	...	...	...
		Pindâri	,,	...	...	...	...	...
		Pinjâri	,,	...	...	...	...	...
		Total Group 49	....	*88*	*32*	*51*	*5*	...
	50. Non-Asiatic races.	European	Christian.	84	42	41	1	...
		Australasian	,,	...	...	...	...	...
		Total Group 50	....	*84*	*42*	*41*	*1*	...
	51. Eurasian	Eurasian	,,	72	40	32	...	...
	52. Christian converts	Native Christian	,,	830	415	401	14	...
		Total Class F	....	**5,293**	**2,561**	**2,635**	**97**	...
		Caste not stated	....	*130*	*49*	*73*	*8*	...
		Grand Total	....	**80,294**	**35,400**	**42,460**	**2,434**	...

di

TABLE E.—(*Continued.*)

District.

Males.

40 and over.					Age not stated.				
Total	Single.	Married.	Widowed.	Civil condition not stated.	Total.	Single.	Married.	Widowed.	Civil condition not stated.
...	...	...	...	...	...	...	...	...	...
...	...	...	...	...	...	...	...	...	...
...	...	...	...	...	...	...	...	...	...
3	...	1	2	...	...	...	...	...	...
...	...	...	...	...	...	...	...	...	...
...	...	...	...	...	...	...	...	...	...
49	3	38	8	...	...	...	...	...	...
...	...	...	...	...	...	...	...	...	...
249	19	209	21	...	...	...	...	...	...
1,245	63	1,066	116	...	...	...	...	...	...
163	14	120	29	...	...	...	...	...	...
...	...	...	...	...	...	...	...	...	...
...	...	...	...	...	...	...	...	...	...
...	...	...	...	...	...	...	...	...	...
...	...	...	...	...	...	...	...	...	...
...	...	...	...	...	...	...	...	...	...
...	...	...	...	...	...	...	...	...	...
...	...	...	...	...	...	...	...	...	...
...	...	...	...	...	...	...	...	...	...
...	...	...	...	...	...	...	...	...	...
1,709	*99*	*1,434*	*176*	...	...	...	...	...	...
39	10	23	6	...	...	...	...	...	...
...	...	...	...	...	...	...	...	...	...
12	2	5	5	...	...	...	...	...	...
...	...	...	...	...	...	...	...	...	...
...	...	...	...	...	...	...	...	...	...
1	...	...	1	...	...	...	...	...	...
53	*12*	*28*	*12*	...	...	...	...	...	...
20	9	8	3	...	...	...	...	...	...
...	...	...	...	...	...	...	...	...	...
20	*9*	*8*	*3*	...	...	...	...	...	...
22	3	16	3	...	...	...	...	...	...
245	39	191	15	...	...	...	...	...	...
2,048	**162**	**1,677**	**209**	...	...	...	...	...	...
81	*12*	*30*	*13*	...	...	...	...	...	...
32,956	**1,350**	**25,635**	**5,971**	...	**6**	...	**1**	**1**	**4**

Class.	Group.	Caste, &c. and sub-division.	Religion.	All Ages. Total.	Single.	Married.	Widowed.	Civil condition not stated.
F.—Races and Nationalities.	48. Asiatic Races of reputed Foreign origin.	Arab	Musalmán.	...	...	...	...	...
		Belúchi	,,	...	...	...	...	...
		Dáyaré		...	...	...	...	...
		Hanifii	,,	...	...	...	...	...
		Khádri	,,	...	...	...	...	...
		Kandhári	,,	...	...	...	...	...
		Mogal	,,	174	51	79	44	...
		Musalmán	,,	...	...	...	...	...
		Pat'hán	,,	970	369	432	169	...
		Shékh	,,	4,750	1,921	1,872	957	...
		Seyad	,,	872	300	388	184	...
		Sharif	,,	...	...	...	...	...
		Armenian	Christian.	...	...	...	...	...
		Burmese	,,	...	...	...	...	...
		Chinese	,,	...	...	...	...	...
		Jews	Jews.	...	...	...	...	...
		Jews	,,	...	...	...	...	...
		Jews.—Israelites	Christian.	...	...	...	...	...
		Pársi	Pársi.	...	...	...	...	...
		Singháli	,,	...	...	...	...	...
		Total Group 48	....	6,766	2,641	2,771	1,354	...
	49. Mixed Asiatic Races.	Labbé	Musalmán.	17	3	14	...	...
		Jám	,,	...	...	...	...	...
		Máplé	,,	1	...	1	...	...
		Méman	,,	...	...	...	...	...
		Pindári	,,	...	...	...	...	...
		Pinjári	,,	...	...	...	...	...
		Total Group 49	....	18	3	15	...	...
	50. Non-Asiatic races.	European	Christian.	60	25	33	2	...
		Australasian	,,	...	...	...	...	...
		Total Group 50	....	60	25	33	2	...
	51. Eurasian	Eurasian	,,	95	29	62	4	...
	52. Christian converts	Native Christian	,,	498	204	215	79	...
		Total Class F	....	**7,437**	**2,902**	**3,096**	**1,439**	...
		Caste not stated	....	196	40	113	43	...
		Grand Total	....	**156,141**	**62,375**	**62,230**	**31,517**	**19**

TABLE E.—(*Continued.*)

District.

Females.

0 to 9					10 to 14				
Total.	Single.	Married.	Widowed.	Civil condition not stated.	Total.	Single.	Married.	Widowed.	Civil condition not stated.
...	...	...	...	...	...	...	...	...	...
...	...	...	...	...	...	...	...	...	...
...	...	...	...	...	...	...	...	...	...
...	...	...	...	...	...	...	...	...	...
...	...	...	...	...	...	...	...	...	...
...	...	...	...	...	...	...	...	...	...
35	35	...	...	...	13	10	3	...	...
...	...	...	...	...	...	...	...	...	...
233	230	3	...	...	106	90	16	...	...
1,457	1,446	9	2	...	446	360	83	3	...
217	208	7	2	...	75	65	7	3	...
...	...	...	...	...	...	...	...	...	...
...	...	...	...	...	...	...	...	...	...
...	...	...	...	...	...	...	...	...	...
...	...	...	...	...	...	...	...	...	...
...	...	...	...	...	...	...	...	...	...
...	...	...	...	...	...	...	...	...	...
...	...	...	...	...	...	...	...	...	...
...	...	...	...	...	...	...	...	...	...
...	...	...	...	...	...	...	...	...	...
1,942	*1,919*	*19*	*4*	...	*640*	*525*	*109*	*6*	...
3	3	...	...	...	...	...	...	...	...
...	...	...	...	...	...	...	...	...	...
...	...	...	...	...	...	...	...	...	...
...	...	...	...	...	...	...	...	...	...
...	...	...	...	...	...	...	...	...	...
...	...	...	...	...	...	...	...	...	...
3	*3*	...	...	...	...	...	...	...	...
19	19	...	...	...	...	...	...	...	...
...	...	...	...	...	...	...	...	...	...
19	*19*	...	...	...	...	...	...	...	...
20	20	...	...	...	...	...	...	...	...
134	127	7	...	...	73	48	25	...	...
2,118	**2,088**	**26**	**4**	...	**713**	**573**	**134**	**6**	...
19	*16*	*3*	...	...	*18*	*10*	*8*	...	...
45,962	**44,473**	**1,477**	**12**	...	**15,179**	**12,041**	**3,017**	**121**	...

Class.	Group.	Caste, &c. and sub-division.	Religion.	15 to 30. Total.	Single.	Married.	Widowed.	Civil condition not stated.
F.—Races and Nationalities.	48. Asiatic Races of reputed Foreign origin.	Arab	Musalmán.	...	...	...	...	...
		Belúchi	,,	...	...	...	...	...
		Dáyaré	,,	...	...	...	...	...
		Hanifi	,,	...	...	...	...	...
		Khádri	,,	...	...	...	...	...
		Kandhári	,,	...	...	...	...	...
		Mogul	,,	81	6	62	13	...
		Musalmán	,,	...	...	...	...	...
		Paṭ'han	,,	433	46	334	53	...
		Shékh	,,	1,897	100	1,523	274	...
		Sayad	,,	373	27	306	40	...
		Shariff	,,	...	...	...	...	...
		Armenian	Christian.	...	...	...	...	...
		Burmese	,,	...	...	...	...	...
		Chinese	,,	...	...	...	...	...
		Jews	Jews.	...	...	...	...	...
		Jews	Christian.	...	...	...	...	...
		Jews—Israelites	,,	...	...	...	...	...
		Pársi	Pársi.	...	...	...	...	...
		Singháli	Buddhist.	...	...	...	...	...
		Total Group 48	....	*2,784*	*179*	*2,225*	*380*	...
	Mixed Asiatic Races.	Labbé	Musalmán.	10	...	10	...	...
		Jám	,,	...	...	...	...	...
		Máplé	,,	1	...	1	...	...
		Méman	,,	...	...	...	...	...
		Pinḍári	,,	...	...	...	...	...
		Pinjári	,,	...	...	...	...	...
		Total Group 49	....	*11*	...	*11*	...	...
	50. Non-Asiatic races.	European	Christian.	38	6	30	2	...
		Australasian	,,	...	...	...	...	...
		Total Group 50	....	*38*	*6*	*30*	*2*	...
	51. Eurasian	Eurasian	,,	59	9	50	...	...
	52. Christian converts	Native Christian	,,	217	25	161	31	...
		Total Class F	....	**3,109**	**219**	**2,477**	**413**	...
		Caste not stated.	....	*108*	*8*	*89*	*11*	...
		Grand Total	....	**65,344**	**5,123**	**49,103**	**11,118**	...

TABLE E.—(Continued.)

District.

Males.

40 and over. Total.	Single.	Married.	Widowed.	Civil condition not stated.	Age not stated. Total.	Single.	Married.	Widowed.	Civil condition not stated.
...	...	...	...	...	...	...	...	...	...
...	...	...	...	...	...	...	...	...	...
...	...	...	...	...	...	...	...	...	...
...	...	...	...	...	...	...	...	...	...
...	...	...	...	...	...	...	...	...	...
...	...	...	...	...	...	...	...	...	...
45	...	14	31	...	...	...	...	...	...
...	...	...	...	...	...	...	...	...	...
196	3	79	116	...	...	...	...	...	...
950	15	257	678	...	...	...	...	...	...
207	...	68	139	...	...	...	...	...	...
...	...	...	...	...	...	...	...	...	...
...	...	...	...	...	...	...	...	...	...
...	...	...	...	...	...	...	...	...	...
...	...	...	...	...	...	...	...	...	...
...	...	...	...	...	...	...	...	...	...
...	...	...	...	...	...	...	...	...	...
...	...	...	...	...	...	...	...	...	...
...	...	...	...	...	...	...	...	...	...
...	...	...	...	...	...	...	...	...	...
1,400	*18*	*418*	*964*	...	...	...	...	...	...
4	...	4	...	...	...	...	...	...	...
...	...	...	...	...	...	...	...	...	...
...	...	...	...	...	...	...	...	...	...
...	...	...	...	...	...	...	...	...	...
...	...	...	...	...	...	...	...	...	...
...	...	...	...	...	...	...	...	...	...
4	...	4	...	...	...	...	...	...	...
3	...	3	...	...	...	...	...	...	...
...	...	...	...	...	...	...	...	...	...
8	...	3	...	...	...	...	...	...	...
16	...	12	4	...	...	...	...	...	...
74	4	22	48	...	...	...	...	...	...
1,497	**22**	**459**	**1,016**	...	...	...	...	...	...
50	*6*	*12*	*33*	...	...	...	...	...	...
29,631	**737**	**8,633**	**20,261**	...	**25**	**1**	...	**5**	**19**

Class.	Group.	Caste, &c. and sub-division.	Religion.	All Ages. Total.	Single.	Married.	Widowed.	Civil condition not stated.
F.—Races and Nationalities.	48. Asiatic Races of reputed Foreign origin.	Arab	Musalmán.	7	3	4	...	...
		Belúchi	,,	...	...	...	...	...
		Dáyaré	,,	...	...	...	...	...
		Hanifi	,,	1	...	1	...	...
		Khádri	,,	...	...	...	...	...
		Kandhári	,,	...	...	...	...	...
		Mogal	,,	119	66	44	9	...
		Musalmán	,,	8	5	3	...	...
		Pat'hán	,,	964	546	371	47	...
		Shékh	,,	6,660	3,720	2,744	196	...
		Sayad	,,	1,186	664	472	50	...
		Sharif	,,	...	...	...	...	...
		Armenian...	Christian.	...	...	...	...	...
		Burmese	,,	...	...	...	...	...
		Chinese	,,	...	...	...	...	...
		Jews	Jews.	1	...	...	1	...
		Jews	Christian.	...	...	...	...	...
		Jews.—Israelites	,,	...	...	...	...	...
		Pársi	Pársi.	2	1	1	...	...
		Singháli	Buddhist.	...	...	...	...	...
		Total Group 48......	....	*8,948*	*5,005*	*3,640*	*303*	...
	49. Mixed Asiatic Races.	Labbé	Musalmán.	8	6	2	...	...
		Jám	,,	...	...	...	...	...
		Mápié	,,	...	...	...	...	...
		Méman	,,	...	...	...	...	...
		Pindári	,,	...	...	...	...	...
		Pinjári	,,	518	258	218	42	...
		Total Gorup 49......	....	*526*	*264*	*220*	*42*	...
	50. Non-Asiatic races.	European	Christian.	15	11	4	...	...
		Australasian	,,	...	...	...	...	...
		Total Group 50......	....	*15*	*11*	*4*	...	...
	51. Eurasian ...	Eurasian	,,	23	13	9	1	...
	52. Christian converts...	Native Christian	,,	128	66	51	11	...
		Total Class F......	....	**9,640**	**5,359**	**3,924**	**357**	...
		Caste not stated......	....	*67*	*34*	*28*	*5*	...
		Grand Total......	....	**209,590**	**117,136**	**81,690**	**10,764**	...

TABLE E.—(*Continued.*)

District.

Males.

0 to 9					10 to 14				
Total.	Single.	Married.	Widowed.	Civil condition not stated.	Total.	Single.	Married.	Widowed.	Civil condition not stated.
2	2	...	...	...	1	1	...	...	...
...	...	...	...	...	...	...	...	...	...
...	...	...	...	...	...	...	...	...	...
...	...	...	...	...	...	...	...	...	...
...	...	...	...	...	...	...	...	...	...
...	...	...	...	...	...	...	...	...	...
39	39	...	...	...	10	10	...	...	...
3	3	...	...	...	2	2	...	...	...
296	296	...	...	...	102	102	...	...	...
2,134	2,128	6	...	...	529	515	14	...	...
397	397	...	...	...	98	93	5	...	...
...	...	...	...	...	...	...	...	...	...
...	...	...	...	...	...	...	...	...	...
...	...	...	...	...	...	...	...	...	...
...	...	...	...	...	...	...	...	...	...
...	...	...	...	...	...	...	...	...	...
...	...	...	...	...	...	...	...	...	...
...	...	...	...	...	...	...	...	...	...
...	...	...	...	...	...	...	...	...	...
...	...	...	...	...	...	...	...	...	...
2,871	*2,865*	*6*	...	...	*742*	*723*	*19*	...	...
...	...	...	...	...	...	...	...	...	...
...	...	...	...	...	...	...	...	...	...
...	...	...	...	...	...	...	...	...	...
...	...	...	...	...	...	...	...	...	...
...	...	...	...	...	...	...	...	...	...
142	142	...	...	...	48	46	2	...	...
142	*142*	...	...	...	*48*	*46*	*2*	...	...
1	1	...	...	...	...	...	...	...	...
...	...	...	...	...	...	...	...	...	...
1	*1*	...	...	...	...	...	...	...	...
3	3	...	...	...	2	2	...	...	...
38	38	...	...	...	5	5	...	...	...
3,055	**3,049**	**6**	...	...	**797**	**776**	**21**	...	...
22	22	...	...	...	4	4	...	...	...
83,781	**83,709**	**71**	**1**	...	**16,621**	**16,290**	**321**	**10**	...

Class.	Group.	Caste, &c. and sub-division.	Religion.	15 to 39 Total.	15 to 39 Single.	15 to 39 Married.	15 to 39 Widowed.	15 to 39 Civil condition not stated.
F.—Races and Nationalities.	48. Asiatic Races of reputed Foreign origin.	Arab	Musalmán.	3	...	3	...	...
		Belúchi	,,	...	...	...	...	...
		Dáyaré	,,	...	...	...	...	...
		Haniff	,,	1	...	1	...	...
		Khádri	,,	...	...	...	...	...
		Kandhári	,,	...	...	...	...	...
		Mogal	,,	52	17	33	2	...
		Musalmán	,,	2	...	2	...	...
		Paṭhán	,,	388	144	232	12	...
		Shékh	,,	2,622	1,022	1,547	53	...
		Sayad	,,	451	169	272	10	...
		Sharíf	,,	...	...	...	...	...
		Armenian	Christian.	...	...	...	...	...
		Burmese	,,	...	...	...	...	...
		Chinese	,,	...	...	...	...	...
		Jews	Jews.	1	...	...	1	...
		Jews	Christian.	...	...	...	...	...
		Jews.—Israelites	,,	...	...	...	...	...
		Pársi	Pársi.	1	1	...	...	...
		Singháli	Buddhist.	...	...	...	...	...
		Total Group 48	...	*3,521*	*1,353*	*2,090*	*78*	...
	49. Mixed Asiatic Races.	Labbé	Musalmán.	4	3	1	...	...
		Jám	,,	...	...	...	...	...
		Máplé	,,	...	...	...	...	...
		Méman	,,	...	...	...	...	...
		Pindári	,,	...	...	...	...	...
		Pinjári	,,	200	66	121	13	...
		Total Group 49	....	*204*	*69*	*122*	*13*	...
	50. Non-Asiatic races.	European	Christian.	14	10	4	...	...
		Australasian	,,	...	...	...	...	...
		Total Group 50	....	*14*	*10*	*4*	...	...
	51. Eurasian	Eurasian	,,	14	8	6	...	...
	52. Christian converts	Native Christian	,,	63	19	37	7	...
		Total Class F	....	**3,816**	**1,459**	**2,259**	**98**	...
		Caste not stated	....	*28*	*8*	*19*	*1*	...
		Grand Total	....	**86,551**	**35,538**	**48,608**	**2,405**	...

TABLE E.—(*Continued.*)

District.

Males.

40 and over.					Age not stated.				
Total.	Single.	Married.	Widowed.	Civil condition not stated.	Total.	Single.	Married.	Widowed.	Civil condition not stated.
1	...	1	...	...	...	...	...	...	...
...	...	...	...	...	...	...	...	...	...
...	...	...	...	...	...	...	...	...	...
...	...	...	...	...	...	...	...	...	...
...	...	...	...	...	...	...	...	...	...
...	...	...	...	...	...	...	...	...	...
18	...	11	7	...	...	...	...	...	...
1	...	1	...	...	...	...	...	...	...
178	4	139	35	...	...	...	...	...	...
1,375	55	1,177	143	...	...	...	...	...	...
240	5	195	40	...	...	...	...	...	...
...	...	...	...	...	...	...	...	...	...
...	...	...	...	...	...	...	...	...	...
...	...	...	...	...	...	...	...	...	...
...	...	...	...	...	...	...	...	...	...
...	...	...	...	...	...	...	...	...	...
...	...	...	...	...	...	...	...	...	...
...	...	...	...	...	...	...	...	...	...
1	...	1	...	...	...	...	...	...	...
...	...	...	...	...	...	...	...	...	...
1,814	*64*	*1,525*	*225*	...	...	...	...	...	...
4	3	1	...	...	...	...	...	...	...
...	...	...	...	...	...	...	...	...	...
...	...	...	...	...	...	...	...	...	...
...	...	...	...	...	...	...	...	...	...
...	...	...	...	...	...	...	...	...	...
128	4	95	29	...	...	...	...	...	...
132	*7*	*96*	*29*	...	...	...	...	...	...
...	...	...	...	...	...	...	...	...	...
...	...	...	...	...	...	...	...	...	...
...	...	...	...	...	...	...	...	...	...
4	...	3	1	...	...	...	...	...	...
22	4	14	4	...	...	...	...	...	...
1,972	**75**	**1,638**	**259**	...	...	...	...	...	...
13	...	*9*	*4*	...	...	...	...	...	...
42,625	**1,589**	**32,690**	**8,346**	...	**12**	**10**	...	**2**	...

Chitaldurg.

Class.	Group.	Caste, &c. and sub-division.	Religion.	All Ages. Total.	Single.	Married.	Widowed.	Civil condition not stated.
F.—Races and Nationalities.	48. Asiatic Races of reputed Foreign origin.	Arab	Musalmán.	6	2	4	...	...
		Belúchi	,,	...	...	...	...	...
		Dáyuré	,,	...	...	...	...	...
		Hanifi	,,	2	1	1	...	...
		Khâdri	,,	...	...	...	...	...
		Kandhâri	,,	...	...	...	...	...
		Mogal	,,	118	51	51	16	...
		Musalmán	,,	6	2	3	1	...
		Paṭ'hán	,,	875	392	346	137	...
		Shékh	,,	6,182	2,483	2,709	990	...
		Sayad	,,	1,085	508	421	156	...
		Sharif	,,	...	...	...	...	...
		Armenian	Christian.	...	...	...	...	...
		Burmese	,,	...	...	...	...	...
		Chinese	,,	...	...	...	...	...
		Jews	Jews.	...	...	...	...	...
		Jews	Christian.	...	...	...	...	...
		Jews.—Israelites	,,	...	...	...	...	...
		Pársi	Pársi.	4	2	1	1	...
		Singhâli	Buddhist.	...	...	...	...	...
		Total Group 48	....	8,278	3,441	3,536	1,301	...
	49. Mixed Asiatic Races.	Labbé	Musalmán.	...	...	...	...	...
		Jám	,,	...	...	...	...	...
		Máplé	,,	...	...	...	...	...
		Méman	,,	...	...	...	...	...
		Pindári	,,	...	...	...	...	...
		Pinjári	,,	437	203	177	57	...
		Total Group 49	....	437	203	177	57	...
	50. Non-Asiatic races.	European	,,	2	...	2	...	...
		Australasian	,,	...	...	...	...	...
		Total Group 50	....	2	...	2	...	...
	51. Eurasian ...	Eurasian	,,	15	10	5	...	...
	52. Christian converts ...	Native Christian	,,	101	47	42	12	...
		Total Class F	....	**8,833**	**3,701**	**3,762**	**1,370**	...
		Caste not stated	....	56	21	26	9	...
		Grand Total	....	**204,394**	**81,371**	**82,973**	**40,050**	...

TABLE E.—(*Continued.*)

District.

Females.

0 to 9					10 to 14.				
Total.	Single.	Married.	Widowed.	Civil condition not stated.	Total.	Single.	Married.	Widowed.	Civil condition not stated.
2	2	...	...	...	...	...	...	...	...
...	...	...	...	...	...	...	...	...	...
...	...	...	...	...	...	...	...	...	...
1	1	...	...	...	—	...	...	...	...
...	...	...	...	...	...	...	...	...	...
...	...	...	...	...	...	...	...	...	...
39	39	...	...	...	11	11	...	...	...
2	2	...	...	...	...	...	...	...	...
321	321	...	...	...	65	59	6	...	...
2,204	2,100	44	...	...	389	267	119	3	...
383	382	1	...	...	130	109	21	...	...
...	...	...	...	...	...	...	...	...	...
...	...	...	...	...	...	...	...	...	...
...	...	...	...	...	...	...	...	...	...
...	...	...	...	...	...	...	...	...	...
...	...	...	...	...	...	...	...	...	...
...	...	...	...	...	...	...	...	...	...
...	...	...	...	...	...	...	...	...	...
...	...	...	...	...	1	1	...	...	...
...	...	...	...	...	...	...	...	...	...
2,952	*2,907*	*45*	...	...	*596*	*447*	*146*	*3*	...
...	...	...	...	...	...	...	...	...	...
...	...	...	...	...	...	...	...	...	...
...	...	...	...	...	...	...	...	...	...
...	...	...	...	...	...	...	...	...	...
...	...	...	...	...	...	...	...	...	...
138	138	...	...	...	54	51	3	...	...
138	*138*	...	...	...	*54*	*51*	*3*	...	...
...	...	...	...	...	...	...	...	...	...
...	...	...	...	...	...	...	...	...	...
...	...	...	...	...	...	...	...	...	...
4	4	...	...	...	6	6	...	...	...
34	34	...	...	...	5	5	...	...	...
3,128	**3,083**	**45**	...	...	**661**	**509**	**149**	**3**	...
14	*14*	...	...	...	*5*	*5*	...	...	...
66,092	**65,148**	**929**	**15**	...	**15,005**	**10,582**	**4,312**	**111**	...

.Chitaldurg

Class.	Group.	Caste, &c., and sub-division.	Religion.	15 to 39 Total.	15 to 39 Single.	15 to 39 Married.	15 to 39 Widowed.	15 to 39 Civil condition not stated.
F.—Races and Nationalities.	48. Asiatic Races of reputed Foreign origin.	Arab	Musalmán.	4	...	4	...	...
		Belúch	,,	...	...	...	...	...
		Dáyaré	,,	...	...	...	...	...
		Hanifi	,,	1	...	1	...	...
		Khádri	,,	...	...	...	...	...
		Kandhári	,,	...	...	...	...	...
		Mogal	,,	46	1	40	5	...
		Musalmán	,,	2	...	2	...	...
		Pat'hán	,,	291	12	245	34	...
		Shékh	,,	2,515	45	2,208	262	...
		Sayad	,,	364	17	298	49	...
		Sharif	,,	...	...	...	...	...
		Armenian	Christian.	...	...	...	...	...
		Burmese	,,	...	...	...	...	...
		Chinese	,,	...	...	...	...	...
		Jews	Jews.	...	...	...	...	...
		Jews	Christian.	...	...	...	...	...
		Jews.—Israelites	,,	...	...	...	...	...
		Pársi	Pársi.	1	1	...	...	...
		Singháli	Buddhist.	...	...	...	...	...
		Total Group 48	....	*3,224*	*76*	*2,798*	*350*	...
	49. Mixed Asiatic Races.	Labbé	Musalmán.	...	...	...	...	...
		Jám	,,	...	...	...	...	...
		Máplé	,,	...	...	...	...	...
		Méman	,,	...	...	...	...	...
		Pindári	,,	...	...	...	...	...
		Pinjári	,,	159	13	133	13	...
		Total Group 49	....	*159*	*13*	*133*	*13*	...
	50. Non-Asiatic races.	European	Christian.	2	...	2	...	...
		Australasian	,,	...	...	...	...	...
		Total Group 50	....	2	...	2	...	...
	51. Eurasian	Eurasian	,,	4	...	4	...	...
	52. Christian converts	Native Christian	,,	51	8	37	6	...
		Total Class F	....	**3,440**	**97**	**2,974**	**369**	...
		Caste not stated	....	24	2	19	3	...
		Grand Total	....	**83,879**	**4,664**	**66,027**	**13,188**	...

TABLE E.—(*Continued.*)

District.

Females.

40 and over.					Age not stated.				
Total.	Single.	Married.	Widowed.	Civil condition not stated.	Total.	Single.	Married.	Widowed.	Civil condition not stated.
...	...	...	...	...	...	...	...	...	...
...	...	...	...	...	...	...	...	...	...
...	...	...	...	...	...	...	...	...	...
...	...	...	...	...	...	...	...	...	...
...	...	...	...	...	...	...	...	...	...
...	...	...	...	...	...	...	...	...	...
22	...	11	11	...	...	...	...	...	...
2	...	1	1	...	...	...	...	...	...
198	...	95	103	...	...	...	...	...	...
1,071	10	338	723	...	3	1	...	2	...
206	...	101	107	...	...	...	...	...	...
...	...	...	...	...	...	...	...	...	...
...	...	...	...	...	...	...	...	...	...
...	...	...	...	...	...	...	...	...	...
...	...	...	...	...	...	...	...	...	...
...	...	...	...	...	...	...	...	...	...
...	...	...	...	...	...	...	...	...	...
...	...	...	...	...	...	...	...	...	...
2	...	1	1	...	...	...	...	...	...
...	...	...	...	...	...	...	...	...	...
1,503	*10*	*547*	*946*	...	*3*	*1*	...	*2*	...
...	...	...	...	...	...	...	...	...	...
...	...	...	...	...	...	...	...	...	...
...	...	...	...	...	...	...	...	...	...
...	...	...	...	...	...	...	...	...	...
...	...	...	...	...	...	...	...	...	...
86	1	41	44	...	...	...	...	...	...
86	*1*	*41*	*44*	...	...	...	...	...	...
...	...	...	...	...	...	...	...	...	...
...	...	...	...	...	...	...	...	...	...
...	...	...	...	...	...	...	...	...	...
1	...	1	...	...	...	...	...	...	...
11	...	5	6	...	...	...	...	...	...
1,601	**11**	**594**	**996**	...	**3**	**1**	...	**2**	...
13	...	*7*	*6*	...	...	...	...	...	...
39,401	**966**	**11,704**	**26,731**	...	**17**	**11**	**1**		...

Class.	Group.	Caste, &c. and sub-division.	Religion.	All Ages. Total.	Single.	Married.	Widowed.	Civil condition not stated.
F.—Races and Nationalities.	48. Asiatic Races of reputed Foreign origin.	Arab	Musalmán.	...	...	...	...	...
		Belúchi	„	2	1	1	...	...
		Dâyaré	„	...	...	...	...	...
		Hanifi	„	13	8	5	...	...
		Khâdri	„	...	...	...	...	...
		Kandhâri...	„	...	...	...	...	...
		Mogal	„	327	191	130	6	...
		Musalmán	„	45	21	23	1	...
		Paṭhán	„	1,825	1,016	737	72	...
		Shékh	„	7,737	4,225	3,245	267	...
		Sayad	„	1,585	890	637	58	...
		Sharif	„	22	16	5	1	...
		Armenian	Christian.	2	...	2	...	...
		Burmese	„	2	1	1	...	...
		Chinese	„	4	...	4	...	...
		Jews	Jews.	1	...	...	1	...
		Jews	Christian.	3	...	3	...	...
		Jews.—Israelites	„	1	1	...	...	...
		Pársi	Pársi.	3	1	2	...	...
		Singhâli	Buddhist.	3	2	1	...	...
		Total Group 48......	....	*11,575*	*6,373*	*4,796*	*406*	...
	49. Mixed Asiatic Races.	Labbé	Musalmán.	500	259	231	10	...
		Jám	„	5	4	1	...	...
		Máplé	„	21	11	10	...	...
		Méman	„	128	78	45	5	...
		Pindári	„	...	...	...	...	...
		Pinjári	„	...	...	...	...	...
		Total Group 49......	....	*654*	*352*	*287*	*15*	...
	50. Non-Asiatic races.	European...	Christian.	3,261	2,734	476	49	2
		Australasian	„	1	...	1	...	...
		Total Group 50......	....	*3,262*	*2,734*	*476*	*49*	*2*
	51. Eurasian ...	Eurasian	„	11,127	772	309	39	7
	52. Christian converts...	Native Christian ...	„	4,715	2,888	1,659	161	7
		Total Class F......	....	**21,333**	**13,119**	**7,528**	**670**	**16**
		Caste not stated......	....	*148*	*81*	*64*	*3*	...
		Grand Total......	....	**50,189**	**28,467**	**19,833**	**1,869**	**20**

TABLE E.—(Continued.)

Station, Bangalore.

Males.

0 to 9					10 to 14				
Total.	Single.	Married.	Widowed.	Civil condition not stated.	Total.	Single.	Married.	Widowed.	Civil condition not stated.
...	...	...	...	...	...	...	...	...	...
...	...	...	...	...	...	...	...	...	...
...	...	...	...	...	...	...	...	...	...
1	1	...	...	...	2	2	...	...	...
...	...	...	...	...	...	...	...	...	...
...	...	...	...	...	...	...	...	...	...
95	95	...	...	...	38	38	...	...	...
4	4	...	...	...	6	6	...	...	...
508	507	1	...	...	167	167	...	...	...
2,033	2,031	2	...	...	893	885	8	...	...
443	442	...	...	...	185	181	4	...	...
8	8	...	...	...	3	3	...	...	...
...	...	...	...	...	...	...	...	...	...
1	1	...	...	...	...	...	...	...	...
...	...	...	...	...	...	...	...	...	...
...	...	...	...	...	...	...	...	...	...
...	...	...	...	...	...	...	...	...	...
...	...	...	...	...	...	...	...	...	...
...	...	...	...	...	1	1	...	...	...
...	...	...	...	...	...	...	...	...	...
3,092	*3,089*	*3*	...	...	*1,295*	*1,283*	*12*	...	...
123	123	...	...	...	39	39	...	...	...
...	...	...	...	...	1	1	...	...	...
4	4	...	...	...	...	...	...	...	...
45	45	...	...	...	17	16	1	...	...
...	...	...	...	...	...	...	...	...	...
...	...	...	...	...	...	...	...	...	...
172	*172*	...	...	...	*57*	*56*	*1*	...	...
462	460	...	...	2	168	168	...	...	...
...	...	...	...	...	...	...	...	...	...
462	*460*	...	...	*2*	*168*	*168*	...	...	...
350	347	...	1	2	178	177		...	1
1,576	1,572	1	1	1	613	609	4	...	...
5,651	**5,640**	**4**	**2**	**5**	**2,311**	**2,293**	**17**	...	**1**
32	*33*	...	...	...	*11*	*11*	...	...	...
13,889	**13,862**	**13**	**8**	**6**	**5,122**	**5,061**	**56**	**4**	**1**

Class.	Group.	Caste, &c., and sub-division.	Religion.	15 to 39 Total.	Single.	Married.	Widowed.	Civil condition not stated.
F.—Races and Nationalities.	48. Asiatic Races of reputed Foreign origin.	Arab	Musalmán.	...	...	...	...	...
		Belúchi	,,	...	...	...	...	...
		Dáyaré	,,	...	...	...	...	...
		Hanifi	,,	8	5	3	...	...
		Khádri	,,	...	...	...	...	...
		Kandhári	,,	...	...	...	...	...
		Mogal	,,	116	52	64	...	...
		Musalmán	,,	25	11	14	...	...
		Pat'hán	,,	739	327	397	15	...
		Shékh	,,	2,998	1,265	1,655	48	...
		Sayad	,,	623	259	353	11	...
		Sharif	,,	9	5	4	...	...
		Armenian	Christian.	1	...	1	...	...
		Burmese	,,	1	...	1	...	...
		Chinese	,,	...	...	...	...	...
		Jews	Jews.	1	...	...	1	...
		Jews	Christian.	3	...	3	...	...
		Jews.—Israelites	,,	1	1	...	...	...
		Pársi	Pársi.	2	...	2	...	...
		Singháli	Buddhist.	3	2	1	...	...
		Total Group 48	....	*4,530*	*1,927*	*2,628*	75	...
	49. Mixed Asiatic Races.	Labbé	Musalmán.	228	95	133	...	...
		Jám	,,	3	3	...	...	...
		Máplé	,,	13	7	6	...	...
		Méman	,,	37	17	19	1	...
		Pindári	,,	...	...	...	...	...
		Pinjári	,,	...	...	...	...	...
		Total Group 49	....	*281*	*122*	*158*	*1*	...
	50. Non-Asiatic races.	European	Christian.	2,297	2,070	219	8	...
		Australasian	,,	...	...	...	...	...
		Total Group 50	....	*2,297*	*2,070*	*219*	*8*	...
	51. Eurasian	Eurasian	,,	403	237	155	9	1
	52. Christian converts		,,	1,639	671	932	33	3
		Total Class F.	....	**9,149**	**5,027**	**3,992**	**126**	**4**
		Caste not stated	....	*84*	*38*	*46*	...	...
		Grand Total	....	**20,804**	**9,510**	**10,910**	**378**	**6**

TABLE E.—(*Continued.*)

Station, Bangalore.

Males.

40 and over.					Age not stated.				
Total.	Single.	Married.	Widowed.	Civil condition not stated.	Total.	Single.	Married.	Widowed.	Civil condition not stated.
...	...	...	...	...	...	...	...	...	...
2	1	1	...	...	...	...	...	...	...
...	...	...	...	...	...	...	...	...	...
2	...	2	...	...	...	...	...	...	...
...	...	...	...	...	...	...	...	...	...
...	...	...	...	...	...	...	...	...	...
78	6	66	6	...	...	...	...	...	...
10	...	9	1	...	...	...	...	...	...
411	15	339	57	...	...	...	...	...	...
1,813	44	1,550	219	...	...	...	...	...	...
335	8	280	47	...	...	...	...	...	...
2	...	1	1	...	...	...	...	...	...
1	...	1	...	...	...	...	...	...	...
...	...	...	...	...	...	...	...	...	...
4	...	4	...	...	...	...	...	...	...
...	...	...	...	...	...	...	...	...	...
...	...	...	...	...	...	...	...	...	...
...	...	...	...	...	...	...	...	...	...
...	...	...	...	...	...	...	...	...	...
...	...	...	...	...	...	...	...	...	...
2,658	*74*	*2,253*	*331*	...	...	...	...	...	...
110	2	98	10	...	...	...	...	...	...
1	...	1	...	...	...	...	...	...	...
4	...	4	...	...	...	...	...	...	...
29	...	25	4	...	...	...	...	...	...
...	...	...	...	...	...	...	...	...	...
...	...	...	...	...	...	...	...	...	...
144	*2*	*128*	*14*	...	...	...	...	...	...
333	35	257	41	...	1	1	...	...	...
1	...	1	...	...	...	...	...	...	...
334	*35*	*258*	*41*	...	*1*	*1*	...	...	...
196	10	154	29	3	1	1	...	...	...
883	32	721	127	3	5	4	1	...	...
4,215	**153**	**3,514**	**542**	**6**	**6**	**6**	**1**	...	...
21	...	*18*	*3*	...	...	...	...	...	...
10,667	**328**	**8,853**	**1,479**	**7**	**7**	**6**	**1**	...	...

Class.	Group.	Caste, &c. and sub-division.	Religion.	All Ages. Total.	Single.	Married.	Widowed.	Civil condition not stated.
F.—Races and Nationalities.	48. Asiatic Races of reputed Foreign origin.	Arab	Musalmán.	...	...	...	...	...
		Bolúchi	,,	...	...	...	...	...
		Dáyaré	,,	...	...	...	...	...
		Hanifi	,,	20	11	7	2	...
		Khádri	,,	...	...	...	...	...
		Kandhári	,,	2	1	1	...	...
		Mogal	,,	313	143	128	47	...
		Musalmán	,,	28	14	12	2	...
		Paṭ'hán	,,	1,698	643	723	332	...
		Shékh	,,	7,564	2,877	3,378	1,308	1
		Sayad	,,	1,514	573	664	277	...
		Sharif	,,	18	5	5	8	...
		Armenian	Christian.	3	1	2	...	...
		Burmese	,,	2	2	...	...	...
		Chinese	,,	...	...	...	...	...
		Jews	Jews.	...	...	...	...	...
		Jews	Christian.	...	...	...	...	...
		Jews.—Israelites	,,	...	...	...	...	...
		Pársi	Pársi.	3	1	2	...	...
		Singhâli	Buddhist.	...	...	...	...	...
		Total Group 48......	....	11,170	4,271	4,022	1,976	1
	49. Mixed Asiatic Races.	Labbé	Musalmán.	397	150	180	58	...
		Jâm	,,	...	...	...	...	...
		Máplé	,,	7	4	3	...	...
		Méman	,,	116	58	43	15	...
		Pindári	,,	...	...	...	...	...
		Pinjári	,,	...	...	...	...	...
		Total Group 49......	....	520	212	235	73	...
	50. Non-Asiatic races.	European	,,	1,723	1,021	520	178	4
		Australasian	,,	...	...	...	...	...
		Total Group 50......	....	1,723	1,021	520	178	4
	51. Eurasian ...	Eurasian	,,	1,622	927	382	205	8
	52. Christian converts ...	Native Christian	,,	5,537	2,548	1,960	1,028	1
		Total Class F......	...	**20,472**	**8,979**	**8,019**	**3,460**	**14**
		Caste not stated......	....	102	31	56	14	1
		Grand Total......	....	**49,892**	**19,763**	**20,892**	**9,220**	**17**

TABLE E.—(*Continued.*)

Station, Bangalore.

Females.

0 to 9.					10 to 14.				
Total.	Single.	Married.	Widowed.	Civil condition not stated.	Total.	Single.	Married.	Widowed.	Civil condition not stated.
...	...	...	...	...	...	...	...	...	...
...	...	...	...	...	...	...	...	...	...
...	...	...	...	...	...	...	...	...	...
8	8	...	...	...	2	2	...	...	...
...	...	...	...	...	...	...	...	...	...
1	1	...	...	...	...	...	...	...	...
101	101	...	...	...	44	38	6	...	...
10	10	...	...	...	4	3	1	...	...
483	482	1	...	...	179	133	44	2	...
2,144	2,137	6	1	...	763	582	181	...	...
453	449	2	2	...	139	96	43	...	...
5	5	...	...	...	1	...	1	...	...
1	1	...	...	...	...	...	...	...	...
1	1	...	...	...	...	...	...	...	...
...	...	...	...	...	...	...	...	...	...
...	...	...	...	...	...	...	...	...	...
...	...	...	...	...	...	...	...	...	...
...	...	...	...	...	...	...	...	...	...
...	...	...	...	...	1	1	...	...	...
...	...	...	...	...	...	...	...	...	...
3,207	*3,195*	*9*	*3*	...	*1,133*	*855*	*276*	*2*	...
111	110	1	...	...	43	27	16	...	...
...	...	...	...	...	...	...	...	...	...
4	4	...	...	...	...	...	...	...	...
37	37	...	...	...	19	19	...	...	...
...	...	...	...	...	...	...	...	...	...
...	...	...	...	...	...	...	...	...	...
152	*151*	*1*	...	...	*62*	*46*	*16*	...	...
420	417	...	...	3	198	198	...	...	...
...	...	...	...	...	...	...	...	...	...
420	*417*	...	...	*3*	*198*	*198*	...	...	...
403	400	...	...	3	226	223	1	...	2
1,556	1,551	5	...	...	610	567	43	...	...
5,738	**5,714**	**15**	**3**	**6**	**2,229**	**1,889**	**336**	**2**	**2**
28	*27*	...	...	*1*	*12*	*4*	*8*	...	...
13,682	**13,570**	**99**	**5**	**8**	**4,944**	**3,797**	**1,131**	**14**	**2**

Class.	Group.	Caste, &c. and sub-division.	Religion.	15 to 39. Total.	Single.	Married.	Widowed.	Civil condition not stated.
F.—Races and Nationalities.	48. Asiatic Races of reputed Foreign origin.	Arab	Musalmán.	...	...	...	...	...
		Belúchi	"	...	...	...	...	...
		Dáyaré	"	...	...	...	...	...
		Hanifi	"	7	1	6	...	...
		Khádri	"	...	...	...	...	...
		Kandhári	"	1	...	1	...	...
		Mogal	"	112	4	102	6	...
		Musalmán	"	9	1	8	...	...
		Pat'hán	"	656	27	560	69	...
		Shékh	"	2,979	154	2,594	230	1
		Sayad	"	592	26	509	57	...
		Sharif	"	6	...	4	2	...
		Armenian	Christian.	2	...	2	...	...
		Burmese	"	1	1	...	...	...
		Chinese	"	...	...	...	...	...
		Jews	Jews	...	...	...	...	...
		Jews	Christian.	...	...	...	...	...
		Jews—Israelites	"	...	...	...	...	...
		Pársi	Pársi.	2	...	2	...	...
		Singháli	Buddhist.	...	...	...	...	...
		Total Group 48......	....	*4,367*	*314*	*3,788*	*364*	*1*
	49. Mixed Asiatic Races.	Labbé	Musalmán.	158	12	135	11	...
		Jám	"	...	...	...	...	...
		Máplé	"	2	...	2	...	...
		Méman	"	39	2	36	1	...
		Pindári	"	...	...	...	...	...
		Pinjári	"	...	...	...	...	...
		Total Group 49......	....	*199*	*14*	*173*	*12*	...
	50. Non-Asiatic races.	European	Christian.	732	344	360	27	1
		Australasian	"	...	...	...	...	...
		Total Group 50......	....	*732*	*344*	*360*	*27*	*1*
	51. Eurasian ...	Eurasian	Christian.	604	293	264	45	2
	50. Christian converts.	Native Christian	"	2,246	409	1,551	285	1
		Total Class F......	....	**8,148**	**1,274**	**6,136**	**733**	**5**
		Caste not stated......	....	*41*	...	*37*	*4*	...
		Grand Total......	....	**20,131**	**2,220**	**15,713**	**2,193**	**5**

TABLE E.—(Continued.)

Station, Bangalore.

Females.

40 and over.					Age not stated.				
Total.	Single.	Married.	Widowed.	Civil condition not stated.	Total.	Single.	Married.	Widowed.	Civil condition not stated.
...	...	...	...	...	...	...	...	...	...
...	...	...	...	...	...	...	...	...	...
...	...	...	...	...	...	...	...	...	...
3	...	1	2	...	...	...	...	...	...
...	...	...	...	...	...	...	...	...	...
...	...	...	...	...	...	...	...	...	...
61	...	20	41	...	...	...	...	...	...
5	...	3	2	...	...	...	...	...	...
380	1	118	261	...	...	...	...	...	...
1,678	4	597	1,077	...	...	...	...	...	...
330	2	110	218	...	...	...	...	...	...
6	...	...	6	...	...	...	...	...	...
...	...	...	...	...	...	...	...	...	...
...	...	...	...	...	...	...	...	...	...
...	...	...	...	...	...	...	...	...	...
...	...	...	...	...	...	...	...	...	...
...	...	...	...	...	...	...	...	...	...
...	...	...	...	...	...	...	...	...	...
...	...	...	...	...	...	...	...	...	...
...	...	...	...	...	...	...	...	...	...
2,463	*7*	*849*	*1,607*	...	...	...	...	...	...
85	1	37	47	...	...	...	...	...	...
...	...	...	...	...	...	...	...	...	...
1	...	1	...	...	...	...	...	...	...
21	...	7	14	...	...	...	...	...	...
...	...	...	...	...	...	...	...	...	...
...	...	...	...	...	...	...	...	...	...
107	*1*	*45*	*61*	...	...	...	...	...	...
364	56	158	150	...	9	6	2	1	...
...	...	...	...	...	...	...	...	...	...
364	*56*	*158*	*150*	...	*9*	*6*	*2*	*1*	...
288	10	117	160	1	1	1	...	...	...
1,125	21	361	743	...	..	...	...	...	...
4,347	**95**	**1,530**	**2,721**	**1**	**10**	**7**	**2**	**1**	...
21	...	*11*	*10*	...	...	...	...	...	...
11,124	**169**	**3,947**	**708**	**2**	**11**	**7**	**2**	**2**	...

Total, including the Civil and

Class.	Group.	Caste, &c., and sub-division.	Religion.	All Ages. Total.	Single.	Married.	Widowed.	Civil condition not stated.
F.—Races and Nationalities.	48. Asiatic Races of reputed Foreign origin.	Arab	Musalmán.	17	6	8	3	...
		Belúchi	,,	2	1	1	...	...
		Dáyaré	,,	1,081	662	404	15	...
		Hanifi	,,	597	306	240	51	...
		Khádri	,,	2	2	...	...	...
		Kandhári	,,	...	...	...	...	...
		Mogal	,,	4,854	2,679	1,949	226	...
		Musalmán	,,	478	258	197	23	...
		Paṭ'hán	,,	19,952	11,089	8,095	768	...
		Shékh	,,	78,930	44,511	32,331	2,086	2
		Sayad	,,	20,201	11,208	8,198	795	...
		Sharif	,,	453	237	182	34	...
		Armenian	Christian.	4	1	3	...	...
		Burmese	,,	2	1	1	...	...
		Chinese	,,	4	...	4	...	...
		Jews	Jews.	10	5	3	2	...
		Jews	Christian.	3	...	3	...	...
		Jews.—Israelites	,,	1	1	...	...	...
		Pársi	Pársi.	18	9	9	...	...
		Singháli	Buddhist.	3	2	1	...	...
		Total Group 48	....	*126,012*	*70,978*	*51,629*	*4,003*	*2*
	49. Mixed Asiatic Races.	Labbé	Musalmán.	2,359	1,271	1,014	74	...
		Jám	,,	5	4	1	...	...
		Mápḷé	,,	151	73	70	8	...
		Méman	,,	128	78	45	5	...
		Pinḍári	,,	1,064	600	432	42	...
		Pinjári	,,	1,199	617	498	84	...
		Total Group 49	....	*4,906*	*2,643*	*2,050*	*213*	...
	50. Non-Asiatic races.	European	Christian.	4,032	3,147	809	74	2
		Australasian	,,	1	...	1	...	...
		Total Group 50	....	*4,033*	*3,147*	*810*	*74*	*2*
	51. Eurasian	Eurasian	,,	1,833	1,151	609	66	7
	52. Christian converts	Native Christian	,,	14,427	8,235	5,691	494	7
		Total Class F	....	**151,811**	**86,154**	**60,789**	**4,850**	**18**
		Caste not stated	....	*2,023*	*1,005*	*871*	*147*	...
		Grand Total	....	**2,483,451**	**1,338,459**	**1,027,547**	**117,361**	**84**

TABLE E.—(*Continued.*)

Military Station, Bangalore.

Males.

0 to 9					10 to 14				
Total.	Single.	Married.	Widowed.	Civil condition not stated.	Total.	Single.	Married.	Widowed.	Civil condition not stated.
2	2	...	...	...	1	1	...	...	...
...	...	...	...	...	...	...	...	...	...
379	379	...	...	...	117	116	1	...	...
126	126	...	...	...	63	63	...	...	...
...	...	...	...	...	...	...	...	...	...
...	...	...	...	...	...	...	...	...	...
1,457	1,457	...	...	...	486	477	9	...	...
127	127	...	...	...	58	57	1	...	...
5,802	5,797	5	...	...	2,047	2,015	32	...	...
21,817	21,778	38	1	...	7,722	7,634	84	3	1
5,811	5,794	17	...	...	2,020	1,961	59	...	...
172	172	...	...	...	37	37	...	...	...
...	...	...	...	...	...	...	...	...	...
1	1	...	...	...	...	...	...	...	...
...	...	...	...	...	...	...	...	...	...
3	3	...	...	...	2	2	...	...	...
...	...	...	...	...	...	...	...	...	...
...	...	...	...	...	...	...	...	...	...
2	2	...	...	...	2	2	...	...	...
...	...	...	...	...	...	...	...	...	...
35,699	*35,633*	*60*	*1*	...	*12,555*	*12,365*	*186*	*3*	*1*
511	511	...	...	...	211	206	5	...	...
...	...	...	...	...	1	1	...	...	...
4	4	...	...	...	6	6	...	...	...
45	45	...	...	...	17	16	1	...	...
332	332	...	...	...	136	136	...	...	...
323	323	...	...	...	114	112	2	...	...
1,215	*1,215*	...	...	...	*485*	*477*	*8*	...	...
606	604	...	...	2	214	214	...	...	...
...	...	...	...	...	...	...	...	...	...
606	*604*	...	...	*2*	*214*	*314*	...	...	...
499	496	...	1	2	223	222	...	...	1
3,951	3,946	3	1	1	1,508	1,488	20	...	...
41,970	**41,899**	**63**	**3**	**5**	**14,985**	**14,766**	**214**	**3**	**2**
465	*465*	...	...	...	*179*	*179*	...	...	...
682,367	**681,612**	**718**	**31**	**6**	**228,742**	**223,207**	**5,449**	**81**	**5**

Total, including the Civil and

Class.	Group.	Caste, &c., and sub-division.	Religion.	15 to 39 Total.	15 to 39 Single.	15 to 39 Married.	15 to 39 Widowed.	15 to 39 Civil condition not stated.
F.—Races and Nationalities.	48. Asiatic Races of reputed Foreign origin.	Arab	Musalmán.	10	3	7	...	...
		Belúchi	,,	...	...	...	...	...
		Dáyaré	,,	346	163	182	1	...
		Hanifi	,,	284	112	161	11	...
		Fhádri	,,	1	1	...	...	...
		Kandhári	,,	...	...	...	...	...
		Mogal	,,	1,914	705	1,158	51	...
		Musalmán	,,	185	70	111	4	...
		Paṭ'hán	,,	7,663	3,030	4,460	173	...
		Shékh	,,	31,631	14,473	16,693	464	1
		Sayad	,,	8,252	3,298	4,782	172	...
		Sharif	,,	159	21	130	8	...
		Armenian	Christian.	3	1	2	...	...
		Burmese	,,	1	...	1	...	...
		Chinese	,,	...	...	...	...	...
		Jews	Jews.	4	...	2	2	...
		Jews	Christian.	3	...	3	...	...
		Jews.—Israelites	,,	1	1	...	...	...
		Pársi	Pársi.	11	5	6	...	...
		Singháli	Buddhist.	3	2	1	...	...
		Total Group 48......	....	*50,471*	*21,855*	*27,699*	*886*	*1*
	49. Mixed Asiatic Races.	Labbé	Musalmán.	1,163	515	635	13	...
		Jám	,,	3	3	...	...	...
		Máplé	,,	116	61	54	1	...
		Méman	,,	37	17	19	1	...
		Pinḍári	,,	406	131	268	7	...
		Pinjári	,,	495	165	310	20	...
		Total Group 49......	....	*2,220*	*893*	*1,286*	*42*	...
	50. Non-Asiatic races.	European...	Christian.	2,745	2,278	456	11	...
		Australasian	,,	...	...	...	...	...
		Total Group 50......	....	*2,745*	*2,278*	*456*	*11*	...
	51. Eurasian ...	Eurasian	,,	771	417	339	14	1
	52. Christian converts ...	Native Christian	,,	6,198	2,648	3,396	151	3
		Total Class F......	....	**62,405**	**28,120**	**33,176**	**1,104**	**5**
		Caste not stated......	....	*949*	*335*	*578*	*36*	...
		Grand Total......	....	**1,029,791**	**413,657**	**590,116**	**26,000**	**18**

TABLE E.—(Continued.)

Military Station, Bangalore.

Males.

40 and over.					Age not stated.				
Total.	Single.	Married.	Widowed.	Civil condition not stated.	Total.	Single.	Married.	Widowed.	Civil condition not stated.
4	...	1	3	...	...	...	...	...	...
2	1	1	...	...	...	...	...	...	...
230	4	221	14	...	...	...	...	...	...
124	5	79	40	...	...	...	...	...	...
1	1	...	...	...	...	...	...	...	...
...	...	...	...	...	...	...	...	...	...
997	40	782	175	...	...	...	...	...	...
108	4	85	19	...	...	...	...	...	...
4,410	247	3,598	595	...	...	...	...	...	...
17,749	617	15,514	1,618	...	11	9	2	...	...
4,118	155	3,340	623	...	...	...	...	...	...
85	7	52	26	...	...	...	...	...	...
	...	1	...	...	...	...	...	...	...
	...	...	...	...	...	...	...	...	...
4	...	4	...	...	...	...	...	...	...
1	...	1	...	...	...	...	...	...	...
...	...	...	...	...	...	...	...	...	...
...	...	...	...	...	...	...	...	...	...
3	...	3	...	...	...	...	...	...	...
...	...	...	...	...	...	...	...	...	...
27,876	*1,081*	*23,682*	*3,113*	...	*11*	*9*	*2*	...	...
474	39	374	61	...	...	...	...	...	...
1	...	1	...	...	...	...	...	...	...
25	2	16	7	...	...	...	...	...	...
29	...	25	4	...	...	...	...	...	...
190	1	154	35	...	...	...	...	...	...
267	17	186	64	...	...	...	...	...	...
986	*59*	*756*	*171*	...	...	...	...	...	...
466	50	353	63	...	1	1	...	...	...
1	...	1	...	...	...	...	...	...	...
1	...	*1*	...	...	*1*	*1*	...	...	...
339	15	270	51	3	1	1	...	...	...
2,763	148	2,271	341	3	7	5	1	1	...
32,431	**1,353**	**27,333**	**3,739**	**6**	**20**	**16**	**3**	**1**	...
490	*26*	*293*	*111*	...	...	...	...	...	...
542,100	**19,752**	**431,158**	**91,177**	**13**	**451**	**231**	**106**	**72**	**42**

SUPPLEMENTARY

Total, including the Civil and

Class.	Group.	Caste, &c., and sub-division.	Religion.	All Ages. Total.	Single.	Married.	Widowed.	Civil condition not stated.
F.—Races and Nationalities.	48. Asiatic Races of reputed Foreign origin.	Arab	Musalmán.	11	4	6	1	...
		Belúchi	,,	...	...	...	...	...
		Dáyaré	,,	1,419	540	540	339	...
		Hanifi	,,	501	168	236	97	...
		Khádri	,,	...	...	...	...	...
		Kandhári...	,,	2	1	1	...	...
		Mogal	,,	4.563	1,760	2,018	785	...
		Musalmán	,,	383	145	177	61	...
		Paṭ'hán	,,	18,627	7,167	8,067	3,393	...
		Shékh	,,	73,617	29,284	30,915	13,410	8
		Sayad	,,	18,472	6,958	8,231	3,283	...
		Sharif	,,	439	18[illegible]	187	[illegible]7	...
		Armenian	Christian.	4	1	3	...	...
		Burmese	,,	2	2	...	...	...
		Chinese	,,	...	...	...	...	...
		Jews	Jews.	11	6	5	...	...
		Jews	Christian.	...	...	...	...	...
		Jews.—Israelites.	,,	...	...	...	...	...
		Pársi	Pársi.	17	9	6	2	...
		Singháli	Buddhist.	...	...	...	...	...
		Total Group 48......	....	118,068	46,230	50,392	21,438	8
	49. Mixed Asiatic Races.	Labbé	Musalmán.	1,358	501	638	319	...
		Júm	,,	...	...	...	...	...
		Máple	,,	27	11	13	3	...
		Méman	,,	116	58	43	15	...
		Pindári	,,	984	374	429	181	...
		Pinjári	,,	981	384	464	133	...
		Total Group 49......	....	3,466	1,328	1,587	551	...
	50. Non-Asiatic races.	European...	,,	2,198	1,234	783	227	4
		Australasian	,,	...	...	...	...	...
		Total Group 50	....	2,198	1,234	733	227	4
	51. Eurasian ...	Eurasian	,,	2,098	1,180	649	261	8
	52. Christian converts ...	Native Christian	,,	13,527	6,081	5,183	2,262	1
		Total Class F......	....	**139,357**	**56,052**	**58,545**	**24,739**	**21**
		Caste not stated......	....	1,701	565	788	347	1
		Grand Total......	....	**3,460,153**	**894,383**	**1,045,356**	**520,315**	**99**

TABLE E.—(*Continued.*)

Military Station, Bangalore.

Females.

0 to 9					10 to 14.				
Total.	Single.	Married.	Widowed.	Civil condition not stated.	Total.	Single.	Married.	Widowed.	Civil condition not stated.
3	3	...	...	...	1	1	...	...	...
...	...	...	...	...	...	...	...	...	...
393	393	...	...	...	111	98	13	...	...
121	121	...	...	...	48	34	14	...	...
...	...	...	...	...	...	...	...	...	...
1	1	...	...	...	...	...	...	...	...
1,336	1,330	6	...	...	415	332	83	...	...
120	120	...	...	...	29	20	9	...	...
5,531	5,458	73	...	...	1,588	1,272	314	2	...
23,493	23,263	220	10	...	6,334	4,521	1,775	38	...
5,339	5,280	55	4	...	1,618	1,329	286	3	...
110	110	...	...	...	67	65	2	...	...
1	1	...	...	...	...	...	...	...	...
1	1	...	...	...	...	...	...	...	...
...	...	...	...	...	...	...	...	...	...
5	5	...	...	...	...	...	...	...	...
...	...	...	...	...	...	...	...	...	...
...	...	...	...	...	...	...	...	...	...
2	2	...	...	...	3	3	...	...	...
...	...	...	...	...	...	...	...	...	...
36,461	*36,093*	*354*	*14*	...	*10,214*	*7,675*	*2,496*	*43*	...
355	354	1	...	...	137	101	36	...	...
...	...	...	...	...	...	...	...	...	...
7	7	...	...	...	3	2	1	...	...
37	37	...	...	...	19	19	...	...	...
304	304	...	...	...	69	53	16	...	...
277	277	...	...	...	90	82	8	...	...
980	*979*	*1*	...	...	*318*	*257*	*61*	...	...
541	538	...	...	3	235	235	...	...	...
...	...	...	...	...	...	...	...	...	...
541	*538*	...	...	*3*	*235*	*235*	...	...	...
552	*549*	...	...	*3*	*261*	*261*	*1*	...	*2*
3,943	3,928	15	...	...	1,398	1,226	160	1	...
42,477	**42,087**	**370**	**14**	**6**	**12,427**	**9,654**	**2,727**	**44**	**2**
380	*376*	*3*	...	*1*	*165*	*140*	*25*	...	...
709,824	**691,382**	**18,171**	**262**	**9**	**205,491**	**136,498**	**67,356**	**1,633**	**4**

Total, including the Civil and

Class.	Group.	Caste, &c., and sub-division.	Religion.	15 to 39. Total.	Single.	Married.	Widowed.	Civil condition not stated.
F.—Races and Nationalities.	48. Asiatic Races of reputed Foreign origin.	Arab	Musalmán.	6	...	6	...	...
		Belúchi	,,	...	...	...	...	...
		Dáyaró	,,	527	44	413	70	...
		Hanifi	,,	212	13	165	34	...
		Khádri	,,	...	...	...	...	...
		Kandhári	,,	1	...	1	...	...
		Mogal	,,	1,767	95	1,485	187	...
		Musalmán	,,	152	5	132	15	...
		Paṭhán	,,	7,275	394	6,112	769	...
		Shékh	,,	28,593	1,317	24,202	3,072	2
		Sayad	,,	7,081	318	6,059	707	...
		Shariff	,,	193	10	162	21	...
		Armenian	Christian.	3	...	3	...	...
		Burmese	,,	1	1	...	...	...
		Chinese	,,	...	...	...	...	...
		Jews	Jews	5	1	4	...	...
		Jews	Christian.	...	...	...	...	...
		Jews—Israelites	,,	...	...	...	...	...
		Pársi	Pársi.	9	4	5	...	...
		Singháli	Buddhist.	...	...	...	...	...
		Total Group 48	....	*45,828*	*2,202*	*38,749*	*4,875*	*2*
	49. Mixed Asiatic Races.	Labbé	Musalmán.	553	45	458	52	...
		Jám	,,	...	...	...	...	...
		Máplé	,,	10	2	8	...	...
		Méman	,,	39	2	36	1	...
		Pindári	,,	357	17	289	51	...
		Pinjári	,,	411	24	356	31	...
		Total Group 49	....	*1,372*	*90*	*1,147*	*135*	...
	50. Non-Asiatic races.	European	Christian.	978	396	535	47	1
		Australasian	,,	...	...	...	...	...
		Total Group 50	....	*978*	*396*	*535*	*47*	*1*
	51. Eurasian	Eurasian	Christian.	894	357	472	63	2
	50. Christian converts.	Native Christian	,,	5,651	867	4,125	658	1
		Total Class F	....	**54,724**	**3,912**	**45,028**	**5,778**	**6**
		Caste not stated	....	*702*	*40*	*534*	*78*	...
		Grand Total	....	**1,003,011**	**57,476**	**793,327**	**152,198**	**10**

TABLE E.—(*Continued.*)

Military Station, Bangalore.

Females.

40 and over.					Age not stated.				
Total.	Single.	Married.	Widowed.	Civil condition not stated.	Total.	Single.	Married.	Widowed.	Civil condition not stated.
1	...	...	1	...	...	...	...	...	...
...	...	...	...	...	...	...	...	...	...
383	...	114	269	...	...	...	...	...	...
120	...	57	63	...	...	...	...	...	...
...	...	...	...	...	...	...	...	...	...
...	...	...	...	...	...	...	...	...	...
1,045	3	444	598	...	...	...	...	...	...
83	...	36	46	...	...	...	...	...	...
4,233	43	1,568	2,622	...	...	...	...	...	...
15,169	172	4,712	10,285	...	28	11	6	5	6
4,431	31	1,831	2,569	...	...	...	...	...	...
69	...	23	46	...	...	...	...	...	...
...	...	...	...	...	...	...	...	...	...
...	...	...	...	...	...	...	...	...	...
...	...	...	...	...	...	...	...	...	...
1	...	1	...	...	...	...	...	...	...
...	...	...	...	...	...	...	...	...	...
...	...	...	...	...	...	...	...	...	...
3	...	1	2	...	...	...	...	...	...
...	...	...	...	...	...	...	...	...	...
25,537	*249*	*8,787*	*16,501*	...	*28*	*11*	*6*	*5*	*6*
311	1	143	167	...	...	...	...	...	...
...	...	...	...	...	...	...	...	...	...
7	...	4	3	...	...	...	...	...	...
21	...	7	14	...	...	...	...	...	...
254	...	124	130	...	...	...	...	...	...
203	1	100	102	...	...	...	...	...	...
796	*2*	*378*	*416*	...	...	...	...	...	...
434	59	196	179	...	9	6	2	1	...
...	...	...	...	...	...	...	...	...	...
434	*59*	*196*	*179*	...	*9*	*6*	*2*	*1*	...
387	12	176	198	1	1	1	...	...	...
2,534	60	871	1,603	...	3	...	3	...	...
29,688	**382**	**10,408**	**18,897**	**1**	**41**	**18**	**11**	**6**	**6**
454	*9*	*176*	*269*	...	...	...	...	...	...
541,370	**8,823**	**166,397**	**366,135**	**15**	**457**	**204**	**105**	**87**	**61**

(LOCAL.)

SPECIAL TABLES.

A

MARRIED

(LOCAL.)

SPECIAL TABLES.

A

MARRIED.

(LOCAL.)

SPECIAL TABLES.—(A) Married.

Provincial.

Age Periods of 1st Marriage.	Total All Religions.			TOTAL HINDU RELIGION.			Brâmhan.			Kshatriya.			Vais'ya.			Lingâyet.		
	Total.	Males.	Females.	Total.	Males.	Females.	Total.	Males.	Females.	Total.	Males.	Females.	Total.	Males.	Females.	Total.	Males.	Females.
Infant	...	...	...	...	...	...	...	...	...	...	...	...	...	...	...	...	...	...
1 year	79	4	75	76	2	74	2	...	2	2	...	2	...	...	...	4	...	4
2 "	365	14	351	363	14	349	18	2	16	8	2	6	3	...	3	38	10	28
3 "	2,484	133	2,351	2,479	132	2,347	153	...	153	33	...	33	10	...	10	407	23	384
4 "	8,778	365	8,413	8,751	364	8,387	516	1	515	101	2	99	109	1	108	1,084	26	1,058
5 to 9	194,811	8,481	186,330	189,170	8,173	180,997	25,533	767	24,766	2,352	107	2,245	3,176	70	3,106	16,542	811	15,731
10 to 14	567,270	75,068	492,202	539,509	72,831	466,678	23,892	8,597	15,295	10,626	1,775	8,851	4,553	1,374	3,179	55,902	5,137	50,765
15 to 19	512,280	250,960	261,320	486,101	240,130	245,971	15,457	15,331	126	7,723	3,688	4,035	2,060	2,060	...	47,676	21,058	26,618
20 to 24	420,468	371,434	49,034	394,162	349,804	44,358	9,541	9,541	...	5,413	5,009	404	1,707	1,707	...	44,941	40,128	4,813
25 to 29	208,427	196,941	11,486	194,794	184,323	10,471	3,484	3,484	...	3,785	3,686	99	864	864	...	17,795	17,046	749
30 to 34	73,340	70,455	2,885	67,738	65,192	2,546	1,192	1,192	...	874	825	49	334	334	...	8,834	8,598	236
35 to 39	20,493	19,212	1,281	18,934	17,743	1,191	293	293	...	201	192	9	67	67	...	2,246	2,156	90
40 to 44	6,144	5,645	499	5,463	5,008	455	98	98	...	69	64	5	29	29	...	807	728	79
45 to 49	2,036	1,809	227	1,832	1,627	205	32	32	...	26	25	1	4	4	...	213	190	23
50 to 54	809	739	70	710	649	61	17	17	...	14	14	...	4	4	...	121	100	21
55 to 59	293	263	30	260	230	30	6	6	...	8	6	2	2	2	...	47	35	12
60 and over ...	229	195	34	197	166	31	6	6	...	3	3	...	...	...	...	44	40	4
Age not stated ...	13,872	5,996	7,876	12,880	5,496	7,384	558	250	308	153	58	95	91	30	61	1,884	861	1,023
Total...	2,032,178	1,007,714	1,024,464	1,923,419	951,884	971,535	80,798	39,617	41,181	31,391	15,456	15,935	13,013	6,546	6,467	198,585	96,947	101,638
2nd Marriage ...	150,392	119,485	30,907	142,840	113,158	29,682	4,424	4,423	1	1,228	1,134	94	868	861	7	15,711	14,341	1,370
3rd and 4th Marriages...	13,308	12,619	689	12,189	11,558	631	480	480	...	125	124	1	141	140	1	1,471	1,427	44

(LOCAL.)

SPECIAL TABLES.—(A) Married.—(*Continued.*)

Provincial.

Age Periods of 1st Marriage.	Other Hindus.			Out-castes.			JAINS.			MUSALMANS.			CHRISTIANS.			OTHER RELIGIONS.		
	Total.	Males.	Females.	Total.	Males.	Females.	Total.	Males.	Females.	Total.	Males.	Females.	Total.	Males.	Females.	Total.	Males.	Females.
Infant ...	...	...	...	...	...	...	...	...	...	...	...	...	...	...	...	...	...	...
1 year ...	53	2	51	15	...	15	...	...	...	3	2	1	...	...	...	...	...	...
2 " ...	250	...	250	46	...	46	...	...	...	2	...	2	...	...	...	...	...	...
3 " ...	1,596	76	1,520	280	33	247	1	...	1	4	1	3	...	...	...	...	...	...
4 " ...	5,722	223	5,499	1,219	111	1,108	18	...	18	8	1	7	1	...	1	...	...	...
5 to 9 ...	119,003	5,074	113,929	22,534	1,314	21,220	593	24	569	4,868	266	4,602	171	18	153	9	...	9
10 to 14 ...	365,676	45,032	320,644	78,860	10,946	67,914	1,505	200	1,305	24,661	1,930	22,731	1,595	107	1,488	...	...	...
15 to 19 ...	333,390	161,755	171,635	79,795	38,238	41,557	1,113	673	410	22,964	9,308	13,656	2,097	845	1,252	5	4	1
20 to 24 ...	265,040	235,445	29,595	67,520	57,974	9,5[illegible]	796	747	49	23,174	18,995	4,179	2,331	1,865	416	5	3	2
25 to 29 ...	135,743	127,970	7,773	33,123	31,273	1,850	565	556	9	11,945	11,088	857	1,110	970	149	4	4	...
30 to 34 ...	44,651	42,917	1,734	11,853	11,326	527	245	213	2	4,924	4,627	297	428	388	40	5	5	...
35 to 39 ...	13,490	12,549	941	2,637	2,486	151	68	68	...	1,314	1,251	63	177	150	27	...	...	...
40 to 44 ...	3,588	3,256	302	873	803	60	22	21	1	585	553	32	74	63	11	...	...	...
45 to 49 ...	1,329	1,160	169	228	216	12	...	...	...	171	150	21	33	32	1	...	...	...
50 to 54 ...	428	404	24	126	110	10	...	...	...	89	81	8	10	9	1	...	...	...
55 to 59 ...	150	138	12	47	43	4	...	...	...	29	29	...	4	4	...	...	...	...
60 and over ...	120	98	22	24	19	5	...	...	...	30	27	3	2	2	...	...	...	...
Age not stated ...	8,015	3,345	4,670	2,179	952	1,227	34	31	3	626	276	350	328	193	135	4	...	4
Total......	1,298,244	639,474	658,770	301,388	153,844	147,544	4,960	2,563	2,397	95,397	48,585	46,812	8,370	4,666	3,704	32	16	16
2nd Marriage ...	96,045	74,719	21,326	24,564	17,679	6,885	314	303	11	6,782	5,644	1,138	456	380	76	...	...	...
3rd and 4th Marriages..	8,176	7,708	468	1,796	1,679	117	34	34	...	992	937	55	93	90	3	...	...	...

(LOCAL.)

SPECIAL TABLES.—(A) Married.—(Continued.)

Bangalore District.

Age Periods of 1st Marriage.	Total All Religions.			TOTAL HINDU RELIGION.			Brâmhaṇ.			Kshatriya.			Vais'ya.			Lingâyet.		
	Total.	Males.	Females.	Total.	Males.	Females.	Total.	Males.	Females.	Total.	Males.	Females.	Total.	Males.	Females.	Total.	Males.	Females.
Infant ...	...	...	...	...	...	...	...	...	...	...	...	...	...	...	...	...	...	...
1 year ...	68	2	66	68	2	66	1	...	1	2	...	2	...	...	...	4	...	4
2 „ ...	181	...	181	181	...	181	12	...	12	2	...	2	1	...	1	19	...	19
3 „ ...	490	...	490	489	...	489	20	...	20	15	...	15	4	...	4	18	...	18
4 „ ...	1,156	33	1,123	1,154	33	1,121	88	...	88	18	...	18	17	...	17	38	...	38
5 to 9 ...	32,642	1,352	31,290	32,427	1,312	31,115	3,755	142	3,613	561	14	547	537	10	527	1,779	86	1,693
10 to 14 ...	96,600	12,816	83,784	90,560	12,413	78,147	4,210	1,498	2,712	2,107	261	1,846	637	230	407	5,374	620	4,754
15 to 19 ...	76,292	42,306	33,986	70,807	40,087	30,720	2,449	2,449	...	1,220	750	470	311	311	...	3,359	2,104	1,255
20 to 24 ...	64,196	57,402	6,794	58,301	53,218	5,083	1,494	1,494	...	1,182	1,123	59	255	255	...	3,040	2,897	143
25 to 29 ...	27,079	25,761	1,318	24,452	23,329	1,123	511	511	...	530	530	...	197	197	...	1,360	1,334	26
30 to 34 ...	10,109	9,693	416	9,000	8,656	344	175	175	...	164	164	...	80	80	...	435	428	7
35 to 39 ...	2,913	2,818	95	2,542	2,464	78	45	45	...	34	34	...	12	12	...	109	109	...
40 to 44 ...	967	876	91	817	739	78	12	12	...	9	9	...	8	8	...	36	33	3
45 to 49 ...	284	258	26	227	206	21	5	5	...	3	3	...	2	2	...	8	8	...
50 to 54 ...	112	99	13	91	79	12	2	2	...	3	3	...	1	1	...	9	6	3
55 to 59 ...	45	38	7	39	32	7	2	2	...	...	...	...	...	...	...	1	1	...
60 and over ...	49	30	19	43	24	19	2	2	...	...	...	...	...	...	...	2	2	...
Age not stated ...	2,192	862	1,330	1,822	686	1,136	66	35	31	31	9	22	25	4	21	102	44	58
Total......	315,375	154,346	161,029	293,020	143,280	149,740	12,849	6,372	6,477	5,881	2,900	2,981	2,087	1,110	977	15,693	7,672	8,021
2nd Marriage ...	21,836	18,030	3,806	20,380	16,826	3,554	617	617	...	267	248	19	202	198	4	871	823	48
3rd and 4th Marriages...	1,873	1,779	94	1,712	1,625	87	68	68	...	34	34	...	35	35	...	60	60	...

SPECIAL TABLES.—(A) Married.—(Continued.)

Bangalore District.

Age Periods of 1st Marriage.	Other Hindus.			Out-castes.			Jains.			Musalmans.			Christians.			Other Religions.		
	Total.	Males.	Females.	Total.	Males.	Females.	Total.	Males.	Females.	Total.	Males.	Females.	Total.	Males.	Females.	Total.	Males.	Females.
Infant	...	...	...	...	...	...	...	...	...	...	...	...	...	...	...	...	...	...
1 year	53	2	51	8	...	8	...	...	...	...	...	...	...	...	...	...	...	...
2 "	125	...	125	22	...	22	...	...	...	...	...	...	...	...	...	...	...	...
3 "	368	...	368	64	...	64	...	...	...	1	...	1	...	...	...	...	...	...
4 "	847	33	814	146	...	146	2	...	2	...	...	...	...	...	...	...	...	...
5 to 9	21,569	884	20,685	4,226	176	4,050	78	3	75	62	36	26	75	1	74	...	...	...
10 to 14	64,816	7,837	56,979	13,416	1,067	14,419	163	20	143	5,318	353	4,965	559	30	529	...	...	...
15 to 19	51,306	27,999	23,307	12,162	6,474	5,688	143	96	47	4,697	1,854	2,843	643	267	376	2	2	...
20 to 24	41,719	37,944	3,775	10,611	9,505	1,106	109	102	7	5,249	3,635	1,614	535	447	88	2	...	2
25 to 29	17,333	16,454	879	4,521	4,303	218	43	40	3	2,345	2,198	147	239	194	45	...	...	...
30 to 34	6,717	6,443	274	1,429	1,366	63	18	18	...	990	943	47	101	76	25	...	...	...
35 to 39	2,036	1,966	70	306	298	8	6	6	...	314	304	10	51	44	7	...	...	...
40 to 44	659	595	64	93	82	11	2	2	...	112	107	5	36	28	8	...	...	...
45 to 49	185	164	21	24	24	...	...	...	...	40	35	5	17	17	...	...	...	...
50 to 54	57	51	6	19	16	3	...	...	...	15	14	1	6	6	...	...	...	...
55 to 59	33	28	5	3	1	2	...	...	...	4	4	...	2	2	...	...	...	...
60 and over ...	33	16	17	6	4	2	...	...	...	5	5	...	1	1	...	...	...	...
Age not stated ...	1,269	460	809	329	134	195	1	1	...	164	68	96	205	107	98	...	...	...
Total....	209,125	100,876	108,249	47,385	24,350	23,035	565	288	277	19,316	9,556	9,760	2,470	1,120	1,250	4	2	2
2nd Marriage ...	14,629	11,969	2,660	3,794	2,971	823	34	34	...	1,288	1,058	230	134	112	22	...	...	...
3rd and 4th Marriages...	1,233	1,161	72	282	267	15	3	3	...	133	126	7	25	25	...	...	...	...

(LOCAL.)

SPECIAL TABLES.—(A) Married.—(Continued.)

Kolar District.

Age Periods of 1st Marriage.	Total All Religions.			TOTAL HINDU RELIGION			Brâmhan.			Kshatriya.			Vais'ya.			Lingâyet.		
	Total.	Males.	Females.	Total.	Males.	Females.	Total.	Males.	Females.	Total.	Males.	Females.	Total.	Males.	Females.	Total.	Males.	Females.
Infant	...	...	...	...	...	...	...	...	...	...	...	...	...	...	...	...	...	...
1 year	2	1	1	...	...	...	...	...	...	...	...	...	...	...	...	...	...	...
2 "	1	...	1	...	...	...	...	...	...	...	...	...	...	...	...	...	...	...
3 "	...	...	...	...	...	...	...	...	...	...	...	...	...	...	...	...	...	...
4 "	1,367	18	1,349	1,364	17	1,347	77	...	77	4	...	4	37	...	37	60	...	60
5 to 9	28,182	928	27,254	26,702	896	25,806	3,579	119	3,460	307	10	297	1,094	24	1,070	543	17	526
10 to 14	74,788	9,695	65,093	70,329	9,239	61,090	3,376	1,258	2,118	1,197	174	1,023	1,393	467	926	1,461	136	1,325
15 to 19	57,083	27,881	29,202	53,736	26,253	27,483	1,887	1,887	...	533	319	214	598	598	...	920	533	387
20 to 24	52,017	48,108	3,909	48,311	44,720	3,591	1,293	1,293	...	525	503	22	469	469	...	924	890	34
25 to 29	25,312	24,672	640	23,499	22,921	578	439	430	...	299	209	...	258	258	...	459	455	4
30 to 34	11,531	11,348	183	10,720	10,560	160	164	164	...	94	94	...	102	102	...	214	212	2
35 to 39	2,517	2,485	32	2,353	2,306	47	36	36	...	17	17	...	20	20	...	64	64	...
40 to 44	882	815	37	813	779	34	11	11	...	10	10	...	8	8	...	21	20	1
45 to 49	211	205	6	197	193	4	1	1	...	1	1	...	1	1	...	12	10	2
50 to 54	89	85	4	81	79	2	3	3	...	1	1	...	2	2	...	5	5	...
55 to 59	26	26	...	26	26	...	...	...	...	...	...	...	1	1	...	4	4	...
60 and over ...	...	...	...	...	...	...	...	...	...	...	...	...	...	...	...	...	...	...
Age not stated ...	1,271	572	699	1,177	522	655	78	36	42	15	6	9	34	18	16	22	13	9
Total...	255,279	126,849	128,430	239,308	116,511	129,797	10,944	5,247	5,697	3,003	1,434	1,569	4,017	1,968	2,049	4,709	2,359	2,350
2nd Marriage ...	14,666	13,540	1,126	13,773	12,779	994	577	577	...	130	127	3	285	285	...	280	273	7
3rd and 4th Marriages...	1,255	1,239	16	1,176	1,161	15	60	60	...	10	10	...	44	44	...	27	26	1

(LOCAL.)

SPECIAL TABLES.—(A) Married.—(Continued.)

Kolar District.

Age Periods of 1st Marriage.	Other Hindus.			Out castes.			JAINS.			MUSALMANS.			CHRISTIANS.			OTHER RELIGIONS.		
	Total.	Males.	Females.	Total.	Males.	Females.	Total.	Males.	Females.	Total.	Males.	Females.	Total.	Males.	Females.	Total.	Males.	Females.
Infant ...	...	...	...	...	...	...	...	...	...	...	...	...	...	...	...	...	...	...
1 year ...	...	...	...	...	...	...	...	...	...	2	1	1	...	...	...	...	...	...
2 ,, ...	...	...	...	...	...	...	...	...	...	1	...	1	...	...	...	...	...	...
3 ,, ...	...	...	...	...	...	...	...	...	...	...	...	...	...	...	...	...	...	...
4 ,, ...	945	14	931	241	3	238	...	...	...	3	1	2	...	...	...	...	...	...
5 to 9 ...	16,708	572	16,136	4,471	154	4,317	40	3	37	1,439	28	1,411	1	1	...	...	...	...
10 to 14 ...	51,288	5,647	45,641	11,614	1,557	10,057	136	25	111	4,025	413	3,612	298	18	280	...	...	...
15 to 19 ...	40,624	18,228	22,396	9,174	4,688	4,486	58	34	24	2,939	1,478	1,461	349	115	234	1	1	...
20 to 24 ...	36,393	33,578	2,815	8,707	7,987	720	47	47	...	3,218	2,963	255	441	378	63	...	...	...
25 to 29 ...	17,996	17,535	461	4,048	3,935	113	29	29	...	1,582	1,532	50	202	190	12	...	...	...
30 to 34 ...	8,487	8,375	112	1,659	1,613	46	24	24	...	708	687	21	79	77	2	...	...	...
35 to 39 ...	1,897	1,856	41	319	313	6	3	3	...	129	124	5	32	32	...	...	...	...
40 to 44 ...	631	605	26	132	125	7	2	2	...	60	57	3	7	7	...	...	...	...
45 to 49 ...	154	154	...	28	26	2	...	...	...	14	12	2	...	...	...	...	...	...
50 to 54 ...	61	61	...	9	7	2	...	...	...	7	6	1	1	...	1	...	...	...
55 to 59 ...	14	14	...	7	7	...	...	...	...	...	...	...	...	...	...	...	...	...
60 and over ...	...	...	...	...	...	...	...	...	...	...	...	...	...	...	...	...	...	...
Age not stated ...	874	385	489	154	64	90	3	3	...	77	38	39	14	9	5	...	...	...
Total......	176,072	87,024	89,048	40,563	20,479	20,084	342	170	172	14,204	7,340	6,864	1,424	827	597	1	1	...
2nd Marriage ...	10,049	9,458	591	2,452	2,059	393	13	13	...	813	688	125	67	60	7	...	...	...
3rd and 4th Marriages...	859	847	12	176	174	2	3	3	...	70	69	1	6	6	...	...	...	...

(LOCAL.)

SPECIAL TABLES.—(A) Married.—(Continued.)

Tumkur District.

Age Periods of 1st Marriage	Total All Religions. Total.	Males.	Females.	TOTAL HINDU RELIGION. Total.	Males.	Females.	Bramhan. Total.	Males.	Females	Kshatriya. Total.	Males.	Females.	Vais'ya. Total.	Males.	Females.	Lingayet. Total.	Males.	Females.
Infant ...	...	...	...	...	...	...	...	...	...	...	...	...	...	...	...	...	...	...
1 year ...	...	...	...	...	...	...	...	...	...	...	...	...	...	...	...	...	...	...
2 " ...	8	...	8	7	...	7	1	...	1	...	...	...	2	...	2	4	...	4
3 " ...	27	4	23	26	4	22	7	...	7	1	...	1	2	...	2	12	...	12
4 " ...	1,283	12	1,271	1,267	12	1,255	33	...	33	8	...	8	20	1	19	57	...	57
5 to 9 ...	25,513	862	24,651	24,815	758	24,057	2,482	62	2,420	223	10	213	658	14	644	1,300	65	1,235
10 to 14 ...	71.217	5.733	62,184	67,909	8,497	59,412	2,462	745	1,717	844	127	717	746	263	483	4,905	294	4,611
15 to 19 ...	59,921	31,845	28,076	57,031	30,554	26,477	1,753	1,742	11	593	320	273	418	418	...	4,091	2,136	1,955
20 to 24 ...	48,706	44,786	3,920	45,764	42,280	3,484	980	980	...	427	409	18	335	335	...	4,147	3,703	444
25 to 29 ...	22,068	21,602	466	20,699	20,286	413	340	340	...	242	241	1	153	153	...	1,082	1,039	43
30 to 34 ...	7,381	7,277	104	7,345	7,241	104	94	94	...	51	49	2	60	60	...	940	933	7
35 to 39 ...	1,751	1,707	44	1,644	1,604	40	15	15	...	15	15	...	20	20	...	218	214	4
40 to 44 ...	566	541	25	518	494	24	9	9	...	1	...	1	6	6	...	64	58	6
45 to 49 ...	128	124	4	117	114	3	2	2	...	...	...	...	...	...	...	16	15	1
50 to 54 ...	44	43	1	39	38	1	...	...	...	...	...	...	...	...	...	2	2	...
55 to 59 ...	13	12	1	12	11	1	1	1	...	...	...	...	...	...	...	1	1	...
60 and over ...	3	3	...	3	3	...	...	...	...	...	...	...	...	...	...	2	2	...
Age not stated ...	901	381	520	855	358	497	36	13	23	1	...	1	3	...	3	91	33	58
Total......	239,530	117,932	121,598	228,051	112,254	115,797	8,215	4,003	4,212	2,406	1,171	1,235	2,423	1,270	1,153	16,932	8,495	8,437
2nd Marriage ...	16,687	14,273	2,414	15,781	13,570	2,211	424	424	...	116	107	9	148	147	1	1,640	1,608	33
3rd and 4th Marriages..	1,328	1,297	31	1,207	1,180	27	37	37	...	12	12	...	10	10	...	141	139	2

(LOCAL) SPECIAL TABLES A. Married.

8

(LOCAL.)

SPECIAL TABLES.—(A) Married.—(Continued.)

Tumkur District.

Age Periods of 1st Marriage.	Other Hindús Total.	Other Hindús Males.	Other Hindús Females.	Outcastes. Total.	Outcastes. Males.	Outcastes. Females.	JAINS. Total.	JAINS. Males.	JAINS. Females.	MUSALMANS. Total.	MUSALMANS. Males.	MUSALMANS. Females.	CHRISTIANS. Total.	CHRISTIANS. Males.	CHRISTIANS. Females.	OTHER RELIGIONS. Total.	OTHER RELIGIONS. Males.	OTHER RELIGIONS. Females
Infant ...	...	...	...	...	...	...	...	...	...	...	...	...	...	...	...	...	...	...
1 year ...	...	...	...	...	...	...	...	...	...	...	...	...	...	...	...	...	...	...
2 " ...	...	...	...	...	...	...	...	...	...	1	...	1	...	...	...	...	...	...
3 " ...	2	2	...	2	2	...	...	...	...	1	...	1	...	...	...	...	...	...
4 " ...	979	8	971	170	3	167	15	...	15	1	...	1	...	...	...	...	...	...
5 to 9 ...	17,961	525	17,436	2,191	82	2,109	103	100	3	593	4	583	2	...	2	...	...	...
10 to 14 ...	50,431	6,178	44,273	8,521	890	7,631	249	25	224	3,010	207	2,803	49	4	45	...	...	...
15 to 19 ...	43,135	22,647	20,488	7,041	3,291	8,750	155	100	55	2,633	1,161	1,472	102	30	72	...	...	...
20 to 24 ...	33,748	31,240	2,508	6,127	5,613	514	135	130	5	2,276	1,974	302	77	65	12	...	...	...
25 to 29 ...	16,072	15,778	294	2,81[illegible]	2,735	75	99	95	4	1,241	1,197	44	29	24	5	...	...	...
30 to 34 ...	5,219	5,145	74	981	960	21	36	36	...	448	428	20	6	6	...	...	...	...
35 to 39 ...	1,155	1,126	29	221	214	7	6	6	...	98	95	3	3	2	1	...	...	...
40 to 44 ...	378	366	12	60	55	5		...	...	47	46	1	1	1	...	...	...	...
45 to 49 ...	79	77	2	20	20	...	...	...	...	9	8	1	3	2	...	...	...	...
50 to 54 ...	25	25	...	12	11	1	...	...	...	5	5	...	...	...	...	...	...	...
55 to 59 ...	8	7	1	2	2	...	...	...	...	1	1	...	...	...	...	...	...	...
60 and over ...	1	1	...	...	...	...	...	...	...	...	...	...	...	...	...	...	...	...
Age not stated ...	605	263	342	119	49	70	8	8	...	33	11	22	5	4	1	...	...	...
Total ...	169,798	83,388	86,410	28,277	13,927	14,350	806	403	403	10,397	5,137	5,260	276	138	138	...	...	...
2nd Marriage ...	11,354	9,611	1,743	2,099	1,673	426	57	57	...	839	638	201	10	8	2	...	...	...
3rd and 4th Marriages ...	879	860	19	128	122	6	6	6	...	113	109	4	2	2	...	...	...	...

(LOCAL.)

SPECIAL TABLES.—(A). Married.—(*Continued.*)

Mysore District.

Age Periods of 1st Marriage.	Total All Religions.			TOTAL HINDU RELIGION.			Brâmhan.			Kshatriya.			Vais'ya.			Lingâyet.		
	Total.	Males.	Females.	Total.	Males.	Females.	Total.	Males.	Females.	Total.	Males.	Females.	Total.	Males.	Females.	Total.	Males.	Females.
Infant ...	...	...	...	...	...	...	...	...	...	...	...	...	...	...	...	...	...	...
1 year ...	...	...	...	...	...	...	...	...	...	...	...	...	...	...	...	...	...	...
2 " ...	15	11	4	15	11	4	1	1	...	4	...	4	...	...	...	10	10	...
3 " ...	1,368	81	1,287	1,368	81	1,287	56	...	56	3	...	3	3	...	3	150	13	137
4 " ...	3,329	109	3,130	3,327	109	3,128	132	...	132	23	1	22	...	...	...	399	12	387
5 to 9 ...	58,912	3,082	55,830	57,471	2,927	54,544	5,814	229	5,585	559	17	542	293	6	287	6,473	206	6,267
10 to 14 ...	147,226	24,768	122,458	142,003	24,352	117,651	5,316	2,279	3,037	2,272	348	1,924	514	141	373	18,358	1,800	16,558
15 to 19 ...	130,056	67,952	62,104	124,622	65,888	58,734	2,220	2,774	46	1,779	761	1,018	223	223	...	15,334	7,569	7,765
20 to 24 ...	99,381	86,054	13,327	94,356	82,013	12,343	2,163	2,163	...	1,224	1,082	142	206	206	...	12,066	11,569	1,497
25 to 29 ...	49,920	45,950	3,970	47,112	43,364	3,748	727	727	...	1,083	1,045	38	78	78	...	7,874	7,581	293
30 to 34 ...	16,806	15,712	1,094	15,420	14,470	950	260	260	...	239	234	5	22	22	...	2,593	2,510	83
35 to 39 ...	6,370	5,806	564	6,025	5,486	539	66	66	...	61	60	1	4	4	...	691	663	28
40 to 44 ...	1,532	1,402	130	1,350	1,226	121	26	26	...	15	14	1	2	2	...	237	225	12
45 to 49 ...	641	605	36	590	558	32	7	7	...	10	10	...	...	...	...	56	53	3
50 to 54 ...	201	188	13	180	169	11	2	2	...	3	3	...	...	...	...	23	21	2
55 to 59 ...	80	74	6	71	65	6	...	...	...	...	...	...	...	...	...	6	6	...
60 and over ...	39	30	9	35	26	9	...	...	...	2	2	...	...	...	...	3	2	1
Age not stated ...	4,900	2,113	2,787	4,718	2,023	2,695	172	77	95	33	12	21	4	...	4	833	421	412
Total......	520,776	254,027	266,749	498,673	242,858	255,815	17,502	8,551	8,951	7,310	3,589	3,721	1,349	682	667	66,106	32,661	33,445
2nd Marriage ...	44,446	31,024	13,422	42,836	29,711	13,125	1,101	1,101	...	267	252	15	73	73	...	4,419	3,756	663
3rd and 4th Marriages...	3,407	3,148	259	3,106	2,867	239	117	117	...	22	22	...	18	17	1	301	293	8

(LOCAL.)

SPECIAL TABLES.—(A) Married.—(Continued.)

Mysore District.

Age Periods of 1st Marriage.	Other Hindus.			Outcastes.			JAINS.			MUSALMANS.			CHRISTIANS.			OTHER RELIGIONS.		
	Total.	Males.	Females.	Total.	Males.	Females.	Total.	Males.	Females.	Total.	Males.	Females.	Total.	Males.	Females.	Total.	Males.	Females.
Infant ...	...	...	...	...	...	...	...	...	...	...	...	...	...	...	...	...	...	...
1 year ...	...	...	...	...	...	...	...	...	...	...	...	...	...	...	...	...	...	...
2 " ...	...	...	...	...	...	...	...	...	...	...	...	...	...	...	...	...	...	...
3 " ...	1,016	44	972	140	24	116	...	...	...	...	...	...	...	...	...	...	...	...
4 " ...	2,303	96	2,207	470	90	380	1	...	1	1	...	1	...	...	...	...	...	...
5 to 9 ...	36,398	1,754	34,644	7,935	715	7,219	132	6	131	1,254	137	1,117	46	9	37	9	...	9
10 to 14 ...	91,367	15,461	75,906	24,173	4,323	19,853	246	28	218	4,719	372	4,347	253	16	212	...	...	...
15 to 19 ...	81,954	43,832	38,122	12,512	[illegible]	11,783	204	115	85	4,972	1,846	3,126	258	99	159	...	...	...
20 to 24 ...	59,813	52,256	7,557	17,813	[illegible]	3,117	134	115	19	4,642	3,724	918	248	201	47	1	1	...
25 to 29 ...	28,507	25,752	2,755	8,823	8,161	662	122	122	...	2,553	2,319	234	129	111	18	4	4	...
30 to 34 ...	9,240	8,568	672	3,076	2,876	200	36	35	1	1,291	1,161	130	44	41	3	5	5	...
35 to 39 ...	4,422	3,966	456	731	727	4	13	13	...	290	283	16	33	21	9	...	...	...
40 to 44 ...	820	730	90	250	229	21	2	2	...	173	167	6	7	7	...	...	...	...
45 to 49 ...	448	[illegible]	24	69	64	5	...	...	...	48	44	4	3	3	...	...	...	...
50 to 54 ...	110	106	4	42	37	5	...	...	...	21	19	2	...	...	...	...	...	...
55 to 59 ...	43	38	5	22	21	1	...	...	...	8	8	...	1	1	...	...	...	...
60 and over ...	25	20	5	5	2	3	...	...	...	4	4	...	...	...	...	...	...	...
Age not stated	2,905	1,183	1,722	771	[illegible]	341	6	4	1	158	73	87	19	13	6	...	...	...
Total......	219,501	154,330	165,171	83,9[illegible]	43,0[illegible]	41,800	835	447	448	20,143	10,157	9,936	1,046	525	521	19	10	9
2nd Marriage ...	29,827	[illegible]	9,939	7,149	[illegible]	2,508	67	59	8	1,463	1,193	270	80	61	19	...	...	...
3rd and 4th Marriages...	2,252	2,053	199	398	362	31	11	11	...	262	242	20	28	2[illegible]	...	...	...	...

(LOCAL.)

SPECIAL TABLES.–(A) Married.

Hassan District.

Age Periods of 1st Marriage.	Total All Religions.			TOTAL HINDU RELIGION.			Brâmhan.			Kshatriya.			Vais'ya.			Lingâyet.		
	Total.	Males.	Females.	Total.	Males.	Females.	Total.	Males.	Females.	Total.	Males.	Females.	Total.	Males.	Females.	Total.	Males.	Females.
Infant ...	...	...	...	...	...	...	...	...	...	...	...	...	...	...	...	...	...	...
1 year ...	1	1	...	...	...	...	...	...	...	...	...	...	...	...	...	...	...	...
2 " ...	...	...	...	...	...	...	...	...	...	...	...	...	...	...	...	...	...	...
3 " ...	125	24	101	124	23	101	29	...	29	1	...	1	...	...	...	14	4	10
4 " ...	330	32	297	329	32	297	87	1	86	3	...	3	1	...	1	16	3	13
5 to 9 ...	11,111	561	10,550	10,870	555	10,315	2,823	98	2,725	85	8	77	157	3	154	1,053	44	1,009
10 to 14 ...	47,972	5,993	41,979	46,415	5,852	40,563	2,366	1,086	1,280	578	145	433	336	84	252	6,469	462	6,007
15 to 19 ...	61,687	23,323	38,364	59,745	22,613	37,132	1,366	1,340	26	603	224	379	133	133	...	7,761	2,590	5,171
20 to 24 ...	45,873	36,942	8,931	44,025	35,513	8,512	794	794	...	301	267	34	100	100	...	6,001	5,027	974
25 to 29 ...	23,713	21,560	2,153	22,704	20,647	2,057	285	285	...	174	164	10	44	44	...	3,098	2,969	129
30 to 34 ...	8,575	8,149	426	8,180	7,769	411	97	97	...	50	48	2	19	19	...	1,247	1,226	21
35 to 39 ...	2,134	1,865	269	1,992	1,735	257	24	24	...	11	11	...	3	3	...	321	308	13
40 to 44 ...	642	587	55	563	518	45	5	5	...	7	7	...	1	1	...	108	105	3
45 to 49 ...	210	194	16	186	172	14	1	1	...	...	...	...	...	...	...	27	24	3
50 to 54 ...	87	72	15	80	65	15	...	...	...	2	2	...	...	...	...	11	10	1
55 to 59 ...	23	22	1	21	20	1	...	...	...	...	...	...	...	...	...	5	4	1
60 and over ...	31	31	...	28	28	...	...	...	...	...	...	...	...	...	...	5	5	...
Age not stated ...	1,501	648	853	1,411	611	800	56	23	33	10	4	6	5	3	2	209	99	110
Total......	204,015	100,004	104,011	196,673	96,153	100,520	7,933	3,754	4,179	1,825	880	945	799	390	409	26,345	12,880	13,465
2nd Marriage ...	18,290	14,096	4,194	17,697	13,626	4,071	442	442	...	96	87	9	47	47	...	1,728	1,603	125
3rd and 4th Marriages...	1,795	1,695	100	1,710	1,612	98	59	59	...	10	10	...	5	5	...	222	207	15

(LOCAL.)

SPECIAL TABLES.—(A) Married.—(Continued.)

Hassan District.

Age Periods of 1st Marriage.	Other Hindus. Total.	Other Hindus. Males.	Other Hindus. Females.	Out-castes. Total.	Out-castes. Males.	Out-castes. Females.	JAINS. Total.	JAINS. Males.	JAINS. Females.	MUSALMANS. Total.	MUSALMANS. Males.	MUSALMANS. Females.	CHRISTIANS. Total.	CHRISTIANS. Males.	CHRISTIANS. Females.	OTHER RELIGIONS. Total.	OTHER RELIGIONS. Males.	OTHER RELIGIONS. Females
Infant ...	...	...	...	...	...	...	...	...	...	...	...	...	...	...	...	...	...	...
1 year ...	...	...	...	...	...	...	...	...	...	1	1	...	...	...	...	...	...	...
2 " ...	...	...	...	...	...	...	...	...	...	...	...	...	...	...	...	...	...	...
3 " ...	57	12	45	23	7	16	...	...	...	1	1	...	[illegible]	...	...	...	...	...
4 " ...	186	22	164	36	6	30	...	...	1	1	...	1	...	...	...	...	...	...
5 to 9 ...	5,569	298	5,271	1,183	161	1,022	20	1	19	206	2	204	15	3	12	...	...	...
10 to 14 ...	28,507	3,066	25,441	8,159	1,009	7,150	178	27	151	1,189	98	1,091	190	16	174	...	...	...
15 to 19 ...	37,744	14,217	23,5[illegible]7	12,133	4,0[illegible]	8,05[illegible]	106	52	54	1,524	529	995	311	128	183	1	1	...
20 to 24 ...	27,425	22,068	5,3[illegible]7	9,384	7,257	2,127	96	81	15	1,344	1,085	259	407	262	145	1	1	...
25 to 29 ...	14,303	12,726	1,5[illegible]7	4,350	4,1[illegible]	241	29	28	1	757	711	46	213	164	49	...	...	...
30 to 34 ...	4,553	4,3[illegible]	209	2,174	2,0[illegible]	89	29	2[illegible]	...	294	285	9	72	66	6	...	...	...
35 to 39 ...	1,213	1,0[illegible]	2[illegible]5	415	[illegible]	31	4	4	...	114	111	3	24	15	9	...	...	...
40 to 44 ...	305	27[illegible]	2[illegible]	137	121	16	5	5	...	62	55	7	12	9	3	...	...	...
45 to 49 ...	119	109	10	39	38	1	...	...	...	18	17	1	6	5	1	...	...	...
50 to 54 ...	43	32	11	24	21	3	...	...	...	5	5	...	2	2	...	...	...	...
55 to 59 ...	9	9	...	7	7	...	...	...	...	2	2	...	...	...	...	...	...	...
60 and over ...	16	16	...	7	7	...	...	...	...	2	2	...	1	1	...	...	...	...
Age not stated ...	777	317	460	354	165	189	3	2	1	54	19	35	29	16	13	4	...	4
Total....	**120,891**	**53,508**	**62,283**	**33,880**	**19,741**	**19,139**	**480**	**239**	**241**	**5,574**	**2,923**	**2,651**	**1,282**	**687**	**595**	**6**	**2**	**4**
2nd Marriage ...	10,927	8,361	2,566	4,457	3,086	1,371	20	20	...	490	382	108	83	68	15	...	...	...
3rd and 4th Marriages...	1,012	962	50	402	369	33	3	3	...	74	73	1	8	7	1	...	...	...

(LOCAL.)

SPECIAL TABLES.—(A) Married.—(Continued.)

Shimoga District.

Age Periods of 1st Marriage.	Total All Religions.			TOTAL HINDU RELIGION			Brâhman.			Kshatriya.			Vaisya.			Lingâyet.		
	Total.	Males.	Females.	Total.	Males.	Females.	Total.	Males.	Females.	Total.	Males.	Females.	Total.	Males.	Females.	Total.	Males.	Females.
Infant	...	...	...	...	...	...	...	...	...	...	...	...	...	...	...	...	...	...
1 year	...	...	...	...	...	...	...	...	...	...	...	...	...	...	...	...	...	...
2 „	3	3	...	3	3	...	1	1	...	2	2	...	...	...	...	...	...	...
3 „	142	...	142	142	...	142	26	...	26	11	...	11	...	...	...	87	...	87
4 „	424	34	390	424	34	390	64	...	64	28	1	27	3	...	3	323	...	323
5 to 9	17,362	678	16,684	16,642	645	15,997	3,589	65	3,524	393	24	369	64	2	62	2,795	198	2,597
10 to 14	54,294	5,789	48,505	50,842	5,531	45,311	3,476	810	2,666	2,458	460	1,998	245	53	192	8,692	834	7,858
15 to 19	48,593	23,325	25,268	45,440	22,108	23,332	3,105	3,076	29	1,901	798	1,103	88	88	...	6,780	2,546	4,234
20 to 24	41,113	37,632	3,481	37,728	34,629	3,099	1,539	1,539	...	1,232	1,146	86	82	83	...	7,173	6,464	709
25 to 29	27,980	26,458	1,522	26,104	24,881	1,223	703	708	...	1,031	982	49	20	20	...	1,995	1,868	127
30 to 34	7,403	7,059	344	6,722	6,417	305	260	260	...	209	169	40	12	12	...	1,550	1,481	69
35 to 39	1,994	1,839	155	1,801	1,664	137	74	74	...	51	43	8	2	2	...	420	387	33
40 to 44	791	607	184	707	593	114	31	31	...	19	16	3	2	2	...	189	145	44
45 to 49	363	236	127	331	210	121	14	14	...	8	7	1	...	...	...	57	45	12
50 to 54	164	147	17	142	128	14	10	10	...	3	3	...	...	...	...	50	38	12
55 to 59	75	62	13	69	56	13	3	3	...	6	4	2	...	...	...	25	15	10
60 and over ..	92	86	6	76	73	3	4	4	...	1	1	...	...	...	...	31	28	3
Age not stated ...	1,218	552	666	1,146	513	633	89	40	49	31	14	17	5	1	4	239	100	139
Total...	202,011	104,567	97,444	188,319	97,485	90,834	12,993	6,635	6,358	7,384	3,670	3,714	523	262	261	30,306	14,149	16,157
2nd Marriage ...	14,444	11,507	2,937	13,295	10,664	2,631	705	705	...	226	195	34	1	...	1	3,100	2,741	359
3rd and 4th Marriages...	1,742	1,645	97	1,588	1,501	87	90	90	...	25	25	...	...	...	...	420	408	12

(LOCAL.)

SPECIAL TABLES.—(A) Married.—(Continued.)

Shimoga District.

Age Periods of 1st Marriage.	Other Hindus. Total.	Other Hindus. Males.	Other Hindus. Females.	Out-castes. Total.	Out-castes. Males.	Out-castes. Females.	JAINS. Total.	JAINS. Males.	JAINS. Females.	MUSALMANS. Total.	MUSALMANS. Males.	MUSALMANS. Females.	CHRISTIANS. Total.	CHRISTIANS. Males.	CHRISTIANS. Females.	OTHER RELIGIONS. Total.	OTHER RELIGIONS. Males.	OTHER RELIGIONS. Females.
Infant	...	...	...	...	...	...	...	...	...	...	...	...	...	...	...	...	...	...
1 year	...	...	...	...	...	...	...	...	...	...	...	...	...	...	...	...	...	...
2 „	...	...	...	...	...	...	...	...	...	...	...	...	...	...	...	...	...	...
3 „	...	...	...	18	...	18	...	...	...	...	...	...	...	...	...	...	...	...
4 „	26	26	...	80	7	73	...	...	...	...	...	...	...	...	...	...	...	...
5 to 9	8,538	317	8,221	1,263	39	1,224	144	4	140	557	26	531	19	3	16	...	...	...
10 to 14	31,156	2,985	28,171	4,815	389	4,426	317	42	275	3,001	203	2,798	134	13	121	...	...	...
15 to 19	28,249	12,535	15,714	5,317	3,065	2,252	267	139	128	2,692	976	1,716	194	102	92	...	...	...
20 to 24	22,639	20,712	1,927	5,063	4,686	377	147	147	...	2,389	2,020	369	249	236	13	...	...	...
25 to 29	18,937	17,979	958	3,413	3,324	89	164	164	...	1,605	1,308	297	107	105	2	...	...	...
30 to 34	3,904	3,746	158	787	749	38	75	75	...	569	530	39	37	37	...	...	...	...
35 to 39	1,037	959	78	217	199	18	23	23	...	165	147	18	5	5	...	...	...	...
40 to 44	387	327	60	79	72	7	9	9	...	69	59	10	6	6	...	...	...	...
45 to 49	227	121	106	25	23	2	...	...	...	29	23	6	3	3	...	...	...	...
50 to 54	70	70	...	9	7	2	...	...	...	21	18	3	1	1	...	...	...	...
55 to 59	31	31	...	4	3	1	...	...	...	6	6	...	...	...	...	...	...	...
60 and over ...	37	37	...	3	3	...	...	...	...	16	13	3	...	...	...	...	...	...
Age not stated ..	626	284	342	156	74	82	13	13	...	56	23	33	3	3	...	...	...	...
Total...	115,864	60,129	55,735	21,249	12,640	8,609	1,159	616	543	11,775	5,952	5,823	758	514	244	...	...	...
2nd Marriage ...	8,172	6,294	1,878	1,088	7,029	359	92	92	...	1,020	717	303	37	34	3	...	...	...
3rd and 4th Marriages...	921	854	67	132	124	8	5	5	...	133	123	10	16	16	...	...	...	...

(LOCAL.)

SPECIAL TABLES.—(A) Married.—(*Continued.*)

Kadur District.

Age Periods of 1st Marriage	Total All Religions. Total.	Males.	Females.	TOTAL HINDU RELIGION. Total.	Males.	Females.	Brámhan. Total.	Males.	Females	Kshatriya. Total.	Males.	Females.	Vais'ya. Total.	Males.	Females.	Lingáyet. Total.	Males.	Females.
Infant ...	...	...	...	...	...	...	...	...	...	...	...	...	...	...	...	...	...	...
1 year ...	2	...	2	2	...	2	1	...	1	...	...	...	...	...	...	...	...	...
2 " ...	21	...	21	21	...	21	3	...	3	...	...	...	...	...	...	5	...	5
3 " ...	48	10	38	48	10	38	7	...	7	...	...	...	1	...	1	9	2	7
4 " ...	137	18	119	137	18	119	20	...	20	3	...	3	24	...	24	17	5	12
5 to 9 ...	7,740	503	7,237	7,400	484	6,916	2,767	25	2,742	94	11	83	152	7	145	542	17	525
10 to 14 ...	28,538	2,888	25,650	27,069	2,754	24,315	1,705	631	1,074	707	162	545	173	40	133	3,108	177	2,931
15 to 19 ...	37,253	15,657	21,571	35,209	14,804	20,405	1,524	1,524	...	696	353	343	104	104	...	4,088	1,183	2,905
20 to 24 ...	33,744	27,831	5,913	31,597	26,044	5,553	1,021	1,021	...	324	300	24	118	118	...	4,620	3,991	629
25 to 29 ...	15,432	14,507	925	14,215	13,318	867	372	372	...	296	296	...	37	37	...	809	735	74
30 to 34 ...	5,042	4,870	172	4,630	4,473	157	103	103	...	34	34	...	15	15	...	768	739	29
35 to 39 ...	1,093	1,040	53	987	940	47	26	26	...	8	8	...	1	1	...	177	173	4
40 to 44 ...	359	339	20	327	308	19	3	3	...	5	5	...	1	1	...	62	56	6
45 to 49 ...	97	91	6	90	86	4	1	1	...	3	3	...	...	...	...	18	17	1
50 to 54 ...	38	36	2	32	31	1	...	...	...	1	1	...	...	...	...	10	9	1
55 to 59 ...	15	15	...	9	9	...	...	...	...	2	2	...	...	...	...	2	2	
60 and over ...	4	4	...	3	3	...	...	...	...	...	...	...	...	...	...	1	1	...
Age not stated ...	961	460	501	867	400	467	50	22	28	20	7	13	4	2	2	205	85	120
Total ...	130,529	68,299	62,230	122,643	63,712	58,931	7,603	3,728	3,875	2,193	1,182	1,011	630	325	305	14,441	7,192	7,249
2nd Marriage ...	9,756	7,838	1,918	9,125	7,299	1,826	448	448	...	70	70	...	42	42	...	1,379	1,351	28
3rd and 4th Marriages...	1,217	1,144	73	1,071	1,010	61	38	38	...	9	9	...	18	18	...	138	136	2

(LOCAL.)

SPECIAL TABLES.—(A) Married.—(*Continued.*)

Kadur District.

Age Periods of 1st Marriage.	Other Hindus.			Outcastes.			Jains.			Musalmans.			Christians.			Other Religions.		
	Total.	Males.	Females.	Total.	Males.	Females.	Total.	Males.	Females.	Total.	Males.	Females.	Total.	Males.	Females.	Total.	Males.	Females.
Infant	...	...	...	...	...	...	...	...	...	...	...	...	...	...	...	...	...	...
1 year	...	...	...	1	...	1	...	...	...	...	...	...	...	...	...	...	...	...
2 years	11	...	11	2	...	2	...	...	...	...	...	...	...	...	...	...	...	...
3 ,, ...	28	8	20	3	...	3	...	...	...	...	...	...	...	...	...	...	...	...
4 ,, ...	57	13	44	16	...	16	...	...	...	...	...	...	...	...	...	...	...	...
5 to 9	3,436	400	3,006	349	21	325	46	...	48	280	18	262	12	1	11	...	...	...
10 to 14	17,646	1,377	16,269	3,730	367	3,363	132	15	117	1,249	110	1,139	88	9	79	...	...	...
15 to 19	22,023	9,519	12,504	6,774	2,121	4,653	124	93	31	1,720	698	1,022	205	92	113	...	...	...
20 to 24	19,668	15,937	3,731	5,846	4,677	1,169	81	78	3	1,712	1,430	282	354	270	75	...	...	...
25 to 29	10,180	9,589	501	2,521	2,319	202	51	50	1	980	939	41	186	170	16	...	...	...
30 to 34	2,632	2,552	80	1,078	1,030	48	21	20	1	310	300	10	81	77	4	...	...	...
35 to 39	559	528	31	216	204	12	8	8	...	72	67	5	26	25	1	...	...	...
40 to 44	176	164	12	80	79	1	2	1	1	25	25	...	5	5	...	...	...	...
45 to 49	57	54	3	11	11	...	...	...	...	5	3	2	2	2	...	...	...	...
50 to 54	14	14	...	7	7	...	...	...	...	6	5	1	...	...	...	...	...	...
55 to 59	5	5	...	...	...	...	...	...	...	5	5	...	1	1	...	...	...	...
60 and over ...	2	2	...	...	...	...	...	...	...	1	1	...	...	...	...	...	...	...
Age not stated ...	406	195	211	182	89	93	1	...	1	52	30	22	41	30	11	...	...	...
Total.....	76,960	40,357	36,603	20,816	10,928	9,888	468	265	203	6,417	3,631	27,86	1,001	691	310	...	...	...
2nd Marriage ...	4,814	3,803	1,012	2,372	1,586	786	21	18	3	566	485	81	44	36	8	...	...	...
3rd and 4th Marriages.	647	607	40	221	202	19	2	2	...	136	126	10	8	6	2	...	...	...

(LOCAL)
SPECIAL TABLES
A.
Married.

(LOCAL.)

SPECIAL TABLES.—(A) Married.—(Continued.)

Chitaldroog District.

Age Periods of 1st Marriage.	Total All Religions. Total.	Males.	Females.	TOTAL HINDU RELIGION. Total.	Males.	Females.	Brámhan. Total.	Males.	Females.	Kshatriya. Total.	Males.	Females.	Vais'ya. Total.	Males.	Females.	Lingáyet. Total.	Males.	Females.
Infant ...	...	...	...	...	...	...	...	...	...	...	...	...	...	...	...	...	...	...
1 year ...	6	...	6	6	...	6	...	...	...	...	...	...	...	...	...	...	...	...
2 " ...	136	...	136	136	...	136	...	...	...	...	...	...	...	...	...	...	...	...
3 " ...	284	14	270	282	14	268	8	...	8	2	...	2	...	...	...	117	4	113
4 " ...	751	19	732	749	19	730	15	...	15	14	...	14	7	...	7	274	6	268
5 to 9 ...	13,350	612	12,738	12,843	596	12,247	724	27	697	130	13	117	221	4	217	2,057	178	1,879
10 to 14 ...	46,635	4,386	42,249	44,382	4,193	40,189	981	290	691	463	98	365	509	96	413	7,535	814	6,721
15 to 19 ...	41,390	18,641	22,749	39,511	17,823	21,688	553	539	11	398	163	235	185	185	...	5,343	2,397	2,946
20 to 24 ...	35,892	33,016	2,876	34,080	31,387	2,693	317	317	...	198	179	19	142	142	...	5,970	5,587	383
25 to 29 ...	16,923	16,431	492	16,009	15,547	462	102	102	...	130	129	1	77	77	...	1,118	1,065	53
30 to 34 ...	6,039	5,913	126	5,711	5,606	105	39	39	...	33	33	...	24	24	...	1,087	1,069	18
35 to 39 ...	1,721	1,672	49	1,590	1,541	49	7	7	...	4	4	...	5	5	...	246	238	8
40 to 44 ...	405	388	17	368	351	17	1	1	...	3	3	...	1	1	...	90	86	4
45 to 49 ...	102	96	6	94	88	6	1	1	...	1	1	...	1	1	...	19	18	1
50 to 54 ...	74	69	5	65	60	5	...	...	...	1	1	...	1	1	...	11	9	2
55 to 59 ...	16	14	2	13	11	2	...	...	...	...	...	...	1	1	...	3	2	1
60 and over ...	11	11	...	9	9	...	...	...	...	...	...	...	...	...	...	...	...	...
Age not stated ...	928	408	520	884	383	501	11	4	7	12	6	6	11	2	9	183	66	117
Total.....	164,863	81,690	82,973	156,732	77,631	79,101	2,759	1,327	1,432	1,389	630	759	1,185	539	646	24,053	11,539	12,514
2nd Marriage ...	10,572	9,177	1,395	9,958	8,683	1,275	110	110	...	56	48	8	70	69	1	2,294	2,186	108
3rd and 4th Marriages.	691	672	19	619	602	17	11	11	...	3	2	1	11	11	...	162	158	4

(LOCAL.)

SPECIAL TABLES.—(A) Married.—(Concluded.)

Chitaldroog District.

Age Periods of 1st Marriage.	Other Hindús.			Outcastes.			JAINS.			MUSALMANS.			CHRISTIANS.			OTHER RELIGIONS.		
	Total.	Males.	Females.	Total.	Males.	Females.	Total.	Males.	Females.	Total.	Males.	Females.	Total.	Males.	Females.	Total.	Males.	Females.
Infant	...	...	...	...	...	...	...	...	...	...	...	...	...	...	...	...	...	...
1 year	...	...	...	6	...	6	...	...	...	...	...	...	...	...	...	...	...	...
2 "	114	...	114	22	...	22	...	...	...	...	...	...	...	...	...	...	...	...
3 "	125	10	115	30	...	30	1	...	1	1	...	1	...	...	...	...	...	...
4 "	379	11	368	60	2	58	...	...	...	2	...	2	...	...	...	...	...	...
5 to 9	8,764	324	8,140	947	50	897	28	1	27	477	15	462	2	...	2	...	...	...
10 to 14	30,465	2,481	27,984	4,429	414	4,015	84	18	66	2,150	174	1,976	19	1	18	...	...	...
15 to 19	28,355	12,748	15,607	4,677	1,791	2,886	56	40	16	1,787	766	1,021	35	12	23	1	...	1
20 to 24	23,485	21,610	1,875	3,968	3,552	416	47	47	...	1,744	1,564	180	20	17	3	1	1	...
25 to 29	12,415	12,157	258	2,167	2,017	150	18	18	...	882	854	28	14	12	2	...	...	...
30 to 34	3,859	3,794	65	669	647	22	6	6	...	314	293	21	8	8		...	...	...
35 to 39	1,166	1,135	31	162	155	7	5	5	...	123	120	3	3	3	...	...	...	...
40 to 44	232	220	12	41	40	1	...	...	...	37	37	...	...	...	...	...	...	...
45 to 49	60	57	3	12	10	2	...	...	...	8	8	...	...	...	...	...	...	...
50 to 54	48	45	3	4	4	...	...	...	...	9	9	...	...	...	...	...	...	...
55 to 59	7	6	1	2	2	...	...	...	...	3	3	...	...	...	...	...	...	...
60 and over ...	6	6	...	3	3	...	...	...	...	2	2	...	...	...	...	...	...	...
Age not stated ...	553	258	295	114	47	67	...	...	...	32	14	18	12	11	1	...	...	...
Total......	110,033	54,862	55,171	17,313	8,734	8,579	245	135	110	7,571	3,859	3,712	113	64	49	2	1	1
2nd Marriage ...	6,275	5,336	939	1,153	934	219	10	10	...	603	483	120	1	1	...	...	...	...
3rd and 4th Marriages.	373	361	12	59	59	...	1	1	...	71	69	2	...	...	...	...	...	...

(LOCAL.)

SPECIAL TABLES

B

WIDOWED.

SPECIAL TABLES.—(B) Widowed.

Provincial.

Age Periods of Widowhood.	Total All Religions.			Total Hindu Religion.			Brāmhan.			Kshatriya.			Vaisya.			Lingāyet.		
	Total.	Males.	Females.	Total.	Males.	Females.	Total.	Males.	Females.	Total.	Males.	Females.	Total.	Males.	Females.	Total.	Males.	Females.
Infant	...	...	...	...	...	...	...	...	...	...	...	...	...	...	...	...	...	...
1 year	...	...	...	...	...	...	...	...	...	...	...	...	...	...	...	...	...	...
2 "	1	...	1	1	...	1	...	...	...	...	...	...	...	...	...	...	...	...
3 "	...	...	...	...	...	...	...	...	...	...	...	...	...	...	...	...	...	...
4 "	8	2	6	7	2	5	...	...	...	...	...	...	...	...	...	...	...	...
5 to 9	3,791	223	3,568	3,774	220	3,554	547	11	536	55	2	53	74	2	72	569	47	522
10 to 14	20,658	978	19,680	20,517	973	19,544	2,521	59	2,462	358	8	350	254	16	238	1,819	141	1,678
15 to 19	43,411	2,772	40,639	42,904	2,723	40,181	2,708	159	2,549	644	43	601	350	38	312	4,734	364	4,370
20 to 24	78,317	9,298	69,019	75,145	8,909	66,236	3,052	419	2,633	1,002	104	898	534	110	424	8,374	1,283	7,091
25 to 29	83,431	13,626	69,805	79,895	13,091	66,804	2,864	612	2,252	1,257	343	914	431	103	328	7,867	1,456	6,411
30 to 34	100,237	18,017	82,220	93,771	17,326	76,445	4,092	1,282	2,810	1,596	355	1,241	594	163	431	8,709	1,795	6,914
35 to 39	78,745	16,177	62,568	75,318	15,574	59,744	3,710	1,277	2,433	1,151	367	784	419	142	277	6,849	1,664	5,185
40 to 44	76,614	16,476	60,138	72,968	15,885	57,083	3,503	1,356	2,147	1,218	374	844	520	171	349	7,857	1,856	6,001
45 to 49	49,423	11,901	37,522	46,859	11,493	35,366	1,970	733	1,237	916	345	571	298	138	160	4,560	1,503	3,057
50 to 54	36,880	9,228	27,652	34,701	8,803	25,898	1,478	545	933	747	306	441	320	96	224	4,024	1,273	2,751
55 to 59	20,631	6,042	14,589	18,765	5,671	13,094	1,024	316	708	254	75	179	199	79	120	2,773	885	1,888
60 and over ...	22,392	8,615	13,777	20,879	8,148	12,731	1,198	446	752	332	107	225	240	99	141	3,166	1,307	1,859
Age not stated ...	11,954	2,044	9,910	11,423	1,965	9,458	492	154	338	183	35	148	97	27	70	2,100	325	1,775
Total.....	626,587	115,492	511,095	598,932	110,780	488,152	29,159	7,321	21,838	9,713	2,464	7,249	4,330	1,184	3,146	63,401	13,896	49,505

(LOCAL.)

SPECIAL TABLES.—(B) Widowed.—(Continued.)

Provincial.—(Concluded.)

Age Periods of Widowhood.	Other Hindús.			Outcastes.			JAINS.			MUSALMÁNS.			CHRISTIANS.			OTHER RELIGIONS.		
	Total.	Males.	Females.	Total.	Males.	Females.	Total.	Males.	Females.	Total.	Males.	Females.	Total.	Males.	Females.	Total.	Males.	Females.
Infant	...	...	...	...	...	...	...	...	...	...	...	...	...	...	...	...	...	...
1 year	...	...	...	...	...	...	...	...	...	...	...	...	...	...	...	...	...	...
2 "	1	...	1	...	...	...	...	...	...	...	...	...	...	...	...	...	...	...
3 "	...	...	...	...	...	...	...	...	...	...	...	...	...	...	...	...	...	...
4 "	7	2	5	...	...	...	...	...	...	1	...	1	...	...	...	...	...	...
5 to 9	2,049	113	1,936	430	45	435	17	3	14	...	...	...	...	...	...	...	...	...
10 to 14	12,496	568	11,928	3,069	181	2,888	57	4	53	84	1	83	...	...	...	...	...	...
15 to 19	27,792	1,603	26,189	6.676	513	6,163	177	13	164	319	35	284	11	4	7	...	...	...
20 to 24	50,371	5,553	44,818	11,812	1,440	10,372	301	38	263	2,673	311	2,362	195	38	157	3	2	1
25 to 29	54,647	8,255	46,392	12,829	2,322	10,507	317	61	256	2,978	425	2,553	243	52	191	1	...	1
30 to 34	6[illegible],215	10,822	54,3[illegible]3	15,535	2,909	12,626	384	106	278	3,789	541	3,245	322	71	251	1	...	1
35 to 39	51.334	9,778	41,556	11.855	2,346	9,509	238	78	160	2,977	462	2,515	211	63	148	2	...	2
40 to 44	43 453	9,793	33,660	11.417	2,338	9 079	276	76	200	3,186	474	2,712	183	41	142	1	...	1
45 to 49	32.139	7,108	25,031	6.976	1,666	5,310	146	47	99	2,323	383	1,940	153	38	115	2	...	2
50 to 54	23.225	5,493	17,732	4.907	1,090	3.817	120	36	84	1,894	357	1,537	165	32	133	...	...	...
55 to 59	12,204	3,594	8,610	2.311	720	1,591	72	28	44	1.705	329	1,376	89	14	75	...	...	...
60 and over ...	13.536	5,270	8,266	2.407	919	1.488	70	33	37	1,364	411	953	79	27	51	...	...	...
Age not stated ...	6,353	1,185	5,168	1,903	289	1,614	14	8	6	439	62	377	73	9	64	...	...	...
Total......	400.122	69,137	330.985	92.207	16,778	75.429	2.189	531	1,658	23,732	3,794	19,938	1,724	385	1,339	10	2	8

(LOCAL.)

SPECIAL TABLES.—(B) Widowed.—(*Continued.*)

Bangalore District.

Age Periods of Widowhood.	Total All Religions. Total.	Males.	Females.	TOTAL HINDU RELIGION. Total.	Males.	Females.	Brâmhan. Total.	Males.	Females.	Kshatriya. Total.	Males.	Females.	Vais'ya. Total.	Males.	Females.	Lingâyet. Total.	Males.	Females.
Infant	...	...	...	...	...	...	...	...	...	...	...	...	...	...	...	...	...	...
1 year	...	...	...	...	...	...	...	...	...	...	...	...	...	...	...	...	...	...
2	...	...	...	...	...	...	...	...	...	...	...	...	...	...	...	...	...	...
3	...	...	...	...	...	...	...	...	...	...	...	...	...	...	...	...	...	...
4	1	...	1	1	...	1	...	...	...	...	...	...	...	...	...	...	...	...
5 to 9	440	23	417	438	23	415	72	3	69	8	...	8	10	...	10	23	1	22
10 to 14	2,680	151	2,529	2,669	151	2,518	310	14	296	64	2	62	16	2	14	154	10	144
15 to 19	5,866	428	5,438	5,847	427	5,420	357	33	325	129	5	124	39	5	34	351	17	334
20 to 24	10,431	1,378	9,053	9,928	1,323	8,605	462	56	406	210	24	186	78	13	65	583	65	518
25 to 29	11,113	1,801	9,312	10,538	1,718	8,821	379	70	309	283	84	199	61	3	58	632	153	479
30 to 34	13,807	2,442	11,365	12,982	2,329	10,653	633	191	442	351	88	263	74	11	63	836	221	615
35 to 39	11,321	2,258	9,063	10,737	2,163	8,574	527	178	349	240	82	158	74	27	47	721	211	510
40 to 44	11,944	2,418	9,526	11,207	2,321	8,886	566	209	357	260	82	178	89	21	68	751	240	511
45 to 49	8,028	1,821	6,207	7,536	1,740	5,796	350	106	244	214	74	140	41	22	19	503	142	361
50 to 54	6,441	1,499	4,942	5,914	1,408	4,506	325	89	236	168	65	103	75	18	57	395	111	284
55 to 59	3,655	1,023	2,632	3,250	941	2,309	179	52	127	54	16	38	60	19	41	211	72	139
60 and over ...	4,331	1,572	2,759	3,938	1,483	2,455	256	84	172	81	24	57	61	27	34	261	111	150
Age not stated ...	1,710	361	1,349	1,579	340	1,239	69	12	57	34	5	29	26	7	19	114	26	88
Total......	91,768	17,175	74,593	86,564	16,367	70,197	4,485	1,099	3,386	2,096	551	1,545	704	178	526	5,535	1,381	4,154

(LOCAL.)

SPECIAL TABLES.—(B) Widowed.—(*Continued.*)

Bangalore District.

Age Periods of Widowhood.	Other Hindus.			Outcastes.			Jains.			Musalmans.			Christians.			Other Religions.		
	Total.	Males.	Females.	Total.	Males.	Females.	Total.	Males.	Females.	Total.	Males.	Females.	Total.	Males.	Females.	Total.	Males.	Females.
Infant ...	...	...	...	...	...	...	...	...	...	...	...	...	...	...	...	...	...	...
1 year ...	...	...	...	...	...	...	...	...	...	...	...	...	...	...	...	...	...	...
2 „ ...	...	...	...	...	...	...	...	...	...	...	...	...	...	...	...	...	...	...
3 „ ...	...	...	...	...	...	...	...	...	...	...	...	...	...	...	...	...	...	...
4 „ ...	1	...	1	...	...	...	...	...	...	...	...	...	...	...	...	...	...	...
5 to 9 ...	279	16	263	46	3	43	2	...	2	...	...	...	...	...	...	...	...	...
10 to 14 ...	1,645	106	1,539	480	17	463	11	...	11	...	...	...	...	...	...	...	...	...
15 to 19 ...	3,894	296	3,598	1,077	72	1,005	19	1	18	...	...	...	...	...	...	...	...	...
20 to 24 ...	6,802	976	5,826	1,793	180	1,614	27	3	24	419	46	373	57	6	51	...	...	...
25 to 29 ...	7,073	1,017	6,056	2,110	391	1,719	26	4	22	404	65	339	85	14	71	...	...	...
30 to 34 ...	8,636	1,349	7,287	2,452	466	1,986	37	11	26	696	87	609	92	15	77	...	...	...
35 to 39 ...	7,256	1,315	5,943	1,917	350	1,567	22	9	13	500	71	429	62	15	47	...	...	...
40 to 44 ...	7,590	1,412	6,178	1,951	354	1,597	29	11	18	647	73	574	61	13	48	...	...	...
45 to 49 ...	5,238	1,153	4,085	1,190	243	947	20	7	13	428	64	364	44	10	34	...	...	...
50 to 54 ...	4,035	974	3,061	916	151	765	20	2	18	473	82	391	34	7	27	...	...	...
55 to 59 ...	2,370	693	1,677	376	88	288	6	2	4	343	69	274	56	11	45	...	...	...
60 and over ...	2,863	1,092	1,771	416	145	271	13	5	8	344	73	271	36	11	25	...	...	...
Age not stated ...	1,075	239	836	261	51	210	3	3	...	101	13	88	27	5	22	...	...	...
Total....	58,759	10,638	48,121	14,985	2,520	12,465	235	58	177	4,415	643	3,772	554	107	447	...	...	...

(LOCAL.)

SPECIAL TABLES.—(B) Widowed.—(Continued.)

Kolar District.

Age Periods of Widowhood.	Total All Religions.			TOTAL HINDU RELIGION.			Brâmhan.			Kshatriya.			Vais'ya.			Lingâyet.		
	Total.	Males.	Females.	Total.	Males.	Females.	Total.	Males.	Females.	Total.	Males.	Females.	Total.	Males.	Females.	Total.	Males.	Females.
Infant	...	...	...	...	...	...	...	...	...	...	...	...	...	...	...	...	...	...
1 year	...	...	...	...	...	...	...	...	...	...	...	...	...	...	...	...	...	...
2 ,, ...	...	...	...	...	...	...	...	...	...	...	...	...	...	...	...	...	...	...
3 ,, ...	...	...	...	...	...	...	...	...	...	...	...	...	...	...	...	...	...	...
4 ,, ...	3	...	3	2	...	2	...	...	...	...	...	...	...	...	...	...	...	...
5 to 9	787	26	761	787	26	761	102	3	99	11	...	11	35	1	34	15	2	13
10 to 14	3,662	186	3,476	3,591	186	3,405	307	9	298	56	1	55	92	5	87	77	2	75
15 to 19	6,715	509	6,206	6,526	488	6,038	315	24	291	69	2	67	118	10	108	121	7	114
20 to 24	10,884	1,497	9,387	10,500	1,442	9,058	475	77	398	102	8	94	182	39	143	223	34	189
25 to 29	10,214	1,920	8,294	9,827	1,860	7,967	429	107	322	102	21	81	125	29	96	224	55	169
30 to 34	12,869	2,712	10,157	12,396	2,637	9,759	589	164	425	171	36	135	168	40	128	245	60	185
35 to 39	10,127	2,366	7,761	9,697	2,279	7,418	456	132	324	116	31	85	133	42	91	201	56	145
40 to 44	10,447	2,418	8,029	9,998	2,331	7,664	495	165	330	133	40	93	184	63	121	272	67	205
45 to 49	6,879	1,651	5,228	6,553	1,580	4,973	345	99	246	89	31	58	101	41	60	144	52	92
50 to 54	5,760	1,366	4,394	5,512	1,313	4,199	285	82	203	88	31	57	103	31	72	105	28	77
55 to 59	2,993	842	2,151	2,853	791	2,062	176	54	122	34	8	26	60	23	37	70	16	54
60 and over ...	3,801	1,439	2,362	3,619	1,380	2,239	185	67	118	31	9	22	90	31	59	79	35	54
Age not stated ...	1,142	245	897	1,088	235	853	45	10	35	14	2	12	27	9	18	20	4	16
Total......	86,283	17,177	69,106	82,949	16,551	66,398	4,204	1,013	3,191	1,016	221	795	1,418	364	1,054	1,796	418	1,378

(LOCAL.)

SPECIAL TABLES.—(B) Widowed.—(*Continued.*)

Kolar District.

Age Periods of Widowhood.	Other Hindus.			Out castes.			JAINS.			MUSALMANS.			CHRISTIANS.			OTHER RELIGIONS.		
	Total.	Males.	Females.	Total.	Males.	Females.	Total.	Males.	Females.	Total.	Males.	Females.	Total.	Males.	Females.	Total.	Males.	Females.
Infant	...	...	...	...	...	...	...	...	...	...	...	...	...	...	...	...	...	...
1 year	...	...	...	...	...	...	...	...	...	...	...	...	...	...	...	...	...	...
2 „	...	...	...	...	...	...	...	...	...	...	...	...	...	...	...	...	...	...
3 „	...	...	...	...	...	...	...	...	...	...	...	...	...	...	...	...	...	...
4 „	2	...	2	...	...	...	...	...	...	1	...	1	...	...	...	...	...	...
5 to 9	516	16	500	108	4	104	...	...	...	...	...	...	...	...	...	...	...	...
10 to 14	2,470	127	2,343	589	42	547	4	...	4	67	...	67	...	...	...	...	...	...
15 to 19	4,639	350	4,289	1,264	95	1,169	9	...	9	171	19	152	9	2	7	...	...	...
20 to 24	7,663	1,008	6,655	1,855	276	1,579	15	1	15	342	43	204	26	6	20	...	...	...
25 to 29	7,173	1,200	5,973	1,774	447	1,327	21	1	20	343	55	291	20	4	16	...	...	...
30 to 34	9,042	1,738	7,304	2,131	599	1,532	20	6	14	407	55	352	46	14	32	...	...	...
35 to 39	7,238	1,576	5,662	1,553	422	1,131	19	6	13	391	68	323	20	13	7	...	...	...
40 to 44	7,349	1,561	5,788	1,565	438	1,127	22	7	15	405	72	333	22	5	17	...	...	...
45 to 49	4,894	1,086	3,808	980	271	709	11	6	5	301	62	239	14	3	11	...	...	...
50 to 54	4,296	991	3,305	635	150	465	15	4	11	223	47	176	10	2	8	...	...	...
55 to 59	2,183	600	1,583	330	90	240	15	9	6	122	42	80	3	...	3	...	...	...
60 and over ...	2,844	1,105	1,739	390	133	257	10	6	4	166	51	115	6	2	4	...	...	...
Age not stated ...	800	175	625	182	35	147	3	1	2	46	9	37	5	...	5	...	...	...
Total ...	61,109	11,533	49,576	13,406	3,002	10,404	165	47	118	2,988	528	2,460	181	51	130	...	...	...

(LOCAL.)

SPECIAL TABLES.-(B) Widowed.-(Continued.)

Tumkur District.

Age Periods of Widowhood.	Total All Religions.			TOTAL HINDU RELIGION.			Brâmhan.			Kshatriya.			Vais'ya.			Lingâyet.		
	Total.	Males.	Females.	Total.	Males.	Females.	Total.	Males.	Females.	Total.	Males.	Females.	Total.	Males.	Females.	Total.	Males.	Females.
Infant ...	...	...	...	...	...	...	...	...	...	...	...	...	...	...	...	...	...	...
1 year ...	...	...	...	...	...	...	...	...	...	...	...	...	...	...	...	...	...	...
2 " ...	...	...	...	...	...	...	...	...	...	...	...	...	...	...	...	...	...	...
3 " ...	...	...	...	...	...	...	...	...	...	...	...	...	...	...	...	...	...	...
4 " ...	2	2	...	2	2	...	...	...	...	...	...	...	...	...	...	...	...	...
5 to 9 ...	320	7	313	317	7	310	29	...	29	5	...	5	4	...	4	39	2	37
10 to 14 ...	3,004	151	2,853	2,982	150	2,832	222	3	219	20	2	18	63	4	59	155	10	145
15 to 19 ...	7,304	435	6,869	7,146	421	6,725	259	18	241	60	4	56	86	12	74	554	61	493
20 to 24 ...	11,553	1,258	10,295	11,163	1,222	9,941	318	61	257	82	5	77	97	20	77	650	188	462
25 to 29 ...	11,805	2,040	9,765	11,385	1,985	9,400	288	77	211	96	35	61	102	34	68	563	171	392
30 to 34 ...	12,922	2,528	10,394	12,448	2,411	10,007	401	125	276	121	26	95	142	52	90	582	124	458
35 to 39 ...	10,278	2,216	8,032	9,889	2,145	7,741	320	122	258	89	27	62	86	35	51	460	150	310
40 to 44 ...	9,098	2,073	7,025	8,711	2,007	6,704	306	113	193	99	33	66	102	40	62	725	101	621
45 to 49 ...	6,204	1,580	4,624	5,964	1,527	4,437	168	84	84	57	28	29	60	27	33	559	152	407
50 to 54 ...	4,112	1,221	2,888	3,924	1,179	2,745	140	63	77	47	24	23		25	32	304	157	147
55 to 59 ...	2,262	795	1,477	2,168	706	1,402	104	32	72	13	6	7	33	16	17	315	95	220
60 and over ...	2,385	1,043	1,312	2,245	995	1,250	113	48	65	23	7	16	22	7	15	373	165	208
Age not stated ...	589	125	464	554	120	434	30	9	21	11	1	10	5	2	3	75	16	59
Total.....	81,838	15,477	66,361	78,898	14,967	63,931	2,758	755	2,003	723	198	525	859	274	585	5,354	1,395	3,959

(LOCAL.)

SPECIAL TABLES.-(B) Widowed.-(Continued.)

Tumkur District.

Age Periods of Widowhood.	Other Hindús.			Outcastes.			JAINS.			MUSALMA'NS.			CHRISTIANS.			OTHER RELIGIONS.		
	Total.	Males.	Females.	Total.	Males.	Females.	Total.	Males.	Females.	Total.	Males.	Females.	Total.	Males.	Females.	Total.	Males.	Females.
Infant ...	...	...	...	...	...	...	...	...	...	...	...	...	...	...	...	...	...	...
1 year ...	...	...	...	...	...	...	...	...	...	...	...	...	...	...	...	...	...	...
2 „ ...	...	...	...	...	...	...	...	...	...	...	...	...	...	...	...	...	...	...
3 „ ...	...	...	...	...	...	...	...	...	...	...	...	...	...	...	...	...	...	...
4 „ ...	2	2	...	...	...	...	...	...	...	...	...	...	...	...	...	...	...	...
5 to 9 ...	214	5	209	28	...	28	3	...	3	...	...	...	...	...	...	...	...	...
10 to 14 ...	2,266	113	2,153	253	18	238	5	...	5	17	1	16	...	...	...	...	...	...
15 to 19 ...	5,453	277	5,176	734	49	685	13	1	12	145	13	132	...	...	...	...	...	...
20 to 24 ...	8,891	821	8,070	1,125	127	998	44	6	38	340	28	312	6	2	4	...	...	...
25 to 29 ...	9,095	1,384	7,711	1,241	284	957	35	7	28	378	47	331	7	1	6	...	...	...
30 to 34 ...	9,790	1,739	8,051	1,412	375	1,037	62	18	44	403	67	336	9	2	7	...	...	...
35 to 39 ...	7,835	1,505	6,330	1,039	308	731	40	10	30	342	60	282	7	1	6	...	...	...
40 to 44 ...	6,532	1,406	5,126	947	311	636	53	17	36	327	48	279	7	1	6	...	...	...
45 to 49 ...	4,492	1,051	3,441	628	185	443	26	8	18	209	43	166	5	2	3	...	...	...
50 to 54 ...	3,009	789	2,220	367	121	246	23	7	16	165	38	127	...	...	...	...	...	...
55 to 59 ...	1,494	542	952	209	75	134	12	4	8	79	24	55	3	1	2	...	...	...
60 and over ...	1,479	678	801	235	90	145	11	5	6	125	41	84	4	2	2	...	...	...
Age not stated ...	378	86	292	55	6	49	1	1	...	32	4	28	2	...	2	...	...	...
Total.....	60,930	10,398	50,532	8,274	1,947	6,327	328	84	244	2,562	414	2,148	50	12	38	...	...	...

(LOCAL.)

SPECIAL TABLES.—(B) Widowed.—(Continued.)

Mysore District.

Age Periods of Widowhood.	Total All Religions. Total.	Males.	Females.	TOTAL HINDU RELIGION. Total.	Males.	Females.	Brâhman. Total.	Males.	Females.	Kshatriya. Total.	Males.	Females.	Vaisya. Total.	Males.	Females.	Lingâyet. Total.	Males.	Females.
Infant ...	...	...	...	...	...	...	...	...	...	...	...	...	...	...	...	...	...	...
1 year ...	...	...	...	...	...	...	...	...	...	...	...	...	...	...	...	...	...	...
2 " ...	...	...	...	...	...	...	...	...	...	...	...	...	...	...	...	...	...	...
3 " ...	...	...	...	...	...	...	...	...	...	...	...	...	...	...	...	...	...	...
4 " ...	...	...	1	1	...	1	...	...	...	...	...	...	...	...	...	...	...	...
5 to 9 ...	869	49	820	861	47	814	128	...	128	11	...	11	6	...	6	109	...	109
10 to 14 ...	3,753	184	3,569	3,741	184	3,557	549	10	539	61	...	61	35	3	32	542	16	526
15 to 19 ...	7,757	524	7,233	7,726	524	7,201	663	38	625	132	7	125	41	5	36	1,089	59	1,030
20 to 24 ...	15,231	1,374	13,857	14,604	1,316	13,288	655	82	573	234	24	210	61	19	42	2,105	159	1,946
25 to 29 ...	17,522	1,912	15,610	16,759	1,820	14,939	631	124	507	272	38	234	32	...	32	2,284	251	2,033
30 to 34 ...	23,425	2,652	20,773	22,333	2,506	19,827	906	228	678	290	38	252	55	1	54	3,161	398	2,763
35 to 39 ...	18,514	2,447	16,067	17,733	2,352	15,381	815	227	588	240	51	189	32	4	28	2,483	360	2,123
40 to 44 ...	18,788	2,831	15,957	17,963	2,726	15,237	811	228	583	264	40	224	57	6	51	2,657	483	2,174
45 to 49 ...	12,170	2,150	10,020	11,627	2,066	9,561	477	150	327	157	34	123	30	6	24	1,656	322	1,334
50 to 54 ...	9,227	1,869	7,358	8,707	1,775	6,932	321	104	217	129	33	96	26	2	24	1,376	284	1,092
55 to 59 ...	5,366	1,258	4,108	4,690	1,156	3,534	246	71	175	84	21	63	13	7	6	741	173	568
60 and over ...	5,539	1,934	3,605	5,223	1,838	3,385	287	100	187	97	26	71	28	13	15	891	292	599
Age not stated ...	4,236	540	3,696	4,055	514	3,541	141	21	120	36	6	30	18	7	11	819	100	719
Total...	142,428	19,724	122,704	136,023	18,822	117,201	6,633	1,386	5,247	2,007	321	1,686	434	73	361	19,916	2,897	17,019

(LOCAL.)

SPECIAL TABLES.—(B) Widowed.—(Continued.)

Mysore District.

Age Periods of Widowhood.	Other Hindus.			Out-castes.			Jains.			Musalmans.			Christians.			Other Religions.		
	Total.	Males.	Females.	Total.	Males.	Females.	Total.	Males.	Females.	Total.	Males.	Females.	Total.	Males.	Females.	Total.	Males.	Females.
Infant ...	...	...	...	...	...	...	...	...	...	...	...	...	...	...	...	...	...	...
1 year ...	...	...	...	...	...	...	...	...	...	...	...	...	...	...	...	...	...	...
2 ,, ...	...	...	...	...	...	...	...	...	...	...	...	...	...	...	...	...	...	...
3 ,, ...	...	...	...	...	...	...	...	...	...	...	...	...	...	...	...	...	...	...
4 ,, ...	1	...	1	...	...	...	...	...	...	...	...	...	...	...	...	...	...	...
5 to 9 ...	483	34	449	124	13	111	8	2	6	...	...	...	...	...	...	...	...	...
10 to 14 ...	2,052	121	1,931	502	34	468	12	...	12	...	...	...	...	...	...	...	...	...
15 to 19 ...	4,568	333	4,235	1,233	80	1,153	31	2	29	...	...	...	...	...	...	...	...	...
20 to 24 ...	9,227	826	8,401	2,322	206	2,116	48	5	43	557	46	511	50	6	44	2	1	1
25 to 29 ...	10,813	1,079	9,734	2,727	328	2,399	49	14	35	657	61	596	58	14	42	1	...	1
30 to 34 ...	14,293	1,423	12,870	3,628	418	3,210	55	15	40	970	111	859	66	17	49	1	...	1
35 to 39 ...	11,352	1,331	10,021	2,808	376	2,432	37	9	28	703	71	632	40	15	25	1	...	1
40 to 44 ...	11,364	1,539	9,825	2,810	430	2,380	30	6	24	765	92	673	29	7	22	1	...	1
45 to 49 ...	7,512	1,187	6,325	1,795	267	1,128	21	4	17	493	69	424	27	11	16	2	...	2
50 to 54 ...	5,523	1,064	4,459	1,332	258	1,014	7	5	2	437	75	362	76	14	62	...	...	...
55 to 59 ...	2,872	681	2,191	734	203	531	9	3	6	659	97	562	8	2	6	...	...	...
60 and over ...	3,155	1,129	2,026	765	278	487	12	5	7	291	89	202	13	2	11	...	...	...
Age not stated ...	2,284	307	1,977	744	70	674	1	...	1	161	26	135	19	...	19	...	...	...
Total....	85,509	11,054	74,455	21,524	3,091	18,433	320	70	250	5,693	743	4,950	384	88	296	8	1	7

(LOCAL.)

SPECIAL TABLES.—(B) Widowed.—(*Continued.*)

Hassan District.

Age Periods of Widowhood.	Total All Religions.			TOTAL HINDU RELIGION.			Bráhman.			Kshatriya.			Vaisya.			Lingayet.		
	Total.	Males.	Females.	Total.	Males.	Females.	Total.	Males.	Females.	Total.	Males.	Females.	Total.	Males.	Females.	Total.	Males.	Females.
Infant	...	...	...	...	...	...	...	...	...	...	...	...	...	...	...	...	...	...
1-year	...	...	...	...	...	...	...	...	...	...	...	...	...	...	...	...	...	...
2 "	1	...	1	1	...	1	...	...	...	...	...	...	...	...	...	...	...	...
3 "	...	...	...	...	...	...	...	...	...	...	...	...	...	...	...	...	...	...
4 "	...	...	...	...	...	...	...	...	...	...	...	...	...	...	...	...	...	...
5 to 9	411	69	342	411	69	342	51	...	51	2	...	2	1	...	1	81	19	62
10 to 14	1,781	143	1,638	1,776	142	1,631	277	5	272	30	1	29	18	...	18	139	22	117
15 to 19	4,074	302	3,772	4,038	295	3,743	221	13	208	45	4	41	12	3	9	628	41	587
20 to 24	7,895	824	7,071	7,639	778	6,861	236	31	205	67	7	60	19	1	18	1,175	176	999
25 to 29	9,080	1,195	7,885	8,808	1,150	7,658	223	44	179	89	27	62	26	10	16	1,014	225	789
30 to 34	10,498	1,596	8,902	10,173	1,544	8,629	315	116	199	113	22	91	34	7	27	1,106	309	797
35 to 39	8,096	1,474	6,622	7,852	1,441	6,411	362	141	221	70	26	44	14	4	10	861	287	574
40 to 44	7,694	1,470	6,224	7,467	1,432	6,035	299	137	162	72	25	47	23	5	18	924	280	644
45 to 49	4,742	1,099	3,643	4,501	1,067	3,434	155	70	85	76	33	43	9	7	2	492	204	288
50 to 54	3,330	741	2,589	3,191	725	2,466	74	51	23	49	17	32	17	8	9	460	159	301
55 to 59	1,905	549	1,356	1,846	536	1,310	92	30	62	18	7	11	10	5	5	307	97	210
60 and over ...	1,914	642	1,272	1,854	624	1,230	119	46	73	13	4	9	13	6	7	328	140	188
Age not stated ...	1,422	224	1,198	1,362	219	1,143	55	12	43	6	1	5	5	...	5	308	51	257
Total ...	62,843	10,328	52,515	60,919	10,022	50,897	2,479	696	1,783	650	174	476	201	56	145	7,823	2,010	5,813

SPECIAL TABLES.—(B) Widowod.—(Continued.)

Hassan District.

Age Periods of Widowhood.	Other Hindus.			Out-castes.			Jains.			Musalmans.			Christians.			Other Religions.		
	Total.	Males.	Females.	Total.	Males.	Females.	Total.	Males.	Females.	Total.	Males.	Females.	Total.	Males.	Females.	Total.	Males.	Females.
Infant ...	...	...	...	...	...	...	...	...	...	...	...	...	...	...	...	...	...	...
1 year ...	...	...	...	...	...	...	...	...	...	...	...	...	...	...	...	...	...	...
2 " ...	1	...	1	...	...	...	...	...	...	...	...	...	...	...	...	...	...	...
3 " ...	...	...	...	...	...	...	...	...	...	...	...	...	...	...	...	...	...	...
4 " ...	...	...	...	...	...	...	...	...	...	...	...	...	...	...	...	...	...	...
5 to 9 ...	206	38	168	70	12	58	...	...	...	...	...	...	...	...	...	...	...	...
10 to 14 ...	932	77	855	380	37	343	5	1	4	...	...	...	...	...	...	...	...	...
15 to 19 ...	2,296	165	2,131	836	69	767	36	7	29	...	...	...	...	...	...	...	...	...
20 to 24 ...	4,485	372	4,113	1,657	191	1,466	49	6	43	176	29	147	31	11	20	...	...	...
25 to 29 ...	5,726	679	5,047	1,730	165	1,565	43	5	38	189	31	158	40	9	31	...	...	...
30 to 34 ...	6,567	927	5,640	2,038	163	1,875	33	12	21	230	26	204	62	14	48	...	...	...
35 to 39 ...	5,038	831	4,207	1,507	152	1,355	22	5	17	177	19	158	45	9	36	...	...	...
40 to 44 ...	4,745	857	3,888	1,404	128	1,276	16	2	14	179	29	150	32	7	25	...	...	...
45 to 49 ...	2,953	601	2,352	816	152	664	8	1	7	200	28	172	33	3	30	...	...	...
50 to 54 ...	1,976	371	1,605	615	119	496	12	3	9	102	13	89	25	...	25	...	...	...
55 to 59 ...	1,146	308	838	273	89	184	7	1	6	38	12	26	14	...	14	...	...	...
60 and over ...	1,109	313	796	272	115	157	2	...	2	50	18	32	8	...	8	...	...	...
Age not stated ...	701	117	584	287	38	249	4	1	3	44	3	41	12	1	11	...	...	...
Total...	37,881	5,656	32,225	11,885	1,430	10,455	237	44	193	1,385	208	1,177	302	54	248	...	...	...

(LOCAL.)

SPECIAL TABLES.—(B) Widowed.—(Continued.)

Shimoga District.

Age Periods of Widowhood.	Total All Religions.			TOTAL HINDU RELIGION.			Bráhman.			Kshatriya.			Vais'ya.			Lingáyet.		
	Total.	Males.	Females.	Total.	Males.	Females.	Total.	Males.	Females.	Total.	Males.	Females.	Total.	Males.	Females.	Total.	Males.	Females.
Infant ...	...	...	...	...	...	...	...	...	...	...	...	...	...	...	...	...	...	...
1 year ...	...	...	...	...	...	...	...	...	...	...	...	...	...	...	...	...	...	...
2 " ...	...	...	...	...	...	...	...	...	...	...	...	...	...	...	...	...	...	...
3 " ...	...	...	...	...	...	...	...	...	...	...	...	...	...	...	...	...	...	...
4 " ...	...	...	...	...	...	...	...	...	...	...	...	...	...	...	...	...	...	...
5 to 9 ...	560	31	549	578	30	548	84	3	81	13	1	12	7	1	6	177	17	160
10 to 14 ...	2,822	76	2,746	2,811	73	2,738	452	7	445	86	...	86	13	1	12	387	49	338
15 to 19 ...	5,279	231	5,048	5,215	229	4,986	504	21	483	135	17	118	15	2	13	953	97	856
20 to 24 ...	9,359	1,324	8,035	8,877	1,244	7,633	405	55	350	194	24	170	23	3	20	1,406	317	1,089
25 to 29 ...	9,907	2,130	7,777	9,381	2,042	7,339	436	105	331	287	97	190	17	7	10	1,134	300	834
30 to 34 ...	11,451	2,775	8,676	10,748	2,655	8,093	632	303	329	368	95	273	27	14	13	1,044	295	749
35 to 39 ...	8,913	2,607	6,306	8,410	2,481	5,929	685	302	383	270	106	164	18	7	11	680	265	415
40 to 44 ...	8,488	2,554	5,934	7,961	2,452	5,509	563	328	211	260	106	154	22	11	11	1,191	387	804
45 to 49 ...	4,988	1,710	3,278	4,664	1,635	3,029	182	118	64	221	100	121	13	10	3	592	321	271
50 to 54 ...	3,714	1,234	2,480	3,392	1,173	2,219	134	82	52	182	98	84	16	6	10	663	[illegible]	276
55 to 59 ...	1,938	649	1,289	1,618	599	1,019	132	44	88	31	10	21	3	1	2	485	190	295
60 and over ...	1,965	860	1,105	1,679	757	922	146	56	90	53	32	21	5	3	2	559	237	322
Age not stated ...	1,280	254	1,026	1,279	254	1,025	79	25	54	62	12	50	3	...	3	331	62	269
Total ...	70,684	16,435	54,249	66,611	15,622	50,989	4,433	1,452	2,981	2,162	698	1,464	182	66	116	9,608	2,830	6,778

(LOCAL.)

SPECIAL TABLES.—(B) Widowed.—(*Continued.*)

Shimoga District.

Age Periods of Widowhood.	Other Hindus.			Outcastes.			Jains.			Musalmans.			Christians.			Other Religions.		
	Total.	Males.	Females.	Total.	Males.	Females.	Total.	Males.	Females.	Total.	Males.	Females.	Total.	Males.	Females.	Total.	Males.	Females.
Infant	...	...	...	...	...	...	...	...	...	...	...	...	...	...	...	...	...	...
1 year	...	...	...	...	...	...	...	...	...	...	...	...	...	...	...	...	...	...
2 years	...	...	...	...	...	...	...	...	...	...	...	...	...	...	...	...	...	...
3 „	...	...	...	...	...	...	...	...	...	...	...	...	...	...	...	...	...	...
4 „	...	...	...	...	...	...	...	...	...	...	...	...	...	...	...	...	...	...
5 to 9	241	...	241	56	8	48	2	1	1	...	...	...	...	...	...	...	...	...
10 to 14	1,429	...	1,429	444	16	428	11	3	8	...	...	...	...	...	...	...	...	...
15 to 19	2,912	21	2,891	696	68	628	64	2	62	...	...	...	...	...	...	...	...	...
20 to 24	5,540	662	4,878	1,309	183	1,126	80	8	72	391	69	322	11	3	8	...	...	...
25 to 29	6,089	1,206	4,883	1,418	327	1,091	97	19	78	418	67	351	11	2	9	...	...	...
30 to 34	6,956	1,509	5,447	1,719	437	1,282	116	29	87	573	92	481	16	1	15	...	...	...
35 to 39	5,368	1,429	3,939	1,389	372	1,017	73	28	45	413	93	320	17	5	12	...	...	...
40 to 44	4,653	1,295	3,358	1,273	355	918	83	20	63	427	79	318	17	3	14	...	...	...
45 to 49	2,949	887	2,062	707	199	508	33	12	21	275	61	214	16	2	14	...	...	...
50 to 54	1,901	595	1,306	487	99	388	32	10	12	290	45	245	10	6	4	...	...	...
55 to 59	836	294	542	131	60	71	9	4	5	308	46	262	3	...	3	...	...	...
60 and over ...	802	366	436	114	63	51	11	8	3	269	93	176	7	3	4	...	...	...
Age not stated ...	687	126	561	117	29	88	...	...	...	1	...	1	...	...	...	...	...	...
Total......	40,366	8,390	31,976	9,860	2,186	7,674	601	144	457	3,364	644	2,720	108	25	83	...	...	...

(LOCAL.)

SPECIAL TABLES.-(B) Widowed.-(Continued.)

Kadur District.

Age Periods of Widowhood.	Total All Religions.			TOTAL HINDU RELIGION.			Brâmhan.			Kshatriya.			Vais'ya.			Lingáyet.		
	Total.	Males.	Females.	Total.	Males.	Females.	Total.	Males.	Females.	Total.	Males.	Females.	Total.	Males.	Females.	Total.	Males.	Females.
Infant ...	...	...	...	...	...	...	...	...	...	...	...	...	...	...	...	...	...	...
1 year ...	...	...	...	...	...	...	...	...	...	...	...	...	...	...	...	...	...	...
2 " ...	...	...	...	...	...	...	...	...	...	...	...	...	...	...	...	...	...	...
3 " ...	...	...	...	...	...	...	...	...	...	...	...	...	...	...	...	...	...	...
4 " ...	...	...	...	...	...	...	...	...	...	...	...	...	...	...	...	...	...	...
5 to 9 ...	163	4	159	163	4	159	66	1	65	3	1	2	4	...	4	35	...	35
10 to 14 ...	1,108	24	1,084	1,103	24	1,079	307	9	298	22	...	22	4	...	4	101	10	91
15 to 19 ...	2,242	143	2,099	2,253	138	2,097	291	6	285	51	3	48	7	...	7	260	20	240
20 to 24 ...	5,703	825	4,878	5,459	796	4,663	380	32	348	74	9	65	23	3	20	930	128	802
25 to 29 ...	6,290	1,305	4,985	5,968	1,235	4,733	368	56	312	89	30	59	18	2	16	796	144	652
30 to 34 ...	7,144	1,648	5,496	6,787	1,571	5,216	457	99	358	125	38	87	33	7	26	832	199	633
35 to 39 ...	5,277	1,287	3,990	5,035	1,242	3,793	344	98	246	77	25	52	17	2	15	537	105	432
40 to 44 ...	4,687	1,095	3,592	4,420	1,058	3,362	350	125	225	78	30	48	11	1	10	544	75	469
45 to 49 ...	2,866	819	2,047	2,634	781	1,853	228	74	152	67	34	33	12	8	4	342	119	223
50 to 54 ...	1,767	465	1,302	1,662	440	1,222	143	45	98	51	24	27	11	1	10	243	58	185
55 to 59 ...	912	307	605	826	297	529	63	22	41	14	3	11	8	2	6	206	69	137
60 and over ...	822	319	503	772	304	468	53	27	26	20	3	17	7	4	3	234	92	142
Age not stated ...	948	171	777	918	161	757	59	10	49	14	8	6	9	1	8	254	22	232
Total.....	39,929	8,412	31,517	37,982	8,051	29,931	3,107	604	2,503	685	208	477	164	31	133	5,314	1,011	4,303

(LOCAL.)

SPECIAL TABLES.—(B) Widowed.—(Continued.)

Kadur District.

Age Periods of Widowhood.	Other Hindús.			Outcastes			JAINS.			MUSALMA'NS.			CHRISTIANS.			OTHER RELIGIONS.		
	Total.	Males.	Females.	Total.	Males.	Females.	Total.	Males.	Females.	Total.	Males.	Females.	Total.	Males.	Females.	Total.	Males.	Females.
Infant	...	...	...	...	...	...	...	...	...	...	...	...	...	...	...	...	...	...
1 year	...	...	...	...	...	...	...	...	...	...	...	...	...	...	...	...	...	...
2 years	...	...	...	...	...	...	...	...	...	...	...	...	...	...	...	...	...	...
3 "	...	...	...	...	...	...	...	...	...	...	...	...	...	...	...	...	...	...
4 "	...	...	...	...	...	...	...	...	...	...	...	...	...	...	...	...	...	...
5 to 9 ...	28	...	28	27	2	25	...	...	...	...	...	...	...	...	...	...	...	...
10 to 14 ...	420	...	420	249	5	244	5	...	5	...	...	...	...	...	...	...	...	...
15 to 19	1,162	62	1,100	464	47	417	2	...	2	3	3	...	2	2	...	...	...	...
20 to 24	2,928	433	2,495	1,124	191	933	25	7	18	209	19	190	10	3	7	...	...	...
25 to 29	3,578	807	2,771	1,119	196	923	35	10	25	265	54	211	22	6	16	...	...	...
30 to 34	3,991	1,017	2,974	1,349	211	1,138	46	13	33	285	58	227	26	6	20	...	...	...
35 to 39	3,051	815	2,236	1,009	197	812	10	[illegible]	6	217	37	180	15	4	11	...	...	...
40 to 44	2,517	694	1,823	920	163	757	28	6	22	227	29	198	12	2	10	...	...	...
45 to 49	1,494	424	1,070	493	122	371	16	5	11	204	28	176	12	5	7	...	...	...
50 to 54	844	210	634	370	102	268	20	5	15	78	18	60	7	2	5	...	...	...
55 to 59	416	143	273	119	58	61	8	4	4	76	6	70	2	...	2	...	...	...
60 and over ...	368	138	230	90	40	50	6	...	6	39	12	27	5	3	2	...	...	...
Age not stated ...	407	79	328	175	41	134	1	1	...	21	6	15	8	3	5	...	...	...
Total ...	21,204	4,832	16,352	7,508	1,375	6,133	202	55	147	1,624	270	1,354	121	36	85	...	...	...

(LOCAL.)

SPECIAL TABLES.—(B) Widowed.—(Continued.)

Chitaldrug District.

Age Periods of Widowhood.	Total All Religions.			TOTAL HINDU RELIGION.			Brámhan.			Kshatriya.			Vais'ya.			Lingáyet.		
	Total.	Males.	Females.	Total.	Males.	Females.	Total.	Males.	Females.	Total.	Males.	Females.	Total.	Males.	Females.	Total.	Males.	Females.
Infant	...	...	...	...	...	...	...	...	...	...	...	...	...	...	...	...	...	...
1 year	...	...	...	...	...	...	...	...	...	...	...	...	...	...	...	...	...	...
2 „	...	...	...	...	...	...	...	...	...	...	...	...	...	...	...	...	...	...
3 „	...	...	...	...	...	...	...	...	...	...	...	...	...	...	...	...	...	...
4 „	1	...	1	1	...	1	...	...	...	...	...	...	...	...	...	...	...	...
5 to 9	221	14	207	219	14	205	15	1	14	2	...	2	7	...	7	90	6	84
10 to 14	1,948	63	1,885	1,944	63	1,881	97	2	95	19	2	17	13	1	12	364	22	342
15 to 19	4,174	200	3,974	4,171	200	3,971	98	4	94	23	1	22	32	1	31	778	62	716
20 to 24	7,231	818	6,413	6,975	788	6,187	121	25	96	39	3	36	51	12	39	1,302	216	1,086
25 to 29	7,403	1,326	6,077	7,129	1,281	5,848	110	29	81	39	10	29	50	18	32	1,120	157	963
30 to 34	8,151	1,694	6,457	7,906	1,645	6,261	159	53	106	57	12	45	61	31	30	803	189	714
35 to 39	6,220	1,522	4,698	5,965	1,471	4,494	141	57	84	49	16	33	45	21	24	903	230	673
40 to 44	5,468	1,617	3,851	5,241	1,555	3,686	114	51	63	52	18	34	32	21	11	793	247	546
45 to 49	3,606	1,131	2,475	3,380	1,097	2,283	67	32	35	35	11	24	32	17	15	272	191	81
50 to 54	2,529	830	1,699	2,309	700	1,609	56	29	27	33	14	19	15	5	10	472	183	289
55 to 59	1,600	619	981	1,514	585	929	32	13	19	6	4	2	12	6	6	438	172	266
60 and over ...	1,635	806	829	1,549	767	782	39	18	21	14	2	12	14	8	6	441	235	206
Age not stated ...	627	124	503	593	122	471	11	2	9	6	...	6	4	1	3	179	44	135
Total......	50,814	10,764	40,050	48,986	10,378	38,608	1,060	316	744	374	93	281	368	142	226	8,055	1,954	6,101

SPECIAL TABLES.—(B) Widowed.—(Concluded.)

Chitaldrug District.

Age Periods of Widowhood.	Other Hindus.			Outcastes.			JAINS.			MUSALMANS.			CHRISTIANS.			OTHER RELIGIONS.		
	Total.	Males.	Females.	Total.	Males.	Females.	Total.	Males.	Females.	Total.	Males.	Females.	Total.	Males.	Females.	Total.	Males.	Females.
Infant ...	...	...	...	...	...	...	...	...	...	...	...	...	...	...	...	...	...	...
1 year ...	...	...	...	...	...	...	...	...	...	...	...	...	...	...	...	...	...	...
2 ,, ...	...	...	...	...	...	...	...	...	...	...	...	...	...	...	...	...	...	...
3 ,, ...	...	...	...	...	...	...	...	...	...	...	...	...	...	...	...	...	...	...
4 ,, ...	1	...	1	...	...	...	...	...	...	...	...	...	...	...	...	...	...	...
5 to 9 ...	82	4	78	23	3	20	2	...	2	...	...	...	...	...	...	...	...	...
10 to 14 ...	1,282	24	1,258	169	12	157	4	...	4	...	...	...	...	...	...	...	...	...
15 to 19 ...	2,868	99	2,769	372	33	339	3	...	3	...	...	...	...	...	...	...	...	...
20 to 24 ...	4,835	455	4,380	627	77	550	12	2	10	239	26	213	4	1	3	1	1	...
25 to 29 ...	5,100	883	4,217	710	184	526	11	1	10	261	42	219	2	2	...	...	...	...
30 to 34 ...	5,940	1,120	4,820	786	210	576	15	2	13	225	45	180	5	2	3	...	...	...
35 to 39 ...	4,194	976	3,218	633	171	462	15	7	8	234	43	191	5	1	4	1	...	1
40 to 44 ...	3,703	1,029	2,674	547	189	358	15	7	8	209	52	157	...	...	...	...	...	...
45 to 49 ...	2,607	719	1,888	367	127	240	11	4	7	213	28	185	2	2	...	...	...	...
50 to 54 ...	1,638	499	1,139	186	60	126	1	...	1	126	39	87	3	1	2	...	...	...
55 to 59 ...	887	333	554	139	57	82	6	1	5	80	33	47	...	...	...	...	...	...
60 and over ...	916	449	467	125	55	70	5	4	1	81	35	46	...	...	...	...	...	...
Age not stated ...	311	56	255	82	19	63	1	1	...	33	1	32	...	...	...	...	...	...
Total ...	34,364	6,646	27,718	4,765	1,227	3,538	101	29	72	1,701	344	1,357	24	12	12	2	1	1

(LOCAL.)

SPECIAL TABLES.

C.

GOTRAS AND SAKHAS.

Name of Gotras.	Total Males.	Rigvédís. Smártás.	Rigvédís. Bhágavata Sampradáya.	Rigvédís. Mádhvás.	Rigvédís. S'rívaishnavás. Tengalé.	Rigvédís. S'rívaishnavás. Vadaghalé.	Yajurvédís. Smártás.	Yajurvédís. Bhágavata Sampradáya.	Yajurvédís. Mádhvás.	Yajurvédís. S'rívaishnavás. Tengalé.	Yajurvédís. S'rívaishnavás. Vadaghalé.	Sámavédís. Smártás.	Sámavédís. Mádhvás.	Sámavédís. S'rívaishnavás.
Kás'yapa	12,074	4,654	528	1,365	37	80	3,450	509	631	257	241	155	16	11
Kaus'ika	4,909	908	114	397	20	218	1,498	179	314	254	872	115	30	60
Káundinya	4,833	1,062	63	336	431	51	1,919	145	405	161	234	22	2	2
A'tréya	5,277	1,790	279	731	9	42	930	143	313	192	617	177	23	1
Bháradvája	13,081	4,311	710	1,891	91	217	3,107	330	824	677	657	194	20	52
S'rívatsa	5,480	1,506	133	419	37	56	1,302	211	472	[illegible]	862	68	10	9
Harita	4,408	1,305	187	611	11	23	1,433	124	373	174	92	55	14	6
Vis'vámitra	6,020	2,608	528	849	13	5	1,537	189	148	49	41	27	13	4
Vádhrayas'va	183	5	4	1	...	1	123	19	13	2	...	11	3	1
Vasist'ha	6,053	2,765	375	1,343	9	13	1,089	105	158	31	34	106	7	17
Jamadagni	1,790	674	88	508	7	5	351	34	87	4	20	4	7	1
S'aunaka	253	31	...	8	...	...	162	2	49	...	1	...	...	...
Gautama	3,063	557	81	342	2	10	1,370	318	265	36	66	9	8	...
Vádhúla	1,670	390	7	17	3	16	654	55	17	165	328	1	5	12
S'álávatsa	67	9	...	2	...	10	21	3	19	2	1	...	...	...
Parás'ara	256	23	...	13	5	3	154	36	9	2	1	...	...	...
Maunabhárgava	1,061	533	115	274	...	...	43	14	25	15	32	3	...	7
Maudgalya	1,111	422	72	317	6	8	58	29	20	36	138	4	1	...
Gárgyáyana	614	100	30	57	3	33	212	6	72	20	33	16	2	...
S'at'hamarshana	554	21	...	4	...	17	50	5	21	21	390	10	...	6
Kanva	150	20	5	46	...	...	32	4	15	10	11	3	...	4
Lóhita	232	42	...	...	41	...	104	19	2	15	9	...	...	...
Paurakutsa	131	7	...	20	3	1	4	...	19	32	45	...	...	...
Vishnuvardhana	174	65	16	60	7	...	16	3	7	...	...	...	...	...
Pútamánasa	187	86	...	55	...	...	9	...	31	...	1	5	...	...
Agastya	418	129	15	155	3	11	73	2	28	...	...	1	2	...
Rat'hítara	92	72	...	3	...	...	12	...	5	...	...	...	...	...
S'ándilya	1,127	251	14	117	1	4	455	15	64	5	133	31	30	7
Rájéndra	11	8	...	...	...	...	3	...	...	...	...	...	...	...
Upamanyu	58	17	3	9	4	...	18	...	8	...	...	...	2	...
Kámsakáyana	51	32	2	2	...	...	13	2	...	...	...	...	...	...
Manayáyana	5	...	...	...	...	...	...	...	...	...	5	...	...	...
Bádaráyana	365	133	4	30	...	2	54	9	92	25	15	1	...	...
Vais'ampáyana	3	1	...	...	...	...	2	...	...	...	...	...	...	...
Dhananjaya	10	10	...	...	...	...	...	...	...	...	...	...	...	...
Sankriti	163	...	1	...	1	...	110	22	2	19	...	7	...	1
Kutsa	232	42	2	3	4	3	95	4	33	32	59	5	...	...
Total	75,216	24,530	3,386	9,085	745	829	20,507	2,577	4,531	2,646	4,207	1,028	195	201

Total Females.	Females. Rigvédis. Smártás.	Rigvédis. Bhágavata Sampradáya.	Rigvédis. Mádhvás.	Rigvédis. S'rívaishnavás. Tengalé.	Rigvédis. S'rívaishnavás. Vadaghalé.	Yajurvédis. Smártás.	Yajurvédis. Bhágavata Sampradáya.	Yajurvédis. Mádhvás.	Yajurvédis. S'rívaishnavás. Tengalé.	Yajurvédis. S'rívaishnavás. Vadaghalé.	Sámavédis. Smártás.	Sámavédis. Mádhvás.	Sámavédis. S'rívaishnavás.
12,077	4,932	605	1,483	30	189	3,158	458	641	171	318	138	14	19
4,984	911	80	419	18	251	1,621	144	329	387	751	82	31	25
4,241	874	68	298	26	26	1,767	172	466	247	267	14	9	7
5,030	1,607	313	665	14	52	843	132	[illegible]	174	711	112	41	4
12,869	4,292	612	1,924	134	121	3,212	222	757	669	570	183	21	63
5,000	907	152	535	24	62	1,464	174	451	334	814	53	17	11
4,063	1,100	197	517	25	28	1,255	115	343	151	128	25	3	14
5,751	2,675	491	729	24	15	1,155	117	174	26	22	14	3	7
160	8	6	2	...	11	98	2	24	...	8	3	7	...
5,539	2,552	318	1,218	18	87	834	146	130	20	70	93	23	5
1,501	550	82	467	...	...	259	32	83	2	2	[illegible]	2	...
220	25	1	7	...	...	128	31	25	...	3	...	...	...
2,859	518	88	333	2	12	1,339	216	218	10	63	23	11	1
1,118	61	2	6	1	11	478	51	25	101	357	21	3	1
67	3	...	4	...	...	30	10	13	6	...	...	...	1
226	18	...	12	4	...	113	17	21	11	...	...	...	...
859	493	61	198	1	5	37	7	20	6	22	3	...	6
1,141	176	31	317	5	...	49	29	17	39	143	23	6	3
518	92	29	51	7	4	219	23	65	3	40	11	4	...
496	17	...	7	...	8	40	3	23	40	344	2	...	12
126	31	1	42	2	6	16	1	18	4	10	1	...	...
228	5	2	2	37	...	138	11	...	17	7	...	8	1
172	32	37	23	...	...	5	1	16	34	24	...	...	...
160	52	29	51	...	...	17	4	7	...	...	...	...	...
156	75	...	34	6	1	4	1	25	2	...	...	7	1
406	117	10	134	...	5	104	16	47	...	1	...	2	...
86	47	2	6	...	...	16	1	14	...	...	...	...	...
1,368	227	28	118	8	21	689	43	55	2	134	17	22	2
8	8	...	...	...	...	...	...	...	...	...	...	...	...
50	15	...	7	...	2	12	5	2	...	...	7	...	...
43	35	...	3	...	...	5	...	...	...	...	...	...	...
4	...	...	...	...	...	...	...	4	...	...	...	...	...
334	190	11	32	...	5	60	10	76	25	15	...	...	...
3	...	...	...	...	...	3	...	...	...	...	...	...	...
14	8	...	...	...	...	...	...	...	...	6	...	...	...
115	1	1	1	...	...	64	31	1	13	...	2	...	1
236	38	...	...	...	1	82	3	22	9	89	1	...	...
72,245	22,901	3,167	9,699	385	914	19,781	2,321	4,383	2,402	4,920	864	224	134

Total Males.	Males.												
	Rigvédis.					Yejurvédis.					Sámavédis.		
	Smártás.	Bhágavata Sampradáya.	Mádhvás.	S'rivaishnavás. Tengalé.	S'rivaishnavás. Vadagalé.	Smártás.	Bhágavata Sampradáya.	Mádhvás.	S'rivaishnavás. Tengalé.	S'rivaishnavás. Vadagalé.	Smártás.	Mádhvás.	S'rivaishnavás.
2,155	775	51	359	8	...	503	26	133	47	102	60	...	2
829	208	15	95	1	10	224	50	60	41	101	13	6	4
1,130	113	5	58	6	...	627	22	174	30	47	8	1	...
1,068	410	22	108	2	4	278	29	93	26	85	7	4	...
2,315	650	72	420	2	5	572	46	256	133	119	33	1	6
1,159	314	9	78	4	4	363	20	119	62	138	15	3	...
640	85	15	98	...	12	274	35	69	18	28	6	...	...
634	203	16	131	1	...	214	21	6	19	17	2	1	...
52	2	4	1	...	...	26	15	4	...	...	...	...	...
777	363	47	214	4	...	62	3	56	2	6	20	...	...
228	64	3	103	...	...	16	3	19	...	19	1	...	...
16	1	...	...	...	...	4	1	10	...	...	...	...	...
403	107	3	52	1	1	175	20	28	2	8	2	4	...
242	42	1	11	...	...	85	...	3	12	88	...	...	...
6	...	...	...	...	...	6	...	...	...	...	...	...	...
38	6	...	...	3	...	29	...	...	...	...	...	...	...
174	103	14	37	...	...	13	...	...	1	3	3	...	...
236	92	4	70	...	...	15	11	2	1	41	...	...	...
89	6	9	12	...	3	45	...	4	4	6	...	...	...
81	...	...	...	...	3	6	1	6	1	61	2	...	1
9	...	1	3	...	...	...	...	5	...	...	...	...	...
1	...	...	...	...	...	1	...	...	...	...	...	...	...
31	...	...	...	...	...	...	...	...	...	31	...	...	...
12	8	...	4	...	...	...	...	...	...	...	...	...	...
60	57	...	3	...	...	...	...	...	...	...	...	...	...
33	...	...	27	...	...	3	...	3	...	...	...	...	...
13	11	...	...	...	...	...	...	2	...	...	...	...	...
206	34	2	31	...	1	100	8	9	2	12	2	...	...
...	...	...	...	...	...	...	...	...	...	...	...	...	...
3	...	...	...	...	...	1	...	...	...	...	...	2	...
8	3	...	2	...	...	3	...	...	...	...	...	...	...
...	...	...	...	...	...	...	...	...	...	...	...	...	...
73	20	...	4	...	2	11	3	14	12	7	...	...	...
...	...	...	...	...	...	...	...	...	...	...	...	...	...
...	...	...	...	...	...	...	...	...	...	...	...	...	...
12	...	...	...	1	...	2	...	...	6	...	3	...	...
100	6	...	1	1	...	55	...	7	17	13	...	...	...
12,833	3,743	293	34	34	45	3,812	310	1,081	445	932	177	22	13

Total Females.	Females. Rigvédis. Smártás.	Rigvédis. Bhágavata Sampradáya.	Rigvédis. Mádhvás.	Rigvédis. S'rívaishnavás. Tengalé.	Rigvédis. S'rívaishnavás. Vadagalé.	Yajurvédis. Smártás.	Yajurvédis. Bhágavata Sampradáya.	Yajurvédis. Mádhvás.	Yajurvédis. S'rívaishnavás. Tengalé.	Yajurvédis. S'rívaishnavás. Vadagalé.	Sámavédis. Smártás.	Sámavédis. Mádhvás.
2,118	780	44	338	19	6	532	43	196	37	83	31	7
559	58	12	72	5	2	194	38	28	40	66	13	6
868	114	3	54	7	...	394	33	158	56	40	3	5
965	333	18	121	...	1	220	25	96	46	103	2	...
2,263	670	81	417	9	2	567	18	241	140	94	19	1
887	152	12	77	4	9	301	19	128	50	107	21	6
580	90	13	84	10	14	228	30	55	22	30	8	...
542	5,194	22	106	1	7	174	2	22	6	5	3	...
27	2	6	2	...	...	11	...	6	...	...	...	...
675	340	43	169	...	...	60	11	31	1	1	19	...
184	62	3	87	...	...	10	8	15	...	2	1	1
18	1	...	...	...	...	11	...	6	...	...	...	...
344	80	2	37	...	2	161	16	26	2	6	5	7
182	9	...	...	1	1	68	2	...	3	98	...	...
9	...	...	...	...	...	6	3	...	...	...	...	...
18	5	...	...	4	...	5	3	1	...	...	...	...
128	65	12	40	...	...	8	...	...	1	...	2	...
306	149	4	71	...	...	12	3	9	2	52	...	4
68	3	2	11	...	...	38	...	5	...	9	...	...
79	...	...	...	...	...	2	...	7	5	59	2	...
10	2	...	3	...	...	...	...	10	1	...	...	...
6	...	...	...	...	...	2	...	...	4	[illegible]	...	...
37	2	...	...	...	...	...	1	1	11	12	...	...
14	8	...	6	...	...	...	...	...	...	...	...	...
61	58	...	2	...	...	1	...	...	...	...	...	...
45	...	...	15	...	...	28	...	...	...	...	...	...
16	4	...	...	...	...	6	...	6	...	...	...	...
170	41	...	23	...	...	83	1	13	2	6	1	...
..	...	...	...	...	...	...	...	...	...	...	...	...
1	...	...	...	...	...	...	...	...	...	...	1	...
11	8	...	3	...	...	...	...	...	...	...	...	...
..	...	...	...	...	...	...	...	...	...	...	...	...
54	11	...	2	...	2	16	4	5	10	4	...	...
..	...	...	...	...	...	...	...	...	...	...	...	...
..	...	...	...	...	...	...	...	...	...	...	...	...
5	...	...	...	...	...	2	...	...	1	...	2	...
80	16	...	...	...	...	47	...	...	...	17	...	...
11,354	3,287	277	1,740	60	46	3,187	255	...	440	814	128	37

Total Males.	Males. Rigvédis. Smártás.	Bhágavata Sampradáya.	Mádhvás.	S'rivaishnavás. Tengalé.	Vadaghalé.	Yejurvédis. Smártás.	Bhágavata Sampradáya.	Mádhvás.	S'rivaishnavás. Tengalé.	Vadaghalé.	Sámavédis. Smártás.	Mádhvás.	S'rivaishnavás.
1,410	412	39	192	2	21	420	46	175	43	47	10	2	1
641	77	12	43	...	8	288	17	69	45	41	16	15	10
713	61	5	39	417	36	98	35	7	14	1	...		...
548	176	20	68	...	4	148	14	47	41	27	2	...	1
1,714	389	63	380	39	27	476	39	141	77	58	20	5	...
813	154	38	39	1	46	303	57	103	36	57	7	6	...
989	177	14	125	4	...	413	23	143	43	8	32	7	...
579	107	49	133	...	1	255	10	9	5	5	4	1	...
64	2	...	...	...	1	43	4	3	2	...	5	3	1
684	227	105	213	...	...	101	8	16	5	...	3	5	1
121	48	21	41	3	...	2	2	3	1	...	...	...	...
73	16	...	...	...	...	55		2	...	...	...	...	...
261	44	5	39	...	...	75	8	67	7	6	7	3	...
197	2	...	...	1	...	77	5	2	85	21	1	...	...
23	1	...	...	...	10	...	...	10	2	...	...	...	...
81	8	...	8	...	...	42	19	3	1	...	...	...	...
216	48	17	126	...	...	13	...	9	3	...	...	...	...
144	32	54	37	1	...	3	4	6	2	5	...	...	...
97	2	3	2	1	...	40	2	36	...	9	...	2	...
141	12	...	...	...	1	14	2	11	13	75	8	...	
7	1	...	...	...	...	5	...	1	...	...	...	...	...
16	...	...	...	...	...	12	2	2	...	...	...	...	...
23	3	...	...	...	...	1	...	6	11	2	...	...	...
26	5	13	8	...	...	2	...	...	...	...	...	...	...
71	12	...	21	...	...	5	...	31	...	...	2	...	...
62	9	7	7	3	...	14	...	20	...	...	...	2	...
47	42	...	1	...	...	4	...	...	...	...	...	...	...
263	21	3	12	...	1	181	5	33	1	...	...	3	...
...	...	...	...	...	...	...	...	...	...	...	...	...	...
...	...	...	...	...	...	...	...	...	...	...	...	...	...
10	...	...	...	...	...	8	2	...	...	...	...	...	...
...	...	...	...	...	...	...	...	...	...	...	...	...	...
113	26	...	6	...	...	28	2	51	...	...	...	...	...
...	...	...	...	...	...	...	...	...	...	...	...	...	...
...	...	...	...	...	...	...	...	...	...	...	...	...	...
12	...	1	...	...	...	...	...	...	10	...	...	...	1
52	7	2	1	...	...	20	2	11	3	6	...	...	...
10,211	2,121	471	1,469	472	116	3,219	308	1,023	450	371	117	54	20

ಹೆಂಗಸರು. Females.

ಒಟ್ಟು ಹೆಂಗಸರು. Total Females.	ಋಗ್ವೇದಿಗಳು. Rigvédis. — ಸ್ಮಾರ್ತರು. Smártás.	ಋಗ್ವೇದಿಗಳು. Rigvédis. — ಭಾಗವತ ಸಂಪ್ರದಾಯ. Bhágavata Sampradáya.	ಋಗ್ವೇದಿಗಳು. Rigvédis. — ಮಾಧ್ವರು. Mádhvás.	ಋಗ್ವೇದಿಗಳು. Rigvédis. — ಶ್ರೀವೈಷ್ಣವರು. S'rivaishnavás. — ತೆಂಗಲೆ. Tengalé.	ಋಗ್ವೇದಿಗಳು. Rigvédis. — ಶ್ರೀವೈಷ್ಣವರು. S'rivaishnavás. — ವಡಗಲೆ. Vadagalé.	ಯಜುರ್ವೇದಿಗಳು. Yajurvédis. — ಸ್ಮಾರ್ತರು. Smártás.	ಯಜುರ್ವೇದಿಗಳು. Yajurvédis. — ಭಾಗವತ ಸಂಪ್ರದಾಯ. Bhágavata Sampradáya.	ಯಜುರ್ವೇದಿಗಳು. Yajurvédis. — ಮಾಧ್ವರು. Mádhvás.	ಯಜುರ್ವೇದಿಗಳು. Yajurvédis. — ಶ್ರೀವೈಷ್ಣವರು. S'rivaishnavás. — ತೆಂಗಲೆ. Tengalé.	ಯಜುರ್ವೇದಿಗಳು. Yajurvédis. — ಶ್ರೀವೈಷ್ಣವರು. S'rivaishnavás. — ವಡಗಲೆ. Vadagalé.	ಸಾಮವೇದಿಗಳು. Sámavédis. — ಸ್ಮಾರ್ತರು. Smártás.	ಸಾಮವೇದಿಗಳು. Sámavédis. — ಮಾಧ್ವರು. Mádhvás.	ಸಾಮವೇದಿಗಳು. Sámavédis. — ಶ್ರೀವೈಷ್ಣವರು. S'rivaishnavás.
1,406	4[illegible]8	49	1[illegible]4	...	1	463	58	4[illegible]8	40	28	11	3	1
632	74	7	34	...	6	281	20	86	39	63	4	10	2
632	45	5	36	...	...	352	47	76	46	17	6	2	...
523	100	30	33	1	31	130	9	61	48	19	...	2	1
1,090	364	71	381	3	6	548	30	135	73	45	23	12	7
747	132	28	55	2	2	294	38	101	26	58	11	...	...
991	158	9	132	10	...	427	15	156	43	25	13	3	...
553	103	41	89	15	6	275	3	11	...	4	5	1	...
41	4	...	...	...	11	19	2	1	...	...	1	3	...
573	196	81	180	...	...	65	2	20	4	7	6	6	...
109	52	16	32	...	...	1	4	3	1	...	...	...	...
58	1	1	...	...	...	42	14	...	...	...	...	...	...
244	47	12	40	...	...	44	12	74	5	7	2	3	...
179	3	...	1	...	...	74	...	4	57	25	13	2	...
21	...	...	...	...	...	9	...	9	3	...	...	...	...
67	3	...	7	...	...	45	...	3	9	...	...	...	...
86	25	17	28	...	1	10	...	5	...	...	...	...	...
119	20	17	59	1	...	3	4	1	7	6	...	...	...
116	2	3	9	...	...	41	...	39	...	14	1	4	...
93	1	...	...	...	...	13	1	11	12	53	...	...	2
3	...	...	...	...	...	2	...	1	...	...	...	...	...
25	1	2	1	...	...	21	...	...	...	...	...	...	...
84	26	37	6	...	...	1	...	5	5	4	...	...	...
27	4	19	3	...	...	1	...	...	...	...	...	...	...
50	8	...	16	...	...	3	1	23	...	...	...	7	1
53	12	4	2	...	...	18	1	13	...	...	...	2	...
33	27	...	1	...	...	5	...	...	...	...	...	...	...
507	20	5	23	...	21	432	40	24	...	...	...	3	...
...	...	...	...	...	...	...	...	...	...	...	...	...	...
...	...	...	...	...	...	...	...	...	...	...	...	...	...
...	...	...	...	...	...	...	...	...	...	...	...	...	...
...	...	...	...	...	...	...	...	...	...	...	...	...	...
97	15	...	7	...	...	25	...	48	2	...	...	...	...
...	...	...	...	...	...	...	...	...	...	...	...	...	...
...	...	...	...	...	...	...	...	...	...	...	...	...	...
12	...	1	...	...	...	...	...	...	10	...	...	...	1
54	8	...	...	...	...	21	...	10	8	6	1	...	...
9,962	1,999	464	1,337	31	65	3,680	301	1,078	445	381	97	69	15

Total Males.	Males. Rigvédis. Smártás.	Bhágavata Sampradáya.	Mádhvás.	S'rivaishnavás. Tengalé.	Vadagalé.	Yajurvédis. Smártás.	Bhágavata Sampradáya.	Mádhvás.	Srivaishnavás. Tengalé.	Vadagalé.	Sámavédis. Smártás.	Mádhvás.	S'rivaishnavás.
969	351	63	186	3	...	203	91	41	3	17	3	1	1
294	54	7	23	...	3	69	15	15	11	89	...	1	7
443	35	9	10	...	...	336	21	25	1	13	1	...	2
538	214	46	65	...	...	86	6	32	12	34	43	...	...
1,552	536	120	216	...	1	412	47	65	51	81	23	...	...
674	65	43	41	...	2	231	88	65	20	115	3	1	...
535	184	42	48	5	1	168	22	24	5	16	...	...	...
429	291	61	9	...	...	57	...	2	8	...	1	...	...
...	...	...	...	...	...	...	...	...	...	...	...	...	...
849	472	40	212	...	...	69	18	13	...	10	14	...	1
176	47	8	57	1	...	28	22	11	1	...	...	1	...
39	6	...	4	...	...	27	...	2	...	...	...	...	...
384	136	58	81	1	...	84	6	13	...	4	...	1	...
59	3	...	1	...	...	40	...	...	2	7	2	...	...
...	...	...	...	...	...	...	...	...	...	...	...	...	...
37	4	...	...	...	...	31	...	1	...	1	...	...	...
147	38	53	44	...	...	6	2	2	...	2	...	...	...
195	57	2	90	...	5	4	4	3	2	26	1	1	...
37	12	10	7	...	...	7	1	...	...	...	...	...	...
91	...	...	...	...	...	2	...	1	1	87	...	...	...
25	...	4	8	...	...	8	...	3	...	...	...	...	2
11	10	...	...	...	...	1	...	...	...	...	...	...	...
...	...	...	...	...	...	...	...	...	...	...	...	...	...
22	...	...	18	4	...	...	...	...	...	...	...	...	...
14	9	...	1	...	...	4	...	...	...	...	...	...	...
46	30	4	...	...	11	...	1	...	...	...	...	...	...
4	4	...	...	...	...	...	...	...	...	...	...	...	...
134	45	2	26	...	...	42	...	7	...	3	2	7	...
...	...	...	...	...	...	...	...	...	...	...	...	...	...
...	...	...	...	...	...	...	...	...	...	...	...	...	...
...	...	...	...	...	...	...	...	...	...	...	...	...	...
...	...	...	...	...	...	...	...	...	...	...	...	...	...
25	5	...	2	...	...	2	...	7	5	4	...	...	...
...	...	...	...	...	...	...	...	...	...	...	...	...	...
...	...	...	...	...	...	...	...	...	...	...	...	...	...
...	...	...	...	...	...	...	...	...	...	...	...	...	...
44	3	...	...	...	...	13	1	6	...	21	...	...	...
7,773	2,521	572	1,239	14	23	1,949	345	341	122	530	91	13	13

Total Females.	Rigvédis. Smártás.	Rigvédis. Bhágavata Sampradáya.	Rigvédis. Mádhvás.	Rigvédis. S'rívaishnavás. Tengalé.	Rigvédis. S'rívaishnavás. Vadagalé.	Yajurvédis. Smártás.	Yajurvédis. Bhágavata Sampradáya.	Yajurvédis. Mádhvás.	Yajurvédis. S'rívaishnavás. Tengalé.	Yajurvédis. S'rívaishnavás. Vadagalé.	Sámavédis. Smártás.	Sámavédis. Mádhvás.	Sámavédis. S'rívaishnavás.
1,031	348	58	188	...	2	260	85	52	4	10	12	1	5
267	38	5	46	...	7	72	9	19	13	72	2	...	7
387	57	4	21	...	...	237	23	17	5	16	2	...	8
466	180	47	59	...	...	73	6	20	6	27	44	1	3
1,430	495	113	225	...	6	378	27	43	29	81	18	7	3
614	59	33	41	...	2	211	91	48	24	91	4	3	4
462	129	38	47	...	4	150	38	18	1	27	1	...	...
301	174	35	104	...	...	37	...	10	1	...	...	...	...
14	...	...	...	...	...	14	...	...	...	...	...	...	...
825	421	38	216	...	...	61	16	21	...	4	46	...	2
153	88	15	40	...	...	31	19	10	...	...	...	...	...
34	7	...	...	...	...	26	...	1	...	...	...	...	...
381	127	54	92	...	...	83	3	11	...	6	5	...	...
63	1	...	...	...	...	42	...	...	6	18	...	...	1
9	2	...	...	...	...	7	...	...	...	...	...	...	...
37	8	...	...	...	...	24	...	5	...	...	...	...	...
132	48	18	55	...	3	4	...	2	2	...	...	...	...
180	47	3	90	...	...	3	2	...	5	29	1	...	...
37	16	11	1	...	...	8	...	...	...	1	...	...	...
79	3	...	...	...	...	2	...	...	1	67	...	...	6
11	1	...	8	...	...	...	...	2	...	...	...	...	...
2	...	...	...	...	...	2	...	...	...	...	...	...	...
...	...	...	...	...	...	...	...	...	...	...	...	...	...
23	...	6	16	...	...	...	...	...	...	...	...	...	...
7	5	...	1	...	...	...	...	1	...	...	...	...	...
37	16	...	5	...	...	14	...	2	...	...	...	...	...
10	3	2	4	...	...	1	...	...	...	...	...	...	...
107	39	2	18	...	...	27	3	4	...	5	...	9	...
...	...	...	...	...	...	...	...	...	...	...	...	...	...
...	...	...	...	...	...	...	...	...	...	...	...	...	...
...	...	...	...	...	...	...	...	...	...	...	...	...	...
...	...	...	...	...	...	...	...	...	...	...	...	...	...
29	3	...	4	...	...	2	4	5	4	7	...	...	...
...	...	...	...	...	...	...	...	...	...	...	...	...	...
...	...	...	...	...	...	...	...	...	...	...	...	...	...
...	...	...	...	...	...	...	...	...	...	...	...	...	...
32	...	...	...	...	...	6	...	3	...	23	...	...	...
7,239	2,265	482	1,284	...	24	1,790	326	299	101	479	135	21	33

	Males.												
	Rigvédis.					Yajurvédis.					Sámavédis.		
				S'rivaishnavás.					S'rivaishnavás.				
Total Males.	Smártás.	Bhágavata Sampradáya.	Mádhvás.	Tengalé.	Vadagalé.	Smártás.	Bhágavata Sampradáya.	Mádhvás.	Tengalé.	Vadagalé.	Smártás.	Mádhvás.	S'rivaishnavás.
2,558	1,080	89	267	23	59	478	13	171	174	128	56	13	7
1,311	295	10	97	4	20	398	19	67	119	225	20	4	27
1,524	619	24	54	8	10	506	24	96	91	89	3	...	...
1,518	518	75	193	7	19	223	43	73	96	158	107	6	...
3,031	1,034	59	286	23	29	684	106	141	333	193	85	12	43
1,302	386	20	132	10	11	142	18	84	194	267	29	...	9
798	163	17	155	...	8	294	10	51	61	21	8	6	1
556	202	3	149	3	3	124	5	21	16	18	8	...	4
51	1	...	...	...	...	39	...	5	...	...	6	...	...
1,011	452	48	304	3	13	95	7	29	20	6	27	1	6
438	254	20	68	...	...	76	1	14	2	...	2	...	1
70	3	...	1	...	...	35	1	30	...	...	...	...	...
391	65	4	55	...	2	131	25	58	17	34	...	...	...
341	14	2	4	...	2	175	28	6	41	69	...	...	...
3	...	...	...	...	...	3	...	...	...	...	...	...	...
63	5	...	4	2	3	33	14	1	1	...	...	...	...
197	138	7	25	...	...	3	2	...	7	8	...	...	7
223	61	3	75	...	...	24	10	1	17	32	...	...	...
179	23	...	15	...	30	61	1	19	12	7	11	...	...
181	2	...	4	...	8	15	2	3	5	142	...	...	...
64	2	...	27	...	...	12	2	5	9	4	3	...	...
113	32	...	...	39	...	19	6	...	15	2	...	...	...
28	1	...	...	8	...	1	...	...	18	10	...	...	...
25	8	...	13	2	...	...	...	2	...	...	...	...	...
34	4	...	26	...	...	...	...	...	...	1	3	...	...
82	14	4	25	...	...	38	1	...	...	...	...	...	...
12	10	...	...	...	...	...	...	2	...	...	...	...	...
183	84	1	28	...	1	43	2	3	1	16	24	8	7
11	8	...	...	...	...	3	...	...	...	...	...	...	...
28	15	3	9	1	...	...	...	...	...	...	...	...	...
11	11	...	...	...	...	...	...	...	...	...	...	...	...
5	...	...	...	...	...	...	...	...	...	5	...	...	...
24	...	...	2	...	...	3	...	12	5	1	1	...	...
3	1	...	...	...	...	2	...	...	...	...	...	...	...
10	10	...	...	...	...	...	...	...	...	...	...	...	...
84	...	...	...	...	...	66	18	...	...	...	...	...	...
55	17	...	...	8	...	7	1	7	9	6	5	...	...
16,518	5,502	389	2,018	131	227	3,733	359	904	1,258	1,442	398	45	112

Total Females.	Females. Rigvédis. Smártás.	Rigvédis. Bhágavata Sampradáya.	Rigvédis. Mádhvás.	Rigvédis. S'rivaishnavás. Tengalé.	Rigvédis. S'rivaishnavás. Vadagalé.	Yajurvédis. Smártás.	Yajurvédis. Bhágavata Sampradáya.	Yajurvédis. Mádhvás.	Yajurvédis. S'rivaishnavás. Tengalé.	Yajurvédis. S'rivaishnavás. Vadagalé.	Sámavédis. Smártás.	Sámavédis. Mádhvás.	S'rivaishnavás.
2,646	1,333	72	332	11	73	439	13	123	49	130	56	1	9
1,563	381	16	147	4	16	496	23	113	138	192	24	9	4
1,381	464	23	63	10	15	445	32	109	119	101	1	...	...
1,447	491	86	174	10	31	224	42	62	64	159	80	24	...
3,228	1,170	70	338	76	85	627	73	150	340	162	81	1	46
1,477	316	21	169	6	18	362	15	88	184	283	3	8	4
748	132	40	137	...	4	283	12	58	48	21	1	...	12
477	187	4	133	1	...	88	6	28	18	...	3	2	7
81	1	...	...	...	...	49	...	17	...	8	2	4	...
917	426	39	283	4	9	95	2	28	5	11	15	...	...
373	189	16	69	...	...	72	1	20	1	...	5	...	...
61	6	...	3	...	...	17	17	18	...	...	...	...	...
264	45	3	36	1	2	61	11	63	2	31	8	1	...
288	19	1	5	...	5	154	16	12	26	47	2	1	...
2	...	...	[illegible]	...	...	2	...	...	...	...	...	...	...
55	2	...	3	...	...	46	...	2	2	...	...	...	...
171	102	6	37	...	...	6	4	1	...	9	...	...	6
200	42	...	68	1	...	24	7	6	18	31	...	...	3
146	17	...	11	2	2	65	17	11	3	10	8	...	...
193	13	...	7	...	5	8	2	5	19	134	...	...	...
53	4	1	22	2	6	4	...	5	3	7	...	...	...
99	4	...	...	37	...	28	9	...	12	...	...	8	1
18	1	...	...	...	...	...	...	...	11	6	...	...	...
21	6	...	11	...	...	2	...	2	...	...	...	...	...
21	1	...	11	6	1	...	...	...	2	...	...	...	...
75	18	...	18	...	...	39	...	...	...	...	...	...	...
17	9	...	...	...	...	...	...	8	...	...	...	...	...
138	30	2	23	3	...	50	...	...	...	20	8	...	2
8	8	...	...	...	...	...	...	...	...	...	...	...	...
23	12	...	3	...	2	...	...	...	...	...	6	...	...
15	11	...	...	...	...	4	...	...	...	...	...	...	...
4	...	...	...	...	...	...	...	4	...	...	...	...	...
12	...	...	3	...	...	1	...	7	2	...	...	...	...
3	...	...	...	...	...	3	...	...	...	...	...	...	...
14	8	...	...	...	...	...	...	...	...	6	...	...	...
73	...	...	1	...	...	43	29	...	...	...	...	...	...
41	7	...	...	...	1	5	...	7	1	20	...	...	...
16,353	**5,455**	**399**	**2,106**	**174**	**280**	**3,742**	**331**	**956**	**1,066**	**1,388**	**203**	**59**	**96**

Total Males.	Rigvédis. Smártás.	Rigvédis. Bhágavata Sampradáya.	Rigvédis. Mádhvás.	Rigvédis. S'rivaishṇavás. Tengalé.	Rigvédis. S'rivaishṇavás. Vadagalé.	Yajurvédis. Smártás.	Yajurvédis. Bhágavata Sampradáya.	Yajurvédis. Mádhvás.	Yajurvédis. S'rivaishṇavás. Tengalé.	Yajurvédis. S'rivaishṇavás. Vadagalé.	Sámavédis. Smártás.	Sámavédis. Mádhvás.	Sámavédis. S'rivaishṇavás.
807	415	37	31	...	...	212	49	6	15	26	16	...	...
895	76	8	6	2	148	225	62	28	24	280	28	3	5
382	64	...	9	...	1	182	33	24	10	54	4	1	...
627	101	10	35	...	13	106	34	7	...	309	5	7	...
1,400	372	44	56	4	81	541	42	24	38	180	16	1	1
442	32	2	21	6	...	126	43	26	35	151	...	...	...
363	151	23	16	...	...	88	17	6	45	5	6	1	5
270	128	40	42	...	...	54	...	...	...	...	3	3	...
16	...	...	...	...	...	15	...	1	...	...	...	...	...
574	339	86	60	...	...	68	13	3	2	6	37	1	9
216	94	3	26	...	...	86	3	3	...	...	1	...	...
4	...	...	1	...	...	3	...	...	...	...	...	...	...
155	24	...	3	...	...	55	42	15	2	14	...	...	...
242	3	...	1	2	2	120	12	1	7	77	...	5	12
...	...	...	...	...	...	...	...	...	...	...	...	...	...
26	...	...	...	...	...	15	11	...	...	...	...	...	...
113	53	7	18	...	...	4	4	4	4	19	...	...	...
106	78	5	2	...	...	6	...	1	3	11	...	...	...
59	12	5	1	...	...	32	2	1	...	6	...	...	...
34	1	...	...	...	1	18	...	...	4	10	...	...	...
4	...	...	4	...	...	...	...	...	...	...	...	...	...
86	...	...	...	...	...	68	11	...	...	7	...	...	...
13	3	...	...	...	...	1	...	...	8	1	...	...	...
41	34	...	5	...	...	1	...	1	...	...	...	...	...
...	...	...	...	...	...	...	...	...	...	...	...	...	...
...	...	...	...	...	...	...	...	...	...	...	...	...	...
...	...	...	...	...	...	...	...	...	...	...	...	...	...
164	18	...	...	...	...	49	1	2	1	86	2	5	...
...	...	...	...	...	...	...	...	...	...	...	...	...	...
1	...	...	...	...	...	1	...	...	...	...	...	...	...
4	4	...	...	...	...	...	...	...	...	...	...	...	...
...	...	...	...	...	...	...	...	...	...	...	...	...	...
60	52	2	1	...	...	2	...	1	2	...	...	...	...
...	...	...	...	...	...	...	...	...	...	...	...	...	...
...	...	...	...	...	...	...	...	...	...	...	...	...	...
55	...	...	...	...	...	42	4	2	3	...	4	...	...
7	...	...	...	...	...	...	...	...	...	7	...	...	...
7,166	2,054	272	338	14	246	2,120	383	156	203	1,249	122	27	32

Total Females.	Females. Rigvédis. Smártás.	Rigvédis. Bhágavata Sampradáya.	Rigvédis. Mádhvás.	Rigvédis. S'rivaishnavás. Tengalé.	Rigvédis. S'rivaishnavás. Vadagalé.	Yejurvédis. Smártás.	Yejurvédis. Bhágavata Sampradáya.	Yejurvédis. Mádhvás.	Yejurvédis. S'rivaishnavás. Tengalé.	Yejurvédis. S'rivaishnavás. Vadagalé.	Sámavédis. Smártás.	Sámavédis. Mádhvás.	Sámavédis. S'rivaishnavás.
809	472	28	40	5	191	43	10	13	47	18	1	1	...
922	61	7	9	2	205	238	38	12	28	313	5	...	4
305	61	8	...	...	...	149	30	45	9	60	2	1	...
702	89	13	38	...	4	108	62	2	1	360	8	6	...
1,283	354	44	45	...	8	548	27	26	36	171	24	...	...
427	40	...	12	2	2	138	1	23	37	171	...	...	1
351	127	25	16	...	6	104	18	6	32	16	...	...	1
337	155	58	35	6	...	57	16	2	...	6	2	...	...
6	1	...	...	...	...	5	...	...	...	...	...	...	...
621	352	38	51	12	76	20	10	1	2	43	...	16	...
92	61	1	14	...	...	11	3	2	...	...	...	...	...
4	...	...	2	...	...	2	...	...	...	...	...	...	...
181	32	5	1	...	...	93	21	13	3	9	...	...	1
230	10	...	...	...	...	90	16	...	5	109	...	...	...
...	...	...	...	...	...	...	...	...	...	...	...	...	...
31	...	...	...	...	...	16	14	1	...	...	...	...	...
118	68	3	23	...	1	3	3	...	3	13	1	...	...
138	86	...	4	3	...	1	13	...	...	8	21	2	...
21	3	5	...	...	...	4	6	...	...	3	...	...	...
31	...	...	...	...	...	15	...	...	3	13	...	...	...
1	...	...	1	...	...	...	...	...	...	...	...	...	...
93	...	...	...	...	...	83	2	...	1	7	...	...	...
11	1	...	...	...	...	1	...	...	7	2	...	...	...
33	25	...	5	...	...	1	1	...	...	...	...	...	...
...	...	...	...	...	...	...	...	...	...	...	...	...	...
...	...	...	...	...	...	...	...	...	...	...	...	...	...
...	...	...	...	...	...	...	...	...	...	...	...	...	...
183	22	...	...	5	...	59	...	1	...	90	6	...	...
...	...	...	...	...	...	...	...	...	...	...	...	...	...
1	...	...	...	...	...	1	...	...	...	...	...	...	...
2	2	...	...	...	...	...	...	...	...	...	...	...	...
...	...	...	...	...	...	...	...	...	...	...	...	...	...
50	40	5	4	...	...	1	...	7	2	...	...	...	...
...	...	...	...	...	...	...	...	...	...	...	...	...	...
...	...	...	...	...	...	...	...	...	...	...	...	...	...
25	1	...	...	...	...	19	2	1	2	...	...	...	...
11	2	...	...	...	...	2	3	2	...	2	...	...	...
7,147	2,065	240	300	35	493	1,812	290	157	218	1,423	70	28	7

O

Total Males	Rigvédis: Smártás	Rigvédis: Bhágavata Sampradáya	Rigvédis: Mádhvás	Rigvédis: S'rivaishnavás: Tengalé	Rigvédis: S'rivaishnavás: Vadagalé	Yajurvédis: Smártás	Yajurvédis: Bhágavata Sampradáya	Yajurvédis: Mádhvás	Yajurvédis: S'rivaishnavás: Tengalé	Yajurvédis: S'rivaishnavás: Vadagalé	Sámavédis: Smártás	Sámavédis: Mádhvás	Sámavédis: S'rivaishnavás
2,639	762	112	[illegible]08	...	...	1,215	251	6[illegible]	9	8	3	...	...
521	87	33	81	11	15	158	13	49	7	32	35	...	...
402	104	9	127	...	1	77	2	65	1	16	...	...	...
389	134	19	124	...	...	37	10	29	15	8	13	...	...
1,320	472	131	254	16	72	182	37	121	11	16	8	...	...
756	442	14	77	11	29	3[illegible]	5	39	9	66	9	...	...
499	253	38	108	2	...	49	6	39	...	6	3	...	...
1,993	822	132	186	4	...	645	156	50	...	...	1	8	...
...	...	...	...	...	...	...	...	...	...	...	...	...	...
1,206	325	43	209	...	...	561	41	23	2	...	...	...	...
370	95	22	107	...	5	109	...	32	...	...	...	...	...
14	1	...	1	...	...	6	...	5	...	1	...	...	...
1,323	115	8	73	...	5	832	210	72	8	...	...	...	...
53	6	...	...	...	2	19	7	4	9	6	...	...	...
14	8	...	...	...	...	1	...	4	...	1	...	...	...
...	...	...	...	...	...	...	...	...	...	...	...	...	...
98	72	1	16	...	...	...	6	3	...	...	...	...	...
37	3	...	12	...	...	3	...	6	7	3	3	...	...
85	12	3	16	...	...	40	...	10	4	...	...	...	...
2	...	...	...	...	...	...	...	...	...	2	...	...	...
33	17	...	...	...	...	3	2	1	1	7	...	...	...
...	...	...	...	...	...	...	...	...	...	...	...	...	...
36	...	...	20	...	1	1	...	13	...	1	...	...	...
18	2	...	10	1	...	1	...	4	...	...	...	...	...
3	...	...	3	...	...	...	...	...	...	...	...	...	...
108	38	...	59	...	...	8	...	3	...	...	...	...	...
5	2	...	2	...	...	...	...	1	...	...	...	...	...
58	24	...	7	1	...	9	...	6	...	7	1	...	...
...	...	...	...	...	...	...	...	...	...	...	...	...	...
3	...	...	...	...	...	...	...	3	...	...	...	...	...
2	2	...	...	...	...	...	...	...	...	...	...	...	...
...	...	...	...	...	...	...	...	...	...	...	...	...	...
13	2	...	...	...	...	...	4	6	1	...	...	...	...
...	...	...	...	...	...	...	...	...	...	...	...	...	...
...	...	...	...	...	...	...	...	...	...	...	...	...	...
...	...	...	...	...	...	...	...	...	...	...	...	...	...
...	...	...	...	...	...	...	...	...	...	...	...	...	...
11,991	3,860	565	1,695	46	130	4,011	734	660	84	180	76	8	2

Total Females.	Females. Rigvédis. Smártás.	Rigvédis. Bhágavata Sampradáya.	Rigvédis. Mádhvás.	Rigvédis. S'rivaishnavás. Tengalé.	Rigvédis. S'rivaishnavás. Vadagalé.	Yejurvédis. Smártás.	Yejurvédis. Bhágavata Sampradáya.	Yejurvédis. Mádhvás.	Yejurvédis. S'rivaishnavás. Tengalé.	Yejurvédis. S'rivaishnavás. Vadagalé.	Sámavédis. Smártás.	Sámavédis. Mádhvás.	Sámavédis. S'rivaishnavás.
2,612	820	145	242	...	18	1,091	177	94	15	3	6	1	...
496	105	13	82	3	7	183	9	40	6	14	34	...	...
350	70	10	97	2	11	82	6	47	12	13	...	...	...
361	108	13	136	2	...	38	3	38	6	11	6	...	...
1,275	[illegible]	102	219	43	9	260	28	104	25	6	10	...	...
495	119	27	158	10	11	102	2	32	6	33	12	...	...
473	242	20	84	4	...	58	21	26	3	5	7	...	...
1,863	747	147	167	...	2	623	112	65	...	...	1	...	...
...	...	...	...	...	...	...	...	...	...	...	...	...	...
1,118	327	35	201	2	2	445	82	16	2	...	4	...	3
335	73	19	105	...	...	112	2	24	...	...	...	...	...
6	...	...	...	...	...	6	...	...	...	...	...	...	...
1,269	117	3	84	1	8	884	138	30	...	4	...	...	...
65	7	...	...	...	...	35	2	9	1	5	6	...	...
9	1	...	3	...	...	1	...	...	3	...	...	...	1
...	...	...	...	...	...	...	...	...	...	...	...	...	...
83	61	...	12	...	...	4	...	6	...	...	...	...	...
32	13	...	10	...	...	1	...	...	5	3	...	...	...
80	17	...	17	...	...	38	...	8	...	...	...	...	...
1	...	...	...	...	...	...	...	...	...	1	...	...	...
32	24	...	...	...	...	2	1	...	1	3	1	...	...
...	...	...	...	...	...	...	...	...	...	...	...	...	...
32	2	...	17	...	...	3	...	10	...	...	...	...	...
17	2	...	10	...	...	...	...	5	...	...	...	...	...
5	...	...	4	...	...	...	...	1	...	...	...	...	...
144	49	6	61	...	5	5	15	...	...	...	...	...	...
4	...	...	1	...	...	3	...	...	...	...	...	...	...
75	22	3	28	...	...	4	1	13	...	4	...	...	...
...	...	...	...	...	...	...	...	...	...	...	...	...	...
2	...	...	...	...	...	...	...	2	...	...	...	...	...
...	...	...	...	...	...	...	...	...	...	...	...	...	...
...	...	...	...	...	...	...	...	...	...	...	...	...	...
16	...	5	...	...	...	4	...	4	3	...	...	...	...
...	...	...	...	...	...	...	...	...	...	...	...	...	...
...	...	...	...	...	...	...	...	...	...	...	...	...	...
...	...	...	...	...	...	...	...	...	...	...	...	...	...
...	...	...	...	...	...	...	...	...	...	...	...	...	...
11,250	3,363	557	1,747	64	76	3,983	599	874	88	105	87	1	4

Total Males.	Males. Rigvédis. Smártás.	Rigvédis. Bhágavata Sampradáya.	Rigvédis. Mádhvás.	Rigvédis. S'rívaishṇavás. Tengalé.	Rigvédis. S'rívaishṇavás. Vadagalé.	Yajurvédis. Smártás.	Yajurvédis. Bhágavata Sampradáya.	Yajurvédis. Mádhvás.	Yajurvédis. Srívaishṇavás. Tengalé.	Yajurvédis. Srívaishṇavás. Vadagalé.	Sámavédis. Smártás.	Sámavédis. Mádhvás.	Sámavédis. S'rívaishṇavás.
1,129	728	119	74	1	...	155	20	12	3	11	6	...	...
317	94	28	34	5	...	113	2	3	5	26	3	[illegible]	4
135	19	10	29	...	1	49	8	3	3	12	1	...	...
369	185	80	29	2	35	7	6	1	23	...	2	...	...
1,285	749	203	77	1	...	177	12	19	29	9	9	...	...
198	48	4	16	...	1	55	3	10	10	5	...	...	...
365	257	17	18	...	...	60	9	...	2	2	...	...	...
1,349	871	196	39	...	...	150	13	46	...	...	4	...	...
...	...	...	...	...	...	...	...	...	...	...	...	...	...
700	471	49	27	2	...	119	14	7	...	6	5	...	...
88	25	11	11	...	...	34	3	3	...	1	...	...	...
...	...	...	...	...	...	...	...	...	...	...	...	...	...
70	34	3	5	...	...	23	5	1	...	...	...	...	...
519	319	4	...	...	1	132	2	1	3	57	...	...	...
8	...	...	2	...	...	1	...	5	...	...	...	...	...
3	...	...	...	...	...	1	2	...	...	...	...	...	...
102	81	15	3	...	...	3	...	...	...	...	...	...	...
126	56	4	...	5	...	3	...	1	4	13	...	...	...
54	30	...	3	...	...	17	...	...	...	4	...	...	...
8	6	...	...	...	...	1	...	...	...	1	...	...	...
...	...	...	...	...	...	...	...	...	...	...	...	...	...
...	...	...	...	...	...	...	...	...	...	...	...	...	...
...	...	...	...	...	...	...	...	...	...	...	...	...	...
26	8	3	...	...	...	12	3	...	...	...	...	...	...
5	4	...	1	...	...	...	...	...	...	...	...	...	...
65	34	...	21	...	...	9	...	...	...	...	1	...	...
9	1	...	...	...	...	8	...	...	...	...	...	...	...
108	52	1	9	...	...	16	6	...	...	9	...	10	...
...	...	...	...	...	...	...	...	...	...	...	...	...	...
23	2	...	...	...	...	16	...	5	...	...	...	...	...
16	12	2	...	...	...	2	...	...	...	...	...	...	...
...	...	...	...	...	...	...	...	...	...	...	...	...	...
16	6	...	1	...	...	8	...	...	...	1	...	...	...
...	...	...	...	...	...	...	...	...	...	...	...	...	...
...	...	...	...	...	...	...	...	...	...	...	...	...	...
...	...	...	...	...	...	...	...	...	...	...	...	...	...
16	9	...	1	...	...	...	...	...	3	3	...	...	...
7,104	4,141	769	400	16	38	1,200	108	117	84	208	31	10	4

Total Females.	Rigvédis. Smártás.	Rigvédis. Bhágavata Sampradáyn.	Rigvédis. Mádhvás.	Rigvédis. S'rívaishnavás. Tengalé.	Rigvédis. S'rívaishnavás. Vadagalé.	Yejurvédis. Smártás.	Yejurvédis. Bhágavata Sampradáyn.	Yejurvédis. Mádhvás.	Yejurvédis. S'rívaishnavás. Tengalé.	Yejurvédis. S'rívaishnavás. Vadagalé.	Sámavédis. Smártás.	Sámavédis. Mádhvás.	Sámavédis. S'rívaishnavás.
907	651	98	61	...	...	141	10	6	2	17	4	...	1
328	159	17	3	2	7	101	7	2	12	14	...	...	4
149	37	15	18	7	...	53	1	3	...	14	...	...	1
423	213	95	28	1	...	38	15	10	...	20	2	1	...
1,270	722	146	73	3	3	253	13	15	24	10	8	...	...
221	65	7	21	2	4	40	5	15	6	55	...	...	
251	198	26	13	...	...	38	5	1	...	1	...	...	...
1,426	1,021	168	32	...	...	190	8	3	...	4	...	...	...
...	...	...	...	...	...	...	...	...	...	...	...	...	...
582	403	37	26	...		75	23	4	6	4	3	1	...
92	34	12	8	...	...	32		5	...	...	...	1	...
...	...	...	...	...	...	...	...	...	...	...	...	...	...
74	35	7	8	...	...	9	12	...	...	...	3	...	...
85	8	1	...	...	1	2	15	...	3	55	...	...	...
11	...	...	1	...	...	...	6	4	...	...	...	...	...
...	...	...	...	...	...	...	...	...	...	...	...	...	...
151	124	4	1	...	...	2	...	...	...	...	...	...	...
128	97	7	...	...	...	5	...	1	2	16	...	...	...
70	34	8	2	...	...	22	...	...	...	3	1	...	...
4	...	...	...	...	2	...	...	...	...	2	...	...	...
...	...	...	...	...	...	...	...	...	...	...	...	...	...
...	...	...	...	...	...	...	...	...	...	...	...	...	...
...	...	...	...	...	...	...	...	...	...	...	...	...	...
23	7	...	...	...	...	13	3	...	...	...	...	...	...
3	3	...	...	...	...	...	...	...	...	...	...	...	...
36	19	...	16	...	...	...	...	...	...	1	...	...	...
4	2	...	...	...	...	1	1	...	...	...	...	...	...
107	49	11	4	...	...	25	1	...	...	7	...	10	...
...	...	...	...	...	...	...	...	...	...	...	...	...	...
23	3	...	4	...	...	11	5	...	...	...	...	...	...
15	14	...	...	...	...	1	...	...	...	...	...	...	...
...	...	...	...	...	...	...	...	...	...	...	...	...	...
24	5	...	...	...	3	10	2	...	...	4	...	...	...
...	...	...	...	...	...	...	...	...	...	...	...	...	...
...	...	...	...	...	...	...	...	...	...	...	...	...	...
...	...	...	...	...	...	...	...	...	...	...	...	...	...
11	5	...	...	...	...	...	...	...	...	6	...	...	...
6,521	3,908	659	324	15	20	1,065	132	69	55	233	21	13	7

Total Males.	Rigvédis. Smártás.	Rigvédis. Bhágavata Sampradáya.	Rigvédis. Mádhvás.	Rigvédis. S'rivaishnavás. Tengalé.	Rigvédis. S'rivaishnavás. Vadaghalé.	Yejurvédis. Smártás.	Yejurvédis. Bhágavata Sampradáya.	Yejurvédis. Mádhvás.	Yejurvédis. S'rivaishnavás. Tengalé.	Yejurvédis. S'rivaishnavás. Vadaghalé.	Sámavédis. Smártás.	Sámavédis. Mádhvás.	Sámavédis. S'rivaishnavás.
416	131	18	118	...	...	101	11	31	3	2	1	...	...
101	17	1	17	...	5	23	1	23	2	8	...	1	3
104	17	1	10	...	2	54	...	11	3	2	5	...	...
220	52	7	109	...	...	17	...	26	1	4	...	4	...
464	109	18	202	3	2	63	1	57	5	1	...	1	2
136	35	3	15	5	3	27	7	20	1	17	3	...	...
219	35	21	18	...	2	67	2	38	...	6	...	...	...
210	74	41	70	5	1	9	1	5	1	...	4	...	...
...	...	...	...	...	...	...	...	...	...	...	...	...	...
252	116	7	104	...	...	14	...	11	...	...	...	...	...
153	47	...	95	3	...	...	...	2	...	...	...	6	...
37	4	...	1	...	...	32	...	...	...	...	...	...	...
76	32	...	34	...	2	5	2	1	...	...	...	...	...
17	1	...	...	...	9	...	1	...	6	...	...	...	...
13	...	...	...	...	...	10	3	...	...	...	...	...	...
8	...	...	1	...	...	3	...	4	...	...	...	...	...
14	...	1	5	...	...	1	...	7	...	...	...	...	...
44	3	...	31	...	3	...	...	...	7	...	...	...	...
14	3	...	1	2	...	...	...	2	...	1	5	...	...
16	...	...	...	...	4	...	...	...	...	12	...	...	...
8	...	...	4	...	...	4	...	...	...	...	...	...	...
5	...	...	...	2	...	3	...	...	...	...	...	...	...
...	...	...	...	...	...	...	...	...	...	...	...	...	...
4	...	...	4	...	...	...	...	...	...	...	...	...	...
...	...	...	...	...	...	...	...	...	...	...	...	...	...
22	4	...	16	...	...	...	...	2	...	...	...	...	...
2	2	...	...	...	...	...	...	...	...	...	...	...	...
16	3	5	1	...	1	3	...	1	...	...	...	2	...
...	...	...	...	...	...	...	...	...	...	...	...	...	...
...	...	...	...	...	...	...	...	...	...	...	...	...	...
...	...	...	...	...	...	...	...	...	...	...	...	...	...
...	...	...	...	...	...	...	...	...	...	...	...	...	...
41	22	2	14	...	...	...	...	1	...	2	...	...	...
...	...	...	...	...	...	...	...	...	...	...	...	...	...
...	...	...	...	...	...	...	...	...	...	...	...	...	...
...	...	...	...	...	...	...	...	...	...	...	...	...	...
8	...	...	...	...	3	...	...	2	...	3	...	...	...
2,620	707	125	900	20	37	435	29	244	28	58	18	14	5

Total Females.	Females.												
	Rigvédis.					Yajurvédis.					Sâmavédis.		
				S'rivaishṇavás.					S'rivaishṇavás.				
	Smártás.	Bhâgavata Sampradáya.	Mádhvás.	Tengalé.	Vaḍagalé.	Smártás.	Bhâgavata Sampradáya.	Mádhvás.	Tengalé.	Vaḍagalé.	Smártás.	Mádhvás.	S'rivaishṇavás.
338	100	11	115	...	70	9	29	2	2	...	...	...	...
167	35	3	26	...	1	56	..	29	10	5	...	...	2
109	26	1	9	...	...	55	...	11	...	6	...	1	...
143	33	2	76	..	5	6	...	10	3	3	...	5	...
412	78	15	193	1	2	61	6	50	2	1	...	...	3
132	24	4	19	...	11	36	3	16	1	16	2	...	...
174	24	17	35	4	...	58	6	25	2	3	...	...	...
192	94	16	63	...	...	12	...	3	1	3	...	...	...
...	...	...	...	...	...	...	...	...	...	...	...	...	...
228	87	7	112	...	...	13	...	9	...	...	...	...	...
166	50	...	112	...	...	...	...	4	...	...	...	...	...
39	10	...	2	...	...	24	...	...	...	3	...	...	...
77	35	2	35	...	...	4	...	1	...	...	...	...	...
26	4	...	...	...	4	13	...	...	...	5	...	...	...
6	...	...	...	...	...	5	1	...	...	...	...	...	...
18	...	...	2	...	...	7	...	...	9	...	...	...	...
10	...	1	2	1	...	...	...	6	...	...	...	...	...
38	12	...	24	...	...	...	...	...	...	1	1	...	...
10	...	...	..	5	2	...	...	2	...	...	1	...	...
16	...	...	...	...	1	...	...	...	...	15	...	...	...
10	...	...	8	...	...	2	...	...	...	...	...	...	...
3	...	...	1	...	...	2	...	...	...	...	...	...	...
...	...	...	...	...	...	...	...	...	...	...	...	...	...
4	...	4	...	...	...	...	...	...	...	...	...	...	...
...	...	...	...	...	...	...	...	...	...	...	...	...	...
19	3	...	14	...	...	...	...	2	...	...	...	...	...
2	2	...	...	...	...	...	...	...	...	...	...	...	...
21	4	5	...	...	...	9	...	...	...	1	2	...	...
...	...	...	...	...	...	...	...	...	...	...	...	...	...
...	...	...	...	...	...	...	...	...	...	...	...	...	...
...	...	...	...	...	...	...	...	...	...	...	...	...	...
...	...	...	...	...	...	...	...	...	...	...	...	...	...
43	26	1	13	...	...	1	...	...	2	...	...	...	...
...	...	...	...	...	...	...	...	...	...	...	...	...	...
...	...	...	...	...	...	...	...	...	...	...	...	...	...
...	...	...	...	...	...	...	...	...	...	...	...	...	...
7	...	...	...	...	...	1	...	...	...	6	...	...	...
2,419	647	89	861	11	96	374	45	179	32	68	6	6	5

Name of Gôtras.	Total Males.	Rigvêdis. Smártás.	Rigvêdis. Bhágavata Sampradáya.	Rigvêdis. Mádhvás.	Rigvêdis. S'rivaishṇavás. Tengalé.	Rigvêdis. S'rivaishṇavás. Vaḍagalé.	Yajurvêdis. Smártás.	Yajurvêdis. Bhágavata Sampradáya.	Yajurvêdis. Mádhvás.	Yajurvêdis. S'rivaishṇavás. Tengalé.	Yajurvêdis. S'rivaishṇavás. Vaḍagalé.	Sámavêdis. Smártás.	Sámavêdis. Mádhvás.	Sámavêdis. S'rivaishṇavás.
Total brought forwd.	76,216	24,589	3,386	9,985	745	829	20,507	2,577	4,531	2,646	4,997	1,028	195	201
Achchyuta	5	1	...	...	...	...	1	...	...	...	...	...	3	...
Dêvarája	92	12	...	6	...	...	61	6	5	2	...	...	...	...
Chôpôgâyana	30	...	...	9	1	...	15	...	...	4	1	...	...	...
Kapi	137	45	3	9	1	1	61	...	17	...	...	...	...	...
Nistundhana	246	25	...	...	...	24	177	17	3	...	...	...	...	...
Vámana	20	3	...	...	...	...	17	...	...	...	...	...	...	...
Kundali	60	5	...	...	...	...	52	...	1	...	...	2	...	...
Santasa	3	3	...	...	...	...	...	...	...	...	...	...	...	...
Gálava	24	7	1	4	...	...	9	1	1	...	...	...	1	...
Svatantrakapi	100	23	...	1	...	...	72	2	2	...	...	...	...	...
Kálakaus'ika	4	...	...	...	...	...	4	...	...	...	...	...	...	...
A'ngirasa	1,497	856	187	53	11	...	282	92	12	...	...	3	...	1
Bárhaspatya	1	1	...	...	...	...	...	...	...	...	...	...	...	...
Mitravasu	1	...	...	...	...	...	1	...	...	...	...	...	...	...
Sánkhyáyana	66	8	1	7	...	...	41	2	6	1	...	...	...	...
Maitrêya	20	3	...	1	...	...	11	5	...	...	...	...	...	...
Sankurshaṇa	8	3	...	...	...	...	3	...	...	2	...	...	...	...
Párt'hiva	50	4	...	2	...	1	8	...	35	...	...	...	...	...
Sankalika	6	...	...	5	...	...	...	...	...	...	1	...	...	...
S'álankáyana	32	10	...	...	...	...	22	...	...	...	...	...	...	...
Môhana	...	...	...	...	...	...	...	...	...	...	...	...	...	...
Kôsala	3	...	...	...	...	...	3	...	...	...	...	...	...	...
Vaikhánasa	8	...	...	...	...	3	...	...	...	...	...	...	...	5
Vyása	16	5	1	...	...	...	8	...	...	...	2	...	...	...
Paulastya	14	9	...	...	...	...	1	...	1	3	...	...	...	...
Kátyáyana	20	5	...	5	...	...	6	...	...	...	...	4	...	...
Ghritasama's'a	6	...	...	...	...	...	6	...	...	...	...	...	...	...
Gauḍasárasvata	43	1	...	42	...	...	...	...	...	...	...	...	...	...
A's'valáyana	15	5	4	1	...	...	1	...	4	...	...	...	...	...
Havikarma	17	4	9	3	...	...	1	...	...	...	...	...	...	...
Mánḍavya	2	...	...	...	...	...	...	...	...	...	1	...	1	...
Ambarísha	2	...	...	...	...	...	2	...	...	...	...	...	...	...
Gôtra and S'ákha not stated	14,067	4,159	290	613	107	153	3,143	85	240	98	327	4,181	210	16[illegible]
Total......	92,831	30,086	3,882	10,746	865	1,011	24,515	2,787	4,858	2,756	5,329	5,218	410	369

Total Females.	Rigvédis. Smártás.	Rigvédis. Bhágavata Sampradáyn.	Rigvédis. Mádhvás.	Rigvédis. S'rivaishnavás. Tengalé.	Rigvédis. S'rivaishnavás. Vadagalé.	Yajurvédis. Smártás.	Yajurvédis. Bhágavata Sampradáyn.	Yajurvédis. Mádhvás.	Yajurvédis. S'rivaishnavás. Tengalé.	Yajurvédis. S'rivaishnavás. Vadagalé.	Sámavédis. Smártás.	Sámavédis. Mádhvás.	Sámavédis. S'rivaishnavás.
72,245	**22,991**	**3,167**	**9,699**	**385**	**914**	**19,781**	**2,321**	**4,383**	**2,402**	**4,920**	**864**	**234**	**184**
3	...	...	1	...	...	2	...	...	...	...	...	...	...
90	9	5	2	...	...	56	6	12	...	...	...	...	...
6	...	2	1	...	...	...	...	...	3	...	...	...	...
146	58	2	12	...	...	47	2	23	...	2	...	...	...
191	9	4	...	...	...	168	10	...	...	...	...	...	...
28	...	...	...	...	...	28	...	...	...	...	...	...	...
63	3	...	...	2	...	53	3	1	...	2	...	...	...
3	3	...	...	...	...	...	...	...	...	...	...	...	...
10	...	3	5	...	...	...	...	2	...	...	...	...	...
90	16	3	9	...	1	56	2	3	...	...	...	...	...
3	3	...	...	...	...	...	...	...	...	...	...	...	...
1,432	850	138	57	...	...	334	34	12	...	2	5	...	...
...	...	...	...	...	...	...	...	...	...	...	...	...	...
3	3	...	...	...	...	...	...	...	...	...	...	...	...
66	20	2	3	...	2	32	1	5	...	1	...	...	...
6	2	...	...	...	...	4	...	...	...	...	...	...	...
9	...	...	...	...	...	...	...	...	...	9	...	...	...
50	5	...	5	...	...	7	...	32	3	...	1	6	...
16	...	...	7	...	3	6	...	...	...	...	...	...	...
60	16	...	...	...	...	35	3	5	1	...	...	...	...
1	...	...	1	...	...	...	...	...	...	...	...	...	...
43	5	...	...	...	...	29	...	...	...	2	7	...	...
6	...	...	...	...	...	1	...	...	...	2	...	...	3
9	5	...	...	...	...	...	...	2	...	2	...	...	...
7	3	...	...	...	...	1	...	...	3	...	...	...	...
23	5	...	4	...	...	9	...	3	...	...	2	...	...
5	...	...	...	...	...	5	...	...	...	...	...	...	...
1	1	...	...	...	...	...	...	...	...	...	...	...	...
13	5	...	5	...	...	...	2	1	...	...	...	...	...
12	1	11	...	...	...	...	...	...	...	...	...	...	...
3	...	...	2	...	1	...	...	...	...	...	...	...	...
...	...	...	...	...	...	...	...	...	...	...	...	...	...
14,902	4,084	257	785	250	302	5,876	133	212	391	240	1,100	230	133
89,554	**28,996**	**3,594**	**10,598**	**637**	**1,223**	**26,530**	**2,517**	**4,096**	**2,803**	**5,182**	**1,979**	**479**	**320**

Total Males.	Rigvédis.					Yajurvédis.					Sámavédis.		
	Smártás.	Bhágavata Sampradáya.	Mádhvás.	S'rívaishnavás. Tengalé.	S'rívaishnavás. Vadagalé.	Smártás.	Bhágavata Sampradáya.	Mádhvás.	S'rívaishnavás. Tengalé.	S'rívaishnavás. Vadagalé.	Smártás.	Mádhvás.	S'rívaishnavás.
12,833	3,743	293	1,926	34	45	3,812	310	1,081	445	932	177	22	13
1	...	...	...	...	...	...	...	...	...	...	...	1	...
2	...	...	...	...	...	2	...	...	...	...	...	...	...
...	...	...	...	...	...	...	...	...	...	...	...	...	...
52	9	...	3	...	...	38	...	2	...	...	...	...	...
1	...	...	...	...	1	...	...	...	...	...	...	...	...
...	...	...	...	...	...	...	...	...	...	...	...	...	...
1	...	...	...	...	...	...	...	1	...	...	...	...	...
...	...	...	...	...	...	...	...	...	...	...	...	...	...
...	...	...	...	...	...	...	...	...	...	...	...	...	...
9	7	...	...	...	...	2	...	...	...	...	...	...	...
...	...	...	...	...	...	...	...	...	...	...	...	...	...
9	4	...	...	...	...	2	...	3	...	...	...	...	...
...	...	...	...	...	...	...	...	...	...	...	...	...	...
...	...	...	...	...	...	...	...	...	...	...	...	...	...
11	1	...	...	...	...	10	...	...	...	...	...	...	...
...	...	...	...	...	...	...	...	...	...	...	...	...	...
...	...	...	...	...	...	...	...	...	...	...	...	...	...
12	...	...	...	...	...	...	...	12	...	...	...	...	...
...	...	...	...	...	...	...	...	...	...	...	...	...	...
...	...	...	...	...	...	...	...	...	...	...	...	...	...
...	...	...	...	...	...	...	...	...	...	...	...	...	...
...	...	...	...	...	...	...	...	...	...	...	...	...	...
1	...	...	...	...	1	...	...	...	...	...	...	...	...
...	...	...	...	...	...	...	...	...	...	...	...	...	...
...	...	...	...	...	...	...	...	...	...	...	...	...	...
5	...	...	...	...	...	5	...	...	...	...	...	...	...
...	...	...	...	...	...	...	...	...	...	...	...	...	...
...	...	...	...	...	...	...	...	...	...	...	...	...	...
...	...	...	...	...	...	...	...	...	...	...	...	...	...
...	...	...	...	...	...	...	...	...	...	...	...	...	...
1	...	...	...	...	...	...	...	...	...	...	...	1	...
2	...	...	...	...	...	2	...	...	...	...	...	...	...
2,306	654	50	404	5	8	650	64	196	60	135	40	36	4
15,246	4,418	343	2,333	39	55	4,523	374	1,295	505	1,067	217	60	17

ಒಟ್ಟು ಹೆಂಗಸರು. Total Females.	ಹೆಂಗಸರು. Females. ಋಗ್ವೇದಿಗಳು. Rigvédis. ಸ್ಮಾರ್ತ. Smártás.	ಭಾಗವತ ಸಂಪ್ರದಾಯ. Bhágavata Sampradáya.	ಮಧ್ವ. Mádhvás.	ಶ್ರೀವೈಷ್ಣವ. S'rivaishnavas. ತೆಂಗಲೆ. Tengalé.	ವಡಗಲೆ. Vadagalé.	ಯಜುರ್ವೇದಿಗಳು. Yajurvédis. ಸ್ಮಾರ್ತ. Smártás.	ಭಾಗವತ ಸಂಪ್ರದಾಯ. Bhágavata Sampradáya.	ಮಧ್ವ. Mádhvás.	ಶ್ರೀವೈಷ್ಣವ. S'rivaishnavas. ತೆಂಗಲೆ. Tengalé.	ವಡಗಲೆ. Vadagalé.	ಸಾಮವೇದಿಗಳು. Sámavédis. ಸ್ಮಾರ್ತ. Smártás.	ಮಧ್ವ. Mádhvás.	ಶ್ರೀವೈಷ್ಣವ. S'rivaishnavas.
11,354	3,287	277	1,740	60	46	3,187	255	1,065	440	814	128	37	18
2	...	...	1	...	...	1	...	...	...	...	...	...	...
3	...	...	...	...	...	3	...	...	...	...	...	...	...
...	...	...	...	...	...	...	...	...	...	...	...	...	...
36	11	...	...	...	...	23	...	...	...	2	...	...	...
...	...	...	...	...	...	...	...	...	...	...	...	...	...
...	...	...	...	...	...	...	...	...	...	...	...	...	...
13	...	...	...	...	...	12	...	1	...	...	...	...	...
...	...	...	...	...	...	...	...	...	...	...	...	...	...
...	...	...	...	...	...	...	...	...	...	...	...	...	...
6	5	...	...	...	...	1	...	...	...	...	...	...	...
...	...	...	...	...	...	...	...	...	...	...	...	...	...
7	...	...	2	...	...	2	...	3	...	...	...	...	...
...	...	...	...	...	...	...	...	...	...	...	...	...	...
...	...	...	...	...	...	...	...	...	...	...	...	...	...
12	1	1	1	...	...	9	...	...	...	...	...	...	...
...	...	...	...	...	...	...	...	...	...	...	...	...	...
...	...	...	...	...	...	...	...	...	...	...	...	...	...
7	...	...	...	...	...	...	...	7	...	...	...	...	...
...	...	...	...	...	...	...	...	...	...	...	...	...	...
...	...	...	...	...	...	...	...	...	...	...	...	...	...
...	...	...	...	...	...	...	...	...	...	...	...	...	...
...	...	...	...	...	...	...	...	...	...	...	...	...	...
...	...	...	...	...	...	...	...	...	...	...	...	...	...
...	...	...	...	...	...	...	...	...	...	...	...	...	...
...	...	...	...	...	...	...	...	...	...	...	...	...	...
3	...	...	...	...	...	3	...	...	...	...	...	...	...
...	...	...	...	...	...	...	...	...	...	...	...	...	...
...	...	...	...	...	...	...	...	...	...	...	...	...	...
...	...	...	...	...	...	...	...	...	...	...	...	...	...
...	...	...	...	...	...	...	...	...	...	...	...	...	...
1	...	...	...	...	1	...	...	...	...	...	...	...	...
...	...	...	...	...	...	...	...	...	...	...	...	...	...
2,912	810	64	480	10	22	864	73	265	96	147	47	19	15
14,356	4,114	342	2,224	70	68	4,105	328	1,341	536	963	175	56	33

Total Males.	Males. Rigvédis. Smártás.	Rigvédis. Bhágavata Sampradáya.	Rigvédis. Mádhvás.	Rigvédis. S'rivaishnavás. Tengalé.	Rigvédis. S'rivaishnavás. Vadagalé.	Yajurvédis. Smártás.	Yajurvédis. Bhágavata Sampradáya.	Yajurvédis. Mádhvás.	Yajurvédis. S'rivaishnavás. Tengalé.	Yajurvédis. S'rivaishnavás. Vadagalé.	Sámavédis. Smártás.	Sámavédis. Mádhvás.	Sámavédis. S'rivaishnavás.
10,211	8,121	471	1,469	472	116	3,219	308	1,023	450	371	117	54	20
...	...	...	...	...	...	...	...	...	...	...	...	...	...
37	4	...	1	...	...	29	...	1	2	...	...	...	...
...	...	...	...	...	...	...	...	...	...	...	...	...	...
3	...	...	2	...	...	1	...	...	...	...	...	...	...
3	...	...	...	...	...	...	3	...	...	...	...	...	...
...	...	...	...	...	...	...	...	...	...	...	...	...	...
...	...	...	...	...	...	...	...	...	...	...	...	...	...
...	...	...	...	...	...	...	...	...	...	...	...	...	...
...	...	...	...	...	...	...	...	...	...	...	...	...	...
...	...	...	...	...	...	...	...	...	...	...	...	...	...
...	...	...	...	...	...	...	...	...	...	...	...	...	...
...	...	...	...	...	...	...	...	...	...	...	...	...	...
...	...	...	...	...	...	...	...	...	...	...	...	...	...
...	...	...	...	...	...	...	...	...	...	...	...	...	...
13	2	...	...	...	...	3	2	6	...	...	...	...	...
7	...	...	1	...	...	2	4	...	...	...	...	...	...
6	3	...	...	...	...	3	...	...	...	...	...	...	...
23	1	...	2	...	1	...	...	19	...	...	...	...	...
...	...	...	...	...	...	...	...	...	...	...	...	...	...
7	...	...	...	...	...	7	...	...	...	...	...	...	...
...	...	...	...	...	...	...	...	...	...	...	...	...	...
3	...	...	...	...	...	3	...	...	...	...	...	...	...
7	...	...	...	...	2	...	...	...	...	...	...	...	...
15	5	...	...	...	...	8	...	...	...	2	...	...	5
1	[illegible]	[illegible]	...	...	...	...	...	...	...	...	...	...	...
...	...	...	...	...	...	...	...	...	...	...	...	...	...
...	...	...	...	...	...	...	...	...	...	...	...	...	...
...	...	...	...	...	...	...	...	...	...	...	...	...	...
...	...	...	...	...	...	...	...	...	...	...	...	...	...
5	...	9	...	...	...	...	...	...	...	...	...	...	...
...	...	...	...	...	...	...	...	...	...	...	...	...	...
...	...	...	...	...	...	...	...	...	...	...	...	...	...
1,348	201	82	196	55	11	396	58	138	50	38	38	16	6
11,693	8,401	562	1,671	527	130	3,671	375	1,187	502	411	155	70	31

ಒಟ್ಟು ಹೆಂಗಸರು. Total Females.	ಹೆಂಗಸರು. Females.												
	ಋಗ್ವೇದಿಗಳು. Rigvédis.					ಯಜುರ್ವೇದಿಗಳು. Yojurvédis.					ಸಾಮವೇದಿಗಳು. Sámavédis.		
	ಸ್ಮಾರ್ತರು. Smártás.	ಭಾಗವತ ಸಂಪ್ರದಾಯ. Bhágavata Sampradáya.	ಮಾಧ್ವರು. Mádhvás.	ಶ್ರೀವೈಷ್ಣವರು. S'rivaishnavás. ತೆಂಗಲೆ. Tengalé.	ಶ್ರೀವೈಷ್ಣವರು. S'rivaishnavás. ವಡಗಲೆ. Vadaghalé.	ಸ್ಮಾರ್ತರು. Smártás.	ಭಾಗವತ ಸಂಪ್ರದಾಯ. Bhágavata Sampradáya.	ಮಾಧ್ವರು. Mádhvás.	ಶ್ರೀವೈಷ್ಣವರು. S'rivaishnavás. ತೆಂಗಲೆ. Tengalé.	ಶ್ರೀವೈಷ್ಣವರು. S'rivaishnavás. ವಡಗಲೆ. Vadaghalé.	ಸ್ಮಾರ್ತರು. Smártás.	ಮಾಧ್ವರು. Mádhvás.	ಶ್ರೀವೈಷ್ಣವರು. S'rivaishnavás.
9,962	**1,999**	**464**	**1,337**	**31**	**65**	**3,680**	**301**	**1,078**	**445**	**381**	**97**	**69**	**15**
...	...	...	...	...	...	...	...	...	...	...	...	...	...
35	7	...	...	...	...	26	...	2	...	...	...	...	...
...	...	...	...	...	...	...	...	...	...	...	...	...	...
5	...	...	1	1	...	...	...	3	...	...	...	...	...
4	...	...	...	...	...	4	...	...	...	...	...	...	...
...	...	...	...	...	...	...	...	...	...	...	...	...	...
...	...	...	...	...	...	...	...	...	...	...	...	...	...
...	...	...	...	...	...	...	...	...	...	...	...	...	...
...	...	...	...	...	...	...	...	...	...	...	...	...	...
...	...	...	...	...	...	...	...	...	...	...	...	...	...
...	...	...	...	...	...	...	...	...	...	...	...	...	...
4	...	...	...	...	...	1	...	1	...	2	...	...	...
[illegible]	...	...	...	...	...	...	...	...	...	...	...	...	...
...	...	...	...	...	...	...	...	...	...	...	...	...	...
4	1	...	...	...	...	...	...	3	...	...	...	...	...
4	...	...	...	...	...	4	...	...	...	...	...	...	...
4	...	...	...	...	...	...	...	...	...	4	...	...	...
45	...	...	3	...	...	7	...	25	3	...	1	6	...
...	...	...	...	...	...	...	...	...	...	...	...	...	...
18	4	...	...	...	...	7	2	5	...	...	...	...	...
...	...	...	...	...	...	...	...	...	...	...	...	...	...
2	...	...	...	...	...	2	...	...	...	...	...	...	...
7	...	...	...	...	...	...	...	...	...	2	...	...	...
9	5	...	...	...	...	...	...	2	...	2	...	...	...
1	1	...	...	...	...	...	...	...	...	...	...	...	...
...	...	...	...	...	...	...	...	...	...	...	...	...	...
...	...	...	...	...	...	...	...	...	...	...	...	...	...
...	...	...	...	...	...	...	...	...	...	...	...	...	...
...	...	...	...	...	...	...	...	...	...	...	...	...	...
11	...	11	...	...	...	...	...	...	...	...	...	...	...
...	...	...	...	...	...	...	...	...	...	...	...	...	...
...	...	...	...	...	...	...	...	...	...	...	...	...	...
1,517	342	70	187	6	10	531	80	160	75	35	35	24	6
11,632	**2,359**	**551**	**1,528**	**38**	**75**	**4,262**	**333**	**1,278**	**523**	**426**	**133**	**99**	**26**

Total Males.	Males.												
	Rigvédis.					Yajurvédis.					Sámavédis.		
				S'rivaishnavás.					Srivaishnavás.				
	Smártás.	Bhágavata Sampradáya.	Mádhvás.	Tengalé.	Vadagalé.	Smártás.	Bhágavata Sampradáya.	Mádhvás.	Tengalé.	Vadagalé.	Smártás.	Mádhvás.	S'rivaishnavás.
7,773	2,521	572	1,239	14	23	1,949	345	341	122	530	91	13	13
...	...	...	...	...	...	...	...	...	...	...	...	...	...
5	...	...	...	...	...	5	...	...	...	...	...	...	...
...	...	...	...	...	...	...	...	...	...	...	...	...	...
...	...	...	...	...	...	...	...	...	...	...	...	...	...
...	...	...	...	...	...	...	...	...	...	...	...	...	...
...	...	...	...	...	...	...	...	...	...	...	...	...	...
...	...	...	...	...	...	...	...	...	...	...	...	...	...
...	...	...	...	...	...	...	...	...	...	...	...	...	...
...	...	...	...	...	...	...	...	...	...	...	...	...	...
...	...	...	...	...	...	...	...	...	...	...	...	...	...
...	...	...	...	...	...	...	...	...	...	...	...	...	...
...	...	...	...	...	...	...	...	...	...	...	...	...	...
...	...	...	...	...	...	...	...	...	...	...	...	...	...
...	...	...	...	...	...	...	...	...	...	...	...	...	...
...	...	...	...	...	...	...	...	...	...	...	...	...	...
...	...	...	...	...	...	...	...	...	...	...	...	...	...
...	...	...	...	...	...	...	...	...	...	...	...	...	...
6	...	2	...	...	...	...	4	...	...	...	...	...	...
...	...	...	...	...	...	...	...	...	...	...	...	...	...
15	3	...	...	...	...	12	...	...	...	...	...	...	...
...	...	...	...	...	...	...	...	...	...	...	...	...	...
...	...	...	...	...	...	...	...	...	...	...	...	...	...
...	...	...	...	...	...	...	...	...	...	...	...	...	...
...	...	...	...	...	...	...	...	...	...	...	...	...	...
...	...	...	...	...	...	...	...	...	...	...	...	...	...
...	...	...	...	...	...	...	...	...	...	...	...	...	...
...	...	...	...	...	...	...	...	...	...	...	...	...	...
...	...	...	...	...	...	...	...	...	...	...	...	...	...
...	...	...	...	...	...	...	...	...	...	...	...	...	...
...	...	...	...	...	...	...	...	...	...	...	...	...	...
...	...	...	...	...	...	...	...	...	...	...	...	...	...
...	...	...	...	...	...	...	...	...	...	...	...	...	...
...	...	...	...	...	...	...	...	...	...	...	...	...	...
771	240	...	...	...	12	192	...	...	...	...	318	3	6
8,570	2,764	574	1,239	14	35	2,158	349	341	122	530	409	16	19

Total Females.	Females. Rigvêdis. Smârtas.	Rigvêdis. Bhâgavata Sampradâya.	Rigvêdis. Mâdhvas.	Rigvêdis. S'rîvaishnavas. Tengalé.	Rigvêdis. S'rîvaishnavas. Vadagalé.	Yajurvêdis. Smârtas.	Yajurvêdis. Bhâgavata Sampradâya.	Yajurvêdis. Mâdhvas.	Yajurvêdis. S'rîvaishnavas. Tengalé.	Yajurvêdis. S'rîvaishnavas. Vadagalé.	Sâmavêdis. Smârtas.	Sâmavêdis. Mâdhvas.	Sâmavêdis. S'rîvaishnavas.
7,239	2,265	482	1,284	...	34	1,790	326	299	101	479	135	21	33
...	...	...	...	...	...	...	...	...	...	...	...	...	...
5	...	...	...	...	...	5	...	...	...	...	...	...	...
...	...	...	...	...	...	...	...	...	...	...	...	...	...
5	3	...	...	...	...	1	...	1	...	...	...	...	...
...	...	...	...	...	...	...	...	...	...	...	...	...	...
...	...	...	...	...	...	...	...	...	...	...	...	...	...
...	...	...	...	...	...	...	...	...	...	...	...	...	...
1	1	...	...	...	...	...	...	...	...	...	...	...	...
...	...	...	...	...	...	...	...	...	...	...	...	...	...
2	...	...	2	...	...	...	...	...	...	...	...	...	...
...	...	...	...	...	...	...	...	...	...	...	...	...	...
2	...	2	...	...	...	...	...	...	...	...	...	...	...
...	...	...	...	...	...	...	...	...	...	...	...	...	...
...	...	...	...	...	...	...	...	...	...	...	...	...	...
15	5	...	...	...	...	9	...	1	...	...	...	...	...
...	...	...	...	...	...	...	...	...	...	...	...	...	...
...	...	...	...	...	...	...	...	...	...	...	...	...	...
2	2	...	...	...	...	...	...	...	...	...	...	...	...
...	...	...	...	...	...	...	...	...	...	...	...	...	...
27	...	...	...	...	...	25	1	...	1	...	...	...	...
...	...	...	...	...	...	...	...	...	...	...	...	...	...
...	...	...	...	...	...	...	...	...	...	...	...	...	...
...	...	...	...	...	...	...	...	...	...	...	...	...	...
...	...	...	...	...	...	...	...	...	...	...	...	...	...
7	...	...	...	...	...	4	...	3	...	...	...	...	...
...	...	...	...	...	...	...	...	...	...	...	...	...	...
...	...	...	...	...	...	...	...	...	...	...	...	...	...
7	5	...	...	...	...	...	2	...	...	...	...	...	...
...	...	...	...	...	...	...	...	...	...	...	...	...	...
...	...	...	...	...	...	...	...	...	...	...	...	...	...
...	...	...	...	...	...	...	...	...	...	...	...	...	...
1,125	*404*	...	...	...	4	589	...	...	...	...	120	3	5
8,437	2,685	484	1,286	...	38	2,423	329	304	102	479	255	24	38

Total Males.	Males. Rigvédis. Smártás.	Rigvédis. Bhágavata Sampradáya.	Rigvédis. Mádhvás.	Rigvédis. S'rívaishnavás. Tengalé.	Rigvédis. S'rívaishnavás. Vadagalé.	Yajurvédis. Smártás.	Yajurvédis. Bhágavata Sampradáya.	Yajurvédis. Mádhvás.	Yajurvédis. S'rívaishnavás. Tengalé.	Yajurvédis. S'rívaishnavás. Vadagalé.	Sámavédis. Smártás.	Sámavédis. Mádhvás.	Sámavédis. S'rívaishnavás.
16,518	**5,502**	**389**	**2,018**	**131**	**227**	**3,738**	**359**	**904**	**1,258**	**1,442**	**398**	**45**	**112**
4	1	...	...	...	...	1	...	...	...	...	...	2	...
36	8	...	...	...	...	23	5	...	...	...	...	...	...
19	...	...	...	1	...	13	...	...	4	1	...	...	...
31	22	...	2	...	...	6	...	1	...	...	...	...	...
54	20	...	...	...	24	7	...	3	...	...	...	...	...
20	3	...	...	...	...	17	...	...	...	...	...	...	...
7	1	...	...	...	...	6	...	...	...	...	...	...	...
3	3	...	...	...	...	...	...	...	...	...	...	...	...
4	...	...	4	...	...	...	...	...	...	...	...	...	...
42	...	...	...	...	...	38	2	2	...	...	...	...	...
4	...	...	...	...	...	4	...	...	...	...	...	...	...
10	...	...	2	1	...	6	...	1	...	...	...	...	...
1	1	...	...	...	...	...	...	...	...	...	...	...	...
1	...	...	...	...	...	1	...	...	...	...	...	...	...
7	3	...	...	...	...	3	...	...	1	...	...	...	...
12	2	...	...	...	...	9	1	...	...	...	...	...	...
2	...	...	...	...	...	...	...	...	...	2	...	...	...
9	1	...	...	...	...	4	...	4	...	...	...	...	...
1	...	...	...	...	...	...	...	...	...	1	...	...	...
...	...	...	...	...	...	...	...	...	...	...	...	...	...
...	...	...	...	...	...	...	...	...	...	...	...	...	...
...	...	...	...	...	...	...	...	...	...	...	...	...	...
...	...	...	...	...	...	...	...	...	...	...	...	...	...
...	...	...	...	...	...	...	...	...	...	...	...	...	...
...	...	...	...	...	...	...	...	...	...	...	...	...	...
...	...	...	...	...	...	...	...	...	...	...	...	...	...
...	...	...	...	...	...	...	...	...	...	...	...	...	...
...	...	...	...	...	...	...	...	...	...	...	...	...	...
...	...	...	...	...	...	...	...	...	...	...	...	...	...
...	...	...	...	...	...	...	...	...	...	...	...	...	...
...	...	...	...	...	...	...	...	...	...	...	...	...	...
...	...	...	...	...	...	...	...	...	...	...	...	...	...
4,638	1,533	...	13	36	70	785	...	...	...	123	1,692	114	72
21,223	**7,100**	**389**	**2,039**	**169**	**321**	**4,656**	**367**	**915**	**1,263**	**1,569**	**2,090**	**161**	**184**

Total Females.	Rigvédis. Smártás.	Rigvédis. Bhágavata Sampradáya.	Rigvédis. Mádhvás.	Rigvédis. S'rivaishnavás. Tengalé.	Rigvédis. S'rivaishnavás. Vadagalé.	Yajurvédis. Smártás.	Yajurvédis. Bhágavata Sampradáya.	Yajurvédis. Mádhvás.	Yajurvédis. S'rivaishnavás. Tengalé.	Yajurvédis. S'rivaishnavás. Vadagalé.	Sámavédis. Smártás.	Sámavédis. Mádhvás.	Sámavédis. S'rivaishnavás.
16,353	5,456	399	8,106	174	280	3,742	331	956	1,066	1,388	303	59	94
1	...	...	...	...	1	...	...	...	...	...	...	...	...
34	2	...	...	...	...	23	5	5	...	...	...	...	...
6	...	2	1	...	...	...	...	...	3	...	...	...	...
43	24	...	7	...	...	8	...	4	...	...	...	...	...
29	2	...	...	...	...	22	5	...	...	...	...	...	...
28	...	...	...	...	...	28	...	...	...	...	...	...	...
16	2	...	...	2	...	9	3	...	...	...	...	...	...
2	2	...	...	...	...	...	...	...	...	...	...	...	...
5	...	...	5	...	...	...	...	...	...	...	...	...	...
31	1	...	...	...	...	27	...	3	...	...	...	...	...
3	3	...	...	...	...	...	...	...	...	...	...	...	...
8	1	...	1	...	...	5	1	...	...	...	...	...	...
...	...	...	...	...	...	...	...	...	...	...	...	...	...
3	3	...	...	...	...	...	...	...	...	...	...	...	...
8	2	...	...	...	2	2	1	...	...	1	...	...	...
...	...	...	...	...	...	...	...	...	...	...	...	...	...
5	...	...	...	...	...	...	...	...	...	5	...	...	...
5	3	...	2	...	...	...	...	...	...	...	...	...	...
9	...	...	...	...	3	6	...	...	...	...	...	...	...
1	1	...	...	...	...	...	...	...	...	...	...	...	...
1	...	...	1	...	...	...	...	...	...	...	...	...	...
41	5	...	...	...	...	27	...	...	...	2	7	...	...
...	...	...	...	...	...	...	...	...	...	...	...	...	...
...	...	...	...	...	...	...	...	...	...	...	...	...	...
...	...	...	...	...	...	...	...	...	...	...	...	...	...
...	...	...	...	...	...	...	...	...	...	...	...	...	...
...	...	...	...	...	...	...	...	...	...	...	...	...	...
...	...	...	...	...	...	...	...	...	...	...	...	...	...
...	...	...	...	...	...	...	...	...	...	...	...	...	...
...	...	...	...	...	...	...	...	...	...	...	...	...	...
...	...	...	...	...	...	...	...	...	...	...	...	...	...
...	...	...	...	...	...	...	...	...	...	...	...	...	...
5,143	2,065	...	...	64	150	2,053	...	...	...	...	730	71	10
21,775	7,571	401	2,123	240	436	5,951	346	968	1,069	1,396	1,040	130	104

Total Males.	Males. Rigvédis. Smártás.	Rigvédis. Bhágavata Sampradáya.	Rigvédis. Mádhvás.	Rigvédis. S'rivaishnavás. Tengalé.	Rigvédis. S'rivaishnavás. Vadagalé.	Yajurvédis. Smártás.	Yajurvédis. Bhágavata Sampradáya.	Yajurvédis. Mádhvás.	Yajurvédis. S'rivaishnavás. Tengalé.	Yajurvédis. S'rivaishnavás. Vadagalé.	Sámavédis. Smártás.	Sámavédis. Mádhvás.	Sámavédis. S'rivaishnavás.
7,166	2,054	222	338	14	246	2,120	383	156	203	1,249	122	27	32
...	...	...	...	...	...	...	...	...	...	...	...	...	...
2	...	...	...	...	...	2	...	...	...	...	...	...	...
...	...	...	...	...	...	...	...	...	...	...	...	...	...
30	11	3	...	...	1	1	...	14	...	...	...	...	...
156	3	...	...	...	...	139	14	...	...	...	...	...	...
...	...	...	...	...	...	...	...	...	...	...	...	...	...
52	4	...	...	...	...	46	...	...	...	...	2	...	...
...	...	...	...	...	...	...	...	...	...	...	...	...	...
19	7	1	...	...	...	9	1	...	...	...	...	1	...
3	...	...	...	...	...	3	...	...	...	...	...	...	...
...	...	...	...	...	...	...	...	...	...	...	...	...	...
30	6	...	1	...	...	21	1	1	...	...	...	...	...
...	...	...	...	...	...	...	...	...	...	...	...	...	...
...	...	...	...	...	...	...	...	...	...	...	...	...	...
13	1	...	1	...	...	11	...	...	...	...	...	...	...
...	...	...	...	...	...	...	...	...	...	...	...	...	...
...	...	...	...	...	...	...	...	...	...	...	...	...	...
...	...	...	...	...	...	...	...	...	...	...	...	...	...
...	...	...	...	...	...	...	...	...	...	...	...	...	...
...	...	...	...	...	...	...	...	...	...	...	...	...	...
...	...	...	...	...	...	...	...	...	...	...	...	...	...
...	...	...	...	...	...	...	...	...	...	...	...	...	...
...	...	...	...	...	...	...	...	...	...	...	...	...	...
1	...	1	...	...	...	...	...	...	...	...	...	...	...
3	...	...	...	...	...	...	...	...	3	...	...	...	...
9	5	...	...	...	...	...	...	...	...	4	...	...	...
6	...	...	...	...	...	6	...	...	...	...	...	...	...
...	...	...	...	...	...	...	...	...	...	...	...	...	...
...	...	...	...	...	...	...	...	...	...	...	...	...	...
...	...	...	...	...	...	...	...	...	...	...	...	...	...
...	...	...	...	...	...	...	...	...	...	...	...	...	...
...	...	...	...	...	...	...	...	...	...	...	...	...	...
1,009	318	...	...	9	31	301	...	...	...	...	305	8	37
8,499	2,400	227	340	23	278	2,659	399	171	206	1,253	429	36	69

ಒಟ್ಟು ಹೆಂಗಸರು. Total Females.	ಹೆಂಗಸರು. Females.												
	ಋಗ್ವೇದಿಗಳು. Rigvédís.					ಯಜುರ್ವೇದಿಗಳು. Yajurvédis.					ಸಾಮವೇದಿಗಳು. Sámavédis.		
				ಶ್ರೀವೈಷ್ಣವ. S'rivaishnavás.					ಶ್ರೀವೈಷ್ಣವ. S'rivaishnavás.				
	ಸ್ಮಾರ್ತ. Smártás.	ಭಾಗವತ ಸಂಪ್ರದಾಯ. Bhágavata Sampradáya.	ಮಾಧ್ವ. Mádhvás.	ತೆಂಗಲೆ. Tengalé.	ವಡಗಲೆ. Vadagalé.	ಸ್ಮಾರ್ತ. Smártás.	ಭಾಗವತ ಸಂಪ್ರದಾಯ. Bhágavata Sampradáya.	ಮಾಧ್ವ. Mádhvás.	ತೆಂಗಲೆ. Tengalé.	ವಡಗಲೆ. Vadagalé.	ಸ್ಮಾರ್ತ. Smártás.	ಮಾಧ್ವ. Mádhvás.	ಶ್ರೀವೈಷ್ಣವ. S'rivaishnavás.
7,147	2,065	240	300	35	493	1,812	299	157	218	1,423	70	28	7
...	...	...	...	...	...	...	...	...	...	...	...	...	...
... 3	...	...	...	...	...	...	...	...	...	...	...	...	...
...	...	...	...	...	...	...	...	...	...	...	...	...	...
34	13	2	...	...	...	5	2	12	...	...	...	...	...
124	...	4	...	...	...	115	5	...	...	...	...	...	...
...	...	...	...	...	...	...	...	...	...	...	...	...	...
34	...	...	...	...	...	32	...	...	...	2	...	...	...
...	...	...	...	...	...	...	...	...	...	...	...	...	...
...	...	...	...	...	...	...	...	...	...	...	...	...	...
5	...	...	...	...	...	5	...	...	...	...	...	...	...
...	...	...	...	...	...	...	...	...	...	...	...	...	...
39	3	...	...	...	...	36	...	...	...	...	...	...	...
...	...	...	...	...	...	...	...	...	...	...	...	...	...
...	...	...	...	...	...	...	...	...	...	...	...	...	...
10	6	...	...	...	...	4	...	...	...	...	...	...	...
...	...	...	...	...	...	...	...	...	...	...	...	...	...
...	...	...	...	...	...	...	...	...	...	...	...	...	...
...	...	...	...	...	...	...	...	...	...	...	...	...	...
...	...	...	...	...	...	...	...	...	...	...	...	...	...
...	...	...	...	...	...	...	...	...	...	...	...	...	...
...	...	...	...	...	...	...	...	...	...	...	...	...	...
...	...	...	...	...	...	...	...	...	...	...	...	...	...
...	...	...	...	...	...	...	...	...	...	...	...	...	...
3	...	...	...	...	...	...	...	...	3	...	...	...	...
9	3	...	4	...	...	...	...	...	...	...	...	...	...
5	...	...	...	...	...	5	...	...	...	...	...	...	...
...	...	...	...	...	...	...	...	...	...	...	...	...	...
...	...	...	...	...	...	...	...	...	...	...	...	...	...
...	...	...	...	...	...	...	...	...	...	...	...	...	...
...	...	...	...	...	...	...	...	...	...	...	...	...	...
...	...	...	...	...	...	...	...	...	...	...	...	...	...
1,151	202	...	...	8	110	490	...	...	...	...	109	9	33
8,561	2,482	246	304	43	603	2,504	306	169	221	1,425	181	37	40

Total Males.	Males. Rigvédis. Smártás.	Rigvédis. Bhágavata Sampradáya.	Rigvédis. Mádhvás.	Rigvédis. S'rivaishnavás. Tengalé.	Rigvédis. S'rivaishnavás. Vadagalé.	Yejurvédis. Smártás.	Yejurvédis. Bhágavata Sampradáya.	Yejurvédis. Mádhvás.	Yejurvédis. S'rivaishnavás. Tengalé.	Yejurvédis. S'rivaishnavás. Vadagalé.	Sámavédis. Smártás.	Sámavédis. Mádhvás.	Sámavédis. S'rivaishnavás.
11,991	3,800	565	1,695	46	130	4,011	734	860	84	189	76	8	2
...	...	...	...	...	...	...	...	...	...	...	...	...	...
7	...	...	...	3	...	...	...	...	4	...	...	...	...
11	...	...	9	...	...	2	...	...	...	...	...	...	...
5	...	...	...	...	...	5	...	...	...	...	...	...	...
26	...	...	...	...	...	26	...	...	...	...	...	...	...
...	...	...	...	...	...	...	...	...	...	...	...	...	...
...	...	...	...	...	...	...	...	...	...	...	...	...	...
...	...	...	...	...	...	...	...	...	...	...	...	...	...
1	...	...	...	...	...	...	...	1	...	...	...	...	...
17	9	...	1	...	...	7	...	...	...	...	...	...	...
...	...	...	...	...	...	...	...	...	...	...	...	...	...
582	227	42	33	...	...	231	40	5	...	...	3	...	1
...	...	...	...	...	...	...	...	...	...	...	...	...	...
...	...	...	...	...	...	...	...	...	...	...	...	...	...
8	1	...	6	...	...	1	...	...	...	...	...	...	...
1	1	...	...	...	...	...	...	...	...	...	...	...	...
...	...	...	2	...	...	...	...	...	...	...	...	...	...
...	...	...	...	...	...	...	...	...	...	...	...	...	...
5	...	...	5	...	...	...	...	...	...	...	...	...	...
7	6	...	...	...	...	1	...	...	...	...	...	...	...
...	...	...	...	...	...	...	...	...	...	...	...	...	...
...	...	...	...	...	...	...	...	...	...	...	...	...	...
...	...	...	...	...	...	...	...	...	...	...	...	...	...
...	...	...	...	...	...	...	...	...	...	...	...	...	...
8	7	...	...	...	...	...	...	1	...	...	...	...	...
6	...	...	5	...	...	1	...	...	...	...	...	...	...
...	...	...	...	...	...	...	...	...	...	...	...	...	...
41	1	...	40	...	...	...	...	...	...	...	...	...	...
14	5	...	4	...	...	...	1	...	4	...	...	...	...
8	4	...	3	...	...	...	1	...	...	...	...	...	...
...	...	...	...	...	...	...	...	...	...	...	...	...	...
...	...	...	...	...	...	...	...	...	...	...	...	...	...
2,990	1,200	78	...	...	12	460	...	...	...	5	1,200	19	16
15,728	5,261	685	1,801	49	142	4,745	776	867	92	185	1279	27	19

Total Females.	Females. Rigvédis. Smártás.	Rigvédis. Bhágavata Sampradáya.	Rigvédis. Mádhvás.	Rigvédis. S'rivaishnavas. Tengalé.	Rigvédis. S'rivaishnavas. Vadagalé.	Yejurvédis. Smártás.	Yejurvédis. Bhágavata Sampradáya.	Yejurvédis. Mádhvás.	Yejurvédis. S'rivaishnavás. Tengalé.	Yejurvédis. S'rivaishnavás. Vadagalé.	Sámavédis. Smártás.	Sámavédis. Mádhvás.	Sámavédis. S'rivaishnavás.
11,250	3,365	557	1,747	64	76	3,983	599	574	88	105	87	1	4
...	...	...	...	...	...	...	...	...	...	...	...	...	...
7	...	...	2	...	...	...	...	5	...	...	...	...	...
...	...	...	...	...	...	...	...	...	...	...	...	...	...
4	1	...	2	...	...	...	...	1	...	...	...	...	...
27	...	...	...	...	...	27	...	...	...	...	...	...	...
...	...	...	...	...	...	...	...	...	...	...	...	...	...
...	...	...	...	...	...	...	...	...	...	...	...	...	...
...	...	...	...	...	...	...	...	...	...	...	...	...	...
5	...	3	...	...	...	...	...	2	...	...	...	...	...
20	7	...	7	...	1	3	2	...	...	...	...	...	...
...	...	...	...	...	...	...	...	...	...	...	...	...	...
516	227	41	24	...	...	209	82	5	...	...	...	...	...
...	...	...	...	...	...	...	...	...	...	...	...	...	...
...	...	...	...	...	...	...	...	...	...	...	...	...	...
5	1	...	2	...	...	2	...	...	...	...	...	...	...
2	2	...	...	...	...	...	...	...	...	...	...	...	...
...	...	...	...	...	...	...	...	...	...	...	...	...	...
...	...	...	...	...	...	...	...	...	...	...	...	...	...
7	...	...	7	...	...	...	...	...	...	...	...	...	...
10	10	...	...	...	...	...	...	...	...	...	...	...	...
...	...	...	...	...	...	...	...	...	...	...	...	...	...
...	...	...	...	...	...	...	...	...	...	...	...	...	...
...	...	...	...	...	...	...	...	...	...	...	...	...	...
...	...	...	...	...	...	...	...	...	...	...	...	...	...
3	2	...	...	...	...	1	...	...	...	...	...	...	...
4	2	...	...	...	...	2	...	...	...	...	...	...	...
...	...	...	...	...	...	...	...	...	...	...	...	...	...
1	1	...	...	...	...	...	...	...	...	...	...	...	...
5	...	...	[illegible]	...	...	...	...	1	...	...	...	...	...
1	1	...	...	...	...	...	...	...	...	...	...	...	...
...	...	...	...	...	...	...	...	...	...	...	...	...	...
...	...	...	...	...	...	...	...	...	...	...	...	...	...
1,749	549	53	54	70	...	700	5	...	150	85	39	50	44
13,646	4,168	657	1,849	134	77	4,927	638	588	238	140	131	51	48

Total Males.	Males. Rigvédis. Smártás.	Rigvédis. Bhágavata Sampradáya.	Rigvédis. Mádhvás.	Rigvédis. S'rívaishṇavás. Tengalé.	Rigvédis. S'rívaishṇavás. Vadagalé.	Yajurvédis. Smártás.	Yajurvédis. Bhágavata Sampradáya.	Yajurvédis. Mádhvás.	Yajurvédis. S'rívaishṇavás. Tengalé.	Yajurvédis. S'rívaishṇavás. Vadagalé.	Sámavédis. Smártás.	Sámavédis. Mádhvás.	Sámavédis. S'rívaishṇavás.
7,104	4,141	749	400	16	38	1,200	108	117	84	206	31	10	4
...	...	...	...	...	...	...	...	...	...	...	...	...	...
2	...	...	2	...	...	...	...	...	...	...	...	...	...
...	...	...	...	...	...	...	...	...	...	...	...	...	...
7	3	...	...	1	...	3	...	...	...	...	...	...	...
4	2	...	...	...	...	2	...	...	...	...	...	...	...
...	...	...	...	...	...	...	...	...	...	...	...	...	...
...	...	...	...	...	...	...	...	...	...	...	...	...	...
...	...	...	...	...	...	...	...	...	...	...	...	...	...
...	...	...	...	...	...	...	...	...	...	...	...	...	...
2	...	...	...	...	...	2	...	...	...	...	...	...	...
...	...	...	...	...	...	...	...	...	...	...	...	...	...
863	619	145	14	10	...	23	51	2	...	...	...	...	...
...	...	...	...	...	...	...	...	...	...	...	...	...	...
...	...	...	...	...	...	...	...	...	...	...	...	...	...
13	...	1	...	...	...	12	...	...	...	...	...	...	...
...	...	...	...	...	...	...	...	...	...	...	...	...	...
...	...	...	...	...	...	...	...	...	...	...	...	...	...
...	...	...	...	...	...	...	...	...	...	...	...	...	...
...	...	...	...	...	...	...	...	...	...	...	...	...	...
2	1	...	...	...	...	2	...	...	...	...	...	...	...
...	...	...	...	...	...	...	...	...	...	...	...	...	...
...	...	...	...	...	...	...	...	...	...	...	...	...	...
...	...	...	...	...	...	...	...	...	...	...	...	...	...
...	...	...	...	...	...	...	...	...	...	...	...	...	...
2	1	...	...	...	...	1	...	...	...	...	...	...	...
...	...	...	...	...	...	...	...	...	...	...	...	...	...
...	...	...	...	...	...	...	...	...	...	...	...	...	...
2	...	...	2	...	...	...	...	...	...	...	...	...	...
...	...	...	...	...	...	...	...	...	...	...	...	...	...
...	...	...	...	...	...	...	...	...	...	...	...	...	...
1	...	...	...	...	...	...	...	...	...	1	...	...	...
...	...	...	...	...	...	...	...	...	...	...	...	...	...
792	193	50	...	...	7	230	...	...	...	15	268	14	16
8,795	4,959	945	418	27	45	1,474	159	119	84	222	299	24	20

ಒಟ್ಟು ಹೆಂಗಸರು. Total Females.	ಹೆಂಗಸರು. Females. — ಋಗ್ವೇದಿಗಳು. Rigvédis. — ಸ್ಮಾರ್ತ. Smártás.	Rigvédis — Bhágavata Sámpradáya.	Rigvédis — ಮಾಧ್ವ. Mádhvás.	Rigvédis — ಶ್ರೀವೈಷ್ಣವ. S'rívaishṇavás. — Tengalé.	Rigvédis — S'rívaishṇavás — Vadagalé.	ಯಜುರ್ವೇದಿಗಳು. Yajurvédis. — ಸ್ಮಾರ್ತ. Smártás.	Yajurvédis — Bhágavata Sampradáya.	Yajurvédis — ಮಾಧ್ವ. Mádhvás.	Yajurvédis — ಶ್ರೀವೈಷ್ಣವ. S'rívaishṇavás. — Tengalé.	Yajurvédis — S'rívaishṇavás — Vadagalé.	ಸಾಮವೇದಿಗಳು. Sámavédis. — ಸ್ಮಾರ್ತ. Smártás.	Sámavédis — ಮಾಧ್ವ. Mádhvás.	Sámavédis — ಶ್ರೀವೈಷ್ಣವ. S'rívaishṇavás.
6,521	3,908	659	324	15	20	1,065	132	69	55	238	21	13	
...	...	...	...	...	...	...	...	...	...	...	...	...	...
5	...	5	...	...	...	...	...	...	...	...	...	...	...
...	...	...	...	...	...	...	...	...	...	...	...	...	...
9	6	...	...	...	...	3	...	...	...	...	...	...	...
...	...	...	...	...	...	...	...	...	...	...	...	...	...
...	...	...	...	...	...	...	...	...	...	...	...	...	...
...	...	...	...	...	...	...	...	...	...	...	...	...	...
...	...	...	...	...	...	...	...	...	...	...	...	...	...
...	...	...	...	...	...	...	...	...	...	...	...	...	...
...	...	...	...	...	...	...	...	...	...	...	...	...	...
...	...	...	...	...	...	...	...	...	...	...	...	...	...
826	617	94	30	...	...	81	1	3	...	...	...	...	...
...	...	...	...	...	...	...	...	...	...	...	...	...	...
...	...	...	...	...	...	...	...	...	...	...	...	...	...
12	4	1	...	...	...	6	...	1	...	...	...	...	...
...	...	...	...	...	...	...	...	...	...	...	...	...	...
...	...	...	...	...	...	...	...	...	...	...	...	...	...
...	...	...	...	...	...	...	...	...	...	...	...	...	...
...	...	...	...	...	...	...	...	...	...	...	...	...	...
4	1	...	...	...	...	3	...	...	...	...	...	...	...
...	...	...	...	...	...	...	...	...	...	...	...	...	...
...	...	...	...	...	...	...	...	...	...	...	...	...	...
...	...	...	...	...	...	...	...	...	...	...	...	...	...
...	...	...	...	...	...	...	...	...	...	...	...	...	...
...	...	...	...	...	...	...	...	...	...	...	...	...	...
...	...	...	...	...	...	...	...	...	...	...	...	...	...
...	...	...	...	...	...	...	...	...	...	...	...	...	...
...	...	...	...	...	...	...	...	...	...	...	...	...	...
...	...	...	...	...	...	...	...	...	...	...	...	...	...
...	...	...	...	...	...	...	...	...	...	...	...	...	...
2	...	...	...	...	...	2	...	...	...	...	...	...	...
...	...	...	...	...	...	...	...	...	...	...	...	...	...
852	261	32	43	64	...	297	15	...	37	15	10	60	18
8,231	4,797	791	397	79	20	1,457	148	73	92	248	31	73	25

Males.

Total Males.	Rigvedis. Smártás.	Rigvedis. Bhágavata Sampradáya.	Rigvedis. Mádhvás.	Rigvedis. S'rivaishnavás. Tengalé.	Rigvedis. S'rivaishnavás. Vadagalé.	Yajurvedis. Smártás.	Yajurvedis. Bhágavata Sampradáya.	Yajurvedis. Mádhvás.	Yajurvedis. S'rivaishnavás. Tengalé.	Yajurvedis. S'rivaishnavás. Vadagalé.	Sámavedis. Smártás.	Sámavedis. Mádhvás.	Sámavedis. S'rivaishnavás.
2,620	707	125	900	20	37	435	29	244	28	58	18	14	5
...	...	...	...	...	...	...	...	...	...	...	...	...	...
1	...	...	...	...	...	...	1	...	...	...	...	...	...
...	...	...	...	...	...	...	...	...	...	...	...	...	...
9	...	...	2	...	...	7	...	...	...	...	...	...	...
2	...	...	...	...	...	2	...	...	...	...	...	...	...
...	...	...	...	...	...	...	...	...	...	...	...	...	...
...	...	...	...	...	...	...	...	...	...	...	...	...	...
...	...	...	...	...	...	...	...	...	...	...	...	...	...
...	...	...	...	...	...	...	...	...	...	...	...	...	...
27	7	...	...	...	...	20	...	...	...	...	...	...	...
...	...	...	...	...	...	...	...	...	...	...	...	...	...
3	...	...	3	...	...	...	...	...	...	...	...	...	...
...	...	...	...	...	...	...	...	...	...	...	...	...	...
...	...	...	...	...	...	...	...	...	...	...	...	...	...
1	...	...	...	...	...	1	...	...	...	...	...	...	...
...	...	...	...	...	...	...	...	...	...	...	...	...	...
...	...	...	...	...	...	...	...	...	...	...	...	...	...
...	...	...	...	...	...	...	...	...	...	...	...	...	...
...	...	...	...	...	...	...	...	...	...	...	...	...	...
...	...	...	...	...	...	...	...	...	...	...	...	...	...
...	...	...	...	...	...	...	...	...	...	...	...	...	...
...	...	...	...	...	...	...	...	...	...	...	...	...	...
...	...	...	...	...	...	8	...	...	...	...	...	...	...
...	...	...	...	...	...	...	...	...	...	...	...	...	...
...	...	...	...	...	...	...	...	...	...	...	...	...	...
...	...	...	...	...	...	...	...	...	...	...	...	...	...
...	...	...	...	...	...	...	...	...	...	...	...	...	...
...	...	...	...	...	...	...	...	...	...	...	...	...	...
1	...	...	1	...	...	...	...	...	...	...	...	...	...
...	...	...	...	...	...	...	...	...	...	...	...	...	...
...	...	...	...	...	...	...	...	...	...	...	...	...	...
...	...	...	...	...	...	...	...	...	...	...	...	...	...
413	58	30	...	2	2	129	...	...	...	11	177	...	4
3,077	772	155	906	22	39	594	30	244	28	69	195	14	9

Total Females.	Females. Rigvédis. Smártás.	Rigvédis. Bhágavata Sampradáya.	Rigvédis. Mádhvás.	Rigvédis. S'rivaishnavás. Tengalé.	Rigvédis. S'rivaishnavás. Vadagalé.	Yajurvédis. Smártás.	Yajurvédis. Bhágavata Sampradáya.	Yajurvédis. Mádhvás.	Yajurvédis. S'rivaishnavás. Tengalé.	Yajurvédis. S'rivaishnavás. Vadagalé.	Sâmavédis. Smártás.	Sâmavédis. Mádhvás.	Sâmavédis. S'rivaishnavás.
2,419	647	89	861	11	96	374	45	179	32	68	6	6	[illegible]
...	...	...	...	...	...	...	...	...	...	...	...	...	...
1	...	...	...	...	...	...	1	...	...	...	...	...	...
...	...	...	...	...	...	...	...	...	...	...	...	...	...
10	...	...	2	...	...	7	...	1	...	...	...	...	...
7	7	...	...	...	...	...	...	...	...	...	...	...	...
...	...	...	...	...	...	...	...	...	...	...	...	...	...
...	...	...	...	...	...	...	...	...	...	...	...	...	...
...	...	...	...	...	...	...	...	...	...	...	...	...	...
...	...	...	...	...	...	...	...	...	...	...	...	...	...
26	3	3	...	...	...	20	...	...	...	...	...	...	...
...	...	...	...	...	...	...	...	...	...	...	...	...	...
...	...	...	...	...	...	...	...	...	...	...	...	...	...
...	...	...	...	...	...	...	...	...	...	...	...	...	...
...	...	...	...	...	...	...	...	...	...	...	...	...	...
...	...	...	...	...	...	...	...	...	...	...	...	...	...
...	...	...	...	...	...	...	...	...	...	...	...	...	...
...	...	...	...	...	...	...	...	...	...	...	...	...	...
...	...	...	...	...	...	...	...	...	...	...	...	...	...
...	...	...	...	...	...	...	...	...	...	...	...	...	...
...	...	...	...	...	...	...	...	...	...	...	...	...	...
...	...	...	...	...	...	...	...	...	...	...	...	...	...
...	...	...	...	...	...	...	...	...	...	...	...	...	...
...	...	...	...	...	...	...	...	...	...	...	...	...	...
...	...	...	...	...	...	...	...	...	...	...	...	...	...
...	...	...	...	...	...	...	...	...	...	...	...	...	...
...	...	...	...	...	...	...	...	...	...	...	...	...	...
...	...	...	...	...	...	...	...	...	...	...	...	...	...
...	...	...	...	...	...	...	...	...	...	...	...	...	...
...	...	...	...	...	...	...	...	...	...	...	...	...	...
...	...	...	...	...	...	...	...	...	...	...	...	...	...
...	...	...	...	...	...	...	...	...	...	...	...	...	...
...	...	...	...	...	...	...	...	...	...	...	...	...	...
53	161	32	21	28	6	139	10	...	33	8	10	3	2
2,916	818	124	884	39	102	540	55	180	65	76	16	9	7

(LOCAL.)

SPECIAL TABLES.

D

PHANAS.

	Castes.	Provincial.			Bangalore.		Kolar.		Tumkur.	
		Total.	Males.	Females.	Males.	Females.	Males.	Females.	Males.	Females.
										A.—18
1	Arasu or Rájapindé ...	1,248	613	635	10	7	25	34	41	38
2	Kómaṭi	21,050	10,809	10,241	2,000	2,066	4,342	3,947	492	429
3	Lingáyet ...	250,997	125,069	125,928	21,201	21,847	21,555	21,996	16,407	14,237
4	Néyigé	20,195	9,752	10,443	3,344	4,506	2,706	2,623	648	489
5	Agasa	63,526	31,136	32,390	4,550	5,117	4,962	4,897	3,970	3,437
6	Hajám	28,052	14,078	13,974	3,050	2,806	3,983	4,070	1,217	1,235
7	Gániga	8,452	4,141	4,311	701	480	934	917	1,192	1,423
8	Golla	27,031	13,723	13,308	444	525	804	1,032	9,398	8,368
9	I'diga	13,323	6,233	7,090	1,123	1,007	710	716	1,423	2,342
10	Kuruba	184,150	89,862	94,288	15,376	16,523	13,428	13,044	14,488	14,425
11	Kumbára ...	32,882	16,822	16,060	1,800	1,560	2,020	1,884	1,103	1,270
12	Darzi	5,821	2,885	2,936	760	670	252	200	177	191
13	Besta	75,624	37,854	37,770	3,442	3,758	1,864	1,916	2,025	1,589
14	Uppára	53,671	25,354	28,317	620	603	1,507	1,403	4,738	4,871
15	Gangadikár Vakkaliga	230,167	109,652	120,515	22,099	22,509	10,285	20,097	47,293	46,859
16	Kunchiṭiga ...	25,852	12,656	13,196	2,099	2,098	1,560	1,599	3,416	3,003
17	Lálagonda ...	4,097	2,084	2,013	901	812	250	262	...	...
18	Morasu	55,927	28,474	27,453	7,000	7,055	12,369	11,322	181	...
19	Reddi	97,869	51,513	46,356	25,250	22,569	5,280	2,281	317	654
20	Nonaba	4,235	2,169	2,066	720	723	525	486	1	4
21	Sáda ...	23,327	8,767	14,560	4,006	4,559	1,002	405	...	...
22	Hallikára ...	55,434	31,461	23,973	9,994	5,628	5,875	4,232	...	47
23	Holaya	482,281	234,836	247,544	31,649	31,235	28,649	29,160	11,544	11,553
24	Others	101,276	49,484	51,792	14,432	13,579	14,186	14,172	12,350	15,067
	Total.....	1,866,487	919,427	947,060	176,571	172,377	139,075	142,647	132,381	131,580
										B.—9
1	Panchála ...	69,575	34,789	34,786	6,213	6,900	4,391	4,341	2,759	3,560
2	Bhéri (Nagarta) ...	212	113	99	4	7	105	86	2	2
3	Néyigé (Déványa) ...	24,393	12,088	12,305	4,414	4,227	641	710	643	952
4	Gániga	18,245	9,404	8,841	2,000	2,000	1,355	1,614	67	90
5	Golla	38,233	20,887	17,346	7,000	4,898	8,456	7,968	3,523	3,355
6	Béda	104,797	51,297	53,500	6,763	7,382	23,852	25,664	16,178	16,035
7	Palli or Tigala ...	33,138	17,317	15,821	7,753	7,152	1,911	1,793	7,451	6,609
8	Mádiga	229,497	112,928	116,569	20,628	21,569	18,688	19,527	22,112	23,971
	Total.....	518,090	258,823	259,267	54,775	54,135	59,429	61,603	52,735	54,579

Mysore.		Hassan.		Shimoga.		Kadur.		Chitaldurg.	
Males.	Females.	Males.	Females.	Males.	Females.	Males.	Females.	Males.	Females.
PHANAS.									
486	509	...	...	8	13	43	34	...	...
1,282	1,300	711	546	507	444	563	504	912	1,005
30,984	32,694	13,707	13,347	7,292	8,422	5,400	9,333	8,529	7,058
1,762	1,318	622	965	...	...	102	133	588	400
7,752	8,271	2,292	2,383	4,312	4,733	1,624	1,900	1,674	1,652
3,495	3,347	760	796	920	886	211	306	440	548
559	750	700	700	...	3	31	32	24	6
1,357	1,552	400	511	19	2	9	4	1,202	1,314
2,262	2,810	561	...	...	...	27	18	127	107
35,931	39,677	8,880	8,931	10	9	609	584	1,140	1,096
6,117	6,138	1,551	1,400	1,300	1,034	1,940	1,846	991	928
335	428	90	100	746	870	312	207	215	270
24,396	23,920	1,649	1,553	2,308	2,763	1,030	1,128	1,131	1,146
18,897	19,018	1,821	1,719	45	15	468	433	258	255
22,038	22,596	6,143	6,215	24	47	150	160	1,560	2,032
1,899	2,899	3,150	3,050	25	23	55	61	452	464
888	836	...	...	...	...	...	...	45	43
6,554	6,658	2,060	2,092	30	33	20	15	260	281
20,250	20,246	340	425	46	87	80	15	70	79
679	686	200	195	...	...	...	...	44	22
3,557	9,088	150	452	2	3	...	2	50	51
14,950	13,556	100	490	22	20	...	...	520	...
86,604	101,626	41,950	42,171	13,769	12,942	17,518	15,216	3,153	3,543
5,468	6,507	1,791	1,444	317	208	427	275	513	540
295,562	326,488	89,628	89,485	31,709	32,535	30,608	29,205	23,960	22,843
PHANAS.									
14,680	13,121	2,329	2,240	1,928	2,310	1,188	1,079	1,356	1,335
...	...	...	...	...	...	2	4	...	...
1,672	1,823	1,703	1,822	1,124	986	1,146	1,190	655	595
5,880	5,007	89	26	...	9	13	29	...	66
900	394	504	319	3	9	31	24	470	379
1,073	928	770	738	14	8	98	110	2,550	2,637
171	259	...	...	...	...	1	8	...	...
11,692	12,032	5,080	5,218	10,088	10,032	6,906	6,129	17,762	18,091
36,087	33,564	10,545	10,363	13,157	13,354	9,332	8,573	22,793	23,103